P9-ASJ-025

Scandinavian Europe

Paul Harding

Mark Elliott, Steve Kokker, Tom Masters, Becky Ohlsen,
Fran Parnell, John Spelman, Andrew Stone

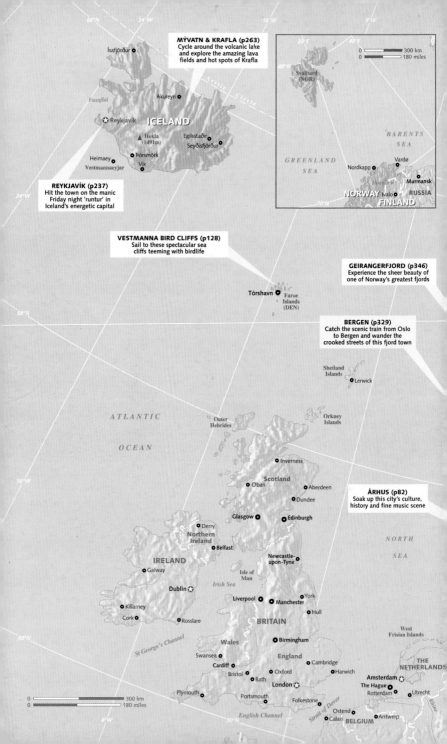

MÝVATN & KRAFLA (p263)
Cycle around the volcanic lake
and explore the amazing lava
fields and hot spots of Krafla

REYKJAVÍK (p237)
Hit the town on the manic
Friday night 'runtur' in
Iceland's energetic capital

VESTMANNA BIRD CLIFFS (p128)
Sail to these spectacular sea
cliffs teeming with birdlife

GEIRANGERFJORD (p346)
Experience the sheer beauty of
one of Norway's greatest fjords

BERGEN (p329)
Catch the scenic train from Oslo
to Bergen and wander the
crooked streets of this fjord town

ÅRHUS (p82)
Soak up this city's culture,
history and fine music scene

Ísafjörður

Akureyri

Reykjavík

ICELAND

▲ Hekla
(1491m)

Egilsstaðir

Seyðisfjörður

Þórsmörk

Heimaey
Vestmannaeyjar

Vík

Faxaflói

Arctic Circle

66°N

66°N

16°W

8°W

24°W

58°N

50°N

16°W

8°W

Svalbard
(NOR)

*BARENTS
SEA*

*GREENLAND
SEA*

Nordkapp

Vardø

Murmansk

NORWAY

Ivalo

RUSSIA

FINLAND

Inarijärvi

20°E

40°E

70°N

0 ___ 300 km
0 ___ 180 miles

Tórshavn

Faroe
Islands
(DEN)

Shetland
Islands

Lerwick

ATLANTIC

OCEAN

Outer
Hebrides

Orkney
Islands

Inverness

Scotland

Oban

Aberdeen

Dundee

Glasgow

Edinburgh

Derry

**Northern
Ireland**

Belfast

IRELAND

Galway

Dublin

Killarney

Cork

Rosslare

Isle of
Man

Irish Sea

Newcastle-
upon-Tyne

Liverpool

Manchester

York

Hull

BRITAIN

Wales

Birmingham

Swansea

England

Cambridge

Cardiff

Oxford

Harwich

Bristol

Bath

London

Plymouth

Portsmouth

Folkestone

English Channel

St George's Channel

Ostend

Calais

Strait of Dover

BELGIUM

Antwerp

West
Frisian Islands

*NORTH
SEA*

**THE
NETHERLANDS**

Amsterdam

The Hague

Utrecht

Rotterdam

Rhine

0 ___ 300 km
0 ___ 180 miles

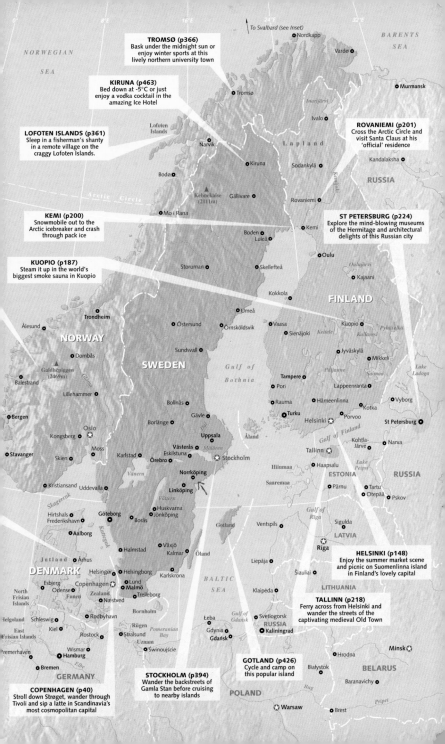

TROMSØ (p366)
Bask under the midnight sun or enjoy winter sports at this lively northern university town

KIRUNA (p463)
Bed down at -5°C or just enjoy a vodka cocktail in the amazing Ice Hotel

LOFOTEN ISLANDS (p361)
Sleep in a fisherman's shanty in a remote village on the craggy Lofoten Islands.

ROVANIEMI (p201)
Cross the Arctic Circle and visit Santa Claus at his 'official' residence

KEMI (p200)
Snowmobile out to the Arctic icebreaker and crash through pack ice

ST PETERSBURG (p224)
Explore the mind-blowing museums of the Hermitage and architectural delights of this Russian city

KUOPIO (p187)
Steam it up in the world's biggest smoke sauna in Kuopio

HELSINKI (p148)
Enjoy the summer market scene and picnic on Suomenlinna island in Finland's lovely capital

TALLINN (p218)
Ferry across from Helsinki and wander the streets of the captivating medieval Old Town

GOTLAND (p426)
Cycle and camp on this popular island

COPENHAGEN (p40)
Stroll down Strøget, wander through Tivoli and sip a latte in Scandinavia's most cosmopolitan capital

STOCKHOLM (p394)
Wander the backstreets of Gamla Stan before cruising to nearby islands

Destination Scandinavia

Rugged and breathtakingly beautiful one minute, flat and featureless the next – there's something undeniably cool about Scandinavia. There's a purity to the air, blondness in the hair and a sense of space you won't find anywhere else in Europe.

There's so much natural beauty in Scandinavia it's difficult to know where to start. Iceland is a volcanic hotspot of lava flows, waterfalls and glaciers. Norway has an overwhelming coastline of dramatic steep-sided fjords and mountains. Finland is a patchwork of lakes and pristine forests. Spy on puffins from clifftops, spot whales breaching at sea or pause as a herd of reindeer crosses your path in Lapland. Parts of northern Scandinavia can seem incredibly remote and empty, but in the south, the cosmopolitan cities of Copenhagen, Stockholm and Helsinki brim with history, architectural highlights, active harbour scenes, nightlife and culture.

Nudging the Arctic Circle, this latitude brings the extremes of near constant daylight in summer and the bluish darkness of long polar nights in winter. While it's natural to imagine snow when you think of this part of the world, southern Scandinavia in summer can be as warm and sunny as southern Europe. Locals live for those summer months when the days are long and there's a buzz of excitement and energy everywhere you go, as summer festivals explode throughout the region. Feeling energetic? You can hike and cycle in virgin forests, canoe through stunning island archipelagos, or in winter (and spring) you can ski, snowmobile or dogsled.

Travel in Scandinavia is easy and getting around can be half the fun. Cruise on a ferry between Helsinki and Stockholm or Tallinn, sail all the way from Bergen in Norway to Seyðis-fjörður in Iceland via the Faroe Islands, or catch Norway's famous *Hurtigruten* coastal steamer beyond the Arctic Circle. The mountainous Oslo–Bergen train trip is one of the world's most scenic.

ANDERS BLOMQVIST

Highlights

DAVID TIPLING

Find yourself face-to-face with fauna on Finland's fells (p147)

Savour a seaside stroll on Nyhavn's quays, Copenhagen (p40)
Denmark

JON DAVISON

WADE EAKLE

Stop, stare and stand back when
Strokkur geyser (p251) erupts,
Iceland

JONATHAN SMITH

Wet your whistle in a weekend *runtur* (pub-crawl) in Reykjavík; p248, Iceland

Soak up the atmosphere in charming Århus (p82), Denmark

JOHN ELK III

Opposite: Marvel at the grandeur of Norway's fjords from the top of Preikestolen (p317)

ANDERS BLOMQVIST

Discover Denmark's northernmost point, Grenen (p99)

HOLGER LEUE

GRANT DIXON

Experience the real meaning of isolation on beautiful Kalsoy (p133), Faroe Islands

Peer into the past in 13th-century Gamla Stan (p398), Stockholm's old town centre, Sweden

JONATHAN SMITH

Find your inner Viking at the Viking Ship Museum (p62), Roskilde, Denmark

OTHER HIGHLIGHTS

- Rock on in summer at Roskilde Festival (p63), Denmark, Northern Europe's biggest music festival
- Admire the astonishing art collection at the Hermitage (p225), St Petersburg
- Strip off for a traditional sauna (p191) in Finland

Escape to the pristine beauty of Norway's fishing villages in Lofoten (p361), Norway

Muddy it up in the steaming waters of the Blue Lagoon (p250), Reykjavík, Iceland

Peer at puffins (p273) in Iceland

JONATHAN SMITH

Step back in time at the amazing Vasamuseet (p399), Stockholm

JONATHAN SMITH

Turn up the heat in the cool nightclubs (p222) of Tallinn, Estonia

Catch some culture at Helsinki's Kiasma Museum of Contemporary Art (p152), Finland

JONATHAN SMITH

ANDERS BLOMQVIST

Hike the blue-ice glaciers of Jostedalsbreen (p344), Norway

ANDERS BLOMQVIST

Wander around the wooden buildings of Bergen's historic Bryggen quarter (p334), Norway

Spread some Christmas cheer with Santa in the Arctic Circle (p205)

JOHN BORTHWICK

GRAEME CORNWALLIS

Thrill to the torrents of Svartifoss waterfall (p269), Skaftafell National Park Iceland

Fortify yourself inside Visby's medieval walls (p451), Sweden

GRAEME CORNWALLIS

Stretch your legs in Vigeland Park (p307), Oslo, Norway

WAYNE W

Visit picturesque Savonlinna (p184), Finland, for its pretty lakes and famous Opera Festival

WAYNE W

Contents

14 CONTENTS

Regional Map Contents

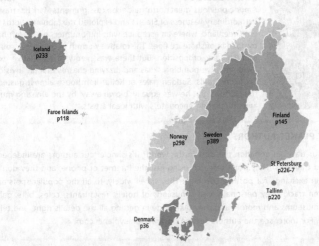

Iceland p233

Faroe Islands p118

Norway p298

Sweden p389

Finland p145

St Petersburg p226-7

Tallinn p220

Denmark p36

The Authors

PAUL HARDING
Coordinating Author, Front Chapters & Finland

Paul first left his comfy job as a newspaper reporter and strapped on a backpack to explore Europe 10 years ago. Mesmerised by the midnight sun, stunned by Scandinavia's pristine environment and wooed by Helsinki's summer energy and nightlife, he has made several trips to Scandinavia, particularly Finland. Covering thousands of kilometres around Finland, he once again snowmobiled on frozen lakes, suffered mild shock from ice swimming after a sauna, managed to survive Vappu in Helsinki (but only just) and even got arrested by Russian police on a side trip to St Petersburg. Fortunate enough to travel and work as a writer and photographer for the past eight years, Paul has contributed to Lonely Planet's *Finland, Iceland* and *Scandinavian Europe* guides, among others.

Life on the Road

It was −6°C and the snow was still heavy on the ground when I arrived in Helsinki (p148) in late March. The Baltic ferries were ploughing though the ice into the harbour and people were skating, kite-surfing and ice-fishing on the frozen lake and inlets. I took an €18 flight to Oulu and made my way up to Kemi (p200), snowmobiled out to the world's only passenger Arctic icebreaker and marvelled as it cut through 20m-thick pack ice in the Gulf of Bothnia, before bedding down in a polar sleeping bag at a hotel made entirely of ice and snow. In Rovaniemi (p205) I visited Santa at the Arctic Circle and drove on icy roads to Inari (p206), where the annual Sami reindeer racing championships were in full swing. Finally, I swallowed my budget and spent the night in a glass igloo at Kakslauttanen (p207) hoping to see the aurora borealis, but on this particular night it wasn't to be. Next time!

Inari
Kakslauttanen
Rovaniemi
Kemi
Oulu

Helsinki

MARK ELLIOTT
Faroe Islands

Among previous 'great north' guidebook assignments Mark has traversed the extraordinary vastness of Siberia and explored the fabulous fjords of southern Greenland, where an escapade with Inuit hunters nearly left him fatally trapped in offshore ice floes. The relative warmth of the Faroes sounded like a much safer proposition. But there was plenty of alternative excitement including dive-bombing skuas and dizzying chasms that lay invisibly across his hiking trails. Sudden gales at Kollur lighthouse almost gusted him off the clifftops. But he was equally 'blown away' by the amazing music scene and stimulating encounters with local artists.

LONELY PLANET AUTHORS

Why is our travel information the best in the world? It's simple: our authors are independent, dedicated travellers. They don't research using just the Internet or phone, and they don't take freebies in exchange for positive coverage. They travel widely, to all the popular spots and off the beaten track. They personally visit thousands of hotels, restaurants, cafés, bars, galleries, palaces, museums and more – and they take pride in getting all the details right, and telling it how it is. For more, see the authors section on www.lonelyplanet.com.

BECKY OHLSEN   Sweden

Becky has her parents to thank for her early exposure to and affection for Sweden. But it was the pickled herring and *snaps* that cinched it. In recent years she's made annual pilgrimages to the motherland and has studied the language enough to be able to enter into conversations that ultimately leave her baffled. She likes the gloom of Swedish art and the gleam of its pop – everything from August Strindberg to ABBA, and Bergman to Pippi Longstocking. Most of all she loves hiking in Norrland forests, sharing the road with reindeer, and eating saffron ice cream in Gamla Stan. Becky has also coauthored Lonely Planet's guide to Sweden.

FRAN PARNELL   Iceland, Directory & Transport

Fran's love of the country began while studying for a masters degree in Anglo-Saxon, Norse & Celtic, and has just kept on growing. It's impossible to choose one favourite spot, but the Westfjords, the Vestmannaeyjar and Grímsey are high on her list, as is Reykjavík with all its Viking history, fine cafés and odd museums. Fran has also worked on Lonely Planet guides to Sweden, Iceland and Reykjavík.

JOHN SPELMAN   Norway

John Spelman spends a lot of time trying to obtain refugee status so that Norway will let him emigrate. Until then, he visits as often as possible to drink tasteless beer, freeload off his generous friends and be overwhelmed by the worlds most stunning landscape.

When Lonely Planet isn't footing the bill, John is a PhD student researching architectural and urban histories, some of them Norwegian. He currently lives in Charlottesville, Virginia. This is the fourth time he has covered Norway for a Lonely Planet title.

ANDREW STONE   Denmark

Andrew first visited Denmark in the mid-1990s to see friends of his in Copenhagen. He returns every year or so just to check that Copenhagen is as effortlessly cool as before, to check out the latest bit of weird architecture, to stock up on hip little design classics and to feed his interest in Denmark's rich Iron Age, Viking and Renaissance history. Andrew is also an author of Lonely Planet's *Denmark* guide.

CONTRIBUTING AUTHORS

Steve Kokker is a die-hard Eastern European lover, having spent most of his time since 1996 living away from his native Montreal, basing himself in his father's homeland of Tallinn, Estonia, and trekking through the Baltic region, Russia and beyond. He's been writing for Lonely Planet since 1998, and was responsible for the Tallinn chapter of this book.

Tom Masters aged 15, travelled around Eastern Europe by train with his intrepid mother, and at 18 finally got to see Russia, his true passion. Since graduating from the University of London with a degree in Russian, Tom has returned more times than he can remember, living in St Petersburg and working throughout the region. Now living in London, he finds himself back in Russia all the time. He wrote the St Petersburg chapter for this book.

Getting Started

Let's make one thing clear: travel throuhout Scandinavia is a breeze. Communicating in English is rarely a problem, transport is efficient and frequent between main towns, standards of living are high and you won't find the crazy crowds that blight summer travel elsewhere in Europe.

On the down side, travel expenses are high, weather can be fickle and distances can be long, especially in the wilds of Arctic Lapland or the Icelandic interior. Scandinavia is a big place; there's a lot of diversity from the Arctic north to the forest and farmland of the south, and midsummer has little in common with midwinter. Depending on where and when you go, you'll probably need to pack winter and summer clothes. No matter how long you plan to travel here, and whatever your budget, a little forward planning will help you squeeze the most out of your trip. There's no point turning up at Bergen to catch the ferry to Iceland in April or planning to see the aurora borealis (northern lights) in September.

WHEN TO GO

Scandinavia has very distinct summer and winter seasons and extremely different climates, especially when comparing the north and the south. For most travellers, the best time to visit is undoubtedly summer – the brief window from June to August – when you can usually be guaranteed some fine weather and long, long hours of daylight. This is the time when camping grounds and hostels are all open, summer festivals are in full swing and there's a buzz of excitement on the streets with lots of shiny, happy Scandinavians. The holiday season begins after Midsummer's Day (usually the third weekend in June). This is when locals take their holidays and vacate the cities en masse for the countryside, but no matter what time of year, Scandinavia rarely feels overcrowded and hotels actually drop their rates in summer. The exceptions are camping grounds and family attractions, which are often packed.

See Climate Charts (p486) for more information.

DON'T LEAVE HOME WITHOUT...

Sleeping bag or sleeping sheet – even if you're not camping you'll sleep cheaper in hostels with your own sheets, and a sleeping bag is a must in Iceland

Insect repellent – for keeping mosquitoes and biting insects at bay in summer, especially in Finland and Iceland

Hat and gloves – for those inevitable cold snaps

Swiss army knife – essential multipurpose tool

Watch – everything in Scandinavia runs on time!

Mobile phone/PDA – it's easy and inexpensive to get hooked up to local prepaid networks in Scandinavia and handy for making bookings or keeping in touch with other travellers

Swimsuit and towel – for soaking in 'hot pots' or thermal springs in Iceland, postsauna swims and spas in Finland, or for the beaches of southern Sweden and Denmark

Credit card – Scandinavians love to pay with the plastic so it's handy to have a credit card for general use or emergencies; essential for car hire

Eye mask, earplugs and torch – useful for sleeping on long summer nights; rowdy hostels; and finding your way in the dark

Sense of adventure and humour – vital for when those fjords and glaciers are lost in fog, when you just missed the last bus by 30 seconds, when you get the bill for that fancy restaurant 'splurge', and for making new discoveries away from the beaten track

Throughout the region, especially in the south, temperatures can be surprisingly warm in summer. Spring and autumn – May, June and September – are also good times to visit. You can still expect fine, sunny days and fewer tourists. Temperature changes can be swift at this latitude – above the Arctic Circle you might find yourself wrapped in layers one day, but wearing only a T-shirt the next. Iceland and the western coast of Norway remain mild thanks to the Gulf Stream, but this also brings rain – hikers and campers should always carry waterproof gear.

Winter (and early spring in the far north) brings its own tourist season, where snowbound activities such as skiing and snowboarding, dogsledding, ice-fishing and snowmobiling are all the rage. Peak ski season in Lapland and the north is generally February to April, when the snow is deep but the gloomy depths of winter are over. True winter (November to January) is the time to view the aurora borealis, but otherwise travel in Scandinavia is a pretty cold, dark and miserable option, when the sauna becomes a sanctuary from the snow and much of the tourist infrastructure outside the main cities shuts down completely. Autumn (late August to September) is the perfect time for hiking and cycling, thanks to the beautiful forest colours.

See the Climate & When to Go section of the country chapters for more information.

COSTS & MONEY

By any standards Scandinavia can be expensive, especially for accommodation, eating out and nightlife, but overall the daily costs of travel are comparable to northern Europe and in some cases cheaper than London or Paris. And there are plenty of free things for travellers to do: hiking, visiting churches, parks and gardens, national parks, fjords, glaciers and beaches which all cost nothing more than the effort to get there. Travel costs vary slightly from country to country – Denmark is probably cheapest, followed by Finland, Sweden, Norway and Iceland. Tallinn and St Petersburg are considerably cheaper than anywhere in Scandinavia.

THE NORTHERN LIGHTS

The haunting sight of curtains of charged light swirling across the sky on a chill Arctic night is an irresistible lure for many travellers. The northern lights, or aurora borealis, are a surreal and exhilarating sight, often visible to observers standing at or above the Arctic Circle (latitude 66°), which includes a large part of northern Scandinavia. They're especially visible around the equinoxes (late September and March), and are particularly striking during the dark winter.

The aurora appears as curtains of greenish-white light stretching east to west across the sky for thousands of kilometres. At its lower edge, the aurora typically shades to a crimson-red glow. Hues of blue and violet can also be seen. The lights seem to shift and swirl in the night sky, as if in a celestial dance.

These auroral storms are created when charged particles (protons and electrons) from the sun bombard the earth. These are deflected towards the north and south poles by the earth's magnetic field. There they hit the earth's outer atmosphere, 100km to 1000km above ground, causing highly charged electrons to collide with molecules of nitrogen and oxygen. The excess energy from these collisions creates the colourful lights we see in the sky.

The ancients had other explanations for the spectacle: the Greeks described it as 'blood rain'; the Inuit attributed the phenomenon to 'sky dwellers'; and the Sami of Lapland believed it was caused by a giant fox swishing its tail above the Arctic tundra.

Like anything in nature, the northern lights can be fickle and certainly don't occur every night. To see them you need at least a cloudless, very cold night and the luck of the heavens.

Once you're in the region, your biggest unavoidable expense is finding a bed, but camping (you can pitch a tent in many places for free) and Scandinavia's excellent network of hostels will keep costs down, and most hotels discount their rates on weekends and in summer. A night on the town in Stockholm, Oslo or Helsinki – say dinner, a few drinks and a nightclub or music bar can easily require a small bank loan, but shopping at markets, filling up on lunch buffets and buying alcohol from supermarkets or state-run liquor stores is relatively cheap. Little things like a cup of coffee, doing your laundry or storing your bag in a locker cost about €2 to €2.50.

Sightseeing costs can add up (museum admissions range from €2.50 to €10) but most capital cities offer good-value discount cards that give free admission to sights for a limited period. An ISIC student card or youth card can cut costs in half.

On a rock-bottom budget – camping or staying in hostels, self-catering, using a rail pass or bus transport – you can squeak by on €30 to €55 a day, which is pretty tight and doesn't allow for much amusement. Staying in private hostel rooms, guesthouses or two people sharing in a cheap hotel, eating at least one sit-down meal a day and seeing a few sights, expect to budget €65 to €80 per person per day. Add to that the 'nonessentials' – shopping, drinking, activities such as cruises, tours and skiing – to come up with your own budget. Travel is a personal thing and everyone spends differently. With €95 a day and some common sense you can travel pretty comfortably.

Norway, Sweden, Denmark, the Faroes and Iceland each have their own kroner, while Finland uses the euro. The easiest way to carry or obtain money in Scandinavia is with debit and credit cards – ATMs (24-hour) linked to international networks (Cirrus, Maestro, Eurocard, Plus, Visa and MasterCard) are common.

READING UP

There are lots of ways to pique your interest, pick up ideas and fuel the dream before your trip. Reading travel books, studying maps and surfing the internet will all help drive that wanderlust.

> 'Most capital cities offer good-value discount cards that give free admission to sights'

Books

Frost on My Moustache: The Arctic Exploits of a Lord and a Loafer by Tim Moore. In this contemporary account following 19th-century traveller Lord Dufferin, British writer Moore hauls himself across the North Atlantic, enduring chronic seasickness, cycling through Iceland's interior, taking a Viking longboat to Norway via the Faroes and finally landing in Spitzbergen. A great read.

Pole to Pole by Michael Palin. The former Monty Python star and his BBC crew travel from the North to South Pole along the 30° line of longitude. The early part of the trip conveniently includes the far north of Norway, Finnish Lapland, Helsinki, Tallinn and St Petersburg. Palin's casual journal-style narrative is typically funny and engaging.

To the Top of the World: Norway's Coastal Voyage by PE Johnson. The author takes the stunning coastal route from Bergen to Kirkenes, stopping in villages along the way. This is a must-read if you're planning this awesome sea journey.

A Year in Lapland: Guest of the Reindeer Herders by Hugh Beach. This is a unique peek into the lives of the Sami reindeer herders, written by an anthropologist who spent a year living among the Sami in the Jokkmokk district of Swedish Lapland.

In Forkbeard's Wake: Coasting Around Scandinavia by Ben Nimmo. With his sailing boat and a quest to retrace the steps of a Norse warrior, British writer Nimmo comes up with a quirky and funny collection of experiences that reveal a lot about Scandinavia and its people.

Just As Well I'm Leaving by Michael Booth. Not strictly about travel in Scandinavia, but this funny travelogue follows the 19th century travels of Denmark's favourite writer, Hans Christian Anderson.

Culture Shock! is a series of short, light-hearted books that delves into the culture, customs, etiquette and foibles of various countries – you may want to pick up the Norway, Finland, Sweden, Denmark or Iceland editions.

For a unique and super cool experience check out the Ice Hotel (p464; www.icehotel.com) in Jukkasjärvi near Kiruna, Sweden or the Snow Castle & Hotel in Kemi (p200; www.snowcastle .net), Finland.

Websites

Go Scandinavia (www.goscandinavia.com) Site of the Scandinavian Tourist Board in North America; links to country sites, tour ideas.

Lonely Planet (www.lonelyplanet.com) This site has destination summaries on all Scandinavian countries, plus the Thorn Tree bulletin board for travellers.

Scandinavia News (www.scandinavianews.com) World News network site with English-language news and views from Scandinavia.

Scandinavia Travel (www.budgettravel.com/scandinavia.htm) Comprehensive site of links and budget travel info for all of Scandinavia.

Scandinavica (www.scandinavica.com) Site devoted to Nordic culture and tourism with links to country sites.

TOP 10 MOVIES

Some of Scandinavia's most famous filmmakers in recent years have included Denmark's Lars von Trier, Finland's Aki Kaurismäki and Sweden's Lasse Hallström.

For more on Scandinavian summer festivals, see www.efa-aef.org/.

- *101 Reykjavík* (2000; director Baltasar Kormákur)
- *Before the Storm* (2000; writer and director Reza Parsa)
- *Buddy* (2003; director Morten Tyldum)
- *Children of Nature* (1991; director Friðrik Thór Friðriksson)
- *Leningrad Cowboys Go America* (1989; director Aki Kaurismäki)
- *My Life as a Dog* (1987; director Lasse Hallström)
- *Songs From the Second Floor* (2000; director Roy Andersson)
- *The Dudesons Movie* (2006; directors Jukka Hilden and Jarno Laasala)
- *The Man Without a Past* (2002; director Aki Kaurismäki)
- *Under the Sun* (1998; director Colin Nutley)

TOP 10 FESTIVALS

Tromsø International Film Festival (mid-January) One of Norway's most exciting cultural festivals (p380).

Jokkmokk Winter Market (February) – Sami celebration in Swedish Lapland (p461).

May Day & Eve (1 May) This is the Labour Day holiday everywhere except Denmark; 30 April is Valborgsmässoafton in Sweden (p470) and Vappu in Finland (p212), with some of the biggest liquid-fuelled student celebrations imaginable.

Midsummer (around 23 June) Celebrated throughout Scandinavia in late June, this a national holiday; Midsummer Eve is usually a big party with bonfires and dancing.

Roskilde Rock Festival (late June/early July) One of Europe's biggest rock music festivals (p63) held in Denmark.

Copenhagen Jazz Festival (July) Ten-day jazz fest (p109) held in Denmark's capital.

World Wife-Carrying Championships (Finland, July) One of Finland's many whacky events (p192).

Savonlinna Opera Festival (July) A month of high culture in the stunning Olavinlinna Castle (p185) in Finland.

Stockholm Pride (late July/early August) Scandinavia's biggest gay and lesbian festival (p471) held in the Swedish capital.

Þjóðhátíð (early August) – this crazy festival celebrating Iceland's independence is held on Vestmannaeyjar island a month after the rest of the country (p281).

RESPONSIBLE TRAVEL

Scandinavia is largely a clean, green environment. Air and water pollution from pulp factories and power plants, deforestation and acid rain are certainly environmental issues facing the Nordic countries, but on the whole travellers will breathe in clean air, see virtually no litter and drink pristine water.

Travellers can have a potentially negative impact, particularly when hiking in forests or national parks. The Right of Common Access (Everyman's Right) is a code that applies in Norway, Sweden, Finland and Iceland, meaning you can walk virtually anywhere, provided you respect private land and behave responsibly. Stick to marked trails, leave flora and fauna alone, and always carry rubbish out with you – don't leave it on trails, at camp sites or around huts. Don't use soap or detergent when washing in streams (use a bucket).

If you're using wilderness huts that require paying a fee on an honesty system (as in Iceland), make sure you pay, and leave the huts as you found them. Don't make campfires on private land, and check local regulations before making a fire anywhere. Never cut down wood for a fire, use only dead wood.

When taking an organised tour, check the credentials and philosophy of the tour company. Are they using knowledgeable local guides? Do they have a responsible attitude to the environment and ecosystem?

In many cities and towns, recycling bins are provided for plastics and paper etc, so use them. In Sweden and Finland there are collection points (at Alko stores in Finland, for instance) for glass and plastic bottles.

If you're driving, particularly in the far north, keep your speed down. Domesticated reindeer herds frequently wander onto the road, and quite apart from your own safety, a dead reindeer is a financial loss to its owner.

Finally, be sensible. Don't exploit the land and its people, learn a few words of the language, and respect local culture.

The best place in Finland for a legendary Finnish smoke sauna is Kuopio (p187).

Itineraries

CLASSIC ROUTES

SCANDI IN A NUTSHELL
Ten Days / Copenhagen to Copenhagen

The obvious place to start your tour of Scandinavia is **Copenhagen** (p40). Spend a couple of days in this cosmopolitan city before catching a train to **Stockholm** (p394) for two days, then take the overnight ferry to **Helsinki** (p148). If you're in a hurry you could spend just the day in Helsinki and catch the ferry back to Stockholm, especially if you book a cabin and get some sleep, or take in some Helsinki nightlife and a day trip to **Porvoo** (p162) or even **Tallinn** (p218). If you're keen to experience some midnight sun (or northern lights in winter or early spring), jump on the overnight train to **Rovaniemi** (p201), right on the Arctic Circle. Returning to Helsinki, then Stockholm take the overnight train to **Oslo** (p302) for the day, then the scenic rail trip to **Flåm** (p342) and the combination boat/bus trip along the Sognefjord to **Bergen** (p329). From here, travel to **Kristiansand** (p321) and take the ferry to **Hirtshals** (p101) in Denmark then return to Copenhagen via **Århus** (p82).

With three weeks or longer spend more time in Sweden, at **Malmö** (p424), **Göteborg** (p432) or **Kalmar** (p446), more time in Norway, with three days in **Fjærland** (p344) and **Geiranger** (p346), or more time in Denmark at **Odense** (p72) and **Ærø** (p81) on the way back to Copenhagen.

A quick city-hop using the train or bus and ferries. If time is very short, you'll be limited to the capitals or you may have to skip Helsinki. Iceland is out of the question!

BALTICS & THE EAST

Three Weeks / Stockholm to Stockholm

Finland, sharing a border and a fair slice of history with Russia, is quite unlike the Scandinavian ideal presented by Sweden, Norway and Denmark. This itinerary combines a brief tour of the Baltics with southern Finland.

Start in Stockholm so you can take advantage of the fantastic overnight **ferries** (p475) to **Helsinki** (p148), with their smorgasbord meals and all-night partying. After a couple of days in the Finnish capital take the ferry (1½ to three hours) to medieval **Tallinn** (p218) in Estonia. Returning to Helsinki (Tallinn can be seen as a day trip if time is short), take the overnight sleeper train to **St Petersburg** (p224). You must have a visa, which can be obtained in Helsinki through specialist agents or at the Russian embassy (allow at least a week). After a few days in this enchanting, Imperial city, return to Helsinki.

If it's summertime, take the train to the Lakeland towns of **Savonlinna** (p184), with its awesome medieval castle and opera festival, or **Kuopio** (p187), home of the world's biggest smoke sauna, or northwest to the dynamic, cultural city of **Tampere** (p173). At any time of year you could also take the overnight train to **Rovaniemi** (p201), cross the Arctic Circle and visit Santa.

Finally, you can return to Sweden by taking the train to **Turku** (p163) then the ferry to Stockholm through the southern archipelago via the **Åland islands** (p169) – stop off at the islands for as long as you wish and maybe take a cycle touring holiday.

The Finnish capital Helsinki offers easy access to the charming and splendidly preserved old town of Tallinn as well as the cultural treasures of St Petersburg. Finland's own attractions include Father Christmas himself and the beautiful Lakeland.

ROADS LESS TRAVELLED

THE VIKING TRAIL   Four to Six Weeks / Copenhagen to Reykjavík

From **Copenhagen** (p40) head to the Viking Ship Museum in **Roskilde** (p61) and the Viking fortress in **Trelleborg** (p64). Cross to Funen, with a trip to **Ladbyskibet** (p77), then to **Århus** (p82) and the Viking burial ground at **Lindholm Høje** (p95) before taking the ferry from **Hirtshals** (p383) to **Kristiansand** (p321) in Norway. Spend a few days in **Bergen** (p330) before taking the train to **Flåm** (p342) and the boat/bus trip along the **Sognefjord** (p342) to see the Viking ruins at **Balestrand** (p343). From Bergen, there is one summer ferry a week to Iceland. You can stop at the **Faroe Islands** (p115) and wait for the following week's ferry, visiting **Vestmanna Bird Cliffs** (p128 and **Mykines p127**; or catch the ferry from **Hanstholm** in Denmark (via the Shetland Islands), instead of Bergen, which gives you two days in the Faroes (see p112).

The ferry continues to Iceland, arriving at **Seyðisfjörður** (p266). From here the best route to Reykjavík is along the south coast past the **Vatnajökull icecap** (p267). In **Reykjavík** (p237), visit the Saga Museum and the Viking village of **Hafnarfjörður** (p251), take a trip to the **Blue Lagoon** (p250), then fly out. If you plan to return by ferry, take a bus trip through the interior to **Akureyri** (p257) then bus back to Seyðisfjörður on the Ring Rd. Remember there's only one ferry a week, so plan for either one or two weeks in Iceland.

Alternatively, fly direct from Copenhagen or Oslo to Reykjavík, and spend a week or more travelling around the Ring Rd.

The Viking Age had its beginnings in Denmark, Norway and Sweden in the 9th century AD, and it was a Viking who settled Iceland. You can still see the remains of Viking fortresses, burial grounds, longboats and churches, while exploring their ancient route.

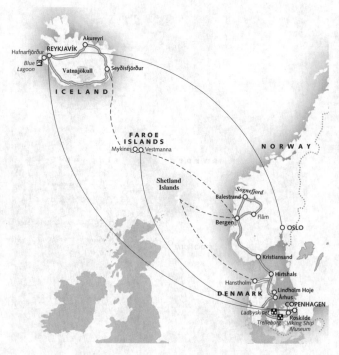

BEYOND THE ARCTIC CIRCLE Three Weeks / Helsinki return or Stockholm

There's something magical and foreboding about the Arctic Circle, the imaginary line at 66°33´N latitude where the sun never truly sets in mid-summer and never peeps above the horizon in winter. The remarkable clarity of light, eerie remoteness, Sami culture and reindeer herds add to the mystique. A trip to Nordkapp (the North Cape), the most northerly point in Europe, is something of a spiritual pilgrimage for many travellers. This trip is best tackled in summer (July–August), when the midnight sun shines and all public transport is running, but September to March is the time to see the northern lights and experience dogsledding and other activities.

Start at **Helsinki** (p148). Take the overnight train to **Rovaniemi** (p201), visit the **Santa Claus Village** (p205) then take a bus up to the Sami village of **Inari** (p206), perhaps stopping to stay in an igloo at **Kakkslauternen** (p207). From here there are direct buses all the way to **Nordkapp** (p372) via Karasjok in Norway. After standing at the top of Europe with a glass of champagne, catch the coastal steamer *Hurtigruten* to the stunning **Lofoten Islands** (p361l) with a possible stop in **Tromsø** (p366). From here you can continue on the steamer all the way to **Bergen** (p330), or get back to the mainland at **Narvik** (p359) and take the train to **Kiruna** (p463) in Sweden. Unfortunately, the famous Ice Hotel will have melted away by summer but you can still visit the Ice Hotel Art Centre in a giant freezer!

From Kiruna head south to Haparanda where you can cross back into Finland at the border town of **Tornio** (p200) – and have a round of midnight golf before returning to Helsinki. Or go to Boden, perhaps via the Sami village of **Jokkmokk** (p461), and catch the train to Stockholm.

Go to the top of Europe, visit a Sami village, play golf through two countries – all possible above 66°33´N.

TAILORED TRIPS

THE GREAT OUTDOORS

Scandinavia's pristine environment begs to be explored at close range – on foot, a bicycle, canoe, skis, skates or dogsled! This itinerary is not a point-to-point tour, but suggestions on where you can enjoy some of Scandinavia's best activities.

Spring/Summer

Flat, rural and not too big, Denmark is a haven for cycling. Popular areas include **Bornholm** (p67), **Funen** (p72), **Langeland** (p80) and the **Lake District** (p90) of Jutland. The Finns are also avid cyclists. The best region for pedalling is the **Åland islands** (p169), but rides anywhere in the eastern Lakeland area and around **Turku** (p163) or **Oulu** (p196) are rewarding. In Sweden head for **Skåne** (p424) or **Gotland** (p451).

Hiking in national parks and forests is sensational in Scandinavia – Iceland and Lapland in particular have some of Europe's last great wilderness areas, and trails, huts and camping grounds are set up for walkers. In Iceland, the **Landmannalaugar-Þórsmörk trek** (p276) is an awesome walk through lava flows and lunar landscapes. In Finland, try **Oulanka National Park** (p199) and treks in **Karelia** (p193). In Sweden, the 450km **Kungsleden** (King's Trail, p465) is a major marked hiking route.

Other summer activities include canoeing, white-water rafting and fishing; see the Activities section of each chapter for information.

Winter/Spring

Skiing – both downhill and cross-country – is a national obsession in Finland, Sweden and Norway, and December to April is the time to go. The best resorts include **Lillehammer** (p328) in Norway, **Åre** (p458) in Sweden, and **Levi** (p208) and **Ruka** (p199) in Finland.

Think of Arctic Lapland and it's not hard to imagine mushing through the snow behind a team of huskies or a reindeer-sleigh. While you'll

have to budget big for these activities, Scandinavia is one of the best places in the world to do it. In Norway, try **Tromsø** (p366) or **Karasjok** (p374) and in Sweden head to **Kiruna** (p463) or **Abisko** (p465). In Finland, **Rovaniemi** (p201) is a magnet for winter activities and there are husky farms organising safaris at **Muonio** (p208) and **Ivalo** (p206).

Other winter highlights to add to your itinerary should include the **Ice Hotel** at Jukkasjarvi near Kiruna in Sweden (p464) and the **Arctic Icebreaker cruise** (p200) at Kemi in Finland.

ON THE RAILS

With a ScanRail Pass (see p513) you can take to the rails and cover a lot of ground in Scandinavia economically, including discounts on ferries. To get the most out of your pass, long (possibly overnight) trips work well, but you can always pay for shorter trips to reach more places. Consider this megacircuit.

Start in **Copenhagen** (p40) and take the train via **Malmö** (p424) to **Stockholm** (p394). Cruise on the overnight ferry (50% discount) to **Helsinki** (p148), then the overnight train to **Oulu** (p196) or **Rovaniemi** (p201), almost at the Arctic Circle – if you have time, consider stops in **Kuopio** (p187) or **Tampere** (p173). Rail down the Gulf of Bothnia coast to **Vaasa** (p180), where you can catch a ferry across to **Umeå** (p459) in Sweden. From here catch a train south to lakeside **Östersund** (p457), then west to **Trondheim** (p352) in Norway. You're now heading toward the spectacular fjords of Norway, where you'll have to combine bus and boat travel with the rail line heads south to **Dombås** (p329) and on to Oslo: detour on the spectacular journey to **Åndalsnes** (p346). Take the bus to **Geiranger** (p346) for the unmissable cruise on **Geirangerfjorden** (p346).

From here you can return to the main train line and Oslo, or make your way through the western fjords to **Bergen** (p330) and take the spectacularly scenic train to **Oslo** (p302) from there. Finally, board the train for **Göteborg** (p432), Sweden, and back to Copenhagen.

ISLAND-HOPPING BY BIKE

Southern Scandi is great for cycling and there are some lovely islands and beaches waiting to be discovered. Grab a set of wheels in **Copenhagen** (p40) and spend a couple of days exploring around the Danish capital. Take the ferry out to **Bornholm** (p67) and spend a few days cycling, stopping at island beaches such as **Dueodde** (p69) and a possible trip to tiny **Christiansø** (p71). Back on the mainland (it's possible to take a ferry direct to Sweden), head up to Kalmar, the jumping off point for the windmill-crammed island of **Öland** (p448), a natural beauty with lots of good camping. Next stop is a ferry from Oskarshamn to the large island of **Gotland** (p451), great for cycling through prehistoric sites. Continue up to **Stockholm** (p394), which has its own amazing archipelago of some 24,000 islands. About 70km north, the port of Grisslehamn is the place for the short ferry hop across to **Eckerö** (p173) in Finland's Åland islands, though a much easier option is to take the ferry direct from Stockholm to **Mariehamn** (p171), the island capital. You could spend a week or more cycling and camping on this beautiful island archipelago, before taking the ferry across to **Turku** (p163) in Finland. Explore Finland's beautiful southeast coast and beaches before taking the train to **Helsinki** (p148) and selling your bike!

Snapshot

For purists, the term Scandinavia encompasses only Denmark, Sweden and Norway – the three kingdoms of the region. Many Finns and Icelanders prefer to regard their republics as being part of the 'Nordic countries'. But it's not just geography that links these countries. They share a long, intertwined history and today share many environmental, social, political and economic issues – inflation, unemployment, immigration…Eurovision.

Sweden, Denmark and Finland are fully-fledged members of the European Union (EU) but Norway and Iceland are holding out. Both countries are members of the European Economic Area (EEA), which allows them to participate in most aspects of the European single market, but oil-rich Norway has sniffed at the idea of becoming a full member, rejecting it most recently in a 1994 referendum. Both Norway and Iceland are extremely protective of their fishing rights and fear they may lose some of their territorial waters and quotas under EU rules. Iceland spent many years during the so-called 'cod wars' with Britain fighting for its 200-mile exclusion zone and doesn't want to lose it now. Finland is the only Nordic country to adopt the euro – Denmark and Sweden have both rejected it at referendums.

In an age of global terrorism, Scandinavia has kept itself a safe distance from international conflict since WWII, although Sweden, Denmark, Finland and Norway all have some form of mandatory military service. Iceland has had the benefit of an American military base since 1951, but the US has announced imminent plans to pack up and move out, 15 years after the end of the Cold War. Presumably they need the troops elsewhere. In 2005, however, peace-loving Denmark managed to set off a chain of world-wide rioting, scores of deaths and the worst national crisis since WWII – all because of the publication of a cartoon. As part of a debate about religion, Islam, self-censorship and freedom of speech, Danish newspaper *Jyllands-Posten* published 12 caricatures of the Prophet Mohammed, any depiction of whom is a serious taboo according to the Islamic faith. The cartoons were reprinted by other European papers, sparking a firestorm of controversy and violence all over the world, but it was the Danes who got the blame. Critics called the cartoons Islamophobic and blasphemous while supporters claim they highlighted the importance of free speech and pointed out that cartoons about other religions are frequently printed. The controversy died down, but for a time Danes around the world feared for their safety.

Such an incident only fuelled the fears of many Scandinavians, not only in Denmark, about growing immigration. It's not that Scandinavians are overtly racist or unwelcoming, but immigration, particularly from asylum-seekers, is still quite new to the region and old attitudes die hard. The usual fears of foreigners taking local jobs, straining the generous welfare system and struggling with language difficulties do exist. In a small minority there's the more serious issue of isolated race-related violence and anti-Muslim sentiment. In Denmark, the government's increasingly hard-line attitude to immigration (such as limiting the right of asylum seekers to migrate to Denmark with their families) led to a censure from the likes of the Council of Europe and the Danish Red Cross over the country's role in upholding international human rights. Iceland (6%) and Finland (2%) have some of the lowest numbers of foreign residents in Europe.

Whales are still getting a hard time of it in Icelandic and Norwegian waters, and the issue is guaranteed to start some finger-pointing and divided opinion. While most of the world opposes whale-hunting, Iceland ended its own 14-year ban on whaling in 2003, allowing a quota of 500 whales to be hunted 'for scientific purposes'. This euphemism may not last since Iceland has plans to start commercial whaling by 2007. Icelanders on the whole support the decision, or at least their government's right to make it. One view is that an overpopulation of whales affects fish stocks, a major issue in Iceland and Norway since it's the backbone of their economy. Others say it's damaging the nation's international standing and, more tangibly, its multimillion-dollar whale-watching industry. In a publicised incident in 2006, a Norwegian ship actually harpooned a minke whale while a sickened boatload of tourists were 'spotting' it! Norway has been culling minke whales since 1993 and you'll find the average Norwegian fisherman willing to argue strongly in favour of it. At present, all whale meat is used for the domestic market, not export.

'Ski' is a Norwegian word and Norway lays claim to having invented the sport.

Declining fish stocks may have something to do with Iceland looking to heavy industry, tourism and technology to boost the economy. The first two don't go hand in hand, and projects such as the Kárahnjúkar hydroelectric project, which will flood a large area of eastern Iceland in order to power a massive new aluminium smelter, are seen by some as environmental suicide. Björk's mother, Hildur Hauksdóttir, famously staged a hunger strike in protest but most Icelanders are resigned to the fact that it's going ahead; it's scheduled to be operational by 2009.

On a lighter note, fascination with the royal families of Denmark, Sweden and Norway rarely wane, but it's been the Danes doing most of the celebrating lately with a royal wedding and royal baby. Crown Prince Frederik married Australian Mary Donaldson in 2004 and the fairytale continued in 2005 with the birth on 15 October of their son Prince Christian Valdemar Henri John. Meanwhile, the Swedes are still waiting for Crown Princess Victoria (heir to the Swedish throne) to hurry up and tie the knot, and the Norwegian Crown Prince and Princess had a second child in 2005.

There are about 1.6 million saunas in Finland – enough to hold the entire population.

Lycra-suited ABBA won Eurovision for Sweden in 1974, and neither the group nor the competition has lost any popularity in Scandinavia since. Eurovision parties are held each May and fans sit glued to TV screens to see if a Nordic country can pull it off again. But who would have thought that a group of heavy rockers, dressed in monster masks and hailing from Rovaniemi in Finland, would win it in 2006? Monster-rock band Lordi stormed the voting with *Hard Rock Hallelujah* and thus Helsinki will host in May 2007 for the first time. If you think that's trivial, the welcome home party for Lordi was estimated to be the biggest ever public gathering in Helsinki – around 90,000 people.

Young Scandinavians take considerable interest if you know a bit about their local music scene. Iceland is a great example. In Reykjavík, just about everyone under 30 seems to be in a band or producing their own CD of 'experimental music'. Everyone has heard of Björk and the Sugarcubes, but does anyone know the legendary Megas? Or the latest big thing, Cynic Guru? In Helsinki you could well bump into famous musicians at a bar or club. Heavy rock bands HIM and Nightwish are doing big things in Europe. In Norway, black metal is the word and Mayhem, Satyricon and Dark Throne some of the bands to see.

Blood on the Snow: The Killing of Olaf Palme by Jan Bondeson, recounts the still-unsolved murder of the Swedish prime minister in 1986.

Sport always makes for a good bar-stool topic. In Finland and Sweden ice hockey really stirs the emotions, especially when the two countries are playing against each other. Sweden hit gold in 2006, becoming the first nation in history to hold both the Olympic and world championship gold in the same year when it beat the Czech Republic in the championship tournament. Finland surprised Canada to take third place.

Denmark

Welcome to the happiest nation on earth. No really, it's official: according to a global survey by something called the World Database of Happiness (we promise we're not making it up), the Danes are the most contented folk on earth.

It's not hard to see why. Denmark (Danmark) is well-ordered, vastly wealthy and its general well being won't take much time to rub off on the visitor. Although smaller than its neighbours and lacking their wild natural grandeur, its appeal lies in a compelling mix of lively, modern cities, historic towns, neatly ordered farmland, graceful beech woods and sleepy islands. These islands are full of medieval churches, Renaissance castles and pretty harbours.

The biggest drawcard is Copenhagen, Scandinavia's largest and most cosmopolitan capital. It is home to superb museums, a vibrant cultural life and a burgeoning bar, café and restaurant scene. The regional capitals hold their own too: Århus and Odense are sophisticated and friendly university cities, brimming with art, music and lively nightlife. Beyond the cities lie treasures include haunting Neolithic burial chambers; the bodies of well-preserved Iron Age people exhumed from their slumber in peat bogs; and atmospheric Viking ruins that reflect the country's dramatic history and once mighty martial and maritime prowess. The sea remains a central part of Denmark's allure. Coastal attractions are numerous, including kilometres of white-sand beaches and a wealth of archipelagos and islands, including magical Bornholm, stuck out in the middle of the Baltic.

FAST FACTS

- **Area** 43,075 sq km
- **Capital** Copenhagen
- **Currency** Danish krone; €1 = Dkr7.45; US$1 = Dkr5.91; UK£1 = Dkr10.82; $A1 = Dkr4.42; CA$1 = Dkr4.88; NZ$1 = Dkr4.14; ¥100 = Dkr5.73
- **Famous for** Hans Christian Andersen, the Little Mermaid, bacon, Carlsberg beer, marauding Vikings
- **Official Language** Danish
- **Phrases** *jah/nie* (yes/no), *tak* (thanks), *farvel* (goodbye), *skål* (cheers)
- **Population** 5.45 million
- **Telephone Codes** country code ☎ 45; international access code ☎ 00
- **Visa** Not required for citizens of the EU, USA, Canada, Australia and New Zealand (see p111)

HIGHLIGHTS

- Soak up the cosmopolitan lifestyle of **Copenhagen** (p40), packed with historical interest, cool cafés, cutting edge-design shopping, cosy little bars and lively clubs.
- Sample the cultural, artistic and historical treasures as well as the lively nightlife of fashionable **Århus** (p82).
- Escape to empty beaches and extensive forests, and relax beside some picture-postcard ports on the idyllic island of **Bornholm** (p67).
- Canoe, cycle and generally take it easy in Jutland's low-key but delightful **Lake District** (p90).
- Watch angry seas collide above luminous **Skagen** (p99), on Denmark's slender northern tip.

ITINERARIES

- **One week** You'll need three days to see the best of the capital, then take a day trip by train to North Zealand's castles or historic Roskilde. Then it's a toss up between the west in Jutland taking in Århus and the north, or east far out to sea on sleepy Bornholm.
- **Two weeks** Follow the one-week route from the capital to Zealand, but go for an extended Jutland option taking in Ribe and the Lake District. Firstly, stop off on Funen, to see Odense and the island's pretty southern towns and the idyllic island of Ærø.

CLIMATE & WHEN TO GO

Compared to its Scandinavian neighbours Denmark has a relatively mild climate. May and June can be a delightful time to visit: the countryside is a rich green and you'll beat the rush of summer tourists (although rain and chill winds can never be ruled out).

July to August is peak tourist season with many open-air concerts, lots of street activity and beach basking. Other advantages to visiting in midsummer include longer opening hours at sightseeing attractions and potential savings on accommodation, as some business-oriented hotels drop their rates. Autumn is pleasant and can be a visual feast of golden colours in wooded areas. Winter is cold, dark and either wet or freezing.

HOW MUCH?

- **Danish pastry** Dkr9
- **Loaf of bread** Dkr12
- **Bottle of wine (takeaway)** Dkr55
- **Royal Copenhagen Porcelain souvenir mug** Dkr590
- **Cappuccino** Dkr25

LONELY PLANET INDEX

- **1L of petrol** Dkr9
- **1L bottle of water** Dkr12
- **Pint of Pilsner beer** Dkr30
- **Souvenir T-shirt** Dkr100
- **Smørrebrød (open sandwich)** Dkr30-70

HISTORY

Denmark was the ancient heart of Scandinavia: prehistoric hunter-gatherers from central and southern Europe moved north to what are now Jutland and Funen as the ice sheets retreated. Neolithic people settled on this new landscape in 4000 BC and by 500 BC Iron Age farms and trading centres were well established.

Only the haunting remnants of burial chambers and vestigial fortifications survive from prehistory. Some of the best are on the island of Møn (see p65). Present-day Denmark traces its linguistic and cultural roots to the arrival of the Danes, a tribe thought to have migrated south from Sweden around AD 500. In the late 9th century, warriors led by the Viking chieftain, Hardegon, conquered the Jutland Peninsula. The Danish monarchy, Europe's oldest, dates back to Hardegon's son, Gorm the Old, who reigned in the early 10th century. Centuries worth of Danish kings and queens are laid to rest in sarcophagi on dramatic display at Roskilde Cathedral (p62). Gorm's son, Harald Bluetooth, completed the conquest of Denmark and spearheaded the conversion of the Danes to Christianity; his story and his legacy is well showcased in the tiny, historical hamlet of Jelling (p89). Successive Danish kings sent their subjects to row their longboats to England and conquer most of the Baltic region. They

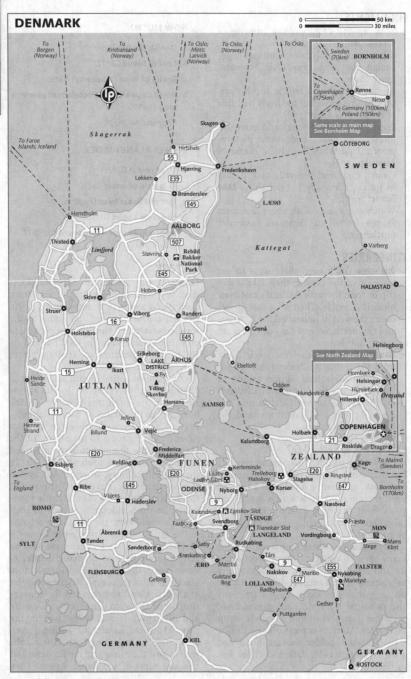

were accomplished fighters, swordsmiths, shipbuilders and sailors, qualities well-illustrated at the excellent Viking Ship Museum in Roskilde (p62).

In 1397 Margrethe I of Denmark established a union between Denmark, Norway and Sweden to counter the influence of the powerful Hanseatic League that had come to dominate the region's trade. Sweden withdrew from the union in 1523 and over the next few hundred years Denmark and Sweden fought numerous border skirmishes and a few fully fledged wars, largely over control of the Baltic Sea. Norway remained under Danish rule until 1814.

In the 16th century the Reformation swept through the country, accompanied by church burnings and civil warfare. The fighting ended in 1536, the Catholic Church was ousted and the Danish Lutheran Church headed by the monarchy established.

Denmark's 'Golden Age' was under Christian IV (1588–1648), with Renaissance cities, castles and fortresses flourishing throughout his kingdom. A superb example is Egeskov (p78) on Funen. In 1625 Christian IV, hoping to neutralise Swedish expansion, entered an ill-advised and protracted struggle known as the Thirty Years' War. The Swedes triumphed and won large chunks of Danish territory.

Literature, the arts, philosophy and populist ideas flourished in the 1830s, and Europe's 'Year of Revolutions' in 1848 helped inspire a democratic movement in Denmark, which overnight and in typically orderly Danish fashion adopted male suffrage and a constitution on 5 June 1849, forcing King Frederik VII to relinquish most of his power and become Denmark's first constitutional monarch. Denmark lost the Schleswig and Holstein regions to Germany in 1864.

Denmark remained neutral throughout WWI and also declared its neutrality at the outbreak of WWII. Nevertheless, on 9 April 1940, an unfortified Denmark faced either a quick surrender or a full-scale invasion by German troops massed along its border. The Danish government settled for the former, in return for an assurance that the Nazis would allow the Danes a degree of autonomy. For three years the Danes managed to walk a thin line, running their own internal affairs under Nazi supervision, until in August 1943 the Germans took outright control. The Danish Resistance movement mushroomed and 7,000 Jewish Danes were smuggled into neutral Sweden.

Although Soviet forces heavily bombarded the island of Bornholm, the rest of Denmark emerged from WWII relatively unscathed. Postwar Social Democrat governments introduced a comprehensive social welfare state in the postwar period, and Denmark provides its citizens with extensive cradle-to-grave social security.

Denmark joined NATO in 1949 and the European Community, now the EU, in 1973. The Danes offer tepid support for an expanding EU. Many fear losing local control to a European bureaucracy dominated by stronger nations. In 1993 they narrowly voted to accept the Maastricht Treaty, which established the terms of a European economic and political union, only after being granted exemptions from common-defence and single-currency provisions. They also voted not to adopt the euro in 2000.

In 2004 the already popular and much-loved royal family gave Danes a reason to celebrate its enduring appeal when the country's most eligible bachelor Crown Prince Frederik married Australian Mary Donaldson in a hugely popular and exhaustively covered fairy-tale wedding.

It has not all been fairytales though. Accustomed to being a blameless paragon of international virtue, Denmark has recently experienced criticism from some unusual quarters. Critics say its increasingly tough immigration laws are proof of creeping xenophobia and racism, earning it a rebuke from the European Council.

In 2006 Danes woke up to find themselves even less popular and widely vilified by Muslims (some of their embassies were the target of fire bombings). The cause? A cartoon by a Danish illustrator depicting the Prophet Mohammed (any image of whom is considered offensive by most Muslims) published in newspapers all over Europe.

PEOPLE

Danes are refreshingly self-effacing and reserved about themselves and their achievements. It springs from a long-standing belief among Danes that no-one should think of him- or herself as being better than the rest and that you should always keep your feet firmly on the ground.

Travellers will find Danes to be relaxed, casual and not given to extremes or to ostentation. They are tolerant of different lifestyles: in 1989 Denmark became the first European nation to legalise same-sex marriages.

Denmark's population is about 5.3 million, with 70% living in urban areas, 1.5 million of them in Copenhagen. Foreign nationals account for 7.8% of Denmark's population.

RELIGION

About 90% of Danes belong to the state-supported National Church of Denmark, an Evangelical Lutheran denomination, but less than 5% of the population are regular churchgoers.

ARTS

Literature

Hans Christian Andersen has long loomed large over Denmark's literary landscape, (see the boxed text, p75). Other notable literary Danes include religious philosopher Søren Kierkegaard, whose writings were a forerunner of existentialism, and Karen Blixen, who penned *Out of Africa* and *Babette's Feast*. One of Denmark's foremost contemporary authors is Peter Høeg, who had international success with his suspense mystery, *Miss Smilla's Feeling for Snow*.

Architecture & Design

Denmark is a leader in industrial design, with a style marked by cool, clean lines applied to everything from architecture to silverware and furniture (during your stay you'll more than likely park yourself on a chair designed by Arne Jacobsen, the godfather of Danish design). Denmark has produced a number of leading 20th-century architects, including Jørn Utzon who designed Australia's Sydney Opera House as well as the concert hall in Esbjerg (p102). The controversial new Copenhagen Opera House is the latest bold (some say grotesque) Danish design statement.

Cinema & TV

Babette's Feast, a film adaptation of Blixen's novel by Danish film director Gabriel Axel, won the Academy Award for Best Foreign Film in 1988. The following year, director Bille August won an Academy Award and the Cannes Film Festival's Palme d'Or for *Pelle the Conqueror,* adapted from the novel by Danish author Martin Andersen Nexø. Gudhjem harbour (p70) in Bornholm was used as a location for the film. In 1997 Bille August directed the film *Smilla's Sense of Snow,* an adaptation of Peter Høeg's novel. In 2000 Danish director and maverick Lars von Trier won the Cannes Film Festival's Palme d'Or for his film *Dancer in the Dark.* Nicolas Winding Refn is one of the upcoming Danish directors, who has produced the *Pusher* trilogy about Copenhagen's underworld.

Visual Arts

Before the 19th century Danish art was mainly formal portraiture, exemplified by the works of Jens Juel (1745–1802). A 'Golden Age' ushered in the 19th century with such fine painters as Wilhelm Eckersberg (1783–1853) and major sculptors such as Bertel Thorvaldsen (1770–1844).

Later in the century the 'Skagen School' evolved from the movement towards outdoor painting of scenes from working life, especially of fishing communities on the northern coasts of Jutland and Zealand. Much of it is exhibited at the Skagens Museum (p99). Leading exponents of the 'Skagen School' were PS Krøyer and Michael and Anna Ancher. In the mid-20th century, a vigorous modernist school of Danish painting emerged, of which Asger Jorn (1914–73) was a leading exponent. Much of his work is on display at the art museum in Silkeborg (p90).

Denmark's towns and cities contain a vibrant selection of home-grown and international contemporary art; even the smallest towns can surprise. Two of the best art museums and galleries outside the capital are the sprawling Brandts Klædefabrik (p73) in Odense and the Aros (p83) gallery in Århus.

Theatre & Dance

The Royal Danish Ballet, which performs in Copenhagen's **Royal Theatre** (☎ 3369 6969; Kongens Nytorv) from autumn to spring, is regarded as northern Europe's finest. The Royal Theatre is also the venue for the Royal Orchestra, Royal Opera and various theatrical performances.

ENVIRONMENT

The ecoconscious Danes are keen recyclers and world leaders in their use and export of alternative energy; almost 20% of Denmark's electricity is now supplied by the wind turbines dotted all over the country and it is the world's largest exporter of these turbines. Keen users of their own pedal power too, Danes are also increasingly interested in sourcing sustainable, organic and fair-trade food and goods, so it's an easy country in which to be environmentally responsible.

The Land

The Danish landmass has been heavily exploited by agriculture and 70% of its land is farmed mainly for barley and root crops, used to feed livestock. With almost 20% of farmland near sea level, many environmentally sensitive wetlands were made arable by draining. EU quotas now make farming such land less viable, and the Danish government has initiated an ambitious plan to restore the wetlands and re-establish marshes and streams throughout the country.

Wildlife

Still commonly seen in Denmark are wild hare, deer and many species of birds, including magpies, coots, swans and ducks. Returning the wetlands should help endangered species such as the freshwater otter make a comeback.

FOOD & DRINK

Staples & Specialities

You could live happily and inexpensively for days on the twin Danish delights of smørrebrød and wienerbrød. Nothing epitomises Danish food more than smørrebrød (literally 'buttered bread'), an open-faced sandwich that ranges from very basic fare to some elaborate sculptural creations. Typically, it's a slice of rye bread topped by roast beef, tiny shrimps, roast pork or fish fillet and various garnishes.

The butter-rich pastry known worldwide as a 'Danish' is called wienerbrød in Denmark, and nearly every second street corner has a bakery with mouth-watering varieties that go exceptionally well with a cup of coffee.

Typical Danish dishes include frikadeller (minced pork meatballs), kogt torsk (poached cod in mustard sauce), flæskesteg (roast pork with crackling), hvid labskovs (beef and potato stew) and hakkebøf (beefburger with fried onions). Then there's the koldt bord, a buffet-style spread of cold foods, including herring dishes, salads, cold cuts, smoked fish and cheeses. Smoked fish (particularly abundant and tasty on Bornholm), pickled herring and fried beef patties (served with a raw egg yolk, pickles and horseradish) are other common specialities.

Where to Eat & Drink

To enjoy a day sipping coffee, having a light lunch, devouring a hearty evening meal or indulging in a night of revelry, you may not have to stir from your seat in many of Denmark's excellent bar/café/restaurant hybrids which can buzz all day and night (in the main cities and towns at least).

Gourmets will be happy in Denmark, where there's an increasingly good (albeit pricey) choice of fine dining places. Copenhagen remains the culinary jewel in Denmark's crown though.

If you're on a tighter budget, never fear. The standard of food in many café/restaurants is impressively high and if you want to try the best, consider splashing out at the top-end places for lunch, when menus and courses are markedly cheaper.

The cheapest restaurant food is generally pizza and pasta; you can eat your fill for about Dkr55 at lunch, Dkr75 at dinner. Dagens ret (daily special) is usually the best deal on the menu, while the børn menu is for children.

Breakfast is usually a light continental buffet with white bread or bagels and a selection of meats or cheeses.

The Danes have increasingly taken to other world cuisines in recent years, including Thai, Japanese and Vietnamese food (most notably in Copenhagen).

Drinks

Denmark's Carlsberg and Tuborg lagers and Pilsners are ubiquitous. The most popular spirit in Denmark is caraway-spiced Aalborg aquavit; it's drunk straight down as a shot, followed by a chaser of beer. Øl (beer), vin (wine) and spirits are reasonably cheap compared to those in other Scandinavian countries. There are a few good microbreweries and pubs selling real ale in Denmark.

DENMARK

COPENHAGEN

pop 1.5 million

Cultured, convivial, cosmopolitan and compact, Denmark's capital Copenhagen (København) is one of the most attractive destinations in Northern European.

Copenhagen is a 1000-year-old city of cobbled squares and copper spires, home to the oldest monarchy in the world and fond of its traditions but, equally, it is a cutting-edge design capital with funky shops at every turn. Striking, modern glass and granite buildings house world-class museums of art and history such as Nationalmuseet (the National Museum) and Statens Museum for Kunst (the National Gallery), both of which now have free admission.

Once you have sated your culture lust, the city has an enticing array of cafés, restaurants and music venues where the locals retire for their dose of *'hygge'*, that untranslatable 'cosiness' that the Danes are so good at fostering. Candles burn day and night, winter and summer and you are never too far from an open fire and a glass of wine.

And just when you think you've got to know Copenhagen, you discover there are beautiful sandy beaches, wooded parks and elegant lakes just minutes away.

HISTORY

For more millennia than anyone can be sure of, Copenhagen was a fisherman's settlement on the shores of what we now call the Øresund Straits, the narrow belt of water between Denmark and Sweden.

Wendish pirates, who marauded the coast in the 12th century, prompted the locals, led by Bishop Absalon, to build a fort on a small island in the harbour – where the modern day Danish parliament stands on Slotsholmen (see p45); you can still see the foundations of the original fort in the cellar museum.

The city of København ('købe' means 'to buy', 'havn' is 'harbour') gradually grew to the north of Slotsholmen, where the restaurants of Gammel Strand now stand, founded on the wealth that came from the herring caught by the local fishermen; but it wasn't until the 15th century that Copenhagen took over as the capital of Denmark from Roskilde.

Denmark's great Renaissance king, Christian IV (1588–1648), transformed Copenhagen into an impressive capital. From there he controlled much of Scandinavia – with numerous ambitious buildings including Rosenborg Slot (p44) and the Rundetårn (p45). Eventually Christian IV brought the country to its knees with overspending and reckless foreign forays.

By the early 19th century the once mighty Danish empire was greatly diminished. Twice in the early 1800s the British navy bombarded the city but its people bounced back with a cultural 'Golden Age', led by the likes of Hans Christian Andersen and Søren Kierkegaard.

ORIENTATION

Whether travellers land at Copenhagen airport, just 12 minutes away from the city centre by train, or arrive from elsewhere in Europe or Scandinavia, most people's first view of Copenhagen is of its Central Station (Hovedbanegården). Just across the street, to the east of the station's main entrance, is Denmark's number one tourist attraction, Tivoli Gardens; beyond that is the town hall square (Rådhuspladsen), from where the

---

COPENHAGEN IN TWO DAYS

Soaking up the cool, casual vibe of the city centre by some easy sightseeing but with ample time for a leisurely smørrebrød lunch and some breaks for drinks in the **city-square cafés** (p50) is a good way to get a feel for Copenhagen's charm. In summer **Tivoli Gardens** (p43) is a good evening destination, especially during the Friday evening concerts.

On the second day choose between the **Nationalmuseet** (p44) and **Statens Museum for Kunst** (p44) and from the many sights around **Slotsholmen** (p45), and then either stroll around the alternative enclave of **Christiania** (p47) or round off the day with a relaxing **canal tour** (p48). In the evening, dine in the centre or strike out for the cafés, restaurants and bars of **Vesterbro** (p51).

city's main shopping street, Strøget (actually several connecting streets and squares), leads to the city's other main square, Kongens Nytorv. From here the ever-bustling quayside of Nyhavn, with its countless cafés, bars and restaurants, leads to the harbour.

INFORMATION
Bookshops
Nordisk Korthandel (www.scanmaps.dk; Studiestræde 26-30; ☻ 10.30am-5.30pm Mon-Fri, 9.30am-3pm Sat) Offers a superb but pricey collection of travel guides and maps. Foreign newspapers are available at the Central Station and a few newsstands on Strøget.

Discount Cards
Copenhagen Card (24hr card adult/child Dkr199/129, 72hr card Dkr429/249, adult card covers 2 children under 10yr) Secures unlimited travel on buses and trains around Copenhagen and North Zealand, and on the city's waterbuses. It also gives free or discounted admission to 60 of the region's museums and attractions. Cards are sold at the Wonderful Copenhagen tourist office, Central Station, major Danske Statsbaner (DSB) stations and at many hotels, camping grounds and hostels. If you want to tick off a lot of sights in a few days this card can be a real bargain but you should be aware that several of the city's attractions are either free or at least free one day of the week. Grab the *Copenhagen Card* guide from the tourist office, which lists the free travel, admission and discounts available or visit www.visitcopenhagen.dk for more information.

Internet Access
Boomtown (☎ 33 32 10 32; www.boomtown.net; Axeltorv 1-3; per hr Dkr30; ☻ 24hr) There's wi-fi access too.
Hovedbiblioteket (☎ 33 73 60 60; 15 Krystalgade; ☻ 10am-7pm Mon-Fri, 10am-2pm Sat) A public library offering free internet access on one of four computers for one hour, but you must book a slot or wait.
Use It (☎ 33 73 06 20; Rådhusstræde 13; ☻ 9am-7pm daily during summer; closed Sat & Sun during winter) Information centre for budget travellers that offers free internet access, within reasonable time constraints. For more on Use It, see Tourist Information.

Laundry
Istedgades Møntvask (Istedgade 45; wash & dry 10kg load Dkr40; ☻ 7am-9pm)

Left Luggage
Central Station (per 24hr small/large locker Dkr25/35, maximum 72hr; ☻ 5.30am-1.00am Mon-Sat, 6am-1am Sun) Lockers are in the lower level near the Reventlowsgade exit.

Use It (☎ 33 73 06 20; www.useit.dk; Rådhusstræde 13; ☻ 9am-7pm mid-Jun–mid-Sep; 11am-4pm Mon-Wed, to 6pm Thu, to 2pm Fri mid-Sep–mid-Jun) Available for storing luggage during the day.

Medical Services
Frederiksberg Hospital (☎ 38 16 38 16; Nordre Fasanvej 57) West of the city centre, has a 24-hour emergency ward.
Steno Apotek (Vesterbrogade 6c; ☻ 24hr) Pharmacy opposite Central Station.

Money
Banks, all of which charge transaction fees, are found throughout the city centre. Banks in the airport arrival and transit halls are open 6am to 10pm daily.

The **Forex exchange booth** (Central Station; ☻ 7am-9pm) has the lowest fees but you will find other exchange shops all along Strøget.

You'll find 24-hour, cash-exchange ATMs that exchange all major foreign currencies for Danish kroner, minus a hefty Dkr25 to Dkr30 fee, at **Den Danske Bank** (Central Station) and **Nordea** (Axeltorv).

Post
Central Station Post Office (☻ 8am-9pm Mon-Fri, 10am-4pm Sat & Sun)
Post Office (Købmagergade 33; ☻ 10am-5.30pm Mon-Fri, to 2pm Sat) Offers poste-restante services.

Tourist Information
Use It (☎ 33 73 06 20; www.useit.dk; Rådhusstræde 13; ☻ 9am-7pm mid-Jun–mid-Sep; 11am-4pm Mon-Wed, to 6pm Thu, to 2pm Fri mid-Sep–mid-Jun) First-class information centre aimed at young budget travellers, but open to all. It stores luggage for free (by day only), holds mail, offers free internet use and provides lots of useful information. *Playtime* is Use It's free annual guide to the city and surrounds.
Wonderful Copenhagen (☎ 70 22 24 42; www .visitcopenhagen.dk; Vesterbrogade 4a; ☻ 9am-4pm Mon-Fri, to 2pm Sat Jan-Apr & Sep-Dec, 9am-6pm Mon-Sat May-Jun, to 8pm Mon-Sat, 10am-6pm Sun Jul-Aug) This tourist information centre distributes the informative *Tourist in Copenhagen* as well as *Copenhagen This Week*, a free city map, and brochures covering all the regions of Denmark.

Travel Agencies
Kilroy Travels (☎ 33 11 00 44; www.kilroytravels.com; Skindergade 28; ☻ 10am-5.30pm Mon-Fri, to 2pm Sat)
Wasteels (☎ 33 14 46 33; Skoubogade 6; ☻ 9am-5pm Mon-Fri, 10am-noon Sat)

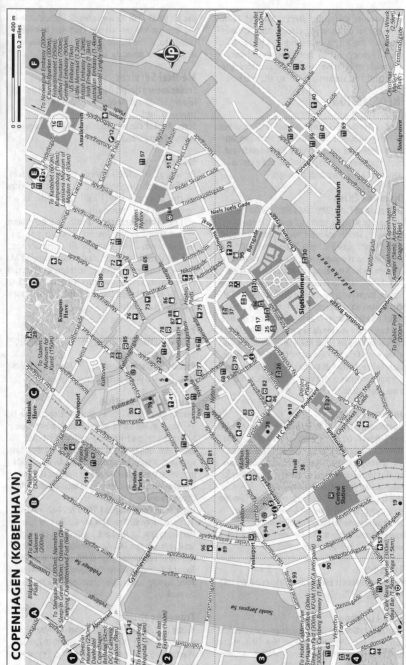

COPENHAGEN (KØBENHAVN)

SIGHTS

Allow at least three days to take in the best of Copenhagen's museums and sights, plus more time if you plan to explore some of its excellent shops. Copenhagen has stunning art, sculpture and history museums as well as myriad specialised, intriguing and just plain weird museums covering everything from erotica to porcelain, and there's probably some erotic porcelain to be found as well. For full details on opening times, addresses and admission fees pick up a copy of *Copenhagen This Week*.

Tivoli

Copenhagen's historic **amusement park** (☎ 33 15 10 01; www.tivoli.dk in Danish; adult/child Dkr75/35; ☯ 11am-11pm Sat-Thu, 11am-1am Fri mid-Apr–mid-Jun & mid-Aug–mid-Sep, 11am-midnight Sun-Thu, 11-1am Fri & Sat mid-Jun–mid-Aug) has been Denmark's number one tourist attraction pretty much since the day it opened over 160 years ago. At first glance, visitors more used to the

scale and glitz of Disneyland might wonder what the fuss is about, but Tivoli Gardens has a unique atmosphere and no-one can deny its appeal, particularly after dark when its wonderful illuminations work their magic. The gardens have an innocent, old-fashioned charm. There are flower beds, food pavilions, amusement rides, carnival games and various stage shows. The newest ride is Himmelskibe, an 80m-high carousel; the Demon, a corkscrewing roller coaster, and the 'dead drop' Golden Tower are two more high-adrenaline, stomach-lurching experiences. It's well worth checking out the free programme of Friday concerts (included in admission prices), with mostly Danish bands but occasionally more widely known artists such as Jamie Cullum or Sting. Fireworks light up the skies at 11.45pm on Saturday. Tivoli Gardens also opens for a short period in the run up to Christmas but with fewer rides and more schmaltz.

DENMARK

Nationalmuseet

For a whistle-stop tour through the history of Denmark, nothing can beat the **Nationalmuseet** (National Museum; ☎ 33 13 44 11; www.natmus .dk; Ny Vestergade 10; admission free; ☺ 10am-5pm Tue-Sun): here you will find the world's most extensive collection of Danish artefacts from the Palaeolithic period to the 19th century. Naturally, the stars of the show are the Vikings, those much maligned, but actually very sophisticated Scandinavian marauders. Highlights include Bronze Age burial remains in oak coffins and various examples of *lur* (musical horns) that were used for ceremony and communication, ancient rune stones, a golden sun chariot, the silver Gundestrip cauldron and Viking weaponry. But the displays don't stop with the Vikings; there are excellent collections covering the Middle Ages and Renaissance period too, plus delightful Egyptian and classical antiquities, as well as frequently changing special exhibitions. There's even a small **Children's Museum**.

Rosenborg Slot

This 17th-century **castle** (☎ 33 15 32 86; www .rosenborgslot.dk; adult/child Dkr65/free; ☺ 10am-4pm May & Sep, to 5pm Jun-Aug, 11am-3pm Oct, to 2pm Tue-Sun Nov-Apr), built by Christian IV in the Dutch Renaissance style, stands at the edge of **Kongens Have** (King's Gardens; admission free). There are glorious marbled and painted ceilings, gilded mirrors, Dutch tapestries, silver lions, and gold- and enamel-ware. The Royal Treasury is in the castle basement, which is home to the Danish crown jewels.

Statens Museum for Kunst

Denmark's national **gallery** (☎ 33 74 84 94; www.smk.dk; Sølvgade 48-50; admission free; ☺ 10am-5pm Tue & Thu-Sun, to 8pm Wed) houses an impressive collection of works from Danish artists, particularly those of the 19th-century 'Golden Age' such as Hammershøj and Eckersburg, in the original building; while the dramatic glass extension contains more modern works from international names like Picasso and Munch as well as more contemporary Danish artists such as Per Kirkeby, Søren Jensen, Michael Ancher, Richard Mortensen and CW Eckersberg.

Ny Carlsberg Glyptotek

This splendid **museum** (☎ 33 41 81 41; www .glyptoteket.dk; Dantes Plads 7, HC Andersens Blvd; adult/ child Dkr50/free, Wed & Sun free; ☺ 10am-4pm Tue-Sun), occupying a grand period building near Tivoli Gardens, has now received a thorough restoration programme. The museum's impressive collection features Etruscan

---

MY COPENHAGEN   *Michael Booth*

I honestly can't think of anywhere I'd rather live than Copenhagen. I like the pace of life here; compared to London, things are much more relaxed and not so relentlessly commercial. The city centre is just so beautiful, with all those Dutch-style town houses and some really quite outrageous public buildings. And I don't just mean things like the new Opera House or the Black Diamond (part of the Royal Library): the Danes have been bonkers architects ever since King Christian built the Rundetårn and invited his friend the Czar of Russia to drive up the tower in his horse-drawn carriage. Check out the dragon's-tail spire of the old Børsen, the original stock exchange building, or the spiralling spire of Vor Frelsers Kirke.

Since I moved here the standard of food has really improved. Although traditional Danish food is tasty, it's also quite heavy but a whole wave of young Danish chefs are rediscovering great local ingredients, such as game, fish and berries, and they're doing inventive, exciting things with these ingredients. Unless you want to spend a fortune, I would avoid the high-end restaurants: you can eat really well in cafés in Nørrebro or Vesterbro for a quarter of the price.

My only warning to visitors is that the Danes don't stand on ceremony. They don't apologise if you step on their foot, like the English do, and they can seem a bit brusque. But I promise you, they don't mean it. And they love speaking English. It took me years to learn Danish, because everyone would always speak to me in my own language.

Michael Booth's book about life in Denmark and his journey in the footsteps of Hans Christian Andersen, *Just As Well I'm Leaving* (p108) is published by Vintage.

art, 18th- and 19th-century paintings from France and Denmark (the Gauguins are particularly notable) and sculpture spanning five millennia (including over 30 works by Rodin). At its heart is a beautiful tropical winter garden with a café.

Danish Design Center
Denmark's **temple to design** (☎ 33 69 33 69; www.ddc.dk; HC Andersens Blvd 27; ☺ 10am-5pm Tue & Thu-Fri, to 9pm Wed, 11am-4pm Sat & Sun; adult/child Dkr40/free, admission free Weds after 5pm) has an excellent permanent exhibition of local design through the decades in the basement and a regularly changing temporary exhibition on the ground floor.

Slotsholmen
An island separated from the city centre by a moat-like canal on three sides and the harbour on the other side, Slotsholmen is the site of **Christiansborg Palace** (☎ 33 92 64 92) home to Denmark's parliament. There are many sites on the island, including a **theatre museum**, a museum housing the **royal coaches**, and a magnificent **Tøjhusmuseet** (armoury museum), but the grandest is the **Slots-og Ejendomsstyrelsen** (Royal Reception Chambers; ☎ 33 92 64 92; www.ses.dk; adult/child Dkr60/25 ☺ guided tours in English 11am, 1pm & 3pm May-Sep, 3pm Tue-Sun Oct-Apr), the ornate Renaissance hall where the queen entertains heads of state.

The **Ruins of Absalon's Fortress** (adult/child Dkr30/15; ☺ 10am-4pm, closed on Mondays during the winter) are the excavated foundations of Bishop Absalon's original castle of 1167 and of its successor, Copenhagen Slot. They can be visited in the basement of the present palace.

Thorvaldsens Museum (☎ 33 32 15 32; Bertel Thorvaldsens Plads; adult/child Dkr20/free; admission free Wed; ☺ 10am-5pm Tue-Sun) features grand statues by the famed Danish sculptor Bertel Thorvaldsen, who was heavily influenced by Greek and Roman mythology. Enter from the direction of Vindebrogade.

The **Royal Library** (☎ 33 47 47 47; Søren Kierkegaards Plads; ☺ 10am-7pm Mon-Sat) dates from the 17th century, but the focal point these days is its ultramodern walkway-connected extension dubbed the 'Black Diamond' for its shiny black granite façade. The sleek, seven-storey building houses 21 million books and other literary items such as Hans Christian Andersen's original manuscripts. The building itself is open for **visits and guided tours** (adult/child Dkr25/10; ☺ 10am-6pm) and has a café and restaurant.

Rundetårn
The **Round Tower** (☎ 33 73 03 73; Købmagergade 52; www.rundetaarn.dk; adult/child Dkr25/5; ☺ 10am-8pm Mon-Sat, noon-8pm Sun Jun-Aug, 10am-5pm Mon-Sat, noon-5pm Sun Sep-May) provides a fine vantage point for viewing the old city. It was built by Christian IV in 1642 as an astronomical observatory. Halfway up the 209m-high spiral walkway is a hall with changing exhibits. The tower houses the oldest functioning observatory in Europe and offers evening **astronomy programmes** (☺ 7-10pm Tue & Wed Sep-Dec, 1-4pm Sun Jun-Aug) and by day you may also be lucky enough to see a dramatic, live projection of the sun too.

Latin Quarter
Also known as Pisserenden (which should need no translation), the historic university quarter is a grid of narrow streets and half timbered town houses to the north of Strøget.

Climb the stairs of the **University Library** (enter from Fiolstræde) to see one quirky remnant of the 1807 British bombardment of Copenhagen – a cannonball in five fragments and the object that it hit, a book titled *Defensor Pacis* (Defender of Peace).

Opposite the university is **Vor Frue Kirke** (☺ 8am-5pm, closed to viewing during services & concerts), Copenhagen's neoclassical cathedral. The building dates from 1829, but stands on the site of earlier churches. Inside are imposing neoclassical statues of Christ and the 12 apostles, the most acclaimed works of the 'Golden Age' sculptor, Bertel Thorvaldsen. A couple of blocks east of the cathedral is the pretty square of **Gråbrdre Torv**, which has several medium-priced restaurants with outdoor seating. On the northern side of the Latin Quarter is **Kultorvet**, a lively square where you'll almost certainly find impromptu street entertainment on sunny days, as well as beer gardens, flower stalls and produce stands.

Gardens
The stretch of gardens along Øster Voldgade offers a refuge from the city traffic. **Kongens Have**, the large public park behind Rosenborg Slot, is a popular sunbathing spot.

FREE COPENHAGEN

Copenhagen is not the cheapest city in the world, so any freebies are most welcome. Following a trial period in early 2006, both the **Nationalmuseet** (p44) and **Statens Museum for Kunst** (p44) now have free admission all the time. And there are plenty of other free museums and sights in the city.

Always free

- Botanisk Have (p45) – botanical gardens northeast of the city centre
- Carlsberg Brewery Visitor Centre (above) – attraction located west of Vesterbro (and you get a free beer at the end)
- Freetown of Christiania (opposite) – a hippy-era enclave by the water
- Frihedsmuseet (opposite) – a collection based on the Danish resistance during WWII, and it's located on the waterfront

Free on Wednesdays

- Geologisk Museum – a museum situated in the northeastern corner of the Botanisk Have (p45)
- Post and Tele Museum – a collection of all things pertaining to the Danish post office (located inside the post office on Købmagergade; p41)
- Thorvaldsens Museum (p45) – a repository of the work and tomb of Denmark's greatest sculptor at the befitting location of Slotsholmen
- Orlogsmuseet – a museum on naval history, beside the canal in Christianshavn (above)
- Tøjhusmuseet (p45) – the armoury museum on Slotsholmen
- Danish Design Center (from 5pm to 9pm only; p45)

Free on other days

- Ny Carlsberg Glyptotek (free on Wednesday and Sunday; p44) – sculpture and painting museum, south of Tivoli Gardens.
- Københavns Bymuseet (free on Friday) – the city museum, on Vesterbrogade

The **Botanisk Have** (Botanical Gardens; main entrance is at Gothersgade 140; ☎ 35 32 22 22; 8.30am-6pm May-Sep, to 4pm Tue-Sun Oct-Apr) on the western side of Rosenborg Slot has fragrant trails. Its **Palmehus** (10am-3pm Mon, Tue, Thu & Fri; 1-3pm Wed, Sat, Sun & public holidays) is a large, walk-through glasshouse growing a variety of tropical plants.

Christianshavn

Most visitors come to the historic canal quarter to the east of the city centre to visit the alternative commune at Freetown of Christiania (opposite), but there is equal pleasure to be had in wandering beside the canals and visiting the quarter's pleasant cafés.

To get there, walk over the bridge from the northeastern side of Slotsholmen or you can take the Metro from Kongens Nytorv or Nørreport direct to Christianshavnstorv.

VOR FRELSERS KIRKE

Close to Freetown of Christiania is the 17th-century **Vor Frelsers Kirke** (☎ 31 57 27 98; www .vorfrelserskirke.dk; Sankt Annæ Gade 29; admission free, tower adult/child Dkr20/10; 11am-4.30pm Apr-Aug, to 3.30pm Sep-Mar, closed during services, tower closed Nov-Mar), which has an impressive baroque altar and an elaborately carved pipe organ, propped up by two unhappy looking decorative elephants. For a panoramic view of the city and across to Sweden, climb the 400 steps of the church's 95m-high spiral tower. The last 160 steps run spectacularly and dizzyingly along the outside rim, narrowing to the point where they disappear at the top.

Carlsberg Brewery

At the recently refurbished **Carlsberg Brewery Visitor Centre** (☎ 33 27 13 14; www.visitcarlsberg .com; Gamle Carlsberg Vej 11; 10am-4pm Tue-Sun), the free self-guided tours provide the low-down on the history of Danish beer. The experience is capped off with a sampling of the present-day product. Take bus No 6A westbound or the S-Tog (S-Train, whose 10 lines pass through Central Station) to Enghave station.

Waterfront

The home of the royal family since 1794 **Amalienborg Palace** (adult/child Dkr50/30; ☺ 10am-4pm) comprises four austere mansions surrounding the central square and guarded by sentries, who are relieved at noon by a ceremonial changing of the guard. You can view the interior of the northwestern mansion, with its royal memorabilia and the study rooms of three kings.

Inland along Frederiksgade is the splendid **Frederikskirken** (☎ 33 15 01 44; www .marmorkirken.dk; admission free, guided tour adult/child Dkr25/10; ☺ 10am-5pm Mon-Thu, noon-5pm Fri-Sun, dome tour 1pm & 3pm mid-Jun–Aug, 1pm & 3pm Sat & Sun Sep-May). It's known universally as Mar-morkirken (Marble Church) and the view from its great dome is spectacular.

Back on Amalienborg Plads, and 500m north along Amaliegade, is Churchill-parken, where you'll find **Frihedsmuseet** (admission free; ☺ 10am-4pm Tue-Sat, to 5pm Sun), with moving relics from the history of the Danish Resistance against Nazi occupation.

About 150m north of the Frihedsmuseet you pass the spectacular **Gefion Fountain** that features the goddess Gefion, ploughing the island of Zealand with her four sons yoked as oxen. Another 400m north along the waterfront is the statue of the unjustly famed **Little Mermaid** (Den Lille Havfrue) – a rather forlorn statue that is actually one of the least interesting of all Copenhagen's many sights.

The **Copenhagen Opera House** (☎ 33 69 69 69; www.operahus.dk; admission Dkr100) on the island of Holmen facing Amalienborg across the harbour is well worth a visit, even if you can't get a ticket (they sell out months in advance). The foyer is open to the public

---

THE 'FREETOWN' OF CHRISTIANIA

Christiania remains just as much a part of the conventional tourist itinerary of Copenhagen as it has been since a group of hippies and political activists founded this 'New Society' in the early 1970s – it's right up there with Tivoli Gardens as one of the 'most-visited' sights in the city and you will see coaches dispersing their tourists daily at the main gate.

But things are not quite as rosy in the alternative community, housed, ironically, in former army barracks by the old city moat and ramparts. The current government is not only hard-right on issues of immigration; it has also cracked down on Christiania's more squalid side. Gone is the world-famous Pusher Street, where soft drugs such as hash and cannabis resin were sold openly; that was wiped out in police raids in 2004.

But drugs, both hard and soft, continue to be widely sold in Christiania and so the raids have continued, making daily life for the people of Christiania tougher than ever and creating increasing bitterness and resentment on both sides. Senior police officers admit their heavy handedness has simply pushed the drug trade further underground, causing far greater social problems than when it was out in the open and monitored by Christiania's leaders. There is little doubt Christiania is a more violent place than it was ten years ago too, with drug turf wars leading to fights and even murders.

You can't help feeling that the tide is turning against Christiania. A Danish TV stunt in which undercover cameras filmed a presenter trying to build his own house in the commune without permission revealed its less welcoming side, not to mention the locals' complete lack of irony: they tore down the interloper's wooden hut and demanded that he leave.

Christiania still has the inexpensive cafés and restaurants, eccentric shops, clubs and galleries that make it well worth a visit and you can pass an absorbing afternoon wandering around the quieter 'residential' areas both in the historic barracks buildings and around the moat, where some of the more elaborate and ingenious makeshift waterside housing has helped create a kind of hippy-trippy mini-Seattle. The **information office** (☎ 32 95 65 07; www .christiania.org; Nyt Forum, Pusher Street; ☺ noon-6pm Mon-Thu, to 4pm Fri) organises guided tours most days in summer.

(there are two restaurants) and you can take a guided tour of Henning Larsen's controversial glass-fronted masterpiece with its vast roof, attacked by critics as ungainly and out of proportion in its waterfront setting.

ACTIVITIES
Swimming & Sunbathing

Weather permitting, there are reasonably good opportunities to swim and sunbathe on stretches of beach around 5km from the city centre at the spectacularly redeveloped **Amager Strand**; take the Metro to Lergravsparken and then walk east for about a kilometre (a new station is scheduled to open at Amagerstrand itself in 2007); or at Bellevue (see p55). But for central swimming you could brave the cold, salty but clean waters of the free public pool at Islands Brygge, right in the heart of the city (open only from June to August), although you might want to grease up, cross channel swimmer style first. Alternatively there's the heated circular indoor pool at the **DGI-byen centre** (☎ 33 29 80 00; www.dgi-byen.dk; Tietgensgade 65, Vesterbro) near the station.

TOURS
Quickshaw Tours

Copenhagen's '**quickshaws**' (☎ 35 43 01 22; www.rickshaw.dk in Danish; 30-min tour Dkr125) are twoseater, open carriages powered by fit young pedal-pushers. They operate daily and can be found at most main squares. They can also be used as taxis – the price starts at Dkr35 and you pay Dkr3 per minute thereafter. Each quickshaw seats two adults and one child.

Canal Tours

The best way to see Copenhagen is from the water. There are several ways to take a boat tour around the city's canals and harbour from April to mid-October. Multilingual guides give a lively commentary in English. **DFDS Canal Tours** (www.canaltours.dk; adult/child Dkr60/25), leave from the head of Nyhavn or the Marriott Hotel. Tours take 50 minutes, passing by the Little Mermaid, Christianshavn and Christiansborg Palace, and leave every half hour between 10am and 5pm. **Netto-Boats** (☎ 32 54 41 02; www.netto-baadene.dk; adult/child Dkr30/5) are cheaper, run the same times and depart from Holmens Kirke and from Nyhavn.

Canal boats also make an excellent, traffic-free alternative for getting to some of Copenhagen's waterfront sites. DFDS Canal Tours charges Dkr50 for a one-day 'waterbus' pass (Dkr25 for children) or Dkr30 per trip from mid-May to mid-September. The boats leave Nyhavn every 30 minutes between 10.15am and 4.45pm (to 5.45pm mid-June to mid-August) and make a dozen stops, including at the Little Mermaid, Nationalmuseet and Vor Frelsers Kirke (with no commentary), allowing you to get on and off as you like. The **HUR public transport system** (www.hur.dk in Danish) has a boat service linking the Royal Library, Nyhavn and Nordre Toldbod, near the Little Mermaid, every 20 minutes until 7pm.

Bear in mind that the tour boats have no roofs and the weather is ever-changing in Copenhagen harbour, so be sure to pack for all eventualities.

FESTIVALS

The **Copenhagen Jazz Festival** (☎ 33 93 20 13; www.jazzfestival.dk) is the city's largest music event, invigorating the whole city with 10 days of music in early July. The festival presents a wide range of Danish and international jazz (Herbie Hancock and Sergio Mendes are both regulars), blues and fusion music in over 500 indoor and outdoor venues, with music wafting out of practically every public square, park, pub and café from Strøget to Tivoli Gardens.

SLEEPING

Copenhagen's range of budget accommodation is much better now than it was a decade or even five years ago. The city boasts several modern, high-quality hostels in prime locations, as well as some good, new budget hotels. Camping options remain limited, however, not least by the weather.

The city's hotel quarter is centred on the area behind Central Station, on and around Istedgade. Here you will find numerous bland business hotels and medium-range chains. This also happens to be the city's red-light district, with some fruity shop window displays and the occasional group of rowdy winos and glazed addicts lingering in shop doorways to spice things up.

The tourist office can book rooms in private homes (Dkr300/450 for singles/doubles; there is a Dkr100 booking fee if you do it via the tourist office when you arrive, otherwise it is free over the phone or internet in advance). It also books unfilled hotel rooms, often at discounted rates. You can also visit the website www.bedandbreakfast.dk for B&B accommodation throughout Denmark.

Budget

Camping Charlottenlund Fort (☎ 39 62 36 88; www .campingcopenhagen.dk; Strandvejen 144, Charlottenlund; camp site per adult/tent Dkr80/25) This is 6km north of the city centre beside a delightful sandy beach overlooking the Øresund sea. Take bus No 14 for a half-hour trip.

Danhostel Copenhagen City (☎ 33 11 85 85; www .danhostel.dk; HC Andersens Blvd 50; dm Dkr150; ☿ all year) The newest and best of Copenhagen's hostels occupies a modern high-rise overlooking the harbour a short walk from the Central Station. With a reception that resembles a boutique hotel, a great café and a 25% discount on the facilities at the DGI-Byen swimming pool and sports centre included in the price, it is a good idea to book well in advance.

City Public Hostel (☎ 33 31 20 70; www.city-public -hostel.dk; Absalonsgade 8; dm Dkr140; ☿ early May–mid-Aug, 24hr reception) A central, well-run hostel with dorms sleeping six to 23; they are both mixed gender and separate gender. Breakfast costs Dkr25, or Dkr20 if it's included with the bed price. There is wi-fi access and an outdoor barbecue area.

Danhostel Copenhagen Bellahøj (☎ 38 28 97 15; www.danhostel.dk/bellahoej; Herbergvejen 8, Bellahøj; dm/d Dkr110; ☿ Feb-early Jan, 24hr reception; P ⌨) This is based in a quiet suburban neighbourhood with 250 dorm beds and a limited number of family rooms (doubles). You can take bus No 2A to Brønshøj from Rådhuspladsen or direct from the airport and get off at Fuglsangs Allé. The night bus is No 82N.

Danhostel Copenhagen Amager (☎ 32 52 29 08; www.danhostel.dk/copenhagen; Vejlands Allé 200, Amager; dm/d Dkr110/340; ☿ early Jan–mid-Dec; P ⌨) Located in an isolated part of Amager just off the E20 this is one of the largest hostels in Europe, with 528 beds in two-, three-, four- and five-bed rooms. Take bus No 5A from Rådhuspladsen to Sundbyvesterplads and change to bus No 77. Until 5pm Monday to Friday, bus No 46 runs from Central Station directly to the hostel.

Danhostel Lyngby (☎ 45 80 30 74; www.lyngbyhostel .dk; Rådvad 1, Lyngby; ☿ all year; dm Dkr115, d Dkr380) This idyllic hostel occupies an early 20th-century factory building in leafy Lyngby, and it's perfect for families. Take the S-train to Lyngby and then catch bus No 182 or 183.

Sleep-In Green (☎ 35 37 77 77; www.sleep-in-green .dk; Ravnsborggade 18; dm Dkr100; ☿ end-May-end-Oct; P ⌨) Located in Nørrebro, close to its cafés and bars, this hotel has 68 dorm beds sleeping eight, 20 or 38. Take bus No 5A, night bus 81N, or the S-train to Nørreport Station, then walk northwest on Frederiksborggade over the lake to Nørrebrogade.

Sleep-In Heaven (☎ 35 35 46 48; www.sleepin heaven.com; Struenseegade 7, Nørrebro; dm Dkr150; ☿ all year). This is a friendly, no-frills kind of place for younger travellers, with two 50-bed rooms and a small back yard. Take bus No 250S from Central Station, or walk there in around 20 minutes.

KFUM (YMCA Interpoint) (☎ 33 31 15 74; Valdemarsgade 15; dm Dkr95; ☿ late-Jul-mid-Aug; ☿ reception 8.30-11.30am, 3.30-5.30pm & 8pm-12.30am) The small 28-bed YMCA is in a quiet part of Vesterbro. Bed sheets (Dkr15), breakfast (Dkr25) and a kitchen are available. It's a 15-minute walk from Central Station (take Vesterbrogade west to Valdemarsgade), or you can take bus No 14 from Rådhuspladsen for around 12 minutes.

Midrange

Hotel Fox (☎ 33 95 77 55; www.hotelfox.dk; Jarmers Plads 3; minimum rate per adult Dkr475). This is the most exciting and radical hotel to arrive in Copenhagen in recent memory, perhaps ever, featuring one-off rooms, each of which are designed by a group of international artists and designers. The hotel reception transforms into a DJ bar by night and is as funky as they come. Located five minutes from the town hall square and Strøget, it's on the fringe of the Latin Quarter.

Cab Inn City (☎ 33 46 16 16; www.cabinn .com; Mitchellsgade 14; s/d/tr/q Dkr510/630/750/870; P ✗ ✄ ⌨) Cab Inns are modern, rather clinical but boast good facilities (including kettle and TV) and reliable levels of comfort (although the ship's cabin (cab-in, geddit?) style means small rooms and rather narrow bunk-style beds). This is the best located of all Copenhagen's Cab Inns, considering it's a short walk south of Tivoli Gardens. There's free foyer internet access.

DENMARK

Cab Inn Scandinavia (☎ 35 36 11 11; www.cabinn .com; Vodroffsvej 57; s/d Dkr510/630; **P**) This Cab Inn has 201 compact rooms in this chain's familiar Spartan style. The rooms are comfortable and have TV and private bathroom.

Cab Inn Express (☎ 33 21 04 00; www.cabinn.com; Danasvej 32-34; s/d Dkr510/630; **P**) A few blocks away from the Scandinavia is the third sister hotel.

Sømandshjemmet Bethel (☎ 33 13 03 70; http:// hotel-bethel.dk; Nyhavn 22; s/d Dkr595/795) Inside the tall, steepled period building in a great location on Nyhavn are bright, pleasant rooms. Some rooms have views of Nyhavn's quays, although you pay more for these.

Square (☎ 33 38 12 00; www.thesquare.dk; Rådhuspladsen 14; s/d Dkr950-2365/1360-2360) This cool new arrival on Copenhagen's town hall square could not be better located nor better equipped with attractive, modern, minimalist rooms and breakfast included. There are cheaper hotels in town, but few offer as much style for the money.

Hotel Rainbow (☎ 33 14 10 20; www.copenhagen -rainbow.dk; Frederiksberggade 25; r with/without bathroom Dkr940/750; **□**) Hotel Rainbow is a small, friendly and exclusively gay hotel in an excellent location right near the Rådhus end of Strøget, so the city's shopping, drinking and clubbing are at your feet. The hotel is on the top floor and has just a few bright and airy rooms. Use the street-level intercom. Book ahead. There is a two-night minimum stay from April to September.

Hotel Christian IV (☎ 33 32 10 44; www .hotelchristianiv.dk; Dronnings Tværgade 45; s/d with bathroom Dkr860/995) This simple, contemporary hotel located in the city centre close to Kongens Have makes every effort with its light, comfortable rooms and added extras like free wi-fi access, use of a nearby fitness centre and bikes for rent (Dkr100 per day).

Tiffany Hotel (☎ 33 21 80 50; www.hoteltiffany.dk; Halmtorvet 1; s/d Dkr945/1145) This is a better class of Vesterbro hotel with its elegant rooms and upmarket airs for reasonable prices (by Copenhagen standards, that is).

Hotel 27 (☎ 70 27 56 27; www.hotel27.dk; Løngangstræde 27; s/d Dkr1095/1295) This very centrally located hotel, just 220m from Tivoli Gardens and the town hall square, chucked out all its chintz during a recent renovation and is now the epitome of a contemporary Danish design hotel with many extras including cable TV and wi-fi internet connection.

Top End

Hotel Skt Petri (☎ 33 45 91 00; www.hotelsktpetri.com; Krystalgade 22; s/d from Dkr1295/1495; **P** ☒ **□**) Copenhagen's coolest luxury hotel, housed in a former department store right in the heart of the shopping district, is a contender for most stylish and best-located hotel in town. The rooms are cosseting, and some have balconies or enchanting city views or both. There's a gym and a magnificent, bright, high foyer just made for sipping cocktails and feeling fabulous in.

Hotel Guldsmeden Bertrams and Carlton (☎ 33 25 04 05/33 22 15 00; www.hotelguldsmeden.dk; Vesterbrogade 107 & 66; s/d Dkr945/1145; **P** ☒ **□**) The excellent Guldsmeden group now has two attractive and welcoming hotels in Copenhagen, both decked out in its characteristic French colonial style and both on Vesterbrogade. The Bertrams is a four star, the Carlton is a three star and thus is a couple of hundred kroner cheaper. Both hotels are a short walk from the city centre but close to the groovy shops, cafés and restaurants of Istedgade and Værndemsvej.

Copenhagen Admiral Hotel (☎ 33 74 14 14; www .admiralhotel.dk; Toldbodgade 24-28; s/d Dkr775/1105, with harbour view Dkr1165/1435; **P** ☒ **□**) This grand place on the waterfront near Nyhavn occupies a renovated 18th-century granary. Its 366 rooms are crisscrossed with thick wooden beams, and blend period charm and modern conveniences. It's reasonably priced when you bear in mind the décor and location. Breakfast is, however, an extra Dkr115.

EATING
Around Strøget

Café Zirup (☎ 33 13 50 60; Læderstræde 32; mains Dkr80-120, brunch Dkr89; ☾ 11am-midnight Mon-Thu, to 2am Fri & Sat, 10am-midnight Sun) Usually packed inside and out, Zirup serves fresh, light fusion food. It's known for its hangover cures.

Huset Med Det Grønne Træ (☎ 33 12 87 86; Gammel Torv 20; ☾ 11.30am-3.30pm Mon-Fri, open Sat during Nov-Feb only) This traditional Danish lunch restaurant in a cellar just off Strøget is a great place to come to get an idea of how Danes used to eat before wraps, bagels and sushi arrived in town. Their smørrebrød are excellent and cheap (Dkr39 to Dkr95) and it has 14 different kinds of schnapps.

La Glace (☎ 33 11 46 46; www.laglace.dk; Skoubougade 3; ☾ 8.30am-5.30pm Mon-Thu, to 6pm Fri, 9am-5pm Sat, 11am-5pm Sun, closed Sun Apr-Sep) The best and oldest cake shop in Copenhagen serves sensational gateaux for Dkr36 a slice and does a wicked hot chocolate.

Peder Oxe (☎ 33 11 00 77; Gråbrødre Torv; mains Dkr100-200) An old favourite with visitors and locals alike in a historic building in the cobbled square just north of Strøget, Peder Oxe serves quality fish and organic meat dishes with a fine salad buffet. There's a cosy wine bar downstairs.

Riz Raz (☎ 33 15 05 75; Kompagnistræde 20; day/evening buffet Dkr59/69; ☽ 11.30am-11pm) Regularly voted one of the city's best cheap eats in the media, Riz Raz offers a great value southern Mediterranean buffet, and plenty of outside seating. There are good meat mains too (Dkr99 to Dkr139). Riz Raz also has a second branch in the Latin Quarter at Store Kanikkstræde 19.

Wokshop Cantina (☎ 33 91 61 21; Ny Adelgade 6; soups Dkr55-95; curry Dkr95; ☽ noon-2pm & 5.30pm-10pm Mon-Fri, 6-10pm Sat) This basement canteen in a street just off Kongens Nytorv (beside the grand Hotel d'Angleterre) serves excellent and cheap Thai staples.

Strøget has an abundance of cheap fast-food joints including hole-in-the-wall kebab joints selling falafels and kebabs for under Dkr30.

The Latin Quarter

Atlas Bar/Flyvefiskeren (☎ 33 15 03 52; Larsbjørnstræde 18; ☽ noon-midnight Mon-Sat) Atlas Bar is an enduringly popular semi-subterranean corner restaurant in the heart of the Latin Quarter. Its globally inspired blackboard menu changes regularly but there is always a good vegetarian option and the portions are generous. You can eat very well here for under Dkr100.

Studenterhuset (☎ 35 32 38 61; Købmagergade 52; sandwiches Dkr30; ☽ noon-midnight Mon-Fri) This is a relaxed student hang-out with drinks and light eats, including vegetarian or meat sandwiches.

Nørrebro

Nørrebro is a great place to eat with countless cool cafés and bars. Head for Elmegade for contemporary takeaways (sushi, bagels, sandwiches, coffee, beer), Blågardsgade for healthy snacks, or Sankt Hans Torv for stylish cafés and ice-cream parlours, and there is the nightclub Rust around the corner.

Kaffe Salonen (☎ 35 35 12 19; Peblinge Dossering 6; ☽ 8am-midnight Mon-Fri; 10am-midnight Sat & Sun) Salonen's floating deck, located on one of the elegant city lakes between the centre and Nørrebro, is its chief attraction, especially during the summer, but the food (standard Copenhagen café fare) is excellent and reasonably priced, such as vegetarian pasta for Dkr89. It also has wi-fi connection.

Nørrebro Bryghus (☎ 35 30 01 30; www.noerrebro bryghus.dk; Ryesgade 3; ☽ 11am-midnight Mon-Wed, 11-2am Thu-Sat, to 10pm Sun; lunch dishes under Dkr100, evening mains around Dkr189) Copenhagen's contemporary beer cathedral brews its own lager, stout, ale and *weiss* beers in-house and serves good brasserie food to a cool, young clientele. The areas to mingle range over two floors with a beer bar and restaurant; over these tower the giant brewing vats.

Vesterbro

Lê Lê (☎ 33 22 71 35; Vesterbrogade 56; ☽ 4pm-10.30pm Wed-Mon) You can eat fantastic, large bowls of noodles and curry for under Dkr100 in this light, modern Vietnamese/Thai restaurant on busy Vesterbrogade (next to Hotel Guldsmeden and close to the City Public Hostel).

Spicylicious (☎ 33 22 85 33; Istedgade 27; www .spicylicious.dk; mains Dkr80-110; ☽ 5pm-midnight) What used to be a fairly traditional Thai place is now a simple, modern Thai-Vietnamese restaurant and takeaway serving delicious rice, noodles, curries and soups for very reasonable prices. It has been voted the best cheap dinner in a recent online poll.

Elsewhere in Central Copenhagen

Cap Horn (☎ 33 12 85 04; Nyhavn 21; mains Dkr110-200; ☽ 9am-11pm) Amid many a middling canalside restaurant, Cap Horn stands out, serving excellent, fresh Danish seafood including a seafood plate with crab claws, double smoked salmon and crayfish terrine for Dkr165.

Cascabel Madhus (☎ 33 93 77 95; Store Kongensgade 80-82; salads Dkr30-50; ☽ 11am-5pm Mon-Fri) This light, bright lunch place is excellent for vegetarians and lies close to Marmorkirken and Amalienborg in the 'royal' part of town.

Produce market (Israels Plads; ☽ 9am-5pm Mon-Fri, to 2pm Sat May–Sep) This is the main city produce market, just a few minutes' walk west of Nørreport Station. On Saturday it doubles as a flea market.

DENMARK

Christianshavn & Christiania

Christianshavns Bådudlejning (☎ 32 96 53 53; Overgaden neden Vandet 29; fish & meat mains Dkr125-140; ⏰ 10am-midnight May-Oct) This deservedly popular place on a canalside deck does tasty sandwiches (Dkr50) and salads (Dkr60 to Dkr70). You can hire rowing boats as well.

Café Wilder (☎ 32 54 71 83; Wildersgade 56; mains Dkr115; ⏰ 9am-midnight) This bohemian corner café serves good salads and pastas by day and French brasserie food by night to a groovy local crowd.

Morgenstedet (Langgaden; mains Dkr35; ⏰ noon-9pm Tue-Sun) This long-established vegetarian and vegan place has a pretty garden in the heart of Christiania. Its dish of the day – usually a curry – is Dkr52.

Spiseloppen (☎ 32 57 95 58; Loppebygningen; fish & meat mains Dkr155-215) The food at this Christiania legend is reliably good. Roast lamb with tzaziki and chips and baked aubergine, or braised turbot with duchesse potatoes are two examples from the ever-changing global menu.

Lagkagehuset (☎ 32 57 36 07; www.lagkagehuset .dk; ⏰ 6am-7pm) One of the best bakeries in town lies right in the heart of Christianshavn and is highly recommended for sandwiches (Dkr39) and salads (Dkr39). It was recently voted best shop in Copenhagen.

Spicey Kitchen (☎ 32 95 20 29; Torvegade 56; ⏰ 2pm-midnight; main Dkr45-70) There are few Indian restaurants in Copenhagen where you can eat as cheaply and as satisfyingly as this and, with its canteen atmosphere, you are sure to strike up a conversation with neighbouring diners.

DRINKING

Visitors are utterly spoilt for choice as far as cafés and bars go in Copenhagen. Many are jack-of-all trade places, they are as good for food as they are for a lively evening spent drinking Pilsner or an afternoon sipping coffee. Nørrebro and Vesterbro (especially along Istedgade, east of the red-light district, and Halmtorvet, closer to the station) are well worth exploring.

Zoo Bar (☎ 33 15 68 69; Kronprinsensgade 7; ⏰ 11am-midnight Mon-Wed, 11am-2am Thu-Sat) This small bar and café attracts an artsy, clubby crowd by night, drawn by its regular DJs who play Thursday to Saturday.

Café Bang & Jensen (130 Istedgade) Small and a fair trek from the centre, this is just one of many hip little bars on this earthy, vibrant street in Vesterbro. We choose this bar-cum-café for its reliably relaxed but buzzing atmosphere.

Charlie's Bar (☎ 33 32 22 89; Pilestræde 33) Charlie's is tiny, cosy, scruffy and hugely popular with Pilsner-sated Danes who worship enthusiastically at this temple to the gods of real British cask ale. There's a small but very well-chosen selection of bitters and stouts and some wonderful and pricey rare single-malt whiskies.

Ideal Bar (☎ 33 25 70 11; Enghavevej 40) A young, hip crowd hangs out here, often for pre-clubbing drinks before heading next door to Vega Nightclub (opposite). The music at Ideal is pumping, danceable and mostly excellent, ranging from hip-hop to more raga-based and African-style sounds.

Kafe Kys (☎ 33 93 85 99; Læderstræde 7; ⏰ 10am-2am) Kys is one of the most popular cafés in town; it's always packed with a young clientele taking a break from shopping or on their way out for the night. It also serves sandwiches and has an extensive cocktail list.

Café Zeze (☎ 33 14 23 90; Ny Østergade 20; ⏰ 8am-midnight Mon-Thu, 8am-2am Fri, 9-2am Sat) During the day this is a great value lunch place for the advertising and fashion people who work in the area. It serves excellent sandwiches for Dkr79. By night Zeze transforms into one of the city's most popular preclub destinations and it throngs at weekends with the city's chic and sexy in their 20s and 30s.

Joe & the Juice (Ny Østergade 11; ⏰ 9am-7pm Mon-Sat) This is one of the few fresh fruit-juice bars in town.

ENTERTAINMENT

Though weekday nights can be a little quiet, Copenhagen really revs into gear from Thursday to Saturday when it turns into a genuine 24-hour party city. Club admission is usually around Dkr50 to Dkr60, but you can often get in for free before a certain time in the evening. Alternatively, you will often find that the café where you had lunch transforms into a DJ bar in the evening – check out Bodega Zeze and Zoo Bar.

Major international rock acts often play the national stadium, Parken in Østerbro, at Forum in Frederiksberg or Valbyhallen in Valby, a little further out of town, although you can just as easily catch the likes of Prince or Jamie Cullum playing at Vega. Visit www.aok.dk for full listings. *Copenhagen This Week* also lists concerts and entertainment schedules in detail.

Live Music

Rust (☎ 35 24 52 00; www.rust.dk; Guldbergsgade 8; admission varies) Rust is a Copenhagen club scene stalwart and continues to pack a university-age crowd in from Wednesdays through to the weekend with DJs and live music in a multilevel location with two dance floors, a lounge bar and cocktail bar. It is located in the heart of groovy Nørrebro, just around the corner from the café square Sankt Hans Torv. The music runs the full gamut from disco to hip-hop, although the club was an electronic pioneer in its infancy. Expect to wait in line at weekends.

Studenterhuset (☎ 35 32 38 61; Købmagergade 52; admission varies) The students' house welcomes all with themed nights (Tuesday is Gay Day; Wednesday is International Evening; Thursday is live jazz, Friday is live rock, and Saturday varies). There's a very cheap beer happy hour from noon to 7pm. During the daytime it's a café serving cheap sandwiches.

Vega (☎ 33 25 70 11; www.vega.dk; Enghavevej 40) Far out at the western end of the Vesterbro district, this place remains one of the city's cooler venues staging hugely popular Friday and Saturday night sessions. Big-name rock bands and underground acts play the 'Big Vega' 1500-capacity venue. Admission is free to the Vega Natklub (11pm to 5am Friday and Saturday) if you arrive before 1am, Dkr70 thereafter.

Copenhagen Jazz House (☎ 33 15 26 00; Niels Hemmingsensgade 10) This is the city's leading jazz spot with a terrific ambience. Danish musicians and occasional international names feature, and after concerts on Thursday, Friday and Saturday nights, the place becomes a lively disco from 1am to 5am (admission Dkr65).

Mojo (☎ 33 11 64 53; Løngangstræde 21; Dkr50; 🕑 8pm-3am) Small, scruffy and friendly, this is a prime spot for blues. Bands play most nights of the week.

Huset (☎ 33 15 20 02; Rådhusstræde 13) Placed in the same courtyard as Use It, you'll find the Huset complex with a cinema, theatre, café and restaurant. There's often music, including good-quality jazz. Many music events are free, but it costs about Dkr50 for special events.

Loppen (☎ 32 57 84 22; Loppebygningen, Christiania; Dkr50-70; 🕑 nightclub 2-5am Fri & Sat) This is a celebrated and much-loved veteran of the Copenhagen live-music scene that hosts bands playing everything from soul to punk rock on various nights, and runs a late disco.

Gay & Lesbian Venues

Copenhagen has a few gay and lesbian bars and clubs, and there's a great ease and confidence about gay life in this most civilised and tolerant of cities. For more information and listings check *Out and About*, a guide to Copenhagen gay life, or the annual *Gay and Lesbian Guide to Copenhagen*, both available in gay cafés and clubs.

Boiz (☎ 33 14 52 70; www.boiz.dk; Magstræde 12-14; 🕑 4pm-3am Mon-Thu, 4pm-5am Fri & Sat) Copenhagen's latest gay venue is on the first floor of Huset and has a lively bar, restaurant and dance floor, with open-air dining in summer.

Club PAN (☎ 33 11 37 84; Knabrostræde 3; Dkr60; 🕑 11pm-6am Thu-Sat) The largest gay club in Denmark with five levels, two dance floors, seven bars and entertaining cross-dressing and karaoke nights.

Oscar (☎ 33 12 09 99; www.oscarbarcafé.dk; Rådhuspladsen 77; 🕑 noon-2am, kitchen noon-10pm) A popular corner café meeting place for gays and lesbians near the Rådhuspladsen. It's a good place to get up to speed with what is happening on the gay scene in Copenhagen.

Kvindehuset (The Women's House; Gothersgade 37) Kvindehuset stages various dance nights for lesbians and has a café and bar.

Masken (Studiestræde 33; 🕑 4pm-2am Mon-Thu, to 5am Fri & Sat, 3pm-2am Sun) Small, smoky and popular with students at weekends, not least because of its special drinks prices, Masken is friendly and puts on no airs or claims to being hip.

Cinemas

There are numerous cinemas showing first-release movies, and most of them lie within 200m of Rådhuspladsen. It is customary in Denmark to show foreign-language films in the original language with subtitles.

DENMARK

SHOPPING

Shoppers are lured to Copenhagen above all by its local designers – whether they are working with textiles, clothing, household objects or art. Wherever you go in the city you will find small, independent designers but even on Copenhagen's main shopping street, **Strøget**, you will find plenty of unique retailers selling glassware, silverware, porcelain, clothing and jewellery. Your one-stop designer shop should be **Illums Bolighus** on Amagertorv, Strøget. Nearby are the **Illum department store** and the **Royal Copenhagen** silver and porcelain stores, which are great for gifts, albeit costly. For cheaper, 'street' clothes and contemporary designs **Istedgade** in Vesterbro is a fertile hunting ground as is the **Latin Quarter** – the latter is also home to many of the city's record shops. Copenhagen's high fashion street is **Kronprinsensegade**, but you will find the cheaper clothing chains on nearby **Købmagergade**.

For an excellent array of stores catering to outdoor pursuits, head to Frederiksborggade north of Nørreport Station. Meanwhile, for high-end antiques Bregade is good, but for a more bric-a-brac feel **Ravnsborggade** in Nørrebro is hard to beat, with over a dozen fascinating junk-antique stores. If the weather drives you indoors, you could head for the city's two malls, Fisketorvet, in Sydhavn and Fields on Amager. Both have a large range of middling clothing and household stores as well as cafés and restaurants.

Nearly everything closes on Sunday, although some grocers and supermarkets remain open in residential areas, such as Istedgade and Nørrebrogade.

GETTING THERE & AWAY

Air

Copenhagen's modern international airport is in Kastrup, 10km southeast of the city centre. Flights connect frequently with most major Danish and Scandinavian destinations. Many airline offices are north of Central Station near the intersection of Vester Farimagsgade and Vesterbrogade.

Boat

The ferry to Oslo, operated by **DFDS Seaways** (☎ 33 42 30 00; www.dfdsseaways.co.uk; Dampfærgevej 30), departs from the Nordhavn area north of the city (past Kastellet).

Bus

International buses leave from Central Station; advance reservations on most routes can be made at **Eurolines** (☎ 33 88 70 00; Reventlowsgade 8).

Car & Motorcycle

The main highways into Copenhagen are the E20, which goes west to Funen and east to Malmö, Sweden; and the E47, which connects to Helsingør. If you're coming into Copenhagen from the north on the E47, exit onto Lyngbyvej (Rte 19) and continue south to get into the heart of the city.

As well as airport booths, the following rental agencies have city branches:

Avis (☎ 33 15 22 99; Kampmannsgade 1)
Budget (☎ 33 55 05 00; Helgolandsgade 2)
Europcar (☎ 33 55 99 00; Gammel Kongevej 13)
Hertz (☎ 33 17 90 20; Ved Vesterport 3)

A fair trek from the centre at Amager Strand, **Rent A Wreck** (☎ 70 25 26 70; Amagerstrandvej 100) hires out battered but usually reliable old wagons from as little as Dkr363 per day. Rates are even more competitive on longer hires. The downside is having to drive around with the company name emblazoned on the doors.

Train

Long-distance trains arrive and depart from Central Station (Hovedbanegården), a huge complex with numerous eateries and all sorts of services. There are even public showers (Dkr15; towel hire Dkr6) located at the underground toilets opposite the police office.

There are three ways of buying a ticket, and the choice can be important depending on how much time you have before your train leaves. *Billetautomats* are coin-operated machines and are the quickest, but only if you've mastered the zone-system prices. They are best for S-train tickets. If you're not rushed, then **DSB Billetsalg** (✆ 8am-7pm Mon-Fri, 9.30am-4pm Sat) is best for reservations. There's a numbered-ticket queuing system. **DSB Kviksalg** (✆ 5.45am-11.30pm) is for quick ticket buying, although queues can build up quite a bit at busy times (ie rush hour). Alternatively you can make reservations at www.dsb.dk, which has an English language option.

GETTING AROUND
To/From the Airport
A train links the airport with Central Station (Dkr27, 12 minutes, three times hourly). The airport is 15 minutes and about Dkr180 from the city centre by taxi.

Bicycle
At Central Station beneath platform 12, **Københavns Cykler** rents out bicycles for Dkr75 a day.

If you just want to ride in the city centre, look for a free-use City Bike; they've got solid spokeless wheels painted with sponsors' logos. There are approximately 125 City Bike racks scattered throughout central Copenhagen, although available bikes are often few and far between. If you're lucky enough to find a bike rack with an actual bike in it, all you have to do is deposit a Dkr20 coin in the stand to release the bike. You can return the bicycle into any rack to get your money back. Except during weekday rush hours, you can carry bikes on S-trains for Dkr10.

Bus & Train
Copenhagen has a large public-transport system consisting of a small but excellent new underground and overground driverless Metro system (trains run a minimum of every three minutes); an extensive metropolitan rail network called S-Tog (S-Train), whose 10 lines pass through Central Station (København H); and a vast bus system, whose main terminus is nearby at Rådhuspladsen.

Buses, Metro and trains use a common fare system based on the number of zones you pass through. The basic fare of Dkr18 for up to two zones covers most city runs and allows transfers between buses and trains on a single ticket as long as they're made within an hour. Third and subsequent zones cost Dkr9 more with a maximum fare of Dkr63 for travel throughout North Zealand. Alternatively get a 24-hour pass allowing unlimited travel in all zones for Dk105/53 per adult/child. Two children under 12 travel free when accompanied by an adult.

On buses, fares are paid to the driver when you board, while on S-trains tickets are purchased at the station and then punched in the yellow time clock on the platform (it is not necessary to punch tickets bought from *billetautomats*).

Trains and buses run from about 5am to 12.30am, though buses continue to run through the night (charging double fare) on a few main routes. For schedule information about buses, call ☎ 36 13 14 15; for trains call ☎ 33 14 17 01.

Car & Motorcycle
With the exception of the weekday-morning rush hour, when traffic can bottleneck coming into the city (and going out around 5pm), traffic is usually manageable. Getting around by car is not problematic other than the usual challenges of finding parking spaces. Still, it's far better to explore sights within the city centre on foot or by using public transport.

For kerbside parking, buy a ticket from a streetside *parkomat* and place it inside the windscreen. Parking costs from Dkr10 to Dkr25 depending on how close you are to the city centre. Overnight kerbside parking is generally free and finding a space is not usually too much of a problem.

Taxi
Taxis with signs saying '*fri*' (meaning 'free') can be flagged down or you can phone ☎ 35 35 35 35. The basic fare is Dkr19 plus Dkr11 per kilometre between 7am and 4pm, Dkr11 between 4pm and 6am, and Dkr14 from 11pm to 7am Friday to Saturday. Fares include a service charge, so tipping is not expected. All taxis accept credit cards.

AROUND COPENHAGEN
Klampenborg
Klampenborg is a favourite spot for family outings from Copenhagen. It is only 20 minutes from Central Station on the S-train's line C (Dkr34). **Bellevue Beach**, 400m east of Klampenborg Station, is a sandy strand that gets packed with sunbathers in summer. A large grassy area behind the beach absorbs some of the overflow. A 10-minute walk west from the station is **Bakken** (☎ 39 63 73 00; Dyrehavevej 62; ⏰ noon-midnight Apr–late-Aug), the world's oldest amusement park. A blue-collar version of Tivoli Gardens, it's a pleasantly old-fashioned carnival of bumper cars, slot machines and beer halls.

DENMARK

Bakken is on the southern edge of **Dyrehaven**, an extensive expanse of beech woods and meadows crossed with peaceful walking and cycling trails. Dyrehaven was established in 1669 as a royal hunting ground and is the capital's most popular picnic area – it's great for cycling and running too. At its centre, 2km north of Bakken, is the old manor house **Eremitagen**, a good vantage point for spotting herds of deer.

Louisiana Museum of Modern Art

Denmark's foremost modern **art museum** (☎ 49 19 07 19; www.louisiana.dk; Gl Strandvej 13; adult/ child Dkr80/free; ☒ 10am-5pm Mon-Tue & Thu-Sun, to 10pm Wed) is housed in several low-level galleries atmospherically located beside the Øresund sea. It is surrounded by beautiful grounds full of sculptures by the likes of Henry Moore and Alexander Calder. The museum's permanent collection features works by Giacometti, Picasso, Warhol, Rauschenberg and many more, and there are outstanding changing exhibitions. It's a terrific spot even if you're not passionate about modern art. There's also a diverting **Children's Wing** and a lakeside **garden**, café and restaurant with fantastic views across the water to Sweden.

The museum is a 10-minute walk north on Strandvej from Humlebæk Station, which is 35 minutes on the S-train's line C from Copenhagen (Dkr63).

Ordrupgaard

For years this modest **country manor** (www .ordrupgaard.dk; Vilvordevej 10, Charlottenlund; ☒ noon-4pm Tue-Sun; adult/child Dkr65/free) to the north of Copenhagen was a quiet, little-visited art museum with a small collection of actually rather fabulous paintings. That all changed when a certain Zaha Hadid was commissioned to design an extension to the museum. Having the world's most famous female architect design a new gallery shone the spotlight on this charming collection of 19th-century art, both Danish (Johannes Larsen, Wilhelm Hammershøj and Joakim Skovgaard are well represented, but there are plenty of others) and international (including Gauguins, Corots and Pisarros). To get here, take the S-train to Lyngby and then bus No 388 will drop you within a two-minute walk.

ZEALAND

It is well worth taking some days out from the hectic pleasures of Copenhagen to explore the rest of the island of Zealand (Sjælland). Head north along the so-called 'whisky belt' beside the Øresund coast and you pass grand villas and posh yacht harbours until you come to Helsingør, the closest point to Sweden (there are ferries). Glowering across the water at the old enemy here is Helsingør Slot, better known as Hamlet's castle, Elsinore.

Turn west along the northern coast and a gorgeous holiday coastline of large, sandy beaches, windswept forests and summer houses lies before you, head inland and there are more castles, and the Viking ships of Roskilde to look forward to. Roskilde also plays host to one of the best music festivals in Europe.

To really get away from the modern world, try going south of Copenhagen to the timeless rural tranquillity of the southern islands where more magnificent beaches and unspoilt countryside awaits.

NORTH ZEALAND

One of the most popular day trips from Copenhagen is a loop tour taking in Frederiksborg Slot in Hillerød and Kronborg Slot in Helsingør. With an early start you might even have time to reach one of the north-shore beaches before making your way back to the city, although it is more rewarding to allow an extra day for wandering between shoreline towns along this idyllic coastline.

If you're driving between Helsingør and Copenhagen, ignore the motorway and take the coastal road, Strandvej (Rte 152), which is far more scenic, although it can get crowded on summer weekends.

Frederiksborg Slot

Hillerød, 30km northwest of Copenhagen, is the site of **Frederiksborg Slot** (☎ 48 26 04 39; adult/child Dkr60/15; ☒ 10am-5pm Apr-Oct, 11am-3pm Nov-Mar), an impressive Dutch Renaissance castle that's spread across three islands. The oldest part of the castle dates from Frederik II's time, though most of the present structure was built by his son Christian IV in the early 1600s. After parts of the castle were ravaged by fire in 1859, Carlsberg beer baron JC Jacobsen spearheaded a drive to restore the castle and make it a national museum.

The sprawling castle has a magnificent interior with gilded ceilings, full wall-sized tapestries, royal paintings and antiques. The richly embellished **Riddershalen** (Knights' Hall) and the **coronation chapel**, where Danish monarchs were crowned between 1671 and 1840, are well worth the admission fee.

The S-train (A and E lines) runs every 10 minutes between Copenhagen and Hillerød (Dkr63), a 40-minute ride. From Hillerød Station follow the signs to Torvet, then continue along Slotsgade to the castle, a 15-minute walk in all. Alternatively, take bus No 701 or 702, which can drop you at the gate.

Helsingør (Elsinore)
pop 35,000

Known the world over as the home of Shakespeare's shilly-shallying hero Hamlet, Helsingør is also a busy, attractive port town, with ferries continuously shuttling across the Øresund Strait to and from Sweden to disgorge thirsty Swedes who stock up on cheaper booze here. The **tourist office** (☎ 49 21 13 33; www.visithelsingor.dk; Havnepladsen 3; ☿ 10am-4pm Mon-Fri, to 1pm Sat Sep- 25 May, to 5pm Mon-Fri, to 3pm Sat 26 Jun-31 Aug) is opposite the train station.

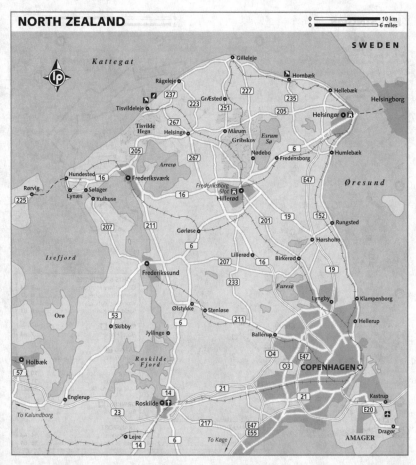

NORTH ZEALAND

SIGHTS

Helsingør's top sight is **Kronborg Slot** (☎ 49 21 30 78; www.kronborg.dk; adult/child Dkr75/15; 🕑 11am-3pm Tue-Sun Jan-Mar, to 4pm Tue-Sun Apr, 10.30am-5pm May-Sep, 11am-4pm Tue-Sun), made famous as the Elsinore Castle of Shakespeare's *Hamlet* (it has been and remains the venue for summer performances of the play in recent decades during the annual Hamlet festival). Kronborg's primary function was not as a royal residence, but rather as a grandiose tollhouse, wresting taxes (the infamous and lucrative 'Sound Dues') for more than 400 years from ships passing through the narrow Øresund. Stand by the cannons facing Sweden and you immediately see what a key strategic military and naval choke point this was. You can cross the moat and walk around the courtyard and walls for free but you will need to pay to enter the castle and see its various museums. These include the Danish Maritime Museum, the Royal Apartments and the Casement (the price quoted above covers all, although you can pick and choose for a lower entrance fee). The castle is on the northern side of the harbour within easy walking distance of the station.

From the tourist office head up Brostræde and along Sankt Anna Gade. This will take you through the **medieval quarter** and past the old cathedral, **Sankt Olai Kirke** (St Anna Gade 12, 🕑 10am-4pm Mon-Sat Apr-Oct, to 2pm Mon-Sat Nov-Mar); the small **City History**

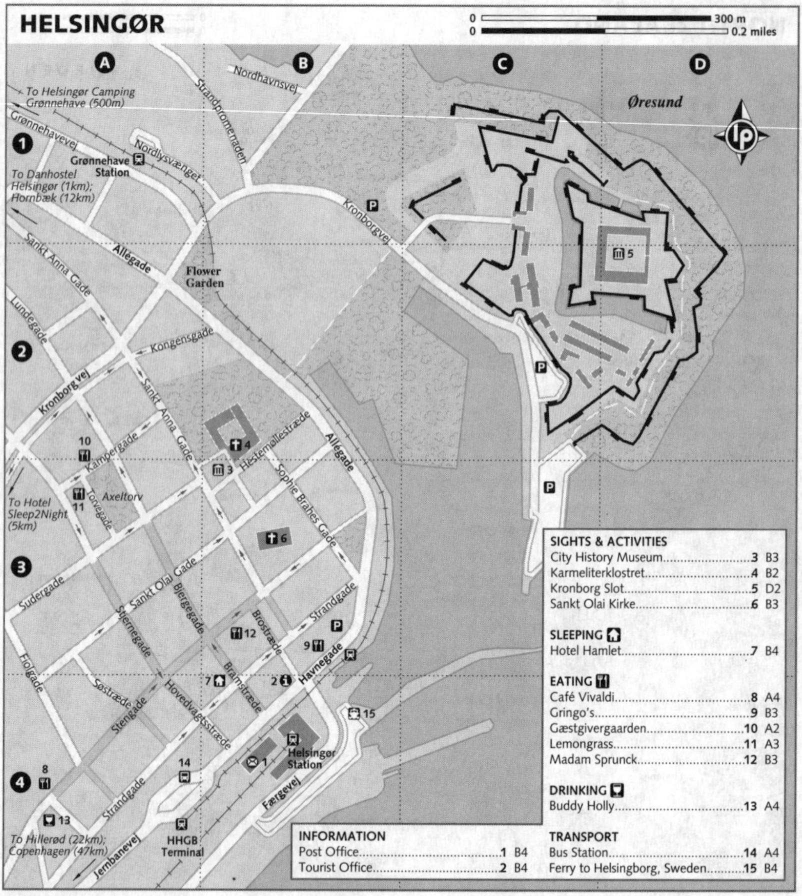
HELSINGØR
0 300 m
0 0.2 miles
A
B
C
D
1
2
3
4
Øresund
To Helsingør Camping Grønnehave (500m)
Grønnehavevej
Grønnehave Station
To Danhostel Helsingør (1km); Hornbæk (12km)
Nordlysvænget
Strandpromenaden
Nordhavnsvej
Kronborgvej
Allégade
Flower Garden
Sankt Anna Gade
Lundegade
Kongensgade
Kronborgvej
Kampergade
Hestemøllestræde
Sophie Brahes Gade
Axeltorv
Tovegade
To Hotel Sleep2Night (5km)
Sudergade
Sankt Olai Gade
Bjergegade
Stjernegade
Brostræde
Strandgade
Havnegade
Bramstræde
Fiolgade
Søstræde
Stengade
Hovedvagtsstræde
Helsingør Station
Færgevej
Strandgade
To Hillerød (22km); Copenhagen (47km)
Jernbanevej
HHGB Terminal
SIGHTS & ACTIVITIES
City History Museum 3 B3
Karmeliterklostret 4 B2
Kronborg Slot 5 D2
Sankt Olai Kirke 6 B3
SLEEPING
Hotel Hamlet 7 B4
EATING
Café Vivaldi 8 A4
Gringo's 9 B3
Gæstgivergaarden 10 A2
Lemongrass 11 A3
Madam Sprunck 12 B3
DRINKING
Buddy Holly 13 A4
INFORMATION
Post Office 1 B4
Tourist Office 2 B4
TRANSPORT
Bus Station 14 A4
Ferry to Helsingborg, Sweden 15 B4

Museum (admission free; noon-4pm); and **Sct Mariæ Kirke and Karmeliterklostret** (guided tours 2pm Mon-Fri adult/child Dkr20/5; church 9am-noon Mon-Wed & Fri 4-6pm Thu), one of Scandinavia's best-preserved medieval monasteries. From here Sudergade leads to the tree-lined, cobbled central square of **Axeltorv**, where you will find several cafés and takeaways. Further out of town are **Danmarks Tekniske Museum** (49 22 26 11; www .tekniskmuseum.dk in Danish; Fabriksvej 25; 10am-5pm Tue-Sun) with historic aeroplanes and motor cars among other exhibits, and **Øresundsakvariet** (35 32 19 70; www.oresundsak variet.ku.dk in Danish; Strandpromenaden 5; 10am-5pm), an aquarium with local sea life.

SLEEPING

Helsingør Camping Grønnehave (49 28 12 12; www.helsingorcamping.dk; Strandalleen 2; camp site per adult/child/tent Dkr60/30/40) A well-spaced beachside camping ground that is east of the hostel and close to one of the area's best beaches.

Danhostel Helsingør (49 21 16 40; www .helsingorhostel.dk; Nordre Strandvej 24; dm/r Dkr150/400-800; Feb-Nov;). The hostel, housed in the imposing red-brick Villa Moltke, is 2km northwest of the centre, by the water with its own beach. It's more welcoming to families than lone travellers.

The tourist office books rooms in private homes for Dkr450 to Dkr800. Singles cost the same as doubles.

Hotel Sleep2Night (49 27 01 00; www .sleep2night.com; Industrivej 19; s/d Dkr570/595) This new, wooden chalet-style accommodation is Denmark's beautifully designed take on the US motel with simple but well-equipped rooms and free internet connections throughout. It's good value but it's a 20-minute journey from the centre of town, to the south of Helsingør. Take bus 805 or 803.

Hotel Hamlet (49 21 05 91; fax 49 26 01 30; Bramstræde 5; s/d Dkr725/995) Hamlet has charming, cosy, old-fashioned rooms with lots of stripped pine panelling and green leather upholstery. It's located right by the harbour and station.

EATING AND DRINKING

Gringo's (49 26 14 47; www.gringos-helsingor.dk in Danish; Stengade 81A; tortillas Dkr99-138; 11am-11pm) Good-value Mexican food is on offer with plenty of outdoor seating in **Færegården**, Helsingør's restaurant complex (which also includes **Kosten**, a more upmarket restaurant, **Bamboo**, a Chinese restaurant, and the tapas and wine bar **Envy** which opens until 6am Thursday to Saturday) and it's close to the station.

Gæstgivergaarden (49 21 19 78; www .gaestgivergaarden.dk in Danish; Kampergade 11) This traditional Danish pub offers a good-value lunch menu. Dishes include half a chicken and chips for Dkr80.

Lemongrass (49 25 15 11; Torvegade 5; mains Dkr89-99; noon-9.30pm) Helsingør's main square has several restaurants and takeaways (there are more of the latter on the high street, Stengade). This Thai place has an extensive menu of authentic dishes for reasonable prices including several vegetarian options.

Madam Sprunck (49 26 48 49 www .madamsprunck.dk; Stengade 48 11.30am-midnight) This Helsingør institution is situated in a charming courtyard. As well as serving great evening meals in its restaurant, it also does a lavish brunch (Dkr120) and a two-course lunch menu for Dkr159. The food is fresh and homemade.

Café Vivaldi (49 26 00 38; Stengade 9; 10am-11pm Mon-Sat, noon-10pm Sun) A part of a small chain, this pleasant French–Italian café at the end of the high street serves salads, sandwiches and omelettes (lunches are Dkr57 to Dkr75 during the day and main courses, such as tortellini, are Dkr99 and chicken curry is Dkr119).

Buddy Holly (26 14 94 64; Svingelport 1, 11pm-5am Fri & Sat). Think wedding night DJs. You'll hear back-to-back mainstream pop and disco designed to get the majority up to dance. Well, you're not in Copenhagen now. There is a dress code.

GETTING THERE & AWAY

Trains departing from Hillerød (Dkr54, 30 minutes) run at least once hourly. Trains from Copenhagen run a few times hourly (Dkr63, 50 minutes). **Scandlines** (33 15 15 15; www.scandlines.dk) and **Sundbusserne** (49 71 02 00; www.sundbusserne.dk) sail frequently throughout the day from Helsingør to Helsingborg, in Sweden. Prices vary, but are roughly Dkr21 to Dkr23 per adult or from Dkr200 if you are taking a car with two passengers.

DENMARK

Zealand's North Coast

There is an innocence and a simplicity to the north coast of Zealand that evokes childhood seaside holidays from decades past with its pretty half-timbered fishing villages, wooded camp sites and miles and miles of excellent sandy beaches. Come July, half of Copenhagen decamps to the north coast for their monthly holiday, however in June and August there is a much smaller crowd.

Hornbæk, the next main town west of Helsingør, has the best and most easily accessible beach on the north coast. The beach is a vast expanse of silky white sand and grassy dunes that run the entire length of the town. From the train station, it's just a five-minute walk directly down Havnevej to the harbour where you'll find a great seafood kiosk and the yacht marina. Simply climb the dunes to the left and you're on the beach. The library doubles as the **tourist office** (☎ 49 70 47 47; www.hornbaek.dk; Vestre Stejlebakke 2A; ☺ 2-5pm Mon, Tue & Thu, 10am-5pm Wed & Fri, to 2pm Sat).

Zealand's northernmost town, **Gilleleje**, has the island's largest fishing port. Visitors usually head straight for the harbour and adjacent sandy beach. The harbour has several wonderful seafood kiosks, selling fresh caught crayfish platters, fish and chips and even sushi. The picnic benches are packed when the sun shines. There is a fish smoking house here too. In the town itself are a smattering of shops and restaurants, but the chief pleasure is simply walking around taking in the characterful thatched houses. The **tourist office** (☎ 48 30 01 74; www.gilleleje.dk; Hovedgade 6; ☺ 10am-6pm Mon-Sat mid-Jun–Aug, to 4pm Mon-Fri & to 3pm Sat Aug–mid-Jun) is in the centre. There are excellent **beaches** either side of the town and others along the coast to the west, especially at Rågeleje, Dronningmølle and at Smidstrup Strand, where conditions are often good for **windsurfing**.

Tisvildeleje is a pleasant seaside village with a long, straggling main street that leads to an even longer beach. The **tourist office** (☎ 48 70 74 51; www.helsinge.com; Banevej 8; ☺ noon-5pm Mon-Fri, 10am-3pm Sat mid-Jun-Aug) is in the train station. Behind the beach is **Tisvilde Hegn**, a windswept forest of twisted trees and heather-covered hills laced with good paths.

SLEEPING & EATING

Rågelige Camping (☎ 48 71 56 40; Hostrupvej 2, Rågeleje; www.camping-raageleje.dk) This is a remote but excellent camping ground that is 10km southwest of Gilleleje. There is a great beach and good facilities.

Camping Hornbæk (☎ 49 70 02 23; www.camping -hornbaek.dk in Danish; Planetvej 4; camp site per adult/ child/tent Dkr62/31/20) This very presentable camping ground is in a pleasant-enough spot behind a small plantation, although it's set a fair way back from the beach.

Hotel Villa Strand (☎ 49 70 00 88; www.villastrand .dk in Danish; Kystvej 2; s/d from Dkr500/750; d with balcony Dkr1250) Villa Strand is a pleasant, quiet place to the west of Hornbæk centre and close to the beach. There are cheaper doubles in garden bungalows and plusher rooms with balconies in the main building.

Hotel Bretagne (☎ 49 70 16 66; Sauntevej 18, Hornbæk; s/d Dkr995/1195) Here is an imposing whitewashed former clinic that is located close to the sea. It has lovely, modern, comfy rooms, and good facilities including wi-fi.

Gilleleje Badehotel (☎ 48 30 13 47; www .gillelejebadehotel.dk; Hulsøvej 15, Gilleleje; d Dkr1390) The grandest of the north coast's bathing hotels is this recently renovated Scandinavian take on a Cape Cod-style place on Gilleleje beach. All rooms have a sea view.

Restaurant Søstrene Olsen (☎ 49 70 05 50; www.sostreneolsen.dk; Øresundsvej 10, Hornbæk; mains Dkr225; ☺ noon-4pm & 5.30pm-11pm Mon-Wed). The best – and most expensive – restaurant in town is in this quaint thatched cottage right by the beach. It's Franco-Danish menu features dishes such as pike perch with fennel and tomato ragout with lobster cappuccino.

Café Ventura (☎ 49 70 13 70; www.café-ventura.dk; AR Friisvej 17, Hornbæk; ☺ opening times vary during the year) There are good burgers, chicken and chilli at this lively Tex-Mex place with open-air seating, on the main road to the beach.

Restaurant Hansens Café (☎ 49 70 04 79; www .hansenscafé.dk; Havnevej 19, Hornbæk; ☺ 4pm to 11pm Mon-Sat; noon-10pm Sun) This half-timbered, thatched cottage restaurant serves traditional Danish food and French inspired dishes such as roast beef with horseradish and pickles for Dkr68, or fried flat fish with mayonnaise and shrimp for Dkr68. Seating is available in the garden in summer.

Adamsen's Fish (Gilleleje Harbour; ☺ 9am-6.30pm Jun-Aug) Adamsen's is the reason why Gilleleje harbour is such a great place to hang out in the summer. Its seafood takeaways – fish cakes Dkr50, sushi Dkr99, shellfish platter Dkr125 – draw the crowds who while away sunny afternoons on the picnic benches here. You can buy fresh fish here too year-round.

Helenekilde Badehotel (☎ 48 70 70 01; www .helenekilde.com; Strandvejen 25, Tisvildeleje; s/d Dkr1295). A beautiful, recently renovated bathing hotel that is built on the cliffs overlooking the beaches at Tisvildeleje; it's about a 10-minute walk from the main street.

Sankt Helene (☎ 48 70 98 50; www.helenekilde .dk; dm/s/d Dkr150/450/470; P 🖥) This modern holiday centre with hostel accommodation, cabins, camping and family rooms is a 10-minute walk from the beach. The most appealing rooms are in the small huts, which are well spaced out on the grounds.

GETTING THERE & AWAY

The train from Helsingør to Hornbæk takes 25 minutes and costs Dkr27; to Gilleleje, it takes 42 minutes and costs Dkr54. To get to Tisvilde by train you must go via Hillerød. From Helsingør this takes just over an hour and costs Dkr63. The Hillerød train runs to Gilleleje and to Tisvildeleje (Dkr42.50), but there's no rail link between the two. Trains run twice an hour during the week and once an hour at weekends. There are also buses, which cost the same but take a little longer; from Helsingør Station, bus No 340 runs to Hornbæk and Gilleleje. Bus No 363 runs between Gilleleje and Tisvildeleje (Dkr27, one hour, every two hours).

ROSKILDE

pop 44,000

Roskilde was a thriving trading port throughout the Middle Ages. It was also the site of Zealand's first Christian church, built by Viking king Harald Bluetooth in AD 980. Today, you could say it is rather stuck in the past. Visitors come here to soak up the atmosphere in the cathedral, which houses the tombs of Danish monarchs from centuries past; and to learn about Viking life in the Viking Ship Museum. Aside from a picturesque location on Roskilde Fjord and a lacklustre high street, you could be forgiven for thinking that was all this former capital of Denmark had to offer. Except that

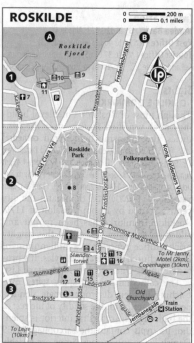

INFORMATION	
Nordea Bank	1 B3
Post Office	2 B3
Tourist Office	3 A3

SIGHTS & ACTIVITIES	
Museum for Samtidskunst	4 A3
Roskilde Domkirke	5 A3
Roskilde Museum	6 A2
Sankt Jorgensbjerg Kirke	7 A1
Site of Medieval Town	8 A2
Viking Ship Museum	9 A1
Waterfront Workshops	10 A1

SLEEPING 🏠	
Danhostel Roskilde	11 A1
Hotel Prindsen	12 B3

EATING 🍴	
Café Satchmo	13 B3
Ce Ci	14 A3
Den Gamle Bagergaarde Bakery	15 A3
Restaurant Bryggergården	16 B3

TRANSPORT	
Jas Cykler Bicycle Shop	17 A3

once a year some fields just outside the city centre play host to the greatest names in contemporary music during the Roskilde Festival – one of the best open-air festivals in Europe.

DENMARK

Information

Nordea Bank (☎ 46 32 32 33; Algade 4)
Post Office (☎ 70 12 40 00; Jernbanegade 3)
Tourist Office (☎ 46 31 65 65; www.visitroskilde.com;
Gullandsstræde 15; ☺ 9am-5pm Mon-Fri, 10am-1pm Sat)

Sights

ROSKILDE DOMKIRKE

Though most of Roskilde's medieval buildings have vanished in fires over the centuries, the imposing twin-spired **cathedral**
(☎ 46 35 27 00; Domkirkepladsen; adult/child Dkr25/free;
☺ 9am-4.45pm Mon-Fri, to noon Sat, 12.30pm-4.45pm
Sun Apr-Sep, 10am-3.45pm Tue-Sat, 12.30pm-3.45pm Sun
Oct-Mar; guided tours 11am & 2pm Mon-Fri, 11am Sat, 2pm
Sun adult/child Dkr20/10) still dominates the city
centre. Started by Bishop Absalon in 1170,
Roskilde Domkirke has been rebuilt and
added to so many times that this mighty
brick edifice represents a millennium of
Danish church architectural styles. It's protected under Unesco's World Heritage List.

The cathedral has tall spiky **spires**, eye-
catching in their disproportionate slender-
ness compared with the solidity of the rest of
the building. The cathedral interior is splendid; its **crypts** contain the sarcophagi of 39
Danish kings and queens. Some are lavishly
embellished and guarded by marble statues of
knights and women in mourning. Others are
simple and unadorned. There's something
quite affecting about being able to stand so
close to the remains of so many of Scandinavia's powerful historical figures. For light
relief, take a look at the 15th-century **clock**
above the entrance, where a tiny St George
on horseback marks the hour by slaying a
yelping dragon (a pair of bellows and three
out-of-tune organ pipes create its yelp).

OTHER ATTRACTIONS

From the northern side of the cathedral,
walk across a field where wildflowers blanket the unexcavated remains of Roskilde's
original medieval town, and continue
through a green belt all the way to the **Viking Ship Museum** (☎ 46 30 02 53; Vindeboder 12;
adult/child Dkr80/free, low season Dkr50; ☺ 10am-5pm).

This well-presented museum contains five reconstructed Viking ships (c
1000), excavated from Roskilde Fjord in
1962 and brought to shore in thousands
of fragments. The fascinating **waterfront
workshops**, a short walk west along the harbour, are a more modern addition to the

museum where Viking ship replicas are
built using Viking-era techniques. The
smells and sounds here are just as they
would have been 1000 years ago.

From May to September, you can take
a **trip** (adult/child excl museum admission Dkr50/
40; ☺ daily from 24 Jun-25 Aug, check with the museum
for others times) on the waters of Roskilde Fjord
in a replica Viking ship. As well as this,
the MS *Svendborg* is a veteran cruiser that
offers sailing tours of the fjord from June
to August.

Further west is the **Sankt Jørgensbjerg
quarter**, where the cobbled Kirkegade walkway leads through a neighbourhood of old
straw-roofed houses into the courtyard of
the 11th-century **Sankt Jørgensbjerg Kirke**.

Roskilde Museum (☎ 46 36 60 44; Sankt Olsgade
18; adult/child Dkr25/free; ☺ 11am-4pm) has displays
on Roskilde's rich history. **Museum for Samtidskunst** (☎ 46·31 65 70; Stændertorvet 3D, ☺ 11am-
5pm Tue-Fri, noon-4pm Sat & Sun; adult/child Dkr30/free),
housed in Roskilde Palace, is a surprisingly
cutting-edge contemporary art space, fond
of perplexing installations by Danish and
international artists.

Sleeping & Eating

The tourist office books rooms in private
homes for Dkr450 for doubles only, plus a
Dkr25 booking fee.

Danhostel Roskilde (☎ 46 35 21 84; www.rova
.dk in Danish; Vindeboder 7; dm/r Dkr150/420; P) This
harbourside hostel is especially smart and
modern, even by Danish hostel standards,
with small three- four- five- or six-bed
dorms. It's adjacent to the Viking Ship
Museum.

Mr Janny Motel (☎ 46 35 43 85; Motelvej 28; d with/
without bathroom Dkr500/400) is a basic 15-room
motel and is the closest accommodation to
the Roskilde Festival.

Scandic Roskilde (☎ 46 32 46 32; www.scandic
-hotels.com; Sdr Ringevej 33; d Dkr813-1305) A large
chain hotel on the outskirts of town. All
rooms have private bathroom and free wi-
fi access.

Restaurant Bryggergården (☎ 46 35 01 03; Algade 15; set menu Dkr88-208) This restaurant offers a good selection of smørrebrød from
Dkr40 to Dkr68 with outdoor seating during summer.

Café Satchmo (☎ 46 35 03 15; Rosenhavestræde 2;
☺ 11am-8pm Mon-Fri, 11am-6pm Sat) This groovy –
or as groovy as things get in Roskilde – jazz

café serves filled pittas (Dkr56 to Dkr63), and salads. It's a few metres off the high street, behind Bryggergården.

Ce Ci (☎ 46 38 48 78; Stændertorvet 8; mains Dkr89-178; ☺ 11am-11pm) Right on the main square is this airy, contemporary Mediterranean café serving bagels (Dkr65) and pasta dishes (Dkr98), as well as evening main courses.

Den Gamle Bagergaarde (Algade 6, ☺ 6am-5.30pm Mon-Fri, 7am-3pm Sat & Sun) is a bakery with good pastries and sandwiches (Dkr29).

Getting There & Around

Trains from Copenhagen to Roskilde are frequent (Dkr63, 25 minutes). From Copenhagen by car, Rte 21 leads to Roskilde; upon approaching the city, exit onto Rte 156, which leads into the centre.

Parking discs are required in Roskilde. There are car parks off Læderstræde, just south of Aldgade, Roskilde Museum and near the Viking Ship Museum.

A bicycle rental shop **Jas Cykler** (☎ 46 35 04 20; Gullandsstræde 3; per day Dkr60), just off Skomagergade, rents out distinctive yellow bikes.

KØGE

pop 33,500

Køge is a pretty town which, if not worth a special visit, offers a pleasant diversion if you happen to be passing through on your way by ferry to Bornholm. The one-time medieval trading centre, 42km south of Copenhagen, retains an engaging cache of historic buildings that line the narrow streets leading off the broad and busy main square, Torvet.

The **tourist office** (☎ 56 67 60 01; www.koegeturist.dk/uk; Vestergade 1; ☺ 9am-5pm Mon-Fri, 10am-1pm Sat) is just off the square.

You can park in Torvet, but for one hour only during the day, but there are longer-term car parks near the train station. Time discs are required.

A short stroll through the central part of Køge takes you to Denmark's oldest **half-timbered building** (c 1527) at Kirkestræde 20, a marvellous survivor with a fine raked roof. Køge's **historical museum** (☎ 56 63 42 42; Nørregade 4; admission Dkr20; ☺ 11am-5pm Tue-Sun Jun-Aug, 1-5pm Mon-Fri, 11am-3pm Sat, 1-5pm Sun Sep-May) is in a splendid building that dates from

---

ROSKILDE FESTIVAL

Once a year, over four days, some of the world's greatest rock and pop acts come to play in a handful of – often quite muddy – fields on the outskirts of a sleepy Danish town 35 minutes west of Copenhagen. It sounds quite improbable unless you've seen it for yourself, but the **Roskilde Festival** (www.roskilde-festival.dk), held each year in early July is Northern Europe's largest music festival.

Everyone from the Beastie Boys to Bowie to Bob Dylan has played the nonprofit-making festival. U2, the Clash, Metallica, Coldplay and Suede have all played famous sets here over the years and the festival continues to draw the highest calibre acts to its six stages. Dylan came again in 2006, along with Guns 'n' Roses, Morrissey and Arctic Monkeys – and around 160 other acts. But you won't just find pop and rock here, there's jazz, hip-hop, folk and even classical music too, plus, of course, all the other accoutrements of open-air festivals – theatre groups, acrobats, beer and burgers.

Many of the acts stay at Mr Janny Motel (opposite), the closest hotel to the festival site, but that gets booked up way in advance. Most visitors, however, choose to camp. There is a vast, free campsite with the usual festival facilities/holes in the ground. Regulars will advise that you turn up a couple of days in advance to pitch your tent, if possible. Don't worry, there is plenty happening thanks to the four day 'warm up' session before the festival proper begins. Ticket prices rise yearly, but at the time of writing they cost Dkr1350 for the full four days – there are no single day tickets.

There is a festival centre set up in Copenhagen's Central Station a week before the festival starts to help people find their way. Trains run direct from the station, and there are festival shuttle buses from Roskilde station to the festival site for Dkr15 one way.

Roskilde Festival 2007 will run from 5 July to 8 July. In 2008 it will run from 3 July to 6 July. You can buy tickets from the festival website, or if they are not sold out, you can buy them at the gate for a couple of hundred kroner extra on the day.

1619. Another gem is **Brogade 23**, decorated with cherubs carved by the famed 17th-century artist Abel Schrøder. Elsewhere best efforts have been made to improve a not very attractive industrial harbour with open air cafés and restaurants

Sleeping

The tourist office can book double rooms in private homes from Dkr450 plus a Dkr25 booking fee.

Hotel Niels Juel (☎ 56 63 18 00; www.hotelnielsjuel.dk; Toldbodvej 20; s/d Dkr825/1077) This harbour-front hotel has modern, light rooms and sea views.

Danhostel Køge (☎ 56 67 66 50; www.danhostel.dk/koege; Vamdrupvej 1; dm/r Dkr140/425; ☺ Mar-Nov; ⓟ ▣) The hostel is 2km northwest of the centre.

Hotel Hvide Hus (☎ 56 65 36 90; www.hotelhvidhus.dk; Strandvejen 111; s/d Dkr825/1275) Well located if a little characterless, this 126 room modern hotel is on the beach with a café and restaurant.

Eating & Drinking

StigAnn (☎ 56 63 03 30; www.stigann.dk; Sankt Gertruds Stræd 2; dinner Dkr175-230, 3-course menu Dkr315) StigAnn serves up superb lunch courses of locally caught seafood (Dkr50-90) and mains, including guinea fowl (Dkr190).

Hugos Vinkjælder (☎ 56 65 58 50; Brogade 19; www.hugos.dk) Køge has a number of pleasant bars, but one of the best is this atmospheric place tucked away off Brogade in the little courtyard of Hugos Gård. It has an eclectic selection of over 70 bottled beers including brews from Eastern Europe to Scotland.

Entertainment

Ritz Rock Cafe (Torvet 22; ☺ café 11am-9.30pm Mon-Sat, 1-9.30pm Sun, club 11pm-6am Fri & Sat) For late night-early morning action, Ritz Rock caters for all tastes in three different dance venues.

Getting There & Away

Køge's train and bus stations are at Jernbanegade 12 on the east side of town. The train station is at the southernmost point of greater ·Copenhagen's S-train network, at the end of the E line. Trains to Copenhagen run at least three times an hour (Dkr63, 35 minutes). The bus to Copenhagen (Dkr63, one hour) leaves from outside the train station.

Bornholmstrafikken (☎ 56 95 18 66; www.bornholmstrafikken.dk) operates the service from Køge, just south of Copenhagen, to Bornholm. The overnight ferry departs daily at 11.30pm and arrives at 6.30am. There are a couple of daytime sailings during the week as well, but these are far more sporadic.

TRELLEBORG

In the countryside of southern Zealand **Trelleborg** (☎ 58 54 95 06; Trelleborg Allé; adult/child Dkr50/free; ☺ 10am-4pm Sat-Thu) is the best preserved of Denmark's four Viking ring fortresses.

The earthen-walled fortress, dating from 980, is divided into four symmetrical quadrants. In Viking times, each quadrant contained four long elliptical buildings of wood that surrounded a courtyard. Each of the 16 buildings, which served as barracks, was exactly 100 Roman feet long (29.5m). You can walk up onto the grassy circular rampart and readily grasp the geometric design of the fortress. Concrete blocks have been placed to show the outlines of the house foundations. Plaques point out burial mounds and other features. It is a fascinating place, but the understandable absence of even vestigial wooden ruins creates a sense of anticlimax overall.

There is a museum, and a separate area is given over to more reconstructions of typical Viking-period buildings. A few costumed interpreters demonstrate old trades and, for a small fee, you can try your hand at baking bread or archery. Spear throwing is free. The museum and office building closes at 4pm, but you can still wander about the grounds in the evening.

Trelleborg is 7km west of Slagelse. To get there, take the train to Slagelse (Dkr63, 33 minutes from Roskilde) and then either catch the hourly bus No 312 to Trelleborg (Dkr18, 12 minutes), take a taxi, or rent a bicycle from a shop near the Slagelse tourist office.

SOUTH ISLANDS

The three islands of Møn, Falster and Lolland mark the southernmost part of Denmark. Though they are just a 1½-hour drive from Copenhagen, these three rural oases can seem centuries removed. Though all three islands are connected to Zealand and each other by bridges, they often appear disconnected from the modern world, which of course is part of their appeal. Cycling holidays are popular here, as is fishing, sailing, bird-watching and hiking, plus there are several good golf courses. There is also a thriving arts scene on Møn although the island is most celebrated for its spectacular chalk sea cliffs, Falster has fine sandy beaches, and Lolland, the largest and least interesting island, has a handful of scattered sights including a drive-through safari park.

Møn

pop 12,000

You don't come to Møn, the easternmost island of the three, for nightlife and museums, but pleasant beaches lie at the end of narrow lanes, the island's medieval churches have remarkable frescoes, and there are numerous prehistoric remains, including a couple of impressive passage graves. The main attractions are the white cliffs and the woods of Møns Klint on the east coast.

One downside is that the island's bus service is sketchy, and to get the best out of Møn, having your own transport is a help.

Stege, the main settlement on Møn, is an everyday place, but it is enlivened by its role as the island's gateway town and main commercial centre. **Møn tourist office** (☎ 55 86 04 00; www.moen-touristbureau.dk; Storegade 2; ☺ 9.30am-5pm Mon-Fri, 9am-6pm Sat mid-Jun–Aug, 9.30am-4.30pm Mon-Fri, 9am-noon Sat Sep–mid-Jun) is at the entrance to Stege and has good information on the entire island.

Stege Kirke (Provstesstræde; admission free; ☺ 9am-5pm Tue-Sun Apr-Sep, to 1pm Oct-Mar) has unique medieval frescoes and a pulpit carved with entertaining visual interpretations of biblical scenes.

MØNS KLINT

The chalk cliffs of Møns Klint, at the eastern tip of the island, were created during the last Ice Age when the calcareous deposits from aeons of compressed seashells were lifted from the ocean floor. The gleaming white cliffs rise sharply for 128m above an azure sea, presenting one of the most striking landscapes in Denmark. The chalk subsoil of the land above the cliffs supports a terrific variety of wildflowers including vivid orchids. There is a strict embargo on picking wildflowers.

Møns Klint is a very popular tourist destination and the wooded arrival point above the cliffs has a busy caféteria, souvenir shops and picnic grounds. But none of this detracts from the natural appeal of the cliffs themselves or the lovely woodland above them.

The woods of Klinteskoven, behind the cliffs, have a network of paths and tracks. From near the caféteria you can descend the cliffs by a series of wooden stairways. It's quite a long descent and a strenuous return up the 500-odd stairs. From the base of the steps, turn south along the narrow beach which leads in about 1km to another stairway at Gråryg Fald. These take you steeply to the top of the cliff, from where a path leads back to the car park. If you turn north at the base of the descent stairway, in just over 1km you'll reach another stairway at Sandskredsfald that again takes you back to the top. In winter, and after heavy rain, unstable lumps of chalk may break off and fall to the beach and you should keep this in mind. Warning notices and barriers should be heeded.

During the summer **boat tours** of the coast around the cliffs run with the MS *Discovery* from Klintholm harbour every two hours from 10am to 4pm (☎ 21 40 41 81; www.sejlkut teren-discovery.dk in Danish).

LISELUND CASTLE

This small, thatched **country manor** (☎ 55 81 20 81; Langebjergvej 6; www.liselundslot.dk; s/d Dkr900/1250) to the north of Møns Klint was built in the late 1800s in the romantic style. The sumptuous parkland surrounding the house is great for picnicking and has various lakes and follies, such as the Chinese Tea Pavilion and Norwegian log cabin. Liselund Ny Slot (the New Liselund Castle) houses a hotel and restaurant. The museum, located in the old house, is open from May to September with guided tours only at 10.30am, 11am, 1.30pm and 2pm.

PASSAGE GRAVES

Møn has a wealth of prehistoric remains, although many are vestigial burial mounds. The best preserved sites are the late-Stone Age passage graves of **Kong Asgers Høj** and **Klek-kende Høj**. Both are on the west side of the island within a 2km radius of the village of Rødvig, from where they are signposted. Kong Asgers Høj is close to the narrow road and parking space is limited. The site is extremely well preserved and comprises a grassy mound pierced by a low passageway that leads to a splendid stonelined chamber. Take a torch and mind your head. **Klekkende Høj** is on a hilltop amid fields. From a car park, follow a signposted track to reach the site. The grave has a double chamber and again you need a torch and some agility to creep inside.

CHURCHES OF MØN

Most of the churches on Møn are medieval and many are graced with the best-preserved primitive frescoes in Denmark. The frescoes depict biblical scenes, often interpreted through light-hearted rustic imagery. These frescoes were obliterated with whitewash by post-Reformation Lutherans fearful of what they saw as too much Roman exuberance. Ironically, the whitewash dealt a blow to bigotry by preserving the frescoes, and 20th-century restoration has revealed them in all their glory. The style of Møn fresco painting owes much to the Emelundemestteren (the Elmelunde Master), an accomplished stylist whose name is unknown. Some of his finest work can be seen at **Elmelunde Kirke** (Kirkebakken 41; admission free; ☑ 8am-4pm Oct-May) on the road to Møns Klint.

CYCLING

Although testing at times, cycling on Møn is rewarding given the island's uncharacteristic hilliness. The tourist office has a route map and an excellent printout guide in English to themed bike tours on the island.

SLEEPING & EATING

Camping Møns Klint (☎ 55 81 20 25; www.campingmoensklint.dk; camp site per adult/child/tent Dkr70/45/20; ☑ Apr-Nov) Located about 3km from the cliffs, the camping ground is in a pleasant woodland setting with swimming pool and tennis courts.

Danhostel Møns Klint (☎ 55 81 20 30; www.danhostel.dk/moen; Langebjergvej 1, Borre; dm/d/tr/q Dkr150/300/390/420; ☑ May–mid-Sep; ℗ ✗) This two-star hostel occupies an enchanting lakeside spot opposite the camping ground.

Præstekilde Klintevej (☎ 55 86 87 88; www.praestekilde.dk; Klintevej, 116, Keldby; s/d Dkr725-925) This modern hotel is convenient for most

of Møn's sights and has an indoor pool and restaurant.

Klintholm Bed and Breakfast (☎ 55 81 24 50; www.klintholm-bb.dk; Klintholm Havnevej 4, Magleby; s/d Dkr425-525) Sofie and Finn Juul run this homesy guesthouse 6km from Møns Klint.

In Stege, there are bakeries and supermarkets and a handful of cafés.

Bryguset Møn (☎ 55 81 20 00; www.bryghusetmoen.dk in Danish; Storegade 18, Stege; ☑ noon-9pm Tue & Wed, to 10pm Thu & Fri, 10am-10pm Sat, to 9pm Sun; burgers, sandwiches & lunch plate Dkr55-125) This new micro brewery is the latest place to eat and drink in the island's capital. It has outdoor seating in summer.

David's (☎ 33 13 80 57; Storegade 11a, Stege; ☑ 10am-5pm Mon-Sat, alternate Fri & Sat evenings during summer; 2-course menu Dkr225) Ambitious modern French–Danish food is on offer here, using locally sourced ingredients for very reasonable prices. Dishes include duck breast with a port wine sauce and Danish summer vegetables.

GETTING THERE & AROUND

From Copenhagen take the train to Vordingborg (Dkr106, 1¼ hours); from there it's a 45-minute ride to Stege on bus No 62 (Dkr39). From late June to mid-August, bus 632 makes the 45-minute run (Dkr18) from Stege to Møns Klint a few times a day. The bus stops at the hostel and camping ground en route. During the rest of the year the bus stops within about 3km of Møns Klint.

Falster

The east coast of Falster is lined with white sandy beaches that attract huge numbers of German and Danish holiday-makers, many of whom own tree-shrouded cabins along the wooded coastline.

The most glorious stretch of beach is at **Marielyst**, which is 12km from the island's main settlement of Nykøbing Falster. The beach draws crowds in summer, but it's so long that you can always achieve some sense of escape. You reach the sea down various lanes that slice through the tree line. Parking is not always easy. The most convenient access and parking is straight on from the junction of the resort's main street, Marielyst Strandvej, with the north–south road, Bøtøvej. There is parking down seaward access lanes at roughly every kilometre as you head south along Bøtøvej from the crossroads. Gedser Odde is the southern most point of Denmark.

The **tourist office** (☎ 54 13 62 98; www.mariel yst.org; Marielyst Strandpark 3; ✆ 9am-4pm Mon-Sat, 10am-2pm Sun mid-Jun–Aug, to 2pm Mon-Fri, 9am-4pm Sat Sep–mid-Jun) is in a modern complex on the western entrance to the resort as you come in from the E55. Go left at the big roundabout. You can rent bicycles from the tourist office for Dkr40 per day.

SLEEPING

Marielyst Camping (☎ 54 13 53 07; www.marie lyst-camping.dk in Danish; Marielyst Strandvej 36; camp site per adult/child/tent Dkr67/35/15) This central camping ground has a long season and is popular with families. It's 400m from the beach.

Danhostel Nykøbing F (☎ 54 85 66 99; www.dan hostel.dk/nykoebingfalster in Danish; Østre Allé 110; dm/r Dkr150/360-520) This is the nearest hostel to Marielyst, being just 1km east of Nykøbing, Falster's train station.

Hotel Nørrevang (☎ 54 13 62 82; www.norrevang .dk; Marielyst Strandvej 32; s/d Dkr795/995). This thatched, half-timbered house 500m from the beach in Marielyst has 26 rooms, a pool, tennis court and restaurant.

GETTING THERE & AROUND

Trains leave Copenhagen several times each hour for Nykøbing F (Dkr133, two hours) on the western side of the island, from where it's a Dkr26 bus ride to Marielyst on the east (25 minutes), or Gedser (35 minutes) further south. From Gedser there are frequent **Scandlines ferries** (☎ 33 15 15 15; www. scandlines.dk) to Rostock, Germany. The trip takes two hours and costs Dkr35 per person. It's Dkr550 for a car with up to five people weekdays and a rather steep Dkr750 at weekends.

Lolland

Perhaps conscious of its comparative lack of natural attractions, Lolland offers instead a couple of diverting attractions.

The main town of **Maribo** has an engaging charm, not least because of its lakeside setting. Maribo's **tourist office** (☎ 54 78 04 96; www .turistlolland.dk in Danish; Torvet; ✆ 10am-5pm Mon-Fri, to 1pm Sat) is on the attractive main square and has masses of information. The town stands amid a scattering of lakes, and its handsome, 15th-century, redbrick **Domkirken** overlooks the gleaming waters of the Søndersø. There

are pleasant lakeside **walks** and Maribo has a number of interesting **museums**.

The biggest draw, at least as far as Danes are concerned, is **Knuthenborg Safari Park** (☎ 54 78 80 89; www.knuthenborg; Birketvej 1, Bandholm; adult/child Dkr115/60; ✆ 10am-5pm).

Danhostel Maribo (☎ 54 78 33 14; www.dan hostel.dk/maribo; Søndre Boulevarde 82; dm/r Dkr100/270; ✆ May–late-Dec; P) Rather a barracklike hostel but well located close to the beach.

The pleasant **Ebsens Hotel** (☎ 54 78 10 44; www.ebsens-hotel.dk in Danish; Vestergade 32, Maribo; s/d without bathroom Dkr350/550, s/d with bathroom Dkr550/750; P) has some strikingly decorated larger rooms.

Vestergade, the main street running west from Torvet in Maribo, has several cafés and restaurant. **Skaanings Gaard Restaurant** (☎ 54 78 22 25; Vesterbrogade 55, Maribo; ✆ noon-midnight) serves a lunch buffet (Dkr99) and has plenty of outdoor seating during summer.

Trains run between Nykøbing F to Maribo (Dkr58, 25 minutes) and on to Nakskov (Dkr65, 47 minutes) every hour Monday to Friday, and less at weekends.

BORNHOLM

pop 45,000

This self-contained little world stuck in the middle of the Baltic 200km east of Copenhagen makes for a wonderful, peaceful escape from Copenhagen's bustle. Lush swathes of wheat fields and extensive forests cover the centre, while the coast is beaded with small fishing villages and stretches of powdery white sand.

Unique among Bornholm's attractions are its four 12th-century round churches, splendid buildings whose whitewashed walls, 2m-thick, are framed by solid buttresses and crowned with black, conical roofs. Each was designed as both a place of worship and a fortress against enemy attacks, with a gunslot-pierced upper storey. All four churches are still used for Sunday services, but are otherwise open to visitors.

HISTORY

Bornholm's history reflects its position at the heart of the Baltic and, in its time, Sweden, Germany and Soviet Russia have occupied it. A Danish possession since the Middle Ages, the island fell into Swedish

DENMARK

hands in the 17th century, but was won back for Denmark by a fierce local rebellion.

The island suffered cruelly in the chaos at the end of WWII. It was occupied by the Nazis, but when Germany surrendered in May 1945 the commander on Bornholm resisted and Rønne and Nexø suffered heavy damage from Soviet air raids. On 9 May the island was handed over to the Soviets who remained *in situ* until the following year, when Bornholm was returned to Denmark.

GETTING THERE & AWAY

Bornholmstrafikken (☎ 33 13 18 66; www.bornholm strafikken.dk; cabins one-way Dkr233, car plus 5 adults Dkr1280) operates ferries between Køge and Rønne. While not as fast as the boat/train option, the overnight sailing (departing daily at midnight and arriving at 6.30am) on the car ferry from Køge is worth considering. Cabins are reasonably inexpensive and it's a good use of time as you travel while you sleep. The downside is the trek out to Køge, about 30 minutes by train south of Copenhagen. A peak (mid-June to August) return ticket per person costs Dkr360.

Bornholmstrafikken also operates the ferry service that runs several times daily between Rønne and Ystad, Sweden (Dkr162 one way or same-day return, 1½ or 2½ hours) and at least once daily between Rønne and Sassnitz, Germany (Dkr150 one way, 3½ hours).

A quicker option is the train-ferry combination from Copenhagen to Rønne via Ystad, Sweden, with **DSB** (☎ 70 13 14 15; www .dsb.dk). This trip goes a few times a day, takes three hours and costs Dkr224. It's also possible to drive to Ystad and cross with a car from there.

The quickest option of all is the 35-minute flight with **Cimber Air** (☎ 74 42 22 77; www.cimber .dk; one-way Dkr1034), with several flights a day between Copenhagen and Bornholm. Book ahead to benefit from cheaper prices.

GETTING AROUND
To/From the Airport

The island's airport, Bornholms Lufthavn, is 5km southeast of Rønne, on the road to Dueodde. Bus No 7 stops on the main road in front of the airport.

Bicycle

Cycling is a great way to get around. Bornholm is crisscrossed by more than 200km of bike trails, many built over former rail routes. You can start right in Rønne, from where bike routes fan out to Allinge, Gudhjem, Nexø, Dueodde and the central forest. Rønne tourist office sells the 60-page English-language *Bicycle Routes on Bornholm* (Dkr45), which maps out routes and describes sights along the way.

In Rønne, **Bornholms Cykeludlejning** (☎ 56 95 13 59; Nordre Kystvej 5; per day/week Dkr70/260), next to the tourist office, has a large fleet of bikes for hire. Bicycles can usually be rented from hostels and camping grounds around the island for about Dkr65 a day.

Bus

A good, inexpensive bus service around the island is operated by **Bornholms Amts Trafikselskab** (BAT; www.bat.dk; day/weekly passes Dkr130/440). Fares are based on a zone system and cost Dkr10 per zone; the maximum fare is for 10 zones. Ask the bus driver about a 'RaBATkort' (10 rides), which can be used by more than one person and saves about 20%. Buses operate all year, but schedules are less frequent from October to April. From May to September, bus No 7 leaves from the Rønne ferry terminal every two hours between 8am and 4pm and goes anticlockwise around the island, stopping at Dueodde beach and major coastal villages before terminating at Hammershus. There are more evening buses in the peak season from late June to the end of August. Other buses make direct runs from Rønne to Nexø, Svaneke, Gudhjem and Sandvig.

Car & Scooter

Motor scooters (per day Dkr245), open-topped mini scoot cars (per day Dkr385) or cars (per day Dkr620) can be rented at **Europcar** (☎ 56 95 43 00; Nordre Kystvej 1, Rønne). The office is in the petrol station just along the road from the ferry terminal. **Avis** (☎ 56 95 22 08), further into town, offers similar rates.

RØNNE

pop 15,000

Rønne is a charming little town with a number of engaging museums and an old quarter of cobbled streets flanked by pretty single-storey dwellings. It is the island's largest settlement and is a popular shopping destination for Swedes on day trips.

The **tourist office** (Bornholms Velkomstcenter; ☎ 56 95 95 00; www.bornholm.info; Nordre Kystvej 3; ☉ 9am-5pm Mon-Sat, 10am-3pm Sun mid-Jun–Aug, 9am-4pm Mon-Fri, to noon Sat Feb-May, Sep & Oct, to 4pm Mon-Fri Nov-Jan) is a few minutes' walk from the harbour and has masses of information on all of Bornholm. There's free internet access at the **public library** (Pingels Allé; ☉ 10am-7pm Mon-Tue & Thu, to 3pm Fri, 1-8pm Wed, 10am-2pm Sat) for which you must book a slot first.

Two very pleasant streets with period buildings are the cobblestoned **Laksegade** and **Storegade**.

Bornholms Museum (☎ 56 95 07 35; Sankt Mortensgade 29; adult/child Dkr35/10; ☉ 10am-5pm Mon-Fri, to 2pm Sat) has a surprisingly large collection of local history exhibits, some interesting displays about Christiansø along with many prehistoric finds and a good maritime section decked out like the interior of a ship. **Hjorths Fabrik** (☎ 56 95 01 60; Krystalgade 5; adult/child Dkr35/10; ☉ 10am-5pm Mon-Sat) is a ceramics museum complete with working features.

The handsome round church, **Nylars Rundkirke**, built in 1150 and decorated with 13th-

century frescoes, is surrounded by Viking rune stones. It's only a 15-minute ride from Rønne on bus No 6.

The tourist office books rooms in private homes for singles (Dkr200) and doubles (Dkr290).

Galløkken Camping (☎ 56 95 23 20; www.gallokken.dk; Strandvejen 4; adult/child Dkr60/30; ☉ mid-May–Aug) is just over 1km south of the town centre. It rents out bikes for Dkr55 to Dkr65 per day. The immaculately kept 140-bed **Danhostel Rønne** (☎ 56 95 13 40; www.danhostel-roenne.dk; Arsenalvej 12; dm/s/d Dkr150/300/400; ℗ ✗) is nearby.

Sverre's Small Hotel (☎ 56 95 03 03; www.sverres-hotel.dk; Snellemark 2; s/d Dkr410/550) offers pleasant, basic, central accommodation near the ferry terminal.

The Kvickly supermarket, which is opposite the tourist office, has a good bakery that opens at 6.30am, and a handy bistro that offers sandwiches (Dkr40 to Dkr55) and hearty hot meals (Dkr65 to Dkr80). You'll find numerous fast-food places on Store Torv. **Strøgets Spisehuz** (☎ 56 95 81 69; Store Torvegade 39; lunch mains Dk80-95, dinner mains Dkr122-160) specialises in excellent Danish meat including a decent steak and chips). Locals vote **Casa Mia** (☎ 56 95 95 73; Antoniestræde 3; pizza Dkr66-72, pasta mains Dkr58-86) the best place for pizza and pasta in town. Rønne isn't much of a party town. Towards the weekend and in summer, there may be some life in **O'Malley's** (☎ 56 95 00 16; Store Torvegade 2), which caters for an older crowd and has an over-21 age limit for its Friday and Saturday late-night discos.

DUEODDE

Dueodde has a vast stretch of white-sand beach backed by woodlands and dunes. The only 'sight' is the slender lighthouse, which you can climb for views of sea and strand that stretch to the horizon. There's no village, just a bus stop with a single hotel, a restaurant, a cluster of kiosks selling ice cream and hot dogs, and necessary public toilets to cope with the rush from tour coaches in summer. It can be a crowded trek for a couple of hundred metres along boardwalks to reach the superb beach. Once there, head left or right for wide-open spaces.

The beachside **Dueodde Vandrerhjem & Campground** (☎ 56 48 81 19; info@dueodde.dk; camp site per adult/child/tent Dkr54/30/25; ⊙ Apr-Oct) is a modern place a 10-minute walk east of the bus stop, or it can be reached by car from the main road. It also has cabins for rent at Dkr170/300 for one/two persons, rising to Dkr800 for eight. There's an indoor swimming pool.

Restaurant Strandhytten (☎ 56 97 82 50, Baunevej 18; lunch mains Dkr150-170, dinner mains Dkr170-290; ⊙ daily lunch & dinner) A short drive north of Duodde. Restaurant Strandhytten occupies a terrific location on the southern coast. Overlooking lapping waves, sand dunes and little else, the Strandhytten offers superior food with a mainly German influence. Big seasonal menus (ten asparagus dishes when we visited), good fish selection, lamb with ratatouille, sirloin steaks, lobster and reasonably priced prosecco make this restaurant a serious contender for best restaurant on Bornholm. There is all-day coffee and cake too.

BORNHOLM'S EAST COAST

Bornholm's east coast tends to be fairly built-up and is punctuated by several settlements, all with some interest as stopping-off places.

Snogebæk is a small shore side fishing village that hangs on to its authenticity because of its small fleet of working boats and its scattering of fishing huts and cabins.

Just north of Snogebæk is the fine beach of **Balka Strand**.

Nexø is Bornholm's second-largest town. It took a hammering from Soviet bombers in WWII and today much of what you see from the harbour outwards is a fairly functional reconstruction. **Nexø-Dueodde Turistinformation** (☎ 56 49 32 00; Åsen 4) is in the centre of town, two blocks inland from the harbour. **Nexø Museum** (☎ 56 49 25 56; Havnen 2; adult/child Dkr25/5; ⊙ 10am-4pm Mon-Fri, 10am-2pm Sat mid-May–mid-Oct) is at the harbour and is packed with maritime flotsam and jetsam including an old-fashioned diving suit, cannons, WWII mines and the inner workings of a lighthouse.

The harbour town of **Svaneke** has award-winning historic buildings, especially those near the village church, a few minutes' walk south of the centre. The **tourist office** (☎ 56 49 70 79; Storegade 24; ⊙ noon-4.30pm Mon-Fri) is in the post office building, two blocks north of the central square.

Sleeping & Eating

Danhostel Svaneke (☎ 56 49 62 42; www.danhostel -svaneke.dk in Danish; Reberbanevej 9; dm/s/d Dkr150/ 400/460; ⊙ Apr-Oct) This quiet complex of bungalow-style chalet dorms and rooms is 1km south of the centre of Svaneke and close to the water.

Hotel Balka Strand (☎ 56 49 49 49; www .hotelbalkastrand.dk; Boulevarden 9; s/d from Dkr625/795; P ⊠ 🖳) A good base in the Snogebæk-Nexø area is this friendly, smart hotel about 200m from Balka Strand beach.

Down by Snogebæk's seafront along Hovedgade, you'll find a cluster of shops selling glassware, organic ice cream, smoked fish and handmade chocolate.

A contender for best smokehouse on the island is **Rogeriet i Svaneke** (☎ 56 49 63 24; Fiskergade 12; counter meals Dkr25-54, lunch/evening buffet meals Dkr84/98). There's excellent, moist, smoked fare including wonderful smørrebrød and tasty fish cakes (Dkr24) to consume inside while you enjoy the view of the massive blackened doors of the smoking ovens or at the outdoor picnic tables. It's by the water at the end of Fiskergade, north of the town centre.

Bryghuset (☎ 56 49 73 21; Torv 5) This friendly place brews three excellent beers, ideal for washing down all that smoked fish. If you haven't already eaten, it also serves decent pub grub.

GUDHJEM

pop 1000

Worth considering as a base on the island, Gudhjem is a compact, attractive seaside village crowned by a squat windmill standing over half-timbered houses and sloping streets that roll down to the pleasant harbour front. It's a popular eating-out place with good accommodation options and good transport links (including to Christiansø). The harbour was one of the settings for the Oscar- winning film *Pelle the Conqueror*, based on the novel of Bornholm writer Martin Andersen Nexø. The **tourist office** (☎ 56 48 52 10; Åbogade 7; ⊙ 10am-4pm Jul-Aug, 1-4pm Mon-Sat Sep & Mar-Jun) is a block inland from the harbour alongside the library. Gudhjem has narrow streets and parking can be difficult. There's a public car park northwest of the harbour.

Stroll the **footpath** running southeast from the harbour for a pleasant coastal view. Gudhjem's shoreline is rocky, though sunbathers will find a small sandy **beach** at Melsted, 1km east. A bike path leads inland 4km south from Gudhjem to the thick-walled, buttressed **Østerlars Rundkirke**, the most impressive of the island's round churches – bus No 3 goes by the church.

Sleeping & Eating

Danhostel Gudhjem (☎ 56 48 50 35; www.danhostel -gudhjem.dk; dm/s/d Dkr150/260/385) Just up from the harbourside bus stop, this hostel is in an attractive spot right by the harbour with small cosy, bright white six-bed dorms. The management also handles the pleasant **Therns Hotel** (☎ 56 48 50 35; www.therns-hotel.dk; Brøddegade 31; s/d Dkr350/550, s/d with bathroom from Dkr500/700).

Jantzens Hotel (☎ 56 48 50 17; jantzenshotel@mail .dk; Brøddegade 33; s/d Dkr525/925) The central Jantzens Hotel is a fine old building that has been refurbished and has stylish rooms and a restaurant.

Restaurant Toldkammeret (☎ 56 48 48 49; Havnegade 19; mains Dkr120-210) Great smørrebrød (four for Dkr120 including tender, pink roast beef with home-made pickles and local salted herring), good seafood and light flavoursome seasonal starters are served on the cosy little harbour-facing terrace.

Gudhjem Rogeri (☎ 56 48 57 08; buffet Dkr871) Further along is this waterfront smoke-house with an all-you-can-eat buffet and some challenging seating, including on the upper floor, which is reached by rope ladder. It has live folk, country and rock music most nights in summer.

You'll find a bakery and a few reasonably priced cafés along Brøddegade, a little inland from the harbour.

SANDVIG & ALLINGE

Sandvig is tucked away under Bornholm's rocky northwestern tip and boasts an excellent sandy beach to add to its distinctive appeal. Bornholm's best-known sight, **Hammershus Slot**, is 3km south on the road to Rønne. The impressive, substantial ruins of this 13th-century castle are the largest of their kind in Scandinavia. They are perched dramatically over the sea, flanked by cliffs and a deep valley. One of the best ways of reaching the castle is by following footpaths from Sandvig through the heather-covered hills of Hammeren – a

wonderful hour-long hike. The trail begins by the camping ground. Sandvig has a mix of attractive old houses and several good eating places. Nearby Allinge has a couple of great historic hotels.

Sleeping & Eating

Danhostel Sandvig (☎ 56 48 03 62; www.danhostel .dk/sandvig; Hammershusvej 94; dm/s/d Dkr150/275/400) This is midway between Hammershus Slot and Sandvig.

Hotel-Pension Langebjerg (☎ 56 48 02 98; Langebjergvej 7; s/d Dkr365/680) This is a good bet out of the several pensions in the village.

Byskriviergarden (☎ 56 48 08 86; www.byskriver gaarden.dk in Danish & German; Løsebækegade 3; s/d Dkr595/710; **P**) An enchanting, white-walled, black-beamed converted farmhouse right on the water in Allinge. The rooms are smartly, if sparsely decorated in contemporary style. Try to get the sea-facing ones. There's a pleasant garden and swimmable, kelp-filled rock pools around the corner if you fancy braving the water.

Café Værftet (☎ 56 48 04 34; Jernbanegade 3; mains Dkr90-140) An unmissable place for good company, delicious Christiansø herring dishes (Dkr38) and meat mains (around Dkr100). It's in an old boathouse whose entire front wall, complete with windows and coverings, can be raised open at the touch of a button from behind the bar; an entertaining event, especially if you've had a few schnapps too many.

CHRISTIANSØ

pop 100

Charmingly preserved, tiny Christiansø (it's about 500m long) is a 17th-century fortress-island an hour's sail northeast of Bornholm. It's well worth making time for a day trip. It has been a seasonal fishing hamlet since the Middle Ages. Christiansø fell briefly into Swedish hands in 1658, after which Christian V decided to turn the island into an invincible naval fortress. Bastions and barracks were built; church, school and prison followed.

By the 1850s the island was no longer needed as a forward base against Sweden and the navy withdrew. Soldiers who wanted to stay on as fishermen were allowed to live as free tenants in the old cottages. Their offspring, and a few latter-day fisherfolk and artists, currently comprise

Christiansø's 100 residents. The entire island is an unspoiled reserve – there are no cats or dogs, no cars and no modern buildings intrude – allowing the rich birdlife, including puffins, to prosper.

If the hectic pace of life on Christiansø is getting to you, try escaping to a smaller island, **Frederickson**, by the footbridge.

There's a small **local history museum** in Frederickson's tower and a great 360° view from Christiansø **lighthouse**. Otherwise the main activity is **walking** the footpaths along the fortified walls and batteries that skirt the island. There are skerries with nesting **sea birds** and a secluded **swimming cove** on Christiansø's eastern side.

In summer, **camping** is allowed in a small field at the Duchess Battery. **Christiansø Gæstgiveriet** (☎ 56 46 20 15; r incl breakfast Dkr800), the island's only inn, has a few rooms with shared bathroom and a restaurant. Booking ahead for a room is advised. There's a small food store and a snack shop.

Christiansøfarten (☎ 56 48 51 76) sails daily to Christiansø from Gudhjem and Monday to Saturday from Allinge between mid-May and mid-September. The mailboat from Svaneke sails Monday to Friday year-round. All boats charge Dkr170 per adult and Dkr85 per child for a return journey. Dogs or other pets are forbidden on Christiansø.

FUNEN

pop 476,000

It is a shame that in the rush from Copenhagen to Jutland many visitors miss the quiet pleasures of the mostly rural island of Funen (Fyn) with its sandy bays, sleepy villages, picturesque fjords and rolling fields.

As well as Funen itself, there are several smaller islands further south still where you really get a sense of escaping from the modern world – chief among them are Langeland and Æro, which are reached via the town of Svendborg.

The island lies between Zealand and the Jutland Peninsula and is connected to the former by the Storebælts Forbindelsen (Great Belt's Bridge) and the latter by the Lillebælts Bro (Little Belt's Bridge).

Store Bælt (Great Belt), the channel that separates Zealand and Funen, is spanned by Europe's longest combined road and

rail bridge, the magnificent Storebæltsforbindelsen (Great Belt Fixed Link). It consists of a four-lane highway that is supported on two sleek suspension bridges connected via the uninhabited island of Sprogø, and an 8km train tunnel, second in length only to the huge UK–France Channel Tunnel. In all, the impressive span, which runs between the industrial towns of Korsør and Nyborg, covers 18km. If you're taking a train, the cost of crossing is included in your train fare; however, if you're driving, there's a costly bridge toll each way (under-6m/over-6m vehicles Dkr200/305) and Dkr105 for a motorbike.

ODENSE

pop 185,000

If overseas visitors stop in Funen, it is usually to visit the birthplace of Hans Christian Andersen in Odense. Denmark's third-largest city takes great pride in being the birthplace of Scandinavia's most famous writer, though after a fairly unhappy childhood, Andersen left Odense with little regret. These days it's a bustling university city with busy, central pedestrianised areas, a fairly lively social scene, a good network of bike lanes, an interesting cathedral and a number of worthwhile museums, including the excellent Andersen museum. Funen's largest produce market is held beside the Koncerthus every Wednesday and Saturday morning.

Information
DISCOUNT CARDS
Odense has a handy 'adventure pass' that allows reduced entry into museums and free local bus transport. You can buy it at the train station or tourist office for adults Dkr120/160, children Dkr65/85 for 24/48 hours.

INTERNET ACCESS
Boomtown Netcafé (☎ 63 11 15 05; Pantheonsgade 4) A plush gamers place with fast internet connection.
Odense Central Library (Odense Banegård Center; ⏲ 10am-7pm Mon-Thu, to 4pm Fri, to 2pm Sat) Offers free use of the internet.

LEFT LUGGAGE
At the train station, left-luggage lockers cost Dkr10 to Dkr20 for 24 hours. Also at the eastern end of Vestergade, close to HC Andersen Hus, is another left luggage place which charges Dkr3 to Dkr6 per hour.

MONEY
Nordea Bank (Vestergade 64)

POST
Post Office (Brandts Passage; ☒ 10am-5.30pm Mon-Fri, to 1pm Sat)

TOURIST INFORMATION
Tourist Office (☎ 66 12 75 20; www.visitodense.com; ☒ 9.30am-4.30pm Mon-Fri, 10am-3pm Sat & Sun mid-Jun–Aug, 9.30am-4.30pm Mon-Fri, 10am-3pm Sat & Sun Sep–mid-Jun) At Rådhus, a 15-minute walk from the train station.

Sights

HC ANDERSEN MUSEUMS

The **HC Andersens Hus** (☎ 65 51 46 01; Bangs Boder 29; adult/child Dkr55/free; 10am-4pm Tue-Sun 16 Aug-15 Jun, 9am-6pm 16 Jun-15 Aug) lies amid the picturesque little houses of the old poor quarter of Odense. It was expanded to mark Andersen's 200th anniversary in 2005 and contains a thorough and lively telling of the amazing life Andersen lived (see the boxed text, p75), put into an interesting historical context and leavened by some good audiovisual material. Andersen was supposedly born on the corner room of the building although the author himself denied this in later life and there is no concrete evidence to support this view. There are often live theatre shows in the small garden to the rear of the museum during June to August.

Next door to the museum is the charming **Fyrtøjet – Et Kulturhus For Børn** (Tinderbox – A Cultural Centre for Children; ☎ 66 14 44 11; Hans Jensens Stræde 21; admission Dkr75; ☒ 10am-5pm mid-Jun–Aug, 11am-4pm Tue-Sun Sep–mid-Jun), where youngsters can explore the magical world of Hans Christian Andersen through storytelling and music (in English as well as Danish during the summer), and by dressing up and pretending to be some of Andersen's most famous characters. There is a good café/restaurant here (sandwiches Dkr65 to Dkr85; two-course menu Dkr135).

HC Andersens Barndomshjem (Munkemøllestræde 3; adult/child Dkr25/free; ☒ 11am-3pm Tue-Sun 16 Aug-15 Jun, 10am-4pm Mon-Sun 16 Jun-15 Aug) has a couple of rooms of exhibits in the small house where Hans Christian grew up. This is the house he describes in his autobiography and which features in a couple of his fairy stories.

SANKT KNUDS KIRKE

Odense's 13th-century, Gothic **cathedral** (☎ 66 12 03 92; Flakhaven; admission free; ☒ 9am-5pm Mon-Sat, noon-5pm Sun) reflects Odense's medieval wealth and stature. The stark white interior has a handsome rococo pulpit, a dazzling, 16th-century altarpiece and a gilded wooden triptych crowded with over 300 carved figures and said to be one of the finest pieces of religious art in Northern Europe.

BRANDTS KLÆDEFABRIK

The former textile mill has been converted into an impressive **cultural centre** (☎ 65 20 70 00; Brandts Passage; www.brandts.dk in Danish; combined ticket adult/child Dkr50/free; ☒ 10am-5pm) with a photography museum (Dkr25), a modern art gallery (Dkr30) and a museum of graphics and printing (Dkr25). The superb exhibition spaces often present excellent temporary exhibitions from artists from all over the world. There's also an appealing roof terrace overlooking town and an excellent artbook/gift shop on the ground floor.

Nearby, in a large loft, is the charming **Tidens Samling** (Times Collection; ☎ 65 91 19 42; Brandt's Passage 29; adult/child Dkr30/20; ☒ 10am-5pm), featuring a series of domestic interiors from various periods between 1900 and the 1980s, and displays on the way Danes dressed, lived and thought in years gone by.

DEN FYNSKE LANDSBY

This is a delightful **open-air museum** (☎ 65 51 46 01; Sejerskovvej 20; adult/child Dkr40/free; ☒ 10am-7pm mid-Jun–mid-Aug, 10am-5pm Tue-Sun Apr–mid-Jun & mid-Aug-Oct, 11am-3pm Nov-Mar), furnished with period buildings authentically laid out like a small country village, complete with barnyard animals, a duck pond, apple trees and flower gardens.

The museum is in a green zone 4km south of the city centre via bus No 42. From May to September you can take a boat (adult/child Dkr35/25) from Munke Mose down the river to Erik Bøghs Sti, from where it's a 15-minute woodland walk along the river to Den Fynske Landsby.

FYNS KUNSTMUSEUM

In a stately, neoclassical building, this **museum** (☎ 65 51 46 01; Jernbanegade 13; adult/child Dkr30/free; ☒ 10am-4pm Tue-Sun) has a serene atmosphere and contains a quality collection of Danish art from the 18th century to the present.

DENMARK

There are small collections of fine sculptures and contemporary art; changing exhibitions are also staged.

CARL NIELSEN MUSEET

This **museum** (☎ 65 51 46 01; Claus Bergs Gade 11; adult/child Dkr25/free; ⏱ 2-6pm Thu & Fri 16 Jun-31 Aug, 4-8pm Thu & Fri 1 Sep-31 May) in Odense's concert

hall details the career of the city's native son Carl Nielsen, Denmark's best-known composer.

JERNBANEMUSEET

Railway buffs should not miss the collection of 19th-century locomotives at the **rail museum** (☎ 66 13 66 30; Dannebrogsgade 24; adult/child

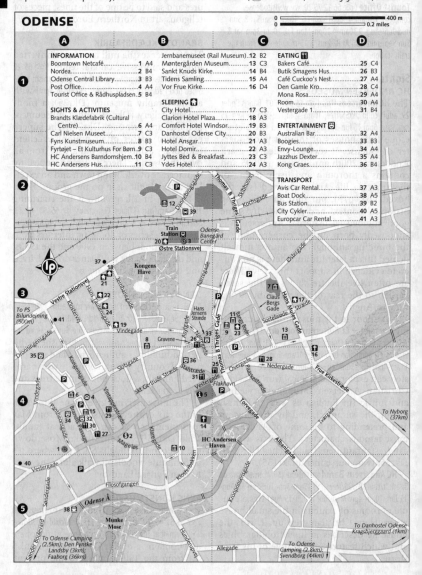

ODENSE

0 _____ 400 m
0 _____ 0.2 miles

INFORMATION
Boomtown Netcafé...................1 A4
Nordea....................................2 B4
Odense Central Library............3 B3
Post Office.............................4 A4
Tourist Office & Rådhuspladsen.5 B4

SIGHTS & ACTIVITIES
Brandts Klædefabrik (Cultural Centre)..................................6 A4
Carl Nielsen Museet.................7 C3
Fyns Kunstmuseum..................8 B3
Fyrtøjet – Et Kulturhus For Børn.9 C3
HC Andersens Barndomshjem..10 B4
HC Andersens Hus..................11 C3

Jernbanemuseet (Rail Museum)..12 B2
Møntergården Museum..........13 C3
Sankt Knuds Kirke.................14 B4
Tidens Samling......................15 A4
Vor Frue Kirke......................16 D4

SLEEPING
City Hotel............................17 B4
Clarion Hotel Plaza...............18 A3
Comfort Hotel Windsor.........19 B3
Danhostel Odense City..........20 B3
Hotel Ansgar........................21 A3
Hotel Domir.........................22 A3
Jyttes Bed & Breakfast..........23 C3
Ydes Hotel...........................24 A3

EATING
Bakers Café..........................25 C4
Butik Smagens Hus................26 B3
Café Cuckoo's Nest...............27 A4
Den Gamle Kro.....................28 C4
Mona Rosa..........................29 A4
Room..................................30 A4
Vestergade 1........................31 B4

ENTERTAINMENT
Australian Bar......................32 A4
Boogies...............................33 B3
Envy-Lounge.......................34 A4
Jazzhus Dexter....................35 A4
Kong Graes.........................36 B4

TRANSPORT
Avis Car Rental....................37 A3
Boat Dock...........................38 A5
Bus Station..........................39 B2
City Cykler..........................40 A5
Europcar Car Rental.............41 A3

Dkr40/16; ☾ 10am-4pm) just behind the train station. There are also mini railways for children of all ages to ride on.

OTHER ATTRACTIONS

Strolling is a pleasure along the busy pedestrianised main street Vestergade and down side streets such as Lille Gråbrødstræd. The central square **Flakhavn**, framed by Odense Rådhuspladsen and Sankt Knuds Kirke, features Svend Wiig Hansen's giant bronze, the reclining *Oceania*. The east side of the city centre has some of Odense's oldest buildings. You can follow a rewarding **walking route** from the centre by crossing the busy Torvegade and strolling down Nedergade, a cobblestoned street lined with leaning, half-timbered houses and antique shops, and then returning via Overgade. En route you'll pass the 13th-century **Vor**

Frue Kirke (☾ 10am-noon Mon-Sat). One of the nicest walks to be had is alongside the river Å (pronounced 'Oh') that runs to the south of the city centre to Munke Mose park. Alternatively you can take the trip with a pleasure boat.

Around the corner, **Møntergården** (☎ 66 14 88 14; Overgade 48-50; ☾ 10am-4pm Tue-Sun), the modest city museum, has various displays on Odense's history from the Viking Age and a couple of 16th- and 17th-century half-timbered houses.

Sleeping

A Cab Inn is due to open in Odense on Østre Stationsvej, close to the station, in October 2007. The tourist office books rooms in private homes for Dkr250/350 for singles/doubles, plus a Dkr35 booking fee.

A FAIRY-TALE LIFE?   Michael Booth

Hans Christian Andersen is probably the biggest selling children's writer of all time. Admittedly he had a head start on JK Rowling, but stories such as *The Little Mermaid, The Emperor's New Clothes* and *The Ugly Duckling,* have been translated into over 170 languages (Chairman Mao was a fan, and put Andersen on the Chinese school curriculum), and are embedded in the global literary consciousness like few others. Even today, over 200 years after his birth, their themes are as relevant and universal as ever.

For the Danes, Hans Christian Andersen is Shakespeare, Goethe and Dickens rolled into one. That may sound a little excessive for a fairy-tale writer, but Andersen was far more than that. As well as single-handedly revolutionising children's literature (*Alice in Wonderland*, the works of Roald Dahl and, yes, even Harry Potter owe him a debt), he wrote novels, plays and several fascinating travel books.

Andersen was born in Odense on 2 April 1805. In three autobiographies he mythologised his childhood as poor but idyllic (his mother was a washerwoman, his father a cobbler) and filled with portents of his fame and success. The truth was his parents were not married when he was conceived and his father died when Andersen was 11.

Soon after the death of his father Andersen left for Copenhagen, an uneducated, gauche 14-year-old following a fairy-tale path. Despite numerous class and educational barriers, he tried and failed to become, variously, a ballet dancer, singer, actor, playwright and novelist, until he eventually found international success with his first volume of short stories.

That success and accompanying wealth were some compensation for what was an otherwise deeply troubled, largely unhappy life. Andersen was a neurotic, sexually ambivalent, highly-strung hypochondriac (he famously carried a length of rope with him wherever he travelled, in case he got trapped by fire in an upstairs room).

It all perhaps goes some way to explaining why he was such a restless nomad to the last. He travelled further than any of his compatriots; most notably in 1840–41 when he journeyed as far as Istanbul, writing about his experiences in the highly accomplished travelogue *A Poet's Bazaar*.

In modern-day Odense, Andersenia is a mini industry. Everywhere you walk you will find his life evoked with statues, museums, shop names and souvenirs. It's probably best not to remind locals that the man himself couldn't wait to get away and fled the city for the gas lights of Copenhagen as soon as he had saved enough money for the coach fare.

Odense Camping (☎ 66 11 47 02; www.camping
-odense.dk in Danish; Odensevej 102; camp site per adult/
child/tent Dkr66/33/20) This camping ground is
3.5km south of the city centre (take bus
No 21 or 22).

Comfort Hotel Windsor (☎ 66 12 06 52; www
.hotel-windsor.dk; Vindegade 45; s/d Dkr895/995) This
reasonably priced hotel is located right
in the city centre. Being more business-
orientated, it has good summer deals (s/d
Dkr595/650)

Danhostel Odense City (☎ 63 11 04 25; www
.cityhostel.dk; dm/s/d Dkr150/350/400; ☒ 🖳) An excellent, modern 140-bed place with four-
and six-bed dorms, a kitchen and laundry
facilities located alongside the train and
bus stations.

Danhostel Odense Kragsbjerggaard (☎ 66 13
04 25; Kragsbjergvej 121; dm/s/d Dkr105/295/420) Occupying a former manor house around a
grassy central square, this 160-bed place is
2km southeast of the centre via bus No 61
or 62.

Jyttes Bed & Breakfast (☎ 66 13 89 36; www
.jyttes-bb.dk; Ramsherred 17; d Dkr350) A cosy B&B
located just along from the HC Andersen
birthplace museum on a cute, cobbled
medieval street. All rooms have TV.

Hotel Ansgar (☎ 66 11 96 93; www.hotel-ansgar
.dk; Østre Stationsvej 32; s/d Dkr595-895/695-995) Another of Odense's more business orientated
venues, also centrally located just down the
road from the station with homely rooms,
each with their own shower.

Hotel Domir (☎ 66 12 14 27; www.domir.dk; Hans
Tausensgade 19; s/d Dkr495/595-795; 🖳) This hotel is
one of the better midrange options in town
with pleasant, good-value rooms, though
some singles are a bit cramped.

Ydes Hotel (☎ 66 12 11 31; Hans Tausensgade 11;
s/d Dkr450/550-745) Near the Hotel Domir is
its sister hotel, which has 26 smaller, but
similarly appointed, rooms.

Clarion Hotel Plaza (☎ 66 11 77 45; www
.choicehotels.dk; Østre Stationsvej 24; s/d Dkr1125/1325;
🅿 ☒ 🖳) Overlooking the green spaces
of Kongens, this comfortable hotel has
friendly service. Its 68 rooms are decorated
in a slightly pastoral Old English style and
are fairly luxurious. There's also wi-fi access
and a gym.

City Hotel (☎ 66 12 12 58; www.city-hotel-odense
.dk; Hans Mulesgade 5; s/d Dkr695/895) A comfortable
modern hotel located near the Carl Nielsen
Museet.

Eating & Drinking

There are numerous, mainly fast-food,
places along Kongensgade and an excellent
bakers at Vestergade 26, the main shopping street.

Room (Brandts Passage 6-8; ☯ 10am-10pm Sun-
Wed, to 3am Thu-Sat) Odense's newest trendy
venue is this light, bright modern Mediterranean styled café/nightclub in the newly
rejuvenated Brandt's Passage area. Serves a
mix-and-match tapas menu – three plates
Dkr70, brunch Dkr78 – with outdoor seating in summer.

Vestergade 1 (☯ 11am-10pm Mon-Fri, 10am-10pm
Sat, 11am-6pm Sun) This is a lovely corner café
at the HC Andersen Museum end of the
main shopping street. It serves excellent
sandwiches (Dkr69-108, a Danish brunch
(Dkr79) and more ambitious Franco-Danish food in the evenings (main courses
Dkr169 to Dkr189).

Bakers Café (Fisketorvet, ☯ 7am-5pm Mon-Fri, to
2pm Sat, to noon Sun) A top-notch bakery and
café close to the HC Andersen Museum
serving elaborate sandwiches (Dkr37 to
Dkr50), salads (Dkr40), breads and cakes.

Café Cuckoo's Nest (☎ 65 91 57 87; Vestergade 73;
☯ 9am-midnight Mon-Wed, to 1am Thu, to 2am Fri & Sat,
10am-11pm Sun) This large, trendy bar/restau-
rant is popular with students and serves an
eclectic menu of sandwiches, salads, burgers
(Dkr55 to Dkr79) and, in the evening, Thai-
French-Danish mains (Dkr109 to Dkr129).

Mona Rosa (Vintapperstræde 4; ☯ noon-10pm) An
Odense institution, this Mexican restaurant
has outdoor seating in summer. The two-
course menu costs Dkr129 to Dkr169.

Den Gamle Kro (☎ 66 12 14 33; Overgade 23;
two-course meal Dkr298) One of Odense's most
atmospheric restaurants is spread throughout several rooms of a half-timbered, 17th-
century house serving heavy, traditional
Danish or French food. It's mostly meat-
based fare, but tasty.

Butik Smagens Hus (☎ 66 12 22 72; Nørregade 32;
☯ 10am-5.30pm Tue & Wed, to 6pm Thu, to 6.30pm Fri,
to 2pm Sat) Gourmet delibar/bakery which
prides itself on sourcing top-quality local
produce (sausages, smoked fish) and is part
of the Danish Slow Food society.

Odense Banegård Center, which incorporates the train and bus stations, has
low-priced options including a **DSB Café**
(☯ 5am-10pm Mon-Fri, 8am-10pm Sat & Sun), a supermarket and a pub.

Entertainment

Envy-Lounge (Brandts Passage 31; ☺ 9.30am-midnight Mon-Wed, to 2am Thu-Sat, 10.30am-11pm Sun) Odense's most glamorous nightlife venue, the Envy lounge-bar is, by day, a cool, light café – the epitome of Scandinavian chic. DJs play in the evenings every Saturday from 10pm.

Australian Bar (☎ 66 11 83 90; Brandts Passage 10) With either live music or dancing happening most nights; it's in the heart of Odense's newly reinvigorated nightlife quarter.

Boogies (☎ 66 14 00 39; Nørregade 21) Popular with students, this dance place is downstairs from a café and opens at midnight, and stays open until 5am on Friday and Saturday. Admission is Dkr40 on Friday and Saturday when there are bands. Upstairs is the Café Birdy serving Mexican and Indian food (mains Dkr48 to Dkr144).

Brandts Klædefabrik (☎ 66 13 78 97; Brandts Passage) has an outdoor amphitheatre that's a venue for free summer weekend concerts, and the **Café Biografen** (☎ 66 13 16 16; Brandts Klædefabrik; tickets Dkr60-70) shows first-run movies on three screens. **Biocity** (Odense Banegård Center) is a cinema.

Kong Graes (☎ 66 11 63 02; Asylgade 7-9) is a dressy late-night dance club for over 20s.

Jazzhus Dexter (☎ 66 11 27 28; Vindegade 65) has good live music (mostly jazz) groups virtually every night of the week from around 8pm.

Getting There & Away

Odense is on the main railway line between Copenhagen (Dkr214, 1½ hours, every 15 minutes), Århus (Dkr187, 1¾ hours, hourly), Aalborg (Dkr286, three hours, hourly) and Esbjerg (Dkr169, two hours, every 30 minutes). The ticket office is open from about 6am to 8.15pm most days, but closes at 4.35pm on Saturday. Buses leave from the rear of the train station.

Odense is just north of the E20; access from the highway is clearly marked. Rte 43 connects Odense with Faaborg; Rte 9 connects Odense with Svendborg. There are several car-rental companies in town:

Avis (☎ 66 14 39 99; Østre Stationsvej 37)

Europcar (☎ 66 14 15 44; Kongensgade 69)

PS Bilundejning (☎ 66 14 00 00; Middlefartvej 1) A competitive local option (from Dkr340 per day) if you don't need to drop the car in another town or city.

Getting Around

In Odense you board city buses at the front and pay the driver (Dkr12) when you get off. You're strongly advised to have the correct change.

Driving in Odense is not difficult outside rush hour, though many of the central sights are on pedestrian streets, so it's best to park your car and explore on foot. You can find substantial parking lots around Brandts Klædefabrik and the Carl Nielsen Museet. Parking costs around Dkr10 for one hour.

Bicycles can be rented at **City Cykler** (☎ 66 13 97 83; www.citycykler.dk; Vesterbro 27; per day Dkr99; ☺ 10am-5.30pm Mon-Fri, to 1pm Sat), west of the city centre.

LADBYSKIBET (LADBY SHIP)

This **historical site** (☎ 65 32 16 67; Vikingevej 123; adult/child Dkr25/free; ☺ 10am-5pm Jun-Aug, to 4pm Tue-Sun Sep-Oct & Mar-May, closed Nov-Feb) comprises the remains of a 22m-long Viking ship that has been skilfully preserved at the place where it was originally excavated in 1935. The ship, which once formed the tomb of a Viking chieftain, was buried in the 10th century. It is the only Viking Age ship burial site uncovered in Denmark to date.

All the wooden planks from the Ladby ship decayed long ago, leaving the imprint of the hull moulded into the earth, along with iron nails, an anchor and the partial remains of the dogs and horses that were buried with their master.

There's a separate visitor centre at the arrival car park with a 1:10-scale model of the ship and background information about the site.

Getting There & Away

In the little village of Ladby, 4km southwest of Kerteminde via Odensevej, turn north onto Vikingevej, a one-lane road through fields that ends after 1.2km at the Ladbyskibet car park. You enter through the little museum from where it's a few minutes' walk along a field path to the mound.

Local bus No 890 (Dkr16, 30 minutes, eight daily Monday to Friday) makes the trip from Kerteminde to the village of Ladby. Check the schedule with the bus driver, as the last return bus is typically around 4pm. Also, you'll have to walk the Vikingevej section to the museum about 20 minutes away.

DENMARK

EGESKOV SLOT

This magnificent **castle** (☎ 62 27 10 16; www
.egeskov.com; combined ticket for all sights except castle adult/child Dkr95/52, plus castle interior Dkr150/77;
☼ 10am-6pm May, Jun, Aug & Sep, to 8pm Jul), complete with moat and drawbridge, is an outstanding example of the lavish efforts that
sprang up during Denmark's Golden Age,
the Renaissance. There are enough sights
and activities here to keep anyone happily
occupied for a day. The castle exteriors are
the best features. The interior is heavily
Victorian in its furnishings and hunting
trophies of now rare beasts. The grounds
include century-old privet hedges, free-
roaming peacocks, topiary, aerial woodland
walkways, English gardens and a bamboo
grass labyrinth.

The castle grounds usually stay open an
hour longer than the castle. Admission to
the grounds includes entry to a large antique **car museum**, which also features some
vintage aircraft swooping from the rafters.

Egeskov Slot is 2km west of Kvændrup
on Rte 8. From Odense take the Svendborg-
bound train to Kvændrup Station (Dkr50)
and continue on foot or by taxi.

FAABORG & AROUND

pop 7,300

Faaborg is a south-facing sun trap and has a
relaxing air even at the height of its tourist
summer season. In the 17th century it was
a bustling harbour town sustained by one of
Denmark's largest commercial fleets. Today,
Faaborg retains many vestiges of that earlier
era in its picturesque, cobblestone streets
and leaning, half-timbered houses. In recent
years Faaborg harbour has been rejuvenated
with smart housing and restaurants and it's
well worth stopping for a drink or lunch before moving on to other towns on Funen or
via the ferry to the southern islands.

Faaborg's **tourist office** (☎ 62 61 07 07; www
.visitfaaborg.dk; Banegårdspladsen 2A; ☼ 9am-5pm Mon-
Sat Jun-Sep, to 4.30pm Mon-Fri, 10am-3pm Sat Oct-May) is
adjacent to the bus station and car park on
the harbour front. You can hire bikes here
for Dkr50 a day.

Sights & Activities

The main square, **Torvet**, is a pleasant spot
to linger. It features the Svendborg sculptor Kai Nielsen's striking bronze fountain
group *Ymerbrønd;* depicting a naked giant

suckling at the udders of a cow (depicting
a Norse fertility myth) – it caused a stir on
its unveiling.

Running east from Torvet is the tree-
lined main shopping street Østergade. Torvegade runs west from Torvet to join the
cobbled Holkegade at a cluster of attractive buildings. They include a neoclassical,
one-time chemist's shop with Tuscan pi-
lasters, and the handsome, 18th-century
merchant's house that is now the town
museum, **Den Gamle Gaard** (Holkegade 1; adult/child
Dkr40/free; ☼ 10.30am-4.30pm mid-May-Oct, 11am-3pm
Sat & Sun Apr–mid-May), complete with period
furnishings.

The small **Faaborg Museum for Fynsk
Malerkunst** (Grønnegade 75; adult/child Dkr40/free;
☼ 10am-4pm Apr-Oct) is a former winery
which contains a fine collection of Funen
art, including works by artists such as Peter
Hansen, Jens Birkholm, and Anna Syberg.
Kai Nielsen's original granite sculpture of
the *Ymerbrønd* is also here. The town landmark is the nearby belltower of **St Nikolai**.

There are numerous daily ferries to the
nearby islands of Avernakø and Lyø (Dkr85
return, bicycle Dkr25, car Dkr145) and a
passenger boat to Bjørnø (Dkr40 return).

There's a small watersports centre at the
Quality Hotel Faaborg Fjord (☎ 62 61 10 10; Svend-
borgvej 175; activities Dkr60-100), 2km out of town,
offering fast water-based fun such as knee-
boarding, high-speed jumping and being
towed along behind a weaving speedboat
astride a big banana.

Sleeping & Eating

The tourist office books rooms in private
homes for Dkr250 for single travellers and
Dkr400 for doubles plus a Dkr25 booking fee. There are a couple of unremarkable cafés and fast-food places in the town
square and more upmarket restaurants on
the harbour front.

Danhostel Faaborg (☎ 62 61 12 03; www.danhostel
.dk/faaborg; Grønnegade 71-72; dm/d Dkr150/300; ☼ Apr-
late Oct) This 69-bed, three-star hostel occupies two handsome historic buildings, close
to the Faaborg Museum and the town's indoor swimming baths.

Hotel Faaborg (☎ 62 61 02 45; www.hotelfaaborg
.dk; Torvet; s/d Dkr750/850; P 🖳) This very central hotel has good, welcoming rooms. Its
restaurant does tasty herring dishes for
Dkr85 and Mediterranean brasserie food.

Hotel Færgegaarden (☎ 62 61 11 15; Christian IX Vej 31; www.hotelfg.dk; s/d with shower Dkr700/850) Faaborg's oldest hotel was refurbished recently and is located close to the harbour and town centre. Its restaurant is orientated to the German tourists who flock here in the summer, featuring dishes such as veal schnitzel and prawn cocktail (two courses Dkr325).

Rødkilde Herregaard (☎ 30 24 10 05; www .roedkilde.dk; Rødkildevej 15, Ulbølle, Vester Skerninge; s/d Dkr700-1000) At the end of a very long, winding private drive, off the road from Faaborg to Svendborg, this delightful B&B takes up a wing of a beautiful historic manor house amid farm land and half-timbered barns. Rooms are pretty and light, with original wooden floors and elegant furnishings. Keenly priced, so be sure to book ahead.

Faaborg Røgeri (☎ 62 61 42 32; Vestkaj; fish dishes Dkr22-59) Situated at the harbour, this place serves cheap, tasty, home-smoked fish.

Getting There & Away

Faaborg has no train service. Bus Nos 961 and 962 from Odense (Dkr58, 1¼ hours) run at least hourly to 11pm. Bus Nos 930 and 962 from Svendborg (Dkr45, 40 minutes, at least hourly) are also frequent throughout the day. Getting to Faaborg by car is straightforward; from the north, simply follow Rte 43, which is called Odensevej as it enters town.

For more information on ferry services to Ærø, see p82.

SVENDBORG

pop 27,000

Svendborg is South Funen's largest municipality and a transit point for travel between Odense and Langeland and Ærø. It can be surprisingly lively in the summer, particularly on the waterfront where yachties and land-bound visitors flock in numbers. It is a major sailing and kayaking centre. You can rent kayaks from the **Sea Kayak Centre** (Skaregaardsvej 9, Skovballe, Tåsinge; ☎ 63 54 19 20; www .havkajakcenter.dk).

The train and bus stations are two blocks northwest of the dock. The **tourist office** (☎ 62 21 09 80; www.visitsydfyn.dk; Centrumpladsen 4; ☼ 9.30am-6pm Mon-Fri, to 3pm Sat mid-Jun–Aug, to 5pm Mon-Fri, to 12.30pm Sat Sep–mid-Jun) has lots of information on South Funen as a whole.

A splendid natural harbour made Svendborg a major port and shipbuilding centre from medieval times onwards and today there is still enough marine heritage to counter-balance the fairly soulless modern docks that dominate the waterfront. The town has a number of maritime training schools to add to its salty ambience.

Sights

At the southern end of Havnepladsen's cobbled quayside, opposite where the Ærø ferry docks, is **Sejlskibsbroen**, a jetty lined with splendidly preserved sailing ships and smaller vessels and with an adjoining marina catering for the great number of yachts that sail local waters. Ask at the tourist centre about the various trips that can be arranged on the old sailing ships.

The town's newest attraction is Naturama (☎ 62 21 06 50; Dronningemaen 30; www .naturama.dk; ☼ 10am-5pm; adult/child Dkr90/free), a large, modern zoological museum.

Just over the bridge from Svendborg is the island of **Tåsinge**, with its pretty harbourside village of Troense and the nearby 17th-century castle **Valdemars Slot** (☎ 62 22 61 06; Slotsalléen 100; www.valdemarsslot.dk; adult/child Dkr65/30; ☼ 10am-5pm May-Sep). The castle was built in the early 1600s by Denmark's great Renaissance king, Christian IV, for his son, but later awarded to the naval hero Admiral Niels Juel; it remains in his family to this day. Its lavish interior is crammed with paintings and eccentric objects. In the grounds are the **Danish Yachting Museum** and **Denmark's Toy Museum**, packed with vintage playthings. The grounds of the castle and the nearby white-sand beach have free access. You can get to Valdemars Slot by bus but a better way is by the MS *Helge*, an old-style ferry that carries passengers from Svendborg to Troense and Valdemars Slot every few hours (Dkr80) from May to September. The castle also has a good Franco-Danish **restaurant** (☼ Weds-Sat; mains from Dkr200) which sells picnic baskets for Dkr118-165.

Sleeping & Eating

The nearest camping grounds are located on Tåsinge.

Danhostel Svendborg (☎ 62 21 66 99; www .danhostel-svendborg.dk; Vestergade 45; dm/r Dkr150/390; P ☒ ☐) Danhostel is in a renovated 19th-century iron foundry in the town centre. Bike hire costs Dkr60.

Hotel Garni (☎ 62 21 17 00; Toldbodvej 5; s/d Dkr550/685) An excellent, basic, cheap hotel located right in the centre of town – part of the more expensive Hotel Svendborg.

Hotel Ærø(☎ 62 21 07 60; www.hotel-aeroe.dk in Danish; Brogade 1; s/d Dkr650/775; **P**) Right by the water, the Ærø has large, modern chalet-style rooms. There's a good restaurant serving traditional fare, including a range of light lunches and smørrebrød (Dkr32 to Dkr82).

Strandbo B&B (☎ 62 23 10 40; www.strandbostudio .dk; Skårupore Strandvej 52, Skårup; s/d Dkr250/600) A little way out of town, this lovely B&B is right on the water with pleasant gardens and an adjacent art gallery.

Restaurant Pakhuset (☎ 62 21 66 97; Havneplads 3a; mains Dkr168-88; ☺ 11.30am-3pm, 5.30-10pm Mon-Sat) This high-end restaurant is housed in a converted 19th-century warehouse right on the harbour front by the historic ships. It serves ambitious French food with the odd Italian influence for what are, actually, quite reasonable prices.

Restaurant 13 (☎ 62 22 07 95; Brogade 13; mains Dkr150; ☺ 6pm-midnight Mon-Sat) Highly recommended by locals, this family-run restaurant serves superb Franco-Danish food at bargain prices.

Getting There & Away

There are trains from Odense to Svendborg (Dkr60, 45 minutes, hourly). Ferries to Ærøskøbing depart five times a day, the last one goes at 10.30pm in summer.

LANGELAND

pop 13,800

The long, narrow island of Langeland, connected by bridge to Funen via Tåsinge, has a satisfying sense of isolation. It has some wonderful sandy beaches, enjoyable cycling and rewarding bird-watching. You can pick up information about the entire island from Langeland's **tourist office** (☎ 62 51 35 05; www .langeland.dk in Danish; Torvet 5, Rudkøbing; ☺ 9am-5pm Mon-Fri, to 3pm Sat mid-Jun–Aug, 9.30am-4.30pm Mon-Fri, to 12.30pm Sat Sep–mid-Jun).

Sights & Activities

Langeland's top sight is the red stucco **Tranekær Slot**, a handsome medieval castle that has been in the hands of the one family since 1672. The castle is not open to the public, but its grounds are home to the **Tickon** (Tranekær International Centre for Art & Nature; admission

to grounds Dkr25), a collection of intriguing art installations created by international artists and sited around the wooded grounds and lake. **Tranekær Slot Museum** and the **Souvenir Museum** are in the castle's old water mill and old theatre respectively. About 1km north of the castle is the **Castle Mill** (☎ 63 51 10 10; Lejbølleveje; adult/child Dkr20/free; ☺ 10am-5pm Mon-Fri & 1-5pm Sat & Sun Jun–mid-Sep, 10am-4pm Mon-Fri & 1-4pm Sat & Sun mid-Sep–May), a 19th-century windmill, with its remarkable wooden mechanics still intact.

Langeland's main town of **Rudkøbing** has a fairly desolate harbour area, but the town centre is attractive and there are some fine old buildings around Rudekøbing Kirke, to the north of Brogade, the street leading inland from the harbour to the main square of Torvet. For beaches, head for **Ristinge** about 15km south of Rudkøbing; for **bird-watching** you'll find a sighting tower at **Tryggelev Nor**, 5km south of Ristinge, and a sanctuary at **Gulstav Bog**, the island's southern tip.

Cycling is a good way to explore Langeland. The tourist office has an excellent English-language edition of a brochure and map (Dkr15) that describes six bike routes on the island. Bikes can be hired at **Lapletten** (☎ 62 51 10 98; Engdraget 1; per day Dkr50).

Sleeping & Eating

The tourist office maintains a list of rooms for rent in private homes with doubles costing about Dkr350 to Dkr400.

Skrøbelevgaard (☎ 62 51 45 31; www .skrobelevgaard.dk; Skrøbelev Hedevej 4; s Dkr450-500, d Dkr675-850) This cosy inn, 4km east of Rudkøbing in the village of Ny Skrøbelev, is a fine option if you enjoy historic settings and the quiet of the countryside. Occupying a 17th-century manor house, Skrøbelevgaard has 10 cosy rooms. The free city bus stops nearby on weekdays.

Danhostel Rudkøbing (☎ 62 51 18 30; www .danhostel.dk/rudkobing; Engdraget 11; dm/r Dkr140/300; camp sites per adult Dkr60; ☺ Apr-end Oct) A pretty basic hostel, which is less than ideally located a way back from the centre or the water. There's also space for tents.

Damgården (☎ 62 59 16 45; www.damgaarden .dk; Emmerbøllervej 5, Emmerbølle, Tranekær; Dkr235 per person) Denmark's first organic B&B offers bright, spacious rooms in a pretty farm house with a large garden and serves great home-made breakfasts. The owners can organise tours and outings.

Getting There & Away

Buses make the 25-minute run from Svendborg to Rudkøbing (Dkr30) at least hourly; most connect onwards to Tranekær. There are daily ferries from Rudkøbing to Marstal in Ærø (one-way per person/car Dkr81/179) and from Spodsbjerg to Tårs in Lolland.

ÆRØ

pop 6800

Ærø is one of the most enchanting of all the islands of the south Fyn archipelago with a gentle coastline and an interior of rolling green hills, patchworked with fields and farmsteads. The winding country roads are punctuated with thatched houses, old windmills, ancient passage graves and dolmens. Most of the villages are to be found on the coast. There are some good, small beaches, one of the best being **Risemark Strand** on the southern tip of the 30km long island; it's a great place to tour by bicycle.

Ærøhas' three main towns are Ærøskøbing, Marstal and Søby. **Ærøskøbing tourist office** (☎ 62 52 13 00; Vestergade 1; ◷ 10am-3.30pm Mon-Sat, to 1pm Sun) is near the waterfront. **Marstal tourist office** (☎ 62 53 19 60; Havnegade 5; ◷ 10am-6pm Mon-Fri, 10.30am-1.30pm Sat, 9.30am-12.30pm Sun) is a few minutes' walk south of the harbour. The island's tourist website is www.arre.dk.

Ærøskøbing

pop 750

The words 'higgledy' and 'piggledy' could have been invented to describe the idyllic town of Ærøskøbing. A prosperous merchants' town in the late 1600s, its narrow, winding cobblestone streets are lined with 17th- and 18th-century houses, many of them gently subsiding, crooked, half-timbered affairs with traditional hand-blown glass windows and decorative doorways beautified by hollyhocks. The tourist office has an illustrated leaflet, with a separate insert in English, describing the finest buildings in the town, many of them very well preserved.

Apart from Ærøskøbing's overall charm, the main tourist attraction is **Flaske Peters Samling** (☎ 62 52 29 51; Smedegade 22; adult/child Dkr25/10; ◷ 10am-5pm), a museum in the former poorhouse with displays of local folk art. There are also examples of the work of ship's cook, Peter Jacobsen, 'Bottle Peter', who crafted 1700 ships-in-a-bottle during his long life. **Ærø Museum** (☎ 62 52 29 50; Brogade 3-5; ; adults Dkr25 ◷ 10am-4pm Mon-Fri, 11am-3pm Sat & Sun) charts the local cultural history.

Søby

This quiet little port has a shipyard, which is the island's biggest employer, a sizable fishing fleet and a busy yacht marina. Five kilometres beyond Søby, at Ærø's northern tip, there's a pebble beach with clear water and a stone **lighthouse** with a view.

Marstal

On the southeastern end of the island, Marstal is Ærø's most modern-looking town and has a web of busy shopping streets at its centre. Marstal has an emphatically maritime history; even its street names echo the names of ships and famous sailors. Its **Søfartsmuseum** (☎ 62 53 23 31; Prinsensgade 1; adult/child Dkr40/free; ◷ 9am-8pm Jul, to 5pm Jun & Aug, 10am-4pm Mar & Sep) has an absorbing collection of nautical artefacts including 250 ships' models and full-size boats. There is a reasonably good **beach** on the southern side of town.

Ancient Ærø

Ærø once had more than 100 prehistoric sites and, although many have been lost, the island still has some atmospheric Neolithic remains, especially in its southeast district, to the west of Marstal. At the small village of Store Rise is the site of **Tingstedet**, the remains of a passage grave in a field behind an attractive **12th-century church**.

At **Lindsbjerg** is the superb hilltop site of a long barrow and two passage graves, one of which has a nicely poised capstone. Just over 1km south of here, following signs and right on the coast, is the fascinating medieval relic of **Sankt Albert's Kirke**. It's within a Viking defensive wall from about the 8th century.

Another striking site is at **Kragnæs**, about 4km west of Marstal. Head through the village of Græsvænge and follow signs for 'Jættestue' along narrow lanes to reach a small car park, from where it's about 600m along field tracks to the restored grave site.

DENMARK

Sleeping

The island's tourist offices have a list of countryside B&Bs around the island for around Dkr230/350 for singles/doubles. There are camping grounds at **Søby** (☎ 62 58 14 70; www.soeby-camping.dk, **Ærøskøbing** (☎ 62 52 18 54; www.arrecamping.dk) and **Marstal** (☎ 63 52 63 69; www.marstalcammping.dk).

Danhostel Ærøskøbing (☎ 62 52 10 44; www .danhostel.dk; dm/r Dkr120/300; ☺ Apr–Sep; P ☒) A solid, modern red-tiled building, this hostel is 1km from town on the road to Marstal.

Danhostel Marstal (☎ 51 35 77 54; www.danhostel .dk; Færgestræde 29; dm/s/d Dkr100/210/250; ☺ May– Sep) South of the harbour, this modest but neatly kept hostel is right by the sea.

Hotel Ærøhus (☎ 62 52 10 03; www.aeroehus.dk; Vestergade 38; s/d Dkr890/1190) In Ærøskøbing, Hotel Ærøhus occupies a large period building close to the harbour. It has comfortable, modern rooms, a smart garden annexe and two tennis courts.

Pension Vestergade 44 (☎ 62 52 22 98; www .pension-vestergade44.dk; Vestergade 44; s/d Dkr450/ 680; P ☒) Next door to the Ærohus is this delightful 18th-century house with very stylish, yet homely interiors.

Toldbodhus (☎ 62 52 18 11; Brogade 8, Ærøskøbing; d Dkr690) This quiet, friendly B&B has wonderfully decorated (if small) rooms, many with local antiques (two have four-poster beds).

Eating & Drinking

All three towns have bakeries, restaurants and food stores.

Hos Grethe (☎ 62 52 21 43; Vertergade 39; mains Dkr45-95; ☺ noon-3pm winter, to 6pm Jun-Aug) Favoured by locals for its home-cooking style and good fish dishes.

Ærøskøbing Røgeri (☎ 62 52 40 07; Havnen 15, Ærøskøbing; ☺ 11am-6pm or until 8pm Jun-Aug) This traditional fish smokehouse in Ærøskøbing harbour serves excellent value plates of fresh-smoked salmon, herring and other fish dishes for Dkr22 to Dkr59 – you eat outside on picnic benches.

Foleys Irish Pub (☎ 62 53 13 23; Strandstræde 39B) Just along the road from Hotel Marstal is Foleys, brimming with Irish beers and a strong, live folk-music programme.

Getting There & Away

There are year-round **car ferries** (☎ 62 52 40 00; www.aeroe-ferry.dk; adult/child/bike/car Dkr 145/78/33/326) to Søby from Faaborg, to Ærøskøbing from Svendborg and to Marstal from Rudkøbing. All run about five times a day and take about an hour. If you have a car it's a good idea to make reservations, particularly at weekends and in midsummer. There's also a **ferry** between Søby and Mommark that runs a few times daily from spring to autumn at comparable prices.

Getting Around

Bus No 990 runs from Søby to Marstal via Ærøskøbing hourly from Monday to Friday, and half as frequently at weekends.

You can rent bikes for Dkr250 a week at the hostel and camping ground in Ærøskøbing and at **Pilebækkens Cykel og Servicestation** (☎ 62 52 11 10; Pilebækken 11) opposite the car park on the outskirts of town.

Søby Cykelforretning (☎ 62 58 18 42; Langebro 4; per day Dkr50) rents out bikes in Søby. The tourist office in Marstal sells a Dkr20 cycling map of a round-island route.

JUTLAND

The Jutland (Jylland) Peninsula is where mainland Europe meets Scandinavia although with little drama; the area where the borders meet is a rather monotonous procession of moor and marsh.

Further north things improve as you hit the pretty, forested Lake District and further north still the windswept western and northern coasts (a windsurfer's dream) lined with vast sandy beaches.

The region was settled originally by the Jutes, a Germanic tribe whose forays included invading England in the 5th century. Not surprisingly Jutland's southern boundary has been a fluid one, last drawn in 1920 when Germany relinquished its holdings in Sønderjylland.

Most of the main cities, including Århus and Aalborg, are along the more sheltered east coast.

ÅRHUS & AROUND

pop 285,000

The cultural and commercial heart of Jutland, Århus has one of Denmark's best music and entertainment scenes, a well-preserved historic quarter and plenty to see and do, ranging from fantastic museums (don't miss Moesgård, p85) and period churches in the centre, to picturesque woodland trails and beaches along the city's outskirts.

The second-largest city in Denmark, it lies midway along Jutland's eastern coastline and has been an important trading centre and seaport since Viking times when it was known as Aros, the 'place at the river's mouth'.

During the medieval period Århus seesawed between prosperity and devastation as rival Vikings and warring kings entangled the city in their campaigns. Today it is home to a thriving university with more than 20,000 students yet retains all the friendliness and ease of a small country town.

Orientation

Århus is fairly compact and easy to get around. The train station is on the southern side of the city centre. The pedestrian shopping streets of Ryesgade, Søndergade and Sankt Clements Torv extend around 1km from the station to the cathedral at the heart of the old city.

Information

BOOKSHOPS

KFM (Store Torv 5) A bookshop with a good range of books including travel guides.

Newspaper Shop (Store Torv 7) Sells international papers and magazines. International newspapers are also sold at the train station.

EMERGENCY

Århus Kommunehospital (☎ 87 31 50 50; Nørrebrogade) has a 24-hour emergency ward.

Emergency (☎ 112) Ambulance and police

INTERNET ACCESS

Boomtown (Åboulevarden 21; per hr Dkr30; ☺ 10-2am Mon-Thu, to 8am Fri & Sat, 11am-midnight Sun)

LAUNDRY

Mønt Vask (St Paul's Gade 64) A coin launderette. An average wash and dry costs Dkr45.

LEFT LUGGAGE

Lockers are available at the bus and train stations. Both charge Dkr10 for 24 hours.

POST

Post Office (Banegårdspladsen; ☺ 9.30am-6pm Mon-Fri, 10am-1pm Sat) Beside the train station.

TOURIST INFORMATION

Tourist Office (☎ 87 31 50 10; www.visitaarhus.com; Banegårdspladsen; ☺ 9.30am-6pm Mon-Fri, to 5pm Sat, to 1pm Sun mid-Jun–mid-Sep, to 5pm Mon-Fri, 10am-1pm Sat May–mid-Jun, 9am-4pm Mon-Fri, to 1pm Sat mid-Sep–Apr) Well stocked with brochures and leaflets on the city and its surroundings, and on the rest of Jutland and Denmark. You can also buy the Århus Passport here, a two-day or weekly pass that include public-transport usage and admissions to various attractions.

TRAVEL AGENCIES

Kilroy Travels (☎ 86 20 11 44; Fredensgade 40) Specialises in discount and student travel and has friendly, helpful staff.

Sights & Activities

AROS

The towering brick walls of Århus's new showpiece **art museum** (☎ 87 30 66 00; www.aros .dk; adult/child Dkr76/free; ☺ 10am-5pm Thu-Sun & Tue, to 10pm Wed) look rather mundane from the outside but inside it's all sweeping curves, soaring spaces and white walls. One of the top three art galleries in Denmark, it is home to a comprehensive collection of 19th- and 20th-century Danish art and a wide range of arresting and vivid contemporary art. There are pieces here from Warhol and Lichtenstein and, in colourfully-lit pickling jars, a work by Danish artist Bjørn Nørgaard consisting of parts of a horse he sacrificed in protest at the Vietnam War (long before British artist Damien Hirst started chopping up animals in the name of art). Perhaps the most compelling exhibit is Ron Mueck's startlingly lifelike giant *Boy*. There are pleasing views over town from the terrace and a good café and restaurant (see p87).

DEN GAMLE BY

The Danes' seemingly limitless enthusiasm for dressing up and recreating history reaches its zenith at Den Gamle By (The Old Town; ☎ 86 12 31 88; www.dengamleby.dk; Viborgvej 2; adult/child Dkr80/free; ☺ 9am-6pm Jul-Aug, 10am-5pm Apr-Jun & Sep-Nov, to 4pm Feb & Mar 10am-5pm, Dec, 11am-3pm Jan). It's an engaging open-air museum of 75 half-timbered houses brought here from around Denmark and reconstructed as a provincial town, complete with a functioning bakery, silversmith and bookbinder. It's on Viborgvej, a 20-minute walk from the city centre. After hours you

DENMARK

ÅRHUS

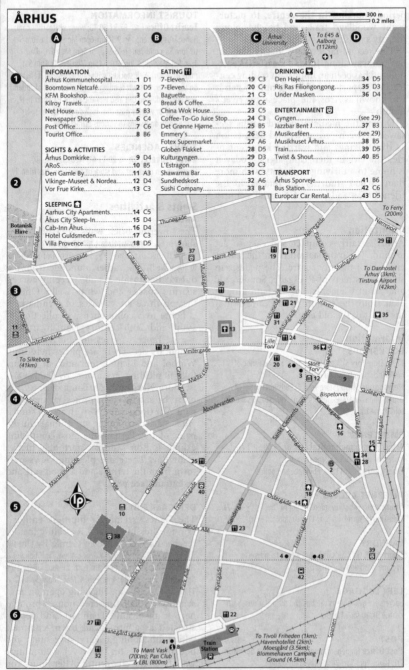

INFORMATION	
Århus Kommunehospital	1 D1
Boomtown Netcafé	2 D5
KFM Bookshop	3 C4
Kilroy Travels	4 C5
Net House	5 B3
Newspaper Shop	6 C4
Post Office	7 C6
Tourist Office	8 B6

SIGHTS & ACTIVITIES	
Århus Domkirke	9 D4
ARoS	10 B5
Den Gamle By	11 A3
Vikinge-Museet & Nordea	12 D4
Vor Frue Kirke	13 C3

SLEEPING	
Aarhus City Apartments	14 C5
Århus City Sleep-In	15 D4
Cab-Inn Åhus	16 D4
Hotel Guldsmeden	17 C3
Villa Provence	18 D5

EATING	
7-Eleven	19 C3
7-Eleven	20 C4
Baguette	21 C3
Bread & Coffee	22 C6
China Wok House	23 C5
Coffee-To-Go Juice Stop	24 C3
Det Grønne Hjørne	25 B5
Emmery's	26 C3
Fotex Supermarket	27 A6
Globen Flakket	28 D5
Kulturgyngen	29 D3
L'Estragon	30 C3
Shawarma Bar	31 C3
Sundhedskost	32 A6
Sushi Company	33 B4

DRINKING	
Den Høje	34 D5
Ris Ras Filiongongong	35 D3
Under Masken	36 D4

ENTERTAINMENT	
Gyngen	(see 29)
Jazzbar Bent J	37 B3
Musikcaféen	(see 29)
Musikhuset Århus	38 B5
Train	39 D5
Twist & Shout	40 B5

TRANSPORT	
Århus Sporveje	41 B6
Bus Station	42 C6
Europcar Car Rental	43 D5

can walk through the old streets for free. It's an interesting time to visit as the crowds are gone and the light is ideal for photography, though you won't be able to enter individual buildings. Bus Nos 3, 14, 25 and 55 will take you there.

The **Botanisk Have** (Botanical Gardens), with its thousands of plants and recreated Jutland environments, occupies the high ground above Den Gamle By and can be reached through an exit from the old town or directly from Vesterbrogade.

ÅRHUS DOMKIRKE

This impressive **cathedral** (☎ 86 20 54 00; Bispetorv; admission free; ☼ 9.30am-4pm Mon-Sat May-Sep, 10am-3pm Mon-Sat Oct-Apr) is Denmark's longest, with a lofty nave that spans nearly 100m. The original Romanesque chapel at the eastern-end dates from the 12th century, while most of the rest of the church is 15th-century Gothic.

Like other Danish churches, the cathedral was once richly decorated with **frescoes** that served to convey biblical parables to unschooled peasants. After the Reformation, church authorities who felt the frescoes smacked too much of Roman Catholicism, had them all whitewashed, but many have now been uncovered and restored. They range from fairy-tale paintings of St George slaying a dragon, to scenes of hellfire.

The cathedral's splendid, five-panel, gilt **altarpiece** is a highlight. It was made in Lübeck by the renowned woodcarver Bernt Notke in the 15th century. In its centre panel, to the left of the Madonna and child, is a gaunt-faced St Clement, to whom Århus Domkirke was dedicated. The ill-fated Clement drowned at sea with an anchor around his neck and became the patron saint of sailors for his pains.

The cathedral's other items worth noting include the bronze baptismal font dating from 1481, the finely carved Renaissance pulpit created in 1588, the magnificent baroque pipe organ made in 1730, the large 18th-century votive ship and the baroque sepulchre in the Marselis family chapel.

VOR FRUE KIRKE

This **church** (☎ 86 12 12 43; Frue Kirkeplads; admission free; ☼ 10am-2pm Mon-Fri, to noon Sat), off Vestergade, has a carved wooden **altarpiece** dating from the 1530s. But far more interesting is

what's in its basement: the **crypt** of the city's original cathedral, dating from about 1060. Enter via the stairway beneath the altar. To enter a third chapel, this one with 16th-century frescoes, go through the courtyard and take the left door.

VIKINGE-MUSEET

There's more than the expected vaults in the bank basement of **Nordea** (☎ 89 42 11 00; Sankt Clements Torv 6; admission free; ☼ 10am-4pm Mon-Wed & Fri, to 5.30pm Thu) where there's a small exhibition of artefacts from the Viking Age town that were excavated at this site in 1964 during the bank's construction. The display includes a skeleton, a reconstructed house, 1000-year-old carpentry tools and pottery, and photos of the excavation.

MOESGÅRD

Visit Moesgård, 5km south of the city centre, for its glorious beech woods and the trails threading through them towards sandy beaches. Visit for the well-presented history exhibits from the Stone Age to the Viking Age at **Moesgård Museum of Prehistory** (adult/child Dkr45/free; ☼ 10am-5pm Apr-Sep, to 4pm Tue-Sun Oct-May). But above all else, visit Moesgård for the museum's most dramatic exhibit: the 2000-year-old **Grauballe Man**, or Graubballemanden, whose astonishingly well-preserved body was found in 1952 at the village of Grauballe, 35km west of Århus.

The superb new display on the Grauballe Man is part history lesson, part forensics lesson. Was he a sacrifice to Iron Age fertility gods, an executed prisoner perhaps, or simply a victim of murder? Either way, the broken leg and the gaping neck wound suggests his death, sometime in the last century BC, was a horribly violent one. His body and skin, tanned and preserved by the unique chemical and biological qualities of the peat bogs, are remarkably intact, right down to hair and fingernails.

Away from all this death and violence, there's an enjoyable **trail** dubbed the 'prehistoric trackway' or Oldtidsstien leading from behind the museum across fields of wildflowers, past grazing sheep and through beech woods down to **Moesgård Strand**, Århus' best sandy beach. The trail, marked by red-dotted stones, passes reconstructed historic sights including a dolmen, burial cists and an Iron-Age house. The museum has a brochure with details. You can walk one way and catch a bus back to the city centre, or follow the trail both ways as a 5km round-trip. It's all well worth a half-day or full-day visit, with a picnic perhaps if the weather behaves itself.

Bus No 6 from Århus train station terminates at the museum year-round, while bus No 19 terminates at Moesgård Strand from May to September; both buses run about twice an hour.

SWIMMING
There are sandy beaches on the outskirts of Århus. The most popular one to the north is **Bellevue**, about 4km from the city centre (bus No 6 or 16), while the favourite to the south is Moesgård Strand.

Tours
A guided 2½-hour bus tour leaves from the **tourist office** (☎ 89 40 67 00 for bookings) at 10am daily from mid-June to early September, giving a glimpse of the main city sights. The Dkr50 tour is a good deal as it includes entry into Den Gamle By and also leaves you with a 24-hour public bus pass.

Festival & Events
The 10-day **Århus Festival** (www.aarhusfestuge .dk) in early September turns the city into a stage for nonstop revelry with jazz, rock, classical music, theatre and dance. The festival has hosted such varied bill toppers as the Rolling Stones, Philip Glass, Anne-Sophie Mutter, Ravi Shankar, the City of Birmingham Symphony Orchestra, New York City Ballet, Günter Grass and many more. Each year the festival has a special theme. Events take place all over the city and there is a fringe element also.

Sleeping
BUDGET
The tourist office books rooms in private homes for around Dkr200/300 per single/double, plus a Dkr25 booking fee.**Århus City Sleep-In** (☎ 86 19 20 55; www.citysleep-in.dk; Havnegade 20; dm Dkr115, d with/without bathroom Dkr400/360; ☒ 24hr reception; ▨ ☒) Run by a youth organisation, the Århus City Sleep-In is in a central former mariners' hotel. It's casual, the rooms are a bit rundown but it's a cheerful place and by far the best budget option in the centre. Sheet hire costs Dkr45 and safety boxes are Dkr20, with Dkr100 deposit. Key deposit is Dkr50. There's a TV and pool table, guest kitchen and laundry facilities. Bike hire costs Dkr50 a day.

Danhostel Århus (☎ 86 16 72 98; www.hostel -aarhus.dk; Marienlundsvej 10; dm/r Dkr108/472; ☒ late Jan–mid-Dec) It may be 4km north of the city centre but its well worth considering for the lovely parkland setting in a renovated 1850s dance hall. It's at the edge of the Risskov

---

DENMARK'S BOG PEOPLE

In the last couple of centuries, hundreds of often amazingly well-preserved bodies of men, women and children have been unearthed by peat cutters in the bogs of Denmark and Northern Europe, mostly from the Iron Age (the early centuries BC and AD).

Each is a compelling historical who- and why-dunnit. The manner of their death is intriguing because these people had not been merely buried after death (cremation was the common funerary ritual at the time). It seems many of them were ritually killed, perhaps as part of religious ceremonies or acts of propitiation linked to the supernatural power the Iron Age people attributed to the bogs.

If it were ritual killing, were these people victims or willing participants? Was it perhaps an honour to be sacrificed? The Windeby Girl, for example, found in 1950 in Germany, aged about 14, had been blindfolded and had her hair carefully cropped, suggesting some kind of ritual.

Others, like the Grauballe Man (see p85) clearly died a nasty, violent death that suggests execution. Others may have simply been waylaid, murdered and dumped. Classical authors at the time such as Tacitus wrote that this was the kind of end met by 'cowards, deserters and homosexuals'.

The most famous, and best preserved, body is that of the Tollund Man in Silkeborg (p90). He died, aged in his 30s, naked but for the beautifully plaited leather noose that strangled him and the leather cap he has worn for 2000 years. It frames an utterly serene face.

Woods and a few minutes from the beach. Bus No 6 or 9 pass nearby.

Blommehaven (☎ 86 27 02 07; www.camping -blommehaven.dk in Danish; camp site per adult/child/tent Dkr62/31/20; ☒ mid-Mar–mid-Sep) The nearest camping ground is right by beaches in the Marselisborg Woods, 6km south of Århus and reached by bus No 19 or 6.

MIDRANGE

Cab Inn Århus (☎ 86 75 70 00; www.cabinn.com; Kannikegade 14; s/d Dkr525/645; ⓟ ☒ ▢) In an ideal central location opposite the Domkirke. The style is standard Cab Inn with small, but comfy and spotless rooms. Parking costs Dkr60. Free internet and wi-fi access.

Hotel Guldsmeden (☎ 86 13 45 50; www .hotelguldsmeden.dk in Danish; Guldsmedgade 40; s/d Dkr595/845, s/d with bathroom from Dkr895/1095; ▢) On the northern side of the city centre, this is our midrange choice in town for friendly staff, delightfully bright French colonial-style rooms with polished wood floors, large four-poster beds with soft white linen, a small garden terrace and a generally relaxed, stylish ambience. Good (mainly organic) breakfasts. There's wi-fi access.

Aarhus City Apartments (☎ 86 27 51 30; www .hotelaca.dk; Fredensgade 18; d from Dkr580; ⓟ) A good midrange option especially for self caterers, these smart, modern one- and two-bedroom apartments right in the city centre have their own kitchen, cable TV and free internet access. There's no reception so you must book ahead.

Havnehotellet (www.havnehotellet.dk; Marselisborg Havnevej 20; d from Dkr495; ⓟ) A bike or bus ride from the city centre, Havnehotellet offers bright, clean, modern comfort overlooking yachts and the sea. A good midrange bet although the single beds are very narrow. Reception hours are short and most guests check in via an electronic reception in the small foyer.

TOP END

Villa Provence (☎ 86 18 24 00; www.villaprovence.dk; Fredens Torv 12; d/ste from Dkr995/1790; ⓟ ☒ ▢) Very central and with beautifully decorated rooms in a lavish Provençal country-house style, this is the place to indulge, with attentive personal service, a predinner snifter in the wine bar, or perhaps its excellent breakfast with French cheese and Spanish charcuterie in the courtyard beneath the linden trees.

Eating

The narrow streets of the old quarter north of the cathedral are thick with cafés serving Danish and ethnic foods. There is a string of slightly more upmarket riverside restaurants and bars with outside seating along the north of Åboulevarden to the west of Sankt Clements Torv bridge.

Globen Flakket (☎ 87 31 03 33; www.globen -flakket.dk; Åboulevarden 18; mains Dkr65-230; ☒ 10am-10pm daily) The best of the riverside café cum restaurants, covering all the bases really well. Upstairs you'll find the cosy bar serving very decent wraps, tapas, burgers, brunch and an evening buffet (Dkr79). Downstairs the rather more formal restaurant turns out finer fare such as guinea fowl with smoked white beans and beetroot salsa or beef tournedos with truffled Madeira sauce.

AroS (☎ 87 30 66 00; mains Dkr140-60; ☒ same as gallery) A good bet for a snack, the art museums downstairs café serves tasty focaccia sandwiches and lovely sweet treats or upstairs for good, simple brasserie food (such as lamb with pearl barley salad and rosemary honey sauce).

Coffee-To-Go Juice Stop (☎ 86 13 69 65; Badstuegade 4; juices small/large Dkr25/30, bagels/sandwiches Dkr34/40; ☒ 9am-6pm Mon-Fri, 9am-2pm Sat) A good juice, fruit salad and sandwich pit stop. It's mainly takeaway, but there are a few seats to rest those cobblestone-weary feet.

Emmery's (☎ 86 13 04 00; Guldsmedgade 24-26; brunch Dkr95, breakfast Dkr23; ☒ 7.30am-6pm Mon-Fri, 8am-4pm Sat & Sun) A stylish and friendly café-cum-delicatessen that serves its own delicious bread, tapas (Dkr95) and sandwiches (Dkr45 to Dkr58), some with vegetarian fillings.

Kulturgyngen (Mejlgade 53; lunch/dinner Dkr38/75; ☒ 11am-9pm Mon-Sat) The café-restaurant of an alternative cultural and youth complex has a great atmosphere and good, often organic food including chilli con carne, sandwiches (Dkr28 to Dkr38) and a choice of vegetarian or meat dinners nightly.

Sushi Company (☎ 86 13 73 83; Vestergade 48; set menu Dkr85-220; ☒ dinner Tue-Sun) A small, unlicenced sushi joint that also serves vegetarian options.

Det Grønne Hjørne (☎ 86 13 52 47; Frederiksgade 60; lunch buffet Dkr69, buffet after 4pm Dkr109) On the corner with Østergade, this restaurant has a superb buffet spread with hearty, warming fare such as lasagne and chilli con carne and several good vegetarian options.

L'Estragon (☎ 86 12 40 66; Klostergade 6; mains Dkr195, 3-course menu Dkr315) The best central fine dining spot in Århus offers very posh French classics accompanied by carefully chosen wines.

If you want fast, cheap and filling take-away fare, some good options include the following: **China Wok House** (Søndergade; lunch box Dkr20); **Shawarma Bar** (Guldsmedgade; pitta-bread sandwiches Dkr25); **Baguette** (Klostergade 17; baguettes Dkr21), close to Emmery's, which does great well-filled baguettes; and **Bread and Coffee** (Banegårdspladsen; pastries Dkr9-20), which serves tasty pastries and is just opposite the train station.

The train station has a DSB café, a snack bar and a small **supermarket** (☒ to midnight). Two blocks west is **Føtex supermarket** (Frederiks Allé), with a cheap bakery and deli, and **Sundhedskost** (Frederiks Allé), the city's largest health-food store. There are a couple of useful branches of **7-Eleven** (cnr Lille Torv & Immervad, Guldsmedgade 33; ☒ 24hr).

Drinking

Under Masken (☎ 86 18 22 66; Bispegade 3) The ethnic masks lining the walls and ceiling may leer and scowl but the real natives in this convivial little basement place are friendly. A good range of bottled lagers and ales.

Ris Ras Filiongongong (☎ 86 18 5006; Mejlgade 24) More of a sitting room than a bar, Ris Ras is intimate, friendly, very small and very popular, so get here early to nab a seat and a hook.

Den Høje (Skolegade 28) There are a number of busy bars in Skolegade, where Den Høje is popular with an easygoing young crowd, not least for its cheap beer. It's open most nights from 7pm to 5am, but is closed on Sunday.

Entertainment

The monthly free publication *What's On in Århus* lists current happenings in detail and is available at the tourist office and other venues around town.

Århus has a vibrant music scene with something for all ages and tastes.

Train (☎ 86 13 47 22; Toldbodgade 6; ☒ until 5am Thu-Sat) One of the biggest venues in Denmark stages concerts by international rock, pop and country stars and there's a late-night disco.

Musikcaféen (☎ 86 76 03 44; Mejlgade 53; ☒ 8.30pm-2am Mon-Sat) and the adjacent Gyngen are alternative and often vibrant venues with rock, jazz and world music. They are a showcase for hopefuls and up-and-coming acts.

Jazzbar Bent J (☎ 86 12 04 92; Nørre Allé 66; ☒ from 3.30pm Mon-Fri) This is a jazz only, very long-established bar with an impressive guest list. Entry is Dkr80 on guest nights.

Twist & Shout (☎ 86 18 08 55; Frederiksgade 29; ☒ 10am-5am Mon-Thu, from 5pm Fri & 10pm Sat) Lively, small, often packed and friendly, this three-floor disco is the place to head for later in the evening. It's not too precious, there's a mix of music from '60s to house (depending on the floor) and everyone has fun.

Musikhuset Århus (☎ 89 40 40 40; Thomas Jensens Allé 2) The city concert hall presents dance, opera and concerts by international performers.

The main gay and lesbian social scene is at **Pan Club** (☎ 86 13 43 80; Jaægergårdsgade 42). To find it, head south down MP Bruuns Gade on the west side of the train station and then go right down Jaægergårdsgade for 300m and it's on the left-hand side of the road.

Getting There & Away

AIR

The airport, in Tirstrup 43km northeast of Århus, has direct flights from Copenhagen and London. Budget carrier Ryanair flies twice daily between London Stansted and Århus on weekdays and once on Saturday and Sunday. See p111 for details.

BOAT

The ferry operator is **Mols-Linien** (☎ 70 10 14 18). It runs car ferries from Århus to Odden (Dkr140 to Dkr235, car and five passengers Dkr525, 65 minutes).

BUS

The bus station (Fredensgade) has a DSB café and a small supermarket. Express buses (☎ 98 90 09 00) run a few times daily between Århus and Copenhagen's Valby Station (adult/child Dkr240/120, students Dkr120 Monday to Thursday only, three hours). Buses run regularly to Silkeborg (adult/child Dkr55/38, 48 minutes, twice hourly) and Aalborg (adult/child Dkr135/78, two hours, five daily).

CAR & MOTORCYCLE

The main highways to Århus are the E45 from the north and south and Rte 15 from the west. The E45 curves around the western edge of the city as a ring road. There are a number of turn-offs from the ring road into the city, including Åohavevej from the south and Randersvej from the north.

Cars can be rented from **Europcar** (☎ 89 33 11 11; Sønder Allé 35).

TRAIN

Trains to Århus, via Odense, leave Copenhagen on the hour from early morning to 10pm (Dkr287, 3¼ hours) and there's a night train at 2am. There are regular trains to Århus (Dkr60, 49 minutes), Aalborg (Dkr150, 1½ hours), and Esbjerg (Dkr206, 2¾ hours). There's a ticket-queuing system at the station: red for internal; green for international. For local journeys, unless you have mastered use of the quicker ticket machines, be prepared for quite long waits at busy times. Friday trains are always very busy and it's advised to reserve a seat for long journeys.

Getting Around

TO/FROM THE AIRPORT

The airport bus to Århus train station costs Dkr80 and takes approximately 45 minutes. Check times to the airport at the stands outside the train station; some services start only in August. The taxi fare to the airport is about Dkr650.

BUS

Most in-town buses stop in front of the train station or around the corner on Park Allé. City bus tickets are bought from a machine in the back of the bus for Dkr17 and are good for unlimited rides within the time period stamped on the ticket, which is about two hours.

You can also buy a 24-hour pass for bus travel in Århus county (adult/child Dkr97/48) or in Århus municipality alone (Dkr55). Or get a one-/two-/seven-day Århus Passet (Dkr97/121/171) that includes both bus travel and entry into Århus museums. You can buy tickets and passes at **Århus Sporveje** (☎ 89 40 10 10; Banegårdspladsen 20; ♥ 10am-6pm Mon-Fri, to 1pm Sat), the city transport service shop across from the train station.

CAR & MOTORCYCLE

A car is convenient for getting to sights such as Moesgårdon on the city outskirts, though the city centre is best explored on foot. There's paid parking along many streets and in municipal car parks, including one on the southern side of Musikhuset Århus. Fees start at Dkr1 for six minutes and Dkr12 for one hour. Overnight (7pm to 8am) is free.

BICYCLE

Look out for free Århusbycykel (www.aarhusbycykel.dk) city bikes in the city centre. One is yours for a Dkr20 deposit.

TAXI

Taxis wait outside the station and at Store Torv. Expect to pay around Dkr60 for destinations within the city.

JELLING

Despite its low-key rural character, the tiny hamlet of Jelling is the location of one of Denmark's most important historic sites, the **Jelling Kirke**. Inside the small whitewashed church are frescoes dating from the 12th century, and outside the door are two impressive and historically significant rune stones.

The smaller stone was erected in the early 900s by King Gorm the Old, Denmark's first king, in honour of his wife, Queen Thyra. The larger one, raised by Harald Bluetooth and dubbed 'Denmark's baptismal certificate', is adorned with the oldest representation of Christ found in Scandinavia and reads: 'Harald king bade this be ordained for Gorm his father and Thyra his mother, the Harald who won for himself all Denmark and Norway and made the Danes Christians.'

Two huge **burial mounds** flank the church; the one on the northern side is said to be that of King Gorm and the other of Queen Thyra, although excavators in the 19th century found no human remains and few artefacts. This could suggest much earlier grave robbing.

During the 1970s archaeologists excavated below Jelling Kirke and found the remains of three wooden churches. The oldest of these was thought to have been erected by Harald Bluetooth. A burial chamber within this site was also uncovered and revealed human bones and gold jewellery that shared characteristics with artefacts previously discovered within the large northern burial mound. One suggestion is that the bones found beneath the church ruins are those of King Gorm and they were moved there from the old pagan burial mound by Harald Bluetooth out of respect for his recently acquired Christian faith. Queen Thyra remains ephemeral. The Jelling mounds, church and rune stones are designated as a Unesco World Heritage Listed Site.

Kongernes Jelling (☎ 75 87 23 50; Gormsgade 23; adult/child Dkr40/15; ☻ 10am-5pm daily Jun-Aug, 10am-5pm Tue-Sun May & Sep, 1-4pm Tue-Sun Nov-Apr) the information and exhibition centre just across the road from the church, offers a good insight into the history of the Jelling monuments and of early Denmark.

Jelling makes a good two-hour side trip off the Odense–Århus run. Change trains at Vejle for the ride to Jelling (Dkr28, 15 minutes). The church is 100m straight up Stationsvej from the Jelling train station.

THE LAKE DISTRICT

The Danish Lake District, the closest thing to hill country in Denmark (so don't imagine anything like England's dramatic Lake District), is a popular outdoor-activity area for Danes, and there is certainly excellent canoeing, biking and hiking to be had amid the woods and on the water. The scenery is placid and pastoral rather than stunning, but the area is delightful all the same and has a distinctive Danish character. The Lake District contains the Gudenå, Denmark's longest river; Mossø, Jutland's largest lake; and Yding Skovhøj, Denmark's highest point. None of these are terribly long, large or high by international standards.

Silkeborg

pop 54,000

Silkeborg overcomes its rather bland modern character with a friendly openness. It is the Lake District's biggest town and is an ideal base for exploring the surrounding forests and waterways. The town has some good restaurants and lively bars and cafés. If you're even slightly interested in Denmark's ancient history, a compelling reason to visit is to see the Tollund Man, the body of a preserved Iron Age 'bog man' (see the boxed text, right), who looks for all the world as if he's merely asleep.

The helpful **tourist office** (☎ 86 82 19 11; www .silkeborg.com; Åhavevej 2A; ☻ 9am-5pm Mon-Fri, 10am-2pm Sat, mid-Jun–Aug, 9am-4pm Mon-Fri, 10am-1pm Sat Sep-Oct & Apr-Mar, 10am-3pm Mon-Fri Nov-Mar) is near the harbour and has lots of leaflets including detailed route descriptions of walks and cycle routes. There's a **Jsyke Bank** (☎ 89 22 22 22; Vestergade 16) branch with ATM. The **Library** (☎ 86 82 02 33; Hostrupsgade 41) is central & well provided with free internet terminals.

SIGHTS

The main attraction at the **Silkeborg Museum** (☎ 86 82 14 99; Hovedgården; adult/child Dkr45/10; ☻ 10am-5pm mid-May–Oct; noon-4pm Sat & Sun Nov–mid-May) is the Tollund Man. He is believed to have been executed in 300 BC and his leathery body, complete with the rope still around the neck, was discovered in a bog in 1950. The well-preserved face of the Tollund Man is hypnotic in its detail, right down to the stubble on his chin. Other attractions include displays on local trades and of fine Danish glasswork.

The **Silkeborg Kuntsmuseum** (Silkeborg Art Museum; ☎ 86 82 53 88; Gudenåvej 7-9; adult/child Dkr45/ free; ☻ 10am-5pm Tue-Sun Apr-Oct, noon-4pm Tue-Fri Nov-Mar) contains some striking work, such as the large ceramic walls by Jean Dubuffet and Pierre Alechinsky that greet visitors at the entrance. It displays many of the works of native son Asger Jorn and other modern artists, including Max Ernst, Le Corbusier and Danish artists from the influential COBRA group. It's 1km south of the town centre.

Situated 2km south of central Silkeborg, **Aqua** (☎ 89 21 21 89; www.aqua-ferskvandsakvarium .dk; Vejsøvej 55; adult/child Dkr85/50; ☻ 10am-6pm Jun-Aug, to 4pm Mon-Fri, to 5pm Sat & Sun Sep-May) is an entertaining aquarium and exhibition centre exploring the ecosystems of the lakes and surrounding area with lots of fishy creatures, otters and fishing birds among imaginative displays.

ACTIVITIES

Outdoor activities are at the heart of the Lake District's appeal. The track of the old railway from Silkeborg to Horsens is now an excellent **walking** and **cycling** trail of about 50km or so. It passes through the beech forest of **Nordskoven**, itself crisscrossed with hiking and bike trails. To reach Nordskoven simply head south down Åhavevej from the

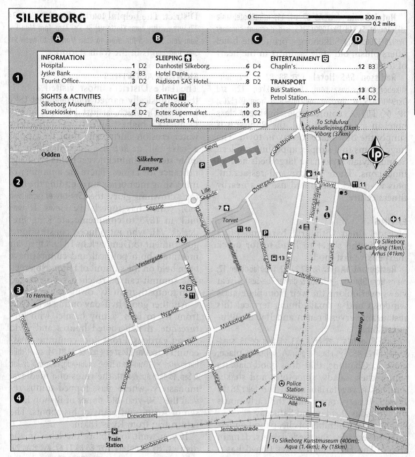

SILKEBORG

INFORMATION		
Hospital	1	D2
Jyske Bank	2	B3
Tourist Office	3	D2

SIGHTS & ACTIVITIES		
Silkeborg Museum	4	C2
Slusekiosken	5	D2

SLEEPING		
Danhostel Silkeborg	6	D4
Hotel Dania	7	C2
Radisson SAS Hotel	8	D2

EATING		
Cafe Rookie's	9	B3
Fotex Supermarket	10	C2
Restaurant 1A	11	D2

ENTERTAINMENT		
Chaplin's	12	B3

TRANSPORT		
Bus Station	13	C3
Petrol Station	14	D2

tourist office, then go left over the old railway bridge down by the hostel. The tourist office has useful leaflets on Nordskoven and on the Silkeborg–Horsens trail.

Canoeing is a marvellous way to explore the Lake District and you can plan trips for several days staying at lakeside camping grounds along the way. The canoe-hire places can help plan an itinerary. You can rent canoes for Dkr75/250 per hour/day at **Slusekiosken** (☎ 86 80 08 93) at the harbour.

Bike hire costs Dkr75 per day at **Schaufuss Cykeludlejning** (☎ 86 81 39 38; Nørreskov Bakke 93), which is about 1.5km from Torvet across Silkeborg Langsø and is reached by bus No 5. **Silkeborg Sø-camping** rents out bikes and canoes from Dkr60 per day.

SLEEPING

Budget and midrange options in town are limited, making B&B accommodation an especially good option. The tourist office publishes a B&B booklet, with singles/doubles costing around Dkr150/300.

Silkeborg Sø-Camping (☎ 86 82 28 24; Århusvej 51; camp site per adult/child/tent Dkr63/31/28) In a lakeside setting 1.5km east of the town centre.

Danhostel Silkeborg (☎ 86 82 36 42; silkeborg@danhostel.dk; Åhavevej 55; dm Dkr150; ☒ Mar-end Nov; ☒ ☒ ☒) The riverbank location, modern facilities and lack of decent alternatives make this hostel very popular, so book ahead. It's east of the train station. There are only dorms, no private rooms.

DENMARK

Hotel Dania (☎ 86 82 01 11; info@hoteldania .dk; Torvet 5; s/d Dkr1090/1265; s/d discount summer Dkr925/1100; ℗) Silkeborg's prime-site hotel offers plush, old-style comfort in the heart of town.

Radisson SAS Hotel (☎ 88 82 22 22; info. silkeborg@radissonsas.com; Papirfabrikken 12; s/d Dkr940/1425, d discount mid-Jun–Aug from Dkr1205; ℗ ⊠ ▣) A comfortable, business-class hotel in a converted mill, the Radisson is simply the best place to stay in town. The huge rooms in a simple, appealing modern Scandinavian style have large beds and all mod cons. There's a bar and restaurant, plus wi-fi and discounted use of a nearby fitness centre.

EATING
Nygade, lined with grill bars and pizza places, is the street to head to for quick inexpensive fast food.

Restaurant 1A (☎ 88 82 22 22; Papirfabrikken 12; mains from Dkr160; ☼ lunch & dinner Tue-Sun) Great views overlooking the weir from plate-glass windows and a small dining terrace, this restaurant serves French and Italian influenced fare.

Café Rookie's (☎ 86 81 33 44; Nygade 18; sandwiches Dkr25-48; ☼ 11am-11pm) A relaxed place, close to Chaplins, that does good ciabatta sandwiches, salads, smoothies and shakes and has a vegetarian menu for Dkr28 to Dkr49. It stays open until the early hours on Thursday, Friday and Saturday.

There are a number of cheap food outlets on Søndergade, the pedestrianised main street. The **Føtex supermarket** (Torvet) has a bakery and an inexpensive café.

ENTERTAINMENT
Nygade is well stocked with music bars and discos including **Chaplin's** (Nygade ☼ Thu-Sat) behind Café Rookie's.

GETTING THERE & AWAY
Hourly or half-hourly trains connect Silkeborg with Skanderborg (Dkr40, 30 minutes) and Århus (Dkr60, 49 minutes) via Ry. There are regular daily buses to Århus (Dkr50, 48 minutes).

Ry
Ry is a smaller town in a more rural setting than Silkeborg and is a good place from which to base your exploration of the Lake District. The helpful **tourist office** (☎ 86 89 34 22; www.visitry.com; Klostervej 3; ☼ 7am-4pm Mon-Fri, 9am-2pm Sat mid-Jun–Aug, to 4pm Mon-Fri, to noon Sat Sep–mid-Jun) is in the train station.

SIGHTS & ACTIVITIES
The Lake District's most visited spot is the whimsically named **Himmelbjerget** (Sky Mountain), which, at just 147m, is one of Denmark's highest hills. It was formed by water erosion during the final Ice Age as a 'false hill' or *kol*, the sides of which are quite steep. Himmelbjerget holds great significance for Danes. There are a number of interesting memorials surrounding the hilltop's crowning glory, the **25m-tower** (admission Dkr5), which has superlative views. It was built in 1875 to commemorate King Frederick VII, who introduced constitutional government to Denmark in 1849. Open-air meetings, both political and cultural have been held on the summit of Himmelbjerget. The summit can be reached via a marked 6km footpath from Ry, or by bus or boat.

Another good, half-day outing is to cycle from Ry to **Boes**, a tiny hamlet with picturesque, thatch-roofed houses and vivid flower gardens. From Boes continue crosscountry to **Øm Kloster** (☎ 86 89 81 94; adult/child Dkr35/10; ☼ 10am-6pm Tue-Sun Jul-Aug, to 5pm May-Jun & Sep, to 4pm Apr & Oct), the ruins of a medieval monastery, where glass-topped tombs reveal the 750-year-old bones of Bishop Elafsen of Århus and many of his abbots. The return trip from Ry is 18km.

If you want to explore the lakes in the district, **Ry Kanofart** (☎ 86 89 11 67; Kyhnsvej 20) rents out canoes for Dkr75/300 per hour/ day. For walking and cycling routes ask at the tourist centre for cycling and walking leaflets (Dkr20). **Cykeludlejning** (☎ 86 89 14 91; Skanderborgvej 19) rents out bikes for Dkr75 a day.

SLEEPING & EATING
The tourist office books rooms in homes from Dkr200/275 for singles/doubles.

Knudhule (☎ 86 89 14 07; www.knudhule.dk in Danish; Randersvej 88; cabins s & d Dkr325, tr & q Dkr350, bungalows Dkr460) Knudhule is an appealing budget holiday camp on a picturesque lake. There are cabins without bathrooms and bungalows (sleeping up to four) with bathrooms. There's also a small restaurant, minigolf, boat hire and swimming/diving platforms on the lake. To get there from the train station, cross the tracks, turn left and go 2.5km; or take the infrequent bus No 311.

The **butcher's shop** opposite the train station has fried fish and a few other takeaway selections. There's a bakery next door.

Pizzeria Italia (☎ 86 89 31 33; Skanderbrgvej 3; fish & meat mains Dkr109-47) There are several restaurants and fast-food places on Skanderborgvej including Pizzeria Italia, which offers tasty pastas (Dkr69) and a three-course menu (Dkr179).

GETTING THERE & AWAY
Hourly trains connect Ry with Silkeborg (Dkr26, 20 minutes) and Århus (Dkr36, 30 minutes).

Viborg
pop 12,700
Quieter and sleepier than Silkeborg, Viborg has a pretty, compact town centre, an important historic and religious heritage and makes a good base for exploring the nearby lakes and surrounding woodland. In 1060 Viborg became one of Denmark's eight bishoprics and grew into a major religious centre. Prior to the Reformation the town had 25 churches and abbeys, though ecclesiastical remnants from that period are few.

ORIENTATION & INFORMATION
The old part of town consists of the streets around Viborg Domkirke. The train station is about 1km southwest of the tourist office.

The **tourist office** (☎ 87 25 30 75; www.visitviborg .dk; Nytorv 9; ☺ 9am-5pm Mon-Fri, to 2pm Sat Jun-Aug, to 5pm Mon-Fri, 9.30am-2.30pm Sat mid-May–mid-Jun, 9am-4pm Mon-Fri, 9.30am-12.30pm Sat Sep-Apr) is in the centre of town.

There is ample and convenient free parking behind the Sankt Mathias Gade Shopping Centre on the south side of town, but you must use a time disc.

The post office and several banks with ATMs line Sct Mathias Gade, just south of the main square.

SIGHTS & ACTIVITIES
The tourist office has excellent printouts, including English-language versions, which describe walks around the town with historical and cultural themes.

The multitowered **Viborg Domkirke** (☎ 87 25 52 50; Sankt Mogens Gade 4; admission free; ☺ 10am-5pm Mon-Sat, noon-5pm Sun Jun-Aug, 11am-4pm Mon-Sat, noon-4pm Sun Apr-May & Sep; 11am-3pm Mon-Sat, noon-3pm Sun Jan-Mar) is one of Denmark's largest granite churches and dominates the town. The first church on the site dated from the Viking period. The interior is awash with frescoes painted over five years (1901–06) by artist Joakim Skovgaard and featuring scenes from the Old Testament and the life of Christ.

Skovgaard Museet (☎ 86 62 39 75; Domkirkestræde 2-4; adult/child Dkr20/free; ☺ 10am-12.30pm & 1.30-5pm May-Sep, 1.30-5pm Oct-Apr) lies to the south of Viborg Domkirke. It also features work by Joakim Skovgaard, but here the scenes are more down to earth and include portraits, landscapes and nudes.

Viborg Stiftsmuseum (☎ 87 25 26 20; Hjultorvet 9; adult/child Dkr25/free; ☺ 11am-5pm mid-Jun–Aug, 1-4pm Tue-Fri, 11am-5pm Sat & Sun Sep–mid-Jun) is a local history museum that tells the story of Viborg's rich past.

Sankt Mogens Gade, between the cathedral and the tourist office, has some handsome old houses, including Hauchs Gård at No 7 and the Willesens House at No 9, both dating back to around 1520.

SLEEPING & EATING
Staff at the tourist office can book rooms in private homes with singles/doubles starting at Dkr250/300 plus a Dkr25 booking fee.

Viborg Sø Camping (☎ 86 67 13 11; www.camping -viborg.dk in Danish; Vinkelvej 36b; camp site per adult/ child/tent Dkr64/32/20; ☺ late-Mar–late-Sep) Viborg is a well-ordered, three-star camping ground at a pleasant, leafy location on the east side of Lake Søndersø.

Danhostel Viborg (☎ 86 67 17 81; viborg@danhostel .dk; Vinkelvej 36; P ✗) Adjacent to Viborg Sø Camping and also handy for lakeside activities (and very quiet) 1km walk from town. Bike hire is available.

Palads Hotel (☎ 86 62 37 00; www.hotelpalads.dk; Sankt Mathias Gade; s/d Dkr895/1095; P ✗) Straddling four sites, this long-established hotel is part of the Best Western chain and has bright, pleasant rooms (some with kitchenettes). It's just a short walk north of the train station.

The huge Sankt Mathias Gade Centre has cafés, a supermarket, fruit shop, a butcher and a baker.

DENMARK

Kafé Arthur (☎ 86 62 21 26; Vestergade 4; mains Dkr165-190) The bare-brick, stripped floors and candlelight make for a smart, cosy setting in which to enjoy the likes of tuna with asparagus and chervil vinaigrette or crab tureen with grilled scallops; it also does a good lunch menu for about Dkr75.

Ristorante Pizzeria Italia (☎ 86 62 42 43; Sankt Mathias Gade 74; buffet lunch Dkr49) This restaurant does tasty pasta and pizza (Dkr45 to Dkr60).

Café Morville (☎ 86 60 22 11; Hjultorvet; brunch Dkr79, mains Dkr158-68) A bustling place on the main square with sleek, modern decor and some good bistro-style dishes such as young grouse breast with herb stuffing and grape sauce (Dkr158).

GETTING THERE & AROUND

Viborg is 66km northwest of Århus on Rte 26 and 41km west of Randers on Rte 16. Trains from Århus (Dk94, 70 minutes) run hourly Monday to Friday, and less frequently at weekends.

The tourist office has a few bikes for hire for Dkr100 a day.

AALBORG

pop 155,000

Don't be put off by the rather dreary industrial hinterland as you approach Aalborg, it's the surprise destination of Jutland with a vibrant nightlife and some worthwhile sites, not least the remarkable Lindholm Høje, Denmark's largest Viking burial ground. Jutland's second largest city has lost chunks of its historical quaintness to industrial and commercial development, although the centre contains enough ancient half-timbered buildings to give you an idea of the kind of affluence its Renaissance merchants enjoyed. By the time you read this, the redeveloped waterfront should afford the city centre some great new public spaces. A new architecture and design museum is also scheduled to open in 2008.

Orientation

Linked by bridge and tunnel, the city spreads across both sides of the Limfjord, the long body of water that cuts Jutland in two. Most of the sights, eating, drinking and sleeping options lie south of the Limfjord. The town centre is a 10-minute walk north on Boulevarden from the train and bus stations.

Information

Boomtown (Nytorv 18-20; per hr Dkr30) Internet access.

Danish Emigration Archives (☎ 99 31 42 20; Arkivstræde 1) Behind Vor Frue Kirke, helps foreigners of Danish descent trace their roots.

Hovedbiblioteket (City library; Rendsburggade 2; ☽ 10am-8pm Mon-Fri, 10am-3pm Sat) Offers free internet access.

Jyske Bank (Nytorv 1)

Laundrette (cnr Rantzausgade & Christiansgade; ☽ 8am-8pm)

Post Office (Algade 42)

Tourist Office (☎ 99 30 60 90; www.visitaalborg .com; Østerågade 8; ☽ 9am-5.30pm Mon-Fri, 10am-1pm Sat mid-Jun–Aug, to 4.30pm Mon-Fri, 10am-1pm Sat Sep–mid-Jun) Friendly and helpful, with masses of information, including a diary of events, What's on in Aalborg.

Sights

OLD TOWN

The whitewashed **Buldolfi Domkirke** marks the centre of the old town, and has colourful frescoes in the foyer. About 75m east of the cathedral is the **Aalborg Historiske Museum** (Algade 48; adult/child Dkr20/free; ☽ 9am-4pm Mon-Fri, to 2pm Sat), with artefacts from prehistory to the present and furnishings and interiors that hint at the wealth Aalborg's merchants enjoyed during the Renaissance.

The alley between the museum and church leads to the rambling **Monastery of the Holy Ghost**, which dates from 1431; the tourist office arranges guided tours in summer (Dkr40). Northeast of the cathedral on Østerågade are three noteworthy historic buildings: the **old town hall** (c 1762), the five-storey **Jens Bangs Stenhus** (built c 1624 by wealthy merchant Jens Bangs) and **Jørgen Olufsens House** (c 1616).

In addition, the half-timbered neighbourhoods around **Vor Frue Kirke** are worth a stroll, particularly the cobbled Hjelmerstald. **Aalborghus Slot**, near the waterfront, is more administrative office than castle, but there's a small dungeon you can enter for free.

NORDJYLLANDS KUNSTMUSEUM

This **regional art museum** (☎ 98 13 80 88; Kong Christian Allé 50; adult/child Dkr40/free; ☽ 10am-5pm Tue-Sun), in a stark, modular building designed by Finnish architect Alvar Aalto, has a fine collection of Danish modern art, including work by Asger Jorn and JF Willumsen.

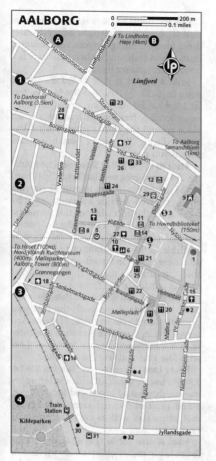

To get to the museum, take the tunnel beneath the train station; it leads to Kildeparken, a green space with statues and water fountains. Go directly through the park, cross Vesterbro and then continue through a wooded area to the museum, a 10-minute walk in all. Alternatively take bus No 5, 8, 10 or 11 from the centre of town.

AALBORG TOWER

The hill behind the art museum has a 105m **tower** (☎ 98 77 05 11; Søndre Skovvej; adult/child Dkr25/15; ☼ 11am-5pm Apr, Jun, Aug & Sep, 10am-7pm Jul) with panoramic views of the city's steeples and smokestacks. It sits on the edge of an expansive wooded area, **Mølleparken**, which has walking trails and a zoo.

LINDHOLM HØJE

The Limfjorden (chalk fjord) was a kind of Viking motorway providing easy and speedy access to the Atlantic for longboat raiding parties. It's perhaps not surprising then that by far the most important piece of Aalborg's historical heritage is a predominantly Viking one. The hugely atmospheric **Lindholm Høje** (admission free; ☼ dawn-dusk) is a Viking burial ground where nearly 700 graves from the Iron Age and Viking Age are strewn around a hilltop pasture ringed by a wall of tall beech trees. Many of the Viking graves are marked by stones placed in the outline of a Viking ship, with two larger end stones as stem and stern. The **museum** (☎ 96 31 04 28; adult/child Dkr30/free; ☼ 10am-5pm

DENMARK

Apr-Oct), adjacent to the field, depicts the site's history while huge murals behind the exhibits speculate on what the people of Lindholm looked like and how they lived. Lindholm Høje is 15 minutes from Aalborg centre on bus No 2.

Sleeping

Accommodation options are pretty good in town, inexpensive compared to other Danish destinations and not generally in massive demand.

Prinsens Hotel (☎ 98 13 37 33; www.prinsen-hotel .dk; Prinsensgade 14; s/d from Dkr545/645; P ⊠ 🖳) Modern, simple rooms (although some are rather small), a good, central location and free extras (such as free internet, wi-fi, solarium and tea and coffee). There's also a sauna and Jacuzzi. Good value

Villa Rosa (☎ 98 12 13 38; www.villarosa.dk; Grønnegangen; r Dkr400-800; P ⊠ 🖳) An elegant B&B inside a pink-walled former Bishop's residence with bright, light rooms, wooden floors, period features and solid bedsteads. Lots of character, very central.

Danhostel Aalborg (☎ 98 11 60 44; www.danhostel .dk/aalborg; Skydebanevej 50; dm/s/d Dkr150/480/500; P 🖳) Handy for boating activities on the fjord but hardly central, the hostel is at the marina 4km west of the centre. It also runs an adjacent camping ground with cabins. Otherwise the facilities are rather basic.

Radisson SAS Limfjord (☎ 98 16 43 33; http:// radissonsas.com; Ved Stranden 14-16; s/d Dkr990/1395, s/d discount mid-Jun–Aug Dkr945/1045; P ⊠ 🖳) The top-end place in town occupying a grandstand position overlooking the fjord. Well-furnished, well-equipped, modern rooms with free wi-fi plus a solarium and gym.

Eating

Eating out in Aalborg has never been better. A clutch of new places dotted around the town centre cater well to all budgets and tastes. If it's just ballast you want with your alcohol, then Jomfru Ane Gade, a lively, pedestrian street jammed solid with fast-food style restaurants and bars, is the place to go.

Pingvin (☎ 98 11 11 66; Brandstrupsgade 11; 4-tapas menu Dkr108, light mains Dkr60-80; ⏲ noon-late Mon-Sat) The locals have quickly embraced this cosy little contemporary wine and tapas bar, serving flavoursome little dishes that are perfect for a light meal.

Cafe Ministeriet (☎ 98 19 40 50; Mølleplads; mains Dkr46-86) Generous portions of fresh café/ diner food including burgers, vegie lasagne, brunch and club sandwiches, and there is a good little summer terrace.

Sushi & Ko (☎ 98 10 98 40; Ved Stranden 11b; menus Dkr70-200; ⏲ 11am-10pm Mon-Fri, noon-10pm Sat, 3-9pm Sun) Sit and enjoy, or pay and take away terrific, fresh sushi from this small place around the corner from Jomfru Ane Gade. Tackle the fierce wasabi-roasted peas if you dare.

Rosdahls (☎ 98 12 05 80; Strandvejen 6; lunch Dkr58-188, 3-/4-course evening menu Dkr375/415; ⏲ 11.30am-3pm & 5.30-10pm Mon-Fri, 10am-10pm Sat) Occupying an impressive waterside warehouse right by the waters the speciality of this romantic place is heavenly, delicate wedges of home-smoked salmon (Dkr75). Good wine is available in the restaurant or to buy in the adjoining shop and staff are knowledgeable. On Saturday there's also a great food market outside.

Mortens Kro (☎ 98 12 48 60; Møllea 4-6; mains Dkr150-95) Hands down both the best and priciest place to eat in town, Mortens Kro serves lavish, inventive fare such as lobster with a cauliflower crème brûlée or beef with foie gras and truffled croutons.

Penny Lane (Boulevarden 10; 10am-6pm Mon-Sat, 9.30-2pm Sun) A great little deli offering its own freshly baked bread and local cheese, cured meat and cured sausage for gourmet picnics as well as cakes to eat in or takeaway.

Schak Nielsen (☎ 98 12 35 92; Algade 23) This fishmonger makes cheap takeaway salmon burgers and a range of other tasty fishy snacks.

Drinking

Wharf (☎ 98 11 70 10; The Wharf, Borgergade 16) This surprising slice of the UK in deepest Jutland is dedicated to cask ale and serving up to 44 different British, Belgian, Irish and German beers the length of its capacious bar. There's also a good selection of rare single-malt whiskies.

Studenterhuset (Student Union; ☎ 98 11 05 22; Gammeltorv 10) A convivial budget drinking and entertainment option. Lined with bookshelves, it's surprisingly upmarket and, well, studious for a students union. There's inexpensive beer, regular live bands and DJ nights.

Entertainment

If it's a flirt, a drink or loud repetitive beats in the form of banging techno, Euro-rock or house music you're after, trawl Jomfru Ane Gade, Aalborg's take-no-prisoners party street. The venues themselves are pretty homogenous, so it's best to explore until you hear your kind of music.

The Irish House (☎ 98 14 18 17; Østerågade 25) A lively Irish pub with live music most nights and a convivial atmosphere.

Huset (☎ 98 16 76 66; Hasserisgade 10) Aalborg's music and cultural centre stages a series of jazz, folk and world music events.

Getting There & Away

CAR & MOTORCYCLE

The E45 bypasses the city centre, tunnelling under the Limfjord, whereas the connecting Rte 180 leads into the centre. To get to Lindholm Høje or points north from Aalborg centre, take Rte 180 (Vesterbro), which bridges the Limfjord.

Avis (☎ 98 13 30 99) is at the train station.

Europcar (☎ 98 13 23 55; Jyllandsgade 4) is a short distance to the west.

TRAIN

Trains run to Århus (Dkr150, 1½ hours, at least hourly) and Frederikshavn (Dkr88, one hour, every two hours). **Express buses** (☎ 70 21 08 88) run to Copenhagen (Dkr230, five hours, daily).

Getting Around

City buses leave from the intersection of Østerågade and Nytorv. The bus fare is Dkr13 to any place in greater Aalborg.

Despite a few one-way streets and the often-confusing outer roads that may have you driving in circles, central Aalborg is a fairly easy place to get around by car. There's metered parking in the city centre (Dkr10/76, one/24 hours) and time-limited, free parking along many side streets, but you need to use a parking disc. If you're unable to find a parking space, there's a large parking garage, **Palads Parking** (Ved Stranden 11).

REBILD BAKKER NATIONAL PARK

Rebild Bakker National Park is a great place to unwind if the urban experience starts to get to you. Relax by hiking through its lovely rolling hills and heathland. Rebild Bakker National Park was founded in 1912 by Danish Americans and is best known for its US-style 4th of July celebration, the largest held outside the USA.

A 4km **trail** begins in a sheep meadow opposite the Lincoln cabin, and numerous other trails crisscross the park and the adjacent Rold Skov, Denmark's largest forest. The Ministry of the Environment publishes a useful leaflet *Rebild Bakker Himmerland* that gives basic directions for a number of rewarding walks. One of the best is the 3km Ravnkilde-Nordre Dybdal trail, which takes in some good views and passes interesting old buildings and ruins.

The **Rebild Festival** is an annual event held on 4 July, celebrating Danish American connections. It commemorates over 300,000 Danish immigrants to the USA during the late 19th and early 20th centuries and the strong familial bonds that survive between the USA and Denmark. There are concerts performed by both military and civilian orchestras and bands, receptions, picnics, dancing as well as rock- and country-music shows.

Safari Camping (☎ 98 39 11 10; Rebildvej 17; adult/child Dkr68/34) is nearby. You can get meals at the park cafeterias. The tiny, quaint, thatch-roofed **Danhostel Rebild** (☎ 98 39 13 40; www .vandrerhjem.net; dm/r Dkr150/375; P) is next to the park entrance.

From Aalborg, Århus-bound trains stop in Skørping (Dkr48, 16 minutes), from where it's 3km to Rebild. Bus No 104 runs between Aalborg and Rebild (Dkr42, 45 minutes, 10 times daily Monday to Friday, six times daily Saturday and Sunday), via Skørping.

FREDERIKSHAVN

pop 34,000

A transport hub rather than a compelling destination, the bustling port town of Frederikshavn nevertheless has a certain appeal, a couple of interesting sights and a pleasant enough pedestrianised centre.

An overhead walkway leads from the ferry terminal to the **tourist office** (☎ 98 42 32 66; www.frederikshavn-tourist.dk; Skandiatorv 1; ☻ 9am-6pm Mon-Sat, to 2pm Sun end-Jun–mid-Aug, 9am-6pm last 2 weeks Jun & Aug, to 4pm Mon-Fri, 11am-2pm Sat Sep–mid-Jun). The train station and adjacent bus terminal are a 10-minute walk to the north.

Sights

BANGSBO

It's well worth exploring this area, about 3km from the centre on the southern edge of town. The main drawcard is **Bangsbo Museum** (☎ 98 42 31 11; Margrethesvej 6; adult/child Dkr40/free; ⊙ 10am-5pm Jun-Aug, 10.30am-5pm Sep-May, closed Mon Nov-May) an old country estate with an interesting mix of exhibits. The manor house displays antique furnishings and collectibles, while the old farm buildings hold ship figureheads, military paraphernalia and exhibits on Danish resistance to the German occupation. The most intriguing exhibit is the Ellingå ship, reconstructed remains of a 12th-century Viking-style merchant ship that was dug up from a nearby stream bed. Bus No 3 from central Frederikshavn stops near the entrance to the estate, from where it's an enjoyable 500m walk through the woods to the museum. The adjoining **Bangsbo Botanisk Have** (Botanical Gardens) have a deer park and make a pleasant place to stroll or enjoy a picnic.

Bangsbo Fort (☎ 98 42 31 11; Understedvej 21; adult/child Dkr30/free; ⊙ 10am-5pm Jun-Aug) about half a mile over the wooded ridge from the gardens is an atmospheric WWII bunker complex housing some big guns and commanding wonderful views across to Frederikshavn and out to sea.

KRUDTTÅRNET

The whitewashed **Krudttårnet** (☎ 98 42 31 11; Kragholmen 1; adult/child Dkr15/5; ⊙ 10.30am-5pm Jun-Sep) is a striking old gun tower and powder magazine, that once formed part of the 17th-century citadel that once protected the port. Various pieces of artillery are on display at the top.

Sleeping & Eating

Unsurprisingly, given the captive custom of those awaiting onward connections, good-value sleeping options are limited, prices higher and standards lower compared to other towns in the region. The tourist office books rooms in private homes from Dkr175/200 for singles/doubles, plus a Dkr25 booking fee.

Danhostel Frederikshavn (☎ 98 42 14 75; www .danhostel.dk/frederikshavn; Buhlsvej 6; dm/s/d Dkr100/250/300; ⊙ Feb–mid-Dec; Ⓟ Ⓧ) A pleasant place with chalet-style, six-bed dorms located 2km north of the ferry terminal.

Hotel Herman Bang (☎ 98 42 21 66; www .hermanbang.dk in Danish; Tordenskjoldsgade 3; s/d Dkr495, s/d with private bathroom from Dkr695/795; Ⓟ) The mid-priced rooms here are bright and comfortable, the most expensive are huge, new and luxurious. Avoid the cheapest which are bland, need new carpets and generally offer poor value. There's an up-market spa next door for beauty and relaxation treatments.

Frank's (☎ 98 42 22 88; www.franks.dk in Danish; Silovej 8; mains Dkr160-90; ⊙ lunch & dinner only) Towering nine stories above the port's gritty industrial heart in a former grain silo, Frank's offers a thrilling bird's-eye view of the dockside loading, unloading and maritime comings and goings. The fine-dining menu doesn't always live up to the views but is strong on fish. Book ahead to bag a window seat.

Møllehuset (☎ 98 43 44 00; Skovalleen 45; mains Dkr70-130; ⊙ 11am-9.30pm Tue-Sat, to 6pm Sun & Mon) An appealing café and restaurant in a leafy setting across the roundabout from the botanic gardens serving simple fresh lunches – such as bagels with smoked salmon and asparagus, and good cheese platters – along with more polished dinners.

Damsgaard Supermarked (Havnegade) Next to the tourist office, Damsgaard has a cheap cafétéria with a harbour view and a good buffet breakfast (Dkr48).

Havne Super (Sydhavnesvej 8) If you're catching a ferry, Havne Super is a supermarket at the harbour with a cafeteria and long hours. Consider picking up provisions if you're going on to expensive Norway.

Getting There & Away

BOAT

From Frederikshavn **Stena Line** (☎ 96 20 02 00) runs ferries six to 10 times daily (Dkr95 to Dkr215, two to 3¼ hours) to Göteborg, Sweden. **Color Line** (☎ 99 56 19 77; www.colorline .com) runs to Oslo once daily (Dkr180 to Dkr460, 8½ hours). Prices vary by season.

BUS & TRAIN

Frederikshavn is the northern terminus of the DSB train line. Trains run about hourly south to Aalborg (Dkr88) and then onto Copenhagen (Dkr343). **Nordjyske Jernbaner** (☎ 98 45 45 10; www.njba.dk) runs smart new trains every two hours (Dkr48) to Skagen.

SKAGEN

pop 10,500

A busy working harbour, fresh seafood, long, sandy beaches, dramatic seascapes and a buzzing holiday atmosphere make Skagen an understandably popular spot at the northern tip of Jutland.

Artists discovered Skagen's luminous light and its colourful, wind-blasted, heath-and-dune landscape in the mid-19th century and fixed eagerly on the romantic imagery of the area's fishing life that had earned the people of Skagen a hard living for centuries. Painters such as Michael and Anna Ancher and Oscar Björck followed the contemporary fashion of painting *en plein air* (out of doors), often regardless of the weather. Their work established a vivid figurative style of painting that became known internationally as the 'Skagen School'.

Today, Skagen is a very popular tourist resort, packed in high summer. But the sense of a more picturesque Skagen survives and the town's older neighbourhoods are filled with distinctive yellow-walled, red-tiled houses.

Skagen gets by on a mix of arts, crafts and conspicuous tourism these days, with plenty of souvenir shops, art galleries and ice-cream parlours. The **Skagen music festival** (www.skagenfestival.dk in Danish) packs the town out with official performers, buskers and appreciative visitors during the last weekend of June. The peninsula is lined with fine beaches, including a sandy stretch on the eastern end of Østre Strandvej, a 15-minute walk from the town centre.

Orientation & Information

Sankt Laurentii Vej, Skagen's main street, runs almost the entire length of this long thin town, and is never more than five minutes from the waterfront. The **tourist office** (☎ 98 44 13 77; www.skagen-tourist.dk; Sankt Laurentii Vej 22; ☼ 9am-6pm Mon-Sat, 10am-4pm Sun late-Jun–early Aug, to 5pm early Jun & late Aug, 9am-4pm Mon-Sat, 10am-1pm Sun May & Sep, earlier closing Oct–May) is in the train/bus station.

Sights

GRENEN

Appropriately for such a neatly kept country, Denmark doesn't end untidily at its most northerly point, but on a neat finger

of sand just a few metres wide. You can actually paddle at its tip where the waters of the Kattegat and Skagerrak clash and you can put one foot in each sea; but not too far. Bathing is strictly forbidden here because of the ferocious tidal currents and often angry seas that collide to create manetossing white horses.

The tip is the culmination of a long, curving sweep of sand at Grenen, about 3km northeast of Skagen along Rte 40. Where the road ends there's a car park, café and souvenir shops, plus, in high summer, what seems like the entire population of Denmark. Crowds head along the last stretch of beach for the 30-minute walk to the tip. A special tractor-drawn bus, the *Sandormen*, leaves from the car park every half-hour, waits for 15 minutes at the beach end, then returns (adult/child return-trip Dkr20/10). From May to September, buses run from Skagen station to Grenen hourly (Dkr15) until 5pm. Taxis, available at the train station, charge about Dkr75 to Grenen.

SKAGENS MUSEUM

This fine **museum** (☎ 98 44 64 44; Brøndumsvej 4; admission Dkr60; ☼ 10am-5pm or 6pm May-Aug, 11am-4pm Tue-Sun Apr, 1-5pm Wed-Fri, 11am-4pm Sat, to 3pm Sun Nov-Mar) showcases the paintings of Michael and Anna Ancher, PS Krøyer, and of other artists who flocked to Skagen between 1830 and 1930, many of them kitchen-sink portraits of the lives and deaths of the fishing community.

MICHAEL & ANNA ANCHER'S HUS

This poignant domestic **museum** (☎ 98 44 30 09; Markvej 2-4; adult/child Dkr50/free; ☼ 10am-6pm mid-Jun–mid-Aug, 10am-5pm May–mid-Jun, 11am-3pm Sep–Apr) occupies the house that the Anchers bought in 1884 and in which their daughter Helga lived until 1960.

SKAGEN BY-OG EGNSMUSEUM

This well-presented, **open-air museum** (☎ 98 44 47 60; Pk Nielsonvej 8-10; adult/child Dkr30/5; ☼ 10am-5pm May-Sep, to 6pm Jul, to 4pm Mon-Fri Mar-Apr & Oct-Nov) depicts Skagen's maritime history, showcasing maritime arts and recreating the period homes of fisherfolk. It's a 15-minute walk from the train station, west down Sankt Laurentii Vej, then south on Vesterled.

DENMARK

TILSANDEDE KIRKE

This whitewashed medieval **church tower** (☎ 98 44 43 71; adult/child Dkr10/5; ☯ 11am-5pm Jun-Sep) still rises above the sand dunes that buried the church and surrounding farms in the late 1700s. The tower, in a nature reserve, is 5km south of Skagen and well signposted from Rte 40. By bike, take Gammel Landevej from Skagen.

RÅBJERG MILE

These undulating 40m-high hills comprise Denmark's largest expanse of shifting dunes and are great fun to explore. Råbjerg Mile is 16km south of Skagen, off Rte 40 on the road to Kandestederne. From May to September, bus No 99 runs six times a day from Skagen Station (Dkr16, 25 minutes).

Sleeping

Hotel accommodation can be scarce at summer weekends and during the Skagen Festival at the end of June. The tourist office books singles/doubles in private homes for around Dkr200/350, plus a Dkr50 booking fee.

Grenen Camping (☎ 98 44 25 46; adult/child Dkr75/43) A fine seaside location, semi-private tent sites and pleasant four-bunk huts, 1.5km northeast of Skagen centre. The only downside is the rather tightly bunched sites.

Danhostel Skagen (☎ 98 44 22 00; www.danhostel.dk/skagen; Rolighedsvej 2; dm Dkr150, s/d from Dkr500/600; ☯ mid-Feb-late Nov; ℗) Well kept, very popular and 1km from the centre, book ahead in the summer. Rates drop sharply in low season.

Marienlund Badepension (☎ 98 44 13 20; www.marienlund.dk; Fabriciusvej 8; s/d with bathroom Dkr460/800) A modern, comfortable, immaculately kept place that is situated on the quieter western side of town near the open-air museum.

Skagen Sømandshjem (☎ 98 44 25 88; Østre Strandvej 2; s/d with bathroom Dkr620/860, without bathroom Dkr460/700) A harbourside hotel that has bright, pleasant rooms.

Brøndums Hotel (☎ 98 44 15 55; www.broendums-hotel.dk in Danish; Anchersvej 3; s/d Dkr575/875, s/d with bathroom Dkr795/1095) This charming hotel in the heart of the old town right across from the Skagens Museum had close associations with Skagen's artists in its day

and retains an old-world sense of decor (slightly chintzy, flowery furnishings), good service and civility. However, it has similarly old-world facilities and plumbing: there's only one TV in the living room and few of the rooms have bathrooms. It's a great, cosy place to relax though, especially in front of a roaring fire and there's a good restaurant (see below).

Eating & Drinking

Perhaps a dozen seafood shacks line the harbour selling good seafood to eat inside, outside or takeaway. Freshly caught prawns are the favourite fare, costing around Dkr75 for a generous helping.

You'll find a couple of pizzerias, a kebab shop, a burger joint and an ice-cream shop clustered near each other on Havnevej. **Super Brugsen** (Sankt Laurentii Vej 28), a grocery store just west of the tourist office, has a bakery.

Restaurant Pakhuset (☎ 98 44 20 00; Rødspættevej 6; light lunches Dkr65-77, mains Dkr150-200) Perhaps the pick of the town in terms of offerings. There's a mix of great fresh fish mains and cheaper light lunches (like fish cakes with remoulade and salad for Dkr72), it has long hours and a superb ambience both outdoors (right among the bustle of the harbour) and indoors (a lovely wooden-beamed interior sprinkled with jovial ship mastheads). Its downstairs café offers the cheaper dishes.

Brøndum's Hotel (☎ 98 44 15 55; Anchersvej 3; mains Dkr120-230) French cuisine is the main influence on the otherwise classic Danish dishes, with lots of fresh seafood such as lobster and turbot as well as tenderloin and chateaubriand. Meals are served in the old-world ambience of the cosy dining room.

Jakobs (☎ 98 44 16 90; Havnevej 4; mains Dkr138-188) Jakobs is a popular restaurant on Skagen's busy main street. It does good home-made brunches (Dkr70), salads and pastas (Dkr45 to Dkr75). By night it's a popular bar staging live music at the weekends (usually cover bands).

Buddy Holly's (Havnevej 16) There's nothing cutting edge or elegant about Buddy Holly's, but the predictable sonic menu of dance and disco classics from the '70s, '80s and '90s gets a 30- and 40-something crowd up and dancing.

Getting There & Away

Nordjyske Jernbaner (☎ 98 45 45 10; www.njba.dk in Danish) runs smart new trains every two hours (Dkr48) to Frederikshavn. A seasonal Skagerakkeren bus (No 99) runs between Hirtshals and Skagen (Dkr37, 1½ hours, six daily mid-June to mid-August). The same bus continues on to Hjørring and Løkken.

Getting Around

Cycling is an excellent way of exploring Skagen and the surrounding area. **Skagen Cykeludlejning** (☎ 98 44 10 70; Banegårdspladsen; per day Dkr75, deposit Dkr200) rents out bicycles and has a stand on the western side of the train station and at the harbour.

Skagen is very busy with traffic in high season. There is free parking for short periods and convenient metered parking (Dkr10 per hour) just by the train station.

HIRTSHALS

pop 7000

A busy, modern little town thanks to a large commercial fishing harbour and ferry terminal, Hirtshals has an easy, friendly character, an excellent aquarium and some fine stretches of beach, although its looks aren't likely to take your breath away. The main street, pedestrianised Nørregade, is lined with a mix of cafés and shops, and with supermarkets that cater to Norwegian shoppers piling off the ferries to load up with relatively cheap Danish meats and groceries. The seaward end of Nørregade opens out into a wide, airy space, Den Grønne Plads (Green Square), which overlooks the fishing harbour and its tiers of blue-hulled boats. There is a **tourist office** (☎ 98 94 22 20; www.visithirtshals.com; Nørregade 40; ⊙ 9.30am-3.30pm Mon-Fri, 9am-2pm Sat mid-Jul-Aug, 10am-3pm Mon-Fri, 9am-2pm Sat Aug-Jun).

Hirtshals' big draw is the **Nordsømuseet** (☎ 98 94 44 44; Willemoesvej 2; adult/child Dkr110/55; ⊙ 10am-6pm mid-Jun–mid-Aug, to 5pm mid-Aug–mid-Jun), an impressive aquarium that recreates a slice of the North Sea in a massive four-storey tank, containing elegantly balletic schools of thousands of fish. Divers feed the fish at 1pm and the seals at 11am and 3pm.

In the surrounding area there are coastal cliffs and a **lighthouse** on the town's western side. If you want beaches and dunes, there's a lovely unspoiled stretch at **Tornby Strand**, 5km to the south.

Sleeping & Eating

Staff at the tourist office can book rooms in private homes starting at Dkr150 plus a Dkr25 booking fee.

Hirtshals Hostel (☎ 98 94 12 48; www.danhostel nord.dk/hirtshals; Kystvejen 53; dm/s/d Dkr150/370/420; ⊙ Mar-Nov) Occupying a bland building and offering basic facilities about 1km from the centre, the saving grace of this hostel is its location a bucket and spade's throw from the beach.

Hotel Hirtshals (☎ 98 94 20 77; info@hotelhirtshals .dk; Havnegade 2; s/d Dkr695/795) On the main square above the fishing harbour, the Hirtshals has bright, comfortable rooms with high, steepled ceilings and good sea views at the front.

There are cafés and a good bakery at the northern end of Hjørringgade, and there are also a couple of pizza and kebab places on Nørregade.

Hirtshals Kro (☎ 98 94 26 77; Havnegade; mains Dkr149-89) A delightful restaurant in a very old *kro* that has retained its character. Not surprisingly the menu offers several tasty seafood dishes including a mixed fish plate for Dkr179.

Getting There & Away

BOAT

The ferry company **Color Line** (☎ 99 56 20 00) runs year-round ferries to the Norwegian ports of Larvik (6½ hours, twice daily from May to September) and Kristiansand (2½, twice daily). Fares on both routes range from Dkr180 midweek in the low season to Dkr420 on summer weekends for passengers.

BUS

From May to September a bus (☎ 70 13 14 15) from Hirtshals Station to Hjørring (Dkr24) stops en route at Tornby Strand six times a day.

TRAIN

Hirtshals' main train station is 500m south of the ferry harbour but there's also a stop near the Color Line terminal. The railway, which is operated by a private company, connects Hirtshals with Hjørring (Dkr24), 20 minutes to the south. Trains run at least hourly. From Hjørring you can take a DSB train to Aalborg (Dkr72) or Frederikshavn (Dkr48).

LØKKEN

pop 1400

Vast lengths of beach and dune lined by neat rows of white beach huts and stout little fishing vessels lure visitors in throngs to Løkken every summer, all but swamping this pretty little town with an intriguing sea trading and fishing heritage. Løkken has something of a reputation as a summer party place attracting teenage party animals from Norway in particular to its campsite and beaches.

The **tourist office** (☎ 98 99 10 09; www.loekken.dk; Harald Fischers Vej 8; 9am-5pm Mon-Sat Jun-Aug, 10am-1pm Sun mid-Jul–Aug, to 4pm Mon-Fri & to 1pm Sat Sep-May) is a few blocks east of Torvet, the central square.

Løkken's **beach** is broad and long and has excellent sand. The town itself has an older neighbourhood to the north of the centre.

The charming little **Løkken Museum** (Nørregade 12; adult/child Dkr15/free; 10am-4pm Mon-Fri, 2-5pm Sun Jun-Aug) and the **Coastal Fishing Museum** (☎ 20 66 13 07; Ndr Strandvej; adult/child Dkr10/free; 10am-4pm Mon-Fri, 2-5pm Sun Jun-Aug), perched above the beach, tell the story of Løkken seagoing.

A string of camping grounds line Søndergade, the street that runs south from Torvet. Most of them charge in the region of Dk75/35 per adult/child in high season.

Hotels and apartment complexes in Løkken are geared to holidaymakers planning longer stays and offer their best prices for weekly bookings, although you might catch an overnight stay for about Dkr600 in the low season. The tourist office can provide a booklet with a brief description of each place and a detailed price list. In the low season it's worth checking out any 'room to let' signs for good deals.

Several places offer cheap fast food on Torvet and along Nørregade and Strandgade, which radiate out from Torvet.

Løkken Fiske-Restaurant (☎ 98 99 02 00; Nørregade 9; mains Dkr135-225) Løkken Fiske has good fish dishes, including a tasty fish soup. It also does fish lunches for Dkr55 and a buffet for Dkr129.

There's also a **Spar** (Kjelgaards Plads; 7am-10pm) supermarket.

Løkken is on Rte 55, 18km southwest of Hjørring. Buses run every couple of hours between Løkken and Hjørring (Dkr30, 30 minutes) and between Løkken and Aalborg (Dkr58, one hour).

ESBJERG

pop 83,000

You won't miss too much if you pass straight through Esbjerg from your ferry or flight, although it's an attractive enough place if you do need or want to stay. A newcomer to Denmark, having been established as a port in 1868 following the loss of the Schleswig and Holstein regions to Germany, Esbjerg is now the country's fifth-largest city. It is the centre of Denmark's extensive North Sea oil activities and the country's largest fishing harbour. Although Esbjerg has its fair share of early-20th-century buildings, if period charm is what you're after then head straight to nearby Ribe.

Information

Central Library (☎ 76 16 20 00; Nørregade 19; internet access free; 10am-7pm Mon-Thu, to 5pm Fri, to 2pm Sat)

Danske Bank (☎ 79 15 72 00; Torvet 18)

Post Office (☎ 79 12 12 12; Torvet 20)

Tourist Office (☎ 75 12 55 99; www.visitesbjerg.com in Danish; Skolegade 33; 9am-5pm Mon-Fri & 9.30am-2.30pm Sat mid-Jun-Aug, 10am-5pm Mon-Fri & 10am-1pm Sat Sep–mid-Jun).

Sights & Activities

The single most worthwhile place to visit in town is the **Esbjerg Kunstmuseum** (☎ 75 13 02 11; Havnegade 20; adult/child Dkr54/free; 10am-4pm), an impressive gallery with an important collection of Danish modern art including work by Asger Jorn.

Also in the town centre, is the small **Esbjerg Museum** (☎ 75 12 78 11; Torvegade 45; adult/child Dkr40/free; 10am-4pm) containing a few historical artefacts from the area and an amber display. It will offer a short diversion if it's raining.

Outshone somewhat by the aquarium in Hirtshals (see p101), and based a little way out of the town centre at Tarphagevej, the **Fiskeri og Søfartsmuseet** (☎ 76 12 20 00; Tarphagevej 2; adult/child Dkr75/35, outside holiday times Dkr115/free; 10am-6pm Jul & Aug, to 5pm Jan-Jun & Sep-Dec), an aquarium and maritime centre has an outdoor seal pool as well as a number of fisheries exhibits including a huge whale skeleton. Take bus No 1 or 6. It's right by a long sweep of bay and beach, overlooked by the towering white sentinels of the sculpture *Man Meets Sea*.

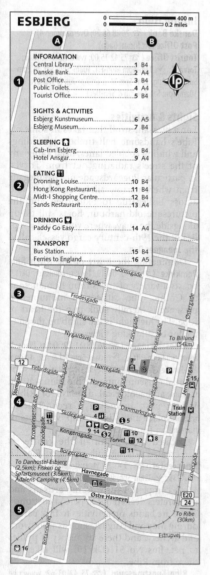

ESBJERG

0 — 400 m
0 — 0.2 miles

INFORMATION
Central Library..........................1 B4
Danske Bank............................2 A4
Post Office...............................3 B4
Public Toilets...........................4 A4
Tourist Office..........................5 B4

SIGHTS & ACTIVITIES
Esbjerg Kunstmuseum..............6 A5
Esbjerg Museum.......................7 B4

SLEEPING
Cab-Inn Esbjerg........................8 B4
Hotel Ansgar............................9 A4

EATING
Dronning Louise.....................10 B4
Hong Kong Restaurant.............11 B4
Midt-I Shopping Centre............12 B4
Sands Restaurant....................13 A4

DRINKING
Paddy Go Easy........................14 A4

TRANSPORT
Bus Station............................15 B4
Ferries to England...................16 A5

Sleeping

There's a good range of reasonably-priced accommodation in town. The tourist office books rooms in private homes at around Dkr175/300 for singles/doubles.

Ådalens Camping (☎ 75 15 88 22; www.adal.dk; Gudenåvej 20; adult/child Dkr77/37; 🛋) The nearest camping to Esbjerg (5km north of the city

via bus No 1 or 7) this place has great facilities including a pool, solarium and Jacuzzi.

Cab Inn Esbjerg (☎ 75 18 16 00; www.cabinn.com; Skolegade14; s/d Dkr525/645; 🅿 ⊠ 🖳) This has clean, functional but good-value, cabin-style rooms (so small dimensions and rather narrow bunk beds) right in the centre. The superior rooms are larger and less clinical. There's free internet access and wifi in the foyer.

Hotel Ansgar (☎ 75 12 82 44; www.hotelansgar.dk; Skolegade 36; s/d Dkr590/750) Ansgar is a friendly place with large, comfortable rooms decorated in simple classic Scandinavian style.

Danhostel Esbjerg (☎ 75 12 42 58; www.danhostel .dk/esbjerg; Gammel Vardevej 80; dm/s/d Dkr150/320/400; 🕙 Feb–mid-Dec) Occupying a handsome former high school 3km northwest of the city centre, this hostel is close to sports facilities including a pool. Take bus Nos 4 and 12.

Eating & Drinking

Most restaurants and grocery stores are east of Torvet on Kongensgade.

Sand's Restaurant (☎ 75 12 02 07; Skolegade 60; lunch Dkr33-75, mains Dkr80-120) You'll find superb, authentic Danish staples such as smørrebrød, Danish hash, meatballs, smoked eel and *pariserbof* (a fried beef patty on bread with a raw egg yolk, pickles and fresh horseradish) in this cosy, old-fashioned dining room.

Dronning Louise (☎ 75 13 13 44; Torvet 19; mains Dkr90-168; 🕙 10am-late Mon-Sat, to 11.30pm Sun; mains Dkr65-120) This jack-of-all-trades place turns out decent sandwiches, burgers and lunch fish plates for Dkr38 to Dkr58, as well as slightly more ambitious brasserie fare and pastries from the café counter.

Midt-I shopping centre (Kongensgade, near Torvet) This has a bakery and cafeteria.

Hong Kong Restaurant (Kongensgade 34; 3-course meals Dkr110-195) It has both restaurant meals and prepares box takeaways for Dkr40 to Dkr55.

Paddy Go Easy (☎ 75 18 07 72; Skolegade 42) A friendly Irish pub just off the main square that is actually run by Irish proprietors.

Getting There & Away

Trains to Copenhagen (Dkr206, 2¼ hours, hourly) run until 10pm.

If you're driving into Esbjerg from the east, the E20 leads into the city centre. If you're coming from the south, Rte 24

DENMARK

merges with the E20 on the city outskirts. From the north, Rte 12 makes a beeline into the city, ending at the harbour.

Ryanair (www.ryanair.com) offers daily flights to Stansted.

DFDS Seaways (☎ 08705 333 000 in UK; ☎ 33 42 30 00 in Denmark; www.dfdsseaways.co.uk) sails from Esbjerg to Harwich (UK) at least three times a week. For full details see p113.

Getting Around

Most city-bound buses (Dkr17) call at the train station. Parking is free in Esbjerg. There's also a convenient car park on Danmarksgade, but it has a two-hour limit; some unlimited parking is available in the car park on Nørregade, east of the library.

LEGOLAND

Children under 12 will love **Legoland** (☎ 75 33 13 33; www.lego.dk; adult/child 3-13 years Dkr210/190; ☺ 10am-8pm Apr-late Oct, 10am-9pm early-Jul–early-Aug), a theme park dedicated to the little plastic blocks from which many of the miniature cities, interactive play areas, safari animals, pirates, princesses, astronauts, Vikings and other displays and attractions are built here (numbering forty-five million blocks in total if you believe the blurb). There are some excellent younger children's amusement rides but for wilder rides suited to older children and adults, Legoland compares unfavourably to Copenhagen's Tivoli Gardens. It's easy to spend an entire day here but since much of the food in the park also tastes as if it's made of reconstituted Lego blocks you may want to bring your own lunch. The rides close two hours before the park does.

There's a frequent bus from Vejle to Legoland (Dkr50, 25 minutes), as well as bus-tour packages from numerous cities, including Esbjerg. Inquire at Esbjerg tourist office.

RIBE

pop 8000

The charming crooked, cobblestone streets of Ribe date from 869, making it one of Scandinavia's oldest and Denmark's most attractive towns. It is a delightful chocolate-box confection of half-timbered, 16th-century houses, clear-flowing streams and water meadows. Almost everything, including the hostel and train station, is within 10 minutes' walk of Torvet, the town square, which is dominated by the huge Romanesque cathedral.

Information

Danske Bank (☎ 76 88 68 20; Overdammen 4)

Post Office (Sct Nicolaj Gade)

Tourist Office (☎ 75 42 15 00; www.ribetourist.dk; Torvet 3; ☺ 9am-6pm Mon-Fri, 10am-5pm Sat, to 2pm Sun Jul & Aug, 9am-5pm Mon-Fri Apr-Jun & Sep-Oct, 10am-1pm Sat Apr-Jun & Sep-Dec)

Sights & Activities

For a pleasant stroll that takes in some of Ribe's handsome half-timbered buildings and winding cobbled lanes, head along any of the streets radiating out from Torvet, in particular Puggårdsgade or Grønnegade from where narrow alleys lead down and across Fiskegarde to Skibbroen and the picturesque old harbour. Boats still tie up alongside the quay, where you'll find a replica of the 19th-century cargo vessel, called the **Johannes Dan**.

Dominating the heart of the town **Ribe Domkirke** (☎ 75 42 06 19; Torvet; admission Dkr12) boasts a variety of styles from Romanesque to Gothic. The cathedral's monumental presence is literally sunk into the heart of Ribe. The highlight is the climb up the steeple for breathtaking views.

Ribes Vikinger (☎ 76 88 11 22; Odins Plads 1; adult/child Dkr60/free; ☺ 10am-6pm Jul & Aug, to 4pm Apr-Jun, Sep & Oct, to 4pm Tue-Sun Nov-Mar) is a substantial museum opposite the train station; it has archaeological displays of Ribe's Viking past, including a reconstructed marketplace and Viking ship, with lots of hands-on features.

Located 3km south of the centre, is a recreated Viking village called **Ribe Vikingecenter** (☎ 75 41 16 11; Lustrupvej 4; adult/child Dkr70/35; ☺ 11am-5pm Jul & Aug, 10am-3.30pm May-Jun & Sep), complete with working artisans and interpreters decked out in period costumes. There are hands-on activities to take part in during May and August, such as woodwork and archery, and there are plenty of ponies to pet. Bus No 51 (Dkr15) will take you there from Ribe.

Ribe Kunstmuseum (☎ 75 42 03 62; www.ribe -kunstmuseum.dk; Sankt Nicolajgade 10; adult/child Dkr40/ free; ☺ 11am-5pm Thu-Sun Jul-Sep, to 4pm Thu-Sun Oct-Jun) has a fine collection of 19th-century 'Golden Age' and 'Silver Age' Danish art, including Ludvig Abelin Schou's dramatic *Death of Chione*.

The town also has a couple of interesting local-history museums, including one at the **Old Town Hall** (☎ 75 42 05 34; adult/child Dkr15/5; ⏱ 1-3pm Mon-Fri), the former debtors' prison, displaying a small arsenal of viciously spiked medieval weaponry and the formidable axe of the town executioner. Make sure you look up at the chimney stacks of the building and you might see a stork's nest, and if you're lucky in spring it's possible to see roosting storks with a clutch of chicks.

There isn't any new-fangled CCTV fad in Ribe; instead, a costumed **night watchman** takes care of security, making the rounds from Torvet at 8pm and 10pm from May to September. You can follow him for free as he sings his way through the old streets.

Sleeping & Eating

The tourist office maintains a list of singles /doubles in private homes from around Dkr250/350.

Weis Stue (☎ 75 42 07 00; www.weisstue.dk; Torvet; s/d Dkr425/625; ⏱ lunch & dinner) This is the poorer, quirkier but no less charming sister to the Dagmar opposite. A small, ancient wooden-beamed house, it has rather small, crooked rooms right above its restaurant, but they have bags of character. The restaurant offers lunch plates of herring, meatballs or lobster (Dkr95 to Dkr125) and seasonal specials that might include half a wild duck with fried potatoes, salad pickles and cream sauce (Dkr175). Breakfast is taken at Hotel Dagmar.

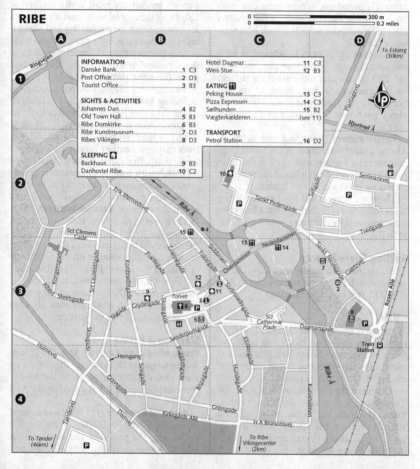

DENMARK

Danhostel Ribe (☎ 75 42 06 20; www.danhostel .dk/ribe; Sankt Pedersgade 16; dm/s Dkr150/315, d Dkr355-488; ⊗ Feb–late-Nov; Ⓟ) The modern, 140-bed hostel has friendly staff and a good, uncrowded location. The new rooms at the top are especially appealing and worth the extra cost.

Hotel Dagmar (☎ 75 42 00 33; www.hoteldagmar .dk in Danish; Torvet; s/d from Dkr925/1125; Ⓟ ⊠) The central Hotel Dagmar claims to be the oldest hotel in Denmark, has plush (if mostly rather small) rooms and a great period atmosphere.

Backhaus (☎ 75 42 11 01; fax 75 42 52 87; Grydergade 12; s/d Dkr250/500, d with bathroom Dkr750) The friendly Backhaus offers a homely, slightly old-fashioned comfort. The rooms at the top have pleasing rooftop views. The restaurant downstairs serves generous portions of home cooking such as fish platters (Dkr135) and pork schnitzel with béarnaise sauce (Dkr120).

Sælhunden (☎ 75 42 09 46; Skibbroen 13; fish & meat mains Dkr46-186; ⊗ café 10am-10pm, lunch & dinner) This handsome, old restaurant is right on the quayside. A tasty lunch of smoked herring or smoked ham costs Dkr75, it's also a good spot for a coffee and a slice of cake (Dkr30).

Vægterkælderen (Torvet; lunch menu Dkr105-135) The basement restaurant in the Hotel Dagmar shares a kitchen with the hotel's classy upstairs restaurant but it has cheaper dishes, including good steaks and fresh fish.

There are several fast-food outlets along Nederdammen, including **Pizza Expressen** (pizza Dkr45) and **Peking House** (lunch Dkr35-85, buffet Dkr129).

Getting There & Away

There are trains from Esbjerg to Ribe (Dkr65, 40 minutes, hourly) and from Århus to Ribe (Dkr207, two hours 40 minutes).

RØMØ

Wide open spaces, ruler-straight horizons, rippling summer-heat hazes and air blown fresh in from the North Sea give the unrelentingly flat island of Rømø a hypnotic quality. Just off the mainland coast, midway between the historic towns of Ribe and Tønder and a 30-minute drive from either, Rømø is connected to the mainland by a 10km causeway that passes over marshlands, where sheep graze happily and wading birds forage for food.

During the 18th century, many islanders were captains of German and Dutch whaling ships working off Greenland. Today, Rømø is a hugely popular holiday destination, especially with visitors from nearby Germany. It has its fair share of caravan parks but also a sprinkling of red-walled, thatch-roofed houses nestling in scrubby pine woods. Vast, sandy beaches line the western shore.

The northern end of the island is an out-of-bounds military zone.

The **tourist office** (☎ 74 75 51 30; www.romo.dk; Havnebyvej 30; ⊗ 9am-5pm mid-Jun–mid-Sep) is on the eastern side of Rømø, 1km south of the causeway exit on to the island.

Sights & Activities

Rømø's **beaches** are most easily reached at Lakolk on the central west coast. Conditions are often perfect for **windsurfing** and **kitesurfing** if you have the right gear, although the sea can be more than a kilometre away from the shoreline at low tide. It's also a good place for **horse riding** on sturdy Icelandic ponies. Several places run pony trekking, including **Rømø Ranch** (☎ 74 75 54 11; Lakolk; per hr Dkr60-80). From June to September look out for spectacular sand sculptures at Lakolk.

The inland section of the island has **trails** through heather moors and wooded areas that offer quiet hiking. There's an **old church** with unique Greenlandic gravestones on the main road in Kirkeby.

The best place to get a feel for Rømø's nautical past is at **Kommandørgården** (☎ 74 75 52 76; Juvrevej 60, Toftum; adult/child Dkr15/free; ⊗ 10am-6pm Tue-Sun May-Sep, to 3pm Tue-Sun Oct), the preserved home of one of Rømø's 18th-century whaling captains, on the northeastern side of the island. Dutch tiles line many of the walls, the woodwork is painted in rococo style and the furnishings come from many countries. A whale skeleton bleaches in the sun outside in the garden.

Sleeping & Eating

Kommandørgårdens Camping (☎ 74 75 51 22; www .kommandoergaarden.dk; Havnebyvej 201; camp site per adult/child/tent Dkr65/35/15; ps) Near the hostel, this camping ground has a swimming pool and spa.

Danhostel Rømø (☎ 74 75 51 88; www.danhostel .dk/sonderborg; dm/r Dkr120/240; ⊗ mid-Mar–Nov) Set among the pines on the southeastern side of Rømø near Havneby, this 91-bed terracotta-walled hostel is centred on a delightful traditional building with a thatched roof and is close to the beach.

Hotel Kommandørgården (☎ 74 75 51 22; www .kommandoergaarden.dk; Havnebyvej 201; s/d Dkr595/795; P ⚘) A resort-style hotel with comfortable cabin-style rooms with fridges and coffee makers; the downside is the setting right by the busy road, but the facilities include a spa, golf packages and a pool.

Otto & Ani's Fisk (☎ 74 75 53 06; Havnepladsen) Right on the harbourside at Havneby, the fish at Otto & Ani's are as fresh as they come and good value too, ranging from Dkr50 for basic fish and chips to Dkr175 for a two-person fish platter.

Kommandørgården (☎ 74 75 52 76; Juvrevej 60, Toftum) There's a good café here offering coffee, cake and light lunches (like a snow-crab platter for Dkr98).

There are grocery stores and a bakery within walking distance of the hostel, and numerous cafés near the beach-road end at Lakolk.

Getting There & Around

Rømø is 14km west of the town of Skærbæk and Rte 11. Buses run from Skærbæk to Havneby (Dkr21, 35 minutes) numerous times a day. From Skærbæk there's a train service to Ribe (Dkr23, 30 minutes), Tønder (Dkr42, 30 minutes) and Esbjerg (Dkr 50, one hour) about once an hour. Car ferries connect Havneby with Germany's island of Sylt (adult/child Dkr53/36, one hour) many times a day.

From May to September, a limited public bus service connects villages on the island. Flat-as-a-pancake Rømø is a good place for cycling; bicycles can be rented in several places for around Dkr55, including the camping grounds.

DENMARK DIRECTORY

ACCOMMODATION

Accommodation in this chapter is listed in order of preference.

Camping & Cabins

Denmark's 516 camping grounds typically charge from Dkr50 to Dkr65 per person to pitch a tent. Many places add about Dkr20 for the tent. A camping pass (available at

any camping ground) is required (Dkr80) and covers a family group with children under 18 for the season. If you do not have a seasonal pass you pay an extra Dkr20 a night for a temporary pass.

Camping is restricted to camping grounds, or on private land with the owner's permission. Camping in a car along the beach or in a car park is definitely prohibited and can result in an immediate fine. Tourist offices usually have brochures listing local camping grounds.

The **Danish Camping Association** (☎ 39 27 88 44; www.campingraadet.dk; Campingrådet, Mosedalvej 15, Valby) inspects and grades Danish camping grounds using a star system and carries a full list on its website.

Hostels

The national Hostelling International office is **Danhostel** (☎ 33 31 36 12; www.danhostel.dk; Vesterbrogade 39, 1620 Copenhagen V).

Most of Denmark's 100 *vandrerhjem* (hostels) in its Danhostel association have private rooms in addition to dormitories, making hostels an affordable and popular alternative to hotels (so book ahead from June to August). Dorm beds cost from about Dkr120 to Dkr150, while private rooms range from Dkr200 to Dkr450 for singles, and Dkr300 to Dkr500 for doubles. Blankets and pillows are provided, but not sheets; bring your own or hire them for Dkr40 to Dkr60. Sleeping bags are not allowed.

Travellers can buy international hostel cards in Denmark for Dkr160 or pay Dkr35 extra a night. Outside Copenhagen, check-in is generally between 4pm and 8pm or 9pm (but a few places close as early as 6pm); the reception office is usually closed and the phone not answered between noon and 4pm. Most hostels close in winter.

You can pick up a free 200-page hostel guide from tourist offices giving information on each hostel. All Danish hostels have an all-you-can-eat breakfast for Dkr45 or less. Nearly all hostels also have guest kitchens with pots and pans where you can cook your own food.

Hotels

Budget hotels start at around Dkr450/600 for singles/doubles. *Kros*, a name that implies country inn but is more often the Danish version of a motel, are generally cheaper by about a third, often occupy pleasing period houses and more often than not offer a sense of homeliness, hospitality and *hygge* (the Danes' wonderfully evocative word for cosiness) that chain hotels cannot hope to compete with. Both hotels and *kros* usually include an all-you-can-eat breakfast.

Rates listed in this chapter include all taxes and are for rooms with toilet and shower, unless otherwise specified. Some hotels offer discount schemes at weekends year-round and from May to September when business travel is light.

Other Accommodation

Many tourist offices book rooms in private homes for a small fee, or provide a free list of the rooms so travellers can phone on their own. Rates vary, averaging about Dkr250/350 for singles/doubles. Standards of accommodation may vary widely and some rooms may be very basic. **Dansk Bed & Breakfast** (☎ 39 61 04 05; www.bbdk.dk; PO Box 53, 2900 Hellerup) handles 300 homes throughout Denmark offering private rooms at similar rates.

ACTIVITIES
Cycling

Cycling is a popular holiday activity and there are thousands of kilometres of established cycling routes. Those around Bornholm, Funen and Møn, as well as the 440km Old Military Rd (Hærvejen) through central Jutland, are among the most popular.

Dansk Cyklist Forbund (DCF; ☎ 33 32 31 21; www .dcf.dk; Rømersgade 7, 1362 Copenhagen K) publishes *Cykelferiekort*, a cycling map of the entire country, as well as more detailed regional cycling maps.

DCF also publishes *Overnatning i det fri*, which lists hundreds of farmers who provide cyclists with a place to pitch a tent for Dkr15 a night. Cycling maps can be purchased in advance from DCF or from tourist offices and bookshops upon arrival.

Walking

Even though Denmark does not have substantial forests, many small tracts of woodland are crisscrossed by pleasant walking trails. The **Skov og Naturstyrelsen** (Forest and Nature Bureau) produces brochures with sketch maps that show trails in nearly 100 such areas. The brochures can be picked up free at public libraries and some tourist of-

fices. Denmark's coastline is public domain lined with scenic walking tracks.

Water Sports

Canoeing possibilities on Denmark's inland lakes, such as canoe touring between lakeside camping grounds in Jutland's Lake District, are superb. You can hire canoes and equipment at many camping grounds or in main centres such as Silkeborg (p90). The lakes are generally undemanding as far as water conditions go, although some experience is an advantage.

Denmark's remarkable coastline offers terrific **windsurfing** and **kitesurfing** possibilities. Good areas are along the northern coast of Zealand at places such as Smidstrup Strand, and in northwest Jutland. The Limfjord area of northwest Jutland is particularly suited to windsurfing and you can pick up an excellent leaflet, *Windsurfing in the Limfjord Area*, from most tourist offices in the area. There's an English version and it pinpoints 28 windsurfing areas by use of small maps.

BOOKS

For travellers, Lonely Planet's *Denmark* is the most comprehensive all-round guidebook available. *Camping Danmark*, a new edition of which is published each year by the Danish Camping Board (Campingrådet), has detailed information on all camping grounds in the country.

Denmark: A Modern History, by W Glyn Jones, gives a comprehensive account of contemporary Danish society.

Just as Well I'm Leaving: Around Europe with Hans Christian Andersen by Michael Booth is both an accomplished biography of Andersen and a funny, entertaining travelogue retracing his footsteps around Denmark and Europe.

Knud Romer's recent *The First to Blink is Afraid to Die,* a novel about racial tensions in southern Denmark, has been critically hailed as a great debut; at the time of this writing, overseas publishers were showing an interest in translating his work into English and other languages.

BUSINESS HOURS

Office hours are generally 9am to 5pm Monday to Friday. Most banks are open from 9.30am to 4pm Monday to Friday (to 6pm Thursday), but some still close earlier.

Stores are usually open 9.30am to 5.30pm Monday to Thursday, to 7pm on Friday, and to 2pm on Saturday.

CHILDREN

It should come as no surprise that Denmark, home of the Lego block, has lots of attractions to entice kids. Legoland itself (p104) is the most visited children's site in Scandinavia, and Denmark abounds with amusement parks. The biggest of these parks, including Tivoli Gardens (p43) are in Copenhagen. Many tourist offices give out brochures focusing on children-oriented activities and attractions.

DANGERS & ANNOYANCES

Denmark is by and large a safe country. Nevertheless, be careful with your belongings, particularly in busy places such as Copenhagen's Central Station. In cities, you'll need to become accustomed quickly to the busy cycle lanes between vehicle roads and the pedestrian pavement, as these lanes are easy to step into accidentally.

DISABLED TRAVELLERS

Overall, Denmark is a user-friendly destination for the disabled traveller. The Danish Tourist Board (www.visitdenmark.com) has to date accredited, in association with local disability organisations, 1300 locations as 'accessible to all' throughout the country. It also publishes *Access in Denmark: a Travel Guide for the Disabled*, in English, with information on accommodation, transport and sightseeing options for disabled travellers.

EMBASSIES & CONSULATES
Embassies & Consulates in Denmark

Australia (☎ 70 26 36 76; www.denmark.embassy.gov .au; Dampfærgevej 26, Copenhagen)
Canada (☎ 33 48 32 00; www.canada.dk; Kristen Bernikows Gade1, Copenhagen)
Germany (☎ 35 45 99 00; www.kopenhagen.diplo.de; Stockholmsgade 57, Copenhagen)
Ireland (☎ 35 42 32 33; Østbanegade 21, Copenhagen)
Norway (☎ 33 14 01 24; www.norsk.dk; Amaliegade 39, Copenhagen)
Poland (☎ 39 46 77 00; www.ambpol.dk; Richelius Allé 12, Hellerup)
Sweden (☎ 33 36 03 70; www.sverigesambassad.dk; Sankt Annæ Plads 15A, Copenhagen)
UK (☎ 35 44 52 00; www.britishembassy.dk; Kastelsvej 36-40, Copenhagen)

USA (☎ 33 41 71 00; www.usembassy.dk; Dag Hammarskjölds Allé 24, Copenhagen)

Danish Embassies & Consulates Abroad

Australia (☎ 03 9866 1242; Suite 3, 492 St Kilda Rd, Melbourne, VIC 3004)
Canada (☎ 613-562 1811; www.danish-embassycanada .com; 47 Clarence St, Suite 450, Ottawa, Ontario K1N 9K1)
Finland (☎ 09-684 1050; www.ambhelsingfors.um.dk; Centralgatan 1A, 00101 Helsinki)
Germany (☎ 030-5050 2000; www.daenemark.org; Rauchstrasse 1, 10787 Berlin)
Ireland (☎ 01-475 6404; www.ambdublin.um.dk; 121 St Stephen's Green, Dublin 2)
Netherlands (☎ 070-302 59 59; www.danishembassy .nl; Koninginnegracht 30, 2514 Den Haag)
New Zealand (☎ 04-537 3099; 273 Bleakhouse Rd, Howick, PO Box 619, 1015 Auckland)
Norway (☎ 22 54 08 00; www.amboslo.um.dk; Olav Kyrres Gate 7, 0244 Oslo)
Sweden (☎ 08-406 75 00; www.ambstockholm.um.dk; Jakobs Torg 1, 11186 Stockholm)
UK (☎ 020-7333 0200; www.amblondon.um.dk/en; 55 Sloane St, London SW1X 9SR)
USA (☎ 202-234 4300; www.denmarkemb.org; 3200 Whitehaven St NW, Washington, DC 20008)

FESTIVALS & EVENTS

Beginning with **Midsummer's Eve** bonfires in late June, Denmark buzzes with outdoor activity throughout the summer. Main attractions are the 180 music festivals that run throughout the country, covering a broad spectrum of music that includes not only jazz, rock and blues but also gospel, folk, classical, country, Cajun and much more.

The acclaimed 10-day **Copenhagen Jazz Festival** (http://festival.jazz.dk in Danish) is held in early July, with outdoor concerts and numerous performances in clubs around the city.

The town of Roskilde hosts an internationally acclaimed **rock festival** (www.roskilde -festival.dk) on the last weekend of June; a single admission fee includes camping space and entry to all concerts.

There are **folk festivals** in Skagen near the end of June and in Tønder in late August. The 10-day **Århus Festival** in early September features music and multicultural events.

GAY & LESBIAN TRAVELLERS

Denmark is a popular destination for gay and lesbian travellers. Copenhagen in particular has an active, open gay community and lots of nightlife options.

Landsforeningen for Bøsser og Lesbiske (LBL; ☎ 33 13 19 48; www.lbl.dk; Teglgårdstræde 13, Copenhagen) is the national organisation for gay men and lesbians. Branch offices in main towns are mentioned in relevant sections. A good English-language website with links to LBL and other gay organisations is www.copenhagen-gay-life.dk.

HOLIDAYS

Summer holidays for schoolchildren begin around 20 June and end around 10 August. Many Danes go on holiday during the first three weeks of July. The following public holidays are observed in Denmark:

New Year's Day (1 January)
Maundy Thursday (Thursday before Easter)
Good Friday to Easter Monday (March/April)
Common Prayer Day (Fourth Friday after Easter)
Ascension Day (Fifth Thursday after Easter)
Whit Sunday (Fifth Sunday after Easter)
Whit Monday (Fifth Monday after Easter)
Constitution Day (5 Jun)
Christmas Eve (24 December from noon)
Christmas Day (25 December)

INTERNET ACCESS

Internet cafés charge about Dkr3 to Dkr45 an hour. Public libraries also have internet -capable computers and visitors generally have free access to them, although you may have to sign up and wait for a free slot. Connections are generally fast. Wi-fi hotspots are mushrooming all over the country, many of them free. **TDC** (http://tdc.dk in Danish) is a network of more than 600 paid-for wi-fi hotspots.

LEGAL MATTERS

Denmark is taking a much harder line on even the 'softest' drugs these days. All forms of cannabis and harder drugs are illegal. If you are arrested for any offence you can be held for up to 24 hours before appearing in court. You have a right to know the charges against you and a right to a lawyer. You are not obliged to answer police questions before speaking to the lawyer.

You can get free legal advice on your rights from the EU legal-aid organisation **EURO-JUS** (☎ 33 14 41 40; ⏰ 9am-6pm Mon-Thu, to 4.30pm Fri). Free legal advice clinics can be found in over 90 places across Denmark. The service is organised by the Danish bar, **Det Danske Advokatsamfund** (☎ 38 38 36 38 or 33 96 97 98).

MONEY

ATMs

Major banks have ATMs which accept Visa, MasterCard and the Cirrus and Plus bank cards. All major credit and debit cards are widely accepted throughout Denmark, although some shops impose a surcharge of up to 5% if you use them, even in the case of debit cards.

Moneychangers

All common travellers cheques are accepted in Denmark. Buy your travellers cheques in higher denominations as bank fees for changing money are a hefty Dkr25 to Dkr30 per cheque, with a Dkr40 minimum. If you're exchanging cash, there's a Dkr25 fee for a transaction. Travellers cheques command a better exchange rate than cash by about 1%.

Post offices will also exchange foreign currency at comparable rates to those at banks.

The Euro

Although Denmark remains outside the Euro zone, acceptance of euros is commonplace. Most hotels and restaurants will take euros, as do many bars, cafés and shops, although you may find reluctance to do so in more remote areas or from very small businesses. Government institutions do not accept euros.

Tipping

Restaurant bills and taxi fares include service charges in the quoted prices, and further tipping is unnecessary.

POST

Denmark has an efficient postal system. Most post offices are open 9am or 10am to 5pm or 5.30pm Monday to Friday and 9am to noon on Saturday. You can receive mail poste restante at any post office in Denmark.

TELEPHONE & FAX

It costs Dkr3 to make a local call at coin phones. You get about twice as much calling time for your money on domestic calls made between 7.30pm and 8am daily and all day on Sunday.

Phonecards (Dkr30 to Dkr100) can be bought at post offices and newspaper kiosks throughout the country.

The country code for calling Denmark from abroad is ☎ 45. To make international calls from Denmark dial ☎ 00 and then the country code for the country you're calling.

TIME

Time in Denmark is normally one hour ahead of GMT/UTC, the same as in neighbouring European countries. Clocks are moved forward one hour for daylight-saving time from the last Sunday in March to the last Sunday in October. Denmark uses the 24-hour clock and all timetables and business hours are posted accordingly.

TOURIST INFORMATION

The tourist board's website is www.visitdenmark.com. There are several Danish tourist offices abroad:

Germany (☎ 01805-326463; daninfo@.dt.dk; Dänemarks offizielle Tourismuszentrale, Glockengießerwall 2, 20095 Hamburg)

Norway (☎ 22 00 76 46; turistinfo@visitdenmark.com; Danmarks Turistkontor, Tollbugaten 27, Postboks 406 Sentrum, 0103 Oslo)

Sweden (☎ 08 611 72 22; info@visitdenmark.se; Danmarks Turistråd, Box 5524, 114 85 Stockholm)

UK (☎ 020-7259 5959; london@visitdenmark.com; Danish Tourist Board, 55 Sloane St, London SW1X 9SY)

USA (☎ 212-885 9700; info@goscandinavia.com; Danish Tourist Board, 655 Third Ave, 18th fl, New York, NY 10017)

VISAS

Citizens of the EU, USA, Canada, Australia and New Zealand need a valid passport to enter Denmark, but don't need a visa for stays of less than three months. If you wish to apply for a visa, do so at least three months in advance of your planned arrival.

WOMEN TRAVELLERS

The **Danish Centre for Information on Women & Gender** (KVINFO; ☎ 33 13 50 88; www.kvinfo.dk in Danish; Christians Brygge 3, Copenhagen) has information on feminist issues, while **Kvindehuset** (☎ 33 14 28 04; Gothersgade 37, Copenhagen) is a help centre and meeting place for women. Dial ☎ 112 for rape crisis or other emergencies.

EMERGENCY NUMBERS

In Denmark, dial the free number ☎ 112 when you need police, fire and ambulance services.

TRANSPORT IN DENMARK

GETTING THERE & AWAY

Air

The profusion of budget carriers and flights into Denmark from elsewhere on the Continent, Ireland and the UK makes flying here very affordable indeed. If you're coming from European destinations consider flying into an airport other than Copenhagen, such as Århus or Billund; air fares can be competitive, and the airports are well connected by bus with neighbouring towns and afford fast access to some great parts of northern and central Jutland.

The budget carrier Ryanair, for instance, has regular, cheap flights from Stansted Airport in England to Århus airport and to Malmö, in Sweden (a short hop by rail from Copenhagen). See the following airport websites for full details.

AIRLINES

Scandinavian Airlines (SAS; ☎ 70 10 30 00; www.scandinavian.net; airline code SK) is the largest carrier serving Denmark, connecting it with much of Europe and the rest of the world.

Many other airlines fly into Denmark including the following ones.

Aer Lingus (airline code EI; ☎ +353 818 365000; www.aerlingus.com)

Air France (airline code AF; ☎ 82 33 27 01; www.airfrance.com)

Alitalia (airline code AZ; ☎ 70 27 02 90; www.alitalia.com)

BMI British Midland (airline code BD; ☎ 70 10 20 00; www.flybmi.com)

British Airways (airline code BA; ☎ 70 12 80 22; www.britishairways.com)

Easyjet (airline code U2; ☎ 70 12 43 21; www.easyjet.com)

Finnair (airline code AY; ☎ 33 36 45 45; www.finnair.com)

Icelandair (airline code FI; ☎ 33 70 22 00; www.icelandexpress.com)

KLM Royal Dutch Airlines (airline code KL; ☎ 70 10 07 47; www.klm.com)

Lufthansa (airline code LH; ☎ 70 10 20 00; www.lufthansa.com)

Ryanair (airline code FR; ☎ +353 818 303 030; www.ryanair.com)

Sterling (airline code NB; ☎ 70 10 84 84; www.sterling.dk)

DENMARK

MAIN DANISH AIRPORTS
Århus (☎ 87 75 70 00; www.aar.dk)
Billund (☎ 76 50 50 50; www.bll.dk)
Copenhagen (☎ 32 31 32 31; www.cph.dk)

Land
GERMANY
The E45 is the main motorway running
between Germany and Denmark's Jutland
Peninsula. There are also three railway
lines linking the two countries (2nd-
class fares from Copenhagen to Frankfurt
are Dkr1732, although be advised fares
booked in advance can be substantially
cheaper than the prices listed here). Eurolines operates buses from Copenhagen to
Berlin (Dkr290, 6½ hours) and Frankfurt
via Hamburg (Dkr770, 15 hours) several
times a week.

NORWAY
Trains operate between Copenhagen and
Oslo; the 2nd-class fare (via Sweden; 7½
hours, one or two daily) is Dkr945. Eurolines offers a daily bus service between Oslo
and Copenhagen (Dkr320, eight hours) via
Göteborg.

SWEDEN
Trains run many times a day between
Denmark and Sweden via a bridge linking
Copenhagen with Malmö (Dkr85, 40 minutes), Dkr365 to Göteborg and Dkr945 to
Stockholm (five hours). If you're travelling
by train, the bridge crossing is included
in the fare, but for those travelling by car,
there's a Dkr220 toll per vehicle. There
are numerous and frequent bus services
between Copenhagen and Sweden, including Eurolines buses to Göteborg (Dkr230,
five hours) and Stockholm (Dkr430, 9½
hours).

Sea
GERMANY
The frequent Rødbyhavn–Puttgarden
ferry takes 45 minutes and is included in
train tickets for those travelling by rail;
otherwise, the cost per adult is Dkr50 and
for a car with up to nine passengers it's
Dkr420.

Bornholmstrafikken operates a ferry
service at least once a day between Rønne
and Sassnitz, Germany (Dkr150 one way,
3½ hours).

ICELAND & THE FAROE ISLANDS
Smyril Lines (in Denmark ☎ 33 16 40 04/96 55 03 60; in
Faroe Islands ☎ 345 900; www.smyril-line.dk) runs every
week from Hanstholm to Tórshavn (Faroe
Islands) and Seyðisfjörður (Iceland) from
mid-May to early September. The boat leaves
Hanstholm at 9pm Saturday, arriving in Tórshavn at 6am Monday. Visitors then have a
two-day stopover in the Faroe Islands (while
the boat makes a run to Lerwick, Shetland,
and Bergen, Norway), before departing from
Tórshavn at 6pm Wednesday and arriving
in Seyðisfjörður at 8am Thursday. The return boat departs from Seyðisfjörður at noon
Thursday, arriving in Tórshavn at 5am Friday and in Hanstholm at 5pm Saturday.

Midsummer fares to Tórshavn start from
€160 with a couchette or sleeping berth
with mattress, but no bedding. Fares to
Seyðisfjörður include couchette (€230) and
cabin bunk (€310); these fares are about
25% less for travel in low season (September to April). There's a 25% discount for
students under 26, on presentation of a
valid student card.

NORWAY
DFDS (☎ 33 42 30 00; www.dfds.dk) operates a
daily overnight ferry between Copenhagen and Oslo. **Colorline** (☎ 99 56 19 77; www
.colorline.dk) sails from Hirtshals to Larvik,
Kristiansand, Stavanger and Bergen; and
from Frederikshavn to Oslo. See the relevant Getting There & Away sections of the
cities for details.

POLAND
Polferries (☎ 33 11 46 45; www.polferries.pl) operates ferries to Świnoujście from both Copenhagen four times a week (from Dkr410,
10 hours) and Rřnne on Saturday (from
Dkr250, five hours).

SWEDEN
Scandlines (☎ 33 15 15 15; www.scandlines.dk) and
Sundbusserne (☎ 49 71 02 00; www.sundbusserne
.dk) sail frequently throughout the day from
Helsingør to Helsingborg, in Sweden. Prices
vary, but are roughly Dkr21 to Dkr23 per
adult or from Dkr200 if you are taking a car
with two passengers.

Other ferries go from Frederikshavn to
Göteborg and Oslo, and Rønne to Ystad.
See the relevant Getting There & Away sec-
tions in this chapter.

UK
DFDS Seaways (in UK ☎ 08705 333 000; in Denmark ☎ 33 42 30 00; www.dfdsseaways.co.uk) sails from Esbjerg to Harwich at least three times a week at 6pm year-round. It takes 19 hours. The cost for passage in a chair ranges from Dkr515 in winter to Dkr1250 in midsummer, while the cheapest bed in a two-person cabin is between Dkr902 and Dkr1935.

GETTING AROUND
Air
Most internal flights cost around Dkr1000 for a standard ticket and can be much cheaper if you book in advance.

Denmark's domestic air routes are operated by the airlines listed here.

Cimber Air (☎ 70 10 12 18; www.cimber.dk) Services include Copenhagen to Aalborg (50 minutes, three times daily), Rønne (Bornholm, 40 minutes, at least four times daily) and Karup (central Jutland, 50 minutes, 12 times daily weekdays, at least twice on weekends).

SAS (☎ 70 10 30 00; www.scandinavian.net) Links Copenhagen with Aalborg, Århus and Billund about a dozen times a day.

Bicycle
Cycling is a practical way to get around Denmark. There are extensive bike paths linking towns throughout the country and bike lanes through most city centres.

You can rent bikes in most towns for around Dkr70 a day, plus a deposit of about Dkr250. Bikes can be taken on ferries and most trains for a modest cost; make sure you pick up the DSB pamphlet *Cykler i tog.*

Boat
A network of ferries links virtually all of Denmark's populated islands. Where there's not a bridge, there's usually a ferry, most of which take cars. All vessels meet strict safety requirements and are punctual and reliable. Specific information is given under individual destination sections. **Scandlines** (☎ 33 15 15 15; www.scandlines.com) operates many domestic ferry services. Timetables are widely available in tourist offices and railway stations.

Bus
All large cities and towns have a local bus system and most places are also served by regional buses, many of which connect with trains. There are also a few long-distance bus routes, including from Copenhagen

to Aalborg or Århus. Travelling by bus on long-distance routes costs about 20% less than travel by train, although it's usually a bit slower than the train.

The main bus companies operating in Denmark include the following:

Abildskou (☎ 70 21 08 88; www.abildskou.dk) Runs from Copenhagen to Aalborg, Silkeborg and Århus.

Bornholmerbussen (☎ 44 68 44 00; www.bat.dk in Danish) Operates the bus services on Bornholm.

Søndergaards Busser (☎ 70 10 00 33; www.sonder gaards-busser.dk) Runs between Copenhagen and Århus.

Thinggaard Expressbusser (☎ 70 10 00 10; www .thinggaardbus.com in Danish) Operates between Copenhagen, Aalborg and Fjerritslev and between Frederikshavn and Esbjerg.

Car & Motorcycle
Denmark is perfect for touring by car. Roads are in good condition and well signposted. Traffic is manageable, even in major cities such as Copenhagen (rush hours excepted).

Access to and from motorways is made easy since roads leading out of city and town centres are sensibly named after the main city to which they're routed. For instance, the road leading out of Odense to Faaborg is Faaborgvej, the road leading to Nyborg is Nyborgvej, and so on.

Denmark's extensive network of ferries carries motor vehicles for reasonable rates. It's always a good idea for drivers to call ahead and make reservations.

AUTOMOBILE ASSOCIATIONS
Denmark's main motoring organisation is **Forenede Danske Motorejere** (FDM; ☎ 32 66 01 00/70 13 30 40; www.fdm.dk in Danish; Firskovvej 32, 2800 Lyngby).

DRIVING LICENCE
A home driving licence, rather than an international one, is sufficient to drive and hire cars in Denmark, although you may also need to supply a passport at hire places.

FUEL & SPARE PARTS
You'll find the best prices for petrol at stations along motorways and at the unstaffed OK Benzin chain, which has self-serve pumps that accept Dkr100 notes as well as major credit cards. It's a small country, so you're never far from a garage and spare parts.

HIRE

You'll generally get the best deal by booking through an international rental agency before you arrive in Denmark. Hire rates for the cheapest cars, including VAT, insurance and unlimited kilometres, begin at about Dkr650 a day, or Dkr450 a day for rentals of two days or more. Most companies offer a special weekend rate that allows you to keep the car from Friday afternoon to Monday morning and includes VAT and insurance for around Dkr1200. Europcar offers unlimited kilometres and generally has the cheapest, most flexible weekend deals, but it's wise to call around and compare.

The largest companies, such as **Europcar** (☎ 70 11 66 99; www.europcar.dk), **Avis** (☎ 33 26 80 00; www.avis.dk) and **Hertz** (☎ 0800-1700; www.hertzdk .dk), have offices throughout Denmark.

INSURANCE

Check with your insurance company that your policy is valid for driving in Denmark before you depart.

ROAD RULES

In Denmark you drive on the right-hand side of the road, seat-belt use is mandatory and all drivers are required to carry a warning triangle in case of breakdowns. Speed limits are 50km/h in towns, 80km/h outside built-up areas and either 110km/h or 130km/h on motorways. Motorcycles and cars must use dipped headlights at all times.

It's illegal to drive with a blood-alcohol concentration of 0.05% or greater and driving under the influence is subject to stiff penalties and a possible prison sentence.

Train

With the exception of a few short private lines, the **Danish State Railways** (DSB; www.dsb.dk) runs all Danish train services.

There are two types of long-distance trains: sleek intercity (IC) trains that generally require reservations (Dkr20) and older, slower interregional (IR) trains that make more stops and don't require reservations. Both cost the same, apart from the InterCity-Lyn, a cushy, pricier express train aimed at businesspeople. Rail passes don't cover reservation fees or surcharges.

Overall, train travel in Denmark is not expensive, in large part because the distances are short. People aged 65 and older are entitled to a 20% discount on Friday and Saturday and a 50% discount on other days. There are also generous discounts for children. Scanrail, Eurail and other rail passes are valid on DSB ferries and trains, but not on the private lines.

Faroe Islands

The forgotten Faroes are just a short flight from the UK, yet they're way off the standard traveller's radar. Adrift in the frothing swells of the north Atlantic, this mysterious 18-piece jigsaw puzzle of islands is at once ancient and very modern. Multicoloured cottages and grass-roofed wooden churches add focus to the grandly stark, treeless moorlands. Timeless networks of cairn-marked footpaths crisscross craggy layer-cake mountains. But even the tiniest once-inaccessible hamlets are now linked by a remarkable series of road-tunnels. And even as you bob around the dramatic fjords on a 70-year-old wooden sloop, your mobile phone is never likely to lose its signal.

The Faroes are a paradise for fell-walkers and ornithologists who accept the pyrotechnically unpredictable climate. Designer-mown by shaggy sheep, fields are blissfully bouncy under-foot. Pastures gleam with the greener-than-green hue of divine billiard tables. Peeping puffins, dive-bombing skuas and wheeling fulmars glide over dizzying chasms. Wave-battered headlands end in plunging cliffs that are as breathtaking as the wild winds that threaten to blow unwary hikers off them.

The proud, stoical Faroese character has been forged from Viking blood, Christian piety, Scandinavian openness and an awe for the humbling nature that's all around. Few communities this small are so alive with art and the Faroes' incredibly vibrant music scene is nothing short of astonishing. So even if the weather proves uncooperative, this self-assured little demi-nation is likely to surprise and delight even the most cynical traveller.

FAST FACTS

- **Area** 1393 sq km
- **Capital** Tórshavn
- **Currency** Danish krone (Dkr); €1 = Dkr7.45; US$1 = Dkr5.91, UK£1 = Dkr10.82, $A1 = Dkr4.42, CA$1 = Dkr4.88, NZ$1 = Dkr4.14, ¥100 = Dkr5.73
- **Famous for** puffins, wool, whales, Viking sagas
- **Official Languages** Faroese, Danish
- **Phrases** *góðan dag* (hello), *takk* (thanks), *farvæl* (goodbye), *orsaka meg* (excuse me)
- **Population** 48,379
- **Telephone Codes** country code ☎ 298; international access code ☎ 00
- **Visa** Not required for citizens of the EU, USA, Canada, Australia and New Zealand (see p140)

HIGHLIGHTS

- Bob beneath the towering bird cliffs on magical boat tours from **Vestmanna** (p128) or from **Gjógv** (p130), the Faroes' prettiest village.
- Gasp at incomparably powerful panoramas of cliffs and headlands viewed from **Kallur lighthouse, Viðareiði, Eiðiskollur, Beinisvørð** or **Glyvraberg** (p133).
- Drive and hike around the charming villages of **northern Eysturoy** (p129).
- Potter amongst puffins on peaceful **Mykines** (p127).

ITINERARIES

Two nights/three days Head straight for Vestmanna for a boat ride along the spectacular bird cliffs. If driving, continue to charming Gjógv with side trips to Saksun and Eiði outbound, Funningur, Elduvík and Kirkjubøur on return. Spend the last night in Tórshavn strolling the historical Tinganes district and exploring the lively pubs.

Ten Days Fly in on a Friday and take the boat the next morning out to the puffin island of Mykines. If bad weather doesn't prevent your escape, take the Sunday helicopter to the capital Tórshavn. Visit the old town, flit up to the Vestmanna Bird Cliffs, explore northern Eysturoy then head for Klaksvík, the launching point for day-trip excursions to Kalsoy and the weather-dependent mail-boat trip to Fugloy. On Friday buzz by helicopter to Froðba on Suðuroy, explore for a day or two then return back to Tórshavn by ferry.

CLIMATE & WHEN TO GO

Theatrical meteorology is part of the Faroes' fascination. Torrential downpours, swirling fogs and vicious storm-force winds are conjured up from nothing as though they were the outcome of witches' spells. Then miraculously the sun bursts through to paint the towering cliffs in dazzling crystal-clear brilliance. Rainfall is very common (280 days per year on average) but unpredictable and often highly localised.

June to August is by far the best time to visit the Faroe Islands. Days are dreamily long and the weather is comparatively passable, though don't expect anything near Mediterranean heat: July temperatures average only 11°C. In winter, time stands still as daytime darkness, closed hotels and shuttered museums add to the stormy sense of a land forgotten. While never fearfully cold (January average 3°C), it can snow as late as May.

HISTORY

According to Irish missionary Brendan, Celtic monks were already living in eremitic seclusion on the Faroes by the 6th century. Their isolation was ended from around AD800 when the first Norse farmers arrived. The farmers' independence dwindled with the often forceful imposition of Christianity, and the isles became part of the Kingdom of Norway in 1035. The first bishops' seat was established in Kirkjubøur.

The Faroese parliament (Løgting) lost further influence after Norway fell to Denmark in 1380. Between 1535 and 1856, all trade was governed by the Danish monopoly for which the great stores of Tinganes were developed. The only Faroese to gain temporary trading rights was Magnus Heinason in 1579, who built Skansin Fort in Tørshavn to protect his ships from pirate attacks.

In 1849 the Danish parliament incorporated the islands as a 'county' of Denmark. This provoked strong independence movements, which were re-ignited by the

---

HOW MUCH?

- **Woollen slippers** Dkr120
- **Sheepskin jacket** Dkr2600
- **Cuddly toy puffin** Dkr500
- **Medium-sized Faroese flag** Dkr200
- **Faroese sweater** Dkr750-1200

LONELY PLANET INDEX

- **1L of blýfrítt (unleaded petrol)** Dkr8.96
- **1.5L bottle of water** Dkr20
- **33cl bottle of Black Sheep beer (in a pub)** Dkr30
- **Souvenir T-shirt** Dkr150
- **Street snack of fish and chips** Dkr40

British occupation of the islands during WWII (see Flag Day box, p136). In 1948 the Danish compromise was to upgrade the Faroes' status to the 'self-governing community within the Kingdom of Denmark' which it remains today. This gave the Faroese legislative power over their own affairs. When Denmark joined the EEC (now EU), the Faroes refused to follow. This smart move protected their fishery-based economy from ruthless EU competition. Following a sharp recession, bank defaults and a population drain in the 1990s, the economy has rebounded impressively in recent years.

PEOPLE

The majority of Faroese are of Nordic Viking origin. They share the reserved politeness of their Scandinavian neighbours, but if you spend some time here you'll discover a rich vein of hospitality. Over 35% of the Faroese population live in the capital Tórshavn at least on weekdays. But on summer weekends many return 'home' and suddenly village populations grow up to fivefold. That explains why villages comprising 40 perfectly-maintained homesteads have official populations of less than 10.

RELIGION

Christianity is fundamental to Faroese culture; 84% of the population belong to the Evangelical-Lutheran Church with around 10% Plymouth Brethren and a small minority of Roman Catholics.

ARTS

William Heinesen and Heðin Brú are the internationally best-known Faroese writers. However, before written Faroese developed (after 1846) the language had been kept alive through a strong tradition of oral epic poetry (kvæði) recited as accompaniment to the classic stomping ringform 'chain dances' which are still a mainstay of summer Ólavsøkan festivities. Today the range of Faroese musical talent is nothing short of astonishing with numerous festivals and a vibrant recording industry. Some of the Faroe Island's best known performers of the moment include Teitor (melancholic folk songs), Eivør Pálsdóttir (jazz/folk inspired ballads) and the uncategorisable band Clickhaze (who launched Eivør's career). Don't miss an opportunity to see ultratalented blues hero Uni Debess (formerly of Gogo Blues) or the spine-tinglingly brilliant Búi Dam (a kind of Faroese Tom Waits). Makrel play a wistful rock that's reminiscent of James, gruff-voiced Petur Pólsen has moments of Pink Floyd–style inspiration, while highly political thrash-punk combo 200 (www .tveyhundrad.net/FO/eng.php) belt out 1976-style two-minute rants screaming for Faroese independence. Select and listen to CDs over an espresso at Leikalund (p131) or choose from hundreds on www.tutl.com (Dkr20/38 per CD delivery fee in Europe/ globally).

Death haunts the powerful canvasses of the islands' most celebrated artist, Sámal Joensen-Mikines, reflecting the harsh life experienced by earlier Faroese generations; you can see his works on display in the National Art Gallery (p121). Numerous modern artists including Astrid Luihn and Zacharias Heinesen prefer brighter Faroese landscapes with an abstract edge and such works feature heavily in the numerous small galleries that abound all around the islands. Dramatic glassworks by Trøndur Patursson illuminate the church of Gøta, while Hans Pauli Olsen's bronze sculptures adorn Tórshavn's park Viðarlundin.

ENVIRONMENT
The Land

Adrift between Iceland and Scotland, these 18 treeless, grassy islands are the remnants of a flatcapped volcanic continent that covered the Atlantic region 100 million years ago. Ice ages have since sculpted characteristic fjords while the sea has etched out numerous sheer cliffs and chasms. The highest peak is Slættaratindur (882m) on Eysturoy.

Wildlife

More than 100 species of birds find summer nesting homes on the Faroe Islands. The coastal cliffs teem with fulmars (havhestur), guillemots (lomvigi), razorbills (álka), various gulls and loveable puffins (lundi). Gannets (súla) are easiest to spot on Mykines. Ubiquitous oystercatchers (tjaldur, the national bird of

FAROE ISLANDS

FAROE ISLANDS

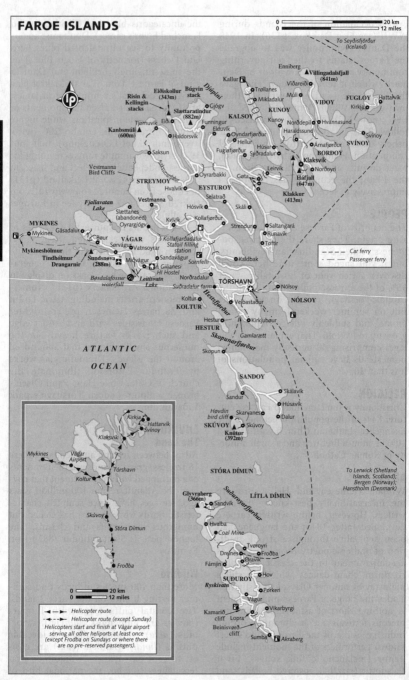

the Faroe Islands) nest on clifftop moors amid the alien warbles of longbilled snipe (*mýrisnípa*) and the dive-bombing antics of predatory great skua (*skúgvur*) and Arctic skua (*kjógvi*), best seen on Skúvoy. Nólsoy has a big colony of storm petrels (*drunnhvíti*).

Ubiquitous sheep, the commonest land mammal, have helped shape the islands' distinctively bare, green appearance. Pilot whales are the best-known inhabitants of Faroese waters (see Grindadráp box, p127) along with various other species of whales, plentiful saltwater fish, extensively farmed trout and salmon plus a few seals, considered to be the reincarnations of ancestral spirits.

Environmental Issues

The marine environment of the Faroe Islands is relatively clean though intensive fish farming (causing water pollution) and dwindling wild fish stocks are significant problems. Visitors should be particularly careful not to disturb nesting birds by walking carelessly through their breeding grounds.

FOOD & DRINK

Traditional Faroese cuisine is a decidedly hearty affair, built around fish, lamb and potatoes. Wind-drying is a classic method of preservation; *turrur fiskur* (dried fish) and *skerpikjøt* (dried mutton) are Faroese specialities. Traditionally no part of the sheep goes to waste. *Seyðahøvd* (sheep's

---

FAROESE CHURCHES

Even the tiniest villages are built around a small, tar-painted, wooden church with a fragrant if plain interior. Most are unpretentious constructions, often with turf roofs. Many were originally erected from driftwood between 1829 and 1847. As the safe return of the fishermen was the biggest worry of traditional Faroese society, churches were typically positioned overlooking the harbour. This permitted worried believers to keep a watchful eye on the sea during services. Even today, model ships are suspended within Faroese churches as a charm to encourage divine boat protection.

---

head) is a delicacy that you might find peering at you from supermarket freezers. Other tourist-frightening staples include baked puffin and *grind og spik* (whale meat and blubber): availability is sporadic and seasonal. Grill-booths and some petrol stations sell hot dogs and burgers. Some offer British-style fish and chips. Vegetarian options are extremely uncommon.

Towns have supermarkets supplemented by small kiosks selling essential groceries until 11pm. Fruit and vegetables are expensive, and fish isn't popular in restaurants: locals catch their own and typically see meat as a going-out food. Only the capital, Tórshavn has much of a selection of dining options, though rural hotels serve set meals and several towns have pizzerias.

Alcohol has only been fully legalised in the Faroe Islands since 1992. It is served at bars, cafés and restaurants and sold (weekdays only) through brewery depots and *rúsdrekkasøla* (state liquor stores), never from grocery shops. The best of several local beers is the rich, dark Black Sheep brew.

TÓRSHAVN

pop 18,100

Named after the Norse god Thor (the god of thunder), Tórshavn is one of the world's smallest capitals, although it's home to over a third of the Faroese population. Behind the harbour and a charming if tiny old-town core lies a compact commercial centre that comes merrily to life on summer weekend nights. Behind this, the town's newer housing and anonymous light-industrial warehouses sweep up towards an inspiringly barren ring of moorland hills.

HISTORY

Due to Tórshavn's central location, the Faroes' first Ting (parliament) was set up here in AD 1000, but poor soils meant that the town remained relatively small until 1856. However, once the Danish trading monopoly was replaced by free trade, Tórshavn rapidly evolved into the islands' main trading hub. It has been growing ever since.

FAROE ISLANDS

ORIENTATION

The Eastern Harbour/ferry terminal is separated from the Western Harbour by the dinky little Tinganes peninsula (old town). Most shops, restaurants and facilities lie directly behind in the area surrounding partly pedestrianised Niels Finsensgøta.

INFORMATION
Internet Access

Býarbókasavnið (Town Library; Map p122;
☎ 302030; Niels Finsensgøta 7; ☒ 10am-6pm Mon-Fri, 10am-1pm Sat)

Føroya Landsbókasavn (National Library; Map p122; ☎ 311626; www.flb.fo; JC Svabosgøta 16; ☒ 10am-8pm Mon-Wed, to 5pm Thu-Fri)

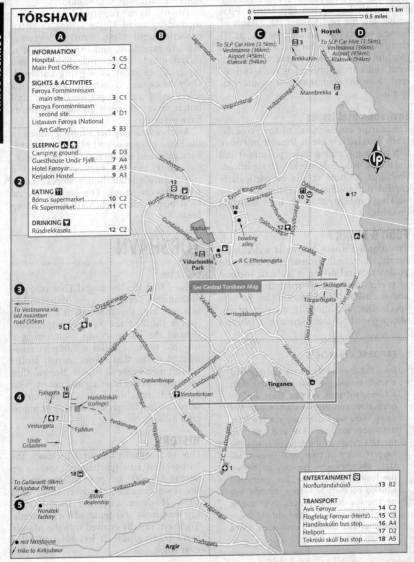

TÓRSHAVN

0 _____ 1 km
0 _____ 0.5 miles

INFORMATION
Hospital...................................1 C5
Main Post Office....................2 C2

SIGHTS & ACTIVITIES
Føroya Fornminnisavn
  main site................................3 C1
Føroya Fornminnisavn
  second site...........................4 D1
Listasavn Føroya (National
  Art Gallery)..........................5 B3

SLEEPING 🏕 🏠
Camping ground......................6 D3
Guesthouse Undir Fjalli..........7 A4
Hotel Føroyar..........................8 A3
Kerjalon Hostel.......................9 A3

EATING 🍴
Bónus supermarket................10 C2
Fk Supermarket......................11 C1

DRINKING 🍷
Rúsdrekkasøla.........................12 C2

ENTERTAINMENT 🎭
Norðurlandahúsið....................13 B2

TRANSPORT
Avis Føroyar............................14 C2
Flogfelag Føroyar (Hertz).....15 C3
Handilsskúlin bus stop..........16 A4
Heliport...................................17 D2
Tekniski skúli bus stop..........18 A5

To SLP Car Hire (3.5km);
Vestmanna (36km);
Airport (45km);
Klaksvík (94km)

Hoyvík

To SLP Car Hire (3.5km);
Vestmanna (36km);
Airport (45km);
Klaksvík (94km)

Brekkutún

Mannbrekka

See Central Tórshavn Map

To Vestmanna via
old mountain
road (35km)

Viðarlundin
Park

bowling
alley

Stadium

Tinganes

Skúlagøta

Tórgarðsgøta

Hoydalsvegur

Handilsskúli
(college)

Vesturgøta

Fjalstun

Undir
Gráasteini

BMW
dealership

To Gallaraett (8km);
Kirkjubøur (9km)

Nonatek
factory

red farmhouse
Hike to Kirkjubøur

Argir

Tourist Office (Map p122; per hr Dkr40) Two internet computers available.

Left Luggage
Big/small lockers (Dkr30/20 for 24hrs) At the Farstodín transport terminal.

Medical Services
Emergency Dental Service (☎ 314544; ☼ 1-2pm Sat & Sun) At the hospital.
Hospital (Map p122; ☎ 313540; JC Svabosgøta) Has a casualty ward.
Emergency Medical Service (☎ 310033) Operates between 4pm and 8am.

Money
Outside banking hours, Hotel Hafnia (Map p122) and the tourist office will exchange cash. ATMs dole out cash till midnight:
Føroya Banki (Map p122; Niels Finsensgøta 15)
Føroya Sparikassi (Map p122; Tinghúsvegur 49)

Post
Central Post Office (Map p122; Posthúsbrekka) Within the new, art-decked City Hall (Snarskivan) building.
Main Post Office (Map p122; Óðinshædd 2)

Telephone
Telecom Shop (Map p122; Telebúðin; Niels Finsensgøta 10) Sells SIM cards.

Tourist Information
Tourist Office (Kunningarstovan; Map p122; ☎ 315788; www.visittorshavn.fo; Mylnugøta; ☼ 9am-5.30pm Mon-Fri, 10am-2pm Sat) Assists with accommodation and tour bookings, sells maps and transport timetables and offers great free brochures including the handy *Tourist Guide: Faroe Islands*. Opens an hour earlier in summer. Within the same atmospheric 1860s building is the city's top bookshop, **HN Jacobsens Bókahandil** (Map p122; ☎ 311036).
National Tourist Board (Map p122; ☎ 316055; www .tourist.fo; Undir Bryggjubakka 17; ☼ 8am-4pm Mon-Thu, to 3pm Fri) Deals more with research and publications. The staff is very knowledgeable about regional attractions.

SIGHTS
Old Tórshavn
The city's tiny but charming historical core is **Tinganes**, a little peninsula delightfully jumbled with pretty turf-roofed cottages and historic red-painted stone-and-timber buildings. Most date from after the devastating 1673 fire. Guides can explain the history of each structure but random

strolling is enough for most visitors. The church **Havnarkirkja** (Bringsnagøta; Map p122) has a distinctive clock tower that peeps above a photogenic row of colourful old **wharf buildings** (Undir Bryggjubakka). Beyond the desert of asphalt that surrounds the modern transport terminal, lie the turf-softened bastions of the ruined **Skansin Fort** (Map p122; admission free; ☼ open all times). It's topped by a little **lighthouse** and four 18th-century cannons. Although rather underwhelming, a five-minute visit is justified by the patchily attractive views.

Føroya Fornminnissavn
The excellent **Føroya Fornminnissavn** (Historical Museum; Map p120; ☎ 310700; www.natmus.fo; adult/child Dkr30/free; ☼ 10am-5pm Mon-Fri, 2-5pm Sat & Sun mid-May–mid-Sep) is split between two sites in Hoyvík, 3km north of the centre.

The **main site** (Brekkutún 6) beautifully displays Faroese artefacts from the Viking Age to the 19th-century with helpfully illustrative photos and notes. In the downstairs treasure room, the 15th-century Kirkjubøur pew-ends include a much photographed carving of the Virgin Mary meeting Elisabeth (mother of John the Baptist). With their halos entwined, the saintly ladies appear to be snogging!

At a wonderfully peaceful **second site** (Kúrdalsvegur) is a superbly preserved 1920s farmstead complete with bell telephone, chuntering grandfather clock, and a full set of turf-roofed outhouses. It's all the more delightful due to its bucolic setting on a low grassy bluff lush with juicy marsh marigolds. It feels a world away from the city yet it's just 300m off major Hvítanesvegur where red buses Nos 2 and 3 drop you off.

Other Museums & Art Galleries
The child-friendly **Náttúrugripasavn** (Natural History Museum; Map p122; ☎ 352300; www .ngs.fo; VU Hammershaimbsgøta 13; adult/child Dkr20/free; ☼ 10am-4pm Tue-Fri & 3-5pm Sat & Sun Jun-Aug, 3-5pm Sun Sep-May) has an informative geological section, a minuscule botanical garden and a gigantic whale's skull.

Viðarlundin, a wonderfully wild park where trees and sculptures mingle, leads to the bright and airy **Listasavn Føroya** (National Art Gallery; Map p120; ☎ 313579; www.art.fo; Gundadalsvegur 9; adult/student/child Dkr60/40/free; ☼ 11am-4pm Mon-Fri, 2-5pm Sat & Sun). Its excellent collection of Faroese modern and contemporary art includes moving, death-haunted canvasses by the great Sámal Joensen-Mikines, allegorical cartoons by William Heinesen and Tita Vinther's entertainingly woolly *Rain*.

Intimate private galleries including **Focus** (Map p122; ☎ 315251; Gríms Kambansgøta 20; ⊗ 2-6pm Mon-Fri, 4-6pm Sat), **Glarsmiðjan** (☎ 216623; Dr Jakobsensgøta; ⊗ 10am-5.30pm Mon-Fri) and **Lydersen** (☎ 213303; JC Svabosgøta; ⊗ by appt) are great places to peruse and potentially purchase more Faroese art.

Wooden Sailing Boats

Moored in the harbour are two beautiful antique wooden sloops, **Westward Ho** and **Norðlýsið** (☎ 218520; www.nordlysid .com). On Tuesday and Thursday in summer Norðlýsið offers **fishing trips** (adult/child Dkr250/125; ⊗ 7pm) and three hour **cruises** (adult/child Dkr200/100) leaving at 9am.

Nólsoy Island
pop 268

The car-free village of Nólsoy isn't especially picturesque but makes a strikingly peaceful contrast to bustling Tórshavn,

whose Tinganes peninsula looks particularly beautiful as you pass by on the ferry *Ritan* (Dkr35, 20 minutes, three to five daily). Around an hour's walk from Nólsoy village, a colony of storm petrels is claimed to be the world's biggest. They're best observed at dusk. Guided **bird tours** (☎ 327175; Dkr300) including basic accommodation are organised through the village hostel-café called Kaffistovan. The village celebrates a big **Ovastevnu festival** in mid-August.

SLEEPING

The limited accommodation options can get booked up early especially when the Smyril Line stopover crowd's in town. Tour agencies (p140) can arrange private rooms and apartments.

Budget

Camping ground (Map p120; Yviri við Strond; camp sites per adult Dkr60; ⊗ mid-May–mid-Sep) This basic site overlooks a wind-battered, rocky beach and has musty little shower blocks. Book through the tourist office.

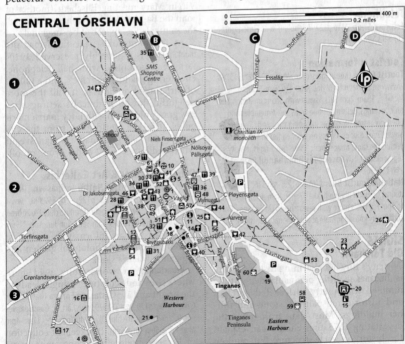

CENTRAL TÓRSHAVN

Bládýpi (Map p122; ☎ 311951; bladypi@hostel.fo; Dr Jakobsensgøta 14-16; dm/s/tw/tr/q Dkr170/350/550/750/950, with bathroom s/tw/tr Dkr500/700/900; ☺ 8am-6pm Mon-Fri, 10am-11am & 4-8pm Sat-Sun;n) Bright, friendly and wonderfully central, rates here include an excellent breakfast. Guesthouse and dorm rooms alike are neat and well equipped. Dorms share spacious sitting areas and an equipped kitchen but double-check the under-mattress slats before crashing (literally) on the bunkbeds. Reception hours are limited.

Kerjalon Hostel (Map p120; dm Dkr165-195; P ☒) This pleasant, unmanned hostel has a good kitchen and coin-laundry but is inconveniently located beside the hilltop Hotel Føroyar, which handles all bookings and check-in. Central Tórshavn's 3km away by road and 25 minutes on foot using the shortcuts. All guests seem to heartily ignore the long list of authoritarian rules.

Midrange

Hotel Streym (Map p122; ☎ 355500; fax 355501; www .hotelstreym.com; Yviri við Strond 19; s/d Dkr595/795; reception ☺ 6.30am-10pm) This semismart business hotel has modern décor, retro scoop-seats and good doubleglazing to reduce road noise. The neat, spacious rooms have desks and are better than those at most top-end options. Rear-facing singles are smaller but quieter.

Guesthouse Skansin (Map p122; ☎ 500606; skansin@hostel.fo; Jekaragøta 8; s/d Dkr440/550, with private bathroom Dkr500/700) Of a mixed bag of well-kept rooms with fridge and TV, the best are those at the top, notably corner-room number 23 which has extensive harbour views. Shared cooking facilities.

Hotel Bólið (Map p122; ☎ 354900; www.bugv .fo/sida16 in Faroese; Niels Finsensgøta 51; s/d Dkr380/480-550; ☒) Above the Smúkkuhjørnið jewellery shop, this handy if style-challenged eight-room guesthouse is more B&B than hotel. Phone ahead to arrange arrival times.

Guesthouse Undir Fjalli (Map p120; ☎ 320527; www.undirfjalli.com; Vesturgøta 15; s/d Dkr490/590; ☺ Jul–mid-Aug) Functional, ensuite student accommodation here is rented to tourists during the summer vacation. Take bus No 1 to Handilsskúlin.

Top End

Rates include breakfast and can drop by over 30% on winter weekends.

Hotel Hafnia (Map p122; ☎ 313233; www.hafnia .fo; Áarvegur 4-10; s/d/ste Dkr995/1195/1595; ☺ closed

FAROE ISLANDS

Christmas) Arguably Tórshavn's best hotel, the Hafnia has discreetly decorated rooms with satellite TV, telephone and minibar. The eyesore that is south façade is less discreet.

Hotel Tórshavn (Map p122; ☎ 350000; www .hoteltorshavn.fo; Tórsgøta 4; s/d/ste Dkr850/990/1500; ☺ closed Christmas) Formerly a bland modernist cube, the hotel's public areas are undergoing a stylishly modernist facelift. However, improvements have yet to reach the small, rather ordinary rooms.

Hotel Føroyar (Map p120; ☎ 317500; www .hotelforoyar.com; Oyggjarvegur; s/d/ste Dkr990/1190/1800) High above the city with super views towards Nólsoy, this turf-roofed palace has trendy touches, a swish reception area and an excellent restaurant serving sushi and scallops. In contrast the reasonably spacious rooms are slightly dowdy for the price. Taxis to town cost around Dkr70. Shuttle-buses run direct to the airport (adult/child Dkr150/75).

EATING

For a town of its size, Tórshavn's has a reasonable selection of dining options, mostly around Sverrisgøta or in upmarket hotels. Restaurants tend to be relatively expensive, but several pubs and cafés serve cheaper meals. Lunch buffets are great money savers.

Restaurants

Most restaurants keep tourists happy with at least one token fish option. Note that menus posted outside often show outdated prices while kitchens may close well before official closing times.

Toscana (Map p122; ☎ 311109; Nólsoyar Pállsgøta 13; mains Dkr170-220) Frank Sinatra's mellow crooning caresses the Chianti-bottle candle-lamps in this cosy little Italian eatery. Toscana specialises in creative meat dishes with tastebud tickling sauces and super rich pastas (Dkr120 to Dkr140) that approach heavenly perfection. Portions are generous: our steak-and-gorgonzola spaghetti contained nearly a whole cow. Bookings advised.

Glitnir (Map p122; ☎ 322525 or 217575; Bøgøta; mains Dkr210-230; ☺ 6pm-10pm Mon-Sat) Gastronomic treats that are nibbled at zinc-and-cream furniture and washed down with wine in fish-bowl glasses make Glitnir the in-

timidating summit of Tórshavn's modernist chic. Curiously, the pub downstairs is a lacklustre local affair.

Merlot (Map p122; ☎ 311121; Magnus Heinasonargøta 20; mains Dkr178-228; ☺ 5pm-10pm Mon-Sat) The highly esteemed chef at Merlot flambées steaks in cognac and poaches salmon in Riesling. The somewhat staid décor comes much more to life in the evening candlelight.

Restaurant Hafnia (Map p122; ☎ 313233; Hotel Hafnia, Áarvegur 4-10; mains Dkr175-310) Huge, mouthwatering seafood buffets (served Tuesday and Thursday evenings in summer, Dkr225) are the greatest drawcard of this upmarket restaurant. Reservations are advised.

Marco Polo (Map p122; ☎ 313430; Sverrisgøta 12; mains Dkr155-215; ☺ lunch 11.30am-2pm) A notionally nautical theme puts the atmosphere slightly beyond that of a typical pub, but the real attraction is a superb-value lunch buffet (Dkr79).

Other recommendations:

Pizzacafé (Map p122; ☎ 350035; www.pizza.fo; Hotel Tórshavn; pizzas from Dkr55; ☺ noon-9.45pm) The capital's most appealing sitdown pizzeria serves beer though it's not on the menu.

Kliché (Map p122; ☎ 322404; www.kliche.fo; Grims Kambansgøta, 1st fl; mains Dkr169-200; ☺ 5pm-midnight) Creditable food and good harbour views undermined by simpering muzak and a lack of atmosphere.

Nan-Tong (Map p122; ☎ 318698; Tinghúsvegur 8, 2nd fl; adult/child Dkr155/55; ☺ 5pm-10pm) Small but tasty Chinese buffet above the cinema.

Rio Bravo (Map p122; ☎ 319767; www.riobravo.fo; Tórsgøta 11; mains Dkr155-185; ☺ 5pm-10pm) Wild west–themed steakhouse.

Quick Eats

For quickly made thincrust pizzas to go, head for **Pizza Kjallarin** (Map p122; ☎ 353353; Niels Finsensgøta; pizzas Dkr55-80; ☺ 5pm-midnight Sun-Thu, to 5am Fri & Sat).

Three fast-food outlets can be found at **Food Court** (Map p122; SMS Shopping Centre).

Self-Catering

For supermarkets, **Miklagarður** (Map p122; SMS Shopping Centre) is the best stocked, though **Bónus** (Map p120; Óðinshædd) and **Fk** (Map p120; Dr Jakobsensgøta & Brekkutún) are marginally cheaper. Bakery-grocery **Frants Restorff** (Map p122; Tórsgøta; ☺ 7am-11pm) opens helpfully long hours.

DRINKING

Dividing-lines between cafés and pubs are somewhat blurred in the Faroes but where there's beer and live music, watch how the characteristic Faroese reserve crumbles. There's only one liquor store called **Rúsdrekkasøla** (Map p120; Smyrílsvegur; 10am-5.30pm Mon-Fri, to 7pm Thu).

Cafés

Gallari Jinx (Map p122; 317101; www.jinx.fo in Faroese; Áarvegur 3; mains Dkr80-140; 11am-midnight) Perched behind big picture windows overlooking the main road, this narrow, artfilled diner-café morphs into a hip youth bar scene at night. The espressos are good while tsatziki or goat's cheese and pesto sandwiches offer salvation for hungry vegetarians.

Café Karlsborg (Map p122; 317464; Undir Bryggjubakka; 9am-8pm; pastries Dkr20-50) Exposed beams, a whitewashed 'rock' wall and plenty of endearingly kitschy knick-knacks make this Tórshavn's most atmospheric harbourside café. Sadly the cappuccinos are half hearted.

Café Kheops (Map p122; Niels Finsensgøta 11; bottomless coffee Dkr12, beers Dkr30) The idiosyncratic copper-panelled bar just about saves this café pub from dull mediocrity.

Pubs

Café Natúr (Map p122; 312625; Áarvegur 7; meals Dkr49-69) The city's most atmospheric café-cum-pub is the hub of Tórshavn's raucous live scene at weekends. They serve a good range of brews and several great-value barmeals. The recommended if misnamed 'Tortilla' is actually a filling burrito-and-salad plate.

Manhattan (Map p122; 319696; Sverrisgøta 15; beers Dkr25; 5pm-midnight, to 4am Fri & Sat) Gentle acoustic live music (mostly covers) is played here nightly in this cosy British-style pub.

Cleopatra (Map p122; Sverrisgøta 12; beers from Dkr25, cocktails Dkr55) This small bar tucked in the eaves above Marco Polo restaurant holds Wednesday night jazz jams.

Tórshøll Pub (Tróndargøta 24) Drinking in this smoky local dive is a daring social experiment. Occasional Faroese folk music.

Cippo (Map p122; Tórsgøta 11) Sports bar with pool tables and fussball.

ENTERTAINMENT

The events-listing pamphlet *Havnartíðindi* is available free from the tourist office.

Norðurlandahúsið (Nordic House; Map p120; 317900; www.nlh.fo; Norðari Ringvegur 10; 10am-6pm Mon-Sat, 2-6pm Sun) This modern, architecturally interesting cultural centre has a turf roof and a mini-Stonehenge in the car park. It frequently houses concerts, plays, exhibitions and conferences. There's a pleasant cafeteria.

Leikhúsið Gríma (Map p122; 318617; www.grima.fo in Faroese; Magnus Heinasonargøta 12) The Faroes' professional theatre troupes hold regular shows and cabaret performances.

Sjónleikarhúsið (Map p122; 311131; Niels Finsensgøta 34; adult/child Dkr300/150, Tue, Jun–mid-Jul) This community centre offers Faroese cultural evenings with chain-dancing, storytelling and a few local nibbles.

Havnar Bio (Map p122; 311956; Tinghúsvegur 8; tickets Dkr75) This two-screen cinema shows original films with Danish subtitles. Upstairs are **Eclipse** (Map p122; Fri night) and **Rex** (Map p122) the city's slightly sleazy nightclubs.

SHOPPING

Several shops sell souvenirs from knitwear to cuddly puffin toys. **Andreas í Vágsbotni** (Map p122; Grims Kambansgøta) also stocks T-shirts and costumed dolls. **Helly Hansen** (Map p122; Havnargøta) has Faroese flags (Dkr200). **Sirri** (Map p122; www.sirri.fo; Áarvegur 10) produces elegant designer garments from organic, dye-free wool and local sheepskins. **Listir** (Map p122; Grims Kambansgøta) sells glass and woollen craftwork. **HCW Tórgarð** (Map p122; Niels Finsensgøta 9) sells CDs of local music.

Photocare (Map p122; Dr Jakobsensgøta 12) downloads digital photos to disk.

GETTING THERE & AWAY

Ferries to Suðuroy and international destinations plus all long-distance buses depart from the Farstøðin transport terminal. The *Ritan* ferry to Nólsoy uses a different jetty.

Airport

Regular bus No 300 from the Farstøðin transport terminal drives via the airport (Dkr90, 55 minutes), see p126. **Airport Shuttle** (223073; www.shuttlebuss.com; Dkr150) minibuses will pick up from hotels and hostels on request at around 6.30am, 9am, 1pm and 3pm. Book a day ahead.

FAROE ISLANDS

GETTING AROUND

Car

Parking is free in marked spaces but in the city centre, most are time-limited: look for a 'P' and the number of minutes or hours (*tíma*) of stay permitted. Display your arrival time using a parking disc, available free of charge from tourist offices and banks. For car rental agencies, see p141.

Public Transport

The three main routes of red city buses (Dkr10 per ride) each operate half-hourly on weekdays (hourly at weekends and evenings) from the central Steinatún stop. Bus No 2 loops anticlockwise passing close to the Hotel Streym, main post office, Føroya Fornminnissavn and Norðurlandahúsið and returning past the SMS Shopping Centre before finally heading south to Argir via the hospital. Bus No 3 does the same loop clockwise then heads west on Landavegur.

The main taxi companies are **Auto** (☎ 311234) and **Bil** (☎ 311444).

THE WESTERN ISLANDS

VÁGAR

If you fly into the Faroes you'll arrive on Vágar (*vow-whar*). Most travellers dash straight off to Tórshavn. But underrated Vágar itself has a spectacular cliffedged western coast that's most entertainingly viewed from the mini-ferry to Mykines (opposite), one of the Faroes most loveable if climatically treacherous getaways.

Airport

The Faroes' only **airport** (☎ 354400; www.floghavn.fo) has a **tourist information desk** (☎ 353300), caféteria and ATM cash machine but no bank. Three minutes' walk west of the terminal, the architecturally dreary **Hotel Vágar** (☎ 332955; www.hotelvagar.fo; s/d Dkr635/855) can exchange cash at mediocre rates. The hotel's rooms are clean, motel-style affairs but its restaurant (lunch specials Dkr68, mains Dkr145-Dkr185, h11am-9pm) has fine food, appealing views towards Mykines and Vágar's only bar (beer Dkr25). Consider prebooking meals. The hotel rents low-tech **bicycles** (half-day Dkr75). These are handy for visiting Bøur but not headlight-equipped for the spooky tunnel to Gásadalur.

PUFFIN PERIL

A great thrill of early-summer hikes around Mykines is being entirely surrounded by thousands of quizzically cute puffins. An enormous colony remains, but the birds' recent behaviour has worried locals. Since around 2003, their young have been dying as parental puffins struggle to find sufficiently accessible fish on which to feed them. Should their young perish, puffins have no reason to linger on the cliffs so increasingly the birds have taken to 'disappearing' from July. The 2005 season was particularly catastrophic and resulted in the cancellation of age-old traditional puffin hunts during 2006. Global warming and herring-stock depletion is implicated.

Sørvágur

pop 970

Just 1km west of the airport, **Sørvágur** curves somewhat blandly around the eastern end of an attractive fjord. Its main attraction is the twice-daily summer boat service to Mykines (opposite) leaving from a harbour at the town's southwestern limit. That's near the petrol station/snack bar, some 150m west of the eccentric **Sørvágs Bygdarsavn** (☎ 333191; 13 Rossatrøðin; admission Dkr30; ☼ by appt), a tatty little museum in a conspicuous blue house.

For acceptable rooms, **Anita Góðadal's B&B** (☎ 332878; Í Gerðinum 11; s/d Dkr350/540) can be booked through Greengate Incoming (www.greengate.fo); it has shared facilities. From the airport walk ten minutes downhill, fork left at the first junction, left again on Garðsvegur, then second left to the top.

AROUND SØRVÁGUR

Picturesque **Bøur** (pop 70) is a bayside huddle of old Faroese homes, several with turf roofs. An intimidatingly tall amphitheatre of *hamrar* (stepped cliffs) stands behind. The 4km trip from Sørvágur is amply justified by spectacular views of **Tindhólmur**, a serrated islet of vertical rock that rises from the frothing waves like a Tolkeinesque fantasy castle. Surreally sliced, Tindhólmur seems to have had its western half mistakenly erased in post-production. It's one of the Faroes' landscape icons.

Another 4km west of Bøur, **Gásadalur** (*gwa-sa-dal-wur*, pop 12) occupies an even grander amphitheatre. The village homes are marginally less photogenic than those of Bøur but beautifully set with Tindhólmur as a delightful backdrop. Road access (no bus) is via a freakily pitch-dark 1½km tunnel. Alternatively a challenging hike via the former **postman's trail** (2½ hours) starts 700m south of the tunnel's eastern entrance. It passes perilously near the first cliff edge then zigzags very steeply up and over the cairn-marked, 425m **Skarð Pass**. Hiking offers superb views but there are loose sections and the route is dangerous in less-than-perfect visibility.

Miðvágur & Sandavágur

Sandavágur with its fanciful 1917 church is 2km from **Miðvágur**, with Vágur's banks, supermarkets and **tourist office** (☎ 333455, 219899; ⏰ 1-3pm Mon-Fri). Between the two, **Á Giljanesi** (☎ 332900; fax 332901; www.giljanes.fo; camp sites per adult Dkr60, dm/s/d Dkr160/250/380) is a no-frills hostel. Though prefabricated and rather cramped, it's good value with a decent kitchen and lovely bay views from even-numbered rooms facing Koltur's craggy rear-end.

AROUND MIÐVÁGUR

A leisurely but very rewarding 50-minute hike follows the eastern bank of lake **Leitisvatn** starting from the main airport road, 1.5km west of Miðvágur petrol station. Rich breeding grounds of oystercatchers, whimbrels and snipes lead to **Bøsdalafossur**, a unique waterfall where the lake water tumbles directly into the foaming seasurf below. For particularly inspiring views of the soaring cliffedged coastline, climb the raised rocks slightly to the east. A slightly boggy upper trail returns directly to Miðvágur police station, offering some glimpsed views across the town towards a spindly rocky spire evocatively nicknamed the **Witch's Finger** (Trøllkonufingur).

Getting There & Away

For flight details see p140 and p141. Bus No 300 runs six to nine times daily between Tórshavn and Sørvágur (Dkr100, one hour) via the airport (Dkr90, 55 minutes) and Miðvágur. One or two daily buses will continue from Sørvágur to Bøur but only by advance request: call ☎ 215610 at least two hours ahead.

Avis and Flogrelag Føroyar (Hertz) have desks within the airport terminal but they are only manned when vehicles have been prebooked (Dkr150 airport supplement).

MYKINES

pop 12

Trafficless Mykines (pronounced *mitch*-iness) is one of the Faroes most charming villages. It's cupped deep within a beautiful green outfield, perched high above a sea-battered jetty where landing can be a minor adventure. Short yet awe-inspiring hikes lead up to sunset-facing bird cliffs. From there the hiking paths pass densely packed puffin burrows to a footbridge that crosses a 35m sea-gorge to **Mykineshólmur**. The walk to Mykineshólmur's 1909 lighthouse (allow three hours return) leads you past the Faroes' only surviving gannet colonies.

Combining snack-bar, basic shop and hostel, **Kristianshús** (☎ 312985; http://heima.olivant. fo/~mykines/indexgb.htm; mykines@post.olivant.fo; camp sites per adult Dkr50, dm/s/d Dkr120/220/440; ⏰ May-Aug) can accommodate up to 30 people in

---

GRINDADRÁP

Hunting long-finned pilot whales (*grind*) is an age-old Faroese tradition called *grindadráp* (see www.whaling.fo). Pods of these whales are herded by boats into a shallow bay where local people stand waiting on the beach. They insert steel gaffs into the whales' blowholes then cut the jugular and carotid blood vessels with long knives. Catastrophic loss of blood pressure causes a rapid death. Hunts are limited by law to prevent wastage and are conducted within rules set by the International Whaling Commission. The method is considered the quickest, least painful way to kill whales. Nonetheless it results in frothing, blood-filled red fjord-water that's a photo-perfect gift to anti-whaling publicists. Anti-whaling campaigners are widely loathed here and many Faroese suggest that objectors could better direct their energy to more pressing concerns such as war and pollution. Pollution may actually be a greater danger to pilot whales than hunting – high levels of mercury and cadmium are now found in the meat reflecting humans' careless treatment of the oceans.

three sections. Rooms above its shop-cafeteria (prebooked 7pm dinner Dkr125) are truly tiny and share a minuscule toilet/shower. The attached cottage offers vastly more spacious if somewhat tattier rooms with shared kitchen facilities and sitting room.

Across the road, sleeping at the homestay-hostel **Yellow House** (☎ 332614; leonsson@kallnet.fo; 3-bed dm Dkr180; ♥ Jun–Aug) can be slightly more awkward to arrange as the owner-family is usually away in Tórshavn.

Helicopters from Vágar (Dkr145) should run Sunday, Wednesday and twice on Friday. From Sørvágur on Vágar, the mostly un-covered mini-ferry **Brynhild** (☎ 333200; Dkr60; 45 minutes) should run at 10am and 4pm in summer (May to August). However, all transport is highly weather-dependent so it's quite possible to find yourself stranded among the puffins. For several days!

STREYMOY
Kirkjubøur
pop 226

Sprinkled along the base of a craggy sea-facing bluff, Kirkjubøur (pronounced *cheer*-chi-ba) consists of roughly a dozen tar-blackened chalet homes, some with turf-rooves and whitewashed stone bases. For centuries this was the Faroes' religious and cultural centre. Behind the whitewashed AD 1111 **St Olav's church** lies the never-completed Gothic shell of **Magnus Cathedral**. Today its hefty basalt walltops are wrapped with protective black-metal cladding which convert the 13th-century ruins into a unique statement of contemporary art.

Built upon the 900-year-old foundation-platform of the long-disappeared bishop's palace is the beautiful turf-roofed farmhouse **Røykstovan** (Smoke Chamber; ☎ 328089; www .patursson.com; adult/child Dkr30/free; ♥ 9am-5.30pm Mon-Sat, 2-5.30pm Sun Jun-Aug or by appt). The exterior is colourfully detailed with 19th century pseudo-Viking carvings. Although a private home (in the Patursson family for 17 generations), two rooms are usually open to public viewing. Their driftwood timbers are scented with history and draped with fascinating artefacts, each telling its own story. By advance arrangement you can even organise a feast at the great banqueting bench fashioned from the life-saving plank of an 1895 shipwreck.

Bus No 101 (Dkr20, 30 minutes, several daily) from Tórshavn runs to Gamlarætt port, 2km northwest of Kirkjubøur. If you request in advance (☎ 343030) the 8.10am and 6.30pm services will make a diversion into Kirkjubøur for you. Alternatively from Tórshavn you could hike along the classic, very well-trodden mountain trail (two hours) that starts down við Sandá near bus No 3's southwestern terminus. **Berg Hestar** (☎ 316896; ♥ by appointment) will take groups the same way riding Icelandic horses . If coming by car the cliff-clinging side-trip towards Syðradalur farm offers some very appealing views over Koltur.

Vestmanna
pop 1238

Deservedly the Faroes' biggest tourist attraction is a breathtaking two-hour **boat tour** (adult/child Dkr200/100, ♥ May–early-Sep) to the soaring **Vestmanna Bird Cliffs**. Boats bob beneath towering cliff faces, past spiky rock pinnacles and through narrow escarpments sometimes squeezing beneath tight stone arches. You'll spy the breeding areas of guillemots and razorbills as screeching fulmars and kittiwakes soar above like thousands of white dots.

Two companies **Lamhauge** (☎ 424155; www.sightseeing.fo) and **Skúvadal** (☎ 424305; www.puffin.fo) offer essentially identical tours using various sized boats to fit passenger numbers (minimum five). Each offers up to five departures daily, most reliably at 9am and 2pm (the most crowded). Both companies use the tourist harbour (former car-ferry port). 900m east of central Vestmanna's post office, banks and commercial port. The **tourist office** (☎ 471500; tourist harbour; ♥ 9am-5pm) sells Skúvadal tickets and books fishing trips with **Magni Blástein** (☎ 581582).

SLEEPING & EATING

Overlooking the tourist harbour, the super-neat six-room guesthouse **Krákureiðrið** (pronounced kraka-*rey*-ree; ☎ 424747 or 764747; jf.egilsnes@kallnet.fo; Niðarivegur 34; s/tw Dkr300/450) has excellent shared showers, a great kitchen and free internet access (with your own computer). The pleasant **Fjørðurkrógvin Restaurant** (☎ 471505; Tourist Office Bldg; set lunch Dkr60; ♥ 10am-6pm) also serves coffee-and-cake sets (Dkr38) to waiting trippers. You can buy groceries from the **Shell Filling Station** (tourist harbour; 🕑 7.30am-11pm Mon-Sat, 9am-11pm Sun). Hidden down steps from the post office is the local pub **Bryggjam** (🕑 5pm-midnight).

GETTING THERE & AWAY

Inconveniently timed public buses from Tóshavn (Dkr50, one hour, three to eight daily) require a change from bus No 300 (airport service) to bus No 100 at the Kollafjarðadalur Statoil petrol station (pronounced *kotla*-furdla). More conveniently, **Øssur Christiansen private buses** (☎ 217752; Dkr120 return; 🕑 variable) and **Tora tours** (www.tora.fo; 🕑 Wed & Sun, Jun-Aug) collect you from Tórshavn hotels, connect with boat trips and add some sightseeing on the way back.

When travelling by car, choose the starkly barren old mountain road (Rte10) and make brief detours to pretty Norðradalur hamlet and to Kvívík with its 1903 church and minimalist Viking longhouse ruins.

Northern Streymoy

Northern Streymoy's hotel-less villages make delightful detours by car but most visitors find they're not quite stunning enough to justify the awkward access by rare buses from Oyrarbakki.

SAKSUN
pop 34

Over 10km of lonely moorland valley leads from Hvalvík to tiny Saksun. Ignore the scrappy look of the first houses and fork right. After another 1km you'll reach the solitary turf-roofed **church** dramatically perched high above a tidal lake, impressively ringed by crags and waterfalls. From road's end look back at the proud **19th-century farmstead** which has an almost medieval appearance. It's strictly private property but in midsummer hosts the **Dúvugarður Folk Museum** (☎ 310700; admission Dkr20; 🕑 2-5pm Fri-Wed mid-Jun–mid-Aug).

TJØRNUVÍK
pop 80

A gently satisfying 13km drive northwest from Oyrarbakki passes a **'forest' of cairns**, an impressive roadside **waterfall** and Haldlorsvík's unique **octagonal church** before following a cliffledge into Tjørnuvík.

Clasped tightly in a rocky claw of backing mountains, the village is a mostly modern huddle hiding just a few turf-roofed cottages. Great views across a black sand beach towards the distinctive sea stacks **Risin and Kellingin** (below), are even finer if you scramble northwest up the steep trail marked by white-painted boulders. Serious hikers could trek south across a partially treacherous mountain trail to Saksun (three to four hours).

NORTHERN EYSTUROY

Lovely landscapes, excellent short hikes and a range of rural lodgings, make this the best region to explore if your time in the Faroes is limited. Gjógv, Elduvík and Funningur villages are especially quaint. Buses do run occasionally (mostly weekdays only, by advanced request) but driving offers vastly more flexibility.

Eiði
pop 670

Architecturally undistinguished Eiði (pronounced *ay-ee*) rises steeply from a wide green isthmus. Behind a quirky 1881 **church**, the old village-core consists of tightly folded alleys hiding the turf-roofed little folk museum **Eiðis Bygdasavn** (☎ 423597; adult/child Dkr30/free; 🕑 2-4pm Wed & Sun Jun-Jul) that quaintly illustrates traditional Faroese lifestyles. Near the top of the village, the extensively renovated **Hotel Eiði** (☎ 423456; www.hoteleidi.fo; s/d Dkr450/650, with private bathroom Dkr600/800) displays the stylish abstract artwork of its charming owner. Eight of the rooms, notably single No 5, offer pleasant views toward the fjord also shared by its convivial restaurant (open noon to 2pm and 6pm to 9.30pm).

The main reason to visit Eiði is to hike 45-minutes from the village's uppermost road-end to **Eiðiskollur** (cairn-marked once you've climbed a small fence). The rewards are lovely headland panoramas and heart-stoppingly steep views down upon the classic twin sea-stacks **Risin and Kellingin**. Folk legends describe the pair as a giant and hag turned to stone while attempting to pull the Faroes over to Iceland! Non-walkers could view Risin and Kellingin using the free binocular stand 3km along the scenic Eiði–Gjógv road or by driving to Tjørnuvik (left).

FAROE ISLANDS

From Oyrarbakki on the Tórshavn–Klaksvík route, bus No 200 (Dkr20, 25 minutes) runs to Eiði eight times every weekday and twice on Sundays.

Gjógv

pop 53

Tourists and local day-trippers alike rave about the picture-postcard beauty of Gjógv (pronounced *jek*-v) village. Divided by a dainty trickle of stream are knots of colourful and tar-blackened cottages. One such cottage is the delightful **Debesar Café** (www.gjogvadventure.fo; coffee & pancakes Dkr30; ☺ 10am-8pm May-Sep) that doubles as a souvenir shop and ticket office for highly recommended **boat tips** (Dkr150) around the towering cliffs to spiky **Búgvin Stack**. Once a few customers have assembled, the boat departs from within a distinctive deep cleft (*gjógv*) for which the village was named. The Debesar Café also sells village hiking maps (Dkr30). Proceeds supposedly support local environmental projects, though a map isn't really necessary for the Gjógv's most attractive short hike – a very obvious stroll past puffin burrows up the western cliffside.

Gjáargarður (☎ 211590; fax 423505; www .gjaarhostel.dk;camp sites per adult Dkr70 dm/d/tr Dkr200/550/700, d/tr with bathroom Dkr650/800; ☺ May-Sep) is an excellent turf-roofed hostel-guesthouse that looks something-like an overgrown Swiss chalet. Some dorm-beds are built cupboard-style into the eaves as in traditional Faroese farmhouses. These are great fun for one person but claustrophobically over-cosy for two. Guesthouse rooms are comfy, rates include a great breakfast and the buffet meals are simply superb.

By advance request (☎ 505520) bus No 201 connects Gjógv to Oyrarbakki twice each weekday (Dkr40, 40 minutes) via the old village of Funningur, home to the Faroes' most photogenic turf-topped church.

Elduvík

pop 60

Facing Kalsoy's jagged northern tip, Elduvík is a dreamily cute snaggle of tar-blackened traditional cottages divided by the meandering mouth of the pretty Stóra stream. **Home Café** (☎ 444815; ☺ Jun–mid-Aug) offers simple coffee-and-cake sets (Dkr30) and has two basic homestay rooms (Dkr200 per person). School buses are the only public transport.

SOUTHERN EYSTUROY

This region offers few pressing incentives to hop off the Klaksvík–Tórshavn bus. However, if driving by you could stop in **Leirvík** to see the new **boat museum** (☎ 443347), or in the triple-centred village of **Gøta**, which is famous for its musicians. The little beach in southern Góta (Suðrugøta) bursts into life during the superb **G! Music Festival** (see below for more information). Opposite the bank in central Gøtugjógv, the 1995 **Gøtu Kirkja** is a church with some superb contemporary glasswork, notably a towering modernist Passion window. Fronting the harbour in northern Góta (Norðragóta) is an 1883 wooden church, which shields from view an unmarked, turf-roofed **Folk Museum** (Blásastova; ☎ 222717, 441440; Tróndargøta 31; adult/child Dkr30/free; ☺ 2-4pm Thu-Tue mid-May–mid-Sep).

Eysturoy's sprawling commercial hub, **Runavík**, has shops, banks and a hotel but limited appeal for tourists.

THE IMPROBABLE G! *Jón Tyril, founder of the G! Festival*

Everyone said it was impossible. Faroese weather and rock festivals couldn't go together. But that's art – doing the impossible. We'd already done the impossible musically with Clickhaze [Jón's seminal Faroese rock band]. So one day after playing Roskilde [the great Danish rock festival], we just decided to go for it. The G! logo came first. Just G! posters; no explanation. People were intrigued. The first year we had just six bands but about 1000 people showed up. Beautiful weather...it was amazing. That was 2002. By the time Europe [1980s Swedish band famous for *Final Countdown*] played in 2005, it was more like 10,000 people. Imagine! That's 20% of the whole Faroese population round this little beach. There were 50 boats, lights all twinkling in fabulous Gøta Bay. And thank goodness there was no wind; bad tides and a storm would have finished us off.

KLAKSVÍK & THE NORTHERN ISLES

KLAKSVÍK

pop 4794

Colourful fishing boats dot the busy, workmanlike harbour of the Faroes' second-largest town. Klaksvík hugs a steep-sided, elongated bay framing the rocky rump of Kunoy which can stay photogenically snow-dusted as late as early-June. As the regional transport hub, Klaksvík makes an obvious base for excursions in the Northern Isles despite a paucity of accommodation options.

Information

Alfa Bókahandil (☎ 455533; Nólsoyar Pálsgøta 2) Bookshop that sells postcards.

Føroya Banki (☎ 456377; Klaksvíksvegur 7) Bank with ATM.

Hospital (☎ 455463; Víkavegur 40-44)

Library (☎ 455757; Tingstøðin; ☀ 1-6pm Mon-Fri) Two computers with free internet access.

Tourist Office (Norðoya Kunningarstova; ☎ 456939; info@klaksvik.fo; Nólsoyar Pálsgøta 32; ☀ 8am-5pm Mon-Fri & 10am-noon Sat Jun-Aug, 10am to noon & 1-4pm Sep-May) Accommodation & tour bookings.

Norðoya Sparikassi (☎ 475000; Ósavegur 1) Bank with ATM.

Photo Care (☎ 457272; Klaksvíksvegur 70) Downloads digital photos to CD.

Post Office (☎ 455008; Klaksvíksvegur 2)

Telecom Shop (Telebúðin; Biskupsstøðgøta 3; ☀ 9am-5.30pm Mon-Fri)

Sights & Activities

Photogenic **viewpoints** abound around the harbour but for the best of all, hike for around an hour up the obvious, if occasionally slightly steep, trail to **Klakkur** (413m). The reward is a truly splendid panorama of both the city (especially magnificent as lights come on at dusk) and the fjord-rent drama of the surrounding islands.

Dragin, a 1940s wooden sailing boat, offers inspiring **sightseeing cruises** (www.dragin.fo; Dkr250, ☀ 6pm daily Jun–Aug) around the Kallur or Enniberg cliffs, weather and passenger-numbers permitting (minimum 10).

The finest feature of Klaksvík's museum, **Norðoya Fornminnissavn** (☎ 456287; Klaksvíksvegur 84; adult/child Dkr20/free; ☀ 1-4pm mid-May–mid-Sep)

is a nostalgic, fully preserved old pharmacy shoproom that operated until 1961.

Next door, **Leikalund** (☎ 457151; www.leikalund.com in Faroese; Klaksvíksvegur 82) is a marvellous bookshop café within a restored old wooden-beamed store that dates from the Danish trading monopoly days. There's no better place to listen to (and buy) CDs of Faroese music over a good espresso. Some weekend nights the atmospheric back-room hosts intimate live concerts. Unmissable.

Architecturally, the modernist 1963 church, **Christianskirkja** (Kirkjubrekka 6) attempts to evoke the ancient Magnus Cathedral at Kirkjubøur (p128). Within there's a superb altar wall depicting the last supper and from soaring rafters hangs a full-sized rowing boat. Free-standing outside, the A-framed **belfry** has a wood-shingle roof and tolls to announce occasional concerts.

The **Föroya Bjór Brewery** (☎ 475454; www.foroya-bjor.fo; ☀ 8.30-5pm Mon-Fri) brews the Faroes' classic Black Sheep ale. Call well ahead (preferably a week) to arrange a free **tour** by appointment. These start from the brewery office, upstairs behind 15 Klaksvíksvegur.

Sleeping

Hotel Sjómansheim (Klaksvíkar Sjómansheim ☎ 455333; Víkarvegur 38; s/tw Dkr395/595, with private bathroom Dkr695/895) Klaksvík's only hotel is big, functional and understaffed but it's clean, handily central and some (pricier) rooms have great bay views. Rates include a substantial breakfast.

The **tourist office** (☎ 456939; info@klaksvik.fo) can arrange two **B&B rooms** (s/d Dkr350/450), some **self-catering apartments** (from Dkr500) and handles payments/bookings for the out-of-centre **camping ground** (Uti-I-Grov; camp sites per adult Dkr60).

Eating & Drinking

Hereford (☎ 456434; Klaksvíksvegur 45; mains Dkr160-225; ☀ 6-10pm Tue-Sun, closed Mon), above welcoming **Café 45** (beers Dkr30; ☀ 10am-10pm), is a convivial steakhouse that uses rough pine walls and wooden dining booths to create a traditional yet contemporary atmosphere. The predictably beefy menu also includes garlic snails and venison medallions.

Pizza 67 (☎ 456767; Klaksvíksvegur 22; dishes from Dkr50; ☀ 5pm-11pm) Klaksvík's predominantly takeaway pizzeria advertises 'Sex, Pizza &

FAROE ISLANDS

Rock'n'Roll'. In fact their pizzas are highly disappointing and the rest boils down to six framed Elvis posters.

The **Hotel Sjómansheim restaurant** (lunch/dinner Dkr80/90; ☽ noon-2pm & 6-8pm) offers simple, filling set meals.

Hjá Jórun (Klingrugarður; ☽ 11am-11pm) The biggest and best of three bakery-cafés with

luscious cakes and a range of open-sandwiches. When sunshine obliges, outdoor seating faces Borðoyarvik Fjord, albeit across a major road.

An unmarked red door in a graffiti-muralled house leads you into **Roykstovan** (Klaksvíksvegur; ☽ 11am-11pm), a rough-edged, suffocatingly smoke-fugged pub: ideal for

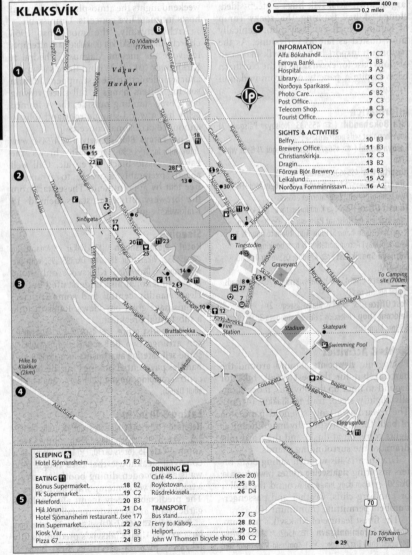

KLAKSVÍK

Vágur Harbour

To Viðareiði (17km)

Sinðgata

Kommunubrekka

Brattabrekka

Hike to Klakkur (2km)

Tingstoðin

Graveyard

Kirkjubrekka
Fire Station

Stadium

Skatepark

Swimming Pool

To Camping site (700m)

Klingrugarður

To Tórshavn (97km)

meeting (and hopefully not fighting with) razzed-up seamen.

Supermarkets include **Fk** (Nólsoyar Pálsgøta 12), **Bónus** (Stangavegur 10) and **Inn** (Klaksvíksvegur; 9am-8pm Mon-Fri, 9am-5pm Sat). Late-night grocery **Kiosk Var** (Klaksvíksvegur; 7am-11pm Mon-Sat, 8am-11pm Sun) also serves hot-dogs.

Buy booze at **Rúsdrekkasøla** (Bøgøta 38; Mon-Fri 2-5.30pm, Thu 2-7pm) or from beneath the brewery.

Getting There & Away

If you pick the right day, a helicopter can whiz you virtually anywhere else in the Faroes (see p140), with scenic hops to Fugloy costing a mere Dkr110. By bus, No 400 to Tórshavn (Dkr90, 1¾ hours, five to 11 times daily) uses the colourfully illuminated 6.8km Norðoya toll-tunnel via Leirvík.

Getting Around

Taxis (590000, 755555) lurk beside the bus stand. **John W Thomsen bicycle shop** (455858; Nólsoyar Pálsgøta 26) rents mountain bikes (Dkr100 per day).

KALSOY

This long, thin succession of abrupt peaks is nicknamed the 'flute' for its many tunnel-holes. For a lovely half-day trip from Klaks-vík take a Syðradalur-bound car ferry ride (Dkr35, 20 minutes, up to six daily) that connects with bus 506 (Dkr30, 40 minutes, up to three daily) to **Trøllanes**, then hike (45 minutes) to **Kallur lighthouse**. Views are truly spectacular, encompassing six different head-lands. However it's a long wait for the next bus back and Trøllanes has neither shop nor accommodation. If you dare subjecting your-self to 25 minutes of heart-pounding sensory deprivation you could walk the totally unlit 2km tunnel from Trøllanes to quietly quaint **Mikladalur** village. Not for the faint hearted.

VIÐOY
Hvannasund
pop 270

The small, nondescript port of **Hvannasund** (pronounced kwana-sund) guards a cross-fjord causeway. It's the starting point for timewarp mail-boat trips to Fugloy (right) and for **Alpha Pilot tour-cruises** (220849; Dkr250; 3pm daily, Jul-Aug) that circumnavigate Fugloy or round Enniberg (see above) ac-cording to currents and weather.

Viðareiði
pop 350

The boxy homesteads of Viðareiði (pro-nounced vee-ar-*oy*-ye) are scattered across a lovely green swale between perfectly py-ramidal **Malinsfjall** (750m) and the soaring amphitheatre of **Villingadalsfjall** (841m). Es-pecially when viewed from Fugloy (below), the resultant U-shaped valley looks like God's skateboarding ramp. Climbing part-way up Villingadalsfjall reveals some magnificent views across the headlands of Borðoy, Kunoy and Kalsoy. Climbing fur-ther you'll encounter steep scree but when fog and low clouds allow, experienced trekkers can scramble over the summit, along a knife-edge ridge and on to **Enniberg**, one of Europe's highest sea-cliffs.

For something much gentler just stroll to Viðareiði's dainty, 1892 **church** and pretty old jetty area at the western end of the village.

Presentable if windlashed, the central **Hotel Norð** (451244; fax 451245; s/d Dkr600/800; Jun-Aug) offers sweeping views from south-facing rooms. The expansive res-taurant (mains Dkr175-205) has an eerily deserted Marie Celeste atmosphere when no groups are in.

Opposite Hotel Nord is a grocery store and four doors away the eight-table house-restaurant **Mastovan Elisabeth** (451275; mains Dkr155-185; noon-9pm) serves roasted puffin in season (July) if you prebook.

Getting There & Away

From Klaksvík bus No 500 runs to Viða-reiði (Dkr30, 30 minutes, three daily) via Hvannasund (Dkr20, 20 minutes). Buses connect with Alpha Pilot tours weekdays only (out 2.20pm, back 6.55pm).

FUGLOY
pop 45

Clinging valiantly to Fugloy's steep south-ern tip, the slopes above **Kirkja** (pronounced *cheer*-cha) face a very attractive array of island views. Somewhat gloomier **Hattarvík** is nestled deep in a sweeping valley that rises steeply to the east-coast bird cliffs. Hattarvík's red-roofed 1899 stone church stares wistfully out across the endless At-lantic surf. Neither village has a protected harbour, and for some travellers the real thrill of visiting Fugloy is the dicey, wave-buffeted landing as one disembarks from

FAROE ISLANDS

the 1959 wooden mail-boat *Másin,* the island's main lifeline. Its schedule varies notoriously according to wind direction, weather and whether a detour to Svínoy is added. However, typically departures are twice daily from Hvannasund to Kirkja (9.15am and 3.15pm) taking around an hour then returning immediately. Always book ahead (☎ 505208) especially if you want to continue to Hattarvík. By picking the right day there's time (sometimes only just) to arrive by helicopter in Hattarvík then walk to Kirkja (around 1½ hours by asphalt road or cliffedge footpath) for the afternoon boat out again. But there's no formal accommodation if you get stranded.

SOUTHERN ISLANDS

SKÚVOY
pop 57

At first glance, Skúvoy's sloping grasslands look just a tad characterless. However, along the west coast, breathtaking **cliffs** plunge dramatically into the surf. And for ornithologists, key attractions are the **great skuas** for which the island was named. In July, these powerful birds swoop menacingly amid oystercatchers and the clouds of fulmars that soar around the very attractive **Høvdin bird cliffs**. Access is on foot from the island's only village, a mostly-tame stroll taking around 45 minutes. Follow the red-painted wooden stakes after the road peters out and make sure you bring a stick to protect your head in case you're dive-bombed!

Skúvoy village is colourful if not the Faroes' most picturesque. There's a gently photogenic **church** beside the heliport and on weekdays the whole place has almost a ghost-town feel. Sweet **Jogvansstova** (from Dkr450) is a vaguely atmospheric if slightly tatty rental-house bookable through Greengate (see p137). It's a bargain though the shower, hidden in the basement garage, is something of a joke. The village lacks a café but the owner of the tiny **shop** (⏱ Tue & Sun) is friendly and very knowledgeable about local ornithology once you get over his initial tetchiness.

For a satisfying day trip, arrive in Skúvoy by helicopter (on Wednesdays you get the

most time) then return to Tórshavn on the 4.30pm boat-bus-ferry-bus combination (Dkr110, 2¾ hours). Prebook the Skúvoy–Sandur section (☎ 505207) in case you're the only passenger. There's no ferry connection between Skúvoy and Suðuroy.

STÓRA DÍMUN
pop 5

This dinky island's central peak dips down at its southern end like a natural ski-jump. Here a small ledge of rich sheep pasture is just enough to sustain a single farm. Ringed by sheer cliffs and lacking a harbour, the island's only practicable access is by helicopter. You'll appreciate the loneliness of the location when landing here very briefly on flights between Froðba and Skúvoy. However there are no tourist facilities so getting off uninvited would be a rude imposition upon the sole resident family.

SUÐUROY

This attractive, friendly island is appealingly untouristed even though its hub, Tvøroyri, offers the Faroes' most atmospheric pub and best-value guesthouse. Although marginally less dramatic than northern Eysturoy, the island's steep, fjord-nibbled undulations offer some excellent short hikes. Several heartstoppingly spectacular viewpoints surveying the plunging west-coast bird-cliffs are easily accessible by road if you're driving. By car you can see most of the sights in a busy 24 hours.

Tvøroyri
pop 1760

Pleasant Tvøroyri (pronounced tver-*oi*-ree) is Suðuroy's main commercial centre and transport hub. Greater Tvøroyri sprawls gently along the northern slopes of Trongisvágsfjørd from pretty Froðba village (2km east) to junction-settlement Trongisvágur (2km west). The Drelnes ferry port (4km by road) is directly across the fjord. As yet streets remain un-named. **Suðuroy Kunningarstova** (Tourist Information; ☎ 372490; sout-inf@post.olivant.fo; ⏱ 9am-4pm Mon-Fri) is based in Tvøroyri's town hall *(kommunia)* but also opens a booth at the Drelnes terminal whenever a ferry arrives. Beside the **post office**, the bank **Føroya Banki** has a single ATM.

SIGHTS & ACTIVITIES

The single greatest attraction of the 1852 grass-roofed **museum** (☎ 372480; admission Dkr20; ⏲ by appt) is the story-telling genius of curator **Einar Larsen** (☎ 228241) who can usually open the museum up if given an hour or two's notice. A rough **cobble-slope**, which was originally used for fish-drying, leads down to the functional commercial port past the restored 1836 **Thomsen monopoly-house** containing the brilliant Kgl Handil pub.

A distinctive three-tiered Norwegian-style 1907 **church** lies beyond the quaint, turquoise **police station**.

Around 1.5km west, **Gallari Oyggin** (☎ 371669; admission Dkr20; ⏲ 3-8pm Tue-Sun) displays somewhat brutal black metallic sculptures and has a small Art Café.

From quaint **Froðba village**, a gently picturesque stroll past some over-hyped **columnar basalt formations** brings you to the attractive low **Skarvatangi headland**. Or more strenuously follow the clear track up to 325m **Nakkur** for extensive clifftop views.

SLEEPING & EATING

Gistingarhúsið Undir Heygnum (☎ 372046; mobile 223925; guesthouse@kallnet.fo; s/d from Dkr250/400) The Faroes' best value if most unpronounceable guesthouse offers gleamingly clean Scandinavian-styled rooms with excellent shared bathrooms, kitchen and a homely living room. It's right at the bayside, just five minutes' stroll east of central Tvøroyri.

Hotel Tvøroyri (☎ 371171; fax 372171; s/d without private bathroom s/d Dkr400/550, s/d with private bathroom s/d Dkr550/650) Beyond the disconcerting welcome of dead-whale photos, this ultra-central blue cube has fresh, tasteful rooms, a comfy top-floor TV room and a flat roof that might one-day make a great café. The restaurant serves set meals by advance order for Dkr85 from lunchtime until 6pm, there's a weekend only pizzeria open from 6.30pm until 10.30pm and a rough-edged basement pub.

Hotel Øravík (☎ 371302; uni@post.olivant.fo; dm/s/d Dkr160/625/940; camp sites per adult Dkr60) This slightly tatty series of shedlike buildings sits beside a gurgling brook in an appealingly

FAROE ISLANDS

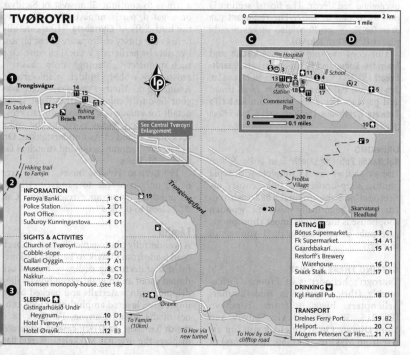

TVØROYRI

0 ——— 2 km
0 ——— 1 mile

Trongisvágur

To Sandvík

Beach   fishing marina

See Central Tvøroyri Enlargement

Hiking trail to Famjin

Trongisvágsfjord

Froðba Village

Hospital

School

Petrol station

Commercial Port

0 ——— 200 m
0 ——— 0.1 miles

Skarvatangi Headland

Øravík

To Famjin (10km)

To Hov via new tunnel

To Hov by old clifftop road

INFORMATION
Føroya Banki	1 C1
Police Station	2 D1
Post Office	3 C1
Suðuroy Kunningarstova	4 D1

SIGHTS & ACTIVITIES
Church of Tvøroyri	5 D1
Cobble-slope	6 D1
Gallari Oyggin	7 A1
Museum	8 C1
Nakkur	9 D2
Thomsen monopoly-house	(see 18)

SLEEPING 🛏
Gistingarhúsið Undir Heygnum	10 D1
Hotel Tvøroyri	11 D1
Hotel Øravík	12 B3

EATING 🍴
Bónus Supermarket	13 C1
Fk Supermarket	14 A1
Gaardsbakarí	15 A1
Restorff's Brewery Warehouse	16 D1
Snack Stalls	17 D1

DRINKING 🍷
Kgl Handil Pub	18 D1

TRANSPORT
Drelnes Ferry Port	19 B2
Heliport	20 C2
Mogens Petersen Car Hire	21 A1

FAROE ISLANDS

FLAG DAY

The *Merkið*, the Faroe Islands' 'national' flag looks rather like a Norwegian one in negative: a red Scandinavian cross, edged with blue on a white ground. Invented by Fámjin students in 1919 it had limited local usage in the 1930s but came into its own in 1940. WWII was at its height and Denmark had fallen to Nazi Germany. The Faroes, however, remained pro-Allies and continued to supply Britain with fish despite considerable wartime dangers. As flying the 'enemy' Danish flag was no longer acceptable to British warships, Hans Mikkelsen, captain of the Faroese ship *Eysturoy* suggested using the *Merkið*. Winston Churchill approved the use of the flag on 25th April, 1940. It was the first international recognition of the flag and the date is still celebrated as Faroese Flag Day.

---

lonely rural hamlet 2.5km south of Drelnes ferry terminal. Double beds are somewhat small and the functional rooms have an over-vivid red decor. The hostel section is due to reopen in 2007. The **restaurant** (fish dinner Dkr198; ⏰ 5pm-10pm) also serves bready pizzas (Dkr60 to Dkr90).

Hot dogs are sold from **snack stalls** and from the **Bónus** and **Fk** supermarkets. **Gaardsbakarí** (☎ 371175; ⏰ 6am-6pm Mon-Fri, to noon Sat, 7am-9am Sun) bakes and delivers fresh bread and pastries. Beers are sold from **Restorff's Brewery Warehouse** (⏰ 10am-noon & 2pm-5.30pm Mon-Fri).

DRINKING

Kgl Handil Pub (☎ 371007; beers Dkr25; ⏰ 9am-11pm with short rest breaks) Complete with sepia photos, shop-drawers, a 19th-century officeroom and the original 1882 cash register, this beautifully restored wooden shophouse is the Faroes' most atmospheric café pub: a must-see even if you're not thirsty.

GETTING THERE & AWAY

Tvøroyri's heliport is at Froðba. Twice-weekly (thrice-weekly in mid-summer) helicopters buzz to/from Tórshavn (Dkr215, 30 minutes) via Skúvoy and Stóra Dimun. On Wednesday you can arrive from Mykines (Dkr360, two hours) or continue to Klaksvík (Dkr360, 40 minutes) and Fugloy (Dkr360, one hour); on Friday arrive from Klaksvík/Fugloy or continue to Vágar/Mykines.

The impressively comfortable Smyril car-ferry sails between Tórshavn and Drelnes port twice a day (adult/student/child/pensioner/car Dkr75/60/35/35/55, two hours) with linking bus services connecting to central Tvøroyri and other Suðuroy villages.

Mogens Petersen (☎ 371466; Shell Petrol Station, Trongisvágur; ⏰ 7.30am-11pm) rents aging Mazdas (Dkr350 per day). That's a great deal but as they have only two available, most tourists bring vehicles on the car-ferry from Tórshavn.

Northern Suðuroy

An attractive road passing Suðuroy's last **coal mine** (a hand-dug tunnel that is not an industrial eyesore) descends to unexpectedly sandy beach-bays at **Hvalba** and **Sandvík**. Both villages frame views of the craggy anduninhabited island of **Lítla Dímun**. However, the greatest attraction of a trip is to continue 3km west of Sandvík on a gated, partly unpaved farm track to the bird-cliffs of **Glyvraberg**. Hike carefully here as the grassy clifftops are sliced almost invisibly by perilously vertical chasms. One such sphincter-tighteningly deep chasm is crossed by wobbly hidden plank-bridge. Assuming no *Monty Python* character asks your favourite colour (or the flight speed details for unladen swallows) you can cross for magnificent views north to the spiky rock-stack island of Ásmundarstakkur. On a clear day, panoramas beyond stretch as far field as Mykines.

Tvøroyri to Hvalba buses (up to five daily) only continue to Sandvík (Dkr30, 30 minutes) by advance reservation. Call ☎ 222690 to book a trip.

Fámjin

A wonderfully photogenic 9km switchback road leads from Øravík to Fámjin. Colourful if architecturally ordinary houses are dotted about an emerald-green bowl-valley dripping with waterfalls and backed by an impressive, layered amphitheatre with echoes of the Grand Canyon. Fámjin's 1876 **church** (key-holder ☎ 371921; donation appropriate) displays the original Mikkelsen **Merkið flag** (see opposite for more information). The 1880 **Krambúðin á Brúgvaroyri** (🕙 3pm-10pm Jun-Sep) is a quaint if slightly over-restored harbour-front shop-café catering to local tourists who drive in to watch Fámjin's magical sunsets.

Bus 703 (Dkr20, 30 minutes) runs up to four times daily from Tvøroyri. The inspiring **hike** from westernmost Tvøroyri (2½ hours) is cairn-marked but only on the upper sections. Another trail continues south with some steep sections to Ryskivatn lake whence a driveable track links on to Vágur.

Southern Suðuroy

Soon to be bypassed by a new tunnel, the old coast road between Øravík and Hov is an inspiring clifftop drive. The overgrown village of **Porkeri** has an attractive turf-roofed **church** dating from 1847. Fjordside **Vágur** is Suðuroy's lacklustre second city. There's a small **museum** (🕾 374342; 🕙 by appt), **tourist office** (🕾 374342; infovag@post .olivant.fo; 🕙 9am-4pm Mon-Fri) and a **wool workshop** (Ullvirkð; 🕾 374006). Although none of these attractions warrants a lengthy stop, if you're stuck **Hotel Bakkin** (🕾 373961; Rte 20; s/d 450/550, with private bathroom Dkr600/680) has some surprisingly acceptable rooms which are hidden behind a smoke-choked local workers' bar. Simple single room No 4 has a fjord-view balcony. Hidden in a 1930s Vágur town-house 700m east, **Pizza Kokkurin** (Rte 20; 🕙 5pm-10pm) bakes the Faroes' best takeaway pizza. The Vágur area's main attraction is the fine **Kamarið Cliff** viewpoint, 3km southwest which is accessed by a narrow asphalt lane. Even finer is the dizzying **Beinisvørð Cliff** plunging 469m into the sea just 20m from a bend in the old mountain route to Sumba (just before the conspicuous communications mast). **Cap Akraberg**, the Faroes' southernmost point, has some puffin burrows and a much-photographed lighthouse but overall it's a disappointing anticlimax dominated by two vast TV masts.

Visiting southern Suðuroy is best by car. Some buses on the Tvøroyri–Vágur route (Dkr40, 50 minutes, up to six daily) will continue to Sumba (twice on weekdays or by advance request on 🕾 228588) but they bypass the main viewpoints by several kilometres.

FAROE ISLANDS DIRECTORY

ACCOMMODATION

Accommodation is relatively limited so it's worth prebooking. Hotels including the self-consciously alcohol-free so-called seamen's homes (*Sjómansheimið*) typically cost from Dkr600/800 per ensuite single/double. Hotels are functionally well equipped rather than inspiring. Cheaper guesthouses (*gistingarhús*) are often better value and typically offer a communal kitchen. However, most have shared bathroom facilities and as guesthouses are rarely staffed, you'll generally need to prearrange arrival times. Youth hostels (*vallaraheim*) charge Dkr120 to Dkr200 for dormitory beds. This assumes you have a sleeping bag without which there's an additional Dkr50 to Dkr65 bed-linen charge. Six hostels affiliated to the **Danish Youth Hostels Association** (www.farhostel.fo) offer Dkr20 discounts for Hostelling International members.

Tourist offices have useful lists of family B&B options (singles/doubles cost from Dkr350/450) and self-catering house or apartment rentals (2-bed flats from Dkr500) though most rental bookings are handled through Tórshavn-based agencies **Tora Tourist Traffic** (🕾 315505; www.tora.fo) and **GreenGate Incoming** (Map p122; 🕾 320520; www .greengate.fo; Undir Bryggjubakka 3).

Camping (typically Dkr60 per person) is only permitted at recognised camping grounds often attached to youth hostels. The inevitably wet and windy weather can make camping challenging.

ACTIVITIES

Bird-watching (see p117) and **hiking** are the greatest attractions of the Faroe Islands. Excellent maps are sold and the tourist board publishes brochures describing key trekking routes. All land is technically private but you're free to use well-established footpaths that are marked (albeit often very indistinctly) by series of ancient cairns. It's extremely bad form not to close gates. Crossing meadows randomly can disturb bird colonies and might result in stuka-attacks from protective skuas. Chasms and

FAROE ISLANDS

cliffedges are predictably treacherous in fog. Don't forget those waterproofs.

Boat cruises are a wonderful way to see the islands' stunning bird cliffs and remarkable needle-shaped rocky islets known as stacks. Many also offer **fishing** trips. The national tourist board produce a detailed pamphlet explaining where licences are necessary (per day/season Dkr300/500), ideal fishing spots and suggested equipment. If bringing your own fishing tackle it should be disinfected (and certified) before leaving home or on arrival at the airport or harbour (costs Dkr300). For a multilingual fish-name listing see www.frs.fo/fish.asp?LangId=0.

Scuba diving is possible with **FaroeDive** (☎ 458939, 218929; www.faroedive.fo) based in Klaksvík.

BOOKS

Liv Kjørsvik Schei's photo-rich book *The Faroe Isles* offers plenty of cultural background. Bradt's *Faroe Islands* travel guide is extremely comprehensive though its town maps are laced with errors. *Tale of Throwd of Gate* is F York Powell's translation of the classic Icelandic Norse narrative, Faereyinga Saga.

BUSINESS HOURS

Shops generally open from 9.30am to 5.30pm Monday to Friday, later on Thursday and 9am to noon (sometimes 2pm) on Saturday. Banks work from 9.30am to 4pm, opening until 6pm on Thursdays.

Eateries typically open around noon and close between 10pm and midnight, though several open evenings only. Pubs and cafés often stay open till 3am at weekends.

CHILDREN

Tórshavn occasionally offers music and theatre shows for kids (ask at the tourist office). Under-14s get bus- and ferry-discounts of up to 50% and free entry to many museums.

EMBASSIES & CONSULATES

The Faroes are represented abroad by Danish embassies (www.um.dk/en/menu/AboutUs/Organisation/MissionsAbroad) who issue all visas. There are Faroese representative offices in the **UK** (☎ +44-20 7333 6707; www.faroes.org.uk) and **Belgium** (☎ +32-2 233 0855; www.faroes.be)

FESTIVALS & EVENTS

Events are listed on www.kunning.fo.

Traditional summer festivals

Many of these colourful events feature rowing competitions, processions in traditional dress, singing and chain dancing:

Jóansøka Located on Suðuroy the weekend following midsummer.

Varmakelda Bonfire and hot-spring fun at Fuglafjørður on Eysturoy on the first weekend of July.

Vestanstevna On Vágar in early July.

Ólavsøka Largest and most exciting traditional festival, celebrating the 10th century Norwegian king Olav the Holy, who spread Christian faith on the isles held on 28-29 July.

Ovastevnu On Nólsoy in mid-August.

Music Festivals

Asfalt Five stages showcase local bands in central Tórshavn in early July.

G!Festival (www.gfestival.com) The Islands' original and biggest music festival held in mid-July features local and international artists on Syðrugøta beach in Gøta.

Summar Festivalur (www.summarfestivalur.fo) At Klaksvík in early August.

GAY & LESBIAN TRAVELLERS

There are no dedicated gay bars or clubs on the Faroe Islands and gay couples are advised to be discreet to avoid upsetting more traditional, religious locals.

HOLIDAYS

Holidays really are holidays in the Faroes: most transport stops running and everything closes down.

New Year's Day (1 January)

Easter (Maundy Thursday to Easter Monday, March/April)

Flag Day (25 April)

Labour Day (1 May)

Common Prayers Day (April/May)

Ascension Day (May/Jun)

Whit Sunday, Whit Monday (May/Jun)

Constitution Day (5 Jun)

Ólavsøka (Faroese National Days & Festival; 28 & 29 Jul)

Christmas Eve (24 December) Some shops open until noon.

Christmas Day (25 December)

Boxing Day (26 December)

New Year's Eve (31 December)

INTERNET ACCESS

There are no internet cafés but major libraries have web-connection offering free time slots that you can book. Beware that some servers illogically treat any e-mail with the

Faroes'.fo ending as spam, so check your 'bulk' inbox.

INTERNET RESOURCES

Faroe Islands Tourist Guide (www.faroeislands.com) General information.

Faroeislands.dk (www.faroeislands.dk) Photos and details of every village.

Framtak (www.framtak.com) Fun mixture including online book sales.

National Tourist Board (www.visit-faroeislands.com) Very extensive tourist information.

Post Office Philatelic Service (www.faroestamps.fo) Surprisingly detailed thematic site including traditional recipes and bird identification photos.

Prime Minister's Office (www.tinganes.fo) Links to all government sites.

MAPS

Tourist offices distribute a free 1:200,000 scale *Faroe Islands Map* that includes basic street plans of larger settlements. Bookshops sell 1:20,000 maps (Dkr90), ideal for hikers, and a comprehensive atlas-booklet of 1:100,000 scale maps (Dkr125), perfect for driving tours.

MONEY

Faroese króna are worth exactly the same as Danish krone (Dkr) and both can be used interchangeably. Technically the same is true throughout the Kingdom of Denmark. However in mainland Denmark some shops refuse Faroese money so play safe and swap any remaining Faroese cash to Danish before departure.

Bigger branches of Føroya Banki and Føroya Sparikassi change travellers cheques and major foreign currencies and have multi-card **ATMs** (6am-midnight). Outside banking hours, hotels and tourist information offices usually exchange money, albeit at poor rates.

Foreigners spending over Dkr300 in shops marked 'Tax-free' can claim back the 25% VAT: fill in a Tax Refund Cheque in the shop and get it stamped by the sales clerk. On departure from the Faroes be prepared to show your purchases to customs who should re-stamp the cheque. Collect your

---

EMERGENCY NUMBERS

For police, fire or ambulance call ☎ 112.

---

refund at the airport's Flogfelag Føroya desk or on board the Norröna ferry.

Tipping isn't customary.

Currency

One króna is equal to 100 oyru (spelt krone, øre in Danish). Notes come in Danish and Faroese designs with denominations of Dkr50, Dkr100, Dkr200, Dkr500 and Dkr1000. Coins are in Danish designs only: Dkr0.25 and Dkr0.50, Dkr1, Dkr2, Dkr5, Dkr10 and Dkr20.

POST

Tórshavn's **central post office** (FR-100 Tórshavn, Faroe Islands; 9am-5pm Mon-Fri) offers reliable poste restante. Village post offices often open much shorter hours. By economy/priority airmail postcards or letters up to 20g cost Dkr7/7.50 to Europe and Dkr9/10 to the rest of the world. Postal rates are fully listed on www.stamps.fo

TELEPHONE

Post offices, some guesthouses and certain restaurants have card phones charging a Dkr0.40 connection charge plus Dkr0.32/0.22 per minute peak/off-peak for local calls. Peak hours are 8am to 6pm Monday to Saturday. Phonecards are sold in post offices and telecom shops. There are no area codes. Dial ☎ 118 for directory inquiries.

Mobile phones use the standard European GSM system (incompatible with most North American hand-phones). Coverage is almost complete. SIM-cards available, from Telebúðin telecom shops in major towns cost Dkr199 including Dkr100 call credit with local calls costing Dkr3/2 per minute peak/off-peak. SMS text-messages cost Dkr0.75. Call ☎ 801020 to check your call credit.

TIME

The local time zone (GMT/UTC in winter) is the same as London, five hours ahead of New York and 11 hours behind Sydney.

TOURIST INFORMATION

There are friendly tourist offices (*kunningarstovan*) in each main town. They can help you find accommodation and tours and dole out free copies of the highly recommended 106-page *Tourist Guide Faroe Islands* plus a

FAROE ISLANDS

very creditable 1:200,000 scale country map produced by the **National Tourist Board** (www.tourist.fo; Undir Bryggjubakka 17, Tórshavn).

TOURS

Tours and bookings are available through local tourist offices and from the following Tórshavn-based organisations:

GreenGate Incoming (☎ 320520; www.greengate.fo; Undir Bryggjubakka 3) Fishing, diving, boat tours and accommodation.

MB Tours (Map p122; ☎ 322121; mb-tours@mb-tours.com; Bryggjubakki 2, Tórshavn) Bus tours.

Smyril Line (Map p122; ☎ 345900; www.smyril-line.fo; J Broncksgøta 37, Tórshavn) Schooner cruises, coach and boat excursions.

Tora Tourist Traffic (☎ 315505; www.tora.fo) Coach tours and accommodation.

VISAS

Citizens of the EU, USA, Canada, Australia and New Zealand need only a valid passport to visit the Faroes for up to three months. Citizens of Nordic countries need only a valid identity card. Those requiring a visa for the Faroes (including South Africans) must have one that specifically identifies the Faroes: ie NOT a standard Danish or Schengen visa. Apply to the Danish embassy in your country of residence.

TRANSPORT IN THE FAROE ISLANDS

GETTING THERE & AWAY
Air

The Faroe Islands' only airport is near Sørvágur on **Vágar** (code FAE; ☎ 354400; www.floghavn.fo), see p126.

AIRLINES FLYING TO AND FROM FAROE ISLANDS

Air Iceland (airline code NY; ☎ 341000; www.airiceland.is)

Atlantic Airways (airline code RC; ☎ 341060; www.atlanticairways.fo)

FaroeJet (airline code F6; ☎ 353333; www.faroejet.fo)

Atlantic Airways, the 'national' airline, flies in twice weekly from London Stansted (from £192 return), some flights stopping en route in Aberdeen or the Shetland Islands. They also serve the Danish cities of Copenhagen

(from Dkr2060 return, at least daily), Aalborg (weekly) and Billund (three weekly) plus Oslo and Stavanger in Norway (both twice weekly in summer). Both Atlantic Airways and Air Iceland have several weekly summer flights to Reykjavík (not Keflavík). FaroeJet flies Vágar to Copenhagen from Dkr995 one way. Quoted fares are for the cheapest, advanced-booking e-tickets including tax.

Sea

Many tourists visit the Faroes during a two-day 'forced' stopover when the weekly car-ferry **Norröna** (www.smyril-line.com) arrives in Tórshavn from Hanstholm (Denmark) then makes side trips to Bergen (Norway) and Lerwick (Shetland Islands) before continuing to Seyðisfjörður (Iceland). Schedules, fares and the order of stops vary seasonally, see p501.

GETTING AROUND

The national transport company **Strandfaraskip Landsins** (☎ 343030; www.ssl.fo in Faroese) publishes a complete timetable (Ferðaætlan Dkr10) of all ferry, bus and helicopter services available from tourist offices and Tórshavn's Farstøðin transport terminal. The same outlets sell SL Visitor Travelcards giving unlimited travel on all buses and interisland ferries (Dkr600/900 for four/seven days). Certain services offer small discounts to students or for 10-trip multitickets.

Note that 'x' on a timetable means 'weekdays'.

Air

At only Dkr85 to Dkr360 per journey, scenic rides in a 9-seater helicopter (tyrlan) are the Faroes' greatest travel-bargain. Book early by phoning **Atlantic Airways** (☎ 341060; ☒ 8am-4pm Mon-Fri) then pay (cash only) on departure. Beware that bad weather can cause cancellations and stops are skipped when nobody has pre-booked.

On each operation day (three weekly or four in mid-summer) helicopters depart from Vágar airport, hopping in quick succession to all other heliports (except on Sunday when Froðba is missed out). The order of stops varies. Most days choppers start with a return hop to Mykines then proceed to Koltur and Tórshavn. Then they do two loops, southern (Skúvoy–Stóra

Dimun–Froðba) and northern (Klaksvík –Svínoy–Kirkja–Hattarvík–Klaksvík) before returning from Tórshavn to Vágar. On Wednesday and Sunday the southern loop is first but on Sunday there's no visit to Froðba. On Fridays the northern loop is first and the day finishes with an extra Mykines return. On midsummer Mondays an extra service runs similar to the Friday route but without the initial trip to Mykines.

Bicycle

Surfaced roads, minimal traffic, light summer nights and stunning scenery all make riding a bicycle (*súkklur*) a tempting proposition. However steep hills, wind, rain and fog argue against it. Road tunnels are cyclists' greatest hazard. Many are freakily dark, others potentially life-threatening due to carbon-monoxide build-up – best avoided.

Good front and rear lighting, extra reflectors, wind- and waterproof-clothing are essential. If things get rough you can pop your bike on certain buses for Dkr30. Mountain bikes can be hired in Klaksvík.

Boat

Apart from Tóshavn-Suðuroy (adult/ student/pensioner/car DKr 75/35/35/55) all domestic vehicle ferries cost adult/student/ pensioner/car Dkr35/15/15/55. They run even in fairly poor weather. The passenger-only boats especially to Fugloy via Svínoy (adult/student/pensioner Dkr35/15/15) and to Mykines (adult/student/pensioner Dkr60/30/30, from May to August) are much more weather dependent. Pay on the boat or connecting bus.

Bus

Bygdaleiðir long-distance bus timetables are sensibly coordinated with ferry services, and combined bus-ferry tickets can be purchased once aboard. Read timetable footnotes very carefully: although buses serve virtually every hamlet, rural services might run only on summer weekdays and even then only if you've pre-booked. If you're the only pre-booked passenger you might find that your 'bus' is actually a taxi (albeit charging standard bus-fares).

Car & Motorcycle

On the bigger islands, driving allows you to see vastly more of the Faroes' appealingly remote villages and valleys in a short time.

DRIVING LICENCE

You can drive in the Faroe Islands with a valid driving licence from EU countries, the US, Canada, Australia and New Zealand.

HIRE

Small hire-cars typically start at Dkr500/2500 per day/week including partial insurance. The minimum age is 20 and you must have held a driving licence for at least one year. Add Dkr150 for airport pick-ups (Dkr800 with the rental company SLP!)

Main Tórshavn rental companies:

Avis Føroyar (☎ 313535, outside office hr 217535; www.avis.fo; Staravegur 1-3, ⊙ 8am-5pm Mon-Fri) Only 100km per day free mileage.

Bilútleigan (☎ 317865, http://heima.olivant. fo/~carrent/) Car delivered to you within Tórshavn.

Flogfelag Føroyar (Map p122; ☎ 340000; www .ff.fo; Hoydalsvegur 17) Hertz agents. Prices rise in summer. Unlimited mileage.

SLP (☎ 357300; www.ognir.fo; Á Hjalla; ⊙ 8am-4pm Mon-Fri) Reasonable deals for weekly rentals but inconveniently located, 5km from Tórshavn.

ROAD RULES & HAZARDS

Driving is relatively easy: road layout is simple, traffic is thin and drivers are relatively considerate. The Vágar–Streymoy and Eysturoy–Borðoy undersea toll-tunnels cost Dkr170 return for small vehicles, paid on a video-surveyed honesty system at designated petrol stations. Driving is on the right-hand side, front and rear seat-belt use is compulsory, and dipped headlights must be kept on at all times. Beware of sheep leaping onto the road; if you hit one, you must call the **police** (☎ 311448) and pay damages. Don't take the sheep-carcass home: by a never-cancelled medieval law, sheep-theft is still technically punishable by death!

Speed limits are 80km/h on open highways, 50km/h through villages. Traffic fines are severe and you can lose your licence on the spot for driving over 110km/h or for exceeding the blood alcohol limit (0.05%).

One-lane tunnels have passing bays (marked 'M') every few hundred metres.

Finland

Squeezed between Sweden and Russia, Finland is one of the most mysterious and misunderstood corners of Scandinavia. But more and more travellers are discovering the serenely beautiful land of lakes and forests that lies beyond the Baltic harbour capital of Helsinki.

Although Finland is riding a wave of hi-tech revolution (think Nokia), for travellers, nature reigns supreme here and for most Finns, happiness is still a ramshackle summer cottage by a lakeshore and a properly stoked sauna. With a population of just over five million, much of Finland can seem very empty and remote, and nowhere is this more evident than Lapland, one of Europe's last great wilderness areas. Reindeer herds wander across fells, and above the Arctic Circle the sun never truly sets in midsummer. Here you'll find the kitsch but cool Santa Claus Village and official post office, and in the bluish haze of winter darkness you can witness nature's greatest lightshow, the aurora borealis (northern lights).

In the south, dynamic cities like Turku and Tampere complement the urban sophistication of Helsinki, and it would take a jaded traveller indeed not to fall for medieval Porvoo or the romantic Lakeland town of Savonlinna.

Finland really comes into its own in the surprisingly warm summer months when Finns emerge from hibernation to savour the long hours of daylight. Some of northern Europe's best music festivals and offbeat events spring to life virtually every day in summer – check out the World Wife Carrying Championships or the World Air Guitar Championships!

Like the land itself, Finns have a reputation for being tough, quiet and mysterious, but take the time to explore their country, steam up in their saunas, and scratch under the surface – you'll find some of the warmest people you'll ever meet, and communicating in English is rarely a problem.

FAST FACTS

- **Area** 338,000 sq km
- **Capital** Helsinki
- **Currency** euro; US$1 = €0.81; £1 = €1.45; A$1 = €0.58; C$1 = €0.64; NZ$1 = €0.54; ¥100 = €0.73
- **Famous for** sauna, reindeer, Formula One drivers, Lordi
- **Official Languages** Finnish, Swedish
- **Phrases** *kiitos* (thank you), *hei* (hello), *anteeksi* (excuse me), *kippis* (cheers)
- **Population** 5.22 million
- **Telephone Codes** country code ☎ 358; international access codes ☎ 00, 990, 994, 999
- **Visas** not required for most visitors for stays of up to 90 days (see p213)

HIGHLIGHTS

- Explore Finland's dynamic harbour capital, **Helsinki** (p148); picnic with locals on Suomenlinna island, dine on an island restaurant, and dance all night at some of Scandinavia's best nightclubs.
- Steam it up in the world's biggest smoke sauna, then jump into the lake at **Kuopio** (p187).
- Experience high culture at the opera festival, held in a medieval castle in the gorgeous Lakeland town of **Savonlinna** (p184).
- Cross the Arctic Circle, visit Santa in his official grotto and take a reindeer-sleigh or husky ride at **Rovaniemi** (p201) in Lapland.
- Plough through pack ice on a genuine Arctic icebreaker and sleep in the Snow Castle at **Kemi** (p200).
- Best trip: take a **lake ferry** between towns – Savonlinna to Kuopio (p187) or Tampere to Hämeenlinna (p178).

ITINERARIES

- **One week** Helsinki demands at least a couple of days and is a good base for a day trip to Tallinn (Estonia) or Porvoo. In summer, head to the eastern Lakeland and explore Lappeenranta, Savonlinna and Kuopio (catch a lake ferry between the latter towns). In winter, take an overnight train or budget flight to Lapland (Rovaniemi) and Oulu for a few days, visiting Santa and mushing with the huskies. Helsinki–Savonlinna–Kuopio–Rovaniemi–Helsinki route is a good option.
- **Two weeks** Spend a few days in Helsinki and Porvoo, visit the harbour town of Turku and lively Tampere. Next stop is Savonlinna and Kuopio in the beautiful eastern Lakeland. Head up to Rovaniemi, and perhaps as far north as Inari. You could also fit in a summer festival, some hiking in North Karelia (Ilomantsi or Lake Pielenin) or a quick cycling trip to Åland.

CLIMATE & WHEN TO GO

The high season for most of Finland is summer (June–August), when the days are long, the climate is surprisingly sunny and warm and festivals abound. This is also when Finns are on holiday, abandoning the towns for their *kesämökki* (summer cottages). May and September are good times to visit the south of the country.

In Lapland, summer means the midnight sun and perpetual daylight but mosquitoes can be annoying if you're hiking. September is a beautiful time for the *ruska* (autumn) colours. October and February to early April are the best times to visit Lapland to view the aurora borealis and enjoy winter activities like skiing, ice fishing and dogsledding.

PEOPLE

Finland is one of Europe's most sparsely populated countries, with 17 people per sq km – a fifth of the population lives in the Greater Helsinki area. There are around 300,000 Swedish-speaking Finns in the west on the Åland islands; and a smaller number of Roma people in the south.

The indigenous Sami population of around 6500 in the far north consists of three distinct groups, each speaking its own dialect. Samis have traditionally been nomads, herding reindeer in the large area of Lapland. Their traditional dwelling, the *kota*, resembles the wigwam of native North Americans, and is easily set up as a temporary shelter. Old traditions are vanishing, though: most Sami now live in permanent villages and use vehicles, snowmobiles and mobile phones to herd their reindeer, rather than migrating with them.

A capacity for silence and reflection are the traits that best sum up the Finnish character (but get a Finn near a stack of duty-free liquor and see if this remains the case!). The image of a log cabin with a sauna by a lake tells much about Finnish culture: independence, endurance (*sisu* or 'guts') and a love of open space and nature.

RELIGION

The majority of Finns – around 86% – are Evangelical Lutherans, 1.1% Orthodox and the remainder unaffiliated. Minority denominations, including Roman Catholic, make up only a few per cent. Finland has some beautiful Orthodox and Lutheran churches, some dating back to the 17th century, but surveys show Finns to have the lowest church attendance record in Europe, at under 4%.

FINLAND

HISTORY

Before arriving on the north of the Baltic coast, the Finns' ancestors appear to have dominated half of northern Russia. They established themselves in the forests, driving the nomadic Sami people to the north, where they remain in an area of Lapland known as Sápmi.

By the end of the Viking era, Swedish traders had extended their interests throughout the Baltic region. In 1155 the Swedes made Finland a province, and Swedish culture was swiftly imposed, beginning with the establishment of the first university in the capital Turku. But the heavy-handedness of Sweden's Protestant monarch, Gustav II Adolf, soon split the country along religious lines, and most Orthodox believers fled to Russia.

In 1809, after a bloody war, Sweden ceded Finland to Russia under Tsar Alexander, allowing it greater autonomy as a Grand Duchy. The capital moved to Helsinki in 1812. Finnish nationalism surged, which suited the tsars until the 1880s, when there was a firm policy to dismantle the Finnish state and incorporate it into Russia.

The communist revolution of October 1917 brought the downfall of the Russian tsar and enabled the Finnish senate to declare independence on 6 December 1917. But divisions between socialists (the Reds) and conservatives (the nationalist Whites) in the new government led to a bloody civil war in which 30,000 Finns died. The conservatives, led by war hero and later president CGE Mannerheim, were victorious, and were gradually replaced by moderate social democrats.

During the Depression of the 1930s Finland gained fame internationally as a brave new nation, as the only country to pay its debts to the USA and as a sporting nation (long-distance runner Paavo Nurmi won seven gold medals in three Olympics).

Anticommunist violence broke out during the 1930s and relations with the Soviet Union remained uneasy. Finland stood firm in the 1939 Winter War, but was forced to cede part of eastern Lakeland (Karelia). Finland resumed hostilities with the Soviets in 1941, winning back large swathes of Karelia in the Continuation War which cost Finland almost 100,000 lives.

ARTS

Architecture & Design

Finland's modern architecture – sleek, functionalist and industrial – has been admired throughout the world ever since Alvar Aalto started making a name for himself during the 1930s. His works can be seen all over Finland today, from the angular Finlandia Hall in Helsinki to the public buildings (library, town hall) and street plan of Rovaniemi. Jyväskylä and Seinäjoki are places of pilgrimage for Alvar Aalto fans.

Earlier architecture in Finland can be seen in medieval churches made from stone but more commonly wood – Kerimaki's oversized church is worth seeing, as are the cathedrals at Turku and Tampere. Low-rise Helsinki boasts a patchwork of architectural styles, including the neoclassical buildings of Senate Square, the rich ornamentation of Art Nouveau (or Jugend), the modern functionalism of Aalto's buildings and the postmodern Kiasma museum.

Finland, like Scandinavia as a whole, is also famous for its design. Aalto again laid a foundation with innovative interior design, furniture and the famous Savoy vase. Finns have created and refined their own design style through the craft tradition and using natural materials such as wood, glass and ceramics. Glassware and porcelain such as Iittala and Arabia are world famous.

HOW MUCH?

- Sauna free-€10
- Museum admission €2-8
- Dogsledding (2hr) €80
- Lake ferry cruise €10-15
- Salmon soup €8

LONELY PLANET INDEX

- 1L of unleaded petrol €1.30
- 1L bottle of water €2
- Pint of beer in bar €5
- Souvenir T-shirt €15
- Snack from a grilli kiosk €2.50-3

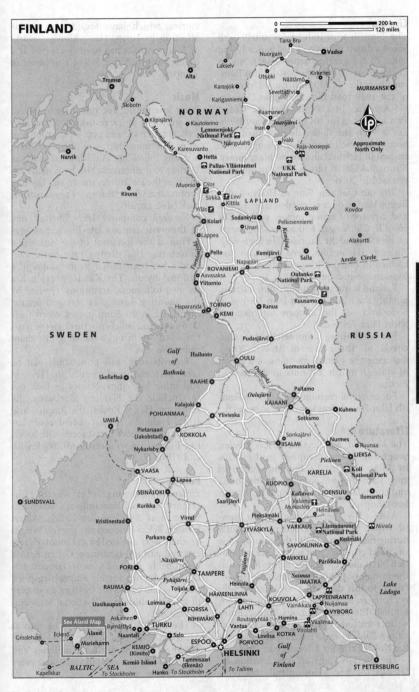

FINLAND

FINLAND

Cinema

The Finnish film industry is small, with about a dozen films produced annually, but some of the greatest achievements are in documentary work. The best-known Finnish filmmaker is Aki Kaurismäki, director of the 1989 road film *Leningrad Cowboys Go America*. In 2002 he won the Grand Prix at Cannes for his film *The Man Without a Past*, the dark tale of a man who becomes homeless after being mugged and bashed in Helsinki and losing his memory. Kaurismäki latest film is *Lights in the Dusk* released in 2006.

The most famous Finn in Hollywood is Renny Harlin, once married to Geena Davis and director of action movies such as *Die Hard II, Cliffhanger,* and scaries *Nightmare on Elm St 4* and the *Exorcist; The Beginning*. An early Harlin film, *Born American,* was banned in Finland for presenting a strong Russians-as-bad-guys view.

Finland hosts some quality film festivals, notably the Midnight Sun Film Festival in Sodankylä and the Tampere International Short Film Festival.

For something completely different, check out the *Dudesons Movie* (2006), featuring the painful madness of a group of young Finnish TV nuts in the style of *Jackass*.

For more information check out the Finnish Film Foundation website at www.ses.fi.

Literature

The *Kalevala*, a collection of folk stories, songs and poems compiled in the 1830s by Elias Lönnrot, is Finland's national epic focusing on Karelia. Translations and compilations can be found in Finnish bookshops.

Aleksis Kivi, perhaps the greatest Finnish writer, was not regarded as a Romantic during his lifetime. Quite the contrary; his so-called crudities met with fierce opposition but it didn't take long before he gained the immense popularity which he has retained to this day. His book *Seven Brothers* is regarded as a foundation of modern Finnish literature. Famous 20th-century writers include Väino Linna (*The Unknown Soldier*) and FE Sillanpää, who won the Nobel Prize for Literature in 1939.

The late Tove Jansson is internationally famous for her Moominland children's stories, which have found a particular affection in Japan. Her whimsical world of Moomintrolls has been re-created as a theme park in Naantali and a museum in Tampere.

Music

Finns love music. You only have to look at the wealth of music festivals – opera, jazz, folk, tango, rock and pop – for proof, and while traditional forms of music still have a strong following, Finnish artists such as Darude and Bomfunk MC have made inroads in the electronic, trance and hip-hop genres, and who can forgot the monstrous rock band Lordi?

Revered composer Jean Sibelius, one of the most famous late-Romantics, was a Finn at the forefront of the nationalist movement. His stirring tone-poem *Finlandia* has been raised to the status of a national hymn. The Karelian region has its own folk music traditions, typified by the haunting *kantele* (a stringed instrument), while the Sami passed down their traditions and beliefs not through the written word but through the song-like chant called the *yoik*.

Finnish rock and pop bands can be seen performing at venues in Helsinki and other big cities. Names to look out for include the Flaming Sideburns, the resurgent Hanoi Rocks, the Rasmus and Irina. Finland's biggest recent contribution is in the heavy metal scene with bands like Eurovision winners Lordi, Nightwish and HIM.

Painting

Finland's 'Golden Age' of art was the 19th-century National Romantic era, when artists such as Akseli Gallen-Kallela, Albert Edelfelt, Pekka Halonen and the von Wright brothers were inspired by the country's forests and pastoral landscape. Gallen-Kallela is probably Finland's most famous artist. He is known for his *Kalevala*-inspired works – don't miss his frescoes on display in the Kansallismuseo (National Museum) in Helsinki.

The best of Finnish art can be seen at Ateneum (National Gallery) in Helsinki, but there are modern art galleries and museums (*taidemuseo*) in just about every Finnish city.

Theatre & Dance

Finns' passion for dance is typified by the tango, which, although borrowed from Latin America, has been refined into a uniquely Finnish style. Older Finns are tango mad and every town has a dance hall or dance restaurant. In summer, outdoor stages are set up for dancing. The annual Tango Festival in Seinäjoki attracts thousands of dancers and performers. A similar form of Finnish dancing is the waltz-like *humppa*.

As with most of Scandinavia, the Finnish theatre season is winter (October–March), when theatre, opera, ballet and concert performances are staged. The exceptions are the summer festivals, such as Kuopio's Dance Festival (p189) and Savonlinna's Ballet Festival (p185).

ENVIRONMENT
The Land

Finland is Europe's seventh-biggest country, with one third of its area lying beyond the Arctic Circle. With 187,888 lakes (and 98,050 islands), fed by a network of rivers and 5100 rapids, Finland's reputation as a land of lakes is undisputed. Compared to Sweden and Norway, it is a flat country with a scattering of fells (forested hills) in the northern Lakeland and Lapland area, some of which are cleared and used for downhill skiing.

Forests cover two-thirds of Finland; the main types of forest are pine, spruce and birch. Much of this forest is managed, and timber-harvesting and the associated pulp-milling is an important industry.

Wildlife

Elk, brown bears and wolves are native to Finland's forests, although sightings are rare. In Lapland, the Sami keep commercial herds of some 230,000 reindeer. Hundreds of species of migratory birds arrive in the Arctic each spring, making Finland a bird-watcher's paradise.

National Parks

Finland boasts over 120,000 sq km of publicly owned lands and waters in 35 national parks – some of the last great wilderness areas in Europe. Some of the best include Oulanka National Park, Urho Kekkonen National Park, Linnansaari National Park, Lemmen-joki National Park and Koli National Park. For more information, contact **Metsähallitus** (☎ 09-270 5221; www.metsa.fi) in Helsinki.

Environmental Issues

While Finland appears quite pristine and much of its forest is protected, logging and forestry is a major part of the economy. Wood and paper products account for about one third of Finnish exports, but the pulp mills cause air and water pollution (some Finnish towns are completely blighted by these smoke-spewing factories), and extensive logging leads to erosion and a loss of old-growth forest. As a result, much of Finland's forest contains only one or two species of commercially valuable trees such as pine and spruce managed for harvesting.

Finland currently has four nuclear reactors, providing some 27% of its power, and the building of a fifth reactor was given the go ahead by parliament in 2002. This controversial decision was based largely on economic grounds and with strict safety and waste management policies, but has been heavily criticised by environmentalists.

FOOD & DRINK

Typically Finnish food is similar to the fare you get elsewhere in Scandinavia and has Swedish and Russian influences – lots of fish such as Baltic herring, salmon and whitefish, along with heavy food such as potatoes, thick soups, stews and dark rye bread. Finns tend to make lunch the main meal of the day. Breakfast can be anything from coffee and a wheat bun to a buffet of cold cuts, porridge, eggs and pickled fish.

Strong beers, wines and spirits are sold by the state network, beautifully named Alko. There are stores in every town and they're generally open from 10am to 6pm Monday to Thursday, till 8pm on Friday and until 2pm on Saturday. The legal age is 18 for beer and wine, and 20 for spirits. Beer and cider with less than 5% alcohol can be bought easily at supermarkets, service stations and R-kiosks.

Staples & Specialities

Simple hamburgers, hot dogs and kebabs are a cheap, common snack, served from grilli kiosks. Fish is a mainstay of the Finnish diet. Fresh salmon, herring and arctic char can be found at markets. *Muikki* and *vendace*, tiny lake fish, are another Finnish treat. In Lappish restaurants, reindeer, elk and snowgrouse feature on the menu.

Regional specialities from Karelia include *vety*, a sandwich made with ham, eggs and pickles, and the Karelian pastie, made with meat or potato folded in a thin, open crust. In Tampere, try *mustamakkara*, a thick sausage made from cow's blood. In Savo, especially Kuopio, a highlight is *kalakukko*, fish baked in a rye loaf. Åland is known for its fluffy semolina pancakes. Seasonal berries are a delight in Finland – look out for cloudberries and lingonberries from Lapland, and market stalls selling blueberries, strawberries and raspberries.

Finns drink plenty of beer *(olut)* and among the best local brews are Lapinkulta, Karhu and Koff. Ciders *(siderii)* are also popular. Uniquely Finnish drinks to sample while here include *salmiakkikoskenkorva*, a home-made spirit that combines dissolved liquorice/peppermint sweets with the iconic Koskenkorva vodka (a potent combination and an acquired taste!); *sahti*, a sweet, high-alcohol beer and cloudberry or cranberry liqueurs.

Where to Eat & Drink
Just about every town has a kauppahalli (market hall), the place to head for all sorts of Finnish specialities, breads, cheeses, fresh fish and cheap sandwiches and snacks. The kauppatori (market square) will also often have food stalls and market produce.

Meals in restaurants *(ravintola)* can be expensive, particularly dinner, but Finns tend to eat their main meal in the middle of the day, so most restaurants and some cafés put on a generous lunch *(lounas)* buffet for €7 to €10. These include all-you-can-eat salad, bread, coffee and dessert, plus big helpings of hearty fare – sausage and potatoes or fish and pasta are common. Most hotels include a free breakfast buffet.

Finns are big lovers of chain restaurants such as Rosso, Amarillo (steaks and Tex-Mex), Koti Pizza and Hesburger (Finland's answer to McDonald's), which can be found in most towns. At Golden Rax Pizza Buffet you can get all-you-can-eat pizza, pasta, chicken wings, salad, drinks

and even dessert for €8 – great for filling up cheaply!

Café culture is growing in Finland – in small towns it's country-style cafés *(kahvila* or *baari)* but in cities cafés are trendy meeting places where lattes, quiche and indulgent cakes are all the rage. Pubs and bars also double as restaurants.

Vegetarians & Vegans
In terms of specifically vegetarian restaurants, there's not a lot around in Finland, Helsinki and Turku have a couple of places, but it's easy to self-cater at markets, or eat only the salad and vegetables at lunch buffets (which is usually cheaper). University cafés and ethnic restaurants (such as Chinese) usually have at least one vegetarian dish on the menu.

HELSINKI

☎ 09 / pop 560,000
A little bit Russian, a little bit Swedish, but undeniably Finnish, Helsinki is a beautiful harbour city looking confidently across the Baltic Sea towards Europe.

Although the capital and nerve centre of Finland, Helsinki doesn't pretend to be a Stockholm or a St Petersburg, but it nevertheless lives up to the tag of 'cool'. It's small and intimate compared to other Scandinavian capitals; a low-rise Nordic city of understated Art Noveau and neo-classical architecture, modern shopping centres, broad boulevards and city parks. Summer beer terraces, boutique shopping and chic nightclubs lend Helsinki a confident, progressive and sophisticated air, but without any pretension. 'Must see' sights are few but Helsinki's appeal in summer is as much in the dynamic atmosphere and upbeat nature of its people as in any particular sight. Strolling around the harbour area, picnicking on Suomenlinna island, cruising around the harbour or joining the throngs of people sunning themselves in the many cafés and island beaches is every bit as good as ticking off the museums. In winter, the 'White City of the North' lives up to its name with a blanket of snow covering the city, and the frozen harbour and lakes provide a focus for skating, skiing and ice-fishing.

FINLAND

HISTORY

Helsinki (Helsingfors in Swedish) was settled in 1550 by the Swedish king Gustav Vasa, who hoped to draw trade away from Tallinn across the Gulf of Finland. In the 18th century the Swedes built a mammoth fortress on the nearby island of Suomenlinna, but it wasn't enough to keep the Russians out. After falling to the tsar in 1808, Helsinki became the seat of the Russian Grand Duchy – although in the process much of the town was wrecked – and in 1812 the capital was moved here from Turku.

ORIENTATION

Helsinki occupies a peninsula, and is linked by bridge and boat to nearby islands. The compact city centre surrounds the main harbour, Eteläsatama, and the kauppatori, which lies between the huge international ferry terminals. The main street axes are the twin shopping avenues of Pohjoisesplanadi and Eteläesplanadi, and Mannerheimintie. Directly north of the centre are the suburbs of Hakaniemi and Kallio.

Maps

You can pick up decent city maps and the *See Helsinki on Foot* walking guide free from the city tourist office. For road atlases, city directories and hiking maps, visit the map shop **Karttakeskus Aleksi** (☎ 0201-340 580; Vuorikatu 14; ⏰ 10am-6pm Mon-Fri) above Kaisaniemi metro.

INFORMATION
Bookshops

Akateeminen Kirjakauppa (Academic Bookshop; ☎ 12141; Pohjoisesplanadi 39; ⏰ 9am-9pm Mon-Fri, 9am-6pm Sat) Finland's biggest bookshop features three floors, an Aalto-designed café and a massive range of books in numerous languages. Big travel section, including maps.

Discount Cards

The Helsinki Card is worthwhile if you plan to do a lot of sightseeing in the capital – at least the top museums, Suomenlinna Island and a sightseeing tour. The pass gives free urban transport (including island ferries), plus free entry to more than 50 attractions in and around Helsinki. A card valid for 24/48/72 hours costs €29/42/53 (children €11/14/17). Buy the card at the city tourist office or at hotels, R-kiosks and transport terminals.

Emergencies

Dial ☎ 112 for all emergencies including ambulance, fire and police; ☎ 10022 for police; and ☎ 10023 for 24-hour medical advice.

Internet Access

Internet access at Helsinki's public libraries is free. Several cafés and bars also have free internet access for customers. If you have your own computer, Helsinki has lots of free wi-fi hotspots.

Helsinki University Library (☎ 1912 3196; Unioninkatu 36; ⏰ 9am-6pm Mon-Fri, 9am-4pm Sat) Email is discouraged but the 2nd floor of this superb library is a serene place to surf the Net.

Lasipalatsi Meeting Point (☎ 3108 5900; Mannerheimintie 22-24; ⏰ 11am-6pm Mon-Fri) Above Café Lasipalatsi is a bank of free terminals and free wi-fi access.

Library 10 (☎ 3108 5000; Elielinkatu 2; free; ⏰ 10am-10pm Mon-Thu, 10am-6pm Fri, noon-6pm Sat & Sun, shorter hr summer) Library on the 1st floor of the main post office; ½ hour internet access is free.

mbar (☎ 6124 5420; Mannerheimintie 22-24; per 20 min/hr €2/5; ⏰ 9am-midnight Mon-Tue, 9am-midnight Wed-Thu, 9am-2am Fri & Sat, 9am-3am Sun) Funky music bar and internet café behind Lasipalatsi where you can email till late; free wi-fi.

Left Luggage

Luggage can be left at the main train station, bus station and ferry terminals. Small/large lockers cost €2/3 for 24 hours, and the train station and Viking Line terminal have left-luggage counters (€2 per piece per day).

Medical Services

Töölö Hospital (☎ 4711; Töölönkatu 40) Private 24-hour medical clinic.

Money

There are currency exchange counters at the airport and the Katajanokka ferry terminal. ATMs ('Otto') are plentiful in the city.

Forex (⏰ 8am-9pm) At Pohjoisesplanadi 27, Mannerheimintie 10 and at the train station, Forex offers good rates and is the best place to change cash or travellers cheques (flat fee €2).

Post

Main post office (☎ 0200-71000; Mannerheiminaukio 1, 00100 Helsinki; ⏰ 7am-9pm Mon-Fri, 10am-6pm Sat & Sun)

Poste restante office (⏰ 8am-6pm Mon-Fri) At the rear of the main post office.

FINLAND

FINLAND

HELSINKI

To Urho Kekkonen Museum (2km); Seurasaari Island (3km)

To Tampere (190km)

To Hartwall Arena (1.5km)

City Winter Gardens

Talvipuutarha Botanical Gardens

Sibelius Park

Töölönlahti

Hietaniemi Beach

Töölö

Hietaniemi Cemetery

Seurasaarenselkä

To Cable Factory (250m)

Ruoholahti

Kamppi

Hietalahden tori

Eira

INFORMATION

Akateeminen Kirjakauppa Bookshop....................................1	E4
Australian Honorary Consulate...2	C3
Canadian Embassy.................(see 4)	
Danish Embassy......................(see 1)	
Dutch Embassy...................(see 116)	
Estonian Embassy....................3	F5
Forex.......................................4	E4
Forex.......................................5	D4
Forex...................................(see 48)	
French Embassy.........................6	F6
Helsinki City Tourist Office.........7	E4
Helsinki Tour Expert...............(see 7)	
Helsinki University Library............8	E3
Karttakeskus Aleksi....................9	E3
Kilroy Travels..........................10	E4
Lasipalatsi Meeting Point........(see 59)	
Library 10............................(see 11)	
Main Post Office & Poste Restante.............................11	D3
mbar.....................................12	D3
Police...................................13	E4
Russian Embassy.....................14	F5
Russian Tours Lähialuematkat....15	F5
Swedish Embassy.....................16	F4
Tikankontti (Forest & Park Service Information).........................17	E4
Töölö Hospital........................18	C2
UK Embassy...........................19	F6
US Embassy............................20	F5

SIGHTS & ACTIVITIES

Ateneum...............................21	E3
Finlandia talo.........................22	D3
Havis Amanda Statue & Fountain............................23	F4
Helsinki Zoo..........................24	H3
Kansallimuseo (National Museum)...........................25	D3
Kiasma.................................26	D3
Kotiharjun Sauna....................27	F1
Mannerheim Museum...............28	F5
Maritime Museum....................29	H3
Old Church............................30	E4
Olympic Stadium.....................31	D1
Opera House..........................32	D2
Parliament House....................33	D3
Senaatintori (Senate Square).....34	F4
Sibelius Monument..................35	B2
Temppeliaukio Church..............36	C3
Tuomiokirkko (Lutheran Cathedral).........................37	F3
Uspensky Cathedral.................38	F4
Yrjönkadun Uimahalli...............39	D4

SLEEPING

Accome Parliament.................40	D3
Eurohostel............................41	G4
Gasthaus Omapohja................42	E3
Hostel Academica....................43	C4
Hostel Erottajanpuisto.............44	E4
Hostel Mekka.........................45	E3
Hostel Stadion........................46	C1
Hotel Arthur..........................47	E3
Hotel Booking Centre...............48	E3
Hotel Linna...........................49	D4
Hotelli Finn...........................50	E4
Marttahotelli.........................51	E5
Matkakoti Margarita.............(see 42)	
Scandic Grand Marina..............52	G4

EATING

Bar Tapasta...........................53	E4
Belge Bar & Bistro...................54	E4
Café Carusel..........................55	E6
Café Ekberg...........................56	D4
Café Engel.............................57	F4
Café Esplanad........................58	E4
Café Lasipalatsi......................59	D3
Café Strindberg......................60	E4
Eatz.....................................61	E3
Fazer....................................62	E4
Forum Shopping Centre............63	D4
Gastone................................64	E4
Hariton.................................65	E4
Kappeli.................................66	E4
Konstan Möljä........................67	C5
Lappi....................................68	E4
Maithai.................................69	E4
New Bamboo Centre.............(see 69)	
Porthania UniCafé...................70	E3
Seahorse...............................71	E5
Vanha Kauppahalli..................72	E2
Vanha Kauppahalli..................73	F4
Ylioppilasaukio UniCafé.........(see 74)	
Zetor....................................74	E4
Zucchini................................75	E4

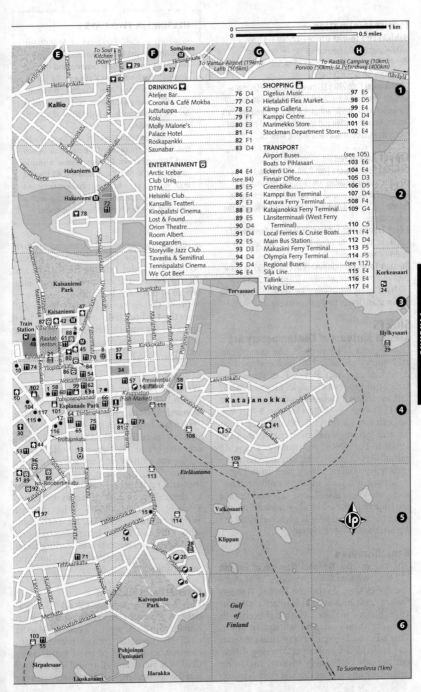

FINLAND

Tourist Information

Helsinki City Tourist Office (☎ 169 3757; www .visithelsinki.fi; Pohjoisesplanadi 19; ☯ 9am-8pm Mon-Fri, 9am-6pm Sat & Sun May-Sep, 9am-6pm Mon-Fri, 10am-4pm Sat & Sun Oct-Apr)

Tikankontti (☎ 270 5221; www.metsa.fi; Eteläesplanadi 20; ☯ 10am-6pm Mon-Fri, 10am-3pm Sat) The Helsinki office of Metsähallitus, the Finnish Forest and Park Service, has information and maps for national parks and hiking areas, cabin rentals and fishing licences.

Travel Agencies

Helsinki Tour Expert (☎ 2288 1500; www.helsinki expert.fi; Pohjoisesplanadi 19) Organises city tours and specialises in travel around Finland and to Tallinn and St Petersburg. There's a desk at the city tourist office and the train station.

Kilroy Travels (☎ 0203-545769; www.kilroytravels.fi; Kaivokatu 10C; ☯ 9am-6pm Mon-Fri, 11am-3pm Sat) Student travel agency.

Russian Tours Lähialuematkat (☎ 668 9570; www .russiantours.fi; Vuorimiehenkatu 3; ☯ 9am-5pm Mon-Fri) Travel agency specialising in Russian tours & organising Russian visas. Close to the Russian embassy.

SIGHTS
Kiasma Museum of Contemporary Art

Like a giant Nike swoosh, the curvaceous and quirky metallic building designed by American architect Steven Holl stands testament to modern Helsinki. **Kiasma** (☎ 1733 6501; www.kiasma.fi; Mannerheiminaukio 2; adult/student/ child €5.50/4/free; ☯ 9am-5pm Tue, 10am-8.30pm Wed-Sun) exhibits an eclectic collection of Finnish and international modern art from the 1960s to the 1990s, and features changing exhibitions of visual arts, multimedia and a theatre for contemporary performing arts.

Kiasma is a local meeting point in summer – its sleek, glass-sided café and terrace are hugely popular, locals sunbathe on the grassy fringes and people gather around the Mannerheim statue outside.

Kansallismuseo

The impressive **National Museum of Finland** (☎ 40501; www.nba.fi; Mannerheimintie 34; adult/student/child €6/4/free; ☯ 11am-8pm Tue-Wed, 11am-6pm Thu-Sun), built in National Romantic style in 1916, looks a bit like a Gothic church with its heavy stonework and tall square tower. This is Finland's premier historical museum and is divided into rooms covering different periods of Finnish history, including prehistory and archaeological finds, church

HELSINKI IN TWO DAYS

Breakfast at Café Esplanad or Strindberg, poke around the *kauppatori* (market square) and stroll up to Senate Square and over to Upensky Cathedral on Katajanokka island. After lunch visit the Kiasma museum, Kansallismuseo or Ateneum. Have a drink on the beer terrace at Kappeli or the high-rise Ateljee Bar.

On day two, grab a bike and head out to the Sibelius monument, Hietaniemi beach and Temppeliauko Church. Throw a picnic together at Vanha Kauppahalli (Old Market Hall) and catch a boat out to Suomenlinna island in the afternoon. End the day with a sauna at the Kotiharjun Sauna in Kallio.

relics, ethnography and changing cultural exhibitions. Look for the imperial throne of Tsar Alexander I dating from 1809, and the display on the reindeer-herding Sami people of northern Lapland.

From the entrance hall, or better still from the 1st-floor balcony, crane your head up to see the superb frescoes on the ceiling arches, depicting scenes from the epic *Kalevala*, painted by Akseli Gallen-Kallela.

Ateneum

With the largest collection of artworks in Finland, the **National Gallery** (☎ 1733 6401; www .ateneum.fi; Kaivokatu 2; adult/student/child €6.50/4/free; ☯ 9am-6pm Tue & Fri, 9am-8pm Wed & Thu, 11am-5pm Sat & Sun) reads like a *Who's Who* of Finnish art. The grand 1887 granite building, opposite the railway station square, houses an absorbing collection of Finnish paintings and sculptures from the 18th century to the 1950s, including works by Albert Edelfelt, Akseli Gallen-Kallela, the von Wright brothers and Pekka Halonen, along with 19th and 20th century international art. Downstairs is a café and reading room. The Ateneum is free between 5pm and 8pm on Wednesday.

Mannerheim Museum

This fascinating **museum** (☎ 635 443; Kalliolinnantie 14; adult/child €7/5; ☯ 11am-4pm Fri-Sun) in Kaivopuisto Park was the home of Marshal CGE Mannerheim, former president and commander-in-chief of the Finnish army, Civil War victor and all-round legend. Such was the national regard for Mannerheim that

FINLAND

the house was converted into a museum less than a year after his death in 1951. Entry includes a mandatory but enthusiastic guided tour, with free plastic booties to keep the hallowed floor clean. The display includes personal possessions, the camp bed he slept in and photographs and mementos from his famous Silk Rd journey•on which he rode the same faithful horse for two years. It's only open three days a week but worth making time for to gain an appreciation of Finland's national psyche.

Cable Factory

The massive red-brick **Kaapelitehdas** (Cable Factory; ☎ 4763 8300; www.kaapelitehdas.fi; Tallberginkatu 1; ☼ information 8am-6pm Mon-Fri), was once used for manufacturing sea cable and later became Nokia's main factory until the 1980s. When Nokia moved out, artists moved in, renting every spare space on offer. Grungy theatre, innovative art exhibitions and bohemian dance performances are staged here now – many are free. The venue has a youthful, experimental and slightly anarchic atmosphere. The building also houses three offbeat museums (free with the Helsinki Card): the **Museum of Photography** (☎ 6866 3621; www.fmp.fi; adult/child €6/free; ☼ 11am-6pm Tue-Sun), covering art photography and photographic culture; the **Hotel & Restaurant Museum** (☎ 6859 3700; adult/child €2/1; ☼ 11am-6pm Tue-Sun), with everything you wanted to know about Finnish bars and restaurants; and the **Theatre Museum** (☎ 6850 9150; adult/child €5.50/2.50; ☼ 11am-6pm Tue-Sun), exploring the history of Finnish theatre. Take tram No 8 or the metro to Ruolahti (about 500m away).

Seurasaari Open-Air Museum

The peaceful, forested island of Seurasaari, northwest of the centre, is home to the sprawling open-air folk museum (☎ 4050 9660; adult/student/child €5/3.50/free; ☼ 11am-5pm daily, to 7pm Wed Jun-Aug, 9am-3pm Mon-Fri, 11am-5pm Sat & Sun late May & early Sep) with more than 80 wooden buildings from the 18th and 19th centuries. Walking trails link the various log houses, chapels, cottages and farmhouses brought here from all over Finland – you'll get a good impression of what rural Finland was like a century ago. In summer, guides dressed in traditional costume demonstrate folk dancing and crafts.

Seurasaari is the best place in Helsinki to see the **midsummer bonfires**, a popular local tradition on Midsummer's Eve.

Near the bridge that connects Seurasaari with the mainland, the **Urho Kekkonen museum** (☎ 4050 9652; Seurasaarentie 15, Tamminiemi; adult/child €5/free; ☼ 11am-5pm mid-May–mid-Aug) was the presidential residence for 30 years. Built in 1904, it housed three presidents, including Mannerheim and Urho Kekkonen, and now shows off Finnish history and art exhibitions. For the museum and Seurasaari island, take bus No 24 from central Helsinki, or tram No 4 and walk.

Suomenlinna

An ideal day or half-day trip from Helsinki is to pack a picnic and take the regular ferry to the island fortress of Suomenlinna (Sveaborg in Swedish). A great deal of Helsinki's history was shaped here – the World Heritage Listed fortress was founded by the Swedes in 1748 to protect against the Russians but following a prolonged attack, Sveaborg was surrendered to the Russians in 1808.

At the bridge connecting the two main islands – Iso Mustasaari and Susisaari – is the **Inventory Chamber Visitor Centre** (☎ 684 1880; ☼ 10am-6pm May-Sep) with tourist information, maps and guided walking tours in summer. In the same building is the illuminating **Suomenlinna Museum** (☎ 40501; adult/student/child €5/4/free), covering the island's history.

You can ramble around the crumbling fortress walls at the southern end of Susisaari island, and there are several museums including the **Ehrensvärd Museum** (☎ 684 1850; adult/child €3/1; ☼ 10am-5pm May-Aug) which preserves an 18th-century officer's home. Three museums relating to Suomenlinna's military history can be visited with a **combination ticket** (adult/student €5.50/2; ☼ 11am-6pm May-Aug) – the most interesting is the **Submarine Vesikko**.

The **church** on Iso Mustasaari was built in 1854 and doubles as a lighthouse – the original gaslight beacon is now electric.

There are several good cafés on Suomenlinna, but many locals like to picnic among the fortress ruins with a few drinks – it can get pretty boozy here on summer weekends. At around 5pm it's worth finding a spot to watch the enormous Baltic ferries pass through the narrow gap.

FINLAND

There's a reasonably well-stocked supermarket near the main ferry terminal and a HI youth hostel. **Suomenlinna Panimoravintola** (☎ 228 5030; Rantakasarmi; lunch €11.50; 🕙 3-10pm Mon-Fri, noon-10pm Sat, noon-6pm Sun) is a fine brewery pub and restaurant right beside the ferry quay.

HKL ferries depart every 20 minutes from the passenger quay at the *kauppatori*. Buy tickets (€3.80 return) for the 15-minute trip at the pier. The Helsinki Card is valid for all ferries and attractions at Suomenlinna.

There's nowhere to hire bikes, but they can be brought across on the ferries.

ACTIVITIES

In summer, join the locals sunning themselves on Helsinki's small islands and beaches. The closest city beach is Hietaniemi, a small and very popular curve of sand west of the centre. Pihlajasaari is the pick of the many islands, with several secluded bays and beaches, including a nudist beach. Get there by boat from the dock next to Café Carusel.

In winter and early spring it's possible to go walking, skating or cross-country skiing on parts of the frozen harbour and on Töölönlahti lake, or try your hand at ice-fishing.

For a sauna and swim, the sleek Art Deco **Yrjönkadun Uimahalli** (☎ 3108 7400; Yrjönkatu 21; admission €4-11; 🕙 men 6.30am-pm Tue, Thu, Sat; women noon-9pm Sun & Mon, 6.30am-9pm Wed & Fri) is a Helsinki institution – a fusion of soaring Nordic elegance and Roman baths. There are separate hours for men and women and, like the saunas, it's compulsory to bathe nude.

Kotiharjun Sauna (☎ 753 1535; Harjutorinkatu 1; adult/child €7/4; 🕙 2-8pm Tue-Fri, 1-7pm Sat), in Kallio, is Helsinki's last public wood-fired sauna and dates back to 1928. It's a real Finnish experience where you can also get a scrub-down and massage. There are separate saunas for men and women.

Walking Tour

Helsinki is an easy and very rewarding city to get around on foot or by bicycle. Start at the **kauppatori**, Helsinki's lively market square. East of the market, on Katajanokka island, you can't miss the magnificent **Orthodox Uspensky Cathedral**. The red-brick exterior supports 13 gilded cupolas ('onion domes'

designed by a Russian architect of the tsar) representing Christ and his disciples.

From the market square walk up the cobbled Sofiankatu to **Senaatintori** (Senate Square), Helsinki's majestic central square. Surrounded by early 19th-century buildings, the square was modelled after St Petersburg's. CL Engel's stately **Tuomiokirkko** (Lutheran cathedral), finished in 1852, is the square's most prominent feature and the steps are a favourite meeting place.

Returning to the market square, check out the fountain and mermaid **statue of Havis Amanda**, designed by artist Ville Vallgren in 1908 and regarded as a symbol of Helsinki. From here the **Esplanade Park** stretches west to the main thoroughfare, Mannerheimintie. Head north to visit **Kiasma**, the **Kansallismuseo** (National Museum) and **Parliament House** (☎ 432 2027; 🕙 guided tours 11am & noon Sat, noon & 1pm Sun). Across the road is Alvar Aalto's angular **Finlandia talo** (Concert Hall). If you have time, continue north (walk along the shore of lake Töölönlahti) to Aalto's **Opera House** on the corner of Mannerheimintie and Helsinginkatu, then turn right to reach the tiny, beautifully manicured **City Winter Gardens**. Also in this area is the **Olympic Stadium**, built for the 1952 Olympics, with a sports museum and a 72m-high tower offering good views over the city.

Returning along Mannerheimintie, detour along Fredrikinkatu to the **Temppeliaukio Church** (the Church in the Rock). Hewn into rock, the church symbolises the modern meanderings of Finnish religious architecture and features a stunning 24m-diameter roof covered in 22km of copper stripping. There are regular concerts and a service in English at 2pm on Sundays.

Walk down Fredrikinkatu, past the new Kamppi Centre, then east on Lönnrotinkatu to the small park where there's a lovely **old church**. This is a popular lunch-time meeting spot in summer. Heading back down Bulevardi (away from the city), you come to Hietalahden tori where there's a market hall and a popular flea market on summer evenings and weekends.

If you have a bicycle, from here you can ride around the southern shoreline of Helsinki (follow Telakkakatu then Merisatamanranta) to **Kaivopuisto park** and return to the kauppatori. Alternatively, head north from Hietalahden tori to Hietaniemenkatu and ride around to **Hietaniemi Beach**, the closest beach to central Helsinki. Continuing north you come to **Sibelius Park** and the steel **monument** to the great Finnish composer. The organlike cluster of steel pipes is said to represent the forest.

TOURS

Helsinki Tour Expert (☎ 2288 1600; www.helsinki expert.fi; adult/child €23/11) runs worthwhile 1½-hour city bus tours in summer on the hour from 10am to 2pm (11am and 1pm in May & September, 11am in winter). Ask which tours are free with the Helsinki Card. They depart from the Esplanade Park, near the tourist office, and taped commentary (in 11 languages) comes via a headset.

Sun Lines (☎ 741 8210; www.sunlines.fi; adult/child €16/8) and **Royal Lines** (☎ 0207-118 333; www.royal line.fi; €16/8) operate 1½-hour archipelago sea cruises, as well as lunch and dinner cruises, with daily departures in summer from the kauppatori.

FESTIVALS & EVENTS

There's something going on in Helsinki year-round. Check with the tourist office for a current programme or check www.hel2.fi.

Vappu (May Day) is celebrated with particular verve in Helsinki. On Vappu Eve (30 April) thousands of students gather around the Havis Amanda fountain to dress up the statue, plant a white cap on her, and so begin a riotous night of partying. On 1 May, crowds of all ages gather for a champagne breakfast and all-day party at Kaivopuisto park.

In late April, the **Espoo Jazz Festival** (www .apriljazz.fi) attracts some big-name local and international performers. On June 6, **Helsinki Day** is celebrated with festivities around town and free concerts in Kaivopuisto park.

The **Helsinki Festival** (www.helsinkifestival.fi) runs for about two weeks in late August-early September with a programme of arts, music and theatre.

SLEEPING

It pays to make bookings or at least call ahead at any time of year – June to August is the peak tourist season but hostels can fill up with school groups and hotels with business travellers outside these months. The **Hotel Booking Centre** (☎ 2288 1400; hotel@helsinkiexpert.fi; ☯ 9am-7pm Mon-Fri, 9am-6pm Sat, 10am-6pm Sun Jun-Aug, 9am-6pm Mon-Fri, 9am-5pm

Sat & Sun Sep-May) in the train station or city tourist office can help in a pinch – they charge a €5 booking fee but can sometimes get cheaper deals on hotels.

Budget

Rastila Camping (☎ 321 6551; rastilacamping@hel.fi; Karavaanikatu 4; camp site per adult €5/10, 2-/4- person cabins €45/64, log cottage €120; Ⓟ) Although 10km from the city centre, this is a lovely camping ground on Vuosaari and it's easily reached by metro (Rastila stop). Facilities include a beach sauna, restaurant and summer youth hostel.

Hostel Erottajanpuisto (☎ 642 169; www .erottajanpuisto.com; Uudenmaankatu 9; dm/s/d/tr €22.50/47/60/78; ☯ 24hr reception; ✕ 🖳) Helsinki's smallest and most laid-back hostel occupies the top floor of a building in a lively street of bars and restaurants close to the heart of the city. Forget curfews, lockouts, school kids and bringing your own sleeping sheet – this is more like a guesthouse with dormitories.

Eurohostel (☎ 622 0470; www.eurohostel.fi; Linnan-katu 9; dm/s/d/tr €23.20/38.60/46.40/69.60; ☯ 24hr reception; 🖳) On Katajanokka island less than 500m from the Viking Line terminal, Eurohostel is a multilevel HI place with plenty of facilities, including free morning sauna, a good café and kitchens on each floor. It's very busy but a bit soulless and the private rooms are poky. Take tram No 4 or 2 from the centre or a 15-minute walk.

Hostel Academica (☎ 1311 4334; www.hostel academica.fi; Hietaniemenkatu 14; dm €18, s/tw/tr €40/60/75, superior s/tw €57/75; ☯ Jun-Aug; ✕ Ⓟ 🖳) In a quiet part of town, this summer hostel is in a student apartment building so there are no large dorms and each room has private bathroom and kitchenette. It's spotless, welcoming and the facilities are excellent, including sauna and uni café.

Hostel Mekka (☎ 630 265; www.hostelmekka.com; Vuorikatu 8B; dm/s/d/tr €24/48.50/58.50/73.50; ✕ 🖳) This rambling, 200-year-old building has plenty of character – high ceilings, ceramic Swedish stove heaters – and a great central location, though it can feel a bit draughty.

Hostel Stadion (☎ 477 8480; www.stadionhostel .com; Pohjoinen Stadiontie 3B; dm €16, s/tw/tr with linen €32/44/66; Ⓟ ✕ 🖳) In the Olympic Stadium complex about 1.5km north of the centre, this is an 'old school' hostel (it's been around since 1962!) with large dorms, daytime lockout from rooms and 2am curfew. It has the cheapest beds in town and some travellers love the busy atmosphere and plentiful facilities (café, laundry, wi-fi internet), while others loathe the austerity and charmless staff. Take tram 7A or 3T to Oopera and walk five minutes.

Midrange

Gasthaus Omapohja (☎ 666 211; Itäinen Teatterikuja 3; s/d €44/65, s/d with shared bathroom €64/85; ☒) A convenient two-minute walk from the train station, this intimate, theatre-inspired guesthouse is Helsinki's cosiest. It's very small, with no common areas and minute shared bathrooms, but it's worth this price. Book ahead.

Matkakoti Margarita (☎ 622 4261; Itäinen Teatterikuja 3; s/d/t €40/54/69, s/d with bathroom €55/70; ☒) Next door to Omapohja, this guesthouse is not as charming and no English is spoken, but it's clean, well priced and worth a try if Omapohja is full.

Hotelli Finn (☎ 684 4360; www.hotellifinn.fi; Kalevankatu 3B; s/d €55/65, s/d with shower €65/80) Although not flash, this small, friendly hotel on the top floor of a central city building offers very reasonable rates for the location. Rooms are compact but tidy, with TV.

Hotel Arthur (☎ 173 441; www.hotelarthur.fi; Vuorikatu 19; s/d/tr €94/113/134, weekend & summer €73/92/112; ☒ 🐾) Close to the train station, Arthur is small enough to feel you're getting some personal attention but big enough to have all the mod-cons, with pleasant décor, spacious rooms, satellite TV and a good restaurant.

Marttahotelli (☎ 618 7400; www.marttahotelli.fi; Uudenmaankatu 24A; s/tw/tr €98/130/150, s/d/tr discount weekends €75/85/100; ℗ ☒) Central but quiet as most rooms face an inner courtyard with free parking. Smallish rooms but sunny décor, well furnished and one of Helsinki's friendliest hotels.

Top End

Helsinki has plenty of big, central business hotels, including the Sokos, Radisson, Scandic and Cumulus chains.

Accome Parliament (☎ 2511 050; www.accome .com; Museokatu 18; studio d from €102; 1-/2-bed apts €128/147, weekends €72/90/103; ☒ 🖳) A step up in style and comfort from many hotels, the apartments here have sleek modern furnishings, kitchenette, internet connections

and cable TV. Prices vary seasonally and there are discounts for longer stays. Great location.

Scandic Grand Marina (☎ 16661; www.scandic -hotels.com; Katajanokanlaituri 7; s/d from €140/180, weekends & summer €95/105; ℗ ☒ 🖳 ♿) In a converted brick harbour warehouse near the Viking Line terminal on Katajanokka, the Grand Marina is an outstanding hotel with one of Helsinki's best outlooks. Facilities are top notch, with spacious, refurbished rooms, business centre, gym and the excellent Makasiini restaurant and bar.

EATING

Helsinki has by far Finland's best range of cafés and restaurants: from Finnish and Russian to Asian and Italian, sushi joints to kebab stands and terrace cafés to fine French dining. Seek out the lunchtime specials if your budget is tight – many restaurants (even the fancy ones) have buffet lunch deals for under €10. Good places to follow your nose include the Esplanade, Mikonkatu, Uudenmaankatu and the tangle of side streets between the train station and Stockmann. In summer, several island restaurants serve lavish seafood dishes.

For everything from Asian noodles to burgers and kebabs, head to the food court in the basement of the **Forum shopping centre** (Mannerheimintie 20), where you'll also find a supermarket and Alko store.

Helsinki University has several student cafeterias around the city, where meals cost under €5. They include **Porthania** (☎ 1311 4298; Hallituskatu 11-13; ☷ 10am-4pm Mon-Fri) and the huge **Ylioppilasaukio** (☎ 260 9491; Mannerheimintie 3B; ☷ 11am-5pm Mon-Sat, noon-5pm Sun), tucked away down an alley next to Zetor.

Restaurants

Zetor (☎ 666 966; www.zetor.net; Mannerheimintie 3-5; mains €7-26; ⊗ 3pm-late Sun-Fri, 11am-late Sat) The deeply ironic pastoral décor at this whacky Finnish restaurant-bar features tractors, milk cans and other farm stuff. The menu is mainly traditional Finnish dishes (reindeer, vendace etc) and steaks and burgers, and it becomes a rock-music bar later in the night. Great fun.

Eatz (☎ 687 7240; Kaisaniemenkatu 2; mains €9-23; ⊗ noon-midnight Mon-Thu & Sun, noon-4am Fri & Sat) The versatile and colourful Eatz manages to serve up everything from Thai and Indian to Mexican and Italian in various themed dining rooms – though you may start to wonder where in the world you are. There's even a sushi bar and an Aussie Outback theme bar.

Lappi (☎ 645 550; Annankatu 22; mains €16-37; ⊗ 5-10.30pm Mon-Fri, 1-10.30pm Sat & Sun) Costumed staff serve up Sami specialities in this delightfully rustic 'log cabin' restaurant. Try sirloin of elk, as well as various reindeer preparations, vendace (lake fish) and cloudberry desserts.

Konstan Mölijä (☎ 694 750; Hietalahdenkatu 14; lunch/dinner buffet €8/14; ⊗ 11am-10pm Mon-Fri, 2-10pm Sat) Great place for hearty, home-style Finnish fare enjoyed in a pleasant atmosphere – much of the maritime décor comes from an old harbour near Vyborg. The buffet always includes reindeer.

Belge Bar & Bistro (☎ 622 9620; Kluuvikatu 5; mains €8-25; ⊗ 11-2am Mon-Thu, 11-3am Fri & Sat, 2-10pm Sun) A steaming bowl of mussels, grilled sausages and those fantastic Belgian beers make this little piece of Brussels a great place for lunch or dinner. Stylish restaurant upstairs and more casual bar and bistro at street level.

Seahorse (☎ 628 169; Kapteeninkatu 11; €11-25; ⊗ 10.30am-midnight Mon-Thu, 10.30-1am Fri & Sat, 10.30am-midnight Sun) Barely changed since the 1930s, Seahorse is as traditional a Finnish restaurant as you'll find anywhere. Smoking locals gather to meet and drink over Baltic herring, Finnish meatballs and cabbage rolls.

Soul Kitchen (☎ 773 2233; Fleminginkatu 26-28; ⊗ 11-2am Mon-Fri, 2pm-2am Sat, 2pm-midnight Sun) In Kallio, Soul Kitchen is a loungey, retro café and bar – the menu is on a record sleeve and the burgers, salads and steaks are some of the best around.

Hariton (☎ 622 1717; Kasarmikatu 44; mains €9-22; ⊗ 11.30am-midnight Mon-Fri, 1-11pm Sat, noon-6pm Sun) Helsinki has some fine Russian restaurants and Hariton is one of the newest and most reasonably priced. Charming dining room with antique furniture, a gallery and varied Orthodox menu, including blini.

Gastone (☎ 666 116; Korkeavuorenkatu 45; mains €7-20; ⊗ 11.30am-midnight Mon-Fri, 2pm-midnight Sat, 3-11pm Sun) Vying for the title of Helsinki's best Italian restaurant, Gastone boasts a diverse list of pasta and antipasto, a fine wine list and an intimate yet not too formal ambience.

Also recommended:

Maithai (☎ 685 6850; Annankatu 31-33; mains €9-17; ⊗ 11am-11pm Mon-Fri, noon-11pm Sat & Sun) An intimate little place and a local favourite for Thai food – only a handful of tables so book ahead.

Bar Tapasta (☎ 640 724; Uudenmaankatu 13; tapas €2.50-5; ⊗ Mon-Thu 11am-midnight, Fri 11-2am, Sat 1pm-2am) Intimate, hole-in-the-wall bar with a welcoming atmosphere and wonderful tapas, including gorgonzola mushrooms and chilli olives. Wash it all down with a jug of sangria.

New Bamboo Centre (☎ 694 3117; Annankatu 29; mains €5-10; ⊗ 11am-9pm Mon-Fri, noon-1pm Sat & Sun) Cheap & filling Asian dishes in simple surroundings.

AUTHOR'S CHOICE

Kappeli (☎ 681 2440; Eteläesplanadi 1; ⊗ 9-2am Mon-Sat, 9am-midnight Sun) Behind the glass and iron façade of this Helsinki institution is an excellent restaurant and café which has been the haunt of Helsinki's artistic elite since 1867. In the stone-walled cellar is an ambient vaultlike bar. Kappeli has a prime position in Esplanade Park – its summer terrace is one of the city's best people watching spots – and the facing stage regularly has free performances in summer.

Cafés

Café Espland (☎ 665 496; Pohjoisesplanadi 37; light meals €3-12, bistro €8-26; ⊗ 8am-10pm Mon-Fri, 9am-10pm Sat, 10am-10pm Sun) Helsinki's most popular café is always crowded. Part breakfast café, bistro, bakery and bar, you can start the morning here with Danish pastries and giant Finnish *pulla* (wheat bun), or enjoy spectacular salads on the terrace.

Cafe Strindberg (☎ 681 2030; Pohjoisesplanadi 33; light meals €4-12; ⊗ 9am-10pm Mon-Sat, 10am-10pm Sun, bar to 1am) This little piece of Paris in

FINLAND

Helsinki has a prime people-watching terrace on the Esplanade. Upstairs is an up-market restaurant but the highlight is the cosy wine bar with squishy leather couches, classical music and candlelight.

Café Ekberg (☎ 6811 8660; Bulevardi 9; buffet breakfast & lunch €7.50; ☼ 7.30am-7pm Mon-Fri, 8.30am-5pm Sat, 10.30am-5pm Sun) Helsinki's oldest café has a spacious, bohemian atmosphere and it's still one of the best places for a smorgasbord breakfast in the city. The lunch buffet is also great value.

Café Carusel (☎ 622 4522; Merisatamanranta 10; dishes €2-10; 10am-10pm) In summer this is a super-busy but unpretentious self-service waterfront café on the edge of Kaivopuisto park. Great focaccias and savoury snacks and a sunny terrace.

Zucchini (☎ 622 2907; Fabianinkatu 4; dishes €5-12; ☼ 11am-5pm Mon-Fri, closed Jul; ✖) Trendy vegetarian café serving quiche, pancakes, soups, salads, juices and a few innovative dishes, including plenty for vegans.

Also recommended:

Fazer (☎ 729 6702; Kluuvikatu 3; cakes from €3; ☼ 8am-10pm Mon-Fri, 9am-10pm Sat; ✖) The best café in town for cakes, pastries, ice cream and jaw-dropping sweets – the Fazer family is Finland's most famous candy maker.

Café Lasipalatsi (☎ 621 6700; Mannerheimintie 22-24; lunch buffet from €8; ☼ 7.30am-10pm Mon-Fri, 9am-10pm Sat, 11am-10pm Sun) With big windows staring across at Kiasma and Helsinki's major city intersection, Lasipalatsi specialises in filling Finnish lunch buffets (11am-4pm). Also an excellent café for free wi-fi access.

Café Engel (☎ 652 776; Aleksanterinkatu 26; ☼ 8am-10pm Mon-Fri, 9am-10pm Sat, 10am-10pm Sun) With a fine outlook opposite Senaatintori (Senate Square) and the cathedral (and appropriately named after its architect), Engel is popular with uni students and the arty crowd.

Self-Catering

In summer there are food stalls, fresh produce and outrageously expensive berries at the kauppatori, but the real gourmet stuff is in the fabulous **Vanha Kauppahalli** (Old Market Hall; Eteläranta 1; ☼ 6.30am-6pm Mon-Fri, 6.30am-4pm Sat, 10am-4pm Sun summer only) at the harbour, where you can get filled rolls, cheese, breads, fish and an array of Finnish snacks and delicacies, plus there's a small Alko. Another good market hall is the **Hakaniemi kauppahalli** (☼ 8am-6pm Mon-Fri, 8am-4pm Sat), a traditional-style Finnish food market near the Hakaniemi metro.

DRINKING

Helsinki has some of Scandinavia's most diverse nightlife. In winter locals gather in cosy bars and the full gamut of clubs. In summer, drinking starts early at the many beer terraces that sprout up all over town. The biggest is along Mikonkatu at the front of Eatz, On the Rocks and Baarikärpänen.

The main areas for nightlife in the centre include the busy Mikonkatu and nearby Yliopistonkatu, and west of the centre around Uudenmaankatu and Eerikinkatu. Also check out the pedestrian strip Iso Rooberinkatu with several good bars and cafés.

For the cheapest beer in Helsinki (from €2 a pint during the seemingly perpetual happy hours), try a pub crawl in the working-class suburb of Kallio (metro: Sörnäinen), north of the centre. There's a string of earthy local pubs along Helsinginkatu such as the grungy local favourite **Roskapankki** (☎ 735 488; Helsingkatu 20) – the name means 'trash bank' – and a growing number of trendy bars and cafés.

Ateljee Bar (☎ 43360; Yrjönkatu 26; ☼ 2pm-late Sun-Fri, noon-2am Sat) Take the lift up to the tiny rooftop bar on the 14th floor of the Sokos Hotel Torni (Helsinki's tallest building) – the views from the terrace (and the toilets) are some of the best in the city.

Palace Hotel (☎ 1345 6660; Eteläranta 10) Another bar with a view is the rooftop terrace of the Palace Hotel which actually has a better outlook over the harbour and cathedrals.

Molly Malone's (☎ 5766 7500; Kaisaniemenkatu 1C; ☼ 10-2am Mon, 10-3am Tue, 10-4am Wed-Sat, noon-2am Sun) Helsinki's rocking Irish pub is packed most nights – there's a live band upstairs, cosy snugs downstairs, and this is a great place to meet travellers, expats and Finns out for a good time.

Corona & Café Mokba (☎ 642 002; Eerikinkatu 11; ☼ 11-2am Mon-Sat, noon-2am Sun) These two quirky bars are owned by filmmakers Aki and Mika Kaurismäki and attract a savvy, grungy crowd. Corona has cool bar staff and about 20 pool tables, so it's popular with drinkers and sharks. Mokba is a tiny Russian-influenced bar with ironic Soviet-era décor, flock wallpaper and almost comically gruff service.

Saunabar (☎ 586 5550; Eerikinkatu 27; ☼ 2am-9pm Mon, 2pm-1am Tue, 2pm-2am Wed-Sat) Feel like a night out and a sauna? Just as the name suggests, this cool student bar has a couple of basement saunas, as well as a decent music bar.

Juttutupa (☎ 774 4860; Säästöpankinranta 6; ⏱ 10-1am Mon-Thu, 10-3am Fri & Sat, 11am-midnight Sun) This imposing granite pub across from Hakaniemi Square is a bit of a local institution and has its own Wednesday night jazz club.

Kola (☎ 694 8983; Helsinginkatu 13; ⏱ noon-2am; 💻) This retro café-bar is part of the new look of the once grungy Kallio district. Loungey, worn furniture, retro art on the walls and chilled music make this a popular hangout with students and a young crowd.

Spårakoff (adult/child €7/3.50; ⏱ hourly 2-8pm, mid-May–mid-Aug) In summer the bright red pub tram trundles around the city on a one hour circuit, departing hourly from the terminus on Mikonkatu (opposite Eatz). Of course, there's a bar on board so it's not a bad way to go sightseeing.

ENTERTAINMENT
Cinemas
Tennispalatsi (☎ 0600-007 007; Salomonkatu 15; tickets €8-10) Helsinki's biggest cinema is a 14-screen multiplex screening mainstream movies.

Kinopalatsi (☎ 0600 9 4444; Kaisaniemenkatu 2) Another large cinema complex in the central entertainment district.

Orion Theatre (☎ 6154 0201; Eerikinkatu 15) Alternative and art-house cinema with a fondness for Woody Allen; screens Finnish Film Archive movies.

Gay & Lesbian Venues
By Scandinavian standards Helsinki has a low-key gay scene.

Lost & Found (☎ 680 1010; Annankatu 6; ⏱ 5pm-4am Mon-Fri, 7pm-4am Sat & Sun) This sophisticated gay-hetero bar is still a hugely popular late-night hang-out with people of all persuasions. Regular shows and the hip Hideaway Bar.

Room Albert (☎ 643 626; Kalevankatu 36) Helsinki's newest gay venue attracts a young, sophisticated crowd.

DTM (☎ 676 315; Iso Roobertinkatu 28; ⏱ 9pm-4am Mon-Sat, noon 4am Sun) Said to be Scandinavia's biggest gay club, DTM (Don't Tell Mama) is more than just drag shows and dance tunes – it's a café, nightclub and meeting place on two floors.

Live Music
Various bars and clubs around Helsinki host live bands.

Tavastia & Semi-final (☎ 774 67420; www.tavastiaklubi.fi; Urho Kekkosenkatu 4-6; tickets €6-25; ⏱ 9pm-2am Sun-Thu, 9pm-3am Fri & Sat) There's always something happening at Finland's biggest rock music club. Live bands, including international acts, hit the stage in this hangar-sized venue. Also check out what's on at Semi-final (same contact and opening times), the smaller sister venue.

Storyville (☎ 408 007; www.storyville.fi in Finnish; Museokatu 8; ⏱ 8am-4pm Mon-Sat) Helsinki's No 1 jazz club attracts a refined older crowd swinging to boogie-woogie, trad jazz, Dixieland and New Orleans most nights. There's a cool outside terrace in summer.

Nightclubs
Helsinki Club (☎ 43 320; www.helsinkiclub.com; Yliopistonkatu 8; ⏱ 10pm-4am) This heaving mainstream dance club is a bit of an institution and pulls in the late-night crowds – including the odd Finnish celebrity – most nights. If you tire of the dancefloor, there's a funky lounge and the iridescent Dome Bar. Minimum age 24.

Club Uniq (☎ 0800-94411; Yliopistonkatu 5; ⏱ 10pm-4am) Across the road from Helsinki Club, the small dance floor gets busy most nights but the novelty vote goes to the tiny Arctic Icebar (open 5pm to 4am; admission €10) inside: don a coat, sip a vodka shot in a balmy -5°C, and watch the ravers outside through the glass wall. Minimum age 24.

On Iso-Rooberinkatu is a growing list of clubs showcasing the latest in cool Helsinki nightlife. **We Got Beef** (☎ 679 268; Iso-Roobertinkatu 21; ⏱ 1pm-2am Sun-Tue, 1pm-3am Wed-Sat) and **Rosegarden** (Iso-Roobertinkatu 10; ⏱ 10pm-4am Wed-Sat) are two worth checking out for DJ club music, drum & bass, dancing or lounging.

Sport
If you're around in winter (September–March), take the chance to see a major ice hockey game. Big matches are played at the huge **Hartwall Arena** (☎ 204 1997, tickets ☎ 0600-10800; www.hartwall-areena.com; Areenakuja 1) in Pasila, north of the centre (tram 7A or 7B). The stadium hosted ice hockey world championships in 1997 and 2004, and is home to Helsinki superleague side Jokerit. You can also catch games at the indoor arena of the Olympic Stadium off Mannerheimintie.

FINLAND

Theatre & Concerts

For concerts and performances, see *Helsinki This Week*, inquire at the tourist office, or check the website of ticket outlet **Lippupiste** (☎ 0600-900 900; www.lippu.fi). Tickets are available through Lippupiste or at the box office at Stockmann department store. Opera, ballet and classical concerts are held at the **Opera House** (☎ 4030 2211; Helsinginkatu 58; tickets from €15), while performances by the Finnish National Theatre are at the **Kansallis Teatteri** (☎ 1733 1331; www.kansallisteatteri.fi in Finnish; Läntinen teatterikuja 1), near the train station.

Big-name rock concerts and international acts often perform at Hartwall Arena.

SHOPPING

Helsinki's main shopping strip is Pohjoisesplanadi, running along Esplanade park, where you'll find chic boutiques of **Kämp Galleria**, the flagship branch of **Marimekko** (☎ 686 0240; Pohjoisesplanadi 31), the trendy Finnish design and homewares store, and **Stockmann** (Aleksanterinkatu 52; 9am-9pm Mon-Fri, 9am-6pm Sat, noon-6pm Sun), Scandinavia's biggest department store with seven floors of everything. Iso Rooberinkatu and Uudenmenkatu are other strips for boutique shops with less pose value.

For music, check out **Digelius Music** (☎ 666 375; Laivurinrinne 2).They stock a range of Finnish music and world music. It's one of those small independent record shops where the staff know everything and they stock obscure CDs like High Fidelity!

The kauppatori at the harbour, has a produce and souvenir market in summer where you can browse for everything from woollen knitwear and Sami dolls, to reindeer antler carvings. **Hietalahti Flea Market** (8am-2pm Mon-Fri, 8am-3pm Sat, 10am-4pm Sun in summer) is the place to hunt for bargains and secondhand gear.

GETTING THERE & AWAY

Air

There are flights to Helsinki from all major European cities. Vantaa airport, one of Europe's most user-friendly terminals, is 19km north of Helsinki.

Finnair (☎ 0203-140160 for reservations; Asemaaukio 3; 8am-8pm Mon-Fri, 10am-5pm Sat) flies to 20 Finnish cities, generally at least once a day but several times daily on routes such as Turku, Tampere, Rovaniemi and Oulu. **Blue1**

(☎ 0600 25831; www.blue1.com) has budget flights to a handful of major Finnish destinations.

Boat

International ferries depart from five main terminals and travel to Stockholm (Sweden), Tallinn (Estonia) and Travemünde (Germany). See p214 for more details.

Ferry tickets can be bought at the terminals or from the ferry companies' offices in the city centre.

Eckerö Line (☎ 228 8544; www.eckeroline.fi; Mannerheimintie 10; Länsiterminaali (West) terminal)

Linda Line (☎ 668 9700; www.lindaliini.ee; Makasiini terminal)

Nordic Jet Line (☎ 0600 01 655; www.njl.fi; Kanava terminal)

Silja Line (☎ 0600-174552; www.siljaline.fi; Mannerheimintie 2; Olympia & Makasiini terminals)

Tallink (☎ 228 311; www.tallink.fi; Erottajankatu 19; West terminal)

Viking Line (☎ 12 351; www.vikingline.fi; Lönnrotinkatu 2; Katajanokka terminal)

From the train station, Kanava and Katajanokka terminals are served by bus No 13 and tram Nos 2, 2V and 4; Olympia and Makasiini terminals by tram Nos 3B and 3T; and Länsiterminaali by bus No 15, or walk from Ruoholahti metro.

Bus

Regional and long-distance buses arrive and depart from the huge new underground **Kamppi Bus Terminal** (24hrs; ticket office 7am-8pm Mon-Fri, 9am-6pm Sat, 10am-6pm Sun), below the Kamppi Centre off Salomonkatu or Frederinkatu. There's a separate set of platforms on the eastern side for buses to Espoo, while express buses to most major towns in Finland leave from long-distance platforms. Destinations include: Tampere (€28.20, 2½ hours), Turku (€25.70, 2½ hours), Savonlinna (€46.30, 5½ hours) and Kuopio (€50.90, seven hours).

Train

Helsinki's large but orderly **train station** (☎ 0600 41902; 24hrs, tickets 6.30am-9.30pm) is central and easy to find your way around. Long-distance and international tickets (to Russia) can be purchased from the hall to the left of the main entrance. A pedestrian tunnel links the train station to Helsinki's metro system (Rautatientori stop).

The train is the best way to get from Helsinki to major centres – express trains run daily to Turku, Tampere, Kuopio and Lappeenranta among others, and there's a choice of day and overnight trains to Oulu, Rovaniemi and Joensuu. There are also daily trains to the Russian cities of Vyborg, St Petersburg and Moscow.

GETTING AROUND
To/From the Airport
Bus No 615 (€3.60, 40 minutes) shuttles between Vantaa airport (all international and domestic flights) and platform No 10 at Rautatientori (Railway Square) next to the main train station. Finnair buses (€5.20, 30 minutes) depart from the Finnair office at Asema-aukio, also next to the main train station, every 20 minutes from 5am to midnight.

There are door-to-door shared **airport taxis** (☎ 0600-555555; www.airporttaxi.fi; 1-2 people €20, 3-4 people €28). A regular taxi costs around €30.

Bicycle
Helsinki is ideal for cycling: the small inner city is flat, and there are well-marked and high-quality bicycle paths. Pick up a copy of the *Helsinki cycling map* from the tourist office.

In summer, the city provides distinctive green 'City Bikes' at some 26 stands within a radius of 2km from the kauppatori – although sometimes you'll wonder where they're all hiding. These bikes are free: you deposit a €2 coin into the stand which locks them, then reclaim it when you return the bike to any stand.

For something a bit more sophisticated and reliable, **Greenbike** (☎ 050-4040 4000; www.greenbike.fi; Bulevardi 32; ☽ 10am-8pm May-Sep) rents quality bikes for €13/20/50 per day/24 hours/week (€20/25/70 for mountain bikes).

Local Transport
Central Helsinki is easy enough to get around on foot or by bicycle, but there's also a metro line and a reasonably comprehensive tram, bus and train network. A one-hour flat-fare ticket for the bus, tram, metro, Suomenlinna ferry and local trains within Helsinki's **HKL network** (www.hel2.fi/HKL) costs €2 from a ticket machine (€2.20 from a tram driver). It allows un-

limited transfers but should be validated in the stamping machine on board when you first use it.

One-/three-/five-day tourist tickets cost €6/12/18. The Helsinki Card gets you free travel anywhere within Helsinki (see Information, p149). The city's green-and-yellow trams are a fun way to get around – tram No 3T from the kauppatori makes for a good sightseeing trip. The metro is also useful for getting to Kallio (Hakaniemi or Sörnäinen).

There are also regional tickets for travel by bus or train to neighbouring cities such as Vantaa and Espoo which cost €3.50 for a single one-hour ticket, or €10/20/30 for 1/3/5 days. Children's tickets are usually half-price.

The *Helsinki Route Map*, available at HKL offices and the city tourist office, is good for making sense of local transport.

AROUND HELSINKI
If your time is short but you want to see a bit of Finland outside the capital, there are a number of easy day trips. The most rewarding is Porvoo, 50km to the east, but if you're interested in the lives of some of Finland's great artists, Espoo and the Museum Rd are worth a look.

Espoo
☎ 09 / pop 221,600
Helsinki's fast-growing, high population satellite city of Espoo is easily reached by bus and train from the capital and offers enough to warrant a long day-trip.

For anyone interested in Finnish art, the big-ticket attraction here is the amazing **Gallen-Kallela Museum** (☎ 541 3388; www.gallen-kallela.fi; Gallen-Kallelantie 27; adult/child €8/4; ☽ 10am-6pm May-Aug, 10am-4pm Tue-Sat, 10am-5pm Sun Sep-Apr), the pastiche studio-castle of Akseli Gallen-Kallela, one of Finland's most notable painters. The Art Nouveau building was designed by the artist and is now a rich museum of his work and life. To get there take tram No 4 from central Helsinki to Munkkiniemi, then walk about 2km, alternatively take bus No 33 (on Saturdays and Sundays only).

Finland is big on indoor pools and spas, but Espoo's **Serena Water Park** (☎ 8870 5555; www.serena.fi/; Tornimäentie 10; day pass €17-19; ☽ 11am-8pm) is the best, with indoor and

FINLAND

outdoor pools, spas, saunas, water-slides and even a winter ski centre. It's pricey but great for families.

Porvoo

☎ 019 / pop 46,000

If you only make one day-trip out of Helsinki, the charming medieval town of Porvoo (known as Borgå in Swedish), 50km away, should be it. This town is Finland's second-oldest settlement (founded in 1346) after Turku. Although the 'new' town centre is drably modern, the distinctly Swedish, cobbled **Old Town**, with its charmingly atmospheric wooden houses, meandering streets and active riverfront is great for exploring.

The **tourist office** (☎ 520 2316; www.porvoo.fi; Rihkamakatu 4; ⏲ 9am-6pm Mon-Fri, 10am-4pm Sat & Sun Jun-Aug, 9.30am-4.30pm Mon-Fri, 10am-2pm Sat & Sun Sep-May; ▣), on the southern edge the Old Town, has plenty of information and a free internet terminal.

SIGHTS

The historic stone and timber **Porvoo cathedral** (⏲ 10am-6pm Mon-Fri, 10am-2pm Sat, 2-5pm Sun May-Sep, 10am-2pm Tue-Sat, 2-4pm Sun Oct-Apr) sits atop a hill looking over the quaint old town. In the small Old Town square, the **Porvoo Historical Museum** (☎ 574 7500; adult/child €5/1; ⏲ 10am-4pm Mon-Sat, 11am-4pm Sat May-Aug, 11am-4pm Wed-Sun Sep-Apr) is housed in two buildings and is packed with local memorabilia, furniture, jewellery and art, including paintings by Albert Edelfelt and sculptures by Ville Vallgren, two of Porvoo's most famous artists. Crossing the old bridge to the west bank of the Porvoonjoki provides a fantastic view of the photogenic, rust-red **shore houses** lining the river bank. These houses were first painted with red ochre to impress the visiting King of Sweden, Gustavus III, in the late 18th century.

On the south side of Porvoo in the Russian-built 19th-century 'Empire quarter', is **Runeberg House** (☎ 582 330; adult/child €5/2; ⏲ 10am-4pm Mon-Sun May-Aug, 10am-4pm Wed-Sun Sep-Apr), the well-preserved, beautiful home of Finland's national poet JL Runeberg. The adjacent **Walter Runeberg Sculpture Museum**, containing 150 sculptures by the poet's son, can be visited on the same ticket.

SLEEPING & EATING

Porvoo Hostel (☎ 523 0012; www.porvoohostel.cjb .net; Linnankoskenkatu 1-3; dm/s/d €15/28/36, linen hire €4) Porvoo's HI hostel, a 10-minute walk southeast of the old town, is in a lovely old building with spotless rooms and a well-equipped kitchen. Reception is closed between 10am and 4pm.

Gasthaus Werneri (☎ 0400-494 876; www .werneri.net in Finnish; Adlercreutzinkatu 29; s/d/tr €35/50/75) This cosy family-run guesthouse, located about 1km east of the old town, is excellent value with just five rooms (shared bathrooms) and a self-contained apartment.

Although there are plenty of places to eat in the new part of town, especially around the kauppatori (market square), Porvoo's most atmospheric cafés, restaurants and bars are in the Old Town and along the riverfront. In summer, the terraces along cobblestoned Välikatu are overflowing with visitors.

Restaurant Timbaali (☎ 523 1020; Välikatu 8; mains €10-24; ⏲ 11am-11pm May-Aug, shorter hrs winter) In the heart of the Old Town, this rustic restaurant is all about escargot – the speciality is locally farmed snails prepared in a variety of innovative ways. There's also a broad menu of gourmet Finnish cuisine, served in quaint dining rooms or the inner courtyard.

Porvoon Paahtimo (☎ 617 040; Mannerheiminkatu 2; ⏲ noon-10pm Mon-Thu, noon-2am Fri, 11-2am Sat, noon-10pm Sun) Right at the main bridge and with a great little terrace hanging over the water, this atmospheric red-brick former storehouse is part cosy bar and part café – fresh coffee is roasted here.

GETTING THERE & AWAY

The bus station is on the kauppatori; buses run every half-hour between Porvoo and Helsinki (€8.40, one hour), but the best way to reach Porvoo in summer is by ferry.

The historic steamship **JL Runeberg** (☎ 019-524 3331; www.msjlruneberg.fi; one way/return €21/31) sails daily at 10am from Helsinki in summer (exact dates vary), returning at 4pm. **Royal Line** (☎ 09-612 2950; www.royalline .fi; one way/return €21/32) has three-hour cruises on a more modern boat between Helsinki and Porvoo daily except Monday from June to mid-August.

SOUTH COAST

The south coast of Finland meanders east and west of Helsinki, revealing harbour towns, marinas, islands and farmland. This is something of a summer playground for Finnish families, with a handful of fading resort towns and the pretty bays, beaches and convoluted islands and waterways of the southern archipelago. Medieval churches, old manors and castles show the strong influence of early Swedish settlers.

TURKU

☎ 02 / pop 175,000

If a city is, as they say, defined by water, then Turku's heart and soul is undoubtedly the lovely Aurajoki (Aura River), a broad ribbon spilling into the Baltic Sea harbour and lined with riverboat bars and restaurants. Turku is Finland's oldest town, but today it's a modern maritime city, brimming with museums and boasting a robust harbourside castle and magnificent cathedral.

For travellers, Turku is one of Finland's most visited cities after Helsinki, thanks to the direct ferries from Stockholm, and this is the place to catch a ferry to the Åland islands or the base for exploring the west coast or southern archipelago.

Once the capital under the Swedes, Turku (Swedish: Åbo) was founded as a Catholic settlement in 1229, and grew into an important trading centre despite being ravaged by fire many times.

Information

DISCOUNT CARDS

Turku Card (24/48hrs €21/28) Gives free admission to most museums and attractions in the region, free public transport, and various other discounts. Available from the tourist office or any participating attraction.

INTERNET ACCESS

Hansa Cyber Café (Hansa Arcade; per min 4c; ☯ 9am-9pm Mon-Fri, 10am-9pm Sat & Sun) Coin-op terminals.

Public Library (☎ 262 3611; Linnankatu 2; ☯ 10am-8pm Mon-Thu, 10am-6pm Fri, 10am-3pm Sat) Free internet access.

Surf City (Aninkaistenkatu 3; per 30 min €1.20; ☯ 3pm-midnight)

MONEY

Forex (☎ 251 0800; Eerikinkatu 12; ☯ 8am-7pm Mon-Fri, 8am-5pm Sat) Exchange bureau on the south side of the kauppatori (market square).

POST

Post Office (☎ 0200-71000; Humalistonkatu 1; ☯ 9am-8pm Mon-Fri)

TOURIST INFORMATION

Turku City Tourist Office (☎ 262 7444; www.turkutouring.fi; Aurakatu 4; ☯ 8.30am-6pm Mon-Fri, 9am-4pm Sat & Sun) Internet access, bike hire, accommodation and information.

Sights & Activities

A great way to soak up Turku's summertime vibe is simply to walk or cycle along the river bank between the cathedral and the castle, crossing via bridges or the much-loved local

FINLAND

WORTH A DETOUR

With your own transport, the tiny but impossibly picturesque village of **Ruotsinpyhtä,** just off highway E18, is a glimpse into Finland's industrial past. At its heart are the quaint brick buildings of the 18th-century *bruk*, the **Strömfors Iron Works**, which is now a museum. The Kyma river became the Swedish–Russian international border in 1743, splitting the village in half.

In the old forge building in the centre of the village is a **café** (☯ 10am-6pm Jun-Aug, 8am-4pm Sep-May), and there's an **information centre** (☎ 618 474) at the nearby hostel. As well as wandering around the ironworks, there's a walking trail circling the lake and you can rent canoes and rowing boats.

Finnhostel Krouvinmäki (☎ 618 474; s/d €26/52; ☯ reception 8am-4pm Mon-Fri) is a wonderful hostel in a renovated former tavern house (1805) opposite the forge buildings. It offers cosy twin rooms (no bunks) and there's a good kitchen and laundry. Call ahead if you're visiting on the weekend.

Ravintola Ruukinmylly (☎ 618 693; pizza & pasta €4.50-9, mains €11.50-19; ☯ 11am-midnight Mon-Thu & Sun, 11-2am Fri & Sat May-Aug), in a 17th-century former mill on a lovely pond, is a rustic restaurant with wood-fired pizzas and some Finnish specialities, including creamy salmon soup.

www.lonelyplanet.com

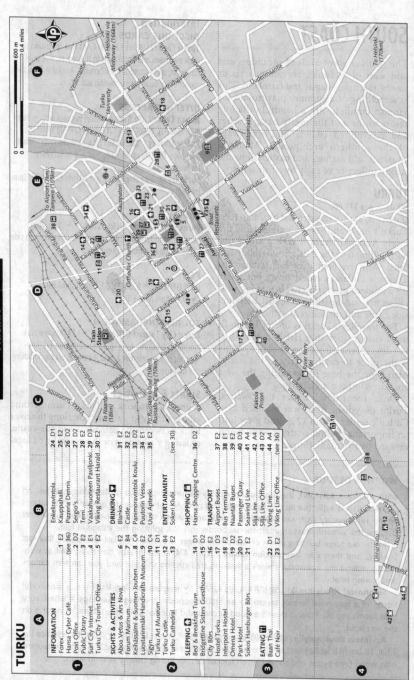

TURKU

pedestrian ferry *(föri)* – pick up a walking tour brochure from the tourist office.

A visit to the lofty **Turku Castle** (☎ 262 0300; Linnankatu 80; adult/child €6/3.50, guided tours €1.50; ☻ 10am-6pm mid-Apr–mid-Sep, 10am-3pm Tue-Sun mid-Sep–mid-Apr), near the harbour, should be your first stop. Founded in 1280 at the mouth of the Aurajoki, the castle has been rebuilt a number of times since. Notable occupants have included Count Per Brahe, founder of many towns in Finland, and Sweden's King Eric XIV, who was imprisoned in the castle's Round Tower in the late 16th century, having been declared insane. Guided tours of the stronghold area are given in English hourly between 11am and 4pm, but do not include the Renaissance rooms on the upper floor, or the extensive museums in the bailey section of the castle, so allow time to explore those yourself.

The open-air **Luostarinmäki Handicrafts Museum** (☎ 262 0350; Luostarinmäki; adult/student & child €4/2; ☻ 10am-6pm mid-Apr–mid-Sep, 10am-3pm Tue-Sun mid-Sep–mid-Apr), in the only surviving 18th-century area of this medieval town, is one of the best of its kind in Finland. In summer artisans work inside its 40 old wooden houses and musicians stroll its paths.

Forum Marinum (☎ 282 9511; www.forum-mari num.fi; Linnankatu 72; adult/child €12/7; ☻ 11am-7pm May-Sep, 10am-6pm Tue-Sun Oct-Apr) is an impressive maritime museum near Turku Castle. As well as a nautically crammed exhibition space devoted to Turku's shipping background, it incorporates three **museum ships**: the mine layer **Keihässalmi**, the three-masted barque **Sigyn** and the impressive 1902 sailing ship **Suomen Joutsen** (Swan of Finland). The ships can be visited independently of the museum for adult/child €5/3, or the museum alone is adult/child €7/4.

The **Aboa Vetus & Ars Nova** (☎ 250 0552; www .aboavetusarsnova.fi/; Itäinen Rantakatu 4-6; adult/student/child €8/7/5.50; ☻ 11am-7pm Apr–mid-Sep, closed Mon mid-Sep–Apr), two museums under the one roof in the Rettig Palace, are respectively an archaeological exhibition and a modern art collection. The fascinating archaeological museum features a slice of medieval Turku – a section of buried streets and housing uncovered during restoration work. In summer there are free guided tours daily at 11.30am and 1.30pm.

The **Turku Art Museum** (☎ 262 7100; www .turuntaidemuseo.fi; Aurakatu 26; adult/child €6/3.50; ☻ 11am-7pm Tue-Fri, 11am-5pm Sat & Sun) houses some of Finland's finest artworks.

The commanding **Turku Cathedral** (☎ 261 7100; Tuomiokirkkokatu 20; ☻ 9am-7pm, to 8pm in summer), dating from the 13th century, is the national shrine and 'mother church' of the Evangelical-Lutheran Church of Finland. Services in English are held every Sunday at 4pm and in summer there are music recitals on Tuesdays and Wednesdays. In the south gallery of the cathedral is a small **museum** (adult/child €2/1) containing church relics and artworks.

Archipelago cruises are popular in summer, with daily departures from Martinsilta bridge at the passenger quay. The best option is the two-hour cruise out to Naantali aboard the steamship **SS Ukkopekka** (☎ 515 3300; www.ukkopekka.fi; one way/return €15/20; ☻ 10am & 2pm Jun-Aug). The same boat also has an evening dinner cruise with buffet meal on Loistokari island from €28.

Festivals & Events

Big events on the Turku calendar include the **Turku Music Festival** in the second week in August and **Ruisrock**, Finland's oldest rock festival, held on Ruissalo island in early July.

Sleeping

BUDGET

Ruissalo Camping (☎ 262 5100; camp sites €12, 2-/4-/5-person r €30/60/80; ☻ Jun-late Aug) Popular camping area on Ruissalo island, 10km west of the city centre. There are no cabins, but there is a villa with comfortable rooms. Take bus No 8 from kauppatori.

Hostel Turku (☎ 262 7680; hostel@turku.fi; Linnankatu 39; dm/s/d €15/35/40, linen hire €4.70; ☻ reception 6-10am & 3pm-midnight) Well located on the river close to the town centre, this warren of rooms is one of the busiest HI hostels in Finland. Well-equipped kitchen, laundry, lockers and bike hire.

Interpoint Hostel (☎ 231 4011; interpoint .hostel@pp.inet.fi; Vähä-Hämeenkatu 12a; dm €8.50, d €21; ☻ 15 Jul-15 Aug) At the Turku YMCA, it's open for one month and is the cheapest place to stay in Turku. It's cheerful and good fun if you don't mind a mattress on the floor and queuing for the solitary shower.

MIDRANGE

Bed & Breakfast Tuure (☎ 233 0230; tuure@netti.fi; Tuureporinkatu 17C; s/d with shared bathroom €37/50; ☲) Don't be fooled by the 'apartment block' façade and dull location, Tuure is a secure, friendly guesthouse close to the bus station, and the best value in town. Bright rooms have shared bathrooms and a good buffet breakfast is served.

Bridgettine Sisters Guesthouse (☎ 250 1910; www.kolumbus.fi/birgitta.turku; Ursininkatu 15A; s/d €42/61; ℗) This clean, simple B&B guesthouse run by the nuns of a Catholic convent is a haven of peace, without being too officious – silence is expected around the corridors and reception areas after 10pm.

Omena Hotel (www.omena.com; Humalistonkatu 7; r €55) In a refurbished Alvar Aalto–designed building, the Omena is a staff-free hotel where you book and pay over the internet (possible even same day) and use a code to get in (access after 4pm). As with others in the chain, the rooms are the quality of hotels twice this price and can sleep up to four if you use the sofa bed.

TOP END

Park Hotel (☎ 273 2555; www.parkhotelturku.fi; Rauhankatu 1; s/d €115/145, s/d weekends & summer €90/120, ste €240; ℗ ✗) All the rooms in this lovely 1902 Art Nouveau building are individually decorated and exquisitely furnished, making this Turku's most romantic hotel by a long shot – check out the top-floor rooms. There's a billiard lounge and tranquil garden.

Sokos Hamburger Börs (☎ 337 381; www.sokos hotels.fi; Kauppiaskatu 6; s/d €129/148, weekends & summer €96; ℗ ☲ ✗ 🖥) This enormous business hotel overlooking the market square is popular for its location alone but it is also packed with facilities including a pool, a whole floor of saunas, functional rooms and a veritable smorgasbord of bars, cafés and restaurants at street level (it is a free wi-fi hotspot).

City Börs (Eerikinkatu 11) Across the road from Sokos is this slightly cheaper sister hotel.

Eating

In summer you can dine in style on the water aboard one of a number of boat restaurants lining the Aurajoki river (see opposite for information).

Vaakahuoneen Paviljonki (☎ 515 3300; Linnankatu 38; mains €7-18, fish buffet €9; ⏲ 11am-10pm May-Aug) This riverfront jazz restaurant is the place to go for great-value food and entertainment in summer. As well as an á la carte menu there's a daily 'archipelago fish buffet' (June to August), plus a changing ethnic buffet such as Thai, Vietnamese and Indian, all served to foot-tapping live trad jazz bands. Recommended.

Enkeliravintola (☎ 231 8088; Kauppiaskatu 16; mains €8-22; ⏲ 1-11pm Tue-Sat, 1-7pm Sun) You can't help feeling the celestial presence in the 'angel restaurant', an atmospheric old café and dinner restaurant serving thoughtfully prepared Finnish cuisine.

Café Noir (☎ 233 2918; Eerikinkatu 8; mains €5-10.50; ⏲ 11am-10pm) It's not flash but this unpretentious first-floor diner and bar is a local classic and one of Turku's cheapest for light meals such as pasta, meatballs and omelettes.

Pizzeria Dennis (☎ 469 1191; Linnankatu 17; dishes €8-15; ⏲ 11am-11.30pm Mon-Thu, 11am-mid Fri & Sat, 12.30-11pm Sun) With its warren of cosy rooms adorned with Chianti bottles and strings of garlic, this place has genuine Italian flavour, innovative slants on pizza, and food that's a cut above most Finnish pizza and pasta restaurants.

Sergio's (☎ 233 0033; Läntinen Rantakatu 27; mains €8.50-21.50; ⏲ 11am-11pm Mon-Fri, 1-11pm Sat) Get a room by the window in this lovely old riverside restaurant. Fine Italian food and wines by candlelight, and tables out the front in summer.

Viking Restaurant Harald (☎ 276 5050; Aurakatu 3; mains €12-22; ⏲ 11am-midnight Mon-Thu, 11am-1am Fri, noon-1am Sat, 1-9pm Sun) This is a fun theme-restaurant where you get to mix with Norse warriors and eat with your hands. Naturally it's heavy on the meat – wild boar fillets and reindeer come served on Viking shields. There are three-course set menus from €28.

There are plenty of cheap eateries on and around Turku's bustling central kauppatori. The **Hansa Shopping Centre** (⏲ 7am-10pm Mon-Sat, 10am-10pm Sun), on the west side of the square has some inexpensive lunch cafés, as well as a supermarket and Alko store. The **kauppahalli** (Eerikinkatu 16; ⏲ 7am-5.30pm Mon-Fri, 7am-3pm Sat) is packed with produce, meat, a sushi bar, and a cool café in a converted train carriage.

Also recommended:

Baan Thai (☎ 233 8290; Kauppiaskatu 15; mains €7-12.50, lunch €6; ☻ 11am-9pm Mon-Thu, 11am-10pm Fri & Sat, noon-9pm Sun) Authentic spicy Thai food with great-value lunch specials.

Teini (☎ 233 0203; Uudenmaankatu 1; mains €10-20; ☻ lunch & dinner) Local institution for traditional Finnish cuisine.

Drinking & Entertainment

In summer the heart of Turku's nightlife scene is along the river. The evening usually begins on the decks of any of half a dozen boats lining the south bank of the river. Although most of these also serve food, they are primarily floating beer terraces with music and lots of shipboard socialising.

If the €5 pints make you wince, first join the hard-up locals gathering on the grassy river bank drinking takeaway alcohol.

Blanko (☎ 233 3966; Aurakatu 1; ☻ 11am-midnight Mon-Tue, 11-2am Wed-Thu, 11-4am Fri, noon-4am Sat, noon-midnight Sun) This ultrachic café by the main bridge is where Turku's hip young things get down to DJs on weekend nights; great sidewalk terrace and excellent tapas and light meals.

Castle (☎ 230 2886; Eerikinkatu 6; ☻ 11-3am) Turku's newest pub is fast gaining a local following. Like all Irish pubs, the emphasis is on fun, live music and an international beer list with Irish stouts on tap.

Turku also has some of Finland's most eccentric bars – try these for an offbeat pub crawl.

Puutorin Vessa (☎ 233 8123; Puutori; ☻ noon-midnight) In the middle of a small square near the bus terminal, this novel bar was a public toilet in a former life – from 1933 to 1968. Toilet humour and memorabilia adorns the walls and you can even have your drink in a tin potty.

Uusi Apteeki (☎ 250 2595; Kaskenkatu 1; ☻ 10-3am) This characterful bar was once an old pharmacy; the antique shelving and desks have been retained, but they are filled with hundreds of old beer bottles.

Panimoravintola Koulu (☎ 274 575; Eerikinkatu 18; lunch buffet €5.50-7.70; mains €10.20-16; ☻ 11am-midnight Mon-Fri, noon-midnight Sat) In an enormous former schoolhouse built in 1889, this is an upmarket restaurant, a brewery pub and wine bar serving good lunches. Creamy home-brewed stout on tap and a big beer garden.

Sokeri Klubi (☎ 276 5700; Aurakatu 3; ☻ 10am-4am) The 'Sugar Club' is popular with a young crowd. Turku's best young DJs and the place to be seen late into the night.

Getting There & Away

Finnair flies regularly to/from Helsinki to the Turku airport, 8km north of the city. **Blue1** (☎ 06000-25831; www.blue1.com) has direct flights to Copenhagen and Stockholm at very cheap internet fares.

From the main **bus terminal** (☎ 0200-4000; Aninkaistenkatu 20) there are hourly express buses to Helsinki (€25.70, 2½ hours), and frequent services to Tampere (€25.70, 2¾ hours), Rauma (€16.80, 1½ hours) and other points in southern Finland.

Express trains run from the **train station** (Ratapihankatu 37) to and from Helsinki (€25.60, two hours) and Tampere (€21, two hours). For Oulu and Rovaniemi you'll need to change in Tampere. There are direct train connections from Turku harbour to Helsinki. Bus No 30 shuttles between the centre and the train station.

Silja Line and Viking Line ferries sail from Stockholm (9½ hours) and Mariehamn (six hours). Seawind Line sails to Stockholm via Långnäs (Åland). All three have offices at the harbour, and Viking Line has an office in the Hansa shopping centre.

Getting Around

Bus No 1 runs to/from the airport and between the centre (€2, 25 minutes). This same bus also goes from kauppatori to the harbour.

The city and regional bus services (both gold and blue buses) are frequent and cost €2 for a single journey or €4.50 for a 24-hour ticket.

Bikes can be hired from the city tourist office for €10/50 per day/week.

AROUND TURKU
Naantali

☎ 02 / pop 13,500

Naantali, 13km from Turku, is one of Finland's loveliest seaside towns, with its gorgeous horseshoe harbour, but that can sometimes be lost on the hordes of Finnish families descending on the star attraction, the extraordinarily popular **Moomin World** theme park (☎ 511 1111; www.muumimaailma.fi; day pass €17; ☻ 10am-6pm Jun–mid-Aug). It's a sort of Disneyland based on the popular children's books written by Tove Janssen and set on an island linked to the mainland by a footbridge.

The village was developed after the founding of a convent in the 1440s. Today the harbour, lined with cafés and restaurants, the delightful cobbled **Old Town** and the huge **Convent Church** are enough incentive for a day trip here from Turku. Outside the tourist summer season, Naantali is practically deserted. Tourist information is available at **Naantali Tourist Service** (☎ 435 9800; www.naantalinmatkailu.fi, Kaivotori 2; ☺ 9am-6pm Mon-Fri, 10am-3pm Sat & Sun Jun–mid-Aug, 9am-4.30pm Mon-Fri mid-Aug–May) near the harbour.

Kulturanta (adult/child €6/4; ☺ guided tour 3pm Tue-Sun 29 Jun-15 Aug), the summer residence of the president of Finland, is a fanciful stone castle on nearby Luonnonmaa island, surrounded by a 56 hectare estate with beautiful, formal rose gardens. It can only be visited by guided tour; book through the tourist office.

SLEEPING & EATING

Although an easy day trip from Turku, spending a night in Naantali is a good way to beat the crowds and the town has some of southern Finland's loveliest guesthouses.

Villa Antonius (☎ 435 1938; Mannerheiminkatu 9; s/d €85/120) In the heart of the old town, Antonius is a romantic boutique B&B with a variety of rooms decked out with historical memorabilia and furnishings. Downstairs is a charming old-world café with light meals, mouth-watering sweets and the house speciality, home-made gingerbread.

Naantali Spa Hotel (☎ 44 550; www.naantalispa .fi; Matkailijantie 2; s/d €127/152) For the last word in pampering, this spa hotel is ranked one of the best in Finland. Luxurious rooms, exotic restaurants, awesome spa and health facilities and there's even a stationary cruise ship docked outside where you can stay in luxury shipboard cabins. It's like something out of Monte Carlo! If this is too much for the budget, nonguests can use the spa and pool facilities for €10 for two hours.

Merisali (☎ 435 2477; Nunnakatu 1; buffet breakfast/lunch/dinner €7/9.50/11.50, Sun lunch €13.50) Just below the Convent Church, this iconic restaurant in an old waterfront spa pavilion has a shaded terrace and a mind-blowing smorgasbord for lunch and dinner, including lavish seafood and salads – pack an appetite!

GETTING THERE & AWAY

There are buses every 15 minutes from Turku's market square (€3.70, 20 minutes), and in summer the steamship *Ukkopekka* cruises between Turku and Naantali several times daily (see p167).

HANKO

☎ 019 / pop 10,600

With its grand wooden Russian villas, sweep of beach and bustling marina, Hanko (otherwise known as Hangö) is easily the pick of Finland's south coast resorts. The town blossomed as a spa resort in the late 19th and early 20th centuries, when it was a popular and glamorous summer retreat for Russian nobles and artists. These cashed-up holidaymakers built lofty wooden villas on the sandy shore east of the harbour and with several of them now converted into charming guesthouses, they continue to attract tourists with a taste for the romantic.

The **tourist office** (☎ 220 3411; www.hanko.fi; Raatihuoneentori 5; ☺ 9am-8pm Mon-Fri, 10am-6pm Sat & Sun Jun-Jul, 9am-5pm Mon-Fri, 10am-6pm Sat & Sun Aug, 8am-4pm Mon-Fri Sep-May) can help with tourist information and the myriad summer activities in town.

Sleeping & Eating

Villa Tellina (☎ 248 6356; www.tellina.com in Finnish; Appelgrenintie 1-2; s/d from €60/80, d with bathroom €100; ☺ Jun–mid-Aug) This quaint but slightly ramshackle villa is close to the beach and town centre. The same owners run two other places, Villa Thalatta and Villa Eva, so this is a good first choice when it's busy.

Villa Doris (☎ 248 1228; Appelgrenintie 23; s/d from €55/85) This stylish Russian B&B dating from 1881 is in the area known as Spa Park. Rooms with shared bathroom are fitted with antique furniture.

Villa Maija (☎ 248 2900; www.villamaija.fi; Appelgrenintie7; s/d from €80/99) Maija is another outstanding 19th-century timber house with loads of Imperial character. The newer rooms have bathrooms and those with sea views have superb glassed-in verandahs or balconies.

Across from the East Harbour is a string of excellent restaurant-bars in converted wooden storehouses, most specialising in seafood, but also pizza and pasta.

Getting There & Away

There are regular daily express buses to/from Helsinki (€22.10, 2¼ hours) and two locals buses from Turku (€20.50, 3½ hours). The train from Helsinki (€20.20, two hours) requires a change to a local train or bus at Karjaa.

Superfast Ferries (www.superfast.com) has a daily international service between Rostock (Germany) and Hanko, departing from Hanko's West Harbour at 9pm (10am on Sunday). The journey takes about 24 hours and costs from €87 one way for a seat only.

ÅLAND

☎ 018 / pop 26,300

The Åland islands comprise a stunning archipelago stretching west like a string of emeralds from the Finnish mainland to within less than 100km of Sweden.

As flat and green as a billiard table (well, maybe not that flat), these islands are made for cycling in the summertime. Ribbons of bicycle paths crisscross the islands, linked by bridges or good old-fashioned ferries, and along the way you'll pass medieval parish churches, ancient ruins and undisturbed fishing villages. Some islands are so remote and pastoral you'll feel like you've stepped back in time. With plenty of camping grounds and guesthouses, you can easily spend a week or more of cycle touring here, and distances between places of interest are mercifully short.

The islands themselves have a fascinating historical and political background. The autonomous, self-governed islands have their own flag, stamps and culture, which leans more to Sweden than to Finland – several Swedish dialects are spoken but few Ålanders speak Finnish. This situation goes back to a League of Nations' decision in 1921 after a Swedish-Finnish dispute over sovereignty. Åland took its own flag in 1954 and has issued stamps (prized by collectors) since 1984. Although Åland joined the EU along with Finland in 1995, it was granted a number of exemptions, including duty-free tax laws which allowed the essential ferry services between the islands and mainland Finland and Sweden to continue operating profitably.

Information

The main tourist office is **Åland Tourist Information** (☎ 24000; www.visitaland.com; Storagatan 8; ✦ 9am-6pm Jun-Aug, 9am-4pm Mon-Fri Sep-May, 10am-3pm Sat Oct-Apr) in Mariehamn. For accommodation bookings, **Ålandsresor** (☎ 28040; www.alandsresor.fi; Torggatan 2) and **Destination Åland** (☎ 0403-008001; www.destinationaland.com; Elverksgatan 5) in Mariehamn handle hotel, guesthouse and cottage bookings for the entire island.

In emergencies call ☎ 112, for police ☎ 10022 and for medical services ☎ 10023.

Getting There & Away

AIR

Finnair (☎ 634500) runs a direct service to/from Stockholm on weekdays and a daily service to/from Helsinki via Turku. **Air Åland** (☎ 117 110; Elverksgatan 10; www.airaland.com), a new company, also has daily flights from Mariehamn to Helsinki (from €44, two hours) and weekday flights to Sweden (€145, 30 minutes). The airport is 4km north of Mariehamn and there's a connecting bus service.

BOAT

The main companies operating between the Finnish mainland and Åland (and on to Sweden) are **Viking Line** (☎ 26011; www.vikingline.fi; Storagatan 2) and **Silja Line** (☎ 16711; www.silja.fi; Torggatan 14). **Eckerö Line** (☎ 28300; www.eckerolinjen.fi; Torggatan 2) and **Birka Cruises** (☎ 27027; www.birkaline.com; Esplanadgatan 7) operate only between Åland and Sweden.

Viking and Silja lines have daily ferries to Mariehamn from Turku (low/high season from €14/23 one way, six hours) and night ferries from Helsinki (low/high season from €24/38) as part of their links with Stockholm. Viking Line also has a ferry between Mariehamn and Kapellskär in Sweden, with bus connections to Stockholm. Eckerö Line sails from Grisslehamn to Eckerö (low/high season from €8.90/5.50, two hours).

Another alternative, if you have the time, are the smaller local ferries that ply the waters from minor Finnish ports to the remote northern and southern archipelago islands of Åland. Free travel for pedestrians and cyclists is possible from mainland Finland via Korppoo (southern route, from Galtby passenger harbour) or Kustavi (northern route, from Osnäs passenger harbour), but only if you break your journey to stay on one or more islands.

FINLAND

www.lonelyplanet.com

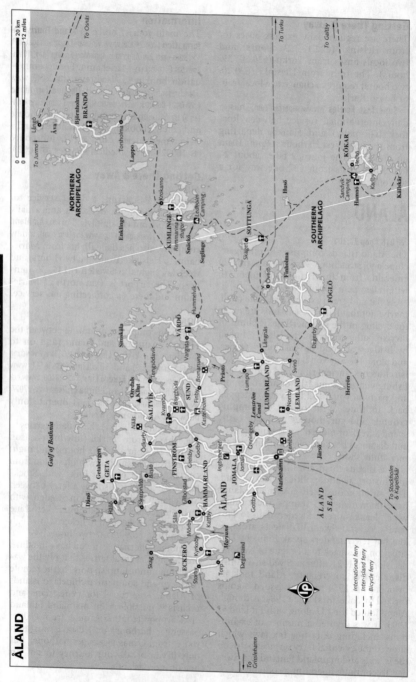

ÅLAND

FINLAND

Legend

International ferry
Inter-island ferry
Bicycle ferry

20 km
12 miles

To Osnäs

To Turku

To Galtby

NORTHERN ARCHIPELAGO

To Jurmo

Långö
Åva
Björnholma
BRÄNDÖ
Torsholma
Lappo
Krokamo
KUMLINGE
Rehmarina Stugor
Snäckö
Seglinge
SÖTTUNGA
Skagö
Enklinge

Hummelvik
Husö
KÖKAR
Sandvik Camping
Hamnö Hellsö
Kaitby
Källskär

SOUTHERN ARCHIPELAGO

Överö
Finholma
FÖGLÖ
Degerby

Simskäla
VÅRDÖ
Vargata
Vangata

Tängsödavik
Öfvrdas
Klint
SALTVIK
Kvarnbo
Bergböla
SUND
Finby
Bomarsund
Kastelholm
Prästö
Långnäs
LUMPARLAND
Lumpo
Svinö
Herrön

Näås
Ödkarby
FINSTRÖM
Grelsby
Godby
Ingby
HAMMARLAND
Pålsböle
Ulfsbystad
Kattby
Morby
Sälis
Marsund
ÅLAND
Gottby
Jomala
Jomalby
JOMALA
Önningeby
Lemström Canal
Lemböte
LEMLAND
Norrby
Järsö

Gulf of Bothnia

Getabergen
GETA
Skarpnåtö
Bastö
Dånö
Hällö

Mariehamn
Mariehamn

ÅLAND SEA

To Stockholm & Kapellskär

Skag
ECKERÖ
Storby
Kyrkoby
Torp
Degersand

To Grisslehamn

Getting Around

BICYCLE

Cycling is the most rewarding way to explore the islands. Some of the main roads have clearly marked separate bike lanes and many of the back roads are virtually traffic-free. You can cover a lot of ground on the main islands in two or three days and with a week or so it's possible to explore as far as the northern and southern archipelagos. **Ro-No Rent** (☎ 018-12 820, 0400-529 315) rents bicycles at Mariehamn and Eckerö harbours for a day/week starting from €7/35 (€13/65 for a mountain bike, and €17/85 for a tandem bike). It also rents boats, canoes, scooters and beach buggies.

BUS

Five main bus lines depart from Mariehamn's regional bus terminal on Torggatan opposite the library. No 1 goes to Hammarland and Eckerö; No 2 to Godby and Geta; No 3 to Godby and Saltvik; No 4 to Godby, Sund and Vårdö (Hummelvik); and No 5 to Lemland and Lumparland (Långnäs).

BOAT

Ferries are constantly plying the shorter straits and are free. For longer routes, ferries run according to schedule and carry cars, bikes and pedestrians.

There are also three bicycle ferries in summer (€6 to €9 with bicycle). For timetables and car-ferry fares, ask at the tourist office or **Ålandstrafiken** (☎ 018-25155; Strandgatan 25, Mariehamn).

MARIEHAMN

☎ 018 / pop 11,000

Mariehamn is Åland's main port and capital, a town of broad avenues lined with linden trees and timber houses set between two large harbours. Coming from Finland, this is the obvious starting point for any tour of the islands. In summer it buzzes with tourists but still manages to retain its village flavour, and the marinas at the East and West harbours are quite pretty when loaded up with gleaming sailing boats. The main pedestrian street, Torggatan, is a colourful and crowded hive of activity, and there are some fine museums – enough to allow a leisurely day's exploration. Outside the summer season you could safely fire a cannon through the town.

Orientation & Information

Mariehamn lies on a peninsula and has two harbours, Västra Hamnen (West Harbour), where the ferries pull in, and Östra Hamnen (East Harbour).

The **tourist office** (☎ 24000; www.visitaland .com; Storagatan 8; ☼ 9am-6pm Jun-Aug, 9am-4pm Mon-Fri Sep-May, 10am-3pm Sat Oct-Apr; ☐), on the main Esplanade, has free internet access and plenty of information on the islands. The **library** (☎ 531 441; Strandgatan; ☼ 10am-8pm Mon-Fri, 11am-4pm Sat) also has free internet access.

The **main post office** (☎ 6360; Torggatan 4; ☼ Mon-Sat) sells collectible Åland postage stamps and changes money.

Sights & Activities

The fine **Ålands Museum & Åland Art Museum** (☎ 25426; Stadhusparken; adult/child €3/2; ☼ 11am-6pm Jun-Aug, 10am-8pm Tue & Thu, 10am-4pm Wed & Fri, noon-4pm Sat & Sun Sep-May), housed together in the same building near the market square, gives an absorbing account of Åland's history and culture, from prehistory to the present, with displays on local music, seafaring, wildlife and festivals. The art museum features a permanent collection of works by Åland artists as well as changing exhibitions.

The stalwarts of Åland are mariners and the best place to get a feel for their exploits is down at the West Harbour. The **Maritime Museum** (☎ 19930; Hamngatan 2; adult/child €5/3; ☼ 9am-5pm May-Jun & Aug, 9am-7pm Jul, 10am-4pm Sep-Apr, noon-4pm Sat & Sun mid-Jan–Apr) is a wonderfully kitsch museum of fishing and maritime commerce and ship figureheads. The central feature of the museum is a re-creation of a ship with mast, saloon, galley and cabins. Anchored outside is the real thing – the museum ship **Pommern** (☎ 531 421; adult/child €4.50/3.50), a beautifully preserved four-masted barque built in Glasgow in 1903. The audio guide (€3.50) can help bring the old ship to life. A combined ticket to the ship and museum is €8/5.

Over at the East Harbour, **Sjökvarteret** (Maritime Quarter; ☎ 16033; www.sjokvarteret.com; adult/child €4/free; ☼ 10am-6pm daily mid-Jun–mid-Aug, 9-11am Mon-Fri mid-Aug–mid-Jun) is a marina, boat-building yard and museum with exhibitions on shipbuilding, craft workshops and a café.

If you want to get out on the water in style, the traditional wooden schooner

FINLAND

Linden (☎ 12055; www.linden.aland.fi) has four-hour lunch (€39) and dinner (€49) cruises daily in July. You can also try your hand at sailing through courses run by the **Åland Sailing Club** (☎ 040-724 5797; Västra Hamnen).

Sleeping

Rates for Mariehamn's hotels and guest-houses peak in July and August, but expect some hefty discounts outside the summer season.

Gröna Uddens Camping (☎ 21121; www.gronaudden.com; Osternäsvägen; camp sites per person/tent €5/5; 2-/4-person cabins from €50/80; ☀ May-Sep; P) In a beachside park 1km south of town, Mariehamn's camping ground has tent and van sites, newly built cabins, bike and canoe rental and saunas on the water's edge.

Gästhem Kronan (☎ 12617; Neptunigatan 52; s/d €41/62; P ✕) Mariehamn has no hostels, but Kronan is a good-value guesthouse with basic but spotless, renovated rooms with shared bathroom. It's in a quiet street a short walk from the ferry terminal. Rooms are discounted outside the June–August high season. The welcoming owners also have another summer-only guesthouse, **Gästhem Neptun** (Neptunigatan 41; s/d €46/67) in the same street, with a better standard of rooms.

Park Alandia Hotel (☎ 14130; Norra Esplanadgatan 3; s/d €80/100; P 🖳) The Park is a modern, comfortable hotel on Mariehamn's main boulevard. A range of modern rooms with TV – some with kitchenette and bathtub – are complemented by a small swimming pool and sauna. Rooms are a bargain on a Sunday when discounted to €60. There's a good restaurant, café and a lively terrace bar at the front.

Eating

Mariehamn has some good cafés and the most active nightlife (such as it is) on the islands. The pedestrian strip Torggatan and the Galleria shopping arcade running off it have several cafés and cheap lunch eateries.

Kaffestugan Svarta Katten (☎ 21599; Norragatan 15; ☀ 10am-5pm Mon-Fri, 11am-4pm Sat) The 'black cat' is a cosy old café and one of the best places to try the local speciality *Ålandspannkaka* (Åland pancakes), made with semolina and served with fruit and whipped cream.

Café Julius (Torggatan 10; ☀ 8am-5pm) On the pedestrian strip, this is another good café that opens early for breakfast.

Dino's Bar & Grill (☎ 13939; Strandgatan 12; mains €9-20; ☀ 10.30am-midnight Mon-Tue & Sun, 10.30-2am Wed-Thu, 10.30-4am Fri & Sat, kitchen till 9pm) Dino's is a popular, earthy pub and meeting spot with hearty pasta and pizza dishes, enormous hamburgers and a brilliant summer terrace in the side courtyard.

Mannechai (☎ 16727; Östra Hamnen; mains €9; ☀ 10.30am-8pm Mon-Thu, 11.30am-8pm Fri & Sat) On a refurbished boat in the East Harbour, this is Mariehamn's only Thai restaurant, serving authentic curries, soups and a salad bar.

Indigo (☎ 16550; Nygatan 1; mains €18.50-26; ☀ 5pm-midnight Mon-Sat, 3-11pm Sun, lunch 11am-3pm Mon-Fri) Mariehamn's most stylish restaurant is in an historic brick and timber building but the menu is contemporary Scandinavian.

FP von Knorring (Östra Hamnen) This boat restaurant has a great beer terrace for sunny afternoons.

AROUND THE ISLANDS
Finström & Sund
pop 950

About 20km north of Mariehamn, the small village of Godby makes a good first stop. A little way north in Grelsby is the island's only brewery, **Stallhagen** (☎ 48500; Getavägen 196), which you can tour Wednesday to Sunday at 2pm in July or by prior arrangement.

Crossing the bridge into the municipality of Sund brings you to Åland's most striking attraction, the medieval 14th-century **Kastelholm** (☎ 432 150; adult/child €5/3.50; ☀ 10am-5pm Jun & Aug, 10am-6pm Jul, 10am-4pm Mon-Fri May & Sep). The beautifully situated castle stronghold can be visited by a guided tour. Next to the castle, **Jan Karlsgarden Museum** (admission free; ☀ 10am-4pm May–mid-Sep, 10am-5pm Jun-Aug) is a typical open-air museum consisting of about 20 wooden buildings, including three windmills, transported here from around the archipelago.

Further east, the ruins of the Russian fortress at **Bomarsund** are accessible all year, as are the cemeteries on Prästö (Priest island). The impressive Russian fortifications date from the 1830s and were destroyed during the Crimean War (1853-56). Near Bomarsund, **Puttes Camping** (☎ 44016; camp site per person €3, cabins €29; ☀ May-Aug) is a large, well-equipped site with a beach sauna, minigolf and cabins.

Eckerö
pop 800

Finland's westernmost municipality, Eck-erö is all blonde hair and tanned bodies in summer, packed with holidaying Swed-ish families making the short hop across from Grisslehamn. The best beach is at **Degersand** in the south, but away from the coast, Eckerö is typical rural Åland, with winding country lanes, tiny villages and two 18-hole golf courses.

The ferry terminal is at Storby village, about 40km (two hours by bicycle) from Mariehamn. The historic **Mail & Customs House** (☎ 38689) now houses a café, post of-fice, bank and the **Mailboat Museum** (☎ 39000; admission €1.70; ☷ 10am-3pm Jun–mid-Aug, 10am-4pm mid-Jun–Jul), which tells the fascinating story of the treacherous archipelago 'mail route' that linked Sweden and Finland. Bus No 1 runs to Mariehamn.

If you're camping, head for **Käringsund Camping** (☎ 38309; Käringsundsvägen 147; camp sites €9, 3-/4-person cabins €35/45; ☷ mid-May–Aug) just north of Storby, or the beachy **Degersands Camping** (☎ 38004; ☷ mid-Jun–mid-Aug) at the southern end of the island. Eckerö is packed with cottage rentals and guest-houses which can be booked from agents in Mariehamn (see p171).

Eastern Archipelago Routes
If you have a bit of time on your hands it's possible to island-hop eastwards through the northeast and southeast archipelago routes using ferry transport (free to pedestrians). Accommodation options are limited com-pared with the main islands so it's useful to carry a tent or make advance bookings.

To the north you can travel through Vårdö then take the 1½-hour ferry ride to Kumlinge. Another 1½ hours by ferry via Lappo brings you to Torsholma on the scattered island group of Brändö. It's then possible to hop via Jurmo all the way to Turku. By public transport, take bus No 4 from Mariehamn to Hummelvik harbour on Vårdö island. From Turku, take a bus to Kustavi, and on to Vartsala island to reach the harbour of Osnäs (Vuosnainen).

To the south, it's an easier trip travel-ling through Lemland and Lumparland to the port of Långnäs, which is a stop on the Viking Line and Sija Line overnight routes to Turku. Local ferries use the port of Svinö

to get across to Degerby on the Föglö is-land group. From there you can hop to the small and sparsely populated island of Sottunga, then take a 1½-hour ferry to the far-flung but picturesque island of Kökar, with hiking trails, a 14th-century abbey and an 18th-century church. By local transport from Mariehamn, take bus No 5 to Lång-näs harbour. From Kökar there are ferries to Galtby harbour on Korppoo island (two hours), then it's 75km by bus to Turku.

SOUTHWESTERN FINLAND

TAMPERE
☎ 03 / pop 199,800

Finland's most dynamic city outside the capital, Tampere is an enthralling post-industrial town beautifully wedged between lakes Näsijärvi and Pyhäjärvi. Long known as the 'Manchester of Finland', this 19th-century manufacturing centre was famous for its powerful textile industry, and dozens of red-brick chimneys from former factories still point skyward, but most have now been transformed into superb cultural centres, bars or restaurants. On a grey day Tampere takes on a sort of Dickensian quality, with steam rising in the air like industrial fog. But don't be put off: Tampere works beauti-fully, combining working-class energy with cool Finnish sophistication.

Information
BOOKSHOPS
Akateeminen Kirjakauppa (☎ 248 0300; Hämeenkatu 6; ☷ 9am-9pm Mon-Fri, 9am-6pm Sat, noon-8pm Sun) English-language books, maps and newspapers.

INTERNET ACCESS
Main Library Metso (☎ 314 614; Pirkankatu 2; ☷ 9.30am-8pm Mon-Fri, 9.30am-3pm Sat, noon-6pm Sun, closed Sun winter) Free internet access in the main library and on 1st floor.
Internet Madi (☎ 2418513; Tuomiokirkonkatu; per hr €3; ☷ 10am-10pm Mon-Fri, 11am-10pm Sat & Sun) Excellent internet café offering CD burning, laptop connec-tions and free coffee.
Vuoltsu Internet Café (☎ 7146 4899; Vuolteenkatu 13; per hr €3; ☷ noon-6pm Mon-Fri Jun-Aug, 1-8pm Sep-May) Youth centre with an internet café near bus station.

FINLAND

MONEY

Forex (Hämeenkatu 14B; 9am-7pm Mon-Fri, 9am-3pm Sat)

TOURIST INFORMATION

Tampere City Tourist Office (☎ 3146 6800; www.tampere.fi/tourism; Verkatehtaankatu 2; 9am-8pm Mon-Fri, 10am-5pm Sat & Sun Jun-Aug, 9am-5pm Mon-Fri Sep-May;) Just off Hämeenkatu by the Tammerkoski, the busy tourist office has two free internet terminals and can help out with accommodation.

Sights

A walk along the banks of the **Tammerkoski rapids** gives a good feel for Tampere's industrial past. From the tourist office, cross Hämeenkatu and walk north along the west bank of the river passing another set of man-made rapids before crossing the bridge at the Finlayson Centre and wandering up to the old Tampella mills and Vapriikki Centre. Return along the east bank, past the Sokos Hotel Tammer and through Koskipuisto, a popular riverside park.

There's quite a lot to see in Tampere in terms of galleries and museums, but some are reserved for those with unique interests – the Coffee Cup Museum, Shoe Museum and, the *pièce de résistance*, the Finnish Museum of Refrigeration, to name a few!

FINLAYSON CENTRE

The Finlayson cotton mill was founded by Scottish industrialist James Finlayson in the 19th century and was the first building in the Nordic countries to boast electric lighting, which went on in 1882. Although the massive red-brick building remains intact, the interior has now been converted into a modern complex of restaurants, bars, shops, exhibition spaces and a cinema. Downstairs, the offbeat **Spy Museum** (☎ 212 3007; adult/child €7/5.50; 10am-6pm Mon-Fri, 10am-4pm Sat & Sun May-Aug, noon-6pm Mon-Fri, 11am-5pm Sat Sep-Apr) explores the world of espionage with an archaic collection of James Bond–type toys, KGB documents and a lie-detector machine – some of it looking a bit comical given today's technology. Also in the complex is the **Central Museum of Labour** (☎ 253 8800; www.tkm.fi; Väinö Linnan aukio 8; adult/child €5/2; 11am-6pm Tue-Sun), aptly devoted to the history of the labour industry and workers' movements;

and the **Rupriikki Media Museum** (☎ 260 4180; www.rupriikki.fi; Väinö Linnan aukio 13; adult/child €4/1; 10am-6pm Tue-Sun), of interest if you have a passion for the history of media and mass communications.

VAPRIIKKI MUSEUM CENTRE

The **Vapriikki Museum Centre** (☎ 020-716 6966; www.tampere.fi/vapriikki; Veturiaukio 4; adult/child €5/1; 10am-6pm Tue & Thu-Sun, 11am-8pm Wed) is Tampere's premier exhibition space, in a renovated Tampella mill factory building. As well as changing exhibitions throughout the year, you'll also find the **Finnish Hockey Hall of Fame**, a small display dedicated to Finland's winter passion, with photos, jerseys, sticks and pucks galore. Pride of place goes to the 1995 World Champions trophy.

LENIN MUSEUM

Don't miss the tiny **Lenin Museum** (☎ 276 8100; www.lenin.fi; Hämeenpuisto 28; adult/child €4/2; 9am-6pm Mon-Fri, 11am-4pm Sat & Sun), which gives a fascinating insight into the life and work of the Russian revolutionary leader who spent some time drumming up support in Tampere; there's a zany gift shop and also the couch he slept on while in Helsinki.

MOOMINVALLEY

In the basement of the public library, **Moominvalley** (☎ 716 6578; Hämeenpuisto 20; adult/child €4/1; 9am-5pm Mon-Fri, 10am-6pm Sat & Sun, closed Mon Sep-May) is a whimsical exhibition based on the children's books of Tove Jansson. It features original drawings and tableaux models from the world of Moomintrolls – a Finnish cultural phenomenon. Kids and fans of Moominworld will love it. In the same building the small **Mineral Museum** (☎ 716 6046; adult/child €4/1) is devoted to glittering rocks and gemstones and has the same hours as Moominvalley, but not the same crowds.

SÄRKÄNNIEMI

Särkänniemi amusement park (☎ 713 0200; www.sarkanniemi.fi; adult/child day pass €29/20; entry-only €5; 11am-9pm Sun-Fri, 11am-10pm Sat Jul-Aug, reduced hours in winter) is great for kids, with carnival rides, an **aquarium** and **planetarium**, a **children's zoo** and the **Dolphinarium**. A pass gives unlimited rides, or you can pay as you go.

TAMPERE

0   500 m
0   0.3 miles

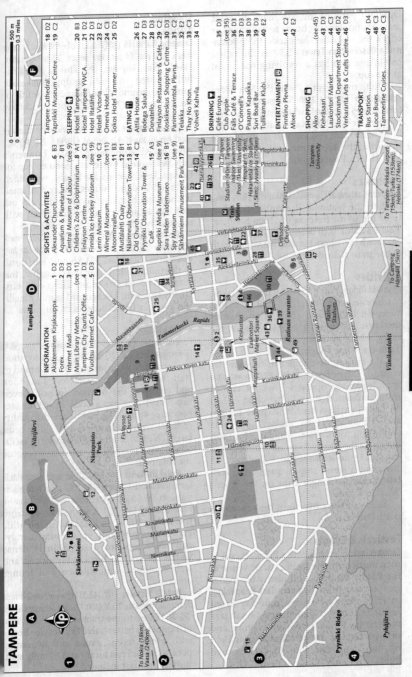

INFORMATION

Akateeminen Kirjakauppa..........	**1** D2
Forex...	**2** D3
Internet Madi................................	**3** D3
Main Library Metso....................	(see 11)
Tampere City Tourist Office......	**4** D3
Vuoltsu Internet Cafe.................	**5** D3

SIGHTS & ACTIVITIES

Alexander Church.........................	**6** B3
Aquarium & Planetarium............	**7** B1
Central Museum of Labour.........	(see 9)
Children's Zoo & Dolphinarium..	**8** A1
Finlayson Centre...........................	**9** C2
Finnish Ice Hockey Museum........	(see 19)
Lenin Museum..............................	**10** C3
Mineral Museum..........................	(see 11)
Moominvalley...............................	**11** B3
Mustalahti Quay..........................	**12** B1
Näsinneula Observation Tower....	**13** B1
Old Church...................................	**14** C2
Pyynikki Observation Tower &	
Café...	**15** A3
Rupriikki Media Museum.............	(see 9)
Sara Hilden Taidemuseo..............	**16** B1
Spy Museum.................................	(see 9)
Särkänniemi Amusement Park....	**17** B1

SLEEPING

Tampere Cathedral......................	**18** D2
Vapriikki Museum Centre............	**19** C2
Hostel Tampere............................	**20** B3
Hostel Tampere YWCA.................	**21** D2
Hotel Iltatähti.............................	**22** D3
Hotel Victoria...............................	**23** E2
Omena Hotel................................	**24** C3
Sokos Hotel Tammer...................	**25** D2

EATING

Attila House.................................	**26** E2
Bodega Salud...............................	**27** D3
Donatello.....................................	**28** D3
Finlayson Restaurants & Cafés....	**29** C2
Koskikeskus Shopping Centre......	**30** D3
Panimoravintola Plevna...............	**31** C2
Telakka..	**32** E2
Thay No Khon..............................	**33** C3
Vohveli Kahvila............................	**34** D2

DRINKING

Café Europa.................................	**35** D3
Club Apple...................................	(see 35)
Falls Café & Terrace.....................	**36** D3
O'Connell's..................................	**37** D3
Paapan Kapakka...........................	**38** D3
Suvi Boat Bar...............................	**39** D3
Tullikamari Klubi..........................	**40** E2

ENTERTAINMENT

Finnkino Plevna...........................	**41** C2
Mixei...	**42** E2

SHOPPING

Alko...	(see 45)
Kehräsaari....................................	**43** D3
Laukontori Market.......................	**44** C3
Stockmann Department Store......	**45** D2
Verkaranta Arts & Crafts Centre..	**46** D3

TRANSPORT

Bus Station..................................	**47** D4
Local Buses..................................	**48** C3
Tammerline Cruises......................	**49** C3

FINLAND

Different parts of the park have different seasons and opening hours so call ahead or check the website. The park's 168m **Näsinneula Observation Tower** (€3.50) is the tallest in Finland and has a revolving restaurant at the top.

Adults may want to visit the **Sara Hilden Taidemuseo** (☎ 714 3500; Särkänniemi; adult/child from €4/1; ☯ 11am-6pm), which is included in the park ticket. It displays changing exhibitions of modern and Finnish art and sculpture from the 4500-strong collection of the Sara Hilden Foundation.

CHURCHES

Tampere Cathedral (Tuomiokirkonkatu; ☯ 9am-6pm), built in the National Romantic style, features the weird frescoes of Hugo Simberg. There is a small but beautifully ornate **Orthodox church** (☯ 9.30am-3pm Mon-Fri May-Aug) south of the train station area.

Activities

Pyynikki Ridge, rising between the two lakes, is a forested area of walking trails with fine views on both sides. There is an **observation tower** (adult/child €1/0.50; ☯ 9am-8pm) on the ridge, which also has a great café serving Tampere's best doughnuts.

Lake cruises are popular in the summer months; **Tammerlines** (☎ 254 2500; www.tammerline.fi; late-Jun-Aug) operates 1½-hour cruises from Laukontori quay (adult/child €12/4) on Lake Pyhäjärvi on Mondays at 1.30pm and 3½-hour return cruises to Nokia (€18/8) on Mondays at 4.30pm. More frequent are the hourly 25-minute **cruises** (adult/child €6/3; ☯ Tue-Sun Jun-Aug) to Viikinsaari. SS *Tarjanne*, a steam ship, departs from **Mustalahti quay** for longer trips on the 'Poet's Way' to Virrat.

Bikes can be rented from the tourist office in summer.

Festivals & Events

Tammerfest in mid-July is a big weekend of rock music with the main concert venue at the Ratina Stadium, and plenty of smaller gigs around town. **Tampere Jazz Happening**, in early November, is a four-day event featuring Finnish and international jazz musicians. Twice a year in autumn and mid-winter, the **Tampere Illuminations** light up the city streets with 40,000 coloured lights.

Sleeping
BUDGET

Camping Härmälä (☎ 265 1355; Leirintäkatu 8; camp sites €11.50 plus €4 per extra person, 3-5-person cabins €30-68; ☯ mid-May–Aug; P) This is a beautifully located and well-equipped lakeside camping ground, though at 5km south of the centre (bus No 1) it's not particularly convenient.

Hostel Tampere (☎ 222 9460; www.hosteltampere.com; Pirkankatu 10-12; dm/s/d €20/38.50/54; P ⛶) Also called Uimahallin Maja, Tampere's only year-round hostel is a good choice for backpackers. Rooms are bright, with linen included and no bunks. There's a small kitchen and breakfast room, but check out Paprilla, a café-bar on the first floor with reasonably priced meals and drinks.

Hostel Tampere YWCA (☎ 254 4020; Tuomiokirkonkatu 12A; dm/s/d €14-16/34/46; ☯ Jun-late Aug; reception closed 10am-4pm; ✕) About 300m north of the train station near the cathedral, this summer hostel is simple, clean and efficiently run, with kitchen and laundry facilities. Neither hostel accepts credit cards.

MIDRANGE

Omena Hotel (☎ 0200-39000; www.omenahotelli.fi; Hämeenkatu 28; r €55; ✕ ⛶) In a great location on Tampere's main strip, this new brand of staff-free hotel is unbeatable value. Book and pay over the internet (possible even same day) and use a code to get in (access after 4pm). The rooms are the quality of hotels twice this price, with fluffy beds, large TV, fridge and coffee-making facilities. They can sleep up to four if you use the sofa bed.

Hotel Iltatähti (☎ 315 161; www.hoteliltatahti.fi; Tuomiokirkonkatu 19; s/d/tr €40/50/55, s/d/tr with private bathroom €55/60/65; ☯ reception 9am-7pm Mon-Fri, noon-6pm Sat & Sun; ✕) A stone's throw from the train station and handy for nightlife and restaurants, this unassuming family-run hotel contains a surprisingly dense warren of rooms. Reasonably priced and well equipped with kitchen and lounge areas.

Hotelli Victoria (☎ 242 5111; www.hotellivictoria.fi; Itsenäisyydenkatu 1; s/d €100/135, s/d discount €80/85; ✕ ⛶) Close to the train station this is one of Tampere's better-value full-service hotels with comfy rooms, sauna and swimming pool, a bar and restaurant and friendly staff. Buffet breakfast included.

TOP END
Sokos Hotel Tammer (☎ 262 6265; www.sokoshotels.fi; Satakunnankatu 13; s/d €119/149, s/d discount from €83/94; ⊗) One of three Sokos hotels in town, this is Tampere's oldest and most stylish address, overlooking the river in a quiet but central location. Modern facilities combine with an old-fashioned elegance and class.

Eating
Cobbled Hämeenkatu is Tampere's broad main street, running east–west from the train station to Hämeenpuisto, and it's along (or just off) here that you'll find most of the city's top restaurants, cafés, bars and the kauppatori (market square), where you can sample Tampere's scary speciality, *mustamakkara* (blood sausage). Also here is the kauppahalli (market hall), but in Tampere it's indistinguishable from the rest of the streetscape.

Another good place for food stalls in summer is the south harbour where there's a weekend market on Laukontori.

RESTAURANTS
Panimoravintola Plevna (☎ 260 1200; Itäinenkatu 8; mains €9-23; ⊗ 11am-midnight Mon, 11-1am Tue-Thu, 11-2am Fri & Sat, noon-11pm Sun) This cavernous German-style brewery pub-restaurant in the old Finlayson textile mill is all polished timber and high ceilings and is one of Tampere's best choices for informal dining. The house speciality here is German sausage such as bratwurst (€8.20 to €15.50), but there are soups, fish and steaks – wash it down with a pint of Plevna's strong stout.

Bodega Salud (☎ 223 4400; Tuomiokirkonkatu 19; tapas from €6, mains €14-28; ⊗ Mon-Fri 11am-midnight, Sat noon-midnight, Sun 1-10pm) Salud is a Tampere institution – a classic Spanish restaurant-bar with everything from tapas plates, paella and the best steaks in town to such delicacies as kangaroo fillet. Great atmosphere.

Telakka (☎ 225 0720; Tullikamarin aukio 3; mains €7-15; ⊗ 11-2am Mon-Tue, 11-3am Wed-Sat, 11-2am Sun, kitchen till 8 or 10pm) In another of Tampere's restored red-brick warehouses, this bohemian bar-theatre-restaurant offers an innovative menu and décor, live music, theatre performances and a bright summer terrace.

Donatello (☎ 222 0169; Aleksanterinkatu 37; buffet €5.50-7; ⊗ 10.30am-9pm Mon-Thu, 10.30am-10pm Fri, 11.30am-10pm Sat, 11.30am-9pm Sun) Lavish all-you-can-eat pizza and pasta buffet for lunch and dinner.

Thay No Khon (Hämeenkatu 29; lunch buffet €7, mains €12.50-15.50; ⊗ 11am-10pm Mon-Fri, noon-11pm Sat & Sun) Cheap and cheerful with tasty Thai dishes, noodles and decent lunch buffet.

CAFÉS & QUICK EATS
The central **Koskikeskus shopping centre** (Hatanpän Valtatie) has lots of fast-food outlets and a few chain restaurants. The **Finlayson Centre** (p174) is another complex of modern restaurants and cafés with a penchant for American-style diners.

Tampere University's student cafeteria in **Attila House** (Yliopistonkatu 38; ⊗ 8.30am-5pm Mon-Fri, lunch Sat) has cheap meals.

Vohveli Kahvila (☎ 214 255; Ojakatu 4; waffles €3-4; ⊗ 9am-8pm Mon-Sat, 10am-8pm Sun) This homey café in a quaint stone house specialises in Tampere's best waffles – the name means 'waffle café' – delicious with whipped cream, fruit and sticky sweet toppings.

Drinking & Entertainment
Tampere has arguably the best nightlife in Finland after Helsinki and locals are blessed with plenty of music venues. In summer, **Suvi Boat Bar** (Laukontori) is a floating beer terrace.

Café Europa (☎ 223 5526; Aleksanterinkatu 29; ⊗ noon-1am Sun-Mon, noon-2am) Still Tampere's coolest bar for the décor alone, with old-world couches, candlelight, and a good summer terrace. There's also a range of international beers and cocktails and a discerning young crowd.

Club Apple (⊗ 10pm-3am Wed-Sat) Upstairs from Café Europa is this small but stylish dance club with DJs playing house, hip-hop and funk. Entry is free before 10pm.

O'Connell's (Rautatienkatu 24; ⊗ 4pm-2am) This unpretentious Irish pub has a strong local following and is a good place to meet travellers, expats and Tampere locals. As well as the dark stuff on tap, there's a back room with big screen for showing sports, free internet and live music on weekends.

Falls Café & Terrace (☎ 223 0061; Kehräsaari; ⊗ 3pm-3am Mon-Fri, noon-3am Sat, 3pm-midnight Sun) In a part of an old brick factory overlooking the Tammerkoski rapids, Falls can be difficult to find but it has a great waterfront terrace, a laid-back atmosphere and live music in summer.

Groove Bar & Cellar (☎ 389 9000; Aleksanterinkatu 22; ⊗ 4pm-4am Mon-Sat, 10pm-4am Sun) Intimate one-room bar with loungey furniture and

FINLAND

board games. Below is a cellar nightclub with DJs playing from 10pm.

Paapan Kapakka (☎ 211 0037; Koskikatu 9; noon-2am Mon-Sat, 4pm-midnight Sun) This small but swinging music bar hosts regular live jazz and blues sessions; the terrace, looking over the Hämeenkatu bridge, is a great place to be in summer.

Mixei (☎ 222 0364; Itsenäisyydenkatu 7-9; ◷ 8pm-2am Tue-Thu, 8pm-4am Fri & Sat) Tampere's No 1 gay club hosts theme parties, live music, DJs on weekends and karaoke on Thursday.

Tullikamari klubi (☎ 3146 6391; Tullikamarinaukio 2; ◷ 11am-midnight Mon-Tue, 11-2am Wed-Thu, 11-4am Fri, noon-4am Sat, noon-midnight Sun) This cavernous club in the old customs house near the train station is Tampere's main indoor venue for rock concerts and music sessions. Big-name Finnish bands sometimes perform here and the cover charge varies from free to €15. It's also the venue for the film festival and jazz events.

Finnkino Plevna (☎ 3138 3831; Itäinenkatu 4; tickets €8) A 10-screen cinema in the old Finlayson factory showing international mainstream movies.

Shopping

Beautiful textiles and handicrafts are sold at the **Verkaranta Arts & Crafts Centre** (Verkatehtaankatu 2; adult/child €2.50/2; ◷ 10am-6pm Mon-Fri, 11am-5pm Sat & Sun) near the tourist office, which also hosts craft exhibitions. There's a café here in a lovely spot overlooking the river.

There is a summer market at **Laukontori** (◷ 6am-5.30pm Mon-Fri, 6am-3pm Sat). **Kehräsaari** (◷ 10am-6pm Mon-Fri, 10am-4pm Sat), in a converted brick factory building east of Laukontori market square, has boutiques selling authentic Finnish designs, handicrafts and clothing. Tampere has a branch of famous **Stockmann Department Store** (☎ 248 0111; Hämeenkatu 4; ◷ 9am-9pm Mon-Fri, 9am-6pm Sat, noon-6pm Sun) with an Alko store.

Getting There & Away

There are frequent daily Finnair services to/from Helsinki; flights to other destinations are via Helsinki. **Ryanair** (☎ 0200-39000; www.ryanair.com) flies from London Stansted, Liverpool, Frankfurt and Riga to Tampere once daily for as little as €30. **Blue1** (☎ 06000-25831; www.blue1.com) has direct flights to Copenhagen and Stockholm at very cheap internet fares if you book early. Tampere's airport,

Pirkkala, is 15km southwest of the centre but all flights are met by a bus.

The **bus station** (☎ 0200-4000; Hatanpäänvaltatie 5-7) is a block south of the Koskikeskus shopping centre. Regular express buses run on Finland's biggest motorway from Helsinki (€28.20, 2½ hours) and to Turku (€25.70, 2¾ hours).

Express trains run hourly to/from Helsinki (€25.60, two hours). Intercity trains go to Oulu (€51.40, five hours) and Turku (€21, two hours); there are direct trains to Pori, Jyväskylä, Vaasa and Joensuu.

You can cruise down to Hämeenlinna by lake ferry in summer. **Suomen Hopealinja** (Finnish Silverline; ☎ 212 4804; www.finnishsilverline.com) operates cruises from Tampere's Laukontori quay daily from July to August, and Tuesday to Saturday in June (€40 one way, 8½ hours).

Getting Around

Tampere's bus service is extensive and a one-hour ticket costs €2. A 24-hour Traveller's Ticket is €6. Bus No 61 goes to the airport (€2, 30 minutes); Ryanair flights are served by a separate bus (€6).

HÄMEENLINNA

☎ 03 / pop 47,500

Historical Hämeenlinna has a scenic outlook at the southern tip of a lake network, dominated by a medieval castle and boasting Finland's only 'urban national park', the beautiful Aulanko. There are enough sights here to keep you busy for a day and it's an easy trip from Helsinki or Tampere.

The **tourist office** (☎ 621 3373; www.hameenlinna .fi; Raatihuoneenkatu 11; ◷ 9am-5pm Mon, 9am-4pm Tue-Fri, also 10am-2pm Sat May-Aug; ▯) has plenty of local information, accommodation bookings and a free internet terminal.

The star attraction here is the medieval **Häme Castle** (☎ 675 6820; adult/child €5/3; ◷ 10am-6pm May–mid-Aug, 10am-4pm mid-Aug–Apr), which was built by the Swedes in the 1260s and converted into a jail in 1837. There are free guided tours and an extensive museum inside. Around the castle are three more **museums** which can be visited on a combined ticket with the castle (adult/child €12/6). The most interesting is the Prison Museum, set in a prison block that only closed in 1997. You can get a feel for Finnish prison life and visit preserved cells that look as if the occupants have just been released.

Finland's most famous composer, Jean Sibelius, was born in Hämeenlinna in 1865 and his childhood home is now an unassuming **museum** (☎ 621 2755; Hallituskatu 11; adult/child €3/1; ⏰ 10am-4pm May-Aug, noon-4pm Sep-Apr) where you can learn something of the man's life and work.

There are no hostels in town, but there's summer camping and cabins at **Aulanko Camping** (☎ 675 9772; dm €15, camp sites €20, cabins €40-65; ⏰ May-Sep) on the edge of the nature park, 6km north of the centre.

Hotelli Emilia (☎ 612 2106; www.hotelliemilia .net; Raatihuoneenkatu 23; s/d/tr €65/87/105, weekends €60/77/93; P ☒) This central hotel is Hämeenlinna's best-value option.

Hämeenlinna is located on the Helsinki–Tampere motorway and rail line, so trains and express buses to both cities are frequent and fast. In summer you can cruise on a lake ferry to or from Tampere (see opposite).

RAUMA
☎ 02 / pop 38,000
Some 600 wooden houses from the 18th and 19th centuries make up Vanha Rauma (Old Rauma), Finland's first Unesco World Heritage Site and the main attraction of this seaside town. With its narrow cobbled streets, cafés, **house museums** (combined ticket €4) and 15th-century stone **Church of the Holy Cross**, the Old Town makes modern-day Rauma worthy of a quick stop along the west coast.

The **tourist office** (☎ 8378 7730; www.visitrauma .fi; Valtakatu 2; ⏰ 8am-6pm Mon-Fri, 10am-3pm Sat, 11am-2pm Sun mid-Jun–Aug, 8am-4pm Mon-Fri Sep–mid-May) publishes a free map and a self-guided walking tour.

Sleeping
Poroholma Camping & Hostel (☎ 8388 2500; Poroholmantie; camp sites per person/tent €4/10, dm €10, s/d €30/45, cottages €45-55; ⏰ mid-May–late Aug) On pretty Otanlahti bay about 2km northwest of the town centre, this pleasant camping ground also has a HI hostel in an old villa, as well as summer cottages.

Kesähotelli Rauma (☎ 824 0130; Satamakatu 20; s/d from €40/52/72; ⏰ Jun-Aug; P ☒) About 1km west of the Old Town, this summer hostel is student accommodation most of the year, so it's clean and the facilities are excellent with private kitchen and bathrooms shared between two rooms.

Hotel Kalatori (☎ 8378 6150; www.hotelkalatori .fi; Kalatori 4; s/d €105/130, weekends & summer €89/100; P ☒ 🖳) This renovated Art Deco warehouse, on the eastern edge of Vanha Rauma, is the closest accommodation to the Old Town. Rooms are bright and airy with bathrooms and pine furniture. There's a good restaurant, the ambitiously named Ravintola Delicio, downstairs.

Eating
Head to the kauppatori (market square), in the Old Town, for cheap food stalls and a colourful market in the summer. Vanha Rauma's quaint charm lends itself to old-world cafés where you can sip coffee in antique and old lace surroundings.

Wähä Tallbo (☎ 822 6610; Vanhankirkonkatu 3; mains €6-20; ⏰ 10.30am-7pm Mon-Fri, 11am-4pm Sat) This old café serves up a full menu and does a good value lunch special.

Wanhan Rauman Kellari (☎ 866 6700; Anundilankatu 8; lunch €10, mains €12-24; ⏰ 11am-10pm Mon, 11am-midnight Tue-Thu, 11-1am Fri & Sat, noon-10pm Sun) On the edge of Vanha Rauma, this stone and timber cellar restaurant is a great place to splurge on Finnish specialities, seafood and steak. The rooftop beer terrace is terrific in summer.

Getting There & Away
Rauma is connected by regular buses to Pori (€11.60, one hour), Turku (€16.80, 1½ hours) and Tampere (€23.30, three hours). The nearest mainline train station is Kokemäki (take a connecting bus).

PORI
☎ 02 / pop 75,900
Pori's biggest claim to fame – apart from having a hamburger named after it – is the internationally renowned **Pori Jazz Festival.** For around 10 days in mid-July, all roads lead to Pori, so pencil it into your trip and try to make it here. Despite being one of Finland's oldest towns, and with a handful of historical buildings remaining, there's not much else of interest to travellers in this modern, industrial port city – the town centre appears to be made up entirely of shopping malls.

The festival is known worldwide among jazz and blues performers, and has hosted truckloads of big names over the past 40 years. And it's not only jazz these days – the

2006 line-up included Sting, Roberta Flack, the Neville Brothers and hip hop star Kayne West. Many scheduled and impromptu performances, jam sessions and street shows are free, creating a nonstop buzz around town. The headliners play on an open-air stage on Kirjurinluoto. For tickets, program details and information contact **Pori Jazz** (☎ 626 2200; www.porijazz.fi; Pohjoisranta 11D, 28100 Pori)

Local sights in town include **Pori Art Museum** (☎ 621 1080; Eteläranta 1; adult/child €3.50/1; ☺ 11am-6pm Tue-Sun, 11am-8pm Wed), one of Finland's better modern art galleries; and the **Juselius Mausoleum** (☎ 623 8746; Käppärä, Maantiekatu; admission free; ☺ noon-3pm daily May-Aug, noon-2pm Sun Sep-Apr), a poignant memorial built by a local businessman for his 11-year-old daughter who died of tuberculosis. The original frescoes inside were painted by Akseli Gallen-Kallela.

Sleeping & Eating

Accommodation during the festival should be booked a year in advance, but the **tourist office** (☎ 621 1271; www.pori.fi; Yrjönkatu 17; ☺ 9am-5pm Mon-Fri, 10am-3pm Sat Jun-Aug, 9am-5pm Mon-Fri Sep-May; ▢), in the Promenade shopping centre, can help organise a cheap bed (around €30 to €45) on a first-come, first-served basis, either in a private home or on the floor of a school classroom.

Yyteri (☎ 634 5700; Yyterinsatojentie; camp sites €9-16, 4-bed cabins €45-55; ☺ May-Aug) This is the nearest camping ground, 18km northwest of Pori.

Hostel Buisto (☎ 633 0646; www.hostelbuisto.net; Itäpuisto 13; s/d/tr €34/48/68) This slick new hostel is the best budget accommodation in the town centre. It's been completely refurbished with colourful rooms (shared bathrooms) and a full kitchen. You'll find it wedged between the fire station and a popular dance restaurant.

Pori's huge market square is the centre of attention, and the main strip, Yrjönkatu, is lined with cafés, restaurants, bars and shops. Be sure to try Porilainen (Pori burger), a local speciality made with onion, sausage, pickles and a bun, available at grillis around town.

During festival time, the waterfront Eteläranta becomes 'Jazz Street', a pulsating strip of makeshift bars and food stalls.

Beerhunters (☎ 641 5599; Antinkatu 1; ☺ 11-2am) Across from the market square, this is a terrific and always busy pub-brewery (try the award-winning 'Mufloni stout') and restaurant with internet access.

Getting There & Away

Pori is well connected by express buses to Turku, Tampere and Helsinki. There are frequent trains to/from Tampere (€14.60, 1½ hours) and one direct service from Helsinki (€32.10, 3¾ hours).

VAASA

☎ 06 / pop 56,900

Vaasa, a bilingual harbour city and the hub of the 'Swedish coast' (so named because of the high number of Swedish speakers) – bills itself, with some justification, as Finland's sunniest city. A lively, bustling place spread over several tight islands, Vaasa lacks the charm and character of some of the smaller towns on the west coast, but it's an important entry or exit point, only three hours from the Swedish mainland by ferry.

The busy **tourist office** (☎ 325 1145; www.vaasa.fi; Kaupungintalo; ☺ 9am-9pm Mon-Fri, 10am-6pm Sat & Sun Jun–mid-Aug, 10am-4pm Mon-Fri mid-Aug–May; ▢), in the town hall building just off Raastuvankatu, books accommodation and rents bikes.

The most interesting of Vaasa's numerous museums and art collections is the **Museum of Ostrobothnia** (☎ 325 3800; Museokatu 3; adult/child €4/2; ☺ 10am-3pm Tue, Thu-Fri, noon-8pm Wed, noon-5pm Sat & Sun), with one of the best collections of art from Finland's Golden Era and artefacts from all over the region. Entry is free on Wednesdays.

On Vaskiluoto island, linked by a bridge to the town centre, is the amusement park, **Wasalandia** (☎ 211 1200; www.wasalandia.fi) and a 'tropical spa', **Tropiclandia** (☎ 211 1300; www.tropiclandia.fi), both popular with Finnish families and great for young kids.

Sleeping & Eating

Hostel Vaasa (☎ 324 1555; www.hostelvaasa.com; Niemeläntie 1; dm/s/d €17.50/40/46; P ☒) On Vaskiluoto island, this hostel is a cut above most with all rooms having attached bathrooms and TV. Handy for the ferries from Sweden and only 1.5km west of the town centre (bus No 5 or 10).

Kenraali Wasa Hostel (☎ 0400-66 8521; www .kenraaliwasahostel.com; Korsholmanpuistikko 6-8; s/d/tr €37/46/50; **P**) More like a guesthouse than a hostel, this friendly place in a former military hospital is quiet and intimate with cosy rooms (shared bathrooms) and a good kitchen.

There's no shortage of restaurants and bars around the kauppatori and Hovioikeudenpuistikko. **Strampen** (☎ 451 4512; Rantakatu 6; mains €12-23; ☒ 11am-midnight Mon-Thu, 1pm-late Fri & Sat) In summer, one of the best places for a meal or drink is this lovely wooden restaurant and terrace bar in the waterfront Hovioikeuden park.

For a drink with a bird's-eye view over the city, head to the **Sky Bar** (☎ 212 4115; Rewell Centre; ☒ 4pm-4am) on the rooftop of the Sokos Hotel Vakuna.

Getting There & Away

There are frequent buses up and down the coast from the **terminal** (☎ 0200-4061; Sepänkyläntie 1). From the **train station** (☎ 037010; Asemakatu 1) there are daily trains to Helsinki (€48.10, 4½ hours, six daily) via Tampere or Seinäjoki.

From May to September there are daily ferries (adult/student/child €55/43/30, three hours) between Vaasa and the Swedish town of Umeå (Uumaja) with **RG Lines** (☎ 320 0300; www.rgline.com). There are no scheduled bus transfers from the ferry terminals at Vaasa or Umeå; call a taxi or take bus No 5 or 10 from Vaasa's Vaskiluoto island to the town centre.

PIETARSAARI (JAKOBSTAD)

☎ 06 / pop 20,000

The quaint town of Pietarsaari (Jakobstad), about 100km north of Vaasa, is distinctively Swedish and the most interesting place to sample the curious world of *parallelsverige* (parallel Sweden) – that part of the Finnish west coast that Swedes consider to be populated by lost brethren.

The **tourist office** (☎ 723 1796; www.jakobstad .fi; Kauppiaankatu 12; ☒ 8am-6pm Mon-Fri, 9am-3pm Sat Jun-Aug, 8am-5pm Mon-Fri Sep-May) is next to the town square. There's free internet access at **After Eight** (☎ 781 6500; Isokatu 6; ☒ 10am-3pm Mon-Fri), a music café and local youth meeting centre.

Skata, the town's historic area filled with 18th-century wooden houses, is just north

of the centre and worth a stroll. In the old harbour area at Gamla Hamn is the pride of Pietarsaari, the **Jacobstad Wapen** (☎ 723 3639; adult/child €4/2; ☒ when in dock mid-May–late Aug), a meticulously built replica of a 17th-century galleon.

Sleeping & Eating

Hostel Lilja (☎ 781 6500; www.aftereight.fi/hostellilja; Isokatu 6; dm/s/d/tr €22.50/40/50/65; **P** ☐ ☒) This stylish, modern hostel in the town centre is attached to the funky After Eight music café. Spotless rooms have that Scandinavian style; there's a TV room, wood-fired sauna and bike rental.

Westerlund Resandehem (☎ 723 0440; Pohjois-nummikatu 8; s/d/tr €27/41/54; ☒) Old-fashioned charm in the heart of the historic Skata part of town make this lovely family-run B&B the first choice for romantics.

There are plenty of cheap places to eat and drink along the partly pedestrian Kävelykatu (Kanalesplanaden), one block north of the market square.

Café Trend (☎ 723 1265; Isokatu 13; ☒ 9am-11pm Mon-Thu, 9-1am Fri & Sat, noon-midnight Sun) On the pedestrian strip, this popular meeting spot is where Pietarsaari's beautiful people crowd the terrace or read magazines over coffee or beer.

Getting there & Away

There are regular buses to/from Vaasa (€16.80, 1½ hours) and to Oulu (€33.60, 3½ hours) via Kokkola (the closest mainline train station).

LAKELAND & THE EAST

If you're looking for quintessential summertime Finland, this is it. Eastern Finland is a romantic region of lakes, rivers, locks and canals. There's more water here than *terra firma* – a glistening patchwork of waterways in summer where a highlight is canoeing or taking a lake ferry between towns. Lakeland encompasses the border region of Karelia, part of which was taken by Russia in the bitter Winter War, and the Savo region of which Savonlinna is the centre. If you've only got the time or money to visit one part of Finland outside Helsinki in the summertime, make this the place.

LAPPEENRANTA

☎ 05 / pop 58,700

On the southern shores of the vast Lake Saimaa, the South Karelian capital of Lappeenranta is an animated Lakeland town with a visible history, a giant sandcastle and a canal that goes all the way to Russia.

Lappeenranta was a frontier garrison town until the construction of the Saimaa Canal in 1856 made it an important trading centre. These days the canal is a major attraction for tourists with boats cruising as far as Vyborg, Finland's second-largest city until it was lost to Russia (along with large swathes of Karelia) in WWII. Finland's largest lake spreads out from Lappeenranta's harbour, but even if you stick to dry land, Lappeenranta is a vibrant town with plenty of historical links in its old fortress, and it's a good place to sample Karelian food and culture.

Information

The **tourist office** (☎ 667 788; www.lappeenranta.fi; Kievarinkatu 1; ☽ 8am-5pm Mon-Fri Jun-late Aug, 10am-4.30pm Mon-Fri late Aug-May; ▣) is on the south side of the market square but is moving to a new location about 100m west, just off Lapeenkatu, in late 2007. From June to August there's a summer **tourist information kiosk** (☽ 9am-8pm) by the harbour.

The **public library** (☎ 616 2346; Valtakatu 47; ☽ 10am-8pm Mon-Fri, 10am-3pm Sat) has free internet terminals (book ahead).

Sights & Activities

The fortifications in **Linnoitus** (Fortress), on a small hill overlooking the harbour, were started by the Swedes and finished by the Russians in the 18th century. Some of the fortress buildings have been turned into interesting **museums** (☎ 616 2255; combined ticket adult/child €7/free; ☽ 10am-6pm Mon-Fri, 11am-5pm Sat & Sun Jun-late Aug, 11am-5pm Tue-Sun late Aug-May). They include the **South Karelia Museum**, with a variety of folk costumes, local history and a scale model of Vyborg as it looked before it fell to the Russians in 1939; the **South Karelia Art Museum**, with a permanent collection of paintings by Finnish and Karelian artists, including a good representation of modern art; and the small **Cavalry Museum**, which exhibits portraits of commanders, uniforms, saddles and guns. There are guided tours (€2.50) at 2.30pm daily in summer.

On the harbour's edge, just north of the fortress walls, is Lappeenranta's latest attraction – an enormous and unmissable **sandcastle** (Hiekkalinna; ☽ 10am-6pm mid-Jun–early Sep). Sand sculptors from around Finland have been constructing the fantasy sculpture – using some three million kilos of sand – since 2003 and it's certainly worth seeing.

In the city centre, the **Wolkoff Home Museum** (☎ 616 2258; Kauppakatu 26; adult/child €4.50/free; ☽ 10am-6pm Mon-Fri, 11am-5pm Sat & Sun Jun-late Aug, 11am-5pm Sat & Sun late Aug-May) is the preserved 19th-century home of a Russian emigrant family. Obligatory guided tours are held on the hour.

There is a public **beach sauna** (admission €4.20/1.50; ☽ 4-8pm Wed & Fri women, Tue & Thu men) on Myllysaari just east of the harbour.

Tours

Short cruises of two to three hours with **Karelia Lines** (☎ 453 0380; www.karelialines.fi; adult/child from €12/5; ☽ noon, 3pm & 6pm) on Lake Saimaa and the canal leave from the harbour daily in summer.

The day cruise along the Saimaa Canal to Vyborg (Russia) is one of Lappeenranta's biggest drawcards, though it's no longer 'visa-free'. **Saimaan Matkaverkk** (☎ 541 0100; www.saimaatravel.fi; Valtakatu 48) arranges the necessary Russian visas but you will need to request one at least a week ahead and provide passport details. EU citizens need only a group visa, but non-EU citizens need an individual visa (which cost around €33 to €44). From mid-May to September, the **MS Carelia** (adult/child €59/44; ☽ Sat late Jun-early Aug €65/44) departs at 8am for the 6½-hour trip and stops for around 4½ hours in Vyborg. The return trip is by bus.

Sleeping

Huhtiniemi Tourist Resort (☎ 451 5555; www.huhtiniemi.com; Kuusimäenkatu 18; tent/per person €12/4, 2-/4-person cottages €32/42, apt from €65; ▣ Ⓟ) This well-kept complex on the shores of Lake Saimaa offers a bit of everything – camping, hostel, cottage and apartment accommodation catering for a range of budgets. On site is the **Huhtiniemi Hostel** (dm €10; ☽ Jun–mid-Aug), with six-bed dorms and the cheapest accommodation in town, and the upmarket **Finnhostel Lappeenranta** (s/d

FINLAND

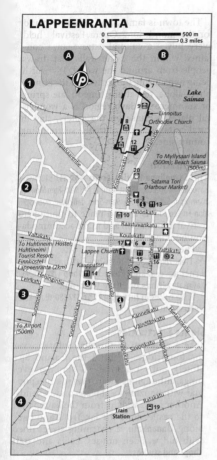

LAPPEENRANTA

Eating & Drinking

In summer, head to Satama tori (Harbour market), just below the fortress walls, where food stalls set up and locals gather. Don't miss trying the delicious Karelian favourite *vety* (a pie or sandwich made with ham, eggs, butter and relish). The kauppatori and **kauppahalli**, just south of the centre, also has Karelian specialities and fresh produce.

Kahvila Majurska (☎ 453 0554; Kristiinankatu 7; ⏰ 10am-7pm, shorter hrs in winter; ✗) In a beautifully furnished 18th-century wooden building at the fortress complex, Majurska oozes old-fashioned charm and does a good range of home-made cakes and quiches.

Kasino Restaurant & Terassi (☎ 415 6063; Ainonkatu 10; lunch buffet €9; ⏰ lunch & dinner) This century-old former casino now houses a stylish harbourside restaurant with an excellent value lunch buffet. It's a bit formal inside, but the terrace hanging over the harbour attracts the summer crowds.

Tiglio's (☎ 411 8311; Raatamiehenkatu 18; pasta & pizza €9.50-13, other mains €12-24; ⏰ 11am-10pm Mon, 11am-11pm Tue-Thu, 11am-mid Fri, noon-mid Sat,

€52/69; ✗), with tidy hotel-style rooms with bathroom and linen, breakfast and a morning swim and sauna included. The resort has a café, pool, and you can rent boats for paddling around the lake. It's located about 2km west of the centre; take bus No 1 or 3 from the centre or No 5 from the train station.

Guesthouse Kantolankulma (☎ 050-328 7595; www.gasthauslappeenranta.com; Kimpisenkatu 19; s/d €52/75; ✗ P) Close to the harbour and town centre, this is a spiffing guesthouse with apartment-style rooms ranging from a studio to four-room apartment, but all have full kitchen with utensils, cable TV and bathroom. Call ahead as it is quite often unstaffed.

noon-11pm Sun) Authentic, relaxed Italian restaurant with tasty, reasonably priced meals and a hefty salad buffet.

Tassos (☎ 678 6565; Valtakatu 41; mains €10-28, lunch buffet €12; 🕙 11am-11pm Mon-Thu, 11am-midnight Fri, noon-midnight Sat) You don't see many Greek restaurants in Finland but at this Greek-Finnish fusion place, pheasant and reindeer share a menu with dolmades and moussaka.

In summer, the best place for a drink is down at the harbour where two boats, **SS Suvi-Saamai** and **Prinsessa Armaada**, welcome you to their busy beer terraces.

In town, Kauppakatu and Valtakatu each have a lively strip of bars and clubs.

Old Park (☎ 678 6563; Valtakatu 36; 🕙 noon-1am Sun-Thu, noon-3am Fri & Sat) is a lively Irish pub that gets very crowded most nights. Downstairs, the **Green Apple** (🕙 8am-3am) is a bright café-pub with a more relaxed crowd, and further still (in the basement) is the **Golden Apple** (🕙 10pm-4am Wed, Fri & Sat, 10pm-3am Thu & Sun), a nightclub where the dance floor is the place to be.

Getting There & Away

Finnair has daily flights between Helsinki and Lappeenranta; take bus No 4 to the airport.

All bus and train tickets can be booked at the central office of **Matkahuolto** (🕙 9am-6pm Mon-Fri), opposite the town park. Regular express bus services include: Helsinki (€33.60, four hours) and Joensuu (€36.10, 4½ hours), while local buses go to Savonlinna (€22.90, four hours, weekdays only) and Imatra (€6.40, one hour). For Kuopio (€32.10) change at Mikkeli. The bus and train stations are together about 500m south of the centre along Ratakatu, though most buses stop in the centre.

Lappeenranta is on the main rail link between Helsinki (€35.60, three hours) and Joensuu (€31.10, 2½ hours). Local services to Savonlinna (€22, 2½ hours) require a change at Parikkala.

SAVONLINNA

☎ 015 / pop 28,700

Split by two stunning lakes and graced with one of the best-preserved medieval castles in the northern countries, Savonlinna is the prettiest of all the eastern Lakeland towns. While others sit on the shores of lakes, Savonlinna seems to float on them.

The town is famous throughout Finland for the month-long Opera Festival held every July – a cultural extravaganza contained within the castle walls that draws people from around the world. It's worth being here during the festival for the atmosphere alone, but at any time in late spring or summer, the Savo region is a wonderful place to cruise on the waters, stay in rural cottages and explore the surrounding countryside.

Information

The **Savonlinna tourist service** (☎ 517 510; www .savonlinnatravel.com; Puistokatu 1; 🕙 9am-8pm Mon-Fri, 10am-8pm Sat & Sun Jul, 9am-5pm daily Aug, 9am-5pm Mon-Fri Sep-Jun) is a good place to find opera festival information and make accommodation bookings.

The **public library** (☎ 571 5100; Tottinkatu; 🕙 11am-7pm Mon-Fri, 10am-2pm Sat) has free internet access. **Knut Posse Bookshop** (☎ 576 960; Olavinkatu 44) has one free terminal.

Hire bikes at **Intersport** (☎ 517 680; Olavinkatu; day/week €10/35).

Sights & Activities

Take a walk out to forested Sulosaari via the footbridges (behind the Casino Spa Hotel) – it's beautiful on summer evenings, although be aware that it's also popular with boozing local teens on weekends. Another good walk is from the kauppatori to the castle along the lakefront and back along **Linnankatu**, a charming street lined with old wooden houses, cafés and **craft shops and studios**.

The late-afternoon reflection of dramatic **Olavinlinna Castle** (☎ 531 164; www.olavin linna.fi; adult/student & child €5/3.50; 🕙 10am-5pm Jun-Aug, 10am-3pm Sep-May) on Lake Pihlajavesi is a memorable sight. The castle was used by both Swedish and Russian overlords, but today is best known as the setting for the month-long Savonlinna Opera Festival. For a tour of the castle, including its original towers, bastions and chambers, join the excellent hourly guided tours.

Across from the castle is the **provincial museum** with a large exhibition space related to local and maritime history, and four **museum ships** (combined ticket adult/child €5/1; 🕙 11am-5pm daily Jul, 11am-5pm Tue-Sun Aug-Jun).

Dozens of 1½-hour **scenic cruises** (€8-12) leave from the harbour near the kauppatori

SAVONLINNA

INFORMATION	
Intersport	1 A3
Knut Posse Bookshop	2 B3
Public Library	3 C4
Savonlinna Tourist Service	4 B3

SIGHTS & ACTIVITIES	
Craft Shops & Studios	5 C4
Museum Ships	6 C4
Olavinlinna Castle	7 D4
Provincial Museum	8 C4

SLEEPING	
Casino Spa Hotel	9 C3
Lossiranta Lodge	10 C3
Perhehotelli Hospitz	11 C4
SS Heinävesi	12 B4
Vuorilinna	13 C3

EATING	
Café Mimosa	14 C4
Café Torppa	15 B3
Huvila	16 B4

Liekkilohi	17 B3
Majakka	18 B3

DRINKING	
Olutravintola Sillansuu	19 B3
Opperra Terassi	20 B3
Terrace Bar	21 B3

TRANSPORT	
Bus Station	22 A3
Cruise boats	23 C4
Passenger Harbour	24 B4

FINLAND

---

daily in summer, and there are ferries to Linnansaari National Park and Punkaharju. **SS Heinävesi** (☎ 514 320) sails to Punkaharju daily at 11am in summer, returning at 3.40pm (one-way adult/child €20/8, two hours).

Festivals

The **Savonlinna Opera Festival** (☎ 476 750; www .operafestival.fi; Olavinkatu 27), held throughout July, is the most famous cultural festival in Finland, with an international cadre of performers, along with concerts of chamber and classical music, all within the walls and covered courtyard of Olavinlinna Castle. The 2006 program included the operas *Carmen* and Mozart's *The Magic Flute*. Tickets cost from €30 to €130 (more for premieres and box seats), but can be picked up for as little as €20 on some nights. Tickets can be booked over the internet. If you arrive in late June you may be able to see performers in rehearsal.

Maintaining the high culture, Savonlinna has a **Ballet Festival** (☎ 555 0200; www.savonlin naballet.net; tickets €45-140), also at Olavinlinna Castle, over the first week in August. In recent years Moscow's Bolshoi Ballet company and Hungarian National Ballet have performed.

The most recent addition to Finland's whacky festival list is the **Mobile Phone Throwing World Championships**, held in Savonlinna in late August since 2000.

Sleeping

Book accommodation well in advance during the opera festival – six months for hotels and a couple of months for hostels, although it's always worth a phone call to see if you can get in on any given day. If you have your own transport there are lots of cottages for rent around Savonlinna.

Vuohimäki Camping (☎ 537 353; myyntipalvelu@ lomaliitto.fi; camp sites tents/per adult/child €12/4/2, cabins €56-82; ◯ Jun-Aug) About 7km west of town, this camping ground on Lake Pihlajavasi fills up quickly in July.

SS Heinävesi (☎ 514 320; cabins upper/lower deck per person €24/27) This small lake cruiser offers cramped harbourside accommodation in twin cabins after the last cruise every evening during summer.

Perhehotelli Hospitz (☎ 515 661; www.hospitz.com; Linnankatu 20; s €65-90, d €75-115; ✗) Savonlinna's most stylish hotel is a stone's throw from the castle; spacious rooms have polished floors, chandeliers, old world charm, and two front rooms have balconies. The restaurant dining room looks more like a ballroom.

Casino Spa Hotel (☎ 739 5430; www.spahotel casino.fi; Kasinosaari; s/d from €87/99, €108/140 Jul-Aug; Ⓟ ✗ ♨) Top-notch rooms with a romantic view of the lake are great value at this price (difficult to get in July), plus you have all the facilities of a spa hotel with spas, saunas, steam bath, gym and pool. It's just over the bridge from the kauppatori train station.

Vuorilinna (s/d €59/69, with bathroom €67/79) Also located at Casino Spa Hotel is this cheaper wing.

Lossiranta Lodge (☎ 511 2323; www.lossiranta.net; Aino Acktén puistotie; d from €90-110, d with sauna €150; Ⓟ ✗) This beautifully designed boutique villa boasts a stunning lakeside location and the closest possible view of Olavinlinna. The five unique rooms are impossibly cute, lovingly designed and surprisingly functional. Recommended but book ahead in summer.

Eating

The lively market at the kauppatori is where to find local pastries such as *omena-lörtsy*, a tasty apple turnover. Also on the kauppatori, **Café Torppa** is a popular student-run kiosk for coffee and late-night snacks.

Liekkilohi (Flamed Salmon; fishy mains €7-10; ◯ to 2am in summer) This bright-red, covered pontoon anchored just off the kauppatori serves portions of flamed salmon and fried vendace – perfect for a very Finnish late-night snack.

Café Mimosa (☎ 532 257; Linnankatu; light meals €6-10) With a view of the castle, this café has a fine terrace and bar, and serves salads, cakes and light meals.

Majakka (☎ 531 456; Satamakatu 11; mains €12-21, lunch from €7; ◯ 11am-1pm Mon-Thu, 11am-midnight Fri & Sat, 11am-10pm Sun) Facing the harbour and making the most of the nautical theme, Majakka is adorned with model lighthouses and ships and is a good place for seafood and Finnish fare. The lunch special is a bargain.

Huvila (☎ 555 0555; www.panimoravintolahuvila .fi; Puistokatu 4; mains €13.50-24; ◯ noon-midnight) The finest place in town to dine or enjoy a beer, this stylish restaurant across the harbour mixes gourmet local food with refined brewing – wash down poached Arctic char or breast of duck with a lovingly brewed Porter ale. The summer terrace looks across the lake to the harbour area. There are two boutique guest rooms upstairs.

Drinking & Entertainment

With only a small student population, Savonlinna is quiet most of the year but explodes into life in July and August. Hotel Seurahuone's top-floor **Terrace Bar** (☎ 5731; Kauppatori 4; ◯ 11am-midnight Mon-Fri, noon-midnight Sat Jun-Aug) is a great place for a drink with a fine view over the town. It's also famous for its fried vendace.

Terraces are also set up all around the harbour – the busiest is **Opperra Terassi** in front of Majakka.

Huvila (see above) is a must for lovers of fine ale, with several types of beer brewed on the premises and some of the best *sahti* (a high-alcohol, sweet Finnish beer) in the country.

Near the main bridge just off Olavinkatu **Olutravintola Sillansuu** (☎ 531 451; Verkkosaarenkatu 1; ◯ 2pm-midnight Sun-Mon, 2pm-2am Tue-Wed, 2pm-2.30am Thu-Sat) an English-style pub is another place for connoisseurs, with a huge selection of international beers and whiskies.

Getting There & Away

AIR

Finnair and FinnComm Airlines fly to Savonlinna from Helsinki from Monday to Friday. The airport is 15km from the centre and a shuttle bus operates during the opera festival (€6).

BOAT

From mid-June to mid-August the lake ferry **MS Puijo** (☎ 555 0120; €75) travels to Kuopio (10½ hours) on Monday, Wednesday, Friday and Saturday at 9am, returning the following day on Tuesday, Thursday and Sunday. This scenic lake journey follows the Heinävesi route, passing through some canals and locks and sailing close to the Valamo Monastery.

BUS

From the bus station located on the western side of Savonlinna there are several daily express buses to the capital Helsinki (€46.30, five hours), Joensuu (€23.30, two hours), Kuopio (€25.70, two hours) and to Lappeenranta (€25.70, two hours). Local buses run services to Kerimäki (€4.80, 35 minutes).

TRAIN

There are trains running from Helsinki (€49.60, five hours) via Parikkala – you must change to a regional train or get a connecting bus service at Parikkala, otherwise you'll wind up in Joensuu. For Kuopio, you need to take a bus to Pieksämäki and then grab a train to Savolinna from there. The main train station is a long walk from Savonlinna's centre; get off at the kauppatori platform instead.

AROUND SAVONLINNA

Punkaharju, situated between Savonlinna and Parikkala, is the renowned sand ridge (*esker*) covered with pines; the surrounding forest and lakes, though, are also beautiful and it is a great area for some cycling or walking.

While you're in town, it's worth making the trip to visit the weird art centre of **Retretti** (☎ 775 2200; adults/student/child €15/9/5; ⏰ 10am-5pm Jun & Aug, 10am-6pm Jul), which has superb summer exhibitions of modern and experimental art in a walk-through artificial cave.

Punkaharju can be reached from Savonlinna by train, bus or, throughout summer, a two-hour cruise (one way adult/child €20/8) to Retretti jetty.

The world's largest wooden church can be found at **Kerimäki**, about 23km east of Savonlinna. It was built in 1847 to seat a congregation of 3300 people.

KUOPIO

☎ 017 / pop 87,800

Surrounded by lakes and forest, with a large hill to view them from, and boasting the world's biggest smoke sauna, Kuopio is the most enjoyable of all the northern Lakeland cities. Along with this beautiful location, the town has a vibrant marketplace, varied nightlife and excellent restaurants. Time your visit for a Tuesday or Thursday so you can steam it up in the smoke sauna, but save time for cruising on the lakes and soaking up the atmosphere of a typical Finnish city.

Information

The helpful **Kuopio Tourist Office** (☎ 182 584; www.kuopioinfo.fi; Haapaniemenkatu 17; ⏰ 9.30am-5pm Mon-Fri Jun-Aug, 10am-3pm Sat Jul, 9.30am-4.30pm Mon-Fri, Sep-May) is behind the impressive town hall north of the kauppatori (market square). Ask about the **Kuopio Card** (adult/child €12), which offers a range of free museum admissions and discounts.

There's free internet access on the 2nd floor of the **public library** (☎ 182 111; Maaherrankatu 12; ⏰ 10am-7pm Mon-Fri, 10am-3pm Sat). Bikes can be rented at the **Hertz office** next to the train station.

Sights & Activities

In a country as flat as Finland, **Puijo Hill** is highly regarded. Take the lift to the top of the 75m-high **Puijo Tower** (adult/child €3.50/2.50; ⏰ 11am-10pm Tue-Sat) for spectacular views of Lake Kallavesi and the surrounding spruce forests. The hill is a popular spot for mountain biking, walking and in winter cross-country skiing, and there's a giant all-season ski jump here where you can often see jumpers in training. There's no public transport but you can walk to the top from the town centre in about 45 minutes.

Time your visit for a Tuesday (or Thursday in summer) so you can sweat in what's said to be the world's largest public **smoke sauna** (☎ 030-60830; Jätkänkämpällä; adult/child €10/5; ⏰ 5-11pm Tue year-round & Thu Jun–mid-Sep) near the Hotel-Spa Rauhalahti. This 60-person log *savusauna* (smoke sauna) is mixed and guests are given towels to wear. Bring a swimsuit for a dip in the lake – devoted locals and brave tourists do so even when the lake is covered with ice, and believe

FINLAND

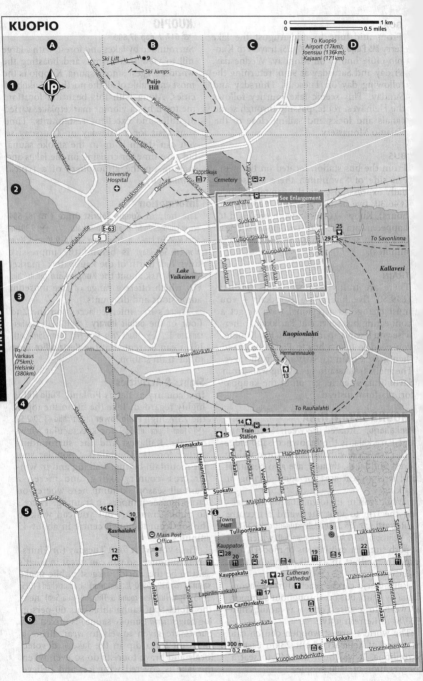

us, it's a singularly exhilarating experience! There's a bar and restaurant serving traditional buffet food and 'lumberjack shows' in summer. Bus No 7 goes from the market square to Rauhalahti every half-hour (€2.60), but the best way to get there in summer is by ferry from Kuopio harbour (adult/child €10/5).

The following city museums can all be visited free with the Kuopio Card. The **Kuopio Museum** (☎ 182 603; Kauppakatu 23; adult/student & child €5/3; ☽ 10am-5pm Mon-Fri, 10am 7pm Wed, 11am-5pm Sat & Sun, closed Mon Sep-Apr) is housed in a lovely Art Noveau castle-like building and combines a natural history museum with cultural history. Pride of place goes to a reconstruction of

a woolly mammoth but there are lots of exhibits relating to the region. The **Old Kuopio Museum** (☎ 182 625; Kirkkokatu 22; adult/child €2.50/free; ☽ 10am-5pm May-Sep, 10am-3pm Tue-Fri, 10am-4pm Sat & Sun Oct-Apr) is a charming set of wooden buildings that make up a folk museum displaying local homes and shops from the 19th century. The **Kuopio Art Museum** (☎ 182 633; Kauppakatu 35; adult/child €3/free; ☽ 10am-5pm, till 7pm Wed, 11am-4pm Sat & Sun) has a collection of Finnish art from the 19th century to the present, including works by Pekka Halonen.

The **Orthodox Church Museum** (☎ 287 2244; Karjalankatu 1; adult/student/child €5/3/1; ☽ 10am-4pm Tue-Sun May-late Aug, noon-3pm Mon-Fri, noon-5pm Sat & Sun late Aug-Apr) is a fascinating museum crammed with collections and artefacts rescued from monasteries, churches and *tsasouni* (chapels) in USSR-occupied Karelia. Take bus No 7 from the market square.

VB Photographic Centre (☎ 261 5599; Kuninkaankatu 14-16; adult/child €3-5/free; ☽ 10am-7pm Mon-Fri, 11am-4pm Sat & Sun Jun-Aug, 11am-5pm Tue, Thu-Fri, 11am-7pm Wed, 11am-3pm Sat & Sun Sep-May) is a quality exhibition of old photos and art by pioneering photographer Victor Barsokevitsch.

Pikku-Pietari Market Alley (Hatsalankatu 24 & Puistokatu 21; ☽ 10am-5pm Mon-Fri, 10am-2pm Sat Jun-Aug) is a charming narrow alley full of renovated shop houses, boutiques, craft galleries and a café which is open during summer.

In summer there are regular lake and canal cruises from the harbour. They include day trips to Heinävesi (€50/25) and Valamo Monastery (€60/30) and cruises on Lake Kallavesi (from €12). Contact **Roll Cruises** (☎ 266 2466, Kauppakatu 1).

Festivals & Events
The main event is the week-long **Kuopio Dance Festival** (☎ 282 1541; tickets 0600-10800; www.kuopiodancefestival.fi) in mid-June. There are open-air classical, ballet and modern dance performances and the town is buzzing at this time. You can also take part in dance workshops and courses. For a week at the start of July, the harbour area is transformed into a food and wine village for the annual **Kuopio Wine Festival** (☎ 044-719 7337; www.kuopiowinefestival.com; tickets €19; ☽ 6pm-1am).

FINLAND

Sleeping

Camping Rauhalahti (☎ 473 000; Kiviniementie; camp site per person/tent €4/7, 2-/4-person cabins from €30/55; ◯ mid-May–Sep) Adjacent to the Rauhalahti spa complex, this upmarket camping ground has a beautiful lakeside location and a truckload of activities for kids, including the nearby pirate theme park.

Hermannin Salit (☎ 364 4961; www.hermannin salit.com; Hermanninaukio 3A; dm/s/d from €20/40/50) Kuopio's best budget option if you want to be within walking distance of the centre. About 1.5km south of the market square, it's a small, simple place with kitchen, lounge and free laundry.

Retkeilymaja Virkkula (☎ 418 2178; Asemakatu 3; dm €15; Jun–early-Aug) About 100m from the train station, this is a conveniently central and cheap summer hostel with large dorms. Reception is open from 6pm.

Rautatie (☎ 580 0569; Asemakatu 1; s/d from €46/75) Conveniently located inside the train station, this is a surprisingly bright, comfortable and peaceful guesthouse.

Spa Hotel Rauhalahti (☎ 030-60830; www.rauh alahti.com; Katiskaniementie 8; s/d €97/124, summer s/d €87/102, apts from €124) This lavish spa hotel is about 6km southwest of the centre and close to the lakeside smoke sauna. Rooms are typical hotel standard and the facilities impressive, including a gym, spa, pool and popular dance restaurant.

Hostelli Rauhalahti (s/d €61/70) A HI-affiliated wing of the Spa Hotel where pairs of rooms share a kitchen and bathroom, and you get to use the hotel facilities. Take bus No 7 from the kauppatori.

Eating

Kuopio's main square dominates the centre of town and here you'll find markets, food stalls and the 105-year-old indoor **kauppahalli** (◯ 8am-5pm Mon-Fri, 8am-3pm Sat). Try the Kuopio speciality *kalakukko*, a local fish baked inside a rye loaf (eaten hot or cold).

Burts Café (☎ 262 3995; Puijonkatu 15; light meals €3-6; ◯ 8am-6pm Mon-Fri, 9am-4pm Sat, 11am-3pm Sun) Burts is an arty café and the best place in town for coffee (with refills), home-made cakes, pastries and light meals.

Café-Restaurant Helmi (☎ 261 1110; Kauppakatu 2; mains €5-8; ◯ 11am-11pm Mon-Thu, 11am-1am Fri & Sat, noon-10pm Sun) In Kuopio's oldest stone building (1850) near the harbour, this atmospheric bar and restaurant specialises in great pizzas. There's often live music in the courtyard at the side.

Vapaasatama Sampo (☎ 261 4677; Kauppakatu 13; meals €8.50-12; ◯ 11am-10pm Sun-Thu, 11am-midnight Fri & Sat) Kuopio's oldest restaurant is famous all over Finland for its *muikku* (whitefish and vendace) – served in various forms, but usually with mashed potato, dill and cucumber. Sampo is very much a typical Finnish pub in the evenings.

WORTH A DETOUR

Finland's only Orthodox monastery, **Uusi-Valamo** (Valamo Monastery; ☎ 017-570 111; www.valamo .fi; Valamontie 42; ◯ 7.30am-9pm) is hidden away in the heart of the eastern Lakeland but manages to draw thousands of pilgrims and tourists annually. The main reason to detour here is to stay overnight and enjoy the tranquil surroundings and beautiful setting. The original Valamo monastery in Russian Karelia was annexed by the Red Army during WWII and shifted to its present-day site in 1940. The two churches here contain a number of priceless icons and there's a small **museum** (◯ 10am-5pm Mon-Sat, noon-5pm Sun mid-Jun–mid-Aug) inside the cultural centre. Like all good monks, the clergy at Valamo produce their own wine using berries such as crowberries, raspberries, strawberries and blackcurrants.

    Valamo Guesthouse (s €30, 2-5-person r per person €25; [P] [✗]) offers clean, simple rooms with share bathroom, while the **Valamo Hotel** (s/d €65/90) has a higher standard of rooms. **Restaurant Trapesa** serves breakfast, lunch and dinner buffets.

    In summer **MS Sergei** (Wed & Sat 2-6pm; one way/return €13/15) cruises through lakes, canals and locks from Valamo to **Lintula Orthodox Convent** (☎ 563 225) which also has accommodation.

    The monastery is 4km north of road No 23 to Joensuu from Varkaus. Buses run direct to Valamo from Joensuu, Savonlinna, Kuopio, Mikkeli and there are a couple of services daily from Helsinki (€55.60, 6½ hours). It's also possible to visit Valamo and Lintula from Kuopio on a **monastery cruise** (adult/child €60/30, eight hr), daily except Sunday. One direction is by bus.

THE FINNISH SAUNA

Nothing is more traditionally or culturally Finnish than the sauna. For centuries it has been a place to bathe, meditate, warm up during cold winters and even give birth, and most Finns still use the sauna at least once a week. Its origins date back over 1000 years, with the earliest saunas dug into hillsides and heated by a fireplace overlaid with stones. The *savusauna* (smoke sauna) in a log cabin is considered by many Finns to be the quintessential experience, but most of Finland's 1.6 million saunas are now electric and many are found in private homes or summer cottages. An invitation to bathe in a family's sauna is a great honour.

Bathing is done in the nude (there are some exceptions in public saunas, which are almost always sex-segregated anyway) and Finns are quite strict about the nonsexual – even sacred – nature of the sauna.

According to sauna etiquette you should wash or shower first. Once inside the sauna (with a temperature of 80° to 90°C), water is thrown onto the stove using a *kauhu* (ladle), producing steam. A whisk of birch twigs and leaves *(vihta)* is sometimes used to lightly strike the skin, improving circulation. Once you're hot enough, go outside and cool off with a cold shower or preferably by jumping into a lake or pool – enthusiastic Finns do so even in winter by cutting a hole in the ice! Repeat the process.

Isa Camillo (☎ 581 0450; Kauppakatu 25; mains €10-22; ☻ 11am-midnight Mon-Thu, 11-1am Fri & Sat, 1-8pm Sun) In a beautifully renovated former bank, this is one of Kuopio's finest restaurants, but is reasonably informal and affordable. The menu is international with plenty of Finnish specialities and there's a good enclosed terrace at the side.

Puijon Torni (☎ 255 5255; mains €15-23; ☻ 11am-1pm Mon-Sat, 3-10pm Sun Jun-Sep) Fancy a reindeer stew with a view? The revolving restaurant atop the Puijo observation tower boasts as good an outlook as anywhere in Finland and the food is good to boot. There's a reasonably priced á la carte menu, and the Finnish three-course set menu (€35) includes whitefish, reindeer and cloudberry dessert.

Drinking & Entertainment

Most of Kuopio's nightlife is conveniently strung along Kauppakatu, running east from the market square to the harbour. At the market end is a block of pubs and clubs that are always jumping on weekends: **Ale Pupi** (Kauppakatu 16), a grungy pub with cheap pints, **Gloria** (Kauppakatu 16) a happening music bar and nightclub on two levels, and the Suomi pop dance club **Giggling Marlin** (Kauppakatu 18), among others.

Henry's Pub (☎ 262 2002; Käsityökatu 17; ☻ 7pm-4am) Around the corner, Henry's is one of the best venues in town for live rock music, with gigs every Friday and Saturday night from 10pm and karaoke on Sunday.

Wanha Satama (☎ 197 304; ☻ 4-10pm Mon-Fri, 11am-10pm Sat, noon-5pm Sun May-Sep) In an historic harbour building, this lively pub is the place to be on a summer's evening, with a sprawling terrace and occasional live music.

Getting There & Away

Finnair and the budget air carrier Blue1 both have direct flights to/from Kuopio every day. The airport is 17km north of town – airport buses leave from the kauppatori (€5 one way, 30 minutes). Airport taxis (☎ 106 400) cost €24 for up to four people.

Kuopio is a transport hub for buses in the southeast region with regular express services to Helsinki (€50.90, 6½ hours), Joensuu (€20.50, 2½ hours), Kajaani (€25.70, 2½ hours) and Savonlinna (€25.70, two hours). The busy main **bus station** is 100m north of the train station.

The train station is about 300m north of the centre on Asemakatu. There are direct services to Helsinki (€51, 5¼ hours) and Kajaani (€21, two hours).

Kuopio is a good base to experience lake travel: from mid-June to mid-August, the lake ferry **MS Puijo** (☎ 266 2466) departs for Savonlinna (€75, 10½ hours) on Tuesday, Thursday and Sunday at 9am, sailing via Heinävesi and Oravi through locks and canals. It makes the return journey from Savonlinna on Monday, Wednesday, Friday and Saturday.

FINLAND

IISALMI & SONKAJÄRVI

☎ 017 / pop 23,500

The pretty little riverside town of Iisalmi, 85km north of Kuopio, is home to the large Olvi brewery, which provides ample excuse for the numerous beer terraces and annual **beer festival** in early July. The tiny village of **Sonkajärvi**, 18km east of Iisalmi, is the place to be in early July when it hosts one of Finland's craziest festivals, the annual **Wife-Carrying World Championships** (see below). The preceding day you can warm up with the **Finnish Barrel Rolling Championships**. It's an entertaining and boozy weekend – accommodation is tight (only available in private homes or by camping in the village) but the **Iisalmi tourist office** (☎ 272 3391; www.iisalmiregion .info; Kauppakatu 22; 9am-6pm Mon-Fri Jun-Aug, 9am-5pm Mon-Fri Sep-May) may be able to help, or try Iisalmi's **YMCA Hostel** (☎ /fax 823 940; Sarvikatu 4C; beds from €18; Jun & Jul; reception 5-11pm).

JOENSUU

☎ 013 / pop 52,300

The provincial capital of North Karelia, Joensuu is mainly a jumping-off point for hikes into surrounding wilderness areas. During school term it's a lively university town with students cruising around on bikes, and there are enough bars and restaurants to keep you occupied in the evening. The gentle Pielisjoki rapids divide the town into two parts: most of the town centre is west of the river, but the bus and train stations are to the east.

The **tourist office** (☎ 248 5319; www.kareliaexpert .com; Koskikatu 5; 9am-5pm Mon-Fri year-round, 11am-4pm Sat May-Sep, 11am-4pm Sun Jul;) is in the Carelicum Centre, which has a good café, free internet and the town's best museum.

The **Carelicum Museum** (North Karelian Museum; ☎ 267 5222; www.pohjoiskarjalanmuseo.fi; Koskikatu 5; adult/student/child €4.50/3/2; 10am-5pm Mon-Fri, 11am-4pm Sat & Sun) is one of the finest museums to be found in the eastern Lakeland area. The exhibits chart the history, traditions and culture of Karelia, part of which is now in Russia.

Held in Joensuu over a weekend in mid-July, **Ilosaarirock** (www.ilosaarirock.fi) is a highly charged annual rock festival.

Sleeping

Linnunlahti Camping (☎ 126 272; www.linnunlahti camping.fi; Linnunlahdentie 1; camp sites €12, 4-6–person cottages €35-42; June–mid-Aug) Just south of the centre and right next to the Ilosaari festival stage, this site has a pleasant lakeside location and good-value cottages.

Partiotalon Retkeilymaja (☎ 123 381; www .youthhostel@lu-joensuu.net; Vanamokatu 25; dm €12-15; Jun-late Aug, reception 9-11am & 4-10pm) Cheapest beds in town, with basic dorms in the slightly run-down old scout hall.

Apartamentos Joensuu (☎ 224 886; Torikatu 47; s/d/tr/q €33/46/57/71; P) This quaint little guesthouse is definitely Joensuu's best-value accommodation. Rooms have bathroom, TV, kitchenette and wi-fi internet connection.

Eating & Drinking

As usual the kauppatori is packed with grillis and stalls selling cheap snacks, such as Karelian pies.

Antique Astoria (☎ 229 766; Rantakatu 32; mains €8-26; 4-10pm Mon, 4pm-midnight Tue-Fri, noon-midnight Sat, noon-10pm Sun) This rustic but stylish riverfront restaurant specialises in Hungarian cuisine such as goulash, as well as cheaper

---

SHE AIN'T HEAVY, SHE'S MY WIFE!

What may have begun as a debauched habit of stealing maidens from neighbouring villages has morphed into one of Finland's maddest but most entertaining events. The Wife-Carrying World Championships, held on the first weekend of July, has put the tiny village of Sonkajärvi on the map. The race is held over a 253.5m obstacle course that includes water hazards, hurdles and hills. Dropping your passenger incurs a 15-second penalty. Under Wife-Carrying competition rules the 'wife' to be carried 'can be your own, the neighbour's, or you may have found her further afield'. All borrowed wives must be returned.

Estonians are still the team to beat – they've won the event eight years in a row. The winners receive, among other prizes, the wife's weight in beer.

Along with the heats, finals and novelty races, this is a big weekend of drinking, dancing and mayhem. Don't miss it!

pizza and pasta dishes. There's a great summer terrace and bar.

Wanha Jokela (☎ 122 891; Torikatu 26, 10-2am Mon-Thu, 10-3am Fri & Sat) The oldest pub in town, this bohemian hang-out is well-known locally; full of characters and cheap beer.

In summer there's plenty of drinking, socialising and live music at the harbour café **Tuulaaki** (Rantakatu; ☻ 11am-3am Jun-Aug), where the passenger ferries dock.

Getting There & Away

Finnair flies daily to/from Helsinki. Joensuu's airport is 11km from town; the bus service costs €5 one way and departs from Sokos Hotel Kimmel opposite the bus station.

The bus and train stations are side by side across the river on Itäranta. Local buses go to Savonlinna (€22.90, three hours), Kuopio (€20.50, 2½ hours), Ilomantsi (€12, 1½ hours, weekdays only) and Lieksa (€14.20, 1½).

Joensuu is well connected by train with direct daily services to/from Helsinki (€54.10, 5¼ hours), Lieksa (€11.50, 1½ hours) and Lappeenranta (€31.10, 2½ hours).

In summer the MS *Vinkeri II* sails to Koli at 9am on Saturday, returning at 11.30am on Tuesday (one way/return €30/45, seven hours). You can also go on from Koli to Nurmes on the same boat, or connect with another ferry to Lieksa, across Lake Pielinen. Book through **Saimaa Ferries** (☎ 481 244; www.saimaaferries.fi).

ILOMANTSI

☎ 013 / pop 6800

Pushing up against the border that separates Finland from Russia, Ilomantsi is Finland's most Karelian, Orthodox and eastern municipality, and the centre of a charming region where a wealth of wilderness hiking opens up before you.

The excellent **tourist office** (☎ 248 5309; www.kareliaexpert.com; Kalevalantie 11; ☻ 9am-5pm Mon-Fri Jun-Aug & 10am-3pm Sat Jul, 9am-4pm Sep-May) can help with just about everything, from cottage reservations to information on trekking routes and hire of camping equipment, snowshoes and cross-country ski gear.

The village centre itself is modern and quite ugly, having been trampled by the Russians, but it's the surrounding region that demands exploration. The **wine tower** (☎ 0400-572 070; adult/child €2/1; ☻ 10am-10pm Jun-

Aug) is worth ascending, for the views and to sample the locally made berry wine.

Parppeinvaara (☎ 881 248; adult/child €3/free; ☻ 10am-6pm Jun-Aug) is the oldest and most interesting of Finland's Karelian theme villages, where you can hear the *kantele* (Karelian stringed instrument) played and try traditional food at the excellent **Parppeinpirtti** (☎ 881 094; lunch €10; ☻ noon-3pm).

Anssilan Monola (☎ 881 181; Anssilantie 7; s/d €28/56, cottage €84-112) This former dairy farm about 4km south of town is run by a friendly family who rent comfy rooms in converted farmhouse buildings. You can eat dinner and breakfast with the family, and camping is possible. Recommended, although it helps to have your own transport.

Ask at the tourist offices about camping and cottages in the surrounding region.

TREKS AROUND KARELIA

Some of the best trekking routes in North Karelia have been linked up to create **Karjalan Kierros**, an 800km loop of marked trails between Ilomantsi and Lake Pielinen. For more information, including maps and trail brochures, contact the Lieksa or Ilomantsi tourist offices, or **Metsähallitus** (☎ 02-0564 5500; www.metsa.fi; Urheilukatu 3A, Lieksa).

Karhunpolku

The **Bear's Trail** (not to be confused with the Bear's Ring in Lapland) is a 133km marked hiking trail of medium difficulty leading north from Patvinsuo National Park near Lieksa, through a string of national parks and nature reserves along the Russian border. The trail ends at Teljo, about 50km south of Kuhmo. You'll need to arrange transport from either end.

Susitaival

The 100km **Wolf's Trail** is a marked trail running south from the marshlands of Patvinsuo National Park to the forests of Petkeljärvi National Park, 21km east of Ilomantsi. This links with the Bear's Trail. It's a three-day trek of medium difficulty (the marshland can be wet underfoot). You will need to be self-sufficient and pre-arrange transport. It passes through some important winter war battlegrounds near the Russian border. There are wolves (and bears) around Ilomantsi but sightings are not common among trekkers.

FINLAND

LAKE PIELINEN REGION

In a land full of lakes, Pielinen, Finland's sixth-largest lake, is pretty special. In summer it's the shimmering jewel of North Karelia, surrounded by some of the most beautiful wilderness areas and action-packed countryside in southeast Finland. Here you can hike, raft, and fish in summer; ski, snowmobile and dogsled in winter. Koli National Park rises in the southeast corner, and the main towns around the lake – Lieksa, Nurmes and Koli – are linked by lake ferry in summer.

Lieksa & Ruunaa

☎ 013 / pop 16,000

The small lakeside town of Lieksa is primarily a base and service town if you're planning any outdoor activities in the region. In winter, husky tours and snowmobile safaris along the Russian border are popular; in summer, hiking, fishing and white-water rafting are all the rage.

The **tourist office** (☎ 248 5312; www.kareliaexpert.fi; Pielisentie 7; ☯ 9am-5pm Mon-Fri Jun-Aug, 9am-2pm Sat Jul, 8am-4pm Mon-Fri Sep-May) is the place to stop for information on accommodation, fishing, canoeing, smoke saunas and national parks, as well as local hiking maps.

One of Finland's largest open-air museums, the **Pielinen Museum** (☎ 689 4151; Pappilantie 2; adult/child €4.50/1.50; ☯ 10am-6pm mid-May–mid-Sep) is a slightly jumbled complex of almost 100 Karelian buildings (many relocated from Russia) and historical exhibits – along with an indoor museum of local war and folk history. The indoor hall is also open in winter.

The **Ruunaa Recreation Area**, 30km east of Lieksa, is a superb, accessible and carefully managed wilderness area perfect for fishing, white-water rafting, wildlife spotting and easy hiking. The drawback is that public transport barely exists, but you should be able to hitch a lift from Lieksa (or go with an organised tour) in summer. The **Ruunaa Nature Centre** (☎ 02-0564 5757; www.ruunaa.fi; ☯ 9am-7pm summer), near the bridge over the Naarajoki (Naara river), has lots of information and is where most boat trips end.

SLEEPING

Kestikievari Herranniemi (☎ 542 110; www.herranniemi.com; Vuonislahdentie 185; dm €12.50, cottages €28-68, B&B s/d €50/68) It's worth going out of the way and catching a train to Vuonislahti, 28km south of Lieksa, for this brilliant lakeside retreat. The welcoming farm property has a restaurant, a dormitory outbuilding, a range of comfortable rooms and cottages, two lakeside saunas, rowing boats and even massage and herbal therapy.

Neitikoski Hiking Centre (☎ 533 170; camp sites €12, 4-6–bed cabins €34-95) At Ruunaa, in addition to accommodation and services at Naarajoki, the Hiking Centre has a large café, camping sites, kitchen, sauna and cabins ranging from simple to luxurious. A boardwalk goes a short distance from here to the Neitikoski rapids, a popular fishing and kayaking spot.

GETTING THERE & AWAY

Buses ply the route around Lake Pielinen, and trains run to Lieksa from Joensuu and Nurmes, but the coolest way to arrive here is by lake ferry from Joensuu (via Koli). A huge 250-person car ferry (adult/child €15/8 one way, car/bicycle €10/2, 1½ hours) runs twice daily between Lieksa and Koli from June to mid-August, departing at 9.30am and 3.30pm, returning at 11.30am and 5.30pm.

Koli National Park

Finns consider the views from the heights of Koli, overlooking Lake Pielinen, as the best in the country – the same views inspired several Finnish artists from the National Romantic era. In summer, the national park offers scenic hiking routes, and there's a ferry service between Koli and Lieksa (1½ hours) or Joensuu (seven hours; see p193). In winter, Koli attracts skiers, with two slalom centres and more than 60km of cross-country trails, including 24km of illuminated track.

There's a regular bus service from Koli village up to the top of the hill. At the top, the modern **Ukko-Koli Heritage Centre** (☎ 688 8400; www.metlakoli.net) has displays and information on the national park and cottages for rent.

The family-run **Koli Hostel** (☎ 673 131; Niinilahdentie 47; dm from €12), on a gravel road 5km from the bus stop, has a kitchen and smoke sauna. If you call ahead you may be able to arrange a pick-up.

Nurmes

☎ 013 / pop 10,000

On the northern shores of Lake Pielinen, Nurmes is another base for wallet-draining activities such as snowmobiling, ice-fishing, dogsledding and cross-country skiing tours in winter, and canoeing and farmhouse tours in summer. It's a more pleasant town in its own right though, with an 'old town' area (Puu-Nurmes) of historical wooden buildings along Kirkkokatu. A highlight is **Bomba House**, part of a delightful re-creation Karelian village 3km east of the centre. Unlike many folk museums in Finland, this one really comes alive with a minivillage featuring a summer market, craft shops and cafés.

The **tourist office** (☎ 248 5316; www.kareliaexpert.com; Välitie 2-4; ☺ 9am-4pm Mon-Fri) is hidden away in the ABC service station on the road to Kuopio, about 2km south of town.

The best places to stay in Nurmes are side by side on the lake shore about 3.5km east of the town centre. **Hyvärilä** (☎ 687 2500; www.hyvarila.com; Lomatie 12; camp sites €13, dm/s/d from €16/30/35, hotel s/d €60/79) is a sprawling lakefront holiday resort with a manicured camping ground, two youth hostels, an upmarket hotel, restaurant and even a golf course.

Bomba Spa Hotel (☎ 687 200; www.bomba.fi; Suojärvenkatu 1; d from €110, apts €110-160), near the Karelian village, is a stylish set-up of rooms and cottages, where you can pamper yourself with the spa and sauna facilities.

There are regular buses from Nurmes to Joensuu, Lieksa, Kajaani and Kuopio; and direct regional trains from Joensuu (€16.40, two hours) and Lieksa (€7.50, 45 minutes). From mid-May to mid-August, the MS *Vinkeri II* cruises once a week to Joensuu (€40, 9½ hours), or you can take the shorter ferry to Koli on Sunday (€20/10). Contact **Saimaa Ferries** (☎ 481 244; www.saimaaferries.fi).

NORTH-CENTRAL FINLAND

KAJAANI

☎ 08 / pop 35,000

Once known as the countrys largest tarproducer Kajaani is the centre of the Kainuu region, and although a pleasant enough riverside city, for travellers it's mainly a transport hub and stopover on the haul between the south and Lapland. An international **jazz festival** in early June brings Kajaani to life.

Kajaani Info (☎ 6155 2555; www.kajaani.fi; Kauppakatu 21; ☺ 8.30am-5pm Mon-Fri, 9am-2pm Sat Jun-Aug, 8.30am-4pm Sep-May; ☐) is the helpful tourist office, just off the tiny town square.

Kajaani's most notable historical claim to fame is that writer Elias Lönnrot, author of the epic *Kalevala*, used Kajaani as a base for his travels. The **Kainuu museum** (☎ 6155 2407; Asemakatu 4; adult/child €2/free; noon-4pm Sun-Tue & Thu-Sat, noon-8pm Wed) has a good section on Lönnrot.

At the Ämmäkoski waterfall, near the remnants of Kajaani castle, is a **tar-boat canal**, a type of lock built in 1846 to enable the boats laden with tar barrels to pass. There are tar-boat shows at 11am on Saturday in July.

Sleeping & Eating

Kartanohotelli Karolineburg (☎ 613 1291; www.karolineburg.com; Karoliinantie 4; s/d from €60/80, d with sauna €100, ste from €130; P ✗) This elegant 19th-century wooden manor house across the river from the centre beats the modern business hotels hand-down for charm and romance. Some of the buildings date back to 1836, but the refurbished hotel rooms are great value, and even if you don't stay the restaurant is worth a visit for lunch or dinner (book ahead).

The partly pedestrianised Kauppakatu – leading from the market square to the town square – is the main street and is lined with numerous cafés, bars and restaurants.

Pikantti (☎ 628 870; Kauppakatu 10; buffet €9; ☺ 10am-5pm Mon-Fri, 10am-3pm Sat; ✗) This unassuming restaurant offers an excellent Finnish lunch buffet of meat, fish, soups and salads but unlike most places it's available all day.

Getting There & Away

Finnair flies to/from Helsinki, and trains connect with Helsinki (€22.30, 7½ hours, five daily), Kuopio (€21, 2¼ hours, four daily) and Oulu (€24.40, 2½ hours, four daily). Buses go to most regional centres including Kuusamo (€36.10, 3½ hours) and Kuhmo (€16.20, 1½ hours).

KUHMO

☎ 08 / pop 6500

Whether you're hoping to spot a brown bear or preparing to hike one of Finland's great trails, Kuhmo is a small piece of civilisation in the heart of real wilderness territory. Like Kajaani, Kuhmo was once a major tar producer, but is now a service town with links to the epic *Kalevala*.

FINLAND

For many travellers, Kuhmo is simply the jumping-off point for the UKK trekking route, the longest marked trekking route in Finland.

The town is also renowned for the annual **Kuhmo Chamber Music Festival** (☎ 652 0936; www .kuhmofestival.fi; Torikatu 39), held from mid-July to August, which attracts musicians from around the world.

The helpful **tourist office** (☎ 6155 5292; www .kuhmo.fi; Kainuuntie 82; ☺ 8am-5pm Mon-Fri, Aug-Jun, 8am-6 or 10pm daily Jul; ☐) is good for both national park and festival information.

Kalevala Village theme park (☎ 652 0114; guided tour adult/child €11/5.50; ☺ 10am-5pm Mon-Sat Jun-Aug, 9am-6pm daily Jul), 3km from the centre, is an interesting open-air museum of Karelian log buildings and artisan displays is linked by a walking track.

If you have any interest in the *Kalevala* or Karelian culture, **Juminkeko** (☎ 653 0670; www.juminkeko.fi; Kontionkatu 25; adult/child €4/free; ☺ noon-6pm Sun-Thu) offers everything from audiovisual presentations, Finland's largest collection of *Kalevala* books, and multimedia translations.

White-water rafting trips on the Lentuankoski rapids can be arranged in June and July. Book through the Kuhmo tourist office.

Sleeping

Kalevala Camping (☎ 655 6388; camp sites €11, 2-/4-person cabins from €27/35; ☺ Jun-late Aug) Near the Kalevala Village theme park, this lakeside camping ground has good facilities including a smoke sauna and boats.

Kuhmon Matkakoti (☎ /fax 655 0271; Vienantie 3; s/d/tr €25/45/60; ℗ ☒) This is a small but good-value guesthouse (share bathroom) near the town centre with friendly owners. Breakfast and sauna included.

Getting There & Away

There are four to five local buses daily to/from Kajaani (€16.20, 1½ hours), where you can pick up road and rail connections to elsewhere west and south. Buses also run to Nurmes (€21.30, 2½ hours) and Joensuu (€38, four hours).

OULU

☎ 08 / pop 124,600

This lively, fast-growing university town looks out on the Gulf of Bothnia and a string of interconnected islands. Hi-tech companies like Nokia have recently set up shop here, lending an affluent, progressive air. For travellers it's not so much that Oulu has any must-see sights, but the summertime energy, superb cycling paths, friendly locals and frenetic nightlife make it worth a stop.

Founded in 1605, Oulu grew prosperous in the 18th-century from tar, which was floated down the river from the Kainuu region and shipped to Sweden for shipbuilding. Although pulp factories are a major industry, it's the IT boom that's leading the way in Oulu now and plenty of professional expats live and work here.

Information
INTERNET ACCESS
Public Library (☎ 558 410; Kaarlenväylä; ☺ 10am-8pm Mon-Fri, 10am-3pm Sat) Internet terminals (book ahead) and a reading room.
Pint Netti Baari (☎ 311 3369; Kauppurienkatu 5; per 10 min €1, free to customers; ☺ noon-3am) Pub with free internet for customers.

TOURIST INFORMATION
Oulu Tourist Office (☎ 5584 1330; www.oulutourism .fi; Uusikatu 26; ☺ 9am-6pm Mon-Fri, noon-4pm Sat & Sun mid-Jun–Aug, 9am-4pm Mon-Fri Sep–mid-Jun). Publishes the useful guide *Look at Oulu*.

UKK TREKKING ROUTE

The 240km Urho K Kekkonen (UKK) route is Finland's longest marked hiking trail, passing through pockets of the now-rare Finnish wilderness on the way from Koli Hill in North Karelia to Iso-Syöte Hill far to the north of Kuhmo. Two of the finest sections of the UKK route are the Kuhmo-Hiidenportti and Kuhmo-Lentiira legs.

The trail is well maintained in the Kuhmo area, with clear markings and *laavu* (simple shelters) spaced every 10km to 20km. In summer, carry a sleeping bag and plenty of mosquito repellent.

You can pick up route maps and information at the Kuhmo tourist office or the **Petola Visitor Centre** (☎ 0205-646 380; Lentiirantie 342; ☺ 9am-5pm daily Jul-Aug, 9am-4pm Mon-Fri Sep-May), near the Kalevala Village theme park in Kuhmo.

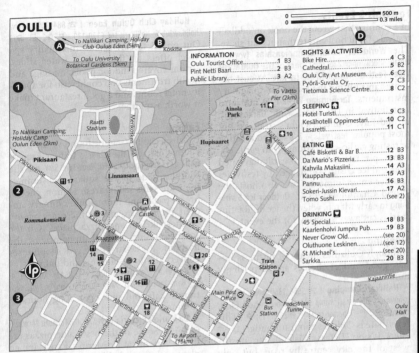

OULU

INFORMATION	
Oulu Tourist Office................1	B3
Pint Netti Baari.....................2	B3
Public Library.......................3	A2

SIGHTS & ACTIVITIES	
Bike Hire.............................4	C3
Cathedral............................5	B2
Oulu City Art Museum...........6	C2
Pyörä-Suvala Oy..................7	C3
Tietomaa Science Centre......8	C2

SLEEPING	
Hotel Turisti........................9	C3
Kesähotelli Oppimestari.....10	C2
Lasaretti............................11	C1

EATING	
Café Bisketti & Bar B..........12	B3
Da Mario's Pizzeria.............13	B3
Kahvila Makasiini.................14	A3
Kauppahalli........................15	A3
Pannu................................16	B3
Sokeri-Jussin Kievari...........17	A2
Tomo Sushi.....................(see 2)	

DRINKING	
45 Special..........................18	B3
Kaarlenholvi Jumpru Pub.....19	B3
Never Grow Old...............(see 20)	
Oluthuone Leskinen.........(see 12)	
St Michael's....................(see 20)	
Sarkka..............................20	B3

FINLAND

Sights & Activities

The imposing, 19th-century **cathedral** (Kirkkokatu; 11am-8pm Jun & Aug, 11am-9pm Jul, noon-1pm Sep-May) was designed by Carl Engel and has Finland's oldest portrait (dating from 1611) hanging in its vestry. The waterside **kauppatori** is one of the liveliest and most colourful in Finland with its red wooden storehouses (now housing restaurants, bars and craft shops), market stalls, bursting summer terraces and its rotund statue of the local constabulary, *Toripoliisi*.

Tietomaa Science Centre (5584 1340; www.tietomaa.fi; adult/child €12.50/10; 10am-8pm Jul–mid-Aug, 10am-6pm mid-Aug–Jun), Scandinavia's largest science museum can occupy kids for the best part of a day with a giant IMAX screen, hands-on interactive exhibits on planets and the human body, and an observation tower.

Oulu City Art Museum (5584 7450; www.ouka.fi/taidemuseo; Kasarmintie 7; adult/student/child €3/1/free; 10am-5pm Tue-Thu, 10am-6pm Fri, 10am-4pm Sat, noon-8pm Sun), on the edge of Ainola Park, is a light-filled gallery displaying changing exhibitions from a large collection of northern Finnish artworks, as well as contemporary art.

Hupisaaret Island is a pleasant town park connected by small bridges, with bike paths, greenhouses, a summer café and the blooming **Ainola Park** – popular for strolling and picnics in summer. About 6km north of the centre, **Oulu University Botanical Gardens** (Kaitoväylä 5; 8am-8pm, greenhouses 8am-3pm Tue-Fri, 11am-3pm Sat & Sun) boasts thousands of exotic plants – including hardy 5m-tall cacti. A pair of greenhouses, named Romeo and Juliet, house tropical species.

Oulu's extensive network of wonderful **bicycle paths** is among the best in Finland and nowhere is the Finns' love of two-wheeled transport more obvious than here in summer. Bikes can be hired from **Pyörä-Suvala Oy** (375 467; Saaristonkatu 27; per day €10) and an excellent route map is available free from the tourist office. A good ride or walk is out to **Pikisaari** via the pedestrian bridge by the kauppatori. It's a favourite picnic and drinking spot for locals in summer. Continue west to Nallikari and Oulu's best beach.

Festivals & Events

In a country that wrote the book on oddball festivals, Oulu hosts more than its fair share. The **World Air Guitar Championships** (www.air guitarworldchampionships.com), part of the **Oulu Music Video Festival** (www.omvf.net) in late August has contestants hitting the stage with imaginary instruments. **Tar-Burning Week** is a midsummer festival in late June, while **Garlic Night**, in mid-July, is one of Oulu's strangest but most popular festivals – it's all about eating or tasting garlic – everything from garlic potatoes, pizzas and bread to garlic-flavoured beer and ice cream – enhanced by festivities and live entertainment. Oulu also hosts the World Championships in **Outdoor Ice Swimming** in early March, when the ice off Raatinsaari is cut away specially for the event.

Sleeping

Although Oulu has plenty of business hotels, good budget choices are surprisingly limited.

Nallikari Camping (☎ 5586 1350; www.nallikari camping.fi; Hietasaari; camp sites per person/tent €4/12, cabins €30, 2-/5-/7-person cottages €62/85/115; P) This lovely site is Oulu's saviour for budget travellers. It's on Hietasaari island, 5km northwest of the city centre by road, but only 3km by foot or bicycle via the pedestrian bridges. Cheap cabins are only available in summer, but the year-round self-contained cottages (with bathroom and kitchen) are a good alternative to hotels.

Kesähotelli Oppimestari (☎ 884 8527; Nahkatehtaankatu 3; s/d €40/58; early-Jun–early Aug; P) Across from the Tietomaa Science Centre, this clean and efficient summer hotel is vacated student accommodation and offers the cheapest rooms in central Oulu.

Hotel Turisti (☎ 563 6100; www.hotellituristi.fi; Rautatienkatu 9; s/d/tr €75/90/100, s/d/tr weekends & summer €55/65/80;) Right opposite the train station, this is a surprisingly bright and tidy place; the spacious rooms have private bathrooms, wi-fi internet, and breakfast is included.

Lasaretti (☎ 884 8300; www.lasaretti.com; Kasarmintie 13; s/d/tr €112/127, weekends & summer €60/70; P) This large, modern hotel complex on Lasaretinsaari island has a bagful of facilities, including spa and pool, tastefully-designed allergy-free rooms and an excellent restaurant. Close to the town centre but with a sense of space.

Holiday Club Oulun Eden (☎ 884 2000; www .holidayclub.fi; Nallikari; s/d €120/130; P) Out on Hietasaari island, this luxury spa hotel offers all the saunas, water slides, atrium covered indoor pools, massage and health treatments you could wish for. Quality hotel rooms and a good restaurant make it worth a splurge.

Eating

Local specialities can be found in the lively kauppatori and the classic indoor **kauppahalli** (8am-6pm Mon-Fri, 8am-3pm Sat) on the southern side of the square. In summer there are stalls selling fresh salmon, cheese, bread, paella and more. Oulu's hungry student population means there are plenty of cheap kebab and pizza places. On the southwest side of the kauppatori, by the harbour, are a string of red shophouses converted into restaurants and pubs.

Kahvila Makasiini (☎ 311 0343; Aittatori 1; 6am-2am Mon-Fri, 7am-midnight Sun) A classic timber café and pub open long hours in summer.

Da Mario's Pizzeria (☎ 379 505; Torikatu 24; pizzas €4.50-5.50) Some of the best-value pizzas are the 25 varieties at De Mario's, a cosy, Italian place with free salad bar.

Café Bisketti & Bar B (☎ 375 768; Kirkkokatu 8; snacks €2.50-6; 8.30am-10pm Mon-Thu, 8.30am-1am Fri & Sat, 11am-10pm Sun) Always overflowing, Bisketti is a top spot for lunch with filled rolls, croissants, quiche and cakes. For something stronger, walk through to the casual wine bar, Bar B.

Tomo Sushi (☎ 312 1665; Kauppurienkatu 5; sushi from €1, dishes €6-13; 11am-6pm Mon-Tue, 11am-8pm Wed-Thu, 11am-10pm Fri & Sat) Delicately prepared sushi plates are the speciality at this authentic little Japanese place. Perfect for a relaxed lunch with miso soup and green tea.

Pannu (☎ 815 1600; Kauppurienkatu 12; mains €9-25; 10.30am-10pm Mon-Thu, 10.30am-11pm Fri & Sat, noon-9pm Sun) In the basement of Stockmann department store, this busy, informal grill restaurant offers a huge range of dishes from fresh fish to wild boar and monster steaks, as well as a speciality line in innovative pizzas. Lunch specials from 10.30am to 2pm weekdays.

Sokeri-Jussin Kievari (☎ 376 628; Pikisaarentie 2; mains €8.50-21 11am-11pm Mon-Thu, 11am-midnight Fri & Sat, noon-10pm Sun) One of Oulu's most atmospheric dining experiences, this pub-restaurant is in a beautiful old wooden storehouse just over the bridge on Pikisaari. The menu is strong on Finnish fish and steak specialities; try elk meatballs (€12), fried *muikki* (whitefish), reindeer stew and crayfish soup.

Drinking & Entertainment

There's plenty going on in Oulu at night – the number of bikes lined up outside pubs and bars on summer weekends is matched only by the numbers of people inside. In summer, the terraces on the market square are a great place to relax with a drink. The main pedestrian strip between the kauppatori and Isokatu is called Rotuaari and along here you'll find plenty of bars and cafés.

Oluthuone Leskinen (☎ 311 7993; Kirkkokatu 10; ☻ 11-2am Sun-Tue, noon-3am Wed-Fri, 11-3am Sat) This friendly British-style pub has a huge range of Finnish and international beers. Try the burnt-flavoured local speciality, tar schnapps – distilled from tar. This is a favourite haunt of expats and locals alike so it's a good place to head first.

Kaarlenholvi Jumpru Pub (☎ 562 4510; Kauppurienkatu 6; ☻ 11am-2am Mon-Tue, 11am-4am Wed-Sat, noon-2am Sun) An Oulu institution, this pub-nightclub and live music venue is always jumping. Inside the vaulted cellarlike building is a warren of cosy rooms, and there's a rowdy summer terrace.

45 Special (☎ 881 1845; Saaristonkatu 12; ☻ 8pm-4am) Oulu's best rock venue and late-night hot spot, with DJs, live bands, Sunday jams, free entry most nights and wall-to-wall people.

On Hallituskatu is a small strip of bars and cafés with terraces that are worth checking out: **Never Grow Old** (☎ 311 3936; Hallituskatu 17), a reggae bar that hits its stride after 10pm; **Sarrka** (Hallituskatu 11), one of Oulu's oldest pubs and wellknown for its meatballs, pancakes and other traditional Finnish grub; and **St Michael's** (☎ 311 7473; Hallituskatu 13-17), an Irish bar.

Getting There & Away

AIR

Blue1 (www.blue1.com) has cheap internet fares from Helsinki daily, as well as direct flights to Stockholm most days. Finnair has daily direct flights from Helsinki. The airport is 15km south of town – take bus No 19 (€2.50, 25 mins).

BUS

Buses connect Oulu with all main centres, though the train is better for most trips. Useful services include Kuusamo (€31.30, three hours), Kajaani (€29.20, three hours) and Kemi (€14.90, 1¼ hours).

TRAIN

Train is the best way to travel north and south: there are direct services to Helsinki (€63.60, seven to 10 hours), Kemi (€14.90, 1¼ hours) and Rovaniemi (€27.70, 2½ hours).

KUUSAMO

☎ 08 / pop 19,000

Kuusamo is a remote frontier town 200km northeast of Oulu and close to the Russian border. There are really only two reasons to detour out here: in summer, it's the base for trekking and canoeing the sublime **Oulanka National Park**; in winter, it's only 30km from **Ruka**, one of Finland's most popular ski resorts.

There are many possibilities for cross-country skiing, hiking and fishing as well as fast, rugged rapids on the **Kitkajoki** and **Oulankajoki**. Inquire about organised tours at the **Kuusamo tourist office** (☎ 850 2910; www.kuusamo.fi; Torangintaival 2). Most tour operators in Kuusamo and Ruka can organise white-water rafting trips in summer, as well as hiring out canoes and kayaks.

Close to the action in Juuma, **Kitkan Safarit** (☎ 0400 280 569; www.kitkansafarit.fi; Juumantie 134) is a reliable operator.

Kuusamon Kansanopisto (☎ 852 2132; Kitkantie 35; dm from €11, s/d €25/34; ☻ Midsummer-Aug, reception 8am-3.45pm Mon-Fri; ℗ ✗) This rambling summer hostel close to Kuusamo's town centre has cheap beds and good facilities.

There's plenty of summer and winter accommodation at Ruka (www.ruka.fi) and camp sites and wilderness huts in Oulanka National Park – inquire at the tourist office.

Finnair flies daily to Helsinki. Buses run daily from Kajaani, Oulu and Kemijärvi.

Oulanka National Park

This is one of the most visited national parks in Finland, thanks mainly to the 80km **Karhunkierros Trail** (Bear's Ring), a spectacular three- or four-day trek through rugged cliffs, gorges and suspension bridges, starting from either the Hautajärvi Visitor Centre or the Ristikallio parking area and

FINLAND

ending at the resort village of Ruka, 25km north of Kuusamo.

There are shelters and free overnight huts on the trail. The *Rukatunturi-Oulanka map* (1:40,000) has trail and hut information.

Juuma is another gateway to the region, with accommodation and accessibility to some of the main sights, such as the **Myllyko-ski** and **Jyrävä** waterfalls. If you don't have the time or resources for the longer walk, you can do the 12km **Little Bear's Ring** from Juuma in around four hours. The trail starts at **Lomakylä Retkietappi** (☎ 863 218), where there are camp sites and cabins.

KEMI
☎ 016 / pop 25,000

An unassuming northern coastal town with smoke stacks and pulp factories caressing the skyline, Kemi has managed to fashion itself into one of the big winter destinations of northern Finland – all thanks to a retired icebreaker and a large pile of ice and snow.

From December to April, Kemi is home to two of Lapland's biggest attractions – the **Arctic icebreaker Sampo**, and the **Snow Castle**.

Plough through the Gulf of Bothnia pack ice on a four-hour cruise aboard the *Sampo*, a genuine Arctic icebreaker ship and the only one in the world that regularly accepts tourists. The trip includes surreal ice swimming in special dry-suits, and it's worth paying the extra for the snowmobile trip to meet the ship. The *Sampo* sails at noon three to four days each week from mid-December to late April and costs a whopping €196 per person. Contact **Sampo Tours** (☎ 256 548; www.sampotours.com; Torikatu 2).

The **Snow Castle** (Lumilinna; ☎ 259 502; www .snowcastle.net; adult/child €7/3.50; ⏰ 10am-8pm Feb-mid-Apr) features an ice restaurant with bar (free to visit), ice tables covered with reindeer fur, ice sculptures, a chapel and 'hotel' rooms (see below).

The **tourist office** (☎ 259 690; www.kemi.fi; Kaup-pakatu 29; ⏰ 10am-6pm daily Feb-Apr & Jul–mid-Aug, 8am-4pm other times), in the Gemstone Gallery at the town harbour, can direct you to a handful of other attractions in town.

Sleeping
Between late January and early April you can spend the night in the **Snow Hotel** (☎ 259 502; s/d €150/220), where heavy-duty Arctic sleeping bags keep you warm in -5°C room

temperature. At this absurd price it's strictly a one-night 'say you've done it' affair.

Hotel Palomestari (☎ 257 117; www.hotellipalom estari.com; Valtakatu 12; s/d €78/108) The pick of Ke-mi's midrange hotels, Palomestari is central and reasonably intimate. There's a sauna with lounge and good views on the top floor and the popular pub Kukko is attached.

Hotel Yöpuu (☎ 232 034; www.hotelliyopuu.com; Eteläntie 227; s/d from €60/68; P ⏼) Yöpuu is a little way out of town on road E4 but it's a comfortable, peaceful and reason-ably priced guesthouse-style hotel with a licensed restaurant.

Getting There & Away
Finnair flies daily from Helsinki to Kemi. The airport is 6km north of town; a taxi will costs around €10.

There are direct trains to/from Helsinki (€70.60, nine to 11 hours), Oulu (€14.90, 1¼ hours) and Rovaniemi (€16, 1½ hours). Frequent buses to/from Tornio (€5.20, 30 minutes) are free with a Finnrail pass.

TORNIO
☎ 016 / pop 23,200

Only a stone's throw – or a well-timed nine iron – from Sweden, Tornio is very much a border town, split from its Swedish twin, Haparanda, by the mighty Tornionjoki. Swedes often trundle across the bridge to take advantage of Finland's slightly cheaper alcohol and an extra hour of daylight!

Tornio is not a place to linger too long but the twin towns share one of the world's most bizarre golf courses, Tornio is home to Lapland's most famous brewery, and 15km north of town are Finland's longest free-flowing rapids – perfect for fishing and white-water rafting. So it's booze, golf and fishing – what more could you want?

Information
The **Green Line Centre** (☎ 432 733; www.haparanda tornio.com; ⏰ 8am-7pm Mon-Fri, 11am-6pm Sat & Sun Jun–mid-Aug, 9am-noon & 1-4pm Mon-Fri mid-Aug–May; ⌨), near the bridge on the Tornio side of the bor-der, houses the tourist office for both towns, with information on Finland and Sweden.

You'll find free internet access at the **public library** (☎ 432 433; Torikatu 2; ⏰ 11am-7pm Mon-Thu, 11am-5pm Fri, 11am-3pm Sat).

Tornio time is one hour ahead of Haparanda time.

Sights & Activities

Interesting sights near the town centre include the beautiful wooden **Tornio Church** (1686) on Seminaarinkatu; the tiny **Orthodox Church** on Lukiokatuthe, built by order of Tsar Alexander I; the **Lapin Kulta Brewery** (☎ 43366; Lapinkullankatu 1; free tours 2pm Tue & Thu Jun–mid-Aug); and the **Aine Art Museum** (☎ 432 438; Torikatu 2; adult/child €2/1; ⊙ 11am-6pm Tue-Thu, 11am-3pm Fri-Sun), with a big collection of Finnish art from the 19th and 20th centuries.

The **Green Zone Golf Course** (☎ 431 711; Näräntie 1; green fees €30-35 for 18 holes, €8 for par 3 course, club hire €10) must be one of the world's coolest courses: not only can you play midnight golf (with the sun shining), but the course actually straddles the border of the two countries (the Tornionjoki). You can tee off in Finland and hit the ball into Sweden, which means if you start at, say, 12.30am, the ball will remain in the air for an hour and land in yesterday. All this novelty, and a round on a reasonable course, can be yours when the snow melts away between late May and late August. To play after 9pm you need to book in advance and a green card is required for a full round but not for the par three course.

Two of the most popular activities in summer are rafting and salmon-fishing on the 3.5km-long **Kukkola rapids**, 15km north of town. **Safaris Unlimited** (☎ 253 405; www.safarisunlimited.fi) can organise a range of trips from around €35 to €60 per person.

Sleeping & Eating

Camping Tornio (☎ 445 945; www.campingtornio.com; Matkailijantie; camp sites €10, cabins d €55; ⊙ May-Sep) Well-equipped site about 3km from town on the road to Kemi.

Vandrarhem Haparanda STF Youth Hostel (☎ 0046 611 71; Strandgatan 26) This well-equipped Swedish STF Youth Hostel just across the bridge in Haparanda is the best choice for hostellers (see p461).

Guesthouse Kaisari (☎ 480 897; www.kaisari.com; Saarenpäänkatu 39; s/d/tr €40/60/80; ✗ P) This unassuming family-run guesthouse is in a pretty part of town. There's a cosy lounge, sauna and breakfast is included. Bathrooms are shared, except in family rooms.

Umpitunneli (☎ 430 360; Hallituskatu 15; lunch €7.50; ⊙ 11am-11pm Mon-Tue, 11-4am Wed-Fri, 1pm-4am Sat, 1pm-2am Sun) For Finnish-style entertainment, head to this classic open-air dance pub where you can see the *humppa*

(Finnish waltz) in full swing on the terrace Wednesday to Saturday in summer; year-round it's a thumping bar and nightclub.

Getting There & Away

From Kemi, take a bus from the train station (€5.20, free with Finnrail pass, 35 minutes). Road No 21 leads from Tornio to the north, and there are local buses to Muonio (€35.60, 3½ hours) and Rovaniemi (€18.60, 2½ hours). If you're heading to Sweden there are buses to Stockholm (€55, 15 hours).

LAPLAND

Extending hundreds of kilometres above the Arctic Circle, Lapland is Finland's true wilderness. For many, this northern extreme is the classic Finland – a mysterious land of clear Arctic air where the midnight sun brings continuous daylight in the brief summer (June to August) and the long, polar nights offer the chance to view the stunning aurora borealis (October to March). From September, the period known locally as *ruska* (autumn) produces exceptional colours of gold, red and brown, and in the far north *kaamos*, the season of eerie bluish light, begins late in October.

Opportunities to get out and experience this sugar-coated wonderland are endless. In winter you can mush with husky-dogs, ski in downhill resorts, cheer for reindeer races on frozen lakes, drill a hole and go ice-fishing or snowmobile through forests. In summer, hike through pristine national parks in endless daylight and raft down whitewater rivers. The only limitation here is your budget.

ROVANIEMI

☎ 016 / pop 57,000

Hovering just below the Arctic Circle, Rovaniemi is Lapland's capital and gateway, a modern town built as much around tourism as any sort of industry, although there's a large student population thanks to the University of Lapland.

The town was completely rebuilt in 1946 after being razed by the Germans and the modern centre is the result of a plan by architectural maestro Alvar Aalto. The main streets are intended to radiate out from Hallituskatu in the shape of reindeer antlers, but this is only obvious from the air.

FINLAND

FINLAND

Apart from the lure of the Arctic Circle, tourists are attracted here by the notion that Santa Claus lives just up the road – a sublime piece of marketing built up from an old Finnish legend. But there's a lot to be said for this latitude: in summer, the midnight sun really does shine, and in winter it's a convenient base for dog- or reindeer-sledding, skiing or snowmobile safaris, and a chance to see the northern lights.

Information

INTERNET ACCESS

Public Library (☎ 322 2463; Jorma Eton tie 6; ☺ 11am-8pm Mon-Thu, 11am-5pm Fri, 11am-6pm Sat & Sun) Free internet (three terminals), maximum 20 minutes, or one hour if you reserve in advance. Reached from Hallituskatu.

MEDICAL SERVICES

Rovaniemi Health Centre (☎ 32241, 322 4900; Sairaalakatu 1)

POST

Main Post Office (Postikatu 1; ☺ 9am-8pm Mon-Fri) Near the train station but there is another branch right in the town centre at Koskikatu 9. Most visitors prefer to send their postcards from the busy Santa Claus post office at Napapiiri.

TOURIST INFORMATION

Santa Claus Tourist Centre (☎ 346 270; www.rova niemi.fi; Rovakatu 21; ☺ 8am-6pm Mon-Fri, 10am-6pm Sat & Sun Jun-late Aug, 8am-5pm Mon-Fri late Aug-May) This small office is an excellent source of information on Rovaniemi and all of Lapland. Internet access per 15 min €2.
Etiäinen (☎ 647 820; ☺ 10am-5pm) At Napapiiri, this is the information centre for the national parks and trekking regions, with information on hiking and fishing in Lapland.

TRAVEL AGENCIES

The following outfits all offer summer and winter activities including snowmobiling, reindeer and husky safaris, and river cruises.
Arctic Safaris (☎ 340 0400; www.arcticsafaris.fi; Koskikatu 6)
Eräsetti Safaris (☎ 362 811; www.erasetti.fi; Santa Claus Village)
Lapland Safaris (☎ 331 1200; www.laplandsafaris .com; Koskikatu 1)
Northern Gate Safaris (☎ 311 042; www.northern gatesafaris.com; Valtakatu 23)
Safartica (☎ 311 485; www.safartica.com; Valtakatu 20)

Sights & Activities

Arktikum (☎ 322 3260; www.arktikum.fi; Pohjoisranta 4; adult/student/child €11/8.50/5; ☺ 9am-7pm mid-Jun–mid-Aug, 10am-6pm early Jun & late Aug, 10am-6pm Tue-Sun Sep-May), with its beautifully designed glass tunnel stretching out to the Kemijoki, spacious layout and engrossing exhibitions, is one of Finland's premier museums. Static and interactive displays focus on Arctic flora and fauna as well as the Sami and other people of Arctic Europe, Asia and North America. Other photographic exhibits examine the lives of ordinary Finns. There's also a theatre screening a short film about the aurora borealis, a library and a good café. Give yourself at least a couple of hours to get around this museum. It's a pleasant walk to Arktikum from the centre of town following the path along the river.

Rovaniemi Art Museum (☎ 322 2822; Lapinkävijäntie 4; adult/child €4/2, free Sat; ☺ noon-5pm Tue-Sat) has changing exhibitions of Finnish modern art.

Rovaniemi has several buildings designed by Alvar Aalto, including the library, town hall and **Lappia-talo** (☎ 322 2495; Hallituskatu 11-13), an impressive concert hall.

Across the Ounasjoki and 3km above the town, the **Ounasvaara Ski Centre** (☎ 369 045; www.ounasvaara.net) has six downhill ski slopes and three ski jumps, plus a summer tobogganing run and the Ounasvaara Sky Hotel. It's a good spot for hiking in summer.

In summer there are two-hour **boat cruises** (☎ 0400-292132; adult/child €10/5; ☺ 2pm, 5pm & 8pm) on the Kemijoki. If the cold gets too much, check out the swimming hall **Vesihiisi** (☎ 322 2592; Nuortenkatu 11) with spas and saunas.

Festivals & Events

Rovaniemi hosts events year-round and is especially busy around Christmas. In late January, the **Arctic Lapland Rally** (www.arcticrally .fi) starts and finishes here, and in mid-March the **Reindeer City Race** flies through the town centre, with riders skiing behind their charges. In summer, **Jutajaiset** (www.juta jaiset.net), a Midsummer festival in late June, is a Lappish arts and folk music event; and there's the **Rovaniemi Rock Festival**, a weekend of concerts in early August.

Tours

Several tour companies in town (see left) specialise in the 'Lapland experience', so you can you easily organise a reindeer sleigh ride or snowshoe walk in winter (November–March) or a river cruise in summer (June–August). In winter and early spring the most popular activities include **snowmobiling** (from €90), and **husky** and **reindeer safaris** (from €105). Summer tours include river cruises from €20, white-water rafting and fishing expeditions from €65 per person.

Sleeping
BUDGET
Ounaskoski Camping (☎ 345 304; Jäämerentie 1; camp sites €5; ☽ Jun-Aug; Ⓟ) Picturesquely situated just across the river from the town centre, Ounaskoski has a lovely, uncrowded location but has tent and van sites only.

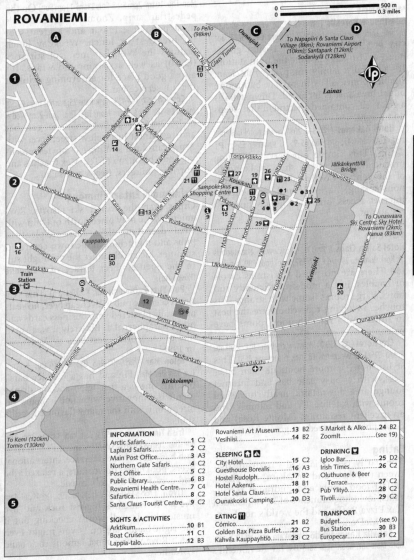

ROVANIEMI

FINLAND

Hostel Rudolph (☎ 321 321; www.rudolf.fi; Koskikatu 41; dm €24.50, s/d €50/75 Apr–mid-Nov, €37/49 mid-Nov-Mar; P ✗) Rovaniemi's HI hostel is an apartment-style building about five minutes' walk north of the centre. It's a bargain since all rooms have their own bathroom, TV and bedding. There's no staff on site; check in at Hotel Santa Claus.

MIDRANGE
Guesthouse Borealis (☎ 342 0130; www.guesthouse borealis.com; Asemieskatu 1; s/d/tr from €45/55/77; apt €185; P ✗ 🖳) Rovaniemi's cosiest guesthouse is virtually opposite the train station. It's a friendly, family-run place with clean, simple rooms, all with private bathroom; buffet breakfast is included. Downstairs is a great self-contained apartment that sleeps up to eight.

Hotel Aakenus (☎ 342 2051; www.hotelliaakenus .net; Koskikatu 47; s/d €60/65-95, d summer €54; P 🖳 ⊛) This simple but very welcoming private hotel is just a short walk north of the centre. Comfortable rooms (most nonsmoking) have TV and free wireless internet access, and there is a sauna and restaurant.

TOP END
Hotel Santa Claus (☎ 321 321; www.hotelsantaclaus .fi; Korkalonkatu 29; s/d €127/152, weekends €89, summer €84) There are no piped Christmas carols or baubles, just a modern, efficiently run hotel. Large rooms (some with strange '70s touches involving red velour) are the best in town and a few 5th-floor rooms have balconies overlooking Koskikatu.

City Hotel (☎ 330 0111; www.cityhotel.fi; Pekankatu 9; s/d €95/120, weekends €85/99, d summer €65) This stylish hotel is more boutique than business, with a busy café bar and internet lounge area downstairs, neatly furnished rooms with satellite TV and minibar, and an excellent restaurant (Monte Rosa) and cellar pub. Who needs to go out?

Eating
The partly pedestrianised Koskikatu (between Rovakatu and Valtakatu) has plenty of fast-food joints and midrange restaurants, including branches of Rosso, Golden Rax Pizza Buffet and the world's northernmost McDonald's.

Kahvila Kauppayhtiö (Valtakatu 24; ⊙ 10.30am-6pm Mon-Sat, noon-5pm Sun) By far Rovaniemi's coolest café, this retro gallery is full of classic old stuff – TVs, a petrol bowser, pinball machine, ancient record players and even an Italian scooter. Relax with a coffee or a light meal on the loungey couches, or access the internet for free. It has a great atmosphere.

ZoomIt (☎ 321 321; Koskikatu; ⊙ 10am-midnight Mon-Thu, 10am-2pm Fri & Sat, 11am-11pm Sun) On the pedestrian strip, ZoomIt is Rovaniemi's most popular café-bar and a great spot for breakfast or lunch. Weekday lunch features the Wok Bar menu of stir fries (€6.50) as well as panini and wraps. It's also a good place for an evening drink at the full service bar.

Cómico (☎ 344 433; Koskikatu 25; nachos from €3.50, mains €6-18; ⊙ 3-10pm Mon, Tue, Thu, 3pm-2am Wed & Fri, 1pm-2am Sat, 1-8pm Sun) Colourful café-bar and restaurant just below street level with American-diner seating, old movies screening and a big menu of Tex-Mex (nachos and burritos), burgers, steaks and salads.

Drinking & Entertainment
Other than the winter ski resorts, Rovaniemi is the only place north of Oulu with a half-decent nightlife – there are plenty of pubs and nightclubs in the town centre. In summer, kick back under the midnight sun in the open-air beer terrace of **Oluthuone** (Koskikatu).

Pub Ylityö (Overtime Bar; Koskikatu 5) This is a tiny, eccentric pub with cheap beer, no seats and walls plastered with business cards and other paraphernalia. Bizarrely it was voted one of the world's best bars by *Newsweek* in 1996!

Igloo Bar (☎ 0400-985 035; Koskikatu; 4-11pm Tue-Sun Dec-Mar) Finland has a few 'ice bars', but this one is a true igloo and the drinks menu is innovative with hot liqueurs on offer along with the many flavoured vodka shots.

Irish Times (☎ 319 925; Valtakatu 33; ⊙ 2pm-2am Sun-Thu, 2pm-3am Fri & Sat) Rovaniemi's best Irish pub has a great heated terrace, international beers, pool tables downstairs, a relaxed vibe and occasional live folk music.

Tivoli (☎ 312 640; Valtakatu 19; ⊙ 10pm-4am Wed-Sat) Rovaniemi's biggest rock and live music club is well worth checking out if the right bands are on – you might even catch Rovaniemi's most famous rock band Lordi here.

Getting There & Away

AIR
Blue1 (www.blue1.com) has the cheapest flights from Helsinki – as low as €18 for the 1½-hour flight when booked by internet. Finnair has daily flights to Rovaniemi from Helsinki, Kemi and Oulu. An airport bus meets all flights, and departs from the central bus station one hour before flight departures (€5).

BUS
Buses are the way to travel further north into Lapland – for Oulu, Kemi and Helsinki, take the train. From the **main bus station** (Lapinkävijäntie) daily services go to Muonio (€33.60, 3½ hours) and Enontekiö (Hetta; €43.70, five hours) in the northwest; Kuusamo (€26.40, three hours) in the east; and north to Sodankylä (€21.40, two hours), Ivalo (€40.80, 4½ hours) and Inari (€46.30, five to six hours), then on to Norway. One bus a day goes all the way to Nordkapp (North Cape; €85.30, 11½ hours) in Norway.

TRAIN
For overnight travel between Helsinki and Rovaniemi (€72.20, sleeper from €79, 10 to 12 hours) the train is quicker, cheaper and more comfy than the bus. There are eight daily trains via Oulu (€27.70, 2½ hours) and Tampere (€62.20, eight hours), including four overnight services.

Getting Around
Rovaniemi's centre is compact and it's easy enough to get around on foot but bicycles can be rented from **Arctic Safaris** (☎ 340 0400; Koskikatu 6; 3/24hr €11/18). Bus No 8 goes from the train station to town.

Major car rental companies have offices in Rovaniemi or at the airport and a car can be a convenient way of exploring northern Lapland. Try **Europcar** (☎ 04-0043 3507; Koskikatu 6) or **Budget** (☎ 312 266; Koskikatu 9).

AROUND ROVANIEMI
Napapiiri
The official **Arctic Circle marker** (Napapiiri) is 8km north of Rovaniemi, and built on top of it is the 'official' **Santa Claus Village** (www.santaclausvillage.info; admission free; ⏰ 10am-5pm Jan-May & Sep-Nov, 9am-7pm Jun-Aug & Dec). The **Santa Claus post office** receives close to a half a million letters each year – he and his helpers

actually reply to almost half of these! Rarely do you get a chance to see such pure commercialism in such a remote location, but as tacky as it sounds, it's all good fun. You can send a postcard home with an official Santa stamp (arrange to have it delivered at Christmas); meet the bearded man in red in his grotto (that's free, but note that Santa is a registered trademark and he can only be photographed by his elves – the cost is from €19!); and there are some excellent souvenir and handicraft shops here. In winter and spring, giant snowmen stand outside and piped Christmas carols give the whole place a kitsch but jolly atmosphere. Bus No 8 goes to the Santa Claus Village hourly from Rovaniemi train station (return €5.40).

Santapark (☎ 333 0000; www.santapark.com; adult/child winter €20/15, adult/family summer €10/30; ⏰ 10am-4pm Tue-Sat early Jun-late Aug, 10am-6pm Tue-Sun Nov-mid Jan), a Christmas-themed amusement park back on the road to Rovaniemi, is strictly for kids.

Ranua Zoo
Although a long detour just to see a zoo, **Ranua Zoo** (☎ 355 1921; www.ranuawildlife.fi; adult/child & student €12/9; ⏰ 9am-7pm Jun-Aug, 10am-4pm Sep-May), 83km south of Rovaniemi on road No 78, is an excellent wildlife park housing over 30 mammal and 30 bird species native to Finland or Scandinavia, including brown and polar bears, lynx, arctic fox and several species of owl. As with any zoo, seeing the animals active is a matter of chance but you'll certainly get a look at the normally elusive *hirvi* – the Finnish elk.

Ranua is most easily reached by bus from Rovaniemi (€22, one hour, two daily).

ROVANIEMI TO INARI
North from Rovaniemi, Hwy 4 (E75) heads up to the vast, flat expanse of northern Lapland and Sápmi, home of the Sami people and domesticated reindeer herds.

Subtle landscape changes become more severe as you head north, and the feeling of entering one of Europe's last great wildernesses is palpable. Snow and icy roads are likely until May. The road passes through Sodankylä, the 'gold village' of Tankavaara and the ski-hiking resort village of Saariselkä, a jumping-off point for the UKK National Park and Saariselkä Wilderness that extends east to the Russian border.

Sodankylä

☎ 016 / pop 9922

The busy market town of Sodankylä is a reasonable place to break the journey between Rovaniemi and northern Lapland, and is renowned for the **Midnight Sun Film Festival** (www.msfilmfestival.fi) held in mid-June.

This is also a base for visiting the **Lampivaara Amethyst Mine** (☎ 624 334; www .amethystmine.fi; Lampivaara Fell; adult/child €14/8; ☽ 11am-5pm Jun-Aug, 11am-4pm Sep, 11am-3pm Tue-Sat Oct & Feb-Apr), 38km south of Sodankylä in Luosto. The only working amethyst mine in Europe can be reached by bus; book at the tourist office.

In the town itself, the **old wooden church** (☽ 10am-6pm Jun-Aug) is worth a look; it's in the cemetery behind the newer stone church. It was built in 1689, making it one of the oldest in Lapland, and the mummified bodies of local priests and their families are buried beneath the church floor.

The **tourist office** (☎ 618 168; www.sodankyla.fi; Jäämerentie 3; ☽ 9am-5pm Mon-Fri, also Sat in summer) is in the same building as the **Andraes Alariesto Gallery** (☎ 618 643; adult/student/child €5/3/2; ☽ 11am-5pm Mon-Fri), which displays art by famous Sami painter Alariesto.

The cosiest place to stay in Sodankylä is **Majatalo Kolme Veljestä** (☎ 611 216; Ivalontie 1; s/d/tr €38/54/65; ✄ Ⓟ), a welcoming family B&B guesthouse with roaring log fire in the lounge, tidy rooms (shared bathroom), guest kitchen and sauna. It's about 500m north of the bus station on the road to Ivalo.

There are plenty of cafés, supermarkets, takeaways and a couple of bars lined up along the main street, Jäämerentie. The best is **Café In CajMar** (☎ 624 383; Jäämerentie 11; snacks €2-5, mains €9.50-23; ☽ 10am-8pm Mon-Sat, noon-6pm Sun).

There are daily buses to/from Rovaniemi (€18.60, two hours) and Ivalo (€25.40, three hours).

Ivalo

☎ 016 / pop 3500

Ivalo is the administrative and commercial centre of the Inari district, but it's a drab, modern centre with no special attractions – Inari, 40km further north, is a better place to stop. Ivalo is merely somewhere to stock up on provisions, make bus connections or

meet some crusty old gold-panners who come to town to trade their gold chips for beer. The **tourist office** (☎ 661 411; Ivalontie 7; ☽ 9am-4.30pm Mon-Fri) is in the Inarilainen agency on the main street.

Kultahippu Hotel (☎ 661 825; www.kultahippu hotel.fi, Petsamontie 1; s/d €60/80, s/d with sauna €75/93; Ⓟ) At the north end of the main street, this rustic hotel is the town focal point. Comfortable rooms upstairs and reasonably priced restaurant and local pub downstairs; attracts all sorts of local characters on weekends.

Kamisak (☎ 667 736; www.kamisak.com; Rovaniementie 915), about 7km south of Ivalo, is an well-established husky farm where you can meet the dogs (€4) or organise dogsledding safaris from a half-day (from €100) to epic five-day journeys.

Express buses from Rovaniemi operate services twice daily (€40.80, 4½ hours), both continuing north into Norway before returning. Gold Line buses run from Ivalo to Saariselka, Inari, Rovaniemi and Murmansk (Russia).

INARI

☎ 016 / pop 550

At first glance there's not a lot to Inari (Sami: Anàr) other than a pub, a large lake and a few shops lining the Arctic Highway. But this tiny village is the hub of the surrounding Sami community and the most interesting point of civilisation in far northern Lapland. Along with a first class cultural museum, this is a renowned centre for genuine Sami handicrafts produced under the name 'Sami Duodji'.

Inari Info (☎ 661 666; www.inarilapland.org; ☽ 9am-7pm Jun-Aug, 10am-4pm Mon-Fri Sep-May) doubles as the post office and Alko store.

Sights & Activities

Don't miss **Side** (☎ 665 212; www.samimuseum.fi; adult/student & pensioner/child €7/6/3; ☽ 9am-8pm Jun-Sep, 10am-5pm Tue-Sun Oct-May), one of the finest cultural museums in Finland. The exhibitions beautifully bring to life Sami origins, culture, lifestyle and present-day struggles with static and audiovisual displays and photographic collections. There's an excellent nature centre covering Lapland, and outside is an open-air museum with Sami buildings, handicrafts and artefacts (open summer only).

There's a marked 7.5km walking track (starting from the Siida parking area) to the 18th-century **Pielpajärvi wilderness church**. If you have a vehicle, there's another parking area 3km closer. In winter or spring you'll need snowshoes and a keen attitude to tackle this walk.

In summer, boat trips leave for the prominent Ukko island, an ancient cult site for the Inari Samis. The two-hour cruises on Inarijärvi are run by **Lake & Snow** (☎ 0400-295731; adult/child €13/7; ◷ 2pm Jun, Aug & Sep, 2pm & 6pm Jul). When the lake is frozen over (November to late April) you can take a snowmobile out to the island (per person €60 to €100).

Inarin Porofarmi (☎ 673 912; www.reindeerfarm .fi) is a reindeer farm run by a Sami family 14km from Inari on the back road to Kittila. You can meet reindeer, try lassoing, see Sami shows, and take reindeer safaris in winter. Most programs require advance notice, so call ahead.

Finland's biggest **reindeer racing championships** are held on the frozen lake in the first week of April, and a big **ice-fishing** competition draws the crowds in mid-April.

Sleeping & Eating
Hotel Inarin Kultahovi (☎ 671 221; www.hotel kultahovi.fi; Saariskoskentie 2; s/d €66/86; P ✕) A short walk from the village centre on the edge of the lovely Alakoski river rapids, this welcoming, family-run hotel is Inari's best, with renovated rooms and a great riverside sauna. There's a good restaurant (mains €9.50 to €26), open 11am to 11pm, offering Lappish specialities and set menus – try the mushroom-filled crepe.

Hotel Inari (☎ 671 026; www.hotelliinari.fi; s/d/tr €42/62/90; P ✕) The local hotel is also the hub of the village – pub, restaurant, Saturday-night disco and all-round local hang-out which can get a bit boisterous on weekends. Upstairs are small but clean rooms with private bathrooms.

Hostel Jokitörmä (☎ 672 725; www.jokitorma.com; camp sites €13, dm €16/19 s/d/tr €30/38/55, cottages €28-88; P ✕) On the Arctic Hwy about 27km north of Inari, this place offers something for everyone with camping, a HI hostel with cosy two- and four-person rooms, and cottages, each with their own kitchen and bathroom facilities. It's a pity it's not closer to Inari, but all buses (including those heading to Nordkapp) will stop here on request.

Getting There & Away
The Arctic Hwy runs through Inari and buses from Rovaniemi ply the route right through to Nordkapp, Tana Bru and Kirkenes (all in Norway) in summer. Buses stop outside the tourist office and although you can't make reservations or buy tickets here, you can pick up timetables and there are no problems getting a seat (pay the driver). Gold Line buses run daily to/from Ivalo (€6.40, 40 minutes), with connections south to Rovaniemi.

LEMMENJOKI NATIONAL PARK
Lemmenjoki is Finland's largest national park (2855 sq km), a remote and wild place and one of Lapland's most diverse environments. Hiking trails extend for over 70km through the vast reserve and there are several free wilderness huts.

SOMETHING SPECIAL

On the Arctic Hwy, about 10km south of the resort village of Saariselken, is one of Lapland's most weird and wonderful places to stay. **Hotel Kakslauttanen** (☎ 016-667 100; www.kakslauttanen .fi; cabins from €100, igloos from €119-158 per person) is a minivillage made up of rustic log cabins, all with their own sauna, fireplace, separate bedroom and kitchenette. But it's the glass igloos that make this place so unique. Situated away from the cabins are some 20 igloos built from 'thermo glass'. Inside is a reclining double bed, private bathroom, enough room to stand comfortably, and a toasty-warm heater. The idea is that, between September and April, you have a good chance of viewing the northern lights from the comfort of your bed. The experience is not cheap, but if you're lucky enough to see the show – or experience a snowstorm – it's priceless. In winter (Dec-Apr), real snow igloos are also built here and you can sleep in -5°C huddled in a polar sleeping bag. There's also an ice chapel and gallery, restaurant and activities such as dogsledding, snowmobiling and cross-country skiing. This is Lapland at its best!

Lemmenjoki Nature Centre (☎ 0205-647793; ⏰ 9am-7pm Jun-Aug, 9am-5pm Sep) is just before the village of Njurgulahti, about 50km southwest of Inari.

As well as hiking trails and opportunities for gold panning, there's a boat cruise along the Lemmenjoki valley in summer, from Njurgulahti village to the Kultahamina wilderness hut at Gold Harbour. A 20km marked trail also follows the course of the river, so you can take the boat one way, then hike back. Accommodation at Njurgulahti includes two camping grounds.

In summer, Gold Line runs at least one bus on weekdays from Inari to Lemmenjoki (€9, one hour).

NORTHWESTERN LAPLAND

Although remote, northwestern Lapland doesn't seem nearly as desolate and empty as its eastern counterpart. For a start it's got 'mountains' and is best known for its ski resorts (Levi, Ylläs and Olos), superb summer hiking (Pallas-Yllästunturi National Park and Kilpisjärvi area), and white-water rafting and canoeing on the fast-flowing Muonionjoki and Tornionjoki rivers, which form the border between Finland and Sweden. Throw in husky dogsledding and you've got plenty of action above the Arctic Circle.

Muonio

☎ 016

For travellers, the little village of Muonio is mainly a centre for hiking and winter activities – nearby is the small Olos ski resort, a serious husky farm and the start (or end) of the four-day trek through the Pallas-Yllästunturi National Park to Hetta. The Munionjoki provides white-water thrills.

Kiela Naturium (☎ 532 280; www.kielanaturium.fi, www.muonio.fi Kilpisjärventie 15; ⏰ 10am-5pm Mon-Sat Jul–early-Sep, 10am-5pm Mon-Fri Sep-Jun) combines tourist information with a nifty 3D-multimedia fells nature display, and a planetarium with aurora borealis show (adult/child €7/5).

About 3km south of the village, **Harriniva Holiday Centre** (☎ 530 0300; www.harriniva.fi; cabins €20-55, s/d €120/140, summer from €68/78) has a vast programme of summer and winter activities, as well as accommodation and a restaurant. This is probably the best place in Finland to organise a husky safari. Harriniva has a husky breeding centre with some 500 dogs (guided tour adult/child €7/4), and in winter and spring there are dogsledding safaris from one hour (adult/child €60/35) to two days (€470/320) staying overnight in a wilderness hut, as well as snowmobile, snowshoe and reindeer safaris. In summer, the centre offers daily guided white-water rafting trips on the Muonio river from €25 for a 1½-hour trip.

Levi

☎ 016

Levi is one of Finland's most popular downhill ski resorts, especially with a young, party crowd. One of the great things about Levi is the accessibility and compact nature of the resort, and the spring skiing here is usually excellent.

The **tourist office** (☎ 639 3300; www.levi.fi; Myllyojoentie 2; ⏰ 9am-4.30pm Mon-Fri, 11am-5.30pm Sat & Sun) should be your first stop for accommodation bookings as well as activities like snowmobile safaris and dogsled treks.

The resort has 45 downhill slopes and 26 lifts, including a gondola. Two lifts operate in summer, and mountain bikes can be hired from the ski rental shop. Ice-fishing on the frozen lake is a popular activity in spring.

Accommodation prices go through the roof in the peak season of February to May and in December – there are 19,000 beds here but book ahead or forget it. In summer (May to September), however, you can get a comfortable cabin sleeping up to five people for as little as €45 a night, and hotel prices drop to rates comparable to anywhere else in Finland.

There are four to seven buses a day from Rovaniemi to Levi (€26.60, 2½ hours).

Hetta & Pallas-Yllästunturi National Park

☎ 016 / pop 700

One of the easiest long-distance walks in Lapland is the excellent 55km trekking route between the northern village of Hetta (also known as Enontekiö) and **Hotelli Pallas** (☎ 532 441; s/d €110/140, summer €52/65; P 🗙). The marked trail passes through Pallas-Yllästunturi National Park, Finland's third-largest, and can easily be completed in four days. There are seven free wilderness huts, but these can be packed with people in summer so it is wise to carry your own tent.

The **Fell Lapland Nature Centre** (☎ 556 215; www.enontekio.fi; Peuratie, Hetta) is the combined local tourist office and a visitor centre for the national park. At the southern end of the trek, the **Pallastunturi Nature Centre** (☎ 0205-647 930; ☺ 9am-5pm daily Jun-Sep, 9am-4pm Mon-Fri Oct-May) at Pallastunturi Fell provides information and can also make hut reservations.

Hetta is the service village for the Sami homeland of Enontekiö, and has plenty of accommodation, including summer camping and cabins.

Hetan Majatalo (☎ 554 0400; www.hetan-maja talo.fi; s/d €60/80) This fine guesthouse in the town centre has Nordic-pine country-style rooms, some with spacious lofts. There are cheaper rooms inside the traditional inn (singles/doubles €42/56).

In summer, there's one daily bus from Muonio to Pallastunturi (€5.20, 45 minutes). Buses to Hetta run daily from Rovaniemi (€43.70, five hours) via Kittilä and Muonio.

Kilpisjärvi
☎ 016

The remote 'left arm' of Finland is home to some of Finland's highest mountains (which aren't very high), however this scenic outpost on the shores of Kilpisjärvi is really only the preserve of serious trekkers or travellers with private transport heading into remote Sweden or Norway. Most people climb the Saana Fell (1029m), or walk (or take a boat taxi) to the **Malla Nature Park**, where you can stand on the joint border of Sweden, Norway and Finland. Serious hikers can walk to the Halti Fell (1328m), the highest in Finland. There are wilderness huts en route but bringing a map is essential. Information, maps and accommodation is available from the hiking centre **Kilpisjärvi Hiking Centre** (☎ 537 771; www.kilpisjarvi.info).

There are two daily bus connections between Rovaniemi and Kilpisjärvi (€55.60, seven hours) both run via Kittilä and Muonio, with one continuing on to Tromsø in Norway.

FINLAND DIRECTORY

ACCOMMODATION

In this chapter, we have classified sleeping options as follows:

- Budget: camping and hostels under €30 per person.
- Midrange: guesthouses, cottages and hotels under €80 a double.
- Top End: €80 and upwards.

Camping

Camping is the cheapest way to travel around Finland – and the best way to get close to the heart of the Finnish countryside. Most camp sites are open only from June to August (ie summer) and popular spots are crowded during July and the Midsummer weekend. Sites cost from €8 to €18. Almost all camping grounds have cabins or cottages for rent, which are usually excellent value from €35 for a basic double cabin to €120 for a cottage with kitchen and bathroom.

If you plan to do a lot of camping, the Camping Card Scandinavia offers useful discounts. Contact the **Finnish Camping Association** (☎ 09-4774 0740; www.camping.fi) for more information.

Finland's *jokamiehenoikeus* (everyman's right) allows access to most land and means you can pitch a tent almost anywhere on public land or at designated free camp sites in national parks. Be sure to ask the owner's permission if you are thinking of camping on private land.

Guesthouses & Holiday Cottages

In large towns and coastal resorts, guesthouses are a cosy choice, often costing only a little more than a double room at a hostel.

Holiday cottages in the countryside are a great way to experience Finland – just as the Finns themselves do. The cottages vary from very basic lakeside cottages with few facilities to luxurious farmhouses. Rental costs vary from about €250 to €700 per week depending on the time of year and size of the property. For listings and booking information, contact **Lomarengas** (☎ 09-5766 3300; www.lomarengas.fi), **Huvila** (www .huvila.net) or any of Finland's regional tourist offices.

Hostels

Finnish hostels are always functional, if a little bland. **Finnish Youth Hostel Association** (SRM; ☎ 09-64 0377; www.srmnet.org) operates 84 hostels. Around half of these are open all year; the rest operate in summer only (June to August) and are usually student accommodation buildings that have been vacated for the school holidays. Always call ahead to book a bed – even during winter, hostels can fill up quickly. Hostel prices quoted throughout this chapter do not include the €2.50 discount given to holders of a valid HI card.

Hotels

Finland has several large business-type hotel chains with all the usual features, including Sokos, Scandic, Cumulus and Radisson – you'll find at least one of these in every large town. In contrast to much of the rest of the world, hotels in Finland offer substantially lower rates on weekends (usually Friday and Saturday nights but sometimes also on Sunday night) and in summer (June to August), when business travel is down, so it's always worth checking out if hotel prices are discounted at these times.

Look out for Omena Hotels (www .omena.com) in Tampere, Turku and Vaasa (two were due to open in Helsinki in 2007). These are staff-free hotels that can only be booked over the internet. They offer excellent rooms sleeping up to four people for the great value price of €55.

ACTIVITIES
Canoeing & Rafting

Finland has so much water in the form of lakes and rivers that it seems a shame to stay on dry land. Canoes and kayaks can be hired in most towns near a lake, often from camping grounds, for around €10 a day. Transport to the start/finishing points of popular river trips can usually be arranged at an extra cost.

Good places for organised **white-water rafting** trips include the rapids around Kuhmo (see p195), the Kitkajoki north of Kuusamo (see p199), the rapids of the Tornionjoki and Munionjoki rivers on the Finland-Sweden border (see p201 and p208), and the Ruunaa Recreation Area in North Karelia (see p194).

Fishing

To fish with a lure you need to buy a one-week (€6) or one-year (€20) fishing licence, available at banks, post offices and the **Forest and Park Service information office** (www.metsa.fi; Eteläesplanadi 20, Helsinki). Fishing in Northern Lapland requires a separate regional licence. In winter and spring, ice-fishing is popular and requires no licence – just bore a hole in the ice and dangle a line.

Hiking

Hiking or trekking (often called fell walking in Finland) is best from June to September, although in July mosquitoes and other biting insects can be a big problem in Lapland. In summer, given the continuous daylight in northern Finland, you can comfortably walk all night if you feel like it, especially in the north. Wilderness huts line the northern trails (they are free and must be shared). According to the law, a principle of common access to nature applies, so you are generally allowed to hike in any forested or wilderness area.

Skiing

Finns love to ski, though a lack of any real mountains means Nordic (cross-country) skiing is favoured. There are some reasonable downhill resorts in the far north, and cross-country trails of varying difficulty (some illuminated) all over the country. From February to April, downhill skiers flock to resorts such as Levi and Ylläs in northwest Lapland, Ruka near Kuusamo or Koli in North Karelia. Expect to pay €20 to €30 a day for lift passes and €25 to hire a complete cross-country or downhill kit (skis or snowboard, boots and poles). The full season runs from October to April. Accommodation prices and crowds are highest in the peak season of spring (February to April).

Swimming & Sauna

What would Finland be without the physically and mentally cleansing sauna? The traditional sauna is a wooden room with benches and a properly stoked wooden stove, although most Finnish saunas now have electric heating. Temperatures should be 80°C to 100°C, and the sauna is taken in the nude. Many hotels – and many hostels and camping grounds – have men's and women's saunas that are free with a night's stay.

Uimahalli (indoor swimming centres) can be found in most towns and they usually have spa and sauna facilities in addition to a pool. *Kylpylä* (spa hotels) are another option for getting hot and wet and some have spectacular facilities as well as massage and hydrotherapy. There are good ones in Turku, Oulu, Kuopio and Savonlinna. In most places nonguests can use the facilities for a fee.

Winter Activities

As well as skiing and snowboarding, Finland offers a range of snowbound activities including dogsledding, snowmobile safaris, ice-fishing and reindeer sleigh tours. Most of these activities are expensive but there's something magic about being pulled through the snow by a team of huskies. The best place to get involved is Lapland: Rovaniemi (see p201) is a major centre for organised tours, and ski resorts such as Levi and Ylläs also offer tours, plus there are husky farms at Ivalo (p206) and Muonio (p208). The Lake Pielinen region, especially Lieksa and Nurmes, is also popular for winter activities. The main season is late winter and spring (January to April).

BUSINESS HOURS

Shops generally open from 9am to 5pm weekdays, and to 1pm on Saturday. Banks are open from 9.15am until 4.15pm weekdays. Many supermarkets and Helsinki department stores stay open until 9pm or 10pm on weeknights and open all day on Saturday.

Cafés are usually open from 9am or 10am to 6pm, however they stay open much later if they're licensed. Restaurants open from around 11am to 10pm with lunch from 11am to 3pm. Pubs open from 11am to 10pm (to 1am or later on Friday and Saturday) and nightclubs stay open as late as 4am.

EMBASSIES & CONSULATES
Finland Embassies & Consulates

Finland maintains embassies in the following countries:

Australia (☎ 02-6273 3800; www.finland.org.au; 12 Darwin Ave, Yarralumla, ACT 2600)

Canada (☎ 613-288 2233; www.finland.ca; 55 Metcalfe St, Suite 850, Ottawa K1P 6L5)

Denmark (☎ 33 13 4214; www.finamb.dk; Sankt Annae Plads 24, 1250 Copenhagen K)

France (☎ 01 44 18 19 20; www.amb-finlande.fr; 1 Place de Finlande, 57007 Paris)

Germany (☎ 030-505030; www.finnland.de; Rauchstrasse 1, 10787 Berlin)

Ireland (☎ 01-478 1344; www.finland.ie; Russell House, Stokes Pl, St Stephen's Green, Dublin 2)

Netherlands (☎ 070-346 9754; www.finlande.nl; Groot Hertoginnelaan 16, 251r EG Den Haag)

New Zealand Honorary Consulate General (☎ 04-499 4599; Level 24, HSBC Tower, 195 Lambton Quay, Wellington) Or contact the Australian embassy.

Norway (☎ 2212 4900; www.finland.no; Thomas Heftyes gate 1, 0244 Oslo)

Russia (☎ 095-787 4174; www.finemb-moscow.fi; Kropotkinskij Pereulok 15/17, 119034 Moskva G-34)

Sweden (☎ 08-676 6700; www.finland.se; Jakobsgatan 6, 10391 Stockholm)

UK (☎ 020-7838 6200; www.finemb-org.uk; 38 Chesham Place, London SW1X 8HW)

USA (☎ 202-298 5800; www.finland.org; 3301 Massachusetts Ave NW, Washington DC 20008)

Embassies & Consulates in Finland

The following embassies are in Helsinki:

Australia (☎ 4777 6640; australian.consulate@tradimex.fi; Museokatu 25B) This is an Honorary consulate; the nearest embassy is in Stockholm.

Canada (☎ 228 530; www.canada.fi; Pohjoisesplanadi 25B)

Denmark (☎ 684 1050; www.ambhelsingfors.um.dk/da; Keskuskatu 1A)

Estonia (☎ 622 0260; www.estemb.fi; Itäinen Puistotie 10)

France (☎ 618 780; www.france.fi; Itäinen Puistotie 13)

Germany (☎ 458 580; www.helsinki.diplo.de; Krogiuksentie 4B)

Ireland (☎ 646 006; ireland@welho.com; Erottajankatu 7A)

Japan (☎ 686 0200; www.fi.emb-japan.go.jp; Eteläranta 8)

Latvia (☎ 4764 7244; embassy.finland@mfa.gov.lv; Armfeltintie 10)

Lithuania (☎ 608 210; embassylt@kolumbus.fi; Rauhankatu 13A)

Netherlands (☎ 228 920; www.netherlands.fi; Errotajankuta 19B)

Norway (☎ 686 0180; www.norja.fi; Rehbinderintie 17)

Russia (☎ 661 876; rusembassy@co.inet.fi; Tehtaankatu 1B)

Sweden (☎ 651 255; www.sverige.fi; Pohjoisesplanadi 7B)

UK (☎ 2286 5100; www.ukembassy.fi; Itäinen Puistotie 17)

USA (☎ 616 250; www.usembassy.fi; Itäinen Puistotie 14A)

FINLAND

FESTIVALS & EVENTS

Finland puts on a barrage of music, arts, cultural, sporting and just plain nutty festivals year-round, but especially between June and mid-August. Midsummer is a big deal in any part of Finland, though for most Finns it's a family time when they disappear to their summer cottages. Pick up the *Finland Festivals* booklet in any tourist office or check out www.festivals.fi.

Air Guitar World Championships (p198) Whacky festival held in Oulu, late August.

Ilosaarirock (p192) Rock Festival in Joensuu, July.

Pori Jazz Festival (p179) Finland's famous jazz festival, held in mid-July.

Ruisrock (p165) Held in Turku in early July.

Savonlinna Opera Festival (p185) Highbrow festival in medieval castle in July.

Vappu (May Day) A big day for Finns, especially students, this holiday is celebrated nationally.

World Wife-Carrying Championships (see p192) Manic two-day festival held in Sonkajärvi in early July.

HOLIDAYS

Finland grinds to a halt twice a year – around Christmas and New Year and during the Midsummer weekend. Plan ahead and avoid travelling during those times. National public holidays are:

New Year's Day 1 January

Epiphany 6 January

Good Friday to Easter Monday March/April

May Day Eve and **May Day** (Vappu) 30 April and 1 May

Ascension Day 40 days after Easter

Whit Sunday Late May or early June

Juhannus Midsummer; third weekend in June

All Saints Day 1 November

Independence Day 6 December

Christmas Eve 24 December

Christmas Day 25 December

Boxing Day 26 December

INTERNET ACCESS

All public libraries offer free internet access, and cafés and tourist offices have at least one terminal that you can use free for 15 minutes or so. Wireless (wi-fi) hotspots are becoming widespread and it's often possible to pick up free signals. Many hotels offer free or paid wi-fi access.

INTERNET RESOURCES

Finland probably has more websites per capita than any other country – all tourist offices have a site and so, it seems, does every other person, place and institution in the country. Good general sites:

Aktivist (www.aktivist.fi/inenglish) A-Z coverage from Alvar Aalto to Vappu with offbeat cultural observations.

Finn Guide (www.finnguide.fi) English site dedicated to all things Finnish, from recipes to nightlife.

Helsingin Sanomat (www.helsinginsanomat.fi) Site of Helsinki's biggest newspaper has an English summary.

Virtual Finland (www.virtual.finland.fi) Excellent site covering all aspects of Finland in five languages.

MONEY

Finland adopted the euro in 2001, and it remains the only Nordic country to have done so. Euro notes come in five, 10, 20, 100 and 500 denominations and coins in five, 10, 20, 50 cents and €1 and €2.

ATMs

There are 24-hour ATMs ('Otto') linked to international networks (Cirrus, Maestro, Visa, MasterCard) in every city, town and almost every village in Finland, so carrying a debit or credit card (and your PIN) is definitely the easiest way to get cash.

Credit Cards

Credit cards are widely accepted and Finns are dedicated users of the plastic – buying a beer or cup of coffee with a credit card is not unusual and it's commonplace to pay for accommodation and restaurant meals in this way. Keeping your credit account in the black will help you avoid bank charges.

Travellers Cheques

Finland's major national banks (Osuuspankki, Nordea and Sampo) will change travellers cheques and have similar rates and charges – up to €7 per transaction. In cities, independent exchangers such as Forex are a better alternative for exchanging cash and travellers cheques (€2 per cheque).

POST

Posti (post offices) are generally open from 9am to 7pm weekdays, and in cities they are also open on Saturday. Stamps (€0.65 for letters and postcards) can be bought at bus or train stations and R-kiosks (newsagents). International parcel post is relatively expensive – from €20 to €40 for up to 5kg depending on the destination. See the website www.posti.fi for more information. Poste restante is offered at the main post offices in cities.

TELEPHONE

Some public phones accept coins, but most accept only plastic Telecards. With just about everyone carrying a mobile phone, public phones don't get much of a work-out these days.

International calls are cheapest if you buy one of the prepaid calling cards from any R-kiosk. Off-peak times are 10pm to 8am on weekdays and all day Satur-day and Sunday. A three-minute call to the USA during peak time will cost about €4. For national directory assistance dial ☎ 020 202; for international assistance call ☎ 020 208.

The country code for calling Finland from abroad is ☎ 358. To make an inter-national call from Finland, first dial an in-ternational prefix (☎ 00, 990, 994 or 999) and then the country code for the country you're calling.

MOBILE PHONES

Finland has one of the world's highest rates of mobile-phone usage, and getting hooked up to the mobile-phone network is easy with the prepaid system using Sonera, DNA or Elisa.

A great option is to bring your own phone and simply buy a SIM card (around €15) from a phone shop or any R-kiosk, then buy recharge cards from the same outlets.

VISAS

A valid passport is required to enter Fin-land, though citizens of EU countries, Norway and Iceland can travel with only an identity card. Most Western nationals don't need a tourist visa for stays of up to three months; South Africans require a Schengen visa. The **Directorate of Immigration** (☎ 09-476 5500; www.uvi.fi) handles visas and work permits.

Australian and New Zealand citizens aged between 18 and 30 can apply for a 12-month working holiday visa under a re-ciprocal agreement – contact the Finnish embassy in your home country.

Russian visas can be obtained from the Russian consulate in Helsinki. You need to leave your passport at the consulate and allow a week to 10 days for processing. Travel agencies in Helsinki can expedite the visa process for a fee.

TRANSPORT IN FINLAND

GETTING THERE & AWAY

Air

Most major European carriers have flights to and from Helsinki's **Vantaa airport** (☎ 0200-14636; www.helsinki-vantaa.fi). Finnair is the na-tional carrier, with direct flights to Helsinki from New York, Toronto, Bangkok, Sin-gapore, Tokyo, Hong Kong and most Eu-ropean capitals. A cheap entry to Finland is with **Ryanair** (www.ryanair.com) from London Stansted, Liverpool, Frankfurt Hahn and Riga to Tampere, or with **Blue 1** (www.blue1.com) which offers cheap internet fares between Helsinki and Amsterdam, Brussels, Copen-hagen, Oslo, Stockholm and as far as Athens and Barcelona.

Airlines flying to and from Finland:

Aer Lingus (airline code EI; ☎ 09-6122 0260; www .aerlingus.ie)

Aeroflot (airline code SU; ☎ 09-659 655; www.aero flot.com)

Air France (airline code AF; ☎ 09-8568 0500; www .airfrance.com)

American Airlines (airline code AA; ☎ 9800 14620; www.aa.com)

Austrian Airlines (airline code OS; ☎ 020-386 000; www.aua.com)

Blue 1 (airline code KF; ☎ 020-386 000; www.blue1.com)

British Airways (airline code BA; ☎ 0800 178 378; www.britishairways.com)

Finnair (airline code AY; ☎ 09-81881; www.finnair.com)

Icelandair (airline code FI; ☎ 09-6126 070; www .icelandair.com)

KLM Royal Dutch Airlines (airline code KL; ☎ 020 353 355; www.klm.com)

LOT Polish Airlines (airline code LO; ☎ 09-6937 9036; www.lot.com)

Lufthansa (airline code LH; ☎ 020-386 000; www .lufthansa.com)

MALEV Hungarian Airlines (airline code MA; ☎ 09-622 0922; www.malev.hu)

Ryanair (airline code FR; www.ryanair.com)

SAS Scandinavian Airlines (airline code SK; ☎ 020-585 6000; www.sas.fi)

Land

BORDER CROSSINGS

There are six road crossings from northern Sweden to northern Finland and another six from Norway to Finland, but there are no border controls or customs formalities. There are six crossings into Russia along Finland's eastern border (the main route is Helsinki–Vyborg–St Petersburg); you must have a valid Russian visa.

BUS
Sweden
The only useful bus route from Finland to Sweden is from the border town of Tornio, where you can get a direct bus to Stockholm (€55, 15 hours) – or just walk across the bridge to Haparanda and you're in Sweden anyway.

Norway
Buses run between Rovaniemi and the Norwegian border, with some buses continuing on to the first Norwegian town – but check timetables as you may be dropped at the border without a connecting bus, especially outside the June to August high season. The main operator is **Eskelisen Lapin Linjat** (☎ 016-342 2160; www .eskelisen-lapinlinjat.com).

The main Nordkapp route will take you from Rovaniemi via Inari and Kaamanen up to Karigasniemi and then across the Norwegian border to Karasjok and Lakselv. Many bus services operate services from Ivalo to Karasjok, and in summer (June to August) there is at least one daily bus travelling all the way to Nordkapp (adult/ student €85.30, 11 hours from Rovaniemi). Two alternative routes, which are not as well served by bus, go through western Lapland, via Hetta and onto Karasjok; or along highway 21 to Kilpisjärvi and along the coast to Alta. The latter route is also the quickest way to Tromsø and anywhere south in Norway.

Russia
Daily express buses run from Turku and Helsinki to Vyborg and St Petersburg (Russian visa required) along highway E18, via the Finnish towns of Porvoo, Kotka and Hamina. Check current timetables and book tickets at the bus station or a travel agency; from Helsinki to St Petersburg there are three daily buses (€55.60, 9½ hours). The train is a more romantic and comfortable way to reach Russia. Note that St Petersburg is Pietari in Finnish, and Vyborg is Viipuri.

CAR & MOTORCYCLE
Vehicles can easily be brought into Finland on the Baltic ferries from Sweden, Estonia and Germany, provided you have registration papers and valid insurance (green card or frontier insurance – check with your local motoring organisation).

See p216 for information about driving in Finland.

TRAIN
The only international train links with Finland are to/from Moscow and St Petersburg in Russia.

There are three daily trains from Helsinki to Russia, travelling via the Finnish stations of Lahti, Kouvola and Vainikkala. You must have a valid Russian visa but border formalities have been fast-tracked so that passport checks are now carried out on board the moving train.

The Russian *Tolstoi* sleeper departs Helsinki daily at 5.42pm, arriving in Moscow at 8.30am the next day (one way in 2nd/1st class €85.80/128.20) via Vyborg (€47/75) and St Petersburg (€58.40/90); it departs from Moscow daily at 10.50pm. Both 1st- and 2nd-class fares include a sleeper berth. The *Sibelius* (a Finnish train) and *Repin* have daily services between Helsinki and St Petersburg (5½ hours) via Vyborg (3¾ hours). The *Sibelius* departs from Helsinki at 7.42am (2nd-/1st-class seats €51.40/81.90, six hours). The Russian *Repin* departs at 3.42pm and has 2nd-class seats (€51.40) or 1st-class sleeping berths (€91). From St Petersburg, departures are at 4.28pm (*Sibelius*) and 7.28am (*Repin*).

Buy Russian rail tickets in Helsinki at the special ticket counter in the central station. Check timetables at www.vr.fi.

Sea
There's no better way to arrive in Helsinki than on board a huge Baltic ferry. These passenger ferries are like miniature cruise ships with cabin accommodation, restaurants, bars, nightclubs, karaoke, gaming rooms and shopping malls, but fares are kept reasonably low by competition and onboard duty-free shopping. Although not the boozy cruises they once were, many Scandinavians still use them simply for overnight or weekend cruises. The ferries dock virtually in the centre of Helsinki.

Many ferries offer 50% discounts for holders of ScanRail and InterRail passes – Silja Line and Viking Line services between Sweden and Finland are free to Eurailpass holders.

Fares vary considerably depending on the season, day of the week (Friday to Sunday is more expensive), whether it's day or overnight and, of course, the class of travel (passenger only or sleeping berth), but all ferry companies have websites in English with detailed timetables and fare information. The main players:

Eckerö Line (www.eckerolinjen.fi, or www.eckeroline.fi)
Åland (☎ 018-28000); Helsinki (☎ 09-228 8544)
Finnlines (☎ 09-251 0200; www.finnlines.fi)
Linda Line (☎ 09-668 9700; www.lindaliini.ee)
Nordic Jet Line (☎ 0600 01 655; www.njl.fi)
RG Line (☎ 06-100 411; www.rgline.com)
Silja Line (☎ 0600-174552; www.silja.com)
Superfast Ferries (☎ 09-2535 0600; www.super fast.com)
Tallink (☎ 0600-15700; www.tallink.fi)
Viking Line (☎ 09-12 351; www.vikingline.fi)

SWEDEN
The Stockholm–Helsinki, Stockholm–Turku and Kapellskär–Mariehamn (Åland) runs are dominated by Silja Line and Viking Line, with daily departures. Viking Line generally has slightly cheaper fares.

On both lines you can buy a passenger-only ticket and sleep in the salons, but it's worth paying extra for a cabin on the Stockholm–Helsinki trip. In the summer high season, overnight crossings (passenger ticket only) from Stockholm start at €36 to Turku (11 to 12 hours) and €47 to Helsinki (16 hours). Cabins start at an additional €42 (€24 in low season).

Eckerö Line sails from Grisslehamn to Eckerö in Åland (€5.50 to €8.90, three hours), and RG Line sails from Vaasa to Umeå (Sweden) one or two times daily from May to end of September (€55, three hours).

ESTONIA
Half a dozen ferry companies ply the Gulf of Finland between Helsinki and Tallinn in Estonia. Car ferries cross in 3½ hours, catamarans and hydrofoils in about 1½ hours, although in winter there are fewer departures and the traffic is also slower due to the ice.

Eckerö Line has only one departure daily but is the cheapest with a day cruise (return)

fare of €28 (€22 in low season). Tallink, Viking Line and Silja Line have regular daily departures from €20 one-way depending on the company, type of boat, the time of year and the day of the week. Linda Line is the cheapest (but smallest) fast boat (one way/return €31/46). Nordic Jet Line is the priciest.

GERMANY
Finnlines has a daily year-round service from Helsinki to Travemünde (26 hours) with bus service to Hamburg. One-way high season rates in a four-person cabin begin at €198.

Superfast Ferries sails between Rostock (Germany) and Hanko on the south coast of Finland (24 hours, daily). The minimum one-way fare in high season for a seat only is €87 or for a cabin €185.

GETTING AROUND
Finland is well served by public transport. A great source to find the best way between two points is the online route planner at Journey.fi (www.matka.fi), which gives you bus and train options and even walking distances between stations and town centres.

Air
Finnair runs a fairly comprehensive domestic service mainly out of Helsinki but also across a few regional centres like Oulu–Rovaniemi. Budget carriers Blue1 and FinnComm Airlines offer the cheapest fares for advance internet bookings.

Full Finnair scheduled fares are not cheap but 'Happy Hour' tickets (book a week in advance, no refunds) are much cheaper and there are summer and weekend specials. Seniors and children aged under 12 receive a 70% discount. If you're aged between 17 and 24 the discount is 50%, but better still you can fly stand-by to anywhere in Finland for €64 or €79 one way, depending on the flight. To qualify you need to arrive at the airport one hour before the flight of your choice and wait to see if there are any seats available.

Blue1 currently flies from Helsinki to Kuopio, Oulu, Rovaniemi and Vaasa for as little as €18 plus taxes (internet booking only).

AIRLINES IN FINLAND
Air Åland (☎ 018-11710; www.airaland.com)
Blue1 (☎ 020-386 000; www.blue1.com)
Finnair (☎ 09-81881; www.finnair.com)
FinnComm Airlines (☎ 4243 2000; www.finncomm.fi)

FINLAND

Bicycle

Finland is flat and as bicycle-friendly as any country you'll find, with miles of bike paths – also used by inline skaters in summer and cross-country skiers in winter. Many Finns use the bicycle as their main form of summer transport around town. The only drawback to an extensive tour is distance, but bikes can be carried on most trains, buses and ferries. The best place for cycling is the Åland islands, where a few days or a week of touring is a breeze.

Daily/weekly hire from €10/50 is possible in most cities, although hiring decent bikes in smaller towns is difficult as there's little demand – check with the local tourist office or try youth hostels or camping grounds. Helmets are advisable but not compulsory. The **Finnish Youth Hostel Association** (SRM; www .srmnet.org) offers a cycling and hostel package that takes in the flat south and lakes for seven/14 days, including bike rental and accommodation (€249/431).

Boat

Lake and river ferries operate from around June to August (lakes are frozen over in winter). They're more than mere transport; a lake cruise taking you from one town to another via southern Finland's sublime system of waterways is a bona fide Finnish experience. The most popular routes include Tampere–Hämeenlinna, Savonlinna–Kuopio, Lahti–Jyväskylä and Joensuu–Koli–Lieksa on Lake Pielinen.

The main coastal sea routes are Turku–Naantali, Helsinki–Porvoo and the archipelago ferries to the Åland islands. Some of the ferries that run between the islands along the coast are free, especially in Åland.

Bus

Dozens of bus companies operate throughout Finland but all long-distance and express bus travel comes under the umbrella of **Oy Matkahuolto Ab** (☎ 09-682 701; www.matkahuolto.fi). Private lines operate local services, but all share the same ticketing system. Major operators include **Express Bus** (www.expressbus.com) and **Gold Line** (www.goldline.fi). Buy tickets on board or book at a bus station or travel agency (Monday to Friday only). Limited services operate on weekends and public holidays.

Fares are based on distance; regular/express adult fares for a 100km trip are €14.20/16.80. Return tickets are about 10% cheaper than two one-way fares. Discounts of 50% (on journeys over 80km) are available for students, but you must have a Matkahuolto student card. Technically you need to be studying in Finland to get one, but travellers have reported getting one with an ISIC card. Children get a discount of 30% (12 to 16 years) or 50% (under 12). On some routes, buses accept train passes.

Car & Motorcycle

Finland's road network is good between main towns, although there are only a handful of multilane motorways emanating from major cities. In the forests you'll find many unsurfaced roads and dirt tracks. There are no road tolls. Fuel is expensive in Finland – at the time of writing a litre of unleaded petrol cost more than €1.30.

HIRE

Car hire in Finland is not cheap, but with a group of three or four it can work out to be reasonably economical, especially if your time is short and you want to get off the main highways. The cheapest way to hire a car is through an internet hire company such as **Web Car Hire** (www.webcarhire.com) which will source a deal from the major rental companies at less than half the standard rates. You can generally pick up a small car with unlimited kilometres for around €30 a day.

Hiring direct from a rental company, expect to pay from €35 per day plus €0.40 per kilometre – from €70 day with unlimited kilometres.

You need only your home driving licence to rent and drive a car in Finland, but most companies require the driver to be at least 21 years old. Major rental companies in Helsinki include:
Avis (☎ 09-441 155; www.avis.fi)
Budget (☎ 09-686 6500; www.budget.fi)
Europcar (☎ 0403-06244; www.europcar.fi)
Hertz (☎ 0200-112 233; www.hertz.fi)
Lacara (☎ 09-719 062; www.lacara.net)
Scandia Rent (☎ 09-2521 2601; www.scandiarent.fi)

ROAD CONDITIONS & HAZARDS

Beware of elk and reindeer, which don't have much respect for car horns and can dash out onto the road unexpectedly. By law, you must notify the police if there is an accident involving these animals. Several thousand accidents involving elk are reported in Finland each year – it's ironic that the only time you may get to see an elk in the wild is when it's careering across the road or through your windscreen. Reindeer are very common in Lapland during spring and summer when they'll often wander along the roads in semidomesticated herds. Slow right down if you see one, as there will be more nearby.

Snow and ice on Finland's roads from September to March or April (and as late as June in Lapland) make driving a hazardous activity without snow tyres (chains are not permitted); cars hired in Finland will be properly equipped.

ROAD RULES

Headlights must be turned on at all times outside built-up areas. Foreign cars must display their nationality and visitors must be fully insured. Wearing seat belts is mandatory for the driver and all passengers. The blood alcohol limit is 0.05%. The speed limit is 50km/h in built-up areas, from 80km/h to 100km/h on highways, and 120km/h on a few motorways. Traffic keeps to the right and, at uncontrolled intersections, give way to traffic approaching from the right.

Train

Finnish trains are efficient, fast, comfortable and cheaper than in Sweden and Norway. From Helsinki, direct trains fan out to all major centres. Crossing the country from east to west may require a change or two, but with a little route planning you can reach most places as far north as Rovaniemi in Lapland.

VR Ltd Finnish Railways (☎ 0600-4192; www.vr.fi) handles rail travel throughout the country. You can search for timetables and fares on its comprehensive website.

CLASSES

The two main types of trains are regional (2nd class only) and express. Other classes include the faster InterCity (IC) trains, and the Pendolino trains which operate fast services on limited major city routes.

Night trains service the longer routes with comfortable one- two- and three-bed sleepers which are only slightly more expensive than a seat-only ticket. For example, the fare for a seat on the train to Rovaniemi is €72.20 – in a three-bed sleeper it's €79. The additional fare for a sleeper in a three-bed compartment in low/high season is €11/16.

COSTS & RESERVATIONS

Reservations can be made at the VR counter at any train station or over the internet (major credit cards accepted).

An open return ticket is valid for 15 days and costs the same as two one-way tickets. Students, seniors and children under 17 pay half fare, and children under six travel free (without a seat). The 50% student discount is officially only available to Finnish students or foreigners studying in Finland.

Ticket prices depend on the distance, the class of travel and season. From Helsinki to Turku express/IC/Pendolino costs €23.40/25.60/30.40. Other express fares include: Helsinki to Tampere (€23.40), Kuopio (€48.60) and Oulu (€61.20). Fares listed in this chapter are IC or express.

TRAIN PASSES

International rail passes accepted in Finland include the Eurailpass, Eurail Flexipass, ScanRail Pass, Euro Domino and InterRail. The Finnrail Pass is a one-month pass good for unlimited travel for 3/5/10 days; 2nd-class travel costs €122/153/220. 1st class is about 50% more. These passes can be bought at VR stations in Finland, or through travel agents. There's also a Holiday Pass (valid June to August) which allows three days of travel in a month for €115.

FINLAND

Tallinn

Tallinn is so much part of the Helsinki experience, it sometimes feels like a distant suburb; 'Tallinski' is a nickname often heard. Not only is the majority of Tallinn's tourists still bargain-hunters from Finland, but the city makes for an obvious addition to travellers exploring eastern Scandinavia. While thoroughly modern and just 80km from Helsinki, it's also, refreshingly, a world apart. Pleasant surprises on all levels abound here.

Boasting a splendidly preserved and lively medieval old town and a gleaming, chrome and glass city centre, Tallinn inspires visitors to poke their heads into ancient courtyards, crane their necks towards Gothic spires, find a cosy cellar café or happening bar, or just hang out at Town Hall Square soaking up the sun and the suds.

Tallinn, Estonia's capital, is one of the coolest spots in Europe, and it's in the mood to strut its new status as the capital of an EU country. Its subtle, quiet charm weaves its way into your heart before you're aware of it.

FAST FACTS

- **Population** 400,000

- **Currency** kroon (EEK); €1=15.65EEK; US$1 = 13.04EEK; UK£1 = 23.26EEK; A$1 = 9.4EEK; CA$1 = 10.9EEK; NZ$1 = 7.9EEK; ¥100 = 10.9EEK

- **Official Language** Estonian

- **Telephone Codes** Estonia country code ☎ 372; no area code for Tallinn

- **Visas** EU nationals and citizens of the US, Canada and Australia do not need a visa to enter Estonia

TALLINN

ORIENTATION & INFORMATION

The medieval Old Town, just to the south of Tallinn Bay, comprises of Toompea (the upper town) and the lower town, which is still surrounded by much of its 2.5km defensive wall. Its centre is Raekoja plats (Town Hall Square). Immediately west of the Old Town is the modern city centre, with shopping plazas and the closest Estonia has to skyscrapers.

The **Tallinn Tourist Information Centre** (☎ 645 7777; www.tourism.tallinn.ee; Niguliste tänav 2; ☼ 9am-7pm Mon-Fri, 10am-5pm Sat & Sun May-Jun, 9am-8pm Mon-Fri, 10am-6pm Sat & Sun Jul-Aug, 9am-6pm Mon-Fri, 10am-5pm Sat & Sun Sep, 9am-5pm Mon-Fri, 10am-3pm Sat Oct-Apr) offers a full range of services. Here you can purchase the Tallinn Card (130EEK to 450EEK), which offers free rides on public transport, admission to museums, free excursions and discounts at restaurants, valid from six to 72 hours. **Estonian Holidays** (☎ 627 0500; www .holidays.ee; Rüütli tänav 28) can help you make travel arrangements.

For maps of the city and region as well as Lonely Planet titles, check out the book shop **Apollo** (☎ 654 8485; Viru tänav 23).

Change money at **Tavid** (☎ 627 9900; Aia tänav 5; ☼ 24hr). To keep in touch, head to the **central post office** (☎ 625 7300; Narva maantee 1; ☼ 7.30am-8pm Mon-Fri, 8am-6pm Sat) or to **Jumping Jacks** (Suur Karja tänav 13; ☼ 11am-9pm; per hr 30EEK) a basement-level, slightly dingy internet connection.

In an emergency, dial ☎ 110 for police and ☎ 112 for fire, ambulance and urgent medical advice. The **First Aid Hotline** (☎ 697 1145) can advise you in English about the nearest treatment centre. For general information, **Info Line** (☎ 626 1111) is very helpful.

SIGHTS
Raekoja Plats & Lower Town

Raekoja plats (Town Hall Square) has been the centre of Tallinn life since markets began here probably in the 11th century. It's dominated by the only surviving Gothic **town hall** (☎ 645 7900; adult/student 35/20EEK; ☼ 10am-4pm Mon-Sat Jun-Aug, by appointment Sep-May) in northern Europe (constructed in the early 14th century, reconstructed 1402–04) and faced by pretty, pastel buildings from the 15th to 17th centuries. Old Thomas, Tallinn's symbol and guardsman, has been keeping watch from his perch

on the weathervane atop the Town Hall since 1530. You can also climb the building's **tower** (adult/student 25/15EEK; ☼ 11am-6pm Jun-Sep). Usually lasting four days, the **Old Town Days** festival in early June sees Raekoja plats come alive with market stalls, concerts, dancing and medieval-themed merry-making.

The **Raeapteek** (Town Council Pharmacy), on the north side of the square, is another ancient Tallinn institution; there's been a pharmacy or apothecary's shop here since at least 1422. An arch beside it leads into narrow Saia käik (White Bread Passage), at the far end of which is the lovely, Gothic **Pühavaimu Kirik** (Holy Spirit Church; ☎ 644 1487; ☼ 10am-3pm, free concerts 6pm Mon), dating from the 14th-century with carvings from 1684 and a tower bell cast in 1433.

A medieval merchant's home at Vene tänav 17, on the corner of Pühavaimu tänav, houses Tallinn's most interesting museum – the **Linnamuuseum** (City Museum; ☎ 644 6553; www .linnamuuseum.ee; Vene tänav 17; adult/student 35/10EEK; ☼ 10.30am-6pm Wed-Mon Mar-Oct, 10.30am-5pm Wed-Mon Nov-Feb), which traces Tallinn's development through to 1940.

From Vene tänav, an arched doorway leads into a cosy courtyard and the world of the **Dominican Monastery** (☎ 644 4606; kloostri @hot.ee; Vene tänav 16/18; adult/student 45/15EEK; ☼ 9.30am-6pm mid-May–mid-Sep), which was founded in 1246 as a base for Scandinavian monks. Today the monastery complex houses Estonia's largest collection of very impressive **stone carvings**, which leave an impression on visitors eager to catch a glimpse of Medieval-looking life; there are often concerts and mysterious activities taking place here.

The majestic **Niguliste Church** (☎ 644 9911; adult/student 35/20EEK; ☼ 10am-5pm Wed-Sun), a minute's walk south of Raekoja plats, is now used to stage concerts and serves as a museum of religious art.

At the foot of the slope below the Niguliste is the carefully exposed wreckage of the buildings that stood here before the Soviet bombing of Tallinn on the night of 9 March 1944.

Pikk tänav, running north from Raekoja plats to the **Great Coast Gate** and the **Paks Margareeta** (Fat Margaret Bastion), the medieval exit to Tallinn port, is lined with many 15th-century houses of medieval

TALLINN

TALLINN

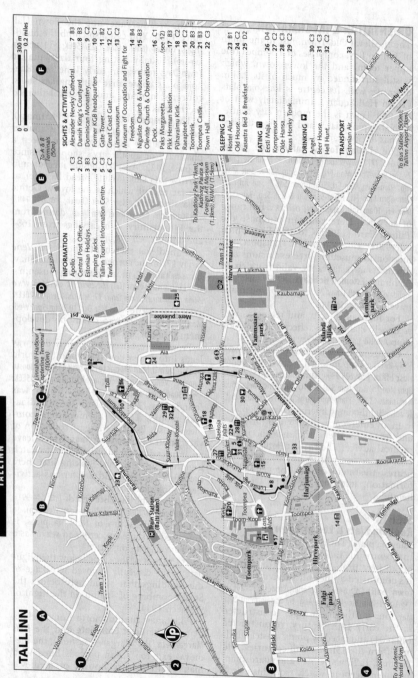

INFORMATION
Apollo..................................... 1 C3
Central Post Office................... 2 D2
Estonian Holidays.................... 3 B3
Jumping Jacks.......................... 4 C3
Tallinn Tourist Information Centre.. 5 C3
Tavid....................................... 6 C2

SIGHTS & ACTIVITIES
Alexander Nevsky Cathedral...... 7 B3
Danish King's Courtyard............ 8 B3
Dominican Monastery................ 9 C2
Former KGB headquarters......... 10 C1
Gate Tower............................. 11 B2
Great Coast Gate..................... 12 C1
Linnamuuseum......................... 13 C2
Museum of Occupation and Fight for
  Freedom.............................. 14 B4
Niguliste Church & Museum...... 15 B3
Oleviste Church & Observation
  Deck................................... 16 C1
Paks Margareeta.................(see 12)
Pikk Herman bastion................ 17 B3
Pühavaimu Kirik...................... 18 C2
Raeapteek.............................. 19 C2
Toomkirik............................... 20 B3
Toompea Castle....................... 21 B3
Town Hall............................... 22 C3

SLEEPING
Hostel Alur............................. 23 B1
Old House.............................. 24 C2
Rasastra Bed & Breakfast......... 25 D2

EATING
Eesti Maja.............................. 26 D4
Kompressor............................. 27 C2
Olde Hansa............................ 28 C3
Texas Honky Tonk.................... 29 C2

DRINKING
Angel.................................... 30 C3
Beer House............................. 31 C3
Hell Hunt............................... 32 C2

TRANSPORT
Estonian Air........................... 33 C3

merchants and gentry. Also here are the buildings of several old Tallinn guilds and some museums.

Near the end of Pikk tänav stands a chief Tallinn landmark, the **Oleviste Church**. This is a great place to start any Tallinn expedition as there's a superb **observation deck** (☎ 621 4421; adult/student 20/10EEK; ☺ 10am-6pm) halfway up its 124m structure offering the city's best views of the Old Town (it's a long and narrow climb up, though – bring a hanky to wipe off the sweat). The Church is dedicated to the 11th-century King Olav II of Norway but it is linked in local lore with another Olav (Olaf), the church's architect who fell to his death from its tower. First built in the early 13th century, it was once the world's tallest building (it used to be 159m high). Near the church on Pikk tänav 59, is the **former KGB headquarters**; the basement windows were sealed to conceal the sounds of cruel interrogations.

Toompea

A regal approach to Toompea is through the red-roofed 1380 **gate tower** at the western end of Pikk tänav in the lower town, and then along Pikk jalg (Long Leg). The still-active 19th-century Russian Orthodox **Alexander Nevsky Cathedral** (☎ 644 3484; ☺ 8am-7pm) dominates Lossi plats at the top of Pikk jalg, sited strategically across from **Toompea Castle**, Estonia's traditional seat of power. The *riigikogu* (parliament) meets in the pink, baroque-style building out front, an 18th-century addition. The state flag flies from the **Pikk Herman bastion**. A path leads down from Lossi plats through an opening in the wall to the **Danish King's Courtyard** where, in summer, artists set up their easels.

The Lutheran **Toomkirik** (Dome Church; ☎ 644 4140; ☺ 9am-5pm Tue-Sun) is Estonia's oldest church, founded in 1219 (though the exteriors date from the early 14th century). From Toomkirik, follow Kohtu tänav to the city's favourite lookout over the Lower Town.

The **Museum of Occupation & Fight for Freedom** (☎ 668 0250; Toompea tänav 8; adult/student 10/5EEK; ☺ 11am-6pm Tue-Sun), is just down the hill from Toompea and contains a new and worthwhile exhibit on Estonia's history of occupation, focusing on the most recent Soviet one.

Kadriorg

Even if you have one day in Tallinn, it's worth heading towards pleasant **Kadriorg Park** located just 2km east of the Old Town along Narva maantee (take tram No 1 or 3 to the last stop). The park and its 1718–36 Kadriorg Palace were designed for Peter the Great for his wife Catherine I. Both the **Kadriorg Palace** (☎ 606 6400; Weizenbergi tänav 37; adult/student 45/25EEK; ☺ 10am-5pm Tue-Wed & Fri-Sun, 10am-9pm Thu May-Sep, 10am-5pm Wed-Sun Oct-Apr) and the **Foreign Art Museum** (adult/student 15/5EEK; ☺ 10am-5pm Wed-Sun) are housed in the same magnificent building and make for a dreamy hour or so – the 17th- and 18th-century foreign art is mainly unabashedly Romantic, and the palace unabashedly splendid.

Nearby is the brand new **KUMU** (☎ 602 6000; Weizenbergi tänav 34; adult/student 75/40EEK; ☺ 10am-5pm Tue-Wed & Fri-Sun, 10am-9pm Thu May-Sep, 10am-5pm Wed-Sun Oct-Apr), the country's largest museum by far. A spectacular, massive structure of limestone and green glass, it contains a large collection of Estonian art as well as constantly changing contemporary exhibits.

SLEEPING

The Tourist Information Centre can help find the right accommodation to fit your budget. **Rasastra Bed & Breakfast** (☎ 661 6291; www.bedbreakfast.ee; Mere puiestee 4) can set you up with a room in a private home from 275EEK per person.

Hostel Alur (☎ 631 1531; www.alurhostel.com; Rannamäe tee 3; dm/s/d/tr from 235/500/720/845EEK, about 15% cheaper Sep-Apr; Ⓟ) Not the liveliest of hostels, but it's clean, friendly, (a bit too) quiet and just a stone's throw from the train station and Old Town. There's 10% discount for ISIC and YHA cardholders.

Academic Hostel (☎ 620 2275; www.academichostel.com; Akadeemia tee 11; d 495EEK) Situated on the edge of the Tallinn Technical University campus grounds, this is a bright, happy, freshly-done-up hostel with a lively atmosphere. With 108 rooms spread out along five colour-coded floors, it feels more like a modern but budget hotel than a typical hostel with a young, vivacious, international clientele.

Old House (☎ 641 1464; www.oldhouse.ee; Uustänav 22 & 26; dm 290EEK, 1-/2-/3-/5-/6-person room 550/650/9

75/1450/1740EEK, guesthouse s/d/tr 450/650/975EEK, apt 1300-2500EEK) This hostel-guesthouse fills two nearly adjacent houses in the Old Town. Walls are paper-thin, but it's pleasant, spotless, filled with friendly travellers and a hearty breakfast is included. Its Old Town luxury apartments make a great splurge. ISIC cardholders get a 10% discount off all rates.

EATING & DRINKING

Beer House (☎ 627 6520; Dunkri tänav 5) A little piece of Austria in the heart of the old town, this multilevelled place is great for a night of revelling in the company of many foreigners and a few locals. Tallinn's only microbrewery is located within and whips up a prize-winning array of delicious and fresh beers (30EEK to 40EEK) – if they don't do you in, the oompah-pah music surely will!

Kompressor (☎ 646 4210; Rataskaevu tänav 3; mains from 40EEK) Eat one of the enormous, stuffed pancakes and you'll be full for the rest of the day. The large hall and casual atmosphere make it a great hang-out too; the big tables make it easy to chat up locals.

Texas Honky Tonk (☎ 631 1755; Pikk tänav 43; mains from 50EEK) No one does Americana quite so well in Tallinn. The menu is mostly Tex-Mex (the burritos are superb), and the atmosphere lively and yippee-ayo-ta-yay fun.

Eesti Maja (☎ 645 5252; www.eestimaja.ee; Lauteri tänav 1; buffet 75EEK, meals from 125EEK; ☺ 11am-11pm) Here's a good place to sample some traditional Estonian fare in a folksy interior. The weekday lunch buffet is a good deal and lets you try some of the heavy, exotic fare without a full-plate commitment.

Olde Hansa (☎ 627 9020; Vana Turg 1; mains from 175EEK; ☺ 11am-midnight) If you'll splurge just once in Tallinn, here's where to do it. This medieval-themed restaurant (more authentic than kitsch!) boasts first and foremost the most ebullient and friendly service in the city, plus exotic meats (elk, wild boar) and home-made delights such as juniper cheese and honey beer. It's a fun atmosphere inside or out on the terrace, and the food and its creative presentation is always first-rate.

Hell Hunt (☎ 681 8333; Pikk tänav 39) A trooper on the pub circuit for years, this place boasts an amiable atmosphere and reasonable prices for locally brewed beer and cider (half-litre for 24EEK).

Angel (☎ 641 6880; Sauna tänav 1) Open to all sexes and orientations, this mainly gay restaurant-bar-club has become one of the liveliest spots in town for fun of all kinds. The upstairs restaurant is noted for its cuisine and sassy waiters.

GETTING THERE & AWAY
Air

The national carrier **Estonian Air** (airline code OV; ☎ 640 1101; www.estonian-air.ee; Vabaduse väljak 10, Tallinn) links Tallinn with some 20 cities in Europe and Russia, and at reasonable prices. A number of other airlines serve the **Tallinn airport** (www.tallinn-airport.ee).

Copterline (www.copterline.ee) runs pricey helicopter flights between Helsinki and Tallinn's Copterline Terminal, at the Linnahall harbour, nearly hourly from 7am to 7pm weekdays (one way 1395EEK to 3100EEK, 18 minutes).

Boat
FINLAND

About 25 ferries, hydrofoils and catamarans cross between Helsinki and Tallinn every day. Ferries make the crossing in 2½ to 3½ hours, hydrofoils in just over an hour. All companies have concession rates. Prices are cheaper from mid-August through until May.

Tallink (☎ 640 9808; www.tallink.ee) operates up to three ferries (from 280EEK) and seven catamarans (from 390EEK) every day. **Lindaline** (☎ 699 9333; www.lindaliini.ee) makes up to eight hydrofoil crossings each way daily (single/return 450/660EEK), leaving from the Linnahall harbour. **Eckerö Line** (☎ 631 8606; www.eckeroline.ee) operates a daily car-carrying catamaran from Terminal B, making the crossing in just 3½ hours (single/return 345/380EEK). **Nordic Jet Line** (☎ 613 7000; www.njl.ee) has several car-carrying catamarans departing from Terminal C, they make the trip in around 1½ hours, seven times a day (from 420EEK). **Silja Line** (☎ 611 6661; www.silja.ee) has both ferries and catamarans leaving from Terminal A (singles from 520EEK) and offers day-trip packages to Helsinki. **Viking Line** (☎ 666 3966; www.vikingline.ee) operates large car ferries, which depart twice a day from Terminal A (from 735EEK).

SWEDEN

Tallink (☎ 640 9808; www.tallink.ee) runs nightly ferries from Tallinn's Terminal D to Stockholm (from 360EEK up to 5740EEK for a luxury suite, 15 hours), as well as daily ferries from Paldiski, 52km west of Tallinn, to Kappelskär near Stockholm (from 375EEK, 12 hours). Tickets should be booked well in advance in Tallinn or Stockholm's **Frihamnen** (Free Harbour; ☎ 08-667 0001).

GETTING AROUND

Tallinn has an excellent public transport network of buses, trolleybuses and trams that operate from 6am to midnight. In Estonia, *piletid* (tickets) are sold from most street kiosks (adult/student 10/7EEK) or can be purchased from the driver (15EEK). Validate your ticket by using the hole-punch inside the vehicle. All public transport timetables are posted on the web at www.tallinn.ee.

Taxis cost from 5.50EEK to 9EEK per kilometre. Try **Iks Takso** (☎ 638 1381) or **Taxi Marabu** (☎ 650 0006). Throughout central Tallinn, the ecologically sound **Velotakso** (☎ 508 8810) offers rides on egg-shaped vehicles run by pedal power and enthusiasm, and charges 35EEK for anywhere within central Tallinn.

St Petersburg

As elegant as Prague and as enchanting as Budapest but with just a smattering of the tourists due to Russia's intransigent visa regime, St Petersburg really will be the next big thing once visa-free travel arrives, although with that looking to be at least a decade away, you still have St Petersburg pretty much to yourself by the standards of other tourist-filled cities in the Baltics.

Long before Eastern Europe became known for its incredible cities, St Petersburg was the most important city in the entire region, capital of one of the world's most powerful empires and centre of countless movements in all fields of art. Since being founded by Peter the Great in 1703, St Petersburg has grown to be Europe's fourth largest city and easily one of its most culturally significant. A 'window on Europe', the city of Dostoyevsky and Shostakovich and the cradle of the Russian Revolution – a trip to St Petersburg makes a fantastic excursion from Scandinavia into a very different world.

FAST FACTS

- **Population** 5 million
- **Currency** Russian rouble (R); €1 = R34; US$1 = R27; UK£1 = R50; $A1 = R20; CA$1 = R24; NZ$1 = R20.19; ¥100 = R23.6
- **Official Language** Russian
- **Telephone Codes** Russia country code ☎ 7; St Petersburg ☎ 812
- **Visa** required by all and can be a real headache – begin preparing well in advance of your trip!

RSBURG

ORIENTATION & INFORMATION

St Petersburg is spread out across many islands, some real and some created through the construction of canals. The central street is Nevsky prospekt (pr), which extends for some 4km from the Alexandr Nevsky Monastery to the Hermitage. The vast Neva River empties into the Gulf of Finland, filtered through a number of islands. Most significant of these are Vasilyevsky and Petrogradsky Islands.

Currency exchange offices are available throughout the city. ATMs are inside every metro station, in hotels and department stores, in main post offices and along major streets. **American Express** (☎ 326 4500; Malaya Morskaya ul 23; ☽ 9am-5pm Mon-Fri) only offers travel services; travellers cheques can be exchanged at most Russian banks (with commission, of course).

There's a mediocre (English-speaking) **tourist office** outside the Winter Palace in a kiosk on Palace Sq.

Nevsky pr boasts two large, excellent internet cafés – **Café Max** (☎ 273 6655; Nevsky pr 90/92; per hr R60; ☽ 24hr; Ⓜ Mayakovskaya) and **Quo Vadis** (☎ 333 0708; Nevsky pr 76; per hr R60; ☽ 9am-11pm; Ⓜ Mayakovskaya), which is entered on Liteiny pr.

In an emergency call ☎ 01 for fire, ☎ 02 for the police and ☎ 03 for an ambulance. The operator will speak Russian only.

SIGHTS
The Historic Heart

Unquestionably your first stop should be **Dvortsovaya Ploshchad** (Palace Sq), where the baroque **Winter Palace** (Zimny dvorets) appears like a mirage under the archway at the start of ul Bolshaya Morskaya. The palace was commissioned from Bartolomeo Rastrelli in 1754 by Empress Elizabeth, and some of its 1057 rooms now house part of the astonishing **Hermitage** (☎ 571 3465; www.hermitage.ru; adult/student & child R350/free, no-flash photo/video ticket R100/350, audio guides R250; ☽ 10.30am-6pm Tue-Sat, 10.30am-5pm Sun; Ⓜ Nevsky Pr), which is one of the world's great art museums. Enter through the courtyard from Palace Sq. To avoid queues in the summer months, you can book tickets online very easily. Entrance is free for all individuals on the first Thursday of every month. The collection is vast and can be overwhelming for a first-time visitor. Ask for an English

map at the information desk in the ticket hall. If your time is limited you should look out for the following highlights: the Jordan Staircase (directly ahead of you when you enter); room 100 (Ancient Egypt), rooms 178–97 (the State rooms for the apartments of the last imperial family); room 204 (the Pavilion Hall); rooms 228–38 (Italian Art, 16th to 18th centuries); room 271 (the Imperial family's cathedral); and concentrate most of your time on the fabulous 3rd floor, particularly rooms 333–50 for late 19th-century and early-20th-century European art, including a huge array of works by Matisse, Picasso, Monet, Van Gogh, Cézanne, Gauguin, Pissaro, Rodin and Kandinsky. There are several cafés and shops within the museum, so you can easily spend a whole day there. Disabled access is now very good – call ☎ 110 9079 if you require any assistance.

Opposite the Winter Palace across the square is the fabulous **General Staff Building** and in the middle of the square, the 47.5m **Alexander Column** commemorates the 1812 victory over Napoleon.

To the west across the road is the gilded spire of the **Admiralty**, former headquarters of the Russian navy. West of the Admiralty is **Ploshchad Dekabristov** (Decembrists' Sq), named after the Decembrists' Uprising of 14 December 1825.

Falconet's famous statue of Peter the Great, the **Bronze Horseman**, stands at the end of the square towards the river. Behind looms the splendid golden dome of **St Isaac's Cathedral** (Isaakievsky Sobor; ☎ 315 9732; Isaakievskaya pl; admission to cathedral adults/students R300/170, to colonnade adults/students R150/100; ☽ 10am-7pm Thu-Tue; Ⓜ Sadovaya/Nevksy pr), built between 1818 and 1858. At this price think twice before going into the cathedral itself unless you like the ornate baroque style. The colonnade is far better value for money giving superb views over the city.

Nevsky Prospekt

The inner part of vast Nevsky pr runs from the Admiralty to Moskovsky Vokzal (Moscow Station) and is St Petersburg's main shopping thoroughfare. The most impressive sight along it is the great colonnaded arms of the **Kazan Cathedral** (Kazansky Sobor; Kazanskaya pl 2; admission free; ☽ 9am-6pm), built between 1801 and 1811.

ST PETERSBURG

CENTRAL ST PETERSBURG

INFORMATION
American Express...................1 C3
Café Max.............................2 F3
Quo Vadis...........................3 D3
Tourist Office......................4 C3

SIGHTS & ACTIVITIES
Admiralty............................5 C3
Alexander Column...............6 C3
Alexander Nevsky Monastery...7 H5
Bronze Horseman..................8 C3
Church on the Spilled Blood....9 D3
Dostoevsky Museum.............10 F4
General Staff Building............11 C3
Hermitage........................(see 21)
Kazan Cathedral...................12 D3
Naryshkin Bastion.................13 D2
Palace Square......................14 C3
Peter & Paul Fortress.............15 D1
Ploshchad Iskusstv (Arts Sq)...16 D3
Russian Museum...................17 D3
St Isaac's Cathedral...............18 C3
St Peter & St Paul Cathedral....19 C1
Smolny Cathedral.................20 H2
Winter Palace......................21 C3
Yusupov Palace...................22 B4

SLEEPING
Five Corners Hotel.................23 E4
Herzen University Hostel.........24 D3
Nevsky Inn.........................25 D3
Nord Hostel........................26 D3
Rachmaninoff Art Hotel..........27 D3

EATING
Fasol................................28 C3
Oliva...............................29 C3
Salkhino...........................30 C1
Sukawati...........................31 D3
Troitsky Most......................32 E4
Vostochny Ugolok................33 D4

DRINKING
Dacha..............................34 D3
Novus..............................35 D3
Tsynik.............................36 C4

Petrovsky Park

To Laima (800m)

Gorkovskaya

Alexandrovsky Park

To Troitsky Most (50m)

Sportivnaya

KRONVERKSKY

MALAYA RIVER

ZAYACHY

Troitsky most

Vasilevsky

University Botanical Gardens

St Petersburg State University

Birzhevoy most

Birzhevaya pl

Dvortsovy most

Ermitazhny most

Mars Field

Dvortsovaya pl

Mikhailovsky Gardens

BOLSHAYA RIVER

pl Dekabristov

Admiralty Gardens

Admiralteysky

Nevsky pr

Gostiny Dvor

most Leytenanta Shmidta

Novaya Gollandiya

Kazansky

Spassky

Potseluev most

Kolomensky

MATISOV

Nikolsky Gardens

Yusupovsky Gardens

Obukhovsky most

Pokrovsky

Izmailovsky Gardens

Sennaya pl

Sadovaya

Semyonovsky most

Pushkinskaya

Vitebsk Station (Vitebsky Vokzal)

Pryazhki

Fontanka

Polsky Gardens

Tehnologichesky Institut

"Olimpia" Gardens

1 Krasnoarmeyskaya ul
13 Krasnoarmeyskaya ul
8 Krasnoarmeyskaya ul
9 Krasnoarmeyskaya ul
10 Krasnoarmeyskaya ul
11 Krasnoarmeyskaya ul
12 Krasnoarmeyskaya ul
2 Krasnoarmeyskaya ul
3 Krasnoarmeyskaya ul
4 Krasnoarmeyskaya ul
5 Krasnoarmeyskaya ul
6 Krasnoarmeyskaya ul
7 Krasnoarmeyskaya ul

nab Obvodnogo kanala

Baltiysky Vokzal (Baltic Station)

Baltiyskaya

Varshavsky Vokzal (Warsaw Station)

Fruzhenskaya

ST PETERSBURG

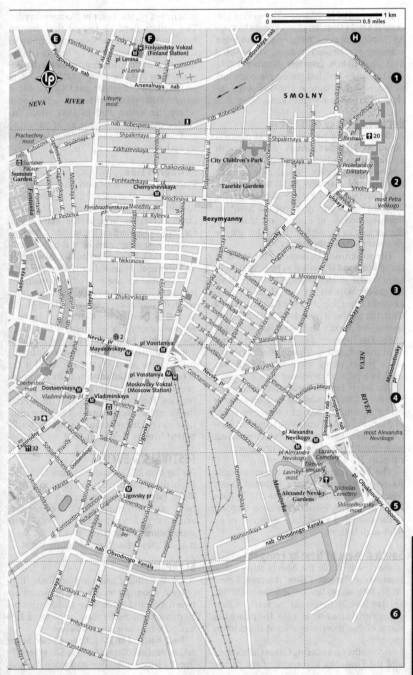

At the end of Nevsky pr is the working **Alexander Nevsky Monastery** (Lavra Alexandra Nevskogo; ☎ 274 0409; adult/student R60/40; ☿ dawn-dusk, to 8pm in summer; Ⓜ pl Alexandra Nevskogo), where you'll find the **Tikhvin Cemetery** (admission R60/40; ☿ 11am-dusk Fri-Wed), last resting place of some of Russia's most famous artistic figures, including Tchaikovsky and Dostoyevsky.

Between Nevsky & the Neva

A block north of Nevsky Prospekt metro is the lovely **Ploshchad Iskusstv** (Arts Sq), with a monument to Pushkin at its centre. The yellow Mikhailovsky Palace, now the **Russian Museum** (Russky Muzey; ☎ 315 1636; Konyushennaya pl; adult/student R300/170; ☿ 10am-8pm Thu-Tue; Ⓜ Gostiny Dvor), housing one of the country's finest collections of Russian art, makes up the far side of the square. Behind it are the pleasant **Mikhailovsky Gardens**.

The polychromatic domes of the **Church on the Spilled Blood** (Khram Spas na Krovi; ☎ 315 1636; Konyushennaya pl; adult/student R300/170; ☿ 10am-8pm Thu-Tue; Ⓜ Gostiny Dvor) are close by. Also known as the Church of the Resurrection of Christ, it was built from 1887 to 1907 on the spot where Alexander II was assassinated in 1881. The interior is incredible and somewhat overwhelming – having been restored since Soviet times when the church was used as a potato warehouse.

The lovely **Summer Garden** (Letny Sad; ☿ 9am-10pm May-Oct, 10am-6pm Oct–mid-Apr, closed mid-Apr to end Apr) is situated between the open space of Mars Field (Marsovo Pole) and the Fontanka River. Laid out for Peter the Great with fountains and pavilions in a geometrical plan, it's a great place to relax.

The best thing about the unmistakable Rastrelli-designed **Smolny Cathedral** (Smolny Sobor; ☎ 278 5596; pl Rastrelli; admission R150; ☿ 11am-5pm Fri-Wed), 3km east of the Summer Garden, is the sweeping view from atop one of its 63m-high belfries.

South & West of Nevsky Prospekt

A short walk down the Moyka River is the fascinating **Yusupov Palace** (Yusupovsky Dvorets; ☎ 314 9883; nab reki Moyki 94; adult/student R300/250; ☿ 11am-5pm). Notorious as the scene of Rasputin's grisly murder in 1916, the palace has some of the most magnificent interiors in the city.

Across the meandering Canal Griboedova and the Fontanka River, east of the palace,

is Sennaya pl, the heart of Dostoevskyville. The author lived in several flats around here, and many of the locations turn up in *Crime and Punishment*. To find out more head to the small, interesting **Dostoevsky Museum** (Muzey Dostoevskogo; ☎ 571 4031; www.md.spb.ru; Kuznechny per 5/2; adult/student R100/50, audio tour in English R100; ☿ 11am-6pm Tue-Sun) in the house where the writer died in 1881 which includes many original pieces of furniture and possessions of the great man as well as a good exhibit about his life.

Petrograd Side

Petrograd Side refers to the cluster of delta islands between the Malaya Neva and Bolshaya Nevka channels. The principal attraction here is the **Peter & Paul Fortress** (Petropavlovskaya Krepost; ☎ 230 0340; admission to grounds free, admission to all buildings adult/student R120/60; ☿ 10am-5pm Thu-Mon, 10am-4pm Tue; Ⓜ Gorkovskaya). Founded in 1703 as the military fortress for the new city, its main use up to 1917 was as a political prison: famous residents include Peter's own son Alexei, as well as Dostoevsky, Gorky and Trotsky. At noon every day a cannon is fired from the **Naryshkin Bastion**, scaring the daylights out of tourists. It's fun to walk along the battlements. Most spectacular of all is the **St Peter & St Paul Cathedral**, with its landmark needle-thin spire and magnificent baroque interior. Here all Russia's tsars since Peter the Great have been buried. The latest addition was Nicholas II and his family, finally buried here by Yeltsin in 1998.

FESTIVALS & EVENTS

City Day is on 27 May and celebrates the founding of the city with mass festivities. The **White Nights** (around the summer solstice in late June) are truly unique. The city comes alive and parties all night as the sun only barely sinks below the horizon, leaving the sky a magical grey-white throughout the night.

SLEEPING

As St Petersburg has a very definite 'high season', room prices are at a premium between May and September. Outside this period, room prices decrease by between 10% and 30% on those quoted below.

Nord Hostel (☎ 517 0342; www.nordhostel.com; Bolshaya Morskaya ul 10; dm/d 825/2250; ☐ ; Ⓜ Nevsky Pr) Run by friendly Russian staff along the lines of a traditional travellers hostel the Nord is a real winner, with by far the best location of any of the city's hostels next to the Hermitage and huge, beautiful dorm rooms (one has its own piano) and a few doubles as well. Book ahead – this is our hostel of choice.

Herzen University Hotel (☎ 314 7472; fax 315 5716; Kazanskaya ul 6; s/d/tr R1950/2600/2800; Ⓜ Nevsky Pr) This well-run Russian hostel with a brilliant location is used to foreigners, although it's very much a university hall of residence and so don't expect your usual hostel vibe, it's mainly popular with groups but its clean and simple rooms (nearly all with ensuite facilities) are a great deal.

Nevsky Inn (☎ 924 9805; www.nevskyinn.ru; Kirpichny per 2, flat 19; s/d R2250/2750; Ⓜ Nevsky Pr) Run by a joint British-Russian management, the Nevsky is one of the best places to stay in the city. Rooms are clean and comfortable and there's a modern kitchen that guests can use, perfectly combining comfort and economy. Highly recommended.

Five Corners Hotel (☎ 380 8181; www.5ugol .ru; Zagorodny pr 13; s/d/ste R4900/5600/6650; ✖ ▢ ; Ⓜ Dostoyevskaya) This place is very stylish indeed. Its suites are some of the coolest in the city and overlook a trendy hub of streets a short walk from Nevsky pr. Staff are polite and efficient and recent expansion to 35 rooms suggests it's deservedly popular. There's free wi-fi throughout.

Rachmaninoff Art Hotel (☎ 327 7466; www .kazansky5.com; Kazanskaya ul 5, 3rd fl; s/d R4000/4850; ✖ ▢ ; Ⓜ Nevsky Pr) Perfectly located and beautifully designed, the Rachmaninoff attracts an in-the-know crowd of arty types staying in the city. Stuffed full of antiques, the understated rooms nonetheless enjoy a thoroughly modern, boutique feel. There's free wi-fi throughout.

EATING

Keep your eyes open for *blini* (Russian pancake) kiosks throughout the city. Their delicious *blini*s are superb value (R20 to R30) and a great snack. Street food is sold around metro stations.

Troitsky Most Kamennoostrovsky pr (☎ 232 6693; Kamennoostrovsky pr 9/2; mains R100-200; Ⓜ Gorkovskaya); Zagorodny pr (☎ 115 1998; Zagorodny pr 38; Ⓜ Vladimirskaya) Superb vegetarian chain with multiple locations across the city. The mushroom lasagne is legendary and the salads delicious.

Fasol (☎ 571 9695; ul Gorokhovaya 17; mains R150; Ⓜ Sennaya pl) Delightful respite from the norms of the Russian eating experience, Fasol combines friendly and efficient service with good food at low prices. It's a cool place to come any time of day, although it's particularly busy in the evening. There's an English menu.

Oliva (☎ 314 6563; Bolshaya Morskaya ul 31; mains R160-300; ☯ 10am-midnight; Ⓜ Nevsky Pr) An authentic Greek addition to the St Petersburg scene, though there is nothing taverna-like about this cavernous place, subtly painted and decorated in an array of Greek styles. The menu is traditional and food is both excellent value and extremely good.

Salkhino (☎ 232 7891; Kronverksy pr 25; mains R300-500; Ⓜ Gorkovskaya) This is our favourite Georgian in town, serving up delicious Georgian fare and a great selection of wines.

Sukawati (☎ 312 0504; Kazanskaya ul 8; mains R250-350; Ⓜ Nevsky Pr) Sleek Indonesian-Japanese fusion place set back behind the Kazan Cathedral. The nasi goreng is delicious, and the whole menu far more imaginative than most Asian restaurants in town.

Vostochny Ugolok (☎ 713 5747; ul Gorokhovaya 52; mains R250-500; ☯ 24hrs; Ⓜ Pushkinskaya/Sennaya pl) A taste of the Caucasus in St Petersburg, the 'Eastern Nook' serves up brilliant trans-Caucasian dishes from Georgian *pkhali* to Azeri *shashlyk*, all in a warm atmosphere of southern hospitality.

DRINKING

Novus (☎ 569 3818; Bolshaya Morskaya ul 8; ☯ 6pm-6am; Ⓜ Nevsky Pr) The current favourite for young expats and travellers, Novus is named after a highly eccentric Latvian hybrid of backgammon and pool. Packed every night, this is a great place to meet a young and beautiful international crowd. Enter through the takeaway downstairs.

Dacha (Dumskaya ul 9; ☯ 6pm-6am; Ⓜ Nevsky Pr) The bar sensation of 2005, when everyone in the city flocked here, indie bar Dacha now looks like an old timer, but still features on many people's list for a night out. The R100 cover charge includes two beers.

Tsynik (☎ 312 9526; per Antonenko 4; ☯ 1pm-3am, until 7am Fri & Sat; Ⓜ Sadovaya) Just as raucous and popular is the grungy cool of Tsynik. Famous for its rowdy crowd and *grenki* (fried garlic black bread), this is the place to be seen misbehaving.

GETTING THERE & AWAY

Daily express buses run from Turku and Helsinki to Vyborg and St Petersburg (Russian visa required) along highway E18, via the Finnish towns of Porvoo, Kotka and Hamina. Check current timetables and book tickets at the bus station or a travel agency; from Helsinki to St Petersburg there are three daily buses (€55.60, 9½ hours). The train is a more romantic and comfortable way to reach Russia. Note that St Petersburg is Pietari in Finnish, and Vyborg is Viipuri.

There are three daily trains from Helsinki to Russia, travelling via the Finnish stations of Lahti, Kouvola and Vainikkala. You must have a valid Russian visa but border formalities have been fast-tracked so that passport checks are now carried out on board the moving train.

The Russian *Tolstoi* sleeper departs Helsinki daily at 5.42pm, arriving in Moscow at 8.30am the next day (one way in 2nd/1st class €85.80/128.20) via Vyborg (€47/75) and St Petersburg (€58.40/90); it departs from Moscow daily at 10.50pm. Both 1st- and 2nd-class fares include a sleeper berth. The *Sibelius* and *Repin* have daily services between Helsinki and St Petersburg (5½ hours) via Vyborg (3¾ hours). The *Sibelius* (a Finnish train) departs from Helsinki at 7.42am (2nd-/1st-class seats €51.40/81.90, six hours). The Russian *Repin* departs at 3.42pm and has 2nd-class seats (€51.40) or 1st-class sleeping berths (€91). From St Petersburg, departures are at 4.28pm *(Sibelius)* and 7.28am *(Repin)*.

Buy Russian rail tickets in Helsinki at the special ticket counter in the central station. Check timetables at www.vr.fi.

GETTING AROUND

The metro (flat fare 12R) is best for covering the large distances across the city. The four lines cross over in the city centre and go out to the suburbs. The most confusing aspect of the system is that all labelling is in Cyrillic. Listen out for the announcements of the station names, or ask locals who will usually go out of their way to help. A further confusion is that two stations sharing an exit will have different names. For example, Nevsky Pr and Gostiny Dvor are in the same place, but as they are on different lines, they have different names.

Around the centre, *marshrutka* minibuses are a very quick alternative to the slow trolleybuses. Costs vary on each route, but the average fare is R18, and is displayed prominently inside each van. To stop a *marshrutka*, simply hold out your hand and it will stop. Jump in, sit down, pass cash to the driver (a human chain operates if you are not seated nearby) and then call out *'ostanovityes pozhalusta!'* when you want to get out and the driver will pull over.

If you'd rather take a cab, holding your arm out will cause nonofficial taxis to stop very quickly. The standard rate for a short distance (1km to 2km) is R50 and then R100 after that, although as a foreigner, expect to have the price raised – always agree on a price before getting into the car. For an official cab, call ☎ 068.

Iceland

Iceland is literally a country in the making, a vast volcanic laboratory where mighty forces shape the land and shrink you to an awestruck speck. The country's natural features – eruptions of lava; gushing geysers; hot springs; tearing fissures and slow, grinding glaciers – are so cinematic that at times they seem unreal. Bathe in turquoise pools, stand behind a toppling cascade or walk across a glaring-white icecap to experience the full weirdness of Icelandic nature.

Iceland's creatures are larger-than-life too: there's no better place on earth to come eye-to-eye with sleek, spouting whales. Fearless little puffins flutter and bill in their millions along the tops of towering sea-cliffs.

The landscape is infectious: hidden energy and a desire to shape the world are Icelandic traits. Vibrant Reykjavík, that clean, green little capital, must contain the world's highest concentration of dreamers, authors, poets and musicians – meet them on the high-spirited *runtur*, the city's wheeling weekend pub crawl.

FAST FACTS

- **Area** 103,000 sq km

- **Capital** Reykjavík

- **Currency** króna (Ikr): €1 = Ikr95.16; US$1 = Ikr76.06; UK£1 = Ikr138.31; A$1 = Ikr56.86; CA$1 = Ikr66.90; NZ$1 = Ikr47.25; ¥100 = Ikr64.86

- **Famous for** fishing, sagas, Björk, the Blue Lagoon, rotten shark meat!

- **Official Language** Icelandic

- **Phrases** *halló* (hello), *gjörðu svo vel* (please), *takk fyrir* (thanks), *skál!* (cheers!)

- **Population** 300,000

- **Telephone Codes** country code ☎ 354; international access code ☎ 00; reverse-charge operator ☎ 533 5309; telephone area codes don't apply

- **Visa** unnecessary for visitors from Australia, Canada, New Zealand, Scandinavia, EU countries, the UK and the USA staying for under three months (see p284)

HIGHLIGHTS

- Cavort with crowds of partygoers on the drunken Reykjavík **runtur** (p248)
- Explore the explosive, lava-strewn wastelands of **Mývatn** and **Krafla** (p262)
- Come eyeball to eyeball with ocean giants on a whale-watching trip in **Húsavík** (p262)
- Be cool in the south – watch baby-blue icebergs float out to sea at **Jökulsárlón** (p268) or walk over a glacier in **Skaftafell National Park** (p268)
- Bathe in turquoise pools in the **Landmannalaugar** (p274) geothermal area

ITINERARIES

- **Three Days** Arrive in Reykjavík on Friday to catch the decadent runtur (p248). Sober up in Laugadalur geothermal pool (p274) before sightseeing. Don't miss the views from Hallgrímskirkja (p240) or Perlan (p241). In summer, sleep is for wimps: squeeze in a midnight horse ride. On Sunday, visit Gullfoss, Geysir and Þingvellir as part of your tour of the Golden Circle (p251). Stop to soak in the Blue Lagoon (p250) on the way back home.
- **One week** Take a whale-watching trip (p240) from Reykjavík harbour, then head for the countryside. Serene Snæfellsnes (p253) lies north; the volcanic Vestmannaeyjar (p270) spot the sea off the southern coast; or else drive east to Europe's largest national park, Skaftafell (p268), for hikes and glacier-walking.

HOW MUCH?

- **Cuddly troll** Ikr1900
- **Postcard** Ikr65
- **Cinema ticket** Ikr800
- **Knitted hat** Ikr1700
- **Whale-watching trip** Ikr3700

LONELY PLANET INDEX

- **1L petrol** Ikr134
- **1L bottle of water** Ikr230
- **Pint of Egils beer** Ikr600
- **Souvenir T-shirt** Ikr1500
- **Hot dog** Ikr200

CLIMATE & WHEN TO GO

Reykjavík's mildish climate can rapidly degenerate into heavy rain, biting wind or fog; May, June and July are the driest months of the year. In the north and east, the weather is better. Blizzards and fierce sandstorms occur in the interior deserts and on the coastal sand deltas. The **Icelandic Meteorological Office** (☎ 902 0600; www.vedur.is/english) provides a daily weather forecast in English.

Mid-June to August is high season, but most highland tours don't operate until July because of snow. At other times, many tourist facilities outside Reykjavík are closed.

Also see p486 for a climate chart.

HISTORY

Irish monks were probably the first people to come to Iceland in around AD 700. Their solitude was rudely shattered by the Age of Settlement (871–930), when a wave of Nordic people descended, driven from the Scandinavian mainland by political clashes. Many raided Ireland and the Scottish islands on the way, bringing Celtic slaves to the new country.

Ingólfur Arnarson, a Norwegian fugitive, became the first official Icelander (AD 871). He settled at Reykjavík (Smoky Bay), which he named after steam he saw rising from geothermal vents. According to 12th-century sources, Ingólfur built his farm on Aðalstræti – an enthralling archaeological excavation recently unearthed what may have been his longhouse (p241).

The settlers rejected monarchy and established the world's first democratic parliament at Þingvellir (Parliament Plains; p251), outside Reykjavík. The country converted to Christianity in the year 1000.

Two hundred years of peace ended during the Sturlunga Period (1230–62), when Iceland's chieftains descended into bloody territorial fighting. The era is epitomised by the life and violent death of historian and political schemer, Snorri Sturluson (p252). Iceland ceded control of the country to Norway in 1262, then was placed under Danish rule in 1397. For the next six centuries, the forgotten country endured a Dark Age of famine, disease and disastrous volcanic eruptions.

In the early 17th century, the Danish king imposed a trade monopoly that was utterly exploited by foreign merchants. In an attempt to bypass the crippling embargo,

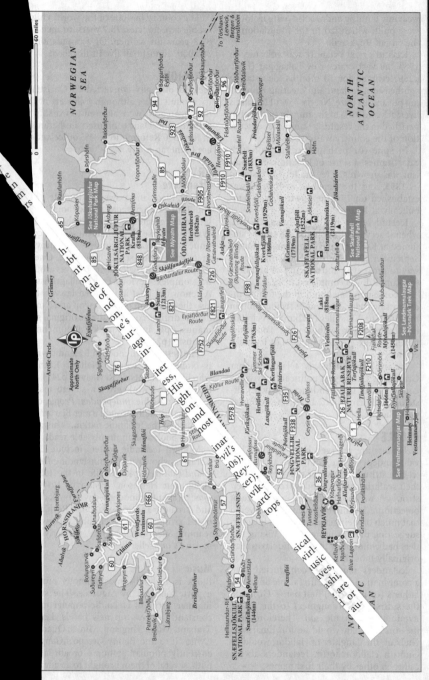

weaving, tanning and wool-dyeing factories were built, which led to the foundation of the city of Reykjavík.

Iceland's next calamity was volcanic. In 1783 the vast crater row Lakagígar (Laki; p269) erupted for 10 months, devastating southeastern Iceland and creating a lingering poisonous haze. Nearly 75% of Iceland's livestock and 20% of the human population perished in the resulting famine; an evacuation of the country was discussed.

In spite (or perhaps because) of such catastrophes, a sense of Icelandic nationalism was growing. Free trade was restored in 1855, and the Republic of Iceland was established on 17 June 1944 (p280), symbolically at Þingvellir.

Iceland began to thrive during WWII, when it serviced British and US troops stationed at Keflavík (the base remained until September 2006). Subsistence farming gave way to prosperity and a frenzy of building; the Ring Rd was completed in 1974.

A corresponding boom in the fishing industry saw Iceland extend its fishing limit in the 1970s to 200 miles (322km), precipitating the 'cod war' with Britain. Today the fishing industry makes up 70% of Iceland's economy.

Iceland's president is Ólafur Ragnar Grímsson. The largest political party is the conservative Independence Party (Sjálfstæðisflokkurinn), led by Prime Minister Geir Haarde.

PEOPLE

Icelanders are reserved but friendly. They value independence, and have a live-and-let-live attitude. However they are proud of their seafaring culture and will express their strong views about whaling in the face of objections. Icelanders recently discovered that much of their genetic makeup is Celtic, suggesting that far more of the Viking settlers had children by their Celtic slaves than originally thought.

Icelanders' names are constructed from a combination of their first name and their father's (or mother's) first name. Girls add the suffix *dóttir* (daughter) to the patronymic and boys add *son*. Therefore, Jón, the son of Einar, would be Jón Einarsson. Guðrun, the daughter of Halldór, would be Guðrun Halldórsdóttir. Icelanders always call each other by their first names.

The country has one of the world's hig est life expectancies: 78.9 years for men a 82.8 years for women. Of a population 300,000, almost half live in Reykjavík.

RELIGION

Iceland officially converted to Christia ity around 1000, although followers of th old pagan gods were allowed to worship private. The Danes imposed Lutheranis in the 1550 Reformation: 84% of Icelande are Lutheran today.

ARTS
Literature

Bloody, black and powerful, the late 12t and 13th-century sagas are without dou Iceland's greatest cultural achieveme Written in terse Old Norse, these epics c tinue to entertain Icelanders and prov them with a rich sense of heritage. One the best known, *Egils Saga,* revolves arou the complex, devious Egil Skallagrímss A renowned poet and skilled lawyer, h also the grandson of a werewolf and a m derous drunk. You can admire original s manuscripts in Reykjavík's Þjóðmenn garhúsið (p241).

The best-known modern Icelandic wr is Nobel Prize–winner Halldór Laxn who lived just outside Reykjavík (p241). darkly comic work gives a superb ins into Icelandic life. *Independent People, c* cerning the fatally proud farmer Bjartur the birth of the Icelandic nation, is his r famous book and an unmissable read.

Modern Icelandic writers include E Kárason, who wrote the outstanding *De Island* (about Reykjavík life in the 195 Hallgrímur Helgason, creator of *101* *kjavík* (about a modern-day city slac and Arnaldur Indriðason, whose Reykja based crime fiction, including the aw winning *Silence of the Grave,* regularly Iceland's bestseller lists.

Music

Björk is Iceland's most famous mu export, followed by Sigurrós. The s ing maelstrom of Icelandic popular m constantly throws up new bands. Le Trabant, Múm, Mugison, Mínus, Quar Cynic Guru and Benny Crespo's Gang currently popular at home or abroa both, several of them brought to a wide dience by the music-documentary *Screaming Masterpiece* (2005).

Bands perform live at venues such as Gaukur á Stöng (p248) and Grand Rokk (p248).

Visual Arts

Various artists have wrestled with Iceland's enigmatic soul, including the prolific Ásgrímur Jónsson (1876–1958). His work, depicting Icelandic landscapes and folktales, can be seen at the National Gallery in Reykjavík (p242). Pop Art icon Erró (b 1932) is honoured with a permanent collection in the Listasafn Reykjavíkur (p242).

Sculptors are well represented: the mystical work of Einar Jónsson (1874–1954; p242) dwells on death and resurrection, and Ásmundur Sveinsson's (1893–1982) sculptures (p242) celebrate Iceland and its stories.

Cinema & TV

Based on Hallgrímur Helgason's book of the same name, Baltasar Kormákur's film *101 Reykjavik* (2000), the painful, funny tale of a Reykjavík dropout's fling with his mother's lesbian lover, won an international audience.

More recently, European art cinemas have screened *Nói Albínói* (2002), Dagur Kari's black comedy about life in an isolated Icelandic valley.

For forthcoming films, see the informative www.icelandicfilmcentre.is.

ENVIRONMENT
The Land

Iceland, a juvenile among the world's land masses, is shaped by desert plateaus (52%), lava fields (11%), *sandur* or sand deltas (4%) and icecaps (12%). Over half of Iceland lies above 400m and its highest point, Hvannadalshnúkur, rises 2119m above sea level. Only 21% of Iceland is considered habitable.

The country's active volcanic zone runs through the middle of the country, from southwest to northeast. Active-zone geological features include lava flows, tubes, geysers, hot springs and volcanoes, and rocks such as basalt, pumice and rhyolite.

There are very few trees. Most of the native flora consists of grasses, mosses, lichens and wildflowers. *Plöntukort Íslands* (Botanical Map; Ikr1290), available from Reykjavík's bookshops, is a good guide.

Wildlife

The wild-eyed Arctic fox is the only indigenous land mammal; introduced species include reindeer and mice. Polar bears occasionally turn up on the north coast, but their life expectancy in Iceland is short.

The lack of land mammals is compensated for by vast numbers of birds and rich marine fauna. Kittiwakes, fulmars and gannets form large coastal colonies (best seen at Látrabjarg, p256); there are hosts of Arctic terns, golden plovers, ducks, swans, divers and geese at Mývatn (p262); and Vestmannaeyjar has huge populations of lovable puffins (p270). The website www.fuglar.is lists what rarities are about. *Fuglakort Íslands* (Bird-watcher's Map; Ikr1290), sold in Reykjavík's bookshops, is a handy reference.

Four different seal species and 12 species of cetacean (including blue whales and dolphins) have been spotted: boat trips run from various coastal towns including Reykjavík (p240), although the best sightings are at Húsavík (p261).

National Parks & Nature Reserves

Iceland's four national parks *(þjóðgarður)* are Skaftafell (p268), Jökulsárgljúfur (p265), Snæfellsjökull (p254), and Þingvellir (p251), a Unesco World Heritage Site. There are countless nature reserves *(friðland)*, the most significant being Mývatn (p262). Parks and reserves are open to visitors at all times. Wild camping is restricted: for further information, contact the government's Environment & Food Agency, **Umhverfisstofnun** (☎ 591 2000; www.ust.is; Suðurlandsbraut 24, IS-108 Reykjavík). Roughly 5% of the total land area of Iceland and the government has the ambitious aim of increasing that percentage ten-fold over time.

Environmental Issues

Historically, sheep farming and timber extraction caused immense environmental damage. It has been estimated that a mere 1% of Iceland's original woodland remains. Large-scale aerial seeding and intensive tree-planting programmes are combatting erosion.

Concerns over declining fish stocks have led the government to invest in other areas, particularly heavy industry. The most controversial project in Icelandic history is the dam being built in the Kárahnjúkar peaks to power an American aluminium smelting plant. Its construction (due for completion 2009) will affect the courses of two glacial rivers and flood a vast area of untouched wilderness.

Iceland is endeavouring to free itself of fossil fuels by 2050, relying instead on hydrogen cells and solar energy.

FOOD & DRINK

Cafés and restaurants in Reykjavík cater to most tastes, but fresh fish, seafood and Icelandic lamb naturally get top billing on most upmarket menus.

The government levies high taxes on alcohol to discourage excessive drinking. Check out Friday-night Reykjavík to see the success of this policy!

Staples & Specialities

Born from centuries of near-starvation, Iceland's traditional dishes reflect a 'waste not, want not' austerity. Specialities include svið (singed sheep's head complete with eyeballs), súrsaðir hrútspungar (pickled ram's testicles) and hákarl (putrefied shark meat, buried and rotted for three months to make it digestible). These gruesome dishes are only eaten nowadays during the February celebration of Þorri. You can try cubes of shark meat at Kolaportið Flea Market (p249), but be warned that the smell alone makes many foreigners ill! Some restaurants serve whale meat (hval), culled during 'scientific' hunts (see the boxed text on below).

More commonly, Icelanders consume lundi (puffin), which looks and tastes like calf liver. Most of the birds are netted on the Vestmannaeyjar (p270). Harðfiskur is an everyday snack: these brittle pieces of wind-dried haddock are usually eaten with butter. Delicious yogurtlike skyr, made from curdled milk, is a unique treat; sugar, fruit and cream are often added to turn it into a rich dessert. Around Mývatn (p262), look out for a regional pudding: hverabrauð (hot-spring bread) is a sweet, dark, sticky loaf, baked in the ground using geothermal heat. Other cakes include kleinur (twisted doughnuts, traditionally deep-fried in lard); and ástar pungar ('love balls'; round, raisin-stuffed doughnuts).

Coffee is a national institution, and most cafés offer free refills. The traditional Icelandic alcoholic brew is brennivín (burnt wine), a sort of schnapps made from potatoes and caraway seeds with the foreboding nickname svarti dauði (black death). Note that if you buy syrmjolk from the supermarket, it's sour milk.

Where to Eat & Drink

Reykjavík has no shortage of cosy cafés (commonly open from 11am until 1am, later at weekends) that turn into bars at night. They're great for lingering coffees, light lunches (from about Ikr800) and late-night beers. Restaurants are more upmarket, often serving gourmet food, with mains from about Ikr2000 to Ikr4500 per person. Some are open for lunch (between 11am and 2pm), and most open nightly (between 6pm and 10pm). In other towns, choice is much reduced and opening times can be shorter.

WEIGHING UP THE WHALE DEBATE

After 150 years of hunting, many whale species are now facing extinction. To give populations a chance to recover, the International Whaling Commission (IWC) called for a suspension of commercial whaling in 1986. Most countries complied; however, Iceland continued by using a loophole: 'scientific' whaling (with whale meat sold to restaurants or rendered down into animal feeds).

Following international pressure, there was a lull between 1989 and 2003, but now Icelandic whalers kill around 30 minkes yearly, and there are plans to begin full-scale commercial hunts in 2007. Many countries have issued formal protests, and conservationists are calling for a boycott of Iceland and Icelandic goods.

Whaling is an emotional topic. Supporters of the hunt (around 70% of Icelanders) believe minke whales are depleting fish stocks and need culling; whereas antiwhalers fear for the animals and for the flourishing whale-watching industry, which brings in about US$18 million annually.

For more information, see the websites of the International Whaling Commission (www.iwc office.org), World Wide Fund for Nature (www.wwf.org) and Greenpeace (www.greenpeace.org).

ICELAND

Every village has at least one *kaupfélagið* (cooperative supermarket), with Bónus and Netto being the cheapest. Petrol stations and grills sell relatively inexpensive fast-food snacks (hot dog and chips cost around Ikr700).

Beer, wine and spirits are available to people aged over 20 years from licensed hotels, bars, restaurants and *vín búð* (state monopoly) stores.

Vegetarians & Vegans
Outside Reykjavík, which has three vegan/ veggie restaurants, choices are limited. Most places offer one veggie dish, but as this usually involves cheese, vegans may have to self-cater.

REYKJAVÍK

pop 115,676
Reykjavík, the pint-size capital of Iceland, is cute, complex and fuelled entirely by coffee. Here you'll find all the cultural trappings of a large 21st-century European city: cozy cafés, top-quality restaurants, fine museums, myriad live bands and state-of-the-art geothermal pools. All these delectable diversions are layered over a foundation of rich Viking history. The froth on top is Reykjavík's eccentric and very excessive *runtur*, a wild pub-crawl that starts on Friday night around small, super-stylish clubs and bars and ends sometime before Monday.

The world's most northerly capital offers a bewitching combination of village innocence and big-city energy. As if that weren't enough, Nature herself adds a powerful extra dimension: ominous mountains and volcanoes line the horizon; the ocean rolls right up to the very edge of town; and the air is as cold and clean as frozen diamonds.

ORIENTATION
Reykjavík's old town lies between Tjörnin, Lækjargata, the harbour and the nearby suburb of Seltjarnarnes. Nearly everything in the city – bars, cafés, restaurants, the post office and the tourist office – is within walking distance of the old settlement. The shopping district extends east along Laugavegur from Lækjargata to the Hlemmur bus station.

INFORMATION
Bookshops
There are three big bookshops offering a superb choice of English-language books, newspapers, magazines and maps.

Eymundsson (Map p242; ☎ 511 1130; Austurstræti 18; ✆ 9am-10pm Mon-Fri, 10am-10pm Sat, 1-10pm Sun)

Iða (Map p242; ☎ 511 5001; Lækjargata 2a; ✆ 9am-10pm)

Mál og Menning (Map p242; ☎ 515 2500; shopping@edda.is; Laugavegur 18; ✆ 9am-10pm Mon-Fri, 10am-10pm Sat & Sun)

Discount Cards
Reykjavík Tourist Card (24/48/72hr Ikr1200/1700/2200) Available at various outlets including the tourist offices. It gives you free entry to galleries, museums, swimming pools and the zoo, and includes a bus pass.

Emergency
Landspítali University Hospital (Map pp238-9; ☎ 543 2000; Fossvogur) 24-hour casualty department.

SEARCHING FOR COD: A FISHERMAN'S TALE *Davíð, Fisherman*

I work on a fishing boat, a longliner with an automated fishing line; it's not done by hand these days. The line, 10km long, is looped onto a reel; when we reach the fishing grounds, you just press a button and it all unwinds. One of my jobs is to feed the baiting machine with pieces of squid and other bycatch; I go through several pairs of chainmail gloves a year!

When the line comes up, we unhook the fish, cut their throats, put them on ice; later we'll gut and clean them. We mostly catch cod, which are filleted on land in the fish-factory. You'll see the women there using ultraviolet lights to hook out the worms.

Some of the big trawlers go out for a month, but we go out for five days at a time. It can be lonely. The married men miss their families, their kids. I've joined a dating agency to meet more women! But the pay is good – we make four times as much as the people who work in the fish factories – and I like being out at sea.

ICELAND

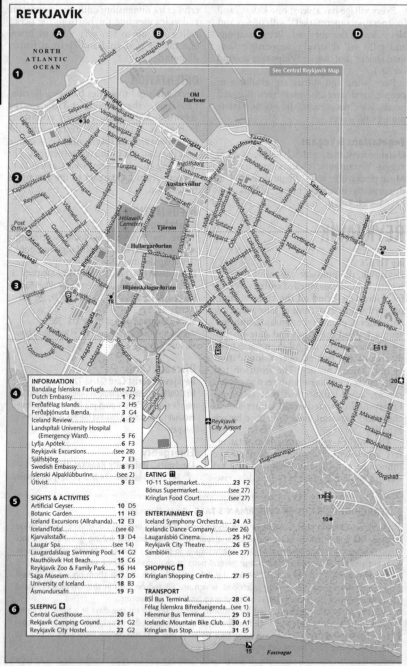

REYKJAVÍK

INFORMATION
Bandalag Íslenskra Farfugla......(see 22)
Dutch Embassy..............................**1** F2
Ferðafélag Íslands........................**2** H5
Ferðaþjónusta Bænda...................**3** G4
Iceland Review..............................**4** E2
Landspítali University Hospital
 (Emergency Ward)......................**5** F6
Lyfja Apótek.................................**6** F3
Reykjavik Excursions...............(see 28)
Sjálfsbjörg....................................**7** E3
Swedish Embassy..........................**8** F3
Íslenski Alpaklúbburinn..............(see 2)
Útivist..**9** E3

SIGHTS & ACTIVITIES
Artificial Geyser...........................**10** D5
Botanic Garden............................**11** H3
Iceland Excursions (Allrahanda)...**12** E3
IcelandTotal...............................(see 6)
Kjarvalsstaðir...............................**13** D4
Laugar Spa...............................(see 14)
Laugardalslaug Swimming Pool....**14** G2
Nauthólsvík Hot Beach.................**15** C6
Reykjavík Zoo & Family Park........**16** H4
Saga Museum...............................**17** D5
University of Iceland.....................**18** B3
Ásmundursafn...............................**19** F3

SLEEPING
Central Guesthouse.......................**20** E4
Rekjavík Camping Ground.............**21** G2
Reykjavík City Hostel....................**22** G2

EATING
10-11 Supermarket.......................**23** F2
Bónus Supermarket....................(see 27)
Kringlan Food Court....................(see 27)

ENTERTAINMENT
Iceland Symphony Orchestra........**24** A3
Icelandic Dance Company...........(see 26)
Laugarásbíó Cinema......................**25** H2
Reykjavík City Theatre..................**26** E5
Sambíóin...................................(see 27)

SHOPPING
Kringlan Shopping Centre.............**27** F5

TRANSPORT
BSÍ Bus Terminal..........................**28** C4
Félag Íslenskra Bifreiðaeigenda...(see 1)
Hlemmur Bus Terminal..................**29** D3
Icelandic Mountain Bike Club.......**30** A1
Kringlan Bus Stop.........................**31** E5

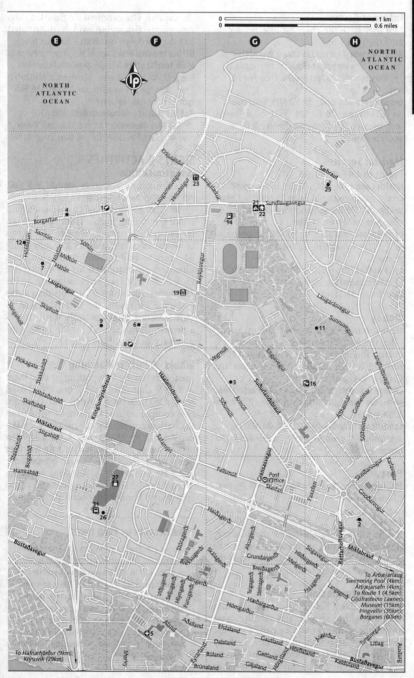

ICELAND

Internet Access

Libraries have the cheapest internet access, at Ikr200 per hour.

Aðalbókasafn (Reykjavík City Library; Map p242; ☎ 563 1717; www.borgarbokasafn.is; Tryggvagata 15; ⏰ 10am-9pm Mon, to 7pm Tue-Thu, 11am-7pm Fri, 1-5pm Sat & Sun)

Ground Zero (Map p242; ☎ 562 7776; Vallarstræti 4; per 15/35/60min Ikr200/300/500; ⏰ 11am-1am Mon-Fri, noon-1am Sat & Sun) A dedicated internet café full of moody teenagers.

Medical Services

Dentist on duty ☎ 575 0505.

Health Centre (Map p242; ☎ 585 2600; Vesturgata 7) Doctor's appointment Ikr700 (under 16s pay 25%).**Lækna-vaktin** ☎ 1770. Nonemergency telephone medical advice between 5pm and 11.30pm.

Lyfja Apótek (Map p242; ☎ 552 4045; Laugavegur 16; ⏰ 10am-7pm Mon-Fri, noon-4pm Sat) Central pharmacy.

Lyfja Apótek (Map pp238-9; ☎ 533 2300; Lágmúli 5; ⏰ 8am-midnight) Late-night pharmacy, near the Nordica Hotel. Bus Nos S2, 14 and 15.

Money

Banks round Austurstræti and Bankastræti offer the best exchange rates. You can exchange foreign currency at hotels, but commission is high. ATMs accept MasterCard, Cirrus, Visa and Electron.

Change Group Has branches at the Keflavik airport and at the main tourist office (Map p242). Commissions from 2.75% to 8.75%.

Landsbanki Íslands (Map p242; ☎ 410 4000; www .landsbanki.is; Austurstræti; ⏰ 9.15am-4pm Mon-Fri) No commission charges.

Post

Main post office (Map p242; Pósthússtræti 5; ⏰ 9am-4.30pm Mon-Fri)

Telephone

Public phones are elusive in mobile-crazy Reykjavík: try the main tourist office, the street opposite Laugavegur 38, and the Kringlan shopping centre.

Tourist Information

Reykjavík has a helpful main tourist office with a booking service, and satellite desks at the bus terminal and city hall. There are several private offices in the city. Pick up the free booklets *Reykjavík This Month* and *What's On in Reykjavík* for events in the capital. The excellent English-language newspaper *Grapevine*, widely distributed, has the lowdown on what's new in town.

BSÍ bus terminal desk (Map pp238-9 ; Vatnsmýrarvegur 10)

Main tourist office (Upplýsingamiðstöð Ferðamanna; Map p242; ☎ 590 1500; www.visitreykjavik.is; Aðalstræti 2; ⏰ 8.30am-7pm Jun–mid-Sep, 9am-6pm Mon-Fri, 9am-2pm Sat & Sun mid-Sep–May)

Raðhús tourist information desk (Map p242; ☎ 563 2005; Tjarnargata 11; ⏰ 8.30am-5pm Mon-Fri, noon-4pm Sat & Sun, closed Sun Sep-May) Inside city hall.

SIGHTS & ACTIVITIES
Hallgrímskirkja

This immense concrete **church** (Map p242; ☎ 510 1000; www.hallgrimskirkja.is; Skólavörðuholt; ⏰ 9am-5pm) is Reykjavík's most attention-seeking building, visible from 20km away. Its sweeping frontage represents columns of volcanic basalt, and took a staggering 34 years to build. Admire the elongated, ultrastark interior; then for an unmissable view of the city, take an elevator trip up the **75m tower** (adult/child Ikr350/50). Outside, a **statue** of Leifur Eiríksson, the first European to visit America, gazes proudly forth. It was a present from the USA on the 1000th anniversary of the Alþing (p251).

Whale- & Puffin-Watching

Iceland is terrific for spotting whales: there is a 98% chance of seeing one (see boxed text, p262). Between April and October, two companies run three-hour trips from the harbour, generally at 9am and 1pm: **Elding** (Map p242; ☎ 555 3565; www.elding.is; adult/7-15yr Ikr3900/1600; ☺) and **Hvalstöðin Whale-Watching Centre** (Map p242; ☎ 533 2660; www.whalewatching.is; adult/7-15yr Ikr3800/1500; ☺). During breeding season (mid-May–mid-August), they also spin round Lundey to look at the puffins.

REYKJAVÍK IN TWO DAYS

Arrive on Friday night to experience the **runtur** (p248). Sober up on Saturday with a quick dip in the **Laugadalur geothermal pool** (opposite). Don't miss the panoramic views at **Hallgrímskirkja** (above), or **Perlan & the Saga Museum** (opposite). Book a **whale-watching trip** (above) for Sunday morning, then visit the **National Museum** (opposite) or chill out at **Nauthólsvík Hot Beach** (opposite).

Geothermal Pools & Spa

Reykjavík's many outdoor swimming pools, heated by volcanic water, are the social hubs of the city: children play, teenagers flirt, business deals are made, and everyone catches up with the latest gossip.

Don't miss out on a dip: the biggest and best facilities are found at **Laugardalslaug** (Map pp238-9; ☎ 553 4039; www.laugar.com; Sundlaugavegur 30; adult/child Ikr280/120, swimsuit/towel hire Ikr300/300; ☯ 6.50am-9.30pm Mon-Fri, 8am-8pm Sat & Sun; ♿), next door to the camping ground, which has an Olympic-size indoor pool, an outdoor pool, seven Jacuzzi-like 'hot pots', steam bath, and a curling 86m waterslide for children. Attached to Laugardalslaug is the new five-star health resort **Laugar** (☎ 553 0000; www.laugarspa.is; admission Ikr3500; ☯ same as pool), with themed saunas, steam rooms and beauty treatments. Catch bus No 14 from Lækjartorg.

Bringing a touch of the Riviera to Reykjavík, the Blue-Flag **Nautholsvík Hot Beach** (Ylströndin; Map pp238-9; ☎ 511 6630; admission free; ☯ 10am-8pm mid-May–mid-Sep) is a dinky crescent of golden sand warmed by 18°C to 20°C geothermal water. There are big crowds in sunny weather. Take Bus No 16.

Perlan & Saga Museum

The huge water tanks on Öskjuhlið hill are also a tourist complex known as Perlan (the Pearl), a popular Sunday afternoon outing for families. Silicon models, thudding axes and bloodcurdling screams bring Iceland's history to life at the excellent **Saga Museum** (Map pp238-9; ☎ 511 1517; www.sagamuseum.is; adult/child/concession Ikr900/450/700; ☯ 10am-6pm Apr-Sep, noon-5pm Oct-Mar). Don't blame the *brennivín* if you see the characters walking round town; they were modelled on Reykjavík inhabitants!

Two **artificial geysers** (one inside and one outside) blast off every few minutes. Upstairs, a **360-degree viewing deck** shares tremendous mountain and city vistas with a café and revolving restaurant. Take bus No 18 from Lækjartorg.

Volcano Show

Eccentric eruption-chaser Villi Knutsen is the photographer, owner and presenter of this awesome **film-show** (Map p242; ☎ 845 9548; vknudsen2000@yahoo.com; Red Rock Cinema, Hellusund 6a; 1hr show adult/child/student Ikr900/250/750, 2hr

show adult/student/child Ikr1150/950/300; ☯ in English 11am, 3pm & 8pm daily, in German 6pm daily, in French 1pm Sat Jul & Aug, in English 3pm & 8pm daily Sep & Apr-Jun, in English 8pm Oct-Mar). His explosive footage captures 50 years' worth of Icelandic volcanoes.

Museums

The city's newest museum **Reykjavík 871+/-2** (Settlement Exhibition; ☎ 411 6370; www.reykjavik871 .is; Aðalstræti 16; adult/12-18yr Ikr600/300; ☯ 10am-5pm; ♿) is a superb combination of archaeology, technology and imagination. Although the exhibition is compact (it's based around a single Viking longhouse), it's completely absorbing. Best are the tiny wraiths – go and see!

The **National Museum** (Map pp238-9; ☎ 530 2200; www.natmus.is; Suðurgata 41; adult/under 18yr/concession Ikr600/free/300, admission free Wed; ☯ 10am-5pm daily May–mid-Sep, 11am-5pm Tue-Sun mid-Sep–Apr, to 9pm first Thu of month; ♿) gives a fine overview of Iceland's history and culture. The strongest section shows off swords and silver hoards from the Settlement Era, but their most treasured artefact is a stunning carved 13th-century church door. Walk or catch bus Nos S1, S3-6, 12 or 14.

The excellent **Þjóðmenningarhúsið** (Culture House; Map p242; ☎ 545 1400; www.thjodmenning .is; Hverfisgata 15; adult/under 16 Ikr300/free, admission free Wed; ☯ 11am-5pm; ♿) offers intelligent displays about the sagas, and the darkened rooms here contain the actual vellums themselves.

Quaint old buildings have been uprooted from various places, then replanted at **Árbæjarsafn** (Open-Air Museum; Map pp238-9; ☎ 411 6300; www.arbaejarsafn.is; Kistuhylur 4; adult/under 18yr Ikr600/ free; ☯ 10am-5pm daily Jun-Aug, by tour only 1pm Mon, Wed & Fri Sep-May), which is a kind of zoo for houses, 4km from the city centre. Kids love running round the creaky timber homes. Take bus No 12.

Out in the suburb of Mosfellsbær, the home of Nobel Prize–winning author Halldór Laxness (1902–98) is now open

ICELAND

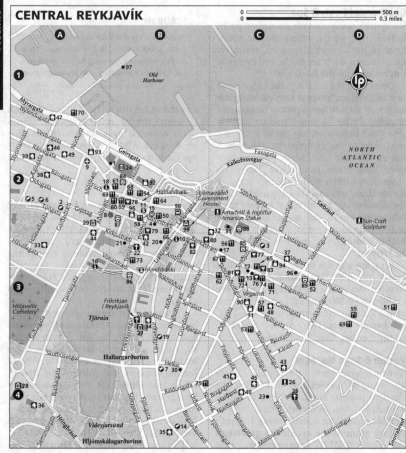

CENTRAL REYKJAVÍK

0   500 m
0   0.3 miles

to visitors. Highlights of the **Gljúfrasteinn Laxness Museum** (586 8066; www.gljufrasteinn.is; Mosfellsbær; adult/under 16yr Ikr500/250; 9am-5pm Jun-Aug, 10am-5pm Tue-Sun Sep-May) include the study where Laxness wrote his defining works, and his beloved Jaguar parked outside. Buses are an extremely awkward way to get there; you really need a car.

Art Galleries

The **National Gallery** (Map p242; 515 9600; www.listasafn.is; Fríkirkjuvegur 7; admission free; 11am-5pm Tue-Sun;) contains works by Iceland's most renowned artists, and provides an interesting glimpse into the nation's psyche: surreal mud-purple landscapes mingle with visions of ogresses, giants and dead men.

The weird symbolist creations of Einar Jónsson, 'Iceland's first sculptor', are objects you'll either love or hate: find out which at the cube-shaped **Einar Jónsson Museum** (Map pp238-9; 551 3797; www.skulptur.is; Njarðargata; adult/under 16yr Ikr400/free; 2-5pm Tue-Sun Jun–mid-Sep, 2-5pm Sat & Sun mid-Sep–Nov & Feb-May, closed Dec & Jan).

Listasafn Reykjavíkur (Reykjavík Art Museum; www.listasafnreykjavikur.is; adult/under 18yr Ikr500/free, admission free Mon) is split over three sites. At the rather wonderful **Ásmundursafn** (Ásmundur Sveinsson Museum; Map pp238-9; 553 2155; Sigtún; 10am-4pm May-Sep, 1-4pm Oct-Apr), you'll find the artist's massive concrete sculptures in the garden (admission free); plus there are smaller, spikier works in wood, clay and metals in the igloo-shaped studio he designed. His themes range from folklore to physics. Bus No 14 passes close by.

Jóhannes Kjarval (1885–1972) was a fisherman until his crew paid for him to study at the Academy of Fine Arts in Copenhagen. His unearthly Icelandic landscapes can be seen inside the angular glass-and-wood **Kjarvalsstaðir** (Map pp238-9; ☎ 552 6131; Flókagata; 🕙 10am-5pm; 🚾). Catch bus No 1.

The third Listasafn Reykjavíkur is **Hafnarhús** (Map p242; ☎ 590 1200; Tryggvagata 17; 🕙 10am-5pm; 🚾), a severe concrete building containing works by political cartoonist Erró, plus changing modern-art exhibitions.

Parks & Gardens

The only attraction aimed at (youngish) children is Reykjavík **Zoo & Family Park** (Map pp238-9; ☎ 585 7800; www.mu.is; Laugardalur; adult/5-12yrs Ikr550/450, 1-/10-/20-ride tickets Ikr170/1500/2800;

🕙 10am-6pm mid-May–mid-Aug, 10am-5pm mid-Aug–mid-May; 🚾). Don't expect lions and tigers: think seals, foxes and farm animals. Nearby are child-size bulldozers, a giant trampoline and minifairground rides.

Next door, the **Botanic Garden** (Map pp238-9; ☎ 553 8870; botgard@rvk.is; Skúlatún 2; admission free; greenhouse 🕙 10am-10pm Apr-Sep, to 5pm Oct-Mar) has sub-Arctic plant species, colourful seasonal flowers, and a café in June to August.

There is no direct route but bus Nos 14, 15, 17, 19 and S2 pass within 400m of both attractions.

Other Sights

Old Reykjavík grew up around **Tjörnin**, a large lake that echoes with the honks and hootings of thousands of geese, swans, ducks and gulls. The pleasant park at the southern end is laced with walking and cycling paths.

Rising on stilts from the northern shore is the postmodern **Ráðhús** (City Hall; Map p242; ☎ 563 2000; Tjarnargata 11; ☒ 8am-7pm Mon-Fri, noon-6pm Sat & Sun; ⓐ). It contains a tourist information desk, café and a huge, impressive 3-D map of Iceland: a mass of mountains, fjords and volcanoes.

The neat grey basalt building on the southern side of Austurvöllur, the main square, houses the Icelandic Parliament, the **Alþingi** (Map p242; ☎ 563 0500; www.althingi.is; Túngata; ⓐ). Next to it is the **Dómkirkja** (Map p242; ☎ 520 9700; Lækjargata 14a; ☒ 10am-5pm Mon-Fri), Iceland's small but perfectly proportioned cathedral.

There are brochures for themed walks, such as statuary and literary figures, that you can follow around Reykjavík and these brochures are available at the tourist office.

SLEEPING

Reykjavík is packed in summer: book accommodation well in advance. Breakfast is usually included in room prices (but not for sleeping-bag accommodation).

Budget

Reykjavík Camping Ground (Map pp238-9; ☎ 568 6944; www.reykjavikcampsite.is; Sundlaugavegur 32; camp sites per person Ikr800, 2-bed cabins per night Ikr4000; ☒ mid-May–mid-Sep, reception 3-6pm; P ⓐ) There's only one camping ground in Reykjavík, and it gets very busy in summer. It holds 650 people, though, so you'd be unlucky not to find a pitch. Laundry and internet facilities.

Reykjavík City Hostel (Map pp238-9; ☎ 553 8110; www.hostel.is; Sundlaugavegur 34; sleeping bag in 6-/4-/2-bed sb Ikr1700/2400/3500, bed linen Ikr600; P ⓐ) Beside the campground, the award-winning youth hostel has many commendable points: it's environmentally friendly, and has helpful staff and excellent facilities (24 hour reception, several kitchens, laundry, large-screen TV room, internet access, wi-fi, bike rental etc). School parties can be a nuisance. Bring ear plugs. Breakfast Ikr800.

Salvation Army Guesthouse (Map p242; ☎ 561 3203; www.guesthouse.is; Kirkjustræti 2; sb/s/d Ikr3100/5500/8000) This is the nearest thing Reykjavík has to a Japanese capsule hotel! The tiny rooms are highly functional and frill-free, but it beats the youth hostel hands-down on location. There's a similar bustling backpackery atmosphere, guest kitchen and lounging area.

Garður Inn (Map p242; ☎ 562 4000, Jun-Aug 551 5900; www.inns-of-iceland.com; Hringbraut; sb Ikr2300-3200, s/d Ikr7500/9900; ☒ Jun-Aug; P) The university campus, about 1km from the centre, has utilitarian rooms once students have left for the summer. The cheapest sleeping-bag accommodation is in 16-person dorms.

Midrange

Tower Guesthouse (Map p242; ☎ 552 5581, 896 6694; www.tower.is; Grettisgata 6; d Ikr9900-13,900, 1-4 person apt Ikr18900-32900, discounts Oct-Apr) This castle-like place has a sweeping spiral staircase and elegant apartments, and you can stargaze from the rooftop Jacuzzi! The guesthouse is popular with gay travellers, and there's the odd phallus-shaped plant pot around, but everyone is welcome. Breakfast isn't provided, but there are kitchen facilities.

Sunna Guesthouse (Map p242; ☎ 511 5570; www.sunna.is; Þórsgata 26; summer s/d from Ikr8400/10,700, winter from Ikr6100/7900, apt Ikr3300-22,500; P ☒ ⓐ) Rooms at this guesthouse are simple and sunny with honey-coloured parquet floors. Those at the front offer good views of Hallgrímskirkja. Families are encouraged to stay at the Sunna; there is a handful of brand-new studio apartments accommodating one to four people.

Three Sisters (Þrjár Systur; Map p242; ☎ 565 2181; www.threesisters.is; Ránargata 16; 1-/2-person apt €98/148, family apt €210; ☒ Jun-Aug; ☒ ⓐ) A twinkly-eyed former fisherman runs the Three Sisters, a lovely townhouse in old Reykjavík, now divided into eight studio apartments. Comfy counterpaned beds are flanked by old-fashioned easy chairs and state-of-the-art flatscreen TVs. Each room comes with a cute fully-equipped kitchen. A short stroll seawards is a second building with sleeping-bag accommodation in six-bed dorms (around Ikr2600).

Guesthouse Butterfly (Map p242; ☎ 894 1864; www.kvasir.is/butterfly; Ránargata 8a; s/d/apt from Ikr6900/8900/13,900; ☒ Jun-Aug) This is on a quiet residential street within fluttering distance of the centre, and has neat, simply furnished rooms. There's a guest kitchen, wi-fi access, and the friendly Icelandic Norwegian owners make you feel right at home. The top floor has two self-contained apartments that have a kitchen and balcony.

Álfhóll Guesthouse (Map p242; ☎ 898 1838; www.islandia.is/alf; Ránargata 8; s/d/tr Ikr6800/9000/11,000

2- to 6-person apt 12,000-18,000; ⊙ Jun-Aug) Almost identical in feel and facilities to neighbouring Guesthouse Butterfly, this place is run by a family of elf enthusiasts.

Castle House & Embassy Apartments (Map p242; ☎ 511 2166; http://hotelsiceland.net; Skálholtsstígur 2a & Garðastræti 40; 1-6 person apt Ikr7600-28,000; ✕) Turn to these pleasant self-contained apartments for satisfyingly central and commendably quiet accommodation. They are much more personal than a hotel, but come with room service. Fresh towels appear daily, and even your washing-up seems to magically clean itself. Breakfast is not included. Be aware that this establishment does change its tariff depending on the demand.

Central Guesthouse (Map pp238-9; ☎ 552 2822; www.central-guesthouse.com; Bólstaðarhlíð 8; summer sb/s/d/tr Ikr2300/4700/5900/7100, winter sb/s/d/tr Ikr1800/3600/4800/6000; ☐) This welcoming place is about 10 minutes' walk from the BSÍ bus terminal and Perlan. Rooms are uncomplicated, light and trim; the attic room, with sloping ceilings and private balcony, has the most character. Breakfast is not included, but there's a guest kitchen.

Gistiheimilið Domus (Map p242; ☎ 561 1200; www.domusguesthouse.is; Hverfisgata 45; summer sb/s/d Ikr2900/9500/11,300, winter sb/s/d Ikr2000/5900/7900) Once the Norwegian embassy, Domus' rooms have stately proportions and antique windows, but vaunt modern touches such as new radio alarms and TVs. The best rooms are on the 1st floor, and feature hardwood floors, leather sofas and artwork on the walls (none have private bathroom). Breakfast is included in accommodation above sleeping-bag level.

Galtafell Guesthouse (Map pp238-9; ☎ 699 2525; www.galtafell.com; Laufásvegur 46; summer s/d/apt from Ikr7900/8900/16,900, winter s/d/apt from Ikr6000/6900/12,000; ✕) Recommended by readers, this new guesthouse has a great location; it is in a quiet, well-to-do suburb within easy walking distance of town. The four spruce apartments each contain a fully equipped kitchen, cosy seating area and separate bedroom, and there's also three double rooms available.

Gistiheimilið Ísafold (Map p242; ☎ 561 2294; isafold@itn.is; Bárugata 11; summer s/d from Ikr7300/9800, winter from Ikr5400/6800) This recommended, rambling old house (a former bakery/rehab centre/bookshop) lies in peaceful old Reykjavík. Sun-filled bedrooms contain washbasins and rustic beds, there are tea-making facilities in the lounge, and solemn Icelandic dolls keep an eye on diners in the attic breakfast room. At the nearby annexe (Bárugata 20), all accommodation comes with private bathrooms (around Ikr1000 extra).

Hótel Leifur Eiríksson (Map p242; ☎ 562 0800; www.hotelleifur.is; Skólavörðustígur 45; summer s/d/tr Ikr14,200/17,400/20,500, winter s/d/tr Ikr9300/11,600/14,200) This hotel glories in one of the best locations in Reykjavík: it's slap on the end of arty Skólavörðustígur, and more than half of the 47 rooms have inspiring views of Hallgrímskirkja. All are decorated with blue carpeting, gauzy curtains and en-suite bathrooms.

Guesthouse Andrea (Map pp238-9; ☎ 552 5515; www.aurorahouse.is; Njarðargata 43; sb/s/d Ikr2900/7000/9000; ⊙ mid-May–Sep) Friendly Siggi runs this hidden place, tucked down a side-street in a quiet residential area. Its five private rooms have spruce wooden floors, and are ideal for self-caterers: each has a sink, cooker, fridge and tiny two-seater table.

Gistiheimilið Aurora (Map p242; ☎ 552 5515; Freyjugata 24) This is also run by the Guesthouse Andrea people, and it is a homely purple townhouse just round the corner. Room No 33, with a balcony and sea view, is the best.

Top End

101 Hotel (Map p242 ☎ 580 0101; www.101hotel.is; Hverfisgata 10; s/d/ste from Ikr27,900/29,900/37,900; ☐ �&) Reykjavík's newest boutique hotel is devilishly divine. Its 38 sensuous rooms – with yielding king- or queen-sized beds, glass-walled showers and rich wooden floors – may mean you boycott the bars and opt for a night in instead. A spa with masseurs, a small gym and a glitterati bar add to the opulence.

Hótel Borg (Map p242; ☎ 551 1440; www.hotelborg.is; Pósthússtræti 11; summer s/d/ste Ikr17,000/28,000/36,000, winter Ikr13,000/21,000/28,000) For those who love slabs of character, this magnificent 1930s Art Deco palace is located in prime position on Austurvöllur square. A wooden elevator rattles up to luxurious rooms, decorated with antique furniture but complete with all mod cons. The buffet breakfast will set you back an extra Ikr1300.

ICELAND

EATING

Reykjavík's eateries vary from hot-dog stands to world-class restaurants. Two things are consistent: high quality, and high prices. The best dishes are generally those made from Iceland's outstanding fresh fish, seafood and juicy mountain-reared lamb. For types of eatery and opening hours, see p236.

Reykjavík's dining places are found along Laugavegur, Hverfisgata and Austurstræti. Tips are always included in the bill. See also Food & Drink (p236).

Restaurants

MIDRANGE

Austur Indía Félagið (Map p242; ☎ 552 1630; Hverfisgata 56; mains Ikr2200-3700; ⊗ 6-10pm Sun-Thu, 6-11pm Fri & Sat) The northernmost Indian restaurant in the world is an upmarket experience, with minimalist interior and a select choice of sublime dishes. One of its finest features, though, is its lack of pretension. The atmosphere is relaxed, and the service warm. Apparently this place is a favourite of Harrison Ford's, and who dares argue with Indy?

Við Tjörnina (Map p242; ☎ 551 8666; www.vidtjornina.is; Templarasund 3; Ikr2000-3600; ⊗ noon-2.30pm Thu & Fri, from 6pm) Tucked away in an alley near Tjörn, this famed seafood establishment serves up beautifully presented Icelandic feasts such as guillemot with port, tender lamb fillet and garlic langoustine. The restaurant itself is cosy and wonderfully distinctive; it feels like a quirky upperclass 1930s drawing room.

Á Næstu Grösum (First Vegetarian; Map p242; www.anaestugrosum.is; ☎ 552 8410; Laugavegur 20b; daily specials Ikr1350; ⊗ 11.30am-10pm Mon-Sat, 5-10pm Sun) This first-rate veggie restaurant, in a cheerful orange room overlooking Laugavegur, offers several daily specials. They use seasonal organic veg, with inventive dressings that give lettuce new appeal; and there's extra spice on Indian nights (Friday and Saturday). Organic wine and beer are available.

Grænn Kostur (Map p242; ☎ 552 2028; www.graennkostur.is; Skólavörðustígur 8; daily special Ikr1100; ⊗ 11.30am-9pm Mon-Sat, 1-9pm Sun) This serves similar organic, vegetarian set meals. It's smaller and harder to find, but persevere!

Hornið (Map p242; ☎ 551 3340; Hafnarstræti 15; 9in pizza Ikr1200-2000, mains Ikr1700-3000; ⊗ 11.30am-11pm) There is an easy-going atmosphere at this bright Art Deco café-restaurant,

with its warm terracotta tiles, weeping-fig plants and decently spaced tables. Pizzas are freshly made before your eyes, the prettily presented pasta meals will set you up for the day, and you can sample traditional Icelandic fish dishes.

Sægreifinn (Map p242; ☎ 867 3660; Verbúð 8, harbour; mains Ikr900-2000; ⊗ 8am-6pm) Eccentric Sægreifinn serves up fresh seafood in what looks almost like a 1950s English chip shop…except for the barrel seats and stuffed seal. The owner is a sprightly old gent, who buys and cooks all the fish himself; lobster soup and smoked fish are particular specialities. He speaks only Icelandic, so make sure you know what you're asking for!

Galileo (Map p242; ☎ 552 9500; www.galileo.is; Hafnarstræti 1; mains Ikr1750-4000; ⊗ 11.30am-11pm Mon-Fri, 1-11pm Sat & Sun) Reykjavík's old falcon house now contains Galileo, a sophisticated Italian restaurant that's perfect for intimate dining – even down to the romantic starry-sky ceiling. Icelandic lamb and fish dishes are served, and pasta, pizza and risotto.

Þrír Frakkar Hjá Úlfari (Map p242; ☎ 552 3939; www.3frakkar.com; Baldursgata 14; mains Ikr2700-4000; ⊗ noon-2.30pm & 6-10pm Mon-Fri, to 11pm Sat & Sun) Owner-chef Úlfar Eysteinsson has built up an excellent reputation at this snug little restaurant; and it's been given the thumbs-up by Jamie Oliver. Specialities include salted cod, anglerfish and *plokkfiskur* (fish stew) with black bread.

TOP END

Einar Ben (Map p242; ☎ 511 5090; www.einarben.is; Ingólfstorg; mains Ikr2600-4500; ⊗ 6-10pm Mon-Thu, to 11pm Fri-Sun) One of the city's finest restaurants, Einar Ben is frequented by diplomats and is renowned for its top-class service and gastronomical marvels. Dishes are Icelandic with a continental twist: think puffin terrine, and lamb Dijon with blueberries and thyme.

Sjávarkjallarinn (Map p242; ☎ 511 1212; www.sjavarkjallarinn.is; Aðalstræti 2; Ikr2900-4500; ⊗ 11.30am-11.30pm Mon-Fri, 5.30-11.30pm Sat & Sun) Not one but two of Iceland's Chef-of-the-Year winners (2004 and 2006) devise exotic dishes at this atmospheric seafood restaurant. Shimmering fish and succulent crustaceans are combined with the unexpected – pomegranate, coconut, lychee and chilli – and served up like miniature works of art.

Cafés

The distinction between cafés and bars is vague; see p248.

Café Paris (Map p242; ☎ 551 1020; Austurstræti 14; snacks Ikr450-870; ☸ 8am-1am Mon-Thu, to 3am Fri, 9am-3am Sat, to 1am Sun) This old favourite has undergone a recent refit and is now better than ever. Leather-upholstered chairs provide a level of bum-comfort previously missing. Although there's a selection of light meals, such as sandwiches, crepes and tacos, people come here for coffee, cakes, chatter, and to check out the crowds.

Café Garðurinn (Map p242; ☎ 561 2345; Klapparstígur 37; soup/mains/both Ikr650/1050/1500; ☸ 11am-6.30pm Mon-Fri, noon-5pm Sat) This tiny but tasteful veggie café is based around seven tables and the hum of civilised conversation. Choice is limited, but it's delicious. We heartily recommend spinach soup and Catalonian tofu balls.

Café Cultura (Map p242; ☎ 530 9314; www .cultura.is; Hverfisgata 18; snacks & light meals Ikr800-1400; ☸ 11.30am-1am Mon-Thu, 11.30am-4am Fri & Sat, 1pm-1am Sun) This arty intercultural café has scratched wooden floors and mosaic tables, and offers well-priced Mediterranean- and Arabic-influenced nosh such as felafel, spicy meatballs and couscous cuisine. There's a tolerant attitude to kids. Free tango lessons start at 8pm Wednesday; and it becomes an equally funky bar at weekends.

Té og Kaffi (Map p242; ☎ 562 2322; www.teog kaffi.is; Laugarvegur 24; snacks Ikr600-1100; ☸ 7.30am-7pm Mon-Fri, 10am-7pm Sat, 11am-6pm Sun) Iceland has created its own indigenous version of Starbucks, complete with barristas and a huge coffee menu. It's popular with families, footsore Saturday shoppers and Lonely Planet readers.

Babalú (Map p242; ☎ 552 2278; Skólavörðustígur 22a) More inviting than your own living room, Reykjavík's newest café is *über*-cute (if smoky). It sells only tea, coffee, hot chocolate and the odd crepe, but once you've settled into one of its snug corners, you won't want to move. In summer there's occasional live music.

Kofi Tómasar Frænda (Koffin; Map p242; ☎ 551 1855; Laugavegur 2; snacks around Ikr600; ☸ 10am-1am Mon-Thu, to 5.30am Fri & Sat, 11am-1am Sun) Subterranean Koffin has a studenty feel. Relax with magazines and a snack (nachos, lasagne, sandwiches, cakes or chocolate-coated marzipan) and watch disconnected feet scurry

along Laugavegur. At night, it turns into a candlelit bar with DJs. Wi-fi hotspot.

Kaffi Hljómalind (Map p242; ☎ 517 1980; Laugavegur 21; www.kaffihljomalind.org; snacks Ikr650-1100; ☸ 9am-11pm Mon-Fri, 11am-11pm Sat & Sun; ☒) This commendable organic and fair-trade café is run on a not-for-profit basis. It looks like a 1950s home with 1970s flourishes (prayer flags, patterned chairs, handpainted cups and saucers), and is a meeting-place for Reykjavík's radicals. Wi-fi hotspot.

Svarta Kaffið (Map p242; ☎ 551 2999; Laugavegur 54; snacks & light meals Ikr800-1300; ☸ 11am-1am Sun-Thu, to 3am Fri & Sat; ☒) Order thick homemade soup (one meat and one veg option daily; Ikr990) at this cavelike café – it's served piping hot in fantastic bread bowls. It's also a whimsical nightspot, with African masks and dim lighting adding a certain frisson.

Vegamót (Map p242; ☎ 511 3040; www.vegamot .is; Vegamótstígur 4; snacks/light meals Ikr800-2190) A long-running café/bar/club, but still a voguish place to eat, drink, see and be seen. There's a startling choice on the 'global' menu, including Mexican salad, sesame-fried monkfish, seafood quesadilla and blackened chicken. The attached takeaway charges 10% less.

Quick Eats

Icelanders swear it's impossible to get a bad hot dog from **Bæjarins Beztu** (Map p242), a van near the harbour, patronised by Bill Clinton! Use the vital sentence *Eina með öllu* (One with everything) for mustard, ketchup, remoulade and onions. The kiosks **Hlölla Bátar** (Map p242; ☸ 11am-2am Sun-Thu, 10am-7am Fri & Sat) and **Emmessís & Pylsar** (Map p242; ☸ 10am-11pm) on Ingólfstorg sell ice cream and hotdogs (Ikr330 to Ikr790).

Head for **Nonnabiti** (Map p242; ☎ 551 2312; Hafnarstræti 18; snacks Ikr280-690; ☸ to 2am) if you want burgers and hot dogs; when you've overdone the fried meat, **Kebabhúsið** (Map p242; ☎ 561 3070; Lækjargata 2; ☸ to 11pm Sun-Thu, to 7am Fri & Sat) offers falafel, and fish and chips (around Ikr800).

Self-Catering

Bónus (☸ 11am-6.30pm Mon-Thu, 10am-7.30pm Fri, 10am-6pm Sat; Laugavegur 59 Map p242; Kringlan Map pp238-9; also ☸ noon-6pm Sun) is the cheapest supermarket. The more upmarket **10-11** (☸ 8am-9pm; Austurstræti Map p242; Hverfisgata Map p242; Laugalækur Map pp238-9) has branches all over the place.

ICELAND

DRINKING

Reykjavík is renowned for its Friday- and Saturday-night *runtur*, when industrious Icelanders abandon work and party with passion (midweek drinking is not part of Icelandic culture). Beer is shockingly expensive. Most people visit a government-owned *vín búð* (the only shops licensed to sell alcohol), tipple at home, then hit the town from midnight til 6am. There's a central **vín búð** (Map p242; Austurstræti 10; 11am-6pm Mon-Thu, to 7pm Fri, to 2pm Sat), and another in Kringlan shopping centre (Map pp238–9).

Some venues have cover charges (about Ikr1000), and 'in' clubs have long queues at weekends. Things change fast; check *Grapevine* or *Reykjavík This Month* for the latest listings. You should dress up in Reykjavík, but there are pub-style places where you won't feel scruffy in jeans. The minimum drinking age is 20.

Bars & Pubs

Often the only difference between a café and a bar is the time of day; see p247.

Sirkus (Map p242; 511 8022; Klapparstígur 3) Our personal favourite, this kooky offbeat bar has dinky fairylights, bus seats in the attic, an annual Tom Selleck Moustache Competition, and a loyal local following. DJs and bands play regularly, and there's a summer garden where you can snatch gulps of fresh air. It's up for demolition, so make the most of it. However it remains in posterity in Björk's music clip 'Triumph of a Heart'.

Kaffibarinn (Map p242; 551 1588; Bergstaðastræti 1) Damon Albarn from Blur has a stake in this *über*-trendy bar, which had a starring role in the cult film *101 Reykjavík*. It's popular with celebs: at weekends you'll need a famous face or a battering ram to get in.

Grand Rokk (Map p242; 551 5522; www .grandrokk.is; Smiðjustígur 6) You'll feel as though you've known this down-to-earth bar all your life. During the day, chess enthusiasts play concentrated matches here; at weekends it's great for live music, luring up to three bands per session. Enjoy it while you can; it's scheduled for destruction in a redevelopment scheme.

Café Oliver (Map p242; 552 2300; www .caféoliver.is; Laugavegur 20a) One of Reykjavík's newest café-bars, Oliver is the most in-vogue place for brunch; and for partying late in super style. DJs pump out the tunes on Thursday, Friday and Saturday, with long queues snaking back from the doors.

Kaffi Sólon (Map p242; 562 3232; www .solon.is; Bankastræti 7a; snacks & light meals Ikr900-2000; 11am-1am Mon-Thu, to 5am Fri & Sat, noon-midnight Sun) Sólon, decked out in white-leather seats and oversized artwork, is a cultivated international bistro during the day and a swish club for a beautiful, martini-drinking set by night. There's long queues, in-demand DJs, moody lighting and (a popular Reykjavík item) a dancefloor containing around 17 people per square metre. It's also a wi-fi hotspot.

Kaffi Brennslan (Map p242; 561 3600; www .brennslan.is; Pósthússtræti 9; snacks Ikr390-1790; til 3am Fri & Sat) All kinds of folk frequent Brennslan, an unpretentious Art Deco café-bar, where conventional tastes mix with Matrix-style leather coats and avant-garde haircuts. It entices a twenties and thirties crowd by offering beers from 20 countries, but never gets so packed that you can't move.

Nelly's (Map p242; 551 2477; Þinghóltstræti 2) By serving the cheapest beer in town (Ikr900 for 1.5L), publike Nelly's naturally pulls in a young, alternative, studenty crowd. DJs and live bands play regularly, it opens until 6am on weekends, and there are daily offers on alcohol.

If Víking beer isn't doing it for you, head for a pint of Guinness at one of Reykjavík's two Irish pubs. **Celtic Cross** (Map p242; 511 3240; Hverfisgata 26), done up like a funeral parlour and with bands in the basement on weekends; and the **Dubliner** (Map p242; 511 3233; Hafnarstræti 4; to 1am Sun-Thu, to 5am Fri & Sat), with live music every night from 10.30pm.

Nightclubs

Hverfisbarinn (Map p242; 511 6700; www .hverfisbarinn.is; Hverfisgata 20; to 1am Thu, to 5.30am Fri & Sat) This trendy bar and club attracts a stylish, studenty crowd, and has long queues at weekends. It is done out in a cool modern-Scandinavian style, which adds to the spacious feel. There's live music on Thursday from 9.30pm, and DJs on Friday and Saturday.

Gaukur á Stöng (Map p242; 551 1556; www .gaukurinn.is; Tryggvagata 22; 8pm-1am Sun-Thu, 8pm-5.30am Fri & Sat) Despite its divey air, stalwart Gaukurinn is one of the most popular taverns in town, particularly with younger drinkers. It was responsible for creating vodka-spiked beer (still available), and is a notorious weekend pick-up joint. It's best as a weeknight venue for catching Icelandic bands (nightly from 11pm).

NASA (Map p242; ☎ 511 1313; nasa@nasa.is; Austurvöllur; admission Ikr1000) The biggest nightclub in Reykjavík, Nasa is a stripped-pine affair filled with Prada-clad crowds. It plays chart music and club anthems, and is also a sometime-venue for live bands. Email for upcoming music.

ENTERTAINMENT
Live Music
Many of the bars, pubs and clubs listed have live band performances, particularly Grand Rokk (opposite), Gaukur á Stöng (opposite), Nelly's Café (opposite) and Nasa (opposite). For listings of live music in Reykjavík, see the excellent English-language newspaper *Grapevine*, available free from cafés and tourist offices.

Two cutting-edge music festivals are **Iceland Airwaves** (www.icelandairwaves.com; ☷ late Oct) and the new **Reykjavík Rocks** (☷ late-Jun/early-Jul) contact the tourist office for details.

Theatre & Classical Music
The **National Theatre** (Map p242; ☎ 585 1200; www.leikhusid.is; Lindargata 7; admission adult/under 16 Ikr2700/2300; ☷ box office 12.30-6pm Mon & Tue, to 8pm Wed-Sun, theatre closed Jul & Aug) puts on around 12 plays, musicals and operas per year, from modern Icelandic works to Shakespeare.

The country's second-largest theatre, **Reykjavík City Theatre** (Map pp238-9; ☎ 568 8000; www.borgarleikhus.is; Listabraut 3, Kringlan; adult/under 12yr Ikr2500/free), also stages classic and contemporary plays. The **Icelandic Dance Company** (☎ 588 0900; www.id.is) is in residence here.

For spooky Icelandic folktales and a demonstration of traditional wrestling, try the English-language performance **'Light Nights'** (☎ 551 9181; www.lightnights.com; Baldursgata 37; tickets adult/7-12yr Ikr2500/1800; ☷ 8.30pm Mon & Tue Jul & Aug) at the **Iðnó Theatre** (Map p242).

The **Iceland Symphony Orchestra** (Map pp238-9; ☎ 545 2500; www.sinfonia.is; Háskólabíó, Hagatorg; tickets Ikr2500-3800) will move to flashy new premises in 2009, but for now it's based at the Reykjavík University cinema. There are around 60 classical performances per season, normally on Thursday at 7.30pm.

Cinemas
Films are shown in their original language with Icelandic subtitles; all cinemas charge adult/under six years Ikr800/450. The newspaper *Morgunblaðið* lists cinema programmes, or click on the 'Í Bíó' tab at www .kvikmyndir.is.

Reykjavík has seven multiplexes, including **Sambíóin** (Map pp238-9; ☎ 588 0800) in the Kringlan shopping centre, and **Laugarásbíó** (Map pp238-9; ☎ 553 2075; Laugarás) near the youth hostel. Central **Regnboginn** (Map p242; ☎ 551 9000; Hverfisgata 54) sometimes shows arts films.

SHOPPING
Laugavegur is the main shopping street; Austurstræti and Hafnarstræti contain tourist stores selling puffin-decorated trinkets; and Skólavörðustígur sells arty-crafty one-offs.

Handknitting Association of Iceland (Map p242; ☎ 552 1890; www.handknit.is; Skólavörðustígur 19) Traditional handmade hats socks and sweaters are on sale here...or buy yarn and knitting patterns and do it yourself!

Kolaportið Flea Market (Map p242; Geirsgata; ☷ 11am-5pm Sat & Sun) Vendors here sell a pleasing tangle of second-hand stuff, while those brave enough can try *hákarl* from the fishmarket.

For cutting-edge Icelandic tunes, try hip record shops **12 Tónar** (Map p242; ☎ 511 5656; 12tonar@12tonar.is; Skólavörðustígur 15), with three floors of music and its own recording label; or **Smekkleysa Plötubúð** (Map p242; ☎ 534 3730; basement, Laugavegur 59; ☷ noon-6pm Mon-Thu, to 7pm Fri, to 5pm Sat).

On the dark side, buy bottles of *brennivín* from **vín búð** (see opposite); or your own Icelandic voodoo doll from **Nornabúðin** (Witch Shop; Map p242; ☎ 552 3540; Vesturgata 12; ☷ 2-6pm Mon-Sat).

GETTING THERE & AWAY
Air
The city airport, Innanlandsflug, serves all domestic destinations, the Faroe Islands and Greenland. Internal flight operator **Flugfélag Íslands** (Air Iceland; ☎ 570 3030; www.air iceland.is) has a desk there, but internet bookings are cheaper.

International flights operate through **Keflavík airport** (www.keflavikairport.com), 48km west of Reykjavík.

ICELAND

Bus

From June to mid-September, there are regular direct services between Reykjavík's **BSÍ bus terminal** (Map pp238-9; ☎ 562 1011; www.bsi .is; Vatnsmýrarvegur 10) and the following places (reduced or no service rest of the year):

Akureyri (Ikr6600, six hours, daily)
Höfn (Ikr7400, eight hours, daily)
Reykholt (Ikr2200, two hours, Friday and Sunday)
Skaftafell (Ikr5400, six hours, daily)
Þorlákshöfn (Ikr1000, one hour, daily)
Þórsmörk (Ikr3700, 3½ hours, daily)

On Friday and Saturday in May, it's possible to get from Reykjavík to Egilsstaðir (Ikr11,100; 11 hours) and Mývatn (Ikr8300, nine hours) in one day, changing in Akureyri. At other times, you'll have to stay overnight in Akureyri (or Höfn).

To reach Húsavík (Ikr8200, eight to 11 hours, daily) change in Akureyri.

For Stykkishólmur (Ikr3300, 2½ hours, daily), change in Vatnaleið.

GETTING AROUND
To/From the Airport

It's a 1km walk into town from the city airport terminal (domestic flights), or there's a taxi rank.

The **Flybus** (☎ 562 1011; www.re.is) to and from Keflavík airport meets all incoming flights. Tickets cost adult/12 to 15 years Ikr1100/550 (credit cards accepted) and the journey to Reykjavík takes around 50 minutes. On the return journey, the bus leaves the BSÍ bus terminal two hours before international departures. Reykjavík City Hostel and the main hotels can arrange transfers to the bus station. Taxis to/from the airport cost around Ikr8000 one way.

Bicycle

Cycling is a great way to buzz round the city (although bicycles seem to be invisible to Reykjavík's car drivers). **Borgarhjól SF** (Map p242; ☎ 551 5653; www.borgarhjol.net; Hverfisgata 50; 10hr/24hr/1 wk Ikr1500/2000/10,500; ☷ 8am-6pm Mon-Fri, 10am-2pm Sat) has bikes for hire, also available from Reykjavík City Hostel and the camping ground (p244).

Bus

Reykjavík's superb **city bus system** (☎ 540 2700; www.straeto.is/english) runs from 7am to 11pm or midnight. A limited night-bus service runs until 2am on Friday and Saturday. Buses only stop at designated bus stops, marked with the letter 'S'. The two central terminals are Hlemmur (Map pp238–9) and Lækjartorg (Map p242).

The fare is adult/six to 12 years Ikr250/75 (no change given). S*kiptimiði* (transfer tickets) are available from the driver if you need to take two buses to reach your destination. The Reykjavík Tourist Card includes a bus pass.

Taxi

Taxi prices are high; flagfall starts at Ikr520. There are usually taxis outside the bus stations, domestic airport, youth hostel, and pubs and bars on weekend nights. Alternatively, call **Borgarbíll** (☎ 552 2440), **BSR** (☎ 561 0000) or **Hreyfill-Bæjarleiðir** (☎ 588 5522). Tipping is not expected.

AROUND REYKJAVÍK
Blue Lagoon

As the Eiffel Tower is to Paris, as Disney World is to Florida, so the **Blue Lagoon** (Bláa Lónið; ☎ 420 8800; www.bluelagoon.is; adult/12-15yr Ikr1400/700, towel/swimsuit/robe hire Ikr300/350/700, spa treatments from Ikr1300; ☷ 9am-9pm mid-May–Aug, 10am-8pm Sep–mid-May; ☷) is to Iceland…with all the positive and negative connotations that implies. Those who say it's too expensive, too clinical, too crowded are kind of right, but ignore them. The Blue Lagoon is a must-see, and you'll be missing something special if you don't go.

Set in a vast black lava field, the milky-blue spa is fed by water (at a perfect 38°C, and at Blue-Flag standards) from the futuristic Svartsengi geothermal plant, which provides an off-the-planet scene-setter for your swim. Add in steaming silver vents and people coated in silica-mud, and you're in another world.

Be careful on the slippery bridges and bring plenty of conditioner to stop your hair going solid. There's a snack bar, top gourmet restaurant and souvenir shop on site, plus roaming masseurs. At the time of research, the lagoon was being extended and will be doubled in size by 2007.

The lagoon is 50km southwest of Reykjavík. Between 10am and 6pm daily, there are six **Reykjavík Excursions** (☎ 562 1011; www .bsi.is) buses from the BSÍ bus terminal (or from your hotel on request). The Ikr3400 cost includes lagoon admission and return fare to Reykjavík (or onward journey to Keflavík airport).

The Golden Circle

Gulp down three of Iceland's most extraordinary natural wonders – Gullfoss, Geysir and Þingvellir – in one day-long circular tour.

Gullfoss (Golden Falls) is a spectacular rainbow-tinged double cascade, which falls 32m before thundering away down a narrow ravine.

Ten kilometres away is **Geysir**, after which all spouting hot springs are named. The **Great Geysir** was plugged in the 1950s, when tourists clogged it with rocks and rubbish, thrown in an attempt to set it off. Since earthquakes in 2000, it has begun erupting again two or three times daily. Nearby, the world's most reliable geyser, **Strokkur** (Butter Churn), spouts every six minutes, when its bulging blue eye bursts into an impressive 15m to 30m plume.

Þingvellir National Park is Iceland's most important historical site: the Vikings established the world's first democratic parliament, the Alþing, here in AD 930. It also has a superb natural setting, on the edge of an immense rift caused by the separating North American and Eurasian tectonic plates. Þingvellir was (finally!) made a Unesco World Heritage–listed site in 2004.

Interesting features, concentrated in a small area of the park, include: **Lögberg** (marked by a flagpole), the podium for the Alþing; the remains of **búðir** (booths) where attending Vikings camped; a **church** and **farm**, now the President's summer house; **Drekkingarhylur**, where adulterous women were drowned; **Þingvallavatn**, Iceland's largest lake; and several fissures, including **Peningagjá** (wishing spring), **Flosagjá** (named after a slave who jumped his way to freedom) and **Nikulásargjá** (after a drunken sheriff discovered dead in the water).

INFORMATION

Just by the turnoff to Þingvellir, the Park Service Centre contains a café and **seasonal tourist desk** (☎ 482 2660; www.thingvellir.is; ⊗ 8.30am-8pm Jun-Aug, 9am-5pm daily May & Sep, to 5pm Sat & Sun Oct-Apr).

Above the park, on top of the rift, is an interesting **multimedia centre** (admission free; ⊗ 9am-7pm Jun-Aug, to 5pm Apr, May, Sep & Oct, to 5pm Sat & Sun Nov-Mar) exploring the area's nature and history.

SLEEPING & EATING

There is a discreet **café** (⊗ approximately 9am-5pm winter, 9am-8pm summer) at each of the three sites.

Geysir camping ground (per person Ikr600) Stay at this camping ground, and you'll get to marvel at the spouting springs before the coach parties arrive. Pay at Hótel Geysir, where you're also entitled to use the hot tub and pool for free.

Þingvellir camping grounds (☎ 482 2660; camp sites per adult Ikr500) The Park Service Centre oversees five camping grounds at Þingvellir. The best are those around Leirar (near the centre).

Hótel Geysir (☎ 480 6800; www.geysircenter.is; summer sb/s/d from Ikr3000/8400/10,200, winter from Ikr2900/8000/9800; P ☮) Accommodation is in spick, span and tasteful alpine-style cabins. There are plans to build new rooms overlooking the geysir field for 2007 or 2008. The hotel can also arrange horse rides, including day trips to Gullfoss (Ikr10,800).

Hótel Valhöll (☎ 480 7100; www.hotelvalholl.is; summer s/d Ikr15,000/21,000, winter Ikr10,000/17,000; P) Valhöll is a large farmhouse in Þingvellir National Park, tucked down at the base of the rift. Some of the rooms are on the small side; positives include peaceful surroundings, a very good restaurant, and the president for your neighbour!

GETTING THERE & AWAY

Golden Circle day tours from Reykjavík cost between Ikr6500 and Ikr7900 (without lunch). Tour operators include Reykjavík Excursions and Iceland Excursions (see p283); you're usually picked up from your accommodation.

From June to August, scheduled buses run from the BSÍ bus station to Gullfoss and Geysir (return Ikr4400, 8.30am and 12.30pm), stopping for at least half an hour at each site.

Hafnarfjörður

pop 22,767

The 'Town in the Lava' rests on a 7000-year-old flow and hides a parallel elfin universe, according to locals. It's worth a quick summer jaunt if you've time to spare.

ICELAND

The dynamic **tourist office** (☎ 585 5500; www
.hafnarfjordur.is; Strandgata 6; ☢ 8am-5pm Mon-Fri year-
round, 10am-3pm Sat & Sun Jun-Aug) is inside the
town hall.

SIGHTS & ACTIVITIES

Hafnarfjörður Museum (☎ 585 5780; admission
Ikr300) is spread across three sites. **Pakkhúsið**
(Vesturgata 8; ☢ 1-5pm daily Jun-Aug, 11am-5pm Sat
& Sun Sep-May) is the main building, with in-
teresting displays on the town's history.
Sívertsen's Hús (Vesturgata 6; ☢ 11am-5pm Jun-Aug)
is an upper-class 19th-century house. At
the other end of the social scale is **Siggubær**
(Sigga's House; Kirkjuvegur 10; ☢ 11am-5pm Sat & Sun
Jun-Aug), a restored fisherman's hut. The
Reykjavík Tourist Card covers admission
to all three.

The tourist office publishes a smashing
sculpture trail map; the highlight is **Hellisgerði**
(Reykjavíkurvegur), a peaceful park filled with
lava grottoes.

In mid-June, the peace is shattered as
Viking hordes invade town for the **Viking
Festival**, with staged fights and traditional
craft demonstrations.

GETTING THERE & AWAY

Hafnarfjörður is a short, easy bus trip from
Reykjavík: take bus No S1 (Ikr220, 30 minutes, every 20 to 30 minutes) from Hlemmur or Lækjartorg bus stations. The **Flybus**
(☎ 562 1011) to/from Keflavík airport also
stops for reserved passengers.

Krýsuvík

For a taste of Iceland's weird countryside,
Krýsuvík, an abandoned village and volatile
geothermal area, makes a fascinating day
trip. The area lies about 20km south of Hafnarfjörður; you'll need your own transport.
At **Seltún**, boardwalks meander round eggy-
smelling, rainbow-coloured steaming vents,
mud pots and solfataras, where the ground
temperature reaches about 200°C.

Just down the road is **Kleifarvatn**, a creepy
1km-deep lake surrounded by volcanic cin-
ders. It's said to be inhabited by a wormlike
monster the size of a whale.

The nearby coast is a bleak stretch of sea-
bird cliffs and black beaches, which stood
in for Iwo Jima in Clint Eastwood's WWII
epic *Flags of Our Fathers* (2006). Dozens of
hiking tracks crisscross through this barren
territory.

THE WEST

UPPER BORGARFJÖRÐUR

A must for saga fans, the lakes and lava
flows of this region feature in *Egils Saga*,
and its author, Snorri Sturluson, lived
here. Upper Borgarfjörður is 90km north
of Reykjavík.

Reykholt & Around

You'd never guess it, but tiny **Reykholt** (www
.reykholt.is), 22km east off the Ring Rd and with
a population of 33, was once a political and
religious power centre. During the bloodthirsty Sturlunga Period (1230–62), it was the
home of Snorri Sturluson, Iceland's greatest
saga writer, historian and social-climber.
Close to the cellar where he was eventually
murdered, you can see his circular medieval
hot tub **Snorri's Pool** (Snorralaug). The museum **Heimskringla** (☎ 433 8000; www.snorrastofa
.is; Reykholt; admission Ikr500; ☢ 10am-6pm daily May-
Sep, to 6pm Mon-Fri Oct-Apr) explores Snorri's fascinating life, and will be augmented in 2007
by an exhibition of recent archaeological
finds.

Deildartunguhver, 4km west of Reykholt, is
Europe's most powerful, prolific and pongy
hot spring, spouting out at 180L per second. About 18km northeast of Reykholt is
Hraunfossar, a 1km-long stretch of 'magic
waterfalls' mysteriously emerging from beneath a lava flow. Just upstream is **Barnafoss**,
where the river Hvítá thunders through a
narrow gorge. According to legend, two
children drowned here when a natural
bridge collapsed.

There's a **camping ground** (☎ 435 1182; Klep-
pjárnsreykir; per person Ikr500) next to a geothermal
swimming pool 6km west of Reykholt. **Hótel
Reykholt** (☎ 435 1260; www.fosshotel.is; Reykholt; sb/
s/d Ikr3200/13,700/17,900 Jun-Aug, Ikr3200/9300/10,700
Sep-May; ℗ ▣) is part of the Foss Hotel
chain. It's a modern place with boxy but
pleasant rooms, sunny staff, a funny Norse-
gods theme, and extras including a restaurant and brand-new 'wellness facility'
(sauna, massages etc). Cheaper rooms with
shared bathrooms are available.

Buses run from Reykjavík to Reykholt
(via Deildartunguhver) on Friday and Sunday at 5pm (Ikr2200, two hours). You'll
need private transport for Hraunfossar and
Barnafoss.

SNÆFELLSNES

[Cue Twilight Zone music...] The peninsula is a magnet for UFOs, and for New Age believers who swear that the glacier Snæfellsjökull (1446m) emits a healing aura. It's certainly atmospheric – shadowy mountains, twisting lava flows, tiny fishing villages and scattered farmhouses all sit under the shadow of the glacier. Jules Verne was impressed enough to use Snæfell as the gateway to the underworld in *A Journey to the Centre of the Earth*. More recently, the whole of the peninsula's tip, was designated a national park.

Stykkishólmur

pop 1167

Quaint coastal Stykkishólmur is the largest village in Snæfellsnes, overlooked by mighty mountains and a striking church. It makes a serene base for boat trips, horse riding and kayaking, or as a picturesque shortcut to the Westfjords – car ferries run via Flatey, an island with 19th-century buildings.

The **tourist office** (☎ 438 1750; Smiðjustígur 3; ☻ 9am-8pm Jun-Aug) is inside the Sæferðir shop/office (see Tours below) by the harbour; out of season, Sæferðir staff can help with inquiries.

SIGHTS & ACTIVITIES

There are admirable views of Breiðafjörður (see boxed text, right) from **Súgandisey**, a basalt islet that shelters the picturesque harbour.

Tarry-smelling **Norwegian House** (☎ 438 1640; norkshus@simnet.is; Hafnargata 5; adult/6-16yr Ikr400/200; ☻ 11am-5pm Jun-Aug) contains a folk museum, café and art gallery.

Visit Breiðafjörður's straits and skerries on guided paddles with **Seakayak Iceland** (☎ 690 3877; http://seakayakiceland.com; bookings via internet); they start from Ikr5500 for a two- to four-hour trip.

You can also hire **bikes** from Sæferðir (per day Ikr1500; below) to explore the peninsula at a leisurely pace.

TOURS

Horse treks, snowmobiling, boat tours, even visits to a nearby farm to see shark-meat being cured; **Sæferðir** (Seatours; ☎ 438 1450; www.seatours.is; Smiðjustígur 3; ☻ 9am-8pm Jun-Aug, 8am-4pm Mon-Fri Sep-May) has all the

local attractions sewn up. Most activities are June to August only, but some are year-round. They also run three-hour **whale-watching trips** (adult/12-15yr Ikr4900/2450; Jun-Aug) from Ólafsvík, 80km along the coast.

SLEEPING & EATING

Camping ground (☎ 438 1750; per person Ikr600; ☻ year-round) A huge but rather exposed spot on the way into town. Basic facilities include a laundry.

Sjónarhóll HI Hostel (☎ 438 1417, 861 2517; www.hostel.is; Höfðagata 1; sb/d Ikr1650/5000; ☻ May-Sep; P) The dorm rooms in this charming hostel have fantastic views of the harbour. You can also catch fish on its Breiðafjörður boat tours, then barbecue them on the patio.

Hótel Stykkishólmur (☎ 430 2100; www.hotel stykkisholmur.is; Borgarbraut 6; s/d Ikr11,900/13,900, Ikr8900/10,900 Apr, May & Sep-Nov Jun-Aug; P ☐) This 33-room hotel is fairly ugly from the outside, but the good-quality rooms all have great views, and there's a smart restaurant and bar.

Narfeyrarstofa (☎ 438 1119; Aðalgata 3; mains Ikr2000-3700) This old house is a welcoming daytime café and evening bar/restaurant. The á la carte menu focuses on locally caught fish and seabirds (such as black guillemot), cooked on the rare side. There's not much for veggies, but kids can eat burgers and chips from the bar menu.

Opposite the camping ground there is a sit-down **bakery** (Nesvegur 1; ☻ 8.30am-6pm Mon-Fri, 8am-4pm Sat).

TROLL TROUBLE

The breathtaking sight of Breiðafjörður's 2700(-ish) islands inspired a legend. Three misanthropic trolls decided to separate the Westfjords from the rest of Iceland. All night, they hacked away huge lumps of earth and hurled the pieces into the nearby fjord. The task was so engrossing that they didn't notice the growing light. As the sun touched them, the two male trolls turned instantly to stone. The trollette almost made it home, when she suddenly remembered that she'd left her cow grazing on Grímsey. Stopping to look at it, both she and Daisy came to a rocky end.

ICELAND

GETTING THERE & AWAY
Daily buses ply between Reykjavík and Stykkishólmur (Ikr3300, 2½ hours), with a change to a connecting bus in Vatnaleið. You also have to change there when travelling between Stykkishólmur and Ólafsvík.

See right for details of the Stykkishólmur–Brjánslækur ferry.

Snæfellsjökull National Park & Around
The tip of Snæfellsnes peninsula, including the glacier, is a national park. The **visitor centre** (☎ 436 6860; ☒ 10am-6pm Jun-Aug) is at Hellnar, an absolutely gorgeous reserve filled with sea birds, 6km outside the main park boundary on the south coast.

The most interesting way up Snæfell is from the western end of the peninsula, along the Móðulækur stream (4WD vehicles can go 4km up the track). This takes you via the red scoria craters of Rauðhólar, the waterfall Klukkufoss and scenic Eysteinsdalur Valley. It takes a couple of days and you may need crampons and ice axes to reach the summit.

ÓLAFSVÍK
As a base, Stykkishólmur has the best facilities, but Ólafsvík (population 1016) is much closer to the park. It has a sheltered **camping ground** (☎ 436 1543; camp sites per adult/tent Ikr300/300; ☒ Jun-Aug) 1km east of the village. Central **Hótel Ólafsvík** (☎ 436 1650; www .hotelolafsvik.is; Ólafsbraut 20; s/d from Ikr11,950/14,800; ☒) has been refurbished and has comfortable business-class rooms. If you don't mind sharing a bathroom, prices fall by almost 50%. The hotel has a restaurant; otherwise there's the **bakery** (Ólafsbraut) and burger-bar **Prinsinn** (Ólafsbraut; from Ikr300; ☒ 10am-11.30pm Mon-Fri, 11.30am-11.30pm Sat & Sun) across the street.

HELLNAR
The spirit of the glacier, Bardur, once lived at tiny Hellnar: he couldn't have chosen a more idyllic spot. The park visitor centre and a small café overlook a dingley bay, echoing with the shrieks of sea birds, and up the hill stands Iceland's only eco-hotel, **Hótel Hellnar** (☎ 435 6820; www.hellnar.is; s/d Ikr10,900/13,900 Jun-Aug, Ikr9800/12,500 May & Sep; ☒ May-Sep; ℗ ☒). Its twin-bedded rooms are clean, bright and monastically simple, the restaurant uses local organic produce, and the guest lounge has marvellous sea views. It's quite common to see whales from the window.

THE WESTFJORDS

The remote Westfjords once had a fearsome reputation for witchcraft, and its abandoned villages, crying sea birds and wild Arctic foxes still cast a haunting spell. You could lose yourself for days in the bleak mountains, or hide away in end-of-the-earth-town Ísafjörður. There is some folklore that people in the Westfjords have been known to swear by rum-soaked seal blubber, horsemeat or a red-haired boy as the best bait for shark fishing!

Getting There & Away

AIR
There are twice-daily flights between Reykjavík and Ísafjörður (Ikr10,500) with **Flugfélag Íslands** (www.airiceland.is; ☎ 570 3030).

BOAT
The **Baldur** (☎ 438 1450; www.seatours.is; Smiðjustígur 3, Stykkishólmur) ferry operates between Stykkishólmur and Brjánslækur (one way per car/passenger Ikr2190/2190, 2½ hours). From June to August, it leaves Stykkishólmur at 9am and 4pm, and Brjánslækur at 12.30pm and 7.30pm. From September to May, it departs Stykkishólmur at 9am Saturday and 1.30pm Sunday to Friday, and Brjánslækur at 12.30pm Saturday, 5pm Sunday to Friday. Ferries link quite badly with buses.

BUS
Scheduled buses in the Westfjords are infrequent, headache-inducing and only possible from June to August.

From Reykjavík to Ísafjörður, you will need to change in Brú and Hólmavík. Buses leave Reykjavík for Brú at 8.30am and 5.30pm, but they only connect with the Brú–Hólmavík service on Tuesday, Friday and Sunday; Reykjavík–Holmavík costs Ikr4900. The bus company **Stjörnubilar** (☎ 456 3518, 893 6356; www.stjornubilar.is) runs the Holmavík–Ísafjorður leg (Ikr4050), at 3pm Tuesday, Friday and Sunday.

Buses also run to the Westfjords via the ferry from Stykkishólmur. There are daily buses from Reykjavík to Stykkishólmur (left), but these don't link well with the ferry; you'll have a few hours to look around, or may even have an overnight stop. On the other side of the water, there are connecting buses from Brjánslækur to Ísafjörður (Ikr2350), running via Látrabjarg and allowing 1¼ hours at the cliffs. In reverse, buses leave Ísafjörður at 9am Monday, Wednesday and Saturday.

If you want to travel between Ísafjörður and Akureyri, you'll also need to change in Holmavík and Brú.

ÍSAFJÖRÐUR
pop 2779

You feel as though you've reached the ends of the earth when you get to Ísafjörður, the Westfjord's largest settlement. Surrounded by vertiginous mountains and deep fjord waters, the town is remote and peaceful…apart from the croaking of conspiracies of ravens.

The Westfjords' largest settlement contains a **tourist office** (☎ 456 5121; www.vestfirdir.is; Aðalstræti 7; ⊙ 8am-6pm daily Jun-Aug, 11am-4pm Mon-Fri Sep-May), several banks, and a **post office** (Hafnarstræti 9). Internet access is available at the immaculate **library** (☎ 456 3296; www.isafjordur.is/bokasafn; Eyrartúni; per hr Ikr200; ⊙ 1-7pm Mon-Fri, to 4pm Sat).

Sights & Activities

The knowledgeable staff at the **Westfjords Maritime Museum** (☎ 456 3293; Neðstíkaupstaður; admission Ikr500; ⊙ 10am-5pm daily Jul & Aug, 10am-5pm Mon-Fri, 1-5pm Sat & Sun Jun), based in three old wooden warehouses, brings the excellent nautical and whaling exhibits to life.

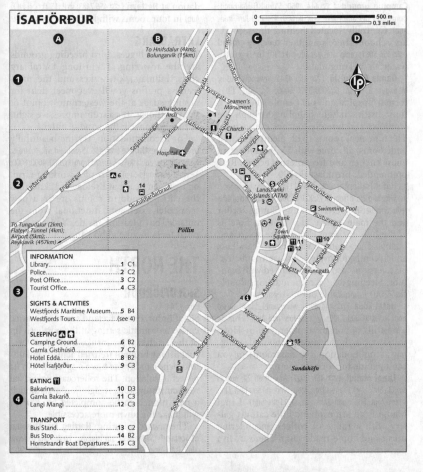

ÍSAFJÖRÐUR

0   500 m
0   0.3 miles

To Hnífsdalur (4km);
Bolungarvík (15km)

Whalebone Arch

Seamen's Monument

Church

Hospital

Park

To Tungudalur (2km);
Flateyri Tunnel (4km);
Airport (5km);
Reykjavik (457km)

Pöllin

Landsbanki Íslands (ATM)

Swimming Pool

Bank
Town Square

Sundahöfn

INFORMATION
Library...1 C1
Police..2 C2
Post Office....................................3 C2
Tourist Office................................4 C3

SIGHTS & ACTIVITIES
Westfjords Maritime Museum.....5 B4
Westfjords Tours....................(see 4)

SLEEPING
Camping Ground...........................6 B2
Gamla Gistihúsið...........................7 C2
Hotel Edda....................................8 B2
Hótel Ísafjörður............................9 C3

EATING
Bakarinn.....................................10 D3
Gamla Bakaríð.............................11 C3
Langi Mangi................................12 C3

TRANSPORT
Bus Stand....................................13 C2
Bus Stop......................................14 B2
Hornstrandir Boat Departures.....15 C3

ICELAND

There are some interesting **hikes** round Tungudalur, 2km west of Ísafjörður; ask at the tourist office, or see the Trekking section on www.vestfirdir.is for detailed walking information. Westfjords Tours (see below) can arrange **kayaking** in the bay. In winter, there's downhill skiing at Tungudalur.

Tours
Westfjords Tours (Vesturferðir; ☎ 456 5111; www .vesturferdir.is; Aðalstræti 7) specialises in Hornstrandir visits, including a four-hour trip to the abandoned village Hesteyri (Ikr4400, Wednesday, Friday and Sunday at 2pm, July to mid-August).

Sleeping & Eating
Camping ground (☎ 444 4960; Skutulsfjarðarbraut; camp sites per adult plus tent Ikr600; ⏲ mid-Jun–mid-Aug) Centrally located behind the secondary school. There's another **camping ground** (☎ 456 5081; camp sites per adult Ikr750) by a pretty waterfall in Tungudalur.

Gamla Gistihúsið (☎ 456 4146; www.gistihus.is; Mánagata 5; sb/s/d Ikr2000/3900/6000; ⌧ 🖳) This former hospital and old people's home is a tonic, with sunlight dappling through the windows and homely touches everywhere. The nine neat rooms (with plentiful shared bathrooms) all come with TV, plus there's a guest kitchen and free internet access. Recommended. Breakfast Ikr800.

Hótel Ísafjörður (☎ 456 4111; www.hotelisafjordur .is; Silfurtorg 2; s/d from Ikr13,900/16,900 Jun-Aug, up to 40% reduction Dec-Feb) Overlooking Skutulsfjörður and the main square, this modern hotel is at the hub of things. Rooms are smart and businesslike, with TVs, radios, minibars and recently renovated shower rooms; deluxe versions also come equipped with bathtubs. Sleeping-bag accommodation (double Ikr7200) is available out-of-season.

Hotel Edda (☎ 444 4960; www.hoteledda.is; sb/s/d from Ikr1700/5800/7200; ⏲ mid-Jun–mid-Aug) This is a no-frills option in summer, run by Hotel Ísafjörður in the secondary school. Sleeping-bag accommodation is in classrooms, or you can upgrade to a private room.

Langi Mangi (☎ 456 3022; Aðalstræti 22; snacks Ikr400-800; ⏲ 11am-11pm Mon-Wed, 11am-1am Thu, 11am-2am Fri, noon-2am Sat, 1-11pm Sun) Langi Mangi is an atmospheric little caff/art gallery with a range of coffees, meandering music and home-made soup. There are live performances at weekends.

Two bakeries, **Bakarinn** (☎ 456 4770; Silfurgata 11; ⏲ 9am-4pm Sun-Fri) and **Gamla Bakaríð** (☎ 456 3226; Aðalstræti; ⏲ 7am-6pm Mon-Fri, 7am-4pm Sat) are good for bread, buns and chocolate frogs.

HORNSTRANDIR
The wildest corner of the Westfjords has a sad history: its elderly inhabitants, left behind with no electricity, roads or telephones, made a collective decision to abandon the peninsula in the 1950s. It's now a spectacular nature reserve, which solitary hikers share only with sea birds and Arctic foxes.

The peninsula is accessible by boat from Ísafjörður, with one-way fares around Ikr4500; contact Ísafjörður tourist office for details. There's basic sleeping-bag accommodation at **Hesteyri** (☎ 456 7183; sb Ikr1500; ⏲ Jul & Aug) in four rooms with kitchen access.

LÁTRABJARG
The world's biggest bird breeding grounds are the towering, 12km-long Látrabjarg cliffs. Fulmars, kittiwakes and the most fearless puffins you'll ever meet fight for nesting space at the westernmost point of the Westfjords. It's a truly impressive sight, but wrap up well; the wind is bitter.

For accommodation, try the beautifully located **guesthouse** (☎ 456 1575; breidavik@patro.is; camp sites per adult Ikr900, sb/s/d from Ikr2000/4000/6000; ⏲ mid-May–mid-Sep), part of a working farm, on a golden beach at Breiðavík, 12km from the cliffs. Nondorm rooms are in a new minihotel extension; functional from the outside, but pleasant inside. You can also pitch tents in a neighbouring field.

THE NORTH

SIGLUFJÖRÐUR
pop 1344
Siglufjörður, one of Iceland's loveliest towns, enjoys a dramatic setting at the northern tip of the Tröllaskagi peninsula. In the past, herring fishing brought frenzied activity and untold riches; today the town's appeal lies in its peaceful isolation. The rollercoasting coastal road currently stops at Siglufjörður, although a new tunnel (to be completed by 2008/9) will make the town more accessible.

The award-winning **Herring Era Museum of Iceland** (Síldarminjasafn Íslands; ☎ 467 1604; www .siglo.is/herring; Snorragata 15; adult/12-16yr Ikr800/400;

10am-6pm Jun-Aug, 1-5pm Sep-May), lovingly created over 16 years, does a stunning job of recreating Siglufjörður's boom days. You can trace the herrings' journey through the museum's three harbourside buildings: from the full-size night-time harbour; to the poignant salting station Roaldsbrakki, looking as though the herring workers have just left; to the huge machinery of the fishmeal and oil processing plant. The museum also functions as the **tourist information centre**.

For hiking, skiing and the lively **Herring Adventure** festival on August bank holiday, check out the town's website www.siglo.is.

The little **camping ground** (Ikr500; Jun-Aug) is situated right by the town square, and has a toilet block and laundry. In a gilt, cherub-decorated 1930s hotel, whose stately proportions hint at wealthier times, you'll find **Gistihúsið Hvanneyri**'s (☎ 467 1378; alla@simnet .is; Aðalgata 10; sb/s Ikr1800/Ikr4000, d Ikr6000-8000) 19 rooms with mountain views. There are a couple of TV lounges, a mighty dining room, and guest kitchen.

BioCafé (☎ 467 1111; Aðalgata 30; mains Ikr1000-1700, 9in pizza from Ikr800; 11.30am-9pm) serves good-value burgers, pizzas, and fish and lamb dishes, and the upstairs bar opens late on Friday and Saturday nights.

The other dining choice in town is **Pizza 67** (☎ 467 2323; Aðalgata; 9in pizza from Ikr900).

From June to September, you can get from Reykjavík to Siglufjörður by bus, but you'll have to change at Varmahlíð and Sauðarkrókur. For good through connections, catch the 9.30am service (Ikr7100) on Monday or Wednesday.

AKUREYRI
pop 16,579

Fertile, sheltered Akureyri (www.akureyri .is), situated alongside Iceland's greatest fjord, has the warmest weather in a cold country. The best restaurants, cafés and cinemas outside the capital nestle beneath a range of snowcapped peaks. It's a place to linger, admiring the flowery gardens, maple trees, shining sculptures and all the bobbing fishing boats and cruise ships.

Information

The **tourist office** (☎ 462 7733; www.nordurland.is; Hafnarstræti 82; 7.30am-7pm mid-Jun–Aug, to 5pm Mon-Fri & 8am-5pm Sat & Sun May–mid-Jun, 10am-4pm Mon-Fri Sep-Apr) can organise tours.

There's a central **post office** (☎ 460 2600; Skipagata 10; 8.30am-4.30pm Mon-Fri) and the fantastic **municipal library** (☎ 460 1250; Brekkugata 17; 10am-6pm Mon & Fri, to 4pm Tue-Thu) has an English book section larger than many UK libraries, plus internet access (per hour Ikr200).

The **Akureyri Hospital** (☎ 463 0100; Spítalavegur) is just south of the botanical gardens, and **Nonni Travel** (☎ 461 1841; www.nonnitravel.is; Brekkugata 5) is the main tour agency.

Sights & Activities

Akureyrarkirkja (Eyrarlandsvegur) was designed by Gudjón Samúelsson, the architect of Reykjavík's Hallgrímskirkja. Although the basalt theme connects them, Akureyrarkirkja looks more like a stylised 1920s US skyscraper than its big-town brother. The church admits visitors in summer; check the board outside the church for opening times.

Akureyri Museum (Minjasafnið Akureyri; ☎ 462 4162; www.akmus.is; Aðalstræti 58; adult/child Ikr400/free; 10am-5pm Jun–mid-Sep, 2-4pm Sat late-Sep–Jul) houses local historical items, including an interesting Settlement Era section. The building is set back from the tranquil garden that set the fashion for Iceland's 19th-century tree-planting.

Children's writer Reverend Jón Sveinsson (1857–1944) spent his childhood in Akureyri and his old-fashioned tales of derring-do have a rich Icelandic flavour. Make sure you visit the higgledy-piggledy wooden **Nonnahús** (☎ 462 3555; www.nonni.is; Aðalstræti 54; adult/under 16yr Ikr350/free; 10am-5pm Jun-Sep), the author's childhood home, and pick up an English translation of his book At Skipalón. You can purchase a **joint ticket** (Ikr550) for Nonnahús and Akureyri Museum.

The most northerly botanical garden in the world is **Lystigarður Akureyrar** (Akureyri Botanical Gardens; ☎ 462 7487; Eyrarlandsvegur; 8am-10pm Mon-Fri, 9am-10pm Sat & Sun Jun-Oct), a delightful spot on sunny days. Opened in 1912, it includes every native Icelandic species, and other tough plants from high altitudes and latitudes.

Akureyri has one of the country's best **swimming pools** (☎ 461 4455; Þingvallastræti 21; adult/6-15yr Ikr310/150, sauna Ikr500; 7am-9pm Mon-Fri, 8am-6.30pm Sat & Sun) with hot pots, saunas and flumes suitable for little kids and big.

ICELAND

Sleeping

BUDGET

Central camping ground (☎ 462 3379; hamrar@
hamrar.is; Þórunnarstræti; camp sites per adult Ikr800;
🕑 mid-Jun–Aug) They are threatening to close
down this central camping ground, but it's
here for the moment, and has improved
security and a fresh splash of paint on the
toilet blocks. It's conveniently located close
to the swimming pool, supermarket and
town.

Hamrar camp site (☎ 461 2264; hamrar@hamrar
.is; camp sites per adult Ikr700; 🕑 Jun–Aug) This huge
camp site, 1.5km south in a leafy setting by
the scout camp at Kjarnaskógur, has newer
facilities and mountain views. Both places
have kitchen and laundry.

Stórholt HI Hostel (☎ 462 3657; www.hostel
.is; Stórholt 1; summer sb/s/d Ikr1800/3900/6600, winter
Ikr1750/2950/5800; 🅿 🖳) This spotless hostel,
15 minutes' walk from the town centre, has
three comfy sitting rooms and three large
kitchens, with a summery decking area
outside. There are two attractive summerhouses (one/seven days Ikr14,280/49,500),
each holding seven people. Bookings pour
in after Easter; don't get left in the cold.

MIDRANGE

Gistiheimilið Salka (☎ 461 2340; salka@nett.is; Skipagata 1; sb d/tr/q Ikr5000/6600/8000, s/d/tr/q Ikr5000/
6600/8100/10,000) Distinctive, large 2nd-
floor rooms filled with books, ornaments,
couches and TVs make Gistiheimilið Salka

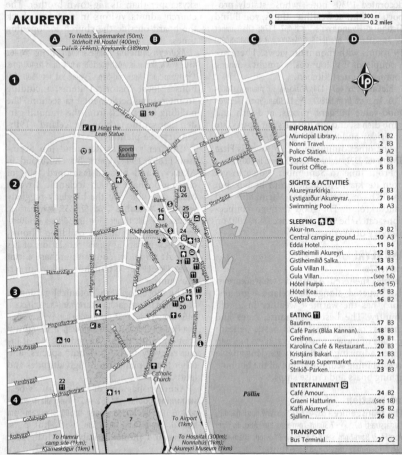

AKUREYRI

0 — 300 m
0 — 0.2 miles

To Netto Supermarket (50m);
Stórholt HI Hostel (400m);
Dalvík (44km); Reykjavík (389km)

Grenivellir

Helgi the
Lean Statue

Sports
Stadium

Bank

Bank

Rádhústorg

Catholic
Church

Pöllin

To Hamrar
camp site (1km);
Kjarnaskógur (1km)

To Airport
(1km)

To Hospital (300m);
Nonnahús (1km);
Akureyri Museum (1km)

feel just like home; there is also a fully equipped kitchen. Recommended.

Sólgarðar (☎ 461 1133; solgardar@simnet.is; Brekkugata 6; sb/s/d Ikr2900/4300/6000) The owner of this place works shifts, so don't be surprised if she's bleary eyed! Her three rooms, one with balcony, overlook a quiet residential street and they're gleaming. Breakfast is available (Ikr800), and there are discounts for stays over three days.

Gistiheimili Akureyri (☎ 462 5588; www.gisti heimilid.net; Hafnarstræti 104; s/d Ikr5300/7300 May-Sep, Ikr4300/5300 Oct-Apr) This largeish place lacks the intimacy of a guesthouse; it's more of a budget hotel with kitchen facilities. The 19 rooms are small but clean, all with satellite TV and washbasins; some have private bathrooms. The sunny, balconied breakfast area (summer only) overlooking bustling Hafnarstræti is the star feature. Breakfast is Ikr850.

Gula Villan (☎ 461 2810; www.gulavillan.is; Brekkugata 8; sb/s/d Ikr3500/5000/6600) At this family-friendly place, you'll find spotless, snow-white rooms with leafy patterns stencilled on the walls. The owners have another buttercup-yellow building (Þingvallastræti 14; open in summer only) opposite the swimming pool. Both houses have kitchens, or you can order breakfast (Ikr950).

Edda Hotel (☎ 444 4000; www.hoteledda.is; Eyrarlandsvegur 28; s/d with bathroom Ikr10,300/12,900, ☯ mid-Jun–late-Aug) Around 200 summer rooms are up for grabs in the grammar school: two-thirds have TVs and private bathrooms. There's a café and large restaurant on site.

TOP END

Hótel Kea (☎ 460 2000; www.keahotels.is; Hafnarstræti 83-5; s/d/tr Ikr14,700/18,900/24,500 Jun-Aug, Ikr11,900/14,900/19,500 Sep-May) Akureyri's top hotel has been going since 1944. Rooms here are business-class with slightly old-fashioned trimmings; the five nicest have balconies overlooking the fjord. Kea is the only hotel in town with facilities for wheelchair users. Hotel Harpa (s/d/tr Ikr12,700/16,100/20,900 June to August, Ikr10,100/12,700/16,600 September to May) shares Kea's restaurant and reception. In some ways its small rooms are superior; they're freshly renovated, with parquet flooring and modern furniture.

Eating

Café Paris (Bláa Kannan; ☎ 461 4600; Hafnarstræti 96; ☯ 9am-10.30pm Mon-Sat, 10am-10.30pm Sun; ☒) This tearoom, with its old wooden interior and swirly-coloured tables, is a peachy place to idle away a morning. In summer, outdoor tables mushroom on the main street, and people flock in for lunch specials (soup, salad and main for Ikr950), often veggie.

Karolína Café (☎ 461 2755; Kaupvangsstræti 23; ☯ 11.30am-1am Mon-Thu, to 3am Fri & Sat, 2pm-1am Sun) Karolína lures a young, crazy-haired crowd with magazines, squashy sofas, alcoholic coffee (Ikr790 to Ikr990) and monthly art exhibitions. Above, the upmarket restaurant (mains Ikr2500 to Ikr4300; open from 6pm) is run by Iceland's Chef of the Year 2003. As you might expect in an important fishing town, the emphasis is on perfectly-presented seafood dishes.

Greifinn (☎ 460 1600; www.greifinn.is; Glerárgata 20; mains Ikr1700-3000; ☯ 11.30am-11.30pm) This is a bustling, lively spot popular with families, birthday parties and work outings. The varied menu includes sizzling Tex-Mex, much-praised pizza and big meaty dishes. A bat-phone button on the table summons the waiter in seconds.

Bautinn (☎ 462 1818; Hafnarstræti 92; soup & salad Ikr1290, mains Ikr1300-3400) Open all day, this restaurant is a favourite for its friendly staff, decent prices and loaded salad bar. There's a large glazed conservatory, and a more shadowy interior if you don't enjoy that goldfish-bowl feeling. Be warned, dishes include everything from pizzas and salad to puffin and whale.

Strikið-Parken (☎ 462 7100; Skipagata 14; mains Ikr2000-3500; ☯ from 11.30am Mon-Sat, from 6pm Sun) Huge windows with panoramic fjord views lend a little magic to this new 5th-floor grill and restaurant. It's a tasteful, minimalist affair, with a small menu of Icelandic seafood and world cuisine: chicken tortilla, salmon with rocket and basil, lobster tails.

Kristjáns Bakarí (Hafnarstræti 100; ☯ 9am-6pm Mon-Fri, 10am-2pm Sat) This bakery sells fresh bread, salad and cakes.

Drinking & Entertainment

There are several pubs in Akureyri, including **Græni Hatturinn** (☎ 461 4646; Hafnarstræti 96). Karolina Café (above) is a popular weekend hangout with a more arty crowd.

ICELAND

Inhabitants shake their booties at **Kaffi Akureyri** (☎ 461 3999; Strandgata 7; ☿ 3pm-1am Sun-Thu, to 4am Fri & Sat), a dressy venue good for live music and dancing; **Café Amour** (☎ 461 3030; Raðhústorg 9; ☿ 11am-1am Sun-Thu, to 4am Fri & Sat), a smoky café/cocktail lounge/wine bar with an upstairs dancefloor and the most garish ceiling you'll ever see; and the very popular **Sjallinn** (☎ 461 2757; Geislagata 14; ☿ to 3am Fri & Sat), a large nightclub with chart tunes, DJs and bands.

Getting There & Away

AIR

In summer, **Flugfélag Íslands** (www.airiceland.is; ☎ 460 7000) has up to seven flights daily between Akureyri and Reykjavík (Ikr10,600). Internationally, **Iceland Express** (☎ 0870 850 0737; www.icelandexpress.com) flies twice a week from London Stansted (around UK£230, three hours).

See right for flights to Grímsey.

BOAT

See right for boats to Grímsey.

BUS

In 2006 the bus company **Trex** (☎ 899 4660; Kaldbaksgata) moved the bus station to its current inconvenient location in the middle of an industrial estate. Akureyri inhabitants want it back outside the tourist office: check the state of the wrangle before departure.

Buses between Akureyri and Reykjavík depart at least once daily (Ikr6600, six hours) year-round. Buses travelling over the Kjölur route to Reykjavík leave daily from 20 June to 31 August (Ikr8200, 10 hours).

A bus to Mývatn (Ikr2200, 1½ hours) runs daily from June to August (four per week during the rest of year), continuing to Egilsstaðir (Ikr2600, two hours), where you can catch another bus (sometimes a good connection, sometimes a five-hour wait) to Seyðisfjörður. Buses to Húsavík (Ikr2100, one hour) depart once or twice daily.

For buses to Dalvík (for the ferry to Grímsey), see right.

AROUND AKUREYRI

South of town is Iceland's most visited 'forest', **Kjarnaskógur**, popular for family outings. A good day walk from Akureyri follows the **Glerárdalur** valley as far as Lambi mountain hut. From Akureyri you

can hike up and down **Mt Sulur** (1213m) in about eight hours; if possible, get a lift to the signposted turnoff (it's a dull walk out of town), from where the summit is a 5km climb.

About 50km east of town is curvy waterfall **Goðafoss**, where Þorgeir Ljósvetningagoði, when asked to decide whether Iceland should adopt Christianity, symbolically threw his statues of the old Norse gods. Buses from Akureyri to Mývatn pass the waterfall.

Grímsey

The main attraction of **Grímsey**, a windblown island 40km from the north coast, is that it's the only part of Iceland that lies (partly) inside the Arctic Circle. A large signpost marks the theoretical line; once you've crossed into polar realms, buy a commemorative certificate from the harbourside café. Abundant birdlife (puffins, razorbills, guillemots, gulls and psychotic Arctic terns) outnumbers the close-knit community by around one million to 100. The boat ride adds to the mystique of reaching this isolated place.

The **Sæfari** (☎ 458 8970; www.saefari.is) sails from Dalvík (44km north of Akureyri) to Grímsey island at 9am on Monday, Wednesday and Friday (return Ikr4340, 3½ hours), returning from Grímsey at 4pm. In summer, connecting buses leave Akureyri at 7.30am on Monday, Wednesday and Friday, returning from Dalvík at 7.30pm (Ikr1000).

There's one daily scheduled evening flight from Akureyri to Grímsey (one way Ikr7700, two hours). Nonni Travel (p257) can arrange day trips by boat or air (Ikr5100 to Ikr14,200).

HÚSAVÍK

pop 2269

Most people visit the 'whale-watching capital of Europe' to do just that; in season, you're almost guaranteed to see these awe-inspiring ocean giants feeding in the Skjálfandi bay.

The **tourist information desk** (☎ 464 4300; inside Kasko supermarket; ☿ 10am-6.30pm Mon-Thu, to 7pm Fri, to 6pm Sat Jun-Aug) is staffed in summer; brochures are available year-round. There's internet access in the **library** (☎ 464 6165; Stórigarður 17; per hr Ikr250; ☿ 10am-7pm Mon-Thu, to 5pm Fri).

Sights & Activities

The fascinating **Whale Centre** (☎ 464 2520; www.icewhale.is; Hafnarstétt; adult/6-14yr/student Ikr600/250/400; ⏱ 9am-9pm Jun-Aug, 10am-5pm May & Sep) deserves a couple of hours' attention, preferably *before* you go whale-watching. It tells you everything about Icelandic whales and whaling, and the hanging gallery of skeletons allows you truly to appreciate their size.

From mid-May to mid-September, **North Sailing** (Norður Sigling; ☎ 464 2350; www.northsailing.is; Gamli Baukur, Hafnarstétt; adult/under 14yr/15-16yr Ikr3800/free/1900) and **Gentle Giants** (Hvalferðir; ☎ 464 1500; www.gentlegiants.is; Garðarsbraut 6; Ikr3700) offer three-hour whale-watching trips on sturdy oaken boats (see the boxed text, op-

posite). There's a 99% chance of sightings; mostly minkes and harbour porpoises, but humpback and blue whales appear occasionally. Buy tickets from the 'lighthouse' ticket booths opposite the church.

Once you've recovered your land legs, **Safnahúsið** (Museum; ☎ 464 1860; www.husmus.is; Stórigarður 17; adult/child Ikr400/100; ⏱ 10am-6pm Jun-Aug, 9am-noon & 1-5pm Mon-Fri, 4-6pm Sun Sep-May), the local museum, has impressive maritime and natural history collections, and admission includes a cup of coffee.

The unique **Icelandic Phallological Museum** (☎ 561 6663; www.phallus.is; Héðinsbraut 3a; Ikr500; ⏱ noon-6pm Jun–mid-Sep) contains 183 penises – pickled, dried and stuffed – from local mammals ranging in size from a hamster to a blue whale. The only willy missing is that of *Homo sapiens*, although four donors have been lined up.

Sleeping

Camping ground (☎ 845 0705; per person Ikr800, 2nd & 3rd nights free) This option, located at the northern edge of town, has heated toilets, washing machines and cooking facilities.

Gistiheimilið Árból (☎ 464 2220; www.simnet.is/arbol; Ásgarðsvegur 2; s/d/tr Ikr6200/9600/13,400 Jun–mid-Sep, Ikr5000/7400/9800 mid-Sep–May) This ex-governor's mansion, on the edge of the park, is the best place to stay in town. It's spacious and welcoming, upper rooms have lovely views of either the harbour or the mountains, and there's interesting ephemera on the walls, including bugles, guns and old photos of Húsavík.

Kaldbaks-Kot (☎ 464 1504; www.cottages.is; off Rd 85; 2-/4-person house Ikr9900/12,900, discounts in low season) For extraordinarily cosy, well-priced accommodation, try these self-contained wooden cottages, 2km south of Húsavík. They contain everything you need (fully equipped kitchen, living room, comfy beds, veranda, TV), have mountain-and-sea views, and there are three hot tubs for starlit bathing.

Guesthouse Baldursbrekka (☎ 464 1005; mariam@simnet.is; Baldursbrekka 20; sb/s/d Ikr2000/2500/5000) The cheapest option, this family home in a quiet cul-de-sac has five dinky rooms, cooking facilities and a garage to hang wet clothes. Breakfast Ikr700. If it's full, the pleasant lady at No 17 opposite has four rooms and a guest kitchen; prices are similar.

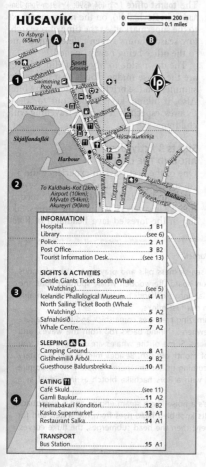

HÚSAVÍK

0 —— 200 m
0 —— 0.1 miles

To Ásbyrgi (65km)

Sólbrekka
Baldursbrekka
Höfðabrekka
Laugarbrekka
Höfðavegur

Sports Ground
Swimming Pool
Auðbrekka
Páskgarður
Ásgarðsvegur
Stóragarður
Grun
Ásgarðsvegur
Búðará
Mararbraut
Garðarsbraut
Túngata
Reykjaheiðarvegur

Skjálfandaflói

Harbour

Húsavíkurkirkja

To Kaldbaks-Kot (2km);
Airport (10km);
Mývatn (54km);
Akureyri (90km)

Eating

Gamli Baukur (☎ 464 2442; www.gamlibaukur.is; Hafnarstétt; mains Ikr990-3500; ☯ 11.30am-9pm Sun-Wed, to 1am Thu, 11am-3am Fri & Sat) Built from driftwood, the Old Tankard is a cosy harbourside restaurant-bar with a nautical theme. It's decorated with copper lamps and compasses, and fresh scallops, cod, shrimp and herring usually feature on the menu (hamburgers are available for the fish-disinclined).

Restaurant Salka (☎ 464 2551; Garðarsbraut 6; mains Ikr900-3000; ☯ 11am-10pm Sun-Thu, 11.30am-11pm Fri & Sat) This historical building, which was once Iceland's first cooperative, houses another good restaurant. Salka also has a bar and an extensive local menu (lobster, shrimp, puffin, lamb), plus pizzas and burgers.

Heimabakarí Konditori (☎ 464 2901; Garðarsbraut 15; ☯ 8am-5pm) Fresh bread, sandwiches and droolworthy cakes are sold at this fantastic bakery. At the time of writing, the bakery was about to open at the harbourside Café Skuld (open 8.30am to 10pm summer), selling tasty baked goods, plus beer and wine.

Getting There & Away

Trex (☎ 899 4660) run one to three daily buses to Akureyri (Ikr2100, 1¼ hours). From mid-June to August, **SBA-Norðurleið** (☎ 550 0700) run two services daily to Reykjahlíð at Mývatn (Ikr1600, 40 minutes), and one service on weekdays to Ásbyrgi (Ikr1800, 1¾ hours).

MÝVATN

Mývatn is the calm, shallow lake at the heart of a volatile volcanic area. Nature's violent masterpieces are everywhere – crazy-coloured mud pots, huge craters, and still-smouldering eruption debris. Once you've had your fill of all the explosive horror, mellow out with cycle rides, bird-watching (geese, Arctic terns, golden plovers, ducks and swans can be seen) and with a bathe in the north's version of the Blue Lagoon.

Reykjahlíð (population 208), at the northern end of the lake, is more an assortment of accommodation than a true town, but it makes the best base (Skútustaðir, at the southern end, also has summer facilities). The **tourist office** (☎ 464 4390; ☯ 9am-9pm Jun-Aug) is in Reykjahlíð, on the main road next to the supermarket. At the time of research, low season hours weren't determined due to the office being newly opened.

The down side to Mývatn (Midge Lake) are the dense midge clouds that appear in summer: on the bright side, they don't bite! Also, if hiking, keep a look out for deep fissures, especially if you are travelling with children.

Sights & Activities

AROUND THE LAKE

One of the best ways to experience the 37-sq-km lake is by bicycle or horse; several places in Reykjahlíð rent them. We recommend a leisurely ride round the shores, taking in the forested lava headland of **Höfði**;

EYE TO EYE: A WHALE ENCOUNTER *Fran Parnell*

On Thursday morning in Húsavík, I'm popping sea-sickness pills and praying to the rain gods to back off. But as I join the other passengers on board the wooden whale-spotting boat, the water is calm and the sun shivers out. We set sail into Skjálfandi bay, snowcapped mountains all around, and within 15 minutes we have seen our first minke.

Over the next two hours, sightings of these amazing creatures come thick and fast. It's a rare moment when there *isn't* a whale visible somewhere: shining backs roll from the waves, and blasts of air spout from blowholes in all directions. Some of the whales are so close that you can even smell their breath – a rancid stench of month-old fish! Besides minkes and a solitary dolphin, we watch five humpbacks repeatedly coming up for air. There's ample time to admire their huge flukes as they dive, each patterned with a Rorschachlike blotch as individual as a human fingerprint.

Just before the boat turns for harbour, there's a noise like a steam engine and a humpback surfaces just metres from where I'm standing. Its knobbled head rises from the water, and for long seconds, a prehistoric eye surveys us gravely; then the head submerges, the fluke curves, and the whale is gone.

pinnacle formations at **Kálfaströnd**; pseudo-craters at **Skútustaðir**, where ponds, bogs and marshlands create havens for nesting birds; the climb up **Vindbelgjarfjall** (529m); and a high-density waterfowl **nesting area** along the northwestern shore (off-road entry restricted between 15 May and 20 July).

One of the most interesting walks begins at **Stóragjá**, a hot spring near the village. After a few minutes, the path comes to a dead end at a pipeline. Turn left and walk several hundred metres until the track turns southward. It crosses a lava field to **Grjótagjá**, a 50°C hot spring in a spooky fissure, then continues to the prominent tephra crater **Hverfell** (sadly scarred by graffiti) and **Dimmuborgir**, a 2000-year-old maze of twisted lava whose highlight is the 'Church', a natural arched cave that really looks manmade.

MÝVATN NATURE BATHS

Ease aching muscles at the **Mývatn Nature Baths** (Jarðbaðshólar; ☎ 464 4411; www.jardbodin.is; adult/8-16yr Ikr1100/550, towel/swimsuit rental Ikr350/350; ⏰ 9am-midnight summer, noon-10pm winter), the north's answer to the Blue Lagoon, 5km east of Reykjahlíð. It's much smaller but is nicely landscaped, with a hot pot and saunas.

NÁMAFJALL & HVERIR

Vaporous vents cover the pinky-orange Námafjall ridge. At its foot, fumaroles and solfataras in the Hverir geothermal field scream steam and belch mud. The area rests on the mid-Atlantic rift (hence all the activity), and can be seen from quite a distance. It's just off the Ring Rd 6km east of Reykjahlíð.

KRAFLA

The colourful, sulphurous mudhole **Leirhnjúkur** is Krafla's prime attraction. From there you can meander round the **Krafla Caldera**, where several different lava flows overlie each other; some from the 1984 eruptions are still smoking.

Nearby **Stóra-Víti** is a 320m-wide explosion crater and lake (now inactive...allegedly). The 30-megawatt **Kröflustöð Power Station** sources steam from 17 boreholes around the volcano; step into the **visitor centre** (Gestastofa; ⏰ 12.30-3.30pm Mon-Fri, 1-5pm Sat & Sun Jun-Aug) for an explanatory film. One

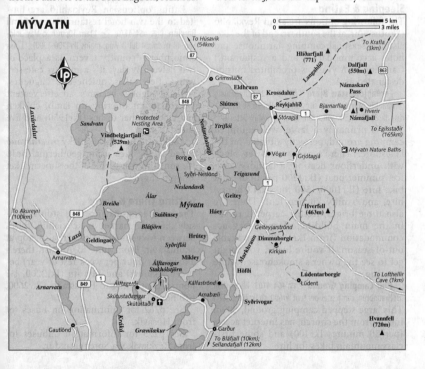

of the power station's preliminary searches produced the whopping crater **Sjálfskapar Viti** (Homemade Hell; near the Krafla car park), when a team drilled into a steam chamber which exploded. Bits of the rig were found 3km away.

Between 20 June and 31 August, a daily Mývatn–Dettifoss bus (see opposite) runs via Krafla.

Tours

From mid-June to September, Hótel Rey-kjahlíð (see below) run daily tours to Det-tifoss via Krafla (Ikr9900, seven hours); to Lofthellir, a lava cave with magnificent natural ice sculptures (Ikr7700, five hours); and to the cratered wasteland of the Askja caldera (Ikr14,400, 12 hours). There's a maximum of eight passengers allowed on each tour, so it is advisable to book tickets in advance.

SBA-Norðurleið (www.sba.is; 3-day tour Ikr20,700; Akureyri ☎ 550 0700; Reykjavík ☎ 550 0770), has tours departing from Akureyri (8.30am), Húsavík (9.45am) or Mývatn (11am) on Monday.

Sleeping & Eating

The following options are all in Reykjahlíð (Skútustaðir, at the southern end of the lake, also has seasonal camping, farmhouse and hotel accommodation and a restaurant.) Camping at Mývatn is prohibited outside designated areas.

Ferðaþjónustan Bjarg (☎ 464 4240; ferdabjarg @simnet.is; Mývatn; camp sites per tent Ikr750, sb Ikr2500, d/tr Ikr8200/10,500 mid-Jun–Aug; ☼ May-Oct; ☐) This is primarily a large, well-equipped camping ground, perfectly situated on the lakeshore. There's a new shower block with underfloor heating, a laundry serv-ice, summer boat (Ikr1200 per hour) and bike hire (Ikr1000/1500 for six/12 hours) hire, and a nifty kitchen tent. There are also three bright, freshly carpeted rooms in the main building; sleeping-bag ac-commodation (from Ikr1750) is available out-of-season. If you're lucky, you might get to see the owner's smokehouse…quite amazing.

Hlíð Camping Ground (☎ 464 4103; hlid@isholf .is; Hraunbrún; camp sites per tent Ikr600, sb Ikr2000; ☐) This large stepped camping ground, 300m inland from the church, has internet access (per 30 minutes Ikr400) and some first-class mountain bikes for hire.

Hótel Reykjahlíð (☎ 464 4142; www.reykjahlid.is; s/d/tr Ikr13,300/16,200/21,200 Jun-Aug, Ikr7300/9900/13,900 Sep-May; ℗ ☐) New owners María and Petur have completely refurbished this lovely lakeside hotel. Its nine light rooms are now a delicate yellow, with billowing curtains, brand-new beds and wi-fi access. The hotel has a bar and á la carte restaurant (open summer only) with the best views in town.

Hótel Reynihlíð (☎ 464 4170; www.reynihlid.is; s/d Ikr15,900/17,900 Jun-Aug & Christmas, Ikr8900/10,900 Sep-May; ℗ ☐) One entire wing of this smartish business hotel has been spruced up: en-suite rooms, with tea-making facilities, are now modern-looking and a restful shade of green. Almost half have lake views. The hotel has an upmarket restaurant serving Icelandic specialities. It also rents out bi-cycles (Ikr1800 per day).

Hraunbrún (☎ 464 4103; sb Ikr2000) For cheap sleeps, try out these six-bed rooms in a portakabin-style building; just pray your neighbours aren't noisy. There are good kitchen facilities and a shower block; check in at Hlíð camping ground.

Eating options in Reykjahlíð are lim-ited to the two hotel restaurants and **Gamli Bærinn** (☎ 464 4170; ☼ 11am-10pm mid-May–mid-Sep, til midnight Jul & Aug; mains Ikr1200-1990). This atmospheric 'country tavern' is a place of two halves. By day, it's a mellow café ser-ving coffee, cakes, quiche and baguettes, while at night it becomes an effervescent bar-restaurant offering up lamb, chicken and smoked char dishes (Ikr1950) and live entertainment.

Look out for dark, sticky *hverabrauð* baked in the area using geothermal heat. It's sometimes available at the supermarket and gift shop.

Getting There & Away

The main long-distance bus stop is out-side the supermarket in Reykjahlíð. Buses between Mývatn and Akureyri also stop at Skútustaðir. From June to August, there's a daily bus (four per week rest of year) be-tween Akureyri and Mývatn (Ikr2200, 1½ hours), continuing to Egilsstaðir (Ikr2600, two hours).

See p262 for information on buses to/from Húsavík.

See p273 for information on buses to/from Reykjavík via Sprengisandur.

JÖKULSÁRGLJÚFUR NATIONAL PARK

Sticky-birch forests, orchids and bizarre rock formations fill the rift of Jökulsárgljúfur National Park (☎ 465 2359; www.ust.is), sometimes called 'Iceland's Grand Canyon'. One highlight is Ásbyrgi, a hoof-shaped chasm formed by a flood of biblical proportions from a glacier 200km away. The swirls, spirals and strange acoustics at Hljóðaklettar (Echo Rocks) are similarly unearthly, and near the park's southern boundary is Dettifoss, Europe's most forcefully-flowing waterfall, where around 200 cu metres of water per second thunder over the edge.

Camping is limited to the large camping ground at Ásbyrgi (camp sites per adult Ikr600, all facilities); and smaller sites at Vesturdalur (camp sites per adult Ikr600, no showers) and Dettifoss (camp sites free, hikers only). The camping grounds are open from June to mid-September. Food is available at the snack bar, supermarket and petrol station at the Ásbyrgi farmstead (Rte 85).

From 20 June to 31 August, daily scheduled buses run from Akureyri (Ikr4900, 3¼ hours) and Húsavík (Ikr2800, 1¾ hours) to major sites in the park. There's also a daily Mývatn–Dettifoss (Ikr1900, 1½ hours) bus via Krafla (Ikr900, 15 minutes), leaving at 11.30am from the supermarket in Reykjahlíð and returning from Dettifoss at 2pm.

THE EAST

Iceland's wild reindeer roam the mountains of the empty east, and Iceland's version of the Loch Ness monster calls the area home. Tiny villages dot the fjords, surrounded by streams of tumbling water. Sadly, the east is also the site of Iceland's controversial aluminium smelter (see p235).

EGILSSTAÐIR

pop 1905

Egilsstaðir is a grey service town and the main regional transport hub. Its saving grace is lovely Lagarfljót (Lögurinn), Iceland's third-largest lake. Since saga times, tales have been told of a monster, the Lagarfljótsörmurinn, who lives in its depths. All amenities are clustered near the central crossroads, including the regional tourist office (☎ 471 2320; www.east.is; ☺ 9am-6pm May, Jun & mid-Aug–mid-Sep, 8am-10pm Jul–mid-Aug; fewer hours at other times) at the camping ground.

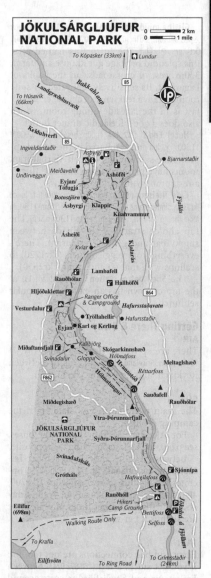

JÖKULSÁRGLJÚFUR NATIONAL PARK

Sleeping & Eating

Camping ground (☎ 471 2320; info@east.is; Kaupvangur 10; camp sites per adult Ikr750, sb Ikr2300, 5-person hut Ikr7000; ☺ year-round; ▯) Camp sites are lined in utilitarian rows, but the facilities are good (including a kitchen, laundry and internet) and there are some dorm beds available.

ICELAND

Gistiheimilið Egilsstaðir (☎ 471 1114; www .egilsstadir.com; s/d Ikr10,500/13,900 May-Sep, Ikr6900/9500 Oct-Apr; P ⛲) The town was named after this splendid heritage guesthouse and farm, 300m west of crossroads, on the banks of Lagarfljót. Its sensitively renovated en-suite rooms retain a real sense of character. Breakfast is in the lakeside dining room, which also does a good Icelandic dinner buffet.

Hotel Edda (☎ 444 4000; sb/s/d Ikr2200/9000/ 11,300; ⛲ Jun–mid-Aug) Based in the school opposite the swimming pool, off Tjarnarbrau, rooms have private bathrooms, and there's a restaurant with panoramic views.

Café Nielsen (☎ 471 2626; Tjarnarbraut 1; lunch Ikr1300, dinner mains Ikr1700-2900; ⛲ 11.30am-11.30pm Mon-Thu, to 2am Fri, 1pm-2am Sat, to 11.30pm Sun) The top choice straddles the divide between smoky bar and genteel restaurant. There's everything from veggieburgers (Ikr1720) to scallops with mango and chilli (Ikr2650).

The **Shell petrol station** (Fagradalsbraut 13) at the top of town has an extremely popular set lunch.

Getting There & Away
AIR
There are up to five **Flugfélag Íslands** (☎ 471 1210; www.airiceland.is) flights daily between Reykjavík and Egilsstaðir (Ikr11,975).

BUS
The main terminal in Egilsstaðir is at the camping ground.

For Akureyri–Mývatn–Egilsstaðir buses, see p260, for Egilsstaðir–Höfn, see opposite.

Between 1 June and 10 September **Ferðaþjónusta Austurlands** (☎ 472 1515, 852 9250) operates a daily bus to Seyðisfjörður (Ikr700, 40 minutes), with two buses on Wednesday and Thursday. At other times of year, there are six buses per week.

TAXI
Ferry and bus connections are not too hot: if you get stuck, a **taxi** (☎ 892 9247) between Egilsstaðir and Seyðisfjörður costs around Ikr8000.

SEYÐISFJÖRÐUR
pop 731

Things get lively when the Smyril Line's ferry *Norröna* sails majestically up the 17km-long fjord and docks at pretty little Seyðisfjörður (www.sfk.is). The picturesque

multicoloured houses, snowcapped mountains and cascading waterfalls make the perfect welcome to Iceland.

The **tourist office** (☎ 472 1551; ⛲ 10am-noon & 1-5pm Mon, Tue, Thu & Fri, 10am-noon & 1-8pm Wed summer, 1-5pm Wed & Thu rest of yr) is inside the ferry terminal.

Sights & Activities
For an unearthly experience, try a guided midnight **kayaking trip** (☎ 865 3741; www.iceland -tour.com; ⛲ Jun-Aug) round the tranquil lagoon (Ikr1500, one hour); more experienced paddlers can go on six-hour/two-day trips (Ikr6000/17,000) to Austdalur or Skálanes. Hlynur also does **mountain-bike tours** (two-hour trips Ikr2000); or hire a bike and go off on your own (half-/one day Ikr1500/2000).

The Seyðisfjörður to Vestdalur **hike** is a fine taste of the countryside, around Mt Bjólfur to the Seyðisfjörður–Egilsstaðir road.

Seyðisfjörður is full of 19th-century **timber buildings**, brought in kit form from Norway: read all about them in the brochure *Historic Seyðisfjörður*, available at the tourist office. For an insight into the town's fishing and telecommunications history, there's a worthwhile museum, **Tækniminjasafn Austurlands** (☎ 472 1596; Hafnargata 44; adult/child Ikr400/free; ⛲ 10am-5pm Jun–mid-Sep, 1-4pm Mon-Fri mid-Sep–May).

On Wednesday evenings in summer, live music performances are held in the pretty **Blue Church** (Ránargata; Ikr1000; ⛲ 8.30pm Jul–mid-Aug).

Sleeping
Camping ground (☎ 861 3097; ferdamenning@sfk.is; Ránargata; camp sites per adult Ikr600) A pleasant, sheltered grassy camping ground with big hedges and picnic benches.

Hótel Aldan (☎ 472 1277; www.hotelaldan.com; Oddagata 6) is shared across three old wooden buildings. Reception and the bar-restaurant (where breakfast is served) are based at Norðurgata 2. Cheaper rooms are at **Snæfell** (Austurvegur 3; s/d/tr Ikr10,800/14,800/16,800 summer, Ikr6500/8800/10,800 winter; P), a creaky, characterful three-storey place with fresh white paintwork, draped muslin curtains and Indian bedspreads to add a splash of colour. **Old Bank** (s/d/tr Ikr12,800/16,800/19,800 summer, Ikr7800/11,800/14,800 winter; P ⛲) houses a truly gorgeous boutique guesthouse with all mod cons. Its luxury rooms are bright,

ICELAND

spacious and furnished with antiques, and beds snuggle under hand-embroidered bedspreads. Triple rooms have wicked alcoves.

Hafaldan HI Hostel (☎ 472 1410; thorag@simnet.is; Ránargata 9; sb dm Ikr1650, sb d Ikr4800, d Ikr6000; ☐) This cheerful arty hostel is split over two sites (facilities are shared). The original building has harbour views, a sunny lounge, newly fitted kitchen, laundry, internet access…and even a snug Mongolian yurt (July and August) in the garden. The central new building used to be the old hospital, but you'd never guess; Indian hangings and funky old furniture make it homely.

Eating

Skaftfell Café (☎ 472 1633; Austurvegur 42; snacks Ikr450-1100, mains Ikr2000-3500; ☺ summer; ☐) This highly recommended, welcoming bistro-bar and internet café is a popular place with local artists and musicians. Snacks include omelette, waffles and toast with caviar, and the freshly caught seafood is great.

Hótel Aldan (☎ 472 1277; Norðurgata 2; mains Ikr2600-3500; ☺ 7am-9.30pm mid-May–mid-Sep) Coffee and light meals are served all day. In the evening, damask tablecloths, crystal wine glasses and flickering candles prettify the tables, and the menu features traditional Icelandic ingredients (lamb, lobster, reindeer, fish) with contemporary salads and sauces. The bar buzzes when the boat comes in.

There's a **snack bar** (☎ 472 1700; Hafnargata 2) at the Shell petrol station and a **Samkaup-Strax supermarket** (☎ 472 1201; Vesturvegur 1; ☺ closed Sun).

Getting There & Away

For bus information, see opposite. Details of the ferry service from mainland Europe are on p293.

THE SOUTH

Getting There & Away

The main bus company in the south is **Austurleið Kynnisferðir** (☎ 562 1011; www.austurleid.is). It runs the following services:

Reykjavík–Kirkjubæjarklaustur–Skaftafell–Jökulsárlón–Höfn (Ikr7400, 8½ hours) June to mid-September; it departs at 8.30am daily from both ends (a reduced service departs later in the day out-of-season). Eastbound from Reykjavík the bus passes Kirkjubæjarklaustur at 1.30pm (Ikr4400), Skaftafell at 2.35pm

(Ikr5400) and Jökulsárlón at 3.30pm (Ikr6200). Westbound from Höfn it passes Jökulsárlón at 10am (Ikr1300), Skaftafell at 11.10am (Ikr2300) and Kirkjubæjarklaustur at 12.40pm (Ikr3300).

Skaftafell–Jökulsárlón (Ikr2300, 9am & 1pm) July and August. Stops for 1½ to 2½ hours at the lagoon before returning.

Höfn–Skaftafell–Egilsstaðir (Ikr4900, four hours) June to August. Departs from Höfn at 8.30am, and from Egilsstaðir at 2pm daily. The bus passes Skaftafell (eastwards towards Egilsstaðir at around 9am, westwards towards Höfn at around 5pm).

Reykjavík–Kirkjubæjarklaustur–Skaftafell, via Landmannalaugar (Ikr8100, 11 hours) Mid-June to August. Departs from Reykjavík at 8.30am and from Skaftafell at 8am daily. The bus passes through Kirkjubæjarklaustur at 6.30pm eastbound and 9am westbound.

STAFAFELL
pop 10

On the southeast coast between nowhere and nowhere, Stafafell is a lovely, lonely hiking area flanked by the **Lón lagoon** and the colourful **Lónsöræfi mountains**.

Wildhaired and welcoming, Bergsveinn is the good-humoured, knowledgeable host of the area's only sleeping choice, **Stafafell HI Hostel** (☎ 478 1717; www.eldhorn.is/stafafell; sb Ikr2000, s/d from Ikr4500/6545) – when he's not tending to his 500 sheep. The hostel is full of light pine fittings and bright sunshine, and has a peaceful feel. Meals are available in summer if reserved in advance, but bring backup food. There's also a **camping area** (camp sites per adult Ikr600) and cottages for hire.

Mountain-bus tours (Ikr5000, ☺ Jun-Aug) to Kollumúli, in the Lónsöræfi mountains, are highly recommended and can be arranged at the HI hostel. The hostel can also advise on about a dozen local **walking routes**.

See left for scheduled buses.

VATNAJÖKULL

Mighty Vatnajökull is earth's largest icecap outside the poles. It's three times the size of Luxembourg (8300 sq km), reaches a thickness of 1km in places, and if you could find a pair of scales big enough, you'd find it weighed an awesome 3000 billion tonnes! Scores of glaciers flow down from the centre as rivers of crevassed ice.

Accommodation is available at the **Jöklasel Hut** (☎ 478 1000; sb Ikr1800), near the edge of the ice.

ICELAND

Tours

From June to August, **Vatnajökull.is** (☎ 894 1616; www.vatnajokull.is) run a trip from Höfn to Jöklasel (near the edge of the ice), leaving at 9.40am. You arrive around 11am, allowing time for a bone-shaking one-hour skidoo ride. It returns via Jökulsárlón (see below), where it's possible to take a boat ride on the lagoon, arriving back in Höfn at 5.15pm. The bus costs Ikr5200. Bus, skidoo and boat ticket combined costs Ikr14,800.

Warning

Hiking around the Jöklasel Hut isn't advised due to dangerous crevasses.

AROUND VATNAJÖKULL
Jökulsárlón

A ghostly procession of luminous-blue icebergs drifts through the 17-sq-km **Jökulsárlón lagoon**, before floating out to sea. This surreal scene (right next to the Ring Rd between Höfn and Skaftafell) is a natural film set: you might have seen it in *Batman Begins* (2005) and the James Bond film *Die Another Day* (2002). The ice breaks off from Breiðamerkurjökull glacier, an offshoot of Vatnajökull.

Boat trips (☎ 478 2222; info@jokulsarlon.is; Ikr2200) among the 'bergs are available from June to August.

See p267 for buses.

Höfn
pop 1662

Tiny Höfn makes a handy base for trips to the glacier. The tourist office is inside the **Jöklasýning Glacier Exhibition** (☎ 478 2665; www.joklasyning.is; adult/under 16yr Ikr600/free; Hafnarbraut 30; ☉ 1-4pm Mon-Fri Oct-Apr, to 6pm daily May & Sep, 9am-9pm daily Jun-Aug), which has two floors of interesting displays on Vatnajökull and the southeastern corner of Iceland as well as some altogether too-strange glacial mice.

The two main companies running summer tours to the glacier are **Arctic-Ice** (☎ 478 1731; www.arctic-ice.is) and **Glacier Jeeps** (☎ 478 1000; www.glacierjeeps.is). The cheapest 3¼-hour Super-Jeep trip costs from Ikr9000, with prices rising for longer tours including skidoo rides. A farmer, Einar Sigurðsson pulls visitors along in a **haycart ride** (☎ 894 0894; www.hofsnes.com; ☉ 11am May-Aug), 10km over glacial sands to Ingólfshöfði, a 76m sheer headland and protected site where there are

loads of sea birds (great skuas, guillemots, fulmar, puffins etc). The headland is named after Ingólfur Arnarson, who spent his first winter in Iceland there.

There's a **camping ground** (☎ 478 1606; camping@simnet.is; Hafnarbraut 52; camp sites per adult Ikr650) with 16 log cabins sleeping up to six people (sleeping bag Ikr2000, whole cabin Ikr6500): it has cooking facilities, but you'll need your own pans.

At the harbour end of town, **Nýibær HI Hostel** (☎ 478 1736; hofn@hostel.is; Hafnarbraut 8; sb Ikr2200; **P**) is a medium-sized place with laundry facilities. Run by the same couple, **Gistiheimilið Hvammur** (☎ 478 1503; hvammur3@simnet.is; Ránarslóð 2; sb Ikr2500, s/d Ikr6500/8800; ☐), overlooking the boat-filled harbour, is the pick of the guesthouses for its smart rooms and internet connection. There are sinks and satellite TV in every room.

For business-class accommodation, try friendly **Hótel Höfn** (☎ 478 1240; www.hotelhofn.is; Víkurbraut; s/d from Ikr12,750/17,500; **P** ☐), where most of the rooms look either out to sea or over the glacier. It also does formal meals, fast food and buffets in its two **dining rooms** (mains Ikr1900-2900; ☉ 9am-9pm).

Kaffi Hornið (☎ 478 2600; Hafnarbraut; mains Ikr1800-4000; ☉ 11am-10pm Mon-Thu, noon-1am Fri & Sat, 3-10pm Sun) This informal log-cabin affair is decorated with old B&W photos of the town. The food is served in stomach-stretching portions; there are a couple of veggie options and a Höfn speciality, garlic-toasted lobster (Ikr4000), as well as burgers, pasta, fish mains and salads.

Buses (see p267) leave from outside Hótel Höfn.

SKAFTAFELL NATIONAL PARK

Europe's largest national park encompasses a breathtaking collection of peaks and glaciers. It's the country's favourite wilderness: 160,000 visitors per year come to marvel at thundering waterfalls, twisting birch woods, and the brilliant blue-white Vatnajökull icecap. Expansion plans are underway; eventually, the Skaftafell and Jökulsárgljúfur (p265) will join to form one 15,000km² megapark – 40% of the entire country.

There is a really helpful **visitor centre** (☎ 478 1627; www.ust.is; ☉ 8am-9pm Jun-Aug, 10am-3pm May & Sep) which shows a cool film about the 1996 *jökulhlaup* (glacial flood) in peak season.

Walking

Skaftafell's main feature is **Svartifoss**, a gloomy waterfall that thunders over black basalt columns. Due to immense pressure in this area, rangers are encouraging visitors to explore elsewhere; for example, the easy one-hour return route to **Skaftafellsjökull**. The trail (wheelchair-accessible) begins at

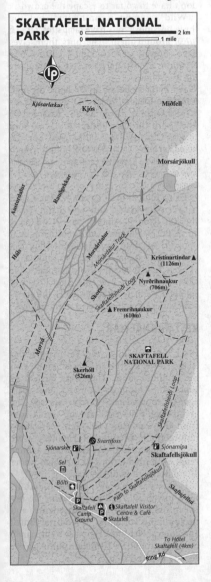

the information centre and leads to the glacier face, where you can see the bumps, groans and brilliant blue hues of the ice. The **Icelandic Mountain Guides** (☎ 587 999; www .mountainguide.is) leads glacier walks in summer (2½ hours Ikr3500, minimum age 10).

In fine weather, the circular walk round **Skaftafellsheiði** is a treat. There are some enjoyable day walks from the camping ground to **Kristínartindar** (1126m), **Kjós** or the glacial lagoon in **Morsárdalur**; plan on about seven hours for each return trip.

Tours

The Laki eruptions of 1783 caused utter devastation to the area. Over 30 billion tonnes of lava spewed from the Laki fissure, the largest recorded flow from a single eruption. The still-volatile **Lakagígar area**, with its spectacular 25km-long crater, is now part of the national park. In July and August, daily 9½-hour **Austurleið Kynnisferðir** (☎ 562 1011; www.austurleid.is) trips from Skaftafell (Ikr7300, at 8am) and Kirkjubæjarklaustur (Ikr5300, at 9am) visit the craters.

Sleeping & Eating

Book all accommodation ahead in summer, as Skaftafell is immensely popular.

Camping ground (☎ 478 1627; camp sites per adult over 16yr Ikr600) Camping is permitted only at this large, gravelly location (with laundry facilities), right by the visitor centre.

Bölti (☎ 478 1626; fax 478 2426; Skaftafellsheiði; sb/d Ikr2200/7500; ☺ May-Sep) This farm, behind the western edge of the camping ground, is superbly located with dizzying views over the *sandur*. There's sleeping-bag accommodation in six-person rooms, plus small cottages with twin beds and cooking facilities; dinner can be supplied if requested in advance.

Hótel Skaftafell (☎ 478 1945; www.hotelskaftafell .is; Freysnes; s/d May-Aug Ikr11,000/14,600, low season Ikr9000/11,100; ☺ Feb-Nov) At Freysnes, 5km east of the park, Skaftafell's 63 rooms (all with bathroom and TV) are functional rather than luxurious. The staff are helpful, and even the rooms in the prefabricated buildings at the back have great glacial views. There's a restaurant, and a pleasant walking trail.

The visitor centre café is the only place to get food inside the park.

Getting There & Away

See p267 for buses.

ICELAND

KIRKJUBÆJARKLAUSTUR

pop 139

Kirkjubæjarklaustur (translated 'church-farm-cloister') is a tiny settlement lost in the staggeringly vast and empty *sandur*. It's full of sights that hark back to its religious beginnings.

There's a **tourist information point** inside the Skaftárskáli petrol station.

Kirkjugólf's regular basalt columns, cemented with moss, were once mistaken for an old church floor rather than a work of nature, and it's easy to see why. The 'floor' lies in a field about 400m northwest of the petrol station.

Systrastapi (Sisters' Pillar) marks the spot where two nuns were reputedly executed and buried, after sleeping with the devil and a few other no-nos. **Systrafoss** is the prominent waterfall located near the hotel. The lake **Systravatn**, a short saunter up the cliffs, was once a place where nuns went to bathe.

See (p269) for information about tours to the **Lakagígar craters**.

Sleeping & Eating

Kirkjubæ II camping ground (☎ /fax 487 4612; camp site per adult Ikr600; ☺ Jun-Aug) Pitch tents on the greensward under a pretty waterfall at this pleasant camping spot above town. Hot showers, kitchen and laundry facilities.

Hótel Klaustur (☎ 487 4900; www.icehotels.is; Klausturvegur 6; s/d from Ikr13,000/16,200) One of the Icelandair chain, the 57-roomed Klaustur looks like a Soviet-bloc hotel, but contains a three-star interior with the usual business-like rooms. The restaurant (mains Ikr1900 to Ikr3900) has an à la carte menu with typical Icelandic mains and some unusual starters – snails, anyone?

Systrakaffi (☎ 487 4848; Klausturvegur 13; light meals Ikr850-1500, mains Ikr1800-3000; ☺ 10am-midnight, to 2am Fri & Sat Jun-Aug, 6-10pm Fri & Sat May & Sep) This ambient little café sells a variety of food including chilliburgers, baconburgers, pizzas and reasonably priced fish and meat dishes, including a bouillabaisselike seafood soup (Ikr1250).

For freshly-made fast-food snacks, there's the **Skaftárskáli petrol station** (☎ 487 4628).

Getting There & Away

See p267 for buses.

ÞÓRSMÖRK

The Woods of Thor is a stunning glacial valley, full of weird rock formations, twisting gorges, a singing cave, mountain flowers and icy streams. Its proximity to Reykjavík (130km) makes it a popular spot in summer, when tents pile up and the camping grounds become partyville. Luckily you don't have to go far to escape the crowds.

Wild camping is prohibited, but the three Þórsmörk huts have **camp sites** (per adult Ikr700) around them. The huts themselves have showers and cooking facilities; reservations are strongly advised, particularly for weekends.

For **Þórsmörk hut** (sb Ikr2000) book through **Ferðafélag Íslands** (☎ 568 2533; www.fi.is; Mörkin 6, IS-108 Reykjavík). Bookings for **Básar hut** (sb Ikr1800) are through **Útivist** (☎ 562 1000; www.utivist.is; Laugavegur 178, IS-101 Reykjavík). For the **Húsadalur huts** (sb/d Ikr1700/4000) book through bus company **Reykjavík Excursions** (☎ 580 5400; www.thorsmork.is, www.re.is; Vatnsmýrarvegur 10, IS-101 Reykjavík).

From June to mid-September, buses run between Reykjavík and Húsadalur (over the hill from Þórsmörk) at 8.30am daily (Ikr3700, 3½ hours) with another bus at 5pm Friday; from mid-June to August, a service runs at 5pm Saturday to Thursday.

Even though Þórsmörk seems tantalisingly close (only 30km from the Ring Rd), you *cannot* drive there without a 4WD: the gravel road surface eventually turns into boulders.

VESTMANNAEYJAR

pop 4172

Black and brooding, the Vestmannaeyjar islands form 15 eye-catching silhouettes off the southern shore. They were formed by submarine volcanoes around 11,000 years ago; except for sulky-looking Surtsey, which rose from the waves in 1963. Ten years later, unforgettable pictures of Heimaey were broadcast across the globe when a huge eruption buried a third of the town under 30 million tonnes of lava.

Heimaey is the only inhabited island. Its little town and sheltered harbour lie between dramatic *klettur* (escarpments) and two ominous volcanoes – blood-red Eldfell and conical Helgafell. Heimaey's cliffs are a breeding ground for 10 million puffin pairs – see the boxed text, p273.

The **tourist office** (☎ 481 3555; www.vestman naeyjar.is; Raðhússtræti; ⏱ 10am-5pm Mon-Fri, 1-4pm Sat mid-May–mid-Sep) is in the same building as the library and folk museum, and is well signposted from the harbour. There are Sparisjóðurinn and Íslandsbanki banks with ATMs near the post office. The library has internet access (Ikr200 per hour).

Sights & Activities

The **Aquarium & Natural History Museum** (Fiska-og Náttúrugripasafn; ☎ 481 1997; Heðarvegur 12; adult/child 6-12yr Ikr400/200; ⏱ 11am-5pm mid-May–mid-Sep, 3-5pm Sun mid-Sep–mid-May) has fishtanks of hideous-looking Icelandic fish as well as a live video link to a puffin colony. There are fascinating photos of Heimaey's 1973 evacuation in the **folk museum** (Byggðasafn; ☎ 481 1194; Raðhússtræti; adult/child 6-12yr Ikr400/200; ⏱ 11am-5pm mid-May–mid-Sep, 3-5pm Sat & Sun mid-Sep–mid-Apr).

The explosive hour-long **Volcanic Film Show** (☎ 481 1045; Heiðarvegur; admission Ikr600; ⏱ 11am, 2pm, 3.30pm & 9pm daily mid-Jun–mid-Aug, by request at other times) plays at the local cinema, and includes footage on whales and puffin rappelling.

Four hundred buildings lie buried under the 1973 lava; on the edge of the flow is an eerie **House Graveyard** where beloved homes rest in peace. **'Pompei of the North'** (www .pompeinordursins.is) is a modern 'archaeological' excavation, where 10 houses are being dug up. So far, only the crumpled concrete remains of **No 25 Suðurvegur** have been unearthed.

Skansinn, the oldest structure on the island, is a ruinous 15th-century fort built by English marauders; nearby is a picturesque replica **Norse stave church** and an old water tower crushed by the 1973 lava.

Opportunities for **hiking** abound, including the walk to Stórhöfði and climbs of Helgafell and Eldfell. It's a treacherous 30-minute climb to the top of **Stóraklif**, 'assisted' by ropes and chains, but worth the terror for the breathtaking views.

Tours

From May to August, **Viking Tours** (☎ 488 4884; www.vikingtours.is; small boats harbour, off Ægis-gata; adult/8-14yr Ikr2700/1700) runs daily boat (10.30am and 3.30pm) and bus (8am and 1pm) tours of the island. If nobody's about, ask in nearby Café Kró.

Sleeping

There are lots of guesthouses to choose from, but they fill up fast after the ferry arrives.

Herjólfsdalur Camp Ground (☎ 692 6952; camp sites per adult Ikr700; ⏱ Jun-Aug) Cupped in the bowl of an extinct volcano, this sheltered, dandelion-dotted camping ground has hot showers, a laundry room and cooking facilities.

Gistiheimilið Erna (☎ 481 2112; www.simnet .is/gisting; Kirkjubæjarbraut 15; sb/made-up bed/apt Ikr1800/3000/12,000) On the edge of the 1973 lava flow, Erna is a great budget choice. It's a friendly family home with cooking facilities, laundry, a Jacuzzi, bikes to borrow, and a TV in every room. The apartment fits eight people.

Gistiheimilið Hreiðrið (☎ 481 1045; http://tour ist.eyjar.is; Faxastígur 33; sb/s/d Ikr2300/3700/6000 summer, Ikr1800/3000/5000 winter) Run by the helpful volcano-show people, Ruth and Sigurgeir, this winning guesthouse has a family feel. Features include wall-to-wall puffins, a well-stocked kitchen, cosy TV lounge and bike hire.

Hotel Þórshamar (☎ 481 3663; www.hotelvest mannaeyjar.is in Icelandic; Bárustígur 2; s/d/ste Ikr10,240/ 14,430/20,110 May-Sep, discounts at other times; 🖳) Iceland's first cinema is now a hotel, with pale, pleasant rooms and facilities including sauna, hot tubs and snooker room. Of the older rooms, No 209 is the best, tucked in the corner with its own balcony; otherwise go for the three new suites, all with big beds, modern décor and dark wood floors. The same family run several cheaper guesthouses – ask the hotel reception for details.

Eating

Fjólan (☎ 481 3663; Vestmannabraut 28; mains from Ikr2000; ⏱ 7am-11pm year-round) Next door to Hótel Þórshamar, this upmarket restaurant has a rather staid air…except for its glitzy gold columns! The buffet breakfast is open to all; after that, traditional home-made Icelandic food is served all day, including probably the best fish on Heimaey.

Lanterna (☎ 481 3393; Bárustígur 11; mains Ikr1500-3500; ⏱ 11am-2pm & 6-10.30pm Fri & Sat Sep-May, 11am-10.30pm daily Jun-Aug) This cosy wood-panelled place, decorated with local B&W photos, specialises in Vestmannaeyjar delicacies and, erm, wienerschitzel. The brave can try puffin served with a sweet sauce; catch of the day costs Ikr1500.

Café Maria (☎ 481 3160; Skólavegur 1; mains Ikr1400-3500; ☺ 11.30am-1.30am Mon-Fri, to 1am Sat & Sun) A stuffed gannet surveys proceedings at this pleasant café-restaurant, which is quiet during the day but busy at night. Pizzas, burgers, savoury crepes, and fresh fish and meat mains are served – plus, yes, puffin.

Pizza 67 (☎ 481 1567; Heiðarvegur 5; pizza Ikr950-1350; ▢) Feathered friends are firmly off the menu: chomp crunchy garlic bread instead in a publike atmosphere.

There's a great sit-down **bakery** (Bárustígur 7) and several cheap service-station grills. For self-catering, there's the central igloo-like **Vöruval supermarket** (☎ 481 3184; Vesturvegur 18; ☺ 8am-7pm daily).

Getting There & Away

Landsflug (☎ 481 3300; www.landsflug.is) flies two or three times daily to as well as from Reykjavík (Ikr7200, 25 minutes).

The **Herjólfur** (☎ 481 2800; www.herjolfur.is) sails May to August from Þorlákshöfn to the Vestmannaeyjar. It leaves at noon and 7.30pm (noon only on Saturday), returning from the island at 8.15am and 4pm from Sunday to Friday (8.15am only on Saturday). The crossing takes 2¾ hours. In the low season, there are fewer departures. The one-way fare per adult/12 to 15 years is Ikr1800/900.

Austurleið Kynnisferðir buses (Ikr1000) connect with the ferry, leaving Reykjavík at 11am and 5.50pm, returning from Þorlákshöfn at 11am and 7pm.

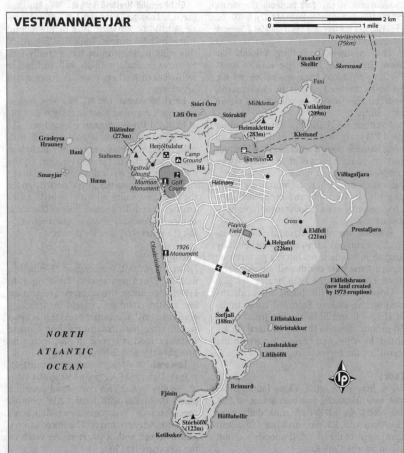

VESTMANNAEYJAR

THE INTERIOR

The desolate interior is so vast, barren and remote that the Apollo astronauts held training exercises here before the 1969 lunar landings. The highlands are truely one of Europe's greatest remaining wilderness areas. There are practically no services, accommodation, mobile-phone signals, bridges, and no guarantees if things go wrong: careful preparations are essential. Routes are only accessible in July and August.

ROUTES OF CENTRAL ICELAND

Historically, the interior routes were used as summer shortcuts between north and south, places of terror to be traversed as quickly as possible. Some *útilegumenn* (outlaws) fled into these harsh highlands: those who survived gained legendary status, like the superhuman Grettir or Fjalla-Eyvindar, an Icelandic Robin Hood/Butch Cassidy figure.

Routes in this section are summer-only, and are strictly for high-clearance 4WD vehicles. It's recommended that vehicles travel in pairs.

Many mountain huts are run by **Ferðafélag Íslands** (☎ 568 2535; www.fi.is; Mörkin 6, IS-108 Reykjavík): accommodation is on a first-come, first-served basis, so book in advance. Facilities tend to be spartan, and if there are kitchens, they generally lack utensils.

Kjölur Route

The Kjölur Rte (35) was once believed to be infested with bloodthirsty outlaws. Today, it's a favourite with visitors: it's greener and more hospitable than the Sprengisandur Rte, and forms a neat shortcut between Reykjavík and Akureyri. The route's name (Keel) refers to the perceived shape of its topography.

Kjölur's main attraction is **Hveravellir**, a geothermal area of fumaroles and multicoloured hot pools at the northern end of the pass. A camping ground and two mountain huts with kitchens are run by **Hveravallafélag** (☎ 452 4200; www.hveravellir.is; camp sites per adult Ikr700, sb Ikr1800).

From mid-June to August, **Trex** (☎ 899 4660; www.trex.is) buses travel over the Kjölur Rte between Reykjavík and Akureyri (Ikr8200, 10 hours), departing at 8am from both ends.

Sprengisandur Route

The Sprengisandur Rte (F26) may be less interesting than Kjölur, but it does offer some wonderful views of Vatnajökull, Tungnafellsjökull and Hofsjökull, as well as Askja and Herðubreið. The bus passes the photogenic waterfall **Aldeyjarfoss**, which topples over clustered basalt columns.

A good place to break your journey is **Nýidalur**, where there's a **camping ground** (camp sites per adult Ikr700), two Ferðafélag Íslands **huts** (☎ Jul & Aug 854 1194; sb Ikr2000; ⌥ Jul & Aug) and numerous hiking possibilities. A recommended, challenging day hike takes you to

---

LITTLE NORTHERN BROTHERS

Iceland is famous for its puffins (*Fratercula arctica*). It's hard not to get dewy-eyed over these expressive, sociable little 'clowns of the ocean'; but really they're as tough as old boots, living out on the stormy winter seas and surviving on salt water.

It's easy to spot puffins: they're the clumsiest things in the air. Wings beat frantically 300 to 400 times per minute to keep them aloft, and the birds often crash-land. Underwater, it's a different story – their flight beneath the waves is so graceful that they were once thought to be a bird-fish hybrid.

Every spring, the puffins return to land to breed. They're discerning birds: 60% of the world's population choose to nest in Iceland. From late May to August, the best places to see them include offshore Reykjavík (p240), Heimaey (p270) and Látrabjarg (p256), where the colonies are wonderfully fearless.

Pufflings start leaving their nests in August. On Heimaey, the young birds are often confused by the town's lights; every year, the children stay up late to collect them and point them seawards. Puffins and their eggs are a traditional part of the Icelandic diet: if you can bring yourself to devour them, you'll find them on menus everywhere, especially in the Vestmannaeyjar.

the **Vonarskarð Pass** (1000m), a colourful saddle between Vatnajökull, Tungnafellsjökull and the green Ógöngur hills.

From mid-July to late August, **Austurleið Kynnisferðir** (☎ 562 1011; www.austurleid.is) buses travel between Landmannalaugar and Mývatn via Sprengisandur. They leave Landmannalaugar at 8.30am on Sunday, Tuesday and Thursday (Ikr7200, 10 hours), and leave Reykjahlíð supermarket (Mývatn) at 8.30am on Monday, Wednesday and Friday.

Daily buses (Ikr4500, four hours) run between Reykjavík (depart 8.30am) and Landmannalaugar (depart 2.45pm), early June to early September.

Öskjuleið Route (Askja Way)

Herðubreið and Askja on the Öskjuleið Rte (F88) are the most visited wonders of the Icelandic desert.

HERÐUBREIÐ

Iceland's most distinctive mountain, Herðubreið (1682m), has been described as a birthday cake, a cooking pot and a lampshade, but the tourist industry calls it (more respectfully) the 'Queen of the Desert'. The track around it makes a nice day hike from **Herðubreiðarlindir Nature Reserve**, a grassy oasis created by springs flowing from beneath the lava. There's a **camping ground** (camp sites per adult Ikr700) and **Þorsteinsskáli Hut** (sb Ikr1800; ☉ Jun-Aug), with basic kitchen, both run by **Ferðafélag Akureyrar** (Akureyri Touring Club; ☎ 462 2720; ffa@ffa.is).

ASKJA

Askja is an immense 50-sq-km caldera, created by a colossal explosion of tephra in 1875. Part of the volcano's collapsed magma chamber contains sapphire-blue **Öskjuvatn**, Iceland's deepest lake at 217m. At its northeastern corner is **Víti**, a hot lake in a tephra crater where the water (around 25°C) is ideal for swimming.

The two **Dreki Huts** (sb Ikr2200) at **Drekagil** (Dragon Ravine), eight kilometres away, accommodate 50 people, and are run by **Ferðafélag Akureyrar** (Akureyri Touring Club; ☎ 462 2720; ffa@ffa.is).

TOURS

Hótel Reykjahlíð at Mývatn run tours to the Askja caldera; see p264 for details.

Kverkfjöll Route

The 108km-long Kverkfjöll Rte (F905, F910 and F902) connects Möðrudalur with the Ferðafélag Íslands' Sigurðarskáli hut. This is 3km from the impressive lower **Kverkfjöll ice caves**, where a hot river flows beneath the glacier, melting shimmering patterns on the ice walls. There are other (less impressive) ice caves higher up the glacier and a **hot waterfall** (30°C) at Hveragil, five hours' return from Sigurðarskáli: ask at the hut for directions.

The 85-bed **Sigurðarskáli hut** (sb Ikr2000) and camping ground can be booked through **Ferðafélag Fljótsdalshéraðs** (☎ 863 5813; ferdafelag@egilsstadir.is).

TOURS

The simplest way to visit Kverkfjöll is with **SBA-Norðurleið** (www.sba.is; 3-day tour Ikr20,700; Akureyri ☎ 550 0700; Reykjavík ☎ 550 0770), with tours departing from Akureyri (8.30am), Húsavík (9.45am) or Mývatn (11am) on Monday in July and August. Tours are just transport and a guide: you must organise your own accommodation and food. Warm clothing, a thick sleeping bag and strong boots are essential.

FJALLABAK NATURE RESERVE

The Fjallabak Route (F208) is a spectacular alternative to the coast road between Hella and Kirkjubæjarklaustur. It passes through the scenic nature reserve to **Landmannalaugar**, an area of rainbow-coloured rhyolite peaks, rambling lava flows, blue lakes and hot springs which can hold you captive for days. Much of the route is along (and in!) rivers and therefore unsuitable for 2WD vehicles.

The star attractions around Landmannalaugar are: **Laugahraun**, a convoluted lava field; the soothing **hot springs** 200m west of the Landmannalaugar hut; multicoloured vents at **Brennisteinsalda**; the incredible red crater lake **Ljótipollur**; and the blue lake **Frostastaðavatn**, just over the rhyolite ridge north of Landmannalaugar. **Bláhnúkur**, immediately south of Laugahraun, offers a scree scramble and fine views from the 943m peak.

Ferðafélag Íslands' **hut** (☎ 854 1192 Jul-Sep; sb Ikr2200) at Landmannalaugar accommodates 78 people on a first-come, first-served basis, and books up quickly with tour groups and club members. Others will probably have to use the **camping ground** (camp sites per adult Ikr700), which has toilet and shower facilities.

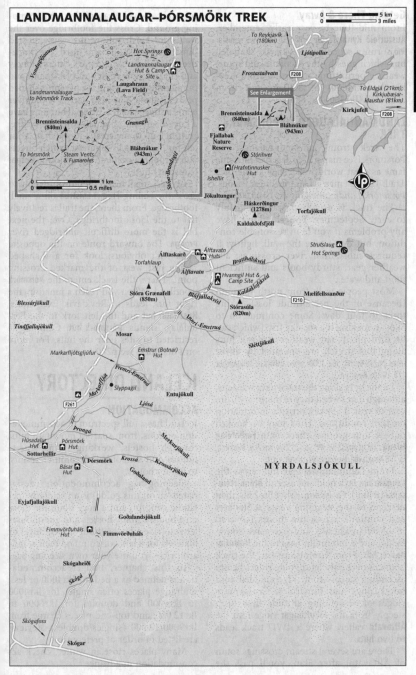

LANDMANNALAUGAR–ÞÓRSMÖRK TREK

Getting There & Away

From mid-June to very early September, **Austurleið Kynnisferðir** (☎ 562 1011; www.austurleid.is) run a scheduled Reykjavík–Skaftafell bus which goes by the scenic inland route, weather permitting, departing from Reykjavík (Ikr4600) at 8.30am and from Skaftafell (Ikr3500) at 8am.

LANDMANNALAUGAR TO ÞÓRSMÖRK TREK

The trek from Landmannalaugar to Þórsmörk (see map p 275) deserves the same fame as great world walks such as the Inca Trail. The best map is Landmælingar Íslands' *Þórsmörk/Landmannalaugar* (1:100,000).

The track is usually passable mid-July to early September. You shouldn't have any problems if you're in reasonable condition, but don't take the walk lightly: it requires substantial river crossings, all-weather gear, sturdy boots and sufficient food and water.

Most people walk from north to south (because of the net altitude loss), taking three to four days. Some continue on to Skógar, making it a six-day trip (which can be difficult if bad weather strikes); huts along this stretch are operated by **Útivist** (Map pp238-9; ☎ 562 1000; www.utivist.is; Laugavegur 178, IS-105 Reykjavík).

Public huts along the track have wardens, although dates when they're there vary from year to year. They can provide information on trail conditions. Huts may be booked out by tour groups: check with **Ferðafélag Íslands** (Map pp238-9; ☎ 568 2535; www.fi.is; Mörkin 6, IS-108 Reykjavík) before you set out.

From Landmannalaugar hut, cross the **Laugahraun** lava field and ascend **Brennisteinsalda** (840m). Cross some rhyolite hills, then descend to the steaming vents at **Stórihver** and continue across the moors (covered in obsidian chunks and extensive snowfields) and a mountain pass to the **Hrafntinnusker hut**. From Hrafntinnusker, the track bounces over parallel rhyolite ridges before ascending steeply to a ridge studded with hot springs and fumaroles. Cross more ridges of descending altitude then drop steeply from the **Jökultungur** ridge into the **Álftavatn** valley, where a 4WD track leads to two **huts**.

There are several stream crossings south of Álftavatn; after 5km, you'll pass the privately owned **Hvanngil** hut and camping ground. Cross the footbridge over the Kaldaklofskvísl, follow the route posted 'Emstrur/Fljótshlíð' and ford the knee-deep Bláfjallakvísl. The track enters a lonely and surreal 5km stretch of black sand and pumice desert, skirting the pyramid-shaped peak, **Stórasúla**. The next barrier is the river **Innri-Emstruá**, which is bridged but may have a knee-deep side channel. After the bridge, continue up to the crest and watch on your left for the 'FÍ Skáli' signpost, which directs you through a desolate desert to the **Botnar** (Emstrur) huts.

Cross a small heath then drop steeply to cross the roiling **Fremri-Emstruá** on a small footbridge. From there, the trail is relatively flat to the Ljósá footbridge. Over the next hill is the more difficult unbridged river **Þrongá**. The onward route on the opposite bank isn't obvious; look for a V-shaped ravine just west of the marked crossing point. There, the track enters the **Þórsmörk** woodland. When you reach a junction, the right fork leads to Reykjavík Excursions' **Húsadalur hut** and the left fork to the Ferðafélag Íslands' **Þórsmörk hut**. Camping is restricted to sites near the huts. For more on Þórsmörk, see p270.

ICELAND DIRECTORY

ACCOMMODATION

Iceland has a full spectrum of accommodation options, from spartan mountain huts, through hostels, working farms, guesthouses and school-based summer rooms, to luxury hotels.

Sleeping-bag accommodation (designated 'sb' in this guide) is a peculiarly Icelandic concept, and a huge boon for those on a budget. Many hostels and guesthouses let you have a bed without sheets, duvet or blankets for a large discount on their standard prices, you use your own sleeping bag.

In this chapter, budget accommodation is defined as a bed for Ikr4000 or less; midrange places offer singles for Ikr4000 to Ikr9000 and doubles for Ikr6000 to Ikr12,000; and top-end places charge from Ikr9000/12,000 (singles/doubles). Reviews are listed in order of preference.

Many places close in winter; check accommodation in advance.

Camping

Make sure your tent is up to the Icelandic weather: storm-force winds and deluges aren't uncommon in summer.

Wild camping is possible in some areas (although not on fenced land without permission, or in national parks and nature reserves), but is often discouraged. With approximately 130 *tjaldsvæði* (organised camping grounds) in towns and at rural farmhouses, there's usually a camp site close at hand. Some have washing machines, cooking facilities and hot showers, others may just have a cold-water tap and toilet block. Camping costs around Ikr700 per person and grounds usually open from June to August.

Standard rules apply: leave sites as you find them, use biodegradable soaps for washing up, carry out rubbish, and bury toilet waste away from surface water.

Campfires are not allowed, so bring a stove. Butane cartridges and petroleum fuels are available in petrol stations and hardware shops. Since they're not allowed on air flights, you might get lucky with other people's leftovers!

A free directory *Útilega: Tjaldsvæði Íslands* (available from tourist offices) lists many of Iceland's camping grounds.

Edda Hotels & Summer Hotels

Once the students leave, many schools become summer hotels, with accommodation ranging from sleeping-bag space in classrooms to standard-looking rooms.

There are 15 **Edda Hótels** (☎ 444 4000; www .hoteledda.is) run on this basis; most have restaurants, and many have geothermal pools. Four are termed 'Edda PLUS' – three-star places where all rooms have private bathrooms, TV and phone. Sleeping-bag accommodation costs from Ikr1700 to Ikr2200 per person, and singles/doubles start at Ikr5800/7200 for a room with washbasin.

Other town and village schools operate their own private summer hotels.

Emergency Huts

ICE-SAR (Icelandic Association for Search & Rescue; ☎ 570 5900; www.icesar.is) and **Félag Íslenskra Bifreiðaeigenda** (Icelandic Automobile Association; ☎ 562 9999; www.fib.is) maintain bright-orange huts on mountain passes and remote coastlines, only to be used in dire emergency (it's illegal to stay there if not). They are stocked with food, fuel and blankets.

Farmhouse Accommodation

Across Iceland, many rural farmhouses offer camp sites, sleeping-bag space, B&B and chalets. Facilities vary: some farms provide meals or have guest kitchens; some have hot pots; and some can organise fishing trips, sheep roundups or horse rental.

Around 150 farmhouses are members of **Ferðaþjónusta Bænda** (Icelandic Farm Holidays; Map pp238-9; ☎ 570 2700; www.farmholidays.is; Síðumúli 2, IS-108 Reykjavík), which publishes an annual listings guide. Twenty-five are wheelchair-accessible; see the website for details.

Guesthouses

There are various types of *gistiheimilið* (guesthouses), from private homes that let rooms to custom-built motels. Most are comfortable and homey, with kitchens, TV lounges, and buffet-style breakfast (either included in the price, or for around Ikr800 extra). Some will also offer sleeping-bag accommodation.

As a general guide, sleeping-bag accommodation costs Ikr1500 to Ikr3500 (usually excluding breakfast); double rooms range from Ikr5000 to Ikr10,500; self-contained flats cost from Ikr6000 to Ikr15,000.

A high percentage of places open from June to August only. Students often take over Reykjavík guesthouses from September to May.

Hotels

Every major town has at least one up-market business-style hotel, usually with bland but comfortable rooms and all the expected amenities. Prices for singles/doubles start at around Ikr9000/11,000, including a buffet breakfast. Two of the largest home-grown chains are **Fosshotels** (☎ 562 4000; www.fosshotel.is), and **Icelandair Hotels** (☎ 444 4000; www.icehotels.is), who also run the Edda chain (left).

Mountain Huts

Sæluhús (mountain huts) sprout up on popular hiking routes, mostly in wilderness areas. Accommodation is of the rough-and-ready variety: sleeping-bag spaces in communal huts. Some huts have cooking facilities, a warden and camping outside.

ICELAND

The huts are open to anyone, but members get a discount. It's highly advisable to book in advance as places fill quickly.

The main mountain-hut provider is **Ferðafélag Íslands** (Icelandic Touring Association; Map pp238-9; ☎ 568 2533; www.fi.is; Mörkin 6, IS-108 Reykjavík). It has 34 huts on its books, although some of these are maintained by local walking clubs. When appropriate, we've given further contact details in this chapter. Sleeping-bag space costs nonmembers from Ikr1200 to Ikr2200; camping (where available) is around Ikr800 per person.

Youth Hostels

Iceland has a network of 26 superb youth hostels, administered by the **Bandalag Íslenskra Farfugla** (Icelandic Youth Hostel Association; Map pp238-9; ☎ 553 8110; www.hostel.is; Sundlaugavegur 34, IS-105 Reykjavík). All hostels have hot showers, cooking facilities, luggage storage and sleeping-bag accommodation, and almost all have family rooms. If you don't have a sleeping bag, you can hire sheets and blankets (Ikr600 per stay). Most are open summer-only, so phone before rolling up out-of-season.

Join **Hostelling International** (HI; www.hihostels.com) before you arrive to benefit from HI member discounts. For a dorm bed, HI members pay around Ikr1900/Ikr2200 (children aged five to 12 years pay half-price), with a surcharge of Ikr1200 if you want a room to yourself. Breakfast (where available) costs Ikr750 to Ikr900 extra.

ACTIVITIES
Dogsledding
For exhilarating, summertime glacier-top action, driving your own huskies is hard to beat. Contact **Dog Steam Tours** (☎ 487 7747; www.dogsledding.is) for further information.

Fishing
Salmon fishing seems like a great idea but a one-day licence may cost anything up to Ikr200,000, making your catch some of the world's most expensive fish! However, you can fish for rainbow trout, sea trout and Arctic char on a more reasonably priced voucher system. Trout fishing runs from April to mid-September but ice fishing is possible in some areas in winter. For further information, contact the **National Angling Association** (☎ 553 1510; www.angling.is).

Hiking, Trekking & Mountaineering
The best way to see the country is undoubtedly on foot, whether on an afternoon hike or a two-week wilderness trek. However, the weather can leave careful plans in tatters: rain, fog and mist are common, and snow may fall in any season at higher altitudes. The www.outdoors.is website gives very good general information about mountaineering and hiking in Iceland.

In the highlands, straightforward hiking only becomes possible in July, August and early September: at other times, routes are impassable without complete winter gear; and in late spring, melting snow turns many tracks into quagmires where whole vehicles have sunk without trace! Unbridged rivers can be difficult to cross at any time of year.

There are stunning hikes and treks all over the country, including in national parks and nature reserves; only the most well-used trails are marked. The most popular walks are in the deserted Hornstrandir peninsula (p256), in the lake-dominated Mývatn area (p262), through Skaftafell National Park (p268), and the Landmannalaugar to Þórsmörk trek (p276) in the highlands. If you are into mountaineering, there are some serious routes, including Hvannadalshnúkur (2119m), Iceland's highest peak.

Use caution when walking with children, especially in fissured areas such as Mývatn and Þingvellir, where narrow cracks in the earth can be hundreds of metres deep. Tough boots are needed for negotiating lava fields.

For details on hiking and mountaineering, contact **Ferðafélag Íslands** (☎ 568 2533; www.fi.is; Mörkin 6, IS-108 Reykjavík), or **Íslenski Alpaklúbburinn** (☎ 581 1700; www.isalp.is/english; Pósthólf 1054, 121 Reykjavík).

Horse Riding
The Icelandic horse (*Equus scandinavicus*) was brought over by the first settlers, and has been prominent in the development of the country. These sweet-natured, small but sturdy animals are perfectly suited to the rough Icelandic terrain and are still used for farm work. They are also ridden recreationally, and are known for their *tölt*, a smooth, distinctive gait which makes riding easy, even for beginners.

You can hire horses through farms and tour agencies throughout the country, with a one-hour/one-day ride costing about Ikr2800/10,000. In September you can also volunteer for the *réttir* (sheep roundup): contact local tourist offices to arrange this.

Horse fanatics might be interested in the **National Horse Festival** (Landsmót; www.landsmot.is /english), which takes place every two years in Skagafjörður in the north of Iceland.

Skiing

Skiers who enjoy out-of-the-way slopes will find some pleasant no-frills skiing in Iceland. In winter, nordic skiing is possible throughout the country, and in the highland areas it continues until early July. The greatest drawbacks are the lack of winter transport in rural areas and bitterly cold winds. Both Reykjavík and Akureyri have winter resorts for downhill skiing (Bláfjöll and Skálafell, the two closest to Reykjavík, get very busy), with ski rental and instructors. A summer ski school operates at Kerlingarfjöll near Hofsjökull in central Iceland.

Snowboarding

The ski resorts nearest to Reykjavík have facilities for snowboarders; Bláfjöll has a dedicated snowboarding track. For four weeks of the year, the **Nikita Iceland Park Project** (www.icelandparkproject.com) runs a snowboarding camp on the Snæfellsnes peninsula, near the glacier.

Swimming

Thanks to an abundance of geothermal heat, every town has at least one *sundlaug* or *sundhöll* (public swimming hall), some with saunas, Jacuzzis and slides. Admission costs around Ikr280/125 per adult/child. There are also natural hot springs, such as those located at Landmannalaugar (p274).

Whale-Watching

Iceland is one of the best places in the world to see whales and dolphins. Quiet oak-hulled boats minimise disruption to the creatures and can get astonishingly close. Regular sailings depart from Húsavík (p261) and Reykjavík (p240), among other places. A three-hour trip costs around Ikr3800, and there are sailings from mid-May to September (in winter, the whales migrate south).

BUSINESS HOURS

Most banks are open from 9.15am to 4pm Monday to Friday. Shops are usually open from 9am to 6pm on weekdays, 10am to noon or 4pm on Saturday. Petrol stations stay open until 10pm generally and supermarkets stay open to 11pm daily. Liquor stores open from 11am to 6pm Monday to Thursday, to 7pm Friday and to 2pm on Saturday. For cafés or bars, these are open from 10am, to 1am Sunday to Thursday and stay open late until 3am or 6am on Friday and Saturday nights, and restaurants are usually open from 6pm to 10pm. Post offices open from 8.30am (or 9am) to 4.30pm (or 5pm) Monday to Friday.

CHILDREN

Icelanders have a relaxed attitude to kids, but there are not many activities provided especially for them. Frequent bad weather may put you off family camping, but everyone can enjoy a ride on a mild-mannered Icelandic horse (opposite).

Children aged two to 11 years pay half fare on Flugfélag Íslands (Air Iceland) flights and tours, and are charged half-price for farmhouse and some other accommodation. Destination Iceland buses and tours charge half fare for ages four to 11. There's a 50% discount at pools, and admission to museums and cinemas varies from full price to free.

Every town has an open-air swimming pool, which will delight waterbabies. Reykjavík contains some attractions suitable for little kids, such as the family fun park and zoo (p243) and feeding the birds on Tjörnin (p243). The most suitable museums for older children are the open-air Árbæjarsafn (p241) and the dramatic Saga Museum (p241).

CUSTOMS

Visitors are permitted to import up to 3kg worth of food provided it doesn't cost more than Ikr13,000 or include animal products. Those aged over 18 years may bring in 200 cigarettes or 250g of other tobacco products. Those aged over 20 years may import duty-free 1L of spirits (22% to 79% alcohol) and 1L of wine (less than 22%); or 1L of spirits and 6L of foreign beer; or 1L of wine and 6L of beer; or 2.25L of wine.

To prevent potential contamination, recreational fishing and horse-riding clothes and equipment require a veterinarian's certificate stating that they have been disinfected. Alternatively, officials can disinfect gear when you arrive (Ikr1800 to Ikr2200).

Vehicle import duty is waived for students and visitors staying less than one month (extendable up to 12 months), but vehicles cannot be sold without payment of duty.

For a full list of customs regulations, see www.tollur.is.

DANGERS & ANNOYANCES

Iceland has a low crime rate, police don't carry guns, and prisoners go home on public holidays. People aren't the danger here; it's nature that you need to be wary of! In geothermal areas avoid thin crusts of lighter coloured soil around steaming fissures and mud pots. Snowfields may overlie fissures, sharp lava chunks, or slippery slopes of scoria (volcanic slag). Don't underestimate the weather: only attempt isolated hiking and glacier ascents if you know what you're doing.

DISABLED TRAVELLERS

Many hotels, restaurants and large shops have facilities for people with disabilities. The airlines can take disabled passengers, as can two of the coastal ferries, the *Baldur* and the *Herjólfur*. Flugfélag Íslands offers discounts to disabled travellers. Facilities aren't available on scheduled bus services, but tours on specially equipped buses can be arranged. For details, contact the tourist information centre in Reykjavík, or the organisation for the disabled, **Sjálfsbjörg** (Map pp238-9; ☎ 550 0300; www.sjalfsbjorg.is; Hátún 12, IS-105 Reykjavík).

EMBASSIES & CONSULATES
Iceland Embassies & Consulates

A full list of Iceland's embassies and consulates is available at www.mfa.is. Icelandic representation abroad includes the following list.

Australia (☎ 02-9365 7345; iceland@bigpond.net.au; 16 Birriga Rd, Bellevue Hill, Sydney, 2000, NSW)
Canada (☎ 613-482 1944; www.iceland.org/ca; 360 Albert St, Ste 710, Ottawa ON K1R 7X7)
Denmark (☎ 33 18 10 50; www.iceland.org/dk; Strandgade 89, DK-1401 Copenhagen K)
Faroe Islands (☎ 30 11 01; info@faroeyard.fo; JC Svabosgøta 31, postbox 65, Tórshavn)

Finland (☎ 09-612 2460; www.islanti.fi; Pohjoisesplanadi 27C, Fin-00100 Helsinki)
France (☎ 01-44 17 32 85; www.iceland.org/fr; 8 Ave Kléber, F-75116 Paris)
Germany (☎ 030-5050 4000; www.iceland.org/de; Rauchstrasse 1, DE-10787 Berlin)
Greenland (☎ 98 12 93; kelly@greennet.gl; c/o Hotel Angmagssalik, Sulup Aqq B725, postbox 117, Tasiilaq)
Ireland (☎ 01-872 9299; jgg@goregrimes.ie; Cavendish House, Smithfield, Dublin)
The Netherlands (☎ 431 3313; robbie@reved.nl; 2nd fl, Strawinskylaan 3037, Amsterdam)
New Zealand (☎ 09-379 4720; ebarratt@sanford.co.nz; c/o Sanford Ltd, 22 Jellicoe St, Auckland)
Norway (☎ 2323 7530; www.iceland.org/no; Stortingsgata 30, NO-0244 Oslo)
Sweden (☎ 08-442 8300; www.iceland.org/se; Kommendörsgatan 35, SE-114 58 Stockholm)
UK (☎ 020-7259 3999; www.iceland.org/uk; 2a Hans St, London SW1X 0JE)
USA (☎ 202-265 6653; www.iceland.org/us; 1156 15th St NW, Ste 1200, Washington, DC 20005-1704)

Embassies & Consulates in Iceland

The following countries have representation in Reykjavík:
Canada (Map p242; ☎ 575 6500; rkjvk@international.gc.ca; Túngata 14)
Denmark (Map p242; ☎ 575 0300; www.ambrey kjavik.um.dk; Hverfisgata 29)
Finland (Map p242; ☎ 510 0100; www.finland.is; Túngata 30)
France (Map p242; ☎ 551 7621; www.ambafrance.is; Túngata 22)
Germany (Map p242; ☎ 530 1100; embager@internet.is; Laufásvegur 31)
Ireland (☎ 554 2355; davidsch@islandia.is; Ásbúð 106, 210 Garðabær)
The Netherlands (Map pp238-9; ☎ 533 1002; holland@holland.is; Borgartún 33)
Norway (Map pp238-9; ☎ 520 0700; www.noregur.is; Fjólugata 17)
Sweden (Map pp238-9; ☎ 520 1230; www.sweden abroad.com; Lágmúli 7)
UK (Map p242; ☎ 550 5100; www.britishembassy.gov.uk; Laufásvegur 31)
USA (Map p242; ☎ 562 9100; www.usa.is; Laufásvegur 21)

FESTIVALS & EVENTS

In addition to the festivals listed opposite, there are various arts festivals and sports tournaments whose dates vary from year to year. For forthcoming live music festivals, see www.musik.is.

February

Þorrablót This midwinter feast is marked with knuckle-whitening meals: see p236 for a sample menu.

Bolludagur (Bun Day; 23 February) Icelanders gorge themselves sick on puff-pastry cream buns. Kids get up early to 'beat' the buns out of their parents with a 'bun wand' (bolluvöndur).

Sprengidagur (Bursting Day; 24 February) The feast continues. The aim is to stuff yourself with saltkjöt og baunir (salted meat and split peas) until you burst. Both are Lenten traditions.

March

Beer Day (1 March) Dating back to the glorious day in 1989 when beer was legalised in Iceland. As you'd expect, Reykjavík's clubs and bars get particularly wild.

April

Sumardagurinn Fyrsti (First Day of Summer) Arrives optimistically early on the first Thursday after April 18, with Reykjavík holding the biggest carnival-style bash. (The First Day of Winter, Fyrsti Vetrardagur, on the third Saturday of October, does not inspire similar merriment.)

May

Reykjavík Arts Festival (www.artfest.is) The city is taken over by local and international theatre performances, films, lectures and music during this two-week event.

June

Sjómannadagurinn The first Sunday is dedicated to seafarers. The Seamen's Union sponsors a party in each coastal town.

Independence Day (17 June) The largest nationwide festival, commemorating the founding of the Republic of Iceland in 1944 with parades and general merriness. Tradition has it that the sun isn't supposed to shine. And it usually doesn't!

Midsummer Celebrated around 24 June in Iceland, but with much less fervour than on the Scandinavian mainland.

August

Þjóðhátíð Vestmannaeyjar This earth-shaking event occurs in Heimaey on the August bank holiday, commemorating the day in 1874 when foul weather prevented the islanders partying when Iceland's constitution was established.

Verslunarmannahelgi Also celebrated on the August bank holiday, the rest of the country celebrates with barbecues, horse competitions, camping and family reunions. Wild boozing takes place in the national parks and at Þórsmörk.

Gay Pride Thousands of people parade carnival-style through the streets of Reykjavík on the third weekend.

Reykjavík Marathon With shorter distances and fun runs for those who like to grit their teeth less.

Culture Night Held on a Saturday in Reykjavík in mid-August, with art, music, dance and a fireworks finale.

September

Réttir In the highlands, the autumn sheep roundup is an occasion for rural camaraderie and festivities.

Reykjavík Film Festival This annual occurance sees blockbusters make way for international art films in cinemas across the city, and talks from film directors from home and abroad.

Reykjavík Jazz Festival (www.jazz.is) Another fun yearly cultural event is the Jazz Festival with jazz concerts around the city.

October

Iceland Airwaves (www.icelandairwaves.com) This four-day event, in Reykjavík near the end of October, is one of the world's most cutting-edge music festivals: don't expect to sleep.

GAY & LESBIAN TRAVELLERS

Icelanders have a fairly open attitude towards gays and lesbians. For specific information, contact the gay and lesbian organisation **Samtökin '78** (Map p242; ☎ 552 7878; office@samtokin78.is; 4th fl, Laugavegur 3, IS-101 Reykjavík), which doubles as an informal gay community centre with a drop-in café (8pm to 11pm Monday and Thursday). See the website www.gayice.is for news and events.

HOLIDAYS

The following annual holidays are observed in Iceland:

New Year's Day 1 January
Maundy Thursday Thursday before Easter
Good Friday to Easter Monday March/April
First Day of Summer 1st Thursday after April 18
Labour Day 1 May
Ascension Day May
Whit Sunday & Whit Monday May
Independence Day 17 June
Shop & Office Workers' Holiday First Monday in August
Christmas Eve 24 December (afternoon)
Christmas Day 25 December
Boxing Day 26 December
New Year's Eve 31 December (afternoon)

INTERNET RESOURCES

Iceland Review – What's On guide (www.whatson.is)
Icelandic Tourist Board (www.icetourist.is)
Icelandic Tourist Board – North America (www.goiceland.org)
Statistics Iceland (www.statice.is)
Visit Reykjavík (www.visitreykjavik.is)

ICELAND

LEGAL MATTERS

Drink-driving laws are very strict in Iceland; one drink can put you over the legal limit of 0.05% blood-alcohol content. The penalty is loss of your licence plus a large fine.

Penalties for possession, use or trafficking of illegal drugs are strict, with long prison sentences and heavy fines.

The legal age for drinking alcohol in Iceland is 20.

MAPS

Ask tourist offices for the free *Map of Reykjavík* and *Around Iceland* booklets (with bags of information plus town plans).

Landmælingar Íslands (National Land Survey of Iceland; ☎ 430 9000; www.lmi.is; Stillholt 16-18, IS-300 Akranes) publishes several series of high-quality maps covering the whole country, purchasable via its website. Most drivers use the general 1:500,000 *Ferðakort Touring Map*. Also useful are the 1:25,000 maps of Skaftafell and Þingvellir, the 1:50,000 maps of Vestmannaeyjar and Mývatn, and the 1:100,000 maps of Hornstrandir, Snæfellsnes, and the Landmannalaugar to Þórsmörk trek.

Landmælingar Íslands maps are available from tourist offices and bookshops all over Iceland.

MEDIA
Magazines

The free fortnightly **Grapevine** (www.grapevine.is) magazine is an excellent read for Icelandic news and reviews. It's available online, or from tourist offices, hotels, bars and even bus stations.

The slicker English-language magazine **Iceland Review** (Map pp238-9; ☎ 5127575; www.iceland review.com; Borgartún 23, IS-105 Reykjavík) is available on subscription for US$40 per year (four issues).

Newspapers

Iceland's main daily newspaper is *Morgunblaðið*. German-, French- and English-language periodicals are available at large bookshops throughout the country.

Radio & TV

The BBC World Service is relayed at FM 94.3 (Reykjavík only). Icelandic TV stations broadcast subtitled British and American programmes during prime time.

MONEY

Icelandic VAT is included in the prices of goods. However, if you spend over Ikr4000 in a shop offering 'Iceland Tax-Free Shopping', you can claim back up to 15%. Shop staff will give you a tax-refund form: hand it in at the tourist office, the airport or the ferry terminal for a rebate. If you spend over Ikr40,000, take your forms and goods to customs before checking in.

Also see (below) for general information about using your debit cards and ATMs abroad.

ATMs

You can draw cash from any bank using MasterCard or Visa; and from Íslandsbanki using Diners Club. Exchange rates for ATM cards are usually good.

Credit Cards

MasterCard and Visa are accepted everywhere; Diners Club and American Express are less commonly used. Icelanders use cards for grocery shopping and other small purchases.

Moneychangers

Travellers cheques in foreign denominations, postal cheques and banknotes may be exchanged for Icelandic currency at banks for a small commission (commission-free at Landsbanki Íslands). Beware of using other exchange offices; commissions can reach 8.75% and exchange rates are lower. Any leftover krónur may be exchanged for foreign currency before departure.

Tipping

As service and VAT are always included in prices, tipping isn't required in Iceland.

POST

The **Icelandic postal system** (Pósturinn; www.postur .is) is both reliable and efficient. An airmail letter or postcard to Europe costs economy/priority Ikr65/75; to places outside Europe it costs Ikr70/95.

Poste restante is available in all cities and villages, but Reykjavík is best set up to handle it. Mail should be addressed with your name to Poste Restante, Central Post Office, Pósthússtræti 5, IS-101 Reykjavík, Iceland.

TELEPHONE

For public telephone boxes in Reykjavík, see p240. Elsewhere, there's usually a phone outside the post office or in the petrol station. Many payphones accept credit cards. Be aware that telephone directories are alphabetised by first name, so Guðrun Halldórsdóttir would be listed before Jón Einarsson.

Mobile Phones

Most European phones are compatible with the GSM network, used in Iceland; for information, contact your phone company. You can generally only pick up a signal in populated places. Mobile phones can also be rented from **Síminn** (☎ 550 6000; www.siminn.is; Ármúli 27, Reykjavík), for around Ikr400 per day plus deposit.

Phone Codes

Direct dialling is available to Europe, North America and elsewhere. After dialling the international access code (☎ 00 from Iceland), dial your country code, area/city code and the telephone number.

For dialling into Iceland from abroad, the country code is ☎ 354. There are no area codes: just follow the country code with the seven-digit number.

Within Iceland, just dial the seven-digit number. Most Icelandic mobile phone numbers begin with the digit '8'.

Directory assistance (international) ☎ 1811
Directory assistance (local) ☎ 118
Operator assistance ☎ 115
Reverse-charge (collect) calls ☎ 533 5019 for assistance

Phonecards

The smallest-denomination phonecard (for use in public telephone boxes) costs Ikr500, and can be bought from post offices and Síminn telephone offices.

> **EMERGENCY NUMBERS**
>
> For police, ambulance and fire services in Iceland, dial ☎ 112.

TIME

Iceland is always on GMT/UTC, and it has no daylight-saving time. So from late October to late March, Iceland is on the same time as London, five hours ahead of

New York and 11 hours behind Sydney. In the northern hemisphere's summer, Iceland is one hour behind London, four hours ahead of New York and 10 hours behind Sydney.

TOURIST INFORMATION

You'll find tourist offices with friendly staff in towns all over the country. Pick up the useful *Around Iceland* (general tourist guide) and *Áning* (accommodation guide); both are annual publications and they're free.

The **Icelandic Tourist Board** (☎ 535 5500; www.icetourist.is; Lækjargata 3, IS-101 Reykjavík) is the umbrella organisation in charge of tourism. The main tourist office in Reykjavík is called **Upplýsingamiðstöð Ferðamála** (Map p242; ☎ 590 1500; www.visitreykjavik.is; Aðalstræti 2).

TOURS

Iceland's many private tour-bus operators are an excellent option if you're short of time, or want to access beautiful but remote locations without hassle. Most companies run in conjunction with adventure-tour operators, so you can also book snowmobile, horse-riding, whale-watching, rafting, hiking, bird-watching, or Northern Lights tours. You can often do the same trips by Super Jeep or Super Truck (prices are at least double those of a bus tour). The following is a brief list of some of the best operators.

Dick Phillips (☎ 01434-381440; www.icelandic-travel .com; Whitehall House, Nenthead, Alston, Cumbria, CA9 3PS) British-based Dick Phillips runs a specialist Icelandic travel service, and has decades of experience leading wild hiking, cycling and skiing trips.

Ferðafélag Íslands (Icelandic Touring Association; Map pp238-9; ☎ 568 2533; www.fi.is; Mörkin 6, IS-108 Reykjavík) Lead summer treks in Hornstrandir, Landmannalaugar and Þórsmörk, and also has some bus tours and cross-country skiing trips.

Iceland Excursions (Allrahanda; Map pp238-9; ☎ 540 1313; www.icelandexcursions.is; Höfðatún 12) The cheapest bus-tour operator, with comprehensive day trips plus horse riding, whale-watching, underground explorations, diving, and self-drive holidays.

IcelandTotal (Map pp238-9; ☎ 585 4300; www.iceland total.com; Lágmúli 4, IS-108 Reykjavík) Inexpensive tours often using small local operators and scheduled bus services. Also organises special-interest tours, eg bird-watching, fishing, cycling.

Nonni Travel (Map p258; ☎ 461 1841; www.nonni travel.is; Brekkugata 5, PO Box 336, IS-602 Akureyri)

ICELAND

Rafting, horse riding, whale-spotting, Super Jeep tours and self-drive trips; specialists in excursions to Greenland.

Reykjavík Excursions (Kynnisferðir; Map pp238-9; ☎ 562 1011; www.re.is; BSÍ Bus Terminal, Vatnsmýrarvegur 10, Reykjavík) The most popular bus-tour operator has summer and winter programmes. Extras include horse riding, snowmobiling, and themed tours tying in with festivals.

Útivist (Map pp238-9; ☎ 562 1000; www.utivist.is; Laugavegur 178, IS-105 Reykjavík) Day trips and weekend hiking tours.

VISAS

The Schengen Agreement means that those from Austria, Belgium, Denmark, Finland, France, Germany, Greece, Italy, Luxembourg, the Netherlands, Norway, Portugal, Spain and Sweden can enter Iceland for up to three months as a tourist with a valid identity card.

Citizens of the European Economic Area (EEA), including Ireland and Great Britain, can visit for up to three months on a passport that is valid for at least four months from their date of arrival.

Citizens from America, Australia, New Zealand, Japan and Canada can travel in Iceland without a visa for up to three months within any six-month period, with the time limit beginning on the first entry to any Schengen Agreement nation.

Other nationalities need a visa before arriving in Iceland.

VOLUNTEERING

A volunteering holiday is a good (and relatively cheap) way of getting intimately involved with Iceland's people and landscape. One of the longest-running projects is the conservation work done by **British Trust for Conservation Volunteers** (BTCV; www.btcv.org) in Skaftafell National Park (see p268).

TRANSPORT IN ICELAND

GETTING THERE & AWAY
Air

Keflavík airport (☎ 425 0600, flight times 425 0777; www.keflavikairport.com), located 48km west of Reykjavík, is Iceland's main gateway. Flights to/from Greenland and the Faroe Islands use Reykjavík domestic airport in the city centre. A couple of international flights per week land at the tiny Akureyri airport, in Iceland's 'second city' in the north.

Fares in this section are general indications only, and are for average-priced high-season return tickets. Cheaper deals are generally available if you are flexible, or if you travel in the low season.

AIRLINES FLYING TO & FROM ICELAND

Only a few airlines have scheduled flights to Keflavík, Reykjavík and Akureyri airports. All have great safety records:

Atlantic Airways (airline code RC; ☎ Faroe Islands 34 10 00; www.atlanticairways.com)

British Airways (airline code BA; ☎ 421 7374; www.britishairways.com)

Flugfélag Íslands (Air Iceland; airline code NY; ☎ 570 3030; www.airiceland.is)

Icelandair (airline code FI; ☎ 505 0700; www.icelandair.net)

Iceland Express (airline code HW; ☎ 550 0600; www.icelandexpress.com)

SAS (airline code SK; ☎ 505 0300; www.scandinavian.net)

CONTINENTAL EUROPE

There are regular direct Icelandair flights to Keflavík from Amsterdam (€300), Copenhagen (Dkr2000), Frankfurt (€300), Oslo (Nkr2000), Paris (€400) and Stockholm (Skr3000), most of which take approximately 3½ hours. Icelandair also has seasonal flights between Keflavík and Barcelona, Berlin, Helsinki, Madrid, Milan, Munich and Zürich, taking between six and nine hours.

Iceland Express flies year-round 14 times weekly between Keflavík and Copenhagen (Dkr2300, three hours). In summer, there are two to four flights weekly between Keflavík and Alicante (€415, four hours), Berlin, Frankfurt, Friedriechshafen (all €450, 3½ hours), Göteborg and Stockholm (both Skr3000, three hours); and between Akureyri and Copenhagen (Dkr3300, three hours).

SAS runs direct flights from Keflavík to Oslo (Nkr3000, 2¾ hours).

GREENLAND & THE FAROE ISLANDS

In summer, Flugfélag Íslands flies from Reykjavík to Greenland: to Kulusuk (Ikr66,000, two hours) six times a week; and to Narsarsuaq (Ikr60,000, two hours) twice weekly.

Flugfélag Íslands and Atlantic Airways fly between the Faroe Islands and Reykjavík (Ikr45,000, 1½ hours) up to four times weekly from April to October.

(Continued on page 293)

DAVID TIPLING

The aurora borealis (northern lights; p22), north-central Finland

Skier hiking in the midnight sun, northern Norway (p350)

CHRISTIAN ASLUND

ANDERS BLOMQVIST

Hikers in Jostedalsbreen National Park (p344), Norway

Patrons at a Copenhagen restaurant (p50) warm up with wine

MARTIN MOOS

Opposite: Skier in the midnight sun, northern Norway (p350)

CHRISTIAN ASLUND

Snowmobiler (p485), Finland

DAVID TIPLING

ANDERS BLO

Snowboarders at Riksgränsen (p466), Sweden

Winter sports in Stockholm (p394), Sweden

JONATHAN SMITH

CHRISTER FREDRIKSSON

ERNEST MANEWAL

ANDERS BLOMQVIST

CHRISTIAN A

Swimmers near Stryn (p345), Norway

HOLGER LEUE

Lighthouse, Jutland (p82), Denmark

Cyclists in Bornholm (p67), Denmark

ANDERS BLOMQVIST

Views around Lake Siljan (p422), Sweden

Tent by the water's edge, Telemark (p325), southern Norway

Jotunheimen National Park (p329), Norway

WAYNE WALTON

Helsinki train station (p160), Finland

NK department store (p410), Stockholm

MARTIN LLADO

Arne Jacobsen furniture (p38) for sale in Copenhagen, Denmark

Oresunds Bridge, Copenhagen (p40), Denmark

ANDERS BLO

JONATHAN SMITH

(Continued from page 284)

UK

Icelandair (☎ 0870 787 4020; www.icelandair.net) has flights to Keflavík from London Heathrow (UK£200, two hours) at least twice daily. Between April and October, there are flights from Glasgow (UK£150, one hour) four or five times per week; and two flights per week from Manchester (UK£380, 1½ hours).

Internet-based airline **Iceland Express** (☎ 0870 850 0737; www.icelandexpress.com) flies twice daily (less frequently in winter) from London Stansted to Keflavík (UK£300, three hours). It also runs two flights per week from London Stansted to Akureyri (UK£230, three hours).

British Airways (☎ 0870 850 9850; www.britishairways.com) are also muscling in on the Iceland routes, and now have a new service from Keflavík to London Gatwick (UK£300, two hours).

From Ireland, the cheapest way is to fly with **Ryanair** (www.ryanair.com) from Dublin to London Stansted, where you can catch the Iceland Express flight to Keflavík.

USA

There are daily Icelandair flights between Keflavík and Boston, and several flights a week between Keflavík and Baltimore/ Washington, Minneapolis, New York and Orlando. A new summer service departs from San Francisco four times weekly. Online return fares from New York to Keflavík cost about US$900; the flight takes around six hours. If you're flying with Icelandair from the US to Britain or Europe, you can include a free stopover in Iceland as part of your travel itinerary.

Sea

CARGO SHIP

Icelandic cargo-shipper **Eimskip** (☎ 525 7000; www.eimskip.com) sails the route Rotterdam–Hamburg–Göteborg–Århus–Fredrikstad–Tórshavn–Reykjavík, which takes eight days, returning to Rotterdam via eastern Iceland and Tórshavn only. The shipper can take up to three passengers on each of its vessels *Dettifoss* and *Goðafoss,* although passengers are not accepted between mid-October to mid-April. The trip from Rotterdam costs €1124 per person (€806 for the return journey), and €488 for a car.

FERRY

You can travel to Seyðisfjörður in eastern Iceland from Bergen (Norway), Hanstholm (Denmark), Lerwick (Shetland Islands, UK) and Tórshavn (Faroe Islands) by the **Smyril Line**'s (www.smyril-line.fo) smart car-ferry *Norröna.* See p502 for the sailing schedule, and for details of the linking ferry from Aberdeen to Lerwick.

GETTING AROUND

Air

There's an extensive network of domestic flights in Iceland, the fastest way to get from place to place. Flexible travel plans are essential, though, since schedules are dependent on the weather.

Flight prices given in the chapter are for full-fare one-way tickets; however, there are often internet offers, and you may be able to snap up standby tickets for up to half-price. There are significant discounts for senior citizens, students and children.

The main domestic airline, **Flugfélag Íslands** (Air Iceland; ☎ 570 3030; www.airiceland.is), has daily flights in summer between Reykjavík and Akureyri (Ikr10,565, 45 minutes), Egilsstaðir (Ikr11,975, one hour) and Ísafjörður (Ikr10,565, 40 minutes). Landsflug operates flights to smaller airstrips in Iceland, including several flights daily from Reykjavík to Vestmannaeyjar (Ikr7180, 30 minutes): book tickets through Flugfélag Íslands.

AIR PASSES

Flugfélag Íslands offers four-/five-/six-sector air passes costing Ikr29,700/33,700/38,700. These are valid for one month and must be bought outside Iceland. There's also a Fly As You Please ticket which gives 12 days of unlimited internal flights for Ikr47,000.

Domestic airport tax (Ikr930) has to be paid on every departure.

Bicycle

Cycling is one of the best ways to view Iceland's incredible landscape. However, gale-force winds, sandstorms, sleet and sudden flurries of snow add to the challenge! Bring the best waterproofing money can buy; and remember, you can always put your bike on a bus if things become intolerable. A mountain bike is probably more practical than a touring rig – you can get off the

Ring Rd onto minor roads and unsurfaced tracks. It is wise to bring plenty of spares and several puncture repair kits. The Kjölur Rte through the interior has bridges over all major rivers, so it's accessible to cyclists.

Domestic airline flights charge Ikr3200 per bicycle. You can carry bikes on the long-distance buses for Ikr600 to Ikr1000, but space may be a problem at busy times.

In areas best suited to cycling, such as Mývatn, Reykjavík and Akureyri, bicycle hire costs around Ikr1700 per day, plus deposit. Children under 15 must wear a helmet by law.

The **Icelandic Mountain Bike Club** (☎ 562 0099; www.mmedia.is/~ifhk/tourist.htm; Brekkustígur 2) and **Icebike** (www.icebike.net) have lots of information and links about touring in Iceland.

Boat

The main car ferries operating in Iceland are *Herjólfur*, between Þorlákshöfn and Vestmannaeyjar (p272); *Baldur*, between Flatey, Stykkishólmur and Brjánslækur (p254); and *Sæfari*, between Dalvík, Hrísey and Grímsey (p260).

Bus

Iceland's long-distance bus network is divided between several private companies who provide routes in different areas of the country. They're overseen by **BSÍ** (Bifreiðastöð Íslands; ☎ 562 1011; www.bsi.is), based in the BSÍ bus terminal on Vatnsmýrarvegur in Reykjavík. The booking desk sells tickets, and distributes the free *Ísland á Eigin Vegum* (Iceland on Your Own) brochure, which contains timetable information for some southern journeys. From June to August, there are regular buses to most places on the Ring Rd, and to larger towns in the Westfjords. During the rest of the year, the service is limited or nonexistent: check with BSÍ or the companies below for details. The main bus companies include the following:

Austurleid+-Kynnisferðir (☎ 545 1717; www .austurleid.is) South and east Iceland.

Flybus (☎ 562 1011; www.flybus.is) Reykjavík to Keflavík airport.

SBK Travel (☎ 420 6000; www.sbk.is) Keflavík and Reykjanes.

Stjörnubílar (☎ 456 3518, 893 6356; www.stjornubilar .is) Westfjords.

Trex-Hópferðamiðstöðin (☎ 587 6000; www.trex.is) West and north Iceland.

BUS PASSES

Bus passes are available from BSÍ, and can save money on long journeys. However, the usefulness of the Omnibus winter and Western Fjords passes are questionable because of sparse bus services.

Full-Circle Passport (Hringmiði; Ikr24,900; ☽ Jun-Aug) Valid for one circuit of the Ring Rd in one direction, stopping wherever you like. An extension (Ikr29,900) allows travel from Reykjavík to Akureyri through the interior (via the Kjölur Rte) instead of the Ring Rd; and between Kirkjubæjarklaustur and Hella via Landmannalaugar instead of the Ring Rd.

Full-Circle Passport/Western Fjords (Ikr37,500) As the Full-Circle Pass, plus one circuit of the Westfjords, reached only via the ferry *Baldur* (from Stykkishólmur).

Omnibus Pass (Tímamiði; 1-/2-/3-/4-week pass Ikr28,700/40,200/51,700/57,400; ☽ mid-May–mid-Sep) Allows unrestricted travel on scheduled buses (excluding interior bus routes). A limited version of the one-week pass is available for Ikr17,300 mid-September to mid-May.

Car & Motorcycle

AUTOMOBILE ASSOCIATION

The Icelandic national motoring association is **Félag Íslenskra Bifreiðaeigenda** (FÍB; ☎ 414 9999; www.fib.is; Borgartún 33, Reykjavík). Membership is only open to Iceland residents. However, if you already have breakdown cover with an automobile association that's affiliated to ARC Europe, you may be covered by the FÍB – check with your home association.

BRING YOUR OWN VEHICLE

It's relatively easy to bring a vehicle on the ferry from mainland Europe. Drivers must carry the vehicle's registration documents, proof of valid insurance (a 'green card') and a driving licence (EU, North American and Australian licences are fine: otherwise you may need an international driving permit). After vehicle inspection, an import permit will be issued which lasts for a month, after which you must export the vehicle or apply for a permit extension. Contact the **Directorate of Customs** (☎ 560 0300; www.tollur.is) for further information. Also see p508.

FUEL & SPARE PARTS

Petrol prices around the country are fixed: unleaded 95 octane (*blýlaust, 95 okt*) costs Ikr134.4 per litre, and diesel Ikr128.3. Leaded petrol and LRP (lead replacement petrol) aren't available. Outside Reykjavík, petrol station opening hours vary, but out-of-hours there's usually a Visa or Master-Card-operated pump. Service stations can be quite widely dispersed; make sure you fill up when you have the chance, and carry a jack, jumpleads, spare tyre etc. Getting stranded on a cold and lonely road is no fun at all.

HIRE

Although rates are expensive by international standards, prices compare favourably against bus or internal air travel. The cheapest vehicles, such as a Toyota Yaris, normally cost around Ikr8900 per day, with unlimited mileage and VAT included. Rental charges for 4WD vehicles are at least twice that. The Reykjavík tourist office keeps details of special offers.

You must be at least 20 years old to hire a car, and will need to show a recognised licence (most firms are happy with your home licence, although you could bring an international driving permit to be on the safe side) and pay by credit card.

ROAD CONDITIONS & HAZARDS

Icelandic highways aren't suitable for high-speeds – they're two-lane affairs, often narrowing to a single-lane over bridges, and there are sometimes long unsurfaced sections. Headlight and radiator protection from dust and rocks is advisable. Road edges are often steeply cambered, with no shoulders or margins. Beware of oncoming cars driving in the middle of the road.

Four-wheel drive vehicles are needed on the F-numbered (interior) highway system.

If you're planning to drive through the interior, do so with an accompanying vehicle – there are no services, and glacial rivers and drifting sand pose real threats. It goes without saying that you'll need full tool/repair kits (and the expertise to use them) and emergency supplies. It's illegal to drive off-road or off-track: Icelandic soil and vegetation are extremely fragile, and damage caused by vehicles can be irreparable.

Current road conditions can be seen on the website of the **Icelandic Meteorological Office** (www.vedur.is/english).

ROAD RULES

Drive on the right and keep your headlights on at all times. The use of seat belts (front and rear) is compulsory. In urban areas, the speed limit is 50km/h or less. On paved/unpaved roads, the speed limit is 90/80km/h. Drink-driving laws are very strict in Iceland and the legal limit is set at 0.05% blood-alcohol content. The penalty for driving over the limit is loss of your licence plus a large fine.

Slow down or give way at blind peaks (marked *blindhæð*) and on single-breadth bridges (marked *einbreið brú*).

Hitching

Lonely Planet does not recommend hitching. Summer hitching is possible but can be inconsistent. The best idea is to find a petrol station, then try to charm drivers who have stopped for a break. At least if waits are long, you can get a coffee! See Hitching in the Transport chapter (p510).

NORWAY

Norway

Visitors leave the world's most expensive country dumbstruck by the staggering array of variety and beauty they encountered in its vast natural landscape. From Finnmark's empty tundra to enormous blue glaciers to the unnerving beauty of narrow fjords, Norway offers terrain for some of the world's most scenic skiing, hiking and fishing. Though if such activities sound mundane, adventure seekers can dive for crabs in the Barents Sea or partake in dogsledding expeditions across frozen Svalbard in the distant polar north.

A country of just 4.6 million people, most of Norway's major cities (there aren't many) are charmingly picturesque with districts of old wooden buildings, harbours of fishing boats and ferries and plenty of café, whose outdoor terraces fill with overeager Norwegians from the very moment the country's long, dark winter comes to an end. Oslo and Bergen are the biggest cities, and each enjoys esoteric museums (think Viking Ships and Leprosy), lively nightlife and public transportation that takes you straight into the wilderness.

FAST FACTS

- **Area** 324,220 sq km
- **Capital** Oslo
- **Currency** krone (Nkr); €1 = Nkr7.96; US$1 = Nkr6.26; £1 = Nkr11.49; A$1 = Nkr4.72; ¥100 = Nkr5.39; NZ$1 = Nkr3.86
- **Famous for** a-ha
- **Official Language** Bokmål and Nynorsk
- **Phrases** hei (hello), takk (thanks), ja (yes), nei (no), stengt (closed)
- **Population** 4.6 million
- **Telephone codes** country code ☎ 47; there are no regional codes; international access code ☎ 00
- **Visa** Not necessary for most nationalities

HIGHLIGHTS

- Sleep in a fisherman's *rorbuer* (shanty) in a remote village on the craggy **Lofoten Islands** (p361)
- Explore lively **Bergen** (p330), whose hilly coastal locale and delightful urban fabric make for a pretty place to drink, eat and club
- Ruin future attempts to appreciate nature by glimpsing the incomparable beauty of **Hardangerfjord** (p340) or **Sognefjord** (p342)
- Hike or ski across the sublime **Jostedalsbreen glacier** (p344)
- Enjoy the scenic countryside on the **Oslo–Bergen train** (p329), a seven-hour race over mountains and snowy plateaus

ITINERARIES

- **One week** Spend a full day in Oslo, then take the train to Bergen. Spend two nights in the city before renting a car for an unrushed jaunt around Hardangerfjord, sleeping in Lofthus. Continue to Sognefjord and stay in Balestrand or Fjærland. Drive to Bergen, return the car, and spend your last day in Bergen or Oslo.
- **Two weeks** After dumping the car in Bergen, take the overnight *Hurtigruten* to Ålesund. Look at Art Nouveau buildings, sleep, and fly to Trondheim. Poke around, take the night train to Bodø and catch a boat to the Lofoten Islands. Sleep here for two nights, then take the

---

HOW MUCH?

- **Hot dog** Nkr15
- **Loaf of bread** Nkr18
- **Bottle of house white** Nkr120
- **Cheese slicer** Nkr20 (in a grocery store, not in tourist shops)
- **Short taxi ride** Nkr90

LONELY PLANET INDEX

- **1L petrol** Nkr9.5
- **1L bottle of water** Nkr15
- **Aass beer** Nkr52
- **Souvenir T-shirt** Nkr65
- **Kebab** Nkr50

---

overnight *Hurtigruten* to Tromsø where you can stay a day or two before returning to Oslo.

CLIMATE & WHEN TO GO

The rainy climate of mainland Norway is surprisingly mild for its latitude; thanks to the warming effects of the Gulf Stream, all its coastal ports remain ice-free throughout the year. Average July temperatures are 16°C in the Oslo area and 11°C in the north, though temperature extremes are possible. In winter, heavy snowfalls are common and make for superb skiing. In January, the average maximum temperature is 1°C in the south and -3°C in the north. However, it can get much colder, especially in areas away from the coast.

Norway is at its best and brightest from May to September. Late spring is a particularly pleasant time: daylight hours are long, and most hostels and sights are open but uncrowded. Peak tourist season is mid-June through August.

HISTORY

Norway's first settlers arrived around 11,000 years ago with the end of the ice age. As the glaciers melted, the earliest hunters and gatherers moved in from Siberia, pursuing migrating reindeer herds. You can see the prehistoric rock drawings of these hunters in the far north on Alta (p370). Shortly afterwards, nomadic European hunters arrived in the south of the country.

Norway's greatest impact on history was during the Viking Age, a period usually dated from the plundering of England's Lindisfarne monastery by Nordic pirates in AD 793. Through the next century, the Vikings conducted raids throughout Europe and established settlements in the Shetland, Orkney and Hebridean islands, the Dublin area (Ireland) and in Normandy (named after the 'North men'). The Viking leader Harald Hårfagre (Fairhair) unified Norway after the decisive naval battle at Hafrsfjord near Stavanger in AD 872; King Olav Haraldsson, adopting the religion of the lands he had conquered, converted the Norwegians to Christianity and founded the Church of Norway in 1024. See Viking artefacts firsthand in Oslo's Vikingskipshuset (p306) and the Viking Museum (p364) in Lofoten.

NORWAY

The Viking Age declined after 1066, with the defeat of the Norwegian king, Harald Hardråda, at the Battle of Stamford Bridge in England. Norwegian naval power was finished off for good when Alexander III, King of Scots, defeated a Viking naval force at the Battle of Largs (Scotland) in 1263.

In the early 14th century, Oslo emerged as a centre of power and a period of growth followed until 1349, when the bubonic plague swept the country, wiping out nearly two-thirds of the population. In 1380, Norway was absorbed into a union with Denmark that lasted more than 400 years.

Denmark ceded Norway to Sweden in 1814. In 1884 a parliamentary government was introduced in Norway and a growing nationalist movement eventually led to a peaceful secession from Sweden in 1905. In a referendum, Norwegians voted in favour of a monarchy over a republic. Having no royal family of its own, Norway's parliament selected Prince Carl of Denmark to be king. Upon acceptance, he took the title Håkon VII and named his infant son Olav, both prominent names from Norway's Viking past.

Norway stayed neutral during WWI. Despite restating its neutrality at the start of WWII, it was attacked by the Nazis on 9 April 1940, falling to the Germans after a two-month struggle. King Håkon set up a government in exile in England, and placed most of Norway's merchant fleet under the command of the Allies. Although Norway remained occupied until the end of the war, it had an active Resistance movement.

The royal family returned to Norway in June 1945. King Håkon died in 1957 and was succeeded by his son, Olav V, a popular king who reigned until his death in January 1991. The current monarch is Harald V, Olav's son, who was crowned in June 1991.

Norway joined the European Free Trade Association (EFTA) in 1960, but has been reluctant to forge closer bonds with other European nations, in part due to concerns about the impact on its fishing industry and small-scale farming industry. In 1972, Norwegians voted against joining the European Community (EC) amid a divisive national debate. It took two decades for membership to once again become a high-profile issue. During 1994 a second national referendum was held, this time on joining the EC's successor, the EU, and voters rejected that proposal as well. For the last decade, the EU issue has waned and waxed in popular opinion, and at time of writing there were no serious proposals to initiate a membership drive.

PEOPLE

Norway has 4.6 million people and one of the lowest population densities in Europe. The majority of modern Norwegians are middle class. Immigration is strictly controlled and only bona fide refugees are admitted. The largest cities are Oslo with 500,000 residents, followed by Bergen, Trondheim and Stavanger.

Most Norwegians are of Nordic origin, and are thought to have descended from central and northern European tribes who migrated northwards around 8000 years ago. In addition, there are about 40,000 Sami (formerly known as Lapps), the indigenous people of the far north of Norway who now make up the country's largest ethnic minority. Some Sami still live a traditional nomadic life, herding reindeer in Finnmark.

RELIGION

Around 86% of Norwegians belong to the Church of Norway, a Protestant Evangelical Lutheran denomination, but most Norwegians only attend church for Christmas and Easter. The Humanist & Ethical Union has around 70,000 members and there are a number of smaller Christian denominations, as well as around 50,000 Muslims and 1000 Jews.

ARTS

Norway's best-known artists include the moody painter Edvard Munch, responsible for *The Scream;* the landscape painter JC Dahl; classical composer Edvard Grieg; sculptor Gustav Vigeland; and famed playwright Henrik Ibsen, who penned *A Doll's House.*

Norway's stave churches are some of the oldest wooden buildings on earth. Named for their vertical supporting posts, these structures are often distinguished by dragon-headed gables resembling ornately carved prows of Viking ships. Of the 500 to 600 stave churches originally built, only about 20 of those remaining retain many original components. Other significant architectural features in the country include

NORWAY

TOP SIX NORWEGIAN ALBUMS

Stop in a record shop to pick these up.

- **Patashnik** by Biosphere is ambient electronic made famous in a regrettable Levi's commercial

- **Blodig Alvor (na na na na na)** The Dum Dum Boys breakout album has a stupid name

- **Melody A.M.** by Royksopp is a groundbreaking dance/pop electronic album

- **Let Them Eat Cake** by Motorsycho sounds kind of like psychedelic '70s rock

- **Anniemal** is top-40 candy pop, but Annie has independent cred when she DJs

- **a-ha** is so totally old school that you don't need some Lonely Planet author telling you what to buy

---

the romantic 'dragon style', found in some historic hotels, and occurrences of the Art Nouveau style, best observed in Ålesund.

Norwegian writers Sigrid Undset and Knut Hamsun (a Nazi collaborator) won the Nobel Prize for Literature in 1928 and 1920, respectively. Undset is best known for *Kristin Lavransdottir,* a trilogy portraying the struggles and earthy lifestyle of a 14th-century Norwegian family, while Hamsun won the Nobel Prize for his novel *The Growth of the Soil.*

Not traditionally a cinematic powerhouse, Norway has recently cranked out several good films, including *Elling* (2001); *Buddy* (2003); and *Beautiful Country* (2004); and *Slipp Jimmy Fri* (Free Jimmy; 2006), an animated flick about an escaped circus elephant pursued by junkies, animal rights maniacs and a Sami. For a Norwegian classic, check out *Ni Liv* (1957), a story concerning the WWII resistance. Information on films and festivals can be found at www.nfi.no.

Classical music and jazz are very popular in Norway and there are annual music festivals around the country, the most significant being in Bergen, Molde and Kongsberg. For details of music festivals, visit www.norwayfestivals.com or contact the Norwegian Tourist Board.

Norway also has a thriving rock scene with most of the action coming out of Ber-

gen, though aficionados should not miss Kristiansand's Quart Festival (p322). It's also largely responsible for black metal (p309).

ENVIRONMENT
The Land
Norway, occupying the western part of the Scandinavian Peninsula, has a land area of 324,220 sq km and shares borders with Sweden, Finland and Russia. The coastline is deeply cut by fjords – long, narrow inlets of the sea bordered by high, steep cliffs. Mountains, some capped with Europe's largest glaciers, cover more than half of the landmass. Only 3% of the country is arable.

With a combination of mountains and a wet climate, it's hardly surprising that Norway has many spectacular waterfalls, including several of the top 10 highest in the world. 'The Land of the Midnight Sun' is more than just a promotional slogan: nearly a third of Norway lies north of the Arctic Circle.

Wildlife
Norway has wild and semidomesticated reindeer herds, thriving elk populations and a scattering of arctic foxes lynxes musk oxen, bears and wolverines. Lemmings occupy mountain areas through 30% of the country. Since the ban on hunting came into force in 1973, polar bear numbers have increased to over 5000. Nearly all are found in Svalbard, though one was recently sighted in Finnmark. Polar bears usually eat seals but have been known to enjoy human flesh. Walruses are rare and are confined to Svalbard, but several species of seal, dolphin and whale may be seen around most western and northern coasts.

Birdlife is prolific in coastal areas and puffins, fulmars and kittiwakes are commonly seen. Rarer species include ospreys, golden eagles and magnificent white-tailed sea eagles. The islands of Runde (p350), Røst and Værøy (p365) are premier places to watch them.

National Parks
Norway's 21 national parks, covering 6.4% of the country, have been established to protect wildlife and distinctive natural features of the landscape. In many cases, they don't attempt to protect any specific features, but rather attempt to prevent

development of remaining wild areas. As a result, park boundaries don't necessarily coincide with the incidence of spectacular natural features, but simply follow contour lines around uninhabited areas.

Compared with their counterparts in the USA and Britain, Norwegian national parks are low profile and lack the traffic and over-developed facilities that have turned other countries' parks into seasonal urban areas. Some parks, notably Jotunheimen and Rondane, are increasing suffering from overuse, but in most places pollution and traffic are kept to a minimum. Norwegians sometimes look askance at foreigners' preoccupation with national parks, since fantastic wilderness areas exist everywhere.

Environmental Issues

Industrial waste is highly regulated, recycling is popular, there's little rubbish along the roadsides and general tidiness is a high priority in both urban and rural environments. Plastic bottles and cans may be exchanged for cash at supermarkets.

Loss of habitat has placed around 900 species of plants and animals on the endangered or threatened species lists, and sport hunting and fishing are more popular here than in most of Europe. Hydroelectric schemes have devastated some mountain landscapes and waterfalls, and over-fishing perpetually haunts the economy.

In 1993 Norway resumed commercial hunting of minke whales in open defiance of an international whaling ban. Norway supports the protection of other threatened species, but the government contends that the estimated 70,000 to 186,000 North Atlantic minke whales can sustain a limited harvest. The annual limit on the number of whales that can be killed is around 1000.

FOOD & DRINK
Staples & Specialities

Norwegian specialities include grilled or smoked *laks* (salmon), *gravat laks* (marinated salmon), *reker* (boiled shrimp), *torsk* (cod), *fiskesuppe* (fish soup), *hval* (whale) and other seafood. Expect to see sweet brown goats' milk cheese called *geitost* and *sild* (pickled herring) alongside the breads and cereals included in breakfast buffets. A fine Norwegian dessert is warm *moltebær syltetøy* (cloudberry jam) with ice cream.

Another popular option is *eplekake* (apple cake) served with fresh cream. *Lutefisk,* dried cod made almost gelatinous by soaking in lye, is popular at Christmas but it's definitely an acquired taste.

If Norway has a national drink, it's coffee and most Norwegians drink it black and strong. Most of the beer you'll drink is watery-tasting pilsner. On the other end of the taste spectrum is Norway's bitter aquavit, which does the job at 40% proof.

Where to Eat & Drink

Common throughout all of Norway is the *konditori,* a bakery with tables where you can sit and enjoy pastries and relatively inexpensive sandwiches. Other moderately cheap eats are found at *gatekjøkken* (food wagons and street side kiosks), which generally have hot dogs for about Nkr15 and hamburgers for Nkr50. Marginally more expensive, but with more nutritionally balanced food, are *kafeterias,* with simple, traditional meals from about Nkr85. In cities, *kafes* almost always function as a hang-out, bar and restaurant. They serve filling 'small dishes' for Nkr80 to Nkr120. Many restaurants feature a *dagens rett* (daily special) for about Nkr100.

By international standards, Norwegian restaurant food is fairly bland and heavy, though the cities of Oslo, Bergen, Trondheim and Stavanger have all made vast cuisine improvements.

Urban bars come in three basic forms. The first breed involves well-dressed Norwegians and cool designs. The second is the 'brown bar', so named because of their dusty wooden interiors – these are usually accused of being dens for alcoholic men, though bohemians have gentrified many of them. The third type is found in the growing numbers of forgettable tourist traps and chain 'Irish' venues. These are easily spotted and avoided.

Vegetarians & Vegans

Being vegetarian in Norway is a challenge. In rural parts of the country, you will live out of a grocery store, though some cafés serve token dishes such as vegetables with pasta. Another easily found option is pizza, though be warned that Norwegian pizza usually tastes lousy. You'll find more options in bigger cities, though most menus are entirely based on fish and meat. Kebab stands serve falafel about half the time. Norwegian restaurants aim to please, and will often attempt to make you a special order if you ask (don't expect fine results though).

Vegans will find Norway almost impossible. The number of places consistently serving vegan food is minuscule.

OSLO

pop 520,000

Norway's capital is easily the country's most cosmopolitan city, offering diverse nightlife options, an array of cafés and bars and some excellent museums, not least the Nasjonalgalleriet and Vikingskipshuset. While Oslo is not as picturesquely stunning as Bergen, its urban fabric does contain the famous Vigeland Park and the city is eminently strollable. For a particularly good urban walk, follow the banks of the Ankerselva where you will encounter several waterfalls and the converted factory buildings that comprise the edge of the trendy Grünerløkka district.

What distinguishes Oslo from many other capitals is its immediate proximity to expansive wilderness areas. Not only is the city at the head of a Fjord (not as impressive as those on the west coast, but a fjord all the same), but a large mountainous forest penetrates the city boundary. The pleasant result is that you can take a subway to ski lifts and an extensive network of trails.

HISTORY

Founded by Harald Hardråda in 1048, it's the oldest Scandinavian capital. In 1299, King Håkon V constructed the Akershus Festning (fortress) here, to counter the Swedish threat from the east. Levelled by fire in 1624, the city was rebuilt in brick and stone on a more easily defended site by King Christian IV, who renamed it Christiania, after his humble self.

In 1814, the framers of Norway's first constitution designated it the official capital of the new realm but their efforts were effectively nullified by Sweden, which had other ideas about Norway's future and unified the two countries under Swedish rule. In 1905, when that union dissolved, Christiania flourished as the capital of modern

Norway. The city reverted to its original name, Oslo, in 1925.

ORIENTATION

Oslo's central train station (Oslo Sentralstasjon, or 'Oslo S') is at the eastern end of the city centre. From there the main street, Karl Johans gate, leads through the heart of the city to Det Kongelige Slott. The neighbourhood of Grünerløkka, hipster-central, is reached by taking Storgata across the Akerselva, while the Grønland immigrant district is just east of Oslo S.

Most central city sights are within a 15-minute walk of Karl Johans gate, as are the majority of Oslo's hotels and pensions (guest houses). Many sights outside Oslo centre, including Vigeland Park and Munchmuseet, are a short tram ride away, and Bygdøy peninsula is a 10-minute ferry ride across the harbour. The trails and lakes of the Nordmarka wilderness are easily reached by T-bane (the underground train system).

INFORMATION
Bookshops

Nomaden (Map pp304-5; ☎ 22 56 25 40; Uranienborgveien 4; ☾ 10am-6pm Mon-Fri, 10am-4pm Sat) Travel guides, maps and gear.

Norli (Map pp304-5; ☎ 22 00 43 00; Universitetsgata 24; ☾ 9am-7pm Mon-Fri, 10am-4pm Sat) Some English-language titles.

Discount Cards

Oslo Card (1/2/3 days Nkr195/285/375) Provides entry to most museums and attractions and travel on public transport. It's sold at tourist offices and hotels. Students and seniors, who get half-price entry at most sights, usually do better buying a public-transport pass (or walking) and paying separate museum admissions.

OSLO IN TWO DAYS

Poke around **Akershus Festning** (p307) before taking a ferry to the **Vikingskipshuset** (p306) and **Norsk Folkemuseum** (p306). Return to relax in Tekehtopa (p312) and wander around **Vigeland Park** (p307)

Spend the morning at **Munchmuseet** (opposite) and stroll through the **Botanisk Hage** (Botanical Gardens; p307) en route to Grønland for some curry. Window-shop on **Bogstadveien**, (p315) then eat **Frogner-seteren's** (p312) mountaintop apple cake.

Internet Access
Deichmanske Bibliotek (Map pp304-5; Henrik Ibsens gate 1; ☺ 10am-8pm Mon-Fri, 9am-3pm Sat Sep-May, 10am-6pm Mon-Fri, 9am-2pm Sat Jun-Aug) Free internet access but expect to wait.
Studenten (Map pp304-5; ☎ 22 42 56 80; Karl Johans gate 45; per hr Nkr60; ☺ noon-8pm Tue-Sat, noon-10pm Sun & Mon)
WTE Internet Café (Map pp304-5; ☎ 22 87 01 60; Thorvald Meyers gate 85; per hr Nkr30; ☺ 10am-9pm Mon-Fri, 11am-9pm Sat & Sun)

Laundry
Selvebetjent (Map pp304-5; Ullevålsveien 15; wash/dry Nkr45/30; ☺ 8am-9pm)

Medical Services
Jernbanetorget Apotek (Map pp304-5; ☎ 22 41 24 83; Fred Olsens gate; ☺ 24hr) Pharmacy opposite Oslo S.
Oslo Kommunale Legevakten (Map pp304-5; ☎ 22 11 80 80; Storgata 40) Medical clinic with 24-hour emergency services.

Money
You'll find banks scattered all over town and most have ATMs accepting international cards. Most have branches along or just off Karl Johans gate near Oslo S.
American Express Amex; (Map pp304-5; ☎ 22 98 37 35; Fridtjof Nansens plass 6; ☺ 9am-4.30pm Mon-Fri, 10am-3pm Sat) Best deal for those changing small sums. Offers best rates with no commission on Amex travellers cheques and around 1% for most other brands of travellers cheques.

Post
Main post office (Map pp304-5; Dronningens gate 15; ☺ 9am-5pm Mon-Fri) To receive mail, have it sent to 'Poste Restante, Oslo Sentrum Postkontor, Dronningens gate 15, N-0107 Oslo'. There's a convenient branch at Oslo S and on Grensen.

Tourist Information
Den Norske Turistforening (DNT, Norwegian Mountain Touring Club; Map pp304-5; ☎ 22 82 28 22; www.dntoslo .no; Storgata 3; ☺ 10am-4pm Mon-Wed & Fri 10am-6pm Thu, 10am-2pm Sat, open 1hr earlier in summer) Provides information and maps on hiking in Norway and sells memberships which include discounted rates on the use of mountain huts along the main hiking routes. You can also book huts and pick up keys.
Oslo Promotion (Map pp304-5; ☎ 24 14 77 00; www .visitoslo.com; Fridtjof Nansens plass 5; ☺ 9am-7pm Jun-Aug, 9am-5pm Mon-Sat Apr-May & Sep, 9am-4pm Mon-Fri Oct-Mar) Its website has extensive information on disabled access to hotels, sights and restaurants.

Use-It (Map pp304-5; ☎ 22 41 51 32; www.use-it.no; Møllergata 3; ☺ 9am-6pm Mon-Fri Jul & Aug, 11am-5pm or 6pm Mon-Fri Sep-Jun) The exceptionally friendly and savvy youth information office (better known as Use-It) is aimed at (but not limited to) the backpacking crowd. It makes (free) bookings for inexpensive accommodation and provides advice from finding Oslofjord fishing spots to hitching. Pick up a copy of its (free) *Streetwise* (a comprehensive guide to Oslo on the cheap), use a (free) phone to make a room reservation anywhere in Norway, or tag along on 'off-track tourism' events, where you might see a football match or take a tour of City Hall guided by the mayor.

SIGHTS
Many sights are clustered together within easy walking distance from Karl Johans gate. Another important concentration is the Bygdøy peninsula, which contains the Vikingskipshuset and more.

Art Museums
For the largest collection of Norwegian art, come to **Nasjonalgalleriet** (Map pp304-5; ☎ 22 20 04 04; www.nasjonalmuseet.no; Universitetsgata 13; admission free; ☺ 10am-6pm Mon, Wed & Fri, 10am-8pm Thu, 10am-4pm Sat, 11am-4pm Sun; ☺). Some of Edvard Munch's best-known works are on display, including *The Scream*, which was brazenly stolen (and later recovered) in 1994. If you dig 19th-century landscape paintings, Johan Christian Dahl keeps it real on the 1st floor.

Dedicated to the life work of Norway's most renowned artist, **Munchmuseet** (Map pp304-5; ☎ 23 24 14 00; Tøyengata 53; adult/student Nkr65/30, free Oct-Mar; ☺ 10am-4pm Mon-Fri, 11am-5pm Sat & Sun Jun–mid-Sep, shorter hrs otherwise; ☺) contains 5000 drawings and paintings that Munch bequeathed to the city of Oslo. Ten years after *The Scream* was stolen from Nasjonalgalleriet, masked gunmen pulled a similar caper on another version of the famous painting here in 2004, it too was recovered in early September, 2006.

For a freakish sensory overload, enter the **Emanuel Vigeland Museum** (Map p310; ☎ 22 14 57 88; www.emanuelvigeland.museum.no; Grimelundsveien 8; adult Nkr30; ☺ noon-4pm Sun) containing his life's work and mausoleum – a specially designed vaulted chamber where you duck under a low door (and thus pay tribute to his ashes, interned above) to enter an eerie nave with almost zero lighting. As your eyes adjust to the dark, you'll begin to discern enormous

NORWAY

CENTRAL OSLO

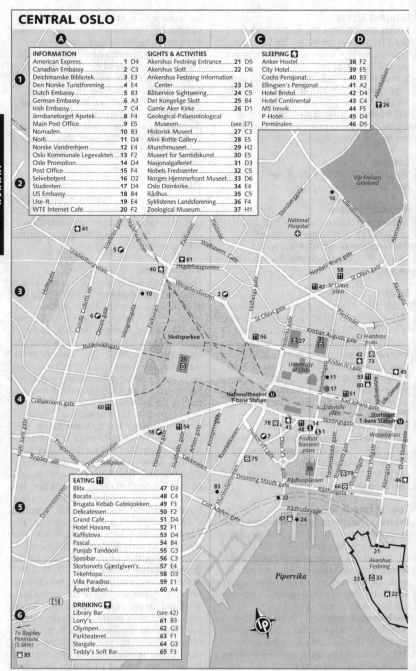

INFORMATION
American Express	1 D4
Canadian Embassy	2 C3
Deichmanske Bibliotek	3 E3
Den Norske Turistforening	4 E4
Dutch Embassy	5 B3
German Embassy	6 A3
Irish Embassy	7 C4
Jernbanetorget Apotek	8 F4
Main Post Office	9 E5
Nomaden	10 B3
Norli	11 D4
Norske Vandrerhjem	12 E4
Oslo Kommunale Legevakten	13 F2
Oslo Promotion	14 D4
Post Office	15 F4
Selvebetjent	16 D2
Studenten	17 D4
US Embassy	18 B4
Use-It	19 E4
WTE Internet Café	20 F2

SIGHTS & ACTIVITIES
Akershus Festning Entrance	21 D5
Akershus Slott	22 D6
Ankershus Festning Information Center	23 D6
Båtservice Sightseeing	24 C5
Det Kongelige Slott	25 B4
Gamle Aker Kirke	26 D1
Geological-Palaeontological Museum	(see 37)
Historisk Museet	27 C3
Mini Bottle Gallery	28 E5
Munchmuseet	29 H2
Museet for Samtidskunst	30 E5
Nasjonalgalleriet	31 D3
Nobels Fredssenter	32 C5
Norges Hjemmefront Museet	33 D6
Oslo Domkirke	34 E4
Rådhus	35 C5
Syklistenes Landsforening	36 F4
Zoological Museum	37 H1

SLEEPING
Anker Hostel	38 F2
City Hotel	39 E5
Cochs Pensjonat	40 B3
Ellingsen's Pensjonat	41 A2
Hotel Bristol	42 D4
Hotel Continental	43 C4
MS Innvik	44 F5
P-Hotel	45 D4
Perminalen	46 D5

EATING
Blitx	47 D3
Bocata	48 C4
Brugata Kebab Gatekjokken	49 F3
Delicatessen	50 F2
Grand Café	51 D4
Hotel Havana	52 F1
Kaffistova	53 D4
Pascal	54 B4
Punjab Tandoori	55 G3
Spasibar	56 C3
Stortorvets Gjæstgiveri's	57 E4
Tekehtopa	58 D3
Villa Paradiso	59 E1
Åpent Bakeri	60 A4

DRINKING
Library Bar	(see 42)
Lorry's	61 B3
Olympen	62 G3
Parkteateret	63 F1
Stargate	64 G3
Teddy's Soft Bar	65 F3

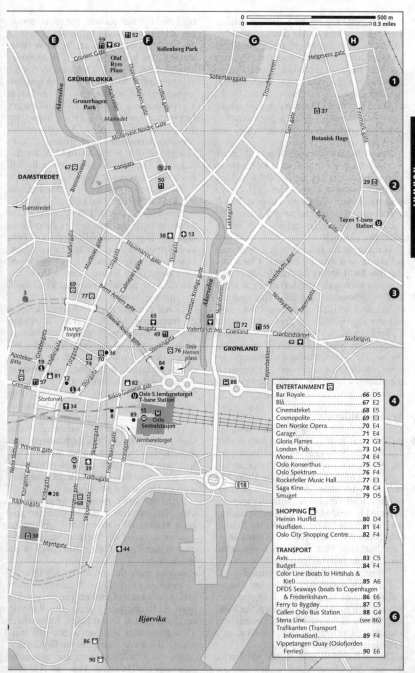

ENTERTAINMENT
Bar Royale	**66** D5
Blå	**67** E2
Cinemateket	**68** E5
Cosmopolite	**69** E3
Den Norske Opera	**70** E4
Garage	**71** E4
Gloria Flames	**72** G3
London Pub	**73** D4
Mono	**74** E4
Oslo Konserthus	**75** C5
Oslo Spektrum	**76** F4
Rockefeller Music Hall	**77** E3
Saga Kino	**78** C4
Smuget	**79** D5

SHOPPING
Heimin Husflid	**80** D4
Husfliden	**81** E4
Oslo City Shopping Centre	**82** F4

TRANSPORT
Avis	**83** C5
Budget	**84** F4
Color Line (boats to Hirtshals & Kiel)	**85** A6
DFDS Seaways (boats to Copenhagen & Frederikshavn)	**86** E6
Ferry to Bygdøy	**87** C5
Galleri Oslo Bus Station	**88** G4
Stena Line	(see **86**)
Trafikanten (Transport Information)	**89** F4
Vippetangen Quay (Oslofjorden Ferries)	**90** E6

NORWAY

frescoes reaching up to a distant ceiling. These depict human life from conception to death (sometimes erotically). Entirely surfaced with smooth stone, the bizarre chamber has such incredible acoustics that visitors are required to wear cloth booties to deaden the echoing thuds created by the slightest footstep. Overheard mobile phone user: Sorry mum, I'm in a pornographic church museum. I can't talk now. Call you later, bye!

Museet for Samtidskunst (Museum of Contemporary Art; Map pp304-5; ☎ 22 86 22 10; Bankplassen 4; admission free; ⌚ 10am-5pm Tue, Wed & Fri, 10am-8pm Thu, 11am-4pm Sat, 11am-5pm Sun) is Norway's principal museum dedicated to post-WWII Scandinavian and international art; here you'll find Norwegian artists with names other than Munch.

Want to see the ridiculous and enormous collection of a wealthy brewer? Check out the **Mini Bottle Gallery** (Map pp304-5; ☎ 23 35 79 60; www.minibottlegallery.com; Kirkegata 10; adult/child Nkr85/35; ⌚ noon-4pm Sat & Sun). This 'gallery' crosses architectural elegance and haunted-house gadgetry with the crass overtures of a puerile club. As you admire tens of thousands of tiny bottles of booze set in an environment whose expensive design surpasses many museums, you're bound to wonder if the place is a joke. The answer comes readily in the toilet.

Bygdøy Peninsula

The magnificent **Vikingskipshuset** (Viking Ship Museum; Map p310; ☎ 22 13 52 80; Huk Aveny 35; adult/child Nkr50/25; ⌚ 9am-6pm May-Sep, 11am-4pm Oct-Apr; ♿) houses three Viking ships excavated from the Oslofjord region. The ships had been brought ashore and used as tombs for nobility, who were buried with all they were expected to need in the hereafter, including jewels, furniture, food and servants. Built of oak in the 9th century, these Viking ships were buried in blue clay, which preserved two of them amazingly well.

The impressive **Oseberg ship**, buried in AD 834 and festooned with elaborate dragon and serpent carvings, is 22m long and took 30 people to row it. A second ship, the 24m-long **Gokstad**, is the world's finest example of a longship. Of the third ship, the **Tune**, only a few boards remain.

Dirt paths wind past sturdy old barns, *stabbur* (storehouses on stilts), rough-timbered farmhouses with sod roofs sprouting wild flowers and a 140 other 17th- and 18th-century buildings at the **Norsk Folkemuseum** (Map p310; ☎ 22 12 37 00; Museumsveien 10; adult/student/child mid-May–mid-Sep Nkr75/45/20, mid-Sep–mid-May Nkr75/40/35; ⌚ 10am-6pm mid-Jun–mid-Sep, short hrs otherwise). There's also a reproduction of an early-20th-century Norwegian town, including a village shop and an old petrol station. A highlight is a restored **stave church**, built around 1200 in Gol and brought to Bygdøy in 1885. Sunday is a good day to visit, as there's usually folk music and dancing at 2pm (summer only).

Take a look a the *Kon-Tiki* balsa raft at the **Kon-Tiki Museum** (Map p310; ☎ 23 08 67 67; Bygdøynesveien 36; adult/child Nkr45/25; ⌚ 9.30am-5.45pm Jun-Aug, 10.30am-5pm Sep-May). Norwegian explorer Thor Heyerdahl sailed from Peru to Polynesia in 1947 on the raft to demonstrate that Polynesia's first settlers could have come from South America. Also displayed is the papyrus reed boat *Ra II*, used to cross the Atlantic in 1970.

Check out the durable *Fram* (1892) at the **Frammuseet** (Map p310; ☎ 23 28 29 50; www.fram.museum.no; Bygdøynesveien 36; adult/child Nkr40/20; ⌚ 9am-6.45pm mid-Jun–Aug, shorter hrs Sep–mid-Jun), which Roald Amundsen used for the first successful expedition to the South Pole in 1911. You can clamber around inside the boat, go down to the hold where the sled dogs were kept and view fascinating photographic displays of the *Fram* trapped in polar ice.

For, uh, boatloads of amazing model ships, check out **Norsk Sjøfartsmuseum** (Norwegian Maritime Museum; Map p310; ☎ 24 11 41 50; Bygdøynesveien 37; adult/student/child Nkr40/25/free; ⌚ 10am-6pm mid-May–Sep, shorter hrs otherwise; ♿), with its film of the Norwegian coast.

Although only minutes from central Oslo, Bygdøy has a rural character and good **beaches**. The royal family maintains a summer home on the peninsula, as do quite a number of Oslo's other well-to-do residents.

Ferries make the run to Bygdøy (Nkr22, 15 minutes, every 20 to 40 minutes) from mid-April to early October. The ferry leaves from Rådhusbrygge 3 (opposite Rådhus) and stops first at Dronningen, from where it's a 10-minute walk up to the folk museum. The ferry continues to Bygdøynes, where the Kon-Tiki, Fram and maritime museums are clustered. You can also take bus No 20 to Bygdøy's sights from the National Theatre. The routes between the sights are signposted.

Frognerparken & Vigeland Park

Frognerparken is a wonderful city **park** (Map p310) with expansive green spaces, duck ponds and rows of shady trees – a fine place for walks and picnics. Its central walkway, **Vigelan Park**, is lined with life-sized statues by Gustav Vigeland (1869–1943). In nearly 200 highly charged works of granite and bronze, Vigeland presents the naked human form in a range of emotions, from screaming pot-bellied babies to entwined lovers and tranquil elderly couples.

The most impressive piece is the monolith of writhing bodies. The circle of steps beneath the monolith is lined with volup tuous stone figures, and the form of the complex recalls Egyptian funerary monu ments. The park is free and always open.

For a more in-depth look at the develop ment of Gustav Vigeland's work, visit the **Vigeland Museum** (Map p310; ☎ 22 54 25 30; www .vigeland.museum.no; Nobels gate 32; adult/child Nkr45/25; ☻ noon-4pm Tue-Sun). The museum was built by the city as a home and workshop for Vige land in exchange for the bulk of his life's work and contains his early statuary, plaster moulds, woodblock prints and sketches.

Nobels Fredssenter

Head inside the brand new **Peace Centre** (Map pp304-5; ☎ 48 30 10 00; www.nobelpeacecenter .org; Brynjulf Bulls Plass 1; adult/child Nkr60/free; ☻ 10am-7pm Jun–mid-Sep, shorter hrs otherwise; ☟) for hi-tech screens flashily exploring themes of peace and conflict. Aside from presenting the his tory of the prize and its patron, Alfred Nobel (a dynamite fellow, har har), you can view exhibits on winners from 1901 to present.

Akershus Slott & Festning

King Håkon V began construction of the earthen walled **Akershus Festning** (Akershus For tress; Map pp304-5; admission free; ☻ 6am-9pm) in 1299. It is strategically positioned on the eastern side of the harbour and the parklike grounds offer excellent views of the city and Oslofjord. The grounds are the venue for a host of concerts, dances and theatrical productions during summer. The **Akershus Festning Information Centre** (Map pp304-5; ☎ 23 09 39 17; ☻ 9am-5pm Mon-Fri, 11am-5pm Sat & Sun mid-

Jun–mid-Aug, 11am-4pm mid-Aug–mid-Jun) recounts the building of the fortress. The changing of the guard occurs at 1.30pm.

In the 17th century, Christian IV reno vated **Akershus Slott** (Akershus Castle; Map pp304-5; ☎ 23 09 35 53; adult/child Nkr40/10; ☻ 10am-4pm Mon-Sat, 12.30-4pm Sun May–mid-Sep) into a Renaissance palace, though the front remains decidedly medieval. In its dungeons you'll find dark cubby-holes where outcast nobles were kept under lock and key, while the upper floors have banquet halls and staterooms.

The chapel is still used for army events and the crypts of kings Håkon VII and Olav V lie beneath it. Tours of the castle (at 11am Mon day to Saturday, and 1pm and 3pm daily) are led by students in period dress, and provide entertaining anecdotal history; otherwise you can wander through on your own.

During WWII, the Nazis used Aker shus as a prison and execution grounds and today it's the site of **Norges Hjemmefront Museet** (Norwegian Resistance Museum; Map pp304-5; ☎ 23 09 31 38; www.nhm.mil.no; adult/child Nkr30/15; ☻ 10am-3pm Mon-Fri, 11am-4pm Sat & Sun, longer hrs mid-Apr-Sep), providing a vivid account of the tyrannical German occupation and the Norwegian struggle against it.

Zoology, Botany & Geology

Next to Munchmuseet is the university's **Zoological Museum** (Map pp304-5; ☎ 22 85 17 00; Sars gate 1; combined ticket with Geological Museum Nkr40; ☻ 11am-4pm Tue-Sun), full of stuffed Norwegian wildlife. Compare the scale of a lemming and polar bear. The adjacent **Geological-Palaeontological Museum** (Map pp304-5) fea tures displays on the history of the solar system, Norwegian geology, and examples of myriad minerals, meteorites and moon rocks. The museums sit in the grounds of the fragrant **Botanisk Hage** (Botanical Gardens; Map pp304-5; ☎ 22 85 17 00; Sars gate 1; admission free; ☻ 7am-8pm Mon-Fri, 10am-8pm Sat & Sun Apr-Sep, shorter hrs Oct-Mar), whose lovely landscaped lawns feature more than 1000 alpine plants as well as tropical and temperate specimens.

City Hall

Oslo's twin-towered, redbrick **Rådhus** (City Hall; Map pp304-5; ☎ 22 46 16 00; Fridtjof Nansens plass; adult/child Nkr40/20, admission free Sep-May; ☻ 9am-5pm May-Aug, 9am-4pm Sep-Apr) features wooden reliefs with scenes from Norse mythology lining its outside entrance, and impressive

NORWAY

frescoes decorating the interior halls and chambers. View the main hall for free from the front corridor, walk around yourself, or take a guided tour in English at 10am, noon and 2pm daily (no extra charge).

Det Kongelige Slott

King Harald V sleeps in **Det Kongelige Slott** (Map pp304-5; Drammensveien 1), the royal palace, peering from a hill over the Karl Johans axis. Guided tours of 15 rooms are available in English, once daily at 2pm (late June to mid-August). Tickets (Nkr100) are difficult to obtain – ask the tourist office for details. The rest of the grounds comprise **Slottsparken**, an inviting public park that's free to enter. If you happen to be around at 1.30pm, watch the changing of the guard.

Historisk Museet

The **History Museum** (Map pp304-5; ☎ 22 85 19 00; www.ukm.uio.no; Frederiks gate 2; admission Nkr40; 🕑 10am-4pm Tue-Sun mid-May–mid-Sep, 11am-4pm Tue-Sun mid-Sep–mid-May) consists of three museums under a single roof. On the ground floor, the **National Antiquities Collection** displays Viking-era coins, jewellery, weapons and bloodthirsty plunder, as well as a medieval church art section that includes the dragon-festooned bits of the 13th-century Ål stave church. The second level has a **numismatic collection of coins** dating from AD 995 and exhibits on indigenous arctic cultures.

Churches

Oslo Domkirke (Olso Cathedral; Map pp304-5; ☎ 22 23 31 46 00; Stortorget 1; admission free; 🕑 10am-4pm) dates from 1697 and it's worth seeing for its elaborate stained glass by Emanuel Vigeland and painted ceiling (completed between 1936–50). The exceptional 1748 altarpiece is a model of the *Last Supper and the Crucifixion* by Michael Rasch. The organ front and pulpit also require your attention.

Built of stone, the medieval **Gamle Aker Kirke** (Map pp304-5; Akersbakken 26; 🕑 noon-2pm Mon-Sat) was built around 1100 and is Oslo's oldest building. It's still used for Lutheran services.

ACTIVITIES
Swimming & Sunbathing

Ferries running to the half a dozen islands in Oslofjord leave from Vippetangen quay, southeast of Akershus Festning. **Hovedøya** (Map p310), the closest island, has a rocky coastline, but its southwestern side is a popular sunbathing area. There are walking paths around the perimeter, some old cannons and the **ruins** (Map p310) of a 12th-century monastery. Boats to Hovedøya leave from Vippetangen once or twice hourly from late May to mid-August, less the rest of the year.

Further south, the undeveloped island of **Langøyene** (Map p310) offers better swimming. It has both sandy and rocky beaches, including one designated for nude bathing. Boats to Langøyene depart late May to mid-August.

The Bygdøy peninsula also has two popular beaches, **Huk** (Map p310) and **Paradisbukta** (Map p310), which can be reached by taking bus No 30 from Jernbanetorget to its last stop. While there are some sandy patches, most of Huk comprises grassy lawns and large, smooth rocks ideal for sunbathing. It's separated into two beaches by a small cove; the beach on the northwestern side is open to nude bathing. If Huk seems too crowded, a 10-minute walk through the woods north of the bus stop leads to the more secluded Paradisbukta.

For freshwater swimming, try the eastern side of lake **Sognsvann** (Map p310), at the end of T-bane line 5, about 6km north of central Oslo.

Hiking

An extensive network of trails leads into Nordmarka from Frognerseteren, at the end of T-bane line 1. One good, fairly strenuous walk is from Frognerseteren to lake Sognsvann, where you can take T-bane line 5 back to the city. If you're interested in wilderness hiking, contact the **DNT office** (p303).

Cycling

One popular outing is to take the *sykkeltoget* (weekend bike train) to Stryken, 40km north of Oslo, and cycle back through Nordmarka. The train leaves Oslo S in the morning on Saturday and Sunday from May to October. For a shorter ride, take the T-bane to Frognerseteren where you can zip downhill by road to the centre or enjoy have access to off-road action.

For Norway-wide information on cycling contact the local club, **Syklistenes Landsforening** (Map pp304-5; ☎ 22 47 30 30; Storgata

23c; 🕑 10am-5pm Mon-Fri, 10am-2pm min-Jun–mid-Aug, shorter hrs otherwise).

Skiing

Oslo's ski season is roughly from December to March. There are over 1000km of ski trails in the Nordmarka area north of Oslo, many of them floodlit; easy-access tracks begin right at the T-bane stations Frognerseteren and Sognsvann. **Tomm Murstad Skiservice** (☎ 22 13 95 00; www.skiservice.no; Tomm Murstdbakken 2), at Voksenkollen T-bane station, hires out downhill (Nkr280 per day) and Nordic gear (Nkr190 per day). The downhill slopes at **Tryvann Skicenter** (☎ 40 46 27 00; www.tryvann.no; day/two-hr/night card Nkr280/205/230; 🕑 Mon-Fri 10am-5pm, 10am-5pm Sat & Sun) are near Voksenkollen Station, from where a ski bus (Nkr20) runs to the lifts. **Skiforeningen** (Ski Society; Map p310; ☎ 22 92 32 00; www.holmenkollen.com; Kongeveien 5) can provide more information.

TOURS

Oslo is so easy to get around that there's little need for organised tours. However, if time is tight, **Båtservice Sightseeing** (Map pp304-5; ☎ 23 35 68 90; www.boatsightseeing.com; Pier 3, Rådhusbrygge; 🕑 late May-late Aug) does a tidy 7½-hour tour of the Bygdøy sites, Vigeland Park, the Holmenkollen Ski Jump, plus a cruise of Oslofjord, for Nkr495; a three-hour version minus the cruise costs Nkr320. Båtservice's frequent 50-minute 'minicruise' of Oslofjord provides city orientation for Nkr100, or is free with the Oslo Card.

The popular **Norway in a Nutshell** (☎ 81 56 82 22; www.fjordtours.com) day tours cost Nkr1825 – they can be booked through any tourist office or directly through NSB at train stations. From Oslo, the typical route includes a rail trip from Oslo across Hardangervidda to Myrdal, a rail descent to Flåm along the dramatic Flåmbanen, a cruise along Nærøyfjorden to Gudvangen, a bus to Voss, a connecting train to Bergen for a short visit, then an overnight return rail trip to Oslo (including sleeper compartment). You can also book one-way tours.

FESTIVALS & EVENTS

Oslo's most festive annual event is the **17 May Constitution Day** celebration, when city residents descend on the royal palace in traditional garb.

In March, the **Holmenkollen Ski Festival** (☎ 22 92 32 00; www.skiforeningen.no) attracts Nordic skiers and ski jumpers from around the world. August sees the **Oslo International Jazz Festival** (☎ 22 42 91 20; www.oslojazz.no), October brings **Films from the South** (☎ 22 82 24 80; www.filmfrasor.no) and April the **Inferno Metal Festival** (www.infernofestival.net).

SLEEPING

When all other options seem unlikely, **Use-It** (p303) can usually find a place, helping travellers book double rooms in private homes for Nkr300 to Nkr500 (excluding breakfast). There's no booking fee. If you arrive on a Saturday or Sunday, when the office is closed, call ahead and they'll give you advance help.

BLACK METAL

Bored of fjords and peace prizes? Perhaps it's time to check out Norway's highly regarded black metal scene, whose notorious, sensational exploits in the mid-1990s raised eyebrows across the globe. At that time, the members of a few big-name bands (Mayhem and Emperor being the most notable) not only committed suicide, but murdered each other, burned stave churches, made trinkets out of fragments of their mates' skulls and beat up bouncers and concert-goers alike. In addition to these and other violent acts, a lot of music was created along the way. Depending on your taste, the goods might sound like a dying Cookie Monster singing through a distortion pedal or liberation from what you perceive to be a Christian-dominated music industry.

While things have calmed down a bit since the gory days, black metal remains popular in Norway. A few of the bands to look out for include Mayhem (much of the previous line-up dead or jailed), Satyricon, Gorgoroth and Dark Throne, and a few of the clubs to view them are **Garage** (p314), **Hulen** (p338), **Rockefeller Music Hall** (p314) and **Blæst** (p356). If you're lucky enough to spend April in Oslo, you must attend the **Inferno Metal Festival** (www.infernofestival.net). If not, try **Bergen's Hole in the Sky** (www.holeinthesky.no) in August. Don't forget your leather pants!

NORWAY

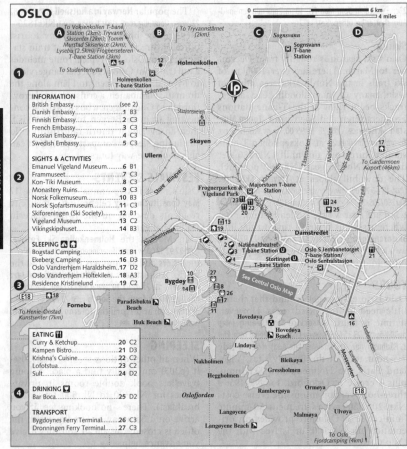

OSLO

0 — 6 km
0 — 4 miles

INFORMATION
British Embassy..........................(see 2)
Danish Embassy.........................**1** B3
Finnish Embassy.........................**2** C3
French Embassy..........................**3** C3
Russian Embassy.........................**4** C3
Swedish Embassy........................**5** C3

SIGHTS & ACTIVITIES
Emanuel Vigeland Museum........**6** B1
Frammuseet................................**7** C3
Kon-Tiki Museum.......................**8** C3
Monastery Ruins........................**9** C3
Norsk Folkemuseum..................**10** B3
Norsk Sjofartsmuseum...............**11** C3
Skiforeningen (Ski Society).......**12** B1
Vigeland Museum......................**13** C2
Vikingskiphuset.........................**14** B3

SLEEPING
Bogstad Camping.......................**15** B1
Ekeberg Camping.......................**16** D3
Oslo Vandrerhjem Haraldsheim..**17** D2
Oslo Vandrerhjem Holtekilen.....**18** A3
Residence Kristinelund **19** C2

EATING
Curry & Ketchup........................**20** C2
Kampen Bistro...........................**21** D3
Krishna's Cuisine.......................**22** C2
Lofotstua..................................**23** C2
Sult...**24** D2

DRINKING
Bar Boca...................................**25** D2

TRANSPORT
Bygdoynes Ferry Terminal.........**26** C3
Dronningen Ferry Terminal.......**27** C3

The tourist offices book unfilled hotel rooms at discounted rates, which can be worth pursuing during the week but are generally close to the rates that you can book directly from hotels on weekends. There's a Nkr35 booking fee. Discounts are offered to holders of hotel passes (p378).

Also worth checking out is www.bbnorway.com, which lists around a dozen B&Bs in Oslo.

Budget

Oslo Fjordcamping (Map p310; ☎ 22 75 20 55; Ljansbrukveien 1; camp sites from Nkr130, static caravan Nkr300) This family-friendly camping ground by the Oslofjord, about 8km south of the city, doesn't have the droves of loud revellers found in Oslo's other main sites. There are showers, a kiosk selling snacks and a nearby restaurant. Take bus No 83 from Oslo S.

Ekeberg Camping (Map p310; ☎ 22 19 85 68; www.ekebergcamping.no; Ekebergveien 65; camp site from Nkr150; ⏰ 7.30am-11pm Jun-early Sep; P) On a scenic hill southeast of the city, Ekeberg provides a great view over Oslo. For this reason, it gets crowded, sometimes unpleasantly. Take bus No 34 or 46.

Bogstad Camping (Map p310; ☎ 22 51 08 00; www.bogstadcamping.no; Ankerveien 117; camp site Nkr140; P) Often overcrowded and rowdy, the campground enjoys a pretty location near a valley of farms and overlooking a golf course with a lake beyond. On-site cafeteria and kitchen (no cooking implements). Take bus No 32.

Perminalen (Map pp304-5; ☎ 23 09 30 81; perminalen@statenskantiner.no; Øvre Slottsgate 2; dm/s/d Nkr295/495/650; ⅏) This central 55-room pension caters to military personnel, but is open to everyone. All rooms have TV, private bathroom and less dirt than the vacuum of space. Rates include linens and breakfast, served in a slick modern room or pleasant interior court.

Anker Hostel (Map pp304-5; ☎ 22 99 72 10; www .anker.oslo.no; Storgata 55; breakfast Nkr60; 4-bed dm/6-bed dm Nkr145/170, 2-person r Nkr430; ⅏) You'll find this utilitarian hostel on a cheerless intersection of wide streets. Aside from this, Anker is excellently located in the centre near Grünerløkka.

Oslo Vandrerhjem Haraldsheim (Map p310; ☎ 22 22 29 65; www.haraldsheim.oslo.no; Haraldsheimveien 4; dm/s/d Nkr205/380/515, dm/s/d with shared bathroom Nkr185/310/430; ☺ closed around Christmas; P ⬚ ⅏) Big bright and busy, this modern hostel is surrounded by acres of athletic fields. Though it's 4km from the centre, you can still make out the Oslofjord in the distance (and a rumbling freeway that's much closer). Take tram No 13 or 17 to the Sinsenkrysset stop.

Oslo Vandrerhjem Holtekilen (Map p310; ☎ 67 51 80 40; www.vandrerhjem.no; Micheletsvei 55, Stabekk; dm/s/d Nkr185/285/470; ☺ mid-May–early Oct; P) This 195-bed hostel sits amid a quiet enclave of trees and grass and is close to the edge of the Oslofjord. It's far enough from the centre (8km west of Oslo) that day cards and Oslo passes won't cover bus fare. Take bus No 151, 153, 161, 162, 252 or 261.

Midrange

MS Innvik (Map pp304-5; ☎ 22 41 95 00; www.msinnvik .no; Langkaia; s/d Nkr400/700) Once a car ferry used as a travelling theatre, the vessel has been reincarnated as a B&B docked in the harbour. It's still a cultural centre, so don't flush your toilet when puppet shows or theatrical events are held below deck.

Residence Kristinelund (Map p310; ☎ 40 00 24 11; www.kristinelund.no; s/d Nkr525/870; ☺ 8.30am-11pm) Set amid a swanky residential neighbourhood of mansions and embassies, this impressive turn-of-the-century building and its flowering grounds provide a hospitable experience in a quiet corner of Oslo.

Ellingsen's Pensjonat (Map pp304-5; ☎ 22 60 03 59; ep@tiscal.no; Holtegata 25; s Nkr300-420, d Nkr490-590) This homey pension set in a quiet

neighbourhood dates from 1890 and many original features (tall ceilings, rose designs, tall thresholds) remain. Rooms are bright and airy. All have a sink and writing table. Bathrooms are shared.

Cochs Pensjonat (Map pp304-5; ☎ 23 33 24 00; fax 23 33 24 10; Parkveien 25; s/d from Nkr400/560) Near the Royal Palace, Cochs' plain pleasant rooms occupy a large turn-of-the-century building with a fine corner location overlooking the beer garden of a café across the street.

P-Hotel (Map pp304-5; ☎ 23 31 80 00; www.p-hotels .no; Grensen 19; s/d Nkr595/695; ⅏) Supremely central and supremely generic, the P-Hotel provides competitively priced private rooms during the business week. No breakfast buffet, instead a bag of snacks is hung on your door.

City Hotel (Map pp304-5; ☎ 22 41 36 10; www.city hotel.no; Skippergata 19; s/d Nkr530/695, s/d with shared bathroom Nkr440/580) There's slight historical ambience in the stairwells, but the rooms are fairly basic in this pleasant budget hotel. The street nearby has become a popular place to make some cash, if you happen to be a lady or man of ill repute.

Top End

Hotel Continental (Map pp304-5; ☎ 22 82 40 00; www .hotel-continental.no; Stortingsgata 24/26; s/d Mon-Fri Sep-Jun Nkr1990/2390, s/d mid-Jun–Aug & Sat & Sun year-round Nkr995/1350; P ⬚ ⅏) A family-run palace dating from 1890, the Continental offers exquisite period rooms with privileged views over interesting monuments. Expect top-notch service and a tear-jerkingly good breakfast. The foyer bar has more Munch lithographs than most museums.

Hotel Bristol (Map pp304-5; ☎ 22 82 60 00; www .bristol.no; Kristian IV's gate 7; s/d Mon-Fri Sep-Jun Nkr1795/1995, s/d mid-Jun–Aug & Sat & Sun year-round Nkr1095/1295; P ⬚) The foyer and lounge provide a glimpse into sumptuous days of steamer trunk travel. These arcaded rooms, lit by crystal chandeliers and furnished with stacks of leather chairs, will make you hanker for some tea and club sandwiches (both available). Upstairs, pleasantly renovated rooms attempt to mirror the elegance below.

Lysebu (Map p310; ☎ 21 51 10 00; www.lysebu .com; Lysebuveien 12; s/d Mon-Fri Sep-Jun Nkr1250/1750, s/d Mid-Jun–Aug & Sat & Sun year-round Nkr940/1250; P ⬚) Given to Denmark as an expression of gratitude for WWII food relief, this tranquil (and swanky) hotel sits near the top of a small, forested mountain with expansive views over distance hills. Take T-Bane line 1 to Voksenkollen (25 minutes).

EATING

Many of the coolest and cheapest dining options can be found in the neighbourhoods of Grünerløkka, the primary enclave for Oslo's young and fashionably dressed, and Grønland, whose population of Asian and Middle Eastern immigrants have established affordable ethnic eating places.

NORWAY

Restaurants

Frognerseteren (☎ 22 46 93 96; Holmenkollveien 200; apple cake Nkr52; ⏲ 10.30am-10.30pm Mon-Sat, 10.30am-9pm Sun) Perched on a mountainside overlooking the city, this 19th-century eatery has big fireplaces, spectacular views and kick-arse apple cake in an impressive building combining the rusticity of large wooden beams with the delicacy of 'dragon-style' ornamentation. Take T-Bane 1 to the Frognerseteren stop.

Lofotstua (Map p310; ☎ 22 46 93 96; Kirkeveien 40; mains Nkr170-220; ⏲ 3-10pm Mon-Fri) Run by a family from the Lofoten islands, this restaurant turns out a changing menu of fantastic fish dishes, in a room that looks sort of like a brown bar.

Kampen Bistro (☎ 22 19 77 08; Bøgata 21; mains Nkr175; ⏲ 2pm-1am) Off the beaten track, this former working-class eatery has been transformed into a slightly stodgy neighbourhood bistro. The good-looking room pleases a local crowd. How about some chicken confit and antipasto?

Curry & Ketchup (Map p310; ☎ 22 69 05 22; Kirkeveien 51; mains Nkr75-99) Waiters wearing black rush through an intimate room to serve quality specials (coconut duck), kormas and curries (mostly chicken and lamb with a few vegetarian dishes). There is no ketchup to be seen.

Pascal (Map pp304-5; ☎ 22 55 00 20; Drammensveien 10; cakes Nkr55, mains Nkr130-270; ⏲ 9am-11pm Mon-Fri, 10am-11pm Sat, noon-5pm Sun) When a visiting Bill Clinton needed a cup of coffee, he procured it here. While most come for locally famous cakes (rich and French), there's also a menu of salads, grilled fish and sandwiches.

Villa Paradiso (Map pp304-5; ☎ 22 35 40 60; Olav Ryes plass 8; mains Nkr119-139; ⏲ 11am-midnight) Make reservations weeks in advance for a weekend dinner of Norway's finest pizza (not difficult in the land of soggy pies). Patrons eat the delicious goods surrounded by big windows and wood panelling.

Sult (Map p310; ☎ 22 87 04 67; Thorvald Meyersgate 26; mains Nkr89-169) Prepares a changing menu of continental fare for patrons who sit at small tables and listen to Elvis Presley. Cod encrusted with pistachios is excellent.

Krishna's Cuisine (Map p310; ☎ 22 60 62 50; Kirkeveien 59B; daily meal/plate Nkr90/70; ⏲ noon-8pm Mon-Sat) Near the Majorstuen T-bane station, Krishna's politely serves a daily vegetarian meal where you might eat corn soup, cucumber salad and a pile of broccoli in yellow curry. Portions are so huge that most just buy a plate of the hot dish.

Stortorvets Gjæstgiveri's (Map pp304-5; ☎ 23 35 63 60; Grubbegata 3; mains Nkr140-235) Norway's oldest restaurant's sagging yellow, wooden walls and pretty interior courtyard provide an excellent backdrop for traditional meals. Don't try for a table on 17 May or Christmas.

Kaffistova (Map pp304-5; ☎ 23 21 42 10; Rosenkrantz gate 8; mains Nkr80-110; ⏲ 10am-8pm Mon-Fri, 11am-5pm Sat & Sun) This cafeteria serves traditional Norwegian food, including reindeer or elk carbonades (locally defined as meat cakes), meatballs and fish cakes; salad is always included.

AUTHOR'S CHOICE

Åpent Bakeri (Map pp304-5; ☎ 22 44 94 70; Inkognito Terrace 1) For stellar breads and pastries, stop by this bakery, easily one of Norway's best. An attached café makes for an elegant spot to eat giant, grainy rolls that you can load up with berry jam and butter (Nkr12) for one of the cheapest breakfasts around. In nice weather, enjoy pavement seating on a quiet, tree-lined street.

Cafés

Tekehtopa (Map pp304-5; ☎ 22 20 33 52; St Olav plass 2; mains Nkr85-135) A former pharmacy, Tekeh topa serves espresso and chevre salads under a beautifully moulded and painted ceiling. It also serves Norway's ubiquitous breed of lousy pilsner, but you'll feel privileged to drink anything at all in a room this nice.

Blitx (Map pp304-5; Pilestredet 30C; sandwiches Nkr8-15; ⏲ 11am-5pm Mon-Fri) Inside a barricaded, graffiti-covered building is an activist

NORWAY

AUTHOR'S CHOICE

Spasibar (Map pp304-5; ☎ 22 11 51 90; St Olavs gate 22; snacks Nkr32-58) Psychedelic '60s table cloths and lots of pinks, oranges and browns provide a suitable backdrop for an outrageous life-size portrait of the Spasibar's artist/workers dressed as cowboys and made out of 255,000 beads. It and everything else in this flea market/gallery/café/music venue (including the PA system) is for sale. Just ask. Proceeds go to an orphanage in Russia. The place serves small plates of chorizo and tandoori chicken, and plenty of beer, on which you'll get a huge discount if you can speak Russian with a convincing accent. An excellent summer garden overlooks Slottsparken. To find it, enter the Kunstacademe on Wergelandsveien and head for the rear of the yellow building.

---

institution with 25 years of squatting history. Friendly, tattooed volunteers run a café serving unbelievably cheap vegetarian and vegan food. Coffee costs Nkr5.

Delicatessen (Map pp304-5; ☎ 22 71 45 46; Søndre gate 8; sandwiches Nkr55-75) One of Grünerløkka's numerous cool-kid cafés, it features sturdy wooden tables and big windows that fold away in the summer to overlook a riverside park across the street. Good Italian sandwiches.

Grand Café (Map pp304-5; Karl Johans gate 31; daily special Nkr140; ⏰ daily special available 11am-6pm Mon-Sat) The café at the Grand Hotel has been serving Oslo's cognoscenti for more than a century. As a reminder, a wall mural depicts the restaurant in the 1890s, bustling with the likes of Munch and Ibsen. The best deal is the traditional daily special.

Quick Eats

Brugata Kebab Gatekjokken (Map pp304-5; Brugata 10; falafel & kebab Nkr29-35; ⏰ 10am-midnight Sun-Thu, 10am-5am Fri & Sat) This florescent-lit hole bucks the trend and turns out excellent falafel and properly cooked lamb on freshly made pita.

Hotel Havana (Map pp304-5; ☎ 23 23 03 23; Thorvald Meyersgate 36; dishes Nkr49-89; ⏰ 10am-6pm Mon-Sat) A Grünerløkka delicatessen serving great takeaway food, enjoy substantial fish burgers (Nkr49) with homemade aioli, or try Brie sandwiches (Nkr49) and fish and chips (Nkr74).

Punjab Tandoori (Map pp304-5; Grønland 24; mains Nkr55-65) Oslo's favourite turbaned man dishes out curries from steam baskets. Immensely popular, the stuff moves so fast that it's always fresh. The room is no frills and sometimes the unlucky get more bones than meat.

Bocata (Map pp304-5; ☎ 22 41 46 62; Stortingsgata 22; snacks Nkr35-95) Come here for takeaway meals of Malaysian-style chicken, sweet and sour pork, spaghetti pesto, and ham sandwiches. Business types pack the counters at lunchtime.

There are numerous cheap pizza, burger and kebab joints along Grønland and Storgata. Fast food abounds in Oslo S.

Self-Catering

Eating can be extremely expensive. One way to save money is to frequent bakeries, many of which sell reasonably priced sandwiches as well as pastries and hearty wholegrain breads. Along Grønland and Storgata, you'll find many small immigrant groceries selling fresh fruit, some of which are open on Sunday.

DRINKING

Parkteateret (Map pp304-5; ☎ 22 35 63 00; Olaf Ryes plass 11) The yellow-and-black foyer of this cool-kid theatre and performance space serves espresso and beer to the fashionably dressed. In summer, excellent pavement seating overlooks one of Grünerløkka's English squares.

Teddy's Soft Bar (Map pp304-5; ☎ 22 17 36 50; Brugata 3A) Established in 1958, Teddy's provides a clear view into the past via its thoroughly unchanged interior. An ancient Wurlitzer sets the tone. While good burgers are served, most come for the suds.

Bar Boca (Map p310; ☎ 22 04 13 77; Thorvald Meyersgate 30) This tiny bar shoots for a stylized 1950s Hawaiian surfer look with a satisfying cool design. The place is packed, serves cocktails made with fresh fruit and is home to someone who clearly spent a lot of time compiling obscure period music.

Olympen (Map pp304-5; ☎ 22 17 28 08; Grølandsleiret 15) A freakish, century-old workers' beer hall, populated by students, artists and drunks, featuring awesomely cheesy cover bands (Bob Jovi) and cheap beer (Nkr33) in a cavernous space full of elaborate wooden booths and huge oil paintings of faded, unrecognisable cityscapes.

Library Bar (Map pp304-5; ☎ 22 82 60 00; Kristian IV's gate 7) Wear your finest tweed (not required) and sit among piles of leather-bound tomes in the Hotel Bristol's old-school drinking den. Crystal chandeliers set the tone. This is also a good place for a fancy luncheon sandwich (Nkr70 to Nkr95). Overcoats must be checked (Nkr20).

Lorry's (Map pp304-5; ☎ 22 69 69 04; Parkveien 12) Overpriced, crappy food in a bar with dirty toilets. Despite this, stuffed moose heads, pleasant heated beer garden and large menu of lager ensure it's well loved. Drunk artists used to pay for their beer with some of the stuff hung on the walls.

Stargate (Map pp304-5; Grønland 2) A cross-roads between east and west Oslo, this watering hole attracts youthful cheap skates, immigrants and guys with too-red noses.

In the summer, you can enjoy a beer in one of Vigeland Park's outdoor cafés.

ENTERTAINMENT

The tourist office's monthly *What's on in Oslo* brochure lists concerts, theatre and special events, but the best publication for night owls is the free *Streetwise*, published annually in English by Use-It (p303). Dress to impress or risk being refused entry to nightspots.

Cinema

Cinemateket (Map pp304-5; ☎ 22 47 45 00; Dronningens gate 16; tickets Nkr60) This art-house cinema screens alternative contemporary films, classics and independent fare.

Saga Kino (Map pp304-5; ☎ 41 51 90 00; Stortingsgata 28; tickets Nkr60) Shows first-run movies in their original languages.

Gay & Lesbian Venues

There are very few strictly gay and lesbian clubs in Oslo. Several places attract mixed crowds and some venues offer a weekly gay night. For details on these nights and special events, pick up the free *Pink Planet* at the tourist office or look in Use-It's *Streetwise*.

London Pub (Map pp304-5; ☎ 22 70 87 00; CJ Hambros plass 5; ☼ 3pm-3am) Oslo's oldest hang-out for the studs, where you can shoot stick and feed jukeboxes. If you feel like serious

dancing, head downstairs where DJs spin every night of the week.

Live Music

Mono (Map pp304-5; ☎ 22 41 41 66; www.cafémono.no; Pløensgata 4) For Indie acts (Gruff Rhys from Super Furry Animals), head to this bar where every surface is black. On nights with no performances, you'll hear the bartender play stuff like Deerhoof.

Garage (Map pp304-5; ☎ 22 17 16 00; www.garage.no; Grønland 18) In addition to Norwegian bands, Garage books international rock acts such as Death Cab for Cutie and the Beautiful People. While the sound system is good, the view is not thanks to a too-low stage.

Den Norske Opera (Map pp304-5; ☎ 81 54 44 88; Storgata 23; 50% student discount) Every month except July, Oslo's opera company stages opera, ballet and classical concerts here.

Also recommended:

Cosmopolite (Map pp304-5; ☎ 22 11 33 09; www.cosmopolite.no; Møllergata 26) Jazz and world music.

Oslo Spektrum (Map pp304-5; ☎ 81 51 12 11; www.oslo spektrum.no; Sonja Henies plass 2) A large concert hall where you can barely see whoever is performing (Guns 'N' Roses).

Oslo Konserthus (Map pp304-5; ☎ 23 11 31 11; ww.oslokonserthus.no; Munkedamsveien 14) Emphasises fine jazz and classical music.

Rockefeller Music Hall (Map pp304-5; ☎ 22 20 32 32; www.rockefeller.no; Torggata 16) Books big-name international contemporary rock (Patti Smith), jazz and more.

Nightclubs

Blå (Map pp304-5; ☎ 22 20 91 81; Brenneriveien 9) A cultural centre inside an old industrial building where you will meet Oslo's best dressed hipsters, Blå also books a ton of jazz acts. There's an outdoor seating area on the river.

Bar Royale (Map pp304-5; ☎ 22 42 28 88; Råhusgata 25) Inside a former public toilet, this cave-like club (previously Skansen, deemed by *Face* to be the world's greatest club) spins House and techno.

Gloria Flames (Map pp304-5; ☎ 22 17 16 00; Grønland 18; ☼ 4pm-3am Sat-Thu, 3pm-3am Fri) King of the Grønland nightclub scene, the DJs and bartenders here play a heavy mix of rock and indie in a blonde-wood room.

Smuget (Map pp304-5; ☎ 22 17 16 00; Grønland 18; ☼ 4pm-3am Sat-Thu, 3pm-3am Fri) If you're into huge crowds, DJs at this pop palace play to the masses, which line up outside like

Vikings assembled to behold the ferocity of Odin or to drink mead from the skull of an enemy to better slack their Viking thirst. Skol!

SHOPPING

For fashionable men's and women's clothes, independent booksellers, record shops and plastic eyeglass frames, head to Bogstadveien, considered by many to be Oslo best shopping street. By doing so, you'll free yourself from the crowds buying rip-off souvenirs off Karl Johans gate. For more cool Scandinavian dudes, try poking around the boutiques of the Grünerløkka district.

If you want a traditional Norwegian sweaters **Husfliden** (Map pp304-5; Møllergata 4) and **Heimen Husflid** (Map pp304-5; Rosenkrantz gate 8), are both large chains selling Norwegian clothing and crafts of good quality, with items ranging from tacky wooden trolls to elaborate folk costumes.

For wine or spirits, there's a Vinmonopolet in the **Oslo City** (Map pp304-5) shopping complex.

GETTING THERE & AWAY
Air

Most flights land at Oslo's main international airport in Gardermoen, 50km north of the city. Oslo Torp is a secondary airport, 123km south of the city.

Boat

Boats to and from Copenhagen, operated by **DFDS Seaways** and from Frederikshavn (Denmark) operated by **Stena Line** use the docks off Skippergata, near Vippetangen.

Boats from Hirtshals (Denmark) and Kiel (Germany), run by **Color Line** dock at Hjortneskaia, west of the central harbour. Connecting buses run to Oslo S, or take tram No 10 or 13.

Bus

Long-distance buses arrive and depart from the **Galleri Oslo bus station**, about a 10-minute walk east from Oslo S.

Car & Motorcycle

The main highways into the city are the E6, from the north and south, and the E18, from the east and west. Unless you're on a motorcycle you'll have to pay a Nkr15 to Nkr25 toll each time you enter Oslo.

All major car-rental companies have booths at Gardermoen airport. The following also have offices in the city centre:
Avis (Map pp304-5; ☎ 81 56 90 44; Munkedamsveien 27)
Budget (Map pp304-5; ☎ 23 16 32 40; Oslo Spektrum)

Train

All trains arrive and depart from Oslo S in the city centre. The reservation desks are open from 6.30am to 11pm daily. There's also an **information desk** (☎ 81 50 08 88) where you can get details on travel schedules throughout Norway. Oslo S has various sizes of lockers for Nkr20 to Nkr50 per 24 hours.

GETTING AROUND
To/From the Airport

FlyToget (☎ 177, 22 17 70 30; www.flybussen.no) runs high-speed trains between Oslo S and Oslo International airport in Gardermoen (adult/student Nkr180/90, 19 minutes, every 20 minutes) between 4.45am and midnight. Alternatively, you can take a northbound local train (Nkr80, 26 to 40 minutes, hourly but fewer on Saturday) or an express airport bus (Nkr120, 40 minutes, three hourly). A taxi costs around Nkr450, though **Oslo Taxi** (☎ 02323) sometimes offers discount rates.

To get to/from Torp Airport, take the **TorpExpressen** (☎ 81 50 01 76; adult/child130/70) bus from the Galleri Oslo Bus Terminal (1½ hours). Departures from Oslo leave three hours before Ryanair departures, and leave from Torp after Ryanair flights arrive. At other times, take an hourly Telemarksekspressen bus (or a taxi; from Nkr150, 10 minutes) between Torp and the Sandefjord train station from where there are connections to Oslo.

Car & Motorcycle

Oslo has many one-way streets, but otherwise traffic is not too challenging. Still, the best way to explore central sights is to walk or take local transport.

Metered street parking (Nkr20 to Nk40 per hour), identified by a solid blue sign with a white 'P', can be found throughout the city centre. Hours written under the sign indicate when the meters need to be fed. Unless otherwise posted, parking is free outside that time and on Sunday. There are many multistorey car parks in the city centre, including those at major shopping centres such as Oslo City and Aker Brygge. Fees range from Nkr70 to Nkr200 per 24-hour period. The Oslo Card gives free parking in municipal car parks.

Boat
Ferries going to Bygdøy leave from Rådhusbrygge every 20 to 40 minutes, while ferries to the islands in Oslofjord leave from Vippetangen.

Public Transport
Oslo has an efficient system with an extensive network of buses, trams, T-bane trains (metro/underground) and ferries. A one-way ticket on any of these services costs Nkr20 if you buy it from a station agent or kerbside machine. You can also buy your ticket from drivers for a Nkr10 surcharge. A *dagskort* (unlimited day ticket) costs Nkr60, but can't be used between 1am and 4am. Weekly/monthly cards cost Nkr160/620 (Nkr80/310 for people under 20 and seniors over 67). Buy them at Trafikanten, staffed T-bane and train stations, and some convenience stores.

Bicycles can be taken on Oslo's trams and trains for an additional Nkr11. While it may seem easy to board the subway and trams without a ticket, if confronted by an inspector you'll be fined Nkr750.

Trafikanten (Map pp304-5; ☎ 81 50 01 76; ☼ 7am-8pm Mon-Fri, 8am-6pm Sat & Sun), below the Oslo S tower on Jernbanetorget, provides free schedules and a handy public-transport map. Dial ☎ 177 from 7am to 11pm for schedule information.

BUS & TRAM
Bus and tram lines extend into the suburbs. There's no central station but most buses and trams converge at Jernbanetorget in front of Oslo S. Most westbound buses, including those to Bygdøy and Vigeland Park, also stop on the southern side of Nationaltheatret.

Service frequency drops dramatically at night, but on Saturday and Sunday only, Nattlinjer night buses No 200 to 218 follow the tram routes until 4am (tickets Nkr50; passes not valid).

T-BANE
The five-line T-bane metro train network, which goes underground in the city centre, is faster and goes further outside the city centre than most bus lines. All lines pass through Nationaltheatret, Stortinget and Jernbanetorget stations.

Taxi
Taxis charge up to Nkr90 at flagfall and from Nkr12 to Nkr18 per kilometre. There are taxi stands at Oslo S, shopping centres and city squares. Any taxi with a lit sign is available for hire. Otherwise, phone **Taxi2** (☎ 02202), **Norgestaxi** (☎ 08000) or **Oslo Taxi** (☎ 02323). Meters start running at the point of dispatch, adding to what will become a gigantic bill.

SOUTHERN NORWAY

The curving south coast exists as a magnet in the summer months for vacationing Norwegian families, who come to the area for its beaches, offshore islands and sailing opportunities. Unless themselves here to pilot masted vessels, first-time foreign travellers generally visit the coast's sleepy wooden towns as a pit shop en route to more exciting locales. The most notable exception is Stavanger, a lively international city conveniently positioned for explorations of surrounding fjords and surfing spots.

STAVANGER & AROUND
pop 106,000
Don't be misled by Stavanger's title 'Oil Capital of Norway' – this is a picturesque city (Norway's fourth largest) of narrow cobbled streets and small white houses. The centre is lively, containing a fine stock of bars, cafés and places to stroll. It's an excellent point from which to begin exploring the Lysefjord.

History
Stavanger was once a bustling fishing centre and, in its heyday, had more than 70 sardine canneries. By the 1960s, the depletion of fish stocks had brought an end to the industry, but the discovery of North Sea oil spared Stavanger from hard times. This is perhaps no great tourist draw, but it has brought prosperity and a cosmopolitan community with nearly 3000 British and US oil people.

Orientation

The adjacent bus and train stations are a 10-minute walk from the harbour, around which most sights cluster.

Information

BOOKSHOP

Gardum (☎ 51 89 44 40; Søregata 22; ☺ 9am-6pm Mon-Thu, 9am-5pm Fri, 9am-4pm Sat) Large travel section.

INTERNET ACCESS

Cafe.com (☎ 51 55 41 20; Søvberg gate 15; ☺ 11am-9pm Mon-Sat, noon-9pm Sun; Nkr55 per hr)

Library (☎ 51 50 72 57; Sølverg gate 2; ☺ 10am-7pm Mon-Thu, 10am-5pm Fri, 10am-3pm Sat) In the Sølvberget Stavanger Kulturhus; provides free internet access (but you'll have to wait and there's a time limit).

TOURIST INFORMATION

Tourist Office (☎ 51 85 92 00; www.visitstavanger .com; Rosenkildetorget 1; ☺ 9am-8pm Jun-Aug, shorter hrs & closed Sun Sep-May) Provides details of Stavanger's 12 annual festivals.

Sights

The bizarre and beautiful **Floro & Fjære** (Flower Island; ☎ 51 11 00 00; www.florogfjare.no; adult/child Nkr590/250; ☺ May-Sep; ☺) blooms brightly with palm trees and exotic plants. Or part of it anyway. The rest is a pile of rocks where grass struggles to grow and sheep struggle to find it. The magical bit is an oasis painstakingly constructed by a horticulturist (and his devoted family) who retired from his nursery to build this 6-acre garden of lush grass, fig cork and lemon trees, thousands of flowers and a slew of tropical plants. For your tariff, you take a pleasant boat ride (20 minutes) past offshore islands, tour the grounds, and enjoy a stellar four-course buffet. Reservations recommended.

Tracing the history of oil formation and extraction in the North Sea, the state-of-the-art **Norsk Oljemuseum** (☎ 51 93 93 00; www .norskolje.museum.no; Kjeringholmen; adult/child Nkr75/35; ☺ 10am-7pm Jun-Aug, 10am-4pm Mon-Sat, 10am-6pm Sun Sep-May; ☺) nicely balances the technical side of oil exploration with archive footage of significant moments in the history of Norwegian oil. Not least among these are the coverage of the Kielland Tragedy, when 123 workers were killed and a 1950s commission report concluding that there was no oil in Norwegian waters. Excellent interactive exhibits for kids.

The following **museums** (☎ 51 84 27 00; ☺ 11am-4pm mid-Jun–mid-Aug, shorter hrs early Jun & late Aug, 11am-4pm Sun Sep-May) have combined same-day admission costs of adult/family Nkr40/90. The main **Stavanger Museum** (Musé-gata 16) has the standard collection of stuffed animals in one wing and local history exhibits in another. More interesting is the **Maritime Museum** (Nedre Strandgate 17), in two restored warehouses, which gives a good glimpse of Stavanger's extensive maritime history. The fascinating **Canning Museum** (Øvre Strandgate 88A) occupies an old sardine cannery, where you'll see ancient machinery in action, learn about the various soul-destroying jobs provided by the cannery and ogle a large collection of old sardine-can labels. There are also two 19th-century manor houses built by wealthy ship owners: the recently restored **Ledaal** (Eiganesveien 45), which serves as the residence for visiting members of the royal family, and the excellent **Breidablikk** (Eiganesveien 40A), a merchant's opulent villa built in 1881.

A fun quarter for strolling about is Gamle Stavanger, on the west side of the harbour, where cobblestone walkways lead through rows of well-preserved early-18th-century whitewashed wooden houses.

Activities

The area's most popular outing is the two-hour hike to the top of the incredible **Preikestolen** (Pulpit Rock), 25km east of Stavanger. You can inch up to the edge of its flat top and peer 600m straight down to the Lysefjord. The tourist board has details on public transport to the trailhead.

A good outing, if you have a vehicle, is to take the **car ferry** (☎ 51 86 87 80; Nkr350, four hr, one daily in mid-Jun to Mid-Aug) from Stavanger to Lysebotn, at the head of the Lysefjord. From there, drive up the mountain pass to Sirdal, along a narrow road that climbs 640m with 27 hairpin turns, for a scenic ride back to Stavanger. Starting at the Øyg-ardsstølen Café car park, near the top of the bends, a strenuous 10km-return hike leads to the second wonder of Lysefjord, the **Kjeragbolten** boulder, or chockstone, lodged between two rock faces about 2m apart but with 1000m of empty space underneath.

SURFING

If you want excellent, unpopulated surf breaks and are willing to brave some cold

NORWAY

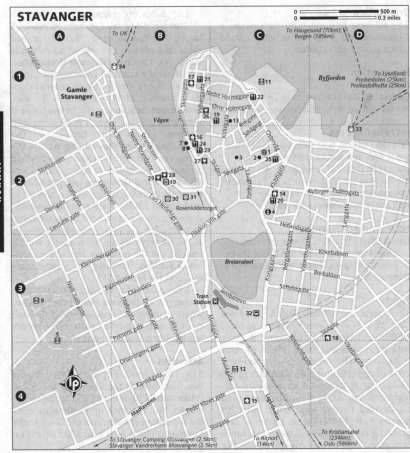

STAVANGER

water, the undeveloped coast around Stavanger attracts purists. For gear purchase, rentals (Nkr350 per day), lessons (Nkr390 gets you gear plus four hours in the water) and advice on where to go, visit **Surf Centrum** (☎ 51 33 11 22; www.surfcentrum.no; ✆ 10am-7pm Mon-Fri, 10am-4pm Sat). The closest surfable spot is 15km to the south.

Tours

If you'd rather look up at Pulpit Rock from the bottom, the **Fjord Tours** (☎ 51 89 52 70; www.fjordpanorama.no) sightseeing boat leaves Stavanger from mid-May through August to cruise the lovely steep-walled Lysefjord, operated by an entertaining bunch of old salts who will point out fish farms along the

way. Tickets (adult/child Nkr280/140) can be purchased at the tourist office.

Sleeping

Because the local hostel is not open year-round, sleeping cheaply in Stavanger can be a challenge. In summer, rooms at all price levels sell out early. For an alternative to the places listed below, the tourist office books rooms in B&Bs (Nkr30 fee). Rooms start at Nkr300.

BUDGET

Stavanger Camping Mosvangen (☎ 51 53 29 71; www.mosvangencamping.no; Tjensvoll 1B; camp sites from Nkr80, dm Nkr120, 2-person cabins Nkr350-400, 4-person cabins Nkr500-600; ✆ May-Sep) Situated in a clearing near lake Mosvangen, you'll find a large field with minimal shade trees and some mass-produced cabins. There's also a dormitory. Nearby walking trails lead to town (3km).

Preikestolhytta (☎ 97 16 55 51; www.preikestol hytta.no; dm/r Nkr210/580; ⏳ Jun-Aug; 🅿) Trees grow from this isolated turf-roofed hostel, 25km out of the city within walking distance of Pulpit Rock and other amazing hikes. The cafeteria works with a culinary school to prepare fine local meals. Book far in advance.

Stavanger Vandrerhjem Mosvangen (☎ 51 54 36 36; stavanger.hostel@vandrerhjem.no; Henrik Ibsens gate 19; dm/d Nkr170/340; ⏳ Jun-Aug) Lakeside and private, two- and four-bed rooms enjoy access to trails around lake Mosvagen and its ducks. Breakfast costs Nkr60.

MIDRANGE & TOP END

Rogalandsheimen Gjestgiveri (☎ 51 52 01 88; Muségata 18; s/d Nkr495/595 Nkr500-550; 🅿 💻) Paintings cover every surface of this charming 19th-century guesthouse. The 13 homey rooms share bathroom facilities and attract artists and musicians.

Skansen Hotel (☎ 51 93 85 00; www.skansenhotel .no; Skansegata 7; s/d Mon-Fri Sep-Jun Nkr845/980, s/d Sat & Sun Nkr560/645, s/d Mid-Jun–Aug Nkr620/705; 💻 ♿) This cool independent place contains simple rooms in a great location near the harbour. The joint's slick Broremann Bar is staffed by a master mixer.

Skagen Brygge Hotell (☎ 51 85 00 00; www.ska genbryggehotell.no; Skagenkaien 30; s/d Nkr1350/1450, s/ d discount Nkr700/850; 🅿 🍽 ♿) A modernised former warehouse containing exceedingly comfortable rooms, half of which have stellar views of the harbour. The breakfast buffet features fresh fruit and French pastry.

Also recommended:

Stavanger Bed & Breakfast (☎ 51 56 25 00; www .stavangerbedandbreakfast.no; Vikedalsgata 1A; s/d Nkr565/670; 🅿) Plain, linoleum-floored rooms in a quiet neighbourhood.

Comfort Hotel Grand (☎ 51 20 14 00; www.choice .no; Kulbbgata 3; s/d Nkr870/770, s/d discount Nkr670/770) Looks grim from the outside, but rooms have high standard interiors.

Eating

Café Sting (☎ 51 89 38 78; Valberget 3; smaller dishes Nkr75-129, mains Nkr155-175) Blessed with a lovely hill-top position and sharing a yard with the Valberg Tower, Sting serves substantial smaller dishes, such as an excellent Creole pasta with shrimp. The clientele is mostly gay on Friday and Saturday nights when there is often a DJ.

Stim (☎ 51 85 00 16; Skagenkaien 28; mains Nkr189-259) A high-end design-team reworked this water-facing warehouse to include green glass stairs, silent video projections of cloudscapes and subtle level changes. For food, try a Cajun fish soup, John Dory or a moderately price three-course splurge (Nkr300).

Resept (☎ 51 55 39 80; Østervåg 43; mains Nkr49-99) This café's décor involves minimal leather couches and solid coloured walls recalling the supergraphics of the '70s. Enjoy vegetarian pasta (Nkr79), Asian noodle soup and DJs.

Food Story (☎ 51 56 37 70; Klubbgata 3; mains Nkr55-99; ☒ 10am-6pm Mon-Wed, 10am-8pm Thu & Fri, 10am-5pm Sat) This deli/restaurant prepares a changing menu of high-end fare, usually organic. Eat raw tuna with citrus fruits, Italian sausages and fancy sauces.

India Tandoori Restaurant (☎ 51 89 39 35; Valberggata 14; lunch mains Nkr78-89, dinner mains Nkr89-199) Authentic northern Indian dishes (several vegetarian) and a particularly good korma navrattan come in a well-decorated room that recalls the subcontinent.

Sjøhuset Skagen (☎ 51 89 51 80; Skagenkaien 16; mains Nkr185-235) For traditionally prepared fish, this creaky-floored choice is a winner. Find exposed wooden frames, models of ships and pavement views over the harbour.

A fish market sits at the harbour, and **Våland Dampbakeri & Conditori** (☎ 51 86 19 23; Nygaten 24) turns out flaky pastry, as it has done since 1913.

Drinking

Cementen (☎ 51 56 78 00; Nedre Strandgate 25) On the 2nd floor with views across the quay, friendly bartenders play kick-arse tunes and sometimes host bands. Pick up a used book (Nkr5 to Nkr10) and Sunday beer special's (Nkr31) in a room that feels like a private library full of drunk hipsters.

Armadillo (☎ 51 89 39 59; Øvre Holmegata 15) Walk straight through Harry Pepper's (a Mexican restaurant) to this hidden neighbourhood pub on the 2nd floor. An excellent collection of worn furniture has been carefully collected from Denmark, and the bar piece is from Dublin. There's no sign.

Gnu (☎ 51 89 73 45; Nedre Strandgate 25) A supergaudy and enormous chandelier hangs over bartenders wearing AC/DC T-shirts, some taxidermy and a foosball table. Toughest, skinniest bouncers in town.

Beverly Hills Fun Pub (☎ 51 89 51 77; Skagenkaien 14A; ☒ noon-2am) Second home to scads of oil-rig workers and international businessmen is Stavanger's most consistently (and inexplicably) crowded bar, even on rainy Monday nights. Despite the name and the startling ratio of four men to every woman, it's not even an expressly gay pub.

Entertainment

Checkpoint Charlie (☎ 51 53 22 45; www.checkpoint .no; Lars Hertervigs gate 5; ☒ 8pm-2am Sun-Fri, 3pm-2am Sat) Friendly dudes tend bar here, where the rock happens on a small stage. Happy-hour beer sells for Nkr36, and it also shows football matches.

Taket (☎ 51 84 37 01; Nedre Strandgata 15) Stavanger's biggest disco plays pop hits to a crowded space whose sense of décor is lost in blackness. Flashing lights over the dance floor reveal that the place is packed with young bodies as well as the tackiness of the floor that various kinds of liquor and biological wastes have been spilled.

Getting There & Away

TO/FROM THE AIRPORT

Buses leave frequently for the airport (14km south of town) from the bus station (Nkr70/110 one-way/return, 20 minutes, several times an hour). A taxi costs Nkr250 to Nkr350.

BOAT

The **HSD Flaggruten** (☎ 51 86 87 80) express passenger catamaran to Bergen (adult Nkr640/840 one-way/return, 4¼ hours) and Haugesund leaves two or three times daily.

BUS

Nor-Way Bussekspress offers connecting services to Oslo (Nkr700, 10¼ hours, one to three daily) and direct to Bergen (Nkr420, 5¾ hours, roughly one an hour).

TRAIN

Stavanger's only railway line runs to Oslo (Nkr833, 7¾ hours, two to four daily) via Kristiansand (Nkr383, three hours, three to seven daily).

MANDAL

pop 12,800

Mandal, Norway's southernmost town, is best known for having the country's finest bathing beach (though water temperatures are significantly warmer in the Oslofjord). There are enough cobbled pedestrian laneways in the centre for an hour or two of village exploration.

The 800m-long **Sjøsanden** beach, about 1km from the centre, is Norway's sandy Copacabana, with a lovely forest backdrop.

At the southernmost point in Norway, 36km west of Mandal, you'll find wild coastal scenery and historical exhibitions at the classic lighthouse, **Lindesnes Fyr** (☎ 38 26 19 02; www.lindesnesfyr.no; Lindesnes; adult/child Nkr30/ free; 🕑 10am-6pm May, 10am-8pm Jun & Sep, 10am-9pm Jul & Aug). Buses from Mandal (Nkr52, one hour) travel to the lighthouse on Monday, Wednesday and Friday in summer. You'll have one hour there before the single return bus departs.

Mandal Tourist Information (☎ 38 27 83 00; Bryggegaten 10; 🕑 9am-7pm Mon-Fri, 10am-4pm Sat & Sun Jun-Aug, 9am-4pm Mon-Fri Sep-May) is a five-minute walk west from the bus station.

Sleeping & Eating

Sjøsanden Ferietun (☎ 38 26 60 37; saferie@online .no; Fr Nansenvei 6; camp sites Nkr100, r from Nkr450, cabins from Nkr550; **P**) Just steps from the beach in a family-friendly complex set within a forest grove. Sells out months in advance.

Kjøbmandsgaarden Hotel (☎ 38 26 12 76; www .kjobmandsgaarden.no; Store Elvegaten 57; s/d Nkr740/970) A former hardware shop dating from 1863. The basic rooms come with private bathroom but don't exhibit much character. Rooms cost 15% less on weekends. It's cafeteria serves traditional Norwegian fare in a wood-floored room with beachy furniture and an upright piano. At night, it's a more expensive restaurant.

Jonas B Gundersen (☎ 38 27 15 00; Store Elvegaten 25; mains Nkr149-164) Serves good pizza (large ones, costing Nkr189 to Nkr209, feed two to three people) in a joint packed with old music instruments and pictures of jazz dudes.

Edgar's Bakeri og Konditori (☎ 38 27 15 55; Torget) Occupying two floors of a charming white building, this place serves excellent *kaneli svingen* (pastry with vanilla filling) and has fine 2nd-floor views of the *torget* (square).

Getting There & Away

Express buses run two to four times daily between Stavanger (Nkr320, 3¾ hours) and Kristiansand (Nkr80, 45 minutes) via Mandal.

KRISTIANSAND

pop 75,000

The fifth-largest city in the country, summertime Kristiansand offers urban life and a small bathing beach right in the town centre. Strollers will enjoy poking around Posebyen, a district containing a large concentration of white houses from the 17th and 18th centuries. Kristiansand also hosts the fantastic Quart Music Festival. It's a busy seaside holiday resort for Norwegians, but foreign tourists with limited time generally prefer Oslo, Bergen and Stavanger.

Kristiansand is Norway's closest port to Denmark and offers the first glimpse of the country for many ferry travellers from the south.

Orientation

The train, bus and ferry terminals are together on the west side of the city centre. Markens gate, a pedestrian street a block inland, is the central shopping and restaurant area.

Information

Cafe.com (Dronningengate 56; per hr Nkr45; 🕑 11am-11pm Mon-Thu, 11am-midnight Fri, noon-5am Sat, 1-11pm Sun) Internet access.

Library (☎ 38 12 49 10; Rådhusgata 11; 🕑 10am-6pm Mon-Thu, 10am-4.30pm Fri, 10am-3pm Sat)

Tourist Office (☎ 38 12 13 14; www.sorlandet.com; Vestre Strandgate 32; 🕑 8am-6pm Mon-Fri, 9am-6pm Sat, noon-6pm Sun mid-Jun–late Aug, 8.30am-3.30pm Mon-Fri late Aug–mid-Jun)

Sights & Activities

The most prominent feature to be seen along Strandpromenaden is **Christiansholm Festning** (Christiansholm Fortress; 🕑 9am-9pm mid-May–mid-Sep), built between 1662 and 1672; there's a fine coastal view from the cannon-ringed wall. From there, walk inland along the tree-lined Festningsgata and turn left onto Gyldenløves gate, passing the **town square** and **Kristiansand Domkirke** (☎ 38 10 77 50; Kirkegata; 🕑 9am-4pm Mon-Fri, 9am-2pm Sat late Jun-early Aug, 10am-2pm Mon-Fri early Jun & late Aug), a huge church which nicely complements the square. You can climb the tower for adult/child Nkr20/10. Organ recitals occur at noon, Tuesday to Saturday.

It's also worth taking a slow stroll around **Posebyen** (old town), which takes in most of 14 blocks at the northern end of Kristiansand's characteristic *kvadraturen* (the city's street pattern).

Baneheia, a wooded park with lakes and trails, abuts the northwest side of the city centre. The 11th-century Romanesque **Oddernes Kirke** (☎ 38 05 87 50), about 1.5km further northeast along E18, contains a rune stone, and a baroque pulpit from 1704; it's open variable hours.

Kristiansand Dyrepark (☎ 38 04 97 00; www .dyreparken.com; adult Nkr85-240, child Nkr70-195; ⊙ 10am-7pm mid-May–early Aug, shorter hr otherwise) has gradually expanded into one of Norway's most popular domestic attractions. Mainly catering to families with children, the park includes water rides, a zoo, a 'Nordic wilderness', a cruise on pirate ships and the fantasy village of Kardamomme By. It's off the E18, 9km east of town.

Festivals & Events

Quart Festival (☎ 38 14 69 69; www.quart.no; day pass Nkr470, 5-day pass Nkr1750), a weeklong music

festival, occurs in June or July. As many as 25 bands play daily and hotels sell out for miles in every direction. See Depeche Mode, Björk and Clap Your Hands Say Yeah! tear it up along with local acts.

Sleeping

Roligheden Camping (☎ 38 09 67 22; www.roligh eden.no; camp sites from Nkr120, 4-person cabins Nkr650; ℗) A popular and good city camp ground. Pathways snake around slightly hilly terrain. It lies near a small, crowded beach 3km east of town. Take bus No 15.

Frosbusdal Rom (☎ 91 12 99 06; www.gjestehus .no; Frobusdalen 2; s Nkr350-400, d Nkr500-700; ℗) Loaded with stained glass and period character, this romantic home from 1917 has

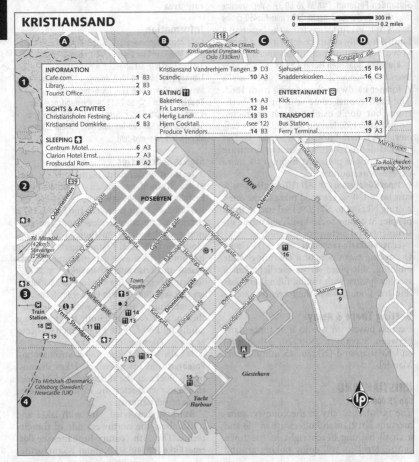

KRISTIANSAND

0 ———————— 300 m
0 ———————— 0.2 miles

INFORMATION	
Cafe.com	1 B3
Library	2 B3
Tourist Office	3 A3

SIGHTS & ACTIVITIES	
Christiansholm Festning	4 C4
Kristiansand Domkirke	5 B3

SLEEPING 🏠	
Centrum Motel	6 A3
Clarion Hotel Ernst	7 A3
Frosbusdal Rom	8 A2

Kristiansand Vandrerhjem Tangen	9 D3
Scandic	10 A3

EATING 🍴	
Bakeries	11 A3
Frk Larsen	12 B4
Herlig Land!	13 B3
Hjem Cocktail	(see 12)
Produce Vendors	14 B3

Sjøhuset	15 B4
Snadderskiosken	16 C3

ENTERTAINMENT 🎭	
Kick	17 B4

TRANSPORT	
Bus Station	18 A3
Ferry Terminal	19 A3

intimate rooms, some with balcony. There's no breakfast, but guests have access to a kitchen and splendid dining room.

Kristiansand Vandrerhjem Tangen (☎ 38 02 83 10; kristiansand.hostel@vandrerhjem.no; Skansen 8; dm Nkr195, s/d Nkr290/460 s/d with shared bathroom Nkr395/595; mid-Jan–mid-Dec; P) The modern hostel offers clean rooms in a quiet, industrialised part of town a few minutes' walk from a small beach.

Scandic (☎ 38 12 86 00; www.scandic-hotels.com; Markens gate 39; s/d Nkr990/1190; P) Smartly refurbished rooms with hardwood floors overlook town through big windows (at least those on higher floors).

Also recommended:

Clarion Hotel Ernst (☎ 38 12 86 00; www.ernst.no; Rådhusgaten 2; s/d Nkr1025/1245; P) Pleasant rooms with glass-roofed courtyard. Too close to nightclubs.

Centrum Motel (☎ 38 02 79 69; www.motell.no; Vestre Strandsgate 49; s/d Nkr490/650; P) Central location, no breakfast, clean ugly rooms with private bathrooms.

Eating & Drinking

Snadderkiosken (☎ 38 02 90 29; Østre Strand gate 78A; dishes Nkr17-55) Follow the crowds to this popular takeaway stand. It offers a vast great-value menu, including such things as meatballs, cod with mashed potato, and sausages.

Frk Larsen (☎ 38 07 14 13; Markens gate 5; mains Nkr 65-120) A popular café filled with mismatched tables, chairs and couches, Frk Larsen serves strong coffee, messy salads and big cakes.

Hjem Cocktail (9pm-midnight Tue, Thu-Sat 9pm-3am) Hidden in a small side room of Frk Larsen, is this incredibly cool white concrete box where seating consists of a red couch and logs. Dress hip.

Herlig Land! (☎ 38 09 06 22; Markensgate 16; mains Nkr130-225) Straddling the ground between café and restaurant, candle-lit Herlig Land! is a good spot to eat chicken that led a happy life until not long before it arrived on your plate. Cheap Sunday specials.

Sjøhuset (☎ 38 02 62 60; Østre Strandgate 12A; mains Nkr215-270) This harbourside favourite with stacks of outdoor seating consistently dishes out superb seafood, such as cod fillets baked with ham and served with caramelised parsnip. The less hungry or the budget-minded should try the shellfish soup (Nkr89).

There are bakeries on Rådhus gate and produce vendors on the southeastern side of the cathedral.

Entertainment

Kick (☎ 38 02 64 44; Dronningens gate 8) With a large dance floor accommodating hundreds, this good-looking disco with its blond wood, luminous white balls and multimedia projections provides an exceedingly popular place to bust it. Arrive a bit early for a voyeuristic balcony seat.

Getting There & Away

Trains run to Stavanger (Nkr383, three hours, three to seven daily) and Oslo (Nkr569, 4¾ hours, three to seven daily).

Nor-Way Busseksress runs to Stavanger (Nkr340, four hours, two to four daily) via Mandal (Nkr75, 40 minutes, two to four daily); to Oslo (Nkr320, 5¼ hours, eight to 10 daily) via Arendal (Nkr100, 1½ hours, eight to 10 daily); and to Bergen (Nkr610, 12 hours, one daily)

For information on ferries to Denmark, Sweden and the UK, see p383.

GRIMSTAD

pop 9500

Grimstad is one of the loveliest of the 'white towns' on the Skagerrak coast and has a charming pedestrianised centre with narrow streets. These streets begin to fill in June, as attendees flock to the Norwegian Short Film Festival. By July, the small town becomes crowded with Norwegians arriving to enjoy their summer holidays. Popular activities include sunbathing on islands, fishing and ice-cream eating.

Today's low-key atmosphere belies Grimstad's past as a major shipbuilding centre – at one point in the 19th century the town had 40 shipyards, and 90 ships were under construction simultaneously.

The **tourist office** (☎ 37 04 40 41; www.grimstad .net; Smith Petersensgata 3; 9am-6pm Mon-Fri, 10am-4pm Sat & Sun Jun-Aug) can suggest various boat trips to the outlying skerries.

Sights

In 1847, Henrik Ibsen started work at Grimstad's Lars Nielsen pharmacy, where he lived in a small room and cultivated his interest in writing. By the time he left Grimstad for university studies in Christiania (Oslo), Ibsen had qualified as a pharmacist's assistant and was on his way to future renown as a writer. Some of his finest works are set in Grimstad's offshore skerries.

The **Grimstad By Museum** (☎ 37 04 46 53; Henrik Ibsens gate 14; adult/child Nkr40/15; ⏱ 11am-5pm Mon-Sat, 1-5pm Sun May–mid-Sep) includes the virtually untouched Lars Nielsen pharmacy and **Ibsenhuset** (the Ibsen house), which contains many of the writer's belongings, such as portraits of mean-looking people.

Sleeping & Eating

Bie Apartment & Feriesenter (☎ 37 04 03 96; www .bieapart.no; Arendalsveien 85; camp sites Nkr210, cabins Nkr550-1200; P ⚄) Not picturesque, this place redeems itself by being the closest option to town, 800m northeast of the centre along Arendalsveien.

Grimstad Hotell (☎ 37 25 25 25; www.grimstadho tell.no; Kirkegata 3; s/d Nkr1045/1245, s/d discount summer & weekends Nkr700/900; P ⚄) An excellent location smack in the town centre. The exterior suggests you'll be sleeping in one of the town's white cuties, but most rooms are part of a bizarre historicist complex.

Apotekergården (☎ 37 04 50 25; Skolegaten 3; mains Nkr225; ⏱ 6-11pm Sun-Thu, noon-1am Fri & Sat) Inside a former pharmacy dating to 1853. Serves swanky tapas and fixed-price menus that run up to Nkr695. It's got some lovely garden seating, though some readers complain of underwhelming food.

There are also a handful of restaurants on the water where you can grab an outdoor beer or eat some fish.

Entertainment

Satisfying nightlife options only exist in the summer. **Club Berg** (☎ 92 83 22 24; Storgata 2) is the perennial favourite, playing host to drunken nights of karaoke, hip-hop, the occasional black metal band and twangy country dudes.

Getting There & Away

The bus station is on Storgata, at the harbour. Eight to 10 daily Nor-Way Bussekspress runs to Oslo (Nkr300, 4½ hours) and Kristiansand (Nkr75, 40 minutes). Nettbuss buses to/from Arendal run once or twice hourly (Nkr40, 30 minutes).

ARENDAL

pop 32,000

Piles of houses smile down from the steep slopes surrounding Pollen, a small bit of flat land that serves as Arendal's centre and harbour. Here you'll find one of the livelier towns on Norway's southern coast with several harbourside cafés whose outdoor seating fills the moment things even begin to resemble warm.

There are many islands to explore in the archipelago off the coast, some appointed with 19th-century lighthouses. Ask **Arendal Turistkontor** (☎ 37 00 55 44; www.arendal.com; Sam Eydes plass; ⏱ 9am-7pm Mon-Fri, 11am-6pm Sat & Sun Jul, 9am-7pm Mon-Fri, 11am-2pm Sat Jun & Aug) for details.

Just a few minutes' walk south of the bus station brings you into the old harbourside area of **Tyholmen**, with its attractively restored 19th-century wooden buildings. Check out the **Rådhus** (☎ 37 01 30 00; Rådhusgata 10; ⏱ 9am-3pm Mon-Fri), originally a shipowner's home dating from 1815, later becoming the town hall in 1844, or the **Aust-Agder Museum** (☎ 37 07 35 00; Parkveien 16; adult/child Nkr25/15; ⏱ 9am-5pm Mon-Fri, noon-5pm Sun late Jun–mid-Aug, to 3pm mid-Aug–mid-Jun),which displays objects brought home by the town's sailors (from 1832), as well as relics of Arendal's shipbuilding, timber and import-export trades.

Sleeping & Eating

For anything inexpensive, you'll have to head out of town.

Nidelv Brygge og Camping (☎ 37 01 14 25; Vesterveien 251, Hisøy; camp sites Nkr60-110, cabins Nkr250-750; P) This field, chock full of caravans staying for months at a time, fronts a calm, swimable estuary. It's 6km west of Arendal. From town, take any half-hourly bus for Kristiansand or Grimstad (Nkr22).

Clarion Hotel Tyholmen (☎ 37 07 68 00; Teaterplassen 2; s/d Mon-Fri Sep-Jun Nkr1480/1680, s/d Sat & Sun Nkr790/990, s/d Mid-Jun–Aug Nkr960/890; P ⚄) Surrounded by boats, this smart harbourside hotel features nice rooms and fine views, close to an enclave of restaurants and cafés.

Ting Hai Hotel (☎ 37 02 22 01; ting@online.no; Østregate 5; s/d Nkr650/890) Just about the least Norwegian hotel experience in Norway, rooms over a decent Chinese restaurant (mains Nkr120) feel like sleeping in Chinatown.

Café Det Lindvedske hus (☎ 37 02 18 38; Nedre Tyholmsvei 7B; dishes Nkr40-110; ⏱ 11am-midnight Mon-Sat, 1pm-midnight Sun) Occupying a 200-year-old building, this café serves salads, pasta and sandwiches, such as a delicious vegetarian number with browned cheese, tomato, avocado, mushrooms and green beans. Booze, coffee and cakes are also offered.

For a tasty snack eat creatures from the waterfront fish market. Plenty of outdoor restaurants bars and a disco line Pollen.

Getting There & Away
Nor-Way Bussekspress runs between Kristiansand (Nkr100, 1¾ hours) and Oslo (Nkr300, four hours) stopping in Arendal eight to 10 times daily. Regional buses connect Arendal with Grimstad (Nkr40, 30 minutes, once or twice hourly) and Kristiansand (Nkr100, 1½ hours, hourly).

Arendal is connected with the main rail system by a trunk line from Nelaug.

RISØR
pop 4500

With its cluster of historic white houses built up around a busy little fishing harbour, Risør is one of the most picturesque villages on the south coast. The harbour is filled with small classic vessels, ranging from old wooden motorboats to oddly designed masted contraptions. Risør is a haunt for artists, and many well-to-do yachties make it their summer base. Don't like boats? Prepare for extreme boredom.

The **Risør Trebåtfestival** (Wooden Boat Festival; ☎ 37 14 81 05; www.risor-woodenboat.no) is the town's biggest annual event. Held in early August, it constitutes an amazing sight: you're unlikely to see so many fabulous boats in such a cute setting anywhere else. During the festival, ships of different classes and ages race one another, sometimes crashing when the wind is strong.

Next to wandering around the town's harbour and the narrow streets, one of the most popular activities is to visit the offshore islands, which can be reached by inexpensive water taxis. The most frequented island, **Stangholmen**, has an old lighthouse with a restaurant.

Though most visitors stay on their boats, there are a few spots for earth dwellers, including the charming **Det Lille Hotel** (☎ 37 15 14 95; www.detlillehotel.no; Kragsgata 12; s Nkr950-1150, d Nkr1150-1450; P), which occupies several small white houses on the water, with individually and exceptionally appointed suites. Parking for boats is available.

The Mediterranean-influenced menu at **Brasserie Krag** (☎ 37 15 14 95; Kragsgata 12; mains Nkr100-210) is best enjoyed at a small pavement table under an awning.

You'll find a couple of moderately priced cafés at the harbour, as well as ice-cream shops, a market and a **bakery** (Kragsgata).

Getting There & Away
Buses (Nkr55, 45 minutes) connect with the train at Gjerstad several times daily. Nor-Way Bussekspress runs between Kristiansand (Nkr150, 1½ hours, eight or nine daily) and Oslo (Nkr300, 3¾ hours, eight or nine daily).

TELEMARK
Most of the Telemark region is sparsely populated and rural, with steep mountains, deep valleys, high plateaus, and countless lakes. Most visitors come for a few stave churches and the Telemark Canal.

Public transport in this region isn't particularly convenient; most buses run infrequently and train lines are largely absent, so sightseeing is best done by car. Telemark's westernmost train station is at Bø; from there, connecting buses lead west to Dalen, Åmot and on to Odda in Hardanger. For tourist information, contact **Telemarkreiser** (☎ 35 90 00 20; www.visittelemark.com).

Telemark Canal
The Telemark canal system, a marvel completed in 1892, covers 105km of scenic lakes, towns and canals with 18 locks, some impressively narrow and wooden. It runs from the industrialised city of Skien to the small town of Dalen. Between May and September, a couple of century-old **sightseeing boats** (☎ 35 90 00 30; www.telemarkskanalen.no) make the sluggish, 11-hour journey (adult/child Nkr400/200 one way).

One kilometre from the Dalen dock, **Buøy Camping Dalen** (☎ 35 07 75 87; www.dalencamping .com; camp site from Nkr130, s/tr Nkr295/345, cabins Nkr525-625; P) separates tenters from caravans. It's common to see elk and beavers. The 'dragon-style' **Dalen Hotel** (☎ 35 07 90 00; www.dalenhotel.no; s/d Nkr950/1200) is a marvellously intact 19th-century wooden beauty with lots of projecting balconies and gables. The restaurant serves high-end international fare. Skien's **HI hostel** (☎ 35 50 48 70; Moflatveien 65; dm/s/d Nkr150/375/505; P &) is a pleasant and tidy modern lodge. To find it, follow signs to 'Skien Fritidspark.'

NORWAY

Trains run every hour or two between Skien and Oslo (Nkr269, 2¾ hours).

Notodden

pop 12,300

Notodden is an industrial town of little note, but the nearby **Heddal stave church** (☎ 35 02 04 00; www.heddal-stavkirke.no; Heddal; adult/child Nkr35/free, Sun services free; 9am-7pm late Jun-late Aug, shorter hrs May & Sep) is Telemark's most visited attraction. It's an impressive structure and possibly dates from 1242, but parts of the chancel date from as early as 1147. Of great interest are the 'rose' paintings, a runic inscription, the bishop's chair and the altarpiece. On Sundays from Easter to November, services are held at 11am (visitors are welcome, but to avoid disruption, you must remain for the entire one-hour service); after 1pm, the church is again open to the public.

The town hosts the renowned **Notodden Blues Festival** (☎ 35 02 76 50; www.bluesfest.no) In early August featuring dozens of bands, such as the Fabulous Thunderbirds and Jeff Healey.

Between Kongsberg and Notodden (Nkr80, 35 minutes), TIMEkspressen buses run once or twice an hour.

Rjukan

pop 3600

The long, narrow industrial town of Rjukan is squeezed into the deep Vestfjord Valley at the base of the 1883m **Mt Gausta**, Telemark's highest peak. The route to the top starts at lake Heddersvann (1173m), 16km southeast of town (by road Fv651). Unless you're here to partake in outdoor activities, you won't find much entertainment.

Ask the **tourist office** (☎ 35 09 12 90; www.visitrjukan.no; Torget 2; ☉ 9am-7pm Mon-Fri, 10am-6pm Sat & Sun late Jun-early Aug, 9am-2.30pm Mon-Fri mid-Aug–mid-Jun) about local activities, including skiing, hiking and fun **rail bicycle rides**.

The **Industrial Workers Museum** (☎ 35 09 90 00; adult/student/child Nkr55/45/30; ☉ 10am-6pm May-Sep, 10am-3pm Tue-Fri Oct-Apr), housed inside a hydroelectric plant dating from 1911, 7km west of Rjukan, details the Norwegian Resistance's daring sabotage of the heavy-water plant used by the Nazis in their atomic efforts.

From the top station of the Krossobanen cable car (Nkr35), above Rjukan, it's an eight-hour walk north to the Kalhovd mountain hut and a network of trails that stretches north and west across the expansive moors of **Hardangervidda**, a bleak and beautiful plateau that makes a popular wilderness hiking area. It contains Norway's largest wild reindeer herd.

The town itself is thin on recommendable places to stay. **Rjukan Gjestegård** (☎ 35 09 05 27; fax 35 09 09 96; Birkelandsgata 2; breakfast Nkr60, dm Nkr175, s/d with shared bathroom Nkr290/450; 🖳) occupies a humdrum postwar building in town where the hostel used to be. The underwhelming **Park Hotel** (☎ 35 08 21 88; www.parkhotell-rjukan.no; Sam Eydes gate 67; s/d from Nkr645/795) has a restaurant.

If you're here to hike, you'll find better options in near the Glaustablikk ski area, accessible by car. **Rjukan Vandrerhjem** (☎ 35 09 20 40; www.kvitaavatn.no; Kvitåvatn; dm/s/d Nkr200/300/450; 🅿 🖳) features a cosy pine lodge, six-bunk huts, and incredible wilderness surrounds.

An express bus runs to Oslo (Nkr290, 3½ hours) via Kongsberg (Nkr150, 1¾ hours), two to five times daily.

BUSKERUD

The mainly forested county of Buskerud stretches northwest from Oslofjord to the central highlands of Norway. Mineral resources, particularly silver, have been thoroughly exploited in Buskerud's hills and mountains.

Kongsberg

pop 18,000

Today's Kongsberg attracts visitors with winter skiing and historic sites left over from its 17th-century glory days. The town was founded in 1624 following the discovery of the world's purest silver deposits in the nearby Numedal Valley. During the resulting silver rush, it briefly became the second-largest town in Norway. The Royal Mint is still in town, but the last mine, no longer able to turn a profit, closed in 1957.

ORIENTATION & INFORMATION

Kongsberg is split into old and new by the falls of the river. The new eastern section of the area has the main shopping district, tourist office and transit stations. Find museums, the hostel and Kirkegata on the old side.

The **Tourist office** (☎ 32 73 50 00; www.visitkongs berg.no; Karsches gate 3; ☺ 9am-7pm Mon-Fri, 10am-4pm Sat & Sun Jul & Aug) serves as a **DNT** agent.

SIGHTS

The **Norwegian Mining Museum** (☎ 32 72 32 00; Hyttegata 3; adult/child Nkr50/10; ☺ 10am-5pm Jul–mid-Aug, shorter hrs mid-Aug–Jun) is in the town centre, just over the bridge on the west side of the Numedalslågen river. Set in an 1844 smelter, it has exhibits on mining and minerals as well as the Royal Mint and the local armaments industry.

The **Lågdal folk museum** (☎ 32 73 34 68; Tillischbakken 8-10; adult/child Nkr40/10; ☺ 11am-5pm mid-Jun–mid-Aug) has a collection of period farmhouses, WWII exhibits and an indoor museum with re-created 19th-century workshops and a fine optics section. It's a 10-minute walk south of the train station: turn left on Bekkedokk and take the walkway parallel to the tracks, following the signs.

In July and August, there are daily tours of the old **silver mines** (adult/child Nkr75/30) at Saggrenda, 8km from Kongsberg, which include a 2.3km train ride through cool subterranean shafts – bring a sweater. Tour times should be checked with the tourist office. The Oslo-Notodden TIMEkspressen bus runs from Kongsberg to Saggrenda (Nkr45, 10 minutes, hourly), then it's a 15-minute walk.

SLEEPING & EATING

Kongsberg HI Hostel (☎ 32 73 20 24; www.kongsberg -vandrerhjem.no; Vinjesgata 1; dm/s/d Nkr195/445/550; ⓟ 🅿 ⓖ) In a new white building, the hostel lies near Kongsberg's baroque church. It is set back from a busy road and the largish grounds contain both a soccer pitch and a childrens' play area.

Quality Hotel Grand (☎ 32 77 28 00; www .choicehotels.no; Chr Augustsgate 2; s/d from Nkr790/920; ⓟ 🅿 ⓖ) The modern rooms in this hotel are not particularly special, but they are in Kongsberg's tallest building so some have nice views over the river's fells.

Christians Kjeller (☎ 32 76 45 00; www.chris tianskjeller.no; Kirkegata 10; mains Nkr190-268) For excellent fillet of reindeer served in an old wainscoted room with ample fireplace, sit upstairs. Below deck, a pub serves cheap fare while occupying a cellar from the 1660s (massive stone walls) where folk bands play. Nice beer garden.

GETTING THERE & AWAY

Trains run to Oslo (Nkr148, 1½ hours, roughly hourly). TIMEkspressen buses connect Kongsberg with Oslo (Nkr149, 1½ hours) and Notodden (Nkr75, 35 minutes, hourly).

CENTRAL NORWAY

The central region of Norway contains Jotunheimen, a popular wilderness area and national park characterised by dramatic ravines and multiple glaciers. The immensely scenic Oslo–Bergen rail line slices east to west, crossing the stark and white snowscape of the Hardangervidda plateau, a cross-country skiing paradise. For a resort town feel, try Lillehammer, close to several downhill slopes and a host of the 1994 Winter Olympics.

HAMAR

pop 28,000

Do you get jazzed over arenas from Olympics past? If so, you're in luck, winter of '94 style. The unimpressive commercial town sits beside **Mjøsa**, Norway's largest lake, which you can use to escape Hamar by riding **Skibladner** (☎ 61 14 40 80; www.skibladner.no), the world's oldest operating paddle steamer (1856), to Lillehammer (Nkr220/320 one way/return; four hours; three weekly).

The **tourist office** (☎ 62 51 75 03; ☺ 8am-6pm Mon-Fri, 10am-6pm Sat mid-Jun–mid-Aug, 8am-4pm Mon-Fri mid-Aug–mid-Jun) is inside the **Vikingskipshuset sports arena**, a graceful structure with the lines of an upturned Viking ship. The staff will be pleased to tell you about the enormous wooden **Northern Lights amphitheatre** built for figure-skating events.

The extensive open-air **Hedmarksmuseet** (☎ 62 54 27 00; Strandveien 100; adult/student/child Nkr70/55/30; ☺ 10am-5pm mid-Jun–mid-Aug, shorter hrs mid-May–mid-Jun & mid-Aug–mid-Sep) includes 18th- and 19th-century buildings, a local folk history exhibit featuring the creepy Devil's Finger, and the fantastic **Hamardomen** (Glass Cathedral), where the ruins of a medieval cathedral are protected within an enormous glass structure.

Seiersted Pensjonat's (☎ 62 52 12 44; www .seiersted.no; Holsetgata 64; s/d Nkr395/695) 18 centrally located rooms have painted furniture. Some share bathrooms.

NORWAY

For gourmet meals in an art gallery, **Artichoke** (☎ 62 53 23 33; Parkgata 21; lunch Nkr72-128, mains Nkr195-235) occupies a former bank building modified by someone who earned good grades in design school.

Drink hooch in **Siste Indre's** (☎ 62 53 55 00; Torggata 53) while relaxing on comfortable leather couches and admiring yellowing pictures of speed skaters. Towards closing time, don't be surprised if someone gets up and starts banging on a piano, while the entire bar sings along.

Trains run to Oslo (Nkr212, 1½ hours, once or twice hourly); to Røros (Nkr444, 3¼ hours, three to five daily), and to Trondheim (Nkr660, five hours, four daily) via Lillehammer.

LILLEHAMMER & AROUND
pop 25,000

Lillehammer, at the northern end of lake Mjøsa, has long been a popular ski resort for Norwegians, and since hosting the 1994 Winter Olympics it has attracted foreign visitors as well.

Lillehammer's centre is small and relatively charming. Storgata, the main pedestrian walkway, is two short blocks east of the adjacent bus and train stations. You'll find more information at the **tourist office** (☎ 61 28 98 00; www.lillehammerturist.no; Jernebanetorget 2; ☻ 9am-8pm Mon-Sat, 9am-6pm Sun mid-Jun–mid-Aug, shorter hrs otherwise).

Sights & Activities

Many tour the former Winter Olympic sites, including **Håkons Hall** (the ice-hockey venue) and the **ski jump**; the tourist office brochure lists opening times.

The **Norwegian Olympic Museum** (☎ 61 25 21 00; www.ol.museum.no; Håkons Hall; adult/student/child Nkr60/50/30, with combined entry to Maihaugen folk museum adult/child Nkr120/55; ☻ 10am-6pm mid-May–mid-Sep, shorter hrs otherwise) provides exhibits on every Olympic Games since 1896.

At Hunderfossen, 15km north of town, speed fanatics can visit the **bobsleigh & luge track** (reservations ☎ 61 05 42 00; www.olympiaparken.no; rides adult/child Nkr190/95) and ride a rubber raft (75km/hr) down the actual Olympic run; in summer, when there's no ice, a 'wheeled bob' is used. For Nkr850, a bobsleigh driver can whisk you down at 120km/h. It is possible to poop your snowpants. Reservations are advised.

Olympics aside, Lillehammer's main attraction is the exceptional **Maihaugen folk museum** (☎ 61 28 89 00; Maihaugveien 1; adult/student/child Nkr90/75/40, with combined entry to Norwegian Olympic Museum adult/child Nkr120/55; ☻ 9am-6pm Jun–mid-Aug, 10am-5pm mid-Aug–Sep, shorter hrs Oct-May), which contains around 180 historic houses, shops, farm buildings and a stave church.

See page 327 for details of the *Skibladner* paddle steamer.

Sleeping & Eating

Lillehammer Camping (☎ 61 25 33 33; Dampsagveien 47; camp sites from Nkr100, cabins Nkr350-650; **P**) On a grassy field overlooknig lake Mjøsa, this camp ground and its modern cabins are 700m south of the *Skibladner* dock. Some large buildings lie behind it, spoiling a sense of isolation.

Gjeste Bu (☎ 61 25 43 21; ss-bu@online.no; Gamlevegen 110; dm Nkr100 s/d from Nkr225/350) Rustic rooms exude loads of character. They are also a real bargain, which is why you must book early. There's a group kitchen, where you'll drink free coffee and meet hikers and skiers. There are shared bathrooms and no breakfast.

Lillehammer Hostel (☎ 61 24 87 00; www.lillehammer.hostel@vandrerhjem.no; dm/s/d Nkr275/475/59; ☻) On the second storey of the train station, modern bunks overlook rail tracks and the lake beyond. Rates include linens. Great for train spotters.

First Hotel Breiseth (☎ 61 24 77 77; www.firsthotels.no; Jernbanegata 1-5; s/d Nkr898/1198; **P**) In a masonry building from 1898, rooms on the top floor contain interesting angles and head-bumping opportunities thanks to a gaggle of dormers. Floors below have typical dimensions. All contain forgettable carpeting.

Nikkers (☎ 61 27 05 56; Elvegata 18; dishes Nkr43-149) For winter beer with a roaring fire and a stuffed elk head – the ski-lodge feel will get you in the proper mood. It serves burritos, salads and minced meat.

Galleri Dryer (☎ 61 25 00 78; Bankgata 15; dishes Nkr59-99) A small café/bar and art gallery with white walls, white chairs and white synthetic sheep skins; stop by for a small menu of French onion soup, a few salads and cake.

Storgata is lined with shops, bakeries and restaurants.

Getting There & Away

Nor-Way Bussekspress runs to Oslo (Nkr304, three hours, three or four times daily). Trains run to Oslo (Nkr282, 2¼ hours, 15 times daily) and to Trondheim (Nkr596, 4¼ hours, four or five times daily).

DOMBÅS

pop 1500

Dombås, a popular adventure and winter sports centre, makes a convenient break for travellers between the highland national parks and the western fjords because it has a few good sleeping options. In town, there isn't much to do except buy fuel and groceries. The **tourist office** (☎ 61 24 14 44; www. dovrenett.no; ☼ 9am-6pm mid-Jun–mid-Aug, shorter hrs otherwise) is by the central car park and commercial complex.

The **Dovrefjell-Rondane Nasjonalparksenter** (☎ 61 24 14 44; ☼ 9am-8pm mid-Jun–mid-Aug, shorter hrs mid-Aug–mid-Jun), at the tourist office, has interesting displays on all Norwegian national parks. **Dovrefjell National Park**, 30km north of town, protects the 2286m-high Snøhetta massif and provides a habitat for arctic foxes, reindeer, wolverines and musk oxen.

In a forested spot with mountain views, the excellent family-run **Dombås Vandrerhjem Trolltun** (☎ 61 24 09 60; www.trolltun.no; dm/s/d Nkr200/365/550; ☎ 7.30am-11pm), in an oversized log cabin, lies near nordic trails and alpine lifts. It also offers hotel rooms (singles /doubles Nkr640/910) in a ski lodge where you can find reindeer meals (Nkr100) and a pub. It's about 1.5km north of the centre and off the E6.

Dombås lies on the railway line between Oslo (Nkr555, four hours, three to four daily) and Trondheim (Nkr345, 2½ hours, three to four daily). The spectacular Raumabanen line runs down the Romsdalen valley from Dombås to Åndalsnes (Nkr193, 1¼ hours, three daily).

JOTUNHEIMEN NATIONAL PARK

The Sognefjellet road between Lom and Sogndal passes the northwestern perimeter of Jotunheimen National Park, Norway's most popular wilderness destination. Hiking trails lead to some of the park's 60 glaciers, up to the top of Norway's loftiest peaks (the 2469m Galdhøpiggen and 2452m Glittertind) and along ravines and valleys featuring deep lakes and plunging waterfalls. There are DNT huts and private lodges along many of the routes. For park information, maps and glacier-walk arrangements contact **Lom tourist office** (☎ 61 21 29 90; www.visitlom.com; ☼ 9am-9pm Mon-Fri, 10am-8pm Sat & Sun mid-Jun–mid-Aug, shorter otherwise). Lom contains a **stave church** dating from 1170, to fairy-tale effect at night.

Dramatic **Galdhøpiggen**, with its cirques, arêtes and glaciers, is a fairly tough eight-hour day hike from Spiterstulen, with 1470m of ascent, accessible by a toll road (Nkr60 per car). **Krossbu** is in the middle of a network of trails, including a short one to the **Smørstabbreen glacier**. From **Turtagrø**, a rock-climbing and hiking centre midway between Sogndal and Lom, there's a three-hour hike to Fannaråkhytta, Jotunheimen's highest DNT hut (2069m), which offers great panoramic views.

DNT's fabulous **Spiterstulen lodge** (☎ 61 21 14 80; www.spiterstulen.no; Lom; camp site per person Nkr50, dm/s/d Nkr170/250/400; Ⓟ), situated at an old *sæter* (summer dairy), lies above the tree-line and makes a great jumping-off point for Galdhøpiggen.

Beautiful Bøverdalen, 18km south of Lom, has a riverside **HI hostel** (☎ 61 21 20 64; boeverdalen.hostel@vandrerhjem.no; dm/s/d Nkr120/210/300; ☼ Jun-Sep), which arranges summer skiing and glacier hiking trips. Breakfast costs Nkr65. Near the head of Bøverdalen, the lovely **Krossbu Turiststasjon** (☎ 61 21 29 22; www.krossbu.no in Norwegian; Krossbu; r Nkr400-600) has 85 rooms, most of them have shared bathrooms.

OSLO TO BERGEN

The Oslo–Bergen railway line is Norway's most scenic, a seven-hour journey past forests and alpine villages, and across the starkly beautiful **Hardangervidda** plateau.

Midway between Oslo and Bergen is **Geilo**, a ski centre where you can practically walk off the train and onto a lift. There's also good summer **hiking** in the mountains around Geilo and the town has an **HI Hostel** (☎ 32 08 70 60; www.oenturist.no; Lienvegen 137; dm/d Nkr160/400-500, breakfast Nkr60), near the train station.

From Geilo the train climbs 600m through a tundralike landscape of high lakes and snowcapped mountains to the tiny village of **Finse**, near the **Hardangerjøkulen** icecap. Finse has year-round **skiing** and is in the middle of a network of summer **hiking trails**. One of Norway's most frequently trodden trails winds from the Finse train station down to the fjord town of **Aurland**, a four-day trek. There's breathtaking mountain scenery along the way as well as a series of DNT and private mountain huts a day's walk apart – the nearest is Finsehytta, 200m from Finse station. There's also a bicycle route from Finse to Flåm (six hours, downhill) on the century-old **Rallarvegen** railway construction road.

Myrdal, further west along the railway line, is the connecting point for the spectacularly steep Flåm railway, which twists and turns its way down 20 splendid kilometres to **Flåm** village on Aurlandsfjorden, an arm of Sognefjorden.

Many people go down to Flåm, have lunch and take the train back up to Myrdal, where they catch the next Oslo–Bergen train. A better option is to take the ferry from Flåm to Gudvangen (via spectacular Unesco protected **Nærøyfjorden**, with its thundering waterfalls and lofty peaks), where there's a connecting bus that climbs a steep valley on the dramatically scenic ride to Voss. From Voss, trains to Bergen run roughly hourly. To include a cruise of the Nærøyfjorden in a day trip from Oslo to Bergen, you'll need to take an early train from Oslo.

BERGEN & THE WESTERN FJORDS

This spectacular region will dazzle your eyeballs with truly indescribable scenery. We'll make a go at it here, but bear in mind that all our superlatives and gushings are actually just understatements. Hardangerfjord, Sognefjord and Geirangerfjord are all variants on the same theme: steep crystalline rock walls dropping with sublime force straight into the sea, often decorated with waterfalls and small farms harmoniously blending into the natural landscape. Summer hiking opportunities exist along the fjord walls and on the enormous Jostedalsbreen glacier. Bergen, a lively city with a 15th-century waterfront, is exceedingly pleasing to behold, and contains some of Norway's finest nightlife and restaurants.

Information on the entire region is available from **Fjord Norge** (☎ 55 30 26 40; www.fjord norway.com).

BERGEN

pop 231,000

Norway's second-largest city contends for the honour of being Norway's most beautiful. Set on a peninsula surrounded by mountains and the sea, the neatly contained centre offers a tangle of crooked streets, picturesque wooden neighbourhoods and hill-top views. Bergen provides ample opportunities to linger in cafés and bars, while a large university population helps to secure Bergen's claim as western Norway's cultural capital, supporting theatres, a philharmonic orchestra and a notable rock scene. Though big by Norwegian standards, the city retains a charming, almost villagelike culture. Drawback: expect rain or showers at least 275 days of the year.

Bergen is a terminus of the scenic Bergen–Oslo train line and a convenient place to stay before prolonged excursions into fjord country. The *Hurtigruten* coastal steamer begins its six-day journey to Kirkenes from the centre.

The **Bergen International Festival** (☎ 55 21 50 60; www.bergenfest.no) held for 12 days in May, is the big cultural event of the year with quality dance, music and folklore events taking place throughout the city.

History

Bergen was the capital of Norway during the 12th and 13th centuries, and in the early 17th century had the distinction of being Scandinavia's largest city, with a population of around 15,000. Bergen's history is closely tied to the sea, as it was one of the central ports of the Hanseatic League of merchants, which dominated trade in northern Europe during the late Middle Ages. The Hanseatic influence is still visible in the sharply gabled row of buildings that lines Bergen's picturesque harbour front.

Orientation

The central area of hilly Bergen remains pleasantly compact and easily manageable on foot. The bus and train stations lie only a block apart on Strømgaten, just a 10-minute walk from the ferry terminals. Most of the restaurants, hotels and museums cluster around Vågen, the inner harbour.

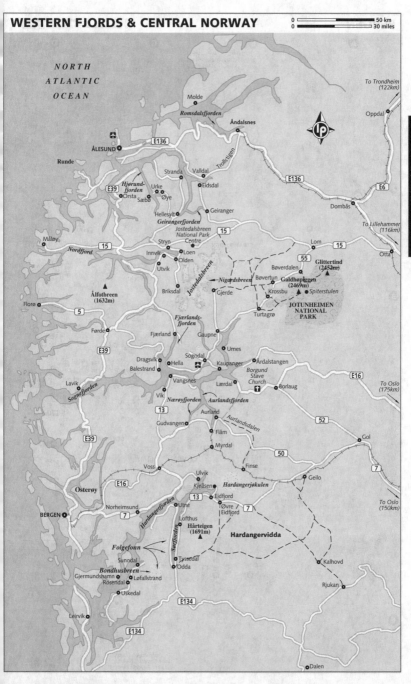

NORWAY

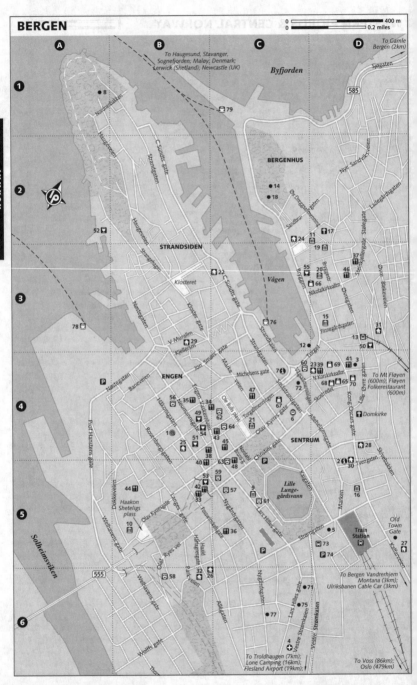

NORWAY

Information
DISCOUNT CARDS
The Bergen Card allows free transport on local buses, free parking and funicular-railway rides as well as admission to most sights. Note that the Schøtstuene and Hanseatic Museum are not covered. A 24-/48-hour Bergen Card costs Nkr170/250 (Nkr70/100 for children) – it's sold at the tourist office.

INTERNET ACCESS
Byens Gtørste Spillehall (Håkonsgaten 15; noon-2am Sun-Thu, noon-4am Fri & Sat; per min Nkr0.50) Cheaper than the internet cafés, with slot machines.
Library (Strømgaten 6; 10am-6pm Mon-Thu, 10am-4.30pm Fri, 10am-4pm Sat, shorter hrs mid-May–Sep) Free internet access.

LAUNDRY
Jarlens Vaskoteque (☎ 55 32 55 04; Lille Øvregaten 17; wash/detergent/dry Nkr45/5/15; 10am-6pm Mon, Tue & Fri, 10am-8pm Wed & Thu, 10am-3pm Sat)

MEDICAL SERVICES
Legevakten Medical Clinic (☎ 55 56 87 00; Vestre Stromkaien 19; emergencies 24hr)
Pharmacy (☎ 55 21 83 84; bus station; 8am-11pm Mon-Sat, 10am-11pm Sun)

POST
Main Post Office (Starvhusgaten at Chrisites gate; 8am-8pm Mon-Fri, 9am-6pm Sat)

TOURIST INFORMATION
DNT office (☎ 55 33 58 10; Tverrgaten 4; 10am-4pm Mon-Wed & Fri, 10am-6pm Thu, 10am-2pm Sat)
Tourist Office (☎ 55 55 20 00; www.visitbergen.com; Vågsallmenningen 1; 8.30am-10pm Jun-Aug, 9am-8pm May & Sep, 9am-4pm Mon-Sat Oct-Apr)

Sights
The waterfront **fish market** at Torget is a good starting point for an exploration of the city's historic district. Bergen has lots of cobblestone streets lined with older homes; one particularly picturesque area good for strolls is near the funicular station on Øvregaten.

BRYGGEN AREA

Bryggen, the old medieval quarter and Unesco World Heritage site on the eastern side of Vågen, is home to museums, restaurants and shops. The alleys that run along the less-restored sides of the long timber buildings reveal an intriguing glimpse of the stacked-stone foundations and rough-plank construction of centuries past.

Some of Norway's creakiest floors are in the timber building (1704) that houses the **Hanseatisk Museum** (Hanseatic Museum; ☎ 55 54 46 90; Finnegårdsgaten 1A; adult/child Nkr45/free; ⏰ 9am-5pm mid-May–mid-Sep, 11am-2pm Tue-Sat 11am-4pm Sun mid-Sep–mid-May) . Period character flourishes, while furnishings and odd bedchambers give a glimpse of the austere living conditions of Hanseatic merchants. The entry ticket is also valid for **Schøtstuene** (Øvregaten 50) where the Hanseatic fraternity once met for their business meetings and beer guzzling.

Norway's tiniest museum, the **Theta Museum** (☎ 55 55 20 80; Enhjørningsgården; adult/child Nkr20/5; ⏰ 2-4pm Tue, Sat & Sun mid-May–mid-Sep), is a one-room reconstruction of a clandestine Resistance headquarters uncovered by the Nazis in 1942. It was hidden in an upper storey at the rear of the Bryggen warehouse with the unicorn figurehead.

The **Rosenkrantztztårnet** (Rosenkrantz Tower; ☎ 55 31 43 80; Bergenhus; adult/student Nkr30/15; ⏰ 10am-4pm mid-May–Aug, noon-3pm Sun Sep–mid-May) was built in the 1560s by Bergen's governor as a residence and defence post. You can climb down to bedrock and then up to the high-ceilinged bedchambers of a 16th century tower. Detours along the way allow you to suffocate in an actual dungeon or peer into ancient toilet chambers.

Håkonshallen (Håkon's Hall; ☎ 55 31 60 67; Bergenhus; adult/student Nkr30/15; ⏰ 10am-4pm mid-May–Aug, noon-3pm Fri-Wed, 3-6pm Thu Sep–mid-May), completed by King Håkon Håkonsson in 1261 for his son's wedding, had its roof blown off in 1944 when a Dutch munitions boat exploded in the harbour. The hall has since been restored using archaeological artefacts. Be pleasantly disoriented while wandering through Escherian stairways, stopping to squint through blurry antique windows for a romantic view of the city.

The site of Bergen's earliest settlement is now **Bryggens Museum** (☎ 55 58 80 10; Dregsalmenning 3; adult/student/child Nkr40/20/free; ⏰ 10am-5pm May-Aug, 11am-3pm Mon-Fri, noon-3pm Sat, noon-4pm Sun Sep-Apr; ⓖ). The 800-year-old foundations unearthed during the construction have been incorporated into the exhibits, along with pottery, human skulls and runes.

ART MUSEUMS

Experience the juxtaposition of form and function from the Renaissance to the present at the **West Norway Museum of Decorative Art** (Vestlandske Kunstindustrimuseum; ☎ 55 33 66 33; www.vk.museum.no; Nordahl Brunsgate 9; adult/student/child Nkr50/40/free; ⏰ 11am-5pm mid-May–mid-Sep, noon-4pm Tue-Sun mid-Sep–mid-May). The eclectic collection (strong in Jugenstil and Modern decorative objects) includes a Lego set, an armchair shaped like a tarantula, Edvard Grieg's table setting and a quilt made from children's raincoats.Three buildings opposite the lake fountain house the **Bergen Art Museum** (Bergen Kunstmuseum; ☎ 55 56 80 00; www.bergenartmuseum.no; Rasmus Meyers Allé 3, 7 & 9; adult/student/child Nkr50/35/free; ⏰ 11am-5pm mid-May–mid-Sep, closed Mon mid-Sep–mid-May; ⓖ), a superb collection of Norwegian art from the 18th and 19th centuries, including many works by Munch and JC Dahl, as well as works by Picasso, Klee and others.

LEPRAMUSEET

Wash your hands before and after visiting the **Lepramuseet** (Leprosy Museum; ☎ 55 32 57 80; Kong Oscars gate 59; adult/child Nkr30/15; ⏰ 11am-3pm mid-May–Aug), an enclosed wooden complex whose wards, church and kitchen appear tranquil from a cobbled, tree-shaded interior court. Not so inside, which is creepy. Buildings date to 1754.

BERGEN AKVARIET

The **aquarium** (☎ 55 55 71 71; www.akvariet.no; Nordnesbakken 4; adult/child Nkr100/50; ⏰ 9am-8pm May-Sep, 10am-6pm Oct-Apr; ⓖ) will provide an entire day's entertainment to travellers with small children. Frolic among outdoor pools and tanks, or if it's raining head inside to check the daily schedule of films and events. Don't miss the collection of confiscated illegal pets on the 1st floor.

BERGENS SJØFARTSMUSEUM

The knowledgeable and garrulous staff at the **Bergen Maritime Museum** (☎ 55 54 96 00; Haakon Sheteligs plass 15; adult/child Nkr30/free; ⏰ 11am-3pm Jun-Aug, 11am-2pm Sun-Fri Sep-May; ⓖ)

will explain the models large and small of Norwegian seafaring vessels. Step inside the 'chart room' to decipher a Morse code message which plays on a continuous loop.

MARIAKIRKEN
With its Romanesque entrance and twin towers, the **St Maria church** (☎ 55 31 59 60; Dreggen 15; adult/child Nkr20/free, admission free Sep–mid-May; ⏱ 9.30am-11.30am & 1-4pm Mon-Fri mid-Jun–mid-Aug, 11am-12.30pm mid-Aug–mid-Jun), Bergen's oldest building, dates from the 12th century. The interior has 15th-century frescoes and a splendid baroque pulpit.

BERGEN ENVIRONS
The open-air **Gamle Bergen** (☎ 55 39 43 04; Sandviken; admission free; ⏱ 9am-5pm May-early Sep, shorter hrs otherwise) presents around 40 buildings from the 18th and 19th centuries, including a dentist's office, bakery and houses. It's 4km north of the city centre and can be reached by bus Nos 20, 21 and 22. Tours cost Nkr60/30 (adult/student) and leave hourly mid-May to August. Entrance to the grounds is free year-round.

If you want to tour to the former lakeside home and workshop of composer Edvard Grieg, take any bus from platform 20, get off at Hosbroen and follow signs to **Troldhaugen** (☎ 55 92 29 92; Troldhaugvegen 65; adult/student/child Nkr60/20/free; ⏱ 9am-6pm May-Sep, shorter hrs Oct-Apr). Although Grieg fans will best appreciate this well-conceived presentation, the main house has excellent period furnishings and is generally interesting.

Activities
For an unbeatable city view, take the **Fløibanen funicular** (☎ 55 33 68 00; Vetrlidsalmenning 21; adult/child Nkr75/35 return; ⏱ 7.30am-midnight May-Aug, 7.30am-11pm Sep-Apr; ♿) to the top of Mt Fløyen (320m). Trails marked with dilapidated signs lead into the forest from the hill-top station. Trails 1 and 3 are the longest, each making 5km loops through hilly woodlands. For a delightful 40-minute walk back to the city, take trail 4 and connect with trail 6. Find a trail map posted in what looks like a public shower behind the mountaintop Fløyen Folkerestaurant (p337).

The **Ulriksbanen cable car** (☎ 55 20 20 20; www.ulriken.no; adult/child Nkr90/45 return; ⏱ 9am-9pm May-Aug, shorter hrs otherwise) to the top of Mt Ulriken (642m) offers a panoramic view of

Bergen, fjords and mountains. The tourist office sells a 'Bergen in a Nutshell' ticket for Nkr150/75 (adult/child) that includes the cable car and a return bus from Bergen. Many take the cable car one way and walk (about three hours) across a well-beaten trail to the funicular station at Mt Fløyen.

Tours
The train station sells the **Norway in a Nutshell** (☎ 81 56 82 22; www.fjordtours.com) ticket combining morning trains from Bergen to Flåm, a ferry along the spectacular Aurlandsfjorden and Nærøyfjorden to Gudvangen, a bus to Voss and a train back to Bergen (Nkr790) in time for a late dinner, or you can continue on to Oslo (Nkr1115), arriving around 10pm.

Sleeping
The tourist office books single/double rooms in private homes from Nkr250/400 (plus Nkr50 booking fee); it can also find you last-minute hotel discounts.

BUDGET
Marken Gjestehus (☎ 55 31 44 04; www.marken-gjestehus.com; Kong Oscars gate 45; 4-/6-/8-person dm Nkr155/175/195, s/d Nkr380/490) Take an old elevator to the 4th floor to find this central hostel. Rooms have wooden floors, spiffy Ikea furniture of recent vintage and big windows. Breakfast can be arranged elsewhere from Nkr55. There's a coin laundry and, often, a decent view.

Dorm.no (☎ 98 23 86 00; www.dm.no; Kong Oscars gate 44; dm Nkr165; ▯) Offers 16 beds with individual reading lamps in an attractive dormitory with linens included. There's a fine rockabilly café/pub, a wood terrace with flowers and chairs, and a spotless, good-looking shared kitchen. Breakfast costs Nkr55.

Intermission (☎ 55 30 04 00; Kalfarveien 8; Nkr150; ⏱ mid-Jun–mid-Aug) This old white house has 37 beds, where the hospitable Christian Student Fellowship serves waffles to guests on Monday and Thursday nights. Laundry facilities are available. Breakfast costs Nkr50.

Bergen Vandrerhjem YMCA (☎ 55 60 60 55; www.bergenhostel.com; Nedre Korskirkealmenning 4; budget/4-/6-person dm Nkr125/160/170, d Nkr600; ⏱ reception 7am-midnight) Perfectly central, dorm dwellers

NORWAY

reside in plain, linoleum-floored bunk rooms sleeping four to six, or in windowless caverns (it gets noisy here) sleeping 15 or 32. Private doubles are also available. Rooftop decks provide views over the water and surrounding garrets. Breakfast costs Nkr50.

Also recommended:

Bergen Vandrerhjem Montana (☎ 55 20 80 70; www.montana.no; Johan Blyttsvei 30; 20-/4-person dm Nkr160/225, s/d Nkr440/660; ☺ 3 Jan–20 Dec) A large institutional hostel 5km away by bus 31. Mountain-top with good view.

Lone Camping (☎ 55 39 29 60; www.lonecamping.no; Hardangerveien 697, Haukeland; camp site Nkr110, 4-person cabin Nkr545) Camp sites lie along along a grassy lakeshore. I'ts 19km east of Bergen by bus No 900 (30 minutes).

MIDRANGE

Skansen Pensjonat (☎ 55 31 90 80; www.skansen -pensjonat.no; Vetrlidsalmenningen 29; s Nkr350-400, d Nkr550-650) Trudge up steep cobbled streets through a pretty neighbourhood to this hilltop house dating from 1918, with its outstanding views. If you're lucky, your period room will have a balcony.

Jacob's Apartments (☎ 98 23 86 00; www.apart ments.no; Kong Oscars gate 44; 1-/2-person apt Nkr590-790/790-890; 🖳) Simple apartments of ample size come with light wood floors and un-adorned neutral-toned walls. All have private kitchens and bathrooms and some an interesting two-floor configuration.

Kjellersmauet Gjestehus (☎ 55 96 26 08; www .gjestehuset.com; Kjellersmauet 22; 1-/2-/4-person apt Nkr500/800/1400) A number of well-equipped apartments with private bathrooms and kitchens. These are homey, and big groups are often given good deals. No breakfast.

Crowded House (☎ 55 90 92 00; www.crowded-house .com; Håkonsgaten 27; s/d Nkr390/590) The 82 spacious, tidy rooms come with modern furniture and free use of laundry facilities. Bathrooms are shared and guests have access to a nice kitchen. The 1st floor holds a lively bar.

TOP END

Steens Hotell (☎ 55 31 40 50; www.steenshotel .no; Parkveien 22; s/d Nkr890/1080, 🅿 🖳) Expect Swedish-style rooms with private bathrooms in a 19th-century home; many have pleasant views over a landscaped park. The real treat is the 1890s dining room, where breakfast is served – check out the gilded wallpaper, an odd wooden chandelier and stained glass depicting butchered meat.

Augustin (☎ 55 30 40 00; www.augustin.no; C Sundtsgata 22; s/d Mon-Fri Sep-Jun Nkr1345/1590, s/d Sat & Sun Nkr700/880, s/d Mid-Jun–Aug 750/1010; 🖳 ⓖ) Bergen's last big family-run hotel, the Augustin dates to 1919, with age showing nicely in a few parlours. Full of contemporary Norwegian art (painting, lamps, furniture), modernised rooms look good and supercute bedspreads come covered with tiny colourful geckos. The basement is a 16th-century taverna (p338).

Hotel Park Pension (☎ 55 54 44 00; www.parkho tel.no; Harald Hårfagresgate 35; s Nkr600-840, d Nkr880-1040; 🅿 🖳) A 19th-century charmer, it's family owned and stuffed to the rafters with grandma's antiques and unusual tools. Spacious rooms come with private bathrooms and breakfast.

Clarion Collection Hotel Havnekontoret (☎ 55 60 11 00; www.choicehotels.no; Slottsgaten 1; s/d Mon-Fri Sep-Jun Nkr1295/1695, s/d Sat & Sun Nkr790/1200, s/d mid-Jun–Aug Nkr595/990; 🖳 🅿 ⓖ) Speculation: the designer of this new hotel was a frustrated goth working within corporate constrains. Rooms are characterised by a purple-and -black colour palette, and the foyer by mild oddness. A chapelesque lounge with painted, vaulted ceiling demonstrates the age of the restored building. Free dinner buffet.

Eating
RESTAURANTS

Curry Curry Nam Nam (☎ 55 96 40 76; Steinkjeller gate 8; mains Nkr55-99; ☺ from 2pm Tue-Sun) Rich curries and vegetarian items (spinach dal, aloo gobi) come steaming and delicious at this tiny restaurant at the convergence of several pretty cobbled alleys. At an outdoor table, smoke a postmeal water pipe for Nkr50.

Krystal (☎ 55 32 10 06; Kong Oscars gate 16; lunch Nkr110-149, 4-course dinner Nkr575) Dimly lit by candles and a frosted Art Deco chandelier, this romantic room changes its seasonal menu every two weeks. Representative dish: king crab with avocado cream. It overlooks a cobbled street and medieval church.

Viva las Vegis (☎ 97 19 72 33; Steinkjeller gate 2; meals Nkr79) Enter this neon-green and Elvis-themed vegetarian restaurant to eat veggie burgers and fabulous baked chips covered in sesame seeds and herbs. Cheap wine (Nkr35) and peanut butter and banana sandwiches (Nkr25).

Zupperia (☎ 55 55 81 44; Nordahl Bruns gate; soup Nkr50-100) From fish to gazpacho, Zupperia

AUTHOR'S CHOICE

Pingvinen (☎ 55 60 46 46; Vaskerelven 20; mains 89-129; ⏱ 2pm-3.30am) A casual hangout with old brick walls and barstool seating, the blackboard of this pub announces the day's four offerings. A reaction against the trend towards fusion and other international food fads, cooks embrace traditional Norwegian cuisine and prepare hearty meals (fish with macaroni; meatloaf with leeks; cabbage in a buttery sauce) with finesse. The fish soup can be described with every superlative in the dictionary. Come here for hipsters and exceptional fare at half the price of the tourist traps. One criticism: occasionally, sides aren't warm enough.

serves 11 kinds of soups with sides of bread. We like the *Husenottsuppe* (oxtail boiled with vegetables).

Zumo (☎ 55 90 19 60; Newmanns gate 25; lunch specials Nkr69; mains Nkr139-169) This Japanese restaurant's pleasing modern design involves every thinkable texture and shade of brown wood. Different grains collide on all surfaces (table, place mat, bathroom sink, floor), and big windows provide a view of the street while you slurp udon or eat raw fish.

Brød & Vin (☎ 55 32 67 04; Christies gate 13; mains Nkr35-75) Eat piles of Asian noodle dishes such as vegetable chop suey (Nkr53) and drink cheap beer (Nkr35) with crowds of Bergen penny pinchers. The room is comfortable, though the filling fare could be tastier.

Fløyen Folkerestaurant (☎ 55 33 69 99; Bellevuebakken 9; pastries & cakes Nkr18-43; ⏱ 11am-8pm May-Sep, 11am-8pm Sat & Sun Oct-Apr) On the summit of Fløyen, this restaurant presides over Bergen with unbeatable views and good hot chocolate. In the warmth of summer, the patio fills with sunbathers and beer drinkers.

CAFÉS

Café Opera (☎ 55 23 08 15; Engen 18; light meals Nkr89-116, sandwiches Nkr30-40) A continental vibe permeates through this early-20th-century café, serving brown rolls with brie, walnut butter and cherries, salads and daily soups. Big corner windows stare at the opera house and you can lounge on 2nd floor couches. DJs at night.

Chaos Coffee Bar (☎ 55 32 15 50; Fosswinckels gate 16; light meals Nkr50-60) Bustling at lunch, this neighbourhood café with its thrift-store assortment of colourful table cloths, lamps and upholstered chairs serves coffee, beer and peppery vegetable pasta to chatting students. Charming service.

Café Jonsvoll (☎ 55 23 00 77; Vaskerelven at Engen; dishes Nkr40-98; ⏱ kitchen 10am-11pm, bar to 3am) Filled with a trendy crowd making use of long plateglass windows and stools. Eat sandwiches, lasagne, quiche (Nkr53) and couscous with marinated vegetables (Nkr98).

Le Rustique (☎ 55 13 47 74; Christies gate 11; sandwiches Nkr45-65; ⏱ 8am-4pm Mon-Fri, 9am-4pm Sat, 11am-4pm Sun) Serves high-calibre, freshly baked baguettes. Also offers smoothies, coffee and French pastries. Good art, but no bathroom.

Studentkafeene (☎ 55 54 50 50; Ivar Aasens gate; lunch Nkr30-40; ⏱ 9.30am-5pm Mon-Thu, 9.30am-4pm Fri late Aug-early Jun) The university's student cafeteria might look ugly, but you can grab pasta with fish (Nkr39), asparagus soup (Nkr19) or a big sandwich with juice (Nkr30) at low prices. Enter the courtyard of the large, yellow brick building behind the red church.

QUICK EATS

Godt Brød (☎ 55 32 80 00; Nedre Korskirkealmenningen 12 or Veste Torggata 2) This bakery does organic breads, pastries and delicious, filling herb dough pizzas topped with marinated vegetables (Nkr35).

Söstrene Hagelin (☎ 55 32 69 49; Olav Kyrres gate 33; dishes Nkr35-89; ⏱ 9am-6pm Mon-Fri, 10am-3pm Sat) Delicious fish pudding, fish casserole and other such delicacies. Filling takeaway fish balls (Nkr35) come with potatoes.

SELF-CATERING

Storsenter, at the bus station, has fast-food outlets, a Vinmonopolet and Rimi and Spar supermarkets. Torget's fish market provides fresh fruit and seafood snacks, including salmon rolls for Nkr15 and boiled crab legs or shrimp for Nkr35 to Nkr75.

Kinsarvik Frukt (Olav Kyrres gate 38) is a small grocery store with a health-food section.

Drinking

Bergen loves to drink. In addition to the following, consider doing it in the cafés mentioned above, or in many of our entertainment recommendations.

Logen Bar (☎ 55 23 38 01; Øvre Ole Bulls plass 6) A hang-out for artists and journalists, the salonlike rooms benefit from tall ceilings and a balcony. Drink here to feel like you're part of a postimpressionist painting. Hard to find: enter, go up one set of stairs, turn left and climb a second stairwell. The conversational mood is deliberately set by a lack of music.

Legal (Christies gate at Nygårdsgaten; bar menu Nkr45-72) The design theme comes from 1960s English rock. Find red lighting, retro flooring, period lamps and tattooed university graduates. The bar menu offers fancy cheese plates and burgers.

Det Lille Kaffekompaniet (☎ 55 32 92 72; Nedre Fjellsmug 2) Hidden on a narrow cobbled street behind the funicular station, this intimate coffee shop brews with skill and serves cakes.

Altona Vinbar (☎ 55 30 40 72; Strandgaten 81; ✆ 6pm-12.30am Mon-Thu, 6pm-1.30am Fri & Sat) A taverna since the 16th-century, the small, cell-like rooms of this wine bar create a subterranean maze connected by incredibly short openings (duck through a hole 1m high). Except for coloured light emitting from some incredible lanterns, the place is candle lit.

Biskopen (Sigurds gate 5) A huge crowd is attracted to the great beer selection at this dark pub filled with books. Thanks to piles of old furniture, it feels like it's been here forever, though really the goods were imported from an airfield in Evenes.

Sjøboden (☎ 55 31 67 77; Bryggen 29; ✆ 6pm-1am Sun-Thu, 6pm-2am Fri & Sat) In a Hanseatic-era building, it's a long, narrow and unpretentious route from entry to bar. Friday nights, your odyssey will involve squeezing through crowds, dodging ceiling-suspended barrels and bumping into a bad two-piece passionately playing 'Summer of 69'. Everyone dances, everyone sings along, and no-one wears cool clothing. Kim Larsen plays here whenever in town.

Naboen (☎ 55 90 62 90; Sigurds gate 4b) This quiet pub serves beer (Bayer Ale Nkr47) that actually has taste. Laid-back regulars quaff it while eating Swedish meatballs and lingonberries (Nkr86) from a fancy restaurant upstairs.

Kafe Kippers (☎ 55 31 00 60; Georgernes Verft) Part of a cultural centre, enjoy outdoor, harbourside tables filled with beer drinkers. The view takes in water, rocky hills, islands and boats. Jazz many nights.

Fotballpuben (☎ 55 90 05 79; Vestre Torggate 9; ✆ from 9am) A long-standing favourite among football freaks, this sports bar provides plenty of scarves, televisions and fans to ensure quality match watching.

Entertainment

For details and schedules of entertainment events, including classical concerts, contact the tourist office (or see www.visitbergen .com). Atop Mt Fløyen, classical concerts are held nightly at 8pm from mid-June to mid-August. Bergen is the epicentre of Norwegian rock.

CINEMA

Bergen Kino (Neumannsgate 3) A 13-screen cinema showing first-run movies.

GAY & LESBIAN

Kafé Fincken (☎ 55 32 13 16; Nygårdsgaten 2A; ✆ 7pm-1.30am Wed & Thu, 7pm-2.30am Fri, 8pm-2.30am Sat, 7pm-12.30am Sun) Contemporary and stylish, this white, black and chrome venue provides a subdued environment to grab a drink.

The frisky should check out the far more flaming **Sailor** (Olav Kyrresgt 28; ✆ 10pm-3am Fri & Sat), a disco whose lively dance floor is apt to have someone actually dressed in a sailor outfit.

LIVE MUSIC

Garage (☎ 55 32 19 80; www.garage.no; Christies gate 14; ✆ from 6pm) Norway's rock headquarters consistently books top bands, including international acts. Concerts are held in a big, black basement space.

Hulen (☎ 55 33 38 38; www.hulen.no in Norwegian; Olaf Ryes vei 47) Carved into the bowels of a hill, Hulen occupies a former bomb shelter. The renowned rock club is over 30 years old.

Logen Teater (☎ 55 23 38 01; www.logen-teater .no; Øvre Ole Bulls plass 6) You'd never know it from the street, but drag yourself inside and you'll find a century-old, two-storied, pillared theatre. Concerts are held several times a month. Expect to see classical performances, pop and rock (Tindersticks, Waterboys).

NIGHTCLUBS

Landmark (☎ 55 31 77 55; Rasmus Meyers Alle 5; ✆ noon-1am Sun-Thu, noon-2am Fri & Sat) This place hosts experimental media artists and DJs (such as pop princess Annie). White carpet, white walls and tall ceilings covered in white cushions create a muted, subtle space of modernist high-design. At night, lighting transforms the room with eerie results. Weekdays, grab a subdued drink. Weekends, dance with Bergen's coolest.

Kameleon (☎ 40 00 59 15; Vågsallmenning 16) Some of Norway's most famous DJs (DJ Torske) spin under the distant ceiling of this old and beautiful former bank, now reinvented as a disco and music venue with a large dance floor.

Studenten (☎ 55 90 23 90; Vaskerlveien; ☺ 10pm-3.30am Thu-Sat) Enter through a dark ally and forbidding steel door near a huge sign proclaiming amazing drink prices (shots Nkr30/30/40 Thu/Fri/Sat). The disco faithfully attracts a young and loud crowd.

Shopping

Two blocks long, intimate Skostredet (Shoe Street) provides two blocks of independent boutiques, many of which sell goods made by hip designers and art-types from Bergen. Stop in **Boogaloo** (☎ 55 32 83 99; Skostredet 16) for hand-sewn bags, cool duds for both genders, and feminine skirts with strong silhouettes by local maker Stina Lunde. In the same store, find **Robot** (☎ 91 69 73 50), selling obscure records and books. Otherwise, browse vintage suits and gowns in **Kless Kapet** (☎ 94 37 58 85; Skostredet 12) or head around the corner to **Tilsammans** (☎ 55 32 55 55; Kong Oscars gate 26) for trendy shoes, hats and silk-screened t-shirts depicting famous dead Italian football referees.

Elsewhere, the chain **Bryggen Husflid** (☎ 55 32 88 03; Bugården) offers quality stock of traditional knit sweaters and mittens in a Bryggen environment.

For protection against all that rain, **Paraply Reparatøren** (☎ 55 32 69 11; 16 Høendergaten) sells designer umbrella, flasks, walking sticks and fancy toilet kits.

The **Galleriet shopping centre**, northwest of the post office, has boutiques, camera shops, a grocery store and a good bookshop, Norli.

Getting There & Away

AIR

The airport is in Flesland, 19km southwest of central Bergen. Direct flights connect Bergen with major cities in Norway, plus a handful of international destinations.

BOAT

Sognefjorden express boats run to Balestrand (Nkr425, four hours, one daily) and Flåm (Nkr585, 5½ hours, one daily). Northbound express boats go to Måløy (Nkr625, 4½ hours, one daily) and southbound express boats to Stavanger (Nkr640/840 one-way/return, 4¼ hours, two daily). These leave from **Strandkaiterminalen** on the western side of Vågen.

The *Hurtigruten* leaves from a newly built terminal east of Nøstegaten.

International ferries dock north of Rosenkrantztårnet.

BUS

Daily express buses run to Odda in Hardanger (Nkr265, 3½ hours, eight daily) and to the western fjord region. Buses also run from to Stryn (Nkr419, seven hours, three daily); to Ålesund (Nkr545, 10 hours, two daily); to Trondheim (Nkr719, 14½ hours, two daily); and to Stavanger (Nkr420, 5¾ hours, seven daily).

TRAIN

Trains run to Oslo (Nkr716, 6½ to 7¾ hours, three to five daily) and to Voss (Nkr148, 1¼ hours, seven to 15 daily). Lockers at the train station cost Nkr15 to Nkr40.

CAR

Avis (☎ 55 55 39 55; Lars Hilles gate 20A; ☺ 7.30am-4pm Mon-Fri, 9am-1pm Sat)

Centrum Bilutleie (☎ 55 21 29 50; Lars Hilles gate 20; ☺ 8am-4pm Mon-Fri)

Hertz (☎ 55 96 40 70; Nygaardsgaten 89; ☺ 8am-4pm Mon-Fri) It has a 2nd office near the airport. Discount with Bergen card.

Getting Around

TO/FROM THE AIRPORT

Flybussen (☎ 177) runs between the airport and Bergen bus station (Nkr70, 45 minutes, at least twice hourly), stopping at many large hotels. Taxis cost Nkr250 to Nkr300.

BUS

City buses cost Nkr20 to Nkr25, while fares beyond the centre are based on the distance travelled. Route information is available by calling ☎ 177. The free bus No 100 runs back and forth between the main post office and the bus station.

NORWAY

NORWAY

CAR & MOTORCYCLE

It's best to park and explore the city centre on foot. Except in spots where there are meters, street parking is reserved for residents. If you see a 'P' for parking but the sign has *'sone'* on it, it's a reserved area. Metered parking has a 30-minute limit in the busiest spots and two hours elsewhere. The parking area at Syndnes allows up to nine hours (free at night). The easiest and cheapest garage to use is **ByGarasjen** (Nkr75 per 24hr; � 24hr).

VOSS

pop 6000

Voss is a year-round sports centre with an attractive lakeside location. Conveniently positioned within a short drive of many top-notch athletic experiences and containing a centre that provides most modern amenities, Voss attracts many adventuresome tourists. Unfortunately, the town's collection of modern buildings are pretty drab. The **tourist office** (☎ 56 52 08 00; www.visitvoss.no; Uttrågata; ⊙ 9am-7pm Mon-Sat, 2-7pm Sun late Jun-early Aug, 9am-2.30pm Mon-Fri mid-Aug–mid-Jun) is a short walk east from the train station.

Voss's second claim to fame is a culinary oddity: deliciously prepared sheep heads. Hundreds of the things are eaten at an annual sheep festival in late September or early October.

Sights & Activities

For bookings or to get an idea about what's available, the tourist office or **Voss Aktivitetsbooking** (☎ 99 47 65 65; ⊙ 10am-5pm Mon-Thu & Sun, 10am-8pm Fri & Sat) can advise on skiing (December to April), white-water rafting (Nkr700), canoeing (Nkr650), waterfall abseiling (Nkr700), riverboarding (Nkr750) and just about any adrenaline inducing behaviour your loved ones would rather not know about, such as bungee jumping from a parasail (Nkr1495).

The **Mølstertunet Museum** (☎ 56 51 15 11; Mølstervegen 143; adult/child Nkr35/free; ⊙ 10am-5pm May-Sep, shorter hrs Oct-Apr), on the hillside north of town, features 16 farm buildings standing in their original positions, which date from the mid-17th to mid-19th centuries and display various aspects of life in earlier times. A **cable car** (Nkr50; ⊙ 11am-5pm mid-May–Aug) whisks you up to the spectacular view from Mt Hangur every 15 minutes.

Sleeping & Eating

Voss Camping (☎ 56 51 15 97; www.vosscamping.no; Prestegardsalléen 40; camp sites Nkr120, cabins Nkr450) Small and lakeside, this crowded spot, a convenient 300m from the tourist office, has a few shade trees that break up its grassy field. It attracts caravans.

Voss Vandrerhjem (☎ 56 51 20 17; voss.hostel@ vandrerhjem.no; Evangervegen 68; dm/s/d Nkr205/445/590; P 回) Modern rooms with private bathrooms throughout and a fine lakeside position, find it 600m west of the train station. Breakfast/dinner costs Nkr45/90. The hostel has bicycles, canoes, kayaks and rowing boats for hire and there's a sauna.

Fleischer's Hotel (☎ 56 52 05 00; www.fleischers .no; Evangervegen; s/d Nkr1125/1490; P 回 ⅀) For historic character, check out this classic behemoth from 1888. With its massive dormers and steep roof peaks, it looks vaguely Swiss. Ye Olde rooms need to tone down the floral curtains.

Indremisjonskaféen (☎ 56 51 14 08; Vangsgata 12; mains Nkr40-100) Serves cakes, sandwiches and bland Norwegian meals in a busy cafeteria. Try the daily soup (Nkr40), which just might be split pea.

Ivar Løne's farm (☎ 56 51 69 65; meal 275-325; ⊙ from 5pm) For a sheep head, visit Ivar's farm. He'll show you around and serve you one of the finest heads to be found, along with homemade beer, cake and coffee. Call ahead. The farm is 5km towards Oslo on the E16.

Getting There & Away

Buses stop at the train station. NSB operates the renowned Bergensbanen to/from Bergen (Nkr148, 1¼ hours, eight to 15 daily) and Oslo (Nkr623, 5½ hours, four or five daily) connect at Myrdal (Nkr90, 45 minutes, eight to 15 daily) with the scenic line down to Flåm.

HARDANGERFJORDEN

A notch less jagged and steep than Sognefjord, Hardangerfjord's slopes support more farms and wildflowers, which picturesquely enhance the green hills as they plunge into the water. The second-longest fjord in Norway, it stretches inland from a cluster of rocky coastal islands to the frozen heights of the **Folgefonn** and **Hardangerjøkulen** icecaps. The area is known for its orchards (apples, cherries and plums) and bursts into bloom from mid-May to mid-June. Route 13 between **Brimnes** and **Lofthus** is particularly pretty farm country, with bleating goats and stands selling eggs, honey and fruit.

The villages along the east coast of the central part of the fjord (also called Kvinnheradsfjorden) are connected to the national road network by an 11km tunnel under the Folgefonn; **Rosendal** and **Sunndal** are popular destinations, with great mountain and glacier scenery. At Rosendal there's the **Baroniet Rosendal** (☎ 53 48 29 99; www.baro niet.no; adult/child Nkr75/10; ⏰ from 11am May-Sep), Norway's only baronial mansion, dating from 1665 and surrounded by flowering gardens and mountains. From Sunndal, an easy walk leads 3km to lake Bondhusvatnet and the glacier **Bondhusbreen**.

On the other side of Folgefonn, **Odda** is an ugly industrial town with a dramatic location. For information on hikes and glacier tours, contact the **tourist office** (☎ 53 65 40 05; www.visitodda.com; ⏰ 7.30am-4pm Mon-Fri) located near the Sørfjorden shore. **Tyssedal**, 6km north of Odda, has a **hydroelectric power plant museum** (☎ 53 65 00 50; adult/student/child Nkr70/35/free; ⏰ 10am-5pm mid-May-Aug, shorter hrs Sep–mid-May) and an impressive **funicular railway**.

At the innermost reaches of Hardangerfjorden you'll find the **Eidfjord** area, with sheer mountains, huge waterfalls, spiral road tunnels and the extraordinary **Kjeåsen**, a deserted farm perched on a mountain ledge about 6km northeast of Eidfjord.

The **Hardangervidda Natursenter** (☎ 53 66 59 00; Øvre Eidfjord; adult/child Nkr80/40; ⏰ 9am-8pm Jun-Aug, 10am-6pm Apr, May, Sep & Oct) has an excellent 19-minute movie, interactive displays and interesting natural history exhibits. For information, contact **Eidfjord tourist office** (☎ 53 67 34 00; www.visiteidfjord.no; ⏰ 10am-8pm Mon-Fri, 10am-6pm Fri & Sat Jun-Aug, shorter otherwise).

At picturesque **Utne**, 55km north of Odda, you'll find an interesting collection of old buildings at the **Hardanger Folk Museum** (☎ 53 67 00 40; www.hardanger.museum.no; adult/child Nkr40/free; ⏰ 10am-4pm May & Jun, 10am-6pm Jul & Aug), and the pretty Utne Hotel.

Helpful regional information can be found at www.hardangerfjord.com.

Sleeping & Eating

In Rosendal, you can stay near the baronial grounds in a **B&B** (☎ 53 48 29 99; s Nkr350-600, d Nkr600-800; **P**), once a 19th-century farmhouse. It's operated by the museum.

Utne Hotel (☎ 53 66 64 00; www.utnehotel.no; Utne Sentrum; s/d Nkr825/1300; ⏰ Mar-Dec) This historic wooden hotel, known for its fabulous décor, was built in 1722 and has been in romantic business ever since. Meals are available in the dining room (three-courses Nkr429). Book ahead.

Getting There & Away

While thorough exploration of Hardangerfjord is best accomplished with a car, those with little time and no wheels would do well to book a round-trip **Fjord Tour** (☎ 81 56 82 22; www.fjordtours.no; adult/child Nkr635/430) from

---

WORTH A TRIP

Lofthus

In the heart of orchard country, the buildings forming Lofthus' tiny centre are oriented along the water edge and not the highway, giving the place a yesteryear feel. Many feel it's the prettiest village on Hardangerfjord. In it you'll find the glitzy and new **Hotel Ullensvang** (☎ 53 67 00 00; www.hotel-ullensvang.no; s/d Nkr1200/1500; ♿), in whose predecessor Edvard Grieg took his holidays, a single café that occasionally books live music and a grocery store.

Back in the 12th-century, the town's orchards stretched up to the mountain ridge and medieval monks' built steps into the mountain to make the hike easier. The steps are still there to make your own hike easier.

To sleep, try **Lofthus Camping** (☎ 53 66 13 64; www.lofthuscamping.com; camp site Nkr135, 2-/4-bed cabin Nkr390/480; ⏰ May-Sep; 🛶). Climb a sliver of a road through 2km of flowering fruit trees before finding this treasure on a grassy bluff with stupendous views over the fjord and the distant glacier Folgefonna. The camp ground lies within an old orchard, and you'll pitch your tent under apple, pear and plum trees (pick and eat freely). Simple cabins cling to the cliff's edge.

Bergen, which combines bus, ferry and train with a three-hour break in Eidfjord.

Hardanger Fjord Cruises (☎ 55 23 87 80; www.hsd .no) operates many of Hardangerfjord's buses and ferries. In summer, there are numerous possibilities for day-trips to Hardangerfjord from Bergen using buses and ferries. These last for up to 12 hours with stops of two to six hours allowing brief explorations of towns and surrounds. Destinations include Rosendal (adult/child Nkr375/255); Lofthus (Nkr460/280); Utne (Nkr460/280) and Eidfjord (Nkr635/430). Tickets can be purchased at major train stations or the Bergen tourist office.

One to three daily Nor-Way Bussek-spress buses run between Bergen (Nkr258, 3¾ hours) and Oslo (Nkr480, 7¼ hours) via Odda and Utne, with connections at Haukeligrend for Kristiansand.

SOGNEFJORDEN

Sognefjorden, Norway's longest (204km) and deepest (1308m) fjord, cuts a deep slash across the map of western Norway. In some places sheer, lofty walls rise more than 1000m above the water, while in others there is a far gentler shoreline with farms, orchards and small towns.

The broad main waterway is impressive, but by cruising into the fjord's narrower arms, such as the deep and lovely Nærøyfjorden (on the World Heritage List) to Gudvangen, you'll have idyllic views of sheer cliff faces and cascading waterfalls.

Tourist information is dispensed by **Sognefjorden** (☎ 57 67 30 83; www.sognefjorden.no).

Getting There & Away

Fjord1 (☎ 55 90 70 70; www.fjord1.no) operates express boats between Bergen and Sogndal (Nkr510; 4½ hours; one daily), as well as a tourist route to Flåm (Nkr585, 5½ hours, one daily) stopping at 10 small towns.

From mid-May to mid-September, Fylkes-baatane runs a second express boat along the same route, except that it terminates in Flåm (Nkr550) instead of Sogndal.

There are numerous local ferries linking the fjord towns and an extensive (though not always frequent) network of buses. They're all detailed in *Sogn og Fjordane Rutehefte* (www.ruteinfo.net/en/index .html), the 208-page timetable which is available at tourist offices.

Flåm

pop 400

A tiny village of orchards and a handful of buildings scenically set at the head of Aurlandsfjorden, Flåm is a jumping-off spot for travellers taking the Gudvangen ferry or the Sognefjorden express boat. It's also the only place on Sognefjorden with rail connections, and is the turnaround point for those doing the 'Norway in a Nutshell' tour, serving as the base station for the dramatic Flåm railway. Though it sees an amazing 500,000 visitors every summer, walk a few minutes from the centre and you'll soon experience solitude. Adventurous visitors arrive from Finse by mountain bike. It's a five- or six-hour downhill ride, obscenely picturesque, and you can return your rented bike in the Flåm centre. Call the **tourist office** (☎ 57 63 21 06; www.visitflam.com; 8.30am-8pm Jun-Aug, 8.30am-4pm May & Sep), at the train station, for details.

The extraordinarily friendly **Flåm Camping & Hostel** (☎ 57 63 21 21; flaam.hostel@vandrerhjem.no; dm/s Nkr135/225, d Nkr345-395; May-Sep; P) has just 31 beds – book early. It's a few minutes' walk from the station: go up the riverside track and over the bridge. If fully booked, they might install you in a large dollhouse, but no promises. At water level on the fringe of the village, **Heimly Pensjonat** (☎ 57 63 23 00; www.heimly.no; s Nkr550-695, d Nkr695-895; P) has ordinary rooms with impressive views.

Near the station, there's a **cafeteria** and the novel **Togrestauranten** (☎ 57 63 21 55; mains Nkr90-135), housed in wooden rail cars, serves traditional Norwegian dishes. For a traditional feast, try the buffet at the high-end **Fretheim Hotel** (☎ 57 63 23 00; www.fretheim-hotel .no; buffet Nkr400), where chefs cure, salt and smoke their own meat and prepare an 'ecological' menu. There's a **Coop** supermarket.

The **Flåmsbana railway** (☎ 57 63 21 00; www .flaamsbana.no; adult/child Nkr175/85; 10 daily) runs to Myrdal, some in sync with the Oslo–Bergen service.

Fjord1 ferries and express boats head out to towns around Sognefjorden. The most scenic trip steams up Nærøyfjorden to Gudvangen (Nkr205, two hours, four daily). Other service runs to Balestrand (Nkr200, two hours, two daily) and Bergen (Nkr585, 5½ hours, one daily). These frequencies for bus boat and trains are during summer season.

Balestrand

pop 800

Quiet Balestrand enjoys a mountain backdrop and fjord views. The beauty of its surroundings and the eerie quality of its summer light attracted a community of landscape painters in the early 19th century, whose work then popularised the area for well-heeled tourists. Today, the low-key farming village remains a favourite destination for travellers, who spend a lot of their time walking and contemplating. The **tourist office** (☎ 57 69 12 55; www.sognefjord.no; 8am-6pm mid-Jun–mid-Aug, 9am-5pm Mon-Fri May, early-Jun & late Aug-Sep) rents bikes.

The road that runs south along the fjord has little traffic and is a pleasant place to stroll. It's lined with apple orchards, ornate older homes and gardens, a **19th-century English church** and **Viking burial mounds**. One mound is topped by a statue of the legendary King Bele, erected by Germany's Kaiser Wilhelm II, who spent his holidays here until WWI.

For a longer **hike**, take the small ferry (Nkr15) across the Esefjord to the Dragsvik side, where there is an abandoned country road that forms the first leg of an 8km walk back to Balestrand.

At **Sjøtun Camping** (☎ 57 69 12 23; www.sjotun.no; camp sites from Nkr50, cabins Nkr230; Jun-Sep), a 15-minute walk south along the fjord, you can pitch a tent amid apple trees or rent a rustic four-bunk cabin. **Balestrand HI Hostel** (☎ 57 69 13 03; www.kringsja.no; dm/d Nkr190/580; late Jun–mid-Aug; P) is a pleasant lodge-style place perched near the water. **Midtnes Pensjonat** (☎ 57 69 11 33; www.midtnes.no; s/d Nkr610/700; P), next to the English church, occupies a charming white house where you'll eat breakfast with great views. There's an attractive terrace and complimentary rowing boat moored steps away.

Consider paying a bit more for a room with fjord-staring balcony.

There's a **supermarket** and a fast-food **café** opposite the dock, and the hostel restaurant serves dinner for Nkr110. For a splurge, eat at **Kvikne's** fjordside dining room.

Buses run to Sogndal (Nkr95, 1¼ hours, three to five daily). Express boats run to/from Bergen (Nkr385, 3½ hours, one to two daily) and Sogndal (Nkr120, 45 minutes, one daily). Between May and September, local ferries run to/from Balestrand (Nkr147, 1¼ hours, two daily).

Sogndal & Around

pop 6600

Sogndal, a modern regional centre, is a starting point for day trips in the area. While it has more amenities than many of the area's smaller towns, it is also far less beautiful. Of most interest is the **Nigardsbreen glacier**, 70km to the north, followed by Norway's oldest **stave church** (dating from 1150 and on the Unesco World Heritage List), in Urnes across the Lustrafjord, and the **Sogn Folkemuseum** near Kaupanger, 11km east of Sogndal. Also in Kaupanger, there's a superb **stave church** dating from 1184. The **tourist office** (☎ 57 67 30 83; Kulturhus, Gravensteinsgaten; 9am-8pm late Jun-Aug, 9am-3pm Mon-Fri Sep–mid-Jun) is about 500m east of Sogndal bus station.

The tourist office books rooms in private homes from Nkr150 per person. There's an **HI Hostel** (☎ 57 67 20 33; sogndal.hostel@vandrerhjem .no; dm/s/d Nkr160/235/370; mid-Jun–mid-Aug), only 15 minutes east of the bus station.

The hotel restaurant **Compagniet** (☎ 57 62 77 00; Hotel Sogndal, Gravensteinsgaten 5; buffet Nkr230; 7am-10.30pm) has formal evening buffets, but there's also a cheaper section with some light meals under Nkr100. For an

---

AUTHOR'S CHOICE

Kvikne's Hotel (☎ 57 69 42 00; www.kviknes.no; s/d in main Bldg Nkr1200/1500, d Nkr1030-2600; Apr-Sep; P) This supremely grand and pristinely preserved timber hotel from the late 19th century boasts a fabulous collection of art and superb craftsmanship in its 'dragon-style' lounges. As you sit in a chair once owned by the landscape painter JC Dahl staring at the summer-lit fjord, you might weep as your mind struggles to comprehend vast interior and exterior beauty. Many rooms have lovely, fjord-oriented balconies – you want one of these. The newer wing – whose rooms are comfortable to a fault – is a grotesque pile of concrete by comparison.

Also enjoy a lavish dinner buffet (Nkr370) that would satisfy the most discerning gourmand and then head to the bar for some aquavit. Book far in advance.

inexpensive meal, try **Kaffir & Co**, a cafeteria in the **Domus** supermarket on Gravensteinsgata.

Buses run to Balestrand (Nkr95, 1¼ hours, three to five daily) and Fjærland (Nkr60, 45 minutes, four to six daily). Twice-daily buses (mid-June to late August) go northeast past Jotunheimen National Park to Lom (Nkr220, 3½ hours) and on to Otta (Nkr295, 4½ hours), on the Oslo–Trondheim railway line.

JOSTEDALSBREEN

With an area of 487 sq km, the many-tongued Jostedalsbreen dominates the highlands between Nordfjord and Sognefjord and is mainland Europe's largest icecap, in some places it is 400m thick. Protected as a national park, the icecap provides extraordinary opportunities for otherworldly glacier hiking.

Nigardsbreen

Among the glacier tongues visible from below, Nigardsbreen ranks among the most dramatic and easily visited, with guided **hikes** from late May to mid-September across the glacier's rippled blue ice. Small avalanches along distant ice walls sound like gunshots as they fall, and ice chips dropping through crevices sound like tinkling bells.

Outings include easy 1½-hour family walks (Nkr160) and challenging four-hour, blue-ice treks (Nkr490), crossing deep crevasses and requiring hiking boots and warm clothing (instruction and technical equipment included); there's also multiday options. More information on summer glacier walks and kayaking on glacier lakes is available from **Jostedal Breheimsenteret** (☎ 57 68 32 50; www.jostedal.com; Jostedal; ☼ 9am-7pm late Jun-Aug, 10am-5pm May & Sep), which books trips and operates a cafeteria and informative **museum** (admission Nkr50).

In the winter, contact friendly **Fimbul Jostedal** (☎ 99 45 09 21; www.fimbuljostedal.no) to learn about multiday courses on avalanche survival, ice climbing and Telemark skiing. It also guides experienced skiers along fabulous and remote glacial terrain. A five-day trip with accommodation in mountain huts costs Nkr3200.

A bus leaves Sogndal at 8.45am (Nkr150, 1½ hours) Monday to Friday for Jostedal Breheimsenteret. A return bus leaves at 6.40pm. Although this will give you time

to do a short hike, if you're doing anything longer you might want to stay at **Nigardsbreen Camping** (☎ 57 68 31 35; Jostedal; camp sites Nkr90, cabins Nkr350; ☼ late-May–Sep), whose basic facilities lie 400m from the Breheimsenteret. About 5km away in Gjerde village, **Jostedal Hotell** (☎ 57 68 31 19; www.jostedalhotel.no; Jostedal; s/d 600/800), an unofficial community centre, has clean rooms and lots of character. Its cafeteria functions as the village pub and has a Friday-night bingo session that attracts droves.

Fjærland
pop 300

The location of this farming village at the head of the beautiful Fjærlandsfjorden, near two arms of the **Jostedalsbreen** icecap, makes it one of the most inviting destinations in Norway. The tiny village is Norway's 'Book Town', with a dozen **bookshops** (www.bokbyen .no; ☼ 10am-6pm May–mid-Sep) selling used stock from an impressive 4km of shelves. Fjærland's centre is called Mundal. Its annual book fair, held the Saturday nearest 23 June pulls in booksellers and antiquarians from around the country.

The **Norwegian Glacier Museum** (☎ 57 69 32 88; Fjærland; adult/child Nkr80/40; ☼ 10am-4pm Apr-Oct) offers hands-on exhibits for children. Learn how fjords are formed and wind your way through a tunnel of mock ice. You can drive within 300m of two arms of the glacier: the **Supphellebreen**, where you can walk up to the glacier's edge and touch the ice; and the creaking, blue-iced **Bøyabreen**, where it's not uncommon to witness ice breaks plunging into the lake beneath the glacier tongue.

Tired? Sleep in the stunning **Hotel Mundal** (☎ 57 69 31 01; www.fjordinfo.no/mundal; Mundal; s Nkr820-1180, d Nkr980-1950; ☼ May-Sep), built in 1891. A wooden beauty, it features a welcoming lounge and lovely tower (drop Nkr1950 and you can sleep in its one panoramic guestroom). The place overlooks the village and fjord from a gentle hill. Eat a traditional four-course meal in the fabulous dining room (Nkr415).

Broke? **Bøyum Camping** (☎ 57 69 32 52; camp sites Nkr125, dm Nkr125, s Nkr250-300, d Nkr300, 6-person cabins Nkr680; **P**) offers simple turf roofed cabins and camp sites on a broad grassy field with mountains rising in the background. Find it near the glacier museum, 2km from the centre. Be sure to visit **Bræ-vasshytta Cafeteria** (☎ 57 69 32 96; snacks Nkr36-75, mains Nkr95-110; May-Sep), built into the moraine of the glacier's most recent advance. As one Lonely Planet author put it 'with the glacier right there and in your face, it's like eating in an IMAX cinema, but for real'.

Four to six daily buses connect Fjærland to Sogndal (Nkr60, 45 minutes) and Stryn (Nkr160, two hours). If driving, prepare for a heart-stopping toll (Nkr150) along Rv5 between Sogndal and Fjærland.

Between May and September, ferries run to/from Balestrand (Nkr147, 1¼ hours, two daily). The morning departure connects in Balestrand with the boat to Flåm and links with the Bergen-bound ferry.

Briksdalsbreen

From the small town of Olden at the eastern edge of Nordfjord, a scenic road leads 23km up Oldedalen to the Briksdalsbreen glacial tongues. It's an extremely accessible plave and as such attracts hordes of tour busses.

Glacier hiking tours are operated by **Briksdal Breføring** (57 87 68 00; www.briksdalsbre .no), near Briksdalsbre Fjellstove, and **Olden Activ** (57 87 38 88; www.briksdalsbreen.com), near the Melkevoll Bretun camping ground. Both organise glacier walks of varying duration (Nkr250 to Nkr350) that include equipment and don't demand previous experience.

It's a 5km return hike to the glacier face, either up a steep path or a longer and gentle cart track. **Oldedalen Skysslag** (57 87 68 05; adult/child Nkr250/125) will be glad to install you on a pony cart.

To sleep, head to Stryn or grab one of six rooms in **Briksdalsbre Fjellstove** (57 87 68 00; www.briksdalsbre.no; s/d Nkr400/800), a cosy mountain lodge run by the climbing company. Eat trout and reindeer (mains Nkr100 to Nkr150) in an attached café.

Between June and August, a bus runs to Stryn (Nkr65, one hour, one to two daily).

Stryn
pop 2100
Since it lies conveniently on several long-distance routes, many travellers break their journeys here. An hour's drive from Briksdalsbreen, it and the neighbouring town of Loen provide a relatively convenient base from which to make glacial excursions, particularly for those who want a restaurant or bar on hand after a day on the ice.

The helpful **tourist office** (57 87 40 40; www.nordfjord.no; 8.30am-8pm Jul, 8.30am-6pm Jun & early Aug, 8.30am-3.30pm Mon-Fri mid-Aug–May) is two blocks south of Tonningsgata, the main drag.

SLEEPING & EATING
Removed from the centre, **Sande Camping** (57 87 45 90; www.sande-camping.no; Loen; camp site Nkr90, cabin Nkr250-400;) provides a breath-taking lakeside setting (in summer, warm enough for a swim), with step mountains rising dramatically beyond. There's a shop, canoe rentals and cafeteria.

Stryn Vandrerhjem (57 87 11 06; www.van drerhjem.no; Geilevegen 14, Stryn; dm/s/d Nkr200/350/450; late May-early Sep;) Nicely perched on a hill with the fjord in the distance, these former German military barracks lie 2km from town. Member guests receive a discount on glacier hikes from Olden Aktiv (left).

Vesla Pensjonat (57 87 10 06; www.veslapensjon .no; Stryn; s/d Nkr600/800;) Boasting a lovely garden, this Victorian place will make you feel like you're living in a gingerbread house. There are plenty of cats to scratch and books on the walls.

Loen has a few worthwhile beds, including those found at **Hotel Alexandra** (57 87 50 00; www.alexandra.no; s/d Nkr960/1480;), a modern hotel where many rooms have good views over the fjord. Its pricey dinner buffet provides a top-notch survey of Norwegian cuisine.

For nightlife, food and caffeine, Stryn is the place to go, with several bars, restaurants and a disco in the Stryn Hotel.

GETTING THERE & AWAY
Buses run from Stryn to Bergen (Nkr435, 7¼ hours, one to two daily) and to Ålesund (Nkr238, 3½ hours, two to four daily). The Ålesund route passes Hellesylt (Nkr80, one hour) where there are boat connections to Geiranger.

NORANGSDALEN & SUNNMØRESALPANE
One of the most inspiring parts of the western fjords is Norangsdalen, a hidden valley west of Hellesylt. The partially unsealed Rv665 road to the villages of Øye and Urke, and the Leknes-Sæbøferry on beautiful Hjørundfjorden are served by

NORWAY

bus from Hellesylt once daily, Monday to Friday mid-June to mid-August.

Hikers and climbers will find plenty of scope in the dramatic peaks of the adjacent Sunnmørsalpane, including the incredibly steep scrambling ascent of Slogen (1564m) from Øye and the superb Råna (1586m), a long and tough scramble from Urke.

GEIRANGERFJORDEN

Added to Unesco's World Heritage List in 2005, this archetypal fjord boasts towering, twisting walls which curve inland for 20 narrow kilometres. Along the way abandoned farms cling to the cliffs and breathtakingly high waterfalls with names such as the Seven Sisters, the Suitor and the Bridal Veil drop straight into the sea from forests above.

The cruise by public ferry between Geiranger and Hellesylt is almost too nice to view.

Geiranger
pop 270

High mountains with cascading waterfalls and cliffside farms surround Geiranger, at the head of the crooked Geirangerfjorden. Although the village is tiny, it's one of Norway's most-visited spots. Nevertheless, it's reasonably serene in the evening when the cruise ships and tour buses have gone.

The **tourist office** (☎ 70 26 30 99; www.geiranger .no; ☻ 9am-7pm mid-Jun–mid-Aug, 9am-5pm mid-May– mid-Jun & mid-Aug–mid-Sep) is beside the pier and details hikes.

SIGHTS & ACTIVITIES

The **Norsk Fjordsenter** (☎ 70 26 18 00; www .fjordsenter.info; adult/child Nkr75/35; ☻ 10am-5pm May-Sep) depicts local culture with tools and uprooted buildings. Learn about the essentials that shape culture in the middle of nowhere: mail packets, avalanches and building roads over impossible terrain.

There's great hiking all around Geiranger to abandoned farmsteads, waterfalls and some beautiful lookout points. One special walk is to **Storseter waterfall**, a 45-minute hike that takes you between the rock face and the cascading falls. You'll get the most spectacular fjord views from **Flydalsjuvet**, about 5km uphill from Geiranger on the Stryn road, and from **Ørnevegen**, about 4km from Geiranger towards Valldal and Åndalsnes.

The highest and most splendid view of the Geiranger valley and fjord is from the **Dalsnibba** lookout (1500m). A bus (Nkr100 return) runs from Geiranger between 15 June and 20 August.

SLEEPING & EATING

Hotels in Geiranger can be quickly booked out by package tours, but cabins and camping spots are plentiful. A dozen camping grounds skirt the fjord and hillsides.

You'll see *Rom* signs around the village advertising rooms at around Nkr200/400 (singles/doubles) – the tourist office maintains a list and can help book one for you.

Grande Fjord Hotell (☎ 70 26 30 90; www.grande fjordhotel.com; s/d Nkr800/980; P ⊠) At a scenic spot on the fjord 2km northwest of the village, the hotel also has cabins and camp sites nearby. The buffet breakfasts (included) and dinners are particularly good here.

The tiny town centre has **Café Ole**, where you can pick up good coffee; **Olebuda**, a decent restaurant; and a supermarket, open even on Sunday. Stop by **Geiranger Galleri** a self-designated 'troll-free zone' representing artists from the Western Fjords.

Also recommended:
Geiranger Camping (☎ 70 26 31 20; www.geirang ercamping.no; camp sites from Nkr80; ☻ 20 May-Sep) Right in the centre of Geiranger.

GETTING THERE & AWAY

From mid-June to late August, buses run to Åndalsnes (Nkr148, three hours). Change at Linge for buses to Ålesund (Nkr172). The Geiranger–Hellesylt ferry (passengers/cars Nkr37/116, one hour, four to 10 daily) runs May to late September.

ÅNDALSNES
pop 2000

By Romsdalsfjorden, Åndalsnes is the northern gateway to the western fjords. Most travellers arrive on the train from Dombås, a scenic route that descends through a deeply cut valley with dramatic waterfalls. Just before reaching Åndalsnes, the train passes **Trollveggen**, a sheer 1500m-high rock face whose jagged and often cloud-shrouded summit is considered the ultimate challenge among Norwegian mountain climbers. Highway E136 between Dombås and Åndalsnes runs parallel to the railway line and is equally spectacular.

The town itself is rather nondescript, but the scenery is fabulous, camping grounds are plentiful and it has one of the finest hostels in Norway. The **tourist office** (☎ 71 22 16 22; www.visitandalsnes.com; ⏰ 9am-6pm Mon-Fri, 10am-6pm Sat, noon-6pm Sun mid-Jun–mid-Aug, 8am-3.30pm Mon-Fri otherwise) is at the train station.

Hiking

The mountains and valleys surrounding Åndalsnes offer excellent hiking – contact the tourist office for details of guided trips. One good trail, which goes to the top of Nesaksla (715m), starts right in town 50m north of the roundabout and makes a fine half-day outing.

Sleeping & Eating

Åndalsnes Camping (☎ 71 22 22 79; www.andalsnescamp.no; camp sites from Nkr80, 4-/7-person cabin Nkr350/750; ℗ ⚑) Dramatically situated on the southeastern side of the scenic Rauma river, find it 2km from the centre. It rents canoes and bikes.

Åndalsnes Vandrerhjem Setnes (☎ 71 22 13 82; aandalsnes.hostel@vandrerhjem.no; dm/s/d Nkr205/370/550; ⏰ late May-early Sep; ℗) This turf-roofed place offers rustic accommodation and a pancakes and pickled herring breakfast. It's 2km from the train station (follow E136 towards Ålesund), just far enough from town to be surrounded by idyllic flowering pastures with fine mountain views.

Grand Hotel Bellevue (☎ 71 22 75 00; www.grandhotel.no; Åndalgata 5; s/d Nkr795/995; ℗ ⚑ ⚑) Perched on a rise in the town centre, the Bellevue delivers on its name: both sides of the hotel overlook stunning water and mountain scenes. Comfortable rooms are bland and yellow, and there's a minigolf course (not challenging at all).

The town centre contains a grocery store, bakery, cafeteria and pizza joint.

Getting There & Away

The train from Dombås runs to Åndalsnes (Nkr193, 1¼ hours, two to four daily), in sync with Oslo–Trondheim trains. Buses to Ålesund (Nkr182, 2¼ hours) meet the trains.

ÅNDALSNES TO GEIRANGER

The **Trollstigen** (Troll's Path) winding south from Åndalsnes is a thriller of a road with hairpin bends and a 1:12 gradient, and to add a daredevil element it's practically one lane all the way. On request, the bus makes photo stops at the thundering, 180m-high **Stigfossen waterfall** on its way up to the mountain pass. At the top, the bus usually stops long enough for you to walk to a lookout with a dizzying view back down the valley.

There are waterfalls galore smoking down the mountains as you descend to **Valldal**. You could break your journey here – there are camping grounds, cabins and a hotel – though most travellers continue on, taking the short ferry ride from Linge across to **Eidsdal**. From there, a waiting bus continues along the **Ørnevegen** (Eagle's Hwy), with magnificent bird's-eye views of Geirangerfjorden during the descent into Geiranger village.

ÅLESUND

pop 44,000

Lucky for you, this pretty coastal town burned to the ground in 1904. The amazing rebuilding created a fantastical downtown centre unlike anything else you'll see in Norway – a harmonious collection of pastel buildings almost entirely designed in the Art Nouveau tradition. All the loveliness is well staged on the end of a peninsula, surrounded by islands, water and hills.

The **tourist office** (☎ 70 15 76 00; www.visitalesund.com; ⏰ 8.30am-7pm Mon-Fri, 9am-5pm Sat, 11am-5pm Sun Jun-Aug, shorter hrs Sep-May) is near the *Hurtigruten* quay. The post office is on Korsegata. For free internet, visit the **public library** (Kremmergaarden, Korsegata).

Sights & Activities

A popular thing to do is to walk the 418 steps up **Aksla** (189m) for a splendid view of Ålesund and the surrounding islands. Take Lihauggata from Kongensgata, pass the **Rollon statue** and begin the 20-minute puff to the top of the hill.

The brilliant **Art Nouveau Centre** (☎ 70 10 49 70; www.jugendstilsenteret.no; Apotekergata 16; adult/student/child Nkr50/40/25; ⏰ 10am-6pm Mon-Fri, 10am-5pm Sat, noon-5pm Sun Jun-Aug, shorter hrs Sep-May), occupies the fabulously restored interior of a former pharmacy. Exhibits explain the town's rebuilding with a weird time machine and presents the work (furniture, paintings, textiles and glass) of well-known continental Art Nouveau masters alongside

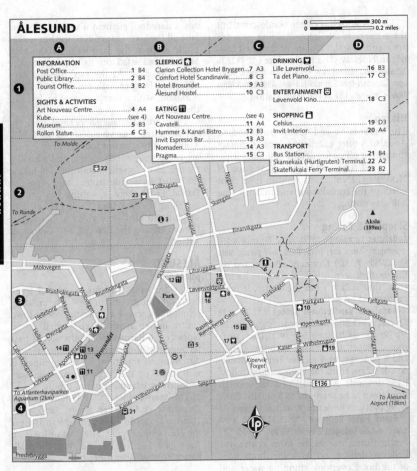

ÅLESUND

INFORMATION	**SLEEPING**	**DRINKING**
Post Office....................1 B4	Clarion Collection Hotel Bryggen...7 A3	Lille Løvenvold....................16 B3
Public Library..................2 B4	Comfort Hotel Scandinavie........8 C3	Ta det Piano......................17 C3
Tourist Office..................3 B2	Hotel Brosundet...................9 A3	
	Ålesund Hostel..................10 C3	**ENTERTAINMENT**
SIGHTS & ACTIVITIES		Løvenvold Kino....................18 C3
Art Nouveau Centre.............4 A4	**EATING**	
Kube.........................(see 4)	Art Nouveau Centre.............(see 4)	**SHOPPING**
Museum........................5 B3	Cavatelli.......................11 A4	Celsius...........................19 D3
Rollon Statue...................6 C3	Hummer & Kanari Bistro........12 B3	Invit Interior....................20 A4
	Invit Espresso Bar...............13 A3	
	Nomaden.......................14 A3	**TRANSPORT**
	Pragma.........................15 C3	Bus Station.......................21 B4
		Skansekaia (Hurtigruten) Terminal..22 A2
		Skateflukaia Ferry Terminal........23 B2

their Norwegian counterparts. A tunnel connects you to **Kube** ( ) whose gleaming white interior strongly counterbalances the wooden splendour next door. It exhibits an eclectic range of art from medieval to contemporary.

The town **museum** (70 12 31 70; Rasmus Rønnebergs gate 16; adult/child Nkr30/10; 11am-4pm Mon-Fri, noon-3pm Sat & Sun mid-Jun–mid-Aug, shorter hrs otherwise) concentrates on local history, including sealing, fishing, shipping, the fire of 1904 and the German occupation during WWII. A few boats are also shown, including the *Uræd* lifeboat, piloted across the Atlantic in 1904.

The aquarium **Atlanterhavsparken** (70 10 70 60; Tueneset; adult/child Nkr85/55; 10am-7pm Sun-Fri, 10am-4pm Sat mid-Jun–mid-Aug, shorter hrs mid-Aug–mid-Jun;), 3km from the centre at the western extreme of the peninsula, introduces visitors to marine life around the Norwegian coast.

Ålesund is a good base for touring the surrounding islands, including the bird island of **Runde** (p350), lighthouses, and Fjords. The tourist office provides a list of sailing times and itinerary suggestions. Ferries depart from the Skateflukaia ferry terminal.

Weekdays in summer there's a scenic bus-ferry day trip (Nkr410) that includes a cruise down Geirangerfjorden, an hour in Geiranger and return to Ålesund via Ørnevegen.

Sleeping

The tourist office keeps lists of a few private rooms that start at around Nkr250 per person.

Hotel Brosundet (☎ 70 12 10 00; www.brosundet .no; Apotekergata 5; s Nkr570-770, d Nkr760-990; ☐) A former warehouse contains modern rooms interestingly punctured by massive timbers. Large pulleys used to haul up fish still exist inside. Sleep inches from the canal.

Clarion Collection Hotel Bryggen (☎ 70 12 64 00; www.choicehotels.no; Apotekergata 1; s/d Mon-Fri Sep-Jun Nkr810/1080, s/d mid-Jun–Aug & Sat & Sun year-round Nkr1425/1650; ☐ ☒ ☒ ☐) This canalside choice occupies a pastel yellow warehouse dating from the town's reconstruction. In addition to breakfast, a basic dinner buffet is included.

Ålesund Hostel (☎ 70 11 58 30; aalesund.hostel@ vandrerhjem.no; Parkgata 14; dm/s/d Nkr225/415/535, ☐) Tidy and central, the hostel offers somewhat industrial rooms where touches of old charm show through. Impressive barrel vaulted breakfast room.

Comfort Hotel Scandinavie (☎ 70 15 78 00; www .choice.no; Løvenvoldgata 8; s Nkr690-1090, d Nkr890-1390; ☐ ☒) While its exterior, stairs and hallways retain lavish *Jugendstil* touches, the rooms of this hotel have been stripped and redone with a conventional modern design.

Eating & Drinking

Art Nouveau Centre (☎ 70 10 49 70; www.jugend stilsenteret.no; Apotekergata 16) Aside from Brie (Nkr60) and tuna sandwiches on grainy bread, the museum's stylish café serves homemade chocolate/marzipan cake (Nkr35) so good that you will evoke Plato.

Hummer & Kanari Bistro (☎ 70 12 80 08; Kongens-gata 19; mains Nk100-250) Downstairs, the bistro serves up ample pizzas and pasta (Nkr90 to Nkr120) with a well-stocked bar beckoning nearby. The more formal restaurant upstairs turns out a daily menu of fish specialities.

Cavatelli (☎ 70 12 27 33; Apotekertorget; dinner mains Nkr180-270) For excellent fish in a candle -lit, tall stemware kind of place, head to Cavatelli, which crosses Art Nouveau and country club. Its canalside terrace is a great place for smokers to dine.

Nomaden (☎ 97 15 89 85; Apotekergata 10; sandwiches Nkr50) Our eyes mist up recalling enormous slabs of moist chocolate layer cake with just the right amount of cherry filling (Nkr35). Eat it yourself in Nomaden's well-lit parlour with wood stove for winter cheer.

Invit Espresso Bar (☎ 70 15 66 44; Apotekergata 9; sandwich Nkr70) This modern espresso bar serves the best steamed drinks in town. Enjoy them with snacks, milkshakes and smoothies on original chairs designed next door, or on a barge on the water.

Pragma (☎ 70 12 61 50) Eat light meals, pastries and coffee in an authentic and carefully restored Art Nouveau interior with excellent vegetal wallpaper. Find it on the 2nd floor of the Storcenter shopping mall.

Lille Løvenvold (☎ 70 12 54 00; Løvenvoldgata 2; ☽ from 11am Mon-Sat, 1pm-1am Sun) Serves beer to a young crowd with rock playing in the background; rooms have couches and are lit with dim red light.

Ta det Piano (☎ 70 10 06 99; Kipervikgata 1B; ☽ from 11am) A bar and café, attracting conversationalists and intellectuals with outdoor seating, occasional live music and constant redecoration. There's a decent bar menu.

Entertainment

Løvenvold Kino (☎ 70 16 24 46; Løvenvoldgata 11) A little changed neobaroque movie house from 1922; come inside for flicks (Nkr80) and original wall paintings.

Shopping

Celsius (☎ 70 10 01 16; Kaiser Wilhelmsgata 52; ☽ 10am-4pm Tue-Fri, 10am-2pm Sat) The small glass studio blows unconventional pieces with vivid colours. The kiln is at the front of the studio, the shop at the back.

Invit Interior (☎ 70 15 66 44; Apotekergata 9; ☽ 8am-5pm Mon-Fri, 10am-5pm Sat) For creative modern furniture and the best of Norwegian kitchen appliances, teapots and cool home goods, head to this design firm and shop.

Getting There & Away

Ålesund has daily flights to Oslo and other Norwegian cities. A taxi to/from the airport costs Nkr350, thanks to numerous tolls. Or take the airport bus (Nkr75, 25 minutes). There are buses to Stryn (Nkr220, 3½ hours, one to four daily) via Hellesylt and to other major coastal and fjord towns. The bus to Åndalsnes (Nkr182, 2¼ hours, two to four daily) is timed to meet arriving and departing trains.

NORWAY

The *Hurtigruten* docks at Skansekaia Terminal.

RUNDE

pop 160

The impressive island of Runde, 27km west of Ålesund, plays host to half a million sea birds of 230 to 240 species, including kittiwakes, fulmars, storm petrels and 100,000 pairs of migrating puffins that arrive in May and stay until late July. You'll see the best bird-watching sites on a 2½-hour boat tour (adult/child Nkr150/100; three sailing daily May to August). Buy tickets at the campground's shop. Ring in advance in high-season.

Runde Camping & HI Vandrerhjem (☎ 70 08 59 16; www.runde.no; camp site Nkr60, dm/s/d Nkr150/250/350), attractively facing the harbourside, has cosy rooms with bunk beds. We particularly like the feel of those in the attic. The grassy camp sites are basic and waterside.

Runde is connected to the mainland by bridge. It can be reached by a pleasurable catamaran-bus combination day trip that gives you six hours on the island. It departs from Ålesund's **Skateflukaia ferry terminal** (Nkr266 return, 2½ hours each way, daily) from mid-June to mid-September. You can also go one way.

NORTHERN NORWAY

With several great cities and some wondrous natural terrain, you'll be mighty pleased with yourself by undertaking an exploration of this huge territory that stretches on either side of the Artic Circle. A vast plateau reaches across much of the interior, while small fishing villages cling to the incredibly steep and jagged Lofoten Islands which erupt vertically out of the ocean. Medieval Trondheim, Norway's third-largest city, provides plenty of culture and charm, while Tromsø, the world's northernmost university town, parties year-round. On some freezing inland mountains you'll find Rorøs, a Unesco-protected copper mining town, and back on the coast is Narvik, an ugly mess of a town with incredible downhill skiing.

An interesting alternative to land travel is the *Hurtigruten* coastal steamer, which pulls into every sizable port passing some of the best coastal scenery in Scandinavia. A good thing, too, since trains only run as far as Bodø.

RØROS

pop 2590

Røros is a wonderful old copper-mining town with a well-preserved historic district, protected under Unesco's World Heritage List. The little hillside town is dominated by a large wooden church, and contains several galleries. The first mine opened in 1644 but in 1977, after 333 years of operation, the company went bankrupt. The town makes for delightful strolling and everything's within easy walking distance. The **tourist office** (☎ 72 41 11 65; Peder Hiortsgata 2; ☼ 9am-3.30pm Mon-Fri, 10.30am-12.30pm Sat) can advise on canoeing, fishing, hiking and skiing.

Sights & Activities

Røros' main attractions are the turf-roofed **miners' cottages** and other centuries-old timber buildings; a prominent green and white 1784 **church** (Kjerkgata; tours adult/child Nkr25/free; ☼ 10am-5pm Mon-Sat, 2-4pm Sun mid-Jun–mid-Aug, tours 2pm) with an excellent baroque interior; **slag heaps**; and the old smelting works, now part of the **Rørosmuseet** (☎ 72 40 61 70; Malmplassen; adult/student/child Nkr60/50/30; ☼ 10am-7pm mid-Jun–mid-Aug, shorter hrs mid-Aug–mid-Jun). The museum features intricate scale models that brilliantly outline the water- and horse-powered smelting process.

Don't miss the now defunct **Olavsguva mine** (☎ 72 41 11 65; Kojedalen; tours adult/student/child Nkr60/50/30; ☼ 10am-5pm mid-Jun–mid-Aug), 13km northeast of town. Subterranean tours pass through the historic Nyberget copper mine, which dates from the 1650s, into the modern Olavsgruva mine, which operated from 1936 to 1970. The ground can be muddy and the air is a steady 5°C – so bring a sweater and good footwear. A car or taxi (Nkr450 return) is needed to get there.

Tours

In winter, the tourist office organises ski tours and excursions by dogsled (Nkr600 to Nkr1000 for two to six hours) or horse-drawn sleigh (Nkr600 per hour for four people). You can also join a winter day trip to the Southern Sami tent camp in

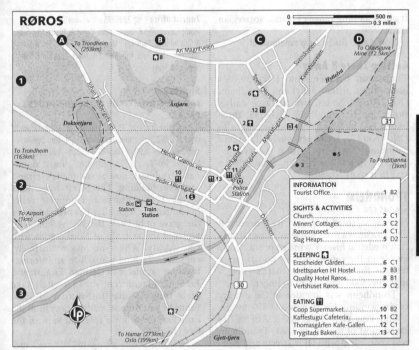

RØROS

INFORMATION
Tourist Office..........................1 B2

SIGHTS & ACTIVITIES
Church...................................2 C1
Miners' Cottages....................3 C2
Rørosmuseet..........................4 C1
Slag Heaps............................5 D2

SLEEPING
Erzscheider Gården.................6 C1
Idrettsparken HI Hostel...........7 B3
Quality Hotel Røros................8 B1
Vertshuset Røros....................9 C2

EATING
Coop Supermarket.................10 B2
Kaffestugu Cafeteria..............11 C2
Thomasgårfen Kafe-Galleri.....12 C1
Trygstads Bakeri....................13 C2

Pinstitjønna, 3km from town and 1km off the road, where you'll dine on reindeer and learn to ice fish and throw axes. The three-hour tour costs Nkr500 per person (minimum 10 people).

Sleeping & Eating

Vertshuset Røros (☎ 72 41 93 50; www.vertshusetroros.no; Kjerkgata 34; s/d from Nkr720/900, 2-person apt per person from Nkr435; P) Many of the inviting rooms have floors painted in a folk style common in the Røros area and they overlook an enclosed backyard surrounded by 18th-century buildings. The intimate dining room (mains Nkr205 to Nkr270) turns out aquavit-marinated reindeer with glazed apples and risotto flavoured with local cheese. There's a cheaper lunch menu.

Erzscheider Gården (☎ 72 41 11 94; www.erzscheidergaarden.no Spell Olaveien 6; s/d Nkr590/890; P) Cosy Erzscheider sits atop a hill, and many of the rooms have fine views across the cathedral's cemetery and the town beyond. It dates from 1780.

Idrettsparken HI Hostel (☎ 72 41 10 89; Øra 25; www.idrettsparken.no; camp sites Nkr145, dm/s/d Nkr250/395/500, cabins s/d Nkr420/650, hotel s/d from Nkr500/650; P) Family run, this pleasant hostel occupies a modern building surrounded by football pitches. Rooms are tidy and comfortable, and some have traditional furniture.

Quality Hotel Røros (☎ 72 40 80 00; www .choicehotels.com; An-Magrittsvei; s/d from Nkr500/700; P ☺ ☻) A 15-minute walk uphill from the train station, generic, clean rooms enjoy views over the valley and low, distant mountains. Trailheads lie nearby.

Thomasgårfen Kafe-Galleri (☎ 72 41 24 70; Kjerkgata 48; snacks Nkr35-50) For a nice read in a rustic room filled with ceramics, grab a table and enhance your experience with apple cake and coffee (Nkr35).

Trygstads Bakeri (☎ 72 41 10 29; Kjerkgata 12) Enjoy great coffee and top-notch blueberry muffins in this bustling town favourite. It has outdoor seating, sandwiches and pastries.

Kafestuggu Cafeteria (☎ 72 41 10 33; Bergmannsgata 18; light meals Nkr60-85, mains Nkr100-120) This cafeteria looks like a ski lodge or a Victorian parlour, depending on where you sit.

NORWAY

It offers a filling range of bland Norwegian usuals.

You'll also find a **Coop supermarket**.

Getting There & Away

Trains run between Oslo (Nkr629, 5¼ hours, three or four daily) and Trondheim (Nkr270, 2½ hours, two to three daily). Buses run to Trondheim (Nkr245, three hours, two to four daily) and overnight to Oslo (Nkr470, six hours, one daily except Saturday). The Røros airport is served by Widerøe from Oslo. It's 1km from town; a taxi to it costs Nkr60.

TRONDHEIM

pop 145,000

Norway's third-largest city, beautiful Trondheim is a lively university town whose rich medieval history remains prominently visible in the centre. While you can get a feel for the city in a day, there's enough nightlife, food and charm to linger.

Trondheim was founded at the estuary of the winding Nidelva in AD 997 by the Viking king Olav Tryggvason. After a fire razed most of the city in 1681, Trondheim was redesigned with wide streets and Renaissance flair by General Caspar de Cicignon. Today, the steeple of the medieval Nidaros Domkirke is still the highest point in the city centre.

Orientation

The central part of town is on a triangular peninsula that's easy to explore on foot. The train station, bus station and coastal-steamer quay are across the canal, a few minutes walk north of the centre.

On and around **Torvet**, the central square, are a produce market, a **statue of King Olav** and the 13th-century stone church, **Vår Frue Kirke**. From Torvet there's a head-on view of the cathedral, Nidaros Domkirke, to the south.

Information

Ark Bruns Bokhandel (☎ 73 51 00 22; Kongens gate 10) Sells English-language books.

Library (Kongens gate; ☼ 9am-4pm Mon-Fri, 10am-3pm Sat Jul–mid-Aug, 9am-4pm Mon-Fri mid-Aug-Jun) Peruse international newspapers. Free internet.

Main Post Office (Dronningens gate 10)

Space Bar (☎ 73 51 55 50; Kongens gate 19; ☼ 10am-2am Sun-Thu, 24hr Fri & Sat; per hr Nkr40) Provides late-night internet access.

Tourist office (☎ 73 80 76 60; www.visit-trondheim .com; Torvet; ☼ 8.30am-10pm Mon-Fri, 10am-4pm Sat & Sun Jul-Aug, 9am-6pm Mon-Fri, 10am-4pm Sat & Sun mid-May–Jun, 9am-4pm Mon-Fri, 10am-2pm Sat & Sun Sep–mid-May)

Sights

NIDAROS DOMKIRKE & ARCHBISHOP'S PALACE

The **Cathedral** (☎ 73 53 91 60; Kongsgårdsgata; adult/child Nkr50/20; ☼ from 9am Mon-Sat, 1-4pm Sun May–mid-Sep, noon-2.30pm Mon-Fri, 11.30am-2pm Sat, 1-3pm Sun mid-Sep–Apr) is Trondheim's most dominant landmark and Scandinavia's largest medieval building. The oldest wing dates to the 12th century, and popular belief holds that the high altar lies precisely over the grave of St Olav, the Viking king who replaced the worship of Nordic gods with Christianity. While you may roam freely, consider attaching yourself to an informative tour (available in German, English and French). Magnificent organ recitals take place from Monday to Saturday at 1pm. From July to August, visitors can climb the cathedral tower for a splendid view of the city (Nkr5).

In addition to walking on the nave's memorial flagstones (naturally, these praise the centuries' old cadavers disintegrating below), be sure to take a gander at the Norwegian royal family's **crown jewels**. The site of coronations, Nidaros Domkirke contains three crowns, the sword of the realm and some other jewel-encrusted trinkets.

An interesting feature of the cathedral is its ornately embellished west wall, lined with statues of biblical characters and Norwegian bishops and kings. Destroyed in the 19th century, the rebuilding of this wing lasted into the 20th century. Though none of the sculptures are original, prominent Norwegian artists helped make them.

Admission includes entrance to the courtyard of the adjacent 12th-century **Archbishop's Palace**. Commissioned around 1160, it's the oldest secular building in Scandinavia. Since the palace can only be admired from the outside, the modern **museum** (☼ 9am-5pm Mon-Fri, 9am-3pm Sat, noon-5pm Sun mid-Jun–mid-Aug, shorter hrs mid-Aug–mid-Jun), in the same compound, provides greater interest. It details the history of the cathedral as it underwent enlargement, modification and multiple conflagrations. Also displayed

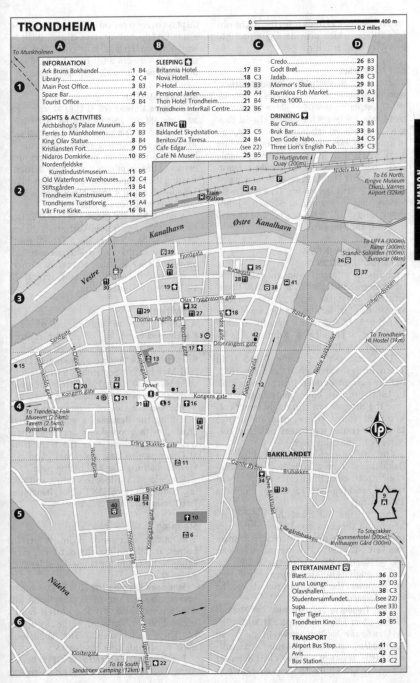

TRONDHEIM

		0 _____ 400 m
		0 _____ 0.2 miles

INFORMATION
Ark Bruns Bokhandel...............**1** B4
Library..................................**2** C4
Main Post Office.....................**3** B3
Space Bar..............................**4** A4
Tourist Office.........................**5** B4

SIGHTS & ACTIVITIES
Archbishop's Palace Museum....**6** B5
Ferries to Munkholmen.............**7** B3
King Olav Statue.....................**8** B4
Kristiansten Fort.....................**9** D5
Nidaros Domkirke...................**10** B5
Nordenfjeldske
    Kunstindustrimuseum..........**11** B5
Old Waterfront Warehouses.....**12** C4
Stiftsgården...........................**13** B4
Trondheim Kunstmuseum........**14** B5
Trondhjems Turistforeig...........**15** A4
Vår Frue Kirke.......................**16** B4

SLEEPING
Britannia Hotel.......................**17** B3
Nova Hotell...........................**18** C3
P-Hotel.................................**19** B3
Pensionat Jarlen.....................**20** A4
Thon Hotel Trondheim.............**21** B4
Trondheim InterRail Centre.......**22** B6

EATING
Baklandet Skydsstation.............**23** C5
Benitos/Zia Teresa..................**24** B4
Cafe Edgar............................(see 22)
Café Ni Muser........................**25** B5

Credo....................................**26** B3
Godt Brød..............................**27** B3
Jadab....................................**28** C3
Mormor's Stue.........................**29** B3
Ravnkloa Fish Market................**30** A3
Rema 1000.............................**31** B4

DRINKING
Bar Circus..............................**32** B3
Bruk Bar................................**33** B4
Den Gode Nabo.......................**34** C5
Three Lion's English Pub...........**35** C3

NORWAY

ENTERTAINMENT
Blæst....................................**36** D3
Luna Lounge...........................**37** D3
Olavshallen............................**38** C3
Studentersamfundet.................(see 22)
Supa....................................(see 33)
Tiger Tiger.............................**39** B3
Trondheim Kino.......................**40** B5

TRANSPORT
Airport Bus Stop......................**41** C3
Avis.....................................**42** C3
Bus Station............................**43** C2

are archaeological finds from the Archbishop's Palace, which provide a glimpse into everyday medieval life.

ART MUSEUMS

The eclectic **Nordenfjeldske Kunstindustrimuseum** (Museum of Decorative Arts; ☎ 73 80 89 50; Munkegata 5; adult/student Nkr50/25; 🕙 10am-5pm Mon-Sat, noon-5pm Sun late Jun-late Aug, 10am-3pm Tue-Sat, noon-4pm Sun Sep–mid-Jun) exhibits a fine collection of contemporary arts and crafts including work by Hannah Ryggen, Norway's highly acclaimed tapestry artist. **Trondheim Kunstmuseum** (☎ 73 53 81 80; Bispegata 7B; adult/student Nkr40/20; 🕙 10am-5pm Jun-Aug, 11am-4pm Tue-Sun Sep-May), has a corridor of Munch's lithographs and displays Norwegian and Danish art from 1850 onward.

HISTORIC BUILDINGS & NEIGHBOURHOODS

Scandinavia's largest wooden palace, the late-baroque **Stiftsgården** (☎ 73 84 28 80; Munkegata; adult/student/child Nkr50/25/25; 🕙 10am-5pm Mon-Sat, noon-5pm Sun, Jun–mid-Aug) was completed in 1778 and is now the official royal residence in Trondheim. Admission is by tour only, on the hour.

The picturesque Gamle Bybro (Old Town Bridge) originally dates from 1681, but the current wooden structure was built in 1861. From it, enjoy marvellous views over the Bryggen, an amazingly intact collection of tall red, yellow, green and orange **18- & 19th-century warehouses** reflected colourfully in the calm river.

On the east side of the bridge lies Bakklandet, a neighbourhood of cobblestone streets containing cafés and plenty of revived working-class residences from the 19th century.

Puff up the hill from this neighbourhood, and there's a good view of the city from the top of the 17th-century **Kristiansten Fort** (☎ 73 99 58 31; Festningsgaten; admission free; 🕙 10am-3pm Mon-Fri, 11am-4pm Sat & Sun Jun-Aug). Though its buildings open only during the summer, the parklike grounds can be viewed year-round.

The **Trøndelag Folk Museum** (☎ 73 89 01 00; Sverresborg Allé; adult/student/child Nkr80/55/30; 🕙 11am-6pm Jun-Aug, 11am-3pm Mon-Fri, noon-4pm Sat & Sun Sep-May), set around the ruins of a medieval castle, is one of Norway's best open-air museums. On a hill with views over town, it displays over 60 period buildings, including a small, 12th-century stave church (visit in winter to understand how cold, dark and miserable services must have been). Catch bus No 8 or 9 from Dronningens gate.

RINGVE MUSEUM

The **Ringve Museum** (☎ 73 87 02 80; www.ringve .no; Lade Allé 60; adult/student/child Nkr75/50/25; 🕙 11am-3pm or 5pm mid-May-mid Sep, 11am-4pm Sun mid-Sep–mid-May) is a fascinating music-history museum set in an 18th-century manor. Music students give tours, demonstrating the antique instruments on display. Take bus No 3 or 4 from Munkegaten 3km northeast of the city centre.

A lavish **botanical garden** (☎ 73 59 22 69; Lade Allé 58; admission free; 🕙 24hrs) surrounds the estate, covering 35 acres near Trondheimfjord. Some sections are strictly geometrical, modelled after Renaissance tastes. Others have sinuous, winding paths typical of 19th-century Romanticism.

Activities

A popular place to sunbathe and picnic is **Munkholmen Island**, site of an 11th-century Benedictine monastery and later converted to a prison, a fort and a customs house. From mid-May to early September, ferries (adult/child Nkr50/30 return) leave from the small harbour east of the Ravnkloa fish market.

The western side of Trondheim is bordered by the **Bymarka**, a woodland area crossed with good skiing and wilderness trails. To get there, take the tram from St Olavs gate to **Lian**, which has good city views, a bathing lake and hiking paths.

For help with wilderness skiing and hiking, contact the local DNT office, **Trondhjems Turistforeig** (☎ 73 92 42 00; Sand gate 30).

Sleeping

The tourist office books rooms in private homes, mostly on the city outskirts, averaging Nkr300/400 for singles/doubles plus a Nkr20 fee.

Sandmoen Camping (☎ 72 59 61 50; www.sand moen.no; camp sites from Nkr130, cabins Nkr650, with shared bathroom Nkr450; 🅿) The nearest camping ground is 12km south of the city on the E6. There's a bar on site. The cabins look mass-produced. Take bus No 46.

Trondheim InterRail Centre (☎ 73 89 95 38; www .tirc.no; Elgesetergate 1; dm Nkr135; 🕙 mid-Jun–mid-Aug;

⬛) During summer recess, university students operate this crash pad. Yeah, you'll sleep on an assortment of military cots and other hastily assembled beds with 15 to 40 others, but the place attracts lots of convivial, laid-back people and its café sometime offers backpackers specials on beer (Nkr25).

Scandic Solisiden (☎ 21 61 46 00; www.scandic -hotels.com/solsiden; Beddingen 1; s/d Mon-Fri Sep-Jun Nkr1095/1295, s/d Sat & Sun & mid-Jun–Aug Nkr680/880; P ⬛ ⬤) Adjacent to a sunny district of cafés and converted warehouse buildings, this good-looking green modern cube with it's pleasing wooden interiors has the most and best disabled rooms in Trondheim.

Britannia Hotel (☎ 73 80 08 00; www.britannia .no; Dronningens gate 5; s/d Mon-Fri Sep-Jun Nkr1500/1700, s/d Sat & Sun Nkr895/1095, s/d mid-Jun–Aug Nkr795/995; P ✖ ⬛ ⬤) Trondheim's oldest (1897) hotel contains Palmehaven, a magnificent and palm-filled Moorish-revival dining hall, and the Lobby Lounge, which looks like a British men's club. Refurbished rooms upstairs attempt to evoke the aura of age.

P-Hotel (☎ 73 80 23 50; www.p-hotels.no; Nordre gate 24; s/d Nkr595/695; ⬛) A recently renovated old hotel, with crisp rooms of Scandinavian design. There is no breakfast buffet, but you do get a sack with food.

Trondheim HI Hostel (☎ 73 87 44 50; trondheim .hostel@vandrerhjem.no; Weidemannsvei 41; dm/s/d from Nkr215/400/500; P ⬛) About 2km east of the train station, this is a plain, comfortable hostel with concrete walls and small windows.

Nova Hotell (☎ 73 80 63 00; www.nova-hotell .no; Cicignons Plass; s/d Mon-Fri Sep-Jun Nkr995/1195, s/d Sat & Sun Nkr595/765, s/d mid-Jun–Aug Nkr650/850; ⬛ ⬤) Finding the reception desk at this combination hotel and movie theatre requires detective work. Proceed past the ticket counter to the 4th floor. Recently refurbished rooms come with subtle herringbone wall coverings and wooden floors.

Thon Hotel Trondheim (☎ 73 88 47 88; www.thon .no/trondheim; Kongensgata 15; s/d Nkr595/795; ⬛ ⬤) This budget hotel occupies two buildings, a turn-of-the-century guy where rooms are carpeted and a modern box where they have wooden floors with simple, smart design. Some on the 6th floor have modest views.

Pensionat Jarlen (☎ 73 51 32 18; p-jarlen@frisurf .no; Kongens gate 40; s/d/6-person apt Nkr400/500/1200) Though barren and utilitarian (think beaten, ugly linoleum), the rooms here are clean, and contain showers and kitchen-

ettes. It's centrally located and, at time of publication, is slated for renovation.

Singsaker Sommerhotel (☎ 73 89 31 00, http:// sommerhotell.singsaker.no; Rogertsgata 1; dm Nkr155, s/d Nkr485/690, s/d with shared bathroom Nkr380/550) Set on a hill amid a grassy neighbourhood of beautiful homes, sleep either privately or in a dark 12-person bunkroom. During the school year only dorm beds are available – the rest of the building becomes a student house. Linen hire is Nkr35.

Eating
RESTAURANTS

Mormor's Stue (☎ 73 52 20 22; N Enkelts Killingsveile 2; mains Nkr62-97) Eat sandwiches (Nkr51), pasta and salads in a house full of lace, parlours and dusty pictures of grandma. The best but most dangerous time to visit is Sunday, when a calorifically evil cake and coffee buffet (Nkr54) ensures every seat is filled.

Tavern (Vertshuset; ☎ 73 87 80 70; Sverresborg Allé 11; mains Nkr130-270) Dating from 1739 and blessed with enormous fireplaces, the menu features items such as roast elk and a superb halibut with hazelnuts and creamed spinach. For atmosphere on a budget, eat some pancakes with jam and bacon (Nkr78).

Kvilhaugen Gård (☎ 73 60 06 60; Blussuvollsbakken 40; mains Nkr195-245; ⏰ from 4pm Tue-Sat, from 2pm Sun) Occupies a lovely hill-top farmstead overlooking the city. It's 300m uphill from the centre, and the traditional food is worth the trip.

Credo (☎ 73 53 03 88; Ørjaveita 4; 3-/5-course meals Nkr350/520) Original concoctions emerge from this decorated kitchen, which beautifully prepares Spanish influenced fair. A bar for the trendy is upstairs.

Benitos/Zia Teresa (☎ 73 52 64 22; Vår Frue strete 4; mains Nkr75-185) Pick between a fancy Italian trattoria or an informal pizza joint under the same, tall, moulded ceiling.

Jadab (☎ 73 52 46 00; Brattørgata 3A; mains Nkr119-195) An Indian place with a large vegetarian menu, it serves so much rice that a side of naan probably won't be needed. For the price, the food and décor are mediocre.

For cheap vegetarian meals with young activists, see **UFFA** (p356).

CAFÉS

Baklandet Skydsstation (☎ 73 92 10 44; Øvre Bakklandet 33; dishes Nkr58-169) A wood-burning stove and hearty fish soup of amazing quality keep people warm in the winter in this old wooden home with listing floor. There's a daily meal for Nkr100.

Ramp (Strandveien at Gregus gate; dishes Nkr50-135) A neighbourhood café/bar attracting few tourists, Ramp serves 'ecological' fare (meaning organic and/or vegetarian). Eat bacon and eggs for breakfast (Nkr59) and lamb burgers or vegetarian pie for dinner. Well furnished with vintage furniture, the bohemian joint often books experimental bands and is a good place for booze. Follow E6 east. Pass the Scandic Hotel and pick up Strandveien on the left side of the rotary.

Cafe Edgar (☎ 73 89 95 00; Elgesetergate 1; dinner Nkr40; ☙ from 5pm Sun-Fri, from 3pm Sat) Full of students, Cafe Edgar prepares an amazingly low-priced daily meal. It's one of many enterprises inside the Studentersamfundet.

Café Ni Muser (☎ 73 53 63 11; Bispegata; light dishes Nkr58-95) The sunlit rooms here look onto a small plaza (on sunny days, it's a beer garden) and attract a crowd of artists and architects. It serves tuna sandwiches, quiche and cake.

QUICK EATS & SELF-CATERING

There's an open-air fruit and vegetable market on Torvet each morning, as well as a **Rema 1000** (Torvet). The **Ravnkloa fish market** (☙ 10am-5pm Mon-Fri, 10am-4pm Sat) provides waterside fish cakes (Nkr75) and fishermen (free). For baguette sandwiches and pastries, try **Godt Brøt** (Thomas Angells gate 16).

Drinking

Den Gode Nabo (☎ 73 87 42 40; Øvre Bakklandet) This bar occupies the lower level of an ancient warehouse. Navigating the cavernous space requires beam-dodging and careful foot placement. Inside, admire several centuries of patchwork carpentry.

Bruk Bar (☎ 73 50 37 08; Kongens gate) A dark room with podlike green chairs, candles and interesting lights illuminates a crowd with hipster hair (receding on a few heads).

Bar Circus (☎ 93 46 11 00; Norde gate 17; ☙ 8pm-2am Thu-Sun) By 11pm the line out the door becomes formidable. On our visit it contained two guys dressed like a pirate and cyborg respectively with blasé attitudes. Inside, listen exclusively to loud rock in a basement with a beer swilling young crowd.

Three Lion's English Pub (☎ 40 00 70 66; Brattøgata 10) An English pub featuring imported

beer on tap, live wide-screen international football, bar meals for around Nkr90 and lots of dark wood.

You would also do yourself a favour by drinking in Ramp, Baklandet Skydsstation or Cafe Edgar (see p355).

Entertainment

Studentersamfundet (☎ 73 89 95 00; Elgeseter-gate 1; ☙ from 5pm) An ideal university student centre that includes a huge maze of bars and organises an excellent calendar of film screenings, discos and cool bands. Thousands of students come on weekend nights, with numerous events occurring simultaneously. During summer recess, it's quiet.

Supa (☎ 73 50 37 08; Kongens gate; ☙ Fri & Sat) Bruk Bar's underground den books weekend DJs spinning some serious House, jungle, drum and bass or R&B for cool kids dismissive of giant clubs.

Tiger Tiger (☎ 73 53 16 06; Fjordgata 56; ☙ 10pm-3am Thu-Sat) Sweaty people wearing designer clothes enjoy this three-storey disco whose theme involves a Disney-esque combo of pretend artefacts 'from' South Africa, India and Polynesia. Very popular, with DJs catering to the masses. No cover on Thursday.

Luna Lounge (☎ 73 60 06 10; TMV Kaia 5; ☙ Fri & Sat) The sweaty might also try this smaller club featuring more sophisticated DJs. Here, the fashionably dressed try to lounge in whatever comfortable furniture they can find. Summer brings scads of outdoor seating. Small dance floor.

Blæst (☎ 73 60 01 01; TMV Kaia 17) Incongruously surrounded by yuppie restaurants in a waterfront redevelopment, Blæst occupies an old warehouse and books international and Norwegian rockers (Sivert Høyem), folk bands and black metal.

Olavshallen (Kjøpmannsgata 44) At the Olavsvartalet cultural centre, Olavshallen is the city's main concert hall, hosting performers ranging from the Trondheim Symphony Orchestra to international rock and jazz musicians.

Uffa (☎ 72 52 48 50; www.uffahus.org; Innherredsveien 69C; ☙ from 4pm Mon-Fri) Long ago, the Sex Pistols played in this centre for activists. It still organises monthly punk shows in a squat white house with interiors covered in graffiti. Uffa hosts many informal political meetings, and you can usually pick up a vegetarian dinner (Nkr25 to Nkr35) around

5pm. Find it east on E6 opposite a green-steepled church.

For cinema, try **Trondheim Kino** (☎ 73 80 88 00; Prinsens gate 2B).

Getting There & Away

AIR
The airport is located in Værnes, 32km east of Trondheim.

BOAT
The *Hurtigruten* docks in Trondheim.

BUS
Nor-Way Bussekspress services run to and from Ålesund (Nkr500, 7¼ hours, one to three times daily), Bergen (Nkr735, 14½ hours, one to two daily), Oslo (Nkr620, nine hours, one to three daily) and Røros (Nkr245, four hours, two to four daily).

CAR & MOTORCYCLE
The E6, the main north–south motorway, passes west of the city centre and tolls total Nkr35, both northbound and southbound (on the Trondheim–Stjørdal section). There's also a Nkr15 toll on vehicles entering the city from 6am to 6pm from Monday to Friday.

For car rentals, there's **Avis** (☎ 73 84 17 90; Kjøpmannsgata 34) and **Europcar** (☎ 73 82 88 50; Thonning Owesens gate 36).

TRAIN
Trains go to Oslo (Nkr797, 6½ to 7½ hours, three to five daily), Bodø (Nkr924, 9¾ hours, two daily) and Røros (Nkr270, 2½ hours, two to three daily). If you're in a hurry to get north, consider taking the overnight train from Oslo, tossing your gear into a locker at the station and spending the day exploring Trondheim before continuing on an overnight train to Bodø (which, incidentally, goes through Hell).

Getting Around

TO/FROM THE AIRPORT
The airport bus, **Flybussen** (☎ 78 82 25 00; Nkr60; 40 min), leaves from the train station, the Britannia Hotel and other hotels frequently from 5am to 8pm.

BUS
The central transit point for all city buses is the intersection of Munkegata and Dronningens gate. The bus fare is Nkr22 (Nkr64 for a 24-hour ticket). Exact change is required.

CAR & MOTORCYCLE
Parking garages throughout town offer better rates and greater convenience than the krone-gobbling streetside meters.

BODØ
pop 42,000

Travellers generally use Bodø as a gateway to the Lofoten Islands and elsewhere in Nordland. Most get off their boat or train, poke around for a few hours and then get on the first ferry. Unless you've got an unusual agenda, you'll be glad to follow suit.

The city's harbour is picturesque, chock full of small fishing vessels with steep granite islands rising behind. The town, hurriedly rebuilt after thorough destruction in WWII, is not. Even so, it has good cafés and the closest thing to nightlife you'll find for hundreds of kilometres.

Information
Library (Kongens gate at Havnegata; 11am-7.30pm Mon, Tue & Thu, 11am-3pm Wed & Fri, 11am-2pm Sat) Free internet.

Ludvig's Brukbokhandel (☎ 75 52 02 99; Dronningens gate 42) Good selection of used books in English.

Post office (Havnegata 9)

Tourist office (☎ 75 54 80 00; www.visitbodo.com; Sjøgata 3; 9am-8pm Mon-Sat, noon-8pm Sun Jun-Aug, shorter hrs Sep-May) has internet terminals (per hour Nkr60) and the worthwhile Bodø Guide.

Sights & Activities
Nordlandsmuseet (☎ 75 52 16 40; Prinsens gate 116; adult/student Nkr35/free; 9am-4pm Mon-Fri, 11am-4pm Sat & Sun May-Aug, shorter hrs Sep-Apr) provides cursory exhibits on Lofoten fishermen, Sami nomads and Bodø's history, much of it oriented around the tragic bombing. The **aviation museum** (☎ 75 50 78 50; Olav V's gate; adult/student Nkr75/50; 10am-7pm Sun-Fri, 10am-5pm Sat mid-Jun–mid-Aug, 10am-4pm Mon-Fri, 11am-5pm Sat & Sun mid-Aug–mid-Jun;), 2km southeast of town, appeals to children and includes some scary simulations of jet-fighter flying. Exhibits include a control tower.

Sleeping
The tourist office books private rooms from Nkr200 per person.

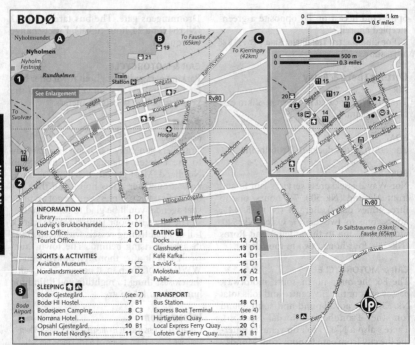

BODØ

Bodøsjøen Camping (☎ 75 56 36 80; Kvernhusveien; camp sites from Nkr130; cabins Nkr250-500) Three kilometres from town via bus No 12, this modern camp ground offers a grassy field for tenters and the grounds have fine views over water and mountain.

Bodø HI Hostel & Bodø Gjestegård (☎ 75 52 04 02 for guesthouse, ☎ 75 52 11 22 for hostel; bodo.hostel@vandrerhjem.no; Storgata 90; dm/s/d Nkr150/250/350) A friendly staff operates this cluttered, clapboarded guesthouse full of small, homey rooms. A hostel occupies an adjacent building. Breakfast costs Nkr60. Bike rental is Nkr50.

Opsahl Gjestegård (☎ 75 42 07 04; Prinsensgata 90; s/d Nkr470/770; 🖳) On a quiet residential street a few blocks from the centre, this white house with yellow trim comes with lots of red and floral wall coverings and mismatched furniture.

Thon Hotel Nordlys (☎ 75 53 19 00; nordlys@ thonhotels.no; Moloveien 14; s/d mid-Jun–Aug Nkr620/820, s/d Sep–Jun Nkr1195/1395; 🅿 🛇 🖳 🕭) Tall windows and newly finished pine floors provide the foundation for the well executed (and generic) modern design you'd expect

from a Scandinavian chain hotel. Half the rooms offer views over the water, the remainder over a parking lot.

Norrøna Hotel (☎ 75 52 55 50; norrona.hotell@ radissonsas.com; Storgata 4B; s Nkr690-860; d Nkr630-860; 🅿 🛇 🖳) Plain, tidy rooms lack luxury. Most stay here because they feel the big hotel conveniences make up for rooms that won't inspire you to stay indoors.

Eating & Drinking

Kafé Kafka (☎ 75 52 35 50; Sandgata 5B; food Nkr69-139; 🕙 11am-1am Mon-Sat, 3pm-midnight Sun) Serving marinated vegetable sandwiches and light fare, this café/bar with its upholstered couches and numerous references to Prague makes for a good place to read. Bands play some weekends.

Molostua (☎ 75 2 05 30; Moloveien 9; mains Nkr85-215; 🕙 from 5pm) Enjoy lots of fish at this red dockside restaurant dishing out regional specialities. It overlooks a pretty part of the harbour.

Løvold's (☎ 75 52 02 61; Tollbugata 9; dishes Nkr35-115; 🕙 9am-6pm Mon-Fri, 9am-3pm Sat) The 2nd-floor cafeteria above a fisherman's outfitter bustles at lunch time, offering daily specials of traditional Norwegian grub to a crowd of sea dogs and old-timers. Big windows have views over the water.

Public (☎ 75 55 83 30; Sjøgata 12; ☹ 8pm-3.30am Sun-Thu, 4pm-3.30am Fri & Sat) Supersized stills from punk-rock shows line the walls of this minimalist bar with black leather stools and a good-sized evening crowd.

For inexpensive food, head to the **docks** for fresh shrimp or **Glasshuset** (Storgata 12), with a supermarket and several fast-food choices.

Getting There & Around

The airport is 2km away, with flights to Svolvær, Trondheim, Tromsø and more. Local buses (Nkr30) marked 'Sentrum-srunden' bring you to town. A taxi costs about Nkr100.

Bodø is the northern terminus of the Norwegian train network, with a service to Trondheim (Nkr924, 10 hours, twice daily). If you're continuing north by bus, be sure to get off before Bodø at Fauske. Connections to Narvik (Nkr467, six hours, twice daily) connect with the train.

The *Hurtigruten* travels to/from Lofoten, stopping in Stamsund (Nkr261, 4½ hours, one daily) and Svolvær (Nkr279, six hours, one daily). OVDS runs car ferries to Moskenes (Nkr440/140 for car and driver/passenger, 3¼ hours, five to six daily) and Hurtigbåt operates express boats to Svolvær (Nkr260, 3½ hours, one to two daily).

AROUND BODØ

The timber-built 19th-century trading station at sleepy **Kjerringøy**, by luminescent turquoise seas and soaring granite peaks 42km north of Bodø, is fantastically preserved as an **open-air museum** (☎ 75 51 12 57; www .kjerringoy.no; adult/child Nkr40/20; ☹ 11am-5pm late May-late Aug) set on a sleepy peninsula. Buses run from Bodøto Kjerringøy (Nkr82, 1½ hours, one daily). In summer, it's possible to do a return trip on the same day.

The spectacular **Saltstraumen Maelstrom**, claimed to be the world's largest, sufficiently boggles the mind. At high tide an immense volume of water violently churns its whirlpool way through a 3km-long strait that empties one fjord into another. The spectacle occurs four times daily. Consult with the **Bodø tourist office** on when to arrive.

NARVIK

pop 14,200

Welcome to what many Norwegians consider to be the country's ugliest town, a coastal city whose waterfront is obliterated by a monstrous transhipment facility, where the ore from the Kiruna mines in Swedish Lapland is off-loaded from rail cars onto ships bound for distant smelters.

While some find a kind of grotesque beauty in this industrial display, most visitors take pleasure in the ski lift just 500m from the centre, as well as the excellent hiking and skiing in the surrounding mountain landscape. Many travellers end up here because it's the terminus of a rail line from Sweden.

Orientation & Information

The train station is at the north end of town and the Lofoten express boat dock is on Havnegata, just over 1km south of the centre, down Kongens gate.

Ask the helpful Narvik **tourist office** (☎ 76 94 33 09; www.narvikinfo.no; Kongens gate 26; 9am-7pm Mon-Fri, 11am-7pm Sat & Sun mid-Jun–mid-Aug, shorter hrs mid-Aug–mid-Jun) for details of local hiking routes.

Sights & Activities

The intelligently handled exhibits at the **Red Cross War Museum** (☎ 76 94 44 26; Kongens gate; adult/child Nkr50/25; ☹ 10am-10pm Mon-Sat, 11am-5pm Sun mid-Jun–mid-Sep, 11am-3pm Mar–mid-Jun) provide a glimpse into the fierce land and naval battles that took place around the town as the Germans and the Allies fought to control the iron-ore trade.

Weather permitting, the **Fjellheisen cable car** (☎ 76 96 04 94; Mårveien; adult/child return Nk100/60; ☹ 10am-1am mid-Jun–Jul, 1-9pm early Jun & Aug) soars 656m for breathtaking views of the midnight sun and the surrounding peaks and fjords.

During ski season, take the cable car to the largest vertical drop in Scandinavia (1000m) on one of Norway's finest downhill mountains. Speed to town while enjoying a stupendous view of the sea glistening in the near distance. Contact the tourist office for information, or see www.skiinfo.no/narvik.

Narvik Wreck Diving (☎ 76 94 41 44) can set you up with diving equipment to check out the local waters, chock-a-block with sunken ships from WWII.

NORWAY

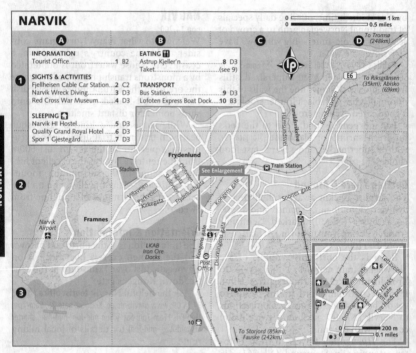

NARVIK

0 ———————— 1 km
0 ———————— 0.5 miles

INFORMATION	
Tourist Office.................1	B2

SIGHTS & ACTIVITIES	
Fjellheisen Cable Car Station...2	C2
Narvik Wreck Diving.............3	D3
Red Cross War Museum.........4	D3

SLEEPING	
Narvik HI Hostel...................5	D3
Quality Grand Royal Hotel 6	D3
Spor 1 Gjestegård.................7	D3

EATING	
Astrup Kjeller'n..................8	D3
Taket...........................(see 9)	

TRANSPORT	
Bus Station......................9	D3
Lofoten Express Boat Dock....10	B3

To Tromsø (248km)

E6 To Riksgränsen (35km); Abisko (69km)

Tours

Arrange sightseeing, fishing and whale-watching on several small boats with the tourist office; during the herring runs between October and December you may see orcas (killer whales). In October and November, **Tysfjord Turistsenter** (☎ 75 77 53 70; www.tysfjord-turistsenter.no/safari; Storjord; Nkr850) runs extraordinary orca-watching cruises from Storjord, about 85km south of Narvik on the E6. The Nor-Way Bussekspress bus to/from Fauske passes less than 1km from Storjord.

Sleeping & Eating

Spor 1 Gjestegård (☎ 76 94 60 20; post@spor1.no; Brugata 2; dm/s/d from Nkr160/450/500) Made for backpackers and in former rail cabins by the tracks, this place has well-kept dorm rooms, friendly hosts, a sauna and a well-equipped, clean kitchen.

Narvik HI Hostel (☎ 76 96 22 00; narvik.hostel@vandrerhjem.no; Dronningens gate 58; dm/s/d Nkr170/350/450;) Centrally located and sharing space with the modern Victoria Hotel, the hostel's rooms come clean and spare with

bunks and institutional flooring. Breakfast is Nkr60 extra.

Quality Grand Royal Hotel (☎ 76 97 70 00; www.choice.no; Kongens gate 64; s/d from Nkr600/800; P) Narvik's most luxurious hotel provides a sauna and rooms with butter coloured walls, good views and ugly ceilings.

Astrup Kjeller'n (☎ 76 96 04 02; Kinobakken 1; mains Nkr150-225) Established in 1903, the heavy stonewalls, dim lighting and intimate nooks of this warm place serves local specialities and a superb fillet of reindeer.

Taket (☎ 76 96 34 30; AFMI shopping centre; mains Nkr70-150) By day you can suck down stir-fired noodles with good window seats. By night, the café turns into a drinking den, and on weekends, a disco.

There are several places to eat within easy walking distance of the tourist office.

Getting There & Away

Narvik's airport is served by SAS BraathensWiderøe from Bodø, Tromsø and Oslo.

Some express bus connections between Fauske and Tromsø require an overnight break in Narvik. Nor-Way Bussekspress runs to/from Bodø (Nkr466, 6½ hours, twice daily) to/from Tromsø (Nkr340, four to five hours, one to three daily) and to/from Svolvær (Nkr433, 5½ hours, one daily).

Trains run between Narvik and Stockholm (Skr649, 20 hours, three daily) via Kiruna (Skr210, three hours, three daily). See the following Lofoten section for information on the express boat to Svolvær.

June to September, express boats sail to/from Svolvær (Nkr310, 3½ hours, one daily) from the Dampskipskaia dock on Havnegata. In winter, boats runs twice a week.

LOFOTEN

The spectacular glacier-carved mountains of Lofoten, separated from the mainland by Vestfjorden, soar straight out of the sea – from a distance they appear as an unbroken line, known as the Lofoten Wall.

Lofoten is Norway's prime winter fishing ground. The warming effects of the Gulf Stream draw spawning arctic cod from the Barents Sea south to the Lofoten waters each winter, followed by migrating north-coast

farmer-fishermen, who for centuries have drawn most of their income from seasonal fishing. Although fish stocks have dwindled greatly in recent years, fishing continues to be Lofoten's largest industry and cod is still hung outside to dry on ubiquitous wooden racks through early summer.

Many of the fishing community's *rorbuer* (winter shanties) and *sjøhus* (former fishermen's bunkhouses) have been converted into luxurious tourist accommodation. They provide some of Norway's most atmospheric places to stay.

The main islands of Austvågøy, Vestvågøy, Flakstadøy and Moskenesøy are all ruggedly beautiful. Artists are attracted by Austvågøy's light and there are art galleries in Svolvær, Kabelvåg and the busy fishing village of Henningsvær. Vestvågøy has Lofoten's richest farmland. Flakstadøy and Moskenesøy have sheltered bays and fjords, sheep pastures and sheer coastal mountains looming above strikingly picturesque fishing villages. Cyclists should be sure to try the unbelievable Kaiser Route (see p362).

NORWAY

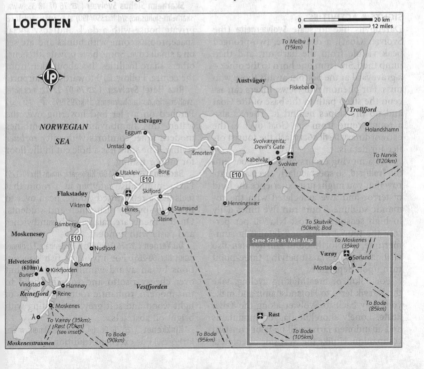

The four main islands are all linked by bridges or tunnels, with buses running the entire length of the Lofoten road (E10) from Fiskebøl in the north to Å at road's end in the southwest.

Tourist information is available at www .lofoten-info.no or www.lofoten.info.

Svolvær

pop 4300

A compact towns of old wooden buildings and modern concrete blocks, the principle town of Lofoten might be two notches less picturesque than its brothers, but it's still a pretty spot from which to base your explorations, with steep mountains rising sharply in the background and a busy harbour. More than other places in Lofoten, in Svolvær you'll find modern conveniences and the best of what passes for nightlife.

On the main square, you'll find a couple of banks, a taxi stand, car rental agency and the regional tourist office, **Destination Lofoten** (☎ 76 06 98 00; www.lofoten.info; Torget; ☺ 9am-9.30pm Mon-Fri, 9am-8pm Sat, 10am-9.30pm Sun mid-Jun–mid-Aug, shorter hrs otherwise).

SIGHTS & ACTIVITIES

Daredevils like to scale **Svolværgeita** (the Svolvær Goat), a distinctive, two-pronged peak visible from the harbour, and then jump the 1.5m from one horn to the other – a graveyard at the bottom awaits those who miss. For phenomenal views, hikers can ascend the steep path to the base of the Goat and up the slopes behind it. There's also a rough route from the Goat over to the extraordinary **Devil's Gate**; ask the tourist office for details.

For a moving excursion, ride a boat into the **Trollfjord**, so spectacularly steep and narrow that you might just experience the kind of terror and awe associated with the romantic sublime. Tours run five times daily in high season and cost Nkr300 per person; the tourist office has details. In summertime, the Northbound *Hurtigruten* also visits and makes a stupefying three-point turn upon departure.

For 83km of breathtaking cycling, take the Narvik ferry to Holandshamn and make your way back to Svolvær along the **Kaiser Route**. Lonely shoreline, jagged mountains and abandoned farms will be your constant companion. Unlike the west side of Lofoten,

this trip takes in parts of the islands that are largely undiscovered by tourists. A long stretch runs parallel to the Trollfjord. The Danish site www.digermulen.de (no English) outlines the journey (click on Kaiserroute), and provides a glimpse of the scenery. Do your preplanning at the tourist office, where you can pick up the handy *Sykkel Guide* (Nkr120) containing topographic maps.

Also contact the tourist office in advance for help booking world-class fishing trips (Nkr400). **Svolvær Sportscenter** (☎ 76 07 58 55; Roald Amundsensgt; 9am-7pm Mon-Fri, ☺ 10am-3pm Sat) sells biking, fishing and hiking gear and rents quality wheels (Nkr185 a day). For a reasonable surcharge, cycle one-way and they'll pick up your rental.

SLEEPING & EATING

Svolvær Sjøhuscamping (☎ 76 07 03 36; www .svolver-sjohuscamp.no; Parkgata 12; r Nkr440-490) On stilts sticking and projecting over the water, this 100-year-old house has small rooms with bunks and pleasant views. Guests share bathrooms and a kitchen. Turn right on the first road past the library.

Skarheim Sjøhus Svolvær (☎ 76 07 18 33; www .skarheim-sjohus.no; s/d Nkr350/490) An immaculate private house with a dock and cosy social space, rooms come with bunks and are set on a small cove. Some have private kitchens, others share facilities. It's about 1km from the centre. Follow E10 towards the airport.

Rica Hotel Svolvær (☎ 76 07 22 22; rica.hotel .svolvar@rica.no; Lamholmen; s/d Nkr795/995; P ☒ ☒) Perched on a pier and hovering over the water, this flamboyant place combines modern hotel comforts with nifty *rorbuer* styling. One suite has a hole cut in the floor for indoor fishing.

Bacalao (☎ 76 07 94 00; Kirkegata; mains Nkr70-125) For a minimalist café/bar in a room that feels like a retro-fitted garage, head over to this hang-out for fishermen and students. On the menu are salads, club sandwiches and pasta with reindeer.

Du Verden (☎ 76 07 70 99; JE Paulengate 12; dinner mains Nkr160-265) For inventive fish concoctions by an award-winning chef (halibut over cheesy risotto and squash), head to this modern, romantic room with tones of light wood and soft grey, contrasting with bright oil abstracts.

Kjøkkenet (☎ 76 06 64 66; Lamholmen; mains Nkr195-250) For excellent traditional fare, this kitchen turns out cod tongues, cured cod with crunchy bits of fat and boiled vegetables, and grilled cod neck. The dining room with its old fireplace looks like grandma's house. There's a dark pub next door.

There's a **bakery** near the square and a **Rimi supermarket** (Torggata) a block inland.

GETTING THERE & AWAY
Svolvær has a small airport (4km from town) where you can catch Widerøe flights to Bodø.

Buses to/from Vesterålen travel between Svolvær and Sortland (Nkr150, 3¼ hours, three or four daily). Buses to Leknes (Nkr120, two hours, three to six daily) make connections to Å (Nkr205, 3½ hours, two to four daily), stopping at points west. The Narvik-Lofoten Ekspressen runs between Svolvær and Narvik (Nkr410, eight to 9¼ hours, one to two daily).

OVDS's express boats ply the waters between Svolvær and Bodø (Nkr260, 3½ hours) and Narvik (Nkr300, 3½ hours), daily except Saturday (but there's no Monday sailing from Svolvær to Narvik).

Svolvær is also a stop for the *Hurtigruten*.

Kabelvåg
If you got off the boat and thought Svolvær's blend of traditional and modern wasn't cute enough, this pleasing village lies only 5km west and is connected by the E10 and a paved walking trail. Narrow channels lined with old warehouses lead to the circular cobbled torget, whose pattern of paving recalls the hulls of small fishing boats themselves docked in the channel.

Behind the old prison, a trail leads uphill to the **statue of King Øystein**, who in 1120 ordered the first *rorbu* to be built to house fishermen who had been sleeping under their overturned rowing boats – not just a kind gesture, as the tax on the exported dried fish was the main source of the king's revenue.

Some of these original *rorbuer* have been excavated as part of the **Lofotmuseet** (☎ 76 06 97 90; www.lofotmuseet.no; Storvågan; adult/student Nkr50/40; ☾ 9am-6pm mid-Jun–mid-Aug, 9am-3pm Mon-Fri mid-Aug–mid-Jun), a regional history museum on the site of the first town in the polar regions.

Nearby, the seafront **Lofoten Aquarium** (☎ 76 07 86 65; Storvågan; adult/student/child Nkr80/60/40;

☾ 10am-7pm mid-Jun–mid-Aug, 11am-3pm mid-Aug-Nov & Feb–mid-Jun) shows you some of the personalities which made Lofoten great, including the heroic cod and some harbour seals in an outdoor tank. You can eat their relatives in the museum café (not the seals).

The **Kabelvåg HI Hostel** (☎ 76 06 98 98; kabelvaag .hostel@vandrerhjem.no; dm/s/d Nkr245/405/605; ☾ Jun–mid-Aug; P) is at a school 1km north of the village centre. Dorms have two, four and ten beds and there's a cafeteria with sporadic opening hours. The **Kabelvåg Hotel** (☎ 76 07 88 00; kabelvaag@dvgl.no; s/d Nkr855/1210; ☾ mid-May–mid-Aug) lies in the centre of town. The original wooden beauty was destroyed by fire in 1995 and has since been convincingly rebuilt with an attractive Art Deco bar.

Sandvika Fjord og Sjøhuscamp (☎ 76 07 81 45; www.sandvika-camping.no; bike/car sites Nkr90/120; cabins Nkr500-1200), 3km and two inlets west of Kabelvåg, sits near the head of a rocky peninsula with good views. Tent sites are few and small, set on grassy patches a bit removed from the RVs. There's a cafeteria on site.

The charming fish, sandwich and pizza pub **Præstenbrygga** (☎ 76 07 80 60; Torget; mains Nkr35-140; ☾ from 11am), affiliated with an outdoor school for college-types and other students, is in the village centre. It often books live music.

From Svolvær you can walk the 5km to Kabelvåg or catch one of the roughly hourly buses (Nkr26, 10 minutes).

Henningsvær
pop 470
Picturesque buildings of red and white crowd the narrow channel that bisects this village, with cod racks perched in the background and fishing boats wherever space allows.

While Henningsvær's nickname, the 'Venice of Lofoten', is a tad overblown, few people would disagree that this bohemian enclave and active fishing village is the brightest and trendiest place in the archipelago. Especially on weekends, the outdoor seating at the waterside bars and restaurants is ideal for observing the lively scene. There are also a couple of **art galleries** and a climbing school.

The climbing school's **Den Siste Viking** (☎ 76 07 49 11; www.nordnorskklatreskole.no in Norwegian; Misværveien 10; dm Nkr180) crosses a Lofoten

NORWAY

rorbuer with an English pub and a Himalayan trekkers' lodge. Its **Klatrekafeen** (⏲ 11am-1am) serves up a small selection of homemade light meals (Nkr75 to Nkr130) and snacks, as well as coffee and desserts. It books some of Lofoten's best music gigs.

In summer, **Johs Giær Sjøhus og Rorbuer** (☎ 76 07 47 19; www.giaever-rorbuer.no; Hellandsgata 790; rorbuer Nkr500-1050; r Nkr400-600; w) lets out workers' accommodation in a modern house on the harbour belonging to the local fish plant. Spruce wood-panels rooms share kitchen and bathrooms. It also has three *rorbuer*.

Henningsvær Bryggehotel (☎ 76 07 47 50; booking@henningsvaer.dvgl.no; Hjellskjæret; s/d from Nkr1050/1200; ♿) abuts the harbour with modern rooms furnished in contemporary stylings. There's a rack of rods by the door if you'd like to catch something.

Buses shuttle between Svolvær (Nkr40, 35 minutes), Kabelvåg (Nkr38, 30 minutes) and Henningsvær two to eight times daily.

Lofotr Vikingmuseum

This 83m-long chieftain's hall, Norway's largest Viking building, has been excavated at Borg, near the centre of Vestvågøy. The **museum** (☎ 76 08 49 00; adult/student/child Nkr90/70/45; ⏲ 10am-7pm mid-May-Aug, 1-3pm Fri Sep-Apr) offers an insight into life in Viking times, complete with a scale-model reconstruction of the building, guides in Viking costume and a replica Viking ship, which you can row daily at 2pm (Nkr20).

Stamsund

pop 1000

The traditional fishing village of Stamsund makes a fine destination largely because of its dockside hostel, a magnet for travellers who sometimes stay for weeks on end. Here, as elsewhere on Lofoten, highlights include hiking and fishing. A popular town activity is to stare at the *Hurtigruten*'s approach.

The wonderful old beach house **Justad Hl Hostel/Rorbuer** (☎ 76 08 93 34; fax 76 08 97 39; dm/s/d Nkr115/250/300, cabins Nkr600-800; ⏲ mid-Dec–mid-Oct; ℗), 1.2km from the quay, attracts many repeat customers drawn by the waterside building, friendly manager (ask about hiking routes) and free loans of fishing gear and row boats. Bike rentals cost Nkr80 to Nkr100 per day.

The village centre contains a supermarket and the **Skæbrygga** (fish mains Nkr150-175) bar and restaurant and little else.

The *Hurtigruten* coastal steamer stops en route between Bodø (Nkr398, 4½ hours) and Svolvær (Nkr132, 1½ hours). In July and August, buses from Leknes to Stamsund (Nkr30, 25 minutes) run up to eight times daily, less often on Saturday and Sunday.

Reine & Hamnøy

The delightful village of Reine, on the island of Moskenesøy, is on a calm bay backed by ranks of mountain cliffs and pinnacles. With its almost fairy-tale setting, it's easy to see the reasons why the village has been voted the most scenic place in all of Norway. Aside from eating some fish, however, the town is pretty deadsville.

For an exceptional panorama of the lagoon, town and island, hike up the precipitous track to Reinebringen (670m), which starts at the tunnel entrance 1.2km south of the Reine turnoff from the E10 and climbs very steeply to the ridge (448m). Experienced hikers can continue to the peak and then drop steeply down a very exposed route to the col of Navaren and on to Navaren's summit (730m).

In summer, ferries run from Reine to **Vindstad** (Nkr64 return, 40 minutes) through the scenic Reinefjord. From Vindstad, it's a one-hour hike over a ridge to the abandoned settlement of **Bunes** on the other side of the island, with a magnificent beach, vast quantities of driftwood and the 610m-high cliff of **Helvetestind**. Here you'll find some extremely basic camping.

The family run **Hamnøy Mat og Vinbu** (☎ 76 09 21 45; Hamnøy; mains Nkr130-165; ⏲ May-Sep) restaurant serves stellar local specialities, including *bacalao* (dried and salted cod), cod tongues, and other fish dragged from the nearby harbour. There's a deck with picnic tables and a cosy dining room.

There's a Coop supermarket in Reine.

All buses from Leknes to Å stop in Reine.

Å

Å is a very special place. It's a preserved fishing village perched on forbidding rocks connected by wooden footbridges. It's shoreline is lined with red-painted *rorbuer*, many of which jut into the sea. Racks of drying cod and picture-postcard scenes occur at almost every turn. Visitors enliven the tiny place in summer, while in winter it's stark, haunting and empty.

SIGHTS & ACTIVITIES

The **Tørrefiskmuseum** (Stockfish Museum; ☎ 76 09 12 11; adult/student Nkr40/25; ☒ 10am-5pm mid-Jun–mid-Aug, 11am-5pm Mon-Fri early Jun & late Aug, otherwise by appointment), inside a cod plant dating from 1920, details the history of the stockfish industry, taking in every step from catching to cooking. Steinar Larson, the gregarious operator, has long family ties to Å, and explains everything cod (and Å) in excited detail.

Many of Å's 19th-century buildings are set aside as the **Norwegian Fishing Village Museum** (☎ 76 09 14 88; admission Nkr40; ☒ 10am-5pm late Jun-late Aug, 11am-3pm Mon-Fri Sep–mid-Jun), complete with old boats and boathouses, a bakery from 1844, Europe's oldest cod-liver oil factory and storehouses.

Walk to the camping ground at the end of the village for a good hillside view of Værøy Island, which lies on the other side of **Moskenesstraumen**, the swirling maelstrom that inspired the fictional tales of, among others, Jules Verne and Edgar Allen Poe.

SLEEPING & EATING

Moskenesstraumen Camping (☎ 76 09 13 44; camp sites from Nkr60, huts Nkr300-500; ℗) This basic campground lies at the south end of Å near an oceanside cliff. Paths and sites wind around granite boulders that seem to erupt from the ground.

Å HI Hostel (☎ 76 09 11 21; www.lofoten-rorbu .com; dm Nkr175, rorbuer Nkr800-1550; ℗) The hostel has accommodation in some of the museum's historic seaside buildings that form the picturesque centre of town. Breakfast is Nkr60 extra.

Å-Hamna Rorbuer (☎ 76 09 12 11; www.lofo tenferie.com dm/d Nkr100/350, rorbuer Nkr600-950; ℗) Also at the museum, this inviting place is run by a crazy guy who knows way too much about stockfish. Pleasant dorms come with a pretty communal space in a restored 1860s home. Cosy wooden *rorbu*, perched magnificently on the rocks, contain four to eight beds each. Off-season you can get the best *rorbuer* for around Nkr350, firewood included.

Brygga restaurant (☎ 76 09 11 21; mains Nkr170-210; ☒ Jun-Sep) The village's only restaurant

cantilevers dramatically over the water and serves fantastic fish. It also serves a vegetarian plate and is a great place to drink beer.

Self-caterers can also buy fresh fish from local fishers and pick up other supplies at the small food shop behind the hostel office.

GETTING THERE & AWAY

Nordtrafikk runs one to three daily buses from Å to Leknes (Nkr107, 1¾ hours), Svolvær (Nkr200, 3¼ hours) and Sortland (Nkr312 plus Nkr30 for a ferry, 5¼ hours).

OVDS runs car ferries from Bodø to Moskenes (Nrr440/140 car and driver/passenger, 3½ hours, five to six daily in high season, less during low season), 5km north of Å. Some of these ferries run via Værøy and Røst.

Værøy & Røst
pop 1400

Lofoten's southern islands of Værøy and Røst have some of the finest **bird watching** in Norway, with large colonies of fulmars, guillemots, kittiwakes and terns. There are puffins as well, but the population has dropped by more than 50% in the past decade as a result of dwindling stocks of herring, the main food source for puffin chicks.

Craggy high and rugged, Værøy has only 775 people, but 100,000 nesting sea birds. **Hiking trails** take in some of the more spectacular sea-bird rookeries. The main trail goes along the west coast, beginning about 300m past the island's airstrip, and continues south all the way to the virtually deserted fishing village of Mostad, passing by steep cliffs, sandy beaches and isolated settlements. This 10km hike makes for a full day's outing and is not too strenuous, but it's exposed to the elements, so is best done in fair weather.

Røst, south of Værøy, enjoys one of the mildest climates in northern Norway, thanks to its location in the middle of the Gulf Stream. Access to the best bird-watching requires a boat, as the largest rookeries are on offshore islands. **Kårøy Sjøhus** (☎ 76 09 62 38; rt-finni@online.no) can arrange all-day boat trips (Nkr250) that cruise past major sea-bird colonies and stop at an 1887 **lighthouse** and a vista point. En route it's common to see seals and there are occasional sightings of orcas. Røst itself is pancake flat and, other than the boat trip, there's not much to do.

The **tourist office** (☎ 76 09 52 10; ✆ 10am-3pm Mon-Sat mid-Jun–mid-Aug) is 200m from the ferry landing at Sørland.

SLEEPING & EATING

Preste Gården (☎ 76 09 54 11; www.pretegaarden .no; Nordland; s/d with shared bathroom Nkr475/690, s/d Nkr400/600) Sleep in an old vicarage next to little onion-domed church in a knotty pine attic or cosy turf-roofed cottage with ocean out front and cliff behind. It's the large house with the flagpole.

Kornelius Kro (☎ 76 09 52 99; korn-kro@online .no; Sørland; r Nkr350-700) Værøy's only nightlife option also has a restaurant, a pub and a few simple but clean cottages out the back. Check out the wood-fired seawater hot tub.

GETTING THERE & AWAY

OVDS ferries run from Bodø to Værøy (Nkr121, four to six hours, one to two daily except Sunday) before continuing to Røst. There are fewer in the low season. A local ferry (☎ 94 80 31 15) provides addition summer service between Værøy, Røst and Moskenes.

VESTERÅLEN

The islands of Vesterålen aren't quite as dramatic as Lofoten, but they're still very attractive to visitors. For tourist information, consult **Vesterålen Reiseliv** (☎ 76 11 14 80; www.visitvesteralen.com; Kjøpmannsgata 2, Sortland).

Vesterålen is connected by ferry from Melbu on Hadseløya to Fiskebøl on Austvågøy (Lofoten). Melbu has a couple of **museums** and a famous **music festival**, featuring classical, jazz and blues, every July. The other main town, **Stokmarknes**, is a quiet market community best known as the birthplace of the *Hurtigruten* coastal steamer.

Nyksund (www.nyksund-info.com) on Langøya is a former abandoned fishing village that's now re-emerging as an artists' colony. There's a great **walk** over the headland from Nyksund to Stø (three hours return), at the northernmost tip of Langøya. Ask the tourist office for details of **whale-watching tours** from Stø.

Andenes on Andøy seems a long way from anywhere, but there's whale-watching,

a whale centre, a natural history centre, a lighthouse and a couple of museums. **Whale Safari** (☎ 76 11 56 00; www.whalesafari.no) runs popular three- to five-hour whale-watching cruises from the whale centre between late May and mid-September. Trips depart at least once daily (at 10.30am) and cost Nkr695. Sightings of sperm whales are guaranteed, or your next trip is free. Dress warm.

Sleeping & Eating

Holmvik Brygge (☎ 76 13 47 96; www.nyksund.com; Nyksund; s/d Nkr300/500) Offers irregular but cosy rooms done up like those in an old fisherman's house. Facilities are shared.

Andenes HI Hostel (☎ 76 14 28 50; andenes .hostel@vandrerhjem.no; Havnegata 31, Andenes; dm/s/d Nkr150/215/325; ✆ Jun-Aug; Ⓟ) The hostel occupies the Lankanholmen Sjøhus, a wonderful old timber-frame building by the sea; breakfast is Nkr60 extra.

Den Gamle Fyrmesterbolig (☎ 76 14 10 27; Richard Withs gate 11, Andenes; s Nkr250-350, d from Nkr300; Ⓟ) So charming that you need to book far in advance, this lighthouse keepers' cottage has four rooms adjacent to the seaside beacon.

There's a bakery and an informal café at the Andenes whale centre, while the restaurant at the Norlandia Hotel serves a good Arctic menu.

Getting There & Away

Sortland is the main transport hub in Vesterålen. Both Sortland and Stokmarknes are stops for the *Hurtigruten* coastal steamer.

Nordtraffik buses from Leknes (Nkr270, four hours) stop in Sortland and continue to Narvik (Nkr200, three hours), with stops in Svolvær (Nrk150, two hours).

In summer, buses connect Sortland with Andenes (Nkr130, two hours, one to four daily) via Risøyhamn.

TROMSØ

pop 52,000

Tromsø, at latitude N69°40′, is the world's northernmost university town. In contrast to some of the more sober communities dotting the north coast of Norway, Tromsø is a spirited place with street music, cultural happenings and more pubs per capita than any other Norwegian town – it even has its own brewery.

A backdrop of snowcapped peaks provides spectacular scenery, excellent hiking in summer and skiing and dogsledding from September to April. Many polar expeditions have departed from Tromsø, earning the city the nickname 'Gateway to the Arctic'. A statue of explorer Roald Amundsen, who headed some of the expeditions, stands in a little square down by the harbour.

Orientation & Information

Tromsø's city centre and airport are on the island of Tromsøya, which is linked by bridges to overspill suburbs on both the mainland and the much larger outer island Kvaløya. Storgata is the principal drag.

The **tourist office** (☎ 77 61 00 00; www.desti nasjontromso.no; Kirkegata 2; ☼ 8.30am-6pm Mon-Fri, 10.30am-5pm Sat & Sun Jun–mid-Aug, 8.30am-4pm Mon-Fri mid-Aug–May) is particularly knowledgeable and attentive. Send or collect your mail from the main **post office** (Strandgata 41). For maps, hiking info and cabin reservation, visit **Troms Turlag DNT** (☎ 77 68 51 75; www.tur istforeningen.no; Grønnegata 32; ☼ 10am-2pm Tue-Wed & Fri, 10am-6pm Thu).

Sights & Activities

Tromsø's daringly designed museum of the Artic **Polaria** (☎ 77 75 01 00; Hjalmar Johansens gate 12; adult/child Nkr80/40; ☼ 10am-7pm mid-May–mid-Aug, noon-5pm mid-Aug–mid-May; ♿) presents panoramic films on Svalbard (caution: these

NORWAY

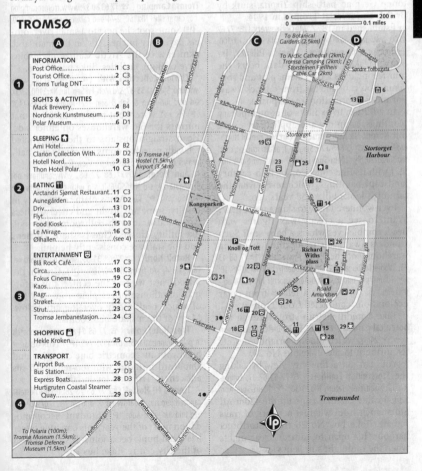

inspire spontaneous and expensive trips to the remote icy netherworld), an aquarium with Artic fish and cohort of bearded seals.

Northern Norway's largest museum, **Tromsø Museum** (☎ 77 64 50 00; www.imv.uit.no; Lars Thøringsvei 10; adult/child Nkr30/15; ☼ 9am-8pm Jun-Aug, shorter hr Sep-May, ☐) simulates the Northern Lights for visitors currently experiencing the midnight sun. It also presents some well-done displays on Arctic wildlife, Sami culture and regional history. Take bus No 28.

Occupying a restored artillery battery with six big Nazi guns, the **Tromsø Defence Museum** (☎ 77 62 88 36; Solstrandveien; adult/child Nkr30/15; ☼ noon-5pm Wed-Sun Jun-Aug, noon-5pm Sun May & Sep) includes a former ammunition store with an exhibition on the 52,600-tonne German battleship *Tirpitz*, sunk by British air forces at Tromsø in 1944.

Established in 1877, **Mack Brewery** (☎ 77 62 45 00; www.mack.no in Norwegian; Storgata 5; tours Nkr100; ☼ tours at 1pm) produces Mack's Pilsner, Isbjørn, Haakon and several dark beers; the tour fee includes a beer stein, pint and souvenir. You can smell it from a block away. For more information, see opposite.

In addition to exhibits of contemporary paintings, sculpture and applied art, check out **Nordnorsk Kunstmueum** (Art Museum of Northern Norway; ☎ 77 64 70 20; Sjøgata 1; adult/student/child Nkr30/20/20; ☼ 10am-5pm Tue-Fri, noon-5pm Sat & Sun; ☐) with its fine collection of 19th-century landscape paintings, which reveal what the far north looked like 150 years ago.

Ever wondered how to skin a polar bear? Want to see a creepy wax figures with dead, zombie eyes whack a baby seal? Such wonders await you inside the low-ceiling warehouse of the **Polar Museum** (☎ 77 68 43 73; Søndre Tollbugata 11; adult/student/child Nkr50/45/10; ☼ 10am-7pm mid-Jun–mid-Aug, shorter hrs mid-Aug–mid-Jun; ☐), as well as artefacts from polar explorations conducted from Tromsø.

Take a midnight sun stroll through the **botanical garden** (☎ 77 64 50 78; Breivika; admission free; ☼ 24hr), which blooms brightly despite its northern locale. Take bus No 20.

You can get a fine city view by taking the **Storsteinen Fjellheis** (☎ 77 63 87 37; Sollieveien 12; adult/child return Nkr70/30; ☼ 10am-5pm Apr-Sep), a cable car that runs up the 420m Mt Storsteinen from where a network of trails radiate. Take bus No 26 from Stortorget harbour. It's open to 1am on clear nights when the midnight sun is in view.

Festivals & Events

The **Tromsø International Film Festival** (☎ 77 75 30 90; www.tiff.no), in mid-January, perhaps the most exciting of Norway's film festivals. Every screening is packed both by locals and A-list types excited to have major screenings in such an exotic place. Check out movies from northern Norway and the Baltic countries, forgotten classics, weird shorts, American independents and more.

TIL (☎ 77 66 38 00; www.til.no) services the town's football mania in a small stadium. Team members have received yellow cards for throwing snowballs. Buy tickets at the Fokus Cinema (opposite).

Sleeping

Tromsø Camping (☎ 77 63 80 37; www.tromsocamping .no; camp sites Nkr150, 2-/4-bed cabins from Nkr400/500; ☐) Some spots lie next to a small river, others have leafy pitches. It's on the mainland, 2km east of the Arctic Cathedral. Cabins have cooking facilities. Take bus No 26.

Clarion Collection With (☎ 77 68 70 00; www .with.no; Sjøgata 35-37; s/d Mon-Fri Sep-Jun Nkr1100/1300, s/d mid-Jun–Aug & Sat & Sun year-round Nkr845/1400 ☐ ☐) A waterfront modern building that mirrors the old warehouses on either side, Head straight upstairs to the glass-roofed relaxation deck. Rooms are comfy and hallways have pictures of sea captains.

Ami Hotel (☎ 77 68 22 08; www.amihotel.no; Skolegata 24; s/d Nkr550/650, s/d with shared bathroom Nkr450/590; ☐ ☐) Ami's plain rooms vary in quality: some are bright and cheery, others worn and drab with bathrooms that look like utility closets. Guests share kitchens and the staff are consistently helpful.

Hotell Nord (☎ 77 68 31 59; www.hotellnord.no; Parkgata 4; s/d from Nkr400/550; ☐) Up on the hillside just west of the centre, this informal guesthouse offers plain rooms, a few of which peak nicely over the city below. Many of them share bathrooms.

Thon Hotel Polar (☎ 77 68 64 80; www.thonhotels .n/polar; Grønnegata 45; s/d Nkr595/795; ☐) This budget hotel with its geometric blue carpeting and chipboard furniture with too-red finish sits adjacent to Tromso's loudest disco.

Tromsø HI Hostel (☎ 77 65 76 28; tromso.hostel@ vandrerhjem.no; Åsgårdveien 9; dm/s/d Nkr170/300/400; ☼ mid-Jun–mid-Aug; ☐) Student accommodation most of the year, this concrete tower has clean bunk-bed rooms. It's 1.5km west of the city centre. Take bus 26.

Eating & Drinking

Aunegården (☎ 77 65 12 34; Sjøgata 29; dishes Nkr118-135, cake Nkr63; ☻ 10.30am-midnight, 1pm-midnight Sun) Serving amazing cakes (try the chocolate truffle with meringue and syrupy hazelnut crust), this café operates out of a former general store from 1830. It makes salads out of greens that are actually green! There's lots of wine and intimate spaces.

Arctandria Sjømat Restaurant (☎ 77 60 07 25; Strandtorget 1; mains Nkr195-260; ☻ from 4pm) Near the harbour and festooned with nautical instruments, this pretty room with white stucco walls and big overhead beams serves an Arctic menu that includes monkfish and reindeer steaks.

Driv (☎ 77 60 07 76; Tollbugata 3; dishes Nkr75-117) This student culture house occupies an old warehouse and serves pizzas and big burgers with great chips. They also books bands, programs events such as the Fucking North Pole Festival (a music and culture festival organised by students) and often serves as a disco. A student ID earns you discounted beer (Nkr42) and 15% off food. Harbourside hot tub in winter.

Knoll og Tott (☎ 77 66 68 80; Storgata 62; sandwich Nkr55; ☻ 10am-6pm Mon-Fri, 10am-4pm Sat) Filling, large sandwiches come on warm baguettes. Take your pick from pepperoni and brie, vegetable (many toppings tasted canned), roast beef and more in a two-storey place with warm yellow walls.

Flyt (☎ 77 69 68 00; Sjøgata 25; dishes Nkr119-159) In a city that sucks for vegetarians, the veggie burger at this café is a tear-jerking find. Otherwise, you'll find the usual meaty light meals. Some nights it turns into a disco with pillows on the floor and a clientele of climbers and guides.

Le Mirage (☎ 77 68 52 34; Storgata 42; mains Nrk79-159; ☻ from 11am) Brown overstuffed faux-leather chairs are the dominant feature in this trendy café/bar long favoured by Tromsø's fashionably dressed. Not loud, it's a good place for conversation. Most use it for the drinks, less for the eats.

Ølhallen (Storgata 4; ☻ 9am-5pm Mon-Wed, 9am-6pm Fri, 9am-3pm Sat) Try Tromsø's own Mack beer at pubs, cafés or here, next to the brewery. It makes up for its pathetic hours with old brick walls and décor from the 1920s. Stuffed polar bears greet visitors by the door, as do drunk guys.

Tromsø's fast-food scene is led by various kebab carts, and a food kiosk at the express boat dock. You can buy fresh boiled shrimp from fishing boats at Stortorget harbour. There are several bakeries.

Entertainment

Tromsø enjoys a thriving nightlife, with many arguing that it's the best scene in Norway. On Friday and Saturday, most nightspots stay open past 4am. Many also serve light meals. See Driv (left) for a student hang-out.

Kaos (☎ 77 63 59 99; Strandgata 22) Hidden in a low-ceiled basement with exposed beams and ripped up brick walls, this cool hangout attracts arthouse DJs and bands. They only let 90 people inside, so show up early. Beer costs Nkr30 before midnight.

Blå Rock Café (☎ 77 61 00 20; Strandgata 14) Live bands and DJs (playing rock, naturally) cause hearing damage in a black-coloured club with Elvis pinball and 50 kinds of beer spilling on the floor. Excellent burgers.

Strøket (☎ 77 68 44 00; Storgata 46) Packed and sweaty on weekends, the three levels of this large disco attracts a young crowd (in May, this means every *Russ* in the city) with it's pop dispensing DJs. The 3rd floor allows a view over the masses.

Ragr (Vestregata 1) The name of Tromsø's queer hang-out comes from Old Norse and shouldn't be translated for fear of making some readers blush. Not a pick-up joint, it's an elegant room of warm woods and some enviable green velvet couches.

C (Storgata 36) Crowded C attracts a broad range of ages – from 19-year-old art students to a mature set with greying hair and sophisticated glasses – with talented weekend DJs and no cover. By day it's a pleasant café.

Strut (☎ 77 68 49 06; Grønnegata 81) Downstairs looks like a pub with pool tables and a piano man singing 'Sweet Home Alabama' (why?). Upstairs is a slicker '70s-inspired disco with a small dance floor and lots of people dressed to look good.

Tromsø Jernbanestasjon (☎ 77 61 23 48; Strandgata 33; ☻ 11am-2am) A brown bar whose name means 'Tromsø's Railway Station', and supports some serious drinking. It's filled with railway artefacts, but the unspoken joke is that this remote city was never even close to being connected by rail.

For films, the six-screen **Fokus Cinema** (☎ 77 75 63 00; Rådhusgata 2) does the job.

Shopping

Hekle Kroken (☎ 77 68 17 89; Storgata 91; ☼ from 11am Mon-Sat) A knitting store selling yarn and pattern books, this shop is mostly frequented by locals. It sometimes sells a limited selection of handmade mittens and sweaters a notch cooler (and more expensive) than the mass-produced stuff (also on hand).

Getting There & Away

Tromsø is the main airport hub for northern Norway, with direct flights to Oslo, Bergen, Bodø, Trondheim, Alta, Hammerfest, Kirkenes and Longyearbyen.

Express buses run to Alta (Nkr460, 6½ hours, one daily), and to Narvik (Nkr360, 4½ hours, three daily), some of them timed to continue to Bodø. The bus to Narvik also has a timed connection to Svolvær, though you can save some time by taking a **TFDS** (☎ 77 64 81 00) ferry to Harstad (Nkr430, 1½ hours, two daily) and then bussing to Svolvær (Nkr265, five hours).

The *Hurtigruten* stops here.

Getting Around

TO/FROM THE AIRPORT

The airport bus (Nkr45/70 one-way/return) can be picked up at the Radisson SAS Hotel; a taxi to the airport costs about Nkr100.

BUS

Thoroughly exploring Tromsø can take time, as the city is spread out and many of the sights are outside the centre. Rides on city buses cost Nkr23.

CAR

If you have your own car, you'll find it convenient for getting around. Tromsø has numerous parking areas spread around the city, including a huge underground car park off Grønnegata.

FINNMARK

Along the jagged coast, deeply cut by forbidding fjords, you'll find numerous isolated fishing villages; Alta with it's Stone-Age rock carvings; Kirkenes, a frontier-like town sharing a border with Russia; and Nordkapp, mainland Europe's northmost point. Or very nearly so; to reach the actual end of the earth, prepare to enjoy an 18km round-trip hike across the eerie peninsula.

Those that head inland will find the vast and empty Finnmarksvidda plateau, a stark expanse with only two major settlements: Karasjok and Kautokeino. They and Finnmarksvidda are part of the heartland of the Sami people (traditionally know as Lapland), where reindeer herding has occurred for centuries. At either, enjoy a dogsled journey across empty tundra half lit under the bruise-blue winter sky.

Drawback: virtually every town in Finnmark was razed to the ground at the end of WWII by retreating Nazis, whose scorched-earth policy was intended to delay the advancing Soviet troops. Unfortunately, the rebuilt towns all look rather grim. Satisfying urban life north of Tromsø does not exist. In the summer, the eerie midnight sun takes over, as do swarms of mosquitoes (at their peak from late June to late July).

You can get information about the entire region from the **Finnmark Tourist Board** (☎ 78 44 00 20; www.visitnorthcape.com).

ALTA

pop 18,000

If anything in Finnmark can be called cosmopolitan, Alta is it. It's easily Finnmark's largest town, and, thanks to the Finnmark Municipal University, it's home to 2000 students. The biggest attraction in town is a collection of Unesco-protected rock carvings, which date to 4000 BC. If this doesn't grab your fancy, wilderness surrounds the city, as do opportunities to go ice fishing or dogsled riding (inquire at the tourist office). Some accuse the place of being an ugly bore.

Orientation & Information

Alta is a sprawling town occupying 15km of coastline. The town's two main centres, Sentrum (it looks like an office park) and Bossekop (hey, at least it's hilly), are 3km apart, connected by the E6. Sentrum's **tourist office** (☎ 78 45 50 00; Parksentret Bldg; ☼ 8.30am-4pm, Mon-Fri, 10am-4pm Sat) is 1km northwest of Sentrum off the E6. Bossekop's **tourist office** (☎ 78 44 50 50; www.altatours.no; Sorekskriverveien; ☼ 10am-8pm Mon-Fri, 10am-5pm Sat, noon-6pm Sun Jun-Aug) has internet access (Nkr15 per 10 minutes). Check your email at the Sentrum **library** (⊙ 10am-6pm Mon-Thu, 10am-3.30pm Fri, 11am-3pm Sat).

Sights & Activities

Alta's main sight is the impressive, World Heritage–protected, **prehistoric rock art** (☎ 78 45 63 30; www.alta.museum.no; Altaveien 19; adult/child Nkr75/free; ⊙ 8am-9pm Jun-Aug, 9am-6pm May & Sep, 9am-3pm Mon-Fri, 11am-4pm Sat & Sun Oct-Apr) at Hjemmeluft, on the E6, 4km southwest of Bossekop. A 3km-long network of boardwalks leads past many of the 3000 rock carvings of hunting scenes, boats, fertility symbols, bears and reindeer that date back as far as 4000 BC. Wait for the snow to melt before visiting, otherwise the rocks are covered. The admission charge includes a guide and the entry to adjacent **Alta Museum**, with regional exhibits.

The Altaelva rushes through the 400m-deep **Sautso**, northern Europe's grandest canyon. The scenic gorge is best seen as part of a tour (Nkr350), which gains you access to the Alta Power Station dam and includes a snack in a traditional Sami *lavvo* (tent). Contact **Alta Tours** (☎ 78 44 95 55; www .altatours.no) for bookings.

Alta is also renowned for its **salmon run**; several local companies organise fishing tours.

Sleeping

Alta Igloo Hotel (☎ 78 43 33 78; www.alta-friluftspark .no; Storelvdalen; per person Nkr1295; ⊙ mid-Jan–mid-Apr) Entirely made of snow and ice (even the drinking glasses), enjoy a pleasurable morning sauna and lights that have been embedded in walls, causing them to glow yellow, blue and red.

Hotel Aurora Borealis (☎ 78 45 78 00; www.hotel aurora.no; Saga; s/d Nkr730/875; P) Cosy, art-filled and secluded, about 6km east of Bossekop by the E6, staff will help plan snowmobile trips (with the option of spending a night in a Sami tent), dogsled excursions or fishing trips, and the kitchen will even prepare what you catch.

Vica Hotell (☎ 78 43 47 11; www.vica.no; Fogdebakken 6; s/d from Nkr1000/1200; P 🖳) In a timber-built former farmhouse in Bossekop, Vica offers free sauna, and outdoor hot tub overlooking snowcapped peaks. The rooms come with knotty pine, and public spaces are filled with stuffed creatures.

Alta HI Hostel (☎ 78 43 44 09; alta.hostel@ vandrerhjem.no; Midtbakkveien 52; dm/s/d Nkr150/255/300; ⊙ late Jun-late Aug; P) Find Alta's hostel in a wooded residential neighbourhood. It's a 10 minutes' walk from the Sentrum bus stop.

Eating

Alpha-Omega (☎ 78 44 54 00; Markedsgata 14-16; lunch Nkr64-104, dinner Nkr89-200) A popular choice on the pedestrian drag in Sentrum, Omega serves excellent tapas and salads. One of these involves a filling piece of salmon baked under a layer of chevre and accompanied with fried onion, mushrooms and greens (Nkr89). For a casual bar, head across the hall to Alpha.

Henrik Restaurant (☎ 78 43 47 11; Fogdebakken 6; mains Nkr170-250) The Vica Hotell's kitchen serves huge portions from an Arctic menu that includes reindeer, elk, cod and a warm soup of cloudberries served with homemade ice cream.

Self-caterers should head to one of Sentrum's three supermarkets.

Getting There & Away

AIR

The **airport** (☎ 78 44 95 55) is 4km east of Sentrum; follow the E6. Norwegian Air, SAS Braathens and Widerøe service the Alta airport. Many domestic flights arrive each day, often routed through Tromsø. Direct flights to Oslo are plentiful.

Taxis (☎ 78 43 53 53) to town cost about Nkr90. The return trip is often inflated with a pick-up charge.

BUS

Nor-Way Bussekspress runs between Tromsø and Alta (Nkr449, 6½ hours, one daily). **FFR** buses run to/from Kautokeino (Nkr193, 2½ hours, four times weekly), Hammerfest (Nkr205, 2¾ hours, three daily) and Nordkapp (Nkr292, 5¾ hours, one to two daily).

HAMMERFEST

pop 9200

Most visitors to Hammerfest arrive by the *Hurtigruten* and have an hour or two to poke around. Unless you have unusual interests, that's about as much time you'll need. The fishing town's oddest experience can be found at the Royal & Ancient Polar Bear Society.

NORWAY

Purporting itself to be Norway's northernmost town (other settlements lie further north, but they are too small to qualify as towns), Hammerfest has suffered as much as that Walrus in the Polar Bear Society: a gale decimated it in 1856, a fire totalled it in 1890 and the Nazi's burned it again in 1944, after which it was rebuilt in the 'Finnmark Ugly' style. Nowadays a newly opened pipe line (the world's longest) sucks in gas from the Barents Sea to a small island in the bay. This will certainly impact the town's economy and depressing landscape.

The **tourist office** (☎ 78 41 31 00; www.hammerfest-turist.no; Havnegata 3; ☑ 10am-5pm mid-Jun–mid-Aug) operates out of the Polar Bear Society.

Sights & Activities

The **Gjenreisningsmuseet** (Reconstruction Museum; ☎ 78 42 26 30; Kirkegata 21; adult/child Nkr40/15; ☑ 9am-5pm mid-Jun–Aug, 11am-2pm otherwise) details the rebuilding of Hammerfest after the German bombings of 1944. As you might guess, such things are neither easy nor pleasurable 600km above the Artic Circle. Nearby, in the town hall, the bizarre **Royal & Ancient Polar Bear Society** (☎ 78 41 31 00; Rådhuset; adult/child Nkr20/free; ☑ 9am-5pm late Jun-early Aug, shorter hrs mid-Aug–mid-Jun) dedicates itself to preserving northern culture and features exhibits on Arctic hunting and local history. Any visitor can become a member (Nkr185) and waive the admission fee for life, get a certificate and a champagne toast. The bone they use to 'knight' you – something a male walrus misses dearly – is a real crowd-pleaser.

Into Nobel Peace Prizes? Stop by **Galleri Syvsterna** (☎ 78 41 01 60; Fjordaveien 27; ☑ Mon-Fri), where local artist Eva Arnesen displays a copy of the one she designed for the 1997 honour awarded to Jody William's campaign against landmines. Her paintings evoke the light of the north.

For lovely views of the town, coast and mountains, climb the 86m-high **Salen Hill**; the 10-minute walking trail begins behind the small park directly up from the town hall. The town keeps some binoculars (free) up top to better enjoy the panorama.

Sleeping & Eating

AF Camping Storvannet (☎ 78 41 10 10; Storvannsveien; cabins Nkr320-340; ☑ late May-late Sep; P) Beside a lake and overlooking an apartment complex, this small site fills up early because it's the only decent option around. About 2km east of the town centre, it offers cooking facilities.

Quality Hotel Hammerfest (☎ 78 42 96 00; www .hammerfesthotel.no; Strandgata 2; s/d from Nkr1100/1300; P ☐) Some rooms overlook the fjord and many resemble cabins on ocean liners. The cosy 'library bar' has been nicely dressed with rich wood panelling and leather couches. Also enjoy the sauna and solarium.

Hotel Skytterhuset (☎ 78 41 15 11; www.skytterhuset .no; Skytterveien 24; s/d Nkr695/895; P ☐) The arms of this hotel, up a hill with views over town, originally served as barracks for Finnish fishwives. Despite the utilitarian history, the modern rooms are cheery and sometimes reindeer chew up the garden. Free sauna.

Odd's Mat & Vinhus (☎ 78 41 37 66; Strandgata 24; mains Nkr190-340; ☑ Mon-Sat) For fantastically prepared Artic game and fish, the rustic digs of the region's favourite restaurant are accented with rope coils and wooden booths.

Sandberg bakery (☎ 78 41 18 08; Strandgata 19; sandwiches Nkr36; ☑ 9am-4pm Mon-Fri, 10am-3pm Sat) serves coffee and pastries tastier than you'll find in other bakeries.

There's a **Coop supermarket** east of the town hall.

Getting There & Away

The *Hurtigruten* coastal steamer stops daily.

FFR (☎ 78 40 70 00; www.ffr.no) operates buses to/from Hammerfest. Go to/from Alta (Nkr205, 2¾ hours, one to three daily) or to/from Kirkenes (Nkr740, 10 to 12 hours, four weekly), via Karasjok (Nkr283, 4½ hours, one to three Sunday to Friday).

NORDKAPP

Nordkapp (North Cape), a coastal plateau at N71°10′21″ latitude, claims to be the northernmost point in Europe and is the main destination for most visitors to the far north (Knivskjelodden is actually the northernmost point – see p373 for details). The sun never drops below the horizon from mid-May to the end of July. To many visitors, Nordkapp, with its steep cliffs and stark scenery, emanates a certain spiritual aura – indeed, long before other Europeans took an interest in the area, Nordkapp was considered a power centre by the Sami people.

It was Richard Chancellor, the English explorer who drifted this way in 1553 on a search for the Northeast Passage, who named North Cape. Following a much-publicised visit by King Oscar II in 1873, Nordkapp became a pilgrimage spot of sorts for tourists.

Nowadays, there's a rip-off Nkr190 entrance fee and a touristy complex with exhibits, eateries, souvenir shops and a post office. The 180-degree theatre runs a rather repetitious short film, but if you want to really appreciate Nordkapp just take a walk out along the cliffs. If the weather is fair you can perch yourself on the edge of the continent and watch the polar mist roll in.

The continent's real northernmost point, **Knivskjelodden** (latitude N71°11′08″) is, thankfully, inaccessible to vehicles and devoid of tourist fluff. To reach it, head to the marked car park about 7km south of Nordkapp, lace up your boots and hike 9km (18km return) to a lovely promontory. It takes about five hours.

Depending on snow conditions, the toll road to Nordkapp is usually open from May to mid-October; the **Road User Information Centre** (☎ 177) gives opening dates.

The closest town of any size is **Honningsvåg**, 35km from Nordkapp with a population of 3500. Here you'll find a **tourist office** (☎ 78 47 70 30; www.northcape.no; Fiskeriveien 4B; ☼ 8.30am-8pm Mon-Fri, noon-8am Sat & Sun mid-Jun–mid-Aug, 8.30am-4pm Mon-Fri otherwise), the hotel **Honningsvåg Brygge** (☎ 78 47 64 64; www.hvg .brygge.no; Vågen 1a; s/d Nkr950/1200), which occupies a nicely converted fishing warehouse, a few restaurants and, unbelievably, a **microbrewery**. Contact the tourist office for area camping options.

Getting There & Away

The *Hurtigruten* stops in Honningsvåg. Northbound ships stop for 3½ hours, long enough for the ship to offer its passengers a Nordkapp tour (Nkr580).

Nor-way Bussekspress runs buses from Alta to/from Honningsvåg (Nkr457, 3¾ hours, one or two daily). FFR runs buses to/from Hammerfest (Nkr351, three hours, one or two daily).

Getting Around

From mid-June to mid-August, local buses run from Honningsvåg (adult/child

Nkr90/45, 45 minutes) to Nordkapp departing at 10.45am and 8.30pm, and setting off from the Cape at 1.15pm and 12.15am (observe the midnight sun at midnight). Avoid so-called 'tours', which may charge considerably more for similar services. And get ready to cry: even bus riders get hit with that Nkr190 toll.

You can also rent a bike from the tourist office (Nkr250/600 per day/three days). Bring a windbreaker for the bleak, exposed ride and, of course, Nkr190 for the pending tear-duct workout.

KIRKENES
pop 4500

Okay you made it – the end of the line for the *Hurtigruten* and the eastern most point in the country. Now what? Kirkenes itself isn't much – after all, it was Norway's most bombed place during WWII, with over 1000 air-raid alarms. A lot of people use it as a jumping-off point into Russia, though be advised that you'd best have your visa in order prior to arrival (see p374). To find the small town centre from the *Hurtigruten* quay, head west (make a right) from the dock and follow the signs. It's about 1.5km. Or just take the waiting shuttle bus.

Information

The **tourist office** (☎ 78 99 25 44; www.kirkenes info.no; Presteveien 1; ☼ 8.30am-6pm Mon-Fri, 8.30am-5.30pm Sat & Sun Jun–mid-Aug, 8.30am-4pm Mon-Fri mid-Aug–May) is exceptionally helpful.

The **library** (☎ 78 99 32 51; Town Sq; ☼ 11am-5pm Mon, Tue & Thu, 11am-3pm Wed & Fri, 11am-2pm Sat) has free internet access.

Sights & Activities

The **Sør-Varanger Grenselandmuseet** (☎ 78 99 48 80; Førstevannslia; adult/student/child Nkr30/15/free; ☼ 10am-6pm mid-Jun–Aug, 10am-3.30pm Sep–mid-Jun) presents the history of the converging cultures in this border region, with displays on WWII history, local geography, religion and Sami crafts.

Check out the particularly worthwhile **Savio Museum**, which features the work of the Sami artist Andreas Savio, whose poignant woodcuts and paintings evoke the tension between indigenous life and nature. It's temporarily inside the Sør-Varanger Grenselandmuseet and shares the same hours.

NORWAY

NORWAY

VISITING RUSSIA

Crossing the border requires dealing with beaurocracy at its worst. Independent travellers first need to obtain an official invitation to visit Russia. You then need to visit a Russian consulate with the invite and your passport at least 14 days in advance. If you plan on crossing in Kirkenes, consider using a service that handles invitations and visas and offers package tours to Russian destinations near Kirkenes. Even from outside Norway, you can send your passport in advance (give them at least 16 days) by certified mail for processing and return.

Government-set fees are based on country of citizenship. For example, a one-day visa cost from Nkr100 for Japanese to Nkr550 for Americans. It escalates according to length of stay. **Grenseland Travel Agency** (☎ 78 99 50 80; www. pasvikturist.no) then charges a processing fee of Nkr500, or Nkr1300 for same day service. It offers weekend trips to Murmansk (Nkr1600), where price includes transport and a hotel room, but not the visa.

For something like help, try Kirkenes's **Russian consulate** (☎ 78 99 37 37; Kirkegata).

The super tourist office will help arrange a ton of activities including snowmobile trips along the border (Nkr950) and night-time dogsled rides (Nkr1075). Our peculiar readers will freak our over underwater trips arranged by **Artic Dive Adventure Resort** (☎ 95 15 07 55; www.artic-dive.no; Jarfjordbotn; ◷ May–Oct). For Nkr750, you get equipment and two dives where you'll try to catch the most big-ass giant crabs imaginable, plus a night's lodging in a seaside cabin. The place is 25km south of Kirkenes.

Sleeping & Eating

Direktørboligen (☎ 78 99 18 09; www.dirboligen.no; Kristen Nygårdsgate 37; s/d from Nkr700/1000) With just six rooms, book ahead to ensure your place in the former residence for the directors of Kirkenes' mining industry. Sophisticated and slick, rooms cantilever over a garden where reindeer sometimes sneak in breakfast. Free sauna and cosy library. It's a 10-minute walk from the centre.

Kirkenes Snowhotel (☎ 78 97 05 40; www.radius -kirkenes.co; s/d Nkr1200/1650; ◷ Dec) Sleep on reindeer pelts inside a small hotel made entirely of ice a kilometre outside town. You'll especially enjoy the sauna.

Rica Arctic Hotel (☎ 78 99 29 29; www.rica.no; Kongensgate 1-3; s/d Mon–Fri Sep–Jun Nkr1195/1300, s/d Sat & Sun Nkr750/900, s/d mid-Jun–Aug Nkr760/960; Ⓟ) This modern block contains decent rooms with generic character (salmon-coloured walls, cheap furniture) and wins points with its heated pool.

Vin og Vilt (☎ 78 99 38 11; Kirkegata 5; mains Nkr165-340) Seasonal Arctic game and fish (reindeer, grouse, crabs) comes in a room that feels like a hunting lodge.

Getting There & Around
AIR

SAS, Braathens, Norwegian Air and Widerøe fly into Kirkenes' airport, a 20-minute (15km) drive from town; flying in/out of Ivolo, Finland, some 250km away, may be cheaper. The airport bus costs Nkr64 and a taxi is about Nkr275.

BOAT
Kirkenes is the terminus of the *Hurtigruten* coastal steamer.

BUS
By land, FFR buses serve Karasjok (Nkr460, 5½ hours, four weekly), Hammerfest (Nkr750, 10¼ hours, four weekly) and Alta (Nkr780, 12¾ hours, three weekly).

CAR
Avis (☎ 78 97 37 05) and **Hertz** (☎ 78 99 39 73) have offices in Hesseng, but they'll deliver cars to you.

KARASJOK
pop 2900

Karasjok is the most accessible Sami town and the site of the Sami Parliament. It has Finnmark's oldest **church** (1807), the only building left standing in Karasjok after WWII. Because of the Nazis' destruction, the centre of today's Karasjok consists of a couple of strip malls connected by the E6 and Rv92.

The **tourist office** (☎ 78 46 88 10; www.koas .no; Porsangerveien; ◷ 9am-7pm Jun–mid-Aug, 9am-4pm Mon-Fri mid-Aug–May), in the Sami Park at the junction of the E6 and route Rv92, can book winter dogsled rides, and arranges salmon fishing, riverboat trips and other summer activities.

The **Sami Park** (☎ 78 46 88 10; Porsangerveien; adult/child Nkr95/60; ⏰ 9am-7pm mid-Jun–late Aug, shorter hrs Sep–mid-Jun) theme park and reindeer farm feels a bit flashy and plastic, though its presentations do a good job presenting the Sami as the normal fellow human beings they are and not exotic anachronisms. The more staid **Sami museum** (☎ 78 46 99 50; Museumsgata 17; adult/child Nkr25/5; ⏰ 9am-6pm Mon-Sat, 10am-6pm Sun early Jun–mid-Aug, shorter hrs mid-Aug–May), just 500m northeast of the town centre, covers Sami history and culture in more academic depth. Visit the **Sami Parliament** (Sámediggi; ☎ 78 47 40 00; Kautokeinoveien 50; admission free), inside a new building with a stunning birch, pine and oak interior. Thirty-minute tours take in a tent-shaped assembly hall and the parliamentary library with its tiny starlike lights.

At **Engholm's Husky** (☎ 78 46 71 66; www.engholm.no; Rv92; cabins Nkr150-300 plus Nkr100 for each guest; Ⓟ), dog-lovers will enjoy the rustic, pelt-furnished cabins in a forested haven near where Sven keeps his sled dogs and pups. Most cabins have a kitchen but no bathroom. There's a free sauna, trails through the woods and a salmon river. It's 6km west of town on the Rv92. Eat an eggy breakfast (Nkr70) and big dinners (Nkr200).

Sven's place also serves as Karasjok's HI-affiliated **Hostel** (dm/s/d Nkr175/300/450).

Gammen (☎ 78 46 74 00; Porsangerveien 1; mains Nkr190-250), at Sami Park, offers traditional dishes in a 'Sami-inspired' dining room. The place consists of four squat, turf-covered huts with a central hearth. There's a grocery store in the town centre.

FFR buses connect Karasjok with Alta (Nkr350, 4¾ hours, six weekly) Hammerfest (Nkr283, 4½ hours, one to three Sundy to Friday) and Kirkenes (Nkr460, 5½ hours, four weekly). Finnish Lapin Linjat buses run to Rovaniemi (Nkr350, eight hours, one daily) via Ivalo (Nkr160, 2½ hours, one daily).

KAUTOKEINO
pop 3000

In Kautokeino, around 85% of the townspeople have Sami as their first language; the town is unlike anywhere else in Nor-

way and it's not uncommon to see locals dressed in traditional garb. Around one-third of the population earns its living working in some aspect of reindeer herding.

Because Kautokeino is a small one-road town, there isn't much to do. Sleepy as it is, some find it preferable to livelier Karasjok, whose developed tourist industry gives it a plastic feel.

The best time to visit is during the **Easter Festival** (www.saami-easterfestival.org), when thousands of costumed Sami participate in championship reindeer racing, theatre and cultural events, and the little town bursts at the seams.

The **tourist office** (☎ 78 48 65 00; ⏰ 10am-4pm Mon-Fri May-Aug) is in a kiosk by the main road through town.

The **Kautokeino Hamlet & Museum** (☎ 78 48 71 00; Boavonjarga 23; adult/child Nkr20/free; ⏰ 9am-7pm Mon-Sat, noon-7pm Sun mid-Jun–mid-Aug, 9am-3pm Mon-Fri mid-Aug–mid-Jun) presents a traditional Sami settlement, complete with an early home, temporary dwellings, a trapping exhibit and several agricultural and pastoral outbuildings.

Inside a cool bit of sloping architecture modelled after drifting snow, **Juhls' Silver Gallery** (☎ 78 48 71 00; www.juhls.no; Galaniitoluodda; admission free; ⏰ 8.30am-9pm mid-Jun–mid-Aug, 9am-6pm otherwise) creates traditional and modern silver jewellery and offers the best of Scandinavian design. The place started 50 years ago, long before anyone dreamed of tourists visiting the town.

Kautokeino Camping (☎ 78 48 54 00; Suomaluodda 16; camp sites Nkr130, cabins Nkr650-800, with shared bathroom Nkr300, motel rooms Nkr500), south of the river, provides a Sami *lavvo* with an open fire. It's operated by an extremely friendly family whose café will often cook up some *bidos*, the traditional reindeer stew served at celebrations.

Alfred's Kro (☎ 78 48 61 18; Hannoluohkka 4; mains Nkr60-135; ⏰ 11am-6pm Mon-Fri, noon-6pm Sat & Sun) offers diners traditional Sami dishes involving reindeer, as well as burgers and Mack draught. **Mara's Pub** occasionally books small bands. With rough wooden floors, booths and benches, the intimate pub is the town's main nightlife spot. Find it beneath Alfred's.

Buses connect Kautokeino with Alta (Nkr193, 2½ hours, four weekly).

SVALBARD

The world's most readily accessible piece of the polar north, and one of the most spectacular places imaginable, Svalbard is *the* destination for an unforgettable holiday. This wondrous archipelago is an assault on the senses: vast icebergs and floes choke the seas, and icefields and glaciers frost the lonely heights. Svalbard also hosts a surprising variety of flora and fauna, including seals, walrus, Arctic foxes and polar bears.

Plan your trip well in advance. When you arrive, you'll almost certainly want to participate in some kind of organised trek or tour, and many need to be booked early. Since travel outside Longyearbyen is both difficult and dangerous, you miss out on a lot if you don't sign up for one.

History

Although known to the Icelanders as early as 1194, the official discovery of Svalbard (then uninhabited) is credited to Dutch voyager Willem Barents in 1596. During the 17th century Dutch, English, French, Norwegian and Danish whalers slaughtered the whale population. They were followed in the 18th century by Russians hunting walrus and seals. The 19th century saw the arrival of Norwegians, who hunted polar bears and Arctic foxes. In 1906, commercial coal mining began and is continued today by the Russians (at Barentsburg) and the Norwegians (at Longyearbyen and Sveagruva). The 1920 Svalbard Treaty granted Norwegian sovereignty over the islands.

Orientation & Information

Longyearbyen, the largest settlement on Svalbard, has an airport with flights to/from Tromsø and Oslo. You'll find a post office, bank (with an ATM) and library. Barentsburg, the Russian settlement, is about 40km west, while Ny Ålesund, a Norwegian research station with an airstrip, is about 100km northwest. Except in settlements, there are no roads.

The **tourist office** (☎ 79 02 55 50; www.svalbard .net; ☻ 8am-6pm Mon-Fri, 9am-4pm Sat, noon-4pm Sun mid-Jun–Aug, shorter hr otherwise) is in central Longyearbyen. For more on travelling in Svalbard, see Andreas Umbreit's *Spitsber-gen: Svalbard, Franz Josef, Jan Mayen*, published by Bradt Publications.

Tours

View dozens of exciting options on the tourist office website. Accommodation, transport and meals are usually included in longer tours, but day tours are also available. Some popular tour operators:

Basecamp Spitsbergen (☎ 79 02 46 00; www.base campexplorer.com; Postboks 316, N-9171 Longyearbyen) Offers unique lodgings including rooms on an ice-locked ship, three-day dog mushing trips from the ship (Nkr12,000), and week-long wilderness expeditions (Nkr24,900).

Spitsbergen Tours (☎ 79 02 10 68; www.terrapolaris .com; Postboks 6, N-9171 Longyearbyen) The oldest locally based operation, owned by Andreas Umbreit. Spend a week in the polar night (Nkr10,500)́, in wintry April (Nkr14,000) or in the summertime high season, when prices range from Nkr7800 if you camp to Nkr20,000 in single room accommodation. Prices include dogsledding expeditions, snowmobile tours, and boat cruises.

Spitsbergen Travel (☎ 79 02 61 00; www.spitsber gentravel.no; Postboks 548, N-9171 Longyearbyen) The giant of the travel scene offers six-day cruises on a former Hurtigruten coastal steamer, putting in at Barentsburg and Ny Ålesund (Nkr7450 to Nkr12,000).

Svalbard Wildlife Service (☎ 79 02 56 60; www .wildlife.no; Postboks 164, N-9171 Longyearbyen) Offers varied tours including a seven-day ski/snow mobile expedition that summits mountains, crosses glaciers and visits an abandoned Russian mining town (Nkr18,500).

Getting There & Away

SAS Braathens fly regularly from Tromsø to Longyearbyen. In summer they offer direct flights to/from Oslo.

LONGYEARBYEN

pop 1500

The frontierlike community of Longyearbyen, strewn with abandoned coal-mining detritus, enjoys a superb backdrop including two glacier tongues, Longyearbreen and Lars Hjertabreen.

The **Svalbard Museum** (☎ 79 02 13 84; Skjæringa; admission Nkr30; ☻ 11am-7pm Mon-Fri, noon-4pm Sat, 1-7pm Sun Jul & Aug, shorter hrs Sep-Jun), occupies a former pigsty, one of the oldest buildings in town. Exhibits cover mining, 17th-century whaling and the history of the archipelago.

Tours

Short day trips are commonly offered, including fossil hunting (Nkr300); mine tours (Nkr590); boat trips to Barentsburg and Pyramidien (Nkr990); dogsledding (Nkr800); glacier hiking (from Nkr490); ice-caving (from Nkr520); kayaking (from Nkr550); horse riding (Nkr420); and snow-mobiling (from Nkr1000). Contact the tourist office.

Sleeping & Eating

Sleeping prices are greatly reduced off-season.

Longyearbyen Camping (☎ 79 02 10 68; www .longyearbyen-camping.com; camp sites per person Nkr80; ☑ late Jun-early Sep) Next to the airport and an hour's walk from town, pitch a tent on some marshy tundra and enjoy the empty expanse around you. There's a building with a kitchen. Tent and sleeping-bag rentals are available.

Basecamp Spitsbergen (☎ 79 02 46 00; www .basecampexplorer.com; s/d Nkr1290/1580) This 15-room hotel provides top accommodation in the centre of town. It shoots for the look of a seal-hunter's cabin (bunks, rough-hewn boards). Each cosy room has a shower, and a common space has a glass roof for polar night viewing.

Gjestehuset 102 (☎ 79 02 57 16; www.wildlife.no; dm/s/d Nkr290/475/790) Sleep in a former miners' lodge, a utilitarian structure sarcastically dubbed 'Millionaire's Residence'. Shared bathroom, kitchen and lounge. It lies at the southern end of town, a 20-minute walk.

Mary-Ann's Polar Rigg (☎ 79 02 37 02; riggen@longyearbyen.net; s/d Nkr595/850) A simple place with a kitchenette and hot tub. Most of the 43 rooms have shared facilities. Linen is Nkr100 extra and breakfast is Nkr95.

Huset (☎ 79 02 25 00; light dishes Nkr135; mains Nkr225-350) For top-notch arctic and French-style meals, hoof it to Huset. It's worth paying the extra quid for their 'Touch of the Arctic' menu, where you'll get to shove Artic char, scallops, reindeer, grouse and dessert down your oesophagus. Lots of wine.

In the central shopping mall, you'll find the Svalbardbutikken supermarket and **Fruene Kaffe og Vinbar** (☎ 79 02 36 50; mains Nkr70-120), a welcoming café serving coffee, pizza and pasta before metamorphosing into a wine bar at 5pm.

Getting Around

Longyearbyen Taxi (☎ 79 02 13 75) charges Nkr120 for a cab trip between the town

and the airport. The airport bus (Nkr40) connects with flights.

AROUND SVALBARD

Independent travel around Svalbard is heavily regulated in order to protect both the virgin landscape and travellers. Travel to the very few settlements is usually done as part of a tour package. One of these settlements is Barentsburg (population 900), a Soviet-era relic. Simultaneously depressing and fascinating, this tiny Russian town still mines and exports coal. A statue of Lenin still stares over the bleak built landscape and the impressive natural landscape that surrounds it.

Tourist cruises might also bring you to **Ny Ålesund**, which, at latitude N79°, is a wild place with scientists and downright hostile Arctic terns. Remnants of past glories include a **stranded locomotive**, previously used for transporting coal, and an **airship pylon**, used by Amundsen and Nobile on their successful crossing of the North Pole in 1926.

NORWAY DIRECTORY

ACCOMMODATION

During summer, it's wise to reserve all accommodation, particularly at hostels. The cheapest lodging costs less than Nkr300, midrange accommodation is less than Nkr650, while top-end luxury can reach Nkr2000.

Camping & Cabins

Camping grounds are abundant. Tent space costs from Nkr80 at the most basic sites to Nkr150 in Oslo. Many camping grounds rent simple cabins with basic cooking facilities from about Nkr300. Bedding is rarely provided, bring your own sleeping bag. Visit www.camping.no to see extensive listings.

Norway has an *allemannsretten* (Right of Common Access) dating back 1000 years. This allows you to pitch a tent anywhere in the wilderness for two nights, as long as you camp at least 150m from the nearest house or cottage and leave no trace of your stay. From 15 April to 15 September, lighting a fire in the proximity of woodlands is strictly forbidden.

NORWAY

The Norwegian Mountain Touring Association, **Den Norske Turistforening** (DNT; Map pp304-5; ☎ 22 82 28 22; www.turistforeningen.no; Storgata 3, N-0101 Oslo), maintains an extensive network of mountain huts, a day's hike apart, in much of Norway's mountain country, ranging from unstaffed huts with just a few beds to large, staffed lodges with more than a hundred beds and generally superb service.

For unstaffed huts, you must pick up keys (Nkr100 to Nkr150 deposit) in advance. There are two types of unstaffed huts: bare bones and chalets stocked with blankets, pillows, firewood, and freeze-dried food for sale (pay by honour system). In these, members/nonmembers pay Nkr145/240 for a bed.

In staffed huts, simply show up – no one is ever turned away, though you might sleep on the floor. Nightly fees for members/nonmembers in a room with one to three beds are Nkr185/240; rooms with four to six beds Nkr145/210; dormitories Nkr95/160; and overflow on the floor Nkr70/135. Breakfast (members/nonmembers Nkr75/95), sandwiches (Nkr10/15), dinner (Nkr175/210) and snacks are served, though members might do better by ordering a full-board option with their room. At all huts, staffed or not, children pay less.

Basic membership for one calendar year costs Nkr425/250/50 for adult/student/child.

Many DNT huts are closed between mid-October and mid-February.

Hostels

Norway has 72 *vandrerhjem* (hostels) affiliated with Hostelling International (HI) and several independent operators. Most have two to six beds per room. Most also have single, double and family rooms at higher prices. Guests must bring their own sleeping sheet and pillowcase, although most hostels hire linen for Nkr50. Nearly all hostels have kitchens where guests can cook their own meals.

The Norwegian Hostelling Association is **Norske Vandrerhjem** (Map pp304-5; ☎ 23 13 93 00; fax 23 13 93 50; www.vandrerhjem.no; Torggata 1, N-0181 Oslo). You can book hostels through their website. Prices listed in this book are those for HI members; nonmembers pay an additional Nkr25 per night.

Hotels

Although standard prices are high, most hotels give substantial discounts on Saturday and Sunday and in summer season (mid-June through until the end of August), which are slow periods for business travel. One important consideration in this land of sky-high food prices is that hotels usually include an all-you-can-eat buffet breakfast, while most pensions do not. Many nationwide chains offer hotel passes which might entitle you to discounts:

Choice Club (www.choicehotels.no) Offers a free pass and is available at Comfort, Quality and Clarion hotels; entitles you to free nights and discounts.

Fjord Pass (www.fjordpass.no) Costs Nkr100 and is valid year-round at 170 Norwegian hotels. Provides significant discounts on nightly rates.

Rica Feriepass (www.rica.no) Offers a free pass from mid-June to mid-August; entitles you to a fifth night free.

Skanplus (www.skanplus.no) Costs Nkr100 and entitles you to weekend and summer discounts in Thon and Norlandia hotels. Every sixth night is free.

Private Rooms & Pensions

Private rooms, usually bookable through tourist offices, average Nkr300/400 for singles/doubles and breakfast isn't normally included. Along highways, you may see *'Rom'* signs, indicating informal accommodation for around Nkr250 (without breakfast).

ACTIVITIES
Hiking

Norway has some of northern Europe's best hiking (over 20,000km of trails), ranging from easy routes in the forests around the cities to long treks through mountains. Due to deep winter snows, hiking in many areas is seasonal; in the highlands, it's often limited to the period of late June to September. The most popular wilderness hiking areas are Jotunheimen, Rondane and Hardangervidda, but no matter where you are a lovely hike will be, too.

There are organised glacier hikes in Briksdal and on Nigardsbreen; Åndalsnes and Lofoten are major centres for mountain climbing. For more information, contact **Den Norske Turistforening** (DNT; p377).

Skiing

'Ski' is a Norwegian word and Norway makes a credible claim to having invented the sport. It's no exaggeration to say that it's the national winter pastime and you're seldom far from a ski run. Norway has thousands of kilometres of maintained cross-country (nordic) ski trails and scores of resorts with excellent downhill runs. The Holmenkollen area near Oslo, Geilo (on the Oslo–Bergen railway line), Narvik and Lillehammer are just a few of the more popular spots. If you're a summer skier, head for the glaciers near Finse, Stryn or Jotunheimen. DNT is a good source of information about skiing.

Rafting

Norway's wild and scenic rivers are ideal for rafting, with trips ranging anywhere from short Class II doodles to Class III and IV adventures and up to rollicking Class V punishment. **Norges Padleforbund** (☎ 21 02 98 35; www.padling.no; Service boks 1, Ullevål stadion, N-0840 Oslo) provides a comprehensive list of rafting operators.

Fishing

Norway's salmon runs are legendary – in June and July, you can't beat the rivers of Finnmark. No licence is required for saltwater fishing. Regulations vary between rivers, but generally you can't keep fish under 30cm in length. In fresh water, a national licence (available from post offices for Nkr200) is mandatory and often a local licence (available from tourist offices, sports shops, hotels and camping grounds for Nkr100 to Nkr300 per day) will also be required. The lengthy book *Angling in Norway*, available in tourist offices for Nkr175, details fees, regulations and choice spots.

BUSINESS HOURS

Opening hours for shops are 10am to 5pm weekdays, 10am to 2pm on Saturday; post offices 9am to 5pm weekdays, 10am to 2pm on Saturdays; banks 8.15am to 3pm weekdays; supermarkets 9am to 9pm weekdays, 9am to 6pm on Saturday; and restaurants 8am to 11am, noon to 3pm and 6pm to 11pm. Opening hours for tourist offices are listed under each city throughout the Norway chapter.

Be aware that many museums have short hours (11am to 3pm is quite common), which can make things tight for sightsee-

ing. On Sunday most stores – including bakeries and supermarkets, and some restaurants – are closed.

EMBASSIES & CONSULATES
Norwegian Embassies

Find up-to-date listings at www.norway.info.

Australia & New Zealand (☎ 02-6273 3444; emb.canberra@mfa.no; 17 Hunter St, Yarralumla, ACT 2600)

Canada (☎ 613-238 6571; www.emb-norway.ca; Royal Bank Centre, Suite 532, 90 Sparks St, Ottawa, Ontario K1P 5B4)

Denmark (☎ 33 14 01 24; emb.copenhagen@mfa.no; Amaliegade 39, DK-1256 Copenhagen K)

Finland (☎ 09-686 0180; emb.helsinki@mfa.no; Rehbindervägen 17, FIN-00150 Helsinki)

France (☎ 01 53 67 04 00; emb.paris@mfa.no; 28 rue Bayard, F-75008 Paris)

Germany (☎ 030-505050; emb.berlin@mfa.no; Rauchstrasse 1, D-10787 Berlin)

Ireland (☎ 01-662 1800; emb.dublin@mfa.no; 34 Molesworth St, Dublin 2)

Netherlands (☎ 070-311 7611; emb.hague@mfa.no; Lange Vijverberg 11, NL-2513 AC The Hague)

Sweden (☎ 08-665 6340; emb.stockholm@mfa.no; Skarpögatan 4, SE-11593 Stockholm)

UK (☎ 020-7591 5500; emb.london@mfa.no; 25 Belgrave Square, London SW1X 8QD)

USA (☎ 212-333 6000; www.norway.org; 2720 34th St NW, Washington DC 20008)

Embassies & Consulates in Norway

Australia Refer to the UK embassy, which handles Australian consular affairs in the absence of an embassy.

Canada (Map pp304-5; ☎ 22 99 53 00; www.dfait-maeci.gc.ca; Wergelandsveien 7, 0244 Oslo)

Denmark (Map p310; ☎ 22 54 08 00; www.amboslo.um.dk; Olav Kyrres gate 7, 0244 Oslo)

Finland (Map p310; ☎ 22 12 49 00; www.finland.no Thomas Heftyes gate 1, 0244 Oslo)

France (Map p310; ☎ 23 28 46 00; www.ambafrance-no.org; Drammensveien 69, 0244 Oslo)

Germany (Map pp304-5; ☎ 23 27 54 00; www.oslo.diplo.de; Oscars gate 45, 0244 Oslo)

Ireland (Map pp304-5; ☎ 22 12 20 00; osloembassy@dfa.ie; Haakon VII's gate 1, 0212 Oslo)

Netherlands (Map pp304-5; ☎ 22 19 71 90; Oscars gate 29, 0244 Oslo)

New Zealand (☎ 66 77 53 30; fax 66 77 53 31; Billingstadsletta 19B, Postboks 113, 1376 Billingstad)

Russia (Map p310; ☎ 22 55 32 78; www.norway.mid.ru; Drammensveien 74, 0244 Oslo)

Sweden (Map p310; ☎ 24 11 42 00; www.swedenabroad.com; Nobels gate 16, 0244 Oslo)

UK (Map p310; ☎ 23 13 27 00; www.britishembassy.gov
.uk; Thomas Heftyes gate 8, 0244 Oslo)
USA (Map pp304-5; ☎ 22 44 85 50; Henrik Isbens gate
48, 0255 Oslo)

FESTIVALS & EVENTS

Norway is chock-a-block with festivals,
which take place in every city, town and
village. Most of these are held during the
summer, and a few of the most popular
are outlined within this chapter's listing.
Among the offerings are festivals dealing
with rock music, wooden boats, film and
cultural spectacles.

Most notable is Norway's Constitution
Day (17 May) when people take to the streets
in traditional dress and attend celebratory
events throughout the country, with the biggest bash in Oslo, where marching bands
and thousands of school children parade
down Karl Johans gate to be greeted by the
royal family. Midsummer's Eve, celebrated
by bonfires on the beach, is generally observed on 23 June, St Hans Day. The Sami
(Lapps) hold their most colourful celebrations at Easter in Karasjok and Kautokeino,
with reindeer races, *joik* (traditional chant-
ing) concerts and other festivities.

For information about all of the country's
largest festivals, check out www.norway
festivals.com.

HOLIDAYS
Public Holidays

New Year's Day 1 January
Maundy Thursday Thursday before Easter
Good Friday March/April
Easter Monday March/April
Labour Day 1 May
Constitution Day 17 May
Ascension Day 40 days after Easter
Whit Monday Eighth Monday after Easter
Christmas Day 25 December
Boxing Day 26 December

Norway practically shuts down during
Christmas and Easter weeks, when you'll
be lucky to find an open bar or grocery
store even in Oslo. See Festival & Events,
above, for information on Constitution Day
and Easter.

School Holidays

Norwegian children enjoy the following
school holidays: eight weeks from mid-June

to mid-August; two weeks over Christmas
and New Year; one week at the end of September or early October; one week at the
end of February; and one week at Easter.

MONEY
ATMs

The machines are ubiquitous and available in almost every town mentioned in
this book.

Currency

The Norwegian krone is most often writ-
ten NOK in international money markets,
Nkr in northern Europe and kr within
Norway.

One Norwegian krone equals 100 øre.
Coins come in denominations of 50 øre
and one, five, 10 and 20 kroner, and bills
in denominations of 50, 100, 200, 500 and
1000 kroner.

Exchanging Money

Some post offices and all banks will exchange major foreign currencies and accept
all travellers cheques, which command a
better exchange rate than cash (by about
2%). Banks open Monday to Friday and
close around 3pm, while post offices open
later (see Post below). You can also change
money in kiosks and hotels, but the rate
won't be as good.

POST

See p379 for opening hours. Postal rates
are high and continue to soar: cards and
letters weighing up to 20g cost Nkr6.50
within Norway, Nkr8.50 to other Nordic
countries, Nkr9.50 to elsewhere in Europe
and Nkr10.5 to the rest of the world. Mail
can be received poste restante at almost all
post offices in Norway.

TELEPHONE & FAX

All domestic numbers consist of eight
digits.

Most pay phones accept Nkr1, Nkr5,
Nkr10 and Nkr20 coins, and will return
unused coins but won't give change so only
insert the minimum amount (Nkr5 for all
calls) to ensure a connection. Directory assistance (☎ 180) costs Nkr9 per minute.
A peak-rate national call costs Nkr7 then
Nkr0.60 per minute. It is more expensive to
call a mobile phone than a landline. Using

a hotel room's phone carries prohibitive charges.

Mobile Phones

GSM mobile telephone networks cover over 80% of Norway's populated areas. There are two main service providers: **Telenor Mobil** (☎ 22 78 50 00) and **NetCom** (☎ 23 88 80 00).

To use your home-county mobile in Norway, contact your carrier about the cost of roaming charges. If you want to use your mobile, but with a Norwegian SIM card, check with your network before leaving home to make sure you won't be blocked from using other carriers. If your phone does accept foreign SIM cards, these can be purchased from any 7-Eleven and from some Narvesen Kiosks. As the connection instructions are entirely in Norwegian, you're better off purchasing the card from a Telehuset outlet, where they'll help you connect on the spot. Cards start at Nkr200, which includes Nkr100 worth of calls.

Mobile phone rental is not possible, though you can buy one with some minutes at Telehuset shops and other phone stores (from Nkr500).

Phone Codes

Norway has no telephone area codes. To make international calls from Norway, dial ☎ 00 then the country code and phone number. The country code for calling Norway from abroad is ☎ 47.

Phonecards

Telekort (phonecards) are sold in Nkr40, Nkr90, Nkr140 and Nkr210 denominations and work out cheaper than using coins. Cards can be purchased at post offices and convenience stores. Credit cards can also be used with many cardphones. For making international calls, your cheapest bet is to forsake Telenor and buy a card issued by a private company. Usually costing Nkr100, these aren't inserted into phones – on the back are local access numbers and a PIN which you dial after following prompts. The cards can be used from a payphone (Nkr5) or private or hotel line (free). Some of the better cards for Western Europe, Australia and North America are EuroCity and Unity. Such cards are hard to find. Look for them in Oslo and Bergen in 'ethnic' grocery stores.

TIME

Time in Norway is one hour ahead of GMT/UTC, the same as Sweden, Denmark and most of Western Europe.

When telling time, note that in Norwegian the use of 'half' means *half before* rather than half past.

Norway observes daylight-saving time, with clocks set ahead one hour on the last Sunday in March and back an hour on the last Sunday in October. Timetables and business hours are posted according to the 24-hour clock.

TOURIST INFORMATION

There are tourist offices in nearly every town in Norway, usually near the train station, dock or town centre. In smaller towns they may be open only during peak summer months, while in cities they're open year-round.

The **Norges Turistråd** (Norwegian Tourist Board; ☎ 24 14 46 00; www.visitnorway.com; PO Box 722 Sentrum, N-0105 Oslo) will send you information on request. You can download brochures from their website.

Useful Norwegian Tourist Board offices abroad:

UK (☎ 020 7389 8800; www.norway.org.uk; 5th fl, Charles House, 5 Lower Regent St, London SW1Y 4LR)
USA & Canada (☎ 212-885-9700; www.norway.org; Suite 1810, 655 Third Ave, New York, NY 10017)

VISAS

Citizens of the USA, Canada, the UK, Ireland, Australia and New Zealand need a valid passport to visit Norway, but do not need a visa for stays of less than three months. The same is true for EU and European Economic Area (EEA – essentially EU and Scandinavia) countries, most of Latin America and most Commonwealth countries.

TRANSPORT IN NORWAY

GETTING THERE & AWAY

Air

Oslo's **Gardermoen airport** (airport code OSL; ☎ 81 55 02 50; www.osl.no) is Norway's principal connection to major European and North American cities. Other international airports, which have limited direct flight connections to international destinations:

Flesland airport, Bergen (code BGO; ☎ 55 99 80 00; www.avinor.no)

Haugesun airport, Karmøy (code HAU; ☎ 33 42 70 02; www.avinor.no)

Kjevik airport, Kristiansand (code KRS; ☎ 38 06 56 00; www.torp.no)

Sola airport, Stavanger (code SVG; ☎ 51 65 80 00; www.avinor.no)

Torp airport, Sandefjord (code TRF; ☎ 33 42 70 02; www.torp.no)

Tromsø airport, Tromsø (code TOS; ☎ 77 64 84 00; www.avinor.no)

Værnes airport, Trondheim (code TRD; ☎ 74 84 30 00; www.avinor.no)

Airlines flying to and from Norway:

Aeroflot (airline code SU; ☎ 23 50 20 01; www.aeroflot.no)

Air France (airline code AF; ☎ 23 50 20 01; www.airfrance.no)

British Airways (airline code BA; ☎ 81 53 31 42; www.britishairways.com)

British Midland Airways (airline code BD; www.flybmi.com)

Finnair (airline code AY; ☎ 81 00 11 00; www.finnair.com)

Icelandair (airline code FI; ☎ 22 03 40 50; www.icelandair.com)

KLM Royal Dutch Airlines (code KL; ☎ 22 64 37 52; www.klm.com)

Lufthansa (airline code LH; ☎ 81 52 04 00; www.lufthansa.com)

Nordic Airlink (airline code LF; ☎ 24 14 87 58; www.flynordic.com)

Norwegian Air (airline code DY; ☎ 81 52 18 15; www.norwegian.no)

Ryanair (airline code XY; ☎ 82 00 07 20; www.ryanair.com)

SAS Braathens (airline code BU; ☎ 91 50 54 00; www.sasbraathens.no)

Spanair (airline code JK; ☎ 81 52 40 00; www.spanair.com)

Sterling (airline code NB; ☎ 81 55 88 10; www.sterling.dk)

Land

BUS

Eurolines (www.eurolines.com) runs buses to Oslo from hundreds of European cities, including Stockholm, Göteborg (Gothenburg) and Copenhagen.

Denmark

The **Säfflebussen** (☎ 771-15 15 15; www.safflebussen.se) from Copenhagen to Oslo (Dkr250,

eight hours, five daily) runs via Malmö in Sweden. **Swebus Express** (☎ 0200 218 218; swebusexpress.se) also runs to/from Copenhagen (Skr450, 8½ hours, four daily).

Finland

The E8 highway runs from Tornio, in Finland, to Tromsø and secondary highways connect Finland with the northern Sami towns of Kautokeino and Karasjok. **Eskelisen Lapin Linjat** (☎ 016-342 2160 in Finland; www.eskelisen-lapinlinjat.com) runs buses from Rovaniemi (Finland) to Karasjok (€59, 6½ hours, year-round), Nordkapp (€96, twelve hours, via Karasjok; summer only) and Tromsø (€68, eight hours, summer only).

Sweden

Nor-Way Bussekspress (☎ 81 54 44 44; www.nor-way.no) runs from Oslo and Göteborg (Skr200, 4¼ hours, five daily) and Malmö (Skr340, 7½ hours, twice daily). **Swebus Express** (☎ 0200 218 218; www.swebusxpress.se.no) runs from Stockholm and Oslo (SKr435, 7½ hours, three daily). **Nordlandsbuss** (☎ 75 55 22 10; www.nbuss.no) runs from Skellefteå and Bodø (Nkr400, nine hours, once daily except Saturday).

CAR & MOTORCYCLE

The main highways between Sweden and Norway are the E6 from Göteborg to Oslo, the E18 from Stockholm to Oslo, the E14 from Sundsvall to Trondheim and the E12 from Umeå to Mo i Rana. Many secondary roads also cross the border.

TRAIN

Sveriges Järnväg (SJ; ☎ 0771-757575; www.sj.se) runs trains from Stockholm (1st/2nd class Skr778/642, six hours, two daily), Göteborg (1st/2nd class Skr698/392, 7½ hours, one daily) and Malmö (1st-/2nd-class Skr945/794, 8½ hours) to Oslo. Journeys from Östersund to Trondheim via Storlien require a change of trains at the border. If you buy tickets seven days in advance, you can usually get a better rate. **Connex** (☎ 771 26 00 00 in Sweden; www.connex.se) trains run between Narvik and Stockholm (Skr649; 20 hours, three daily) via Kiruna (Skr210, three hours, three daily).

Sea

DENMARK

DFDS Seaways (☎ 22 41 90 90 in Norway, ☎ 33 42 33 42 in Denmark; www.dfdsseaways.com) runs daily overnight ferries between Copenhagen and Oslo, with fares ranging from €80 to €400 depending on what time of year you travel and what kind of cabin you select.

Color Line (☎ 81 00 08 11 in Norway, ☎ 99 56 19 77 in Denmark; www.colorline.com) runs ferries between Hirtshals and Kristiansand (4½ hours, two to five daily); Larvik (6¼ hours, two to five daily); Stavanger (12 hours, three weekly); and Bergen (21 hours, three weekly). **Oslo ferries** run to/from Frederikshavn (9½ hours, one daily) and to/from Kiel (5½ hours, five weekly). Fares are the same for all routes – depending on the day of the week and the time of year, they range from €24 to €65 for passengers and from €59 to €264 for cars. Overnight routes require that you book a cabin for an additional charge.

Fjord Line (☎ 81 53 35 00 in Norway, ☎ 97 96 14 01 in Denmark; www.fjordline.com) sails from Hanstholm to Bergen (Nkr540, 16 hours, four weekly), stopping in Egersund en route. Cabins, cars and folding deck chairs cost extra.

Stena Line (☎ 23 17 91 00 in Norway, ☎ 02010 in Denmark; www.stenaline.com) operates daily ferries between Frederikshavn and Oslo (€47, 12 hours, six weekly). Cars cost extra.

ICELAND & FAROE ISLANDS

See **Smyril Line**, p502.

SWEDEN

DFDS Seaways (☎ 22 41 90 90 in Norway, ☎ 0526-62000 in Sweden; www.dfdsseaways.com) runs overnight ferries from Helsingborg to Oslo (passenger/car €65/120, 14 hours, one daily) and from Göteborg to Kristiansand (passenger/car €22/55, seven hours, three days weekly).

Color Line (☎ 81 00 08 11 in Norway, ☎ 0526-62000 in Sweden; www.colorline.com) runs between Strömstad (Sweden) and Sandefjord (€24, 2½ hours, two to six daily).

UK

Fjord Line (☎ 55 54 88 00 in Norway, ☎ 01595-690845 in UK; www.fjordline.com) sails from Newcastle to Bergen (€60 to €120, two to three weekly, from 21 hours). Some run to Stavanger. For cars and up to four passengers, packages begin at €240.

GETTING AROUND

Public transport in Norway is usually quite efficient, with trains, buses and ferries often timed to link effectively. The handy *NSB*

Togruter, available free at train stations, has rail schedules and information on connecting buses. Boat and bus departures vary with the season and the day, so pick up the latest *ruteplan* (timetables) from regional tourist offices. The Norwegian Tourist Board also publishes a free, annual national transport timetable.

When planning your route, particularly if heading into more remote areas, keep in mind that Saturday and Sunday bus services are often greatly reduced, and some are nonexistent on Saturday. Nearly every boat, bus and train offers a substantial discount (usually 50%) to students. Always ask when buying a ticket.

Air

Norway has nearly 50 airports, with scheduled commercial flights from Ny Ålesund (Svalbard) in the north to Kristiansand in the south. Air travel is worth considering, even by budget travellers, due to the great distances involved in overland travel.

Norway's main domestic airlines are:

Coast Air (☎ 81 54 44 42; www.coastair.no)
Norwegian Air (☎ 81 52 18 15; www.norwegian.no)
SAS Braathens (☎ 91 50 54 00; www.sasbraathens.no)
Widerøe (☎ 81 00 12 00; www.wideroe.no)

Bicycle

Given its great distances, hilly terrain and narrow roads. Norway is not ideally suited for extensive touring by bicycle. A big headache for long distance cyclists will be tunnels, and there are thousands of them.

A number of regions, however, are good for cycling. The *Sykkelguide* series of booklets, with maps and English text, is available from larger tourist offices for Nkr120 each – routes include Lofoten, Rallarvegen and the North Sea Cycle Route (from the Swedish border at Svinesund to Bergen). Bike rentals are easy to find; for example, from some tourist offices, hostels and camping grounds (usually around Nkr150 to Nkr200 per day). For further information, contact **Syklistenes Landsforening** (☎ 22 47 30 30; post@slf .no) or visit www.bike-norway.com.

Rural buses, express ferries and nonexpress trains carry bikes for an additional fee (around Nkr100), but express trains don't allow them at all and international trains treat them as excess baggage (Nkr250). NorWay Bussekspress charges half the adult

NORWAY

fare to transport a bicycle. If you plan to take your bike on long-distance trains, you must make a reservation well in advance.

Boat

An extensive network of ferries and express boats links Norway's offshore islands, coastal towns and fjord districts. See specific destinations for details.

CANAL

Southern Norway's Telemark region has an extensive network of canals, rivers and lakes. There are regular ferry services or you can travel using your own boat. See p325.

HURTIGRUTEN COASTAL STEAMER

For more than a century Norway's legendary **Hurtigruten** (☎ 81 03 00 00; www.hurtigruten .no) has been the lifeline for villages scattered along the western and northern coasts. The modern steamers still carry supplies and mail, though the passenger desks now resemble those found on cruise liners.

One ship heads north from Bergen every night, pulling into 35 ports on its 11-day journey to Kirkenes and back. With agreeable weather, expect spectacular scenery.

Many (but not all) ships accommodate deck-class travellers. Those that do have baggage rooms, shower rooms, 24-hour cafeterias and coin laundry, though you'll struggle to sleep among the 24-hour activity in the public lounges. Most passengers prefer cabins (Nkr300 to Nkr1000 per night).

Sample fares for trips from Bergen are Nkr1194 to Trondheim, Nkr2049 to Svolvær, Nkr2449 to Tromsø and Nkr3798 to Kirkenes. At many ports of call, you can leave the ship for several hours. Cars are carried for an extra fee. Students, children, seniors over 67 and accompanying spouses all receive 50% discount.

There are some great low-season deals: from September to April, passengers get 40% discount off basic fares for sailings on any day except Tuesday, with return journeys at a further 50% reduction on the return portion of the ticket.

Bus

Nor-Way Bussekspress (☎ 82 02 13 00; www.nor-way .no), the main carrier, has routes connecting every main city. There's a host of local

buses companies; most of them operate within a single county.

Most local and some long-distance bus schedules are drastically reduced on Saturday. Sunday and low-season schedules may also be reduced – and nonexistent in some cases. For a complete listing of timetables (and prices for major stops) pick up a copy of the free *Rutehefte* from larger bus stations. Tourist offices and bus stations have smaller timetables for routes passing through town.

BUS PASSES

Nor-Way Bussekspress offers nontransferable passes valid for 21 consecutive days (Nkr2300). With it, you can travel on the Oslo airport bus for free.

In Nordland, several Togbuss (train-bus) routes offer half-price fares to Eurail, InterRail and ScanRail passholders. It runs between Fauske and Bodø, Narvik, Tromsø, Svolvær and Harstad. InterRail and ScanRail passes get half-price bus tickets to/from the western fjords, between Oslo and Åndalsnes, Ålesund, Molde and Måløy, as well as various other routes in southern Norway.

COSTS

Tickets are sold on the buses or in advance at the station. Fares are based on the distance travelled, averaging Nkr150 for the first 100km. Many bus companies quote prices excluding any ferry costs. Most bus companies offer child, student, senior, group and family discounts of 25% to 50% – always ask.

RESERVATIONS

Advance reservations are almost never required in Norway, and Nor-Way Bussekspress even has a 'Seat Guarantee – No Reservation' policy. Unless there's more than 12 in your party – then you might be stuffed.

Car & Motorcycle

If you plan to drive through mountainous areas in winter or spring, check first to make sure the passes are open, as some are closed until May or June. The **Road User Information Centre** (☎ 175) can tell you about the latest road conditions. Main highways, such as the E16 from Oslo to Bergen and the E6 from Oslo to Kirkenes, are kept open year-round. Cars in snow-covered areas should have studded tyres or carry chains.

If you plan to travel along Norway's west coast, keep in mind that it isn't only mountainous, but deeply cut by fjords. While it's a spectacular route, travelling along the coast requires numerous ferry crossings, which can be time-consuming and costly. For a full list of ferry schedules, fares and reservation phone numbers, consider investing in a copy of *Rutebok for Norge,* the comprehensive transport guide available in larger bookshops. Some counties publish free booklets detailing bus and ferry timetables – tourist offices usually stock copies.

AUTOMOBILE ASSOCIATIONS

For motoring information, contact the national automobile club, **Norges Automobil-Forbund** (NAF; ☎ 22 34 14 00; www.naf.no; Storgata 2, N-0105 Oslo). For 24-hour breakdown assistance call the NAF on ☎ 81 00 05 05. Ask your home automobile association for a Letter of Introduction (Lettre de Recommendation), which entitles you to services offered by affiliated organisations in Norway.

DRIVING LICENCE

Short-term visitors may hire a car with only their home country's driving licence.

FUEL

Leaded and unleaded petrol is available at most petrol stations. Regular unleaded averages Nkr9 per litre in the south, and can be well over Nkr10 per litre in the north. In towns, there are some 24-hour petrol stations, but most close by 10pm or midnight. In rural areas, many stations close in the early evening and don't open on weekends. Many don't take foreign credit cards.

HIRE

Major car-rental companies, such as Hertz, Avis, Rent-a-Wreck and Europcar, have offices at airports and in city centres. Car rentals are expensive: the walk-in rate for a compact car with free 200km is about Nkr1000 a day, including VAT and insurance. You're likely to get much better deals by booking with an international agency before you arrive in Norway.

One relatively good deal is the weekend rate offered by major car-rental companies,

which allows you to pick up a car after noon on Friday and keep it until 10am on Monday for about Nkr1400 – make sure it includes unlimited kilometres.

To rent a car you must be at least 21 years old with at least one year's driving experience and hold a valid driver's licence.

INSURANCE

Third-party car insurance (unlimited cover for personal injury and Nkr1 million for property damage) is compulsory and, if you're bringing a vehicle from abroad, you'll have fewer headaches with an insurance company Green card, which outlines the coverage granted by your home policy. Ensure your vehicle is insured for ferry crossings.

ROAD RULES

In Norway, traffic keeps to the right. All vehicles, including motorcycles, must have their headlights on at all times. The use of seat belts is mandatory and children under the age of four must have their own seat or safety restraint. You're required to carry a red warning triangle in your car for use in the event of breakdown. Motorcycle helmets are mandatory; motorcycles cannot park on the pavement and must follow the same parking regulations as cars.

On motorways and other main roads, the maximum speed is generally 80km/h (a few roads have segments allowing 90km/h or 100km/h), while speed limits on through roads in built-up areas are generally 50km/h. Mobile police units lurk at roadsides. In particular, watch for signs designating *Automatisk Trafikkontrol,* which means that there's a speed camera ahead. Big, ugly and grey, these boxes will nab you for even 5km/h over the limit. Fines range from Nkr1000 to well over Nkr10,000.

Tolls are common on highways, bridges and tunnels. Make sure you have plenty of cash (and loose change) to pay for tickets; if you pass an automatic toll station without paying, call in at the next petrol station or tourist office and ask for assistance on how to pay in retrospect and avoid a whopping fine. Rental-car agencies will automatically add fines (including speed-camera tickets) to your credit-card bill.

Drink-driving laws are strict in Norway: the maximum permissible blood alcohol concentration is 0.02% and violators are subject to severe fines and/or imprisonment.

The speed limit for caravans (and cars pulling trailers) is usually 10km/h less than for cars. There are a few mountain roads where caravans are forbidden and numerous other roads that are only advisable for experienced drivers, as backing up may be necessary to allow approaching traffic to pass. For a map outlining these roads, and caravan rules, contact **Vegdirektoratet** (☎ 22 07 35 00; Gaustadalleen 25, N-0371 Oslo).

Hitching

Hitching is legal but uncommon.

Train

Norway has an excellent, though somewhat limited, national rail system. **NSB** (Norges Statsbaner, Norwegian State Railways; ☎ 81 50 08 88; www .nsb.no) operates most lines.

Second-class travel is comfortable. Komfort-class travel, which costs Nkr75 more, isn't worth the extra tariff, unless you really dig free coffee.

Discounted Minipris tickets are sometimes available. Extremely cheap, you could travel from Oslo to Bergen for Nkr199 or to Stavanger for Nkr299. These tickets may only be purchased online, at least a day in advance. Buy early – these sell out.

The Norway Rail Pass (US$218/258/298 for three/four/five days' travel within one month) allows unlimited train travel for three to eight days within Norway. Purchase before or after you arrive in Norway. The Flåm line isn't covered (there's a 30% discount). There's a 50% discount on Bergen–Stavanger ferries.

Regular fares from Oslo are Nkr716 to Bergen, Nkr692 to Åndalsnes, Nkr833 to Stavanger and Nkr797 to Trondheim. On many long-distance trains reservations (Nkr35) are mandatory.

Second-class sleepers provide high standard compartments. These cost Nkr750 and have two beds.

Most train stations have luggage lockers for Nkr15 to Nkr40 and many also have a luggage-storage room.

Sweden

From berserker Vikings to the Nobel Peace Prize in just a few short centuries – Sweden really has earned its reputation as a model for progressive society. It's earned most of its other reputations, too: the population is overwhelmingly gorgeous, the standard of living is among the highest in Europe, the interior design is clean-lined and functional, and people really do eat meatballs on a regular basis.

But it's a little more complicated than that. There are plenty of surprises for the traveller, from the diversity and grit of cities like Göteborg (Gothenburg) and Malmö, to the rugged beauty of the national parks in Norrland, to the huge number of pre-Viking relics just lying around in the countryside, to Östersund's mysterious lake monster.

FAST FACTS

Area 449,964 sq km

Capital Stockholm

Currency €1 = Skr9.19; US$1 = Skr7.13; UK£1 = Skr13.34; A$1 = Skr5.32; CA$1 = Skr6.51; NZ$1 = Skr4.49; ¥100 = Skr6.34

Famous for Vikings, Volvos, Ericsson, ABBA, meatballs, tennis players, IKEA

Official Languages Swedish, plus the officially protected minority languages Romani, Finnish, Yiddish, Meänkieli (Tornedal) and Sami (actually three languages)

Phrases hej (hello), hej då (goodbye), ja (yes), nej (no), tack (thanks)

Population 9.02 million

Telephone Codes country code ☎ 46; regional codes: Stockholm ☎ 08, Göteborg ☎ 031; international access code ☎ 00

Visa Not needed for most visitors for stays of up to three months (see p473)

HIGHLIGHTS

- Tour the urban waterways, explore top-notch museums and wander the cobblestone backstreets of Gamla Stan in **Stockholm** (p398)
- Enjoy a frosty beverage – and a frozen bed – at the ultra-cool **Ice Hotel** (p464), near Kiruna
- Let your hair down with holidaying Swedes on **Gotland** (p451), the perfect cycling and camping destination
- Celebrate Midsummer in the heartland villages surrounding the lovely **Lake Siljan** (p422)
- Admire the picturesque farmsteads and cosmopolitan cities that dot the green fields of **Skåne** (p424)

ITINERARIES

- **One week** Spend three days in Stockholm and Uppsala, and two days in and around Göteborg before continuing south to the dynamic cities of Malmö and Lund. Alternatively, explore the Stockholm region more thoroughly, including day trips to Drottningholm and Birka and a couple of days in the archipelago, before heading to Uppsala via Sigtuna.
- **Two weeks** As above, but include a trip northwards to the Lake Siljan region, then further up to Härnösand to explore the quaint fishing villages and dramatic cliffs of Höga Kusten. Alternatively, camp and cycle on Gotland for a few days.

CLIMATE & WHEN TO GO

Sweden is at its best during summer and autumn (late May to September). Summers are short and intense, and daylight hours are long. This is particularly true anywhere north of Stockholm, where the change in seasons is dramatic. Many youth hostels, camping grounds and attractions open only in high summer (late June to early August). This period is also when most Swedes are holidaying, so finding accommodation in areas favoured by the locals (eg Dalarna, Gotland and Öland) may prove difficult. Travel in winter takes some planning, but there are good opportunities for activities such as skiing or dogsled and snowmobile safaris. The big cities are in full swing all year, but smaller towns hibernate when the temperature drops (the notable exceptions being popular ski resorts). The south,

particularly Skåne, is known for its mild climate, as is Gotland.

For climate charts, see the Regional Directory (p466).

HISTORY

Written records in Sweden survive only from the late Middle Ages, but the number of ancient fortifications, assembly places, votive sites and graves is impressive.

The Viking Age was getting under way by the 9th century and vast repositories of Roman, Byzantine and Arab coins attest to the wealth and power Swedish Vikings accumulated over the next century. Vikings travelled mostly to the east, making their mark in Russia, as well as trading with (and pillaging) Byzantine territories.

Internal squabbles whiled away the bulk of the Middle Ages until Denmark intervened and, together with Norway, joined Sweden in the Union of Kalmar in 1397 (signed at Kalmar's grand castle; see p446). Danish monarchs held the Swedish throne for a while.

A century of Swedish nationalist grumblings erupted in rebellion under the young nobleman Gustav Vasa. After being crowned Gustav I in 1523, he introduced the Reformation and a powerful, centralised nation-state. A period of expansion began and resulted in Sweden's control over much of Finland and the Baltic countries.

King Karl XII's adventures in the early 18th century cost Sweden its Baltic territories and the crown much prestige. The next 50 years were marked by greater parliamentary power, but Gustav III led a coup that interrupted this development. Unrestricted royal power was undone by aristocratic revolt in 1809 and Finland was lost to Russia. That same year produced a constitution that divided legislative powers between king and Riksdag (Parliament). Napoleon's marshal Bernadotte was chosen to fill a gap in the succession and, as Karl Johan, became regent. Thus began the rise of liberalism and Sweden's policy of neutrality. In 1814 the military enforcement of the union with Norway was Sweden's last involvement with war.

Sweden declared itself neutral at the outbreak of WWI, but a British economic blockade caused food shortages and civil unrest. Consensus was no longer possible,

SWEDEN

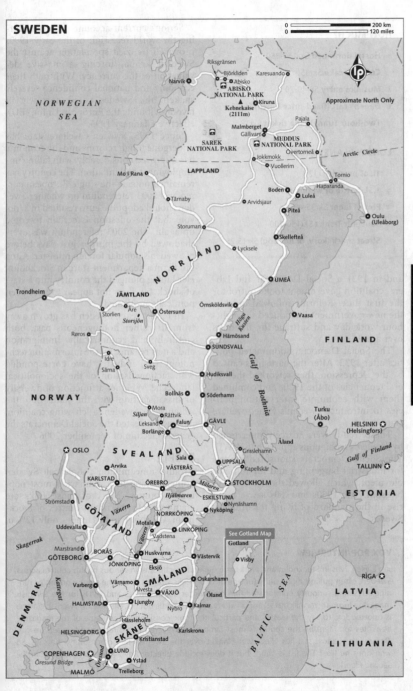

HOW MUCH?

■ **Hostel dorm bed** Skr150-350

■ **Coffee & cake** Skr35

■ **Museum entry** Skr40-70

■ **Dagens rätt (fixed-price lunch)** Skr65

■ **Two-hour Tunnelbana ticket** Skr18

LONELY PLANET INDEX

■ **1L of petrol** Skr12

■ **1.5L bottle of water** Skr15

■ **Pint of lager** Skr35-48

■ **Souvenir T-shirt** Skr150-200

■ **Street snack (korv, or hot dog)** Skr15-25

and in 1921 a Social Democrat and Liberal coalition government took control for the first time. Reforms followed quickly; the new government introduced the eight-hour work day and suffrage for all adults over age 23.

The Social Democrats dominated politics after 1932. After the hardships caused by the Depression, they reworked the liberal tendencies of the 1920s and combined them with economic intervention policies to introduce Sweden's famed welfare state.

These trends were scarcely interrupted by Sweden's ambiguous approach to WWII. The Social Democrats sponsored models for industrial bargaining and for full employment, which allowed the economy to blossom. The 1950s and '60s saw a rapid rise in the standard of living for ordinary Swedes.

Serious current-account problems during the world recession of the early 1990s provoked frenzied speculation against the Swedish krona, forcing a massive devaluation of the currency. With both their economy and national confidence severely shaken, the Swedes voted narrowly in favour of joining the European Union (EU), effective 1 January 1995.

Since 1995, Sweden's welfare state has undergone tough reforms and the economy has improved considerably, with falling unemployment and inflation. The country has remained outside the single European currency; a 2003 referendum on whether Sweden should adopt the euro resulted in a 'no' vote, but the question is certain to come up again. The 2003 referendum was overshadowed by the murder just days before of Sweden's popular foreign minister, Anna Lindh, in a department store in Stockholm. Her killing plunged the country into a state of shock, but does not appear to have been politically motivated.

In recent years, Sweden has grown away from its rather homogeneous past, both culturally and economically. Immigration and a new reliance on the information technology (IT) industry have corresponded with factionalisation of the sociopolitical landscape. Whether a function of diversity or dissatisfaction with the status quo, the Alliance for Sweden, a left-wing coalition, narrowly defeated the Social Democrats the general election of September 2006

PEOPLE

Around nine million people call Sweden home, making it Scandinavia's most populous country. Most of those folks are crammed into the urban centres of Stockholm, Göteborg and Malmö – only 12% of

VOX POP/INTERVIEW

Jan Elvsén lives in Stockholm and works as a general practitioner in various health centres across Sweden, often pulling night shifts for one or two weeks straight. When he's not working or running, Elvsén, a seriously opinionated film buff, writes about movies and DVDs for the Swedish magazine **Ingmar** (www.ingmar.se) and a variety of other media outlets. His take on Swedish cinema is unorthodox, to say the least – and particularly ironic considering the name of the magazine he writes for. Mention the country's most famous and revered film director and Elvsén frowns. 'Bergman's shadow still lies like a wet blanket over the Swedish film community,' he says. So who does he like? The list is short, but it does include director Roy Andersson *(Songs from the Second Floor)*.

the population lives in Norrland, which takes up two-thirds of the country's geographical area. There are around 17,000 Sami in Sweden, largely concentrated in the north. More than 20% of Sweden's population are foreign-born or have at least one non-Swedish parent. Most immigrants have come from other European countries. Of non-European immigrants, the largest group consists of Middle Easterners, mostly from Iraq, Turkey and Iran. There are an estimated 40,000 Roma people in Sweden. Other well-represented countries include Poland, Chile and Somalia.

RELIGION

Some 87% of the Swedish population is Lutheran, although only about 10% regularly attend church services.

ARTS

Sweden today is probably better known for design and pop music than fine arts. Thanks to IKEA, words like 'spartan' and 'clean-lined' are mandatory in any discussion of Swedish aesthetics. The self-assembled bookshelves and affordable bold-print curtains didn't come out of nowhere, of course – artists such as Josef Frank, Carl Malmsten

and Bruno Mathsson are among the early progenitors of Swedish interior design. Also influential is the trifecta of glassworks, Kosta Boda and Orrefors, the products of which can be spotted somewhere in most Swedish households.

By some counts the third-largest exporter of music in the world (after the US and UK), Sweden hosts about 120 music festivals every year, from medieval and baroque to folk, jazz and rock. No discussion of Swedish pop is complete without mention of ABBA; more recent exports include Sahara Hotnights, Hellacopters, The (International) Noise Conspiracy, The Hives, Refused, Timbuktu, In Flames and The Soundtrack of Our Lives. Domestic sensations like Amy Diamond and Elena Paparizou dominate Swedish radio.

For an interesting and thorough summary of Swedish music history, along with factsheets on other topics such as design and architecture, check out www.sweden.se.

In the literary world, stormy dramatist August Strindberg (Miss Julie) and Nobel laureate Selma Lagerlöf are probably the biggest names. But the best-loved Swedish writer is Astrid Lindgren, creator of the resourceful, pigtailed Pippi Longstocking.

SWEDEN

THANK YOU FOR THE MUSIC

If asked to name Sweden's most famous exports, ABBA would top many people's list.

During the 1970s ABBA, consisting of two couples, became one of the most successful popular music acts of the decade. The individual members were all show-business veterans in their native Sweden, and their wholesome image, perfectly constructed pop songs and strong melodies took the world by storm.

ABBA, an acronym of their names (Agnetha, Björn, Benny and Anni-Frid – more commonly known as Frida), won the Eurovision Song Contest in 1974 with 'Waterloo', which went on to top the charts in several countries. ABBA went from success to success: they toured the world, made a film and recorded hit after hit.

ABBA's last year together was 1982. By then the fairy tale was over and both couples had divorced but, in the words of one of their songs, 'the music still goes on'. Recent years have seen something of an ABBA revival, with successful cover versions of ABBA anthems, ABBA tribute bands, the group's elevation to the status of gay icon, and popular movies featuring ABBA music and impersonations. In 1992 the compilation album *ABBA Gold* was released and became the group's biggest seller (to date it has sold a staggering 25 million copies worldwide). A stage show based on their music, *Mamma Mia!* (written by Benny and Björn), still sells out regularly in Stockholm. The show's soundtrack, with all the group's hits performed in Swedish, went gold in 2005. *ABBA: The Movie* won a Swedish Grammy award in 2006. Despite this revival success, no reunion is on the cards (the media reports that band members knocked back an offer of US$1 billion to regroup).

There are hundreds of ABBA websites on the internet; a good place to start is the endearing www.abbasite.com, which includes a 'Today in ABBA' section.

Vilhelm Moberg is a renowned documentarian of Swedish working-class life *(The Immigrants* and *The Emigrants)*. Contemporary authors to look for include Henning Mankell, author of a crime series featuring morose detective Kurt Wallander *(Dogs of Riga)*; and spy novelist Jan Guillou *(Evil)*.

The beret-crowned Ingmar Bergman, though supposedly retired from filmmaking, remains one of the most important film directors of all time. New Swedish directors making names for themselves include Lukas Moodysson, Roy Andersson and Josef Fares.

Carl Larsson, Anders Zorn and Bruno Liljefors are among the best-known Swedish painters – visitors to nearly any art museum in the country will see examples of their work.

In the scientific realm, the two biggest Swedish influences are Carl von Linné, the 18th-century botanist who pioneered modern plant taxonomy under Latin classifications; and Alfred Nobel, the inventor of dynamite and other explosives, whose will founded the Nobel Institute and the international prizes in 1901.

ENVIRONMENT
The Land
Sweden covers an area of 449,964 sq km, and its maximum north–south extent is 1574km. This size allows for a little diversity: flat and open Skåne is similar to Denmark, but further north the landscape is hillier and heavily forested. The rocky west coast is most notable for its fjords and skerries, although they scarcely compare with the barrage of rocky islets that shield Stockholm. The islands of Öland and Gotland consist of flat limestone and sandstone.

There are approximately 100,000 lakes in Sweden. Lake Mälaren is the heart of the country, although Vänern is by far the biggest of the south and central lakes. In Norrland there's an almost uniform expanse of forest cut by rivers and narrow lakes. The trees thin out in Jämtland and Lappland and the mountains assert themselves, providing a natural frontier with Norway in the northwest.

Geographical divisions in Sweden are complex. The two kingdoms which united in the 11th century form the southern half of the country: Götaland in the south and Svealand in lower central Sweden. Anything north of Svealand is called Norrland. The 25 historical regions (based on common dialect), called *landskap,* remain as denominators for people's identity and a basis for regional tourist promotion. Regional administration is based on 21 *län* (counties), which are responsible for things such as *länstrafik* (regional public transport) and *länsmuseum* (county museums).

Wildlife
Large numbers of elk (moose) and deer live in the forests, and in Norrland there are sizable herds of reindeer (no longer truly wild, as each animal belongs to a local Sami community). Other animals peculiar to the north are the arctic fox and lemmings, small, hardy rodents famous (mistakenly so) for leaping off cliffs en masse. European brown bears, Scandinavia's only surviving wild bear population, number about 1000 and live mainly in the remote northern areas; visitors can see them at the Grönklitt Björnpark (p423) outside Orsa in the Lake Siljan area.

National Parks
Nature-loving Swedes led Europe in setting up national parks in the early 20th century; there are now 28 throughout the country (the biggest and best are in Lappland). Rules vary locally, but the constant is that all people have access to open areas (see p469). In 1996, the 9400-sq-km Laponia area was placed on the World Heritage List – it includes the national parks Stora Sjöfallet, Sarek, Padjelanta and Muddus. See the website of **Naturvårdsverket** (www.environ.se), the Swedish environmental protection agency, for coverage of national parks.

Environmental Issues
Ecological consciousness in Sweden is very high and reflected in concern for native animals, clean water and renewable resources. Swedes are fervent believers in sorting and recycling household waste – you'll be expected to do the same in some hotels, hostels and camping grounds. Most plastic bottles and cans can be recycled – supermarket disposal machines give Skr0.50 to Skr1 per item.

FOOD & DRINK

There's a lot more to Swedish food than meatballs and a crazed Muppet chef.

Staples & Specialities

Classic Swedish *husmanskost* (home-style Swedish food) is based on simply prepared combinations of meat, potatoes and fish. Many traditional restaurants specialise in *husmanskost*, but other restaurants often include a *husmanskost* section (or even just a dish) on the menu. Typical *husmanskost* dishes are *pytt i panna*, a meat-and-potato hash served with pickled beets and a fried egg; fried or pickled herring, called *sill* or *strömming* depending on which coast it comes from; *lax* (salmon) in several forms, from grilled to smoked to *gravad* (salt-and-sugar cured); game such as elk and reindeer; and of course the requisite *köttbullar* (Swedish meatballs), normally served with mashed potatoes and lingonberry sauce.

Where to Eat & Drink

Swedes don't typically go out for *frukost* (breakfast); most start their day with coffee and a pastry or cereal with yogurt. Most hotels and some hostels provide extensive breakfast buffets laden with cereals and yogurt plus bread, fruit, cold cuts, cheese and the like.

Most cafés and restaurants serve a daily lunch special called *dagens rätt* or *dagens lunch* at a fixed price (typically Skr65 to Skr75) between 11.30am and 2pm. The price usually includes main course, salad, bread, cold drink and coffee, and it's one of the most economical ways to sample up-market Swedish cooking.

To counter the mid-afternoon slump, Swedes enjoy *fika*, an almost mandatory coffee break. *Konditori* are old-fashioned bakery-cafés where you can get a pastry or a *smörgås* (sandwich) from Skr25, but there are also many stylish, modern cafés where you can enjoy people-watching over pricier Italian coffees, gourmet salads, bagels and muffins.

For a quick, inexpensive snack, it's hard to beat a *grillad korv med bröd* – a grilled hot dog on a bun (Skr15 to Skr25), available from countless stands and carts, with the price depending on proximity to major tourist attractions. Variations include *kokt* (boiled) *korv* and several types of *rulle*, which are hot dogs wrapped in pitta-style bread with *mos* (mashed potatoes), onions, shrimp salad and lots of other unlikely things.

Dinner options in medium and large cities are extensive. Pure vegetarian restaurants do exist but they're not common; however, there will usually be at least one vegetarian main-course option on the menu. Due to the strict licensing laws, most pubs and bars in Sweden serve a good range of meals too. Some upscale restaurants have a less formal bar section with a cheaper menu.

Nonsmokers have been breathing easier since 2005, when Sweden implemented a ban on smoking in bars and restaurants.

Alcoholic Drinks

Lättöl (light beer, less than 2.25% alcohol) and *folköl* (folk beer, 2.25% to 3.5% alcohol) account for about two-thirds of all beer sold in Sweden and can be bought in supermarkets everywhere. *Mellanöl* (medium-strength beer, 3.5% to 4.5% alcohol), *starköl* (strong beer, over 4.5% alcohol) and wines and spirits can only be bought at outlets of the state-owned alcohol store, called Systembolaget, which is open until about 6pm on weekdays and slightly shorter hours on Saturday (Friday afternoon queues can be long!). You must be aged 20 or over to make a purchase. Alcohol prices are kept high as a matter of government policy; the result sees many Swedes travelling to Denmark, the Åland islands or even Finland to stock up, though prices are slowly beginning to equalise as Sweden shifts its policies towards compliance with those of the EU.

Habits & Customs

When invited to someone's house for a meal, it's polite to bring flowers or a bottle of wine. Guests should take their shoes off in the foyer, even if the host or hostess says it isn't necessary. Table manners don't differ much from those in most of Europe. It's polite to make eye contact with everyone when toasting. Locals tend to eat breakfast at home, lunch between 11.30am and 2pm (taking advantage of the *dagens rätt* bargains) and the evening meal between 6pm and 8pm, often later in larger cities.

STOCKHOLM

☎ 08 / pop 758,148

Known for its impeccable style and a population as conspicuously beautiful as its surroundings, Stockholm is a thoroughly attractive destination. Whether you're wandering the narrow, crooked streets of Gamla Stan or trolling the broad shopping avenues of the modern commercial neighbourhoods, it's hard not to wonder if the whole city's been art-directed. The famously clean, blue water sparkles under the midsummer sun, practically begging locals and visitors alike to take a dip. Winter is equally pretty, as snowfall makes the big, square buildings of the city's historic core look like frosted cakes and the cold air brightens the eyes of people wandering its streets. The view of majestic waterfront buildings and Gala Stan's cobblestone warren of narrow streets as seen from the heights of Södermalm is hard to beat.

But the city is far from a museum piece. Its design and fashion industries race to be cutting-edge, and the populace can be determinedly fast-paced. Best of all, Stockholm is compact enough that a visitor can easily appreciate all of these elements at once.

ORIENTATION

Stockholm is built on 14 islands, with the modern city centre on the main island. The business core is composed of Norrmalm and Vasastan (the boundaries between these two are debatable); the most chic, and historically wealthiest, part of town is Östermalm, to the east.

The tourist office is in the eastern part of Norrmalm; the popular garden Kungsträdgården (often referred to as 'Stockholm's living room') is almost next door. Off the western edge of Norrmalm is the mostly residential island of Kungsholmen.

Smack in the middle of Stockholm is the island housing the historic Gamla Stan (old town). Two smaller, satellite islands are linked to it by bridges: Riddarholmen to the west; and Helgeandsholmen to the north, occupied by the Swedish Parliament building.

To the east of Gamla Stan is the island of Djurgården (known as 'Animal Park'), where many of Stockholm's better-known museums are located. The small island of Skeppsholmen sits between Djurgården and Gamla Stan; it's home to more museums and the well-known youth hostel STF Vandrarhem af Chapman.

Södermalm, the city's funky, Bohemian area, inhabits the large island to the south of Gamla Stan. It's linked by the car-and-pedestrian bridge Centralbron as well as by the rather baffling traffic snarl called Slussen.

There are some pleasant picnic and bathing spots around Långholmen, the parklike island to the west of Södermalm.

Maps

The *What's on Stockholm* tourist booklet, available free from tourist offices and many hotels, has basic map pages, but *Stockholms officiella turistkarta* (official tourist map, Skr25 from Sweden House) covers a larger area and is easier to read.

A huge range of guidebooks and maps for driving, hiking or sailing in Sweden and across Scandinavia is available at the tourist office in **Sweden House** (Sverigehuset; Map p402; ☎ 789 2490; www.stockholmtown.com; Hamngatan 27), online through **Swedish Lantmäteriet** (www.lantmateriet.se), or at the following shops:

Kartbutiken (Map p402; ☎ 202303; Kungsgatan 74; ☼ Mon-Sat)

Kartcentrum (Map p402; ☎ 411 1687; Vasagatan 16; ☼ Mon-Sat)

INFORMATION
Bookshops

Akademibokhandeln (Map p402; ☎ 613 6100; Mäster Samuelsgatan 28) A good selection of both fiction and nonfiction in English.

Press Stop (Map p402; ☎ 644 3510; Götgatan 31) This shop in Södermalm is attached to a coffee shop and has a wide range of international magazines.

Sweden Bookshop (Map p402; ☎ 453 7880; www.swedenbookshop.com; Slottsbacken 10; ☼ Mon-Fri) This store in Gamla Stan offers the broadest selection of English-language books on Sweden (also available online).

Discount Cards & Packages

Stockholm a la Carte (☎ 663 0080; www.destination-stockholm.com) Discount hotel-and-sightseeing packages; can be booked online.

Stockholm Card (www.stockholmtown.com; adult 24/48/72hr Skr270/420/540, child Skr120/160/190) Available from tourist offices, a number of camping grounds, hostels and hotels, and Storstockholms Lokaltrafik (SL) public transport centres, the card gives free entry to about 75 attractions (including Skansen), free city parking in metered spaces, free sightseeing by boat and free travel on public transport (including the lift, Katarinahissen, but excluding local ferries and airport buses).

Emergency

Emergency (☎ 112) Free number for fire brigade, police and ambulance.

Police stations Kungsholmen (Map pp396-7; ☎ 401 1300; Kungsholmsgatan 37; ⊗ 24hr); Södermalm (Map p402; ☎ 401 0100; Torkel Knutssonsgatan 20; ⊗ 24hr)

Internet Access

Nine (Map pp396-7; ☎ 673 6797; Odengatan 44; per hr from Skr35; ⊗ 10am-1am) The computer area is downstairs through the café.

Sidewalk Express (www.sidewalkexpress.se in Swedish; per hr Skr19) A chain of roving internet kiosks at numerous central locations (Centralstationen, Cityterminalen, Arlanda and Bromma airports, inside some convenience stores and coffee shops). Vouchers are purchased from vending machines next to the monitors (coins only). See the website for locations in Stockholm and elsewhere in Sweden.

Internet Resources

Local (www.thelocal.se) News and features about Sweden in English.

Stockholm's Museums (www.stockholmsmuseer .com) Has a drop-down menu with links to all museum homepages.

Stockholm: the Official Visitors Guide (www.stock holmtown.com) Excellent tourist information in English (and many other languages).

Laundry

Laundry options are limited and it's best to find a hotel or hostel with facilities.

Tvättomat (Map pp396-7; ☎ 346 480; Västmannagatan 61; per load from Skr70 ⊗ 8.30am-6.30pm Mon-Fri, 9.30am-3pm Sat; Ⓜ T-Odenplan)

Media

There are a number of useful publications for visitors – the best overall guide is the monthly **What's on Stockholm** (www.stockholmtown .com), available free from tourist offices and many hotels and downloadable online, with sections on nightlife, shopping, restaurants, museums, activities, events and sightseeing.

Medical Services

CW Scheele Apotek (Map p402; ☎ 454 8130; Klarabergsgatan 64; ⊗ 24hr) Central pharmacy near Centralstationen.

Sankt Eriks Sjukhus (Map pp396-7; ☎ 654 1117; Flemminggatan 22; ⊗ 8am-8.30pm) Emergency dental treatment is available here. Outside these hours, dial ☎ 644 9200 for the dentist on duty.

Södersjukhuset (Map pp396-7; ☎ 616 1000; Ringvägen 52; ⊗ 24hr) Large hospital in Södermalm handling casualties from the central city area.

Money

There are ATMs all over town, including a few inside Centralstationen, and by the post office (usually with long queues). There are banks around Sergels Torg and along Hamngatan.

Forex (Map p402; www.forex.se; Centralstationen; ⊗ 7am-9pm) Other branches are scattered throughout the capital; at all of them the charge is Skr15 per travellers cheque.

Post

Post office (Map p402; Centralstationen; ⊗ 7am-10pm Mon-Fri, 10am-7pm Sat & Sun) Next to Hotelcentrallen office.

STOCKHOLM IN TWO DAYS

A good way to get familiar with any city is to look down on it, so make a beeline for Slussen and ride to the top of **Katarinahissen** (p401), the big elevator, for a stunning view. From here, stretch out the view and your legs with a stroll along the edge of the **Söder Heights** (p401). Back down at Slussen, catch a ferry across to **Djurgården** (p399) to explore the best of the city's museums in a wonderful, parklike setting. Head back over the Djurgården bridge to Stureplan for shopping, supper and nightlife. Start the next day early with a wander through the old town, **Gamla Stan** (p398), to beat the tourist rush. Peek into **Storkyrkan** (p399), then take a tour of **Kungliga Slottet** (the Royal Palace; p398), and try to be near the outdoor courtyard at midday for the Changing of the Guard. Take an afternoon **cruise** (p401) of Stockholm's waterways for another interesting perspective on the capital. If there's any juice left in your tank, prowl the cool pubs and cafés of **Södermalm** (p407) for an evening meal and offbeat entertainment.

SWEDEN

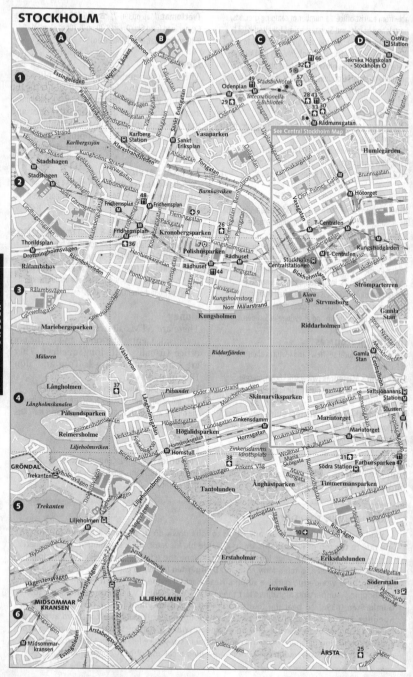

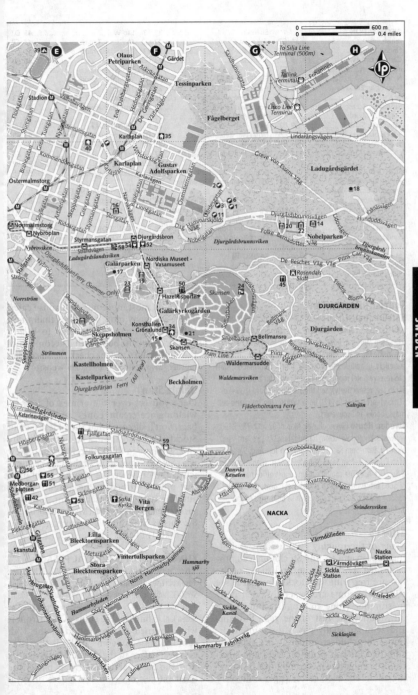

0 ___ 600 m
0 ___ 0.4 miles

To Silja Line Terminal (500m)

Tallink Terminal

Lisco Line Terminal

SWEDEN

Tourist Information

Hotellcentralen (Map p402; ☎ 789 2456; hotels@svb .stockholm.se; Centralstationen; ☻ 8am-8pm Jun-Aug, 9am-6pm Mon-Sat, noon-4pm Sun Sep-May) This busy office inside the main train station is convenient for arriving travellers. In addition to providing tourist information, staff can reserve hotel rooms and hostel beds (for a Skr60 or Skr25 fee, respectively), sell the Stockholm Card (p394) or SL transport passes (p412), book sightseeing tours and sell maps, books and souvenirs.

Sweden House (Sverigehuset; Map p402; ☎ 789 2490; www.stockholmtown.com; Hamngatan 27; ☻ 9am-7pm Mon-Fri, 9am-5pm Sat, 10am-4pm Sun Jun-Aug, 9am-6pm Mon-Fri, 10am-4pm Sat & Sun May & Sep, 9am-3pm Sat & Sun Oct-Apr) The capital's main tourist office has lots of good brochures and can book hotel rooms, theatre and concert tickets, and packages such as boat trips to the archipelago.

SIGHTS

Many of the roughly 70 museums and attractions in and around Stockholm can now be visited free of charge, and many of the rest are free with the Stockholm Card (see p394). Museums are generally open daily in summer (June to August) but closed on Monday the rest of the year. Students and seniors usually pay a discounted entrance fee; children under 16 are generally admitted for half-price (or free) and small children enter free if accompanied by a paying adult. Disabled access is generally very

good, and most museums also house cafés. There are many more museums than those listed below; for a full list, refer to *What's on Stockholm*, the booklet that accompanies the Stockholm Card, or check the **Stockholms museer** (www.stockholmsmuseer.com) website.

Gamla Stan

Once you get over the armies of tourists wielding ice-cream cones and shopping bags, you'll discover that the oldest part of Stockholm is also its most beautiful. The city emerged here in the 13th century and grew with Sweden's power until the 17th century, when the castle of Tre Kronor, symbol of that power, burned to the ground. While ambling along Västerlånggatan, look out for **Mårten Trotzigs Gränd** (Map p402) by No 81: this is Stockholm's narrowest lane, at less than 1m wide.

KUNGLIGA SLOTTET (ROYAL PALACE)

The 'new' **palace** (Map p402; ☎ 402 6130; www .royalcourt.se; Slottsbacken; adult/child per attraction Skr90/35, adult/child combined ticket Skr130/65; ☻ 10am-4pm mid-May–Aug, noon-3pm Tue-Sun Sep–mid-May, closed Jan) is built on the ruins of Tre Kronor, which burned to the ground in the 17th century. Its 608 rooms make it the largest royal palace in the world. Many visitors find the **State Apartments** (Map p402) the most interesting, with two floors of royal pomp and portraits of pale princes (these may occasionally be closed to the public).

Crowns are displayed at **Skattkammaren** (the Royal Treasury; Map p402), near **Slottskyrkan** (the Royal Chapel; Map p402). **Gustav III's Antikmuseum** (Gustav III's Museum of Antiquities; Map p402) displays Mediterranean treasures acquired by that eccentric monarch. **Museum Tre Kronor** (Map p402) is in the palace basement and features the foundations of 13th-century defensive walls and exhibits rescued from the medieval castle.

The **Changing of the Guard** takes place in the outer courtyard at 12.15pm Monday to Saturday, and 1.15pm on Sunday and public holidays.

OTHER ATTRACTIONS

Near the palace, **Storkyrkan** (Map p402; ☎ 723 3021; admission free) is the Royal Cathedral of Sweden, consecrated in 1306. The most notable feature is the life-sized *St George & the Dragon* sculpture, dating from the late 15th century. On nearby Stortorget is the excellent **Nobelmuseet** (Map p402; ☎ 232506; Stortorget; adult/child Skr60/20; ☺ daily mid-May–mid-Sep, Tue-Sun mid-Sep–mid-May), presenting the history of the Nobel Prize and past laureates.

The large collection of royal memorabilia at **Livrustkammaren** (Royal Armoury; Map p402; ☎ 5195 5544; www.livrustkammaren.se; Slottsbacken 3; admission free; ☺ 10am-5pm Jun-Aug, 11am-5pm Tue-Sun Sep-May) includes ceremonial costumes and colourful carriages. **Kungliga Myntkabinettet** (Royal Coin Cabinet; Map p402; ☎ 5195 5304; www.myntkabinettet.se; Slottsbacken 6; admission free; ☺ 10am-4pm Oct-Jun, 9am-5pm Jul-Sep) is opposite the palace and covers the history of money and finance.

The island of Riddarholmen has some of the oldest buildings in Stockholm. **Riddarholmskyrkan** (Map p402; ☎ 5903 5009; Wrangelska Backen; adult/child Skr20/10; ☺ 10am-4pm mid-May–Aug, noon-3pm Sat & Sun Sep), with its striking iron spire, houses the royal necropolis. Nearby, the beautiful **Riddarhuset** (House of Nobility; Map p402; ☎ 723 3990; www.riddarhuset.se; Riddarhustorget; adult/child Skr50/25; ☺ 11.30am-12.30pm Mon-Fri) displays 2325 coats of arms.

The site of **Medeltidsmuseet** (Map p402; ☎ 5083 1790; Strömparterren; admission free; ☺ daily Jul-Aug, Tue-Sun Sep-Jun), the museum of medieval Stockholm, had been allocated as parking space for members of the nearby.

Riksdagshuset (Parliament House; Map p402; ☎ 786 4872; Riksgatan 3A), but excavations in the late 1970s revealed well-preserved foundations of the medieval town and it's now a museum. Riksdagshuset has free one-hour guided tours in English at 12.30pm and 2pm Monday to Friday from late June to August, and they're fascinating to anyone with an interest in how political systems work.

Djurgården

The royal playground, Djurgården is an urban oasis of parkland with some of Stockholm's best attractions. To get here, take bus No 47 from Centralstationen or the regular Djurgården ferry services from Nybroplan or Slussen (see p412). Beyond the large tourist haunts are plenty of small gems, including some excellent art collections. You can rent bikes (see p411) by the bridge, and cycling is the best way to explore the island.

SKANSEN

You could easily spend all day at this 'Sweden in miniature'. **Skansen** (Map pp396-7; ☎ 442 8000; www.skansen.se; adult Skr50-80, child Skr20-30; ☺ 10am-8pm May, 10am-10pm Jun-Aug, 10am-5pm Sep, 10am-4pm Oct-Apr) was the world's first open-air museum (it opened in 1891). Today over 150 traditional houses (with staff in period costume) and other exhibits from all over Sweden occupy the attractive hill top. There's also a handicraft precinct, an unusual **zoo** (Map pp396-7) full of Nordic animals, and daily activities taking place on Skansen's stages in summer (including folk dancing and music). Skansen is the place to head to if you're in Stockholm for any of the country's major celebrations (eg Walpurgis Night, Midsummer, the Lucia festival, Christmas season and New Year's Eve; see p470), though keep in mind that everyone else in town will be here, too.

VASAMUSEET

The flagship *Vasa* sank within minutes of being launched in 1628. Some 300 years later it was painstakingly resurrected, and the long process of restoration and preservation began. This acclaimed **museum** (Map pp396-7; ☎ 5195 4800; adult/child Skr80/40; ☺ 10am-5pm Sep-May, 8.30am-6pm Jun-Aug), behind Nordiska Museet and on the western shore of

SWEDEN

Djurgården, allows you to simultaneously look into the lives of 17th-century sailors and appreciate a brilliant achievement in marine archaeology.

Guided tours in English run hourly from 10.30am in summer and at least twice daily at other times. On Wednesday between 5pm and 8pm there's a Skr20 discount on entry. At the moorings behind the museum are the icebreaker *Sankt Erik* and the lightship *Finngrundet*.

OTHER ATTRACTIONS

Nordiska Museet (National Museum of Cultural History; Map pp396-7; ☎ 5195 6000; www.nordiskamuseet.se; Djurgårdsvägen 6-16; admission free; ☉ 10am-5pm Jun-Aug, 10am-4pm Mon-Fri, 10am-5pm Sat & Sun Sep-May) is housed in an enormous Renaissance-style castle, with notable temporary exhibitions and vast Swedish collections of fine arts and handicraft dating from 1520 to the present day.

Junibacken (Map pp396-7; ☎ 5872 3000; www.junibacken.se; adult/child Skr110/95; ☉ 9am-7pm Jul, 10am-5pm Jun & Aug, 10am-5pm Tue-Fri, 9am-6pm Sat & Sun Sep-May) re-creates the fantasy scenes of Astrid Lindgren's children's books, which should stir the imaginations of young children and the memories of adults familiar with her characters.

More family fun can be had at **Gröna Lund Tivoli** (Map pp396-7; ☎ 5875 0100; www.gronalund.com; adult/child Skr60/30), a fun park with dozens of rides and amusements – the Åkbandet day pass (Skr240) gives unlimited rides; individual rides range from Skr15 to Skr60. Big-name concerts are often held here in summer. The park is open from noon to 11pm on most days between mid-May and September; hours vary during the rest of the year.

Central Stockholm

The fashionable, high-heeled heart of modern-day Stockholm beats in bustling Norrmalm. Near T-Centralen station is **Sergels Torg** (Map p402), a severely modern public square (though it's actually round) bordered on one side by the imposing Kulturhuset. Norrmalm is also home to the beloved public park **Kungsträdgården** (Map p402), where locals gather in all weather. The park is home to an outdoor stage, winter ice-skating rink and restaurants, cafés and kiosks. Vasastan is the somewhat quie-

ter, more residential area that extends to the north of Norrmalm.

Sweden's largest art museum, the excellent **Nationalmuseum** (Map p402; ☎ 5195 4300; www.nationalmuseum.se; Södra Blasieholmshamnen; admission free; ☉ 11am-5pm Wed-Sun, 11am-8pm Tue) houses the national collection of painting and sculpture but hosts other exhibitions, including design and handicrafts.

The main national historical collection is at **Historiska Museet** (Museum of National Antiquities; Map pp396-7; ☎ 5195 5600; Narvavägen 13; admission free; ☉ daily mid-May–mid-Sep, Tue-Sun mid-Sep–mid-May). Displays cover prehistoric, Viking and medieval archaeology and culture; don't miss the incredible Gold Room with its rare treasures, including a seven-ringed gold collar.

The giant, boxy **Kulturhuset** (Map p402; ☎ 5083 1508; Sergels Torg) houses temporary exhibitions (often with entry fee), a theatre, bookshop, design store, reading room, several cafés, a comics library and bar. It's open daily, although some sections are closed on Monday.

Skeppsholmen

Across the bridge by the Nationalmuseum are more museums, including the sleek, impressive **Moderna Museet** (Map pp396-7; ☎ 519 55200; www.modernamuseet.se; admission free; ☉ closed Mon), which boasts a world-class collection of modern art, sculpture, photography and installations, temporary exhibitions and an outdoor sculpture garden. Adjacent to Moderna Museet is **Arkitekturmuseet** (Map pp396-7; ☎ 587 27000; admission free; ☉ closed Mon), which is housed in an extraordinary building and contains displays on Swedish and international architecture.

Kungsholmen

The main visitor sight here is the landmark **Stadshuset** (City Hall; Map p402; ☎ 5082 9058; Hantverkargatan; admission by tour only Skr60; ☉ tours 10am, 11am, noon, 2pm & 3pm Jun-Aug, 10am & noon Sep-May), resembling a large church, with two internal courtyards. Inside are the mosaic-lined Gyllene Salen (Golden Hall), Prins Eugen's own fresco re-creation of the lake view from the gallery, and the Blå Hallen (Blue Hall), where the annual Nobel Prize banquet is held. You can walk down the staircase just like the Nobel laureates do, only without putting in all that hard work.

To feel even more important, climb Stadshuset's 106m-high **Stadshustorn** (Tower; Map p402; ☎ 5082 9058; adult Skr20; ☺ daily May-Sep, Sat & Sun Apr), with 365 steps, for a great view of the city.

Södermalm

Södermalm is perhaps Stockholm's most interesting neighbourhood. Historically home to many of the city's artists, Söder (as locals call it) is still the part of town where artistic and alternative types hang out – if you're looking for, say, a straight-edge vegan all-ages punk club, this is where you'll find it. The scene on the street is scarcely less exciting than the gorgeous views over Stockholm from the island's northern cliffs (called the Söder Heights).

The best place to start is at the top of **Katarinahissen** (Map p402; Slussen; adult Skr5), an old lift that goes up from Slussen. At the top is one of the city's best restaurants, Eriks Gondolen (p407). Wooden staircases also wind steeply up the hillside, though these can be treacherous in winter.

For evening walks, head towards the northern cliffs for the old houses and fine panoramas.

Stockholms Stadsmuseum (Map p402; ☎ 5083 1600; Slussen; admission free; ☺ 11am-5pm Tue-Sun) covers the history of the city and its people, and is worthwhile once you've developed a romantic attachment to Stockholm.

Ladugårdsgärdet

North of Djurgården, in the vast parkland, are more fine museums and attractions. To get to Ladugårdsgärdet, take bus No 69 from Centralstationen.

The very good **Etnografiska Museet** (Museum of Ethnography; Map pp396-7; ☎ 5195 5000; www.etnografiska.se; Djurgårdsbrunnsvägen 34; admission free; ☺ 11am-5pm) brings the entire world under one roof. **Sjöhistoriska Museet** (National Maritime Museum; Map pp396-7; ☎ 5195 4900; www.sjohistoriska.nu; Djurgårdsbrunnsvägen 24; admission free; ☺ 10am-5pm Tue-Sun) exhibits extensive maritime memorabilia. **Tekniska Museet** (Museum of Science & Technology; Map pp396-7; ☎ 450 5600; Museivägen 7; adult/child Skr60/30; ☺ 10am-5pm Mon-Fri, 11am-5pm Sat & Sun) contains exhaustive exhibits on Swedish inventions and their applications.

The 155m-high TV tower, **Kaknästornet** (Map pp396-7; ☎ 667 2180; adult/child Skr30/15; ☺ 9am-10pm May-Aug, 10am-9pm Sep-Apr), has an observation deck from which you can enjoy stunning 360-degree views.

ACTIVITIES

Summer sees locals and visitors taking advantage of the fine weather; many head for the coast and the islands of the archipelago (with good swimming spots) or organise picnics in the parks. Winter also sees some outdoor activity, including ice-skating on a rink set up in Kungsträdgården.

Eriksdalsbadet (Map pp396-7; ☎ 5084 0250; Hammarby slussväg 20; adult/child Skr65/30; ☺ 6.30am-8pm Mon-Thu, 6.30am-7pm Fri, 9am-6pm Sat & Sun) has indoor and open-air swimming pools in the far south of Södermalm, plus gym, aerobics and other activities.

From the restaurant-bar **Djurgårdsbrons Sjöcafé** (Map pp396-7; ☎ 660 5757; Djurgårdsbron; ☺ May-Sep), by the bridge leading to Djurgården, you can rent bikes (Skr65/250 per hour/day), as well as inline skates, kayaks, canoes, rowing boats and pedal boats.

TOURS

Stockholm Sightseeing (Map p402; ☎ 5871 4020; www.stockholmsightseeing.com; main terminal, Strömkajen) runs frequent cruises from early April to mid-December around the central bridges and canals from Strömkajen (near the Grand Hôtel), Nybroplan or Stadshusbron. The two-hour 'Under the Bridges of Stockholm' (Skr170) covers the most territory, passing under 15 bridges and through two locks. The land-based sister operation is **City Sightseeing** (Map p402; ☎ 5871 4020; www.citysightseeing.com), which offers year-round 1½- to 3½-hour coach tours of the city (departing from Gustav Adolfs Torg) from Skr170 to Skr395, and one-hour walking tours around Gamla Stan (Skr90, daily July and August).

You can also take a one-hour, English-language guided walk through Gamla Stan with an authorised guide (Skr70). From June to August these tours start at 7.30pm Monday, Wednesday and Thursday, and from September to May at 1.30pm Saturday and Sunday. Meet at the Obelisk at Slottsbacken (Map p402), outside the royal palace; no reservation is needed.

SWEDEN

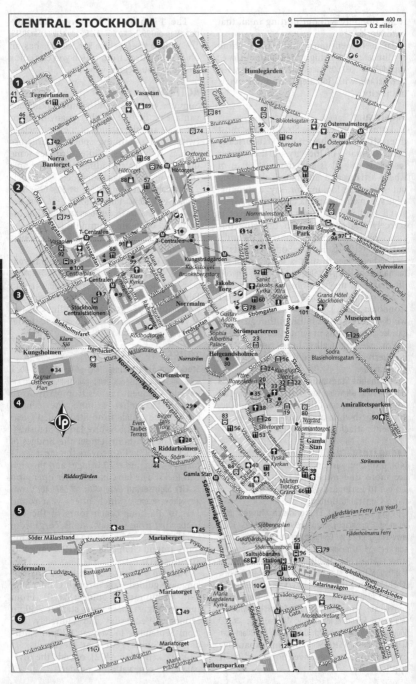

SLEEPING

Options are spread out all over the city, and all are accessible by public transport and close to a neighbourhood of bars and cafés.

Most hostels fill up during the late afternoon in summer so arrive early or book in advance. May is also a busy time for hostels, with many Swedish school groups visiting the capital. For a Skr25 fee, **Hotellcentralen** (Map p402; ☎ 789 2456; hotels@svb.stockholm.se; Centralstationen) can assist you in getting a bed in a hostel. Keep in mind that reception desks for many hostels have limited hours; check on websites or when you book.

A number of agencies can arrange good-value apartment or B&B accommodation (many with a two-night minimum). The going rate in the city centre is Skr200 to Skr500 for a single, Skr500 to Skr800 for a double. Agencies (with detailed websites) include the following:

Bed & Breakfast Agency (☎ 643 8028; www.bba.nu)
Bed & Breakfast Service (☎ 660 5565; www.bed breakfast.se)

Budget

Bredäng Camping (Map p414; ☎ 977071; bredang camping@telia.com; Stora Sällskapets väg; camp sites Skr180-210, 4-bed cabin Skr650-850, hostel dm/d Skr160/450; Ⓜ T-Bredäng) Cabins and hostel beds are also available at this pleasant lakeside location 10km southwest of the city centre. The camping ground is open from April to late October, while the hostel is open year-round.

Östermalms Citycamping (☎ 102903; Östermalms Idrottsplats, Fiskartorpsvägen; camp sites Skr210; Ⓨ mid-Jun–mid-Aug; Ⓜ T-Stadion) This is Stockholm's most

SWEDEN

central camping ground (1.5km from the city centre). Take the metro or bus No 55.

STF Vandrarhem af Chapman & Skeppsholmen (Svenska Turistföreningen Map p402; ☎ 463 2266; www .stfchapman.com; Skeppsholmen; dm/d Skr245/550; 🖳) Anchored off Skeppsholmen (bus No 65), this boat is a popular hostel, with bunks below and great views from on deck. On dry land beside the boat, with the same reception and prices, is Skeppsholmen Hostel, with kitchen and laundry facilities. Breakfast is Skr70.

STF Vandrarhem Fridhemsplan (Map pp396-7; ☎ 653 8800; info@fridhemsplan.se; St Eriksgatan 20; dm/s/d Skr240/435/585; Ⓜ T-Fridhemsplan; 🖳) One of the few hostels you'll see with egg chairs in the foyer and modern art on the walls, this 150-room STF on Kungsholmen epitomises the Swedish approach to hostelling (ie good facilities, great décor, excellent value). There's parking (Skr95 per day), and breakfast is Skr60.

STF Vandrarhem Långholmen (Map pp396-7; ☎ 720 8500; www.langholmen.com; Långholmsmuren; dm/d Skr250/480) Off the northwestern corner of Södermalm is the small island of Långholmen, home to large parklands and this former prison complex. Hostel beds are in jail cells. Hotel-standard rooms are also available, plus there's an on-site café and restaurant and a prison museum. Breakfast is Skr80. Take the metro to Hornstull, walk north along Långholmsgatan and turn left onto Högalidsgatan, then head north across the footbridge.

Mälaren den Röda Båten (Map p402; ☎ 644 4385; www.theredboat.com; Söder Malärstrand, Kajplats 6; dm/s/d Skr210/430/530) This red-painted boat in northern Södermalm is probably the cosiest of Stockholm's handful of floating hostels. It features a rustic interior, a good summer restaurant, but no self-catering kitchen.

STF Vandrarhem Zinkensdamm (Map pp396-7; ☎ 616 8100; www.zinkensdamm.com; Zinkens väg 20; dm/s/d Skr240/485/560; Ⓜ T-Zinkendamm; 🖳) This large, well-equipped and welcoming complex (with adjacent hotel) is in a quiet location in the green, western end of Södermalm. It offers an on-site café, breakfast (Skr55), sauna and bike rental. Breakfast is included in the hotel-room tariff.

City Backpackers (Map p402; ☎ 206920; www .citybackpackers.se; Upplandsgatan 2A; dm from Skr210, d Skr560; 🖳) About 500m from Central-

stationen and deservedly popular with backpackers. It has clean rooms, friendly staff and facilities including kitchen, sauna, laundry, lockers and courtyard, plus free internet access. No breakfast is offered and prices double on Friday and Saturday.

Hostel Bed & Breakfast (Map pp396-7; ☎ 152838; www.hostelbedandbreakfast.com; Rehnsgatan 21; dm/s/d Skr200/425/590; Ⓜ T-Rådmansgatan; 🖳) Cosy basement hostel, with breakfast included. Good facilities including kitchen and laundry. Also a large, cheap summer annexe here with 40 beds (June to August, Skr145).

Abbe's Hostels (☎ 300350; www.abbes.se; dm Skr220-260, d Skr500-640); Abbe's Hostel Stora Nygatan (Map p402; Stora Nygatan 38); Abbe's Hostel Skeppsbron (Map p402; Skeppsbron 40); Abbe's Hostel Kungsholmen (Map pp396-7; Fleminggatan 19); Abbe's Hostel Globen (Map pp396-7; Gullmarsvägen 92) Abbe offers new, small, basic hostels scattered around the city centre (including two in prime spots in Gamla Stan and another on Kungsholmen). There are no kitchen facilities or breakfast served, and reception is only staffed from 3pm to 6pm.

Other budget options:

M/S Rygerfjord (Map p402; ☎ 840830; www.ryger fjord.se; Söder Malärstrand, Kajplats 12; dm Skr195-210, d Skr530; Ⓟ) Boat with small hostel cabins, plus onsite restaurant.

Östra Reals Vandrarhem (Map pp396-7; ☎ 664 1114; www.ostrareal.com; Karlavägen 79; dm Skr150-195, d Skr575; ☿ mid-Jun–mid-Aug; Ⓟ 🖳) In an old school, without kitchen facilities or breakfast offered.

STF Vandrarhem Backpackers Inn (Map pp396-7; ☎ 660 7515; www.backpackersinn.se; Banérgatan 56; dm Skr180-215; ☿ late Jun–mid-Aug; Ⓟ 🖳) Around 300 beds in a school building. No kitchen facilities, but breakfast is available (Skr50).

Hotel Formule 1 (Map p414; ☎ 744 2044; www .hotelformule1.com; Mikrofonvägen 30; r Skr350; Ⓜ T-Telefonplan; Ⓟ) Supercheap, small, uninspiring rooms for up to three people (one flat rate, excludes breakfast). Bathroom facilities shared. About 4km southwest of the city centre.

Midrange

In the midrange price category (Skr650 to Skr1500 for a weekday double, including breakfast), you'll find a number of homey places in mostly residential locations a little off the tourist path (but with good transport connections), without all the trimmings of the grander hotels. See also the combined hotel/hostel options listed in the Budget section.

Hotellcentralen (Map p402; ☎ 789 2456; hotels@svb .stockholm.se; Centralstationen) can find you suitable hotel accommodation for a fee of Skr60.

Hotel Tre Små Rum (Map pp396-7; ☎ 641 2371; www.tresmarum.se; Högbergsgatan 81; r Skr695; Ⓜ T-Mariatorget) In a quiet part of Södermalm, this charming place has small, comfortable rooms, shared bathrooms and rental bikes (Skr85). Great value and location.

Rex Hotel (Map pp396-7; ☎ 160040; www.rex hotel.se; Luntmakargatan 73; s/d Skr1390/1590, discount Skr790/990; 🖳) Inside an 1866 townhouse is this no-nonsense boutique hotel, with colourful modern rooms, excellent facilities and ultra-friendly staff. It's the understated sibling of the stylish Hotel Hellsten across the street (right).

Columbus Hotell (Map pp396-7; ☎ 5031 1200; www .columbus.se; Tjärhovsgatan 11; s/d Mon-Fri Skr1250/1550, s/d Sat & Sun Skr950/1250, annex s/d Skr695/895; Ⓜ T-Medborgarplatsen) A Södermalm option set around a cobblestone courtyard and by a park, close to nightlife. The excellent budget rooms are in the 3rd-floor 'annex' (no lift) and have phone, TV and shared bathroom.

Hotel Gustav Vasa (Map pp396-7; ☎ 343801; www.gustavvasahotel.se; Västmannagatan 61; s Skr649-1149, d Skr949-1449; Ⓟ) The Gustav Vasa is right on Odenplan in the north of town and housed in a building dating from 1899. There's an antique lift and a variety of rooms – the cheapest are well appointed and have private bathrooms located outside the room, in the corridor. Some of the larger rooms have beautiful ceramic stoves. Parking costs Skr125.

Pensionat Oden (☎ 796 9600; www.pensionat .nu; s Skr630-995, d Skr700-1295) Pensionat Oden City (Map p402; Kammakargatan 62), Pensionat Oden Södermalm (Map p402; Hornsgatan 66), Pensionat Oden Vasastan (Map pp396-7; Odengatan 38) A chain of affordable *pensions* (boarding houses) in character-rich old buildings with attractive rooms. Prices vary according to season, room size and facilities.

Mälardrottningen (Map p402; ☎ 5451 8780; www .malardrottningen.se; Riddarholmen; Mon-Fri s/d from Skr1130/1250, Sat & Sun from Skr930/1050) This classy vessel, launched in 1924 and now anchored off Riddarholmen, was once the world's largest motor yacht and belonged to Barbara Hutton. The deep blue carpets, dark-wood fittings and restaurant (with a bar in the bridge) create a great maritime atmosphere. All cabins have private bathrooms.

August Strindberg Hotell (Map p402; ☎ 325 006; www.hotellstrindberg.se; Tegnérgatan 38; s/d from Skr895/1495, discount Skr695/995) This quiet, family-run hotel offers 27 rooms and personalised service. Entry through a street-front apartment block takes you to the hotel, set in a pretty courtyard. There's an inviting breakfast room and some garden seating. Rooms vary in size and style but all are pretty.

Top End

There's no shortage of Stockholm hotels that fall into this category (Skr1500 and upwards for a weekday double). The listed price, however, is rarely the lowest available – always ask about special deals and discounts when booking, and remember that even the poshest hotels usually offer steep discounts at weekends and in summer.

Hotel Hellsten (Map pp396-7; ☎ 661 8600; www .hellsten.se; Luntmakargatan 68; s/d from Skr1490/1890, discount Sat & Sun Skr990/1190) The minute you walk in, you know this new boutique hotel is something special. The long black hallway leading to reception feels more like a posh nightclub than a crash pad. The foyer, bar and rooms are equally spectacular, each with individually chosen décor to give you the impression you're staying at the manor house of an artistic friend. All the rooms are gorgeous, but the exposed roof beams and skylights give the superior rooms the most atmosphere.

Rival Hotel (Map p402; ☎ 5457 8900; www.rival .se; Mariatorget 3; s/d from Skr1990/2190, discount Sat & Sun Skr1240/1390) ABBA's Benny Andersson is a co-owner of this fabulous, hopping place in Södermalm's prettiest square. All rooms have plasma TVs and DVD players, plus gleaming hardwood floors and huge pictures of Swedish film stars on the walls. The complex includes a vintage 1940s movie theatre, café, swanky cocktail bar and well-preserved retro architecture throughout. Summer rates (singles/doubles Skr650/1300) are a bargain.

Scandic Hotel Hasselbacken (Map pp396-7; ☎ 5173 4300; www.scandic-hotels.com/hasselbacken; Hazeliusbacken 20; s/d Skr1690/1990, discount Skr990/1190) There's only one hotel on the pretty green island of Djurgården, and it's hard to imagine a lovelier setting for a stay in Stockholm. This 1925 building is in the heart of the area's attractions, and facilities (and the on-site restaurant) are first-rate.

SWEDEN

Rica City Hotel Gamla Stan (Map p402; ☎ 723 7250; www.rica.se; Lilla Nygatan 25; s/d Skr1710/1895, discount Skr890/1150) One of only five hotels on Gamla Stan (all understandably popular). A classy place in a great location, housed in a 17th-century building and with elegant, unfussy décor – including pictures of Swedish royalty on the walls – and good service.

EATING

Like nearly every other aspect of life here, Stockholm's restaurant scene constantly seeks to be at the forefront of fashion. If there's a food trend happening, you can bet that all the hot restaurants in town are offering a take on it. A great way to sample the options is to visit during the **Smaka på Stockholm** (Taste of Stockholm; www.smakapastockholm .se) festival. This food festival, usually in late May or early June, is staged in Kungsträdgården. Besides sampling from the kitchens of local restaurants, you can also take in a number of performances.

Stockholm has thousands of eateries to cater to all tastes and budgets, ranging from inexpensive lunch cafeterias and old-style *konditori* to five-star gourmet establishments; the city is also home to colourful market halls that are tourist attractions in their own right.

Gamla Stan

Tourists, not surprisingly, love Gamla Stan and many dine on Västerlånggatan, but be sure to check out the offerings along Stora Nygatan and Österlånggatan – the area around Köpmantorget is home to many classy favourites.

Chokladkoppen (Map p402; ☎ 203170; Stortorget 18; snacks from Skr35, mains Skr40-85) In a pair of gorgeous Renaissance buildings from the 1650s you'll find the gay-friendly café Chokladkoppen and its next-door sibling, Kaffekoppen. Servers run from one to the other, candelabras drip wax onto thick wooden tables inside, and the outdoor patio is always buzzing.

Zum Franziskaner (Map p402; ☎ 411 8330; Skeppsbron 44; lunch from Skr75, mains Skr97-200) Founded by German monks, this wonderful, museum-like place is said to be the oldest restaurant in town. It serves enormous plates of German and Austrian classics (sausages, schnitzel) as well as Swedish *husmanskost* meals such as grilled herring and *pytt i panna* (meat-and-potato hash served with pickled beets and a fried egg).

Café Art (Map p402; ☎ 411 7661; Västerlånggatan 60; sandwiches Skr35-75) Once hip, but now comfortable, this brick vault makes a nice hideout from busy Västerlånggatan and serves filling, inexpensive lunches and pastries.

Hermitage (Map p402; ☎ 411 9500; Stora Nygatan 11; mains Skr65-85) One for the herbivores: Hermitage rustles up fine vegetarian fare from around the world. The *dagens lunch* is great value.

Sundbergs Konditori (Map p402; ☎ 106735; Järntorget 83; lunch specials Skr70) One of the oldest *konditori* in Gamla Stan is this lovely café on the square, which offers filling lunches and decadent pastries to go with coffee poured from a giant samovar.

Djurgården

Rosendals Trädgård (Map pp396-7; ☎ 5458 1270; Rosendalsterassen 12; light meals Skr40-120; ☺ from 11am May-Sep, Tue-Sun Mar-Apr & Oct) One of the island's hidden gems and enormously popular with locals, this biodynamic garden is home to a fantastic café (inside a greenhouse) serving light lunches and delectable homemade sweet treats. Not to be confused with Rosendals Wärdshus, a more upscale (and also lovely) restaurant atop a hill.

Wärdshuset Ulla Winbladh (Map pp396-7; ☎ 663 0571; Rosendalsvägen 8; lunch Skr80, à la carte mains Skr195-265) With so many places on the touristy island of Djurgården, you won't go hungry. For fine food in an old villa with a lovely garden setting, head to this place along the northern loop road. The menu features superbly prepared traditional meals, including meatballs, herring and crayfish tails.

Central Stockholm

Tranan (Map pp396-7; ☎ 52 72 81 00; Karlbergsvägen 14; starters Skr55-125, mains Skr95-265) A neighbourhood joint beloved by locals – and for good reason – Tranan has a comfortable, low-key vibe that makes its gorgeously prepared seafood and *husmanskost* (home-style Swedish food) an even more delightful surprise. With candlesticks and red-checked tablecloths inside and a terrace that faces the bustling Odenplan, it's a relaxing place to enjoy a fine meal completely free of pretence.

Operakällarens Bakfickan (Map p402; ☎ 676 5808; Karl XIIs Torg; mains Skr95-220; ❤ Mon-Sat) Not far from Kungsträdgården is Kungliga Operan (Stockholm's opera house), housing the late-19th-century, superposh restaurant Operakällaren, the lively Café Opera (more a nightclub than a café) and the intimate Bakfickan – the 'back pocket' of Operakällaren. This casual restaurant features great service, Art Nouveau décor and stools around the bar, and serves gourmet-quality *husmanskost* at moderate prices.

Östermalms Saluhall (Map p402; Östermalmstorg; ❤ Mon-Sat) A classed-up counterpart to Hötorgshallen, this covered market hall contains gourmet food stalls and some excellent dining nooks. It's the perfect place to fill a picnic basket.

Örtagården (Map p402; Östermalmstorg; buffet Skr125; ❤ lunch & dinner Mon-Sat) Upstairs in Östermalms Saluhall is a separate vegetarian restaurant, with a vast lunch buffet in a gardenlike setting.

Hötorgshallen (Map p402; Hötorget) This chaotic (for Sweden) basement food hall hides one of the best places in Stockholm to eat seafood, tucked away amid stalls selling the day's fresh catch. There's also a tantalizing collection of speciality food shops, baked goods, produce stalls and Mediterranean fast-food counters.

Sturehof (Map p402; ☎ 440 5730; Stureplan 2; mains Skr105-295) One of Stockholm's busiest restaurants, particularly in summer when the terrace is perpetually hopping. Sturehof has a modern menu vast enough to satisfy every taste, including lots of seafood and some reasonably priced *husmanskost* options.

Sturekatten (Map p402; ☎ 611 1612; Riddargatan 4; lunch Skr35-85) Pleasantly haunted by the tea parties of a million little old Swedish ladies, this traditional café consists of room after room of antiques – and we're not just talking about the clientele.

Lao Wai (Map pp396-7; ☎ 673 7800; Luntmakargatan 74; dagens lunch Skr75, dinner mains from Skr155; ❤ lunch Mon-Fri, dinner Tue-Sat) Luntmakargatan is home to some great Asian eateries, including this minimalist restaurant with strictly vegetarian Chinese food – spices coax miraculous flavours out of various tofu and vegetable combinations.

Sabai Sabai (Map p402; ☎ 790 09 13; Kammakargatan 44; mains Skr59-179) This elaborately decorated Thai place, full of bamboo, wood carvings and tropical murals, is often named as the best Thai in town. It's always packed, so call ahead.

Sirap (Map pp396-7; ☎ 612 9419; Surbrunnsgatan 31A; meals Skr35-95) One of the few places in Stockholm that serves full, cooked breakfasts – the pancakes are recommended.

Café Piccolino (Map p402; Kungsträdgården) Among the stalls on the edge of Kungsträdgården is this long and lean café with large windows to capture the sun (and the passing parade).

Kungshallen (Map p402; Hötorget) Opposite Hötorgshallen is this enormous fast-food court, best for those days when you need a meal that's quick, cheap and not necessarily an adventure.

The handiest central supermarket is **Hemköp** (Map p402; Klarabergsgatan 50; ❤ 8am-9pm Mon-Fri, 10am-9pm Sat & Sun), in the basement of the Åhlens department store, and there's a **Systembolaget** (Map p402; Klarabergsgatan 62; ❤ 10am-8pm Mon-Fri, 10am-3pm Sat) nearby for buying alcohol.

Kungsholmen
The best eat street on this island is Scheelegatan, with some interesting international options.

Thelins Konditori (Map pp396-7; ☎ 651 1900; St Eriksgatan 43; pastries from Skr35) Walk past the showcase of immaculate pastries (collecting a few on the way, of course) and sip coffee in a sweetly antique, red-velvety back room decorated with small white lampposts.

Mamas & Tapas (Map pp396-7; ☎ 653 5390; Scheelegatan 3; tapas from Skr40, mains Skr98-158) Delirious with kitsch, this energetic place is a little overpriced for dinner but an excellent stop for snacks and drinks of an evening.

Södermalm
This area is home to some great restaurants and cafés – start by branching off the main drag, Götgatan, and then explore further afield for less crowded, more interesting options.

Crêperie Fyra Knop (Map p402; ☎ 640 7727; Svartensgatan 4; crepes Skr42-90; ❤ dinner) Snuggle into this intimate hideaway just off Söder's main drag for inexpensive and delicious crepes, both sweet and savoury.

Hermans (Map pp396-7; ☎ 643 9480; Fjällgatan 23A; lunch Skr68-98) Best in summer for its gardenlike veranda, Hermans loads you up on vegetarian food while you sit perched atop the hillside feeling like the king or queen of all you survey.

Östgöta Källaren (Map pp396-7; ☎ 643 2240; Östgötagatan 41; lunch Skr65-85, mains Skr72-190) A popular neighbourhood restaurant-bar with lots to recommend it – a dimly lit romantic atmosphere, friendly service and unpretentious *husmanskost*, plus it's a nice place to linger over a drink or two. If you're feeling goth, peek into the Vampire Lounge downstairs.

Marie Laveau (Map p402; ☎ 668 8500; Hornsgatan 66; mains Skr95-248; ☽ dinner Tue-Sat) A chic but lively new hang-out near Pensionat Oden, this restaurant named for the voodoo queen has a bar/lounge area, a fancier restaurant side and a nightclub. There are huge windows draped in red velvet curtains, edgy artwork on the walls, and an upscale French-influenced menu of seasonal dishes.

Eriks Gondolen (Map p402; ☎ 641 7090; Stadsgården 6; mains Skr185-295) Top of the heap – figuratively and literally. Eriks Gondolen is at the top of Katarinahissen, with a spectacular view of the city and a menu of gourmet offerings. The grill bar has a lower-priced bistro menu. It's worth getting up here even just for a drink, though it can be obnoxiously crowded on weekends. Reservations strongly recommended.

Söderhallarna (Map pp396-7; Medborgarplatsen; ☽ Mon-Sat) This modern food hall includes a vegetarian restaurant, deli, cheese shop, Asian supermarket and a pub. It's not the most atmospheric place, however, so make plans to enjoy your lunch in the outdoors on Medborgarplatsen.

Jerusalem Royal Kebab (Map pp396-7; Götgatan 61; kebabs & felafels Skr28-50; ☽ 24hr) Kindly lining the stomachs of Söder's intrepid bar-goers is this no-nonsense kebab outlet, often cited as the best in town.

Nystekt Strömming (Map p402; Södermalmstorg; plates from Skr35) Line up at this van outside metro T-Slussen for a platter of genuinely Scandinavian fast food: fried herring and potatoes.

DRINKING

It seems that almost every decent restaurant in Stockholm has a cool bar attached. Many cafés bring in a DJ in the evening and, *voila*, another groovy bar is born. In Södermalm, check the Götgatan, Östgötagatan and Skånegatans area, and around Medborgarplatsen. In Kungsholmen, visit Scheelegatan and Flemminggatan, and in the northern centre try the Tegnérgatan and Rörstrandsgatan areas. For fashionable latenight bars and clubs frequented by the city's beautiful people, head to Stureplan. The following drinking venues are generally open daily until 1am.

Foggy Dew (Map p402; ☎ 207641; www.foggydew.se; Sveavägen 39; pub snacks from Skr62) Named for the song that got gentle folkie Burl Ives thrown in jail, this lively Irish pub is big on character and full of characters. About 50:50 Swedes and expats, it's a welcoming place to catch up on the local chatter and sink a few.

Soldaten Svejk (Map pp396-7; ☎ 641 3366; www.svejk.se; Östgötagatan 35) Your best bet for seeing accordions and really cool moustaches is at this comfortable Czech pub in Södermalm, with huge beer mugs and hearty food.

Pet Sounds Bar (Map pp396-7; ☎ 643 8225; www.petsoundsbar.se; Skånegatan 80; mains from Skr119) A strong contender for coolest new hang-out in Stockholm, this place, opened by the folk who run the nearby Pet Sounds record shop, has a sleek black-tiled bar, B&W rock photos on the walls and good DJ nights.

Mosebacke Etablissement (Map p402; ☎ 5560 9890; www.mosebacke.se; Mosebacketorg 3) Even if you're not partaking in Mosebacke's many cool club nights, its terrace bar in summertime is a fantastic place to relax.

Ice Bar (Map p402; ☎ 5056 3000; Vasaplan; ☽ 4.30pm-midnight Mon-Fri, 3pm-midnight Sat) It's worth feeling like a tourist for a visit to the Ice Bar; whether it's worth the Skr125 entry charge is another question, but you do get to see a mini version of the famed Ice Hotel, filled with sculptures and shivering cuties in puffy coats. The temperature is a constant -5°C and the vodka comes in glasses made of ice. Refills are Skr85.

El Cubanito (Map pp396-7; ☎ 650 1238; Scheelegatan 3) A worn-in bodega feel and pressed-tin bar make this small Cuban joint feel authentic and worlds away from snowy Stockholm.

Akkurat (Map p402; ☎ 644 00 15; Hornsgatan 18) This old beer hall has a great patio for summertime drinking, plus a good selection of microbrewed beer and delicious plates of mussels.

Grodan Grev Ture (Map p402; ☎ 679 6100; Grev Turegatan 16; mains from Skr95) Drinks and swanky seafood dishes at this très chic bar are merely an excuse to sit outdoors and be looked at.

Tures (Map p402; Sturegallerian shopping mall) Just across the street from Grodan Grev Ture, inside a highbrow shopping mall, is this surprisingly comfortable place with its sleek red-tinted design flourishes.

Two outdoor restaurant-bars on the bridge leading across to Djurgården, the **Sailor's Cafe** (Map pp396-7; Strandvägskajen 27) and its neighbour, **Djurgårdsbrons Sjöcafé** (Map pp396-7; ☎ 660 5757; Djurgårdsbron), are perfect for long leisurely drinks and summertime people-watching.

ENTERTAINMENT

'På Stan' (On the Town) is an arts-and-culture supplement found in the Friday edition of **Dagens Nyheter** (www.dn.se in Swedish), one of Stockholm's two main daily newspapers. **Nöjesguiden** (www.nojesguiden .se) is a free, monthly, music-focused entertainment paper with lots of club listings. Both these publications are written in Swedish only but most of the listings and advertisements for events are easy enough to understand.

The **Ticnet** (www.ticnet.se) website has information in English about larger events.

Theatre

Stockholm is a theatre city, with outstanding dance, opera and music performances; for an overview, pick up the free **Teater Guide** (www.iti.a.se) from tourist offices or online. For tickets, contact the tourist office, theatre box offices or **Biljett Direkt** (☎ 0771-707070; www.ticnet.se). Operas are usually performed in their original language, while theatre performances are invariably in Swedish.

Kungliga Dramatiska Teatern (Map p402; ☎ 667 0680; www.dramaten.se; Nybroplan) The Royal Theatre (aka Dramaten), an unmissable Art Nouveau building resembling a large, gilded wedding cake, stages a range of plays and is the unofficial home of Ingmar Bergman.

Konserthuset (Map p402; ☎ 5066 7788; www.kon serthuset.se; Hötorget) This large blue building on Hötorget is a main venue for classical concerts and other musical events, including the Royal Philharmonic Orchestra.

Kungliga Operan (Map p402; ☎ 248240; www.op eran.se; Gustav Adolfs Torg) The royal opera house is the place to go for opera and classical ballet.

Nightclubs

Most of Stockholm's best clubs charge an entrance fee, at least at the weekend, of around Skr100. At many, you're also required to check your coat at the door (Skr10 to 35).

La Habana (Map pp396-7; ☎ 166465; Sveavägen 108) Salsa is big in Stockholm, and this is one of the least pretentious places to sample it; the small basement bar features cigars, rum and dangerously attractive barkeepers.

Kvarnen (Map pp396-7; ☎ 643 0380; Tjärhovsgatan 4) If this bar were a hairstyle, it would be a mullet: business up front, party in the back. DJ nights range from reggae to house. Queues are constant and the doormen are not to be trifled with – just hand over your coat and don't fuss.

Spy Bar (Map p402; ☎ 5450 3704; Birger Jarlsgatan 20; admission Skr125; ☿ Wed-Sat) Once Stureplan's crown jewel, 'the Puke' (so nicknamed because *spy* is Swedish for 'vomit') may have lost some of its gleam, but its prime location on Stureplan is still pretty cool, and these days you might actually stand a chance of getting in.

Live Music

Live jazz is popular in the capital and the **Stockholm Jazz Festival** (www.stockholmjazz.com) is held annually in mid-July. Summer sees outdoor concerts performed at places such as Gröna Lund Tivoli (p399).

Glenn Miller Café (Map p402; ☎ 100322; Brunns gatan 21) This intimate place is the most likely venue for live shows that even local jazz snobs won't sneer at.

Jazzclub Fasching (Map p402; ☎ 5348 2960; www .fasching.se; Kungsgatan 63) Well-known and reliable, Fasching attracts fairly big-name acts from around the world.

Stampen (Map p402; ☎ 205793; www.stampen.se; Stora Nygatan 5) More for good-time boogiers than strict jazz aficionados, this Gamla Stan standby is a fun place to watch Nordic types get their groove on.

Mosebacke Etablissement (Map p402; ☎ 5560 9890; www.mosebacke.se; Mosebacketorg 3) This excellent bar, club and concert venue atop the ridge of Södermalm hosts all sorts of music and performers.

Nalen (Map p402; ☎ 5052 9200; Regeringsgatan 74) This grand, old-school dance hall puts on a wide range of concerts and club nights. Its small basement club, Alcazar, has live rock and pop bands most nights.

Gay & Lesbian Venues

The gay scene is well established in Stockholm, although Sweden's famous open-mindedness means that nonheteros are welcome in almost all bars and clubs, and there is no real 'gay district'. The best source of sass and information is the free monthly mag **QX** (www.qx.se).

Lady Patricia (Map p402; ☎ 743 0570; www.lady patricia.se; Stadsgårdskajen 152) Patricia is a ship that's been moored near Slussen and converted into a nightclub; it's known for gay nights (complete with drag shows) that draw partiers of all persuasions every Sunday.

Popular gay restaurant-bars on Gamla Stan include **Mandus** (Map p402; ☎ 206055; Österlånggatan 7) and **Torget** (Map p402; ☎ 205560; Mälartorget 13).

SHOPPING

Stockholm's fascination with style and design means there are endless opportunities to pick up clothing and interior-design items from top-notch names. Swedish-made crafts tend to be of a uniformly high quality. Some of the best souvenirs include the country's famous glassware; painted wooden horses from Dalarna; intricately carved woodwork; linen tablecloths and handtowels; and amber and silver jewellery. If you're planning to spend up and you come from outside the EU, see p472 for details on tax-free shopping.

Look out for *hemslöjd* signs, indicating handicraft sales outlets. Another good place to buy traditional items is at Skansen (p399).

Shops in Stockholm are generally open 10am to 6pm Monday to Friday, 10am to 5pm Saturday and noon to 4pm Sunday, although smaller shops are often closed on Sunday and have limited Saturday hours.

DesignTorget (www.designtorget.se) Kulturhuset (Map p402; ☎ 5083 1520; basement, Kulturhuset, Sergels Torg) Södermalm (Map p402; ☎ 462 3520; Götgatan 31) A great place to pick up bargain gifts, this Stockholm chain is a showcase for the work of both established and up-and-coming young designers.

Filippa K (Map p402; ☎ 5458 8256; Grev Turegatan 18) Stockholm clothing designer Filippa K has several boutiques in town, including this one at the end of a long, sloping hallway; walk down it and hope you shrink like Alice in Wonderland.

Svensk Hemslöjd (Map p402; ☎ 232115; Sveavägen 44) The flagship store for the Society of Swedish Handcrafts, here you'll find everything from textiles to pottery made by Swedish artisans.

Svenskt Hantverk (Map p402; ☎ 214726; Kungsgatan 55) A similar range of goods is available here, with special prominence given to the famous carved wooden Dalarna horses.

NK (Map p402; ☎ 762 8000; Hamngatan) The best selection of souvenirs can be found in the basement of NK department store. There's also a gourmet grocery here.

Other handy department stores include **Åhlens** (Map p402; ☎ 676 6000; Klarabergsgatan 50) and **PUB** (Map p402; ☎ 402 1611; Drottninggatan 72-76).

GETTING THERE & AWAY
Air

See p473 for information on international flights to Sweden, and p476 for domestic flights.

Stockholm's main airport, **Arlanda** (Map p414; ☎ 797 6000), is 45km north of the city centre and has all the facilities you could need, including **Sidewalk Express** (per hr Skr19) internet terminals. **Bromma airport** (Map p414; ☎ 797 6874), 8km west of Stockholm, is a minor airport used for some domestic flights. Two airports are used by some low-cost carriers and sometimes labelled as 'Stockholm', despite being a fair distance from the capital: **Skavsta airport** (☎ 0155-280 400) is 100km south of Stockholm, near Nyköping, and **Västerås airport** (☎ 021-805600) is near Västerås, about 105km northwest of Stockholm. Transport connects the city with all airports (see opposite). Infor-

---

BSTOCKHOLM'S TOP FIVE SHOPPING STREETS

Biblioteksgatan (Map p402) Big-name fashion-designer boutiques in the Östermalm area.

Drottninggatan (Map p402) A central pedestrian mall full of the practical, the affordable, and the blatantly blue-and-yellow.

Götgatan (Map pp396-7, Map p402) The main artery through Södermalm, lined with offbeat shops and galleries.

Hamngatan (Map p402) Department store NK on one side, shopping centre Gallerian on the other.

Västerlånggatan (Map p402) Gamla Stan's mecca for souvenirs (tacky and otherwise).

mation about facilities at each airport can be found on the website of Sweden's civil aviation authority, **Luftfartsverket** (www.lfv.se).

Boat

See p475 for details of international ferry connections from Stockholm and areas surrounding the city to Finland (Helsinki and Turku), Estonia (Tallinn) and Latvia (Riga). When booking tickets, inquire about buses run by the ferry companies from Cityterminalen to their harbours.

Frihamnen, about 3km northeast of the city centre, is the arrival and departure point for **Tallink** (Map p402; ☎ 666 6001; www.tallink.ee; Klarabergsgatan 31) ferries to/from Tallinn. To get to Frihamnen, take a connecting bus from Cityterminalen operated by the ferry company, or town bus Nos 1, 72 or 76.

Silja Line Office (Map p402; ☎ 222140; www.silja .com; Kungsgatan 2) ferries depart for Helsinki and Turku from Värtahamnen, north of Frihamnen – take the connecting bus, walk from T-Gärdet or take local bus No 76 from T-Ropsten.

Viking Line (Map p402; ☎ 452 4000; www.viking line.fi; Cityterminalen) ferries sail to Turku and Helsinki from the terminal in northeast Södermalm (Map pp396–7). Take the connecting bus from Cityterminalen or walk 1.5km east of T-Slussen.

Bus

Cityterminalen (Map p402; ☒ 3.30am-midnight) is above and next door to Centralstationen (follow the signs from within the main station hall, or use the street entrance on Klarabergsviadukten). From Cityterminalen there are long-distance buses to most major towns in Sweden and international destinations; airport buses (to Arlanda, Bromma, Skavsta and Västerås, see right); and ferry buses (to connect with the services of Silja Line, Viking Line, Destination Gotland and Tallink; see p475 for international ferry details). Cityterminalen has good facilities, including ATMs, foreign exchange, stores, cafés, lockers and internet access.

Train

Stockholm is the hub for the national services of **Sveriges Järnvag** (SJ; ☎ 0771-757575; www .sj.se), see p479. Direct trains to/from Copenhagen, Oslo, Storlien (for Trondheim) and

Narvik arrive and depart from Centralstationen (Stockholm C), as do the SL *pendeltåg* (commuter) services that operate within Stockholm county (see p412). The central hall at **Stockholm Centralstationen** (Map p402; ☒ 5am-12.30am) has all manner of facilities, including restaurants, shops, lockers, ATMs, internet access and public toilets and showers.

Train ticket offices are open as follows:
Domestic 7.30am to 8pm Monday to Friday, 8.30am to 6pm Saturday, 9.30am to 7pm Sunday
International 10am to 6pm Monday to Friday

GETTING AROUND
To/From the Airports
ARLANDA

The **Arlanda Express** (Map p402; ☎ 020-222224; www.arlandaexpress.com) train travels between Arlanda and Centralstationen (Skr200, 22 minutes) at regular intervals from around 5am to midnight (every 15 minutes from 6am to 10.30pm).

A cheaper option is the **Flygbussarna** (☎ 600 1000; www.flygbussarna.se) bus service to/from Cityterminalen (Skr95, 40 minutes). From the airport, Flygbus drivers can arrange to have a Flygtaxi meet you at one of several drop-off points and take you directly to your door (from Skr140); call ☎ 686 1010 to arrange a lift to the airport.

OTHER AIRPORTS

There are **Flygbussarna** (☎ 600 1000; www.flygbus sarna.se) bus services from Cityterminalen to Bromma airport (Skr69, 15 to 20 minutes), Skavsta airport (Skr130, 80 minutes), and Västerås airport (Skr130, 75 minutes).

Bicycle

Stockholm has an extensive network of bicycle paths; tourist offices sell cycling maps but they're not usually necessary. Top day trips include: Djurgården; a loop going from Gamla Stan to Södermalm, Långholmen and Kungsholmen (on lakeside paths); Drottningholm (return by steamer); and Haga Park. Some long-distance routes are marked all the way from central Stockholm.

Bicycles can be carried free on SL local trains during off-peak times (ie not from 6am to 9am and 3pm to 6pm Monday to Friday), but they're not allowed in Central-stationen or the metro.

SWEDEN

Djurgårdsbrons Sjöcafé (Map pp396-7; ☎ 660 5757; Djurgårdsbron), by the bridge to Djurgården, rents bikes for Skr65/250 per hour/day and has options for longer rentals. Not far away, **Cykel & Mopeduthyrningen** (Map pp396-7; ☎ 660 7959; Strandvägen kajplats 24), by the OK-Q8 petrol station, also rents bikes for around the same price.

Boat

Djurgårdsfärjan city ferry services, operated by SL, connect Djurgården with Nybroplan and Slussen, with many trips calling in at Skeppsholmen.

Strömma Kanabolaget (Map p402; ☎ 5871 4000; www.strommakanalbolaget.com) operates ferries between Nybroplan and Djurgården (Skr18 to Skr30; every 20 minutes 10am to 8pm daily mid-May to mid-August, weekends and holidays April to mid-May and mid-August to September). Strömma Kanabolaget also runs boats to Drottningholm (see p415) and Birka (see p416).

Waxholmsbolaget (Map p402; ☎ 679 5830; www .waxholmsbolaget.se) runs boats year-round between Djurgården and Slussen (adult/child Skr30/20, every 10 to 20 minutes from 7am Monday to Friday and from 9am on weekends, running to midnight, from late April to mid-September, less frequently in the low season). Trips are free with the SL Tourist Card, but not with the Stockholm Card.

Car & Motorcycle

Driving in central Stockholm is not recommended: small one-way streets, congested bridges and limited parking all present problems and car parks (P-hus) charge up to Skr50 per hour (the fixed evening rate is usually more reasonable). There's also a complicated new tax on driving in the heart of the city, implemented to help ease congestion. If you have a car, one of the best, hassle-free options is to stay on the outskirts of town and catch public transport into the centre.

Public Transport

Storstockholms Lokaltrafik (SL; ☎ 600 1000; www .sl.se) runs all tunnelbana (T or T-bana) metro trains, local trains and buses within Stockholm county. At T-Centralen (Map p402) there are SL information offices in the lower level of the station hall and at the Sergels Torg entrance. Both offices issue timetables

and sell SL transport passes and the Stockholm Card. You can call for schedule and travel information from 7am to 9pm Monday to Friday and 8am to 9pm weekends.

The Stockholm Card (p394) allows you to travel on all SL trains and buses in greater Stockholm, as well as providing free entry to many city attractions. A cheaper alternative is to buy an SL Public Transport pass (Skr60/180 for 24/72 hours), covering transport only. If you want to explore the county in rather more detail, bring along a passport photo and get yourself a 30-day SL pass (adult/child Skr600/360).

A new fare system for Stockholm's public transport means each trip takes a coupon good for two hours, with no zone limits. Coupons are available individually for Skr20, or in packs of 10 for Skr180 (available at SL offices and Pressbyrå newsagents). International rail passes aren't valid on SL trains.

BUS

Bus timetables and route maps can be complicated but are worth studying. Inner-city buses can be replaced by the tunnelbana or by walking, but useful connections to suburban attractions radiate from Sergels Torg, Fridhemsplan (on Kungsholmen), Odenplan and Slussen: bus No 47 runs from Sergels Torg to Djurgården (stopping out the front of Centralstationen); bus No 65 goes from Centralstationen to Skeppsholmen (for STF Vandrarhem af Chapman hostel); and bus No 69 runs to the Ladugårdsgärdet museums and also to Kaknästornet.

Check where the regional bus hub is for different outlying areas. Islands of the Ekerö municipality (including Drottningholm Palace) are served by bus Nos 301 to 323 from T-Brommaplan. Buses to Vaxholm (No 670) and the Åland ferries (bus No 640 to Norrtälje then No 637 to Grisslehamn or No 631 to Kapellskär) depart from T-Tekniska Högskolan. Odenplan is the hub for buses to the northern suburbs, including Haga Park.

METRO

The most useful mode of transport in Stockholm is the tunnelbana (T), which converges on T-Centralen and is connected by an underground walkway to Centralstationen. There are three main through lines with branches – check that the approaching train is actually going your way.

TRAIN

Local trains (called *pendeltåg*) are useful for connections to Nynäshamn (for ferries to Gotland); Märsta (for buses to Sigtuna and Arlanda airport); and Södertälje. There are also services to Nockeby (from T-Alvik); Lidingö (from T-Ropsten); Kårsta, Österskär and Näsbypark (from T-Tekniska Högskolan); and Saltsjöbaden (from T-Slussen).

TRAM

Djurgårdslinjen No 7 (Map pp396-7; ☎ 660 7700; www.ss.se; adult/child Skr25/13) is a historical tram running between Norrmalmstorg and Skansen on weekends from April to December (daily June to August), passing most attractions on Djurgården. Separate fees apply for Stockholm Card–holders, but the SL Tourist Card is valid.

Taxi

There's usually no problem finding a taxi in Stockholm; costs are about Skr35 for flagfall, then Skr8 to Skr9 per kilometre (more expensive late on Friday and Saturday nights). A trip within the city shouldn't cost more than Skr200. Reputable firms:
Taxi 020 (☎ 020-939393)
Taxi Kurir (☎ 300000)
Taxi Stockholm (☎ 150000)

AROUND STOCKHOLM

Most locals will tell you that the one thing not to miss about Stockholm is leaving it – whether for a journey into the lovely rock-strewn archipelago or an excursion into the surrounding countryside. Within easy reach of the capital are idyllic islands, Viking gravesites, cute fishing villages and sturdy royal palaces.

NORTHERN SUBURBS

One of Stockholm's loveliest attractions is **Millesgården** (Map p414; ☎ 446 7594; www.millesgarden.se; Carl Milles väg 2, Lidingö; adult/child Skr80/free; ☑ 11am-5pm mid-May–Sep, noon-5pm Tue-Sun Oct–mid-May), a superb sculpture park and museum of works by Carl Milles. It's on Lidingö island with great views to the mainland; take the metro to T-Ropsten then bus No 207.

The extensive **Naturhistoriska Riksmuseet** (Map p414; ☎ 5195 4040; www.nrm.se; Frescativägen 40; admission free; ☑ 10am-7pm Tue-Fri, 11am-7pm Sat & Sun; Ⓜ T-Universitet), founded by Carl von Linné in 1739, is the national museum of natural history, and includes the Imax theatre and planetarium **Cosmonova** (Map p414; ☎ 5195 5130; adult/child Skr75/50; ☑ 10am-8pm Tue-Sun).

The large parks that extend from Djurgården in the south form **Ekoparken** (www.ekoparken.com), a 27-sq-km national city park and the first such protected city area in the world. The area is perfect for cycling tours.

Haga Park (Map p414) is also pleasant for walks and bicycle tours with attractions including the royal **Gustav III's Pavilion**, **Butterfly House** and colourful **Copper Tent**. To reach the park, take bus No 515 from Odenplan to Haga Norra.

FJÄDERHOLMARNA

These tiny islands (the 'Feather Islands') offer an easy escape from the city – they're just 25 minutes away by boat (off the east coast of Djurgården) and are a favourite swimming spot for locals. Take one of the boats (Skr80 return, buy tickets on board) that leave from either Nybroplan (half-hourly) or Slussen (hourly) from May to early September. There are a couple of restaurants here and the last boats leave the islands at around midnight, making them a perfect spot to enjoy the long daylight hours.

FERRY PORTS

Nynäshamn, 50km south of Stockholm, is the main gateway to Gotland (see p451 for more); there are also regular ferries to Gdańsk (Poland). Regular local (SL) trains run from Stockholm to Nynäshamn; you can use SL passes, but international rail passes are not valid. There are also direct bus services from Stockholm's Cityterminalen to connect with the Gotland ferries (Skr85), leaving 1¾ hours before ferry departure times.

Ferries sail between tiny **Kapellskär** (90km northeast of Stockholm) and Turku (Finland) via the Åland islands (see p475). The ferry companies offer a direct bus from Stockholm Cityterminalen to meet the ferries, but you can also take bus No 640 from T-Tekniska Högskolan to Norrtälje and change there to No 631, which

SWEDEN

runs every two hours or so (infrequent at weekends).

The quickest and cheapest ferries to the Ålands depart from **Grisslehamn**, about 100km from Stockholm; SL passes apply on bus No 637, which runs regularly from Norrtälje. **Eckerö Linjen** (☎ 0175-25800; www .eckerolinjen.fi) ferries sail from Grisslehamn to Eckerö (Åland; Skr50/80 low/high season, bicycles free, two hours, five daily). The company runs regular bus connections from Uppsala and from T-Tekniska Högskolan (Stockholm) to Grisslehamn two hours before most boat departures (Skr110/140 low/high season, including ferry ticket).

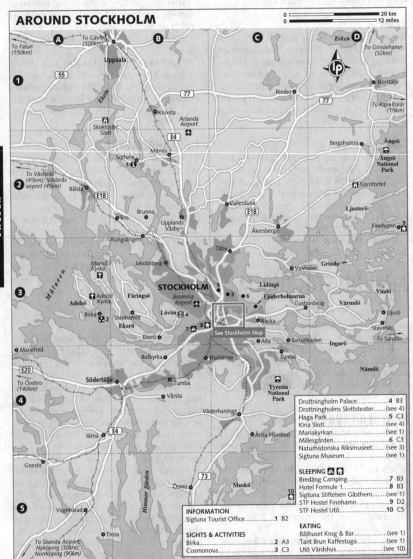

AROUND STOCKHOLM

0 — 20 km
0 — 12 miles

Drottningholm Palace	**4** B3
Drottningholms Slottsteater	(see 4)
Haga Park	**5** C3
Kina Slott	(see 4)
Mariakyrkan	(see 1)
Millesgården	**6** C3
Naturhistoriska Riksmuseet	(see 3)
Sigtuna Museum	(see 1)

SLEEPING
Bredäng Camping	**7** B3
Hotel Formule 1	**8** B3
Sigtuna Stiftelsen Gästhem	(see 1)
STF Hostel Finnhamn	**9** D2
STF Hostel Utö	**10** C5

INFORMATION
Sigtuna Tourist Office	**1** B2

SIGHTS & ACTIVITIES
Birka	**2** A3
Cosmonova	**3** C3

EATING
Båthuset Krog & Bar	(see 1)
Tant Brun Kaffestuga	(see 1)
Utö Värdshus	(see 10)

SWEDEN

VAXHOLM
☎ 08 / pop 9500

Vaxholm, about 35km northeast of the city, is the gateway to the central and northern reaches of Stockholm's archipelago and it swarms with tourists in summer. It has a collection of quaint summerhouses that were fashionable in the 19th century. The oldest buildings are in the Norrhamn area, a few minutes' walk north of the town hall, but there's also interesting architecture along Hamngatan (the main street), plus galleries, boutiques, souvenir shops and cafés.

Take bus No 670 from T-Tekniska Högskolan or one of the frequent **Waxholmsbolaget** (Map p402; ☎ 679 5830; www.waxholmsbolaget.se) boats from Strömkajen (outside the Grand Hôtel; Skr65).

STOCKHOLM ARCHIPELAGO
☎ 08

The archipelago is the favourite time-off destination for Stockholm's locals, and summer cottages on rocky islets are popular among the well-to-do. Depending on which source you read, the archipelago has anything between 14,000 and 100,000 islands, although the common consensus is 24,000; many are worth visiting and you could almost choose your destination via the dartboard method. The **Stockholm** (www.stockholmtown.com) website has a large section devoted to the archipelago, and the **Archipelago Foundation** (www.skargardsstiftelsen.se) is another great resource.

The biggest boat operator is **Waxholmsbolaget** (Map p402; ☎ 679 5830; www.waxholmsbolaget.se). Timetables and information are available online or from offices outside the Grand Hôtel on Strömkajen in Stockholm and at the harbour in Vaxholm. Its Båtluffarkortet (Skr300) is a pass valid for five days giving unlimited rides plus a handy island map; if you have a 30-day SL card, it costs Skr490 to add on 30 days of unlimited ferry travel. Bikes can be taken on the ferries for a fee, but it's a better idea to hire at your destination.

It's also worth checking what **Cinderella Båtarna** (☎ 5871 4000; www.cinderellabatarna.com) has to offer. Its boats also go to many of the most interesting islands from Stockholm. If your time is short, a recommended tour is the Thousand Island Cruise offered by **Strömma Kanabolaget** (Map p402; ☎ 587 14000; www.strommakanalbolaget.com), running daily between July and mid-August. The full day's excursion departs from Stockholm's Nybrokajen at 9.30am and returns at 8.30pm; the price (Skr775 to Skr900) includes lunch, dinner and guided tours ashore. The tour visits a number of islands, and there are several opportunities for swimming.

While many islands can be visited on a day trip, you'll get a better experience and fewer crowds if you stay overnight. Most main islands have hostels, but they tend to open only in summer and they're often booked out months in advance. For information on cottage rental (usually on a weekly basis), contact **Destination Stockholms Skärgård** (☎ 5424 8100; www.dess.se).

Chichi **Sandhamn** village on Sandön is popular with sailors and day-trippers; if you'd like to stay overnight, **Sands Hotell** (☎ 5715 3020; www.sandshotell.se; s/d Skr1400/1650) has style and all the modern luxuries you'd expect.

Finnhamn has excellent swimming spots, but book in advance to stay at the **STF hostel** (Map p414; ☎ 5424 6212; www.finnhamn.se; dm/s/d Skr275/410/550); it has 80 beds but they fill up quickly.

Utö, far out in the southern archipelago, is popular among cyclists. Reception for the STF hostel is at the nearby **Utö Värdshus** (☎ 5042 0315; www.uto-vardshus.se; dm Skr325; ☼ May-Sep), ranked among the best restaurants in the archipelago. It also offers an array of hotel and cottage accommodation; see the website for details.

EKERÖ DISTRICT
☎ 08 / pop 22,600

Some 20km west of Stockholm and surprisingly rural, the **Ekerö district** (www.ekeroturism.se) consists of several large islands in Lake Mälaren, the Unesco World Heritage Listed sites of Drottningholm and Birka, and a dozen medieval churches.

Drottningholm

The main Renaissance-inspired **Drottningholm Palace** (Map p414; ☎ 402 6280; www.royalcourt.se; adult/child Skr70/20; ☼ 10am-4.30pm May-Aug, noon-3.30pm Sep, noon-3.30pm Sat & Sun Oct-Apr), with its geometric baroque gardens, was built late in the 17th century, about the same time as, and clearly in the model of, Versailles. The highlights are the baroque Karl X Gustav Gallery,

Hedvig Eleanora's fiercely blue bedroom and the painted ceilings of the state bedchamber. The palace is home to the Swedish royal family, and you can either walk around the wings open to the public on your own or take a one-hour guided tour (no additional charge; English tours at 11am, noon, 1pm and 3pm daily from June to August, reduced schedules during the rest of the year).

The unique **Drottningholms Slottsteater** (Map p414; ☎ 5569 3100; www.drottningholmsslottsteater.dtm.se; tours Skr60/40; ⏰ noon-4.30pm May, 11am-4.30pm Jun-Aug, 1-3.30pm Sep) is the original 18th-century court theatre and is well worth a tour, especially the backstage sound-effects department; ask about opera, ballet and musical performances here in summer.

At the far end of the gardens is the 18th-century **Kina Slott** (Map p414; ☎ 402 6270; adult/child Skr60/25; ⏰ 11am-4.30pm May-Aug, noon-3.30pm Sep), a lavishly decorated 'Chinese pavilion' that was built as a gift to Queen Lovisa Ulrika. Admission includes an entertaining guided tour.

It can add up to an expensive day out if you wish to see everything at Drottningholm. Given the separate admission charges for each attraction, it's a good idea to use the Stockholm Card. You can bring a picnic and enjoy it in the gardens, or dine in one of the two restaurants by the palace. If you're not short of time you could cycle out here, otherwise take the metro to T-Brommaplan and change to bus Nos 301 or 323. The most pleasant way to get to Drottningholm is by boat: **Strömma Kanalbolaget** (Map p402; ☎ 5871 4000; www.strommakanalbolaget.com) has boats that depart from Stadshusbron in Stockholm daily from May to mid-September (Skr95/125 one way/return).

Birka

At the fascinating Viking trading centre of **Birka** (Map p414; ☎ 5605 1445; www.raa.se; ⏰ May-Sep), a Unesco World Heritage Site on Björkö in Lake Mälaren, archaeologists have excavated the ancient settlement's cemetery, harbour and fortress. Cruises to Birka run from May to mid-September; the return trip with **Strömma Kanalbolaget** (Map p402; ☎ 5871 4000; www.strommakanalbolaget.com) from Stadshusbron, Stockholm, is a full day's outing (Skr255). A visit to the museum and a guided tour in English of the settlement's burial mounds and fortifications are included in the price.

SIGTUNA

☎ 08 / pop 6500

About 40km northwest of Stockholm is the picturesque lakeside town of Sigtuna, the oldest surviving town in Sweden. It was founded in about 980; the first Swedish coins were struck here in 995. There's a popular **Medieval Festival** in July and good holiday markets throughout December. The friendly **tourist office** (Map p414; ☎ 5948 0650; www.sigtuna.se/turism; Stora gatan 33) can help with inquiries, tours and tickets to local events.

Ten runestones still stand in various places around Sigtuna, and 150 more dot the surrounding landscape. Stora gatan is probably Sweden's oldest main street, and there are ruins of 12th-century churches around town. The mid-13th-century **Maria-kyrkan** (Map p414), Sigtuna's most arresting sight, contains restored medieval paintings. The friendly **Sigtuna Museum** (Map p414; ☎ 5978 3870; Stora gatan 55; adult/child Skr30/free; ⏰ noon-4pm Jun-Aug, noon-4pm Tue-Sun Sep-May) displays finds from excavations of the area.

If you're looking to stay overnight, there's little budget accommodation in town. Those with their own wheels should look for signs advertising *stugor* (cabins) at local farmhouses (usually Skr200 to 300) or ask at the tourist office. **Sigtuna Stiftelsen Gästhem** (Map p414; ☎ 5925 8900; www.sigtunastiftelsen.se; Manfred Björkquists allé 2-4; s/d Skr800/950) is a pretty place run by a Christian foundation.

There are a number of good cafés and restaurants to choose from, plus supermarkets for picnic supplies (and tables by the lake, among the ducks). Don't miss the delightful **Tant Brun Kaffestuga** (Map p414; ☎ 5925 0934; Laurentii gränd 3; snacks Skr20-40), a 17th-century café with a worryingly saggy roof and pretty courtyard just off Stora gatan. **Båthuset Krog & Bar** (Map p414; ☎ 5925 6780; Strandvägen; mains Skr180-240; ⏰ dinner Tue-Sun) is a classy restaurant and bar, on a pontoon in the lake by the guest harbour.

Travel connections are easy from Stockholm. Take a local train to Märsta, from where there are frequent buses to Sigtuna (bus Nos 570 or 575, half-hourly). In summer there are cruises on Lake Mälaren from Stockholm and Uppsala (stopping at the fine baroque castle Skokloster, around 26km by road northwest of Sigtuna).

SVEALAND

This area, the birthplace of Sweden, offers the visitor much evidence of the region's long history, including rune stones so plentiful you're likely to stumble over a few. Pre-Viking burial mounds in Gamla Uppsala light the imaginations of myth-builders and history buffs. There's also the old mine in Falun, which accidentally provided the means for all those little cottages dotting the landscape to be painted red. And in Mora, the definitive Swedish king's path towards the crown is still retraced today, by thousands of skiers each year in the Vasaloppet.

UPPSALA

☎ 018 / pop 191,100

Uppsala's huge pink castle and prominent *domkyrka* (cathedral) give it an instantly recognisable silhouette. The fourth-largest city in Sweden, it's a university town where young people and old buildings meet over coffee. About 70km from Stockholm, it makes a good excursion and has decent budget accommodation. You can soak up history and beer in equal measure.

Gamla (Old) Uppsala flourished as early as the 6th century. The cathedral was consecrated in 1435 after 175 years of construction and the castle was first built in the 1540s, although today's edifice belongs to the 18th century. The city's university was founded in 1477 and is Scandinavia's oldest.

Information

Forex (Fyristorg 8; ☉ Mon-Sat) Currency exchange next door to the tourist office.

Port 22 (Sankt Olofsgatan 32; per hr Skr40) Internet access. Enter through the courtyard.

Public library (cnr Sankt Olofsgatan & Svartbäcksgatan; ☉ Mon-Sat) Offers free internet access, but expect long waits.

Tourist office (☎ 27 4800; www.uppsalatourism .se; Fyristorg 8; ☉ 10am-6pm Mon-Fri, 10am-3pm Sat year-round, noon-4pm Sun late Jun–mid-Aug) Close to the cathedral. Ask about the summer-only Uppsala Card (Skr100 for 24 hours), which gives you free admission to many of the town's sights plus free local transport.

UNT City Internet Café (cnr Fyristorg & Drottninggatan; per hr Skr25; ☉ Mon-Sat) Internet access right by the tourist office, inside the *Upsala Nya Tidning* newspaper office, with tealight candles charmingly decorating the computers.

Sights

GAMLA UPPSALA

A great excursion for imaginative history buffs, especially in nice weather, is Gamla Uppsala – the city's beginnings, consisting of three great **grave mounds** 4km north of the modern city and well signposted (take bus No 2 from Stora Torget). The mounds are said to be the graves of legendary pre-Viking kings and lie in a cemetery including about 300 smaller mounds and a great heathen temple. Even more fascinating is all the myth-making that has grown up around the grave mounds. A 17th-century professor, Olof Rudbeck, argued that Gamla Uppsala was actually the ancient sunken city of Atlantis, just for example.

For more myths, rumours and some of the actual science surrounding the site, visit **Gamla Uppsala Historical Centre** (☎ 239300; www.raa.se/olduppsala; adult/child Skr50/30; ☉ 11am-5pm May-Aug, noon-3pm Sun Sep-Apr). The museum has exhibits of ancient artefacts excavated from Gamla Uppsala and the nearby archaeological sites. Guided tours will help you get more out of your visit – these are held at 3pm daily from May to August and are included in the entry price of the museum.

Christianity arrived in the 11th century and with it the bishops and other church officials. From 1164 the archbishop had his seat in a cathedral on the site of the present **church**, which, by the 15th century, was enlarged and painted with frescoes.

Next to the flat-topped mound Tingshögen is the **Odinsborg Inn**, known for its horns of mead and the Viking feasts at its restaurant, but it's also home to a small café. **Disagården** (admission free; ☉ mid-May–Aug), a farm and village museum, is a few minutes from the church.

UPPSALA SLOTT

Originally constructed by Gustav Vasa in the mid-16th century, **Uppsala Slott** (castle; ☎ 727 2485; adult Skr60; ☉ tours 1pm & 3pm Jun-Aug) features the state hall where kings were enthroned and a queen abdicated. It's open by guided tour only. Midsummer and other holidays are frequently marked by ringing the **Gunilla klockan**. The **Botanic Gardens** (admission free; ☉ 7am-9pm May-Aug, 7am-7pm Sep-Apr) are below the castle hill and include the Carl Linnaeus orangery.

OTHER SIGHTS

The Gothic **Domkyrka** (admission free; Domkyrkoplan; ☯ 8am-6pm) dominates the city, just as some of those buried there dominated their country, including St Erik, Gustav Vasa, Johan III and Carl von Linné. Inside, visit the **treasury** (☎ 187201; adult/child Skr30/free; ☯ daily May-Sep, Tue-Sun Oct-Apr) in the north tower.

Gustavianum Museum (☎ 471 7571; www.gustavianum.uu.se; Akademigatan 3; adult/child Skr40/30; ☯ Tue-Sun), the university museum, has an excellent antiquities collection and features an old 'anatomical theatre'. **Uppland Museum** (☎ 169100; Sankt Eriks Torg; admission free; ☯ Tue-Sun), in an 18th-century mill, houses county collections from the Middle Ages.

Carolina Rediviva (☎ 471 3900; Dag Hammarskjöldsväg 1; adult Skr20; ☯ daily mid-May–mid-Sep, Mon-Sat mid-Sep–mid-May) is the old university library and has a display hall with maps and historical and scientific literature, the pride of which is the surviving half of the 6th-century *Codex Argentus* (Silver Bible).

The **Linné Museum** (☎ 471 2576; Svartbäcksgatan 27; adult/child Skr30/free; ☯ noon-4pm Tue-Sun Jun–mid-Sep) exhibits memorabilia of von Linné's work in Uppsala, and its **gardens** (adult/child Skr30/free; ☯ May-Sep), with more than 1000 herbs, were designed according to an 18th-century plan.

Just west of the Botanic Gardens is the fascinating **Bror Hjorth's hus** (☎ 567030; Norbyvägen 26; adult/child Skr30/free; ☯ noon-4pm Tue-Sun). The home and studio of the Swedish sculptor and

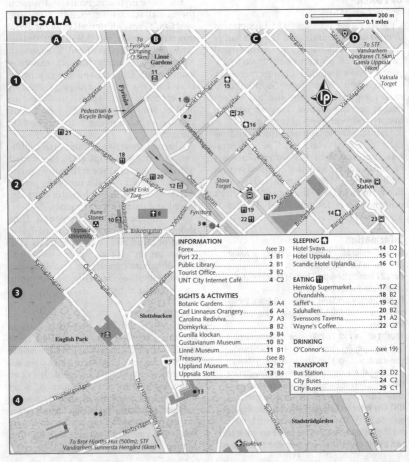

UPPSALA

0 ——————— 200 m
0 ——————— 0.1 miles

To Fyrishov Camping (1.5km)

Linné Gardens

To STF Vandrarhem Vandraren (1.5km); Gamla Uppsala (4km)

Vaksala Torget

Pedestrian & Bicycle Bridge

Stora Torget

Train Station

Sankt Eriks Torg

Fyristorg

Rune Stones

Uppsala University

Biskopsgatan

Slottsbacken

English Park

Stadsträdgården

To Bror Hjorths Hus (500m); STF Vandrarhem Sunnersta Herrgård (6km)

Sjuktius

INFORMATION	
Forex	(see 3)
Port 22	1 B1
Public Library	2 B1
Tourist Office	3 B2
UNT City Internet Café	4 C2

SIGHTS & ACTIVITIES	
Botanic Gardens	5 A4
Carl Linnaeus Orangery	6 A4
Carolina Rediviva	7 A3
Domkyrka	8 B2
Gunilla klockan	9 B4
Gustavianum Museum	10 B2
Linné Museum	11 B1
Treasury	(see 8)
Uppland Museum	12 B2
Uppsala Slott	13 B4

SLEEPING	
Hotel Svava	14 D2
Hotel Uppsala	15 C1
Scandic Hotel Uplandia	16 C1

EATING	
Hemköp Supermarket	17 C2
Ofvandahls	18 B2
Saffet's	19 C2
Saluhallen	20 B2
Svenssons Taverna	21 A2
Wayne's Coffee	22 C2

DRINKING	
O'Connor's	(see 19)

TRANSPORT	
Bus Station	23 D2
City Buses	24 C2
City Buses	25 C1

painter (1894–1968) are jam-packed with his work and collections, as well as rotating exhibits of current Scandinavian artists.

Sleeping

Fyrishov Camping (☎ 727 4960; www.fyrishov.se; Idrottsgatan 2; camp sites Skr130, 4-bed cabins from Skr695) This well-equipped, family-friendly camping ground is 2km north of the city, on the river at Fyrisfjädern and neighbouring a huge pool and sports complex. Take bus Nos 4, 6, 25 or 50.

Hotel Uppsala (☎ 480 5000; www.profilhotels.se; Kungsgatan 27; hostel dm/s/d Skr250/435/600, hotel s/d from Skr1050/1275;) It looks dull from the outside, but this hotel has some excellent-value rooms with all the trappings you'd normally find in a more expensive place, and rooms are discounted to Skr700. There are also hostel rooms, a laundry, wheelchair access, a good restaurant and lounge, and free internet access.

STF Vandrarhem Sunnersta Herrgård (☎ 324220; Sunnerstavägen 24; hostel dm/s/d Skr235/385/470, hotel s/d Skr590/680) Some 6km south of the centre in a beautiful green setting is this old manor house. Hostel rooms are small, or you can pay extra for a 'hotel' room – a larger room (still with shared bathroom) with linen and breakfast included. Bike rental is available. Take bus Nos 20 or 50.

STF Vandrarhem Vandraren (☎ 104300; www.vandraren.com; Vattholmavägen 16; s/d Skr295/485; mid-Jun–mid-Aug) This is a second, summer STF hostel 2km north of town. It's a student residence the rest of the year and facilities, including private bathroom for each room, are top-notch. Bike rental is available. Take bus Nos 2, 20, 24 or 54.

Hotel Svava (☎ 130030; www.hotelsvava.com; Bangårdsgatan 24; s/d Skr1325/1625, discount Skr675/800) Opposite the train station, this hotel (now part of the Comfort Inn chain) has all the facilities of an upper-range business-style hotel, and offers good weekend and summer prices.

Eating & Drinking

There are several eateries on and around the pedestrian mall and Stora Torget, and around the cathedral. Visitors can also head to Sysslomansgatan for some good choices.

Saffet's (☎ 124125; Stora Torget 1; meals Skr59) When it comes to quick sustenance and cheap food, Saffet's has the works – burgers, enchiladas, baked potatoes, fish and chips, and kebabs.

Svenssons Taverna (☎ 100908; Sysslomansgatan 14; mains Skr80-185; dinner Mon-Fri, lunch & dinner Sat & Sun) Pottery Barn meets the Ancient Mariner in the decorating scheme of this upscale eatery, with a nice outdoor patio and a menu of gourmet Swedish staples.

Ofvandahls (☎ 132404; Sysslomansgatan 3-5) This is a classy *konditori* full of old-world charm.

Wayne's Coffee (☎ 710012; Smedsgränd 4) Wayne's has good coffee and café fare in stylish modern surrounds.

Hemköp supermarket (Stora Torget) In the basement of Åhlens the central shopping centre, this supermarket is open until 10pm nightly.

Saluhallen (Sankt Eriks Torg; Mon-Sat) The indoor produce market is between the cathedral and the river. Pop in for a browse and a bite to eat – it houses great stalls and cafés.

O'Connor's (☎ 144010; Stora Torget 1; mains Skr59-180) Upstairs from Saffet's, O'Connor's is much as you'd hope for in an Irish pub anywhere in the world – crowded, lively, friendly and well stocked with Guinness. There's also live music most nights.

Getting There & Away

The **bus station** (Kungsgatan) is outside the train station. Bus No 801 (the Flygbus) departs at least twice an hour for nearby Arlanda airport (Skr80). **Swebus Express** (☎ 0200-218218; www.swebusexpress.se) runs regularly to Stockholm (Skr55), Örebro (Skr185) and Falun (Skr135). Frequent **SJ trains** (☎ 0771-757575; www.sj.se) run to/from Stockholm (Skr47 to 62); all train services to/from Gävle, Östersund and Mora stop in Uppsala. SL coupons or passes take you only as far as Märsta from Stockholm.

Getting Around

A local bus ticket costs from Skr20 and gives unlimited travel for two hours – just enough for a visit to Gamla Uppsala. Catch a city bus from Stora Torget or outside **Scandic Hotel Uplandia** (Dragarbrunnsgatan). **Upplands Lokaltrafik** (☎ 0771-141414) runs regional transport within the county; if you're staying long in the area, ask about rebate cards and the various passes available.

You can hire a bicycle at Fyrishov Camping (left) or the STF hostels (left), or inquire at the tourist office.

SWEDEN

ÖREBRO

☎ 019 / pop 125,000

A castle that looks like it's floating on water, pretty gardens to wander through at leisure, people bicycling everywhere – Örebro has to be one of the most post-card-friendly towns in Sweden. There's a river lined with pink-and-green houses drifting lazily through the city centre, and a bustling square that's a great place for people-watching.

The **tourist office** (☎ 212121; www.orebro.se/turism; ⏰ 10am-6pm Mon-Fri, 10am-4pm Sat & Sun Jun-Aug, 10am-6pm Mon-Fri, 10am-2pm Sat & Sun Sep-May) is inside the castle. The **library** (Näbbtorgsgatan) is south of the town centre and has internet access, as does **Video Biljarden** (Järntorget; per hr Skr35; ⏰ 11am-midnight).

Sights

Admission to the once-powerful **Slottet** (☎ 212121; adult/child Skr50/free), now fully restored, includes a castle tour (in English at 1.30pm and 3.30pm daily mid-June to mid-August; the rest of the year, all tours are in Swedish at 1pm on weekends). Tickets can be purchased from the tourist office.

Outside the castle is the **Örebro Länsmuseum** (☎ 602 8700; Engelbrektsgatan 3; admission free; ⏰ 11am-5pm), the combined regional and art museums.

A pleasant stroll east of the castle along the river will take you through Stadsparken. Bikes are available to rent from May to September from the **kiosk** (Hamnplan) on the river's edge.

In Stadsparken, the **Stadsträdgården** green-house precinct has a great café and, further east, there's the excellent **Wadköping** museum village, which has craft workshops, a bakery and period buildings. You can freely wander around here at any time, but the shops, exhibitions and museums are generally open from 11am to 4pm Tuesday to Sunday.

The commercial centre and some grand buildings are around Stortorget, including the 13th-century **St Nikolai kyrka** (⏰ Mon-Sat).

Sleeping & Eating

STF Vandrarhem Örebro (☎ 310240; www.hepa.se in Swedish; Kaptensgatan 1; dm/s/d from Skr185/315/370) This hostel is very well hidden, some 1.6km northeast of the train station (get hold of a map before setting off). It has good facilities, including some en-suite rooms, and bike hire is available. Take bus Nos 16 or 31.

Livin' Lägenhetshotell (☎ 310240; www.livin.nu in Swedish; apt per night for 1 week Skr400) Next door to Vandrarhem Örebro and run by the same management is this complex of bright, modern apartments. Each apartment has a fully equipped kitchen, bathroom and living area, and can sleep up to four (at a push).

First Hotell Örebro (☎ 611 7300; www.firsthotels.se; Storgatan 24; s/d from Skr1095/1495, discount Skr595/995) In a good location close to the bus and train stations, as well as the castle, this classy hotel offers comfortable rooms in a variety of sizes, and good discounted rates.

Restaurang & Café Stadsträdgården (☎ 139835; Floragatan 1; lunch buffet Mon-Fri/Sat & Sun Skr75/98) Make a beeline for this lovely area in Stadsparken, with a restaurant (lunch only) and café (open until 4pm) surrounded by lush plant life inside a greenhouse.

Slottskällaren (☎ 156960; Drottninggatan 1; lunch Skr79, mains Skr110-250) For something a little more formal, this elegant restaurant located inside the Elite Hotel (right by the castle) serves good-value lunches and posher dinners, including a decent vegetarian selection.

Bishop's Arms (☎ 156920; Drottninggatan 1; pub meals under Skr100) Also part of the hotel, this English-style pub has an outdoor terrace that overflows with bright young things in summertime.

Getting There & Away

You're well placed to go almost anywhere in southern Sweden from Örebro by long-distance buses, which leave from opposite the train station. **Swebus Express** (☎ 0200-218218; www.swebusexpress.se) has connections in all directions: to Norrköping; Karlstad and Oslo; Mariestad and Göteborg; Västerås and Uppsala; and Eskilstuna and Stockholm.

Train connections are similarly good. Direct **SJ trains** (☎ 0771-757575; www.sj.se) run to/from Stockholm every hour; to get to Göteborg, take a train to Hallsberg and change there. Other trains run daily to Gävle and Borlänge (where you can change for trains to Falun and Mora).

FALUN

☎ 023 / pop 54,600

Falun, traditionally the main centre of Dalarna, is a cluster of crooked pedestrianised streets and a main square, intriguingly slanted, that's capped by an imposing church. The town is synonymous with mining and with Stora, perhaps the world's oldest public company (first mentioned in 1288), and the mine is now World Heritage Listed and accessible to visitors. The popular **Falun Folkmusik festival** (www.falufolk .com) features world music as well as Nordic folk traditions and is held over four days in mid-July.

The **tourist office** (☎ 83050; www.visitfalun.se; Trotzgatan 10-12; ⏰ daily mid-Jun–mid-Aug, Mon-Sat mid-Aug–mid-Jun) can help with information. There's free internet at the **library** (Kristinegatan 15), and **Billiard & IT Café** (Falugatan 4; per hr Skr40; ⏰ Mon-Sat) is a central internet café.

Sights & Activities

The **Kopparberget copper mine** (☎ 782030; www .kopparberget.com; mine tour & museum adult/child Skr100/50, museum only Skr20/free) was the world's most important by the 17th century and only closed in 1992 (it's now on Unesco's World Heritage List). As a by-product, the mine also provided the red coating that became the characteristic house paint of the age and is still in popular use today throughout Sweden. The mine and museum are west of town at the top end of Gruvgatan (take bus No 709). You can go on an interesting one-hour tour of the bowels of the disused mine (bring warm clothing) or just check out the museum; call in advance to find out the times of English-language tours. On weekdays from October to April it's necessary to book tours in advance.

Carl Larsson-gården (☎ 60053; www.carllarsson .se; tour adult/child Skr90/40; ⏰ 10am-5pm daily May-Sep, 11am-5pm Mon-Fri Oct-Apr) is the beautiful early-20th-century home of the artist Carl Larsson and his wife Karin in the pretty village of Sundborn (13km from Falun; bus No 64). It's a bright, lively house with superb colour schemes, decoration and furniture. Tapestries and embroidery woven by Karin Larsson reveal she was as skilled an artist as her husband. Admission is by 45-minute guided tour only; call in advance for times of English tours.

There's more folk culture at **Dalarnas Museum** (☎ 765500; Stigaregatan; adult/child Skr40/20), along with some cutting-edge temporary exhibits of Swedish artists. This fine museum features local culture and art, and Nobel-winning novelist Selma Lagerlöf's study is preserved here.

The baroque interiors of **Kristine kyrka** (Stora Torget) show some of the riches that arrived in Falun, but don't miss the late-14th-century **Stora Kopparbergs kyrka**, the oldest building in town, off Mariabacken and a bit north of the centre.

Falun is a winter-sports centre with plenty of **ski runs**, **nordic courses** and **toboggan runs**, particularly in the Lugnet area, to the northwest. Take bus Nos 705 or 713.

Sleeping & Eating

STF Vandrarhem Falun (☎ 10560; www.stfvandrarhem .falun.just.nu; Vandrarvägen 3; dm/s/d Skr185/225/410) This large hostel is 3km east of the town (bikes are available for hire), with excellent facilities. Take bus Nos 701 or 712 to Koppartorget, from where it's a 10-minute walk.

Falu Fängelse Vandrarhem (☎ 795575; www .falufangelse.se; Villavägen 17; dm/s/d Skr200/300/400) A more central option is this friendly, well-equipped hostel, where accommodation is in the simple cells of an old prison, used up until the mid-1990s.

Hotel Falun (☎ 29180; www.hotelfalun.nu; Trotzgatan 16; s/d from Skr540/740, discount Skr490/590) There are a few good hotel choices right by the tourist office, including this small place offering comfortable modern rooms with private toilet and shared shower (or you can pay extra for rooms with full private bathroom).

Café Kopparhattan (☎ 19169; Stigaregatan; lunch from Skr75) This café is the pick of the town's lunchtime haunts, attached to Dalarnas Museum – it was being renovated at the time of research. Choose from tempting sandwiches, soups and cakes, or feel virtuous and fill up at the great-value vegetarian buffet.

Banken Bar & Brasserie (☎ 711911; Åsgatan 41; lunch Skr75, mains Skr115-225) A classy place with a grand interior, formerly a bank. The menu includes a *gott & enkelt* (good and simple) category featuring the likes of *gravad lax* (cured salmon), burgers and pasta (Skr105 to Skr130), plus fancier creations such as bouillabaisse or rack of lamb.

SWEDEN

Getting There & Away

Falun isn't on the main railway lines – change at Borlänge when coming from Stockholm or Mora. **Swebus Express** (☎ 0200-218218; www.swebusexpress.se) has buses on the Göteborg–Karlstad–Falun–Gävle route, and also has connections to buses on the Stockholm–Borlänge–Mora route (some run via Uppsala).

Traffic in the region is run by **Dalatrafik** (☎ 0771-959595; www.dalatrafik.se) and covers all corners of the county of Dalarna. Tickets cost Skr17 for trips within a zone, and Skr17 extra for each new zone. A 31-day *Länskort* (County Card) costs Skr900 and allows you to travel throughout the county. Regional bus No 70 runs regularly on the Falun–Rättvik–Mora route.

LAKE SILJAN REGION

This pretty, traditional area in the county of Dalarna is a popular summer- and winter-sports destination, with reasonable-sized towns offering good facilities and attractions. Siljansleden (the Siljan Trail) extends for more than 300km around Lake Siljan and has **walking** and **cycling** paths – maps are available from tourist offices. Another way to enjoy the lake is by boat: in summer, MS *Gustaf Wasa* has a complex schedule of lunch, dinner and sightseeing cruises from the main towns of Mora, Rättvik and Leksand. Inquire at any of the area's tourist offices for a schedule. Also check out the **Siljan** (www.siljan.se) website. Tourist offices in the area can all help with accommodation, including cottages in the idyllic countryside.

In summer the area is busy with events: Leksand's **Midsummer Festival** is the most popular in Sweden. **Musik vid Siljan** (www.musikvidsiljan.se) is a week-long event taking place in early July with something to suit most tastes, including chamber, jazz and traditional folk music. The stunning Dalhalla venue in Rättvik (right) hosts an **opera festival** in early August.

Rättvik & Around

☎ 0248

Rättvik (population 10,900) has sandy lakeside beaches for summer and ski slopes for winter. Don't miss the longest wooden pier in Sweden, the 625m **Långbryggan** out over the lake. Views from surrounding hills are excellent. Try the 725m-long **rodel run** (☎ 51300; 1/3 rides Skr45/110; ☼ Jun-Aug), a sort of summer bobsled chute in the hills east of town that's lots of fun. The **tourist office** (☎ 797210; rattvik@siljan.se; Hwy 70; ☼ daily mid-Jun–mid-Aug, Mon-Fri mid-Aug–mid-Jun) is at the train station.

By the lake northwest of the train station, the 13th-century **church**, rebuilt in 1793, has 87 well-preserved **church stables**, the oldest dating from 1470. Further north is **Gammelgården** (☎ 51445; tours Skr45; ☼ mid-Jun–mid-Aug), an open-air museum with a good collection of furniture painted in local style.

Inviting all sorts of bad puns about rocking out, **Dalhalla** (☎ 797950; www.dalhalla.se), an old limestone quarry 7km north of Rättvik, is used as an open-air concert venue in summer. The setting is stunning and allegedly was discovered by an opera singer testing acoustics. Tickets start around Skr165, see tourist offices in the area for a programme of concerts, or check the website.

Tiny **Tällberg**, midway between Rättvik and Leksand, is a pretty village of wooden buildings scattered like a handful of rubies along a hillside, and it's nearly as expensive if you want to stay the night. It has a population of around 200 and no fewer than eight upmarket hotels (most with attached restaurants), plus a few galleries and boutiques. But it's a lovely place to enjoy lunch and have a wander – don't miss the huge pink Dala horse on someone's front lawn. See the **Tällberg** (www.infotallberg.nu in Swedish) website, which has links to all the hotels. Bus No 58 between Rättvik and Leksand stops in the village regularly, and it's worth going just for the scenic landscape along the route.

On the lakeshore near the train station is **Siljansbadets Camping** (☎ 51691; www.siljansbadet.com; camp sites Skr105-155, 4-bed cabins from Skr310). **Rättviksparken** (☎ 56110; www.rattviksparken.fh.se in Swedish; camp sites Skr110-150, cabins from Skr330) is by the river off Centralgatan (1km from the train station). Both camping grounds are large, well equipped and crowded in high season; book ahead if you're planning to travel between mid-June and mid-August.

By Rättviksparken camping ground is the highly rated hostel **STF Vandrarhem Rättvik** (☎ 10566; rattviksparken@rattviksparken.fh.se; Centralgatan; dm/s/d from Skr175/195/350), in a charming complex of old wooden buildings.

Behind the OK-Q8 petrol station on the main road to Leksand, about 3km south of town, is the not-quite-camouflaged **Hotell Vidablick** (☎ 30250; www.hantverksbyn.se; Faluvägen; s/d from Skr600/850), offering rustic hotel accommodation sneakily disguised in grass-roofed huts. There's a restaurant on site.

The cheapest eateries are opposite the train station, and Storgatan is home to a few supermarkets. You might want to head to Tällberg or Mora for other evening options, as Rättvik doesn't excel in the restaurant department. The cute **Restaurang Anna** (☎ 12681; Vasagatan 3; mains Skr95-160; ☺ Tue-Sun) is the best option for finer dining in Rättvik. It's a good midrange place in a pretty wooden cottage serving up Swedish and international dishes, including fish, lamb, pork and reindeer.

Buses depart from outside the train station. The **Dalatrafik** (☎ 0771-959595; www .dalatrafik.se) bus No 70 runs between Falun, Rättvik and Mora. Direct trains from Stockholm and Mora stop at Rättvik.

Mora

☎ 0250 / pop 20,000

The popular legend is that, in 1520, King Gustav Vasa fled on skis from Mora after hiding from the Danes. (Historians now tend to think it's more likely he travelled on snowshoes, but that's not as glamorous.) Two good yeomen of Mora chose to brave the winter and follow. **Vasaloppet**, the huge ski race that ends in Mora, commemorates Gustav's journey on the first Sunday every March. It involves 90km of gruelling nordic skiing and about 15,000 people.

The **tourist office** (☎ 592020; mora@siljan.se; Stationsvägen; ☺ daily mid-Jun–mid-Aug, Mon-Fri mid-Aug–mid-Jun) is at the train station.

The ski race that puts Mora on the map is comemmorated in **Vasaloppsmuseet** (☎ 39225; Vasagatan; adult/child Skr30/10; ☺ daily mid-May–Aug, Mon-Fri Sep–mid-May), with interesting displays about the event and the story behind it. Mora's other big draw is the **Zornmuseet** (☎ 592310; www.zorn.se; Vasagatan 36; adult/child Skr60/2), celebrating the works and private collections of the Mora painter Anders Zorn. The highlight is an enormous self-portrait done almost entirely in black, a test run for one commissioned by the Uffizi. The Zorn family house, **Zorngården** (☎ 592310; Vasagatan

36; tours adult/child Skr50/15), between the church and the museum, is an excellent example of a wealthy artist's house, reflecting Zorn's National Romantic aspirations. Access to the house is by guided tour only, every 30 minutes, in Swedish unless requested in advance.

The Dalahästar (Dala horses) are wooden horses painted in bright, cheerful colours, and to many they represent the original, genuine symbol of Sweden, more powerful than the Swedish flag. The most reputable of the Dalahästar are made by **Nils Olsson Hemslöjd** (☎ 37200; ☺ daily mid-Jun–mid-Aug, Mon-Sat mid-Aug–mid-Jun) at Nusnäs, 10km southeast of Mora (bus No 108). Here you can inspect the workshops and buy up big at the souvenir outlet.

Outside the town of Orsa (16km north of Mora) is **Grönklitt Björnpark** (☎ 46200; www.orsa gronklitt.se; adult/child Skr95/55; ☺ mid-May–mid-Sep), where you can see bears, wolves and lynxes in fairly natural surrounds. The bears are usually fed around noon, when you'll get a great view of them. To get here, take bus No 104 from Mora to Orsa, then bus No 118 to the park.

SLEEPING & EATING

Mora Parken (☎ 27600; www.moraparken.se in Swedish; Hantverkaregatan; camp sites from Skr155, cabins from Skr270) This busy, family-friendly camping ground has good facilities in a great spot by the river northwest of the church.

Målkull Ann's Pensionat (☎ 38196; www.maalkull ann.se; Vasagatan 19; r from Skr600) Housed in a series of more and less rustic buildings is this B&B in the centre of town, with a good range of accommodation choices (with and without private bathroom). Call ahead, as reception hours vary a lot depending on the season.

STF Vandrarhem Mora (☎ 38196; Fredsgatan 6; dm/s/d from Skr205/395/530) This excellent hostel is owned by Ann of Målkull Ann's Pensionat and booked through the Pensionat's office.

Hotell Kung Gösta (☎ 15070; www.trehotell.nu in Swedish; Kristinebergsgatan 1; s/d from Skr995/1150, discount Skr695/895; ☐ ☐) This large hotel, conveniently located opposite the main train station, has business-style rooms. There's a free internet terminal in the hotel foyer.

Kristineberg Hostel (☎ 15070; www.trehotell .nu in Swedish; Kristinebergsgatan 1; dm from Skr130, s/d with private bathroom Skr445/620; ☑) Kung Gösta's hostel annexe has en-suite rooms, kitchen facilities, a huge lounge area, linens and breakfast included.

There are a few old-style cafés on Kyrkogatan, plus fast-food joints and supermarkets. All the hotels also have pub-restaurants.

Claras Restaurang (☎ 15898; Vasagatan 38) This place next to Zornmuseet has been a reliable place for light meals and pizzas and was undergoing renovations at the time of research.

GETTING THERE & AWAY

All **Dalatrafik** (☎ 0771-959595; www.dalatrafik.se) buses use the **bus station** (Moragatan 23). Bus No 70 runs to Rättvik and Falun. Bus No 170 goes to Särna, Idre and Grövelsjön, near the Norwegian border.

Mora is an **SJ** (☎ 0771-757575; www.sj.se) terminus and the southern terminus of *Inlandsbanan* (the historic train that travels through Norrland), which runs north to Gällivare in summer (see p479). The main train station is about 1km east of town, by the lake. The more central Mora Strand is a platform station in town but not all trains stop there, so check the timetable.

You can rent bikes from **Intersport** (☎ 593 939; Kyrkogatan).

SKÅNE

Everyone loves Skåne. It would be hard not to. Wearing its proximity to Denmark on its sleeve, **Skåne** (www.skanetur.se) offers the mildest weather on Sweden's mainland and some of the most beautiful pastoral scenery you'll find outside of a frame. Sometimes called Scania, this area was Danish until the mid-17th century – the influence of the Danish is still easily detected in the dialect and architecture. Many natives of Skåne feel more strongly tied to nearby Copenhagen than Stockholm – and they certainly go that direction more often for entertainment.

Being so flat and lovely, Skåne is popular with cyclists; there are numerous attractions in the gently rolling landscape and more hostels than any other region of Sweden. Other treats include castles, historic cities and the pretty coastline.

MALMÖ

☎ 040 / pop 265,000

Malmö is as pretty as it is dynamic, with a well-preserved old town circled by a canal, plus a castle complex, numerous parks and wide, walkable avenues. It's connected to the rest of Europe by the impressive, 7.8km-long Oresunds bridge to Copenhagen. South of the centre is the lively square Möllevång-storget, the focus of a working-class neighborhood that played a strong role in the early labour movement. It's now lined with multi-ethnic shops, restaurants and pubs.

Orientation

The old town is the city centre and is encircled by a canal. There are three main squares here: Stortorget, Lilla Torg and Gustav Adolfs Torg. Malmöhus castle, in its park setting, guards the west end. Across the canal on the northern side you'll find the bus and train stations.

Information

Dot.Spot (Kalendegatan 13; per hr Skr10-18; ☾ noon-6am) Cool, industrial-designy internet café.

Forex (Centralstationen; ☾ 7am-9pm) Currency exchange.

Library (Regementsgatan; ☾ closed Sun May-Aug)

Malmö Card (1/2/3 days Skr130/160/190 for) Allows free bus transport, free entry to several museums and discounts at other attractions; available from the tourist office.

Post Office (Skeppsbron 1; ☾ 7am-7pm Mon-Fri) Near the train station.

Tourist office (☎ 341200; www.malmo.se; Central-stationen; ☾ 9am-7pm Mon-Fri, 10am-5pm Sat & Sun Jun-Aug, 9am-6pm Mon-Fri, 10am-2pm Sat & Sun May & Sep; 9am-5pm Mon-Fri, 10am-2pm Sat & Sun Oct-Apr) Inside the train station. Pick up the useful, free booklet *Malmö this Month*.

Zeze (Engelbrektsgatan 13; per hr Skr30) Internet café open until 11pm or midnight daily; cheaper rates after 6pm.

Sights & Activities

The cobbled streets and interesting buildings around **Lilla Torg** are restored parts of the late-medieval town – the oldest of the half-timbered houses here was built in 1597. The houses are now occupied by galleries, boutiques and restaurants.

The main museums of Malmö are based in and around **Malmöhus** (☎ 344437; www .malmo.se/museer; Malmöhusvägen; adult/child Skr40/10; ☾ 10am-4pm Jun-Aug, noon-4pm Sep-May). You can walk through the royal apartments, see the **Stadsmuseum** with its Malmö collection, and see works by important Swedish artists such as John Bauer and Sigrid Hjerten at the **Konstmuseum** (admission Skr40). There's also an **aquarium** and **Naturmuseum**. The old **Kommendanthuset** arsenal is opposite the castle and **Teknikens och Sjöfartens Hus** is to the west. The latter is a well-presented technology and maritime museum displaying aircraft, motor vehicles, steam engines and a submarine.

Boat tours of the canals run regularly from late April through September from the kiosk of **Rundan** (☎ 611 7488; www.rundan.se; tours adult/child Skr75/40), by the canal, opposite Centralstationen.

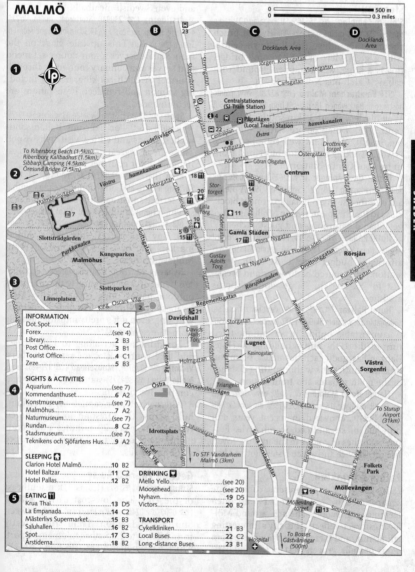

SWEDEN

Ribersborg is a long sandy beach backed by parkland about 2km west of the town centre. Out in Öresund, reached by a 200m-long pier, is the naturist **Ribersborgs Kallbadhus** (☎ 260366; www.ribban.se; admission Skr50), dating from 1898. There's a cold, open-air, saltwater pool and wood-fired sauna, and separate sections for men and women. Take bus No 32.

Sleeping

Sibbarp Camping (☎ 155165; Strandgatan 101; camp sites Skr150-190, cabins from Skr280) By the beach about 5km southwest of the town centre, with a great view of the Öresund bridge, this is a large, well-equipped ground with cabins. Catch bus Nos 12B or 12G.

STF Vandrarhem Malmö (☎ 82220; www.malmo hostel.com; Backavägen 18; dm/s/d from Skr175/325/460) Well hidden, about 3.5km south of the city centre (get a map before setting off), this big, bright, clean and well-equipped place is worth seeking out. Catch bus No 21 from in front of Centralstationen.

Bosses Gästvåningar (☎ 326250; www.bosses.se; Södra Förstadsgatan 110B; s/d/tr Skr315/450/550) A pleasant guesthouse in a regular apartment block, close to the cheap eateries on Möllevångstorget. Shared bathrooms and guest kitchens.

Hotel Pallas (☎ 611 5077; home.swipnet.se/Hotell _Pallas; Norra Vallgatan 74; s Skr450, d from Skr550) An affordable budget hotel close to the train station, with shared bathrooms and breakfast for Skr30. The 'large' double rooms are huge.

Hotel Baltzar (☎ 665 5700; www.baltzarhotel.se; Södergatan 20; s/d from Skr980/1300, discount Skr700/850) A comfortable option in an antique-filled turn-of-the-19th-century building, the Hotel Baltzar has good facilities and a bountiful breakfast buffet. It's within spitting distance of the main squares and train station.

Clarion Hotel Malmö (☎ 71020; www.choicehotels .se; Engelbrektsgatan 16; s/d Skr1525/1890, discount Skr790/ 990) Nicely renovated in recent years and now full of streamlined Scandi style. Features splashes of colour in the inviting foyer, friendly service and a nice restaurant and bar.

Eating & Drinking

Lilla Torget is a picturesque cobblestone square lined by restaurant-bars and often teeming with people. The area around Möllevångstorget reflects the city's interesting ethnic mix, and there's cheap food here from a mix of stalls, grocers, restaurants and bars.

Saluhallen (Lilla Torg; ⊙ Mon-Sat) One of the best lunchtime pit stops, with an excellent range of food stalls offering something to appeal to every taste, including pasta, sushi, kebabs and Vietnamese food.

La Empanada (☎ 120262; Själbodgatan 10; mains Skr35-50; ⊙ 11am-9pm Mon-Sat) Recommended cheap and cheerful cafeteria, with a huge menu of mainly Mexican dishes, plus pasta and even Swedish meatballs.

Årstiderna (☎ 230910; Stortorget; mains Skr225, 4-course menu Skr525; ⊙ 11:30am-midnight Mon-Fri, 5pm-midnight Sat) This upscale place on the main square serves a four-course set menu that serves as a culinary tour guide through gourmet Swedish cooking, usually including salmon and reindeer. Reservations are recommended.

Spot (☎ 124331; Stora Nygatan 33; dishes Skr49-75; ⊙ lunch Mon-Sat) For delicious Italian sandwiches, salads and coffee, visit stylish Spot. There are also great gelati available, and an Italian deli for gourmet picnic.

Krua Thai (☎ 122287; Möllevångstorget 14; lunch Skr65, mains Skr60-85) Long-standing eatery with a nice terrace and ornate wood-carved interior, serving cheap and plentiful Thai dishes.

Mästerlivs supermarket (Engelbrektsgatan; ⊙ 7am-9pm). Buy groceries at this central supermarket. The best produce market is on Möllevångstorget.

Nyhavn (☎ 128830; Möllevångstorget; mains Skr55-109) One of several bars with enormous outdoor patios on a corner facing Möllevångstorget, this is a good place for people-watching, even if it's pretty indistinguishable from its neighbours.

For drinking, get along to Lilla Torget and take your pick of the restaurant-bars. **Victors** (☎ 127670), **Moosehead** (☎ 120423) and **Mello Yello** (☎ 304525) stand side by side and compete for custom.

Alternatively, for capital-city diversions, head across the Öresund to Copenhagen (trains run every 20 minutes until midnight, then hourly until around 5am). See p474 for details.

Getting There & Away

Sturup airport (☎ 613 1100) is 31km southeast of the city. The low-cost carrier **Ryanair** (☎ 0900-202 0240; www.ryanair.com) flies between Sturup and London. Trains run directly from Malmö to Copenhagen's main airport, which has a better flight selection (p112).

SJ (☎ 0771-757575; www.sj.se) services (including X2000) run regularly to/from Göteborg and Stockholm, all via Lund.

Skånetrafiken (☎ 0771-777777; www.skanetrafiken.se) operates the local buses and trains in the southern region and sells a variety of value cards and passes. Local (purple) trains run to Helsingborg, Lund, Ystad and other nearby destinations. International rail passes are accepted.

Long-distance buses depart from a **bus terminal** (Skeppsbron) about 500m north of the train station. **Swebus Express** (☎ 0200-218218; www.swebusexpress.se) runs daily to Stockholm, Göteborg and Oslo. Trains are best for trips across the Öresund bridge – it takes just 35 minutes, see p474.

Getting Around

Malmö Lokaltrafik information kiosks are at main bus hubs, including Centralplan and Gustav Adolfs Torg. Local buses are green (regional buses are yellow); tickets cost Skr15 for one hour's travel. Bicycles can be rented from **Cykelkliniken** (☎ 611 6666; Regementsgatan 12; per day/week Skr120/600).

LUND

☎ 046 / pop 99,600

This comfortable and pretty place feels as friendly as a university town should. You can take a highbrow or a lowbrow approach to Lund, focusing on history and academics or lounging in student cafés – a little of both is best.

Lund is Sweden's second-oldest town, founded by the Danes around 1000. Much of the medieval town can still be seen. The university was founded in 1666 and today has 35,000 students. In summer it's a fairly quiet place, with the students on holiday and the tourist buses visiting.

The **tourist office** (☎ 355040; www.lund.se; Kyrkogatan 11; ☽ daily Jun-Aug, 10am-5pm Mon-Fri, 10am-2pm Sat Sep-May) is opposite the cathedral. The **library** (Sankt Petri Kyrkogatan 6; ☽ closed Sun May-Aug) has free internet access.

Sights & Activities

The spectacular **Kulturen** (☎ 350400; www.kulturen.com; Tegnerplatsen; adult/child Skr50/free; ☽ daily mid-Apr–Sep, Tue-Sun Oct–mid-Apr) claims to be the world's second-oldest open-air museum (it opened in 1892). Its impressive collection of about 40 buildings fills two blocks

and includes period homes from the 17th century and countless displays. Nearby, **Hökeriet** (☎ 350400; cnr St Annegatan & Tomegapsgatan; admission free; ☽ May-Sep) is an old-fashioned general store.

The magnificence of Lund's Romanesque **domkyrka** (cathedral) is well known, but for a real surprise visit at noon or 3pm (1pm and 3pm Sunday and holidays) when the astronomical clock strikes up. Just opposite the cathedral is the **Domkyrkomuseet**, where you can learn more about it, and the attached **Historiska Museet** (☎ 222 7944; Kraftstorg; ☽ 11am-4pm Tue-Fri) has pre-Viking Age finds. Combined entry to the two museums is Skr30/free for adults/children. There are a number of galleries, plus small, special-interest museums and archives in town, many attached to university departments. Inquire at the tourist office.

The **main university building**, which faces Sandgatan, is worth a glance inside, and Scanian rune stones are arranged in the park nearby. The **Botanic Gardens** with tropical **greenhouses** are east of the city centre.

Sleeping & Eating

Private rooms can be booked at the tourist office from around Skr250 per person plus a Skr50 fee.

STF Vandrarhem Tåget (☎ 142820; www.trainhostel.com; dm from Skr175) Take the overpass from the bus station to access this unusual hostel. Guests sleep in railway carriages set in parkland, with three bunks to a room.

Hotell Oskar (☎ 188085; www.hotelloskar.com; Bytaregatan 3; s/d Skr1295/1595, discount Skr795/995) This small, elegant boutique hotel has well-equipped rooms (with kettle, stereo, cable TV and DVD) right in the heart of town, each with furniture by noted Scandinavian designers. It's next door to the delightful Ebbas Skafferi; go there to inquire about rooms.

Grädhyllan Café, Restaurang & Hotell (☎ 157230; www.graddhyllan.com; Bytaregatan 14; s/d Skr595/850, discount Skr500/700) Book early to stay at central Grädhyllan, a lovely place offering four rooms above a café-restaurant at remarkably good prices.

Ebbas Skafferi (☎ 134156; Bytaregatan 5; dagens lunch Skr64; ☽ breakfast, lunch & dinner) This courtyard café with a great lunchtime selection is one of the most appealing places in town. A breakfast buffet is also available (Skr55).

SWEDEN

Govindas (☎ 120413; Bredgatan 28; lunch Skr35-65; ⓨ lunch Mon-Sat) Join the earnest student-types at friendly Govindas for the good-value vegetarian lunch deals.

Fellini (☎ 137020; Bangatan 6; mains Skr85-200) Fashionable Fellini, opposite the train station, serves up good Italian nosh, including gourmet pizzas for under Skr100 (less if you order takeaway), plus pasta, meat and fish dishes, and the all-important tiramisu and gelato. It's just as nice for a simple glass of wine.

GlassKulturen (Stortorget) The locals will stand in line all afternoon to get a sample of the frozen delights this little ice-cream nook churns out; 50,000 Lund-ites can't be wrong, right?

Saluhallen (Mårtenstorget; ⓨ Mon-Sat) This typical Swedish market hall is a great place to scrounge up some cheap and filling food, from pasta to Thai dishes and kebabs.

Getting There & Away

There are frequent **SJ** (☎ 0771-757575; www .sj.se) and regional train (*pågatågen*) departures from Lund to Malmö (15 minutes);

some trains continue to Copenhagen. All long-distance trains between Stockholm and Malmö stop in Lund. Buses leave from outside the train station. Buses go to Copenhagen, Stockholm, Göteborg, daily. See www.swebussexpress.se for updated timetables. For local bus info, contact Skånetrafiken on ☎ 771-777777 or on the web at www.skanetrafiken.se.

TRELLEBORG
☎ 0410 / pop 38,600

Trelleborg has Sweden's main ferry connections with Germany, but if you're arriving in Sweden here there's no reason to linger in town long – it's better to move on to Malmö or Ystad. The **tourist office** (☎ 733320; www.trelleborg.se; Hamngatan 9; ⓨ daily Jun-Aug, Mon-Fri Sep-May) is near the harbour. If you need a place to stay, **Night Stop** (☎ 41070; www.ho telnightstop.com; Östergatan 59; s/d/tr Skr199/299/399) is diagonally opposite the town museum, about 500m from the tourist office.

Bus No 146 runs every half-hour or so between Malmö and Trelleborg's bus station, 500m from the ferry terminals.

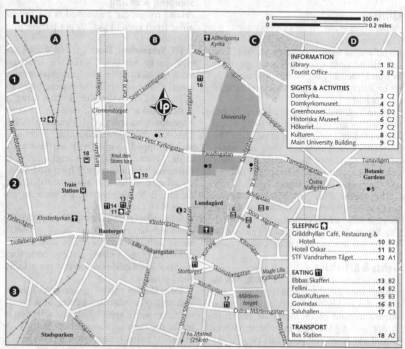

LUND

0 — 300 m
0 — 0.2 miles

INFORMATION
Library...............................1 B2
Tourist Office...................2 B2

SIGHTS & ACTIVITIES
Domkyrka.........................3 C2
Domkyrkomuseet.............4 C2
Greenhouses.....................5 D2
Historiska Museet............6 C2
Hökeriet..........................7 C2
Kulturen...........................8 C2
Main University Building....9 C2

SLEEPING
Gräddhyllan Café, Restaurang &
  Hotell.........................10 B2
Hotell Oskar.....................11 B2
STF Vandrarhem Tåget......12 A1

EATING
Ebbas Skafferi.................13 B2
Fellini.............................14 B2
GlassKulturen..................15 B3
Govindas.........................16 B1
Saluhallen.......................17 C3

TRANSPORT
Bus Station......................18 A2

SWEDEN

There are two ferry terminals, both behind the tourist office. **Scandlines** (☎ 0410-65000; www.scandlines.se) and TT-Line shuttle regularly across to the German ports of Sassnitz, Rostock and Travemünde. See p476 for information.

YSTAD
☎ 0411 / pop 26,200

A supremely attractive little town of half-timbered houses and meandering cobblestone streets, Ystad is also home to the melancholy fictional detective Kurt Wallander in Henning Mankell's *Dogs of Riga*. But most visitors will find no trace of the morose in this pretty medieval town. Photogenic houses line Stora Östergatan: most are from the latter half of the 18th century, but the façade of the beautiful **Änglahuset** (Stora Norregatan) dates from around 1630.

The **tourist office** (☎ 577681; www.visitystad .com; ⦿ daily late Jun-late Aug, Mon-Fri late Aug-late Jun) is opposite the train station. Next door is the large **Konstmuseum** (Art Museum; ☎ 577285; adult/child Skr30/free; ⦿ Tue-Sun). Don't miss the tiny, ornate medieval **Sankta Maria kyrka** (Stortorget; admission free) or the historical **Ystads Stadsmuseum** (☎ 577286; St Petri Kyrkoplan; adult/ child Skr30/free) in the old monastery church of Gråbrödraklostret.

One of Skåne's most intriguing attractions is **Ales Stenar** (adult/child Skr20/10), a ship setting made of 59 carefully arranged stones in the middle of a field 19km east of Ystad. The origins of the mysterious oval formation are most likely early Iron Age. It measures 67m along its long axis. Take bus No 322, and look for signs to Kåseberga, the nearby village.

Those with their own wheels can choose B&B or cottage options along the scenic coastal roads east or west of Ystad; inquire at the tourist office.

The small **Stationen Vandrarhem** (☎ 0708-577 985; www.turistlogi.se; dm/s/d Skr195/250/390) is centrally located in a renovated railway building at Ystad's train station. The well-equipped **STF Kantarellen Vandrarhem** (☎ 66566; www.tur istlogi.se; Fritidsvägen; dm/s/d Skr195/295/345) is 2km east of Ystad in a beachside recreation area. Bikes can be rented here. Take bus No 572.

Hotell Bäckagården (☎ 19848; www.backagar den.nu; Dammgatan 36; s/d from Skr590/720) is a cosy guesthouse in a 17th-century home behind the tourist office.

There are some lovely eating options among the historic buildings. For soup and sandwiches, seek out the charming **Book Café** (☎ 13403; Gåsegränd; ⦿ Tue-Sat) – inside there's a room full of mismatched furniture and books; outside is a leafy courtyard.

Bryggeriet (☎ 69999; Långgatan 20; lunch Skr75, mains Skr138-215) is an atmospheric restaurant and pub in an old brick brewery; there are copper beer kettles behind the bar, and cast-iron equipment lying around a gardenlike central courtyard.

Buses depart from outside the train station. To get to Trelleborg by bus, first take bus No 303 to Skateholm then transfer to bus No 183. *Pågatågen* trains run roughly hourly to/from Malmö.

Ferries run regularly between Ystad and Poland, and to the Danish island of Bornholm (see p476 and p475, respectively). The ferry terminal is just south of the train station.

HELSINGBORG
☎ 042 / pop 84,500

The busy port of Helsingborg is perched on the Öresund coastline, with Denmark only 20 minutes away by ferry. Many travellers leave town without seeing any more than the train station, but it's an appealing place with seaside character, quality budget accommodation and great parkland.

The **tourist office** (☎ 104350; Rådhuset; ⦿ daily May-Aug, Mon-Sat Sep-Apr) can help with inquiries. **First Stop Sweden** (☎ 104130; Bredgatan 2; ⦿ daily Jun-Aug, Mon-Fri Sep-May), near the car-ferry ticket booths, gives advice for new arrivals from Denmark.

Sights & Activities

The eye-catchingly modern **Dunkers Kulturhus** (☎ 107400; www.dunkerskulturhus.se; Kungsgatan 11; admission free; ⦿ 10am-5pm Tue-Sun), just north of the transport terminals, houses the **town museum** and **art museum** (combined entry adult Skr70), plus a concert hall, restaurant and café. Take a stroll along the northern waterfront from here to admire the sleek apartment buildings and restaurants, all part of a successful harbour redevelopment project.

You can access the square medieval tower **Kärnan** (☎ 105991; adult/child Skr20/10; ⦿ daily Jun-Aug, Tue-Sun Sep-May) from steps near the tourist office. The tower is all that remains of a

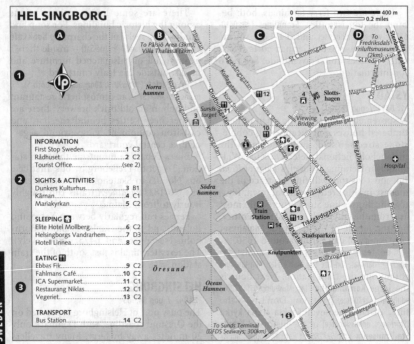

HELSINGBORG

INFORMATION
First Stop Sweden.................1 C3
Rådhuset.............................2 C2
Tourist Office.....................(see 2)

SIGHTS & ACTIVITIES
Dunkers Kulturhus.................3 B1
Kärnan................................4 C1
Mariakyrkan........................5 C2

SLEEPING
Elite Hotel Mollberg...............6 C2
Helsingborgs Vandrarhem........7 D3
Hotell Linnea.......................8 C2

EATING
Ebbas Fik...........................9 C2
Fahlmans Café....................10 C2
ICA Supermarket.................11 C1
Restaurang Niklas................12 C1
Vegeriet............................13 C2

TRANSPORT
Bus Station........................14 C2

14th-century castle; the view from the top (34m) overlooks Öresund to the Danish heartland.

Historic **Mariakyrkan** (Mariatorget) is worth a visit for its medieval features and choral and organ concerts.

Fredriksdals Friluftsmuseum (☎ 104500; admission free-Skr60) is off Hävertgatan, 2km northeast of the centre. It has a pretty manor, gardens, a café and a museum village – it's a lovely place for a stroll and is free or half-price in the low season. Highlights of the summer programme here include performances in the baroque open-air theatre. Take bus Nos 1 or 7.

North of the town, the **Pålsjö area** houses a fine park, the 16th-century Pålsjö Slott (closed to the public) and a nature reserve.

Sleeping

If you're visiting on a weekend or during summer, bear in mind that many upmarket hotels discount heavily at this time (double rooms around Skr800 to Skr900).

Villa Thalassa (☎ 380660; www.villathalassa.com; Dag Hammarskjöldsväg; dm Skr190, d from Skr440) This recommended hostel, 3km north of the city centre, is 500m from the bus stop at Pålsjöbaden. The villa and gardens are a delight, and there are three sleeping options in modern annexes and wooden huts. Take bus No 219 from Knutpunkten.

Helsingborgs Vandrarhem (☎ 145850; www.hbgturist.com; Järnvägsgatan 39; dm/s/d Skr165/245/370) This central hostel, inside a nondescript building about 200m from Knutpunkten, has high-quality rooms and good facilities.

Hotell Linnea (☎ 372400; www.hotell-linnea.se; Prästgatan 4; s/d from Skr965/1120, discount Skr750/895) The pick of the town's midrange offerings is this charming central hotel, with pretty décor and friendly management.

Elite Hotel Mollberg (☎ 373700; www.elite.se; Stortorget; s/d from Skr1120/1390, discount Skr650/750) You'll find a large number of upmarket options on Stortorget; try this grand place.

Eating & Drinking

Vegeriet (☎ 240303; Järnvägsgatan 25; mains Skr49-75; ☼ Mon-Fri) Vegetarians will rejoice at this café-restaurant, with menu items such as soup, curry, lasagne, tortilla and stir-fried dishes.

WORTH A TRIP

Hovdala Slott & Restaurant Mikkelsen (☎ 0451-186 15; www.restaurangmikkelsen.se in Swedish, www
.hovdalaslott.se; Hässleholm; starters from Sk65, mains Skr95-230) Most of Sweden's museums and attractions have a restaurant attached, but very few of them are up to this standard. Restaurant
Mikkelsen, inside Hovdala Slott – itself a fascinating lesson in the successful restoration of a
monument – has developed an ambitious menu that's served in an equally fine dining room. In
both the food and the décor, history melds seamlessly into the modern. Simple dishes such as
cured herring or *gravad lax* join more complicated takes on tradition – sautéed wild boar, leg of
lamb, and a classic Skåne dish of egg custard with bacon and lingonberries. Ingredients are all
locally sourced, and most of the herbs and spices used are taken from the castle's garden. There's
a Sunday lunch buffet and a three-course set menu. The restaurant has gained a reputation as
one of the top places to eat in Skåne; booking ahead is advised. The castle is just outside of
Hässleholm; from the town center, head southwest along Hovdalavägen and look for signposts.
Any tourist office in the region will have maps.

Restaurang Niklas (☎ 280050; Norra Storgatan 16;
lunch from Skr89, bistro mains Skr170-250; ☺ Tue-Sat)
This gastronomic temple – home of the
popular TV cooking show host – is among
Sweden's best restaurants, with cuisine
inspired by the French, elegant modern
décor, a wine bar, bistro and fine-dining
area (set menus in the latter from Skr495
for four courses).

Ebbas Fik (☎ 281440; Bruksgatan 20; ☺ Mon-Sat)
All done up in shocking turquoise rockabilly, Ebbas is a 1950s-style joint with a
killer jukebox.

Fahlmans Café (☎ 213060; Stortorget 11) There
are some cool cafés in town – this is the
most traditional, serving sandwiches, quiche
and pastries.

ICA supermarket (Drottninggatan 48) Self-caterers
should head here.

Getting There & Away

The main transport centre is Knutpunkten; the underground platforms serve
both the **SJ** (☎ 0771-757575; www.sj.se) and
pågatågen trains departing for Stockholm,
Göteborg, Copenhagen, Oslo and nearby
towns. At ground level and a bit south,
but still inside the same complex, is the
bus station where regional **Skånetrafiken**
(☎ 0771-777777; www.skanetrafiken.se) buses
dominate, but daily long-distance services run to various destinations, including
Göteborg and Oslo.

Knutpunkten is the terminal for frequent
ferries across to Helsingør in Denmark, and
there are regular ferries to/from Oslo; see
p475 and p476, respectively, for full details
of these services.

GÖTALAND

This region has a rich history and plenty
to offer the visitor. For one, it's home to
Sweden's second city, Göteborg (also known
as Gothenburg), with an amusement park
for the kids that's matched by a huge range
of grown-up entertainment, from art museums to nightclubs. Norrköping, an urban-
restoration achievement, is an industrial city
that has turned its workmanlike heart into
a lovely showpiece. Linköping's medieval
cathedral is one of Sweden's largest, and in
Vadstena there's the abbey established by the
country's most important saint, Birgitta. If
historic or cosmopolitan delights don't do
it for you, there are also the quaint fishing
villages and overwhelming natural beauty of
the Bohuslän coast. The two largest lakes in
Sweden – Vänern and Vättern – are also in
Götaland, and are linked by the remarkable
Göta Canal.

VARBERG

☎ 0340 / pop 53,100

A town built for sunsets, Varberg has plenty
of hang-out space along the waterfront and
some gorgeous views from the **medieval fortress** (☎ 82830; adult Skr30-50, child Skr10), which
has guided tours and excellent museums.
You might also want to brave the brisk
Nordic weather and swim at **Kallhusbadet**
(☎ 17396; adult/child Skr45/25; ☺ daily mid-Jun–mid-
Aug, Sat & Sun mid-Aug–mid-Jun), a striking bathing
house built in Moorish style on stilts above
the sea. The **tourist office** (☎ 88770; www.turist
.varberg.se; Brunnparken; ☺ daily Midsummer–mid-Aug,

SWEDEN

Mon-Sat May-Jun & Aug, Mon-Fri Sep-Apr) is in the centre of town.

The top-notch **Fästningens Vandrarhem** (☎ 88788; vandrarhem@turist.varberg.se; dm/s/d from Skr175/260/435) is within the fortress and offers single rooms in old prison cells or larger rooms in other buildings. Call ahead, as reception hours are very limited. Most dining options are along the pedestrianised Kungsgatan, but the fortress café offers the best sea views in town.

Ferries from the Danish town of Grenå dock near the town centre (see p475 for ferry information). Trains and buses between Göteborg and Malmö (and on to Copenhagen) stop regularly at the train station.

GÖTEBORG

☎ 031 / pop 475,000

Göteborg (pronounced roughly 'yoo-te-bor', and sometimes called Gothenburg), Sweden's second-largest city, has a hip, cosmopolitan feel, an eminently strollable central boulevard and Scandinavia's biggest amusement park. If that's not enough fun for you, it's also surrounded by some of the prettiest stretches of coastline in Sweden. The city's heavy architecture gives it a wonderfully moody atmosphere, especially in grey weather. Best of all, it's diverse enough to offer plenty of options to the budget traveller.

Orientation

The heart of the city is bordered by canals, well suited to sightseeing cruises. A branch snakes its way to Liseberg amusement park in the southeast. The huge Nordstan shopping centre lies just north of the canal system, opposite Centralstationen and its modern neighbour, Nils Ericson Terminalen, the regional and long-distance bus station.

From the centre of the city, Kungsportsavenyn crosses the canal and leads southeast to Götaplatsen. Known as the 'Avenyn', this is the heart of the city with boutiques, restaurants, theatres, galleries and cafés.

The shipyards (now closed) and much of the heavy industry (including Volvo) are on the northern island of Hisingen, reached by bridge, tunnel and regular boat traffic.

Information

DISCOUNT CARDS & PACKAGES

The good-value Göteborg Pass gives free entry to Liseberg and a number of city at-

tractions, city tours, and parking and public transport. It costs Skr210/295 for 24/48 hours and is available from tourist offices, hotels, hostels and numerous Pressbyrån newsagents.

Göteborgspaketet (Göteborg Package) is a hotel package with prices from Skr485 per person per night, and including the Göteborg Pass for the number of nights you stay. Book the package in advance on the **Göteborg** (www.goteborg.com) site or with the tourist office.

EMERGENCY

Emergency (☎ 112) Free number for fire brigade, police and ambulance.

Police station (☎ 739 2000; Ernst Fontells Plats) Off Skånegatan, near Nya Ullevi stadium.

INTERNET ACCESS

IT-Grottan (Chalmersgatan 27; per hr Skr29-43; ☽ to midnight) Cheaper hourly rate before 6pm.

Sidewalk Express (www.sidewalkexpress.se; per hr Skr19) A chain of internet kiosks at central locations (Centralstationen, Landvetter airport, inside the 7-Eleven store at Vasaplatsen); vouchers are purchased from vending machines.

MEDICAL SERVICES

Apoteket Vasan (☎ 802 0532; Nordstan complex; ☽ 8am-10pm)

Östra Sjukhuset (☎ 343 4000) Large hospital near tram terminus No 1, northeast of town.

MONEY

Banks with ATMs attached are to be found scattered all over town, including inside the Nordstan complex and Centralstationen.

Forex (www.forex.se; Kungsportsavenyn 22; ☽ 9am-7pm Mon-Fri, 10am-4pm Sat) The exchange company has a number of branches throughout Göteborg, including one in Centralstationen.

TOURIST INFORMATION

Tourist offices (☎ 612500; www.goteborg.com) Branch tourist office (Nordstan; ☽ 10am-6pm Mon-Fri, 10am-4pm Sat, noon-3pm Sun); Main tourist office (Kungsportsplatsen 2; ☽ 9am-6pm daily Jun-Aug, 9am-5pm Mon-Fri, 10am-2pm Sat Sep-May)

Sights

LISEBERG

This **fun park** (☎ 400100; www.liseberg.se; admission Skr60, child under 7 free) is dominated by its futuristic spaceportlike tower. The ride to the top, some 83m above the ground, climaxes in a spinning dance and a breathtaking view of the city. The other amusements and rides seem tame by comparison but there's no lack of variety. You can buy a pass for Skr270 that allows you to ride the attractions all day, otherwise individual rides cost between Skr10 and Skr50. There are often summer shows and concerts staged here. Opening hours are complex but the season generally runs from late April to early October (and also in the weeks leading up to Christmas) – check the website. Tram No 5 takes you there.

MUSEUMS
After Liseberg the museums are Göteborg's strongest attractions. If several take your fancy, purchase the Göteborg Pass.

By Liseberg is the striking **Universeum** (☎ 335 6450; www.universeum.se; Södra Vägen; admission Skr135-145; ☺ Tue-Sun mid-Aug–Apr, daily May–mid-Aug), a huge and impressive 'science discovery centre' featuring everything from rainforests to a shark tank. It has great displays and hands-on experiments, but it's not cheap to visit (use the Göteborg Pass).

The **Stadsmuseum** (☎ 612770; Norra Hamngatan 12; adult/under 20yr Skr40/free; ☺ daily May-Aug, Tue-Sun Sep-Apr) has archaeological, local and historical collections, including Sweden's only original Viking ship.

The main art collections are at **Konstmuseet** (☎ 611000; Götaplatsen; adult/child Skr40/free; ☺ Tue-Sun), with impressive collections of Nordic and European masters (notable for works by Rubens, Van Gogh, Rembrandt and Picasso) and touring exhibitions.

The excellent **Röhsska Museet** (☎ 613850; Vasagatan 37; adult Skr40; ☺ noon-5pm Tue-Sun) covers modern Scandinavian design and decorative arts, but also contains classical and Oriental items, and a design store and popular café.

Göteborgs Maritima Centrum (☎ 105950; Packhuskajen; adult Skr70; ☺ Mar-Oct), by the opera house north of the centre, says it's the largest floating ship museum in the world and usually displays 13 historical ships, including the submarine *Nordkaparen*.

The main museum of maritime history, **Sjöfartsmuseet** (☎ 612900; Karl Johansgatan 1; adult/child Skr40/free; ☺ 10am-5pm May-Aug, 10am-5pm Tue-Sun Sep-Apr), is near Stigbergstorget about 2km west of the city centre. There's an interesting aquarium attached. Take tram Nos 3, 9 or 11.

Just off Linnégatan in Slottsskogsparken, **Naturhistoriska Museet** (Natural History Museum; ☎ 775 2400; adult/child Skr80/20; ☺ 11am-5pm May-Aug, 11am-5pm Tue-Sun Sep-Apr), has a collection of some 10 million specimens of wildlife from around the world. Take tram Nos 1 or 2.

OTHER SIGHTS
Göteborg's churches aren't very old but they're a truer reflection of Swedish architecture than Stockholm's Italian imitations. The classical **domkyrkan** (cathedral; Västra Hamngatan) was consecrated in 1815 – two previous cathedrals were destroyed by town fires. One of the most impressive buildings in Göteborg, **Masthuggskyrkan** (Storebackegatan; ☺ Mon-Fri) was completed in 1914, and its interior is like an upturned boat. The church is also a great viewpoint for the western half of the city.

Feskekörka (Rosenlundsgatan; ☺ Mon-Sat Jun-Aug, Tue-Sat Sep-May) is called the Fish Church due to its curious appearance. It isn't a church at all – it's a fish and seafood market, and a perfect stop for lunch or a snack.

The **Haga district**, south of the canal, is Göteborg's oldest suburb, dating back to 1648. In the 1980s and '90s, the area was thoroughly renovated and now includes shops and restaurants.

There are some lovely green oases in the city, including **Trädgårdsföreningen** (Nya Allén; adult/child mid-Apr–mid-Sep Skr15/free, mid-Sep–mid-Apr free), laid out in 1842 and home to a couple of pretty cafés, a rosarium and a **palm house**. In Göteborg's southwest is **Slottsskogsparken**, the 'lungs' of the city; the **Botanic Gardens** – the largest in Sweden – are nearby.

Tours
Börjessons (☎ 609670; www.paddan.com) operates most sightseeing tours in and around Göteborg. From June to August there are one-hour city bus tours (adult/child Skr120/60), leaving regularly from outside Stora Teatern, across the canal from the tourist office, but perhaps the most popular way to pass time in Göteborg is to take a boat cruise on the Göta älv, or further afield to the sea. From May to September Börjessons' Paddan boats tour the canals and harbour from Kungsportsbron, near the tourist office. The 50-minute tours (adult/child/family Skr95/60/250) depart regularly from 10am; tours after 3pm are free for Göteborg Passholders.

SWEDEN

GÖTEBORG

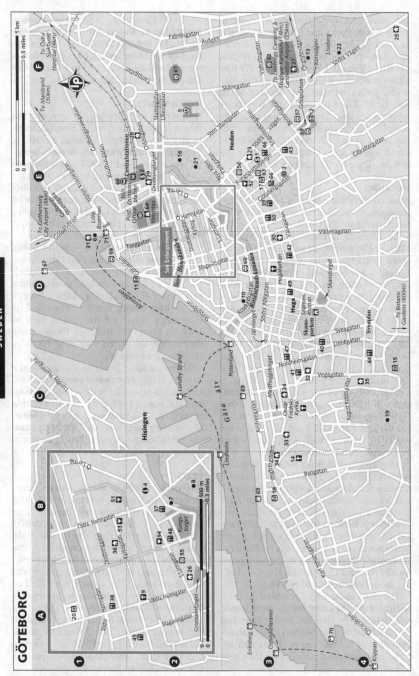

Holders of the Göteborg Pass also pay nothing to join a Börjessons' cruise from Lilla Bommen to the ruins of **Nya Älvsborg fortress** near the river mouth.

Sleeping

Göteborg has several exceptional hostels; most are clustered in the central southwest area, in apartment buildings that sometimes inspire little confidence from the outside, but inside offer accommodation of a high standard. All are open year-round.

Most hotels offer great discounts at weekends and in summer. The tourist office can arrange **private rooms** (s/d from Skr175/225) for a Skr60 booking fee.

BUDGET

Lisebergs Camping & Stugbyar Kärralund (☎ 840200; www.liseberg.se; Olbergsgatan; camp sites Skr100-325) The closest camping ground to town, this one is geared for families. It has a wide range of cabins, cottages and hostel beds for rent. Prices have a ridiculously complex schedule of rates. Take tram No 5 to Welandergatan.

STF Vandrarhem Slottsskogen (☎ 426520; www .sov.nu; Vegagatan 21; dm/s from Skr165/305; ☻ 24hr; ☐) Slottsskogen is regarded as one of Sweden's best hostels, so book early. It's a friendly, social place with breakfast buffet, bike hire, laundry, sauna and lounge. Take tram Nos 1 or 2 to Olivedalsgatan.

Göteborgs Mini-Hotel (☎ 241023; www.minihotel .se; Tredje Långgatan 31; dm/d Skr130/360) This decent option has well-priced renovated rooms (all with TV and fridge) and shared bathroom facilities, plus laundry and self-catering kitchen.

Masthuggsterrassens Vandrarhem (☎ 424820; www.mastenvandrarhem.com; Masthuggsterrassen 10H; dm/ s/d Skr170/290/440) A clean, well-run spot near the ferries to/from Denmark. Take tram Nos 3, 9 or 11 to Masthuggstorget and check the signs (upstairs, behind the supermarket).

STF Vandrarhem Stigbergsliden (☎ 241620; www.hostel-gothenburg.com; Stigbergsliden 10; dm/s/d Skr180/310/420) Another welcoming, well-run STF hostel, this time in a renovated 19th-century seaman's house. It has a good kitchen, laundry, TV room and garden, plus bike hire. Take tram Nos 3, 9 or 11 to Stigbergstorget.

Göteborgs Vandrarhem (☎ 401050; www.gote borgsvandrarhem.se; Mölndalsvägen 23; dm/s&d from Skr200/500) A well-equipped, well-run place,

SWEDEN

just south of Liseberg, which is convenient for the big attractions. Take tram No 4 to Getebergsäng.

Linné Vandrarhem (☎ 121060; www.vandrarhem met-linne.com; Vegagatan 22; dm/s/d Skr190/380/400) Down the road from STF Slottsskogen is another budget option – it looks huge and rather Soviet from the outside but has bright, clean rooms and good communal facilities. Take tram Nos 1 or 2 to Olivedalsgatan.

MIDRANGE & TOP END

Vanilj Hotel (☎ 711 6220; www.vaniljhotel.entersol.se; Kyrkogatan 38; s/d from Skr995/1145, discount Skr695/795) This is an excellent choice – a small, cosy and personal place above a lovely café and courtyard, situated along a narrow cobblestone street in the heart of town. There's typically Swedish streamlined décor, friendly staff, good breakfasts and shopping at the front door.

Hotel Odin Residence (☎ 745 2200; www.hotel odin.se; Odinsgatan 6; s/d apt from Skr1300/1500, discount s/d Skr895/995) This hotel, part of the Clarion Collection chain, has spacious apartments filled with the kind of decor and gadgets you'd kill for at home, and all rooms come equipped with everything you need for a long, happy stay, including a full kitchen, lounge, TV and stereo. Cheaper rates are offered for stays of longer than a week.

Hotel Gothia Towers (☎ 750 8800; www.gothia towers.com; Mässans Gata 24; s/d from Skr1795/2095, discount Skr995/1095) This 23-storey, 704-room hotel (the largest in Scandinavia, and popular for conventions) is top of the tree in Göteborg. The interior is stylish and modern, and there are popular restaurants and bars on the premises. Summer and weekend prices are quite reasonable. The hotel is opposite Liseberg and only a few minutes' walk to Kungsportsavenyn; take tram No 5.

Hotell Barken Viking (☎ 635800; www.liseberg .se; Gullbergskajen; crew quarters s/d Skr595/850, officer's cabins Skr1395/1595, discount officer's cabins Skr995/1195) This is a fabulous boat hotel with lots of history and an interesting location (near Lilla Bommen and the opera house, best accessed by walkway from the northern part of Nordstan). Crew quarters have shared bathroom facilities and bunkbeds. You can pay extra for a little more luxury and private facilities in a surprisingly spacious officer's cabin. The deck is home to a restaurant and bar.

City Hotel (☎ 708 4000; www.cityhotelgbg.se; Lorensbergsgatan 6; s/d with shared bathroom from Skr495/595, with private bathroom from Skr795/995) If you want to taste the nightlife, this place is for you – it's within stumbling distance of Kungsportsavenyn. Weekend and summer discounts see rates reduced by Skr50 to Skr100.

Hotel Opera (☎ 805080; www.hotelopera.se; Norra Hamngatan 38; budget s/d Skr750/1150, discount Skr595/995, standard s/d Skr1095/1450, discount Skr695/1095) An appealing option, conveniently located close to the train station and bus terminal. Budget rooms are in an older part of the hotel and are small but perfectly adequate. All rooms have private facilities, TV and phone.

Hotel Vasa (☎ 173630; www.hotelvasa.se; Viktoriagatan 6; s/d from Skr895/995, discount Skr645/845) An attractive, family-run place handy to the cafés of Vasagatan. Rooms are pleasant and range in size and luxury (some have a Jacuzzi); winning features are the courtyard garden and very friendly owners.

Hotel Flora (☎ 138616; www.hotelflora.se; Grönsakstorget 2; s/d Skr990/1195, discount Skr650/850) This comfortable, affordable hotel has just doubled its size and modernised many of its rooms. There's also a stylish ground-level restaurant-café.

Eating

Kungsportsavenyn is lined with all kinds of restaurants, cafés and bars, and alfresco dining is popular when the sun shines. Nearby, Vasagatan is close to the student heartland and has excellent cafés, Linnégatan (close to most of the hostels) has a great selection of eateries, and Magasingatan is a good place to check out the latest on the Göteborg scene.

CAFÉS

Brogyllens Konditori (☎ 138713; Västra Hamngatan 2; snacks Skr30-52) Essentially a museum of pastry, this showpiece café and bakery is easy on the eyes and palate both. Linger over coffee and cake in a seat under the grand chandeliers.

Eva's Paley (☎ 163070; Kungsportsavenyn 39; meals Skr40-65; ⏱ to 11pm) A huge corner place open late and serving good-value dishes including panini, baked potatoes, pasta, salads and seriously good muffins – an institution on Avenyn.

R.O.O.M. (☎ 606630; Magasingatan 3; dishes Skr35-90; ⏱ Mon-Sat) Get inspired at this great interiors store – and if your knees go weak from looking at the price tags, you can repair to the funky café and enjoy a more affordable Caesar salad or Thai curry soup.

Kalaya (☎ 123998; Olivedalsgatan 13; dishes Skr59-69) Not far from the hostel area, Kalaya has authentic Thai cuisine, including soup, noodle and curry choices.

Cafe Mio (☎ 133600; Vasagatan 24; dishes Skr55-65) Next door to Espresso House is this cozy little Italian café with filling meals at good prices.

For a quick snack while you stroll, **Café Garbo** (☎ 774 1925; Vasagatan 40; specials from Skr45) and **Espresso House** (☎ 39750; Vasagatan 22) are two of several comfortable hang-outs facing the leafy Vasagatan boulevard.

RESTAURANTS

Cyrano (☎ 143010; Prinsgatan 7; mains Skr75-200) A highly regarded French bistro-style restaurant, where three-course set menus cost from Skr155. There's also a selection of good French á la carte dishes, and simpler pizzas (Skr75 to Skr95).

Sjöbaren (☎ 711 9780; Haga Nygata 25; mains Skr99-239) This cosy spot in the rejuvenated Haga district offers well-prepared seafood in nautical surrounds (inside) or a pleasant courtyard garden. Opt for items in the 'Swedish classics' category such as *gravad lax* with potatoes, fish soup or seafood pasta.

Ruby Nuevo Latino Bar (☎ 7515400; Kungsport-savvenyn 24; mains Skr89-195) A newish spot along the main drag, the Ruby is perpetually abuzz with diners and spectators; nestle into the 'red corner' for some tapas, or have a drink on the terrace and watch the human traffic go by. Food is served late.

Smaka (☎ 132247; Vasaplatsen 3; mains Skr89-195) Smaka (meaning 'taste') serves traditional Swedish *husmanskost* including classics such as herring, meatballs, or *gravad lax*.

Den Lilla Taverna (☎ 128805; Olivedalsgatan 17; mezes Skr35-65, mains Skr69-99) A welcoming place with authentic Greek dishes, plus a great array of *mezes* (starters) perfect for sharing.

Brasserie Lipp (☎ 105830; Kungsportsavenyn 8; mains Skr75-239) You're spoilt for culinary choice along Kunsportsavenyn, although prices can be higher than in other parts of town. Brasserie Lipp is a classic, classy eatery and has good light meals on its menu, including Caesar salad and a club sandwich, plus more substantial main courses.

QUICK EATS

Saluhallen (Kungstorget; ☿ Mon-Sat) This is a classic old market hall where you can buy a huge range of delicatessen foods. There are also superb budget eateries: Alexandras is renowned for its Greek soups and stews (Skr30 to Skr40) and Kåges Hörna serves up bargain meals – chicken salad, lasagne and burgers for Skr35 to Skr40.

Saluhall Briggen (Nordhemsgatan; ☿ Mon-Sat) Not as busy as the central Saluhallen but also housing a good array of lunch stalls is this place, not far from the hostel district.

Crepe Van (Linnégatan; crepes Skr25-45; ☿ 4-10pm Mon-Thu, 4pm-3.30am Fri & Sat) This takeaway van near McDonald's offers sweet and savoury crepes from afternoon until the wee hours.

Aldardo (☎ 132300; Kungstorget 12; snacks Skr25-55; ☿ Mon-Sat) Right by the tourist office, this busy deli sells authentic Italian fast food – pizza *al taglio* (by the slice) and pasta dishes.

SELF-CATERING

Hemköp supermarket (☿ 8am-10pm) Self-caterers should head to this supermarket in the Nordstan complex.

Saluhallen (Kungstorget; ☿ Mon-Sat) This is the perfect place to put together your picnic pack. Outside Saluhallen you'll find fresh produce stalls and food vans.

Drinking

You'll find some good pubs and bars along the main thoroughfares. For more choices, stroll down Kungsportsavenyn and take your pick.

Ölhallen 7:an (☎ 136079; Kungstorget 7) Portraits of long-gone barflies haunt the walls of this well-worn Swedish beerhall, which hasn't changed in about 100 years and hopefully never will.

Dubliner (☎ 139020; Östra Hamngatan 50B) This is as authentic an Irish pub as you'll find on the Continent. It has live music nightly in summer. Pints of Guinness flow, and bar meals include Emerald Isle staples such as fish and chips or beef-and-Guinness pie.

O'Leary's (☎ 711 5519; Östra Hamngatan 36) Opposite the Dubliner, this is an American-style sports bar with TV screens and bar snacks.

Lounge(s) (☎ 711 1541; Kungsportsavenyn 5; ☿ Thu-Sat) Muscle or flirt your way past imposing doormen in headsets to sip pretty cocktails in this chic lounge full of Göteborg's beautiful people.

SWEDEN

Entertainment

Biopalatset (☎ 174500; Kungstorget) One of many cinemas around town, this 10-screener behind Saluhallen shows new releases. Showtimes are listed in newspapers.

Göteborgs Stadsteatern (City Theatre; ☎ 615050; Götaplatsen) Culture vultures should head to the end of Avenyn for dramatic performances (usually in Swedish) at the Stadsteatern.

Göteborgs Konserthus (Concert Hall; ☎ 726 5300; Götaplatsen) Home to the local symphony orchestra, this is at the other end of Avenyn.

GöteborgsOperan (☎ 131300; Christina Nilssons gata) It's worth investigating what's on at this striking opera house at Lilla Bommen harbour, which stages ballet, opera and assorted musical performances.

Nefertiti (☎ 711 1533; Hvitfeldtsplatsen 6) This cool venue near Feskekörka is a well-established location for live jazz, blues and ethnic music; it also has a nightclub, restaurant and café.

Göteborgers are avid sports fans. Outdoor stadiums include Nya Ullevi for football matches and Scandinavium for ice hockey.

Kungsportavenyn is the place to go for clubbing. Popular options:

Avenyn 10 (Kungsportsavenyn 10-12) One of the biggest clubs in town.

Bubbles (Kungsportsavenyn 8) As descriptive a name as any nightclub ever had.

Valand (cnr Kungsportsavenyn & Vasagatan) Vintage music hall blending silly and sophisticated, with its imposing architecture and hilarious pair of Greek statues guarding the door.

Getting There & Away

AIR

Landvetter airport (☎ 941000) is 25km east of the city with services to many European cities. **Göteborg City Airport** (☎ 926060; www.goteborgcityairport.se) is a minor airport 10km northwest of the city, used by **Ryanair** (☎ 0900-202 0240; www.ryanair.com).

BOAT

Göteborg is a major entry point for ferries, with several terminals. For more details on ferry services and fares to Denmark, Germany and the UK, see p475.

The **Stena Line** (☎ 704 0004; www.stenaline.se) Denmark terminal near Masthuggstorget (tram No 3, 9 or 11) has several daily departures for Frederikshavn.

Faster and more expensive is **SeaCat** (☎ 720 0800), with catamarans to Frederikshavn departing daily in summer from near Sjofartsmuseet (tram No 3 or 9 to Stigbergstorget).

Near Chapmans Torg is the **Stena Line terminal** for car ferries to Germany.

DFDS Seaways (☎ 65 06 80; www.dfdsseaways.se) sails twice weekly to Norway and the UK from Skandiahamnen on Hisingen (tram No 6 to Frihamnen).

BUS

The modern bus station, Nils Ericson Terminalen, is next to the train station. **Eurolines** (☎ 031-100240; www.eurolines.com) and Swebus Express share an office here.

Swebus Express (☎ 0200-218218; www.swebusexpress.se) operates frequent buses to/from most major towns. There are services to/from Stockholm (concession/full price Skr250/360, six hours, up to 10 daily) and Oslo (concession/full price Skr160/225, 3½ hours, up to six daily).

Svenska Buss (☎ 0771-676767; www.svenskabuss.se) and **Säfflebussen** (☎ 0771-151515; www.safflebussen.se) also run on the major routes.

There's a **Tidpunkten office** (☎ 0771-414300; Nils Ericson Terminalen) that gives advice and sells tickets for city and regional public transport.

TRAIN

Centralstationen serves **SJ** (☎ 0771-757575; www.sj.se) and regional trains, with direct trains to Malmö, Copenhagen, Oslo and Stockholm, plus other destinations in the southern half of Sweden. **Connex** (☎ 0771-260000; www.connex.se) night trains travel to the far north. Direct train services to Stockholm depart approximately hourly.

Getting Around

Buses, trams and ferries make up the city public transport system; there are Tidpunkten information booths inside Nils Ericson Terminalen, on Drottningtorget and at Brunnsparken. The easiest way to cover lengthy distances in Göteborg is by tram. There are 11 lines, all converging near Brunnsparken, one block from the train station. An individual transport ticket costs Skr20. 'Value cards' (Skr50 to Skr100) reduce the cost considerably. Holders of the Göteborg Pass travel free.

Cykelkungen (☎ 184300; Chalmersgatan 19) offers bike rental for Skr120/300/500 for one day/three days/one week.

MARSTRAND
☎ 0303 / pop 1300

Pretty **Marstrand** (www.marstrand.nu), with its wooden buildings, island setting and relaxed air, conveys the essence of the Bohuslän fishing villages that dot the coast from Göteborg to the Norwegian border, and provides an idyllic area for sailing, cycling or driving. Car traffic is banned on the island itself, so those with their own wheels should take the frequent passenger ferry from Koön, 150m to the east.

Like many other places along the coast, Marstrand has become an upmarket weekend destination for sailors and city slickers. The 17th-century **Carlstens Fästning** (☎ 60265; adult/child Skr70/25; ۞ Jun-Aug) fortress reflects the town's martial and penal history; entry price includes a guided tour.

Marstrands Varmbadhus Båtellet (☎ 60010; mar strandsvarmbadhus@telia.com; dm Skr295, d Skr625-775) offers simple hostel accommodation 400m from the ferry dock; the attached **restaurant** (۞ daily Jun-Aug, Sat & Sun Sep-May) serves lunch specials and á la carte selections, with a great view.

There are numerous eating options along the harbour, including fast-food stalls (one sells fresh fish and chips for Skr50), cafés and upmarket restaurants.

Marstrand is about an hour from Göteborg by bus and makes an excellent day trip. Take bus No 312 from Nils Ericson Terminalen (Skr50 one way), then cross to Marstrand by the passenger ferry (Skr15 return).

If you have your own transport and are heading north to Norway, get off the E6 and take Hwy 160 from Stenungsund for a pretty slice of Swedish coastal life.

STRÖMSTAD
☎ 0526 / pop 11,250

A model fishing village that's especially popular with Norwegians on holiday, Strömstad lies about 30km south of the border and has the relaxed atmosphere you'd expect to find in a seaside resort. There are good attractions, including museums, beaches and boat trips to nearby islands. The Koster islands, decorated with clusters of cute little red fishing huts, are the most westerly in Sweden and are popular for cycling.

The **tourist office** (☎ 62330; www.stromstadtour ist.se; Torget, Norra hamnen; ۞ daily Jun-Aug, Mon-Fri

Sep-May) is between the two harbours on the main square. There are lots of camping grounds and cabins in the area, and the first-class **STF Crusellska Vandrarhemmet** (☎ 10193; www.crusellska.com; Norra Kyrkogatan 12; dm/s/d Skr205/345/490; ۞ Mar–mid-Dec) is deservedly popular – book ahead.

Try the fresh local *räkor* (shrimp) and delicious seafood in the many restaurants, or purchase from local fishmongers. Next to the tourist office is **Laholmens Fisk** (Norra Kyrkogatan), selling baguettes filled with seafood (around Skr50). Not far away is **Göstases** (☎ 10812; Strandpromenaden; mains Skr49-145), with cosy nautical décor, lots of outdoor seating and a good menu of local sea creatures.

Strömstad is the northern terminus of the local train system, with regular trains to/from Göteborg. **Swebus Express** (☎ 0200-218218; www.swebusexpress.se) buses between Göteborg and Oslo also stop here. There are regular ferries between Strömstad and Sandefjord in Norway; see p476 for details.

NORRKÖPING
☎ 011 / pop 122,900

Norrköping has a peculiar industrial beauty, thanks to its 19th-century textile mills and factories along the Motala river. The architecture intermingles attractively with the city's canals, locks and waterfalls, and the rest of the downtown core has a pleasant old-fashioned feel as well.

The well-stocked **tourist office** (☎ 155000; www.destination.norrkoping.se; Dalsgatan 16; ۞ 10am-5pm Mon-Fri year-round, 10am-2pm Sat Jul), by the strikingly modern Louis de Geer Konserthus, can help with visitor information. The **library** (Södra Promenaden 105) has free internet access, or you can try the cheap **Norrköpings Biljard och IT Café** (Prästgatan 48; per hr Skr15; ۞ to 1am).

Sights
KOLMÅRDEN
With about 750 animals from all continents and climates, this **zoo** (☎ 249000; www.kolmarden .com; ۞ daily May-Aug, Sat & Sun Sep) is billed as the largest in Europe. The complex is divided into two areas: the main **Djurparken** (zoo; adult/child Skr215/120), with its enjoyable dolphin show; and **Safariparken** (adult/child Skr110/80), which you drive around. A separate **Tropicarium** (☎ 395259; www.tropicarium .se; adult/child Skr70/50) opposite the entrance

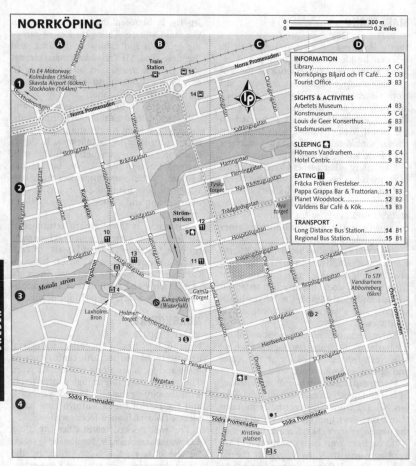

NORRKÖPING

0 ——— 300 m
0 ——— 0.2 miles

INFORMATION	
Library...................................1	C4
Norrköpings Biljard och IT Café....2	D3
Tourist Office............................3	B3
SIGHTS & ACTIVITIES	
Arbetets Museum.....................4	B3
Konstmuseum............................5	C4
Louis de Geer Konserthus..........6	B3
Stadsmuseum...........................7	B3
SLEEPING	
Hörnans Vandrarhem..................8	C4
Hotel Centric............................9	B2
EATING	
Fräcka Fröken Frestelser...........10	A2
Pappa Grappa Bar & Trattorian...11	B3
Planet Woodstock....................12	B2
Världens Bar Café & Kök............13	B3
TRANSPORT	
Long Distance Bus Station.........14	B1
Regional Bus Station.................15	B1

includes sharks, alligators and reptiles. A general 'maxi' ticket for the zoo and safari park costs Skr275/160 per adult/child. The **cable car** (Skr80/40) around the park gives a better view of the forest than of the animals.

You'll need all day to take in the zoo fully. Kolmården is 35km north of Norrköping, on the north shore of the bay Bråviken (regular bus Nos 432 or 433; Skr54). There's camping and hotel accommodation out here too – see the website for details.

OTHER SIGHTS
Pedestrian walkways and bridges lead around Norrköping's ingenious system of locks and canals along the riverside. The industrial past is exhibited at the city museum,

Stadsmuseum (☎ 152620; Västgötegatan 19-21; admission free; ☺ Tue-Sun). Sweden's only museum of work, the excellent **Arbetets Museum** (☎ 189800; admission free; ☺ 11am-5pm), is just across the bridge from the Stadsmuseum in a 1917 building designed to mirror the island it sits on; named Strykjärnet (flatiron), it has seven sides, seven floors and a total of 7,000 square metres of floor space. A modern addition to the riverside scenery is the extraordinary **Louis de Geer Konserthus** (☎ 155030; Dalsgatan 15), a concert hall and conference centre that's home to good restaurants.

The **Konstmuseum** (☎ 152600; Kristinaplatsen; adult/child Skr40/free; ☺ Tue-Sun), the large art museum south of the centre at Kristinaplatsen, has some important early-20th-century works.

Summer-only attractions include short guided tours on vintage trams; inquire at the tourist office.

Sleeping

Hörnans Vandrarhem (☎ 168271; Hörngatan 1; dm/s/d from Skr170/350/480) This hostel is in the heart of town, above a footy-friendly Scottish pub, and offers spacious, comfortable rooms, some with kitchenettes and all with cable TV.

STF Vandrarhem Abborreberg (☎ 319344; www .abborreberg.se; dm/s/d from Skr195/240/385; ☺ May-Sep) Beautifully situated by the coast 6km east of town, this hostel has beds in little cottages scattered through the surrounding park; there's also a café and a seaside pagoda that invites picnicking. Take bus Nos 101 or 111 to Lindö.

Hotel Centric (☎ 129030; www.centrichotel.se; Gamla Rådstugugatan 18; s/d Skr725/825, discount Skr465/675; 🖵) This basic hotel is in a central location, and has slightly dated but comfortable rooms and good facilities including free internet access. There's parking available for Skr55.

Eating & Drinking

There are plenty of eateries in the shopping district along Drottninggatan, and also in the student quarter around Kungsgatan. This is also where you'll find supermarkets.

Fräcka Fröken Frestelser (☎ 238823; Kungsgatan 43; light meals Skr45-75; ☺ breakfast, lunch & dinner) The name is a tongue-twister but this cool café's great selection of sandwiches, light meals and cakes is easier to wrap your mouth around. It's also on a busy corner, making its large windows ideal for people-watching.

Världens Bar Café & Kök (☎ 134510; Västgötegatan 15; dishes Skr45-75) A funky and colourful restaurant-bar serving simple dishes – and music – from around the world. It's popular for lunch (from Skr45), and open until late (until 11pm or 1am); the wooden patio is a lovely hang-out on a warm summer evening.

Pappa Grappa Bar & Trattorian (☎ 180014; Gamla Rådstugugatan 26; mains Skr105-235; ☺ dinner Mon-Sat) It's worth booking a table for this cosy, low-lit cellar restaurant-bar, one of the town's best options and deservedly popular. It offers authentic Italian dishes and great desserts.

Planet Woodstock (☎ 188111; Gamla Rådstugugatan 11; dishes Skr40-70) This backpacker's dream was undergoing renovation and expansion at the time of research, but it's known for a crunchy, granola-type atmosphere and reliably huge, inexpensive meals. There are several other inviting spots on the same corner.

Getting There & Around

The regional bus station is next to the train station in the north of town; long-distance buses leave from a terminal across the road. **Swebus Express** (☎ 0200-218218; www.swe busexpress.se) and **Svenska Buss** (☎ 0771-676767; www.svenskabuss.se) have frequent services to destinations including Stockholm, Göteborg, Jönköping, Kalmar and Örebro. Norrköping is on the main north–south railway line, and **SJ trains** (☎ 0771-757575; www.sj.se) run roughly hourly north to Stockholm and south to Malmö. Frequent regional trains and buses run south to Linköping.

Trams cover the city and are quickest for short hops, especially along Drottninggatan from the train station. The fare for trams and city buses is Skr18.

LINKÖPING

☎ 013 / pop 134,000

The highlight of a visit to this university city is the open-air museum Gamla Linköping. Another big draw is the medieval cathedral, an impressive standout amid the modern city with its emphasis on the aircraft industry.

The **tourist office** (☎ 206835; www.linkoping.se) is inside the city **library** (Östgötagatan 5), not far from the cathedral; there's also free internet access here. **Gamer Palace** (Drottninggatan 36; per hr Skr19; ☺ 1pm-10pm Mon-Thu, 1pm-11pm Fri, 10am-midnight Sat, 1-8pm Sun) is an internet café conveniently close to the hostel.

Sights & Activities

The enormous, copper-roofed **domkyrka** (cathedral; ☺ 9am-6pm) with its 107m spire is the landmark of Linköping and one of Sweden's oldest and largest churches. Learn more about its history and architecture at the museum inside the castle just across the way, the **Slotts- & Domkyrkomuseum** (Castle & Cathedral Museum; ☎ 122380; adult/child Skr40/free; ☺ Tue-Sun late Apr–mid-Oct).

On the opposite side of the busy Stora Torget, down a pedestrianised street, is **Sankt Lars Kyrka**, which has live music concerts some evenings.

Just north of the cathedral, **Östergötlands Länsmuseum** (County Museum; ☎ 230300; Vasavägen;

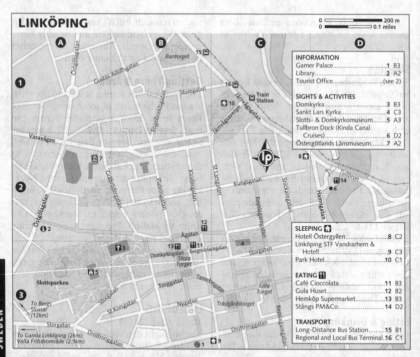

LINKÖPING

INFORMATION
Gamer Palace	**1** B3
Library	**2** A2
Tourist Office	(see 2)

SIGHTS & ACTIVITIES
Domkyrka	**3** B3
Sankt Lars Kyrka	**4** C3
Slotts- & Domkyrkomuseum	**5** A3
Tullbron Dock (Kinda Canal Cruises)	**6** D2
Östergötlands Länsmuseum	**7** A2

SLEEPING
Hotell Östergyllen	**8** C2
Linköping STF Vandrarhem & Hotell	**9** C3
Park Hotel	**10** C1

EATING
Café Cioccolata	**11** B3
Gula Huset	**12** B2
Hemköp Supermarket	**13** B3
Stångs PM&Co	**14** D2

TRANSPORT
Long-Distance Bus Station	**15** B1
Regional and Local Bus Terminal	**16** C1

adult/child Skr20/free; ⏰ Tue, Wed, Sat & Sun) houses an extensive collection of art by a variety of European painters, including Cranach's view of Eden, *Original Sin*, and a collection of Swedish art reaching back to the Middle Ages.

The best attractions are just outside the centre. Some 2km west of the city is **Gamla Linköping** (☎ 121110; admission free), one of the biggest living-museum villages in Sweden. Among the 90 quaint houses are about a dozen theme museums, many handicraft shops, a small chocolate factory, a restaurant and a café. You can wander among the 19th-century buildings at will – the village and most museums are open daily. Just 300m through the forest behind the old village is the **Valla Fritidsområde** (admission Skr20), a recreation area with domestic animals, gardens, a children's playground, minigolf, a few small museums and many old houses. To get there take bus Nos 202 or 214.

Bergs Slussar, 12km northwest of Linköping (take bus Nos 521 or 522; Skr30) is one of the most scenic sections of the Göta Canal, with seven locks and a height gain

of 19m. It's a great excursion on a sunny day, and there are cafés and restaurants by the canal.

Linköping boasts its own canal system, the 90km **Kinda Canal**. There are 15 locks, including the deepest in Sweden. A variety of cruises from mid-May to September run along the canal. The trip on **M/S Kind** (☎ 0141-233370) leaves the Tullbron dock on Tuesday, Thursday and Saturday from late June to early August and heads south to Rimforsa (Skr330; return by bus or train included).

Sleeping

Linköping STF Vandrarhem & Hotell (☎ 359080; www.lvh.se; Klostergatan 52A; dm/s/d Skr205/390/410, hotel s/d Skr675/780, discount Skr495/590) There's something for every budget at this bright, central youth hostel complex. As well as comfortable hostel rooms, there are good hotel rooms (many come with kitchenettes) and some excellent, spacious apartments (from Skr 600).

Hotell Östergyllen (☎ 102075; www.hotelloster gyllen.se; Hamngatan 2B; s/d Skr450/750, with shared bathroom Skr395/550) It doesn't look like much from the outside, but inside is a small, pleasant hotel with a lovely breakfast room. It's conveniently located about 150m from the train station.

Park Hotel (☎ 129005; www.fawltytowers.se; Järnvägsgatan 6; budget r from Skr490, s/d Skr890/1090, discount Skr590/790) A quirky place in a tilty yellow house that claims it's 'Linköping's Fawlty Towers', this hotel directly opposite the train station has friendly owners and good rooms, including a budget option with showers off the corridor.

Eating & Drinking

Most places to eat and drink are on the main square or nearby streets, especially along buzzing Ågatan.

Café Cioccolata (☎ 131880; Hantverkaregatan 1; snacks Skr35-55) A central café with cool interiors, outdoor seating, strong coffee and a great selection of panini or ciabatta sandwiches.

Gula Huset (☎ 138838; Klostergatan 19; lunch from Skr70, mains Skr79-219) On a warm day the courtyard area at the 'Yellow House' beckons. There are cheaper pasta and vegetarian options, plus a range of hearty Swedish fish and meat mains, including reindeer steak.

Stångs PM&Co (☎ 312100; Södra Stänggatan 1; lunch Skr75, mains Skr200-270; ☻ lunch Tue-Fri, dinner Tue-Sat) Down by the Kinda Canal dock, off Hamngatan in the city's northeast, is this highly rated waterside restaurant. The dinner menu here is impressive (with prices to match) and the lunch-time deal is excellent value.

Hemköp supermarket (Stora Torget) This supermarket in the basement of the Filbytersgallerian shopping complex.

Getting There & Away

The **regional and local bus terminal** (Järnvägsgatan) is adjacent to the train station. Long-distance buses leave from 500m north of the train station. Linköping is on the main north–south railway line and **SJ trains** (☎ 0771-757575; www .sj.se) stop roughly every hour.

Regional (and local) traffic is run by **ÖstgötaTrafiken** (☎ 0771-211010; www.ostgotat rafiken.se); there's an information office at the station. Journeys cost from Skr20; the 24-hour *dygnskort* (Skr110) is valid on all buses and local trains within the county

(buy this if you're travelling to Vadstena, opposite).

VADSTENA
☎ 0143 / pop 7600
Saint Birgitta was Sweden's most prominent saint – the published record of her 'celestial revelations' was a popular page-turner during the Middle Ages. In the 1340s she established an order of nuns here in Vadstena (confirmed by the Vatican in 1370), and the town remains completely devoted to her. The abbey competes for the visitor's interest with the equally impressive castle. The historic monuments, charming alleys and relaxed atmosphere in the old town (and by the lake) makes Vadstena one of the nicest spots in Sweden. The **tourist office** (☎ 31570; www.vadstena.com; ☻ daily mid-May–mid-Sep, Mon-Fri mid-Sep–mid-May) is inside the castle.

Sights & Activities

The Renaissance castle, **Vadstena Slott** (☎ 315 70; Slottsvägen; adult/child Skr30/10), looks straight over the harbour and lake beyond. It was the mighty family project of the early Vasa kings and in the upper apartments there are some items of period furniture and paintings. There are daily tours from mid-May to mid-September. The superb 15th-century **Klosterkyrkan** (Abbey Church; Lasarettsgatan; admission free; ☻ mid-May–mid-Sep), consecrated in 1430, has a combination of Gothic and some Renaissance features. Inside are the accumulated relics of St Birgitta and medieval sculptures. Near the church is the **Sankta Birgitta Klostermuseum** (☎ 10031; adult/child Sk50/10; ☻ daily late May–mid-Sep, Sat & Sun mid-Apr–May & mid-Sep–mid-Oct), the old convent founded by St Birgitta.

The area around Vadstena is full of history and deserves a closer look. Cycling is an option as the scenic flatlands around Vättern lend themselves to the pedal. A series of ancient legends is connected with **Rökstenen**, Sweden's most impressive and famous rune stone, by the church at Rök, just off the E4 on the road to Heda and Alvastra.

Sleeping & Eating
STF Vandrarhem Borghamn (☎ 20368; www.borghamns vandrarhem.nu; Borghamnsvägen 1; dm/s/d Skr195/325/440) This large complex is in a lovely, quiet lakeside setting 15km southwest of Vadstena. It's about

750m from the bus stop at Borghamn (take bus No 610), and bike rental is available, plus there's an on-site café.

STF Vandrarhem Vadstena (☎ 10302; www.va-bos taelle.se; Skänningegatan 20; dm/s/d from Skr225/325/405) This inviting central hostel is open year-round, but outside the high season (June to August) it's essential to book in advance.

27ans Nattlogi (☎ 76564; www.27ansnattlogi .se in Swedish; Storgatan 27; s/d Skr500/650, with private bathroom Skr600/790) This cosy B&B is nicely central and has simple, comfortable rooms (some with private facilities, some shared) and a courtyard with gardens.

Restaurang På Hörnet (☎ 13170; Skänningegatan 1; mains & snacks Skr40-100; ◌ Wed-Sun) This cool corner bar-restaurant at the end of the main drag has a checkered floor, pretty carved bar-back and great bar snacks such as buffalo wings, marinated feta cheese and calamari – not to mention a lot of beer on tap.

Mi Casa (☎ 14101; Storgatan 9; lunch specials Skr65-75, mains Skr109-139) Mi Casa is a bright, modern, family-friendly restaurant-café. There's a lunch-time buffet as well as the regular lunch menu of enormous pasta salads; in the evening there are bistro meals, tapas dishes (Skr20 to Skr35) and cheerful service. In summer there are a few outdoor tables in the back.

Old-style cafés line Storgatan for an afternoon pit stop, and there's a central supermarket on Rådhustorget for picnic supplies.

Getting There & Around

Only buses run to Vadstena: bus No 661 regularly links the town with Mjölby, and from Mjölby you can catch trains to Linköping and Stockholm. **Swebus Express** (☎ 0200-218218; www.swebusexpress.se) bus No 855 runs on Friday and Sunday between Stockholm and Vadstena via Linköping.

Sport Hörnan (☎ 10362; Storgatan 8) rents bikes.

SMÅLAND

This is one of the nicest regions of Sweden to visit, especially if you have your own wheels – much of Småland consists of thick, forested wilderness interlaced with narrow roads and tiny villages. It's the home of glassmaking, and as such is perhaps the most scenic place in the country

to shop for dishware. There's also the pretty town of Kalmar, home to an impressive castle and an important point on Sweden's history timeline. From there it's a quick jaunt over to the long, skinny island of Öland, a popular summer destination full of camping grounds, hostels and windmills.

Småland was also the homeland of many emigrants to the USA, so it's an important destination for those tracing their Swedish roots.

See the **Småland** (www.visit-smaland.com) website for more about the region.

VÄXJÖ

☎ 0470 / pop 74,100

Växjö might be difficult (or impossible) to pronounce (try to say 'vex shoe' while sneezing), but it's easy to navigate, and it puts you right where you want to be for explorations of the Glasriket (opposite). It has supermarkets, shops, petrol stations – all the services you might need to stock up on before setting out. The **tourist office** (☎ 41410; www.turism.vaxjo.se; Stadsbiblioteket, Västra Esplanaden 7; ◌ daily Jul–mid-Aug, Mon-Fri mid-Aug–Jun) inside the library has maps and brochures and can advise travellers about what to see in the region.

Millions of North Americans have roots in Sweden, many of them in Småland. Those who return shouldn't miss **Svenska Emigrantinstitutet – Utvandrarnas Hus** (House of Emigrants; ☎ 20120; www.swemi.nu; Södra Järnvägsgatan; adult/child Skr40/5; ◌ daily May-Aug, Tue-Sat Sep-Apr), which has archives, information and historical exhibitions on the beckoning USA. It's just behind the train-and-bus station, close to **Smålands Museum** (☎ 704200; www.smalandsmuseum.se; Södra Järnvägsgatan; adult/ child Skr40/20; ◌ daily Jun-Aug, Tue-Sun Sep-May), with an absorbing exhibition of glass from Glasriket.

STF Vandrarhem Växjö (☎ 63070; www.vaxjovan drarhem.nu; Evedals Brunn; dm/d from Skr155/400) is a lovely hostel 6km north of the centre, in a popular lakeside recreational area (take bus No 1C, which unfortunately only runs from June to August, Skr17).

First Hotel Cardinal (☎ 722800; www.firsthotels .com; Bäckgatan 10; d from Skr995, discount Skr695) is a large, well-equipped hotel in the centre of town, with a range of rooms and rates.

For sustenance, head to Storgatan or try the classy **Wibrovski** (☎ 740410; Sandgärdsgatan

19; mains Skr165-235; ☻ dinner Mon-Sat), where you can dine in an old timbered house or from a hanging basket chair on the patio. At Smålands Museum, **Café Momento** (☎ 39129; dishes & snacks Skr35-99) is a great lunch or coffee spot. There's an excellent selection of baguettes, salads and cakes, and a pretty courtyard.

Getting There & Away

Växjö lies between Alvesta and Kalmar and is served by **SJ trains** (☎ 0771-757575; www.sj.se) that run roughly hourly. Buses to other parts of the county also depart from the train station, with destinations including Oskarshamn and Kosta. **Svenska Buss** (☎ 0771-676767; www.svenskabuss.se) runs daily between Stockholm and Malmö via Norrköping, Linköping and Växjö.

GLASRIKET

One of the most impressive things to see in Sweden is traditional glass-blowing, and there's no better place to see it than here, in its birthplace, the so-called 'Kingdom of Crystal'. The rest of the scenery's not bad either – dense forests, quaint red houses and intricately winding roads. It's no surprise that the area known as **Glasriket** (www .glasriket.se) is the most visited area of Sweden outside of Stockholm. Visit the area anytime outside of the June-to-August high season, though, and you'll feel like the first person to discover it. There are at least 15 glass factories (look for signs saying '*glasbruk*') scattered around the wilderness, but if you're short on time you should visit at least one or two of the big three – Kosta, Boda and Orrefors. Factory outlets offer substantial discounts on seconds, and most of the larger places offer a shipping service.

Nybro

☎ 0481 / pop 19,800

Nybro's **tourist office** (☎ 45085; www.nybro.se; Stadshusplan; ☻ daily Jun-Aug, Mon-Fri Sep-May) is inside the town hall and can help with information about the town and region. Of the glass factories in the immediate surrounds, traditional **Pukeberg** (☎ 80029; www .pukeberg.se) is a worthwhile stop for its quaint setting and high quality. About 2.5km west of the town centre is the 200m-long *kyrkstallarna* building, old church stables that

now house the excellent folklore museum **Madesjö Hembygdsgård** (☎ 17935; adult/child Skr30/5; ☻ mid-May–mid-Sep).

Nybro Lågprishotell & STF Vandrarhem (☎ 10932; Vasagatan 22; dm/s/d from Skr195/345/445; ☻ Mar–mid-Dec), south of the centre near Pukeberg, is the local STF hostel. It's clean and comfortable and has a kitchen on each floor. You can also rent bikes here (Skr50 per day).

The more upmarket, governmental-looking **Stora Hotellet** (☎ 51935; rumsbokning @telia.com; Mellangatan 11; s/d Skr1190/1450, discount Skr795/1090) is on Stadhusplan, just by the tourist office. It's home to the best eating options in town, with both a pub and a restaurant.

SJ trains (☎ 0771-757575; www.sj.se) between Alvesta and Kalmar stop here every hour or two. Regional bus No 131 runs regularly to/from Kalmar.

Kosta, Boda & Orrefors

These three tiny Småland villages are home to the three biggest names in Swedish glass production. Each namesake company is open daily and each factory complex has an outlet store, museum or gallery, glass-blowing demonstrations and tourist information for the area. Admission to most attractions costs Skr20, or free with the Glasriket Pass (Skr95).

Kosta is the largest village and is where Glasriket started in 1742. At times it looks like the biggest tourist trap in southern Sweden, but it can be appreciated if you concentrate on the finesse and quality of the local craftsmanship and not on the tourist buses and discount stores, or if you go between seasons, when you may well be the only visitor. Boda is a quaint little village with a large factory outlet, a few other homewares shops and little else. Founded in 1864, the Boda glass factory is now part of the internationally renowned **Kosta Boda company** (☎ 0478-34500; www.kosta boda.com; ☻ 10am-8pm Mon-Fri, 10am-6pm Sat & Sun mid-Jun–Aug, 10am-6pm Mon-Fri, 11am-4pm Sat & noon-4pm Sun Sep–mid-Jun) Much the same range is available at these two factories.

Orrefors (☎ 0481-34195; www.orrefors.com; ☻ 0478-34500) was founded in 1898. The factory complex is impressive (make sure you check out the gallery) and there's a good hostel nearby.

Across the road from the factory in Kosta, **Kosta Värdshus** (☎ 0478-50006; www.kostavardshus .com; Storavägen; s/d from Skr450/750) serves inexpensive lunches and offers simple, comfortable accommodation. There's also **Kafe Kosta** (meals around Skr50), inside the factory's outlet store, serving sandwiches, cakes and hot meals – nice if you're looking to try out some of that glassware before you buy.

STF Vandrarhem Boda (☎ 24230; boda.van drarhem@telia.com; dm/s/d Skr185/215/345; ☺ May–mid-Sep) in Boda is not far from the factory and well signposted.

The friendly, well-equipped **STF Vandrarhem Orrefors** (☎ 30020; dm/s/d Skr165/275/365; ☺ May-Aug) in Orrefors is conveniently located near the factory area. At the factory complex you can dine at Orrefors Värdshus (lunch and snacks available) but there's also a summertime stall selling hot dogs and ice cream. You can also get pizzas and kebabs from Pizzeria Alexandra in the village.

If you're here from June to August, ask about *hyttsill* parties at the glass factories, where traditional meals are prepared using the furnaces and cooling ovens. The menu includes herring, smoked sausage, bacon and baked potatoes, as well as the regional speciality *ostkaka* (cheesecake). The cost starts at around Skr325 per person including drinks. Contact the regional tourist offices or the glassworks for more information.

Getting There & Around
Glasriket is fairly isolated and is not that easy to explore without transport. Bicycle tours are great if you follow the minor roads; there are plenty of hostels and you can camp almost anywhere in the countryside. From mid-June to mid-August bus No 138 runs a few times daily (not on Sunday) from Kalmar to Nybro, Orrefors and Kosta (and vice versa). Regular (year-round) bus No 139 connects Nybro and Orrefors; Kosta is served by regular bus No 218 from Växjö.

OSKARSHAMN
☎ 0491 / pop 26,200
There's not a lot to Oskarshamn (from a visitor's perspective) other than some important boat connections to Gotland. Hantverksgatan is one of the main streets, where you'll find the **Kulturhuset** (Hantverksgatan 18) housing the **tourist office** (☎ 88188;

www.oskarshamn.se; ☺ daily Jun-Aug, Mon-Fri Sep-May) and the town library, which has free internet access.

If you're staying overnight, the well-run **STF Vandrarhem Oskarshamn** (☎ 88198; vandrarhemmet@oksarshamn.se; Åsavägen 8; dm/s/d Skr250/350/455) is a few hundred metres from the train station and well positioned for the Gotland ferries.

Local trains run from Nässjö, and regional buses make a regular run on the coastal Kalmar–Oskarshamn–Västervik route (the Oskarshamn–Kalmar section is Skr70). **Swebus Express** (☎ 0200-218218; www .swebusexpress.se) has three daily buses between Stockholm and Kalmar that stop at Oskarshamn. Regular boats to Visby on Gotland depart from near the train station.

KALMAR
☎ 0480 / pop 35,000
For a long time the port of Kalmar was the key to Baltic power, and the short-lived Scandinavian union agreement of 1397 was signed at its grand castle. Kalmar was vital to Swedish interests until the 17th century and its cobbled streets and impressive edifices retain a strong historical flavour. It's also the gateway to the long, skinny island of Öland.

Information
IT-Caféet (Kaggensgatan 40B; ☺ 8am-4pm Mon-Thu, 8am-3pm Fri) Internet access.
Library (Tullslätten 4) Has free internet access.
Tourist office (☎ 417700; www.kalmar.se/turism; Ölandskajen 9; ☺ daily Jun-Aug, Mon-Sat May & Sep, Mon-Fri Oct-Apr)

Sights & Activities
The once-powerful Renaissance **Kalmar Slott** (☎ 451490; adult/child Skr75/20; ☺ Apr-Sep), which is located in a magnificent setting by the sea south of the railway, was the key to Sweden before the lands to the south were claimed from Denmark. The panelled King Erik chamber is the highlight of the castle's interior, while another chamber exhibits punishment methods used on women in crueller times. For art-lovers the nearby **Konstmuseum** (☎ 426282; Slottsvägen 1D; adult/child Skr40/free) is worth a look, while the pretty streets of the **Gamla Stan** area to the northeast of the castle are lovely for wandering.

The highlight of **Kalmar Länsmuseum** (County Museum; ☎ 451300; www.kalmarlansmuseum .se; Skeppsbrogatan 51; adult/child Skr50/free), in the old steam mill by the harbour, is the exhibition of finds from the flagship *Kronan*, which sank controversially off Öland in 1676 – a disaster to match the sinking of the *Vasa*, which sank in 1628 and is now on show in Stockholm at the spectacular Vasamuseet (p399).

A few blocks away, in the imposing but somewhat empty main square, is the baroque **domkyrka** (Stortorget), which – like most of the buildings designed by Tessin, the leading 17th-century architect working for the Swedish crown – looks like a gigantic birthday cake.

Sleeping

Svanen STF Vandrarhem & Lågprishotell (☎ 12928; www.hotellsvanen.se; Rappegatan 1; dm Skr195, hotel s/d Skr520/625) In a lovely setting by the water, facing the city's appealing silhouette, Svanen is a well-equipped hostel and hotel on the island of Ängö (connected by road to the centre; take bus No 402). There are good, clean rooms available with or without private bathroom – the hotel rooms cost only a little more than the hostel, and breakfast is included. Canoe hire is available.

Söderportsgården (☎ 12501; www.soderportsgar den.se in Swedish; Slottsvägen 1; s/d Skr495/695, 3-/4-bed apt Skr950/1190; ⏰ mid-Jun–mid-Aug) In a great location right by the castle, this student

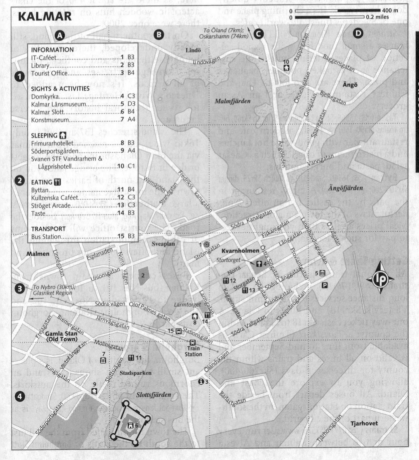

residence offers good, simple, summertime-only accommodation. There's also a good café-bar here (with regular live music), and prices include breakfast.

Frimurarhotellet (☎ 15230; www.frimurarehotellet .com; Larmtorget 2; s/d Skr1040/1260, discount Skr720/895, summer Skr770/945) A pretty, older-style hotel with 34 en-suite rooms, a super friendly staff and free coffee and cookies in the foyer, this place is right in the heart of the action. Bike rental is available.

Eating

Kulzenska Caféet (☎ 28882; 1st fl, Kaggensgatan 26; sandwiches Skr25-40) This place goes on forever, with room after room of tiny coffee nooks furnished with grandmotherly antiques but generally populated by students quietly doing homework. It's a charming place and one of Sweden's finest old-world cafés.

Ströget arcade (Storgatan 24) This arcade houses a small food hall, with a good selection of places offering lunch-time sustenance such as baked potatoes, baguettes and pizza. There are also lots of Thai and Chinese restaurants here, and an Asian grocery.

Taste (☎ 15565; Södra Långgatan 5; lunch Skr69, bistro mains Skr90-150) A fresh, modern café and restaurant-bar with good-value hot lunches and a bistro menu of classics such as Caesar salad, pasta and burger options.

Byttan (☎ 16360; Stadsparken; lunch Skr75, dinner Skr160-200; ☉ May-Sep) A classy restaurant in the park by the castle, Byttan offers wonderful views of the town's major attraction. Meal prices are less than you might expect to pay for such a location.

Getting There & Away

All regional traffic is run by **Kalmar Län-strafik** (☎ 0491-761200), including the Rasken long-distance services (Oskarshamn Skr70, Västervik Skr118) and buses to Öland. A one-way ticket costs Skr18 to Skr118 within the county; a *Turistkort* (Tourist Card) is available from June to mid-September and is valid on all buses and trains within the county for three/seven days (Skr200/400), allowing you to explore the coast and Öland. All buses depart from beside the train station on Stationsgatan, in the southwestern part of the city grid.

SJ trains (☎ 0771-757575; www.sj.se) run every hour or two between Kalmar and Alvesta

(with connections to the main north–south line), and to Göteborg.

ÖLAND

☎ 0485 / pop 23,000

This has to be the easiest possible way to visit a Swedish island – you can actually drive to it. Öland acts as a long, skinny offshore camping ground – it's a popular summer holiday destination for Swedes, and it's full of camping grounds and hostels. Much of the island is designated a haven for nature. There are lighthouses dotting the key points at the northern and southern tips. But what it's really famous for are the windmills. You can play out your Don Quixote fantasies with abandon here, as there are about 400 of the characteristic wooden huts on rotating bases; there were once 2000.

On the southern half of the island, still mostly undeveloped, there are relics of human settlements and conflicts, including Iron Age fortresses and graveyards of all periods. It's now been added to Unesco's World Heritage List, recognised for its long cultural history and diverse landscapes.

The island stretches 137km (but is only 16km wide) and is reached from Kalmar via the 6km Ölandsbron, once the longest bridge in Europe. The bridge lands you on the island just north of Färjestaden ('ferry town' – the prebridge name), where there's a large **tourist office** (☎ 560600; www.olandsturist .se; ☉ daily May-Aug, Mon-Fri Sep-Apr) beside the road. The tourist office will book rooms or cabin accommodation throughout the island and offers numerous brochures and maps.

Buses connect all main towns from Kalmar (bus Nos 101 to 106 all cross the bridge to Färjestaden; Nos 101, 102 and 106 go to Borgholm). Kalmar–Borgholm costs Skr46.

Borgholm & Around

Borgholm, the 'capital' of Öland, is a pleasant small town with shops, cafés and an enormous ruined castle on the outskirts. The small **tourist office** (☎ 89000; Sandgatan 25; ☉ Mon-Sat Jun–mid-Aug, Mon-Fri mid-Aug–May) is at the bus station.

The town is dominated from the hill just to the south by the ruins of **Borgholms Slott**

(☎ 12333; adult/child Skr50/free; ⏱ May-Sep). This castle was burnt out and abandoned early in the 18th century after being used as a dye works. There's a museum inside; the ruins are often used as a venue for summer concerts and festivals.

Sweden's most famous 'summer house', **Solliden Slott** (☎ 15355; www.sollidensslott.se; parks & pavilion exhibitions adult/child Skr60/30; ⏱ mid-May–mid-Sep), 2.5km south of the town centre, is used by the Swedish royal family. It has beautiful parks and pavilion exhibitions, plus a café.

VIDA Museum (☎ 77440; www.vidamuseum.com; adult/child Skr40/free; ⏱ daily May-Sep, Sat & Sun Apr & Oct-Dec) is a strikingly modern museum and art gallery in Halltorp, about 9km south of Borgholm on road 136, with graphics, textiles, paintings, sculpture and more from some of the best-known artists working in Sweden.

SLEEPING & EATING
The tourist offices in Borgholm and Färjestaden can help you find inexpensive private rooms in the area.

Kapelludden Camping & Stugor (☎ 560770; www.kapelludden.se; Sandgatan; camp sites from Skr170; 6-person cabin Skr860-1220; ⏱ late Mar-early Oct; 🛒) This is the handiest camping ground to Borgholm, just north of the bus terminal. It's a huge place (with some 450 camp sites) and has five-star, family-oriented facilities, including a swimming pool.

Ebbas Vandrarhem & Trädgårdscafé (☎ 103 73; Storgatan 12; dm from Skr155) Just outside the centre of Borgholm is this well-equipped hostel, in a manor house set in a pretty garden.

Guntorps Herrgård (☎ 13000; www.guntorpsher rgard.se; Guntorpsgatan; s/d Skr895/1095) A delightful old farmhouse east of town, near the

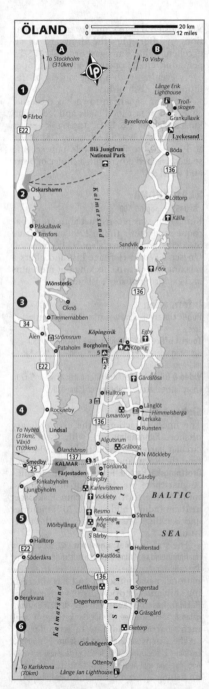

INFORMATION	
Tourist Office	1 A4

SIGHTS & ACTIVITIES	
Borgholms Slott	2 A4
Solliden Slott	(see 2)
VIDA Museum Konsthall	3 A4

SLEEPING 🏠 ⛺	
Ebbas Vandrarhem & Trädgårdsgafe	(see 5)
Guntorps Herrgård	4 B3
Kappelludden Camping & Stugor	5 A3

EATING	
Pubben	(see 5)

SWEDEN

STF hostel. There's quality accommodation on offer, plus the drawcard of an excellent-value smorgasbord (Skr175/75 per adult/child, open to all) from 6pm every evening, with a huge variety of traditional Swedish dishes.

The main square in town has the usual collection of fast-food stalls and ice-cream kiosks. **Pubben** (☎ 12415; Storgatan 18; ☼ from 6pm Sun-Thu, from 3pm Fri & Sat Jun-Aug, Wed-Sat Sep-May) is a classic English-style pub serving snacks, washed down with a choice of beers and whiskies.

KARLSKRONA

☎ 0455 / pop 60,600

Karlskrona was reconstructed in grand baroque style after a fire in 1790 and became Sweden's greatest naval port. It's now on Unesco's World Heritage List and offers a relaxing day or two checking out museums and exploring offshore islands.

Information

Public Library (Borgmästeregatan 8) Has free internet access.

Tourist office (☎ 303490; www.karlskrona.se/tourism; Stortorget 2; ☼ daily mid-Jun–mid-Aug, Mon-Sat mid-Aug–mid-Jun)

Video & Biljard Café (Admiraltetsgatan 4; per hr Skr20) Cheap internet access until 10pm or 11pm daily.

Sights & Activities

The finest attraction is the extraordinary offshore **Kungsholms Fort**, with its curious circular harbour, established in 1680 to defend the town, and the impregnable tower **Drottningskär kastell**. From mid-June to mid-August there are daily four-hour guided tours to the fort, sailing from Fisktorget at 10am (adult/child Skr140/70); inquiries and bookings are made through the tourist office.

The striking **Marinmuseum** (☎ 53902; www .marinmuseum.se; Stumholmen; adult/child Skr50/free; ☼ daily Jun-Aug, Tue-Sun Sep-May) is the new national naval museum and has interesting ship and historical displays. Nearby is **Båtmanskasernen Konsthall** (☎ 303422; Bastionsgatan 8; admission free; ☼ Tue-Sun), once a seamen's barracks and now an art gallery.

The extensive **Blekinge Museum** (☎ 304960; Fisktorget 2; adult/child Skr40/free; ☼ daily mid-Jun–mid-Aug, Tue-Sun mid-Aug–mid-Jun) features exhibits on fishing, quarrying and the local shipping

trade, plus there's a baroque garden, a lovely courtyard café and a host of other things.

Touring Karlskrona's **archipelago** is a pleasant way to spend a sunny afternoon. A three-hour tour taking in the eastern islands costs from Skr110/50 per adult/child; contact **Skärgårdstrafiken** (☎ 78330; Fisktorget) for timetables and information.

Sleeping & Eating

STF Vandrarhem Karlskrona-Trossö (☎ 10020; www.karlskronavandrarhem.se; Drottninggatan 39; dm/s/d from Skr175/275/370) Good central hostel with all the facilities you need, plus a decent outdoor area.

Hotell Siesta (☎ 80180; siesta.hotell@telia.com; Borgmästaregatan 5; s/d from Skr655/1050, discount Skr600/750) A good midrange option, right near Stortorget and offering fresh, modern rooms.

The northern side of the huge Stortorget and the street behind it, Ronnebygatan, are home to a good choice of eateries and lots of outdoor seating in fine weather.

Montmartre (☎ 311833; Drottninggatan 28; mains Skr65-140) A nice little Italian restaurant (with attached museum), serving pizza for around Skr70, plus a range of pasta, meat and fish dishes.

King's Crown (☎ 10088; Stortorget; lunch Skr70, bar snacks & light meals Skr35-140) Take a break from sightseeing at this English-style pub by the tourist office, and enjoy a bar meal of nachos, steak sandwiches or baked potatoes. There's also a more upmarket dining area, with a menu featuring items such as seafood and reindeer fillet (mains Skr150 to Skr230).

Getting There & Away

The bus and train stations are just north of the town centre, on Kungsplan. **Svenska Buss** (☎ 0771-676767; www.svenskabuss.se) runs services once daily except Saturday between Stockholm and Malmö via Oskarshamn, Kalmar and Karlskrona. Train connections are better, running regularly to Copenhagen via Kristianstad and Malmö. Regular trains also run to Emmaboda, and from there to Kalmar or Växjö and on to Göteborg.

Stena Line ferries to Gdynia (Poland) leave from Verkö, 10km east of Karlskrona (take bus No 6). See p476 for more information on this ferry service.

GOTLAND

☎ 0498 / pop 57,400

Historically rich and economically right on the money, Gotland is a budget traveller's dream. Cycling around the mostly flat island and camping free in forests is a truly wonderful way to see the island's hundred-plus medieval churches and prehistoric sites. Other attractions include the unusual *raukar* limestone formations (remains of 400-million-year-old coral reefs), particularly at the northern tip of Fårö. You can scarcely take three steps on Gotland without stumbling over a runestone or an ancient burial site (see p455), typically marked with large stones arranged into the shapes of Viking ships or piled up. There's also a great network of hostels scattered around the island – that's if you can be persuaded to leave its stunning port city of Visby, a walled beauty that's on Unesco's World Heritage List. You could easily pass a week here seeing the highlights, eating well in the high-quality restaurants and relaxing on a beach. Book ahead in summer, though, because it's also on the list of practically every holidaying Swede.

Good websites for travellers heading to Gotland include www.gotland.net and www.gotland.info.

VISBY

☎ 0498 / pop 21,400

Like a living museum, albeit a museum taken over by throngs of partying Swedes each summer, Visby is a labyrinth of cobblestone streets surrounded by medieval town walls. From mid-May to mid-August cars are banned in the old town, making it safer and more pleasant to stroll this gorgeous Hanseatic port city to your heart's content. The Hanseatic League was an alliance that held a trade monopoly over the Baltic region. It reached the height of its power in the 1300s.

The city's summer highlight is the costumes, performances, crafts, markets and reenactments of **Medeltidsveckan** (Medieval Week; www.medeltidsveckan.com), held during the first week of August. Book accommodation well in advance if you wish to visit at this time.

The **tourist office** (☎ 201700; www.gotland.info; Hamngatan 4; ☺ daily May-Sep, Mon-Fri Oct-Apr) can help with brochures, maps and visitor information, but doesn't book accommodation. The **library** (Cramérgatan; ☺ Mon-Sat) offers free internet access.

Sights

The old town is a noble sight, with its **13th-century wall** of 40 towers. Set aside enough time to stroll the perimeter (3.5km), and meander around Visby's narrow roads and pretty lanes. Ask at the tourist office about guided walking tours, conducted in English a few times a week in summer (Skr85), or buy a copy of *Visby on Your Own* (Skr35) for a self-guided tour.

The **ruins** of 10 medieval churches are all within the town walls and contrast with the old but sound **Cathedral of St Maria**, north of Stora Torget. **Gotlands Fornsal** (☎ 292700; Strandgatan 14; adult/children under 16 Skr60/free; ☺ daily May-mid-Sep, Tue-Sun mid-Sep-Apr) is one of the largest and best regional museums in Sweden, with a notable collection of runestones and early grave findings. Extraordinary 8th-century, pre-Viking picture stones, human skeletons from chambered tombs, silver treasures and medieval wooden sculptures are highlights. Don't miss the display of a skull found with a hatchet stuck through it. Allow a couple of hours if you want to fully appreciate the displays. The nearby **Konstmuseum** (☎ 292775; Sankt Hansgatan 21; adult/child Skr40/free; ☺ daily May-mid-Sep, Tue-Sun mid-Sep-Apr) displays varying art exhibitions.

Sleeping

Moderately priced accommodation in and around Visby is in demand; we recommend booking well in advance if possible. Gotland's hotel prices work opposite to most hotel rates in Sweden: prices increase on summer weekends and in the peak tourist months.

It's possible to book all types of accommodation (hotels, hostels, cottages) and/or holiday packages for the entire island through large agencies such as **Gotlands Resor** (☎ 201260; www.gotlandsresor.se) and **Gotlands Turistservice** (☎ 203300; www.gotlandsturistservice.com).

Norderstrands Camping (☎ 212157; www.norderstrandscamping.se; camp sites Skr100-175, 4-bed cabins Skr450-650; ☺ mid-Apr–mid-Sep) By the sea, 800m north of the ring wall (which is connected by a walking/cycling path), this camping ground is just at the edge of Visby and has killer views of the water.

SWEDEN

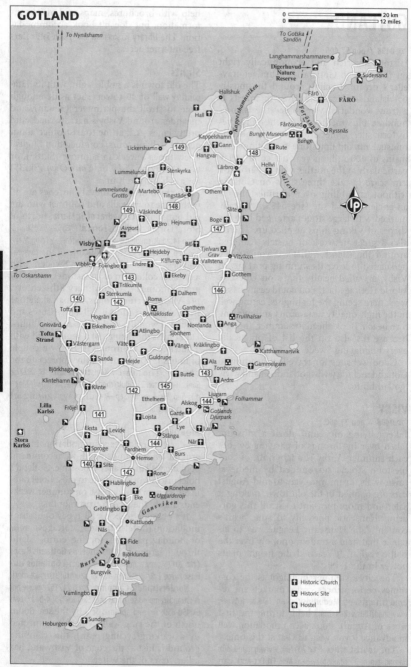

GOTLAND

SWEDEN

| 0 | 20 km |
| 0 | 12 miles |

To Nynäshamn

To Gotska
Sandön

Langhammarshammaren

Digerhuvud
Nature
Reserve

Sudersand

Fårö

FÅRÖ

Hallshuk

Fårösund

Ryssnäs

Hall

Kappelshamnsviken

Kappelshamn

Bunge Museum

Bunge

Gann

Rute

Lickershamn

Hangvar

Lärbro

Hellvi

Lummelunda

Stenkyrka

Othem

Valleviken

Lummelunda
Grotto

Martebo

Tingstäde

Slite

Väskinde

Bro

Hejnum

Boge

Airport

Bäl

Visby

Hejdeby

Tjelvars
Grav

Vitviken

Vibble

Fole

Källunge

Vallstena

Endre

Follingbo

Ekeby

Gothem

Träkumla

Dalhem

Stenkumla

Roma

Ganthem

Trullhalsar

Tofta

Romakloster

Norrlanda

Anga

Hogrän

Eskelhem

Atlingbo

Sjonhem

Gnisvärd

Väte

Vänge

Kräklingbo

Katthammarsvik

Tofta
Strand

Västergarn

Sanda

Hejde

Guldrupe

Ala

Gammelgarn

Björkhaga

Buttle

Torsburgen

Klintehamn

Klinte

Ardre

Lilla
Karlsö

Fröjel

Ethelhem

Alskog

Ljugarn

Folhammar

Eksta

Levide

Lojsta

Garde

Gotlands
Djurpark

Stora
Karlsö

Sproge

Fardhem

Lye

Lau

Silte

Hemse

Stånga

När

Burs

Rone

Hablingbo

Havdhem

Eke

Ronehamn

Grötlingbo

Uggarderojr

Näs

Kattlunds

Gansviken

Fide

Björklunda

Öja

Burgsvik

Burgsviken

Vamlingbo

Hamra

Hoburgen

Sundre

Historic Church

Historic Site

Hostel

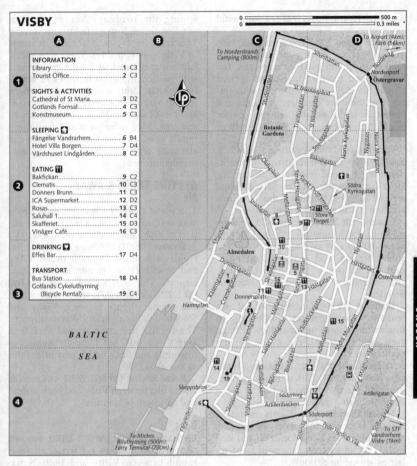

VISBY

INFORMATION
Library.....................................**1** C3
Tourist Office..........................**2** C3

SIGHTS & ACTIVITIES
Cathedral of St Maria...............**3** D2
Gotlands Fornsal.....................**4** C3
Konstmuseum.........................**5** C3

SLEEPING
Fängelse Vandrarhem..............**6** B4
Hotel Villa Borgen...................**7** D4
Värdshuset Lindgården............**8** C2

EATING
Bakfickan..............................**9** C2
Clematis...............................**10** C3
Donners Brunn.......................**11** C3
ICA Supermarket....................**12** D2
Rosas...................................**13** C3
Saluhall 1..............................**14** C4
Skafferiet..............................**15** D3
Vinäger Café.........................**16** C3

DRINKING
Effes Bar..............................**17** D4

TRANSPORT
Bus Station...........................**18** D4
Gotlands Cykeluthyrning
(Bicycle Rental)..................**19** C4

SWEDEN

STF Vandrarhem Visby (☎ 269842; carl.tholin@tjelvar.org; Fältgatan 30; dm/d from Skr175/475; ☺ mid-Jun–mid-Aug) This is southeast of the town centre off Lännavägen, in a school residence and therefore only open in the high season. Facilities include kitchen and laundry.

Fängelse Vandrarhem (☎ 206050; Skeppsbron 1; dm Skr200-300; ☺ May-Sep) A deservedly popular hostel near the harbour, this former prison has beds in converted cells. Facilities include kitchen, TV room and sauna, and an outdoor bar in summer.

Värdshuset Lindgården (☎ 218700; www.lindgarden.com in Swedish; Strandgatan 26; s/d low season Skr750/900, high season Skr1070/1295) Right in the middle of town, with eight spacious en-suite bedrooms in a beautiful garden set-

ting, this hotel is also attached to a good restaurant with al fresco dining.

Hotel Villa Borgen (☎ 279900; www.guteinfo.com/villaborgen; Adelsgatan 11; low season s/d Skr890/1010, high season Skr1050/1260) Another reasonably priced option for central Visby, with pleasant rooms set around a pretty, quiet courtyard off a street filled with cafés and boutiques. The lowest prices are on weekends in the low season (Skr710/850).

Eating & Drinking

There's no shortage of quality restaurants, cafés and bars around the old town squares, on Adelsgatan or at the harbour.

Rosas (☎ 213514; Sankt Hansgatan 22; light meals Skr30-70) In a pretty half-timbered house with sunny courtyard, Rosas makes a wonderful lunch spot.

Donners Brunn (☎ 271090; Donnersplats; mains Skr95-245; ☑ dinner) Among the finest restaurants in town and good for a splurge. The Swedish and international menu (priced around Skr230) is adventurous and tempting, and there are cheaper vegetarian and *husmanskost* dishes; alternatively, opt for one of the set menus from Skr380 (for three courses). Book ahead.

Bakfickan (☎ 271807; Stora Torget 1; lunch Skr75, mains Skr75-198) The menu at this unpretentious, highly rated restaurant on buzzing Stora Torget features well-prepared fish and seafood including fish soup, salmon, prawns and herrings in a few different guises.

Clematis (☎ 210288; Strandgatan 20; ☑ dinner mid-Jun–mid-Aug) In summer, step back in time some 700 years by visiting Clematis, a restaurant serving food cooked according to medieval recipes, accompanied by music and entertainers (including the occasional fire-eater).

Skafferiet (☎ 214597; Adelsgatan 38; light meals Skr45-65) An excellent café, as inviting as Rosas with its cosy interior and low ceilings, great sandwiches and cakes, and popular outdoor area.

Vinäger Café (☎ 211160; cnr Hästgatan & Mellangatan; lunch buffet Skr59) This stylishly modern, unsigned place is frequented by a young and fashionable crowd.

Saluhall 1 (Skeppsbron) Hang-outs around the harbour are popular on warm summer days and evenings. Do as the locals do and stop by here for an ice cream at one of Sweden's largest ice-cream parlours.

ICA supermarket (Stora Torget; ☑ 8m-8pm Mon-Sat, 10am-8pm Sun) There's this store for self-caterers. Alternatively, there are large supermarkets outside the town walls (head to Österväg, through Österport gate).

Effes Bar (☎ 215111; Adelsgatan 2; mains Skr60-130; ☑ Wed-Mon) A unique pub-bar that's built into the town wall, this is a great place for a laid-back meal or drink; there's a bar menu, outdoor courtyard, pool tables and regular live music.

AROUND THE ISLAND

Renting a bicycle and following the well-marked **Gotlandsleden cycle path** is one of the best ways to spend time on the island. It loops all around the island, sometimes joining the roadways but more often winding through quiet fields and forests. You can hire cycles at several locations in Visby (see opposite). There's an excellent hostel network along the cycle route, with particularly good facilities in **Bunge**, **Lummelunda**, **Lärbro** and the small northern islet of **Fårö** (home of Ingmar Bergman! and lots of sheep). The passenger ferry to and from Fårö is frequent and free; don't miss a chance to see the sunset from the elaborate rock formations at Langhammarshammaren.

GETTING THERE & AWAY
Air

The island's **airport** (☎ 263100; www.lfv.se) is 4km northeast of Visby. A taxi from the airport to Visby should cost around Skr100.

Skyways (☎ 0771-959500; www.skyways.se) has regular scheduled flights between Visby and Stockholm's Arlanda and Bromma airports. The local airline is **Gotlands Flyg** (☎ 222222; www.gotlandsflyg.se in Swedish), which has regular flights between Visby and Stockholm's Bromma and Skavsta airports. The regular fare costs around Skr600 to Skr800 one way, but there are numerous discounts and deals which may offer fares as low as Skr300.

Malmö Aviation (☎ 0771-550010; www.malmoaviation.se) flies between Visby and both Malmö and Göteborg in summer.

Boat

Destination Gotland (☎ 0771-223300; www.destinationgotland.se) operates car ferries all year-round between Visby and both Nynäshamn and Oskarshamn. Departures from Nynäshamn are from two to six times daily (about five hours, or three by high-speed catamaran). From Oskarshamn there are one or two daily departures (about three hours).

Regular one-way adult tickets cost from Skr228/301 for the ferry/catamaran, but from mid-June to mid-August most crossings go up in price – some overnight, evening and early-morning sailings in the middle of the week retain the cheaper fares, and tickets booked via the internet are cheaper. There are child, student and senior discounts available, plus budget tickets (these must be booked at least 21 days before departure).

To transport a bicycle costs Skr40; a car usually costs about Skr300/400 on the ferry/catamaran, although on many crossings during the peak summer these prices increase, and the spaces fill up quickly – make sure you book well in advance if you're planning to travel with a car in the peak summer period.

GETTING AROUND

There are over 1200km of roads in Gotland, typically running from village to village through the pretty landscape. There's also a dedicated cycle path, the Gotlandsleden (see opposite for more information). Bicycle tours are highly recommended, and bikes can be hired from a number of places in Visby. **Gotlands Cykeluthyrning** (☎ 214133; info@ gotlandscykeluthyrning.com; ☙ mid-May–Aug), just behind Saluhall 1 not far from the harbour, rents bikes from Skr65/325 per day/week. For cycling/camping trips it also offers rental of three-person tents (Skr100/400 per day/week).

There are also a few car-rental agencies on the island if you prefer to drive around. **Mickes Biluthyrning** (☎ 266262; www .mickesbiluthyrning.se; Visby harbour) offers affordable rates (from Skr250/1500 per day/week) for older cars.

Kollektiv Trafiken (☎ 214112; www.gotland.se /kollektivtrafiken in Swedish) runs buses via most villages to all corners of the island. A one-way ticket costs between Skr12 (for a short journey of less than 4km) and Skr59 (for journeys of more than 51km). Carrying a bicycle on board the bus will cost you an additional Skr40.

NORRLAND

Norrland, the northern half of Sweden, is remote enough that travellers here aren't likely to see the tour-bus crowd – or, for that matter, much of anyone else. The population is sparse – reindeer outnumber cars on the roads, and much of the landscape consists of deep green forest. It's a paradise for nature lovers who enjoy hiking, skiing and other outdoor activities. Some of the best long-distance hiking trails in Sweden are here, along with the most rugged of the country's national parks. Accommodation tends to be budget-friendly, too, leaning more towards camping and hostels than proper hotels.

The area has what amounts to its own separate identity from the rest of Sweden. It's associated with early pioneers' struggles to produce the timber and iron ore necessary for building the railways that opened up the region.

The north is home to the Sami, and it's here that you'll find the Ájttemuseum in Jokkmokk, one of the best places to learn about their culture. Several villages have well-preserved open-air museums that demonstrate traditional Sami culture.

For quirk-seekers, Norrland offers some true gems: a rarely glimpsed monster lurking in a lake, a disappearing hotel made of ice, and a golf course that flits between Sweden and Finland, to name a few. Inlandsbanan, the historic railway line from Mora to Gällivare via Östersund, Storuman, Arvidsjaur and Jokkmokk, is a fun if not particularly fast way to see the north (see p479).

SWEDEN

ISLAND ATTRACTIONS

There are hundreds, perhaps thousands of prehistoric sites around Gotland, many of them signposted, including stone ship-settings, burial mounds and remains of hill-top fortresses. Keep your eyes open for the information boards along roadsides. You can visit these sites, as well as the numerous nature reserves, any time, free of charge.

Nowhere else in northern Europe are there so many medieval churches in such a small area. There are 92 of them outside Visby; more than 70 have medieval frescoes and a few have rare medieval stained glass. In addition, Visby has a dozen church ruins and a magnificent cathedral.

Each village had a church built between the early 12th and the mid-14th centuries, until wars ended the tradition. Each church is still in use, and all of the medieval villages still exist as entities. Most churches are open from 9am to 6pm daily, mid-May to late August. *The Key to the Churches in the Diocese of Visby* is a useful English-language brochure available free from tourist offices.

SUNDSVALL

☎ 060 / pop 93,000

Much of Sundsvall was reduced to ashes by the great fire of 1888, but the town centre was rebuilt in grand style over the following 10 years. It's a pleasant place to spend a day or two, admiring the impressive architecture and enjoying one of Norrland's biggest and liveliest towns. It's also a convenient base for exploring the delightful Höga Kusten, especially with your own transport. The **tourist office** (☎ 610450; www.sundsvallturism.com; Stora Torget; ☽ Mon-Sat) can help with traveller inquiries.

Kulturmagasinet (☎ 191800; Sjögatan; ☽ Mon-Sat), down near the harbour, is a magnificent restoration of old warehouses. The buildings now contain a café, the town library and **Sundsvall Museum** (☎ 191803; adult/child Skr20/free), which has exhibits of local and natural history. The library here offers internet access.

Up on the hill **Norra Stadsberget** (150m), there's a viewing tower, walking tracks, and a typical **friluftsmuseum** (outdoor museum; admission free), a collection of old-fashioned local houses. The southern hill, **Södra Stadsberget** (250m), has an extensive plateau that's good for hiking, with trails up to 12km long. Buses run to each hill every couple of hours in summer.

Sleeping & Eating

The intersection of Nybrogatan and Rådhusgatan is a good area to go looking for reasonably priced hotels.

STF Vandrarhem Sundsvall (☎ 612119; www.norraberget.se; Gaffelbyvägen; dm/s/d from Skr150/250/300; 🖳) This excellent hostel is above the town on Norra Stadsberget and has simple older rooms plus slightly more expensive rooms with en suite and TV. The uphill walk to the hostel is pleasant but not much fun with heavy bags; ask about buses when booking.

Baltic Hotel (☎ 140440; Sjögatan 5; s/d from Skr1100/1250, discount Skr525/700) This fairly stylish older building near Kulturmagasinet has bright, modern rooms in a great location and good weekend/summer discounts.

Café Tinells (☎ 56149; Sjögatan 7; mains Skr40-65) This sleek café serves traditional pastries, tempting sandwiches and quiche, and good coffee in chic, modern surrounds.

Saigon Palace (☎ 173091; Trädgårdsgatan 5; lunch from Skr65, mains Skr70-125) This comfortable place has a great lunch buffet and a huge menu of satisfying Chinese and Vietnamese dishes.

Getting There & Away

Buses arrive at and depart from the bus station, known as Navet, in the northern part of town near Kulturmagasinet. **Ybuss** (☎ 0771-334444; www.ybuss.se in Swedish) runs daily to Östersund, Umeå and Stockholm. **Norrlandskusten** (☎ 0771-511513) bus No 100 runs several times daily between Sundsvall and Haparanda via Umeå, Luleå and most northern coastal towns.

Trains run south to Stockholm via Uppsala and west to Östersund (and from there on to Trondheim, Norway); change at Ånge for northern destinations. The **train station** (Köpmangatan) is just east of the centre.

HÖGA KUSTEN

☎ 0613

One of the most attractive parts of Sweden's coastline, Höga Kusten (meaning the High Coast) is a hilly area with many lakes, fjords and offshore islands. Although in most parts the scenery is not as dramatic as the name might suggest, the region as a whole has been listed as a Unesco World Heritage Site, recognised as a unique area largely shaped by the combined processes of glaciation, glacial retreat and the emergence of new land from the sea (this retreat continues today at a rate of 0.9m per hundred years).

Höga Kusten stretches from north of Härnösand to Örnsköldsvik, both pleasant but unremarkable towns with decent facilities. There's a **tourist office** (☎ 50480; www.hogakusten.com) inside Hotell Höga Kusten, just north of the spectacular E4 suspension bridge over Storfjärden (which is about 70km north of Sundsvall), where you can pick up information on attractions and accommodation options in the tiny villages; be sure to pick up a free map highlighting the scenic driving routes (marked with brown and white signs). There's also useful information on the internet at www.turistinfo.kramfors.se.

Unfortunately, there's little by way of public transport (buses cruise along the E4 highway but don't make it into the region's villages). Hence, this area is virtually impossible to explore without your own set of wheels.

As well as the striking landscapes, the region's other major attractions are the many well-preserved fishing villages, the pick of them being Barsta, Bönhamn and Norrfällsviken, and the lovely offshore islands, especially Högbonden and Ulvön, both accessible by boat.

Ferries to Högbonden (☎ 0706-818284; adult/child return Skr80/40) go from Barsta every two hours from 9.30am to 5.30pm, returning 45 minutes later, mid-June to mid-August, and from Bönhamn every two hours from 9.45am to 5.45pm mid-June to mid-August. **Ferries to Ulvön** (☎ 0613-10550; adult/child return Skr150/50) leave from Ullånger (9.30am), Docksta (10.15am) and Mjällomslandet (10.45am), arriving at 11.30am and returning at 3pm from Ulvöhamn, from June to August.

The odd attraction that is **Mannaminne** (☎ 20290; www.mannamine.com; adult/child Skr40/free; ☯ daily Jun-Sep, Sat & Sun Oct-Nov & Mar-May), near tiny Häggvik, encompasses an eccentric collection of just about everything from farming to emigration and technology. There's also a good café – get the fried herring if they have it – and a handful of souvenir and craft shops. Walk up the steep hill behind the museum for the best view in the area (35 minutes return).

Skuleberget Naturum (☎ 40171; admission free; ☯ daily Jun-Aug, Mon-Thu Sep-May), by the E4 just north of the village of Docksta, has exhibitions and lots of information on the area. The steep mountain **Skuleberget** (285m) soars above the *naturum*; ask about hiking routes, the chairlift and rock-climbing routes.

Sleeping & Eating

There are a few cafés scattered throughout the region, but it's a nice idea to pick up supplies before setting off and take advantage of the scenic waterside picnic spots. There are supermarkets in Ullånger, Nordingrå, Docksta and Mjällom.

Norrfällsviken Camping (☎ 21382; www.norrfallsvikenscamping.com; camp sites Skr120, cabins/cottages from Skr350/600; ☯ May-Oct; ☲) The idyllic village of Norrfällsviken has this well-equipped camping ground with cottages, plus the excellent fish restaurant and pub Fiskarfänget (☎ 21142), with a takeaway counter as well as service in a wood-panelled room or a large deck over the water – the kind of place you never want to leave.

Hotell Höga Kusten (☎ 722270; www.hotellhoga-kusten.se; s/d Skr845/1095, discount Skr500/750) Stay at this large, modern hotel just off the E4. It's by the huge bridge and offers stunning views. There's also a café here and a restaurant, Bridge Brasserie & Bar, with a huge range of snacks (Skr40 to Skr100) and meals (Skr8 to Skr210), plus a kids' menu.

Mannaminne (☎ 20290; www.mannaminne.se in Swedish; s/d Skr250/500, cabin d/tr/q Skr300/350/400) As well as its bizarre assortment of museum exhibitions, Mannaminne, near Häggvik, has B&B accommodation and cabins for hire. There's a café as well, and music and theatre performances in summer.

Vandrarhem Högbonden (☎ 23005, 23100; www.hogbonden.se in Swedish; dm Skr265-285; ☯ May-Oct) This is a superb getaway on the island of Högbonden, reached by boat from Bönhamn and Barsta (Skr80 return). There's a kitchen here (bring all supplies with you), and also a café in summer; breakfast is served for Skr70 but order it ahead of time. You'll need to book well in advance.

ÖSTERSUND

☎ 063 / pop 58,400

This pleasant town by Lake Storsjön, in whose chilly waters is said to lurk a rarely sighted monster, has good budget accommodation and is a relaxed and scenic place and an excellent gateway town for further explorations of Norrland. The **tourist office** (☎ 144001; www.turist.ostersund.se; Rådhusgatan 44; ☯ daily Jun-Aug, Mon-Fri Sep-May) is opposite the town hall, one block from the bus station.

Sights & Activities

Don't miss **Jamtli** (☎ 150100; www.jamtli.com; admission Skr60-90; ☯ daily Jun-Aug, Tue-Sun Sep-May), 1km north of the town centre. This is the highlight of Östersund, combining the lively exhibitions of the regional museum and a large museum village with staff in period clothing. The regional museum exhibits the curious **Överhogdal tapestry**, a Viking relic from around 1100 that's perhaps the oldest of its kind in Europe and may even predate the famous Bayeaux tapestry.

Some of the attractions lie on the adjacent island of Frösön, reached by road or footbridge from the middle of Östersund (the footbridge is from the pleasant Badhusparken – nearby you can rent bikes, inline skates and canoes). The island features the animals at **Frösö Zoo** (☎ 514743; adult/child Skr150/80; ☯ mid-Jun–late Aug) and the restored, late-12th-century **Frösöns kyrka** (☉ Jun-Aug), with its characteristic separate bell tower. For skiers there are slalom and nordic runs on the island at Östberget, where there's a **viewing tower** (adult/child Skr10/5; ☉ mid-May–mid-Sep) giving fine views.

Ask at the tourist office about monster-spotting **lake cruises** (Skr65-95; Jun-Sep). Take your binoculars.

Sleeping & Eating

STF Vandrarhem Jamtli (☎ 122060; vandrarhem met@jamtli.com; dm/s/d Skr185/280/380) Take the opportunity to live among Östersund's major attraction: this small, quaint hostel is inside the Jamtli museum precinct. Catch bus No 2.

STF Vandrarhem (☎ 34130; micke2@algonet.se; Södra Gröngatan 36; dm/s/d Skr210/375/420; ☉ late Jun-early Aug) This second, summer-only STF hostel offers excellent apartments (all with bathroom, kitchen and TV) and is not far from the train station.

Vandrarhemmet Rallaren (☎ 132232; rallaren @hotmail.com; Bangårdsgatan 6; dm/s/d Skr175/225/380) For tired and weary Inlandsbanan passengers, this small, clean and modern hostel is very conveniently located next to the train station.

Pensionat Svea (☎ 512901; Storgatan 49; s/d from Skr450/550) A homey and affordable guesthouse close to the heart of town. Bathroom facilities are shared, breakfast is included and there's also a guest kitchen. Check-in is at Hotel Jämteborg, opposite.

Paviljong Thai (☎ 130099; Prästgatan 50B; lunch Skr65, mains Skr75-149) There's a good lunch buffet and hefty portions of great Thai cuisine here, with all the favourite noodle, curry and seafood dishes on the menu.

Brunkullans Krog & Bar (☎ 101454; Postgränd 5; lunch Skr70, dinner mains Skr140-200; ☉ lunch Mon-Fri, dinner Tue-Sat) A classy eatery with friendly staff and an outdoor patio, this gourmet establishment serves an excellent-value lunch buffet.

Getting There & Away

The train station is a short walk south from the town centre, but the main **regional bus station** (Gustav III Torg) is central. Local buses usually run to both. Local bus Nos 1, 3, 4, 5 and 9 go to Frösön.

Bus No 45 runs south to Mora twice a day (5¼ hours). In summer the Inlandsba-

nan train runs once daily to Gällivare (14 hours) or Mora (six hours). Bus No 156 runs west to Åre and bus No 63 runs twice daily northeast to Umeå.

Direct trains run from Stockholm via Uppsala and Gävle, and some continue west to Storlien (from where you can catch trains to Trondheim, Norway). You can also catch a train east to Sundsvall.

ÅRE & AROUND

☎ 0647 / pop 9600

The **Åre** (www.skistar.com/are) area is arguably Sweden's top mountain-sports destination. The area has 40 ski lifts that serve 100 pistes and 1000 vertical metres of skiable slopes, including a superb 6.5km downhill run (day pass about Skr300). The skiing season is from November to early May, but conditions are best from February, when daylight hours increase; Easter is a hugely busy time. There are also cross-country tracks in the area, a big après-ski scene, and winter activities such as dogsledding, snowmobile safaris and reindeer sleigh rides.

When the weather warms up, Åre also offers great summer outdoor recreation, including hiking, kayaking, rafting, fishing and mountain biking. The area west of Åre is popular among fell walkers: there's a network of STF wilderness huts and lodges here for enthusiasts.

The **tourist office** (☎ 17720) is in the train station. Most facilities are around the main square, which you reach by walking through the park opposite the train station.

Sleeping

In winter it's best to book accommodation and skiing packages via **Åre Resor** (☎ 17700; www.skistar.com/are); the same company also organises summer packages, but independent travellers at this time of year shouldn't have too many problems finding accommodation. The low season, when almost all hotels and restaurants are closed, is after the snow has melted in May, and between the summer and winter seasons (October until around Christmas).

Like the hotels, many restaurants in the area are closed in summer, but there are still some good choices, primarily centred on the main square (where you'll also find supermarkets).

Åre Ski Lodge (☎ 51029; s/d/tr Skr190/290/390; ☽ May-Sep) On the E14 above the town, next to the fire station, is this cosy Austrian-style ski lodge offering great summer prices and facilities such as sauna and kitchen.

STF Vandrarhem Åre (☎ 30138; info@brattlands garden.com; dm/s/d from Skr175/175/305; ☽ Jun-Sep & mid-Dec-Apr) This hostel is actually 8km east of Åre, signposted off the E14. It has good facilities and enjoys great views.

Åre Continental Inn (☎ 17170; www.areinn.se in Swedish; d from Skr800; ☽ May-Sep) This huge, 130-room complex offers reasonable summer rates for its fairly basic rooms. Facilities are first-rate, however, and include pool, sauna and gym as well as restaurants and bars. The hotel is about 5km east of Åre and operates a shuttle bus to town.

Villa Tottebo (☎ 50620; Parkvägen 1; mains Skr105-250) In a pretty red cottage opposite the train station, this is one of the leading restaurants in Sweden's north, and there's an inviting bar upstairs.

Getting There & Away

Regional bus No 156 runs from Östersund and connects Åre to the nearby winter-sports centre of Duved (much quieter and more family-oriented than Åre). Regular trains between Stockholm and Storlien, via Östersund, stop at Åre. Storlien is the terminus for **SJ trains** (☎ 0771-757575; www.sj.se); change here for Norwegian trains to Hell and Trondheim.

UMEÅ

☎ 090 / pop 105,000

Umeå is a big, bustling town that sticks out amid the quiet expanses of Norrland. The busy port has ferry connections to Finland. It's among the fastest-growing towns in Sweden and has some 22,000 students, making it an agreeable place to just hang out for a spell en route north. The **tourist office** (☎ 161616; www.umea.se/turism; Renmarkstorget 15; ☽ daily mid-Jun–mid-Aug, Mon-Fri mid-Aug–mid-Jun) can help with visitor inquiries and offers free internet access.

The **Gammlia** (☎ 171800; admission free; ☽ daily Jun-Aug, Tue-Sun Sep-May) complex, 2km east of the town centre, is home to several good museums and shouldn't be missed. It includes the cultural history and Sami collections of the regional **Västerbottens Museum** (adult/child Skr20/free); the open-air

Friluftsmuseet (admission free; ☽ mid-Jun–mid-Aug), with old houses and staff in period clothes; and the modern-art museum **Bildmuseet** (admission free).

There are interesting offshore islands plus a number of activities in the surrounding area, including fishing, white-water rafting, jet-boating and canoeing in or on the local rivers, horse riding and a variety of **walking trails** (from two hours to three days). The tourist office can help organise these.

Sleeping & Eating

Compared with other towns in the north, Umeå doesn't have much by way of central budget accommodation.

STF Vandrarhem Umeå (☎ 771650; info@vandrar hemmet.se; Västra Esplanaden 10; dm/d Skr210/420) This place is run with militaristic precision and has a great central location.

Hotel Pilen (☎ 141460; Pilgatan 5; s/d Skr550/750, discount Skr450/550) A small, family-run place, with somewhat dated décor but comfortable rooms, in a quiet area some 600m from the town centre.

Royal Hotel (☎ 100730; www.royalhotelumea .com; Skolgatan 62; s/d Skr1240/1440, discount weekends Skr650/880, discount summer Skr550/765) An upmarket option with great summer rates, the Royal has all the facilities you'd expect, with a highly regarded restaurant, Greta, on site.

Lottas Krog (☎ 129551; Nygatan 22; mains Skr108-198; ☽ Mon-Sat) A friendly, cosy restaurant-pub with something for everyone on the extensive menu, from great snacks under Skr100 to meals such as fish and chips, Mexican fajitas or roast lamb; Lottas is also a popular drinking spot.

Rex (☎ 12 60 50; Rådhustorget; mains Skr100-200) This fancy bar in the back of the town hall has an immensely long list of knowledgeably executed cocktails to go wtih its top-notch fare.

Blå (☎ 132300; Rådhusesplanaden 14; mains Skr94-132) A large, glossy place with a menu of favourites, Blå turns into a fashionable bar and nightclub as the evening progresses.

Getting There & Away

The long-distance **bus station** (Järnvägsallén) is opposite the train station, just north of the centre. Umeå is the main centre for **Länstrafiken Västerbotten** (☎ 020-910019), the regional bus network. Direct buses run to Mo i Rana in Norway; other daily destinations include Östersund and Luleå. **Connex** (☎ 0771-260000; www.connex.se) trains leave daily from Umeå to connect with the north–south trains between Stockholm and Luleå.

There are daily ferries between Umeå and Vaasa in Finland (see p475). A bus to the harbour leaves from near Umeå's tourist office an hour before ferry departures. Local buses leave from Vasaplan on Skolgatan.

LULEÅ
☎ 0920 / pop 72,000

Luleå is the capital of Norrbotten, Sweden's largest county and accounting for one quarter of the country's total area. It may be an important transport hub on your journey north, and there are interesting diversions and good-value accommodation. Storgatan is the main pedestrian mall; the **tourist office** (☎ 293500; www.lulea.se; Storgatan 43; ☺ daily Jun-Aug, Mon-Sat Sep-May) will help with inquiries; and the **library** (Kyrkogatan) has free internet access.

The most famous sight in Luleå is the Unesco World Heritage Listed **Gammelstad**, or 'Old Town', which was the medieval centre of northern Sweden. The stone church (dating from 1492), 424 wooden houses (where the pioneers stayed overnight on their weekend pilgrimages) and six church stables remain. The open-air museum **Hägnan** (☺ Jun-Aug) and a nature reserve are nearby. There's a small **tourist office** (☎ 293581; www.lulea.se/gammelstad; ☺ daily Jun-late Aug, Tue-Thu late Aug-Jun) at Gammelstad, and it organises guided tours (Skr30) of the church village in summer. Take local bus No 6 to Kyrkbyn.

Norbottens Museum (☎ 243500; Storgatan 2; admission free; ☺ Tue-Sun) is worth a visit, particularly for the Sami section and some very interesting short films on the northern lights and Sami identity. In summer there are **boat trips** to the surrounding archipelago; schedules vary but are available at the tourist office.

Sleeping & Eating
Luleå Vandrarhem & Mini Hotell (☎ 222660; luleavandrarhem@telia.com; Sandviksgatan 26; dm/s/d Skr175/265/380) This budget option doesn't look like much from the outside, but inside there's clean and comfortable accommodation. The large dorms are not so great (with tri-level bunks) – the twin rooms are a far better option. Bikes are available for hire.

Park Hotell (☎ 211149; www.parkhotell.se in Swedish; Kungsgatan 10; s/d from Skr500/700, discount Skr400/550) This small hotel offers pleasant but somewhat basic rooms. Prices given here are for rooms without bathroom – an extra Skr200 or so will get you a private bathroom.

Comfort Hotel Max (☎ 220220; www.choicehotels .se; Storgatan 59; s/d Skr1250/1350, discount Skr550/750) A huge bargain at weekends and in summer, this well-equipped business hotel offers discounted rates that include breakfast and a dinner buffet.

Roasters (☎ 88840; Storgatan 43; lunch Skr70, snacks Skr35-75) There are good cafés on either side of the tourist office, including this stylish spot with extensive lunch options, grilled focaccia and ciabatta, strong coffee and outdoor seating.

Corsica (☎ 15840; Nygatan 14; mains Skr60-98) This restaurant-bar is slightly dingy but full of character and has a huge menu of reasonably priced selections – pizza, pasta, kebabs, salads, fish and steak.

Getting There & Away
The **airport** (☎ 244900; www.lfv.se) is 9km southwest of the town centre. There are around a dozen flights daily between Stockholm and Luleå, with **SAS** (☎ 0770-727727; www.scandinavian.net) and **Nordic Airlink** (☎ 08-528 068 20; www .flynordic.com), and **Skyways** (☎ 0771-959500; www .skyways.se) flies directly to/from Göteborg. Take the airport bus from the bus station (Skr45).

Länstrafiken Norrbotten (☎ 020-470047; www .ltnbd.se) buses travel around the 100,000-sq-km county. Individual fares start at Skr17, travel cards are Skr270/410 for 20/40 trips, and bicycles are carried for Skr50. Bus No 100 is one of the most useful for travellers – it runs services between Haparanda, Luleå, Skellefteå, Umeå and Sundsvall four times daily. Bus No 21 travels up to Arvidsjaur, and bus No 44 to Jokkmokk and on to Gällivare.

Direct **Connex** (☎ 0771-260000; www.connex.se) trains from Stockholm and Göteborg run at night only. Most trains from Narvik and Kiruna terminate at Luleå.

HAPARANDA

☎ 0922 / pop 10,400

Considering that its very name sounds like something fun to do, it's no surprise that Haparanda is a gateway to some of the best outdoor activities in the north. The small settlement was founded in 1821 as a trading town to replace Sweden's loss of Tornio (spelt Torneå in Swedish) to Russia (now in Finland, p200). These days the two border towns function almost as one entity – both the krona and the euro are accepted at most places; Tornio is one hour ahead of Haparanda.

There is an extremely efficient and well-equipped joint Haparanda-Tornio **tourist office** (☎ 12010; infokiosk.haparanda.se; ☯ daily Midsummer–mid-Aug, Mon-Fri mid-Aug–Midsummer) on the 'green line' between the countries – look for the mess of flags sticking up near the bridge. A smaller summer tourist office operates inside Haparanda's Stadshotellet.

There are few sights in Haparanda and the church looks like a grain silo, but one noteworthy attraction is the unique golf course. The **Green Zone Golf Course** (☎ 10660) is right on the border of the two countries; during a full round of golf the border is crossed four times.

The scenic **Kukkolaforsen** rapids, on the Torne älv 15km north of Haparanda, are well worth a visit (take bus Nos 53 or 54). There's a **tourist village** (☯ Midsummer–mid-August) here that includes a camping ground and cabins, restaurant, café, fish smokehouse, saunas and a museum.

Vandrarhem Haparanda (☎ 61171; Strandgatan 26; dm/s/d Skr160/250/320) is an excellent hostel near the water and not far from the town centre. Some rooms have private bathroom, plus there's a sauna, laundry and self-catering facilities. Alternatively, you can opt for a meal at the on-site restaurant.

The large and once-grand **Stadshotellet** (☎ 61490; www.haparandastadshotell.se; Torget 7; s/d from Skr1090/1390, discount Skr650/850) is the focus of the town, and its pub-restaurant, the **Gulasch Baronen** (mains Skr70-120) offers reasonably priced meals in a convivial atmosphere. You can find some budget beds for about Skr300 here in summer.

A regular bus service connects Haparanda and Tornio (Skr15). There are regional buses from Luleå and towns further south, and daily bus No 53 travels north along

the border via the Kukkolaforsen rapids, Övertorneå and Pajala, then continues west to Kiruna.

ARVIDSJAUR

☎ 0960 / pop 7100

The settlement of Arvidsjaur, on the Inlandsbanan railway, was an early Sami market. **Lappstaden**, a well-preserved Sami church village, contains almost 100 buildings as well as forestry and reindeer-breeding concerns. Tours are Skr30/free for adults/children but operate only in July. The **tourist office** (☎ 17500; www.arvidsjaurlappland.se; Östra Skolgatan 18C; ☯ daily Jun-Aug, Mon-Fri Sep-May), behind the main street, has useful information.

The town is buzzing in winter, when test drivers from around Europe put their cars through their paces in the tough weather conditions, and there are loads of cold-weather activities available, including dog-sledding and snowmobile safaris. Inquire at the tourist office for more details, and for information on the range of summer options, including hiking, excursions, steam trains and fishing.

Cosy **Lappugglans Turistviste** (☎ 12413; Västra Skolgatan 9; dm Skr150) and the stylish **Rallaren** (☎ 070-682 3284; Stationsgatan 4; r per person Skr150; ☯ Midsummer-Aug), both near the train station, have excellent accommodation; the latter is a restored wooden house adjacent to an artist's gallery.

Kaffestugan (☎ 10725; Storgatan 21; lunch Skr60) is a popular café by the main square, with good daily lunch specials plus an assortment of cakes, sandwiches and light meals.

The daily bus between Gällivare and Östersund (No 45) stops at the **bus station** (Storgatan). Bus No 200 runs daily between Skellefteå and Bodø (Norway) via Arvidsjaur. The Inlandsbanan train can take you north to Gällivare via Jokkmokk, or south to Mora via Östersund.

JOKKMOKK

☎ 0971 / pop 5900

The small town of Jokkmokk, also on the Inlandsbanan railway, is just north of the Arctic Circle and started as a Sami market and mission. Its primary attraction is a worthwhile one indeed – the best museum of Sami culture in Sweden.

Since 1605 the **Jokkmokk Winter Market** (www.jokkmokksmarknad.com) has taken place here; the three-day event attracts some 30,000 people and starts on the first Thursday in February, when you can shop seriously for Sami handicrafts.

The Jokkmokk **tourist office** (☎ 22250; www.turism.jokkmokk.se; Stortorget 4; ☺ daily mid-Jun–mid-Aug, Mon-Fri mid-Aug–mid-Jun) can help with visitor information. The **Ájtte museum** (☎ 17070; Kyrkogatan 3; adult/child Skr50/free; ☺ daily May-Sep, Sun-Fri Oct-Apr) is a highlight, providing the most thorough introduction to Sami culture anywhere in Sweden. It also offers exhaustive information on Lappland's mountain areas, with maps, slides, videos and a library. A visit is recommended for planning wilderness trips (there are good opportunities for trekking in the areas surrounding Jokkmokk).

Naturfoto (☎ 55765; ☺ Jun-Aug), at the main Klockartorget intersection, exhibits and sells work by a local wilderness photographer, Edvin Nilsson. There are a number of Sami handicraft studios around town – ask at the tourist office.

About 7km south of Jokkmokk you'll cross the **Arctic Circle**; on road No 45 there's a summertime café and camping ground here.

Sleeping & Eating

STF Vandrarhem Jokkmokk (☎ 55977; www.jokk mokkhostel.com; Åsgatan 20; dm/d Skr175/450; ☐) Behind the tourist office, this comfortable hostel has laundry, sauna, yard, internet facilities and bikes for rent. It's a favourite with Inlandsbanan travellers and worth booking in advance in summer.

Hotell Gästis (☎ 10012; www.hotell-gastis.com in Swedish; Herrevägen 1; s/d/tr Skr850/995/1200, discount Skr650/750/900) It doesn't look too promising from the outside, but this hotel offers decent value with pleasant but unremarkable rooms, sauna and a good restaurant, with lunch specials and à la carte dinners.

Ájtte museum restaurant (Kyrkogatan 3; lunch from Skr65) A meal at the museum restaurant is recommended to reinforce the learning experience – you can try local and Sami specialities, including the fresh local fish or a sandwich with reindeer meat.

Café Piano (☎ 10400; Porjusvägen 4; lunch Skr65, mains Skr60-120; ☺ Mon-Sat) One of the town's best options, with a grand piano inside, a large garden outside and an extensive menu, including inexpensive pizza, pasta and wok meals.

Getting There & Away

Buses arrive and leave from the **bus station** (Klockarvägen). Bus Nos 44 and 45 run daily to/from Gällivare, and bus No 45 runs to Arvidsjaur once daily and further south to Östersund. Inlandsbanan trains stop in Jokkmokk; for main-line trains, take bus No 43 to Murjek (up to six a day) or bus No 44 to Boden and Luleå.

GÄLLIVARE & MALMBERGET

☎ 0970 / pop 19,700

The town of Gällivare and its northern twin Malmberget are surrounded by forest and dwarfed by the bald Dundret hill. It's not the most immediately appealing place for a stopover but is important as the northern terminus for the Inlandsbanan railway, and there are good opportunities for summer and winter activities.

The **tourist office** (☎ 16660; www.gellivare.se; Centralplan; ☺ Mon-Fri) is by the train station. **Dundret** (821m) is a nature reserve with superb views; you can view the midnight sun here from 2 June to 12 July. In winter there are four nordic courses and 10 ski runs of varying difficulty, and the mountaintop resort organises numerous activities including snowmobile safaris and northern lights tours.

In Malmberget, 5km north of Gällivare, **Kåkstan** is a historical 'shanty town' museum village dating from the 1888 iron-ore rush. Bus No 1 to Malmberget departs from opposite the Gällivare church. The Gällivare tourist office has details of tours to the **LKAB iron-ore mine** (tours Skr200; ☺ Midsummer-early Aug).

STF Vandrarhem Gällivare (☎ 14380; www.ex plorelapland.com; Barnhemsvägen 2; dm from Skr195) is across the footbridge from the train station. Accommodation is in well-equipped cabins; bikes can be hired and a variety of activities organised (multiday wilderness treks in summer, dogsled tours in winter; see the website for details).

The large **Quality Hotel Gällivare** (☎ 55020; Lasarettsgatan 1; s/d Skr1090/1450, discount Skr690/890), opposite the train station, is your best bet for dining in Gällivare – either at the restaurant (lunch for Skr68) or the cosier pub (mains Skr95 to Skr230). Both have a decent menu of cheaper dishes (pasta, burgers) and local specialities such as elk fillet or arctic char.

Getting There & Away

Regional buses depart from the train station. Bus No 45 runs daily to Östersund (Skr410) via Jokkmokk and Arvidsjaur; bus No 93 serves Ritsem and Kungsleden in Stora Sjöfallet National Park (from mid-June to mid-September only); bus Nos 10 and 52 go to Kiruna; and bus No 44 runs to Jokkmokk and Luleå.

Connex (☎ 0771-260000; www.connex.se) trains come from Luleå and Stockholm (sometimes changing at Boden), and from Narvik in Norway. More exotic is the Inlandsbanan, which terminates at Gällivare; the full journey from Östersund to Mora costs Skr762.

KIRUNA

☎ 0980 / pop 23,900

Kiruna is the northernmost town in Sweden and, at 19,446 sq km, it's the largest municipality in the country. The area includes Sweden's highest peak (Kebnekaise, 2111m), a remarkable attraction in the form of a hotel made from ice, and several fine national parks and trekking routes (see Abisko, p465). It's worth making the effort to get up here, especially for nature lovers, hikers or anyone interested in Sami culture.

This far north, the midnight sun lasts from 27 May to 14 July and there's a bluish darkness throughout December and New Year.

The helpful **tourist office** (☎ 18880; www.lap pland.se; Lars Janssonsgatan 17; ⊙ 8.30am-8pm Mon-Fri, 8.30am-6pm Sat & Sun May-Sep, closed Sun Oct-Apr) is next to the Scandic Hotel and has loads of detailed brochures, as well as a few computers for internet access. Staff can arrange various outdoor activities including Sami experiences year-round; rafting, hiking, horse riding, rock climbing and fishing in warmer weather; and ice-fishing, dogsledding and snowmobile safaris in winter.

The **library** (Biblioteksgatan), behind the bus station, offers free internet access.

A visit to the Ice Hotel (p464) is a must. Also worthwhile in Kiruna is a visit to the depths of the **LKAB iron-ore mine** (☎ 18880; tours adult/child Skr220/50), 540m underground. Two-hour English-language tours depart from the tourist office regularly from June to August, and during other months if there's enough interest. Make inquiries and book-

ings through the tourist office. **Kiruna kyrka** (Kyrkogatan), the town church, looks like a gigantic Sami tent; it's particularly pretty against a snowy backdrop.

Sleeping & Eating

Kiruna has lots of good-value accommodation options, especially in summer. The tourist office brochures include full details, including prices.

STF Vandrarhem Kiruna (☎ 17195; Bergmästaregatan 7; dm/s/d Skr205/345/470) This large, functional hostel has a central location, good facilities (including sauna) and an adjacent Chinese restaurant.

Yellow House (☎ 13750; www.yellowhouse.nu; Hantverkaregatan 25; dm/s/d Skr150/300/400) Another

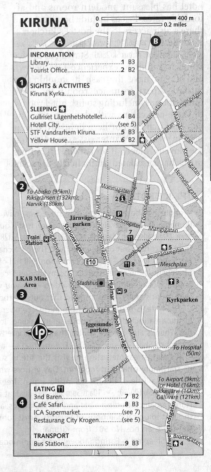

KIRUNA

INFORMATION	
Library	1 B3
Tourist Office	2 B2

SIGHTS & ACTIVITIES	
Kiruna Kyrka	3 B3

SLEEPING	
Gullriset Lägenhetshotellet	4 B4
Hotell City	(see 5)
STF Vandrarhem Kiruna	5 B3
Yellow House	6 B2

EATING	
3nd Baren	7 B2
Café Safari	8 B3
ICA Supermarket	(see 7)
Restaurang City Krogen	(see 5)

TRANSPORT	
Bus Station	9 B3

good budget option, the more homey Yellow House has a comfortably worn-in feel, with facilities including sauna, kitchen, laundry and TV in each room. Breakfast is Skr50, and there's a garden to relax in if the weather holds.

Gullriset Lägenhetshotellet (☎ 10937; www .fabmf.se/gullriset in Swedish; Bromsgatan 12; apt Skr400-700) About 1.5km from the tourist office, this bargain option is perfect for self-caterers and those who fancy more space than a hotel room offers. Rent an apartment sleeping up to four people, with kitchen, bathroom and cable TV.

Hotell City (☎ 66655; www.hotellcity.se; Bergmästaregatan 7; s/d Skr750/850, discount Skr650/750) In the same building as the STF hostel, this new hotel has pleasant, modern rooms and affordable rates. Prices include breakfast, and there's also access to the hostel's kitchen.

Ice Hotel (☎ 66800; www.icehotel.com; Marknadsvägen, Jukkasjärvi; r from Skr2800) Staying at the Ice Hotel is a unique experience (see below), and if you have the cash it shouldn't be missed. Apart from ice rooms there are other options, including stylish hotel rooms, or three-bed cabins with skylights enabling you to watch the northern lights from your bed in winter. Winter is expensive but the novelty makes it worthwhile. Summer prices have escalated dramatically in recent years, and don't represent good value given the range of affordable accommodation in Kiruna.

Ice Hotel Restaurant (☎ 66884; Marknadsvägen, Jukkasjärvi; mains Skr190-280) This quality restaurant opposite the accommodation complex in Jukkasjärvi specialises in local produce – try the arctic char or reindeer, and for dessert try the cloudberry mousse or elk cheese parfait! Some meals even come on plates made of ice. The lunch buffet (in summer) costs Skr95. It's open daily from June to September and at various times during the rest of the year.

3nd Baren (☎ 66380; Föreningsgatan 11; lunch Skr65, mains Skr69-189) At this moderately priced restaurant and lively drinking spot, you can try local specialities like reindeer, or play it safe with steak or pasta. There's a good outdoor patio to catch the late sunshine.

Café Safari (☎ 17460; Geologsgatan 4; light meals Skr20-60) Kiruna is not well endowed with great eateries. This is easily the nicest café, with good coffee, cakes and light meals such as sandwiches, quiche and baked potatoes.

Restaurang City Krogen (☎ 10900; Bergmästaregatan 7; lunch buffet Skr55, meals Skr92-140) This restaurant is attached to the STF hostel, offering classic Chinese dishes, cheap lunches, takeaway meals and kids' options.

THE ICE HOTEL

It might not be as exciting as it once was, now that similar hotels exist in Canada, Alaska and Romania, but the Ice Hotel in Jukkasjärvi is still quite a spectacle. The **hotel** (☎ 66800; www.icehotel .com; Marknadsvägen; day visit adult Skr130; r from Skr2800), 18km east of Kiruna, is rebuilt each winter from ice carved out of the local river. There's a chapel, a bar – where you drink vodka from a glass made purely of ice – and an exhibition hall full of – surprise – ice sculptures. But the main draw, obviously, is the hotel itself. In rooms made of ice, guests lie on beds covered with reindeer skins and inside sleeping bags designed to keep you warm despite the -5°C to -8°C temperatures. (If that sounds chilly, keep in mind that outside the hotel it can be as low as -30°C.)

The hotel is usually open from mid-December to late April (weather permitting). Things to do in the area include snowmobile safaris, skiing, ice-fishing, dogsledding and other winter activities. There's also the **Ice Globe Theatre** (nonguests from Skr450, guests Skr300, ☻ mid-Jan–early Apr), a replica of Shakespeare's Globe Theatre that's – again, surprise – built out of ice.

It's almost as interesting to visit the site in summer, when the melted hotel has left behind its startlingly small, flat footprint. Day visitors who have missed the main attraction can still experience a little of the magic. Inside a giant freezer warehouse, called the **Ice Hotel Art Center** (adult/child Skr100/50; ☻ 10am-5pm Jun–mid-Aug), at a temperature of -5°C, some features of the Ice Hotel remain, including a bar and ice sculptures; a recent exhibit consisted of sculptures based on the mythological paintings of Swedish artist John Bauer. The entry fee includes warm clothing. Get there on bus No 501 from Kiruna.

See Sleeping & Eating (above) for accommodation and meal details.

ICA supermarket (Föreningsgatan; 9am-7pm Mon-Fri, 10am-4pm Sat, 11am-4pm Sun) There's a supermarket next to 3nd Baren.

Getting There & Away

The small **airport** (68000; www.lfv.se), 9km east of the town, has daily nonstop flights to/from Stockholm with **SAS** (0770-727727; www.scandinavian.net). An airport bus (Skr50) connects with most flights.

Regional buses in this vast region are run by **Länstrafiken Norrbotten** (020-470047; www.ltnbd.se). Buses operate from the **bus station** (Hjalmar Lundbohmsvägen), opposite the Stadshus, and serve all major settlements. Bus No 91 runs two or three times daily to Riksgränsen via Abisko.

Regular trains connect Kiruna with Luleå, Stockholm (overnight) and Narvik (Norway). Trains to Narvik call at Abisko and Riksgränsen.

ABISKO

 0980 / pop 180

This village is a hiker's dream, with access to some of the best wilderness trails in Sweden mere steps away. It also has one of the best viewpoints for catching a midnight sunset. On top of that, the village itself is welcoming and pretty, and there's an excellent hiker-friendly hostel here.

The 75-sq-km **Abisko National Park**, on the southern shore of scenic Lake Torneträsk, is well served by trains, buses and the scenic mountain highway between Kiruna and Narvik. It's the soft option of the northern parks – distinctly less rugged and more accessible. There are some great short hikes.

The popular **Kungsleden** (King's Trail) follows the Abiskojåkka Valley, and day trips of 10km or 20km are no problem from Abisko village. With planning and preparation, committed hikers can walk the entire Kungsleden, which extends 450km south from Abisko to Hemavan (with huts and lodges along most of the route) and offers diversions to the summit of **Kebnekaise** or the magical national park of **Sarek** (note that Sarek is rugged and for experienced hikers only; it has no huts and few bridges).

Waterproof boots are essential at any time of the year; the snow doesn't melt until June. July, August and September are recommended for hiking, although in July there's still some boggy ground where mosquitoes

breed. It can still get cold very quickly, despite the midnight sun. Winter escapades are too risky for the uninitiated due to blizzards, extreme cold and avalanches.

The **Naturum** (40177; www.abisko-naturum.nu), next to the STF lodge in Abisko, provides information on the region, including help with hike preparation.

The **Linbana** (return ticket Skr140; 9.30am-4pm) chairlift takes you to 900m on Njulla (1169m) for breathtaking views.

In Björkliden, 8km northwest of Abisko, the resort **Björkliden Fjällby** (64100; www.bjorkliden.com) offers a full range of summer and winter activities and even has a nine-hole golf course. Tours are also organised by STF at Abisko Turiststation (below); both places offer outdoor gear for hire.

Sleeping & Eating

Abisko Fjällturer (40103; www.abisko.net; dm Skr150) This small hostel is a backpackers' delight. It has simple, comfortable accommodation and a wonderful wooden sauna, but the treat is in the reasonably priced activities on offer. The friendly owners keep a team of sled dogs, and for Skr700 in winter you get a night's hostel accommodation plus the chance to drive a sled, pulled by dogs, for about 10km. There are also half- and full-day sled trips (Skr1000/1700), and popular week-long sled trips from late February to early April (Skr9800 including meals and accommodation). Book early for longer trips. In summer you can take mountain walks with the dogs (Skr300 with a night in a dorm).

STF Abisko Turiststation (40200; www.abisko.nu; dm/s/d Skr290/620/980; Mar-Apr & mid-Jun–mid-Sep) Another excellent option, kept to the usual high STF standards. Trekking gear can be hired here, and there's a variety of accommodation options, guided tours, a shop with basic groceries, a pub and a restaurant (breakfast/lunch/dinner Skr75/75/195; half- and full-board arrangements are available). Accommodation prices are reduced by Skr100 for HI/STF members.

STF huts (dm members Skr185-275, dm nonmembers Skr285-375) Self-service huts along Kungsleden are spread at 10km to 20km intervals between Abisko and Kvikkjokk; ask at Abisko Turistation for information and take a sleeping bag. Day visitors are charged Skr40/50 for members/nonmembers, campers pay Skr60/80.

SWEDEN

Kebnekaise Fjällstation (☎ 55000; info@kebnekaise .st.se; dm/s/d from Skr320/850/1000; ☯ Mar-Apr & mid-Jun–mid-Sep) The excellent 100km trek from Abisko to Nikkaluokta runs via this STF lodge. Meals are available, and guided tours to the summit of Kebnekaise are offered. HI and STF members pay Skr100 less than the prices listed.

There's a supermarket in Abisko village for self-caterers, and a café-restaurant nearby.

Getting There & Away
In addition to trains between Luleå and Narvik (there are stations at Abisko Östra and Abisko Turiststation), bus No 91 runs from Kiruna to Abisko. Bus No 92 travels from Kiruna to Nikkaluokta (two to three a day), at the Kebnekaise trail heads. Kvikkjokk is served by bus No 47 that runs twice daily on weekdays to/from Jokkmokk.

RIKSGRÄNSEN
☎ 0980 / pop 50

The best midnight (or daytime) skiing in June in Scandinavia awaits you at this rugged frontier area (Riksgränsen translates as 'National Border'), 132km from Kiruna. You can briefly visit Norway at full speed on downhill skis! Rental of downhill gear/snowboards costs from Skr285/315 per day, and a day lift pass is Skr300; the skiing season can run until Midsummer.

There's not much to the tiny settlement here, but you can visit Sven Hörnell's **wilderness photography exhibition** (☎ 43111; www.sven -hornell.se; ☯ Feb-Sep) at his gallery and shop. The exhibition itself is free, and there's an audiovisual show for a fee (3pm daily mid-June to August, call for other times); commentary is in Swedish only, but you don't have to understand the language to appreciate the stunning Norrland photography.

Riksgränsen Ski & Spa Resort (☎ 40080; www .riksgransen.nu; r per person from Skr655; ☯ mid-Feb–Sep) is a large resort that's popular with skiers and offers organised wilderness activities in both the skiing and summer seasons. Rooms and apartments are available.

From Kiruna, bus No 91 runs via Abisko to Riksgränsen (two or three a day). Three daily trains run on the Luleå–Kiruna–Narvik route, and Riksgränsen is the last train station in Sweden before the train rushes through tunnels and mountain scenery back to sea level at Narvik in Norway.

SWEDEN DIRECTORY

ACCOMMODATION
In this chapter, we have classified sleeping options as follows:
- Budget: a bed in these establishments (usually hostels and budget guesthouses) should cost under Skr300 per person.
- Midrange: Skr650 to Skr1500 for a double room on a weekday. This price range covers small, comfortable hotels in the major cities, but some more luxurious options in smaller towns.
- Top End: Skr1500 and upwards for a weekday double.

Cabins & Chalets
Daily rates for *stugor* (cabins and chalets, often found at camping grounds or in the countryside) offer good value for small groups and families, and range in both facilities and price (Skr200 to Skr800). Some cabins are simple, with bunk beds and little else (you share the bathroom and kitchen facilities with campers); others are fully equipped with their own kitchen, bathroom and even living room. Local and regional tourist offices have listings of cabins and cottages that may be rented by the week; these are often in idyllic forest, lakeside or coastal locations and offer the chance for a true Swedish holiday experience. See the **Stuga** (www.stuga.nu) website for further information.

Camping
Sweden has hundreds of camping grounds and a free English-language guide with maps is available from tourist offices. Some camping grounds are open in winter, but the best time for camping is from May to August. Prices vary with facilities, from Skr100 for a basic site to Skr200 for the highest standards. Most camping grounds have kitchens and laundry facilities, and many grounds are popular family holiday spots and have the works – swimming pool, minigolf, bike and canoe rental, restaurant, store etc.

You are required to have the (free) Svenskt Campingkort to stay at Swedish camping grounds. Apply at least one month before your journey to **Sveriges Camping & Stugföreta-gares Riksorganisation** (SCR; fax 0522-642430; Box 255,

SE-45117 Uddevalla), or on the internet at www
.camping.se. If this isn't possible, you'll be
given a temporary card on arrival. The annual stamp on your card costs Skr100 and
is obtainable at the first camping ground
you visit.

Visit www.camping.se for lots of useful
information. See also the boxed text (p469)
for advice on free camping in Sweden.

Hostels

Forget all your preconceptions about hostels being dingy, scruffy and the domain
of noisy young backpackers. Swedish hostels are exceptional: clean, well equipped,
nicely decorated (this is the land of Ikea,
after all, so practical, attractive furniture
is readily available) and very good value.
Dorm beds, singles, doubles and family
rooms are usually available; some rooms
have a private bathroom and/or TV. The
majority are nonsmoking establishments.
There's almost always a kitchen for guests'
use, and often a laundry (which is handy,
as laundrettes are almost nonexistent in
Sweden). Breakfast is often available (Skr50
to Skr70), but normally has to be arranged
the night before. Linen is available for rent,
but bring sleeping sheets, a pillow case and
a towel from home to save money. You'll
be expected to clean your room upon departure (if you don't want to do this, you
can pay the hostel a 'cleaning fee').

Sweden has well over 475 *vandrarhem*
(hostels) and some 315 are 'official' hostels affiliated with **Svenska Turistföreningen**
(STF, Swedish Touring Agency; ☎ 08-463 2100; www
.svenskaturistforeningen.se; Box 25, SE-10120 Stockholm),
part of Hostelling International (HI). STF
produces a free detailed guide to its hostels,
but the text is in Swedish only (although
the symbols are generally easy to understand). All hostel details are also found
on the organisation's website, with some
information in English. Holders of HI cards
stay at STF hostels for between Skr100 and
Skr280 per bed per night. Nonmembers pay
Skr45 extra per night or can join up at hostels (membership costs Skr285 for adults,
Skr110 for those aged 16 to 25, free for
children). In this chapter we have listed the
prices at STF hostels for nonmembers.

Around 160 hostels belong to the 'rival'
Sveriges Vandrarhem i Förening (SVIF; ☎ 0413-553
450; www.svif.se; Box 9, SE-45043 Smögen). No mem-

bership is required; rates and facilities are
similar to those of the STF. Pick up the free
guide at tourist offices or SVIF hostels.

Also look out for other hostels that are not
affiliated with either STF or SVIF, and note
that some camping grounds have hostels.

Hostels in Sweden have a unique and
frustrating problem: they're hard to get into
outside reception opening times. Most of
the day (and much of the winter) the doors
are firmly locked. The trick is to phone
and make a reservation during the (usually short) reception hours. These vary, but
are generally from 5pm to 7pm. You may
have to write down the four-digit entrance
door code and ask where the room key will
be. Theoretically, you could stay overnight
without seeing another person until you
pay in the morning. From June to August
you can expect longer reception hours, but
a reservation is recommended during this
busy period. May is also a busy time for
hostels in major cities such as Stockholm
and Göteborg.

Be careful in December and check that
the hostel is open at Christmas and New
Year. Not all hostels are open year-round –
some are in student residences and only
open for the seven-week summer break
(from around Midsummer to early or mid-
August). Others are only open in the busier
months from May to September.

There are numerous mountain huts and
lodges, especially in Lappland, run by STF.
These are popular with hikers and outdoor
enthusiasts; more information is available
on STF's website.

Hotels

There are few cheap hotels in Sweden.
However, almost all Swedish hotels offer
good-value weekend and summer (mid-
June to mid-August) rates, often below
Skr800 for a quite luxurious double (up to
50% cheaper than their regular prices). See
individual reviews for discount prices. All
hotels have nonsmoking sections (most
are entirely nonsmoking). Rates usually
include a breakfast buffet. Some packages
are good value if you plan ahead: Stockholm, Göteborg and Malmö offer cut-price
'packages' that include a hotel room, free
entry to the major attractions of the city
and free local transport (see the Information sections under each city). Tourist

offices and travel agents can usually provide details about package deals.

Ask at a tourist office for the free brochure **Hotels in Sweden** (www.hotelsinsweden.net), or check the website. Discount schemes for 'frequent stayers' are generally run by the big chains; eg **Radisson SAS** (www.radissonsas .com), **Scandic** (www.scandic-hotels.com), **First** (www .firsthotels.com) and **Elite** (www.elite.se). Appealing to those on a budget are the two cheapest (and somewhat characterless) hotel chains, **Formule 1** (www.hotelformule1.com) and **Ibis** (www .ibishotel.com). At the other end of the scale, **Countryside Hotels** (www.countrysidehotels.se) offers accommodation in historic establishments ranging from castles and mansions to monasteries and spas.

ACTIVITIES

The image of wholesome, outdoorsy Swedish people is pretty spot-on (well, except for all the coffee they consume and cigarettes they smoke). The Swedes are huge naturelovers and are active year-round, on bike paths, forest jogging tracks, rivers and lakes, mountain trails, and the snow and ice.

Anyone getting out and about in the Swedish countryside should become familiar with Sweden's very democratic right of public access – see opposite.

Canoeing & Kayaking

Sweden's superb wilderness lakes and whitewater rivers are a paradise for canoeists and kayakers. The national canoeing body is **Svenska Kanotförbundet** (☎ 0155-209080; www .kanot.com; Rosvalla, SE-61162 Nyköping). It provides general advice and produces *Kanotvåg*, a free annual brochure listing the 75 approved canoe centres that hire canoes (averaging Skr200/800 per day/week) throughout the country. According to the right of common access, canoeists may paddle or moor virtually anywhere provided they respect the basic privacy of dwellings and avoid sensitive nesting areas within nature reserves. More good information is available on the **Kanotguiden** (www.kanotguiden.com) website, which also lists rental centres.

Hiking

Hiking is popular everywhere and the mountain challenge of the northern national parks is compelling. However, these parks are rarely snow-free and the jewel,

Sarek, is only for experienced hikers. Good equipment is vital.

Easy walking trails are common throughout Sweden. Many counties have a network of easy trails connecting sites of interest, and many municipalities have their own wilderness tracks (some off-the-beatentrack routes have free huts or shelters). The best hiking time is between late June and mid-September, but conditions are better after early August, when the mosquitoes have gone.

For information on organised group walks and the STF mountain huts, which are placed at intervals averaging about 20km along popular trails such as Kungsleden, contact STF (p467). You may stay the night (or camp nearby) for a fee which is slightly higher than STF hostel rates. There are also nine STF mountain lodges with shops, showers and restaurants. The free STF hostel guide includes details of mountain huts and lodges. Conditions are self-service, similar to STF hostels, and you should bring sheets (sleeping bags in huts).

Skiing

Cross-country (nordic) skiing opportunities vary depending on the snow and temperatures, but the northwest usually has plenty of snow from December to April (although not a lot of daylight in December and January). Practically all town areas (except the far south) have marked skiing tracks, often illuminated. There are large ski resorts catering mainly for downhill skiing in the mountainous areas of the west – Åre (p458) is the biggest and busiest (especially around Easter). The **Go Ski** (www.goski.com) and the **Alps** (www.thealps.com) websites have good pages reviewing the Swedish ski fields.

Other Activities

Opportunities for countless other activities exist, including cycling, rock climbing, mountaineering, fishing, horse riding, golf, sailing and rafting in summer; and skating, ice fishing, ice climbing, snowmobile safaris and dogsledding in winter. Tourist offices should be able to provide information, and you should check out the 'what to do?' pages on the **Visit Sweden** (www .visit-sweden.com) website.

SWEDEN

BUSINESS HOURS

Businesses and government offices open from 8.30am or 9am to 5pm Monday to Friday, although they can close at 3pm in summer. Banks usually open at 9.30am and close at 3pm, but some city branches open from 9am to 5pm or 6pm. Post offices are usually open 9am to 5pm Monday to Friday and shorter hours Saturday; the office in Centralstationen in Stockholm has longer hours (varying by season).

Most museums have short opening hours and many tourist offices are closed at weekends in the low season, from mid-August to mid-June.

Normal shopping hours are 9am to 6pm Monday to Friday and 9am to between 1pm and 4pm on Saturday, but department stores are open longer and sometimes also on Sunday. Some supermarkets in large towns will open until 7pm or 9pm. In restaurants, lunch often begins at 11.30am and is over by 2pm, and the restaurant will reopen again at 6pm for dinner. Cafés are usually open long hours (from 8am or 9am sometimes through until 9pm).

Frustratingly, many hostels, especially those hostels belonging to the STF network, are closed between 10am and 5pm (see p467).

'Summer' in this chapter is generally used to refer to the busy, brief summer season that runs from around mid-June to early or mid-August. This is when Swedish schools and many industries and offices are closed, and the Swedes flock en masse to their summer houses, the beach, lakes, mountains etc. Even some restaurants in larger cities are closed during this period. However, all is not lost – this is when hotels offer great bargains, with discounts of up to 50% on their standard rates (to fill rooms usually taken by business travellers).

CUSTOMS

Going through customs rarely involves any hassles, but rules on illegal drugs are strictly enforced. Duty-free allowances for travellers from outside the EU are: 1L of spirits or 2L of fortified wine; 2L of wine; and 200 cigarettes. The limits on goods brought into Sweden from another EU country are far more generous: up to 10L of spirits or 20L of fortified wine; 90L of wine; 110L of beer; plus 800 cigarettes. People aged under 20 years are not allowed to bring in alcohol. More information is on the website of the Swedish customs authority, **Tullverket** (www .tullverket.se).

DISABLED TRAVELLERS

Sweden is one of the easiest countries to travel around in a wheelchair. People with disabilities will find special transport services and adapted facilities of a generally high standard, ranging from trains and taxis to hotels and grocery stores. For information about facilities, contact the national organisation for people with disabilities, **De Handikappades Riksförbund** (☎ 08-685 8000; www.dhr.se; Katrinebergsvägen 6, Box 47305, SE-10074 Stockholm).

DISCOUNT CARDS

A HI membership card means discounts at STF hostels and mountain lodges (nonmembers pay an additional Skr45 per night,

---

RIGHT OF PUBLIC ACCESS

The right of public access to the countryside (called *allemansrätten*) means that in Sweden, by law, you're allowed to walk, boat, ski or swim on private land as long as you stay at least 70m from houses and keep out of gardens, fenced areas and cultivated land. You can camp for more than one night in the same place, and you may pick berries and mushrooms. You must not leave any rubbish nor take living wood, bark, leaves, bushes or nuts. Fires may be set where safe (not on bare rocks) with fallen wood. Use a bucket of water to douse a campfire even if you think that it's out. Cars may not be driven across open land or on private roads. Close all gates. Do not disturb farm animals or reindeer.

If you have a bicycle or car, look for free camp sites around unsealed forest tracks off secondary country roads. Make sure your spot is at least 50m from the track and not visible from any house, building or sealed road. Dry pine forests are your best bet. Bring drinking water and food, although running creek water can be used for washing (don't pollute the water with soap or food waste).

or can join in Sweden). Students should bring an International Student Identity Card (ISIC) card, although a number of discounts only apply to people with a Swedish student card. Still, students receive discounts on many forms of transport (including some airlines, ferry operators and local public transport), and on admission to museums, sights, theatres and cinemas. Children under 16 and seniors (usually 65 and over) normally receive similar discounts.

There are good-value discount cards available in the major cities (Stockholm, Göteborg and Malmö) that cover all local transport and most sightseeing needs for visitors for a set period (usually up to 72 hours). See the Information sections under each city for details.

EMBASSIES & CONSULATES
Swedish Embassies & Consulates

A list of Swedish diplomatic missions abroad (and links) is available at **Sweden Abroad** (www.swedenabroad.com).

Australia (☎ 02-6270 2700; 5 Turrana St, Yarralumla ACT 2600)

Canada (☎ 613-241 8553; www.swedishembassy.ca; 377 Dalhousie St, Ottawa ON K1N 9N8)

Denmark (☎ 33 36 03 70; www.swedenabroad.com /copenhagen; Sankt Annæ Plads 15A, DK-1250 Copenhagen K)

Finland (☎ 09-6877 660; www.swedenabroad.com /helsinki; Pohjoisesplanadi 7B, 00170 Helsinki)

France (☎ 01 44 18 88 00; www.swedenabroad .com/paris; 17 rue Barbet-de-Jouy, F-75007 Paris)

Germany (☎ 030-505060; www.swedenabroad .com/berlin; Rauchstrasse 1, 10787 Berlin)

Ireland (☎ 01-474 4400; www.swedenabroad.com /dublin; 13-17 Dawson St, Dublin 2)

Netherlands (☎ 070-412 0200; www.swedenabroad .com/thehague; Jan Willem Frisolaan 3, 2517 JS Den Haag)

New Zealand (☎ 04-499 9895; sweden@xtra.co.nz; 13th fl, Vogel Bldg, Aitken St, Wellington)

Norway (☎ 24 11 42 00; www.swedenabroad.com/oslo; Nobels gate 16, NO-0244 Oslo)

UK (☎ 020-7917 6400; 11 Montagu Place, London W1H 2AL)

USA (☎ 202-467 2600; www.swedenabroad.com /washington; Suite 900, 1501 M St NW, Washington DC 20005)

Embassies & Consulates in Sweden

The diplomatic missions listed here are in Stockholm, although some neighbouring countries also have consulates in Göteborg, Malmö and Helsingborg:

Australia (Map p402; ☎ 08-613 2900; 11th fl, Sergels Torg 12)

Canada (Map p402; ☎ 08-453 3000; 7th fl, Tegelbacken 4)

Denmark (Map p402; ☎ 08-406 7500; Jakobs Torg 1)

Finland (Map pp396-7; ☎ 08-676 6700; Gärdesgatan 9-11)

France (Map p402; ☎ 08-459 5300; Kommendörsgatan 13)

Germany (Map pp396-7; ☎ 08-670 1500; Skarpögatan 9)

Ireland (Map pp396-7; ☎ 08-661 8005; Östermalmsgatan 97)

Netherlands (Map p402; ☎ 08-556 933 00; Götgatan 16A)

Norway (Map pp396-7; ☎ 08-665 6340; Skarpögatan 4)

UK (Map pp396-7; ☎ 08-671 3000; Skarpögatan 6-8)

USA (Map pp396-7; ☎ 08-783 5300; Dag Hammarskjöldsväg 31)

FESTIVALS & EVENTS

The Swedes love their traditional festivals and celebrate in style year-round.

Valborgsmässoafton (Walpurgis Night on 30 April) celebrates the arrival of spring with bonfires and choral singers. Upper-secondary-school leavers with their white caps are a common sight; the festivities have developed from a mixture of traditional bonfires on the eve of May Day and student celebrations at Lund and Uppsala.

The **National Day** is 6 June (Gustav Vasa was elected King of Sweden on 6 June 1523).

Midsommar (Midsummer) on the first Saturday after 21 June, is *the* festival of the year. Decorating and raising the Midsummer pole and dancing around it are traditional activities on Midsummer's Eve, and most people head for the countryside for this. For the folk touch, the Lake Siljan region (p422) is a good place to celebrate, but folk costumes, singing, music, dancing, pickled herring washed down with schnapps, strawberries and cream, and beer drinking, are common almost everywhere. At the other end of summer, **crayfish parties** in August celebrate the end of the season.

Luciadagen (the Lucia festival) on 13 December, is also popular. Oddly, it seems to merge the folk tradition of the longest night and the story of St Lucia of Syracuse. A choir in white, led by Lucia (who wears a crown of lit candles), leads the singing.

Many towns host popular Christmas markets in December. **Christmas Eve** is the main day of celebration during this season; it's when the gifts are opened and the big celebratory meal is taken.

If you're in Stockholm for Valborgsmässoafton, Midsommar, Luciadagen, Christmas or New Year's Eve, a great place to participate in the festivities is the Skansen open-air museum on Djurgården (p399) in Stockholm. Just don't plan on doing anything much on the days surrounding these holidays, as they are often claimed as 'squeeze days' and are effectively additional holidays.

Almost every Swedish town hosts a summer festival between May and September. Music, dancing, eating, drinking, competitions and fun for children are regular features of these events, which can last for up to a week. You can find more information on music festivals (opera, choir, folk, jazz and chamber music) online at **Svenka Musikfestivaler** (www.musikfestivaler.se).

GAY & LESBIAN TRAVELLERS

Sweden is famous for its liberal attitudes and there are laws allowing same-sex 'registered partnerships', which grant most of the standard marriage rights. The organisation concerned with equality for lesbians and gays is **Riksförbundet för Sexuellt Likaberättigande** (RFSL; Map pp396-7; ☎ 08-457 1300; www.rfsl.se; Sveavägen 57-59, Stockholm).

One of the capital's biggest parties is the annual **Stockholm Pride** (www.stockholmpride.org), a five-day festival celebrating gay culture, held in late July/early August and based mainly in Tantolunden, a large park in Södermalm.

A good source of information is the free, monthly magazine **QX** (www.qx.se) giving gay and lesbian information and listings (only in Swedish). You can pick up a copy at many clubs, stores and restaurants, mainly in Stockholm, Göteborg, Malmö and Copenhagen. Its website has some excellent information and recommendations in English.

HOLIDAYS

There are plenty of public holidays in spring and early summer. The Midsummer holiday brings life almost to a halt for three days: transport and other services are reduced, so plan ahead. Some hotels are closed from Christmas to New Year. Note: many businesses will close early the day before a public holiday and all day the day after.

Public holidays in Sweden:
New Year's Day 1 January.
Epiphany 6 January.
Good Friday to Easter Monday March/April.
Labour Day 1 May.
Ascension Day May/June (39th day after Easter).
Whitsunday & Monday Late May or early June.
Midsummer's Day First Saturday after 21 June.
All Saints' Day Saturday, late October or early November.
Christmas Day 25 December.
Boxing Day 26 December.

Christmas Eve, New Year's Eve and Midsummer's Eve are not official holidays, but are generally nonworking days for most of the population.

INTERNET ACCESS

Internet cafés typically charge around Skr30 to Skr40 per hour online. Facilities can be rare outside big cities, because many Swedes have internet access at home or school. Many internet cafés, where they do exist, are testosterone-filled amusement arcades rather than traveller hang-outs. Most tourist offices have a computer terminal available for visitor use (sometimes free but usually with a Skr10 to 20 charge per hour). Look out for the free 'drop-in' terminals at many libraries, available for 15 minutes at a time.

INTERNET RESOURCES

Most Swedish organisations have their own websites, and many of these have pages in English. Every town also has its own site – usually this is found by simply entering 'www.', then the town's name, followed by '.se'; eg **Örebro** (www.orebro.se) or **Luleå** (www.lulea.se).

Following are some helpful websites:
CityGuide Sweden (www.cityguide.se) Detailed information pages for nearly 80 Swedish cities.
Local (www.thelocal.se) Swedish news and feature articles written by locals, in English.
Naturvårdsverket (www.environ.se) Site of the Swedish environmental protection agency, with good coverage of the country's national parks.
Svenska Institutet (www.si.se) The Swedish Institute is a public agency entrusted with disseminating knowledge abroad about Sweden. This site is full of detailed information on countless topics.
Svenska Turistföreningen (www.svenskaturistforeningen.se) STF maintains a network of 300 quality hostels throughout the country.

Swedish Travel Tourism Council (www.visit
-sweden.com) This site has loads of useful travel information in many languages.

Virtual Sweden (www.sweden.se) Svenska Institutet
maintains this 'official gateway to Sweden' with excellent
links in various categories (including culture, nature and
environment, and sports and leisure).

MONEY

You should encounter few problems if you
carry cash in any convertible currency or internationally recognised travellers cheques.
The national ATM networks usually accept
international Visa, Plus, EC, Eurocard,
MasterCard or Cirrus cards.

Forex (www.forex.se), with branches in the
biggest cities and most airports and ferry
terminals, is one of the cheapest and easiest places to exchange money and charges
Skr15 per cheque. Banks charge up to Skr60
per cheque. You can buy foreign notes for
no fee at Forex.

Currency

The Swedish krona (plural: kronor), usually
called 'crown' by Swedes speaking English, is
denoted Skr and divided into 100 öre (prices
are rounded to the nearest 50 öre). Coins are
50 öre and one, five and 10 kronor, and notes
are 20, 50, 100, 500 and 1000 kronor.

Taxes & Refunds

The main additional cost for the traveller
is *mervärdeskatt* or *moms,* the value-added
tax (VAT) on goods and services, which is
included in the marked price. This varies
but may be as much as 25%.

At shops that display the sign 'Tax Free
Shopping', non-EU citizens making single
purchases of goods exceeding Skr200 (including *moms*) are eligible for a VAT refund of 15% to 18% of the purchase price.
Show your passport and ask the shop for
a 'Global Refund Cheque', which should
be presented along with your unopened
purchases (within three months) at your
departure point from the country (before
you check in), to get export validation.
You can then cash your cheque at refund
points, which are found at international airports and harbour terminals. The *Tax Free
Shopping Guide to Sweden* is available from
tourist offices free of charge. Contact **Global
Refund Sweden** (☎ 020-741741; www.globalrefund
.com) for more information.

Tipping

Service charges are usually included in
restaurant bills and taxi fares, but it's
common to tip about 10% in a restaurant
or round up the taxi fare (particularly if
there's luggage). Cloakrooms usually cost
about Skr20.

POST

Mailing letters or postcards up to 20g
within Sweden costs Skr5.50, and Skr10 to
overseas destinations. A package weighing
2kg costs Skr180/250 by airmail to Eu-
rope/outside Europe. Airmail will take a
few days to reach European destinations,
a week to most parts of North America,
and perhaps a little longer to Australia and
New Zealand.

In recent years **Posten** (www.posten.se), the
Swedish postal service, moved to new
premises all over the country; service outlets opened in some 3000 new venues, many
in supermarkets and petrol stations. These
outlets offer all that most travellers will
need; eg stamps *(frimärken),* letter *(brev)*
and package *(paket)* services. You can also
buy stamps from many tourist offices,
convenience stores, bookshops and newsagents; look for the yellow post symbol on a
pale blue background, which indicates that
some postal facilities are offered.

Receiving poste restante mail under the
new postal system is difficult for travellers. As many of the large, old-style post
offices have closed or relocated, there is
no central 'holding place' in most towns.
The person sending you mail will need to
specify which post outlet you will be collecting mail from, with a specific address
and postal code.

TELEPHONE

Travellers may notice a lack of public
telephones in Sweden; some 70% of the
population owns a mobile phone, so the
number of public phones has dwindled in
recent years (travellers might find it useful
to bring their mobile telephone from home
and buy an inexpensive Swedish SIM card
and pay-as-you-go plan). There are scarcely
any coin phones; all public telephones take
Telia phonecards. These cards cost Skr35,
Skr60 or Skr100 (giving 30, 60 or 120 cred-
its, respectively), and even they can be hard
to find outside of the major cities. Many

Telia booths also accept credit cards (with expensive rates).

For directory assistance dial ☎118118 (for numbers within Sweden) or ☎118119 (international), but note that these services aren't free. To place a collect call, dial ☎020-0018.

Phone Codes

Calls to Sweden from abroad require a country code (☎46) followed by the area code and telephone number (omitting the first zero in the area code). For international calls dial ☎00 followed by the country code and the local area code.

Swedish phone numbers have area codes followed by varying numbers of digits. You must use the area code when dialling from outside that area. Numbers beginning ☎020 or ☎0200 are free (but not from public phones or mobiles). Numbers beginning ☎077 are roughly the same price as a local call. Mobile phone numbers usually begin with ☎070.

TIME

Sweden is one hour ahead of GMT/UTC, but summer time (from the end of March to the end of October) is another hour ahead. The 24-hour clock is widely used.

TOILETS

Public toilets in parks, shopping malls, libraries and bus or train stations are rarely free in Sweden. Except at the larger train stations (where an attendant is on duty), pay toilets are coin operated, and usually cost Skr5. The exception is museums, where toilets usually are free and well-maintained.

TOURIST INFORMATION

The official website for the **Swedish Travel Tourism Council** (www.visit-sweden.com) contains a great deal of useful information in many languages.

Sweden has about 350 local tourist information offices. Most are open long hours in summer and short hours (or not at all) during winter, and a few exhibit nomadic tendencies. The offices in large towns stock brochures from all around Sweden. The **FörTur** (www.turism.se) website lists Sweden's tourist information offices and their contact details.

VISAS

Citizens of the EU, Norway and Iceland can enter Sweden with a passport or a national identification card (passports are recommended). Nationals of Nordic countries can stay and work indefinitely but others require residence permits for stays of between three months and five years.

Citizens of Australia, New Zealand, Canada and the US can enter and stay in Sweden without a visa for up to three months. Australian and New Zealand passport-holders aged between 18 and 30 can also qualify for a one-year working holiday visa.

Citizens of South Africa and other African, Asian and some Eastern European countries require tourist visas for entry; these are only available in advance from Swedish embassies (allow at least two months), and cost Skr225/275 for permits allowing a maximum 30/90 days. It may be hard to extend your stay once you're in Sweden.

Migrationsverket (☎ 011-156000; www.migrationsverket.se; SE-60170 Norrköping) is the Swedish 'migration board' and it handles all applications for visas and work or residency permits. Its website is full of useful information for visitors with visa questions.

TRANSPORT IN SWEDEN

GETTING THERE & AWAY
Air

The major international airport in Sweden is Stockholm's **Arlanda airport** (☎ 08-797 6000), with direct flights linking the country to major Scandinavian towns, European and North American cities, and a few Asian destinations. Göteborg's **Landvetter airport** (☎ 031-941000) and Malmö's **Sturup airport** (☎ 040-613 1000), as well as a few other minor airports, also have direct international flights (especially to/from large cities within Scandinavia). A wealth of information on airports and airlines is available at the website of Sweden's civil aviation authority, **Luftfartsverket** (www.lfv.se).

When planning your travel, note that Copenhagen's airport (p112) is just 25 minutes by train from Malmö in southern Sweden.

The national carrier is Scandinavian Airlines System, better known as **SAS** (airline code SK; ☎ 0770-727727; www.scandinavian.net), with a very good safety record.

SWEDEN

AIRLINES FLYING TO & FROM SWEDEN

Some of the main international airlines flying into and out of Sweden:

Aeroflot (airline code EI; ☎ 08-505653; www.aeroflot.com)
Air France (airline code AF; ☎ 08-519 999 90; www.airfrance.com)
Alitalia (airline code AZ; ☎ 08-237320; www.alitalia.com)
Austrian Airlines (airline code OS; ☎ 0200-727373; www.aua.com)
British Airways (airine code BA; ☎ 0770-110020; www.britishairways.com)
Finnair (airline code AY; ☎ 020-781100; www.finnair.com)
Iberia (airline code IB; ☎ 08-566 125 00; www.iberia.com)
Icelandair (airline code FI; ☎ 08-690 9800; www.icelandair.net)
KLM Royal Dutch Airlines (airline code KL; ☎ 08-587 997 57; www.klm.com)
LOT Polish Airlines (airline code LO; ☎ 08-243490; www.lot.com)
Lufthansa (airline code LH; ☎ 0770-727727; www.lufthansa.com)
Skyways (airline code JZ; ☎ 0771-959500; www.skyways.se)
SN Brussels Airlines (airline code SN; ☎ 08-797 9400; www.flysn.com)
Swiss (airline code LX; ☎ 08-587 704 45; www.swiss.com)
Thai Airways (airline code TG; ☎ 08-598 836 00; www.thaiairways.com)

Budget airlines also cover Scandinavian and continental European destinations:

Blue1 (airline code KF; www.blue1.com) Flights to Finnish destinations from Stockholm and Göteborg.
Fly Me (airline code; ☎ 0770-790790; www.flyme.com) From Stockholm to Helsinki, and Göteborg to Nice and Mallorca.
FlyNordic (airline code LF; ☎ 08-528 068 20; www.flynordic.com) From Stockholm to Copenhagen and Oslo.
Ryanair (airline code FR; ☎ 0900-202 0240; www.ryanair.com) From Stockholm, Göteborg & Malmö to London (Stansted) and other locations including Glasgow and Frankfurt.
SAS Snowflake (☎ 0771-661000; www.flysnowflake.com) From Stockholm to destinations in southern Europe incl Rome, Lyon, Athens and Lisbon.
Sterling (airline code NB; ☎ 08-587 691 48; www.sterlingticket.com) From Stockholm and Göteborg to European destinations including Barcelona, Paris, Milan and Prague.

Land

Direct access to Sweden by land is possible from Norway, Finland and Denmark (from Denmark via the remarkable Öresund toll bridge). Border-crossing formalities are nonexistent.

Train and bus journeys are also possible between Sweden and the continent – these vehicles go directly to ferries. Include ferry fares (or Öresund tolls) in your budget if you're driving from continental Europe.

Eurolines (☎ 031-100240; www.eurolines.com), the long-distance bus operator, has an office inside the bus terminals in Sweden's three largest cities: Stockholm, Göteborg and Malmö. Full schedules and fares are listed on the website.

CONTINENTAL EUROPE

Eurolines services run between Sweden and several European cities. The Stockholm to London service (from Skr1299, approximately 30 hours, two to five weekly) goes via Malmö, Copenhagen, Hamburg and Amsterdam or Brussels. There are also services from Göteborg to Berlin (Skr610, approx 12 hours, two daily).

Berlin Night Express (www.berlin-night-express.com) is a direct overnight train between Berlin and Malmö (Skr750/1100 or €85/120 for a couchette/bed one way, 8½ hours, three to seven times a week) via the Trelleborg–Sassnitz ferry. Trains connect points north of Malmö or beyond Berlin. See the website for booking details, or in Sweden book through **SJ trains** (☎ 0771-757575; www.sj.se).

DENMARK

Eurolines (☎ 031-100240; www.eurolines.com) runs buses between Stockholm and Copenhagen (Skr538, nine hours, two to four daily), and between Göteborg and Copenhagen (Skr280, 4½ hours, three to five daily). **Swebus Express** (☎ 0200-218218; www.swebusexpress.se) and **Säfflebussen** (☎ 0771-151515; www.safflebussen.se) both run regular buses on the same routes, and have discount fares for travel from Monday to Thursday. All companies offer student, youth (under 26) and senior discounts.

Trains are the quickest option, especially from southern Sweden, and run between Copenhagen and Malmö (from Skr85, 35 minutes, every 20 minutes) via the Öresund bridge.

The Swedish national rail company, **Sveriges Järnväg** (SJ; ☎ 0771-757575; www.sj.se), runs X2000 trains between Copenhagen and Stockholm (from Skr447, five hours, up to 14 a day) via Norrköping, Linköping, Lund and Malmö. Three high-speed services operate between Copenhagen and Göteborg (3½ hours) via Helsingborg, Lund and Malmö (slower InterCity trains take 4½ hours, seven daily). Prices vary dramatically depending on when you buy your ticket – for best prices, purchase at least one day before departure.

For drivers, tolls across the Öresund bridge are Skr285 one way for a car up to 6m. See the **Öresundbron** (www.oeresundsbron .com) website for more information, and if the prices seem too steep, consider taking a ferry between Helsingborg and Helsingør (right).

FINLAND

There are seven crossing points along the river border. Bus services on the Swedish side are run by **Länstrafiken Norrbotten** (☎ 020-470047), who also run the 'Bothnian Arc X-press', a daily bus service along the northern coast into Finland, from Skellefteå or Luleå on to Haparanda, Tornio and Kemi, finishing in Oulu.

Tapanis Buss (☎ 0922-12955, 08-153300; www .tapanis.se) runs overnight coaches between Stockholm and Tornio via Haparanda (Skr515, 15 hours, twice weekly).

NORWAY

The major bus companies operate on routes connecting Stockholm and Oslo, and Göteborg and Oslo (many of the services from Oslo to Göteborg continue on to Malmö and Copenhagen).

Eurolines (☎ 031-100240; www.eurolines.com) has regular daily services between Oslo and Copenhagen via Göteborg, Helsingborg and Malmö. Göteborg to Oslo costs from Skr220 (four hours).

Swebus Express (☎ 0200-218218; www.swebus express.se) runs services between Stockholm and Oslo (from Skr392, 7½ hours, three daily) and between Göteborg and Oslo (from Skr230, four hours, up to six daily).

Säfflebussen (☎ 0771-151515; www.safflebussen .se) runs the Stockholm–Oslo route (from Skr305, five daily), and Göteborg to Oslo (from Skr180, 10 daily).

Many *länstrafiken* (regional transport networks) run buses to within a few kilometres of Norway's border. **Länstrafiken Norrbotten** (☎ 020-470047) operates services between Kiruna and Narvik in summer (Skr241, 2½ hours, one or two daily).

Sea

BALTIC COUNTRIES

Tallink (☎ 08-666 6001; www.tallink.ee) sails daily between Sweden and Estonia on two routes: Stockholm–Tallinn (from €45, 15 hours) and Kapellskär–Paldiski (from €28, 10 to 11 hours). Tallink also sails daily between Stockholm and Riga in Latvia (from €29, 17½ hours).

Lisco Line (☎ 0454-33680; www.lisco.se) sails between Klaipeda in Lithuania and Karlshamn, near Karlskrona in southern Sweden (from Skr625, 14 hours, three to six weekly).

DENMARK

The quickest and most frequent services are between Helsingør and Helsingborg (Skr20 to Skr22, 20 minutes). Three companies operate on this busy route: **HH-Ferries** (☎ 042-19 8000; www.hhferries.se), **Scandlines** (☎ 042-186300; www.scandlines.se) and **Sundsbussarna** (☎ 04238 58 80; www.sundsbussarna.se).

Stena Line (☎ 031-704 0000; www.stenaline.se) has five to 10 sailings daily between Göteborg and Frederikshavn (from Skr130, 3¼ hours). Stena Line also sails three or four times daily between Grenå and Varberg (from Skr115, four hours). It's cheaper to travel between 10pm and 6am, or from Monday to Thursday. Prices also increase in summer.

BornholmsTrafikken (☎ 0411-558700; www .bornholmstrafikken.dk) sails from Ystad to Rønne (Bornholm) from €22. There are conventional (2½ hours) and fast (70 minutes) services, two to nine times daily.

FINLAND

Daily services throughout the year are available on Stockholm to Turku and Stockholm to Helsinki routes (all via the Åland islands). Note that Helsinki is called Helsingfors in Swedish, and Turku is known as Åbo. There are two major ferry operators, and it's considerably more expensive to travel either from Thursday to Saturday, or in peak season. Both ferry companies offer bus services to and from their ports.

Silja Line (☎ 08-222140; www.silja.com) sails daily (overnight) from Stockholm to Helsinki (from €92, around 15 hours) and to Turku (from €18/36 day/night crossing, 11 hours).

Viking Line (☎ 08-452 4000; www.vikingline.fi) operates a daily service on the same routes. An overnight trip from Stockholm to Helsinki costs from €33. Stockholm to Turku sailings cost from €14/19 for a day/night crossing.

Further north, **RG Line** (☎ 090-185200; www.rgline.com) operates a connection from Umeå to Vaasa (Skr450, four hours, daily).

GERMANY

Scandlines (☎ 0410-65000; www.scandlines.se) sails between Trelleborg and Rostock (from Skr185, 5¾ hours, three daily) and Trelleborg and Sassnitz (from Skr120, 3¾ hours, three daily).

Stena Line (☎ 031-704 0000; www.stenaline.se) offers overnight cruises between Göteborg and Kiel (from Skr390, 13½ hours) every day of the week.

NORWAY

Color Line (☎ 0526-62000; www.colorline.com) operates ferries between Strömstad and Sandefjord (from €16, 2½ hours, two to six daily).

DFDS Seaways (www.dfdsseaways.com; Göteborg ☎ 031-650650; Helsingborg ☎ 042-266000) runs overnight ferries between Copenhagen and Oslo, via Helsingborg. Fares between Helsingborg and Oslo (14 hours) vary according to the season and day of the week, starting at €44.

POLAND

Polferries (☎ 040-121700; www.polferries.se) operates between Świnoujście and Ystad (from Skr490, seven to nine hours, daily) and also between Gdańsk and Nynäshamn (from Skr560, 18 hours, three weekly). Children under seven ride free. **Unity Line** (☎ 0411-556900; www.unityline.pl) also operates on the Świnoujście–Ystad route (from Skr550, nine hours, daily).

Stena Lines (www.stenaline.se; ☎ 031-704 0000) operates ferries to Gdynia from Verkö, 10km east of Karlskrona. A car and five people costs from Skr750; the passenger-only fare is from Skr365.

UK

DFDS Seaways (☎ 031-650650; www.dfdsseaways.com) sails from Göteborg to Newcastle (from €29, 25 hours, twice weekly) via Kristiansand (Norway).

GETTING AROUND

Although Sweden takes time and money to travel through, public transport is well organised using 24 different *länstrafik* (regional networks); they're heavily subsidised and offer good bargains. The general confusion of having so many operators is partly solved by the **Resplus system** (☎ 0771-878787; www.resplus.se), where one ticket is valid on trains and on *länstrafik* buses. Handy local timetables are available on the website and for free or at nominal cost from tourist offices or the operators.

Air

Sweden's half-dozen domestic airlines mostly use Stockholm's Arlanda airport as a hub (p473), although Stockholm's Bromma airport also sees some domestic action. The domestic network is extensive and local airlines are safe and very efficient, but full-fare tickets can be quite expensive. Substantial discounts are available, such as for internet bookings, student and youth fares, off-peak travel, or return tickets booked at least seven days in advance. Major domestic flight destinations include Stockholm, Göteborg, Malmö, Luleå, Kiruna and Visby (on Gotland). Fares for popular routes such as Stockholm–Göteborg can be found for as little as Skr195 with the budget airlines.

AIRLINES IN SWEDEN

Fly Me (☎ 0770-790790; www.flyme.com) Flies from Stockholm to Göteborg and Malmö (and Helsinki).

Malmö Aviation (☎ 0771-550010; www.malmoaviation.se) Flies between Stockholm (Bromma), Göteborg, Malmö and Umeå, and to Gotland in summer.

Nordic Airlink (☎ 08-528 068 20; www.flynordic.com) Flies from Stockholm to Göteborg, Umeå and Luleå (and to Oslo and Copenhagen).

SAS (☎ 0770-727727; www.scandinavian.net) Has daily domestic flights serving the country from Malmö to Kiruna (all through Stockholm Arlanda).

Skyways (☎ 0771-959500; www.skyways.se) Runs a larger network than SAS, including a few direct flights between northern and southern destinations that don't fly via Stockholm (eg Göteborg direct to Umeå or Luleå).

AIR PASSES

If you're flying into Sweden from continental Europe with SAS, you can buy Visit Scandinavia Airpass flight coupons (up to a maximum of eight) allowing one-way travel on direct flights between any two

Scandinavian cities serviced by SAS and other affiliated operators. Fare schedules under the pass are complicated but it takes all flights within and between Scandinavian countries to around €70 to €80. Non-European residents can participate in a similar scheme, the Visit Scandinavia/Europe Airpass. See p496 for more details on these passes.

Bicycle

Sweden is a flat country and it's ideal for cycling, with Skåne and Gotland particularly recommended. Cycling is an excellent way to look for points of interest and quiet spots for free camping. The cycling season is May to September in the south, and July and August in the north.

You can cycle on all roads except motorways (green sign, with two lanes and a bridge) and roads for motor vehicles only (green sign with a car symbol). The reasonably quiet and safe secondary roads are good for cycling.

You can take a bicycle on some *länstrafik* trains and most regional buses (free, or up to Skr50), and bikes are transported free or for a small fee on many ferries. Long-distance buses usually do not accept bicycles, and nor does SJ.

You'll find bike-rental outlets in most major towns; multigear bikes can cost up to Skr200/800 per day/week. Some country areas, towns and cities have special cycle routes – check with local tourist offices for information and maps. The well-signposted, 2600km-long Sverigeleden is the national route (extending from Helsingborg in the south to Karesuando in the north), linking points of interest with suitable roads (mostly with an asphalt surface) and bicycle paths.

Boat

Sweden's national road authority, Vägverket, operates dozens of car ferries across short stretches of water, but many are slowly being replaced with bridges. These ferries are part of the road network and are free.

An extensive boat network opens up the attractive Stockholm archipelago, and boat services on Lake Mälaren, west of Stockholm, are busy in summer (see p415). Boat passes are available for exploration of the Stockholm archipelago. Gotland is served by regular ferries from Nynäshamn and Oskarshamn (see p454), and there are summer services to many other small islands off the coast.

The canals provide cross-country routes linking the main lakes. The longest cruises, on the historic Göta Canal from Söderköping (south of Stockholm) to Göteborg, run from mid-May to mid-September and take at least four days. The **Göta Canal Steamship Company** (☎ 031-806315; www.gotacanal.se) operates three old ships over the whole distance with fares from Skr12,995/17,990 for singles/doubles, including full board and guided excursions. The company also offers two-day cruises on probably the most picturesque section of the canal, from Motala to Söderköping (from Skr4675/6750 per single/double). Other companies offer day trips and short cruises on sections of the canal – tourist offices in the area can help (Linköping and nearby Söderköping are good places to inquire).

Bus

Sweden has a safe, reliable and extensive bus network. Travellers heading to the north of the country, in particular, will rely heavily on this form of transport to get around. You can travel by bus in Sweden either on national long-distance routes, or using any of the regional *länstrafik* networks.

LONG-DISTANCE BUS COMPANIES

The following companies operate on long-distance routes. If you're under 26, a student or a senior (over 65), it's worth asking for a discount, but most transport companies will only give student prices to holders of Swedish student cards (the exception is Swebus Express, where you can use ISIC cards). Advance bookings are required for all but Swebus Express – it always guarantees a seat.

Säfflebussen (☎ 0771-151515; www.safflebussen.se) A small network, running daily on major routes (eg Stockholm–Malmö, Stockholm–Göteborg, Göteborg–Malmö). Also serves Oslo, Copenhagen and Berlin. Fares are 30% cheaper from Monday to Thursday.

Svenska Buss (☎ 0771-676767; www.svenskabuss .se) This network connects many southern towns with Stockholm.

Swebus Express (☎ 0200-218218; www.swebus express.se) Has the largest 'national network' of buses, but only serves the southern half of the country (as far north as Mora in Dalarna). Fares for journeys over 100km are 30% cheaper between Monday and Thursday most weeks (not public or school holidays).

Ybuss (☎ 0771-334444; www.ybuss.se) Daily journeys from Stockholm north along the coast as far as Umeå (via Uppsala, Gävle, Sundsvall), and to Östersund.

BUS PASSES

Länstrafik is usually complemented by the regional train system, and one ticket is valid on any bus, local or regional. Rules vary but transfers are usually free within one to four hours. Most counties are divided into zones; travel within one zone will cost from Skr15 to Skr20. Every time you enter a new zone, the price increases, but there's usually a maximum fare.

Timetables explain all the various discount schemes. There are good-value daily or weekly passes and many regions have 30-day passes for longer stays, or a special card which is valid for travel from Midsummer to mid-August (the major school holiday period). The *Värdekort* (Value Card), which you can 'top up' at any time, is also quite good value: you pay, say, Skr200 for over Skr250 worth of travelling. Always ask how the regional discount pass works: you may have to run the ticket through a machine, press buttons, tell the driver where you want to go, get your ticket stamped or something else of that kind.

Car & Motorcycle

Sweden has good roads and there are no public toll roads or bridges in the country. You usually only need a recognised full driving licence, even for car rental. If bringing your own car, you'll need your vehicle registration documents. Insurance Green Cards are recommended. Fuel and spare parts are widely available, but may be pricey.

Parking can be tricky to find (and very expensive) in the larger cities. Look for parking signs: times (using the 24-hour clock) will indicate when an *avgift* (payment) is required. *Billetautomat* (automatic ticket machines) usually cost from Skr5 to Skr15 per hour during the day, but may be free in the evenings and at the weekend. Cities have multistorey car parks *(P-hus)* that charge between Skr15 and Skr40 per hour.

AUTOMOBILE ASSOCIATIONS

The Swedish national motoring association is **Motormännens Riksförbund** (☎ 020-211111, 08-690 38 00; www.motormannen.se; Sveavägen 159, SE-10435 Stockholm). In case of an emergency, it can help you contact your home club or to find assistance locally.

HIRE

To rent a car you normally have to be at least 18 (sometimes 25) years of age, you need to show a recognised licence (in some cases, an International Driving Permit) and you may be required to pay by credit card.

International car rental chains are expensive, with prices starting from around Skr600 per day for smaller models, but shopping around can turn up some reasonable deals. Fly-drive packages can bring some savings, and weekend or summer packages may also be offered at discount rates. All the major firms (for example Avis, Hertz, Europcar) have desks at Stockholm's Arlanda airport and offices in major cities.

Mabi Hyrbilar (☎ 020-110 1000; www.mabirent.se in Swedish) is a good national company with branches in many major cities and competitive rates. Rates for the smallest car are Skr160 per day plus Skr1.60 per kilometre, or Skr320 per day including 150km. For weekly rentals, prices start at Skr1995, including 1000km. Motorcycles can also be rented through Mabi.

Cars can be hired from many large petrol stations (look for signs saying *hyrbilar* or *biluthyrning*) at reasonable rates, but must be returned to the hiring point. **OK-Q8** (☎ 020-850850; www.okq8.se in Swedish) has small cars from Skr315 per day (including 100km allowance) or Skr550 per day (unlimited kilometres). Weekend rental makes sense for travellers wishing to explore areas not well served by public transport (eg Glasriket from Kalmar, Bohuslän from Göteborg or Höga Kusten from Sundsvall); prices start at Skr595 (including 300km allowance) or Skr895 (with unlimited kilometres) for a whole weekend. **Statoil** (☎ 0770-252525; www .statoil.se in Swedish) has similar prices. Websites for these companies are in Swedish only, but you'll probably be able to navigate through to *priser* or *prislistor* (prices) for *hyrbilar*.

ROAD HAZARDS

In the northern part of Sweden, privately owned reindeer and wild elk are serious road hazards, particularly around dawn and dusk. Look out for black plastic bags tied to roadside trees or poles – this is a sign from local Sami that they have reindeer herds grazing in the area. Report all incidents to police – failure to do so is an offence. Sandboxes on many roads may be helpful in mud or snow. Also, if driving in Göteborg and Norrköping watch out for trams.

ROAD RULES

The basic rules of the road conform to EU standards. In Sweden, you drive on and give way to the right. Headlights should always be dipped, but must be on at all times when driving. Seat belt use is obligatory for the driver and all passengers. The maximum blood-alcohol limit is a stringent 0.02%, and random breath tests are not uncommon. The maximum permitted speed on all motorways and remote highways is 110km/h. Other speed limits are 50km/h in urban areas, 70km/h outside urban areas and 90km/h on motorways. The speed limit for cars towing caravans is a maximum of 80km/h. Police often use hand-held radar equipment and cameras to detect speeding, and will impose on-the-spot fines.

On many highways you will see broken lines defining wide-paved edges. The vehicle being overtaken is expected to move into this area to allow faster traffic to pass by safely.

Local Transport

In Sweden, local transport is always linked with the regional *länstrafik* – rules and prices for city buses may differ slightly from long-distance transport, but a regional pass is valid both in the city and on the rural routes. There's usually a flat fare of around Skr15 to Skr20 in towns.

Stockholm has an extensive underground metro system, and Göteborg and Norrköping run good tram networks. Göteborg also has a city ferry service.

Train

Trains are certainly the fastest way to get around, although many destinations in the northern half of the country cannot be reached by train alone.

The national network of **Sveriges Järnväg** (SJ; ☎ 0771-757575; www.sj.se) covers most main lines, especially in the southern half of the country. Its flag carriers are the X2000 fast trains running at speeds of up to 200km/h, with services from Stockholm to major destinations. InterCity (regional and interregional) trains also run on many of these routes; InterCity fares are cheaper and the journey times longer. **Connex** (☎ 0771-260000; www.connex.se) operates train services in the far north and offers services from Stockholm and Göteborg north as far as Kiruna and across to Narvik in Norway. In addition, several counties run small regional train networks as part of their *länstrafik* service.

There are huge variations on fares depending on time of travel, type of service and concession rate and how far in advance you book your trip. Full-price tickets are expensive, but you'll receive a substantial discount for booking at least a day before departure (ask for the *'just nu'* fare). Students (with a Swedish CSN or SFS student card if aged over 26) and people aged under 26 get up to a 30% discount on the standard adult fare. All SJ ticket prices are reduced in summer, from late June to mid-August, and also during off-peak travel times (10am to 2pm and after 7pm Monday to Thursday, Friday and Sunday until noon, and all day Saturday). On X2000 and InterCity trains, an adult passenger can be accompanied by two children, at no extra charge. X2000 tickets include a seat reservation. Bicycles can be carried on many *länstrafik* trains and on Öresund trains (running between Malmö and Copenhagen), unlike on SJ trains (which won't carry them).

INLANDSBANAN

From mid-June to early August, **Inlandsbanan** (Inland Railway; ☎ 0771-535353; www.inlands banan.se) offers one of the great rail journeys in Scandinavia. The 1067km route stretches from Mora to Gällivare; travel is slow (the train travels at 50km/h) and it takes six hours from Mora to Östersund (Skr379) and 14 hours from Östersund to Gällivare (Skr762). A special card allows two weeks' unlimited travel on the route for Skr1395 (mid-June to mid-July) or Skr1195 (mid-July to early August). InterRail Card users under 26 can travel free, while ScanRail card-holders receive a 25% discount on the two-week pass (but not on individual tickets).

TRAIN PASSES

The Sweden Rail Pass, Eurodomino tickets and InterRail, Eurail and ScanRail passes are accepted on all SJ train serv-ices and most other operators, such as regional trains. Exceptions to this include the local SL *pendeltåg* trains which run around Stockholm, and the Inlandsbanan train (although some passholders get a discount on Inlandsbanan – see left for more information).

X2000 and overnight trains require all rail passholders to pay a supplement, usu-ally about Skr50 extra (including an ob-ligatory seat reservation). The reservation supplements for non-X2000 trains aren't obligatory, and there are no supplements required for regional *länstrafik* trains.

Regional Directory

CONTENTS

Please note that this chapter gives a general overview of the whole Scandinavian Europe region. For information relevant to one particular country, see the Directory section at the end of each country chapter.

Some subjects are covered in *both* places (eg general accommodation options are discussed below, but price ranges plus contact details for useful accommodation organisations appear in each country Directory). We've added cross references where appropriate.

ACCOMMODATION

Throughout this book, accommodation is divided into budget, midrange and top-end categories. Our choices are listed in order of preference, with favourites first (although in budget sections, camp sites are at the top of each list, no matter what!). See the individual country Directories for an overview of local options, and a rundown of prices and useful associations.

The cheapest places to stay are camping grounds, then hostels and student accommodation. Cheap hotels are virtually unknown in far-northern Europe, but guesthouses, pensions, private rooms, farm accommodation and B&Bs can be good value. Self-catering flats and cottages are worth considering if you're with a group, especially if you're staying in one place for a while.

During peak holiday periods, accommodation can be hard to find and it's advisable to book ahead. Even camping grounds, especially popular big-city ones, can fill up.

If you arrive in a country by train, there's often a hotel-booking desk at the train station. Tourist offices tend to have extensive accommodation lists and the more helpful ones will go out of their way to find you somewhere to stay. There's usually a small fee for this service, but it can save a lot of running around. Agencies offering private rooms can be good value; you may lack privacy, but staying with a local family brings you closer to the spirit of the country.

B&Bs, Guesthouses & Hotels

There's a huge range of accommodation above the hostel level. B&Bs, where you get a room and breakfast in a private home, can often be real bargains. Pensions and guesthouses are similar, but usually slightly more upmarket.

BOOK ACCOMMODATION ONLINE

For more accommodation reviews and recommendations by Lonely Planet authors, check out the online booking service at www.lonelyplanet.com. You'll find the true, insider lowdown on the best places to stay. Reviews are thorough and independent. Best of all, you can book online.

Above this level are hotels, which are always much more expensive than B&Bs and guesthouses; in cities, luxury five-star hotels have five-star prices. Categorisation varies from country to country.

Check your hotel room and the bathroom before you agree to take it, and make sure you know what it's going to cost – discounts are often available at certain times (eg at weekends in Finland, Norway and Sweden) and for longer stays. Also ask about breakfast – it's usually included in the price of the room, but sometimes it's compulsory and you must pay extra for it (which can be a real rip-off).

If you think a hotel is too expensive, ask if they have a cheaper room. If you're with a group or are planning to stay for any length of time, it's always worth trying to negotiate a special rate.

Camping

Scandinavians love their tents! Camping is cheap and immensely popular throughout the region. There's usually a charge per tent or site, per vehicle and per person. National tourist offices have booklets or brochures listing camping grounds all over their country. See p487 for information on the Camping Card International and the Camping Card Scandinavia, both of which offer benefits and discounts.

In most larger towns and cities, camp sites are some distance from the centre. If you're on foot, the money you save by camping can quickly be outweighed by the money spent commuting in and out of town.

Some camping grounds rent small cabins or chalets (common except in Iceland and the Faroes); otherwise you'll need a tent, sleeping bag and cooking equipment.

Camping other than in designated camping grounds is not always straightforward. In Denmark and the Faroes, it's illegal without permission from the local authorities (the police or local council office) or from landowners (don't be shy about asking!). As always, take care to keep toilet activities away from all surface water and use biodegradable soaps for washing up.

There's a concept in Sweden, Norway, Finland, and to a more limited extent Iceland, of a right of public access to forests and wilderness areas. In these countries, within the framework of the regulations, camping for one night is legal; but there are important restrictions. See the Right of Common Access (p484) section, and the Directories of the relevant country chapters for additional information. Tourist offices usually stock official publications in English explaining your rights and responsibilities.

Hostels

Hostels offer the cheapest roof over your head in Scandinavia, and you don't have to be young to use them. Most hostels are part of national YHAs (Youth Hostel Associations), known collectively across the world as **Hostelling International** (HI; www.hihostels.com). Some Scandinavian hostels are run privately, although the majority are affiliated with HI.

Technically you're supposed to be a YHA or HI member to use affiliated hostels (indicated by a blue triangle symbol) but in practice most are open to anyone. You may have to pay a bit extra without an HI card but this can be offset against future membership. Stay for six nights as a nonmember and you automatically become a member. Prices given throughout this book are member prices. To join HI, ask at any hostel, contact your local or national hostelling office, or register over the internet.

In Scandinavian countries, hostels are geared for budget travellers of all ages, including families with kids, and most have dorms and private rooms. Specially adapted rooms for disabled visitors are becoming more common, but check with the hostel first.

You must use a sleeping sheet and pillowcase or linen in most Scandinavian countries – simply using your own sleeping bag is not permitted – but you can often hire or buy these on the spot. Many hostels (exceptions include most hostels in Iceland and the Faroes) serve breakfast, and almost all have communal kitchens where you can prepare meals.

Some hostels accept reservations by phone or fax but not usually during peak periods; they'll often book the next hostel you're headed to for a small fee. The HI website has a booking form, where you can reserve a bed in advance – however, not all hostels are on the network. Popular hostels in capital cities can be heavily booked in summer and limits may be placed on how many nights you can stay.

Many hostel guides are available, including HI's annually updated *Official International Youth Hostels Guide 2006* (UK£9.99, €15.95). For further information on Scandinavian hostels, including price ranges, see the Directories in the individual country chapters.

University Accommodation

Some universities and colleges rent out their students' rooms to tourists from June to mid-August; in Finland this kind of accommodation is usually affiliated with HI (see p210). These will often be single or double rooms and cooking facilities may be available. Enquire directly at the college or university, at student information services or at local tourist offices.

ACTIVITIES

A love of the outdoors seems hard-wired into the Scandinavian brain. With such amazingly varied geography and vast wilderness areas, it's not really surprising. Outdoor activities include bird-watching, windsurfing, skiing, snowmobiling, skating, climbing, dogsledding, fishing, hiking, horse riding, mountaineering, kayaking, whitewater rafting, cycling, whale-watching, and way-out white-knuckle sports like snowkiting.

For more information, see the relevant country chapters.

Bird-watching

Scandinavia's large, unspoilt areas are fantastic places to spot huge varieties and numbers of birds. In coastal areas, kittiwakes, fulmars and puffins are common. Rarer species include golden eagles and sea eagles. Even reluctant twitchers will be wowed by the Vestmanna (p128) and Látrabjarg (p256) bird cliffs, in the Faroes and Iceland, respectively. Other good areas include the Danish islands Møn, Falster and Lolland (p64); the Norwegian islands Runde (p350), Værøy and Røst (p365); and Oulanka National Park (p199) in Finland.

Boating

The Vikings' trade and communication routes – the lakes, rivers and meandering coastlines of Scandinavia – present a variety of boating options unmatched anywhere in the world. You can ride the rapids in a Finnish canoe (p210); take a trip on an Arctic icebreaker (p200); kayak around the feet of Icelandic mountains (p266); chug round peaceful lake Mjøsa in Norway (p327) on the world's oldest paddle steamer; or cruise from Helsinki to Stockholm (p215) – manifold possibilities! Country chapters contain more details.

Cycling

Along with hiking, cycling is the best way to get into the scenery and chat to the locals. It's also a fantastic way to whizz around cities without getting throbbing feet or stuck in traffic.

Popular cycling areas include much of Denmark, which sets the world standard for cycling infrastructures; greater Oslo; the islands of Gotland in Sweden; and Åland in Finland. Cycling in certain areas of Iceland can be tough, with blasting sandstorms or endless fjords. In western Norway – as beautiful as it is – there are tunnels galore which prohibit cyclists, the snaking roads to/from mountain passes are killers and, unless you want to pedal an extra 50km around a fjord, you'll have to add on ferry costs. The Faroes also have their fair share of hazardous, nonventilated tunnels and tortuous inclines.

Many long-distance routes (see individual country chapters for details) can be linked together to form an epic Scandinavia wide cycle tour. A popular route is to start from Kiel in Germany, then make your way through Denmark, north along the west coast of Sweden and into Norway. (Note that bikes are banned on the Øresund toll bridge between Denmark and Sweden.) In the UK, the Cyclists' Touring Club (p505) can provide members with route sheets prepared by experienced riders who have pedalled their way around Scandinavia.

If you come from outside Europe, you can often bring your bicycle along on the plane for a surprisingly reasonable fee – check out any restrictions with your carrier. Alternatively, this book lists places where you can rent one (the minimum rental period is usually half a day).

See p505 and the individual country chapters for more information on bicycle touring and tips on places to visit.

Hiking

Keen walkers could spend several lifetimes exploring the region's hundreds of trails – there are enough national parks and nature reserves to make it a veritable paradise. Routes are usually well marked, and accommodation is available along the way. As always, be sure to bring enough food, appropriate clothing and equipment with you, and consult local weather forecasts before setting off.

The Right of Common Access law in effect in Sweden, Norway, Finland and to a lesser extent Iceland allows anyone to walk virtually anywhere, while respecting home-owners' and commercial premises' privacy. Most tourist offices in the first three countries have leaflets outlining what rights and responsibilities you have.

Huge national routes such as Kungsleden in Sweden (p465) and the UKK trekking route (p196) in Finland are popular, as are provincial or regional routes (spanning hundreds of kilometres) and extensive tracks through national parks. Local and regional tourist offices distribute free maps for shorter routes and sell excellent trekking maps for the national parks.

Horse Riding

Another way to see the breathtaking Scandinavian countryside is from the back of a horse. Most stables offer short rides for beginners, with longer treks for experienced riders. Iceland has its own breed of horse, the Icelandic pony, and a great equine tradition (p278). On the Faroes, you can trek between Torhavn and Kirkjabour on Icelandic ponies (p128).

Husky Sledding

Hurtling over the snow, pulled by a team of near-wolves, has to be one of life's most exhilarating experiences. Husky sledding is particularly popular in northern Finland, around Rovaniemi (p202), Muonio (p208) and Levi (p208); in Røros (p350), and various towns in Finnmark and Svalbard, in northern Norway, and in the far north of Sweden. You can also ride with a team over an Icelandic glacier (p278).

Skiing

A long snow season makes winter sports, particularly skiing, popular Scandinavian pastimes. The longest downhill (alpine)

WORLD HERITAGE LIST

Scandinavia is rich in sites that have made the Unesco list of 'cultural and national treasures of the world's heritage'. Sites mentioned in this book are as follows.

Denmark

- Jelling Kirke, burial mounds and runic stones (p89)
- Kronborg Slot (p58)
- Roskilde Domkirke (p62)

Finland

- Fortress of Suomenlinna (p153)
- Vanha Rauma (Old Rauma; p179)

Iceland

- Þingvellir National Park (p251)

Norway

- Bryggen (p334)
- Mining town of Røros (p350)

- Rock carvings of Alta (p371)
- Urnes' stave church (p343)
- West Norwegian Fjords – Geirangerfjorden (p346) and Nærøyfjorden (p330)

Sweden

- Agricultural landscape of southern Öland (p448)
- Birka and Hovgården (p416)
- Church village of Gammelstad, Luleå (p460)
- Falun mining area (p421)
- Hanseatic town of Visby (p451)
- Höga Kusten (High Coast; p456)
- Naval port of Karlskrona (p450)
- Royal Domain of Drottningholm (p415)

slopes are in Sweden and Norway, although it's quite an expensive activity (compared to skiing at other European resorts), once the costs of ski lifts, accommodation and evening drinking sessions have been factored in. Cross-country (nordic) skiing has a bigger following, and there are many world-class trails in the region.

Åre in Sweden (p458) is probably the single best area for alpine skiing. The top resorts in Norway are Geilo (p329) and Lillehammer (p328), where telemark skiing, a form of free-heel downhill skiing, is also popular. Finnish ski areas are fairly well equipped – the emphasis is on cross-country skiing – with Ylläs (p208) being one of the best resorts. Several towns in Iceland have lifts and trails.

Renting equipment for downhill skiing is easily organised. However, for cross-country skiing, travellers will normally have to rely on friendly locals to lend them equipment – or plan on buying their own skis, poles and boots. (Flea markets are the probably the cheapest and most likely places to look.)

Skiing – especially cross country – should only be attempted after studying trails and routes (wilderness trails are identified by colour codes on maps and signposts). Practically all towns and villages illuminate some skiing tracks. Wear appropriate clothing and carry food, extra clothing and emergency supplies, such as matches and something to burn. Skiers should be extra careful about darkness. In Scandinavia, days are very short in winter and, during the winter months of December and January, there's no daylight at all in the extreme north.

The skiing season generally lasts from early December to April. Snow conditions can vary greatly from one year to the next and from region to region, but January and February, as well as the Easter holiday period, tend to be the best (and busiest) months. Snow cannons for producing artificial snow are common.

Snowboarding & Snowkiting

The biggest downhill ski resorts (see above) usually make provisions for snowboarders. It's possible to try out the new sport snowkiting in Luleå (Sweden), Geilo (Norway) and Langjökull (Iceland) – see the website www.snowkiting.com for more details.

Snowmobiling

If zipping through the untouched snowy wilderness on a deafening, bone-shaking, 190km/h machine sounds like fun, there are many places in Scandinavia where you can indulge in two-stroke pleasure. Snowmobile outfits are particularly prevalent in the far north of Finland, Norway and Sweden, with the season generally running from November to April; you can ride on Icelandic glaciers year-round. There's usually no minimum age for passengers, but if you want to drive, you'll need your driving licence. See the country chapters for further details.

Whale-watching

Norway, Iceland and the Faroes are often severely criticised for their policies on hunting whales (see the boxed texts on p127 and p236), so it's perhaps an encouraging sign that whale-watching tours are on the increase, in Norway and Iceland at least (pilot whales in the Faroes that come too close to shore are killed).

All three countries offer spotting trips from around May to October, with a wonderfully high chance of seeing cetaceans. Common species are minke, sperm and killer whales, white-beaked dolphins and the ubiquitous harbour porpoise. Humpback whales appear in certain seasons, and blue whales surface from time to time. In Iceland, Húsavík (p261) is the acknowledged hotspot; in Norway, you're practically guaranteed to see sperm whales on trips around the Vesterålen islands (p366).

Windsurfing & Kitesurfing

The beaches of Denmark, particularly on the West Jutland coast, attract crowds of windsurfers and kitesurfers in summer. Wetsuits enable keener surfers to continue their sport throughout the colder months. Sailboards can be rented in some tourist centres, and courses are sometimes on offer for beginners. See p108 for more details.

BUSINESS HOURS

Pubs generally open from 4pm to 11pm, and normal hours for restaurants and cafés are noon to 10pm daily. Variations are noted throughout the text.

CHILDREN

Most of Scandinavia is very child-friendly, with domestic tourism largely dictated by children's needs. Iceland and the Faroes are exceptions: children are liked and have lots of freedom, but they're treated as mini-adults and there aren't many attractions tailored particularly for them. In Denmark, Finland, Norway and Sweden, you'll find excellent theme parks, water parks and holiday activities. Many museums have a dedicated children's section with toys, games and dressing-up clothes.

Car-rental firms hire out children's safety seats at a nominal cost, but advance bookings are essential. Similarly, highchairs and cots (cribs) are standard in many restaurants and hotels, but numbers may be limited. The choice of baby food, infant formulas, soy and cow's milk, disposable nappies (diapers) etc is wide in most Scandinavian supermarkets.

In the Faroes and more rugged areas of Scandinavia, a baby carrier rather than a pram is crucial.

For tips and anecdotes on successful travel with the underage crowd, check out Lonely Planet's *Travel with Children*, by Cathy Lanigan.

CLIMATE

Generalisations about the weather over an area of approximately 2,500,000 sq km are something of an impossibility! Temperatures range from -50°C in the Arctic Circle in winter to summer temperatures of over 30°C in some parts of Sweden. Large chunks of Scandinavia lie within the Arctic Circle, yet the presence of the Gulf Stream makes coastal areas much warmer than you might expect at such a northerly latitude. See the climate charts, and tune in to local weather reports for conditions once you're on the road.

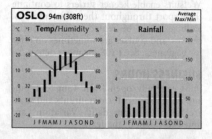

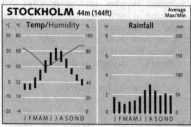

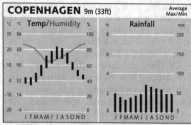

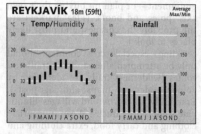

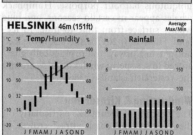

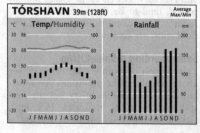

DANGERS & ANNOYANCES
Drugs
Always treat drugs with a great deal of caution. There's a fair amount of dope available in Scandinavia, sometimes quite openly, but that doesn't mean it's legal: a bit of hash can cause a lot of bother. Don't try to bring drugs home with you – energetic customs officials could well decide to take a closer look at your luggage.

Remote Areas
In remote rural areas, hypothermia, injury and getting lost are serious hazards. Never underestimate the wilderness; always take proper equipment and seek local knowledge. People living in isolated places may be suspicious of outsiders, and winter darkness can lead to unpredictable behaviour and alcohol abuse.

Theft
Theft, usually pickpocketing, is only really a problem in major Scandinavian cities like Oslo, Copenhagen and Stockholm. Take care of your belongings and remember that the greatest threat can often be from fellow tourists, who thieve from others to fund their trips.

The most important things to guard are your passport, other important documents, tickets and money – in that order. It's always best to carry these next to your skin or in a sturdy leather pouch on your belt.

Train-station lockers or luggage-storage counters are useful places to stash your bags (not valuables) while you get your bearings in a new town. Be very suspicious about people who offer to help you operate your locker.

Carry your own padlock for hostel lockers and watch out for thieves who strike at night in hostel dorms – keep your money and passport well out of reach. Be careful, even in hotels: don't leave valuables lying around your room.

Parked cars, especially those with foreign number plates and/or rental-agency stickers, are prime targets for petty criminals. If possible, remove the stickers (or cover them with local football club stickers or something similar), leave a local newspaper on the seat and try to make it look like a local car. Don't ever leave valuables in the car, and remove all luggage overnight.

In case of theft or loss, always report the incident to the police and ask for a statement, or your travel insurance won't pay up.

Wildlife
Wild animals pose a small risk. Polar bears and wolves roam the arctic archipelago of Svalbard (Norway). Arctic terns in coastal regions defend their nests aggressively – hold a stick up above your head, as they divebomb the highest part of you.

Clouds of mosquitoes, midges and blackflies can be a real annoyance in some parts of Scandinavia. You might look a fool, but a mosquito head-net (often found for sale in petrol stations) will save you from a faceful of flies.

DISABLED TRAVELLERS
Scandinavia leads the world in terms of facilities for wheelchair-users, but getting around can still be awkward. By law, for example, every new restaurant in Finland must have a wheelchair-accessible toilet; however, that leaves plenty of older restaurants to contend with! There are ramps to practically all public buildings, most department stores, shopping centres and many private shops. Some train carriages are fitted with special lifts for wheelchairs. Iceland and the Faroes are a little further behind the rest of the region – check access issues before you travel.

If you have a physical disability, get in touch with your national support organisation (preferably the 'travel officer' if there is one) and ask about the countries you plan to visit. They often have complete libraries devoted to travel, and they can put you in touch with travel agents who specialise in tours for the disabled. Scandinavian tourist office websites (see 'Tourist Information' in the individual country directories) generally contain good information on disabled access.

DISCOUNT CARDS
Camping Card International
The **Camping Card International** (www.campingcardinternational.com) is basically an ID card you can leave behind a camping ground's reception desk instead of your passport. It incorporates third-party insurance for any damage you may cause, and you may also get small discounts at some amusement parks,

museums and camping grounds. They're obligatory in Denmark (you can also use the Camping Card Scandinavia) and at some Swedish camping grounds (others are affiliated with the Camping Card Scandinavia), valid in Finland and Norway, but not commonly recognised in Iceland or the Faroes.

You can buy one before you leave home from any organisation affiliated with the Fédération Internationale de Camping et de Caravanning (FICC), Fédération Internationale de l'Automobile (FIA) or Alliance Internationale de Tourisme (AIT) – these are usually your country's major automobile associations and/or camping and caravanning groups. The cards are valid for one year and cover up to 11 people.

Camping Card Scandinavia

Similar to the Camping Card International, **Camping Card Scandinavia** (www.camping.se) acts as an ID card, offers discounts at certain camping grounds and attractions, and has built-in third-party insurance.

It's valid in Denmark, Norway and Finland and at most Swedish camp site, and in some other European countries. One card covers you whether you're an individual, a couple or a family with children under 18.

Order the card through the website before you leave home, or pick up a temporary card directly from camping grounds in Scandinavia. The card is 'free' but you have to pay a small fee for a validity sticker, which means your card is valid for one year.

Hostel Card

While not mandatory in Scandinavia, a **Hostelling International** (HI; www.hihostels.com) card gives a sizable discount every time you check in to an affiliated hostel. It's best to buy the card from your national hostelling association before you set off, although in Scandinavia some hostels will issue one on the spot or after six stays (generally more expensive than getting one at home). See p482 for more details on hostelling in the region.

Senior Cards

Museums and other sights, public swimming pools, spas and transport companies frequently offer discounts to retirees, pensioners and to those over 60 (sometimes slightly younger for women; and over 65 in Sweden). Make sure you bring proof of age; the ever-proper and always polite Scandinavian ticket-collector is not going to admit that you look a day over 39.

If you're going to be travelling by train, those aged over 60 are entitled to discounted Euro Domino passes (p511) and senior versions of the ScanRail pass (p511).

Student & Youth Cards

The most useful of these cards is the International Student Identity Card (ISIC), a plastic ID-style photocard, which provides discounts on numerous forms of transport (including airlines, international ferries and local public transport), reduced or free admission to museums and sights, and cheap meals in some student restaurants – a good way of cutting costs in expensive Scandinavia. Full-time students from the age of 12 upwards are eligible. If you're under 26 but not a student, you can apply for an International Youth Travel Card (IYTC), with similar benefits. Both are available through student unions, hostelling organisations or youth-oriented travel agencies: see the website of the International **Student Travel Confederation** (www.istc.org) for further details.

Also available to anyone aged under 26 is the **Euro26 card** (www.eyca.org), which goes by various names in different countries – see the website for more information.

These cards don't automatically entitle you to discounts and some companies and institutions don't recognise them – but you won't find out until you try.

ELECTRICITY

Most of the region runs on 220V, 50Hz AC. Check the voltage and cycle (usually 50Hz) used in your home country. Most appliances that are set up for 220V will handle 240V quite happily without modifications (and vice versa); the same goes for 110V and 125V combinations.

It's always preferable to adjust your appliance to the exact voltage if you can (some modern battery chargers and radios will do this automatically). Just don't combine 110/125V and 220/240V without a transformer (which will be built into an adjustable appliance).

Several countries outside Europe (eg the USA and Canada) run on 60Hz AC, which will affect the speed of electric motors even after the voltage has been adjusted to European values, so CD and tape players (where motor speed is all-important) will be useless. However, appliances such as electric razors, hair dryers, irons and radios will be fine.

The standard plug is the so-called 'europlug' with two round pins, although some plugs in the Faroes have three pins and some in Iceland have two slanted prongs. Adaptors are available from most supermarkets in Scandinavia. Many europlugs and some sockets don't have provision for earth since most local home appliances are double insulated; when provided, earth usually consists of two contact points along the edge.

EMBASSIES & CONSULATES

See the individual country Directories for specific embassy and consulate addresses.

It's important to realise the things your own embassy can and can't do to help you. Generally speaking, it won't be much help in emergencies if the trouble you're in is your own fault in any way. Remember that you are bound by the laws of the country you are in. Your embassy will not be sympathetic if you end up in jail after committing a crime locally, even if such actions are legal in your own country.

In genuine emergencies you might get some assistance, but only if other channels have been exhausted. For example, if you need to get home urgently, a free ticket is exceedingly unlikely – the embassy would expect you to have insurance. If you have all your money and documents stolen, it might assist with getting a new passport, but a loan for onward travel is out of the question.

GAY & LESBIAN TRAVELLERS

This book lists contact addresses and gay and lesbian venues in the individual country chapters, and your national gay and lesbian organisation should be able to give you more information before you travel. The *Spartacus International Gay Guide* (US$33), published by Bruno Gmünder Verlag (Berlin), is an excellent international directory of gay entertainment venues. It's updated every two years, so it's best used in conjunction with more up-to-date listings in local papers – venues can change with great speed.

Denmark, Iceland, Norway and Sweden allow gay and lesbian couples to form 'registered partnerships', which grant every right of matrimony except access to church weddings, adoption and artificial insemination. Finland, too, is tolerant of homosexual couples. However, public displays of affection are uncommon in Norway, and it's a good idea to be discreet in the Faroes, where a conservative society and strongly held religious beliefs may cause problems for gay and lesbian couples.

HOLIDAYS

Midsummer's Eve (the longest day of the year) is celebrated in late June across Scandinavia, generally with fervour and large bonfires! For holidays particular to each country, see the Directories at the end of each country chapter.

INSURANCE
Private Travel Insurance

A travel insurance policy to cover theft, personal liability, loss and medical problems is strongly recommended. There's a variety of policies available and travel agencies will have recommendations. International travel policies handled by STA Travel and other student travel organisations are usually good value. Check the small print; some policies specifically exclude 'dangerous activities' such as skiing, motorcycling, mountaineering or even hiking.

Travel insurance also covers cancellation or delays in travel arrangements, for example, if you fall seriously ill two days before departure. The cover will depend on your insurance so ask your insurer to explain where you stand. Ticket loss is also covered by travel insurance.

Buy insurance as early as possible. If you buy it the week before you are due to fly, you may find that you're not covered for delays to your flight caused by strikes or other industrial actions that may have been in force before you took out the insurance.

Paying for your airline ticket with a credit card often provides limited travel accident insurance, and you may be able to reclaim the payment if the operator doesn't deliver. In the UK, for instance, institutions issuing credit cards are required by law to reimburse consumers if a company goes into liquidation and the amount involved is more than UK£100. Ask your credit-card company what it is prepared to cover.

An insurance policy that pays doctors or hospitals directly may be preferable to one where you have to pay on the spot and claim back later. If you have to claim later, make sure the foreign health centre or hospital gives you all the necessary documentation you'll need for insurance purposes. Some policies ask you to call back (reverse charges) to a centre in your home country where an immediate assessment of your problem can be made. Check if the policy covers ambulances and an emergency flight home.

Worldwide cover to travellers from over 44 countries is available online at www .lonelyplanet.com/travel_services.

Reciprocal Medical Insurance Agreements

Citizens of the European Economic Area (EEA) are covered for emergency medical treatment in other EEA countries (including Denmark, Finland, Iceland, Norway and Sweden) on presentation of a European Health Insurance Card (EHIC), which replaced the E111 form in January 2006. Enquire about EHICs at your health centre, travel agency or (in some countries) post office well in advance of travel. UK citizens can find out more on the website www .dh.gov.uk/PolicyAndGuidance/HealthAd viceForTravellers, and can apply for a card online at www.ehic.org.uk.

Australian Medicare has a reciprocal healthcare agreement (covering emergency treatment only) with eight European countries, including Finland, Norway and Sweden.

The cost of repatriation will not be covered by the EHIC or Australian Medicare, and sometimes other services are also exempt – for example, ambulance costs or emergency dental treatment. You will usually have to pay on the spot for your medical care, but should be able to reclaim most of your expenses – just insist on receipts for everything.

Private travel insurance is still advisable because of the flexibility it offers, and because it usually covers big expenses such as repatriation. For further information about health insurance, see p514.

Car Insurance
See p509.

INTERNET ACCESS

Free web-based email accounts like **Hotmail** (www.hotmail.com) or **Yahoo!** (http://mail.yahoo.com) are the easiest way to email when you're abroad. Once you've set up an account, you can get to that all-important inbox from any internet-connected computer in the world.

If you're bringing your own laptop, make sure you've got a universal AC adaptor (which will stop the computer's innards frying if the power supply voltage varies) and a plug adaptor for each country you visit (cheaper if bought at home).

For more information on travelling with a laptop, see the World Wide Phone Guide on the internet at www.kropla.com or TeleAdapt at www.teleadapt.com.

Internet Cafés

You'll find internet cafés throughout Scandinavia: many are listed in the country chapters in this book. In general, libraries provide a free or very cheap internet service, although there may be a waiting list and locals may have priority. You can also find public internet access in some post offices, tourist offices, hostels, hotels and universities.

Wireless Hotspots

Scandinavia is rife with wireless (wi-fi) hotspots. An astonishing number of cafés, bars, hostels and hotels, particularly in cities, offer the service for free. Most modern laptops have built-in wireless LAN, which means you don't require a modem, jacks or other fiddly bits and pieces. If you set up your computer within a hotspot, it should automatically pick up a signal (you may need a password) and you'll be able to surf the internet. Even if your laptop is an older model without built-in wireless, you can buy a wireless adaptor which plugs into a USB port on your laptop and does the job perfectly. As with most things in the region, wireless USB adaptors are relatively expensive, so it's better to pick one up at home.

LEGAL MATTERS

See the individual country Directories for specific legal matters, including drinking laws, drug laws and traffic restrictions.

MAPS

Good maps are easy to come by in Scandinavian Europe, but you might want to buy a few beforehand, especially if you're driving, cycling or have some hefty treks planned. The maps in this book are a useful first reference when you arrive in a city.

Michelin do a general road map of Scandinavia. Some people prefer the meticulous larger-scale Freytag & Berndt, Kümmerly + Frey or Hallwag maps, which have been recommended for Scandinavian countries. Falk Plan city maps are very usable and detailed, and the Falk map of Scandinavia is particularly good.

In Scandinavia, tourist offices are an excellent source for free and up-to-date maps, often in English-language versions. Local automobile associations also provide detailed, free maps to their members.

The following shops sell Scandinavian maps, including motoring maps and topographic maps for hikers, by mail order:

Map Land (☎ 03-9670 4383; www.mapland.com.au; 372 Little Bourke St, Melbourne, VIC 3000, Australia)

Map Shop (☎ 0800 085 4080, 01684-593146; www .themapshop.co.uk; 15 High St, Upton-upon-Severn, Worcestershire, WR8 0HJ, England)

Omni Resources (☎ 336-227 8300; www.omnimap .com; 1004 S Mebane St, PO Box 2096, Burlington, NC 27216-2096, USA)

MONEY

All Scandinavian currencies are fully convertible. Most foreign currencies can be easily exchanged but US dollars, pounds sterling and euros are the best to carry. You may well decide, however, that other currencies suit your purposes better. You lose out through commissions and customer exchange rates every time you change money, so if you only visit Sweden, for example, you may be better off buying some kronor before you leave home. See the relevant country Directories for further details.

ATMs

Credit and cash cards (eg Visa, Cirrus, Plus, Eurocard) are accepted widely throughout Scandinavian Europe; always make sure you know which ATMs abroad will accept your particular card by checking first with your bank at home. Remember that ATMs aren't completely fail-safe. If one

SCANDINAVIA & THE EU		
Country	EU member	Currency
Denmark	yes	Danish krone (Dkr)
Faroe Islands	no	Faroese króna (Fkr) & Danish krone (Dkr)
Finland	yes	euro (€)
Iceland	no	Icelandic króna (Ikr)
Norway	no	Norwegian krone (Nkr)
Sweden	yes	Swedish krona (Skr)

swallows your card it can be a major headache. Note that many ATMs in Europe will not accept PINs of more than four digits.

Withdrawals may incur a 'loading fee' (conversion fee) of around 2.75%, plus a transaction fee (usually a flat rate of about $US2 to $US5, or a percentage of at least 2%) – check charge rates with your card provider. It's often more economical if you make fewer but larger withdrawals. If you travel abroad a lot, look into opening an account with a bank that doesn't charge rip-off fees!

Charge cards such as American Express and Diners Club may also be hooked up to ATM networks.

Cash

Nothing beats cash for convenience…or risk. If you lose it, it's gone forever and very few travel insurers will come to your rescue. For tips on carrying your money safely, see p487.

It's still a good idea, though, to bring some local currency in cash, if only to tide you over until you get to an exchange facility or find an ATM. Some extra cash in an easily exchanged currency (eg US dollars or pounds sterling) is also a good idea. Remember that banks will always accept foreign-currency paper money but very rarely coins, so you might want to spend (or donate) local coins before you cross a border.

Credit Cards

A credit card can be an ideal travelling companion. Make sure you know what to do in case of theft (usually you need to call a telephone hotline).

Credit and debit cards are very popular in Scandinavia; Visa is the most common, followed by MasterCard. They are more widely accepted than charge cards (such as American Express and Diners Club) because they charge merchants lower commissions. Their major drawback is that they have a credit limit based on your regular income, and this limit can stop you in your tracks if you're charging major expenses such as long-term car rental or long-distance airline tickets and travelling extensively. You can avoid this by depositing money into your card account before you begin your travels.

Other drawbacks are that many banks slap a 'loading fee' of around 2.75% onto each transaction that you make abroad, which can really add up. Also, interest is charged on outstanding accounts, either immediately or after a set period (always immediately on cash advances), and the card can be very difficult to replace if lost abroad in remote areas.

Although it's rare in this region, fraudulent shopkeepers have been known to make several charge-slip imprints with customers' credit cards when they're not looking. They then simply copy the signature from the signed slip. Try not to let the card out of your sight, and always check your statements carefully.

Moneychangers

Travellers should avoid banks in Scandinavian countries (except in the Faroes and Iceland, where banks are often a better option) in favour of *bureaux de change* (eg Forex) or post offices, which tend to offer better rates and charge lower fees or com-

---

CREDIT & DEBIT CARD TIP

Let your bank know when you'll be going abroad. Unusual spending patterns, for example, a large cash withdrawal in Norway instead of your usual £20-per-week in Northampton, may lead to the bank freezing your card.

---

missions than banks. They generally have longer opening hours than banks, which are closed at weekends and on public holidays (see the Directories in the individual country chapters for lists). However, most airports, central train stations, some fancy hotels and many border posts have banking facilities outside working hours. If you're visiting several countries, buy a cheap pocket calculator, cut out the list of exchange rates from a newspaper, and stick it to the back of the calculator for easy reference.

Tipping

For the most part, tipping isn't required in Scandinavia, although if you round up the bill or leave a little something in recognition of good service, it won't be refused.

Travellers Cheques

The main advantage of travellers cheques over cash is the protection they offer against theft, although they are losing their popularity as more travellers withdraw their hard-earned money directly via ATMs. American Express, Visa and Thomas Cook cheques are widely accepted and have efficient replacement policies for lost and stolen cheques.

It's vital to keep a record of your cheque numbers and which ones you have used, in case of theft. Keep your list separate from the cheques themselves.

Cheques denominated in US dollars, euros and pounds sterling are the easiest to cash. When you change them, don't just look at the exchange rate; ask about fees and commissions as well. There may be a per-cheque service fee, a flat transaction fee, or a percentage of the total amount irrespective of the number of cheques. In most European countries the exchange rate for travellers cheques is slightly better than the exchange rate for cash.

TAXES & REFUNDS

A kind of sales tax called value-added tax (VAT) applies to most goods and services throughout Scandinavia. International visitors can usually claim back the VAT on purchases (above a set minimum amount) that are being taken out of the country. Remember, though, that travellers who reside in an EU country are not entitled to a refund on VAT paid on goods bought in another EU country (eg a Briton returning home with goods from Finland, Sweden or Denmark). The procedure for making the claim is usually pretty straightforward. For guidance, see the relevant country chapters.

PHOTOGRAPHY & VIDEO

Scandinavia is extremely photogenic, but the local climate and when/where you travel will dictate what film to take. In autumn, when the sky can often be overcast, photographers should use high-speed film (rated 200 or 400 ASA). In bright conditions, eg in sunny weather or if there's lots of settled snow, slower film (with an ASA of 50 to 100) is the answer.

It's worth noting that if you're taking pictures in reflective conditions, eg of icebergs, water or snow, you need to overexpose your shots; otherwise automatic cameras think it's brighter than it really is, resulting in dark photos. Batteries tend to run out quickly in cold conditions, so carry a spare set. Try to avoid exposing your camera and films to extremes of temperature.

If you're using a digital camera, check that you have enough memory to store your snaps – two 128MB cards will probably be enough. If you do run out of memory space your best bet is to burn your photos onto a CD. Increasing numbers of processing labs now offer this service. To download your pics at an internet café you'll need a USB cable and a card reader. Some places provide a USB on request, but be warned that many of the bigger chain cafés don't let you plug your gear into their computers, meaning that it's back to plan A – the CD.

For more pointers, check out Lonely Planet's *Travel Photography*, by internationally renowned travel photographer Richard I'Anson. It's a full-colour guide designed to be taken on the road.

Still and video film and camera equipment is available throughout Scandinavia, but it would be advisable to bring as much as possible with you, as prices can be exorbitant. Print processing is generally available in towns and cities.

POST

Airmail typically takes about a week to reach North American or Australasian destinations. Postage costs vary from country to country. Postal services are very efficient in Scandinavia.

You can collect mail from post office poste restante sections, although this can be a tricky process in Sweden; see p472 for details. Ask people writing to you to print your name clearly on the envelope, under-line your surname and use capital letters. When collecting mail, bring along your passport for identification. If an expected letter is not waiting for you, ask post office staff to check under your first name as letters are sometimes misfiled. Unless the sender specifies otherwise, mail will always be sent to the main post office of any city.

You can also have mail (but not parcels) sent to you at American Express offices so long as you have an American Express card or travellers cheques. When you buy American Express travellers cheques you can ask for a booklet listing all their office addresses worldwide.

SOLO TRAVELLERS

Scandinavia is well developed and one of the safest places to travel in Europe, so travelling alone should pose no problems. Inhabitants of Scandinavia are often thought to be pleasant but not particularly gregarious, so you may have to brush up your social skills if you want to make friends locally.

Hostels and camping grounds are good places to meet other travellers.

TELEPHONE & FAX

You can call abroad from almost any phone box in Scandinavia. Reverse-charge (collect) calls are usually possible, and communicating with the local operator in English should not be much of a problem. In some countries you can avoid the local operator, and dial direct to your home operator.

You can send faxes and telegrams from most of the larger post offices and some hotels and public telephone offices.

Mobile Phones

Most populated parts of Scandinavia use GSM 900/1800, which is compatible with the rest of Europe and Australasia, but not with the North American GSM 1900 or the totally different system in Japan (although some North American GSM 1900/900 may work here). If you have a GSM phone, check with your service provider about using it in Scandinavia, and beware of calls being routed internationally (very expensive for a 'local' call). Local telephone companies and national tourist offices can advise on coverage.

Rental of mobile phones is possible everywhere except Norway, and is particularly easy in mobile-centric Finland. Purchasing a mobile phone is always an option, but it's an expensive option and you'll be unable to use your existing number. Another option is to buy a local SIM card with a rechargeable account – this is particularly good value in Sweden, Iceland and Finland.

Phone Codes

To call abroad you simply dial the international access code (IAC) for the country you are calling from (most commonly 00 in Europe), the country code (CC) for the country you are calling, the local area code (usually dropping the leading zero if there is one) and then the number. If, for example, you are in Norway (which has an international access code of 00) and want to make a call to Sweden (country code 46) in the Stockholm area (area code 08), number ☎ 123 4567, then dial ☎ 00-46-8-123 4567. Again, www.kropla.com has a comprehensive list of international dialling codes.

Phonecards

Public telephones accepting stored-value phonecards are the norm and, in some places, coin-operated phones are almost impossible to find. Phonecards are readily available from post offices, telephone centres, news stands or retail outlets. These cards solve the problem of having the correct coins for calls. More and more public telephone kiosks are giving callers the opportunity to pay by credit card. Beware of public telephones in bars and restaurants – most will eat up your money at an incredible rate.

TIME

Scandinavian Europe sprawls across six time zones. See the individual country Directories for details.

TOURIST INFORMATION

Tourist information offices in Scandinavia are located at train stations or centrally (often in the town hall or central square) in most towns. They tend to be open for longer hours over the summer and reduced hours over the winter; smaller offices may only be open during the peak months of summer.

TELEPHONE CODES

Country	☎ CC	☎ IAC	☎ IO
Denmark	45	00	141
Faroe Islands	298	00	808080
Finland	358	00, 990, 994, 999	020208
Iceland	354	00	1811
Norway	47	00	1882
Sweden	46	00	118119

CC – country code (to call into that country)
IAC – international access code (to call abroad from that country)
IO – international operator (to make inquiries)

Facilities are generally excellent, with piles of regional and national brochures, helpful free maps and friendly employees. Staff are often multilingual, speaking several tongues including Scandinavian languages, English, German and French. They will book hotel and transport reservations and tours; a small charge may apply.

VIDEO SYSTEMS

If you want to record or buy videos to play back home, they won't work if the image registration systems are different. Most of Europe and Australia uses PAL (France and Poland use SECAM), which is incompatible with NTSC in North America and Japan.

Similarly, if you're thinking of buying DVDs, remember that Scandinavia uses Region 2 coding (covering Europe, the UK, Japan, the Middle East, South Africa) and so may not be compatible with your DVD player at home. Even if your DVD player is Region 2, discs bought in Scandinavia still may not be playable because of NTSC/PAL incompatibility (eg Region 2 Scandinavian discs will not play on Region 2 Japanese DVD players).

VISAS

There's a wide variety of visas available, including tourist, transit, business and study visas. Transit visas are usually cheaper than tourist or business visas, but they only allow a very short stay (one or two days) and can be difficult to extend. Often you can get the visa at the border or at the airport on arrival; check first with the embassies or consulates of the countries you plan to visit.

It's important to remember that visas have a 'use-by date', and you'll be refused entry after that period has elapsed. Visa requirements do change, and you should always check with the individual embassies or consulates or a reputable travel agency before leaving home. If you wish to apply for a visa while still at home, make sure you do it at least three months in advance of your planned arrival. If you plan to get your visas as you go along rather than arranging them all beforehand, carry spare passport photos.

Citizens of the UK, the USA, Canada, Ireland, Australia and New Zealand don't require visas if visiting a Scandinavian country for less than three months; South Africans, on the other hand, need a visa to enter all Scandinavian countries. With a valid passport most travellers will be able to visit Scandinavian countries for up to three (sometimes even six) months, provided they have some sort of onward or return ticket and/or 'sufficient means of support' (money). Except at international airports, it's unlikely that immigration officials will give you and your passport more than a cursory glance.

Many EU countries have abolished passport controls between their borders and an identity card should be sufficient, but it's always safest to carry your passport.

For more specific visa information, refer to the individual Directories in the country chapters.

WEIGHTS & MEASURES

The metric system is used in Scandinavia. Decimals are indicated by commas and thousands are indicated by points.

WOMEN TRAVELLERS

Scandinavia is one of the safest places to travel in all of Europe and women travellers should experience little trouble; however, use common sense when dealing with potentially dangerous situations such as hitching or walking alone at night. Recommended reading is the *Handbook for Women Travellers* by M & G Moss.

WORK

Officially, a citizen of the EU is allowed to work in other EU countries, although the paperwork isn't always straightforward for longer-term employment. Other country/nationality combinations require special work permits that are almost impossible to arrange, especially for temporary work. However, Australian and New Zealand passport holders aged between 18 and 30 can qualify for a one-year working holiday visa in some Scandinavian countries: see the individual country Directories for details.

That doesn't prevent enterprising travellers from topping up their funds occasionally, and not always illegally. Your national student-exchange organisation may be able to arrange temporary work permits to several countries through special programmes.

If you do find a temporary job, the pay may be less than that offered to locals, although this is not always the case in Scandinavia. Teaching English can pay well, but such work is hard to come by. Other typical tourist jobs (such as working in a restaurant, hotel or fish-processing plant) may come with board and lodging, and pay that's little more than pocket money, but you'll have a good time partying with other travellers.

Work Your Way Around the World by Susan Griffith gives good, practical advice on a wide range of issues. Another useful title is *The Au Pair & Nanny's Guide to Working Abroad* by Susan Griffith and Sharon Legg.

Selling goods on the street is generally frowned upon and can be tantamount to vagrancy, apart from at flea markets.

If you play an instrument or have other artistic talents, you could try busking (street entertainment). It's fairly common in many major cities. In Sweden, you'll need to get a busking permit, which is available from the police, although not everybody actually has the permit. In Copenhagen, acoustic music is allowed without a permit in pedestrian streets and squares between 4pm and 8pm on weekdays and noon to 5am at the weekend. Most other Scandinavian countries require municipal permits that can be hard to obtain. Talk to other buskers first.

Transport in Scandinavian Europe

CONTENTS

GETTING THERE & AWAY

ENTRY REQUIREMENTS

Citizens of the UK, the USA, Canada, Ireland, Australia and New Zealand do not need to apply for a visa if they are visiting a Scandinavian country for less than three months. With a valid passport, most travellers will be able to visit the region for up to three (sometimes even six) months, provided they have some sort of onward or return ticket and/or 'sufficient means of support' (ie money) for the lenght of their stay.

Many EU countries have abolished passport controls between their borders, requiring only an identity card, but it's always safest to carry your passport. If it's about to expire, renew it before you go – some countries insist that it's valid for a specified minimum period (usually three months but sometimes up to six) after your visit.

Flights, tours and rail tickets can be booked online at www.lonelyplanet.com /travel_services.

WARNING

The information in this chapter is particularly vulnerable to change. Check directly with the airline or a travel agency to make sure you understand how a fare (and the ticket you may buy) works and be aware of the security requirements for international travel. Shop carefully. The details given in this chapter should be regarded as pointers and are not a substitute for your own careful, up-to-date research.

AIR

Increased competition among airlines is great news for travellers. There are plenty of cheap tickets from 'no-frills' airlines which sell budget tickets direct to customers.

London is one of the best centres for picking up inexpensive, restricted-validity tickets through discount operators (see p498). Various classes of cheap air tickets and passes are also available on routes within Scandinavian countries (see p505), subject to restrictions. European 'gateway' cities include Amsterdam, Athens, Berlin, Copenhagen, Frankfurt, London, Oslo, Stockholm and Vienna.

Before booking a flight, wheelchair travellers should check the airline's lifting policy, whether it's possible to take a wheelchair with spillable battery on board, and whether the airline requires a 'fit to travel certificate'.

Bicycles are generally accepted as luggage if they're in a bike bag – check conditions with your airline.

Airports & Airlines

Major hubs in Scandinavia include Denmark's **Kastrup International Airport** (☎ 45 32 31 32 31; www.cph.dk), Finland's **Helsinki-Vantaa Airport** (☎ 358-2001 4636; www.helsinki-vantaa.fi), Iceland's **Keflavík Airport** (☎ 354-425-0600; www .keflavikairport.com), Norway's **Oslo Airport** (☎ 47 815 50 250; www.osl.no) and Sweden's **Arlanda Airport** (☎ 46 879 70 000; www.lfv.se).

The main international airlines flying into and out of Scandinavia and Continental Europe are given below. Telephone numbers are for help desks and booking offices in the hub country; for an airline's representatives in other countries, check their website.

Air Canada (airline code AC; ☎ 1-888-247-2262; www .aircanada.ca) Hub: Toronto, Canada.

Air France (airline code AF; www.airfrance.com) France (☎ 08 20 82 08 20) Australia (☎ 1 300 390 190 toll free) Hub: Charles de Gaulle, Paris, France.

Atlantic Airways (airline code RC; ☎ 341000; www .atlantic.fo) Hub: Vágar, Faroes.

Austrian Airlines (airline code OS; ☎ 051789; www .aua.com) Hub: Vienna, Austria.

Blue1 (airline code RF; ☎ 20 585 6000; www.blue1.com) Hub: Helsinki-Vantaa, Finland.

British Airways (airline code BA; ☎ 0870 850 9850, ☎ 0191 490 7901; www.britishairways.com) Hub: Heathrow, UK.

Cathay Pacific (airline code CX; ☎ 2747 1888; www .cathaypacific.com) Hub: Hong Kong.

City Airline (airline code CF; ☎ 31-600 385; www .cityairline.com) Hub: Göteborg, Sweden.

EasyJet (airline code U2 ☎ 0870 600 0000; www .easyjet.com) Hub: Luton, London, UK.

Finnair (airline code AY; ☎ 600 140 140; www.finnair .com) Hub: Helsinki-Vantaa, Finland.

Flugfélag Íslands (Air Iceland; airline code NY; ☎ 570 3030; www.airiceland.is) Hub: Keflavík, Iceland.

FlyMe (airline code SH; ☎ 0770 790 790; www.flyme .com) Hub: Göteborg, Sweden.

Fly Nordic (airline code 6B; ☎ 08-585 54 400; www .flynordic.com) Hub: Arlanda, Sweden.

Icelandair (airline code FI; ☎ 505 0100; www.icelandair .net) Hub: Keflavík, Iceland.

Iceland Express (airline code FHE; ☎ 550 0600; www .icelandexpress.com) Hub: Keflavík, Iceland.

KLM (airline code KL; ☎ 20 474 7747; www.klm.com) Hub: Schipol, Amsterdam, Netherlands.

Lufthansa (airline code LO; ☎ 020-1805 83 84 26; www .lufthansa.com) Hub: Frankfurt, Germany.

Norwegian Air Shuttle (airline code DY; ☎ Norway 815 21 815, outside Norway 21 49 00 15 ; www.norwegian .no) Hub: Oslo, Norway.

Qantas (airline code QF; ☎ 13 13 13; www.qantas.com .au) Hub: Sydney, Australia.

Ryanair (airlinr code FR; ☎ 01-1812 1212; www.ryanair .com) Hub: Dublin, Ireland.

SAS (Scandinavian Airlines; airline code SK; ☎ 70 10 20 00; www.scandinavian.net) Hub: Kastrup, Denmark.

Skyways (airline code JZ; ☎ 0771 95 95 00; www .skyways.se) Hub: Arlanda, Sweden.

Sterling Airlines (airline code NB; ☎ 70 10 84 84; www.sterling.dk) Hub: Kastrup, Denmark.

Swiss (airline code SR; ☎ 0848 700 700; www.swiss.com) Hub: Zurich, Switzerland.

Thai Airways (airline code TG; ☎ 2628-2000; www .thaiairways.com) Hub: Bangkok, Thailand.

Tickets

For 'full-service' airlines, it's usually cheaper to buy tickets from a travel agency rather than directly from an airline. For extra peace of mind, use a bonded agency, such as one covered by the Air Transport Operators Licence (ATOL) scheme in the UK. Firms such as STA Travel, which has offices worldwide, are not going to disappear overnight and they offer good prices to most destinations.

For budget airlines turn to the internet, which has made booking cheap tickets a breeze. Usually the low-cost carriers' websites offer one-way tickets that are exactly half the cost of the return fare, so you can easily fly into one place and leave from another.

Flights to Scandinavia are most expensive in July and August and at Christmas. Prices given below are approximate high-season return fares.

Asia

Singapore and Bangkok are the discount plane-ticket capitals of Asia. Not all agencies are reliable: ask for advice from other travellers before buying tickets.

Finnair has direct daily flights from Helsinki to Bangkok (€1700, 10 hours), Beijing (€1000, eight hours), Shanghai (€1400, nine hours); and several flights per week to Tokyo (€1300, 9½ hours). Finnair also flies Helsinki–Singapore (€1800, 13 hours) and Oslo–Singapore (Nkr19,600, 13 hours) with a stopover in Bangkok.

Thai Airways flies from Bangkok to Stockholm (Skr11,300, 10½ hours) and to Copenhagen (Dkr31,500, 11 hours).

SAS has flights from Tokyo to Copenhagen (Dkr17,500, 11½ hours).

Aeroflot offers inexpensive deals from India to Europe.

Recommended agencies:

Four Seas Tours (☎ 2200 7777; www.fourseastravel .com/english; Hong Kong)

No 1 Travel (☎ 03 3205 6073; www.no1-travel.com; Japan)

STA Travel (www.statravel.com); Bangkok (☎ 02 236 0262; www.statravel.co.th); Hong Kong (☎ 2736 1618; www.statravel.com.hk); Japan (☎ 03 5391 2922;

www.lonelyplanet.com

www.statravel.co.jp in Japanese); Singapore (☎ 6737 7188; www.statravel.com.sg)
STIC Travels (www.stictravel.com); Delhi (☎ 11 233 57 468); Mumbai (☎ 22 221 81 431)

Australia

Flights to Scandinavian capitals require stopovers, usually in Singapore or Bangkok and a European city. Return fares cost around A$3000, and take 26 hours. Air France, Qantas and KLM offer some good deals.

Some travel agencies, particularly smaller ones, advertise cheap air fares in the travel sections of the weekend newspapers. Well-known travel agencies with offices throughout Australia:
Flight Centre (☎ 133 133; www.flightcentre.com.au)
STA Travel (☎ 1300 733 035; www.statravel.com.au)

Canada

Airlines flying to Scandinavia include Finnair, British Airways, Northwest Airlines and Air Canada. Flights leave from all major cities including Montreal, Ottawa, Toronto and Vancouver, and take around 14 hours, with one change in Frankfurt, London or New York. Prices varied quite substantially at the time of research (average C$2000 plus tax), so shop around.

Travel Cuts (☎ 1 866 246 9762; www.travelcuts.com) is Canada's national student travel agency, with offices in major cities.

For online bookings try www.expedia.ca and www.travelocity.ca.

Continental Europe

Several European cities, particularly Amsterdam, Athens and Berlin, offer bargain flights. Various Scandinavian budget airlines, with numerous cheap internet deals, fly to European towns and cities: Sterling Airlines, who fly from Stockholm, Oslo and Helsinki, are the biggest; Blue 1 (a subsidiary of SAS) fly from Helsinki; Norwegian Air Shuttle fly from Oslo.

Icelandair serves the USA via Reykjavík from numerous European cities. Budget airline Iceland Express has year-round flights to Reykjavík and Akureyri from Copenhagen; and seasonal flights to Reykjavík from Alicante, Berlin, Frankfurt and Friedrichshafen, for around €400 to €500 including taxes.

Atlantic Airways fly to the Faroes from Denmark (two hours) and Iceland (one hour), and from Norway (Oslo and Sta-

vanger, two hours) in the summer. Flights cost around €320.

Across Europe many travel agencies have ties with STA Travel. Agencies in important transport hubs:

FRANCE
Anyway (☎ 0892 302 301; www.anyway.fr in French)
Lastminute (☎ 0899 785 000; www.lastminute.fr in French)
Nouvelles Frontières (☎ 0825 000 747; www.nouvelles-frontieres.fr in French)
OTU Voyages (☎ 01 55 82 32 32; www.otu.fr in French) Specialises in student and youth travel.
Voyageurs du Monde (☎ 08 92 23 56 56; www.vdm.com in French)

GERMANY
Expedia (☎ 01805 900 560; www.expedia.de in German)
Just Travel (☎ 089 747 3330; www.justtravel.de)
Lastminute (☎ 01805 284 366; www.lastminute.de in German)
STA Travel (☎ 069 743 032 92; www.statravel.de in German) For travellers under the age of 26.

ITALY
CTS Viaggi (☎ 199 501150; www.cts.it in Italian) Specialises in student and youth travel.

NETHERLANDS
Airfair (☎ 0900 771 7717; www.airfair.nl in Dutch)

SPAIN
Barcelo Viajes (☎ 902 200 400; www.barceloviajes.com in Spanish)

New Zealand

British Airways, KLM, Qantas and Swiss are some of the airlines flying to Scandinavia, usually with stopovers in southeast Asia and/or Europe. Return fares cost around NZ$3500 and take 26 hours. The site www.travel.co.nz is recommended for online bookings.

It's easiest and cheapest to book flights via an agency such as:
Flight Centre (☎ 0800 243 544; www.flightcentre.co.nz)
STA Travel (☎ 0508 782 872; www.statravel.co.nz)

UK & Ireland
NO-FRILLS AIRLINES
Currently, three no-frills airlines offer cheap flights to major entry points in Scandinavia.

Ryanair flies from London Stansted to nine airports in Denmark, Norway, Swe-

den and Finland; from Glasgow Prestwick
to Oslo and Stockholm; from Liverpool to
Oslo and Tampere; and from Newcastle to
Oslo. Some promotional fares cost from as
little as UK£30, including taxes, although
most are around £120 in peak season.

EasyJet flies from London Stansted to
Copenhagen for around UK£100 return.

Iceland Express flies from London-Stan-
sted to Keflavík (Iceland) from UK£69 return, although most peak-season prices are
around £230; a new service to Akureyri (Iceland) was due to start in October 2006.

From Ireland, the cheapest way to Scandinavia is to catch a flight from Ryanair to
London Stansted, then pick up one of the
above no-frills flights.

FULL-SERVICE AIRLINES

SAS was offering some very good deals at
the time of writing, including peak-season
return flights from London to airports in
Denmark, Finland, Norway and Sweden
(from around UK£100 return).

City Airline flies from Birmingham and
Manchester to Göteborg; internet offers
start from UK£130 return, including tax.

Atlantic Airways has flights from Aberdeen to Vágar (Faroe Islands) for around
GB£70; see p140 for details. They also
have weekly summer flights from London,
changing in the Shetlands.

Another option is Icelandair, which flies
to the USA from London, Manchester and
Glasgow via Keflavík. The cheapest tickets
(around UK£160) are available on the internet, with further discounts if you sign
up for Icelandair's free Netclub.

DISCOUNT TRAVEL AGENCIES

Discount air travel is big business in London. Agencies advertise in the travel pages of
the weekend papers, *Time Out*, the *Evening
Standard* and the free magazine *TNT*.

Recommended travel agencies:

ebookers (☎ 0800 082 3000; www.ebookers.com)
Flight Centre (☎ 0870 499 0040; www.flightcentre.co.uk)
North-South Travel (☎ 01245 608 291; www.north
southtravel.co.uk) Donates a portion of its profits to
projects in the developing world.
Quest Travel (☎ 0871 423 0135; www.questtravel.com)
STA Travel (☎ 0870 163 0026; www.statravel.co.uk) For
travellers under the age of 26.
Trailfinders (☎ 0845 050 5940; www.trailfinders.com)
Travel Bag (☎ 0870 814 4440; www.travelbag.co.uk)

USA

There are myriad flight options from the
USA to Europe. To start with, check out
weekly travel sections in larger newspapers,
where you'll find travel agencies' advertisements. You should be able to fly return
from New York and/or Boston to Copenhagen, Helsinki, Oslo or Stockholm for
around US$2000 in high season, although
there are frequent offers of up to two-thirds
lower than this. The journey takes around
10 hours. Open-jaw tickets allow you to
land in one city and return from another
at no extra cost.

Icelandair flies from New York, Boston,
Baltimore/Washington, Minneapolis, Or-
lando, and San Francisco (summer only), via
Keflavík in Iceland to many European des-
tinations including Glasgow, London, Oslo,
Stockholm and Copenhagen. It has some
of the best deals (eg New York–Keflavík
US$650 at the time of writing), and also al-
lows a free stopover of up to seven days in
Reykjavík on transatlantic flights.

If you're planning to fly within Scandinavian Europe, SAS sells various internal
air passes (see p505) if you travel across
the pond with them. They depart from Chi-
cago, New York, Seattle and Washington to
Copenhagen and Stockholm.

Airhitch (www.airhitch.org) specialises
in internet purchases of standby tickets to
Europe from the east coast/west coast for
US$450/590 return. Destinations are by
region (not a specific city or country), so
you'll need to be flexible.

DISCOUNT TRAVEL AGENCIES

Discount travel agencies are known as consolidators in the USA, and San Francisco
is the consolidator king. Other good deals
can be found in Los Angeles, New York and
other big cities. Track down consolidators
through the *Yellow Pages* or the major daily
newspapers.

Travel agencies recommended for online
bookings:

Cheap Tickets (☎ 1 888 922 8849; www.cheap
tickets.com)
Expedia (☎ 1 800 397 3342; www.expedia.com)
Lowestfare.com (☎ 1 800 678 0998; www.lowestfare
.com) Website-based.
Orbitz (☎ 1 888 656 4546; www.orbitz.com)
STA Travel (☎ 1 800 781 4040; www.sta.com)
Travelocity (☎ 1 888 709 5983; www.travelocity.com)

LAND

Bus

Without a rail pass, it's generally cheapest to get from Europe to Scandinavia by bus. Some coaches are quite luxurious with stewards, air-conditioning, toilet and snack bar. Small bargain-price bus companies regularly appear and disappear – ask student and discount travel agencies for the latest companies.

Eurolines (www.eurolines.com), a conglomeration of 32 coach companies, is the biggest and best-established express-bus network, and connects Scandinavia with the rest of Europe. Most buses operate daily in summer and between two and five days per week in winter; advance ticket purchases are usually necessary. Eurolines' representatives in Europe:

Bohemia Euroexpress International (☎ 224 218 680; www.bei.cz in Czech; Křižíkova 4-6, 18600 Prague 8, Czech Republic)

Bus Éireann (☎ 01-836 6111; www.eurolines.ie; Bus Éireann Travel Centre, Busáras Bus Station, Store Street, Dublin 1).

Deutsche Touring (☎ 01805 790 303; www.eurolines.de; Am Römerhof 17, 60486 Frankfurt am Main)

Eurolines Austria (☎ 01-798 29 00; www.eurolines.at; Busstation Wien-Mitte, Erdbergstrasse 202, 1030 Vienna, Austria)

Eurolines France (☎ 08 92 89 90 91; www.eurolines.fr in French; Gare Routière Internationale, Boite 313, 28 ave du Général de Gaulle, F-93541 Bagnolet, Paris, France)

Eurolines Italy SRL (☎ 39 055 35 71 10; www.eurolines.it in Italian; Via GS Mercadente 2b, 50144 Firenze, Italy)

Eurolines Nederland (☎ 020-560 8788; www.eurolines.nl; Amstel Station, Julianaplein 5, 1097 DN Amsterdam, Netherlands)

Eurolines Scandinavia Denmark (☎ 07 010 00 30; www.eurolines.dk; Halmtorvet 5, Copenhagen, Denmark); Norway (☎ 2217 2000; www.eurolines.no; Bussterminalen, Schweigaardsgate 6, 0185 Oslo); Sweden (☎ 031 100 240; www.eurolines.se; Busstop, Cityterminalen, Klarabergsviadukten 72, SE-11164 Stockholm, Sweden)

Eurolines Spain (☎ 902 40 50 40; www.eurolines.es in Spanish; Estación Sur de Autobuses, c/Méndez Alvaro, Madrid, Spain)

Eurolines UK Ltd (☎ 0870-580 8080; www.nationalexpress.com/eurolines; 52 Grosvenor Gardens, London, SW1W 0AG, UK)

Sample Eurolines fares: London to Copenhagen (from UK£95 return) and Frankfurt to Copenhagen (€190 return). There's a 10% discount for those under 26 years or over 60 years.

The Eurolines Pass allows unlimited travel to 40 cities across Europe; the Scandinavian cities included are Copenhagen, Göteborg, Oslo and Stockholm. Between late June and mid-September, a 15-/30-day pass costs €329/439 (€279/359 for those under 26 years and over 60; cheaper at other times).

From St Petersburg in Russia, daily express buses run to Helsinki (see p214 for details). A Russian visa is required.

Car & Motorcycle

Driving to Scandinavia usually means taking a car ferry (opposite). The only land borders in the region are between Finland/ Norway and Russia, or between Denmark and Germany. It is possible to drive through Denmark into Sweden using bridges and tunnels.

If you're driving from the UK, you can put your car on a direct ferry to Scandinavia (p504); or get to mainland Europe using the Channel Tunnel car-carrying train, **Eurotunnel** (☎ 0870 535 3535, 01303 282 061; www.eurotunnel.com), then from mainland Europe drive northwards.

See p508 for more information about required paperwork.

Hitching & Car-Ride Services

For local hitching conditions and laws, see the individual country chapters.

After hitching, the cheapest way to head further north in Europe is as a paying passenger in a private car. Car-sharing is particularly well-organised in Germany. After paying a reservation fee to a city-based **Mitfahrzentrale agency** (www.mitfahrzentrale.de in German), you're then linked up with people driving in your direction (petrol money is also due to the driver). Local tourist information offices can help you locate agencies, or in larger German cities, dial the city area code and ☎ 19444.

A list of European car-ride agencies can be found at www.allostop.com under the section 'Carpooling in Europe'.

Train

The monthly *Thomas Cook European Timetable* is the train traveller's bible. It's available from Thomas Cook outlets in the

UK (£13.99), or you can order a copy from www.thomascookpublishing.com.

The **Man in Seat 61** (www.seat61.com) is a slow-travel hero with a wonderfully helpful website about rail journeys.

For further information about rail passes, see p511.

ASIA

Travelling across Asia by train costs about the same as flying – but it's a real adventure. Three routes cross Siberia: the Vladivostok-Moscow Trans-Siberian route (packages around US$650, seven days); the Beijing-Moscow Trans-Manchurian route (packages around US$650, seven days); and the popular Beijing-Moscow Trans-Mongolian route (six days), where a 2nd-class sleeper in a four-berth compartment costs around US$540 excluding visas and meals. Trains then run daily from Moscow to Helsinki (p214), usually requiring a change at St Petersburg.

Prices vary enormously, depending on where you buy the ticket and what's included – prices quoted here are only a rough indication. **Monkey Business** (☎ 8610 6591 6519; www.monkeyshrine.com) in Beijing organises all-inclusive packages and visas for trips starting in Beijing; for the Hong Kong office call ☎ 2723 1376. More expensive packages can be bought in Europe; one well-known UK operator is **Regent Holidays** (☎ 0117-925 4866; www.regent-holidays.co.uk).

Lonely Planet's *Trans-Siberian Railway* is a comprehensive guide to the route; also see www.seat61.com.

CENTRAL EUROPE

Hamburg is the main European gateway for Scandinavia but direct trains also run from Berlin. There are several direct trains daily to Copenhagen from Hamburg (2nd-class €76, five hours); the hour-long ferry trip is included in the ticket price. Direct trains from Berlin run daily to Malmö (2nd-class €130, 8½ hours), via the Sassnitz to Trelleborg ferry (3¾ hours).

In Germany, the Sparpreis fare structures are a good deal: use them to cheapen the rail journey to northern Germany. Sparpreis 25 and Sparpreis 50 give 25% and 50% respectively off long-distance return fares if booked at least three days in advance, with certain restrictions on times of travel and point of departure/return.

In Poland, take a train to Gdynia or Świnoujście for a ferry to Sweden (see p476). For Polish timetables and prices, see www.intercity.com.pl.

A useful website for planning European train journeys is www.europeanrail.com.

UK

Going by train to Scandinavia can be more expensive than flying, but it's more of an experience. The Channel Tunnel makes land travel possible between Britain and continental Europe. **Eurostar** (☎ 0870 518 6186, 01233 617575; www.eurostar.co.uk) passenger services connect London with Calais, Paris, Lille and Brussels. From Brussels connect to Hamburg, which is the main gateway to Scandinavia.

From London, a 2nd-class return ticket costs from UK£250 to Copenhagen (via Cologne or Hamburg), and around UK£450 return to Oslo and Stockholm (via Copenhagen). Contact **Deutsche Bahn UK** (☎ 0870 243 5363; www.bahn.co.uk) for details of frequent special offers, and for reservations and tickets.

For more information on international rail travel (including Eurostar services), contact the **Rail Europe Travel Centre** (☎ 0870 8371 371; www.raileurope.co.uk; 178 Piccadilly, London W1).

SEA

Prices given in this section are sample starting prices, based on a foot-passenger travelling one way in high season, using the cheapest-available sleeping option (usually a reclining seat or couchette – see p510 for a definition). Booking a cabin, travelling on weekends or night boats, or taking a vehicle will obviously up the cost; travelling outside June to August will lower it. Book as early as possible to take advantage of limited cheaper tickets.

See the transport sections of the country chapters for information about boat-train links within Scandinavian Europe. See also p511 for rail passes and their validity on ferries.

Ferry Companies

The following details cover the larger ferry companies operating to Scandinavia.

COLOR LINE

The Norwegian company **Color Line** (www.color line.com) have year-round routes from Norway to Denmark (all €60, except Bergen–Hirtshals which costs €90) and Germany.

From Hirtshals in Denmark you can get to four Norwegian towns: Kristiansand (4½ hours), Larvik (6½ hours), Stavanger (11 hours), and Bergen (21 hours). From Frederikshavn in Denmark, boats run to Larvik (six hours) and Oslo (6½ hours). Boats also run to Oslo from Kiel in Germany (€110, 20 hours).

It's possible to take a car on these ferry services (around €100 one-way); if you have a full car, packages (around €350 for vehicle and five people) are more economical. Booking agencies:

Denmark Frederikshavn (☎ 99 56 19 77; Postboks 30, DK-9900 Frederikshavn); Hirtshals (☎ 99 56 19 77; Postboks 30, DK-9850 Hirtshals)

France (☎ 01 42 85 64 50; c/o Scanditours, 36 rue de St-Pétersbourg, 75008 Paris)

Germany (☎ 0431-7300 300; Postfach 2646, D24025 Kiel)

Norway (☎ 81 00 08 11; Postboks 1422 Vika, N-0115 Oslo)

DFDS SEAWAYS

DFDS Seaways (www.dfdsseaways.com) operates year-round routes between Denmark, Norway, Sweden and the UK. Prices below are per person, based on four people sharing the cheapest cabin. Cars cost from UK£75.

Boats run from Oslo to Copenhagen (from Nkr370, 16 hours), via Helsingborg in Sweden (14 hours); from Harwich in the UK to Esbjerg in Denmark (from UK£60, 19 hours); and from Newcastle in the UK to Göteborg in Sweden (from UK£80, 26 hours), via Kristiansand in Norway (19 hours). Booking agencies:

Denmark (☎ 33 42 30 80; Sundkrogsgade 11, DK-2100 Copenhagen Ø)

Germany (☎ 01805-304 350; Högerdamm 41, D-20097 Hamburg)

Norway (☎ 21 62 13 40; Postboks 365 Sentrum, N-0102 Oslo)

Sweden (☎ 031-650650; Kajskjul 107, Frihamnen, Box 8895, SE-40272 Göteborg)

UK (☎ 08702 520 524; Scandinavia House, Parkeston, Harwich, Essex, CO12 4QG)

FJORD LINE

Fjord Line (www.fjordline.com) sails from Denmark and the UK to western Norway.

Ferries run at least four times per week from Hanstholm in Denmark to Egersund in Norway (€40 with reclining seat, seven hours). Some of these services continue from Egersund up the Norwegian coast

to Haugesund (€55, 13 hours) and Bergen (€60, 17 hours).

There are also one or two ferry services per week from Newcastle in the UK to Stavanger in Norway (from €130 per person based on four-person cabin, 20 hours), continuing up the coast to Haugesund and Bergen.

Prices are up to 50% lower for children, students and seniors. Booking agencies:

Denmark (☎ 97 96 30 00; Coastergade 10, DK-7730 Hanstholm)

Germany (☎ 040-3769 3350; Kleine Johannisstrasse 10, D-20457 Hamburg)

Norway (☎ 815 33 500; Skoltegrunnskaien, Postboks 7250, N-5020 Bergen)

UK (☎ 0870 143 9669, 0191-296 1313; Norway House, Royal Quays, North Shields, Tyne & Wear, NE29 6EG)

SILJA LINE

Silja Line (☎ 0600 174552; www.silja.com; Keilaranta 9, Espoo, 02060 Silja) runs ferry routes between Sweden, Finland and Estonia; in June 2006 they were being bought out by Tallink, although this probably won't affect routes and schedules.

SMYRIL LINE

From March to mid-October, Smyril Line (www.smyril-line.com) operates the car ferry *Norröna* weekly between Hanstholm (Denmark), Bergen (Norway), Lerwick (Shetland Islands, UK), Tórshavn (Faroe Islands) and Seyðisfjörður (eastern Iceland)…although not necessarily in that order! High-season passengers from Hanstholm must disembark for two days in the Faroes while the boat makes side trips to Norway and the Shetlands. At the time of writing, there were controversial plans to abandon the Lerwick leg.

It's a convoluted route: check out the Smyril Line website for full details, or better still, talk to a booking agent about your intended journey.

Fares are highest between mid-June and mid-August, when a one-way adult fare (including a rather claustrophobic couchette) from Hanstholm to Seyðisfjörður costs €230. If your budget will stretch a little further, we recommend the very pleasant cabins: prices start at €320. Bringing a vehicle is not much more expensive than paying for two foot passengers. There's a small charge for bicycles, and there are discounts available for seniors, students, disabled travellers and children. Booking agencies:

Denmark (☎ 96 55 03 60; www.smyril-line.dk; Trafikhavnsgade 7, DK-7730 Hanstholm)

Faroe Islands (☎ 345900; www.smyril-line.com; J Broncksgøta 35, PO Box 370, FO-110 Tórshavn)

Iceland (☎ 570 8600; www.smyril-line.is; Sætúni 8, 105 Reykjavík)

Norway (☎ 55 59 65 20; www.smyril-line.no; Slottsgaten 1, Postboks 4135, Dreggen, N-5835 Bergen)

UK (☎ 01595-690845; www.smyril-line.com; The Gutters' Hut, North Ness Business Park, Lerwick, Shetland, ZE1 0LZ)

Passengers from mainland UK can connect with the Smyril Line by taking one of the daily **NorthLink Ferries** (☎ 0845 600 0449; www.northlink ferries.co.uk) services (UK£31.20, 13 hours) from Aberdeen via Kirkwall (Orkney) to Lerwick in the Shetland Islands.

STENA LINE

Stena Line (www.stenaline.com) runs daily ferry services between Denmark and Sweden, Denmark and Norway, Germany and Sweden and, Poland and Sweden. Some boats sail overnight, with prices around double those quoted below for day sailings.

From Frederikshavn (Denmark), you can sail to Oslo in Norway (Dkr270, 6½ hours) and Göteborg in Sweden (Dkr185, 3¼ hours). Express ferries (Dkr260, two hours) also run the latter route in summer. From Grenå (Denmark), there are twice-daily ferries to Varberg in Sweden (Dkr185, four hours).

From Kiel (Germany), there are daily ferries to Göteborg in Sweden (€70, 13½ hours).

From Gdynia (Poland) there are one or two ferries per day to Karlskrona in Sweden (Skr670, 10½ hours).

Booking agencies:

Denmark (☎ 96 20 02 00; www.stenaline.dk in Danish; Trafikhavnen, DK-9900 Frederikshavn)

Germany (☎ 01805-91 66 66; www.stenaline.de in German; Schwedenkai 1, D-24103 Kiel)

Norway (☎ 02010; www.stenaline.no in Norwegian; Postboks 764, Sentrum, N-0106 Oslo)

Poland (☎ 058-660 92 00; www.stenaline.pl in Polish; Kwiatkowskiego 60, PL-81-156 Gdynia)

Sweden (☎ 031-704 0000; www.stenaline.se in Swedish; Box 94, SE-43222 Varberg)

UK (☎ 0870 570 7070; www.stenaline.co.uk; Station Approach, Stena House, Holyhead, Anglesey LL65 1DQ)

Baltic Countries

There are regular sailings from Estonia, Latvia and Lithuania across the Baltic Sea to Sweden and Finland. In addition to the information below, see the Sweden (p475) and Finland (p214) transport sections.

ESTONIA

Silja Line sails two to six times daily from Tallinn to Helsinki (€48, 3½ hours).

Tallink (Estonia ☎ 640 9808, www.tallink.ee; Finland ☎ 600 15700, www.tallink.fi; Sweden ☎ 08-666 6001, www.tallink.se) sails several times daily from Tallinn to Helsinki (€25, 3½ hours); once daily in summer via Mariehamn to Stockholm (from €65 per person based on four people sharing, 16 hours); and from Paldiski in Estonia to Kapellskär (from €28 per person based on four people sharing, 10 hours), north of Stockholm.

LATVIA

Scandlines (Latvia ☎ 360 7358; Sweden www.scandlines.se; ☎ 04-218 6100) runs three services per week between Ventspils and Karlshamn in Sweden (from €85 per person based on four people sharing, 17 hours) and five per week between Ventspils and Nynäshamn (€75 for reclining seat, 11 hours), also in Sweden. Prices include two meals!

Tallink sails between Stockholm and Riga three times weekly (Skr365 based on four people sharing, 18 hours).

LITHUANIA

DFDS Tor Line (in Sweden ☎ 0454-33680, in Lithuania 46-395051; www.dfdstorline.com) shuttles daily between Klaipėda (Lithuania) and Karlshamn in Sweden (from Skr710, 16 hours).

Germany

The **Scandlines** (☎ 04-218 6100; www.scandlines.se) train, car and passenger ferry from Puttgarden to Rødbyhavn in Denmark (the quickest way to Copenhagen) runs every half-hour around the clock and takes 45 minutes (€7). Frequent Scandlines ferries also run from Rostock to Gedser (€10, two hours) in Denmark.

From Kiel, there are daily Stena Line ferries to Göteborg in Sweden (€70, 13½ hours) and Color Line ferries to Oslo in Norway (€110, 20 hours).

Five large Scandlines ferries run in each direction daily between Sassnitz (eastern

Germany) and Trelleborg (€15, four hours), south of Malmö in Sweden. Three ferries run from Rostock to Trelleborg in Sweden (€24, six hours).

Finnlines (☎ in Finland 09-251 0200, in Germany 0451 150 7443; www.finnlines.fi) has a daily service from Travemünde to Helsinki (from €200 per person based on four people sharing, 34 hours); and to Malmö (€25, nine hours) – for these ferries, ☎ 04-5028 0520 in Germany, ☎ 04-017 6800 in Sweden.

TT Line (☎ in Sweden 0410-56200; www.ttline.com) has daily ferries to Sweden (mostly overnight) between Travemünde and Trelleborg (from €75, seven hours); and between Rostock and Trelleborg (€30, 5½ hours).

See also the relevant transport sections in the individual country chapters.

Poland

Regular ferries cross the Baltic Sea between Poland and Sweden. Stena Line has one or two ferries daily from Gdynia to Karlskrona (Skr670, 10½ hours).

Unity Line (☎ in Sweden 0411-556900, in Poland 091-359 5592; www.unityline.pl; Pl Rodla 8, 70-419 Szczecin) has a daily ferry (Skr550, eight hours) between Świnoujście and Ystad in Sweden.

Polferries (☎ in Sweden 46-401 21700, in Poland 091-322 4396; www.polferries.pl; ul Bema 9/2, 72-600 Świnoujście) links Gdansk with Nynäshamn in Sweden (from Skr670, 18 hours) three times per week. It has one night boat, which operates daily from Świnoujście to Ystad in Sweden (Skr540, seven hours).

It also has four or five departures per week from Świnoujście to Copenhagen (Skr450, 10½ hours), and one on Saturdays to Rønne in Denmark (Skr250, 5¼ hours).

The UK

For the weekly Smyril Line sailing between Lerwick (Shetland Islands) and Seyðisfjörður (Iceland), with additional legs to Denmark, the Faroes and Norway, see p502.

From Newcastle, Fjord Line runs ferries year-round to Stavanger (19½ hours) in Norway, continuing to Haugesund (22 hours) and Bergen (24 hours). High-season fares start from £90.

DFDS Seaways has ferries from Harwich to Esbjerg in Denmark (from UK£60, 19 hours) and from Newcastle to Kristiansand (from UK£80, 19 hours) and Göteborg (from UK£80, 27 hours, twice weekly).

See the relevant transport sections in the individual country chapters for more details.

Transatlantic Passenger Ships & Freighters

If you want to sail from the USA to Europe, you'll have to suffer the privations of a luxury cruise ship! Cunard Line's **QM II** (☎ in Canada & the USA 1 800 728 6273, in the UK 0845 071 0300) sails between New York and Southampton in the UK around 26 times per year, taking six nights/seven days per trip. The cost of a one-way crossing starts at US$1800. From June to August, the company does three different northern cruises, calling in at Iceland and/or Norwegian villages and towns, including Oslo and Bergen. Most travel agencies can provide the details.

A more adventurous alternative is as a paying passenger on a freighter, which will typically carry six to 12 passengers. They're less luxurious than dedicated cruise ships, but provide a real taste of life at sea. Costs normally hover around US$100 a day; vehicles can often be included for an additional charge. Although it's out of date and out of print, *Travel by Cargo Ship* by Hugo Verlomme is still a valuable reference.

TOURS

For special-interest trips (canoeing, birdwatching, cycling), see the country chapters in this book, contact your local activity club, check out classified ads in hobby mags, or consult the national tourist offices of the country you're headed for. In the UK, the Cyclists' Touring Club (see opposite) run occasional cycling tours in Scandinavia.

If your time is limited, consider using one of the following tour operators:

Australia

Bentours (☎ 02-9241 1353; www.bentours.com.au; Level 7, 189 Kent St, Sydney 2000) With 25 years experience covering the highlights of Denmark, Norway, Sweden, Finland and Iceland/Greenland, with fjord cruises and trips to St Petersburg and Moscow.

France

Grand Nord Grand Large (☎ 01-40 46 05 14; www .gngl.com in French; 15 Rue du Cardinal Lemoine, 75005 Paris) A 'polar voyage' specialist, with trips to northern Finland, Norway (including Svalbard), Sweden, the Faroes and Iceland.

Germany

Norden Tours (☎ 040-3770 2270; www.norden-tours.de in German; Kleine Johannisstrasse 10, D-20457 Hamburg) Wide range of Scandinavian tours, including cruises.

Nordwind Reisen (☎ 08331-87073; www.nordwin dreisen.de in German; Maximilianstrasse 17, D-87700 Memmingen, Nordwind) Specialist tours to Iceland, Greenland and Spitzbergen; some winter tours to Sweden and Finland.

Norway

Brand Cruises (☎ 52 85 31 03; www.brand.no; Postboks 33, N-4291 Kopervik) Norwegian cruises, including Svalbard.

UK

Arctic Experience: Discover the World (☎ 01737 -214214; www.arctic-experience.co.uk; 29 Nork Way, Banstead, Surrey, SM7 1PB) Summer and winter wilderness, wildlife and activity holidays in the Faroes, Iceland, Sweden and arctic Norway.

Dick Phillips (☎ 01434-381440; www.icelandic-travel com; Whitehall House, Nenthead, Alston, Cumbria, CA9 3PS) Mr Phillips has decades of experience leading rigorous, wild hiking and skiing trips in Iceland.

USA

Scantours (☎ 1 800 223 7226; www.scantours.com) Comfortable, hotel-based excursions and cruises throughout Scandinavia, with trips to St Petersburg.

Travcoa (☎ 1 866 591 0070; www.travcoa.com; 2424 SE Bristol St, Ste 310, Newport Beach, CA 92660) Hotel-based tours visiting the highlights of Scandinavia.

GETTING AROUND

Getting around the populated areas of Scandinavia is generally a breeze, with efficient public transport systems and snappy connections. Remote regions usually have trustworthy but infrequent services.

AIR

Domestic networks in Scandinavia are safe and reliable. Internal flights can be expensive, but they're often cheaper than land-based alternatives for longer journeys, and of course can save days of travelling time. Companies running internal airline routes offer reduced rates for internet bookings. For domestic carriers, see the country transport sections.

Travelling between airports and city centres isn't a problem in Scandinavia thanks to good bus and train networks.

Air Passes

Visitors flying **SAS** (☎ in North America 1 800 221 2350,   in the UK 0870 607 2727 , 020 8990 7159; www .scandinavian.net;) on a return ticket to Norway, Sweden or Finland from outside Europe can buy Visit Scandinavia/Europe Airpass coupons (starting at US$65 each), as can US travellers flying with United Airlines.

Visitors (but not residents of Denmark, Finland, Norway or Sweden) flying SAS return to Scandinavia from inside Europe can buy similar Visit Scandinavia Airpass coupons (starting at €69 each).

The passes allow one-way travel on direct flights between any two Scandinavian cities serviced by SAS, Blue 1, Skyways, **Widerøe** (☎ 81 00 12 00; www.wideroe.no) and other operators, with stopovers limited to one in each city. You can buy up to eight tickets which are valid for three months. Children fly for around 70% of the adult price. Tickets can be purchased after arriving in Scandinavia if you have a return SAS international ticket.

BICYCLE

A tour of northern Europe by bike is an exciting prospect, giving you the chance to see vast areas of wilderness under your own steam. One organisation that can help you gear up in the UK is the wonderful **Cyclists' Touring Club** (CTC; ☎ 0870 873 0060; www.ctc.org .uk; Parklands, Railton Rd, Guildford, Surrey, GU2 9JX). It can help members with cycling conditions, routes, itineraries, maps and specialised insurance. It also organises occasional **tours** (www.cyclingholidays.org) to Denmark and the Norwegian fjords.

English-language books about cycling in Scandinavia are virtually nonexistent. *Europe by Bike*, by Karen and Terry Whitehill, is a little out of date but its descriptions of 18 cycling tours include two for Scandinavia (from Kiel across Denmark to Sweden and from southern Sweden to Stockholm via the Åland islands). *The Essential Touring Cyclist* by Richard A Lovett is full of useful general advice.

The North Sea Cycle Route covers parts of Denmark, Sweden, Norway and the Shetland Islands: see www.northsea-cycle.com for information.

Make sure you take sufficient tools and spare parts, as replacements may be pricey and hard to find. Panniers are essential, and

RAILWAYS & FERRIES

- RAILWAYS
- FERRY ROUTES
- MAJOR STATIONS/ INTERCHANGES

of course a bike helmet is always a good idea. Take a decent lock and use it when you leave your bike unattended; theft is not uncommon in places like Helsinki and Copenhagen.

It's easy to hire bikes throughout Scandinavia, sometimes from train station bike-rental counters, and in some cases it's possible to return them to another outlet so you don't have to double back. On slower trains and local buses in Scandinavia, bikes can usually be transported as luggage, either free or for a small fee. Fast trains and long-distance buses rarely take bikes. Cycling across the Øresund bridge between Denmark and Sweden is prohibited.

For an overview of cycling in Scandinavian Europe, see p483 and the individual country chapters.

BOAT

Ferry

You can't really get around Scandinavia without using ferries extensively (although many Swedish services are being replaced by bridge links). The shortest routes from Denmark (Jutland) to Norway and from southern Sweden to Finland are ferry routes. Denmark is now well connected to mainland Europe and Sweden by bridges.

Ferry tickets are cheap on competitive routes, although transporting cars can be costly. Bicycles are usually carried free. On some routes, train pass holders are entitled to free or discounted travel (p511).

Weekend ferries, especially on Friday nights, are significantly more expensive. Teenage travellers are banned from travelling on some Friday-night ferries due to problems with excessive drunkenness.

For further information about the many ferry options available between the destinations in this book, see the transport sections of the individual country chapters. Also see 501 for ferry companies running services between Scandinavian countries.

Steamers

Scandinavia's main lakes and rivers are served by both diesel-powered boats and steamers during the summer. Treat these extended boat trips as relaxing, scenic miniholidays; if you view them merely as a way to get from A to B, they can seem quite expensive.

Sweden has the largest fleets in Scandinavia. Most leave from Stockholm and sail east to the Stockholm archipelago (p415) – a maze of 24,000 islands and islets – and west to historic Lake Mälaren (p415) – home base of the Swedish Vikings a millennium ago. You can also cruise the Göta Canal (p477), the longest water route in Sweden.

The legendary Hurtigruten (p384) links Norway's coastal fishing villages. In Finland, steamships ply Lake Saimaa (p182) and its canal; there are also diesel-engine boats.

BUS

Buses provide a viable alternative to the rail network in Scandinavian countries, and are the only option in Iceland and the Faroes. Compared to trains, they're usually cheaper (Finland is the exception) and slightly slower. Connections with train services (where they exist) are good.

Bus travel tends to be perfect for getting around cities and for short hops, and is sometimes your only choice in remote rural areas (particularly northern Sweden).

Bus Passes

Eurolines offers a variety of city 'loops' and the Eurolines Pass – see p500 for more details.

See the transport section in the country chapters for details of internal bus passes, or contact one of the main long-distance bus operators listed here.

DENMARK
Søndergaards Busser (☎ 70 10 00 33; www.sonder gaards-busser.dk)
Thinggaard Expressbusser (☎ 98 11 66 00; www .thinggaardbus.com in Danish)

FAROE ISLANDS
Strandfaraskip Landsins (☎ 343030; www.ssl.fo)

FINLAND
Oy Matkahuolto Ab (☎ 09-682 701; www.matka huolto.fi)

ICELAND
BSÍ (Bifreiðastöð Íslands; ☎ 562 1011; www.bsi.is)

NORWAY
Nor-Way Bussekspress (☎ 815 44 444; www .nor-way.no)

SWEDEN

Säfflebussen (☎ 0771-151515; www.safflebussen.se in Swedish)

Svenska Buss (☎ 0771-676767; www.svenskabuss.se in Swedish)

Swebus Express (☎ 0200-218218; www.swebus express.se)

Ybuss (☎ 0771-334444; www.ybuss.se in Swedish)

Reservations

Advance reservations are rarely necessary. However, you do need to prepurchase your ticket before you board many city buses, and then validate your ticket on board. See the individual country chapters for specific details.

CAR & MOTORCYCLE

Travelling with your own vehicle is the best way to get to remote places and gives you independence and flexibility. Drawbacks include being isolated in your own little car-bubble, and stressful city-centre driving.

Scandinavia is excellent for motorcycle touring, with good-quality winding roads, stunning scenery and an active motorcycling scene – just make sure your wet-weather gear is up to scratch. The best time for touring is May to September. On ferries, motorcyclists rarely have to book ahead as they can generally be squeezed in. Anyone considering Scandinavia on two wheels should read *The Adventure Motorbiking Handbook,* by Chris Scott, which gives sound advice on motorcycle touring worldwide.

Bringing Your Own Vehicle

Proof of ownership of a private vehicle should always be carried (this is the Vehicle Registration Document for British-registered cars) when touring Europe. You may also need a *carnet de passage en douane,* which is effectively a passport for the vehicle and acts as a temporary waiver of import duty. The *carnet* may also need to specify any expensive spare parts that you're planning to carry with you, such as a gearbox. Contact your local automobile association for further information.

Vehicles crossing an international border should display a sticker showing their country of registration. (The exception is cars with Euro-plates being taken into another European Union country). It's compulsory to carry a warning triangle in most places, to be used in the event of breakdown. You must also use headlamp beam reflectors/convertors on right-hand-drive cars.

Driving Licence

An EU driving licence is acceptable for driving throughout Scandinavia, as are North American and Australian licences (in general). If you have any other type of licence, you should obtain an International Driving Permit (IDP) from your motoring organisation before you leave home.

If you're thinking of going snow-mobiling, you'll need to bring your driving licence with you.

Fuel & Spare Parts

Fuel is heavily taxed and very expensive in Scandinavia. Most types of petrol, including unleaded 95 and 98 octane, are widely available; leaded petrol is no longer sold. Diesel is significantly cheaper than petrol in most countries. Always check the type of fuel being supplied – usually pumps with green markings and the word *Blyfr* on them deliver unleaded fuel, and black pumps supply diesel.

Recommended accessories are a first-aid kit, a spare bulb kit, and a fire extinguisher. In Iceland, it's wise to carry general spare parts, including a fan belt and clutch cable, and learn how to make basic repairs; garages and passing motorists can be few and far between. Contact your automobile association or, in the UK, contact the **AA** (☎ 0870 600 0371, 0161 495 8945; www.theaa.com) or the **RAC** (☎ 0870 572 2722, 020 8917 2500; www.rac.co.uk) for more information.

Hire

Renting a car is more expensive in Scandinavia than in other European countries, and the variety of deals, terms and conditions can be mind-boggling. However, there are a few pointers that can help you through the morass. The big international firms – Hertz, Avis, Eurodollar, Budget, and Europe's largest rental agency, Europcar – will give you reliable service, a good standard of vehicle, and the (usually chargeable) option of returning the car to a different outlet when you've finished with it.

Try to prebook your vehicle, which always works out cheaper. If you've left it too late, look for national or local firms, which can often undercut the international companies substantially. It's generally more expensive to hire cars from airport-rental stands than to pick one up in town.

Fly/drive combinations are worth looking into; for example, SAS and Icelandair often offer cheaper car rentals to their international passengers. The ScanRail 'n' Drive package gives you a five-day rail pass and a car for two days to be used within 15 days in Denmark, Norway and/or Sweden. Prices start at US$410 for an adult on 2nd-class trains and an economy car (US$720 for two adults), with an option of retaining the car for US$59 per day.

Holiday Autos International (www.holidayautos.com) usually has good rates for rental, but you need to prebook. It has offices around Europe, including Denmark, Norway and Sweden. Ask in advance if you can drive a rented car across borders.

If you fancy chancing a banger, the US firm **Rent-a-Wreck** (www.rent-a-wreck.com) has franchises in Denmark, Finland, Iceland and Sweden.

Be sure you understand what's included in the price (unlimited or paid kilometres, injury insurance, tax, collision damage waiver etc) and what your liabilities are. Always take the collision damage waiver, although you can probably skip the injury insurance if you and your passengers have decent travel insurance.

The minimum rental age is usually 21, sometimes even 23, and you'll probably need a credit card (or a mountain of cash) for the deposit.

Motorcycle and moped rental isn't particularly common in Scandinavian countries, but it's possible in major cities.

Insurance

Third-party motor insurance is a minimum requirement in most of Europe. Most UK car-insurance policies automatically provide third-party cover for EU and some other countries. Ask your insurer for a Green Card – an internationally recognised proof of insurance (there may be a charge) – and check that it lists all the countries you intend to visit. You'll need this in the event of an accident outside the country in which the vehicle is insured. Also ask your insurer for a European Accident Statement form, which can simplify things if worse comes to worst. Never sign statements you can't read or understand – insist on a written translation and only sign it if it's acceptable.

A European breakdown-assistance policy, such as those provided by the AA or the RAC, is a good investment: expect to pay about UK£60 for 14 days' cover. It's also worth asking your motoring organisation for details of reciprocal services offered by affiliated organisations around Europe.

Road Conditions & Hazards

Conditions and types of roads vary widely across Scandinavia, but it's possible to make some generalisations. The fastest routes are four- or six-lane dual carriageways, which tend to skirt cities and plough through the countryside in straight lines, often avoiding the most scenic areas. Motorways and other primary routes, with the exception of some roads in Iceland, are universally in good condition.

Road surfaces on minor routes are not so reliable, although normally adequate. These roads are narrower and progress is slower, but in compensation, you'll pass through more scenic places along the way.

Norway has some particularly hair-raising roads; serpentine examples climb from sea level to 1000m in what seems no distance at all on a map. These rollercoasters will use plenty of petrol and strain the car's engine and brakes, not to mention your nerves! Driving a camper van on these kinds of routes is not recommended.

In Norway, there are tolls for some tunnels, bridges, roads and entry into larger towns, and for practically all ferries crossing fjords. Roads, tunnels, bridges and car ferries in Finland and Sweden are usually free, although there's a hefty toll of €32 (Skr290/Dkr235) per car on the Øresund bridge between Denmark and Sweden.

During winter in Scandinavia, snow tyres are compulsory. The tyre chains common in the Alps are allowed in Norway, but are illegal elsewhere.

Suicidal stock, including sheep, elk, horses and reindeer, is a potential hazard. If you are involved in an animal incident, you must report it to the police by law.

Road Rules

You drive on the right-hand side of the road in all Scandinavian countries. Seatbelt use is compulsory for all passengers and headlights must be switched on at all times (except in built-up areas in Finland). Vehicles from the UK and Ireland need their headlights adjusted to avoid blinding oncoming traffic (a simple solution on older headlight lenses is to cover up the triangular section of the lens with a headlight deflector, available from motoring accessory shops). Priority is usually given to traffic approaching from the right.

It's compulsory for motorcyclists and their passengers to wear helmets. Check first if you're thinking of parking motorcycles on pavements (sidewalks). This is illegal in some countries, although the police usually turn a blind eye as long as pedestrians aren't obstructed.

Take care with speed limits, which vary from country to country. Many driving infringements are subject to on-the-spot fines in Scandinavian countries. If you receive a fine for any driving offence, make sure to get a receipt.

Drink-driving regulations are strict: one drink can put you over the limit. The maximum blood-alcohol concentration (BAC) is 0.01% in Norway (the strictest in Europe), 0.02% in Sweden and 0.05% in the rest of Scandinavia.

Your national motoring organisation may distribute free booklets summarising Scandinavian motoring regulations.

HITCHING

Hitching is never entirely safe in any country in the world, and we don't recommend it. Travellers, particularly women, who decide to hitch are taking a small but potentially serious risk – even in 'safe' Scandinavia. People who do choose to hitch will be safer if they travel in pairs and let someone know where they're planning to go.

Hitching is neither popular nor particularly rewarding in most of the region. That said, with a bit of luck, hitchers can end up making good time in some areas, but obviously your plans need to be flexible in case you suddenly become invisible to passing motorists. Don't try to hitch from city centres; take public transport to suburban exit routes.

Hitching is usually illegal on motorways – stand on the entrance ramps.

It's sometimes possible to arrange a lift privately: scan student notice boards in colleges or contact car-sharing agencies (see p500).

TOURS

See the individual country chapters for details of recommended, locally organised tours.

TRAIN

Trains in Scandinavia are comfortable, frequent and punctual. As with most things in the region, prices are relatively expensive, although European train passes can make travel affordable. Finland has the cheapest rail service. There are no trains in Iceland or the Faroes, nor in most of far-northern Norway.

If you plan to travel extensively by train, get the *Thomas Cook European Timetable* (see p500), which gives a complete listing of train schedules and indicates where supplements apply or where reservations are necessary.

Express Trains

Fast trains in Europe, or ones that make few stops, are usually identified by the symbols EC (Eurocity) or IC (Intercity). There are national variations: in Norway, some expresses are called Signatur trains; in Finland they're Pendolino express trains; and in Sweden they're known as X2000. Supplements usually apply on fast trains and it's wise (sometimes obligatory) to make reservations at peak times and on certain lines.

Overnight Trains

If you don't fancy sitting upright all night with a stranger dribbling on your shoulder, overnight trains usually offer couchettes or sleepers. Again, reservations are advisable, particularly as sleeping options are generally allocated on a first-come, first-served basis.

Couchettes are basic bunkbeds numbering four (1st class) or six (2nd class) per compartment and are comfortable enough if lacking a little privacy. In Scandinavia a bunk costs around US$25 to US$35 for most international trains, irrespective of the length of the journey.

Sleepers are the most comfortable option, offering beds for one or two passengers in 1st class and two or three passengers in 2nd class. In Norway, when individual travellers book a bed for one they'll be booked into a compartment with two other people of the same sex. Denmark has six-person compartments, as well as single and double cabins; charges vary, but these tend to be significantly more expensive than couchettes.

Most long-distance trains have a dining car or snack trolley – bring your own nibbles to keep costs down.

Costs

Full-price tickets can be expensive, but there are generally lots of discounts, particularly if you book ahead. European rail passes are worth buying if you plan to do a reasonable amount of inter-country travelling within a short space of time.

Seniors and travellers under 26 years of age are eligible for discounted tickets, which can cut international fares by between 15% and 40%: see below for details.

Reservations

It's a good idea (and sometimes obligatory) to make reservations at peak times and on certain train lines, especially long-distance trains. Check the individual country chapters for particulars.

Train Passes

There are a variety of passes available, for students, people under 26, seniors and those who intend to do a lot of train travel. Numerous agencies issue youth tickets in Europe, including **STA Travel** (www.statravel com) and **Wasteels Rejser** (☎ 33 14 46 33; www wasteels.dk in Danish; Skoubogade 6, DK-1158 Copenhagen K, Denmark).

Supplements (eg for high-speed services) and reservation costs are not covered by passes, and terms and conditions change – check carefully before buying. Pass-holders must always carry their passport on the train for identification purposes.

EURAIL

In Scandinavia, the ScanRail pass (p513) is usually a better deal than the Eurail pass, so the following information is mainly for travellers visiting other parts of Europe too

(however, see details of the new Eurail National Pass and Selectpass below).

Eurail (www.eurail.com) passes can only be bought by residents of non-European countries (residents of Algeria, Morocco, Tunisia, Turkey and Russian Federation countries are ineligible to buy passes). It's always wise to buy a pass before you leave home: you *can* buy them inside Europe, but they're 20% more expensive and there are very few sales outlets. You can buy passes online; the website also has a list of sales agents.

Eurail passes are valid for unlimited travel on national railways and some private lines in Austria, Belgium, Denmark, Finland, France (including Monaco), Germany, Greece, Hungary, Ireland, Italy, Luxembourg, the Netherlands, Norway, Portugal, Spain, Sweden and Switzerland (including Liechtenstein). The passes do *not* cover the UK.

Eurail is also valid on ferries running between Ireland–France, Italy–Greece, and Silja Line routes between Germany, Sweden and Finland.

In addition to the passes listed below, there's a **Eurail Regional Pass**, offering unlimited rail travel in two countries, and valid for five, six, eight or 10 days within a two-month period; however, the only Scandinavian region covered is Germany–Denmark. Eurail have also created a new **Eurail National Pass**, providing unlimited rail travel in a single country, valid for between three and 10 days within a one-month period depending on the country – versions of this pass exist for Denmark, Finland, Norway and Sweden. For both these types of pass, you can choose to travel 1st or 2nd class; Saver and Youth versions are also available.

On most Eurail passes, children aged between four and 11 get a 50% discount on the full adult fare.

Eurail passes include the following:

Eurailpass (15-/21-day pass US$605/785, 1-/2-/3-month pass US$975/1,378/1,702) For those aged over 26; valid for unlimited 1st-class travel.

Eurailpass – Saver (15-/21-day pass US$512/668, 1-/2-/3-month pass US$828/1,172/1,450) For two to five people travelling together; valid for unlimited 1st-class travel.

Eurailpass – Youth (15-/21-day pass US$394/510, 1-/2-/3-month pass US$634/896/1,108) For those aged under 26; valid for unlimited 2nd-class travel.

Eurailpass Flexi (10-/15-day pass US$715/940) For those aged over 26; valid for 10 or 15 days' 1st-class travel within a two-month period.
Eurailpass Flexi – Saver (10-/15-day pass US$608/800) For two to five people travelling together; valid for 10 or 15 days' 1st-class travel within a two-month period.

Eurailpass Flexi – Youth (10-/15-day pass US$465/611) For those aged under 26; valid for 10 or 15 days' 2nd-class travel within a two-month period.
Eurail Selectpass (three-country 5-/6-/8-/10-day pass US$383/423/503/580, four-country 5-/6-/8-/10-day pass US$428/468/548/625, five-country 5-/6-/8-/10-/15-day

Country	Transport	Route	Company	ScanRail Discount
Denmark	Train	Hjørring-Hirtshals	Nordjyske Jernbaner	50%
Denmark	Train	Frederikshavn-Skagen	Skagensbanen	50%
Denmark/Germany	Ferry	Rødby-Puttgarden Mitte See	Scandlines	free
Denmark/Norway	Ferry	Copenhagen-Oslo	DFDS Seaways	25%
Denmark/Sweden	Ferry	Helsingør-Helsingborg	Scandlines	free
Denmark/Sweden	Ferry	Grenå-Varberg	Stena Line	30%
Denmark/Sweden	Ferry	Frederikshavn-Göteborg	Stena Line	30%
Denmark/UK	Ferry	Esbjerg-Harwich	DFDS Seaways	25%
Finland	Bus	Kemi-Tornio	Veljekset Salmela	free
Norway	Train	Myrdal-Flåm	The Flåm Railway	30%
Norway	Bus	Åndalsnes-Ålesund	Nettbuss Ålesund AS	50%
Norway	Bus	Åndalsnes-Molde	Veøy Buss AS	50%
Norway	Bus	Mosjøen-Sandnessjøen	Helgelandske AS	50%
Norway	Ferry	Bergen-Haugesund-Stavanger (day sailing)	Flaggruten A/S	50%
Norway	Ferry	Hardangerfjord & southern Hordaland	HSD Sjø AS	50%
Norway/Denmark	Ferry	Larvik-Hirtshals (day sailing)	Color Line	50%
Norway/Denmark	Ferry	Oslo-Hirtshals (day sailing)	Color Line	50%
Norway/Denmark	Ferry	Kristiansand-Hirtshals (day sailing)	Color Line	50%
Norway/Denmark	Ferry	Larvik-Frederikshavn (day sailing)	Color Line	50%
Norway/Denmark	Ferry	Oslo-Frederikshavn	Stena Line	50%
Norway/Denmark	Ferry	Bergen-Haugesund-Egersund-Hanstholm	Fjordline	small discount
Norway/Sweden	Ferry	Sandefjord-Strömstad (day sailing)	Color Line	50%
Norway/UK	Ferry	Bergen-Haugesund-Stavanger-Newcastle	Fjordline	small discount
Sweden	Train	Östersund-Storlien	Nabo-Tåget	50%
Sweden	Train	Mora-Östersund-Gällivare	Inlandsbanan	25% off Inland-banan Card
Sweden/Germany	Train	Berlin-Malmö-Berlin	SJ/GVG	small discount
Sweden/Finland	Bus	Luleå-Haparanda-Tornio	Länstrafiken i Norrbotten	free
Sweden	Ferry	Nynäshamn-Visby	Destination Gotland	check for discount
Sweden	Ferry	Oskarhamn-Visby	Destination Gotland	check for discount
Sweden/Finland	Ferry	Stockholm-Helsinki	Silja Line/Viking Line	50% (on limited cabins)
Sweden/Finland	Ferry	Stockholm-Turku	Silja Line/Viking Line	50% (on limited cabins)
Sweden/ Norway/UK	Ferry	Göteborg-Kristiansand-Newcastle	DFDS Seaways	25% (limited number)

pass US$473/513/593/670/850) For those aged over 26; valid for five, six, eight, 10, sometimes 15 days' 1st-class travel through three, four or five countries within a two-month period. Countries must be connected by either rail or ferry.

Eurail Selectpass – Saver (three-country 5-/6-/8-/10-day pass US$325/360/428/493, four-country 5-/6-/8-/10-day pass US$363/398/465/530, five-country 5-/6-/8-/10-/15-day pass US$400/435/503/568/723) For two to five people travelling together; valid for five, six, eight, 10, sometimes 15 days' 1st-class travel through three, four or five countries within a two-month period. Countries must be connected by either rail or ferry.

Eurail Selectpass – Youth (three-country 5-/6-/8-/10-day pass US$249/275/325/375, four-country 5-/6-/8-/10-day pass US$278/304/354/404, five-country 5-/6-/8-/10-/15-day pass US$306/333/383/433/553) For those aged under 26; valid for five, six, eight, 10, sometimes 15 days' 2nd-class travel through three, four or five countries within a two-month period. Countries must be connected by either rail or ferry.

EURO DOMINO

The Euro Domino pass (called a Freedom pass in Britain) is available to people who have been living in Europe for at least six months. It's valid in most of the same countries covered in the zonal Inter Rail pass (see the following section; France, Italy and Spain are not participating).

Adults (travelling 1st or 2nd class) and people under 26 can travel within one country for three to eight days within a one-month period. Examples of adult/youth prices for eight days in 2nd class are UK£102/77 for Denmark, UK£165/123 for Finland, UK£248/189 for Norway and UK£214/149 for Sweden. Children aged between four and 11 travel for half price; and seniors receive a discount of around 15% on adult fares. The websites www.raileurope.co.uk and www.eurodomino.com contain full details.

INTER RAIL

Inter Rail (www.interrailnet.com) passes are valid for unlimited 2nd-class travel in 30 countries in Europe and North Africa, and are available to European residents of at least six months' standing – passport identification is required. Terms and conditions vary slightly from country to country, but in the country of origin there's only a discount of around 50% on normal fares, rather than free travel.

The Inter Rail pass is split into eight zones. Zone A is Ireland and the UK; B is Finland, Norway and Sweden; C is Austria, Denmark, Germany and Switzerland; D is Bosnia-Hercegovina, Croatia, the Czech Republic, Hungary, Poland and Slovakia; E is Belgium, France, Luxembourg and the Netherlands; F is Morocco, Portugal and Spain; G is Italy, Greece, Slovenia and Turkey; H is Bulgaria, Macedonia, Romania and Yugoslavia.

The price for any one zone is UK£223/145 (if aged over/under 26) for 16 days and UK£295/205 for 22 days. A global pass is better value, allowing one month's travel in all zones for UK£405/285.

SCANRAIL

ScanRail (www.scanrail.com) is a pass covering rail travel in Denmark, Norway, Sweden and Finland, with discounts on some private railways, ferries, boats and buses. It's very important to buy your ScanRail pass outside Scandinavia, or you'll face huge restrictions regarding the days you can travel. The pass comes in two versions (children aged four to 11 travel for half the adult fare):

ScanRail Flexi Pass (adult 5-/8-/10-day pass UK£174/210/234, under-26 5-/8-/10-day pass UK£120/145/162, over-60s 5-/8-/10-day pass UK£153/185/207) For unlimited 2nd-class travel on any five, eight or 10 days within a two-month period.

ScanRail Consecutive Pass – 21 days (adult/under 26/over 60 UK£270/188/237) For unlimited 2nd-class travel over 21 consecutive days.

ScanRail passes are valid on the following major Scandinavian train networks: DSB and Arriva (Denmark); VR (Finland); NSB (Norway); the Arlanda Express (Arlanda Airport-Stockholm), Connex, SJ, Tågkompaniet and some regional services (Sweden). Some other rail and ferry services are discounted or free – see the table for more information.

Health

CONTENTS

Travel in Scandinavia presents very few health problems. The standard of health care is high and English is widely spoken by doctors and medical clinic staff, tap water is safe to drink, the level of hygiene is high and there are no endemic diseases. The main health issues to be aware of are extreme climates (with the potential for hypothermia, frostbite or viral infections such as influenza) and biting insects such as mosquitoes, though they're more an annoyance than a health risk.

BEFORE YOU GO

Prevention is the key to staying healthy while abroad. A little time spent planning before departure, particularly if you have pre-existing illnesses, will save trouble later: see your dentist before a long trip; carry a spare pair of contact lenses and glasses, and take your optical prescription with you. Bring your medications in their original, clearly labelled containers. A signed and dated letter from your physician describing your medical conditions and necessary medications, including their generic names, is also a good idea.

Specific travel vaccinations are not required for visitors to Scandinavia but you should be up to date with all normal childhood vaccinations.

INSURANCE

Citizens of the European Economic Area (EEA) are covered for emergency medical treatment in other EEA countries (including Denmark, Finland, Iceland, Norway and Sweden) on presentation of a European Health Insurance Card (EHIC), which replaced the E111 form in January 2006. Enquire about EHICs at your health centre, travel agency or (in some countries) post office well in advance of travel. Citizens from other countries should find out if there is a reciprocal arrangement for free medical care between their country and the country visited. Health insurance is still recommended, especially if you intend to go hiking or skiing. Make sure you get a policy that covers you for the worst possible scenario, such as an accident requiring an emergency flight home. Find out in advance if your insurance plan will make payments directly to providers or reimburse you later for overseas health expenditures.

ONLINE RESOURCES

The WHO's publication *International Travel and Health* is revised annually and is available online at www.who.int/ith/. Other useful websites include www.mdtravelhealth.com (travel-health recommendations for every country; updated daily), www.fitfortravel.scot.nhs.uk (general travel advice for the layperson), www.ageconcern.org.uk (advice on travel for the elderly) and www.mariestopes.org.uk (information on women's health and contraception).

FURTHER READING

'Health Advice for Travellers' (called the 'T7.1' leaflet) is an annually updated leaflet by the Department of Health in the UK that's available free from post offices. It contains some general information, legally required and recommended vaccines for different countries, reciprocal health agreements and information on how to apply for an EHIC. Lonely Planet's *Travel with Children* includes advice on travel health for younger children. Other recommended references include *Traveller's Health* by Dr Richard Dawood and *The Traveller's Good Health Guide* by Ted Lankester.

IN TRANSIT

DEEP VEIN THROMBOSIS (DVT)

Blood clots may form in the legs during plane flights, chiefly because of prolonged immobility. The longer the flight, the greater the risk. The chief symptom of DVT is swelling or pain in the foot, ankle or calf, usually but not always on just one side. When a blood clot travels to the lungs, it may cause chest pain and breathing difficulties. Travellers with any of these symptoms should immediately seek medical attention.

To prevent the development of DVT on long flights you should walk about the cabin, contract the leg muscles while sitting, drink plenty of fluids and avoid alcohol and tobacco.

JET LAG & MOTION SICKNESS

To avoid jet lag (common when crossing more than five time zones) try drinking plenty of nonalcoholic fluids and eating light meals. Upon arrival, get exposure to natural sunlight and readjust your schedule (for meals, sleep and so on) as soon as possible.

Antihistamines such as dimenhydrinate (Dramamine) and meclizine (Antivert, Bonine) are usually the first choice for treating motion sickness. A herbal alternative is ginger.

IN SCANDINAVIA

AVAILABILITY & COST OF HEALTHCARE

Good healthcare is readily available and for minor self-limiting illnesses pharmacists can give valuable advice and sell over-the-counter medication. Major cities in Scandinavia have a 24-hour pharmacy. The staff can advise when more specialised help is required and point you in the right direction to find it. The standard of dental care is good, but it is sensible to have a dental check-up before a long trip.

TRAVELLER'S DIARRHOEA

Tap water and food is generally safe throughout Scandinavia, but a change in diet can sometimes cause diarrhoea.

If you develop diarrhoea, drink plenty of fluids, preferably an oral rehydration solution such as Dioralyte. A few loose stools don't require treatment, but if you have more than four or five stools a day you should start taking an antibiotic (usually a quinolone drug) and an antidiarrhoeal agent (such as loperamide).

ENVIRONMENTAL HAZARDS
Hypothermia

Proper preparation will reduce the risks of getting hypothermia. Even on a hot day in the mountains, the weather can change rapidly. Hikers should carry waterproof clothing, wear warm layers and inform others of the route taken.

Acute hypothermia follows a sudden drop of temperature over a short time. Chronic hypothermia is caused by a gradual loss of temperature over hours.

Hypothermia starts with shivering, loss of judgment and clumsiness. Unless rewarming occurs, the sufferer deteriorates into apathy, confusion and coma. Prevent further heat loss by providing shelter, warm dry clothing, hot sweet drinks and shared bodily warmth.

Frostbite is caused by freezing and subsequent damage to bodily extremities. It is dependent on wind chill, temperature and length of exposure. Frostbite starts as frostnip (white numb areas of skin) from which complete recovery is expected with rewarming. As frostbite develops, the skin blisters and then becomes black. The loss of damaged tissue eventually occurs. Adequate clothing, staying dry, keeping well hydrated

---

HEADING

It's usually a good idea to consult your government's travel-health website before departure, if one is available:

Australia www.smartraveller.gov.au
Canada www.travelhealth.gc.ca
UK www.dh.gov.uk/PolicyAndGuidance/Health AdviceForTravellers/
USA www.cdc.gov/travel/

and ensuring adequate calorie intake is the best way to prevent frostbite. Treatment involves rapid rewarming. Avoid refreezing and rubbing the affected areas.

Insect Bites & Stings

Mosquitoes are found in most parts of Scandinavia, particularly in Lapland during summer and around lake areas such as eastern Finland. Malaria is not a problem but irritation and infected bites are possible. Use a DEET-based insect repellent.

In northern Iceland, midges and black-flies can be a real annoyance in summer.

Bees and wasps only cause real problems to those with a severe allergy (anaphylaxis). If you have a severe allergy to bee or wasp stings, carry an 'epipen' or similar adrenalin injection.

Bed bugs lead to very itchy lumpy bites, but Scandinavian hotels and hostels are generally immaculate. Spraying the mattress with crawling-insect killer after changing bedding will get rid of them.

Scabies are tiny parasitic mites that live in the skin, particularly between the fingers. They cause an intensely itchy rash. Scabies are easily treated with lotion from a pharmacy.

WOMEN'S HEALTH

Emotional stress, exhaustion and travelling through different time zones can all contribute to an upset in the menstrual pattern. If using oral contraceptives, remember some antibiotics, diarrhoea and vomiting can stop the pill from working and lead to the risk of pregnancy. Tampons and similar products are widely available in Scandinavia at pharmacies and supermarkets.

Travelling during pregnancy is usually possible but always seek a medical check-up before planning your trip. The most risky times for travel are during the first 12 weeks of pregnancy and after 30 weeks.

Language

CONTENTS

This language guide contains pronunciation guidelines and basic vocabulary to help you during your travels in Scandinavian Europe. For a more detailed guide to the languages in this region, pick up a copy of Lonely Planet's *Scandinavian Phrasebook*.

DANISH

While the majority of Danes speak English, any effort to learn a few basic words and phrases will be greatly appreciated by the people you meet.

Danish has a polite form of address, using the personal pronouns *De* and *Dem*. The Danish translations in this book mostly use the informal pronouns *du* and *dig*, except where it's appropriate and/or wise to use the polite form. In general, you should use the polite form when speaking to senior citizens and officials, and the informal the rest of the time.

Nouns in Danish have two genders: masculine and neuter. In the singular, the definite article ('the' in English) is suffixed to the noun: -*en* (masculine) and -*et* (neuter). In the plural -*ne* is used for the indefinite ('some' in English) and -*ene* for the definite, regardless of gender.

PRONUNCIATION

You may find Danish pronunciation difficult. Consonants are drawled, swallowed and even omitted completely, creating, in conjunction with vowels, the peculiarity of the glottal stop or *stød*. Its sound is rather as a Cockney would say the 'tt' in 'bottle'. Stress is usually placed on the first syllable or on the first letter of the word. In general though, the best advice is to listen and learn. Good luck!

Vowels

a	as in 'father'
a, æ	as in 'act'
å, o &	
u(n)	a long rounded 'a' as in 'walk'
e(g)	as the sound of 'eye'
e, i	as the 'e' in 'bet'
i	as the 'e' in 'theme'
ø	as the 'er' in 'fern'
o, u	as the 'oo' in 'cool'
o	as in 'pot'
o(v)	as the 'ou' in 'out'
o(r)	as the 'or' in for' with less emphasis on the 'r'
u	as in 'pull'
y	say 'ee' while pursing your lips

Consonants

sj	as in 'ship'
ch	a sharper sound than the 'ch' in 'cheque'
c	as in 'cell'
(o)d	a flat 'dh' sound, like the 'th' in 'these'
ng	as in 'sing'
g	a hard 'g' as in 'get', if followed by a vowel
h	as in 'horse'
k	as the 'c' in 'cat'
r	a rolling 'r' abruptly cut short
w	similar to the 'wh' in 'what'
j	as the 'y' in 'yet'

ACCOMMODATION

hotel	*hotel*
guesthouse	*gæstgiveri*
hostel	*vandrerhjem*
camping ground	*campingplads*

Do you have any rooms available?	*Har I ledige værelser?*
How much is it per night/ per person?	*Hvor meget koster det per nat/ per person?*
Does it include breakfast?	*Er morgenmad inkluderet?*

I'd like ...	Jeg ønsker ...
a single room	et enkeltværelse
a double room	et dobbeltværelse

| one day/two days | en nat/to nætter |

CONVERSATION & ESSENTIALS

Hello.	Hallo/Hej. (informal)
Goodbye.	Farvel.
Yes.	Ja.
No.	Nej.
Please.	Må jeg bede/Værsgo.
Thank you.	Tak.
That's fine/You're welcome.	Det er i orden/Selv tak
Excuse me/Sorry.	Undskyld.
Do you speak English?	Taler De engelsk?
How much is it?	Hvor meget koster det?
What's your name?	Hvad hedder du?
My name is ...	Mit navn er ...

EMERGENCIES – DANISH

Help!	Hjælp!
Call a doctor!	Ring efter en læge!
Call the police!	Ring efter politiet!
Go away!	Forsvind!
I'm lost.	Jeg har gået vild.

SHOPPING & SERVICES

a bank	en bank
a chemist/pharmacy	et apotek
the ... embassy	den ... ambassade
my hotel	mit hotel
the market	markedet
a newsagent	en aviskiosk
the post office	postkontoret
the tourist office	turistinformationen

| What time does it open/close? | Hvornår åbner/lukker det? |

TIME, DAYS & NUMBERS

What time is it?	Hvad er klokken?
today	i dag
tomorrow	i morgen
morning	morgenen
afternoon	eftermiddagen

Monday	mandag
Tuesday	tirsdag
Wednesday	onsdag
Thursday	torsdag
Friday	fredag

| Saturday | lørdag |
| Sunday | søndag |

SIGNS – DANISH

Indgang	Entrance
Udgang	Exit
Åben	Open
Lukket	Closed
Forbudt	Prohibited
Information	Information
Politistation	Police Station
Toiletter	Toilets
Herrer	Men
Damer	Women

0	nul
1	en
2	to
3	tre
4	fire
5	fem
6	seks
7	syv
8	otte
9	ni
10	ti
100	hundrede
1000	tusind

TRANSPORT

What time does ... leave/arrive?	Hvornår går/ankommer ...?
the boat	båden
the bus (city)	bussen
the bus (intercity)	rutebilen
the tram	sporvognen
the train	toget

| Where can I hire a car/bicycle? | Hvor kan jeg leje en bil/cykel? |

I'd like ...	Jeg vil gerne have ...
a one-way ticket	en enkeltbillet
a return ticket	en tur-retur billet

1st class	første klasse
2nd class	anden klasse
left luggage office	reisegodsoppbevar ingen
timetable	køreplan
bus stop	bus holdeplads
tram stop	sporvogn holdeplads
train station	jernbanestation (banegård)

Directions

Where is ...?	Hvor er ...?
Go straight ahead.	Gå ligefrem.
Turn left/right.	Drej til venstre/højre.
near/far	nær/fjern

FAROESE

Faroese is a Germanic language derived from old Norse, closely related to Icelandic and some Norwegian and Swedish dialects. In 1890, a standard written version of Faroese, *Føroyskt*, was made official and given equal status with Danish in public and government affairs.

All Faroese speak Danish, can handle Norwegian and Swedish, and some speak English. Nearly every Faroese learns Danish at school (and many also learn English and German), but foreign languages have had little impact on everyday life.

PRONUNCIATION

In most cases, Faroese words are stressed on the first syllable. Grammar is very similar to that of Icelandic, but pronunciation is quite different due to a mix of Icelandic, Danish, and even Gaelic influences, eg the name of Eiði village is inexplicably pronounced 'oy-yeh'; the nearby village of Gjógv is referred to as 'Jagv'; the capital, Tórshavn, gets the more or less Danish pronunciation, 'torsh-hown'.

Vowels & Diphthongs

a, æ	short, as the 'u' in 'cut'; long, as the 'ai' in 'hair'
á	short, as the 'o' in 'hot'; long, as the 'oi' in French moi
e	as in 'get'
i, y	short, as the 'i' in 'hit'; long, as the 'i' in 'marine'
í, ý	as the 'ui' in Spanish muy
o	as in 'hot'
ó	short, as the 'a' in 'ago'; long, as the 'o' in 'note'
ø	as the 'a' in 'ago'
u	as in 'pull'
ú	short, as a sharp 'u' – purse your lips and say 'ee'; long, as the 'ou' in 'you'
ei	as the 'i' in 'dive'
ey	short, as the 'e' in 'get'; long, as the 'ay' in 'day'
oy	as the 'oy' in 'boy'

Consonants

ð	silent in final position, otherwise taking on the value of surrounding vowels
ðr	as the 'gr' in 'grab'
dj	as the 'j' in 'jaw'
ft	as the 'tt' in 'bitter'
g	silent in final position, otherwise taking on the value of surrounding vowels
ggj	as the 'j' in 'jaw'
hv	as 'kv'
hj	as the 'y' in 'yellow'
ll	as the 'dl' in 'saddle'

ACCOMMODATION

hotel	hotell
guesthouse	gistingarhús
youth hostel	vallarheim
campground	tjáldplass

Do you have any rooms available?	Eru nøkur leys kømur?
How much is it (per person/per night)?	Hvussu nógv kostar tað (fyri hvønn/eina natt)?
Does it include breakfast?	Er morgunmatur innifalinn?

I'd like (a) ...	Eg vil fegin hava ...
single room	eitt einkultkamar
double room	eitt dupultkamar

CONVERSATION & ESSENTIALS

Hello.	Hey/Halló/Góðan dag.
Goodbye.	Farvæl.
Yes.	Ja.
No.	Nei.
Please.	Gerið so væl.
Thank you.	Takk fyri.
Excuse me/Sorry.	Orsaka.
Do you speak English?	Tosar tú eingilskt?
How much is it?	Hvussu nógv kostar tað?
What's your name?	Hvussu eita tygum?
My name is ...	Eg eiti ...

SHOPPING & SERVICES

bank	banka
chemist	apotekið
the ... embassy	... ambassaduni
market	handilsgøtuni
the post office	posthúsinum
a public toilet	almennum vesi
the tourist office	ferðaskrivstovuni/ turistkontórinum

EMERGENCIES – FAROESE

Help!	Hjálp!
Call a doctor!	Ringið eftir lækna!
Call the police!	Ringið eftir løgregluni!
Go away!	Far burtur!
I'm lost.	Eg eri vilst/vilstur. (m/f)

SIGNS – FAROESE

Atgongd	Entrance
Útgongd	Exit
Neyðútgongd	Emergency Exit
Bannað	Prohibited
Upplýsingar	Information
Løgregla	Police

TIME, DAYS & NUMBERS

What time is it?	Hvat er klokkan?
today	í dag
tomorrow	í morgin
morning	morgun
afternoon	seinnapartur
night	nátt
Monday	mánadagur
Tuesday	týsdagur
Wednesday	mikudagur
Thursday	hósdagur
Friday	fríggjadagur
Saturday	leygardagur
Sunday	sunnudagur
1	eitt
2	tvey
3	trý
4	fíra
5	fimm
6	seks
7	sjey
8	átta
9	níggju
10	tíggju
20	tjúgu
100	hundrað
1000	túsund

TRANSPORT

boat	bátur
bus	bussur
map	kort
road	vegur
street	gøta
village	bygd
I'd like a ...	Kundi eg fingið ...
one-way ticket	einvegis ferðaseðil
return ticket	ferðaseðil aftur og fram

FINNISH

Finnish is a Uralic language spoken by just six million people, the vast majority of whom live in Scandinavia and in Russian Karelia. The most widely spoken of the Finno-Ugric family is Hungarian, but its similarities with Finnish are few. Suomi refers to both the Finnish-speaking part Finland and its language.

Staff at hotels, hostels and tourist offices generally speak fluent English. Bus drivers or restaurant and shop staff outside the cities may not, but they'll always fetch a colleague or bystander who does. You can certainly get by with English in Finland, but don't assume that everyone speaks it.

Swedish is spoken on Åland, as well as on the west ('Swedish') coast and around Helsinki and Turku, and all Finns learn Swedish at school.

PRONUNCIATION

Finnish pronunciation is more or less consistent – there is a one to one relationship between letters and sounds. There are nine vowels: a, e, i, o, u, y, ä, å and ö (the å has been adopted from the Norwegian and Swedish alphabets). The final letters of the alphabet are å, ä and ö (important to know when looking for something in a telephone directory).

Vowels

y	as the 'u' in 'pull' but with the lips stretched back (like the German 'ü')
å	as the 'oo' in 'poor'
ä	as the 'a' in 'act'
ö	as the 'a' in 'ago'

Consonants

z	pronounced (and sometimes written) as 'ts'
v/w	as the 'v' in 'vain'

h   a weak sound, except at the end of a
     syllable, when it is almost as strong
     as 'ch' in German *ich*
j   as the 'y' in 'yellow'
r   a rolled 'r'

Double consonants like **kk** in *viikko* or **mm**
in *summa* are held longer.

ACCOMMODATION

hotel	*hotelli*
guesthouse	*matkustajakoti*
youth hostel	*retkeilymaja*
camping ground	*leirintäalue*

Do you have any rooms available?	*Onko teillä vapaata huonetta?*
How much is it per night/per person?	*Paljonko se on yöltä/hengeltä?*
Does it include breakfast?	*Kuuluko aamiainen hintaan?*

I'd like ...	*Haluaisin ...*
a single room	*yhden hengen huoneen*
a double room	*kahden hengen huoneen*

one day	*yhden päivän*
two days	*kaksi päivää*

CONVERSATION & ESSENTIALS

Hello.	*Hei/Terve.*
Moi. (informal)	
Goodbye.	*Näkemiin.*
Moi. (informal)	
Yes.	*Kyllä/Joo.*
No.	*Ei.* (pronounced 'ay')
Please.	*Kiitos.*
Thank you.	*Kiitos.*
That's fine/You're welcome.	*Ole hyvä.* *Eipä kestä.* (informal)
Excuse me/Sorry.	*Anteeksi.*
Do you speak English?	*Puhutko englantia?*
How much is it?	*Paljonko se makasaa?*
What's your name?	*Mikä teidän nimenne on?*
My name is ...	*Minun nimeni on ...*

SHOPPING & SERVICES

bank	*pankkia*
chemist/pharmacy	*apteekki*
... embassy	*...-n suurlähetystöä*
market	*toria*
newsagent	*lehtikioski*
post office	*postia*
stationer	*paperikauppa*

tourist office	*matkailutoimistoa/ matkailutoimisto*
What time does it open/close?	*Milloin se aukeaan/ suljetaan?*

> ### EMERGENCIES – FINNISH
>
> | | |
> |---|---|
> | Help! | *Apua!* |
> | Call a doctor! | *Kutsukaa lääkäri!* |
> | Call the police! | *Soittakaa poliisi!* |
> | Go away! | *Mene pois! (Häivy!)* |
> | I'm lost. | *Minä olen eksynyt.* |

TIME, DAYS & NUMBERS

What time is it?	*Paljonko kello on?*
today	*tänään*
tomorrow	*huomenna*
morning	*aamulla*
afternoon	*iltapäivällä*
night	*yö*

Monday	*maanantai*
Tuesday	*tiistai*
Wednesday	*keskiviikko*
Thursday	*torstai*
Friday	*perjantai*
Saturday	*lauantai*
Sunday	*sunnuntai*

0	*nolla*
1	*yksi*
2	*kaksi*
3	*kolme*
4	*neljä*
5	*viisi*
6	*kuusi*
7	*seitsemän*
8	*kahdeksan*
9	*yhdeksän*
10	*kymmenen*
100	*sata*
1000	*tuhat*

TRANSPORT

What time does ... leave/arrive?	*Mihin aikaan ... lähtee/saapuu?*
the boat	*laiva*
the bus (city/intercity)	*bussi/linja-auto*
the tram	*raitiovaunu/raitikka*
the train	*juna*

I'd like a one way/ return ticket.	*Saanko menolipun/ menopaluulipun.*

SIGNS – FINNISH

Sisään	Entrance
Ulos	Exit
Avoinna	Open
Suljettu	Closed
Kielletty	Prohibited
Opastus	Information
Poliisiasema	Police Station
WC	Toilets
Miehet	Men
Naiset	Women

Where can I hire a car?	*Mistä mina voisin vuokrata auton?*
Where can I hire a bicycle?	*Mistä mina voin vuokrata polkupyörän?*
1st class	*ensimmäinen luokka*
2nd class	*toinen luokka*
left luggage	*säilytys*
timetable	*aikataulu*
bus/tram stop	*pysäkki*
train station	*rautatieasema*
ferry terminal	*satamaterminaali*

Directions

Where is ...?	*Missä on ...?*
Go straight ahead.	*Kulje suoraan.*
Turn left.	*Käänny vasempaan.*
Turn right.	*Käänny oikeaan.*
near/far	*lähellä/kaukana*

ICELANDIC

Icelandic belongs to the Germanic language family that includes German, Dutch and all the Nordic languages except Finnish. Its closest 'living relative' is Faroese. Both Icelandic and Faroese are derived from Old Norse and they've changed little since the time of the Vikings.

Icelandic grammar is very complicated; the suffixes which are added to nouns and place names to indicate case may render a place name quite unrecognisable. This can lead to a great deal of confusion, especially when you're trying to read bus timetables and find names of towns spelt several different ways. For example, the sign that welcomes visitors to the town of Höfn reads *Velkomin til Hafnar. Hafnar* is the dative of Höfn.

Fortunately, it's not essential for foreigners to speak Icelandic. The second language of most young people is English, then Danish (and therefore Swedish and Norwegian to some degree) and German. Some people also learn French, Italian or Spanish. Other Icelanders will normally know enough English and German to exchange pleasantries.

PRONUNCIATION

Stress generally falls on the first syllable of a word. Double consonants are given a long pronunciation.

Vowels & Diphthongs

a	long, as in 'father' or short, as in 'at'
á	as the 'ou' in 'out'
au	as the word 'furry' without 'f' or 'rr'
e	long, as in 'fear' or short, as in 'bet'
é	as the 'y' in 'yet'
ei, ey	as the 'ay' in 'day'
i, y	as the 'i' in 'hit'
í, ý	as the 'i' in 'marine'
o	as in 'pot'
ó	as the word 'owe'
u	a bit like the 'u' in 'purr'
ú	as the 'o' in 'moon', or as the 'o' in 'woman'
ö	as the 'er' in 'fern', but without a trace of 'r'
æ	as the word 'eye'

Consonants

ð	as the 'th' in 'lather'
f	as in 'far'. When between vowels or at the end of a word it's pronounced as 'v'. When followed by **l** or **n** it's pronounced as 'b'.
g	as in 'go'. When between vowels or before **r** or **ð** it has a guttural sound as the 'ch' in Scottish loch.
h	as in 'he', except when followed by **v**, when it's pronounced as 'k'
j	as the 'y' in 'yellow'
l	as in 'let'; when doubled it's pronounced as 'dl'
n	as in 'no'; when doubled or word-final it's pronounced as 'dn' (unless **nn** forms part of the definite article *hinn*)
p	as in 'hip', except when followed by **s** or **t**, when it's pronounced as 'f'
r	always rolled
þ	as the 'th' in 'thin' or 'three'

ACCOMMODATION

hotel	hótel
guesthouse	gistiheimili
youth hostel	farfuglaheimili
camping ground	tjaldsvæði

Do you have any rooms available?	Eru herbergi laus?
How much is each night per person?	Hvað kostar nóttin fyrir manninn?
Does it include breakfast?	Er morgunmatur innifalinn?

I'd like ...	Gæti ég fengið ...
a single room	einstaklingsherbergi
a double room	tveggjamannaherbergi

one day	einn dag
two days	tvo daga

CONVERSATION & ESSENTIALS

Hello.	Halló.
Goodbye.	Bless.
Yes.	Já.
No.	Nei.
Please.	Gjörðu svo vel.
Thank you.	Takk fyrir.
That's fine.	Allt í lagi.
You're welcome.	Ekkert að þakka.
Excuse me/Sorry.	Afsakið.
Do you speak English?	Talar þú ensku?
How much is it?	Hvað kostar það?
What's your name?	Hvað heitir þú?
My name is ...	Ég heiti ...

EMERGENCIES – ICELANDIC

Help!	Hjálp!
Call a doctor!	Náið í lækni!
Call the police!	Náið í lögregluna!
Go away!	Farðu!
I'm lost	Ég er villtur/villt. (m/f)

SHOPPING & SERVICES

bank	banka
chemist/pharmacy	apótek
... embassy	... sendiráðinu
market	markaðnum
newsagent/stationer	blaðasala/bókabúð
post office	pósthúsinu
tourist office	upplýsingaþjónustu fyrir ferðafólk

SIGNS – ICELANDIC

Inngangur/Inn	Entrance
Útgangur/Út	Exit
Opið	Open
Lokað	Closed
Bannað	Prohibited
Upplýsingar	Information
Lögreglustöð	Police Station
Snyrting	Toilets
Karlar	Men
Konur	Women

TIME, DAYS & NUMBERS

What time is it?	Hvað er klukkan?
today	í dag
tomorrow	á morgun
in the morning	að morgni
in the afternoon	eftir hádegi

Monday	mánudagur
Tuesday	þriðjudagur
Wednesday	miðvikudagur
Thursday	fimmtudagur
Friday	föstudagur
Saturday	laugardagur
Sunday	sunnudagur

0	núll
1	einn
2	tveir
3	þrír
4	fjórir
5	fimm
6	sex
7	sjö
8	átta
9	níu
10	tíu
20	tuttugu
100	eitt hundrað
1000	eitt þúsund

TRANSPORT

What time does ... leave/arrive?	Hvenær fer/kemur ...?
the boat	báturinn
the bus (city)	vagninn
the tram	sporvagninn

I'd like ...	Gæti ég fengid ...
a one-way ticket	miða/aðra leiðina
a return ticket	miða/báðar leiðir
bus stop	biðstöð

LANGUAGE

ferry terminal	ferjuhöfn
timetable	tímaáætlun
I'd like to hire a car/bicycle.	Ég vil leigia bíl/reiðhjól.

Directions

Where is ...?	Hvar er ...?
Go straight ahead.	Farðu beint af áfram.
Turn left.	Beygðu til vinstri.
Turn right.	Beygðu til hægri.
near/far	nálægt/langt í burtu

NORWEGIAN

Norway has two official languages – Bokmål and Nynorsk – but the differences between the two languages are effectively very minor. In this language guide we have used Bokmål – it's by far the most common language travellers to Norway will encounter.

English is widely understood and spoken, especially in the urban areas and in most tourist destinations. In the rural areas (where Nynorsk predominates) you may come across people who speak very little English. If you show an effort to speak Norwegian, it will help a great deal in connecting with the Norwegians you meet.

PRONUNCIATION
Vowels & Diphthongs

a	long, as in 'father'; short, as in 'cut'
å	as the 'aw' in 'paw'
æ	as the 'a' in 'act'
e	long as in 'where'; short, as in 'bet'; when unstressed, as the 'a' in 'ago'
i	long, as the 'ee' in 'seethe'; short, as in 'hit'
o	long, as the 'oo' in 'cool'; short, as in 'pot'
ø	long, as the 'er' in 'fern'; short, as the 'a' in 'ago'
u, y	say 'ee' while pursing your lips
ai	as the word 'eye'
ei	as the 'ay' in 'day'
au	as the 'o' in 'note'
øy	as the 'oy' in 'toy'

Consonants & Semivowels

| d | at the end of a word, or between two vowels, it's often silent |

g	as the 'g' in 'get'; as the 'y' in 'yard' before ei, i, j, øy, y
h	as in 'her'; silent before v and j
j	as the 'y' in 'yard'
k	as in 'kin'; as the 'ch' in 'chin' before ei, i, j, øy and y
ng	as in 'sing'
r	a trilled 'r'. The combination rs is pronounced as the 'sh' in 'fish'.
s	as in 'so' (never as in 'treasure'); as the 'sh' in 'she' before ei, i, j, øy and y

ACCOMMODATION

hotel	hotell
guesthouse	gjestgiveri/pensionat
youth hostel	vandrerhjem
camping ground	kamping/leirplass

Do you have any rooms available?	Har du ledige rom?
How much is it per night/person?	Hvor mye er det pr dag/person?
Does it include breakfast?	Inklusive frokosten?

I'd like ...	Jeg vil gjerne ha ...
a single room	et enkeltrom
a double room	et dobbeltrom

| one day | en dag |
| two days | to dager |

EMERGENCIES – NORWEGIAN

Help!	Hjelp!
Call a doctor!	Ring en lege!
Call the police!	Ring politiet!
Go away!	Forsvinn!
I'm lost.	Jeg har gått meg vill.

CONVERSATION & ESSENTIALS

Hello.	Goddag.
Goodbye.	Ha det.
Yes.	Ja.
No.	Nei.
Please.	Vær så snill.
Thank you.	Takk.
You're welcome.	Ingen årsak.
Excuse me/Sorry.	Unnskyld.
Do you speak English?	Snakker du engelsk?
How much is it?	Hvor mye koster det?
What's your name?	Hva heter du?
My name is ...	Jeg heter ...

SHOPPING & SERVICES

bank	*banken*
chemist/pharmacy	*apotek*
... embassy	*... ambassade*
market	*torget*
newsagent	*kiosk*
post office	*postkontoret*
tourist office	*turistinformasjon*

TIME, DAYS & NUMBERS

What time is it?	*Hva er klokka?*
today	*i dag*
tomorrow	*i morgen*
in the morning	*om formiddagen*
in the afternoon	*om ettermiddagen*

Monday	*mandag*
Tuesday	*tirsdag*
Wednesday	*onsdag*
Thursday	*torsdag*
Friday	*fredag*
Saturday	*lørdag*
Sunday	*søndag*

0	*null*
1	*en*
2	*to*
3	*tre*
4	*fire*
5	*fem*
6	*seks*
7	*sju*
8	*åtte*
9	*ni*
10	*ti*
100	*hundre*
1000	*tusen*

TRANSPORT

What time does ...	*Når går/kommer ...?*
leave/arrive?	
the boat	*båten*
the (city) bus	*(by)bussen*
the intercity bus	*linjebussen*
the train	*toget*
the tram	*trikken*

I'd like ...	*Jeg vil gjerne ha ...*
a one-way ticket	*enkeltbillett*
a return ticket	*tur-retur*

1st class	*første klasse*
2nd class	*annen klasse*

left luggage	*reisegods*
timetable	*ruteplan*
bus stop	*bussholdeplass*
tram stop	*trikkholdeplass*
train station	*jernbanestasjon*
ferry terminal	*ferjeleiet*

Where can I rent a	*Hvor kan jeg leie en*
car/bicycle?	*bil/sykkel?*

SIGNS – NORWEGIAN

Inngang	Entrance
Utgang	Exit
Åpen	Open
Stengt	Closed
Forbudt	Prohibited
Opplysninger	Information
Politistasjon	Police Station
Toaletter	Toilets
Herrer	Men
Damer	Women

Directions

Where is ...?	*Hvor er ...?*
Go straight ahead.	*Det er rett fram.*
Turn left.	*Ta til venstre.*
Turn right.	*Ta til høyre.*
near/far	*nær/langt*

SWEDISH

Swedish belongs to the Nordic branch of the Germanic language family and is spoken throughout Sweden and in parts of Finland. Swedes, Danes and Norwegians can understand each others' languages. Most Swedes speak English as a second language.

Definite articles in Swedish ('the' in English) are determined by the ending of a noun: *-en* and *-et* for singular nouns and *-na* and *-n* for plural.

If you learn a few common phrases, your attempts will be greatly appreciated by Swedes, who aren't used to foreigners speaking Swedish.

Sami dialects, which fit into three main groups, belong to the Uralic language family, and are ancestrally related to Finnish, not Swedish.

EMERGENCIES – SWEDISH

Help!	Hjälp!
Call a doctor!	Ring efter en doktor!
Call the police!	Ring polisen!
Go away!	Försvinn!
I'm lost.	Jag har gått vilse.

PRONUNCIATION

Vowels

The vowels are pronounced as short sounds if there's a double consonant afterwards, otherwise they are long sounds. Sometimes Swedish **o** sounds like the **å**, and **e** similar to the **ä**. There are, however, not as many exceptions to the rules of pronunciation as there are in English.

a	long, as in 'father'; short, as the 'u' in 'cut'
o, u	long, as the 'oo' in 'cool'; short, as in 'pot'
i	long, as the 'ee' in 'seethe'; short, as in 'pit'
e	long, as the 'ea' in 'fear'; short, as in 'bet'
å	long, as the word 'awe'; short as the 'o' in 'pot'
ä	as the 'a' in 'act'
ö	as the 'er' in 'fern', but without the 'r' sound
y	try saying 'ee' while pursing your lips

Consonants

The consonants are pronounced almost the same as in English. The following letter combinations and sounds are specific to Swedish:

c	as the 's' in 'sit'
ck	as a double 'k'; shortens the preceding vowel
tj/rs	as the 'sh' in 'ship'
sj/ch	similar to the 'ch' in Scottish loch
g	as in 'get'; sometimes as the 'y' in 'yet'
lj	as the 'y' in 'yet'

ACCOMMODATION

hotel	hotell
guesthouse	gästhus
youth hostel	vandrarhem
camping ground	campingplats

Do you have any rooms available?	Finns det några lediga rum?
Does it include breakfast?	Inkluderas frukost?
How much is it per night/person?	Hur mycket kostar det per natt/person?

I'd like ...	Jag skulle vilja ha ...
a single room	ett enkelrum
a double room	ett dubbelrum

for one/two nights	i en natt/två nätter

CONVERSATION & ESSENTIALS

Hello.	Hej.
Goodbye.	Adjö/Hej då.
Yes.	Ja.
No.	Nej.
Please.	Snälla/Vänligen.
Thank you.	Tack.
You're welcome.	Det är bra/Varsågod.
Excuse me/Sorry.	Ursäkta mig/Förlåt.
Do you speak English?	Talar du engelska?
How much is it?	Hur mycket kostar den?
What's your name?	Vad heter du?
My name is ...	Jag heter ...

SHOPPING & SERVICES

bank	bank
chemist/pharmacy	apotek
... embassy	... ambassaden
market	marknaden
newsagent/stationer	nyhetsbyrå/pappers handel
post office	postkontoret
a public telephone	en offentlig telefon
tourist office	turistinformation

What time does it open/close?	När öppnar/stänger de?

TIME, DAYS & NUMBERS

What time is it?	Vad är klockan?
today	idag
tomorrow	imorgon
morning	morgonen
afternoon	efter middagen

Monday	måndag
Tuesday	tisdag
Wednesday	onsdag
Thursday	torsdag
Friday	fredag
Saturday	lördag
Sunday	söndag

0	*noll*
1	*ett*
2	*två*
3	*tre*
4	*fyra*
5	*fem*
6	*sex*
7	*sju*
8	*åtta*
9	*nio*
10	*tio*
100	*ett hundra*
1000	*ett tusen*

TRANSPORT

What time does ... leave/arrive?	*När avgår/kommer ...?*
the boat	*båten*
the city bus	*stadsbussen*
the intercity bus	*landsortsbussen*
the train	*tåget*
the tram	*spårvagnen*

I'd like ...	*Jag skulle vilja ha ...*
a one-way ticket	*en enkelbiljett*
a return ticket	*en returbiljett*
1st class	*första klass*
2nd class	*andra klass*

left luggage	*effektförvaring*
timetable	*tidtabell*
bus stop	*busshållplats*
train station	*tågstation*

Where can I hire a car/bicycle?	*Var kan jag hyra en bil/cykel?*

SIGNS – SWEDISH

Ingång	Entrance
Utgång	Exit
Öppet	Open
Stängt	Closed
Förbjudet	Prohibited
Information	Information
Polisstation	Police Station
Toalett	Toilets
Herrar	Men
Damer	Women

Directions

Where is ...?	*Var är ...?*
Go straight ahead.	*Gå rakt fram.*
Turn left.	*Sväng till vänster.*
Turn right.	*Sväng till höger.*
near/far	*nära/långt*

Behind the Scenes

THIS BOOK

Scandinavian Europe is part of Lonely Planet's Europe series, which includes Eastern Europe, Western Europe, Mediterranean Europe, Central Europe and Europe on a Shoestring. Lonely Planet also publishes phrasebooks to these regions.

This guidebook was commissioned in Lonely Planet's London office, and produced by the following:

Commissioning Editor Sam Trafford, Ella O'Donnell
Coordinating Editor Emma Gilmour
Coordinating Cartographer David Connolly
Coordinating Layout Designers Jessica Rose, Evelyn Yee
Managing Editors Imogen Bannister, Martin Heng
Managing Cartographer Mark Griffiths
Assisting Editors Louise Clarke, Kate Daly, Kate Evans, Melissa Faulkner, Monique Choy, Rosie Nicholson, Lauren Rollheiser
Assisting Cartographers Julie Dodkins, Karina Vitiritti, Jody Whiteoak
Assisting Layout Designers Wibowo Rusli, Carlos Solate
Cover Designer Marika Kozak
Colour Designer Yvonne Bischofberger
Project Manager Glenn van der Knijff
Language Content Coordinator Quentin Frayne
Thanks to Sin Choo, Sally Darmody, Mark Germanchis, Ali Lemer, Katie Lynch, Jacqueline McLeod, Trent Paton, Alan Murphy, Suzannah Shwer, Tashi Wheeler, Celia Wood

THANKS
PAUL HARDING

As always, I received a warm welcome from the Finns and met many travellers along the way.

Thanks to Peter and Anita and Kaisa in Helsinki, Markku, Jussi and friends in Savonlinna, the friendly folks at Sampo in Kemi, Tom in St Petersburg, my fellow ice-jumping sauna-goers in Kuopio, Simon, Tony, and staff at tourist offices who helped out. Most of all thanks to Hannah at home for support and chats. Thanks also to Sam, Ella, Emma, Mark and everyone at Lonely Planet.

MARK ELLIOTT

Thank you to the whole LP team notably Sam Trafford for getting me on the road to puffin-land and to Ella O'Donnell for fighting for those much needed extra pages. In the Faroes special 'thank you's' to the urbane Solarn Solmunde for introductions into the fabulous world of Faroese music, Jón Tyril and Elisabeth for unforgetable hospitality and great all-round insights, Uni Debess for blues perfection, Mikako Inada in Skúvoy, Einar in Suðuroy, Peter Tilley (your round!), Afenginn for inspiration, and dozens of other delightfully helpful folks throughout the islands.

Most of all eternal thanks and love to my beloved wife, parents and siblings.

BECKY OHLSEN

Becky would like to thank Ella O'Donnell, Sam Trafford and all of the authors on this book; Christina & Joel Ohlsen, Arne & Elisabeth Odeen, Peter Kvarnestam, Mick Lavin, DK Holm, Jan Elvsen, Jennifer Spratly, Charlotta Roth, and the Sang-Froid Riding Club.

THE LONELY PLANET STORY

The story begins with a classic travel adventure: Tony and Maureen Wheeler's 1972 journey across Europe and Asia to Australia. There was no useful information about the overland trail then, so Tony and Maureen published the first Lonely Planet guidebook to meet a growing need.

From a kitchen table, Lonely Planet has grown to become the largest independent travel publisher in the world, with offices in Melbourne (Australia), Oakland (USA) and London (UK). Today Lonely Planet guidebooks cover the globe. There is an ever-growing list of books and information in a variety of media. Some things haven't changed. The main aim is still to make it possible for adventurous travellers to get out there – to explore and better understand the world.

At Lonely Planet we believe travellers can make a positive contribution to the countries they visit – if they respect their host communities and spend their money wisely. Every year 5% of company profit is donated to charities around the world.

FRAN PARNELL

Huge thanks to everyone who helped during research and writing of the Iceland chapter: all the tourist office staff, particularly María at Höfn and Guðmundur at Húsavík; other travellers who shared their tips and comments; Sigmar at Sæferðir in Stykkishólmur; and Ragnar Kristjánsson, ranger at Skaftafell National Park. It's always fun catching up on Reykjavík gossip with Jón Trausti Sigurðarson at Grapevine. For fisherman's vodka, translation services and a fun Florence Nightingale's day, thanks to Liva, the Vestmanneyjar's midwife. And for a surreal but wonderful stay at the Icelandair Hotel in Borgarnes, thank you to Unnur and the rest of the staff.

Thank you too to the Lonely Planet in-house crew: Mark Griffiths, Emma Gilmour and especially Ella O'Donnell for supreme patience – and for increasing the wordcount! At home, thanks to Stuart for everything x.

JOHN SPELMAN

Thanks to Cathrine Solberg and David Dudek for the perpetually open door; to Solveig and Christian for warm socks and aquavit; and to the depravity of Michael Gibson. More gratitude to Margete for Bergen insights and generosity; to Jannicke Risjord and friends; to David Aasen Sandved for years helping a guy he's only meet twice; to Irene Alvheim and Siri Giil; to Bente Saxon, Lisbeth Fallan, and Gunhild Vevik; to Claudia Debrunner and Jørn Jensen; and to Black Metal specialist Megan Knight. Thanks also to my comrades at LP -- Ella O'Donnell, Emma Gilmour, Paul Harding, Sam Trafford and Mark Griffiths -- your kindness makes deadlines less dreadful and your critical eyes constantly save me from embarrassment.

Thanks especially to Lisa Conathan, my favourite research assistant.

ANDREW STONE

British author and journalist Michael Booth has lived in Denmark for a decade now and knows every cool little bar, restaurant, hotel and shop worth knowing about in Copenhagen. He very generously shared every last tip on these as well as his erudition on all things Hans Christian Andersen with me for this edition. Thanks Michael. The Danish tourist offices around the country were as efficient and helpful as ever but special thanks go to Pernille at Destination Bornholm for her organising powers and to Anne Sofie Olesen at Aalborg Tourist Bureau for all her help.

OUR READERS

Many thanks to the travellers who used the last edition and wrote to us with helpful hints, useful advice and interesting anecdotes:

Rachel Allen, Laure Arnold, James Batten, Yau Fai Chau, Mike Curtis, Valeria Di Grado, Rizzo Di Premuda, Peter Feldchen, Lin Fritschi, Jay Geller, Lynne Grabar, David Graham, Kari Gudjonsson, Terry Harper, Anders Jeppsson, Tore Jungnelius, Christoph Kalthoff, Karles Karwin, Jan Klovstad, Tero Lahtinen, Ed Lambert, Mairi Mcgregor, Cari Merkley, Richard Morris, Nicole Mueller, Petter Muri, Serhat Narsap, Palava Pensas, Tim Portley, Steinunn Ragnarsdóttir, Jun Suk Rho, Niki & Kevin Richardson, Stephanie Rowatt, Bruce Rumage, Leonard Scuderi, Nikolai Selch, Oxana Shveykina, Hakon Skanhaug, Merz Tanja, Janice & Robin Tausig, Cameron Tickner, Hanna Toivonen, Ryan Tracey, Alicia Trezise, Miguel Victoria, Thomas Vikberg, Teya Vitu, Mirjam Weber, Fernando Zaidan, Christoffer Zieler

ACKNOWLEDGMENTS

Many thanks to the following for the use of their content:

Map data contained in colour highlights map © Mountain High Maps 1993 Digital Wisdom, Inc.

SEND US YOUR FEEDBACK

We love to hear from travellers – your comments keep us on our toes and help make our books better. Our well-travelled team reads every word on what you loved or loathed about this book. Although we cannot reply individually to postal submissions, we always guarantee that your feedback goes straight to the appropriate authors, in time for the next edition. Each person who sends us information is thanked in the next edition – and the most useful submissions are rewarded with a free book.

To send us your updates – and find out about Lonely Planet events, newsletters and travel news – visit our award-winning website: **www.lonelyplanet.com/feedback**.

Note: We may edit, reproduce and incorporate your comments in Lonely Planet products such as guidebooks, websites and digital products, so let us know if you don't want your comments reproduced or your name acknowledged. For a copy of our privacy policy visit www.lonelyplanet.com/privacy.

BEHIND THE SCENES

Index

000 Map pages
000 Photograph pages

12pm 1pm 2pm 3pm 4pm 5pm 6pm 7pm 8pm 9pm 10pm 11pm 12am

Mon/Sun
International Date Line

Svalbard (Norway)
Zemlya Frantsa-Iosifa (Russia)
Novaya Zemlya (Russia)
Severnaya Zemlya (Russia)
KARA SEA
LAPTEV SEA
Novosibirskie Ostrovo (Russia)
EAST SIBERIAN SEA
BARENTS SEA

Sweden 1pm
Norway
Finland 2pm
3pm
Denmark
Latvia
Germany Poland Belarus
France Austria Ukraine
Italy Romania
Greece Turkey
Tunisia MEDITERRANEAN SEA Syria
Algeria Libya Egypt
Niger Chad Sudan
Nigeria Eritrea Yemen
Central African Republic Ethiopia
Congo Kenya Somalia
Gabon Congo (Zaire)
Angola Tanzania
Namibia Zambia Malawi
Botswana Zimbabwe Mozambique
South Africa

4pm 5pm
Russia 7pm 9pm
3pm
4pm 6pm
Kazakhstan Mongolia
Uzbekistan Kyrgyzstan
Turkmenistan China 8pm
Iran 3.30pm Afghanistan 4.30pm
Iraq Pakistan 5pm Tibet (China) Nepal 5.45pm
Saudi Arabia India 5.30pm
Oman 4pm Myanmar 6.30pm
ARABIAN SEA BAY OF BENGAL 5.30pm Thailand Vietnam
Maldives Sri Lanka
Indonesia

North Korea
South Korea Japan
EAST CHINA SEA Taiwan
SEA OF OKHOTSK 10pm 11pm 12am

BERING SEA 2am 3am

NORTH PACIFIC OCEAN

Northern Mariana Is (US) 9pm
Marshall Is (US) 12am

Federated States of Micronesia 11pm
Palau
Kiribati
Nauru EQUATOR

Philippines
Malaysia
East Timor
Papua New Guinea
Solomon Is

SOUTH PACIFIC OCEAN

Vanuatu
New Caledonia (Fr) Fiji

Seychelles 4pm
Cocos (Keeling) Is (Aust) 6.30pm
Mauritius
Reunion (Fr)
Madagascar
INDIAN OCEAN

Australia 9.30pm

Lord Howe Is (Aust) 10.30pm
Norfolk Is (Aust) 11.30pm

New Zealand

Prince Edward Is (S. Africa)
French Southern & Antarctic Territories (Fr)
Heard & McDonald Is (Aust)
SOUTHERN OCEAN
TASMAN SEA

1pm 2pm 3pm 4pm 5pm 6pm 7pm 8pm 9pm 10pm 11pm 12am

540

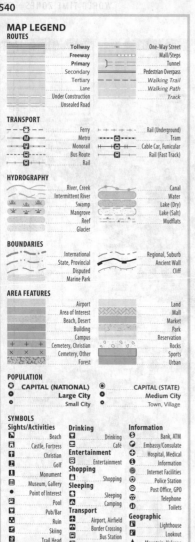

MAP LEGEND

ROUTES

Tollway	One-Way Street
Freeway	Mall/Steps
Primary	Tunnel
Secondary	Pedestrian Overpass
Tertiary	Walking Trail
Lane	Walking Path
Under Construction	Track
Unsealed Road	

TRANSPORT

Ferry	Rail (Underground)
Metro	Tram
Monorail	Cable Car, Funicular
Bus Route	Rail (Fast Track)
Rail	

HYDROGRAPHY

River, Creek	Canal
Intermittent River	Water
Swamp	Lake (Dry)
Mangrove	Lake (Salt)
Reef	Mudflats
Glacier	

BOUNDARIES

International	Regional, Suburb
State, Provincial	Ancient Wall
Disputed	Cliff
Marine Park	

AREA FEATURES

Airport	Land
Area of Interest	Mall
Beach, Desert	Market
Building	Park
Campus	Reservation
Cemetery, Christian	Rocks
Cemetery, Other	Sports
Forest	Urban

POPULATION

CAPITAL (NATIONAL)	**CAPITAL (STATE)**
Large City	**Medium City**
Small City	Town, Village

SYMBOLS

Sights/Activities
- Beach
- Castle, Fortress
- Christian
- Golf
- Monument
- Museum, Gallery
- Point of Interest
- Pool
- Pub/Bar
- Ruin
- Skiing
- Trail Head
- Windsurfing
- Zoo, Bird Sanctuary

Eating
- Eating

Drinking
- Drinking
- Café

Entertainment
- Entertainment

Shopping
- Shopping

Sleeping
- Sleeping
- Camping

Transport
- Airport, Airfield
- Border Crossing
- Bus Station
- Cycling, Bicycle Path
- General Transport
- Parking Area
- Petrol Station
- Taxi Rank

Information
- Bank, ATM
- Embassy/Consulate
- Hospital, Medical
- Information
- Internet Facilities
- Police Station
- Post Office, GPO
- Telephone
- Toilets

Geographic
- Lighthouse
- Lookout
- Mountain, Volcano
- National Park
- Pass, Canyon
- River Flow
- Waterfall

LONELY PLANET OFFICES

Australia
Head Office
Locked Bag 1, Footscray, Victoria 3011
☎ 03 8379 8000, fax 03 8379 8111
talk2us@lonelyplanet.com.au

USA
150 Linden St, Oakland, CA 94607
☎ 510 893 8555, toll free 800 275 8555
fax 510 893 8572
info@lonelyplanet.com

UK
72–82 Rosebery Ave,
Clerkenwell, London EC1R 4RW
☎ 020 7841 9000, fax 020 7841 9001
go@lonelyplanet.co.uk

Published by Lonely Planet Publications Pty Ltd
ABN 36 005 607 983

© Lonely Planet Publications Pty Ltd 2007

© photographers as indicated 2007

Cover photograph: Arctic fox searching for food in snow laden forest,
Blickwinkel/Photolibrary. Many of the images in this guide are available for licensing from Lonely Planet Images: www.lonelyplanetimages
.com.

Printed through Colorcraft Ltd, Hong Kong.
Printed in China